The Nonprofit Sector

THE NONPROFIT SECTOR

A Research Handbook

SECOND EDITION

EDITED BY
WALTER W. POWELL AND RICHARD STEINBERG

Yale University Press
New Haven & London

Set in Times Roman with Optima display by
Technologies 'N Typography, Inc.
Printed in the United States of America.

Library of Congress Cataloging-in-Publication Data

The nonprofit sector : a research handbook / edited by Walter W. Powell and Richard Steinberg.—2nd ed.
p. cm.
Includes bibliographical references and index.
ISBN-13: 978-0-300-10903-0 (cloth : alk. paper)
ISBN-10: 0-300-10903-2 (cloth : alk. paper)

1. Nonprofit organizations—Management. 2. Nonprofit organizations. 3. Charitable uses, trusts, and foundations. I. Powell, Walter W. II. Steinberg, Richard.
HD62.6.N67 2006
338.7'4—dc22 2006009076

A catalogue record for this book is available from the British Library.

The paper in this book meets the guidelines for permanence and durability of the Committee on Production Guidelines for Book Longevity of the Council on Library Resources.

10 9 8 7 6 5 4 3

TO

Gabriel G. Rudney, Burton A. Weisbrod, *and* John Simon,

for their efforts in creating the field of nonprofit studies

Contents

Preface to the Second Edition

We are very pleased to present this second edition of *The Nonprofit Sector: A Research Handbook.* Some time has passed since the first edition, and scholarly analysis of the nonprofit sector has advanced considerably. We took this opportunity to update and refocus the discussion through twenty-seven new or revised chapters. In doing so, we filled in some conspicuous gaps from the first edition. We widened the coverage of nonprofit industries or fields of endeavor to include religious and membership organizations. We expanded the discussion of philanthropy to include a chapter on economic theories of giving and another on work in the nonprofit sector, including volunteering. We made some progress toward covering the burgeoning literature on nonprofit organizations outside the United States, although clearly more work remains to be done. Some chapters were revised to address international issues, and we commissioned additional chapters on the history of philanthropy in the West, cross-national comparisons of the scope and dimensions of the nonprofit sector, and international nongovernmental organizations. Finally, we added a chapter on the legal framework for nonprofit organizations.

Some chapters from the first edition were omitted—those having to do primarily with the management of nonprofit organizations. This choice was dictated by space limitations as well as the emergence of another volume that covers the subject, *The Jossey-Bass Handbook of Nonprofit Leadership and Management,* 2nd ed., by Robert D. Herman and Associates (San Francisco: Jossey-Bass, 2004). Those chapters that border on management issues (notably the chapter on nonprofit governance) focus on social science research topics rather than providing guidance on good practice.

As the field continues to grow, future editions of this handbook will too. Topics included in the current chapters may well be expanded into chapters of their own. For example, we may someday see chapters dedicated to anthropological, psychological, and consumer behavior theories of giving; non-Western traditions of philanthropy; cross-national comparisons of tax and regulatory regimes; nonprofit think tanks, environmental organizations, primary and secondary educational institutions, disaster relief agencies, self-help groups, and immigrant societies; or cross-sectoral comparisons. New chapters dedicated to the roles of nonprofit organizations could discuss the redistributive, affiliative, expressive, entrepreneurial, misanthropic, and social capital roles played by the sector. We might expand further into the humanities, with chapters on ethics, cross-cultural dimensions of philanthropy, and even representations of philanthropy in literature, pop culture, and other media.

We have tried to minimize unnecessary redundancy but asked our authors to make each chapter self-contained, providing sufficient background for the reader to follow the argument without reading other chapters. Our authors were asked to keep the bulk of their discussion accessible to readers who are not trained in the respective disciplines and fields, but a small amount of detailed content was allowed for those who will appreciate it. Where appropriate, we asked authors to include international and comparative perspectives, small and informal organizations, and discussion of the "dark sides" of philanthropy and nonprofit organizations.

Acknowledgments

Funding and support were provided by the McCormick Tribune Foundation, the Aspen Institute's Nonprofit Sector Research Fund, the Center for Social Innovation at the Stanford University Graduate School of Business, and the Center on Philanthropy at Indiana University. Many individuals were helpful at the planning stage for this project, including Dwight Burlingame, Paul DiMaggio, Peter Dobkin Hall, Leslie Lenkowsky, Janet Huettner, Kevin Robbins, Kathryn Steinberg, Eugene Tempel, Mary Tschirhart, Burton Weisbrod, and James Wood. Numerous individuals commented on drafts of individual chapters, including Alan Abramson, Helmut Anheier, Wolfgang Bielefeld, John Boli, Evelyn Brody, Arthur Brooks, Eleanor Brown, Jeffrey Brudney, Dwight Burlingame, Mark Chaves, Jeannette Colyvas, Tom Davis, Benjamin Deufel, Marion Fremont-Smith, Philip Grossman, David Hammack, Zeke Hasenfeld, Robert Herman, Jerome Himmelstein, Alan Hough, Hokyu Hwang, Estelle James, Stan Katz, Sheila Kennedy, Dan Kessler, Jennifer Kuan, Leslie Lenkowsky, Tami Mark, Kathleen McCarthy, Deborah Minkoff, Adil Nadjam, Colleen O'Neal, Kelley Porter, Anne Preston, Nancy Robertson, Patrick Rooney, Kerstin Sahlin-Andersson, Adrian Sargeant, Marc Schneiberg, Mark Davidson Schuster, Steven Schwartz, W. Richard Scott, Erik Shokkaert, David Horton Smith, David Suarez, Andrew Walsh, Natalie Webb, Burton Weisbrod, Mark Wilhelm, Dennis Young, and Mayer Zald. The editors thank Tanya Chamberlain and Natalie Harvey for secretarial assistance.

Introduction

RICHARD STEINBERG
WALTER W. POWELL

Any society has a multiplicity of tasks and an accompanying variety of ways to accomplish them. Some tasks are undertaken by individuals, others by organizations, formal and informal. Organizations are multidimensional, and these dimensions vary widely from organization to organization. This volume focuses on one such dimension, the structure of ownership, and one kind of entity, the nonprofit organization. The chapters herein assess which tasks are undertaken by nonprofit organizations, either alone or in combination with or competition with other kinds of entities, and explore the reasons for these patterns. The authors analyze the common elements linking advocacy, charitable assistance, higher education, health care, arts performances, residential nursing care, and religious ceremonies, all of which are often provided by nonprofit organizations. They also examine patterns of convergence or differentiation when nonprofits compete with the other sectors. Finally, the authors assess whether nonprofit organizations should receive special regulatory privileges and tax breaks or whether virtue should serve as its own reward.

This volume makes the constructive argument that, despite considerable diversity and sometimes fuzzy boundaries, nonprofit studies is a coherent and valuable line of scholarly inquiry. To sustain this argument, we first need to define our terms.

SCOPE

Nonprofit organizations are ubiquitous. Many people are born in a nonprofit hospital, attend a nonprofit university, send their children to a nonprofit day-care center, worship at a nonprofit religious institution, watch the performances of nonprofit symphonies and dance companies, visit their parents in a nonprofit nursing home, and face the end of their life in a nonprofit hospice. Some need the services of nonprofit job-training organizations, soup kitchens, family counseling, and housing assistance agencies. People hope that nonprofit health-research associations will find cures and treatments for the ails they study, that nonprofit think tanks and advocacy groups will foster a better society, and that international nongovernmental organizations will promote the spread of human rights and economic development. We fear that some nonprofits will divide us into warring factions, that tax breaks will be wasted on largely unaccountable and antidemocratic organizations, or that the wrong side will win the advocacy wars. What factors define this diverse collection of organizations and causes?

Following Hansmann (1980), we define a *nonprofit organization* as one that is precluded, by external regulation or its own governance structure, from distributing its financial surplus to those who control the use of organizational assets. Nonprofit boards have some ownership rights, such as the right to direct the use of resources, but not others, such as the rights to profit from that use of resources and to sell these rights to others for a profit (Ben-Ner and Jones 1995). Other definitions are available, of course, and we consider them later, but this definition has the virtue of being embodied in the nonprofit corporation statutes of all fifty states in the United States. Salamon and Anheier have also found the concept of nondistribution useful in their efforts to define a set of institutions cross-nationally (1992; also Anheier and Salamon, this volume). Nondistribution has the additional virtue of defining things in terms of what they are rather than what they are not (Lohmann 1989), even if the label *nonprofit* does not immediately bring the nondistribution definition to mind. Finally, Hansmann's definition has the virtue of defining an organizational type by its structure of control rights rather than by a possibly inaccurate self-statement of purpose.

Next, we define the *nonprofit sector* as the collection of private entities defined as nonprofit. Hall (this volume) argues that the shift in focus from "*what* voluntary associations, charitable trusts, eleemosynary corporations, cooperatives, religious bodies, and other nonproprietary entities and activities did" to "ownership form as the framework for enquiry" is a modern definition that some scholars have criticized. We shall return to the question of whether this focus is indeed useful.

In most chapters, the nonprofit sector is clearly distinguished from for-profit and government sectors. *For-profit firms* provide full ownership rights—that is, the rights to direct, profit from, and sell ownership—to those in control of organizational assets. In democratic regimes, *government agencies* are owned by an electorate and its chosen representatives. Weisbrod (1988) notes that most governments restrict their officeholders from receiving distributions of budgetary surplus, so he regards government agencies as public nonprofits. If, instead, we regard the electorate as the ultimate owners of government assets, profit distribution does occur. Either way, government is distinguished by its monopoly on legitimate coercive power and the rules and procedures that are necessary so that this power is seen as legitimate and appropriate (Clemens, this volume).

Most leading theories of the role of the nonprofit sector adopt this concept of a trichotomy of sectors—nonprofit, for-profit, and government. Each sector responds to failures to deliver the appropriate quantity or quality of services or to make those services available to appropriate constituencies. This collection of theories has become known as *three-failures theory* (detailed in Steinberg, this volume). For-profits are good at meeting consumer needs when two conditions are met. First, consumers must be well informed about the quality and quantity of their purchase, or at least protected from any misperceptions by regulation, reputation, and warranties. Second, purchases must be individually, rather than collectively, consumed. Violation of the first condition is known as *contract failure* (Hansmann 1980), and when this occurs, nonprofits are likely to be more trustworthy because the profit-distribution motive is removed. Violations of the second condition are often used to justify government expenditures, but such expenditures must accord with the majority wishes of the electorate. The minority desiring that more be spent on collectively consumed services or wanting these services provided in a different way (say, with a religious focus) view government's attention to the majority as a source of *government failure* and, in response, may choose to support nonprofits with their donations (Weisbrod 1975). As a result, nonprofits suffer from philanthropic insufficiency, amateurism, paternalism, and particularism, the chief forms of *voluntary failure.* Government agencies and for-profit firms provide goods and services that are poorly provided by nonprofits, and this completes the circle of three-failure theory (Salamon 1987).

Nonprofits are further categorized in various ways, one of which is relevant here. *Charitable organizations* (in common usage, not the legal sense) are organizations concerned with helping those in need of food, shelter, and other necessities of life. In the legal sense, charitable organizations include those organizations that help the needy but also include churches, schools, hospitals, and social service organizations, which generally benefit an indefinite class of individuals. They are distinguished from *mutual benefit organizations,* such as labor unions, trade associations, and social clubs, which are also nonprofit but benefit a specific class of members. Charitable organizations are treated more favorably under tax and regulatory laws, so that favored churches are counted as charitable even though they usually have members that benefit from religious services. Most chapters in this book concern charitable organizations (in the legal sense), but Tschirhart's chapter examines mutual benefit organizations.

THE BOUNDARIES OF THE SECTOR

Three problems occur when we define our field in terms of nondistribution (see, for example, Bilodeau and Steinberg 2006). The first is the challenge of constructing an operational definition of profit distribution. Questions arise with respect to who is a controlling party, what is a distribution of profit (rather than a payment to a resource supplier), and what is excessive executive compensation. There are also issues relating to when self-dealing (purchases from companies owned by nonprofit board members) is impermissible and how nonprofit assets can be lawfully used by for-profit entities (either when the nonprofit converts its status or when it enters into joint ventures like those between nonprofit universities and biotechnology firms). The way in which these questions are answered can have powerful effects on the distinctive roles and behaviors of nonprofit organizations.

Second, the boundaries of many organizations are unclear. Coase (1937) defined the boundary of a firm as the division between internal nonmarket transactions and external market transactions. This definition works well for for-profit firms; however, nonprofits often provide services to clients for free, a nonmarket transaction with agents that are clearly outside the organizational boundary. In addition, when nonprofits are members of a for-profit shell corporation, possess for-profit subsidiaries, or participate in joint ventures with for-profit firms, it can be extremely hard to isolate the nondistributing parts and ensure they function as an independent entity.

A third challenge in some cases is distinguishing private nonprofit organizations from public government agencies. What constitutes separation from government, especially in cases where an organization receives nearly all its resources from purchase-of-service contracts with the government? Is it hiring and firing power, or the freedom to decide objectives and methods of implementation? When does public regulation amount to a taking of nonprofit property? The formal dividing line was quite vague and fluid earlier in the history of the United States (Hall 1987), and the rapid growth of exclusively government-funded social service agencies in the 1960s made the problem more evident (Smith and Lipsky 1993).

This book is mostly about the nonprofit sector, but some

chapters concern philanthropy, or the volunteering of time, money, and property. Most donations to formal organizations are given to nonprofits, but the other two sectors also benefit from donations and volunteering and some philanthropy is given directly to individuals (Havens, O'Herlihy, and Schervish; Leete; both this volume). Further, many nonprofits receive the bulk of their revenues from commercial sales and contracts, benefiting from little or no philanthropy (Boris and Steuerle; Anheier and Salamon; both this volume). The concepts of nonprofit and philanthropic overlap only in part, but that overlap seems sufficient to warrant the attention we have paid to philanthropy in this volume.

To this point, we have defined philanthropy loosely as consisting of gifts of time, money, or property. When we look at the category more closely, we see that like the boundaries of the nonprofit sector, the boundaries of philanthropy are also blurry. Writers have defined *philanthropy* as "voluntary action for the public good" (Payton 1984) or "love to mankind; practical benevolence towards men in general; the disposition or active effort to promote the happiness and well-being of one's fellow-men" (*Oxford English Dictionary* 1989). Some definitions of philanthropy include both the act and the institutions that facilitate that act *(philanthropies),* but here we focus on the first meaning.

There is, of course, the difficulty of dividing philanthropy from *misanthropy,* or voluntary action *against* the public good. This challenge is particularly true for gifts supporting advocacy, where voluntary action supports causes that the opposition views as against the public good. At various times and places, gifts to religious denominations, labor unions, private foundations, and social movements have been declared, by governmental authorities, to be against the public good. The lively debate over this dividing line, however, makes voluntary action, thought by many participants to be for the public good, into an element for scholarly inquiry.

To define philanthropy as people, actions, and institutions doing what they think is good for others is too all-encompassing, however. In a nuanced discussion of the meaning of philanthropy, Van Til asks, "Does the concept include all thoughts, words, and deeds that involve the love of fellow humans (the first dictionary definition)? Or should it be restricted to the transfer of funds from one such being to another (which raises the question of its distinction from charity)? And if the latter, should it then be further restricted to such transfers as are mediated by formal institutions (those we earlier saw identified by *Webster's* as 'philanthropies')?" (1990:21). Most chapters in this volume employ the more restrictive definition, including donations and volunteering directed to formal organizations.

MULTIPLE DEFINITIONS AND CATEGORIZATIONS

There are many ways to divide the world into categories and many labels attached to these categories. Our focus is on nonprofit organizations and philanthropy, but a variety of alternative nomenclatures are found in the literature and may confuse some readers. Therefore, we provide a catalog of commonly used terms in order to distinguish the synonyms from the alternative partitions. Consider first the variety of labels attached to the broad terrain of nonprofit organizations. As noted, nonprofit (or not-for-profit) organizations are defined by the structure of ownership. *Nongovernmental organizations* (NGOs) have various definitions, but it is common to define them similarly to private nonprofit organizations (Boli, this volume). Likewise, the term *third sector* is often used synonymously with nonprofits, voluntary sector organizations, or other terms defined below. The International Society for Third-Sector Research (ISTR) defines its terms implicitly, listing its mission as "promoting research and education in the fields of civil society, philanthropy, and the nonprofit sector" (http://www.istr.org/about). This definition combines analysis of organizations and individuals in a way similar to this volume.

Voluntary organizations are those that receive substantial contributions of time (volunteering), below-cost goods or services, or money. As noted earlier, many nonprofit organizations receive little or no donations and some for-profit organizations and government agencies receive substantial contributions of time and money. Nevertheless, some writers regard the voluntary sector as synonymous with the nonprofit sector, while others restrict the term to the first definition, resulting in some confusion.

Independent sector organizations are those categorized under the U.S. Internal Revenue Code as section 501(c)(3) or 501(c)(4) organizations, consisting of all charitable (in the legal sense) and some mutual benefit nonprofits. As detailed later in this book, independent sector organizations are hardly financially independent, and nominally independent organizations are dependent on the state (and vice versa) in a variety of ways (Boris and Steuerle; Smith and Grønbjerg; both this volume). *Tax-exempt entities* include various sorts of profit-distributing and nondistributing organizations that are exempt from the U.S. Federal Corporate Income Tax (Simon, Dale, and Chisolm, this volume).

Nonmarket institutions include government agencies, nonprofit organizations, consumer cooperatives, social clubs, unincorporated associations, and the like. This category is the organizing principle adopted by the Public Choice Society. In contrast, the International Centre of Research and Information on the Public and Cooperative Economy (CIRIEC) is dedicated to the study of the "public, social, and cooperative economy." The *social economy* includes "private companies that . . . provide goods, services, insurance or finance, in which the distribution of surpluses and the decision-making processes are not directly linked to the share capital of each member" as well as "those economic agents whose main function is to produce services not intended for sale, for particular groups of households, financed by the voluntary contributions of families" (Barea Tejeiro 1990:400). This concept includes cooperatives, mutuals, credit unions, labor-managed firms, and associations, some of which distribute their profits according to democratic decision-making processes.

Ben-Ner (1986) distinguishes organizations that are controlled by patron- or demand-side stakeholders (nonprofits and consumer cooperatives) from those that are controlled by supply-side-stakeholders (firms and producer cooperatives), the key distinction being whether the supplier of resources consumes the resulting services.

Several concepts relate to philanthropy and philanthropic acts. Schervish broadens the topic to include the *economy of caring:* "[A] broad definition of philanthropy . . . encompasses all those activities of giving and volunteering by which an individual responds directly to those moral signals that communicate need. Excluded would be those social relationships in which an individual responds to the material medium of needs voiced through dollars (as in the commercial sphere) or through campaign contributions and votes (as in the political sphere). . . . [This definition includes] certain forms of intra-family transfers of time and money, gifts of money to individuals, political contributions of time and money, and various business expenditures designed to provide benefits to employees and customers that exceed market standards" (1993:224). To this list, one might add donations of blood, organs, and genomic materials.

From psychology, we have the study of *pro-social behavior,* defined by Eisenberg and Mussen as "voluntary actions intended to benefit others" regardless of the motive behind those actions. This includes *altruism,* defined as "voluntary actions intended to benefit others that are intrinsically motivated," as a subset of pro-social behavior, where intrinsic motivations include concern and sympathy for others (1989:3).

From anthropology, we have the *gift relationship,* defined by contrast to commodity exchange. O'Neal explains, "As anthropologists now understand, the gift entails a threefold obligation to give, receive and repay, and the exchange of gifts establishes relations among giver, receiver and gift. The gift is comprised of objects, services and symbolic emblems that include goods, property, money, work, persons, food, hospitality, names, titles, and other signs of honor and status" (2002:3) Anthropologists conceive of gifts in a fashion that does not neatly correspond to ideas of philanthropy, giving, and volunteering. The gift is defined in terms of systems of obligation rather than "voluntary action for the public good" or "active effort to promote the happiness and well-being of one's fellow-men," and gift-giving can even be an act of hostility, designed to bankrupt or dishonor the recipient who cannot reciprocate. The anthropological perspective fosters a better understanding of some of the possible darker sides of philanthropy.

Four concepts cut across the dividing lines of individuals and organizations: social capital, civil society, voluntary action, and the commons. The concept of social capital entered contemporary social science discourse with contributions by Loury (1977), Bourdieu (1980), and Coleman (1988). These writers defined social capital as a resource for individuals stemming from family relations and community social organization. More recently, some writers, such as Putnam, define social capital in terms of the networks themselves: "Whereas physical capital refers to physical objects and human capital refers to properties of individuals, social capital refers to connections among individuals—social networks and the norms of reciprocity and trustworthiness that arise from them" (2000:19).

The concept of *civil society* has been around since Hobbes (1651), and after long neglect has reentered the literature. Edwards discusses the multiplicity of common definitions, elaborating on the most relevant: "Civil society has become a notoriously slippery concept. . . . [One part of the literature] sees civil society as a part of society distinct from states and markets, formed for the purposes of advancing common interests and facilitating collective action. Most commonly referred to as the 'third sector,' civil society in this sense contains all associations and networks between the family and the state, except firms" (2004:vi–viii).

Voluntary action was the original defining concept for the Association for Research on Voluntary Action and Nonprofit Organizations (ARNOVA; formerly the Association of Voluntary Action Scholars, or AVAS). ARNOVA defined voluntary action as "all kinds of noncoerced human behavior, collective or individual, that is engaged in because of a commitment to values other than direct, immediate remuneration. Thus, voluntary action includes . . . a focus on voluntary association, social movements, cause groups, voluntarism, interest groups, pluralism, citizen participation, consumer groups, participatory democracy, volunteering, altruism, helping behavior, philanthropy, social clubs, leisure behavior, political participation, religious sects, etc." (*Journal of Voluntary Action Research* 1985, inside cover).

Lohmann objects to defining the sector in terms of what it is not. Instead, he presents the *commons,* which denote "the economic dimensions of a large and diverse set of voluntary collective action by service clubs; artistic, scientific, and amateur athletic societies; social and political movements; religious and philosophical groups; and other groups that form the core of the voluntary sector" (1989:373). The definition has evolved, so that Dart refers to the commons as "an organizational space containing activity focused on prosocial behaviors, mutuality, voluntary labor, and the production of collective goods" (2004:292).

ORGANIZATION OF THE BOOK

The chapters are organized around six themes. The first part discusses the history and scope of the nonprofit sector. The next part considers nonprofits and the marketplace, including the many and varied ways in which nonprofits engage in economic production, participate in various output and input markets, and compete or collaborate with for-profit firms. The third part considers nonprofits and the polity. The authors consider political theories of nonprofit organization and issues of competition, collaboration, and opposition between state and private nonprofit organizations. We also include in this section the tax treatment of nonprofits and donors, government regulation of nonprofits, and the governance role of transnational nongovernmental organizations.

The fourth and largest part focuses on those domains of modern life where nonprofits play a significant role in providing goods and services. These chapters cover foundations, health care, social services, the arts, higher education, religion, and urban community organizations. The fifth part examines participation in the nonprofit sector and assesses factors that explain the extent and nature of engagement in the sector. These chapters discuss membership associations, patterns of giving, and motives for giving. The concluding part contains three chapters on the themes of mission and governance.

History and Scope of the Nonprofit Sector

The first chapter, by Kevin Robbins, assembles the various threads of the philanthropic tradition in Western history and illustrates how these diverse strands have become intertwined. He first traces patterns of spiritual, social, and moral imperatives behind philanthropy. Second, he follows the evolution of charitable purposes and uses toward today's focus on the general quality of life and on the misfortunate, marginalized, and disfranchised. He then considers the history of regulation of philanthropy. Finally, he portrays the beginnings of the scientific philanthropy movement, with its emphasis on efficient institutions and managerial practices. He finds evidence on these themes from ancient Jewish, Greek, Roman, early Christian, Byzantine, late medieval and early modern, and modern European cultures.

In chapter 2, Peter Dobkin Hall argues that today's nonprofit sector is the result of the federal tax code, which, in the 1950s, organized the complex domain of eleemosynary corporations, charitable trusts, and mutual benefit associations into one section of the code. He surveys the evolution of these organizations and activities from colonial times to the present, tracing the origins of the private sector, the differentiation of charitable and noncharitable corporations, the evolution of philanthropic giving and volunteering, and the partnership between government and nonprofit enterprise following the expansion of the welfare state. Hall's account covers the role of nonprofits and their predecessors in American religious life, industrialization, social movements, and political reform, portraying the capacity of these institutions to facilitate both grassroots empowerment (as in the civil rights movement) and elite hegemony (as in the recent conservative revolution).

There are many myths about the nonprofit sector in the United States that can only be answered with the data summarized by Elizabeth Boris and Eugene Steuerle. Contrary to popular opinion, most nonprofit organizations are not concerned with helping the needy. In addition, donations and volunteer labor provide only a small share of nonprofit resources. About 85 percent of these donations come from living individual donors rather than corporations, foundations, and charitable bequests. We also learn that nonprofit organizations produced 4.2 percent of gross domestic product in 2000, but because of volunteers, interactions with government, and the influence of these things on civil society, the sector's impact is far greater than its measured production of goods and services. The quality of data on the nonprofit sector has improved considerably since the publication of this handbook's first edition, but there are still major gaps in our knowledge of even such basic statistics as the number of organizations.

Helmut Anheier and Lester Salamon take on the challenging topic of the international scope of the nonprofit sector. They find a marked increase in the availability of data on the size and scope of the sector; they also find that the sector itself is growing rapidly. Correspondingly, the nonprofit sector has moved to the center of many policy debates around the world. The authors' prior research contributed enormously to the development of a consistent set of cross-national statistics; nevertheless, international comparisons remain plagued by different definitions, varying legal status, and diverse forms of record keeping. Regardless, the patterns that are emerging highlight the inadequacies of existing theories on the role of nonprofit organizations and suggest key themes for future theorizing.

Nonprofits and the Marketplace

Richard Steinberg details the most developed theoretical approach to nonprofits, the three-failures theory, summarizing empirical work that tests various predictions of the theory. Then he highlights two shortcomings of the approach: first, the lack of a well-integrated supply side and, second, the excessive focus on economic efficiency to the exclusion of distribution, the cultivation of consumer preferences, and the expressive and affiliative functions of many nonprofit organizations. He then outlines an approach to remedy these defects. Although limited progress has been made toward implementing that approach, several lines of research are promising. He concludes with illustrations of how economic theories can contribute to the design of good public policies toward nonprofits.

Eleanor Brown and Al Slivinski examine the many markets that nonprofits participate in, competing or collaborating with other nonprofits, for-profits, and (to a lesser extent in this chapter) government agencies. Nonprofits participate in output markets, where their goods and services are sold or given away, but they also participate in resource and input markets for acquiring labor, capital, and grants and donations. The authors carefully point out the ways in which organizations that are motivated by various missions compete differently from those motivated by profits, and discuss empirical evidence that validates these distinctions.

Laura Leete provides a comprehensive picture of the nature of the nonprofit labor force in the United States, including both paid workers and volunteers. She summarizes studies that compare nonprofit workers with those in other sectors with respect to pay, executive compensation, working conditions, and career mobility. She examines the challenges of managing and motivating volunteers and looks at the relationship between volunteer labor and gifts of money to see whether they supplement or substitute for each other.

Finally, she considers several policy implications of these studies, including the tax treatment of donations of volunteer time, employment discrimination policy, and policies that regulate the family-work tradeoff.

Joseph Galaskiewicz and Michelle Sinclair Coleman offer a roadmap to the growing and highly varied terrain of nonprofit-business partnerships. This terrain encompasses far more than corporate donations to charity, although that subject is well covered in the chapter. Galaskiewicz and Coleman find that corporate donations continue even during recessions and periods of merger-mania and that corporate motives are quite complicated. Partnerships also arise for strategic, commercial, and political reasons, taking a variety of forms including product donations, cause-related marketing, and joint ventures. Collaboration across sectors is not easy because for-profits and nonprofits have such different missions and cultures. Each partner must consider the costs and benefits of collaboration, including financial benefits but also legitimation, organizational learning, the risk that nonprofits will lose sight of their core mission, the risk that corporations will alienate their customers (or that nonprofits will lose their donors) if the partnership is tainted by controversy, and the added cost and complexity of decision making.

Nonprofits and the Polity

Elisabeth Clemens looks at political theories of nonprofit organization. Nonprofit organizations and associations are political constructions, but they operate outside the formal political sphere. The market model of democracy serves as a prominent political theory of nonprofits, but many other theories of politics color the claims we make about nonprofit organizations and their role in civil society. Clemens begins by discussing the disputed role of nonprofit organizations in generating greater political participation. Next, she discusses arguments that participation generates incivility and apathy and evaluates whether nonprofit-engendered participation is truly helpful to democratic processes. She concludes with a discussion of the politics of partnership between government agencies and nonprofit organizations.

Steven Rathgeb Smith and Kirsten Grønbjerg discuss and analyze the multifaceted and complex relationships between nonprofits and governments. They begin by discussing the roles of collaboration in service delivery and policy formation. Next they present three models of government-nonprofit relations. The first approach, demand/supply, is akin to three-failures theory but also incorporates transactions costs; Smith and Grønbjerg provide different perspectives on this theory from the other chapters in this volume. Second is the civil society/social movement approach, which focuses on the impact of government and the nonprofit sector on civil society as well as the effect of social movements and nonprofits on government and public policy. The third, neo-institutionalist approach, is explicitly comparative, focusing on the profound effects on institutional structures and the processes by which social and organizational structures become institutionalized. The three approaches span several disciplines, with the first closely linked to economic models, the second to sociological and political models, and the third to cross-disciplinary approaches to large-scale institutions.

Evelyn Brody examines the legal foundation of nonprofits, finding that the law is a relatively weak force constraining nonprofit operations. As long as organizations pursue charitable purposes, honor donor intent, and refrain from private inurement, no laws tell the entity or its managers how to "do" charity. Specifically, the law endows a charity's board with full governance authority, generally granting only the state attorney general with standing to sue for breach of fiduciary duties. This autonomy is sensible, Brody argues, because we probably do not want the state to run charities, but it often leads to insufficient attention by both nonprofit managers and charity regulators. Within this broad framework, Brody discusses the right of association, permissible nonprofit purposes, the choice of organizational form, modification of gift restrictions, fiduciary duties, and mandated public disclosures. She concludes with a brief discussion of peer and self-regulatory efforts to improve charity governance and operations.

In our longest chapter, John Simon, Harvey Dale, and Laura Chisolm offer a comprehensive analysis of the tax treatments of donations and nonprofit entities. Chief justice John Marshall, citing Daniel Webster, is oft quoted for his decision in *McCulloch v. Maryland* (1819): "That the power to tax involves the power to destroy . . . [is] not to be denied." Thus, the conditions that determine whether nonprofit and donor activities are or are not taxed have powerful effects on the role and health of the nonprofit sector. The authors consider the ways in which tax policy intersects with such vital issues as federal "subsidy" of charities and donors, nonprofit political activity, church autonomy, nonprofit/for-profit joint ventures, fiduciary abuses, executive compensation, and "unfair" competition with for-profit firms. The design of tax policies toward donors and nonprofit organizations has been hampered by ambiguous or absent legislative intent and conflicting theories of the appropriate definition of taxable income, the role of nonprofit organizations, and the use of tax policies to obtain objectives that we cannot, or choose not to, regulate in more straightforward ways. The authors organize their discussion around four functions of tax policy: support, equity, regulation, and border patrol, and thereby impose order on this complex and fundamental set of issues.

Craig Jenkins notes the tremendous growth in the number and scope of nonprofit advocacy groups in the United States. There are many reasons for this increase, including the mobilization of previously excluded and marginalized groups, elite philanthropy, and a more permeable political system. He discusses the factors that account for the survival and maintenance of nonprofit advocacy organizations. Finally, he considers evaluation: advocacy can be evaluated as something that affects the formation of policies or as an embedded process focused on ensuring broad and inclusive access. The new nonprofit advocates have had success by both measures, but major inequities in political representation and access remain.

John Boli provides a comprehensive overview of those voluntary associations, confederations, and councils that transcend national boundaries. He charts the growth of these international nongovernmental organizations (INGOs) from an initial spurt in the late nineteenth century through a slowdown during the two world wars to a sharp acceleration thereafter. The most prominent INGOs are devoted to such issues as human and women's rights, environmental quality, development, and disaster relief, but these constitute a small proportion of the total. Most INGOs are lesser known and found in technical, scientific, business, professional, and infrastructure domains. Membership in INGOs is growing most quickly among the poorer and more peripheral countries of the world. INGOs operate in the absence of a world government, having relations and effects on nation-states, intergovernmental organizations, and transnational corporations.

Key Activities in the Nonprofit Sector

Foundations are critical intermediaries in the nonprofit world, offering financial support and expertise, while exerting control and guidance. Kenneth Prewitt discusses the various ways of classifying foundations: by legal status, funding priorities, geographic scope, and change strategies promoted. He then surveys alternative funding strategies and discusses the history of foundations in America (and, more briefly, Europe). His emphasis is on the role of institutions—on what foundations do better than the state, the market, or other kinds of nonprofit organizations.

Health care is the most resource-intensive domain of nonprofit activity in the United States; it is also where many of the largest nonprofits are located. Yet this is no secure bastion of nonprofit enterprise. Nonprofit hospitals, nursing homes, mental health centers, health insurers, and hospices face intense competition from for-profit and in many cases government health organizations, challenging both their financial viability and public legitimacy. Mark Schlesinger and Bradford Gray survey this intersectoral competition with three key questions in mind. First, what difference does sector make? The authors survey hundreds of studies on the question, arguing that inconsistent results across studies do not reflect an absence of differences (as some scholars contend). Rather, the extent to which nonprofit and for-profit behavior differs depends on the nature of the service, the market conditions under which organizations operate, and the external constraints on their behavior. Second, why are perceptions of the nonprofit sector among both the public and academics so often at variance with these patterns of performance? Schlesinger and Gray attribute these misperceptions to a limited public understanding of ownership and an academic literature that is fragmented across disciplines. Third, why do nonprofit market shares vary so dramatically across health subsectors and over time? Schlesinger and Gray contend that these patterns can be best understood by a life-cycle theory of ownership in the context of changing medical technology. The authors conclude by discussing the policy relevance of these statistical results and the contribution of studies of health-care organizations to nonprofit studies more generally.

Social care has long been a cornerstone of the nonprofit sector; before governments provided social services, charitable hospices, almshouses, churches, and communities offered care to the needy and indigent. With the growth of the modern state, the position of nonprofits in delivering social care has become more complex. Jeremy Kendall, Martin Knapp, and Julien Forder guide us through this new territory, assessing the role of the social service sector in Western democracies. Social care is different from other charitable realms in part because the quality of ongoing and personal relationships between the caregiver and client is such a prominent determinant of the quality of service. In other ways, social care raises the same questions common to many topics in this section about cross-sectoral differences in behavior and determinants of sectoral shares, and we learn what light social care organizations can shed on these questions.

The realm of the arts captures the full gamut of nonprofit enterprise, from famous, established museums and their vast holdings of cultural treasures to experimental organizations pursuing avant-garde expressions that may never become part of cultural memory. The arts, broadly defined, also include elements of popular and folk culture, produced by for-profit firms or displayed in governmental museums. Paul DiMaggio surveys this landscape, from established organizations to minimalist ones, explaining why nonprofits are such a major presence in some activities and why market provision is more salient in others. He also explores the effect of nonprofit ownership on organizational behavior. Finally, he analyzes how the arts and cultural domains evolve in the face of demographic, social, and technological change.

Many of our readers either study at or work for an institution of higher education and so may find that the chapter by Patricia Gumport and Stuart Snydman speaks to their current experiences. Higher education provides a natural experiment with which to test the various theories on the roles of the sectors. Trends in the United States are particularly evocative, as differences in the finance, mission, and governance of public and private institutions of higher education are blurred by a variety of forces. Competition for resources has led many private and public universities to behave like commercial enterprises, and joint ventures with for-profit firms (particularly in the field of biotechnology) have become an important and controversial source of revenue. For-profit colleges and universities have entered the marketplace and are growing rapidly, providing a new challenge for the nonmarket missions of incumbents. New hybrid organizational forms are emerging that challenge presumed distinctions between the sectors.

The most active nonprofit realm with regard to individual participation is religion. Wendy Cadge and Robert Wuthnow offer a tour of this landscape, noting its powerful historical roots as well as its many surprising, contemporary forms. The literatures on religion and nonprofit organization have developed separately, but scholars have recently noted the connections. There is a long history of sometimes contentious, sometimes cooperative, sometimes indistinct relations between religious institutions and the state. Most recently, the controversy over government funding of explicitly religious social service agencies through "charitable choice" programs has raised constitutional issues and tested claims regarding religious service delivery.

The nonprofit sector also appears in settings where markets have failed and the state has retreated, as evident in disadvantaged urban areas. Sarah Deschenes, Milbrey McLaughlin, and Jennifer O'Donoghue consider the role of neighborhood organizations in the healthy development of low-income urban youth. Neighborhood-based community organizations operate where schools, health-care facilities, and social service agencies have failed and provide the tools, attitudes, competencies, and connections essential to healthy youth development. Neighborhood organizations do not just supplement government; they provide a different focus on deinstitutionalized means, individualized problem definition, and progressive working relationships. The authors discuss attributes of successful neighborhood organizations—organizational structure, funding, and interorganizational relationships—that enable or constrain their effectiveness.

Who Participates in the Nonprofit Sector and Why?

Most of our chapters focus on public-benefit nonprofits. Mary Tschirhart surveys the literature on the rest of the nonprofit sector—those agencies that provide services to members, active or passive. She notes that many of the issues surrounding membership organizations are common to all nonprofits, then focuses on four issues unique to this subsector. First she discusses the various taxonomies applied to the subsector. Next she evaluates claims about the value of association. Then she summarizes literature on the determinants of member entry, retention, and participation. Finally, she analyzes member governance, organizational structures, and trends.

In the first edition of this handbook, Christopher Jencks (1987) described "Who Gives to What?" This time, John Havens, Mary O'Herlihy, and Paul Schervish also ask "how much" and "how." They discuss gifts from living donors to nonprofit organizations, charitable bequests, and several aspects of informal giving to individuals outside the family. As in the earlier chapter by Jencks, they summarize what is known about amounts given by various socioeconomic and demographic groups and about the composition of recipient nonprofits. They also discuss a variety of institutional forms, some new, that facilitate giving, including family and private foundations, donor-advised funds, charitable gift annuities, and charitable trusts.

The next chapter, by Lise Vesterlund, summarizes mostly economic theories on motivations for giving. She argues that by understanding donor motivations, we can design better public policies and improve nonprofit and campaign management. First, she looks at empirical studies summarizing donor reactions to changes in their income and in donor cost per dollar contributed. Vesterlund argues that such studies help in the design of tax policy toward donations and in forecasting future donations. Next, she summarizes the many taxonomies of motivation that have been developed, highlighting the importance of an overriding distinction between motivations keyed on the provision of nonprofit outputs *(public motivations)* and those keyed on personal and psychological benefits to the act of giving *(private motivations).* Surprisingly, publicly motivated donors *free ride,* giving too little and benefiting from the contributions of others, whereas privately motivated donors supply the socially optimal level of donations. She summarizes evidence on the frequency of various motivations as revealed in statistical studies of natural data and in laboratory studies with human subjects acting as donors. Finally, she looks at newer and broader theories of giving that emphasize social norms, network interactions, repeated interaction, information revelation, and alternative mechanisms such as raffles and matches.

Mission and Governance

Debra Minkoff and Walter Powell look at how the nonprofit mission is beset with the twin pulls of dedication to a goal and the opportunities and contingencies posed by the environment, assessing the forces that enable organizations to retain fidelity to their mission or alter it in the face of external pressures. They outline dominant responses by organizations in the face of challenges to their mission, and analyze the organizational factors that influence whether nonprofits bend or break in response to winds of change.

Nonprofit assets are controlled by a board of directors that cannot personally profit from their decisions. Board-member motivations must therefore come from other sources, and these motivations shape the evolution of nonprofit mission and effectiveness. Francie Ostrower and Melissa Stone examine nonprofit governance, finding that boards defy sweeping generalizations, that context matters, and that the study of boards should be integrated with broader studies of philanthropy, nonprofit organization, and civic participation. They survey the legal context of regulating boards, then discuss the determinants and consequences of board composition, board-staff relations, and board roles and effectiveness. They conclude with a more detailed discussion of nonprofit boards in health-care industries.

In recent years, a host of forces such as funding crises, declining government service provision, new technologies, and more entrepreneurial managers have led nonprofits to engage in activities that would have not been considered previously. Howard Tuckman and Cyril Chang assess whether these varied commercial ventures enhance or distort nonprofit mission. They begin with motivations for commercialization and provide alternative definitions of the phenomenon. Under some definitions, outsourcing is seen as a commercial activity, bringing the same risks and rewards as commercial ventures. They focus on the chief asserted disadvantage of commercial activity—mission drift—but also on ways that commercial activity can benefit mission attainment. These factors are examined in detail in the context of three examples: distance learning, technology transfer, and business incubators.

THE FIELD OF NONPROFIT AND PHILANTHROPIC STUDIES

The chapters in this volume make the case that private nondistributing organizations behave differently, are organized differently, and play a different role in society than distributing organizations and governments. There are certainly vast differences among the many kinds of nonprofits such that they may, for some purposes, be studied separately (as they are in graduate programs related to health care, arts, or higher education administration and in schools of social work). But common themes arise throughout this book, themes that define the growth of a coherent field of study.

Nondistribution of profits affects the sources of revenue, nature of property rights, and constraints under which organizations operate. Because of the nondistribution constraint, nondistributing organizations often receive donations while profit-distributing entities do not. Publicly traded profit-distributing organizations can secure capital by selling ownership rights as shares of dividend-yielding stock; nondistributing organizations cannot, for dividends constitute a distribution of profit. This affects nonprofit capital structures but also frees nonprofits from the constraining threat of takeover bids. Thus, nonprofits can safely behave in ways not open to distributing entities, either by pursuing socially beneficial activities not rewarded by markets or by squandering resources through indolence, inattention, and incompetence. Nondistributing organizations are treated differently under our tax and regulatory laws, amplifying their tendencies to depart from profit maximization. Finally, nonprofit entrepreneurs and workers differ from their for-profit counterparts in motivation; self-selecting into the sectors on the basis of the differing constraints and regulations. This too amplifies the differences in behavior across the sectors.

While this volume consciously excludes chapters on the management of nonprofit organizations, nondistribution of profits does affect most aspects of management (see also Young 2004). Finance theories appropriate to for-profit organizations need to account for the differences in capital structure resulting from nondistribution and regulatory differences. Nonprofit success is evaluated in terms of mission, rather than a simple bottom line. Hence, rules for capital budgeting and benchmarking need to be adjusted. Nonprofits receive restricted and temporarily restricted funds, and accounting practices must reflect that. Nonprofit revenues come from donors, customers, and bondholders; consequently, stakeholder conflicts must be managed carefully. Nonprofit marketing includes fundraising and social marketing as well as impression management. The laws of nonprofit corporations and trusts diverge in many particulars from business law. Human resource management necessarily includes recruitment and retention of volunteers. Finally, although the expressed, or instrumental, mission of the organization is paramount, the expressive and affiliative dimensions of management are also critical (Mason 1996; Frumkin 2002).

ACKNOWLEDGMENTS

The authors thank Dwight Burlingame, Jeannette Colyvas, Denise Gammal, Julie Hatcher, Hokyu Hwang, Leslie Lenkowsky, Caroline Simard, Kathryn Steinberg, and David Suarez for comments on earlier drafts of this introduction.

REFERENCES

Barea Tejeiro, J. 1990. "Concepto y agentes de la economía social." *Revista CIRIEC-España* 8:109–117. As translated by J. L. Monzón Campos in "Contributions of the Social Economy to the General Interest." *Annals of Public and Cooperative Economics* 68 (1997): 397–408.

Ben-Ner, Avner. 1986. "Nonprofit Organizations: Why Do They Exist in Market Economies?" In *The Economics of Nonprofit Institutions: Studies in Structure and Policy,* ed. Susan Rose-Ackerman. New York: Oxford University Press.

Ben-Ner, Avner, and Derek Jones. 1995. "Employee Participation, Ownership, and Productivity: A Theoretical Framework." *Industrial Relations* 34 (4): 532–554.

Bilodeau, Marc, and Richard Steinberg. 2006. "Donative Nonprofit Organizations." In *Handbook of the Economics of Giving, Altruism, and Reciprocity,* ed. J. Mercier-Ythier and S. C. Kolm. Amsterdam: Elsevier/North-Holland.

Bourdieu, P. 1980. "Le capital social: Notes provisaires." *Actes de la Recherche en Sciences Sociales* 3:2–3.

Coase, Ronald H. 1937. "The Nature of the Firm." *Economica* 4 (16): 386–405.

Coleman, James. 1988. "Social Capital in the Creation of Human Capital." *American Journal of Sociology* 94:S95–S121.

Dart, Raymond. 2004. "Being 'Business-Like' in a Nonprofit Organization: A Grounded and Inductive Typology." *Nonprofit and Voluntary Sector Quarterly* 33:90–310.

Edwards, Michael. 2004. *Civil Society.* Cambridge, UK: Polity.

Eisenberg, Nancy, and Paul H. Mussen. 1989. *The Roots of Prosocial Behavior in Children.* Cambridge: Cambridge University Press.

Frumkin, Peter. 2002. *On Being Nonprofit.* Cambridge, MA: Harvard University Press.

Hall, Peter Dobkin. 1987. "A Historical Overview of the Private Nonprofit Sector." In *The Nonprofit Sector: A Research Handbook,* ed. Walter W. Powell. New Haven: Yale University Press.

Hansmann, Henry. 1980. "The Role of Nonprofit Enterprise." *Yale Law Journal* 89:835–901.

Hobbes, T. 1651. *Leviathan.* Repr., Oxford: Blackwell, 1651.

Jencks, Christopher. 1987. "Who Gives to What?" In *The Nonprofit Sector: A Research Handbook,* ed. Walter W. Powell. New Haven: Yale University Press.

Lohmann, Roger A. 1989. "And Lettuce Is Nonanimal: Towards a Positive Economics of Voluntary Action." *Nonprofit and Voluntary Sector Quarterly* 18:367–383.

Loury, Glenn. 1977. "A Dynamic Theory of Racial Income Differences." In *Women, Minorities, and Employment Discrimination,* ed. P. Wallace and A. LaMond. Lexington, MA: Lexington Books.

Mason, David E. 1996. *Leading and Managing the Expressive Dimension: Harnessing the Hidden Power Source of the Nonprofit Sector.* San Francisco: Jossey-Bass.

O'Neal, Colleen G. 2002. "Toward a Theory of the Modern Gift (Or, Alternatively) Anthropology's Gift and Nonprofit Sector Research" (unpublished paper, draft of Feb. 25).

Oxford English Dictionary, 2nd ed. 1989. Oxford: Oxford University Press.

Payton, Robert. 1984. "Major Challenges to Philanthropy." Paper presented at the annual meeting of Independent Sector, Washington, DC.

Putnam, Robert D. 2000. *Bowling Alone: The Collapse and Revival of American Community.* New York: Simon and Schuster.

Salamon, Lester M. 1987. "Of Market Failure, Voluntary Failure, and Third-Party Government: Towards a Theory of Government-Nonprofit Relations in the Modern Welfare State." *Journal of Voluntary Action Research* 16:29–49.

Salamon, Lester M., and Helmut K. Anheier. 1992. "In Search of the Nonprofit Sector I: The Question of Definitions." *Voluntas* 3 (2): 125–151.

Schervish, Paul G. 1993. "The Dependent Variable of the Independent Sector: A Research Agenda for Improving the Definition and Measurement of Giving and Volunteering." *Voluntas* 4 (2): 223–232.

Smith, Steven Rathgeb, and Michael Lipsky. 1993. *Nonprofits for Hire: The Welfare State in the Age of Contracting.* Cambridge, MA: Harvard University Press.

Van Til, Jon. 1990. "Defining Philanthropy." In *Critical Issues in American Philanthropy,* ed. Jon Van Til and Associates. San Francisco: Jossey-Bass.

Walzer, Michael. 1991. "The Concept of Civil Society." *Dissent* (Spring): 393–404.

Weisbrod, Burton A. 1975. "Toward a Theory of the Voluntary Nonprofit Sector in a Three-Sector Economy." In *Altruism, Morality, and Economic Theory,* ed. Edmund S. Phelps. New York: Russell Sage Foundation.

———. 1988. *The Nonprofit Economy.* Cambridge, MA: Harvard University Press.

Young, Dennis R., ed. 2004. *Effective Economic Decision-Making by Nonprofit Organizations.* New York: The Foundation Center.

I

HISTORY AND SCOPE OF THE NONPROFIT SECTOR

1

The Nonprofit Sector in Historical Perspective: Traditions of Philanthropy in the West

KEVIN C. ROBBINS

Although it can be claimed that the formation of a distinct nonprofit sector is a comparatively recent achievement in the political economy of modern Western states, the actors, values, and institutions driving that process forward have a long and neglected history. It is the purpose of this chapter to survey that history selectively, interconnecting those key agents of change over time that have contributed to forming major parts of the nonprofit sector as it now exists in the United States and abroad. This chapter also explores how ancient and innovative forms of Western philanthropy have shaped and continue to inform the operations of charitable organizations within the modern nonprofit sector. Few scholars have subjected historic forms of philanthropy to long-term comparative analysis (Moreau-Christophe 1851; Lallemand 1906–1912). However, the huge archives that charitable actors and institutions created and carefully preserved in the past are now attracting more and more attention from historians (Hall 1988; Himmelfarb 1991). These inquiries are fueled by new sets of questions historians ask that link past charitable practices to modern philanthropic movements.

Modern charitable nonprofit organizations owe their inception and continued support to the public-spirited generosity of philanthropists who feel that contributions to the commonwealth are spiritual or moral imperatives. Historians want to know what are the deeper religious and ethical wellsprings of this benevolent behavior over time. In many Western and developed countries, large majorities of the population (up to 70 percent) make regular charitable donations (Lane, Saxon-Harrold, and Weber 1994). Significant proportions of these residents (up to 25 percent) also volunteer their time and energy to serve others. What key forces over time impelled such large numbers of people to behave so charitably?

Philanthropic agencies seek to sustain the integrity of the communities they serve by enhancement of the general quality of life and provision for the misfortunate, marginalized, and disenfranchised. How did charitable actions in the past gain this inclusive and specifically civic character aimed at the expansion of civil rights? Organized charitable activity is now very lawful, carefully regulated by federal and state governments. Lawmakers regularly work in close partnership with private philanthropic entities to achieve socioeconomic or sociocultural reforms, often across international borders. How did prior states over the span of Western civilization police, discipline, and direct the charitable impulses of their citizens? With the rise of the state in the West, how did private philanthropists apply their donations to serve what they perceived to be the greater and changing needs of the nation? Who benefited and who suffered from historic alterations in the direction, legal regulation, culling, and control of philanthropic resources? Finally, the advent of highly organized and professionalized, even "scientific," philanthropy in the nineteenth century makes it imperative to ask: Who were the historic proponents of this transformation? What were their methods? What, ultimately, did the highly analytical managers of expert philanthropy achieve?

In quest of answers for such questions, historians are now constructing a more "environmental" or multidimensional history of philanthropy informed by scholars' closer attention to the many artifacts amassed by charitable organizations and voluntary associations over time. Vital evidence comes from institutional archives stuffed with charity's revealing paperwork. The many artworks and purposefully impressive buildings charities acquired now get more attention (Markus 1993). Critical written sources here include newly discovered religious documents, prime to the canons of several faiths; various law codes governing charitable acts, foundations, and associations; notarized records of gifts made during the lifetime of donors; and posthumous benefactors' last wills and testaments, surviving in greater numbers from the Middle East and Europe after the year 1000 CE. These laws and legal records, analyzed quantitatively in bulk, track shifting flows of philanthropic capital. Such recoverable patterns of past benefits further reveal the charitable preoccupations and investments of individual or corporate donors. They measure donors' fidelity to religious and secular codes of giving (Robbins 1997).

This chapter draws upon the new history of philanthropy. Attentiveness to past constructions and performances of "philanthropy" yields keener and more distinct meanings of the term to compare with its current connotations and practice inside the nonprofit sector. Cognizant of this history, modern actors and analysts of the sector can better measure both its loyalty to older traditions of philanthropy and its currently distinctive dimensions.

CHARITY AS MORAL IMPERATIVE IN ANCIENT JEWISH LIFE

In a quest to uncover the religious and ethical motors driving private philanthropy in support of the nonprofit sector, ancient Judaism is an appropriate place to start. Semitic religious codes unequivocally asserted charitable action to be indispensable in forging Jewish identity and divine worship. This principle resonated throughout ancient Hebrew society, making philanthropy incumbent upon all believers. Jewish conceptions of charity endowed the needy with potent rights to assistance and molded Hebrew conceptions of community, place, and time. Religious teachers coordinated arguments to describe charity simultaneously as a duty, a human stewardship of God's gifts, an empathy between rich and poor promoting social peace, and a distinctive tribal virtue. Jews responded with the creation and refinement of enduring communal institutions for charitable action.

Acts of benevolence *(gemilut hasadim)* take a central place in Jewish conceptions of the sacred, the just, and the godly community always enacting a covenant with the divine (Cassel 1887; Frisch 1924; Lehmann 1897). Among these simultaneously humanitarian and liturgical good deeds, the Talmud extols *tsedaqah,* alms or assistance to the needy. Connected semantically and spiritually with Hebrew expressions of righteousness, integrity, and justice *(tsedeq)* for all, the charitable imperative inspires complementary virtues. Charity reinforces the structure of society while compensating for disparities in wealth and power among the social ranks in early Judean temple-kingdoms (Sanders 1992).

Such generosity acknowledges one's moral obligation to worship a generous God through sharing with the less fortunate those personal benefits He alone confers. The first five books of the Bible, composing the Torah, or Pentateuch, and datable from 900 to 600 BCE, reiterate God's eminent domain over all of creation. These texts limit the status of the propertied to that of beneficiary and steward of the worldly goods ultimately donated by Jehovah ("for the land is mine; for you are strangers and sojourners with me," Leviticus 25:23). Moses repeatedly described God as a special avenger of orphans, widows, and refugees. These praises entail Israelites to render material and spiritual assistance promptly to the bereft ("Love the stranger therefore; for you were strangers in the land of Egypt," Deuteronomy 10:19). Jewish sages ruled that the poor of Israel had the strict right to claim support from their neighbors, an entitlement to aid they derived from scripture (Hamel 1990). A key objective here was to use individual and then communal gifts to sustain the Jewish poor while helping them find work and achieve financial independence.

Judaism's stark equation of misanthropy with faithlessness requires believers to be givers (Loewenberg 2001). Certain benefactions are incumbent upon the pious. Rituals of giving organize ancient Jewish calendars and give deeper ethical meaning to the flow of time. Obligatory shared meals and ceremonial gift exchanges mark the days of celebration and atonement that measure the lunar year. These events strengthen personal bonds of conviviality and deference to superior givers. Landowners had to reserve untouched field corners for the gleanings of the poor at the close of each growing period. Triennially, Israel's townspeople and peasantry raised special tithes for the poor. The poor also received all untended field produce during every seventh, or sabbatical, year, in which the land lay fallow. Laws of the jubilee in every seventh and fiftieth year ordained (but did not compel) cancellations of loans, forgiveness of debts, and the manumission of Jewish slaves. Rabbinical courts *(battei din)* enforced provision of these cyclical aids and could compel the recalcitrant to participate. The first and second divisions of the Mishnah, a comprehensive code of regulations for Jewish communities compiled between 200 BCE and 200 CE, explain these liberalities (Danby 1933; Klein 1979). Charity here works as an ordering principle that makes entire cosmologies, chronologies, and bodies of law more intelligible to the living heirs of past patrons and protégés.

Generations of rabbis emphasized pertinent Bible passages such as Deuteronomy 15:7–8: "If there is among you a poor man, one of your brethren . . . you shall not harden your heart or shut your hand against your poor brother, but you shall open your hand to him." The rabbinate ruled that "open your hand" entailed charitable assistance from rich to poor beyond customary gleanings and tithes for the needy. Only the morally oblivious saw a test of piety in the choice to give or not to give. Real tests of Jewish piety are found in donors' efforts to provide the right relief and to serve the unfortunate efficiently and without shame. Lessons in this regard fill Talmudic literature from 200 to 600 CE (Prockter 1991). Jewish teachers consistently construed promises to act charitably as religious vows that must be generously fulfilled. Voluntary donors who act anonymously, who succeed in organizing others in systems of mutual aid, and whose wise gifts save beneficiaries from total destitution get high praise in this literature. Discretionary charity persistently informs the hierarchy of all Jewish virtues, as the later ethical writings of Maimonides attest (1135–1204 CE; Twersky 1980). Charity is not only a virtue in itself; it is the crucial practice underlying other virtues of the Jews: piety, compassion for the weak, love of justice, and devotion to communal survival.

To honor God, succor themselves, and build communities worthy of divine protection, Jews progressively created institutions of charitable action between 100 BCE and 200 CE (Hamel 1990; Loewenberg 2001). According to Loewenberg, these developments mark an early transition from individual charity to concerted action in quest of social justice. As early as the Second Temple era (536 BCE–70 CE), Jews accommodated communal charitable action within the sacred precinct of the Jerusalem Temple. Secret chambers for collection and distribution of charity occupied a part of the most sacred sanctuary. Donors could leave their gifts secretly in one room. Beneficiaries collected the offerings in a second room unseen by contributors and protected from shame.

Judean political and economic upheavals of the second century BCE greatly increased the numbers of the poor, migrant, fugitive, and destitute. Jewish institutions of relief expanded at this time to include communal soup kitchens *(tamhui)* where travelers were especially welcome. Jews also started collective charity funds *(kuppah)* providing weekly assistance to the resident poor from contributions made by local householders. Material artifacts from these organizations, including engraved collection boxes and homely eating utensils, enrich the archaeological record of Jewish philanthropy from late antique to early modern times. The Talmud advised needy and wandering scholars to settle only in localities with an operational *kuppah.* This indicates that these relief agencies had broader, salutary material and cultural repercussions.

Socially, the worthy men who became charity fund managers *(gabbai tsedaqah)* accumulated intangible status advantages for themselves and their kin. The daughters and granddaughters of an accomplished *gabbai* might marry into prestigious priestly families without the close scrutiny of pedigree normally imposed on such aspiring brides. The overseer's moral authority in fund-raising was backed by Jewish local courts that could compel an individual's participation in communal charity collections. Charitable service here could legitimate both the authority of community elders and the structures of government they served.

At the turn to the Common Era, rabbinical judgments enshrined in Jewish religious law *(halakha)* began stipulating acceptable material limits to charitable behavior, prescribing nullifications to the jubilees under certain conditions, and condoning donors' scrutiny and selection of recipients for aid (Collins 1905). Field corners to be left to gleaners, for example, were set at one-sixtieth of the surface area of each farmer's holding. Tithes and charitable acts accomplished within the sacred boundaries of Jerusalem gained greater acclaim. The role of Jewish charity in setting gradations of social rank and the protocols of priestly office intensified. More punctilious but also more debatable philanthropic acts invigorated Jewish sectarianism antedating the rise of Christianity. These controversies catalyzed broader dissent among disaffected Jews against established political, religious, and charitable institutions. Jewish converts to early Christianity took inspiration from these complaints and embarked on a quest for their own "true charity." Thus arguments over proper philanthropy sparked rebellion and the genesis of a new faith.

GREEK CLASSICAL FORMS OF PHILANTHROPY AND THE NURTURE OF INCLUSIVE CIVIC IDEALS

Modern revisions of the history of ancient Greece show philanthropy as a cultural phenomenon that thoroughly shaped the sociology and politics of fractious civic communities (Morris 1986). Since we owe directly to the Greeks the very term *philanthropy* as a designation of exceptional generosity, findings from Greek history enable deeper appreciation of the practice's many cultural and power-political implications (De Ruiter 1932). Focused on Hellenic cities from 200 BCE through 200 CE, the noted research of the French historian Paul Veyne presents the behavior of Greek civic benefactors as a curious amalgam of volition, duty, and constraint—a "predicament" in which the holders of great wealth were caught (Veyne 1969, 1976). Since such nominally "private" wealth was usually appreciated as a real trust in which all members of the civic community held a share, the propertied had to distribute their surplus resources generously. Greek patrons were expected to embellish and glorify the city as a whole. Failure to do so could antagonize rival clans, political factions, and the entire citizenry. Ordinary Greek townsmen served as jurors in city courts and this made wealthy litigants especially wary of angering them. Miserly rich men courted popular rebuke, legal frustrations, and public dishonor. With varying degrees of enthusiasm, the propertied sponsored municipal building projects, the upkeep of warships, civic arsenals, temples dedicated to the gods, and various festivals including superb dramatic competitions (Francotte 1905; Schmitt-Pantel 1992). Enduring productions and celebrations of Greek drama thus constitute one of the most influential traditions of compulsive philanthropy shaping the culture of Western civilization.

Greek urbanites called such civic benefactions or public services incumbent on the rich "liturgies" *(leitourgiai).* They devised official protocols governing the annual or cyclical acceptance and proper execution of these benevolent duties (Lewis 1960, 1963). Some Greek town councils expected wealthy citizens to take up as many as 120 liturgies per year.

Impressed by the ubiquity of such benefactions in classical Greek cities, Veyne has coined the term *euergetism* to describe such pervasive employment of private liberality for public benefit.

Compelling Greek philosophical precepts also required great men to make constant performances of generosity to the city. These gift acts showed an elite's determined progress toward the humane ideal of self-betterment (Buchanan 1962). Competitive patrons used conspicuous civic donations to display the perfection of their distinctively liberal souls. The public came to expect this generosity—which even included the application of private fortunes toward defense and other government operations—from the self-improvement efforts of the wealthy. This was not the exercise of noblesse oblige (giving as a by-product of a status achieved), but rather an individual quest for a noble soul through acts of generosity. These donations also enabled city fathers to display an endearing solicitude for public welfare, earning them popular sympathy upon which they could later draw to advance themselves in civic affairs or in lawsuits tried before favorable citizen juries (Davies 1965; Rhodes 1986).

Under euergetism, the elite viewed stinginess as nonexistence and misanthropy as ignoble suicide. Failure to give on the part of the great was entirely uncivilized, warranting mockery by peers and plebs. Considering the alternatives, then, Greek philanthropy was less a choice than an imperative for civic benefactors. Acts of incumbent liberality enabled paragons of generosity to display their accumulating superiority over less gifted ranks of the urban population. Such philanthropy reinforced the social, political, and cultural hierarchies of antagonistic Greek civic communities.

In his delineation of the complex types and motives of giving by notable Greek urbanites, however, Veyne cautiously assesses the significance of these systemic liberalities in sustaining the classical cities. He notes that euergetism often yielded short-lived presents that were not essential to the effective operation of coercive Hellenic civic governments. Thus Veyne refuses to accord these presents any flat functional status as merely primitive means of exchange, taxation, redistribution, or political legitimization, reinforcing oligarchies while disenfranchising most citizens. These benefits did not originate within a "sector" of the classical world nor did they operate as some external corrective or fix to the "system" of antique political economy.

According to Veyne, several conjoining factors produced the unique and opportune outgrowth of Hellenic philanthropy. First, Greeks regarded private wealth as a public trust. Second, ruling elites vied for honor via personal donations to embellish civic administration. Third, aspiring citizens emulated elite donors' gift behavior to gain status for themselves. Fourth, ordinary Greek citizens asserted their traditional entitlement to notables' benefactions. In return, plebeians skillfully offered deference to the generous while humiliating recalcitrant donors. Finally, insurmountable popular animus toward taxation for civic amenities made their provision incumbent upon wealthy donors. Euergetism was more than just extraneous or occasional "bread and circuses," then; it became the essential "system" of Greek city-states. This was a vital and dynamic philanthropic modus vivendi, peaceably integrating the various ranks of urban populations through the exchange of gifts. Investigating the creative force of euergetism shows how it effected enduring moral and social contracts between potentially antagonistic strata of urbanites. As Veyne insists, this makes it essential to regard ancient philanthropy, its institutions, and its material artifacts as the formative elements in a historical sociology of political pluralism.

In ancient Athens, great private patrons underwrote the city's famous regular drama festivals. They vied to commission new works from playwrights. Other patrons furnished trained teams of actors to perform the plays before audiences that united different ranks of the citizenry. Such prestigious liturgies show classical philanthropy's persistent powers of symbolic and synthetic representation (Wilson 2000). These stage works drew lessons from the behavior of archetypically good and bad citizens in other imaginary cities, blending multiple art forms to treat the civic audience with memorable enactments of didactic plays and choruses. Perfected in costly rehearsals subsidized by private patrons, these edifying, often tragic spectacles let thronging crowds watch the effects of good order and terrible disorder unfolding in fictional communities. Audiences judged each play, and the patrons of the winning production got to erect (at personal expense) beautiful monuments commemorating themselves as triumphant philanthropists. Regular commissions for such resplendent public mementos gave Greek craftsmen special incentives to produce impressive original works. Here, artisans synthesized and recombined in novel ways decorative elements from other building types. The grand drama patron's imposing outdoor trophy became one of the most stylistically innovative and expressive of all Greek plastic art forms. These monuments to self-interested political generosity filled the streets and squares of sacred urban theater precincts, powerfully shaping the entire built environment and cultural ethos of Hellenic cities for centuries.

One sees here concrete evidence of philanthropy's ancient role as a modulator of contention for prestige within and among distinct social groups. Classical philanthropy channeled urbanites' competitiveness toward more broadly beneficial joint accomplishments—such as drama contests in subsidized theaters that brought large numbers of the public together in one sacred space. Such philanthropic events reinforced the privileged and cultured identity citizens shared. On this scale, antique philanthropy became highly symbolic, generating ideally inclusive forms in art, society, and politics.

So public an art of philanthropy could generate as many disputes as it forestalled. Greeks responded with adroit judicial maneuvers firmly establishing legal regulation of ostensibly charitable acts as an integral part of Western civic culture. This was especially true in classical Athens (500–300 BCE), where assumption of liturgies by the wealthy was compulsory but no less celebrated as a manifestation of honorable philanthropy. A rich man nominated by ruling peers to undertake any liturgy could file a motion *(skepsis)* protesting his exemption, ineligibility, or comparative inability for public service with the requisite generosity. Outright refusal of the charge would have been self-abnegating and unthinkable in addition to being illegal. Through a quasi-judicial litigation procedure known as an *antidosis,* the nominee for any liturgy also had the right to challenge any other citizen he thought richer to take up the charge. If the challengee refused, the challenger could trade estates with his opponent so that he might fulfill the obligation with possibly superior resources. Preliminary steps toward private resolution of the matter via exchange included preparation of detailed estate inventories by both parties. Failure to respond to the challenge, calculated dereliction in drawing up inventories, or disinclination to pursue settlement would transform the contest into a delicate case of state adjudication *(diadikasia).* In this instance, a citizen's tribunal, without assigning the roles of plaintiff or defendant, attempted to determine which party had a better claim to the liturgy (Gabrielsen 1987; Goligher 1907; Todd 1993). A rich man risked his honor, however, by rejecting a liturgy outright or by accepting the charge only under court order. Such jeopardy continually led to private settlement of the matter.

The genius of this legislation lay in the processes by which dispensations from liturgical expenditure were duly accorded to men claiming inability to pay, replacements found to take up the charge, and shirkers policed. Via the antidosis procedure, the state encouraged maintenance of these tasks as essentially private, not public, endeavors. City fathers did not apply the blunt and potentially divisive instruments of democratic statutory law. Rather, they relied on elite peer pressures to regulate the civic philanthropic duty of rich citizens. Ancient philanthropy fostered and relied upon such creative, completely calculated, and balanced public-private partnerships to sustain munificent urban polities.

ROMAN RULES ON MAJOR GIFTS, FOUNDATIONS, VOLUNTARY ASSOCIATIONS, AND PUBLIC BENEVOLENCE

As conquerors, heirs, and cautious emulators of the Greeks, the Romans assumed better regulation of philanthropy to be among their greatest obligations as a civilized and conservative people. Great Latin authors such as Cicero (*On Duties,* composed circa 44 BCE) and Seneca (*On Benefits,* composed circa 60 CE) put forth rigorous manuals on the arts of giving and receiving gifts. They told prospective donors and their beneficiaries about the best motives, forms, and objectives of charitable practices now deemed essential for preserving society. Roman paralegal scribes and jurists contributed to a growing corpus of legal instruments enabling patrons to consolidate and extend their gifts in perpetuity. Roman emperors burdened subordinates with commands to supervise and control voluntary associations and fraternal or mutual aid societies proliferating in all the cities of their vast realm. The same emperors arrogated to themselves the prestigious right of making certain magnificent gifts to the people of Rome including great aqueducts, fountains, and enormous bath complexes. These demonstrated the imperial family's superb power to manipulate primordial elements such as water and fire for public benefit. And at Rome, statesmanship itself gained a more benevolent aura. Apologists for imperial expansion capitalized upon older Greek notions of *philanthropia* to claim that Roman rulers extended a beneficial respect for international law and the welfare of the ruled that legitimated their imperium. Cognizance and enforcement of international human rights took shape in this stream of philanthropic political propaganda.

Roman efforts to systematize a practical ethics of giving took their most cogent form in the didactic works of such stoic philosophers as Seneca in *On Benefits.* Good gifts must be distinguished from bad gifts. There is a right way and a wrong way to acknowledge a present. Seneca's philanthropic treatise posits direct linkage between faulty giving by aspiring benefactors and proliferation of ingratitude among beneficiaries. Ingratitude, according to Seneca, is terrible. It threatens the integrity of Roman civilization, held together by the "glue" of gratitude gifts inspire. This glue binds patrons to protégés at all levels of society. Prospective donors need thorough instruction in how to give in order to generate maximum gratitude. Seneca contributes a handy guidebook to proper benefaction, demanding all patrons to choose their beneficiaries and their benefits with exacting premeditation.

"No gift can be a benefit unless it is given with reason. . . . Thoughtless benefaction is the most shameful sort of loss" (Seneca 1935). Allegiance to this axiom makes heavy demands on donors from whom Seneca expects the establishment of clear priorities in giving. Selection and distribution of necessities for the unfortunate must take precedence over delivery of mere embellishments to life or frivolous, ephemeral entertainments. Indiscriminate Greek modes of liberality are now condemned as grossly irresponsible. They neither satisfy real public needs nor generate the deep gratitude between benefactor and beneficiary essential to maintain the vertical patronage chains holding entire communities together. Highly discriminate Roman givers must also know and choose their beneficiaries very carefully. Donors should elect to assist those honest souls capable of recognizing and repaying with gratitude the honor of generosity done to them. While Seneca reasserts the obligation of the fortunate to give, he stipulates that they are never without choice in selecting the means and objectives to fulfill that duty. The goal of all such calculation is to impress the recipient's mind so powerfully with the magnanimity of the aptly timed, appropriate gift that an image of the donor will linger there forever. Such potent mental images of generosity should bring forth from the recipient acts of commensurate serial benevolence. Mastering the psychology of perpetual gift exchange thus developed as a peculiarly Roman political art incumbent upon all good patrons. The donor's ability to judge the character of others becomes essential to the successful consummation of this philanthropy. Seneca advocates a very judgmental generosity. In Seneca one thus finds classical anticipations of subsequent arguments that Western philanthropy must become a data-driven, discriminatory science in which the machinations of the head regulate the impulses of the heart.

Roman wills and public inscriptions commemorating testamentary gifts show how ancient legal instruments secured the operations of trusts, foundations, and voluntary associations (Duncan-Jones 1974; Rickett 1979). Legal historians now trace the early development of foundations as a curious outgrowth of dying elite Romans' vanity. Their fear of personal oblivion, mistrust of surviving kin, and anxiety over eventual family neglect of traditional funeral rites for ancestors called forth new agencies of perpetual giving. Preserving a cult of the dead became the chief objective of early Roman foundations. In this service, Western conceptions of trusteeship gained judicial breadth and strength.

The key testamentary provision anticipating a law of foundations is the bequest of money or property to another for maintenance in perpetuity of the testator's tomb and memorial services (Le Bras 1936). Roman testators normally went outside immediate family and, initially, endowed other individuals and their heirs with funds for such duty in the form of a private trust. Over time, however, dying benefactors showed greater preference to endow more stable corporate bodies such as cities and *collegia,* meaning various burial clubs, craft or commercial guilds, and neighborhood associations (Bruck 1949; Feenstra 1956). By conveying endowments for personal commemoration to these organizations, worried patricians helped to solidify the material resources and legal rights of corporations, akin to foundations, operating for broader public benefit (De Visscher 1949). However, while Romans did invest corporate agencies with fiduciary responsibilities (devoting certain resources to fixed goals over time), Roman law of the classical era did not yet accord any distinct judicial personality to independent foundations themselves (De Visscher 1955). Romans thus moved slowly from private trusts toward corporate forms of charitable action. The needs of individual Romans for a more serviceable justice, protecting their own souls in perpetuity, drove this transformation first expressed in Roman common law (Bruck 1955). New classical instrumentalities primed for the practice of philanthropy did not come from generous state provision (or positive law). They emerged from inventive and selfish popular demand focused by periodic crises of public confidence in established social institutions and moral norms. Such complex conjunctures typically catalyze epochal changes in Western charitable practices.

The makers of Roman statute law soon gave their subjects new pretexts for richer and more broadly beneficial gifts by will. The emperor Nerva (imperium 96–98 CE) authorized Roman municipalities to receive and hold in trust the gifts of individual donors intended to accomplish private and public benefits (Hands 1968). Subsequent codes of civic administration required conservation of capital in such foundations. Roman law stipulated the inalienability of such resources and required application of foundation revenues to the purposes set by donors. Consolidation of this legislation (200–300 CE) increased endowments and bequests, enabling more male and female urbanites to become living or posthumous patrons of entire cities or specific civic amenities (Nicols 1989). Other urban corporations, such as the popular mutual benefit clubs, commercial guilds, and collegia, progressively acquired statutory rights to administer and execute foundations. These powers enhanced the local stature and legitimated the authority of these collectivities shaping the civil society of Roman towns. But they also complicated imperial politics by fanning official suspicions that such organizations might impede or subvert autocratic central government.

Research on voluntary associations in the Greco-Roman world shows how their fortunes waxed and waned under rapidly oscillating bouts of imperial favor and disdain (Kloppenborg and Wilson 1996). Even simple burial societies among the poor and philosophical study groups among the better off could evolve in dangerous directions. The propensity of members to use these assemblies in forging urban political factions and potent lobbies for specific socioeconomic interest groups attests to the vitality and controversy of classical associational life. However, the proven power of this dynamic sector to catalyze violence and disorder within urban communities often elicited imperial agents' fearful surveillance and destructive intervention. So, for example, although the emperor Nerva enacted laws strengthening corporations and foundations, his immediate successor, Trajan (imperium 98–117 CE), considered even volunteer companies of firemen potentially seditious. Trajan therefore tried to prohibit all types of voluntary associations (Cotter 1996). Associations that did survive imperial censure operated only locally and symbiotically with the vigilant state (Walker-Ramisch 1996). While truly revolutionary associations were unknown, however, the collegia, with their close ranks, bylaws, and internal self-governance, could offer members both satisfying camaraderie and a semblance of political empowerment. The fact that the early Christian church gained converts rapidly among the members of Roman associations suggests that voluntary associations inspired innovative behavior in both spiritual and secular matters (Meeks 1983).

The growing desire of Roman emperors to be seen as the greatest of all public benefactors led to their regulation of potentially competitive benevolent associations. Emperors built their reputations as superior donors especially by subsidizing construction of elaborate aqueduct networks and enormous bath complexes in the center of Rome and other cities (Boatwright 2000). Research on the vast architectural and symbolic scale of this largesse indicates that most munificent emperors did not give the Roman people baths out of a genuine solicitude for public welfare (Fagan 1999; Yegul 1992). Such magnificent presents became manifestations and legitimizations of plenteous imperial power, demonstrating each donor's fidelity to the generous duties of the great for apparent public benefit. Dynastic rivalries for greater glory between successive imperial clans mostly drove indulgent bath building. Great baths also went up after periods of political upheaval when new ascendants to power used impressive gift projects to demonstrate firmer command at the apex of empire. Through highly functional gift buildings embellished to impress but open to all social ranks, Roman emperors fabricated spaces in which the illusion of a single Roman collectivity could be recurrently staged. At Rome, imperial philanthropy contributed to the imagery of solicitous authoritarian politics and symbolic communal integrity (Duncan-Jones 1974; Nicols 1989).

The Romans also appropriated Greek ideals of philanthropia to enlarge the moral claims of clement imperial government. This version of classical philanthropy asserted that Romans were very attentive to the common human rights of their increasingly diverse subjects (Bauman 2000). Propagandists of empire, desperate to combat allegations from conquered authors (mainly eloquent Greeks) that Roman rule was both impious and inhumane, developed the clever counterargument that some peoples were naturally meant to be ruled and actually benefited from subordination. But this contention required rulers to constantly consider their many subjects' welfare and moderate their rulership accordingly. As Bauman notes, "In this way severity and morality were reconciled: to rule called for severity, but the ruler's moral obligations promoted philanthropy" (25). Herein one finds the "moralization of the imperial idea" through philanthropic discourse.

Philosophers and historians of the imperial age amplified this line of argument by celebrating a Roman art of international diplomacy sustained by strong devotion to the binding obligations of sworn treaties. Through these pacts, Romans made allies of their defeated opponents and hospitably welcomed them to share in the general benefits of imperial affiliation. Here, propagandists of empire also skillfully turned earlier Greek connotations of the word *philanthropy* to Roman advantage, alluding to proper reception of ambassadors, appropriate conduct for diplomatic negotiations, and the mutual, serial benefits to be derived from reciprocal respect for peace treaties. From Greek sources, Roman polemicists also exploited a meaning of philanthropia as gracious restraint by aggrieved parties in the due punishment of selfish treaty breakers. Imperial writers cited historic examples of such Roman clemency toward treacherous allies as exemplary of the humane values sanctioning expansion of Roman sovereignty.

Such charitable self-justification carried with it inescapable corollaries. The exportation to the Mediterranean world of Roman standards of benevolence in statecraft implied that aliens, even defeated prior enemies, could claim eligibility for fair treatment and humane government equal to that of Roman citizens. The philanthropic universalization of a protective empire entailed prudent extension to weaker foreigners of the basic civil rights justifying the alleged superiority of Rome's hegemonic but benevolent civilization. Appeals to Roman law as the ideal vehicle to effect this benefit gave new Latin understandings of "philanthropy" a legal and utilitarian cast as a type of practical social justice. Roman political operatives emerged as custodians of the ruled, legally bound to respect and nurture their wards' best interests. Imperialism celebrated (or cloaked) as a form of enlightened trusteeship resonated well with contemporary efforts by Seneca and others to give private benefactors fixed rules for meeting the rightful needs of the weak and misfortunate. As Bauman concludes, these Roman essays in "philanthropy" consolidated the fundamental human rights of the vanquished while justifying the contemporary power politics of imperium. Philanthropy as a means of empowerment for the disenfranchised via the expansion of civil rights has very ancient roots in Western civilization.

CHRISTIAN REGIMES OF PHILANTHROPY

The development of Christianity has profoundly influenced the motives of philanthropists, the formation of voluntary associations, and the ethos of self-sacrifice for individual spiritual growth and communal improvement. Investigations of Christian origins emphasize the importance of selflessness, voluntary poverty, alms deeds, and hospitality in the lives of Jesus and the church his first acolytes constructed. Biblical scholars' quests to recover Jesus's original teachings have uncovered early commandments for believers to abandon all material possessions by almsgiving. Early disciples were also ordered to become more self-deprecating by alms seeking, courting rejection and abuse at every door. Here, church members' cathartic identification with small groups of fellow believers, through loyal sharing of resources and total devotion to care of the needy, is also seen as the building block of a new faith (Johnson 1998). Early Christians worked together to universalize a personal charitable imperative previously restricted to elite members of Greco-Roman societies.

Historians of Christianity are accumulating evidence of an early Jesus movement integrated by novel philanthropies inimical to Jewish, Greek, and Roman modes of government and giving. Charitable practices are among the essential means by which Christians distinguished themselves from Jews, captured enthusiastic Greek disciples, institutionalized churches, and parried frequent Roman efforts to destroy the young sect. Christian authorities used faithful giving to discipline ordinary believers. Simultaneously, clerics rewrote many times over their doctrines on the proper means and ends of philanthropy. There is no such thing as a consistent or uniform "Christian charity."

By prodding Mediterraneans of the first century CE to recognize the miseries of the poor as a proper target for philanthropy, proselytes to Christianity altered classical balances of power between benefactors and beneficiaries. Christian givers capitalized on the popular acclaim generated by their philanthropies to enhance their own status as patrons and power brokers within ancient polities (Veyne 1976). From 200 to 400 CE, Christians strove to break a near monopoly on major public gifts by pagan elites. Christian bishops aggressively pursued this strategy, using massive gifts of food to curry popular favor as "lovers of the poor." Christian polemicists called this "philanthropy." Competing Christian sects regularly employed such calculated acts of generosity in the struggle for greater influence on the politics and culture of antique cities (Brown 1992, 2002). To discipline their growing flocks more effectively, senior clerics developed a Christian theology of sin and atonement where new emphasis fell on individual almsgiving as a means of penance conducive to individual salvation.

Periodic bouts of tolerance toward the church from weakening Roman authorities strengthened the power of ecclesiastics. Clerics gained advantages in written Roman law, enhancing churches' gift income and protecting their charitable assets from spoliation by jealous secular powers. The Christian church gained an independent legal persona while true foundations developed as bulwarks of its material security and spiritual authority. After 300 CE, the progressive fusion between state and Christian church in the Eastern Roman (Byzantine) Empire yielded more advantageous imperial property rights to clerics. Faithful emperors now endowed a host of new philanthropic institutions, such as hospitals, sustaining Byzantium's vibrant urban culture. These institutions operated in accord with Christian regulations of proper and targeted benevolence. Drawing upon such accomplishments, Western European churchmen of the Middle Ages built up their own innovative organs of charitable action, such as monasteries, while propounding novel ideas about how charity could best sustain Christian communities.

No brief survey of these developments can do justice to the richness and variety of Christian opinions about charity and the proper enactments of that virtue. The following paragraphs, roughly chronological in order, thus offer only highly selective samples of these crucial historic forces shaping the motivations and ambitions of donors for centuries.

The letters of Paul (composed 50–60 CE) give the earliest information about Christian doctrine and ritual practices in the formative years of Christianity. Through his correspondence, Paul exported to many nascent churches in Mediterranean cities the self-deprecating and ecumenical principles of early Christian charity. Paul explained: "By one Spirit we were all baptized into one body, Jews and Greeks, slaves or free—and all were made to drink one Spirit" (1 Cor. 12:12–13). By this assimilation, the Christian assumes constant obligations to others. "You are not your own," Paul tells Corinthian Christians (1 Cor. 5:19). He tells the Philippians: "Do nothing from selfishness or conceit but in humility count others better than yourselves" (Phil. 2:3). The Romans get the news that "none of us lives to himself. . . . Let us then pursue what makes for peace and mutual uplift. . . . Love does no wrong to a neighbor; therefore love is the fulfilling of the law" (Rom. 13:10, 14:7, 14:19). Finally, Paul advises the Colossians: "Above all things clothe yourselves in charity, which binds everything together in perfect harmony" (Col. 3:14). Through his letters, Paul propounds an intensified Christian ideal of the community as a social body identified with the all-encompassing body of Christ (Dodd 1951). For early Christians, obligatory service to all others was an empowering form of worship as a personal imitation of the benevolent Christ figure (Jacobs-Malina 1993).

Paul's letters can also be read as primers on a radical social ethic, demanding that all Christians become tireless benefactors (Winter 1994). This advice is emancipatory for ordinary believers in that it encourages all new Christians to renounce forever their status as a mere client of some other patron. Paul attacks patrician systems of patronage that solely advance the interests of pagan or Jewish elites. Former protégés must now aspire to become protectors of their neighbors no matter how humble they all may be. Paul is raising up entirely new communities of donors empowered spiritually and philanthropically through the church.

In his epistles, Paul promotes this development by stipulating the care with which Christians should seek to discover the real needs of their fellows. Paul worked diligently to institutionalize effective Christian giving. He did so by instituting weekly church collections among the faithful and orchestrating international fundraising campaigns on behalf of poorer churches and the impoverished in Jerusalem. According to Paul, contributors would gain a greater sense of personal agency and moral power through material support of collective good works, winning recruits to beleaguered congregations (Dodds 1965; Meeks 1993). The need to centralize and coordinate their individual charitable efforts, transcending ethnic and civic boundaries, brought Christians together into larger assemblies, thereby building up the church and its administrative infrastructures (Lampe 1987).

The striking variety of lessons about giving conveyed in early Christian literature show how debates over proper charitable practices generated new faiths throughout the ancient world. What is the significance of the three synoptic gospels (Matthew, Mark, and Luke, composed 65–85 CE) opening the New Testament with regard to the history of Christian charity? These books relate the life of Jesus, often retelling the same events although not always in the same order nor with the same detail. In Mark, Jesus distinguishes himself by repeated acts of healing, exorcism, and miraculous provision of sustenance and protection to his followers (for example, multiplying loaves and fishes, Mark 6:38–44, and aiding travelers aboard ship by walking on the Sea of Galilee, Mark 6:47–51). Jesus heals the withered hand of a suffering man in a synagogue on the Sabbath, asking rhetorically: "Is it lawful on the Sabbath to do good?" (Mark 3:4). Here, he puts active service of human needs above rigid observation of Jewish law requiring rest on the holy day ("The Sabbath was made for man, not man for the Sabbath," Mark 3:27). Referring to this incident, one New Testament scholar comments, "The Law is to be obeyed to the fullest extent possible . . . but in obeying the Law what really matters is human need" (Ehrman 2000).

Awed disciples and outraged Jewish priests witness Jesus's radical, subversive intensification of the individual charitable imperative that Judaism itself first established (Johnson 1999). The sacred rhythms of Jewish charity, however, now clash with Jesus's examples of more timely benevolent action. Jesus amplifies these calls by demanding that each follower become "a servant of all" (Mark 9:35) and prepare for discipleship by giving away all personal possessions to the poor (Mark 10:21). This order contradicts Talmudic rulings that no benefactor ever part with more than a fifth of his wealth in doing good (Loewenberg 2001). The acolyte's premeditated impoverishment makes rich, Greek-style largesse to gain honor equally impossible. Fundamental tenets of Christianity formed as its exponents did battle with more ancient regimes of philanthropy.

The evangelist Luke may have communicated some of the most provocative and enduring lessons from Jesus about Christian charity. The beatitudes in Luke (where Jesus announces, "Blessed are you poor . . . Blessed are you who hunger now, Blessed are you who weep now," Luke 6:20–21) elevate the afflicted to a special level of sanctity and compassion. This reveals a strong early Christian concern for redressing contemporary social ills through personal charitable contributions, sparing believers from the many corruptions wealth causes (Brown 1997; Ehrman 2000). Luke also communicates Jesus's command to love your enemies and to give to every beggar generously and without expectation of return (6:27–31). Total disinterest in the character of one's beneficiaries and in their capacity to acknowledge or repay a benefit breaks all the rules stoical Romans set for politically correct generosity yielding gratitude to donor from recipient. Very iconoclastic forms of philanthropy drive the Jesus movement.

Special remarks on Christian charity found in Luke and Matthew include the parable of the Good Samaritan (Luke 10:29–37), the story of poor Lazarus and the rich man, Dives (Luke 16:19–31), and Jesus's instructions to give alms unknowingly and in secret (Matthew 6:1–4). Here faithful readers got their Lord's reply to the simple question "who is my neighbor?" The wounded Jewish traveler, untouchable by the Hebrew priest and Levite punctiliously observing caste laws of purity, is succored by the Samaritan, a foreigner, whose charity thus transcends boundaries of ethnicity and social rank. This is the Christian role model of true compassion. Similarly, Dives roasts in hell for his neglect to rescue Lazarus, who died on the rich man's doorstep, getting more pity from the master's dogs. The fate of such hard-hearted men as Dives who refused to consider their neighbors shows the ultimate recompense of selfishness and ethnocentrism. The Christian God embodied in such early gospel parables as the Good Samaritan advocates a more universal charity that is neither self-seeking nor ostentatious. Almsgiving that is always done in secret defeats the self-promoting purposes of much elite Greco-Roman giving

The growing Christian church was not merely a refuge for the poor and miserable. Wealthier, more learned townsmen also joined new Christian congregations. They employed their administrative talents and personal gifts to strengthen and guide the church. Through their control of sacred offices, especially bishoprics, Christian notables competed directly with old pagan elites for power and prestige within late antique cities. However, prelates also became more determined to shape the church into an authoritarian institution, guaranteeing orthodoxy among adherents. Flocks of believers had to be more tightly disciplined. Here, churchmen used shifting forms of Christian charity to regulate a delicate balance between new freedoms of expression and new duties of obedience among the faithful.

By presenting themselves through impressive acts of public welfare as "lovers of the poor," bishops further expanded the social imagination of contemporaries, making room for the needy in the conduct of civic affairs (Brown 2002). Championing the cause of the poor, Christian bishops created a new form of moral leadership within antique towns. Simultaneously, high-ranking churchmen relied upon acts of philanthropy to mobilize popular support for the extension of their own autocratic governing authority (Brown 1992). Paradoxically, in the name of a religion that claimed to challenge the values of the elite, upper-class Christians gained greater control over brethren from lowlier social ranks. They did this by conscious manipulation of the church's charitable resources and cultivation of their own image as benefactors. At a minimum, regular church food doles kept the needy in one place. Episcopal licensing of beggars also helped to make the itinerant more tractable. Thus bishops began to challenge pagan governors' former monopoly over the maintenance of public order. Philanthropy here appears as a crucial agency by which great rival social factions vying for political power contest and supplant one another. Success in this spirited police action required clerical patrons to exercise their disciplinary skills via charitable acts and discourse on authorized forms of Christian charity.

Myriad heresies violently divided Christians, and competing mystery cults flourished in decadent late antique Roman cities. Here, church agents became increasingly preoccupied by the necessary but costly policing of humble parishioners and the defense of orthodoxy by all available philanthropic means. Strategic modulations in official Christian doctrines on wealth, charity, and the power politics of giving quickly ensued. Original sources of the era show changes of great magnitude in church teachings about the proprieties of money, gifts to the church, and alms rightly understood and applied didactically to recipients. Increasingly divergent opinions among professed Christians about the social utility of wealth, poverty, and alms catalyzed disputes within and between congregations. "Christian charity" could divide as well as gather the faithful.

Notable bishops among the "fathers of the church," such as St. Clement of Alexandria, St. Augustine of Hippo, and St. John Chrysostom, provided the most useful rewritings of Christian doctrine to accommodate wealth within the church and to strengthen orthodoxy by charity. Clement's *The Rich Man's Salvation* (circa 200 CE) is a marvelous tract in which the author rejects all fundamentalist readings of the gospels (Clement of Alexandria 1960). Clement asserts that Jesus never really endowed the poor with any sanctity at all, arguing that the poor are much too wretched, stupid, and needing of constant correction by their betters. According to Clement, Jesus could never have meant literally any of the censures he spoke in the Bible about the vile rich and their ineligibility for salvation. On the contrary, Clement asserts that the real beauty of wealth is not to corrupt but "to minister" (that is, to serve and to guide). He invites the rich to donate generously to the church and submit to its teachings. Their submission bestows spiritual rewards while enlarging the sociopolitical stature of new clerical intermediaries in formerly direct gift exchanges.

Certain charity managers historically have bid to accumulate their own social capital through interventions between givers and receivers. When successful in these ambitions, controllers of philanthropy have often gained greater wealth and power, changing the sociopolitical hierarchies of their communities. Attentiveness to the rising or declining fortunes of charity brokers helps to gauge the full historic effects of the philanthropic regimes they helped to create.

An early apotheosis of self-promoting Christian reconceptualizations of almsgiving can be found in the sermons of St. John Chrysostom, bishop of Constantinople from 396 to 398 CE (Chrysostom 1998; Kelly 1995). To this great, inventive Christian orator, alms are many things: "the Queen of Virtues who quickly raises human beings to the heavenly vaults," "your ransom from the bondage of sin," and "salvation of the soul." According to St. John, once catapulted to heaven by copious good gifts, consistent almsgivers can rightly "boast" to the divine assembly—"with a boldness exceeding that of the angels"—of their unimpeachable character and complete immunity from damning judgment. The Christian's duty to give remains unabated here. However, advertising alms as infallible hygiene for the individual donor's soul makes motives for giving more self-centered. Christian charity is now performed to augment the donor's own spiritual capital. This conception of alms progressively substitutes eternal personal preferment for self-abnegating communal integration as the prime driver and reward of philanthropists (Garrison 1993).

Eclipsed by the church fathers' eloquence, an original scriptural message of a more rigorous beggary for grace would come back to inspire later insurrectionary movements for reform within the Western European Catholic Church. Such humble men as St. Francis of Assisi, St. Dominic, and Thomas à Kempis became philanthropic subversives by advocating a return to apostolic poverty and self-abnegating alms seeking. Unfortunately, new orders of mendicant monks who embraced poverty and begging as a profession—the "voluntary poor"—began to compete with all the old ranks of the involuntary poor for a share of total alms given. Competing Christian versions of true charity rarely assured the truly needy of effective relief (Wolf 2003).

Clerical redefinitions made gifts a critical agency of doctrinal orthodoxy and parochial discipline. These views gained greater force within an unfolding Christian moral economy directly connecting sin and charity as inversely proportional forces locked in perpetual cosmic battle. Growing quantities of evil might ultimately reduce even the sum total of God's grace, his free, charitable gifts of redemption, and foredoom more human souls to hell. In this exquisite calculus of salvation, the containment of sin by all available means became imperative to preserve Christendom. Influential church catechists harped upon this theme, emphasizing that true Christian charity must now have essentially redemptive and corrective effects. St. Augustine, bishop of Hippo from 396 to 430 CE, contributed his popular instructional manual for novice Christians (translated as *Faith, Hope, and Charity,* circa 420–423 CE). He built this text around the general proposition that "almsgiving without purpose of amendment is useless" (Augustine 1947). Under the category of acceptable methodical alms, Augustine included reproaches to the immoral, chastisement of miscreants, and physical punishment of the incorrigible. A fine almsgiver is anyone "who corrects with blows or restrains by any kind of disciplinary measure another over whom he has authority" (Augustine 1947). Senior ecclesiastics' insistence on the essential role of alms in protecting and policing entire Christian communities reconnects private philanthropic action with the politics of the public sphere. Imperative correctional use of alms within a Christian cosmology of dueling sin and grace amplifies the ethical duties of philanthropists. They must become pious public figures determined to shape the moral discipline, behavior, and imagination of their brethren.

Secular potentates in the Eastern Roman (Byzantine) Empire moved quickly to expropriate the disciplinary and material resources of enriched Christian churches (Constantelos 1991). Alliances of convenience and conflicts of interest between lay and ecclesiastical authorities in the eastern and western remnants of the Roman Empire produced innumerable documents detailing these interactions. Innovations in Byzantine law enabled self-governing, propertied foundations to develop as independent legal entities free from the tutelage of other powers, both sacred and secular (Philipsborn 1951; Rickett 1979; Saleilles 1907). Expert legal historians have ascribed these novelties to a culture in which "donation advances to the fore as the noblest transaction of christianized Roman civil law" (Bruck 1944).

Crucial here is the emperor Constantine's general law of 321 CE endowing the Catholic Church with the perpetual right to stand as heir to and receive legacies from Roman and Hellenic testators (Duff 1926). Widening flows of gift capital to the church enabled construction of diverse affiliated charitable institutions. Churchmen supervised the building of hospitals, orphanages, and almshouses and endowed funds for poor relief and the ransom of Christian captives. The birth of the modern hospital (and a host of associated modern fundraising techniques) has been linked to this concentration of charitable resources for restorative public service in the Byzantine Empire (Miller 1985). Hospitals benefited disproportionately from Greek Christians' extolling medical practice as the finest form of love in action. Institutionalized medicine reshaped the meaning and practice of philanthropy.

By enactments of the subsequent Byzantine emperor Justinian (imperium 527–565 CE), philanthropic organizations progressively obtained the capability themselves to receive gifts and legacies directly. They also gained exemptions from most forms of imperial taxation. Indeed, by this era, the noun *philanthropy* in Greek also meant the tax-exempt status emperors conferred on select charities (Brown 2002). For centuries, these tax privileges to charities also earned Byzantine emperors the title of "Your Philanthropy," employed by grateful and solicitous subjects. From this early date, fiscal immunities became integral to the definition and ethos of Western philanthropic institutions.

Moreover, Byzantine charitable institutions also progressively won emancipation from supervision and control by clerics. They did so through enlarged individual endowments, staff expansion, and refinement of their internal administrative procedures by legal means. Charities' own resources had once been construed collectively as the "patrimony of the poor" under necessary supervision by bishops. Now greater rights of independent fundraising, purposeful capital accumulation, and self-administration for charities broke the former episcopal monopoly of control. Church-affiliated foundations without a clear and separate legal persona became independent foundations exercising a hard-won personality in riskier power-political environments (Feenstra 1955; Gaudemet 1955). Lay administrators in more foundations fought for greater professional autonomy. They developed idiosyncratic strategies for cultivation of more private donors. Charity managers now found it politically expedient to accord lay givers expanded influence over the operation of private philanthropic institutions. Donor-advised funds have an ancient pedigree.

The administrators of Byzantine organized philanthropies also were enjoined by law to convert all gifts of movable property as rapidly as possible into immovable holdings. They quickly invested all gifts in landed estates. This secured future revenue in support of mission from the sale of agricultural produce. Official prohibitions against all sales or other lasting alienations of these endowment properties show no fear in late antiquity of expanding mortmain. The privilege of mortmain allowed charities forever to remove such productive resources as land from sale through markets. Kings and philanthropists once deemed mortmain, the right of charitable organizations to build endowments through accumulation of inalienable landed property, essential to support pious or humanitarian institutions. By 1100 CE, certainly in the Byzantine world, the lineaments are visible of a private philanthropic "sector" in dynamic and challenging coexistence with the forces of market, state, and church.

LATE MEDIEVAL AND EARLY MODERN REGIMES OF ORGANIZED BENEVOLENCE

The most provocative and rapidly expanding corpus of historical research on nearly modern philanthropic institutions concerns the politics of public welfare and donor behavior in resurgent Western European cities after 1200 CE. The extensive archives, rich material embellishments, and impressive physical structures amassed by urban charitable organizations in early modern Europe permit extensive investigation of why and how urbanites became benefactors and beneficiaries in new ways at this time. Larger numbers of citizens and their shifting stratifications produced new forms of sacred and secular philanthropy. Changing modes of urban commercial and political interaction altered popular beliefs about charity's proper forms. Religiously inspired crises of conscience and conflicts among townspeople caused them to question older styles of benevolence. The cultural history of philanthropy necessarily assumes multiple dimensions in these built urban venues of dynamic experiment in charitable activity to sustain cities and, later, nations.

For the Western European world, new measures now exist of lay urbanites' venturesome development of their own practical agencies for neighborhood and community betterment. Charitable confraternities now became important. A confraternity was a club of ordinary citizens who joined together to accomplish pious and charitable works satisfying their need for immediate, personal enactments of neighborly Christian virtues. Confraternity members more often aimed to enhance the social rather than the spiritual capital of all citizens. From 1200 CE, the proliferation of male and female confraternities among the laity as key vehicles of urban charity helped to assuage citizens' new moral dilemmas. Confraternities directly challenged (and progressively supplanted) older modes of communal care sponsored by the Catholic Church. The Catholic Church directly sponsored some confraternities; many others possessed only a chaplain and were loosely tied to clerical networks of influence (Henderson 1994).

Growing civic economies and the decline of feudalism in the countryside sparked massive human migrations toward cities. More Europeans simply walked away from traditional forms of Catholic charity, centrally administered from monasteries implanted deep in the vast rural world. Townspeople responded by developing their own more feasible and emotionally satisfying hybrid philanthropies less directly tied to religious requirements for charitable acts.

New modes of philanthropic activity drew force from proliferating clerical and lay inquiries about the true numbers and types of the poor. The poor constituted a category of humanity Christians had long been taught to regard with equanimity and compassion but that now appeared to be growing without limit. Fears of submersion (and perversion) by numberless poor drove propertied Europeans to intensify scrutiny of the miserable in a quest to ascertain precisely those subcategories of the needy best susceptible to rescue and improvement by concentrated alms. New media of communication (such as printing) and of representation (such as satirical printmaking) alternately facilitated and confounded effective rationalization of philanthropy. Books and prints circulated simultaneously more elaborate schemes of poor relief and more grotesquely stereotypical (and misleading) images of the poor themselves (Jutte 1994).

The questions of how to give properly and who to give to

had no certain, immutable answers (some readers of this era turned back to Seneca for advice). Agents of centralized poor relief through royally chartered or privately administered relief organizations amalgamated, expropriated, and often destroyed the earlier plurality of confraternal charitable groups. These philanthropic police actions heightened the urban social tensions that older caring agencies were designed to mitigate. Radical, multiliterate theologians drove the religious reformations of the sixteenth century forward with inflammatory sermonizing about donations good and bad. Quarrelsome churchmen battled to clarify and reestablish Jesus's prime teachings on Christian duties, charity, and the gifts of grace. Gifts became the texts and pretexts announcing unprecedented religious schisms throughout Europe (Davis 2000).

In reformed Protestant nations such as England, state-sponsored destruction of most preexisting Catholic charitable organizations and confiscation of their endowments made poor relief incumbent upon poorer local governments. This transformation increased official efforts to assure efficient use of all private monies donated for public improvements (Slack 1988, 1999). State policing of private foundations for charitable purposes became imperative. Parliamentarians during Queen Elizabeth's reign responded with the Statute of Charitable Uses (1601). This legislation gave a definition of legal charity that has remained influential in all lands touched by British law. The statute's original intent was not to define a charity, however, but to provide new judicial tools for discovery and correction of frauds involving private foundations. Armed with such legislation, Europeans now embarked on a permanent quest to find the "deserving poor" and to rationalize the operations of philanthropies intended to diminish their number (Riis 1981).

The European urban confraternity has become an important focal point in revisionary histories of early modern charitable activity and public welfare through voluntary associations (Bagliani 1987; Banker 1988; Flynn 1989; Terpstra 1995; Weissman 1982). Weissman's pathbreaking analysis of the ritual brotherhood via confraternal membership achieved by Renaissance Florentines applies the insights of cultural anthropology to an understanding of late medieval and early modern donor behavior. Crucial here is Weissman's description of the agonistic, psychically disturbing character of civic life, especially for commercially and politically active males inhabiting packed, factionalized, and risky Renaissance cities. On a daily basis, townspeople faced densely conflicting duties. They were honor-bound to compete with one another for personal status advancement but also craved trustworthy allies necessary for careers in business and politics. They saw enlargement of family patrimonies and social connections as essential, but they also feared that too much success would elicit the ruinous envy of gossiping neighbors and the attentions of undercover civic tax agents, hunting concentrations of wealth in every neighborhood. They sought to achieve literary ideals of good repute through ample generosity to friends, but inwardly they feared the advantages one's gifts gave to other players in a zero-sum game of status rivalry.

Confronted by so much stress, many male urbanites sought emotional relief through membership and service in charitable confraternities. Here, members were united—if only weekly—in peaceable, guileless, reassuring brotherhoods for alms deeds conducive to civic peace. The psychosocial benefits volunteers accrued in joining novel charitable organizations drove historic innovations in religious and philanthropic practices. The rise of urban confraternities definitively broke a near monopoly on provision of charitable service formerly belonging to the monasteries and orders of the Roman Catholic Church (Mollat 1986). Weissman's work shows Renaissance philanthropies offering alternatives and challenges to the existing sociopolitical order. Lay brothers and sisters in their Renaissance service organizations adroitly converted voluntary charitable acts into enhanced worldly social capital for themselves.

Subsequent investigations of early modern confraternities by Flynn (in Spain) and Terpstra (in the north Italian city of Bologna) show the power of these community-based organizations in catalyzing effective opposition to outside authorities' plans for change in local government and philanthropy. City confraternities became hotly contested sites in battles over the policing of urban society and welfare, energizing ordinary citizens, civic magistrates, and encroaching early modern European monarchs. According to Cavallo (1995), princes covetous of more influence over civic politics and wealthy citizenries targeted older urban charitable groups for destruction. Nobles also resorted to sponsorship of their own competitive philanthropic or hospitable associations to build up political support networks and reliable municipal clienteles against rebellious commoners. A polity's real needs thus rarely inspired such calculated and increasingly centralized foundations. And these endeavors threatened the capacity of such charitable agencies to offer alternatives to existing sociopolitical orders.

Cavallo's excellent research on the motives of early modern donors also provocatively suggests that intensifying competitions for power and preferment among urbanites drove a vogue for status enhancement through more private giving to prominent charitable institutions such as hospitals. Hospitals became "an arena in which city elites could put their prestige on display through their charitable acts" (Cavallo 1995:100). This movement weakened older collective, anonymous, and compulsive modes of benefaction while promoting philanthropy's own distinguished status as the voluntary action of urbane notables. Surviving confraternities now played a larger role as local art patrons, employing architects, painters, and artisans to build their clubhouses and make appropriate symbols of their service.

Historians of early modern European philanthropy have also given close attention to contemporary texts and images representing the misfortunate and needy (Cubero 1998; Geremek 1994; Jutte 1994; Mollat 1986; Starobinski 1997). These media circulated more vicious fictions and uglier images depicting the poor as degraded, duplicitous, and depraved savages whose own personal foibles precipitated their destitution. Such stimuli impelled former suppliers of alms to redirect their charities toward larger, centralized, and repressive secular institutions for rehabilitation of the needy. In pictures and in print, the poor were now rapidly losing the special sanctity once ascribed to them. In Europe from 1500 to 1700, such reorientations of assistance became ecumenical. Catholic and Protestant givers alike refused to satisfy beggars at the door or serve them in confraternities. Philanthropists increasingly preferred to patronize disciplinary institutions (such as workhouses, orphanages, general hospitals, and charity schools) whose full-time officers and instructors could promise more economical and effective acquisition of orderly public welfare through social reform (Jutte 1980; Fehler 1999). By the sixteenth century, the secularization and professionalization of Western European philanthropy had greatly accelerated (Sauvel 1954).

In the language of their gifts and testaments, benefactors now spoke far less about saving their own souls or boasting to angels through donations and far more about making worthy investments training needy people for productive self-sufficiency and enhancing the worldly social security of all. This process has been recently described as a "capitalization of charity." European philanthropists after 1600 CE often construed charitable donations as their own voluntary capital placements entitling them to tangible returns and to some degree of enduring control over funds provided to entrepreneurs running charitable organizations (Safely 1997). This attitude is attributable to the Reformation that divided European communities into antagonistic camps of Protestants and Catholics, each having to develop and fund their own charitable organizations. The splintering of religious communities placed a new premium on more efficient use of the limited funds raised for charity among smaller religious sects. European clerics, equating bad gifts with the spread of heresy, counseled potential givers toward greater prudence in deciding—as a free choice—when, if ever, to make any philanthropic gift. The possession of wealth, in itself, no longer obligated the wealthy to give. Such arguments abrogated charity's traditional lien on property (Andrew 1992).

The advent of charity as investment capital made the jobs of program officers in philanthropic organizations harder. Charity as capital volatilized streams of private donations, accelerating the pace at which donors demanded hard evidence of positive welfare outcomes and shifted their support at will among more numerous and competitive relief organizations to maximize their gifts' public benefit (Innes 1996). Increasingly, charity administrators found that they had to solicit and skillfully manage a mix of private donations, public subventions, and legitimate institutional earnings in order to accomplish their missions. Philanthropists and charity managers thus actively participated in the development of contemporary market economies and state instruments of police. Post-Reformation European charity organizations, in their quest for operational efficiency, promoted the calculating and experimental business practices intrinsic to capitalism's success (Cunningham and Innes 1998). This new symbiosis of charity and political economy gained strength as European avatars of individualism, such as Michel de Montaigne, railed against the offensive dependencies and exaggerated reciprocal obligations fostered by older modes of European gift exchange. Montaigne recommended instead escape from the coils and expected reciprocities of patronage through the "relief of contract" and explicit quantifications of service (Davis 2000).

Europeans' desire to replace the whim of patronage with legally enforceable adherence to principle in philanthropic action also informs the famous Elizabethan Statute of Charitable Uses. The preamble to this act specifies which charitable causes could be legally endowed through trusts, including aid of the poor, care of veterans, nurture of orphans, advancement of learning, and promotion of religion (Jones 1969; Jordan 1959). This act issued from a parliament determined to maximize the amount of private monies available to promote social welfare, sparing the state from such expense and diminishing the chances of popular rebellion by the poor. The legislation mostly stipulates how lawful commissions of inquiry under government aegis may be formed in any county to discover "any breach of trust, falsity, nonemployment, concealment . . . or conversion" of endowed charitable funds. Early legal commentators on the statute accordingly emphasize and explain at length the inquisitorial powers and procedures it conveys to local commissioners combating manifold frauds against charitable gifts and endowments (Herne 1660). Government supposition of malfeasance in the operation of private philanthropies dates back a long way. Delegating its powers of surveillance, the Elizabethan state partnered with lawyers and philanthropists in creating a more secure legal environment for the private service of public welfare. The statute not only defines charitable uses, it also announces the state's prerogative to police an early semblance of the nonprofit sector.

NATIONALIZING THE CHARITABLE IMPERATIVE AND THE RISE OF "SCIENTIFIC PHILANTHROPY" IN MODERN EUROPE

Across Europe, amateur givers' sympathies for safe, cautious, and respectable philanthropic investments first reinforced localized giving and then steered more gifts and bequests into permanent private foundations (Jordan 1959). Donors subjected these assets to close management via restrictive living deeds of gift and stringent testamentary bequests. However, deepening pools of mercantile wealth led to more speculation in philanthropy after 1700. Such endeavors enabled status-conscious bourgeois benefactors to challenge nobles' traditional lock on high social prestige and governing power. Aspiring middle-class donors made competitive use of their disposable capital via self-promoting and increasingly patriotic charitable activity (Shapely 1998). Early modern European philanthropy, energized by battles for influence among increasingly competitive elements within factionalized socioeconomic elites, became a kind of civil war by other means while also fueling more interstate rivalries.

Feuding European states' violent contests for empire on a global scale in the eighteenth century redefined public welfare (foreign and domestic). High-stakes warfare imposed new exigencies on all uses of productive material resources, including their charitable deployment. Growing consciousness among power-political players of the emerging national interests to be served, or more likely abused, by domestic philanthropic regimes raised the dangers of self-indulgent and inflexible giving. How the operations of any existing or proposed charitable institution served the mutable hegemonic needs of the state in armed struggle for global domination via colonial adventure became an issue of paramount importance among astute trustees. This concern reshaped definitions and provisions of philanthropy that underwent what may be termed a thorough "nationalization" (if not "imperialization") during the early modern period (Andrew 1989). After 1750, British philanthropists, for example, proved themselves very adept at forming novel, privately endowed hospitals and paramilitary schools. They designed these institutions to increase the procreative powers of poor English women and to enlist their surviving offspring, legitimate or not, in armed colonial campaigns abroad (Taylor 1979).

Growing European disputes over the purposes and logistics of charitable institutions resulted in fierce, revolutionary eighteenth-century debates over the laws governing private philanthropic activity. Legislators took aim at myriad obsolete foundations with missions vitiated by dynamic sociocultural changes. Governors deplored fixed endowments yielding paltry sums for charity incommensurate with the real problems of the day. Many statesmen also deeply distrusted charity officers and trustees, accusing them of embezzling funds under their control and robbing the nation of vital resources. Government restrictions on mortmain became a pan-European phenomenon at this time, altering the meaning and practice of philanthropy. By nearly coincident parliamentary bill in England (1736), royal edict in France (1749), and imperial decree in the Habsburg domains (1755), legislators rewrote laws of mortmain to prohibit transfers of real estate by testamentary gift to the endowments of private foundations. New strictures also regulated life gifts of property to such beneficiaries. Donors now had to obtain costly and deliberate official approval for such acts. The endowed foundation, once a key agency of philanthropic action, fell into deepening disrepute, infuriating comfortable and defensive trustees but galvanizing statesmen to regulate private charities more stringently (Brody 1997).

A vital objective of legislators here was to protect noble families' patrimonies (and contingent sociopolitical influence) from gross ruin by any one family member's vain benefactions. Great impetuous or testamentary gifts of property to charitable endowments were especially to be feared. But governors' rulings had other effects and implications. With endowment by major gifts, capital conversions, and real estate transfers discouraged, landed elites began to lose an older preeminence in charitable action. Aristocrats now faced more adroit competition in philanthropic leadership from notable merchants and professional men with greater liquid assets more easily convertible to (and coveted for) charitable purposes and distinction. The rise of the activist bourgeois trustee is a later eighteenth-century phenomenon, especially in England, undoubtedly linked to alterations in statutory policing of major gifts (including bequests) and charity management (Innes 1996; Shapely 1998). Philanthropic organizations found themselves more reliant on continual and increasingly competitive fundraising campaigns, held annually, quarterly, or seasonally. In order to adapt and survive, philanthropies had to appeal to a more socially diverse array of potential contributors. Organized charities used all available resources of communication and publicity to create a more democratic but frenetic culture of gift solicitation and service. They more often urged donors to give for patriotic reasons rather than to satisfy personal or religious motives (Andrew 1989).

Attracted by the philanthropic hubbub, journalists for growing mass-circulation European daily newspapers covered charitable institutions more critically. Reporters investigated charitable operations, censured program failures, and championed populations ignored by existing organizations. Public opinion, channeled by the press, pushed European philanthropic experimentation after 1800 in new directions. Exponents of these reforms established intrepid "scientific philanthropy" as the dominant paradigm for all modern regimes of giving and public service. They promoted greater efficiency among charitable institutions and encouraged deeper quasi-anthropological and sociological data-driven knowledge of the populations to be served. Philanthropists mounted expeditions to such places as "darkest London" and "deepest Paris" in hopes of discovering what really needed to be done to rescue the poor, improve charity, and better society as a whole (Himmelfarb 1991). This exploratory social science explicitly modeled itself on contemporary Western imperial ventures to colonize the inhabitants of the Southern Hemisphere. Imperial and scientific philanthropy launched many experiments in the domestic colonization of the poor. Europe's needy were more often defined as primitives requiring guidance toward the proper lifeways of civilized, sober, and competitive market societies. Philanthropy could now be construed as furnishing mandatory instruction in home economics for the masses.

Eighteenth-century governors across Europe found older, lethargic forms of philanthropy unjustifiable. They deemed outmoded and counterproductive the endowment of land and resources to perpetual charitable foundations because donors could never accurately foresee society's true needs long after their own demise. Ecclesiastical and secular foundations previously exercising mortmain now came under sweeping official attack (Kenny 1880; Owen 1964; Jones 1969). In England and France, the new legislation appears to have been motivated, in part, by the strengthening anti-clerical attitudes of statesmen anxious to free the economies and charities of their secularizing countries from the "dead hand" (the literal meaning of *mortmain*) of the church.

In England in the 1730s, however, parliamentarians also grew alarmed by "the prevailing madness of perpetuating one's memory by leaving a large estate to some charity" (Cobbett 1811:1142). On the floor of the House of Commons, statesmen railed against the conceits of donors whose impetuous charitable contributions, they believed, impoverished noble families, cheated descendants of rightful inheritances, and destabilized society. Members of Parliament denounced "those pretences drawn from piety, charity, and a compassion for the poor . . . that only . . . cloak the vanity, pride, and ambition of private men who have got into, or expect to get into the management of what they call a charitable foundation" (Cobbett 1811:1154). English governors put the natural rights of heirs above the natural rights of donors. They expressly made philanthropy a matter of national security by arguing that, in case of invasion, only private property owners could be counted on to defend their holdings valiantly. Philanthropists who transferred private lands to the endowments of faceless charities harmed the nation because charity officers could not be trusted to fight for lands they only held in trust and did not own.

In France, revisions of mortmain legislation also aimed to weaken the territorial and charitable prerogatives of the church. But the endeavor took more inspiration from official animus toward the presumed vanities and self-glorifying pretensions of private founders avidly converting gifts to fame while the nation starved for more flexible and productive capital. In his article "Foundations," published in Denis Diderot's widely influential *Encyclopaedie* (1755), Anne-Robert-Jacques Turgot, the future French royal comptroller-general of the economy, denounced the founders of all charitable agencies for fixed purposes as vain and presumptuous fools whose costly creations inexorably progressed to obsolescence (Marais 1999; Tissier 1891). Turgot contended that a founder's charitable enthusiasm could never be sustained over time. Unscrupulous successors would misuse or abuse the original endowment and cheat the nation of any future benefit. Statesmen had to regulate the public's vain charitable impulses, harnessing them to the polity's evolving needs (Stephens 1895).

Turgot asserted civil government's "incontestable right" to supervise, alter at will, expropriate, and—preferably—destroy all existing foundations in France. Louis XV, in his new edict on mortmain of 1749, did not go so far as to ban all foundations, but he did assert the necessity of royal authorization and periodic review for all such organizations, now fully accountable to the crown. The king ordered the trustees of such entities to convert their immovable endowed properties into cash for direct purchases of negotiable state bonds, thereby rendering the charities more economically beneficial to the kingdom as a whole. This was another instance of philanthropy's "nationalization" in early modern times.

Leading European utilitarian philosophers and political economists of the nineteenth century, such as John Stuart Mill, found such arguments especially persuasive. Mill's widely circulated tract "Corporation and Church Property" had multiple journal and pamphlet editions from 1833. In it he attacked the inviolability of most public charitable trusts, promoted increased state scrutiny of all foundations, and sanctioned eventual state intervention to alter founders' bequests for better practical effect. Mill urged that the landed properties of all charitable endowments in mortmain be rapidly brought to market and sold at auction, and the proceeds directly invested in stocks and other commercial securities for redistribution to the charities under government supervision (Mill 1833). These mounting arguments for the essential liquidity of all philanthropic endowments show nineteenth-century Europeans to be preoccupied by defining the right relationship between amalgamated philanthropies, states, and markets. This is the regime of public scrutiny and public expectation under which the modern nonprofit sector has developed.

New urban print media, including daily newspapers, monthly magazines, and increasingly professional journals, broadcast and amplified nineteenth-century Europeans' dissensions over the proper means and objectives of philanthropic activity. City readerships, avid for news and cheap entertainment, made the fortunes of journalists adept in such newly popular genres of expression as exposés and human interest stories. Each of these became venues of heated public debate over philanthropy and its place in modern societies. Enterprising newspapermen, such as Henry Mayhew, deployed teams of reporters and informants to bring back printable daily news from all ranks of metropolitan society, especially the needy (Mayhew 1861–1862). This investigative reporting gave poverty a human face. It also pointed out gross discrepancies between the real needs of all the various classes of laboring poor people and the woefully ineffectual relief dispensed by crusading but unsupervised and uninformed volunteer philanthropists. This was the inept and supercilious group responsible for what Charles Dickens disgustedly called "the charity business."

Such reportage encouraged the professionalization of philanthropy. Frustrated metropolitan benefactors, including civil servants, learned professional men, academicians, and philanthropists, sought to develop alternative modes of disciplined work for public service. They advocated far more careful, methodical, and quantitatively accurate surveys of urban populations and their material attributes and wants. The success of these endeavors was in large part due to the development of new serial publications under the patronage of voluntary professional associations, including the Statistical Society of London (founded 1835) and the National Association for the Promotion of Social Science (founded 1857). The serials published an astonishing diversity of writings on new analytical strategies and means of data accumulation to advance efficiently systematized private philanthropy and to measure the beneficial outcomes of bureaucratized public welfare. A thoroughly modern regime of "scientific philanthropy" gained encouragement and legitimacy in these publications from voluntary associations of experts in social reform.

Even a brief survey of philanthropy's history in the West shows the densely interconnected social, economic, legal, political, religious, artistic, and psychological dimensions of the subject. Over time, philanthropists and the institutions they created to perpetuate their generosity have played central roles in the building of cities and the articulation of civic values. Charitable actors and organizations have long been essential in the formation, communication, and teaching of religious principles. Donors did not merely build churches. Their generous, at times selfless behavior also catalyzed doctrinal disputes and generated sectarian movements that led to entirely new religions. Rituals of giving worked in part to differentiate castes and reinforce social hierarchies, especially in cities. Givers' ambitions and anxieties contributed to the development and revision of Western law codes. Ceremonies of just donation also moderated class tensions and became an important theater for symbolizing social norms and contracts. Using charity as conspicuous compassion, contenders for supreme governing power sought to demonstrate their moral aptitude for rulership.

More broadly, entire systems or regimes of philanthropy have clashed and modified continuously in Western history. Particular eras, such as the fifth century BCE, the first century CE, late antiquity, the fourteenth century CE, the Reformations, and the nineteenth century, stand out as periods of great human experimentation to redefine and better administer philanthropy. Vital contemporary trend lines that emerge from these experiments can be summarized as the rationalization, secularization, capitalization, nationalization, and professionalization of philanthropy and its agents. Within this dynamic, the scrutiny of donor behavior and potential recipients of aid increases dramatically. Endorsements of spontaneous, indiscriminate largesse drop off and the paradigm of socially responsible generosity moves toward stringent premeditation and selectivity in giving. Self-assertion increasingly supplants self-denial as a spring for benevolence with a greater attendant risk that philanthropists may be denounced as vain, self-serving egoists. The economic and political obsolescence of aristocrats, hastened by enterprising and rebellious merchants, renders noblesse oblige impractical as an ideology of modern giving. The status of donor, even patron, is democratized to admit a far wider array of competitors for social distinction via thoughtful giving and rigorous selection of worthy beneficiaries. Existing charities bureaucratize and new cadres of expert philanthropists form to counsel wise giving and steward the liquid capital amassed by "nonprofit" organizations. A more diverse body of donors is recruited in a culture of perpetual fundraising and more frenetic gift solicitation enabled by the evolving mass media of print and communication.

Attentiveness to the long history of individual and collective charitable action in the West enables better understanding of how the nonprofit sector and its supporters behave today. Such knowledge leads to many new topics of research. Heavily reliant on the benevolence of private givers and volunteers, many modern charitable nonprofits survive in large part because of the compulsions toward external or communal service experienced by private donors. Historical analysis suggests that donor motives are usually, if not always, plural in nature and do not derive solely from benefactors' most religious or ethical precepts. However, knowledge of charity's essential place but varying strength or intensity in different codes of Western religious practice over time can help in comprehending the deeper springs and directions of gift flows, most of which have gone and still go to religious organizations. Just as likely, tacit self-interest, fear of humiliation, rampant patriotism, and a poignant quest for psychic or worldly comfort may combine to produce the human actions and emotions of confraternity and compassion. What is the mix of emotions and motives that drive donor behavior now? How charitable institutions incorporate and modify the ideals that supporters bring to them also requires more careful attention and historical insight because those processes are potentially crucial to the maintenance—and the disturbance—of social order.

Prior civilizations, such as the Greeks, had no qualms whatsoever about identifying as "philanthropic" donor behaviors that were both overtly and tacitly coerced by the communities in which benefactors lived. The Greeks' own elaborate lexicon of *philanthropy,* in which the word took on multiple new meanings over time, should prompt us to wonder about the accuracy, scope, and limitations of the term as used in our modern tongues today. Where did all the ancient meanings of philanthropy go? And what do current definitions of the term tell us about the historic philanthropies we have accepted and those we have rejected in shaping the operations of the nonprofit sector?

As both beneficiary and target of accumulated legal privileges and judicial investigations over time, the current nonprofit sector exists in dynamic symbiosis with the forces of justice and state government. European and American archives document a long quest for a law of charity in the West. That jurisprudence, now luxuriant, is the net result of cross-fertilizations between positive and customary law occurring in the legal histories of several ancient and modern cultures, including Greece, Rome, Byzantium, medieval Christian Europe, and England. Examples from these civilizations show philanthropy's historic power to integrate human communities and to moderate their socioeconomic tensions. These phenomena suggest that charities have contributed their own informal laws or implied contracts, creating commonwealths by articulating the needs of minorities and smoothing relations between different social strata. Do modern philanthropies, often bureaucratically organized and expertly managed, continue to exert these pacific powers?

Has the more recent advent of scientific philanthropy, with its rational and professional pretensions, enhanced or diminished philanthropy's capacity for popular and consensual peacemaking? As epitomes of Renaissance philanthropy, civic confraternities are celebrated for offering alternatives to the existing social order. Can the same be said for those modern nonprofits that, under a regime of rationalized and nationalized philanthropy, only manage to survive through the sale of services and direct grants or contracts from governments? From a comparative historic perspective, does the sector now subvert or sustain the status quo?

Finally, philanthropists have been instrumental in expanding (and occasionally contracting) the moral imaginations of their contemporaries. Can the professionalized and bureaucratized agents of an expanding and increasingly competitive modern nonprofit sector, now far more vulnerable to harsh media scrutiny, achieve similar public trust and influence? Historic charitable organizations contended to set and to reset the bounds of civilization, often by striving to exemplify civilized behavior in their own operations and assistance. Retracing the steps by which they did so primes us to recognize whether and how they may do so now.

REFERENCES

Adler, Betsy. 1999. *The Rules of the Road: A Guide to the Law of Charities in the United States.* Washington, DC: Council on Foundations.

Andrew, Donna. 1989. *Philanthropy and Police: London Charity in the Eighteenth Century.* Princeton, NJ: Princeton University Press.

———. 1992. "*Noblesse Oblige:* Female Charity in an Age of Sentiment." In *Early Modern Conceptions of Property,* ed. John Brewer and Susan Staves, 275–300. London: Routledge.

Augustine. 1947. *St. Augustine: Faith, Hope, and Charity.* Trans. Louis Arand. Repr., New York: Newman Press, 1978.

Bagliani, Agostino. 1987. *Le mouvement confraternal au moyen âge: France, Italie, Suisse.* Geneva: Librairie Droz.

Banker, James R. 1988. *Death in the Community: Memorialization and Confraternities in an Italian Commune.* Athens: University of Georgia Press.

Bauman, Richard A. 2000. *Human Rights in Ancient Rome.* London: Routledge.

Boatwright, Mary T. 2000. *Hadrian and the Cities of the Roman Empire.* Princeton, NJ: Princeton University Press.

Brody, Evelyn. 1997. "Charitable Endowments and the Democratization of Dynasty." *Arizona Law Review* 39:873–948.

Brown, Peter. 1992. *Power and Persuasion in Late Antiquity: Towards a Christian Empire.* Madison: University of Wisconsin Press.

———. 2002. *Poverty and Leadership in the Later Roman Empire.* Hanover, NH: Brandeis University Press.

Brown, Raymond. 1997. *An Introduction to the New Testament.* New York: Doubleday.

Bruck, Eberhard F. 1944. "Ethics vs. Law: St. Paul, the Fathers of the Church, and the 'Cheerful Giver' in Roman Law." *Traditio* 2:97–114.

———. 1949. "Foundations for the Deceased in Roman Law, Religion, and Political Thought." In *Scritti in onore di Contardo Ferrini,* vol. 4, 1–42. Milan: Societa Editrice Vita e Pensiero.

———. 1955. "Les facteurs moteurs de l'origine et du developpement des fondations grecques et romaines." *Revue internationale des droits de l'antiquité* (3rd series) 2:159–166.

Buchanan, James. 1962. *Theorika: A Study of Monetary Distributions to the Athenian Citizenry.* Locust Valley, NY: J. J. Augustin.

Cassel, David. 1887. *Die Armenverwaltung im Alten Israel.* Berlin: Muller.

Cavallo, Sandra. 1995. *Charity and Power in Early Modern Italy: Benefactors and Their Motives in Turin, 1541–1789.* Cambridge: Cambridge University Press.

Chrysostom, St. John. 1998. *St. John Chrysostom on Repentance and Alms Giving.* Trans. Gus G. Christo. Washington DC: Catholic University Press of America.

Clement of Alexandria. 1960. *Clement of Alexandria.* Trans. G. W. Butterworth. Loeb Classical Library. Cambridge, MA: Harvard University Press.

Cobbett, William. 1811. *Cobbett's Parliamentary History of England.* Repr., New York: AMS Press, 1966.

Collins, Edwin, trans. 1905. *The Duties of the Heart by Rabbi Bachye.* London: John Murray.

Constantelos, Demetrios. 1991. *Byzantine Philanthropy and Social Welfare.* New Rochelle, NY: Aristide Caratzas.

Cotter, Wendy. 1996. "The Collegia and Roman Law: State Restrictions on Voluntary Associations, 64 BCE–200 CE." In *Voluntary Associations in the Graeco-Roman World,* ed. John S. Kloppenborg and Stephen G. Wilson, 74–89. New York: Routledge.

Cubero, José. 1998. *Histoire du vagabondage.* Paris: Editions Imago.

Cunningham, Hugh, and Innes, Joanna, eds. 1998. *Charity, Philanthropy, and Reform.* London: Macmillan.

Danby, H. D., trans. 1933. *The Mishnah.* Oxford: Oxford University Press.

Davies, J. K. 1965. *Wealth and the Power of Wealth in Classical Athens.* Repr., Salem, NH: Ayer, 1992.

Davis, Natalie. 2000. *The Gift in Sixteenth-Century France.* Madison: University of Wisconsin Press.

De Ruiter, S. Tromp. 1932. "De Vocis Quae Est 'Philanthropia' Significatione atque Usu." *Mnemosyne* 59:271–306.

De Visscher, Fernand. 1949. "Le notion du 'corpus' et le regime des associations privées à Rome." In *Scritti in onore di Contardo Ferrini,* vol. 4, 43–53. Milan: Societa Editrice Vita et Pensiero.

———. 1955. "Les fondations privées en droit roman classique." *Revue internationale des droits de l'antiquité* (3rd series) 2:192–218.

Dodd, C. H. 1951. *Gospel and Law: The Relation of Faith and Ethics in Early Christianity.* Cambridge: Cambridge University Press.

Dodds, E. R. 1965. *Pagan and Christian in an Age of Anxiety.* Repr., Cambridge: Cambridge University Press, 1990.

Duff, P. W. 1926. "The Charitable Foundations of Byzantium." In *Cambridge Legal Essays,* ed. G. G. Alexander, 83–99. Cambridge, UK: Heffer and Sons.

Duncan-Jones, R. P. 1974. "The Procurator as Civic Benefactor." *Journal of Roman Studies* 64:79–85.

Ehrman, Bart D. 2000. *The New Testament: A Historical Introduction.* New York: Oxford University Press.

Fagan, Garrett. 1999. *Bathing in Public in the Roman World.* Ann Arbor: University of Michigan Press.

Feenstra, R. 1955. "Le concept de fondation du droit romain classique jusqu'à nos jours: Théorie et pratique." *Revue internationale des droits de l'antiquité* (3rd series) 2:245–263.

———. 1956. "L'histoire des fondations: A propos de quelques etudes recentes." *Tijdschrift voor Rechtsgeschiedenis* 24:381–448.

Fehler, Timothy. 1999. *Poor Relief and Protestantism: The Evolution of Social Welfare in Sixteenth-Century Emden.* Aldershot, UK: Ashgate.

Flynn, Maureen. 1989. *Sacred Charity: Confraternities and Social Welfare in Spain, 1400–1700.* Ithaca, NY: Cornell University Press.

Francotte, Henri. 1905. "Le pain à bon marché et le pain gratuit dans les cites grecques." In *Melanges Nicole: Recueil de mémoires de philologie classique et d'archéologie offerts à Jules Nicole,* 135–157. Geneva: Imprimerie W. Kündig and Fils.

Frisch, Ephraim. 1924. *An Historical Survey of Jewish Philanthropy from the Earliest Times until the Nineteenth Century.* New York: Macmillan.

Gabrielsen, Vincent. 1987. "The Antidosis Procedure in Classical Athens." *Classica et Medievalia* 38:7–37.

Garrison, Roman. 1993. *Redemptive Almsgiving in Early Christianity.* Sheffield, UK: JSOT Press.

Gaudemet, Jean. 1955. "Les fondations en occident au Bas-Empire." *Revue internationale des droits de l'antiquité* (3rd series) 2:275–286.

Geremek, Bronislaw. 1994. *Poverty: A History.* Oxford: Blackwell.

Goligher, W. A. 1907. "Studies in Attic Law II: The Antidosis." *Hermathena* 14:481–515.

Hall, Peter D. 1988. "Private Philanthropy and Public Policy: A Historical Appraisal," In *Philanthropy: Four Views.* New Brunswick, NJ: Transaction Books.

Hamel, Gildas. 1990. *Poverty and Charity in Roman Palestine: First Three Centuries CE* Berkeley: University of California Press.

Hands, A. R. 1968. *Charity and Social Welfare in Greece and Rome.* Ithaca, NY: Cornell University Press.

Henderson, John. 1994. *Piety and Charity in Renaissance Florence.* Oxford: Oxford University Press.

Herne, John. 1660. *The Law of Charitable Uses Set Forth and Explained.* London: T. Twyford.

Himmelfarb, Gertrude. 1991. *Poverty and Compassion: The Moral Imagination of the Late Victorians.* New York: Knopf.

Innes, Joanna. 1996. "The 'Mixed Economy of Welfare' in Early Modern England: Assessments of the Options from Hale to Malthus (c. 1683–1803)." In *Charity, Self-Interest and Welfare in the English Past,* ed. Martin Daunton, 139–180. New York: St. Martin's Press.

Jacobs-Malina, Diane. 1993. *Beyond Patriarchy: Images of the Family in Jesus.* Mahwah, NJ: Paulist Press.

Johnson, Luke T. 1998. *Religious Experience in Earliest Christianity.* Minneapolis, MN: Fortress Press.

———. 1999. *The Writings of the New Testament: An Interpretation.* Minneapolis, MN: Fortress Press.

Jones, Gareth. 1969. *History of the Law of Charity.* Repr., Holmes Beach, FL: W. W. Gaunt and Sons, 1986.

Jordan, W. K. 1959. *Philanthropy in England, 1480–1660.* London: George Allen and Unwin.

Jutte, Robert. 1980. "Poor Relief and Social Discipline in Sixteenth-Century Europe." *European Studies Review* 11:25–52.

———. 1994. *Poverty and Deviance in Early Modern Europe.* Cambridge: Cambridge University Press.

Kelly, J. N. D. 1995. *Golden Mouth: The Story of John Chrysostom, Ascetic, Preacher, Bishop.* Grand Rapids, MI: Baker Books.

Kenney, Courtney S. 1880. *The True Principles of Legislation with Regard to Property Given for Charitable and Other Public Uses.* London: Reeves and Turner.

Klein, Isaac. 1979. *The Code of Maimonides: Book 7, The Book of Agriculture.* Yale Judaica Series, vol. 21. New Haven: Yale University Press.

Kloppenborg, John S., and S. G. Wilson, eds. 1996. *Voluntary Associations in the Greco-Roman World.* London: Routledge.

Lallemand, Leon. 1906–1912. *Histoire de la charité.* 4 vols. Paris: Alphonse Picard.

Lampe, Peter. 1987. *Die stadtromischen Christen in der ersten beiden Jahrhunderten.* Tübingen, Ger.: Mohr.

Lane, Jacqueline, Susan Saxon-Harrold, and Nathan Weber, eds. 1994. *International Giving and Volunteering.* London: Charities Aid Foundation.

Le Bras, Gabriel. 1936. "Les fondations privées du haut empire." In *Studi in onore di Salvatore Riccobono,* vol. 3, 23–67. Palermo, It.: Arti Grafiche G. Castiglia.

Lehmann, Joseph. 1897. "Assistance publique et privée d'après l'antique legislation juive." *Revue des études juives* 58:i–xxxviii.

Lewis, Naphtali. 1960. "Leitourgia and Related Terms." *Greek, Roman, and Byzantine Studies* 3:175–184.

———. 1963. "Leitourgia and Related Terms (II)." *Greek, Roman, and Byzantine Studies* 6:226–230.

Loewenberg, Frank M. 2001. *From Charity to Social Justice: The Emergence of Communal Institutions for Support of the Poor in Ancient Judaism.* New Brunswick, NJ: Transaction Books.

Malina, Bruce. 1981. *The New Testament World: Insights from Cultural Anthropology.* Atlanta, GA: John Knox Press.

———. 1996. *The Social World of Jesus and the Gospels.* London: Routledge.

Marais, Jean-Luc. 1999. *Histoire du don en France de 1800 à 1939: Dons et legs charitables, pieux et philanthropiques.* Rennes: Presses Universitaires de Rennes.

Markus, Thomas. 1993. *Buildings and Power.* London: Routledge.

Mayhew, Henry. 1861–1862. *London Labor and the London Poor.* Repr., London: Penguin Books, 1985.

Meeks, Wayne A. 1983. *The First Urban Christians: The Social World of the Apostle Paul.* New Haven: Yale University Press.

———. 1993. *The Origins of Christian Morality: The First Two Centuries.* New Haven: Yale University Press.

Mill, J. S. 1833. "Corporation and Church Property." In *Collected Works of John Stuart Mill.* Vol. 4, *Essays on Economics and Society,* ed. J. M. Robson, 195–222. Repr., Toronto: University of Toronto Press, 1967.

Miller, Timothy J. 1985. *The Birth of the Hospital in the Byzantine Empire.* Repr., Baltimore: Johns Hopkins University Press, 1997.

Mollat, Michel. 1986. *The Poor in the Middle Ages.* New Haven: Yale University Press.

Moreau-Christophe, L. M. 1851. *Du problème de la misère et de sa solution chez les peuples anciens et modernes.* Paris: Guillaumin et Cie.

Morris, Ian. 1986. "Gift and Commodity in Ancient Greece." *Man* 21:1–17.

Newby, Howard. 1978. *Property, Paternalism, and Power: Class and Control in Rural England.* Madison: University of Wisconsin Press.

Nicols, J. 1989. "Patrona Civitatis: Gender and Civic Patronage." *Studies in Latin Literature and Roman History* 5:117–142.

Owen, David. 1964. *English Philanthropy, 1660–1960.* Cambridge, MA: Harvard University Press.

Philipsborn, Alexander. 1951. "Les éstablissements charitables et les théories de la personnalité juridique dans le droit romain." *Revue internationale des droits de l'antiquité* 6:141–159.

Prockter, L. J. 1991. "Alms and the Man: The Merits of Charity." *Journal of Northwestern Semitic Languages* 17:69–80.

Rhodes, P. J. 1986. "Political Activity in Classical Athens." *Journal of Hellenic Studies* 106:132–144.

Rickett, C. E. F. 1979. "Charitable Giving in English and Roman Law: A Comparison of Method." *Cambridge Law Journal* 38:118–147.

Riis, Thomas, ed. 1981. *Aspects of Poverty in Early Modern Europe.* Stuttgart, Ger.: Klett-Cotta.

Robbins, Kevin C. 1997. *City on the Ocean Sea: La Rochelle, 1530–1650: Urban Society, Religion, and Politics on the French Atlantic Frontier.* Leiden, Neth.: Brill Academic Publishers.

Safely, Thomas M. 1997. *Charity and Economy in the Orphanages of Early Modern Augsburg.* Boston: Humanities Press.

Saleilles, R. 1907. "Les piae causae dans le droit de Justinian." *Melanges Girardan,* 513–551.

Sanders, E. P. 1992. *Judaism: Practice and Belief, 65 BCE–66 CE.* London: SCM Press.

Sassier, Philippe. 1990. *Du bon usage des pauvres: Histoire d'un thème politique.* Paris: Fayard.

Sauvel, T. 1954. "Les foundations: Leurs origines, leur evolution." *Revue du droit public* 60:325–351.

Schmitt-Pantel, Pauline. 1992. *La cité au banquet: Histoire des repas publiques dans les cités grecques.* Rome: Ecole Française de Rome.

Seneca. 1935. "On Benefits." *Moral Essays,* vol. 3, trans. John Basore. Loeb Classical Library. Repr., Cambridge, MA: Harvard University Press, 1989.

Shapely, Peter. 1998. "Charity, Status, and Leadership: Charitable Image and the Manchester Man." *Journal of Social History* 32:157–177.

Slack, Paul. 1988. *Poverty and Policy in Tudor and Stuart England.* London: Longman.

———. 1999. *From Reformation to Improvement: Public Welfare in Early Modern England.* Oxford: Oxford University Press.

Starobinski, Jean. 1997. *Largesse.* Chicago: University of Chicago Press.

Stephens, W. Walker. 1895. *The Life and Writings of Turgot.* London: Longmans.

Taylor, James S. 1979. "Philanthropy and Empire: Jonas Hanway and the Infant Poor of London." *Eighteenth-Century Studies* 12:285–305.

Terpstra, Nicholas. 1995. *Lay Confraternities and Civic Religion in Renaissance Bologna.* Cambridge: Cambridge University Press.

Theissen, Gerd. 1978. *Sociology of Early Palestinian Christianity.* Philadelphia: Fortress Press.

Tissier, Théodore. 1891. "Etude sur les dons et legs aux establissements publics ou d'utilité publique dans le droit ancien." *Nouvelle revue historique du droit français et etranger* 15:529–560.

Todd, S. C. 1993. *The Shape of Athenian Law.* Oxford: Oxford University Press.

Twersky, Isadore. 1980. *Introduction to the Code of Maimonides (Mishnah Torah).* New Haven: Yale University Press.

Veyne, Paul. 1969. "Panem et circenses: L'euergetisme devant les sciences humaines." *Annales E.S.C.* 24:785–825.

———. 1976. *Bread and Circuses: Historical Sociology and Political Pluralism.* Repr., London: Penguin Books, 1990.

Walker-Ramisch, Sandra. 1996. "Graeco-Roman Voluntary Associations and the Damascus Document: A Sociological Analysis." In *Voluntary Associations in the Graeco-Roman World,* ed. Johns S. Kloppenborg and Stephen G. Wilson, 128–145. New York: Routledge.

Weissman, Ronald. 1982. *Ritual Brotherhood in Renaissance Florence.* New York: Academic Press.

Wilson, Peter. 2000. *The Athenian Institution of the Khoregia: The Chorus, the City, and the Stage.* Cambridge: Cambridge University Press.

Winter, Bruce W. 1994. *Seek the Welfare of the City: Christians as Benefactors and Citizens.* Grand Rapids, MI: Eerdmans.

Wolf, Kenneth. 2003. *The Poverty of Riches: St. Francis of Assisi Reconsidered.* Oxford: Oxford University Press.

Yegul, Fikret. 1992. *Baths and Bathing in Classical Antiquity.* Boston: Architectural History Foundation and MIT Press.

2

A Historical Overview of Philanthropy, Voluntary Associations, and Nonprofit Organizations in the United States, 1600–2000

PETER DOBKIN HALL

The terms *nonprofit sector* and *nonprofit organization* are neologisms. Coined by economists, lawyers, and policy scientists in the decades following World War II as part of an effort to describe and classify the organizational domain for tax, policy, and regulatory purposes, the meaning varies depending on the identity and intentions of the user.

Defined narrowly, the terms refer to entities classified in section 501(c)(3) and 501(c)(4) of the Internal Revenue Code of 1954 and subsequent revisions: nonstock corporations and trusts formed for charitable, educational, religious, and civic purposes which are exempt from taxation and to which donors can make tax-deductible contributions. The terms can also refer to the broader range of organizations in section 501(c)—categories that include political parties, trade associations, mutual benefit associations, and other entities that enjoy various degrees of exemption, accord donors various kinds of tax relief, and are constrained in distributing their surpluses in the form of dividends.

Most broadly construed, the terms refer to the larger universe of formal and informal voluntary associations, nonstock corporations, mutual benefit organizations, religious bodies, charitable trusts, and other nonproprietary entities. Some of these are classified as exempt organizations by the Internal Revenue Service (IRS); others, such as religious bodies (which are not required to incorporate or apply for tax-exempt status) and informal organizations (which David Horton Smith [2000] calls the "dark matter" of the nonprofit universe), are not.

None of the contemporary definitions does justice to the complex historical development of these entities and activities. Every aspect of nonprofits that we consider distinctive—the existence of a domain of private organizational activity, the capacity to donate or bequeath property for charitable purposes, the distinction between joint stock and nonstock corporations, tax exemption—was the outcome of unrelated historical processes that converged and assumed significance to one another only at later points in time.

Processes of development and change are continuous and ongoing. The institutional and organizational realities we attempt to capture in creating such synoptic terms as *nonprofit sector* are, at best, of only temporary usefulness. Because such frameworks may incentivize collective behavior (as when entrepreneurs come to understand the economic benefits associated with nonprofit ownership or the tax benefits of charitable giving), they may actually serve to accelerate processes of growth and change. It is no accident that the impressive proliferation of registered tax-exempt nonprofits in the United States from fewer than 13,000 in 1940 to more than 1.5 million at the end of the century coincided with legislative and regulatory policies that defined and systematically favored nonprofits and those who contributed to their support. Nor is it a coincidence that ownership of hospitals shifted from predominantly public and proprietary in 1930 to nonprofit by the 1960s to proprietary by the century's end with changes in tax and health policy.

Under these circumstances, any attempt to produce a definitive historical account of the development of the nonprofit sector is problematic. At best, one can chronicle the emerging and converging institutions, practices, concepts, and shifting allocations of collective tasks between public and private actors.

CHARITABLE, EDUCATIONAL, RELIGIOUS, AND OTHER NONPROPRIETARY ACTIVITIES BEFORE 1750

The land area now occupied by the United States was the object of rivalry between several European powers. Spain occupied a huge area of North America, stretching from today's Florida, Alabama, and Louisiana in the Southeast through Texas, New Mexico, and Arizona in the Southwest and California on the West Coast. France occupied Canada and much of Maine and the territories composing the Louisiana Purchase. The Dutch held New York. The Swedes established a small colony on the Delaware River. And a variety of British settlements, most of them initially ventures by private trading companies, occupied the East Coast between Maine and Georgia.

Settlement began at a time when European law was still emerging from the shadow of feudalism. Statutes were uncodified and judicial decisions only spottily reported. Customary and local law continued in effect, resistant to efforts to impose national uniformity on centuries-old patchworks of parliamentary enactments, royal decrees, and decisions by a variety of lay and ecclesiastical courts. Accordingly, the legal and institutional heritage of the Old World that colonists brought with them varied, depending on where they had come from and the nature and extent of their encounters with the legal systems of their native lands (Billias 1965).

Religion and material circumstances affected the ways in which colonists drew on Old World institutions and practices. In the farther reaches of the Spanish empire, where colonial administrators were few and far between, clergy tended to assume judicial responsibilities, bringing to the task notions of the law that owed more to Scripture and local custom than to the laws of Spain or Mexico (Saunders 1995, 1998; Rosen 2001). Beyond administrative centers like Montreal, the French took a similarly casual view of legal formality, freely adapting Old World practices to New World exigencies (Banner 1996).

The legal and governmental institutions of British North America developed very differently from those of the French and Spanish colonists, who governed substantial native populations as agents of the papacy or the Crown. In contrast, the English settled in areas with sparse native populations, and as inhabitants of colonies established by joint stock companies (such as Massachusetts and New York) or proprietorships (such as Pennsylvania and New Hampshire) their primary task was crafting institutions of self-government. This orientation to self-government was evident even in royal colonies (such as Virginia and the Carolinas), where governors appointed by the Crown held sway with the assent of elected legislative assemblies.

The English brought with them a rich heritage of self-governing corporate institutions. Townships, the basic political building block outside the South, were treated under the law as municipal corporations, with citizens electing boards of selectmen. Churches—even Catholic congregations before the appointment of an American bishop in the 1790s—were governed by boards of deacons, elders, or vestrymen elected by their congregations. The handful of colleges—Harvard (1636), the College of William and Mary (1693), Yale (1701), Columbia (1754), Brown (1764), Dartmouth (1769), and the College of Charleston (1770)—were governed by boards of self-perpetuating and ex officio (either elected officials or clergy) trustees, fellows, and overseers.

Like the French and the Spanish, the English settlers also shaped their Old World legal and institutional heritage to suit circumstances and their religious and political inclinations. In Congregationalist Massachusetts and Connecticut and in Anglican Virginia, where churches were supported by taxation and dissenters were forbidden to practice their faiths, religion was tightly bound to the interests of government. In colonies such as Rhode Island and Pennsylvania, where religious toleration was the rule, self-supporting and self-governing congregations enjoyed an autonomy that anticipated the status of voluntary associations of the nineteenth century.

While evidently familiar with associational and corporate forms of collective action, the colonists were slow to embrace them. Corporate institutions such as Harvard and Yale were regarded as governmental or quasi-governmental entities (Whitehead 1973). Purely private corporations in the modern sense were virtually unknown, since colonial governments lacked the authority and legal knowledge to issue charters. By the middle of the eighteenth century, fraternal organizations (such as the Freemasons) and other informal clubs and associations (such as Benjamin Franklin's famous Junto) began to appear. But on the rare occasions when they sought to formalize their status—as did a group of Connecticut physicians who sought to incorporate as a medical society—their efforts were firmly rejected.

Charitable and educational activities that had primarily been the responsibility of the church in England were parceled out variously in the colonies (Trattner 1979; Katz 1996). In Virginia, as in England, parishes took care of the poor and ignorant. In New England, these responsibilities were exercised by municipal authorities. In larger cities such as New York, Boston, and Philadelphia, city governments operated specialized facilities—almshouses—to care for the dependent and disabled—out of which came the Bellevue hospitals of New York (1731) and Pennsylvania (1751; Rothman 1971).

Because colonial legal codes did not clearly distinguish between public/private and proprietary/nonproprietary domains, corporations and associations (when they existed at all) served public rather than private purposes. These included maintaining public order and providing education, poor relief, and (in most colonies) religious services. Government meant a very different thing in colonial America than it does today; although colonial governments and municipalities collected taxes and enacted laws, they usually entrusted the actual tasks of caring for the poor, healing the sick, and educating the ignorant to families who could provide these services at the lowest cost. In New England villages, for example, the poor and dependent were often auctioned off to the lowest bidder. Where churches were tax-supported, the tasks of levying and collecting these taxes were carried out by the churches themselves, acting under authority delegated to them by government (McKinney 1995). Many of the early almshouses were contracted out to managers who could operate them at the lowest cost to the public.

In colonial America, public and private domains were so imperfectly delimited that, in New England, it took until the 1670s for private property rights to be clearly established—and another 125 years passed before common law conceptions of property rights were universally accepted (Nelson 1975; Horowitz 1977). Legislatures generally refused to grant equity jurisdiction to colonial courts, and without them, trusts—charitable and testamentary—were unenforceable, resulting in the misdirection or failure of early charitable trusts (*Prescott v. Tarbell* 1804; Bowditch 1889; Curran 1951; Hall and Marcus 1998).

In addition to substantial gifts from abroad, there was a modest tradition of indigenous philanthropy. The bequests of clergyman John Harvard in 1638 to the colony ("towards erecting a Colledge") and Boston merchant Robert Keayne in 1656 to the town of Boston ("for a Conduit and a Town House Comprising a Market Place, Court Room, Gallery, Library, Granary, and an Armory") and to Harvard College (which received books and real estate) suggest that while charitable giving was not unknown in colonial America, government was more likely than any private body to be its recipient (Bailyn 1970). Such institutions as Harvard, William and Mary, and Yale were regarded as public corporations, subject to legislative oversight and supported significantly in the form of legislative grants of money, real estate, and "privileges" (which could range from the levying of special taxes to a monopoly on the operation of ferries) (Sears 1922; Foster 1962; Harris 1970).

Both the growth of trade and the integration of the colonies into the British commercial system in the late seventeenth and early eighteenth centuries initiated a wholesale transformation of legal, political, social, and religious institutions. For much of the first century of settlement, the English settlers of North America had been cut off from Europe by the Puritan Revolution and by incessant religious warfare on the continent. After the restoration of the Stuart monarchy in 1665, the Crown and Parliament began to look to the colonies as sources of cheap raw materials and growing markets for manufactured goods. Because trade regulations restricted the colonists' production of certain manufactured goods, which British merchants were eager to exchange for certain commodities (timber, fish, tobacco, furs), growing numbers of Americans entered into a market economy, creating growing differences in wealth and upsetting traditional patterns of deference and mutual responsibility.

Natural population increase, supplemented by renewed immigration, disrupted older forms of community. Trade brought epidemics of smallpox and other diseases, as well as an increasingly visible population of poor and dependent people for whom the public was expected to take responsibility. These changes forced Americans of the early eighteenth century to rethink the meaning of scriptural injunctions about loving one's neighbor. Influenced by Newtonian cosmology, Boston minister Cotton Mather (1663–1728) reframed doctrines of charity in *Bonifacius* (1710), advocating "friendly visiting" of the poor, the use of voluntary associations for mutual support, and philanthropic giving by the rich to relieve the poor and support schools, colleges, and hospitals. The first American to be elected to the prestigious Royal Society (an early association of scientists), Mather was influenced by the growth of urban charities in England and the ideas of British Enlightenment philosophers and scientists (Wright 1994).

Mather's ideas had a profound influence on Benjamin Franklin (1706–1790), who, after leaving Boston for Philadelphia in 1723, would carry out many of them (Franklin 1961). As a journeyman printer in London in the 1720s, Franklin acquired firsthand knowledge of the flourishing voluntary associations being created by the merchants and artisans of the rising middle class (Jordan 1960). He joined the Freemasons in London—and organized the first American lodge on his return. Freemasonry would spread rapidly in the colonies and would serve a key role—as one of America's only translocal organizations—in carrying forward the movement for independence from Great Britain (Dumenil 1984; Clawson 1989; Fischer 1994). He subsequently organized an influential young men's association, the Junto, which served as a model for young men's and mechanic's societies throughout the colonies; a volunteer fire company; and a circulating library—as well as the privately supported academy which eventually became the University of Pennsylvania.

Although voluntary associations and philanthropic giving began to appear in such urban centers as Boston and Philadelphia by the middle of the eighteenth century, cities were only one of the taproots out of which American voluntarism would grow. In rural areas, economic changes led to important changes in religious belief and practice. While the cosmopolitan Cotton Mather drew on Newtonian physics to redefine the moral universe and to plot a course toward religious rationalism, the backcountry theologian Jonathan Edwards (1703–1758) drew on the ideas of English philosopher John Locke to recast Calvinism in ways that stressed the spiritual sovereignty and moral agency of the individual—and to develop a sophisticated psychology of conversion. The preaching of Edwards and other evangelicals helped to spark a nationwide religious revival—the Great Awakening—which challenged the power of government over religious matters and, in doing so, gave politics a spiritual dimension by legitimating resistance to political tyranny (Bushman 1967).

The Awakening's emphasis on liberty of conscience led many Americans to break away from the religious establishment, embracing the new evangelical creeds being preached by itinerant Baptist and Methodist evangelists. Efforts by the religious establishment to protect its prerogatives stimulated the political activism of the clergy. The increasingly politicized clergy played an important role as revolutionary leaders, fueling political engagement and associational activity at the community level.

REVOLUTION AND REPUBLIC, 1750–1800

Voluntary associations played key roles in the American Revolution and in subsequent efforts to organize republican government. The Freemasons spread rapidly, with lodges and influential members in virtually every town of any size by the 1770s. As the only secular translocal organization of the era—and the only transcolonial one—the Freemasons linked together many of the leaders of the revolutionary struggle. Freemasonry would provide an organizational model for more explicitly political groups, such as the Sons of Liberty (Fischer 1994).

Religious groups also played important roles. While churches had not yet developed translocal denominational structures to any great extent, informal ties between settled clergy and itinerant evangelical preachers and missionaries, who went from town to town holding religious services and seeking converts, helped to spread news of political events and to infuse political ideas with powerful religious messages ("resistance to tyrants is obedience to God").

The centrality and effectiveness of voluntary associations in the Revolution served to kindle hostility toward them after the war, as Americans sought to establish governmental and legal institutions based on democratic principles. Democratic theory as it existed in the late eighteenth century viewed associations as inimical to popular government, not only because any combination of citizens was viewed as a threat to the political rights of individuals, but also because people feared that such associations representing special interests could capture control of elected governments. James Madison's famous tenth essay in the *Federalist Papers* (1787) was addressed to the hazard that "factions"—associations representing special interests—posed to democratic government. A decade later, after having crushed armed rebellions by tax resisters and suffered virulent abuse by the anti-Federalist opposition, which was organized as "democratic societies," George Washington warned in his 1796 Farewell Address against "all combinations and Associations, under whatever plausible character, with the real design to direct, controul[,] counteract, or awe the regular deliberation and action of the Constituted authorities." These associations, he asserted, "serve to organize faction, to give it an artificial and extraordinary force; to put in the place of the delegated will of the Nation, the will of a party; often a small but artful and enterprising minority of the Community." They are likely, he declared, "in the course of time and things, to become potent engines, by which cunning, ambitious and unprincipled men will be enabled to subvert the Power of the People, and to usurp for themselves the reins of Government; destroying afterwards the very engines which have lifted them to unjust domination" (Washington 1796).

During the last quarter of the eighteenth century, most states outside New England enacted laws restricting the powers of corporations, repealing sections of British common law relating to charities, and restricting the ability of citizens to give property to charities (Davis 1917). Southern states, influenced by Jefferson's concerns about "un-republican" institutions, were particularly hostile to private corporations, associations, and charities. Virginia disestablished the Anglican Church and confiscated their assets (*Terrett v. Taylor et al.* 1815; Hirchler 1939). New York created the Regents of the University of the State of New York, which exercised regulatory authority over all educational, professional, and eleemosynary organizations (Whitehead 1973). Pennsylvania annulled the Elizabethan Statute of Charitable Uses and, by declining to give its courts equity powers, discouraged the establishment of charities, since without equity jurisdiction, courts could not enforce trust provisions (Liverant 1933).

Even such states as Connecticut and Massachusetts, which would become the national centers for the chartering of corporations and the founding of private charities after 1800, were ambivalent about them in the decades immediately following the Revolution: Connecticut limited the amount of property eleemosynary corporations could hold, while Massachusetts declined for decades to grant its courts the equity powers needed to enforce charitable and other trusts (Curran 1951). Like other Americans of the time, Massachusetts Attorney General James Sullivan worried about the hazards that "the creation of a great variety of corporate interests" posed for republican institutions (Sullivan 1802).

Sullivan's misgivings were not far-fetched. In New England, which had chartered two-thirds of the 300 corporations in existence by 1800, business and eleemosynary entities had been generally chartered by conservative legislatures to help established elites resist the democratic masses, who were themselves using associational vehicles to mobilize politically (Davis 1917). As the nation completed its first decade under the federal Constitution, the institutions of republican government still seemed extraordinarily fragile. And of all the forces threatening its stability, none seemed so potently dangerous—to conservatives and liberals alike—as associations (which could accumulate unlimited political power) and corporations (which could accumulate unlimited economic power).

The nub of the problem was the essentially unresolvable tension between voice and equality posed by the Constitution, with its simultaneous commitments to majoritarian decision making and to inviolable individual rights. On the one hand, without such intermediary organizations as voluntary associations, government, though *de jure* the servant of the people, was *de facto* the master of the people—since without intermediary collectivities, the people had no way of making their influence felt, save at election time (see Tocqueville 1988). On the other hand, the existence of these associations seemed incompatible with democratic institutions, since organized collectivities—operating beyond the control of government, especially if invested with property rights—both made some citizens "more equal" than others and threatened to undermine the egalitarian foundation of the new governmental order.

At the end of the eighteenth century, indigenous philanthropy and voluntarism were still embryonic. Most philanthropy was devoted to public institutions—municipal governments, schools and colleges, and religious congregations (most of which were tax-supported). Voluntary participation in organizations was restricted to fraternal associations, local social clubs, a handful of medical societies, and the secretive political societies that would eventually form the basis for political parties. The absence of a legal infrastructure to enforce charitable trusts, as well as broad hostility toward corporations, discouraged private initiatives professing to benefit the public.

PUBLIC AND PRIVATE CHARITY AND ASSOCIATIONS, 1800–1860

Ambivalent as citizens were about voluntary associations, the conditions of political and economic life in early America compelled people to embrace them. For political and religious dissenters, associations were the only means available for counteracting the conservative political elites that dominated public life. Similarly, these elites, once displaced, embraced associations and eleemosynary corporations to maintain and extend their public influence when they could no longer do so through the ballot box. A developing economy required larger, more broadly capitalized enterprises and ways of spreading risk, which were only possible through joint stock companies—much of the capital for which would come from the invested endowment funds of charitable, educational, and religious institutions (White 1955; Hall 1974). The hazards and uncertainties of urban life could be mitigated through fraternal associations which helped members and their families financially in times of illness and death (Beito 2000; Kaufman 2002). Associations of artisans protected their members from exploitation and sought to ensure that they received fair prices for their work. By the 1820s, when Alexis de Tocqueville visited the United States, Americans were using associations for all sorts of purposes and were beginning to donate impressively large sums of money to private institutions.

Religion played a particularly important role in fueling the proliferation and acceptance of associational activity and giving for public purposes. The dismantling of religious establishments and increasing religious toleration fueled sectarianism—the splitting off of new religious groups from old ones. At the same time increasingly universal religious toleration permitted many Americans to abandon religion entirely. By 1800, it is estimated that fewer than one in five Americans belonged to any religious body (Finke and Stark 1992). The rising number of unchurched citizens was viewed by the pious as both a threat to democracy and a challenge to their powers of persuasion. A second Great Awakening, begun in the 1790s, brought together the major Protestant groups in a cooperative effort in which associations would become essential parts of their "evangelical machinery" (Foster 1960; Wosh 1994).

The Search for an American Law of Charity

Given the primitive state of American law in the early nineteenth century, it was inevitable that the increasing number of voluntary associations and growing range of purposes they served, as well as the swelling amounts of property being given for charitable, educational, and religious purposes, would produce political controversy, acrimonious litigation, and landmark court rulings (Wyllie 1959; Miller 1961). The federal system, which limited the power of the central government and allowed states wide latitude to set their own policies, ensured that the outcome of this process would reflect the diversity of preferences already characteristic of the American people.

The most famous of these struggles involved New Hampshire's Dartmouth College. Founded in 1769 under a royal charter on a gift from the Earl of Dartmouth, the college remained stalwartly Congregationalist in a state in which religious dissenters had become the dominant political force. In 1816, the state's newly elected Baptist governor, William Plumer, with encouragement from Thomas Jefferson, took control of the college and proceeded to reorganize it as a public institution. Its twelve-member self-perpetuating board was replaced by twenty-one gubernatorially appointed trustees and twenty-five legislatively appointed overseers who enjoyed veto power over the trustees (Jefferson 1856:440–441). The president of the college was required to report annually to the governor on its management, and the governor and his council were empowered to inspect the college every five years and report on its condition to the legislature.

When the old board of trustees contested the action, the New Hampshire Supreme Court upheld the state, drawing on the generally accepted doctrine that corporations, as creations of the legislature, were entirely subject to the state's will (*Trustees of Dartmouth College v. William H. Woodward* 1817). The story might have ended there had not influential U.S. senator and Dartmouth alumnus Daniel Webster (1782–1852) suggested that the ousted board of trustees appeal to the U.S. Supreme Court on the grounds that the state had violated Article II, Section 10 of the Constitution, which forbade states from impairing the obligation of contracts. The Court, which had been wrestling with a succession of suits involving eleemosynary corporations, accepted the case for review and evidently viewed it as an opportunity for a landmark decision.

In representing the old trustees, Webster conceded that the college's charter, like that of any corporation, was an act of government. But, he suggested, individuals had been encouraged by that grant of corporate powers to make donations and bequests to trustees of the institution. Though the use was public, Webster argued, this did not diminish the private character of the donated property: the gifts were made to the trustees and, as such, constituted private contracts between the trustees and the donors—contracts which the Constitution prohibited the states from abrogating.

The court, with a single dissent, accepted Webster's argument. The case, Chief Justice John Marshall asserted, did not involve the corporate rights of the college. If it did, the New Hampshire legislature might "act according to its own judgement, unrestrained by any limitation of its power imposed by the Constitution of the United States." Rather, it involved the individual rights of the donors who had given property to Dartmouth's trustees. The charter, Marshall stated, was not a grant of political power, an establishment "of a civil institution to be employed in the administration of government," or a matter of government funds. It was, rather, a "contract to which the donors, the trustees, and the Crown (to whose rights and obligations New Hampshire succeeds) were the original parties. It is a contract made on a valuable consideration. It is a contract for the security and disposition of property. It is a contract on the faith of which real and personal estate has been conveyed to the corporation. It is then a contract within the letter of the Constitution and within its spirit also" (*Trustees of Dartmouth College v. William H. Woodward* 1819). As such, Marshall ruled, Dartmouth's charter could not be altered by the legislature "without violating the Constitution of the United States."

Despite the ruling in the Dartmouth College case, legal doctrines on the status of eleemosynary corporations remained confused. Although the Court affirmed the Constitution's prohibition of states' impairing the obligation of contracts, the decision did not require states to treat charitable corporations favorably. Even today, many states remain hostile to charities despite the Dartmouth ruling.

Even the Supreme Court itself seemed ambivalent about the issue: in the same term in which it decided for Dartmouth College, it also affirmed the power of the Commonwealth of Virginia to hold invalid a charitable bequest by one of its citizens to establish a religious charity in another state (*Philadelphia Baptist Association v. Hart's Executors* 1819). It was not until 1844 that private charity received an unambiguous blessing from the federal courts, when the Supreme Court heard the Girard will case (*Francois Fenelon Vidal et al. v. The Mayor, Aldermen, and Citizens of Philadelphia, et al.* 1844). The case involved the will of Stephen Girard (1750–1831), a multimillionaire Philadelphia merchant who had left the bulk of his estate to the city for public works and for the establishment of a school for orphans. The central issue in this case involved the status of charitable bequests in states that had repealed the Statute of Charitable Uses. In the erroneous belief that the power to establish charitable trusts stemmed from this statute, earlier court decisions had upheld the power of states that had annulled it to limit or prohibit such trusts. But by the 1840s, advances in legal scholarship permitted the attorneys for the Girard estate to show that the Elizabethan statute had, in fact, merely been the codification of a long series of previous acts and precedents and that, as a result, the status of charitable trusts was unaffected by the repeal of the 1601 statute. Although the decision in the Girard will case secured under federal law the right of individuals to create charitable trusts, this decision did not affect particular states which chose to limit their activities. Nor did it particularly stress the importance of private philanthropy, since most of the objects of Girard's legacy were public institutions.

By the end of the nineteenth century, the legal and regulatory treatment of philanthropic and charitable institutions and voluntary associations fell into two broad categories (Zollmann 1924). A handful of states, almost all of them in New England, embraced a "broad construction" of charity under which virtually any kind of not-for-profit associational activity was not only permitted but encouraged through tax exemptions. For example, Massachusetts's 1874 charities statute extended property tax exemption to any "educational, charitable, benevolent or religious purpose" including "any antiquarian, historical, literary, scientific, medical, artistic, monumental or musical" purpose; to "any missionary enterprise" with either foreign or domestic objects; to organizations "encouraging athletic exercises and yachting"; to libraries and reading rooms; and to "societies of Freemasons, Odd Fellows, Knights of Pythias and other charitable or social bodies of a like character and purpose" ("An Act" 1874). Trustees who managed charitable funds were both permitted broad authority in financial management and protected from claims by donors and beneficiaries.

Most other states favored a "narrow construction" of charity, which restricted the kinds of activities that could be legally deemed charitable and required even those to demonstrate their redistributional and noncommercial intent as a condition for tax exemption. Thus, for example, Pennsylvania's nineteenth-century charities statute required that such entities advance a charitable purpose (as defined in the statute), donate or render gratuitously a substantial portion of its services (limiting a charity's ability to charge fees), benefit a substantial and indefinite class or persons who are legitimate subjects of charity, relieve government of some of its burdens, and operate entirely free of private profit motives (see *Episcopal Academy v. Philadelphia et al., Appellants* 1892 and Zollmann 1924). Clearly, many of the kinds of entities designated as charitable under Massachusetts law would not have been regarded as such in Pennsylvania.

Where charities and tax laws favored private initiatives, philanthropic and voluntary enterprises flourished. Where the law discouraged them, they did not (Bowen et al., 1994; Schneider 1996). In the Northeast and upper Midwest, privately supported schools, colleges, and charities were founded in great numbers. In the South and West, public institutions—state universities and public hospitals being the most notable examples—were established instead.

The Rise of Voluntary Associations

Even as early as the 1830s, Alexis de Tocqueville took note of the extraordinary variety of voluntary associations and ways in which they were used by different groups. "The affluent classes of society," he wrote, "have no influence in political affairs. They constitute a private society in the state which has its own tastes and pleasures." "The rich," he continued, "have a hearty dislike of the democratic institutions of their country." Deprived of direct political influence by their small numbers, the "chief weapons" used by the wealthy to make their views known were newspapers and associations, which they used to "oppose the whole moral authority of the minority to the physical power that domineers over it" (Tocqueville 1945, 1:187). Speculating on the social and political consequences of industrialization, Tocqueville foresaw the emergence of an "aristocracy of manufactures" whose members would take on the power of "administrators of a vast empire" (Tocqueville 1945, 2:169). Though politically disempowered, this aristocracy would exercise its power through the private institutions that were becoming increasingly central to the nation's development. By midcentury, such metropolitan centers as Boston, New York, and Philadelphia boasted constellations of cultural, educational, and charitable institutions tightly linked by interlocking boards of directors. These not only enabled moneyed elites to extend their cultural and political influence but also, to the extent that institutional endowments were among the largest capital pools of the period, served as arenas for collective economic decision making. It was no accident that Massachusetts, whose charity-friendly laws permitted such institutions as Harvard and the Massachusetts General Hospital to accumulate substantial endowments, became an early center of investment banking—based on the strategic investment of these funds in the textile industry and western railroads (White 1957).

In describing the temperance movement, Tocqueville noted the marked differences between the organizations used by the wealthy to pursue their agendas and those used by average citizens. "The first time I heard in the United States that a hundred thousand men had bound themselves publicly to abstain from spirituous liquors," he wrote, "it appeared to me more a joke than a serious engagement, and I did not at once perceive why these temperate citizens could not content themselves with drinking water by their own firesides. I at last understood that these hundred thousand Americans, alarmed by the progress of drunkenness around them, had made up their minds to patronize temperance. They acted just the same way as a man of high rank who should dress very plainly in order to inspire the humbler orders with a contempt of luxury. It is probable that if these hundred thousand men had lived in France, each of them would singly have memorialized the government to watch the public houses all over the kingdom" (1945, 2:110). The temperance groups were organized as federations of state and local organizations that coordinated their activities nationally through staffed headquarters, newspapers, and periodic convenings of delegates (Putnam and Gamm 1999; Skocpol 1999a; Skocpol 1999b).

The increasing use of associations by ever larger numbers of Americans helped to clarify the distinctions not only between public and private domains of activity but also between commercial and noncommercial organizations. Early corporation statutes drew little distinction between joint stock companies and membership associations (Dunlavy 2000). Over time, as Americans grew more familiar with the possibilities of associational and corporate forms, their experiments were eventually codified in the law.

In the course of this process, many of the activities that we today think of as especially suited for nonprofits—arts, culture, education, and health care—were as likely to be produced by commercial enterprises as by noncommercial ones. Not until the end of the century, when rising taxes on real estate and other organizational assets and the imposition of inheritance taxes created financial incentives to adopt the not-for-profit corporate form, did the distinction between proprietary and nonproprietary firms emerge with any clarity. The efforts of urban elites in the post–Civil War decades also helped to clarify the distinction, as wealthy cultural entrepreneurs organized nonprofit orchestras and museums, closely tied to nonprofit universities, to help define and solidify the collective identity of the social groups to which they belonged (Fox 1963; Story 1980; Horowitz 1976; DiMaggio 1986; Bender 1987; Wooten 1990).

By the 1850s, Americans had largely overcome their suspicion of voluntary associations and private charity. Elites, displaced by religious disestablishment and the political mobilization of the "common man," turned to philanthropy and associational activity as alternatives to electoral politics (Bledstein 1976). The learned professions, especially medicine and engineering, formed national associations to define and uphold professional standards and to promote the diffusion of knowledge: the American Statistical Association was founded in 1839; the American Psychiatric Association in 1844; the American Medical Association in 1847; the American Society of Civil Engineers in 1852; and the American Institute of Architects in 1857 (Wiebe 1967; Haskell 1977; Haskell 1984; Calhoun 1965; Hatch 1988; Brint 1994; Kimball 1995). As they were drawn into the industrial system, artisans and laborers began organizing mutual benefit associations to provide social insurance and assert their political and economic rights. Evangelical Protestants used associations both to proselytize and to advance such social reforms as temperance, sabbatarianism, and work among the poor. Farmers used associations to promote agricultural improvements and to broaden markets for their products. Socially excluded groups, such as free blacks and immigrants, established their own congregations and fraternal associations. Barred from electoral politics, women used associations to create a "separate sphere" of educational, religious, and cultural activity (McCarthy 1982; Blair 1989; Ginzberg 1990; Scott 1991; Sander 1998). Electoral politics became firmly grounded in associational forms and economic activity was increasingly carried out through incorporated associations, while social life for Americans rich and poor became increasingly defined by participation in religious and secular associations.

The sheer variety of association forms in this period makes it difficult to generalize about them. Some were genuinely private and independent of government. Others were quasi-governmental, receiving government funds or having governing boards on which government officials sat ex officio. Some served the interests of the privileged; others served the needs of common people. They both enabled majorities to assert their power and protected minorities from assaults on their liberties. Organizationally, they ranged from ad hoc community-level gatherings to elaborately formalized trusts and corporations. Some were supported by sales of services and government funding, others by donations, endowment income, or some combination thereof. Although the vast majority of associations were purely voluntary, the largest ones—colleges, hospitals, and such entities as the American Bible Society and the American Tract Society—were being run by cadres of salaried employees (Bacon 1847; Wosh 1994).

By the 1830s, recognizably modern forms of fund-raising had begun to emerge, as institutions actively solicited contributions and bequests from local and national constituencies and such public figures as the evangelist Lyman Beecher (1775–1862) toured eastern cities raising funds for schools and colleges in the newly settled western states. Increasingly well-informed about current events, Americans were quick to respond to disasters and liberation movements with generous "subscriptions." An 1845 survey of Boston charity gives a good idea of the range of organizations and causes to which citizens donated money: in addition to generous support for major institutions such as schools, colleges, libraries, and hospitals, Bostonians gave money to build churches and seminaries; to sustain domestic and foreign missionary societies; to erect public monuments; to relieve the suffering of fire victims in Mobile, Alabama, in Fall River and Pittsfield, Massachusetts, and in Hamburg, Germany; for the abolition of slavery; and for the "diffusing of information among immigrants" (Eliot 1845).

Tocqueville's exuberant proclamation that "Americans of all ages, all conditions, and all dispositions constantly form associations" was in many ways an exaggeration (1945, 2:106). While associations of various kinds proliferated in the first half of the nineteenth century, their growth was both geographically selective (with particular concentrations in the Northeast and upper Midwest) and was closely associated with religious demography, particularly variants of Calvinist Protestantism. Colleges and hospitals—which would eventually rank among the most important private institutions—were relatively small and marginal operations. Total enrollment at Yale—the largest college in the country—ranged between three hundred and six hundred until after the Civil War, and its endowment was less than a quarter of a million dollars (Pierson 1983). Both Harvard and Yale, with significant representation of elected officials on their governing boards, were not private institutions as we understand the term, though both would replace the ex officios with elected alumni representatives by 1870 (Hall 2000). The hospitals and medical schools languished, thanks to competition from unlicensed practitioners, rival schools of practice, and proprietary entities. Without a credible scientific basis on which to ground claims for professional authority, physicians were little more than businessmen. Voluntary associations in this period were overwhelmingly church related: religious congregations composed the largest part of the nonproprietary domain; private schools, colleges, and most private charities were invariably church related, even after disestablishment. Hospitals, fraternal associations and other mutual benefit organizations, and the few libraries extant before the Civil War were uniquely secular.

In the first half of the nineteenth century, while voluntary entities were assuming a recognized place in public life, the majority of the work of caregiving, healing, educating, and even worshipping took place in the primary institutions of family and community, rather than in associational or corporate settings. But as economic and social change eroded traditional communities and family ties, Americans were increasingly willing to experiment with new kinds of formal organizations.

Most of these were voluntary associations that enabled people to spread risk or pool resources to provide mutual benefits—such as building and loan societies and fraternal organizations that offered death and sickness benefits (Beito 2000). Some—the so-called utopian communities—attempted to create corporate cooperatives in which members held property in common and allowed their lives to be regulated by the collective (Noyes 1870; Bestor 1971; Kanter 1972). Some of these, such as the Oneida and Shaker communities, were religiously based. Others, such as the Fourierists and Robert Owen's New Harmony community, drew their inspiration from new socialist critiques of capitalism. In the years between 1830 and 1860, several hundred of these communities were established.

PRIVATE INSTITUTIONS AND THE CREATION OF THE MODERN STATE, 1860–1920

American institutional life on the eve of the Civil War was diverse, incoherent, and charged with possibilities. The economy was becoming increasingly urban and industrial, with growing metropolitan areas competing to dominate the commerce of surrounding regions through networks of roads, canals, and railroads—some publicly financed, others privately subscribed, and still others funded with a mix of public and private investment. Still, there was no national economy as such: few railroads or canals crossed state lines, and capital was scarce and localized, except for ventures in which European investors took an interest. Most goods and services were produced in small, locally owned plants that distributed their products locally and regionally rather than nationally.

Slavery, Voluntary Associations, and the Nationalization of Political Culture

The only real exception to this pattern of localism was the cotton industry, a complex network of interdependencies involving slavery, plantation agriculture, textile production, and the financial services, transportation, and manufacturing activities that sustained it. King Cotton made its influence felt in both the North and South. Many of the great fortunes of Boston, New York, and Philadelphia philanthropists were derived from direct or indirect participation in the slave economy.

While Americans had owned slaves since colonial times, in the closing years of the eighteenth century many believed it to be a declining institution. The invention of the cotton gin in 1793, which made it possible to cheaply process varieties of cotton that grew well in the American South, changed all this. Cheaper American cotton found a ready market in Britain's growing textile industry, which had been dependent on cotton imported from India. As the international and domestic market for cotton grew, the slave trade and commodity agriculture based on slave labor became fabulously profitable. And as cotton agriculture flourished, southern slave owners and their northern allies began to press for the expansion of slavery into western territories and into such areas as Texas that were still under Spanish rule.

The cotton industry proved to be not only a major source of philanthropic funding but also a fertile source of associational activity, often in opposition to the growing influence of slavery supporters over national policy. Many Americans, particularly in the North, were troubled by the seeming conflict between slavery and a republic founded on the idea of inalienable human rights—a contradiction to which the British antislavery movement was quick to call attention. Organized antislavery agitation began in the 1780s, with the establishment of the Pennsylvania Society for the Abolition of Slavery, one of whose founders was Benjamin Franklin. In 1787, free blacks in Philadelphia founded the Philadelphia Free African Society, which soon had counterparts in Boston, New York, and Newport, Rhode Island.

In 1816, a prestigious group which included diplomat and future president James Monroe, Bushrod Washington (George Washington's nephew and a member of the U.S. Supreme Court), general and future president Andrew Jackson, lawyer Francis Scott Key, and senators Daniel Webster and Henry Clay organized the American Colonization Society, which proposed resettling freed slaves in Africa (Fox 1919; Bevan 1991; Smith 1993). With a $100,000 federal grant, the group acquired land in Africa (today's Liberia) and in 1820 began sending shiploads of emancipated slaves there. Over a period of twenty years, nearly three thousand settled in Liberia. The Colonization Society was an unusual alliance of southern slaveholders who feared the influence of free blacks on those still in bondage and northerners who opposed slavery on moral grounds. This accommodation, like the orderly process by which new states were admitted to the Union in a manner that preserved the political balance between free and slave states, would break down after 1831, when southerners, terrorized by the bloody Nat Turner slave rebellion, adopted harsh racial codes that made slavery even more oppressive than it had ever been.

The increasing oppressiveness of slavery as an institution and the growing political aggressiveness of slavery's defenders helped to push those who opposed slavery toward more extreme positions. While most opponents continued to favor gradual emancipation and colonization, a vocal activist element began agitating for immediate abolition. Organizations such as the American Anti-Slavery Society (AASS; founded in 1833) split into factions: conservatives formed the American Foreign and Domestic Anti-Slavery Society, while radicals retained control of the original organization. Under the leadership of journalist William Lloyd Garrison (1805–1879), the AASS flooded the country with mass mailings—to the point that Congress attempted to enact legislation forbidding the mailing of antislavery literature. The polarization of political positions on slavery led to the breakup of the major national religious denominations and such ecumenical organizations as the American Tract Society.

Conflict over slavery produced both national and local organizations and stimulated philanthropic contributions to promote emancipation and aid emancipated slaves. The Underground Railroad, an informal network of abolitionists, helped escaped slaves find their way to free states and, after the enactment of the federal Fugitive Slave Act in 1850, to Canada. After the passage of the Kansas-Nebraska Act in 1854, which left the question of whether new states in the Nebraska Territory would be slave or free up to their inhabitants, both abolitionists and advocates of slavery donated money, guns, and supplies to groups willing to settle in these states and do battle for their particular causes. These terrorist gangs, led by such men as abolitionist John Brown (who was later hanged for leading a slave rebellion in Virginia) and slaveholder Charles W. Quantrill (who would lead Confederate guerilla bands during the Civil War), carried the possibilities of voluntary association to its furthest extremes, committing bloody crimes under the color of higher purposes.

The emergence of slavery as the central issue in American politics helped to nationalize public life, shifting power to national associations, national political organizations, and publications that commanded national audiences. This helped other reform issues to command national attention and to elicit action by the federal government. Among the more notable of these was the movement for more humane treatment of the insane, led by New Englander Dorothea Dix (1802–1887; Marshall 1937; Wilson 1975; Snyder 1975). After leading successful crusades in several states, in the late 1840s Dix began lobbying Congress to appropriate federal funds for the purpose. In 1854, Congress passed a bill authorizing the appropriation of more than twelve million acres of federal lands for the benefit of the insane, blind, deaf, and dumb. But when it reached the desk of President Franklin Pierce, he vetoed it, declaring, "I can not find any authority in the Constitution for making the Federal Government the great almoner of public charity throughout the United States" (Pierce 1854). The "Pierce Veto," as it is known to historians of social welfare, expressed a conservative view of federal powers and responsibilities that would generally characterize federal involvement with welfare issues until the twentieth century.

In 1828, British aristocrat James Smithson's half-million-dollar bequest to the federal government for the establishment of an institution "for the increase and diffusion of knowledge among men" elicited a protracted debate that similarly reflected political leaders' uncertainty about the power of the federal government. The bequest was bitterly attacked by southern congressmen, who doubted that the federal government had the legal capacity either to receive the bequest or to establish such an institution. At the same time, the bequest was enthusiastically supported by those who believed that the federal government should actively promote economic growth and saw a national institution devoted to scientific research as a potentially important stimulus to development. It took nearly two decades for Congress to decide what to do with the bequest (Rhees 1859; Goode 1897).

Although slow to expand its own role, the federal government was extraordinarily effective in creating conditions favorable to the growth of nongovernmental activity. The reorganization of the postal system in the 1840s created a cheap and efficient means for Americans and the voluntary associations they were busily creating to communicate with one another and to spread word about their causes. Federal authority over interstate commerce improved navigation and transportation, which helped Americans and their ideas move rapidly into national circulation. Americans committed to social reform and religious evangelism took advantage of the new infrastructure to create associations that transcended state and local boundaries—and that were, in their federated structures, modeled on the national government (Skocpol 1999b).

Evangelical Protestants, especially those with New England roots, were particularly aggressive in taking advantage of cultural and commercial opportunities to promote nationalist agendas. Their embrace of nationalism was a product both of religious ideology—which led them to view the settlement of North America as a divinely mandated "errand into the wilderness"—and of demography—particularly the extraordinarily high level of migration from New England's unproductive and crowded farmlands to the rich lands of the South and West.

By the 1840s, a flood of immigrants from Germany and Ireland broadened the range of voluntary and philanthropic endeavors. German immigrants brought with them their own associational traditions, founding athletic, musical, and social organizations wherever they settled, which helped to maintain their common culture. The Irish were less associationally active because of the Catholic Church's hostility toward associations over which it had no direct control. This was in part a consequence of its effort to affirm ecclesiastical authority over the laity, who in the absence of a North American bishop had established early Catholic congregations in the United States, supporting them with voluntary donations and hiring and firing priests—much as their Protestant counterparts did. With the appointment of an American bishop, the church began cracking down on "laymen acting in church affairs on their own initiative, abetted by vagrant priests who had no regard for ecclesiastical authority" (Ellis 1987, 2:160). Because it took thirty years and a series of highly publicized and acrimonious lawsuits for the hierarchy to suppress "lay trusteeism," the church was reluctant to sanction organizations that might rekindle sentiments of religious independence. Catholics were forbidden to join secret associations (such as the Freemasons) and, though the church tolerated the establishment of Catholic temperance, patriotic, and devotional societies, their role in the growth of American associational and philanthropic activity would remain overshadowed by Protestant initiatives until the twentieth century. Despite these strictures, the church itself—through schools, hospitals, orphanages, and other charities run by religious orders and the dioceses—assumed an enormously important role in American social welfare, particularly in the cities where the Catholic population was concentrated (Dolan 1985, 1987; Oates 1995).

Elites, Philanthropy, and Voluntary Associations

In the decades leading up to the Civil War, the educated elites felt increasingly isolated and powerless as they confronted the growth of immigrant populations, the rise of corrupt urban political machines, and the penetration of market values into every aspect of American life. The disestablishment of religion had diminished the authority of the clergy, as Americans felt free to worship as they pleased—or not worship at all. Physicians and lawyers who had struggled (with some success) in the early years of the century to restrict admission into their professions to educated and credentialed practitioners found their efforts undone by Jacksonian legislatures, which placed them in competition with quacks of every description and with ambitious young men, trained as apprentices, who succeeded in persuading increasingly politicized judges to admit them to the bar. Though it would be decades before businessmen would begin to think of themselves as professionals, those allied with established elites worried about the turbulence occasioned by unscrupulous and speculative business practices (see Chandler 1952).

While associational action could never fully restore the authority of professional and commercial elites, it could afford them a measure of public stature by reorganizing the market for their services. In addition to establishing private hospitals, the professional elites organized these hospitals as charitable institutions (which clearly set them apart from the proprietary hospitals), associated them with university-based medical schools, and restricted ward privileges to holders of medical degrees, thereby creating enclaves of practice protected from market forces. The stature of these enclaves was enhanced as university-affiliated hospitals, such as Massachusetts General Hospital, were able to claim credit for scientifically based medical advances, such as anesthesia and asepsis, and were able to expand their influence through medical journals. Although wealthy laymen increasingly dominated the governing boards of benevolent institutions, the continuing presence and involvement of clergy helped to distinguish clerical leaders from the mass of preachers—and these leaders were also active in establishing new specifically church-oriented organizations, ranging from schools of theology to publishing ventures and domestic and foreign missions (Scott 1978; Cherry 1996). Businessmen created credit reporting agencies which assessed creditworthiness not only in commercial terms but in moral and political ones.

During the Civil War, elites performed heroically not only on the battlefield but in support roles. The centerpiece of their efforts was the U.S. Sanitary Commission, a privately funded national federation that assumed responsibility for public health and relief measures on the battlefield and in military encampments (Frederickson 1965). Rigorously professional and relentlessly bureaucratic, the commission sought to replace politics and sentimentality with disinterested, science-based expertise (Giesberg 2000). Through its local chapters, which raised funds and produced medical supplies, the commission also helped to maintain public enthusiasm for wartime policies. Just as the officer corps proved to be an invaluable training ground for men who took leading roles in managing the large firms that dominated the national economy after the war, so the Sanitary Commission produced cadres of experts to take the lead in helping to reform and reorganize the public welfare system in the postwar decades. Their unsentimental approach to suffering, which included focusing on its causes rather than its alleviation, would give rise to a revolution in American social welfare, under the banners of "charity organization" and "scientific philanthropy" (Watson 1922; Katz 1996).

The older diversity of institutional traditions did not simply disappear in the face of such innovative and powerful organizations as the Sanitary Commission. Throughout the war, the commission's efforts were vehemently opposed by the U.S. Christian Commission, an evangelically oriented organization that placed individual spirituality and the relief of individual suffering ahead of utilitarian considerations of efficiency and effectiveness (Moss 1868). Where the Sanitary Commission was concerned with solving problems, the Christian Commission was concerned with helping people. Where the Sanitary Commission focused on the worthiness of relief recipients, the Christian Commission focused on need. Where the Sanitary Commission used professionals and experts to provide services, the Christian Commission recruited well-intentioned volunteers to relieve suffering. The two approaches would clash repeatedly both during the war and after, as veterans of the two groups became involved in the effort to "reconstruct" the devastated South and, later, in initiatives to address poverty in the nation's growing cities.

Reconstruction, Racism, and the Transformation of Voluntarism

Reconstruction was the most ambitious government initiative to be undertaken by the federal government before the New Deal of the 1930s (Fleming 1906). Not only did the South's economy and infrastructure lie in ruins, but millions of emancipated slaves—jobless, landless, and uneducated—had to be integrated into a new political and economic system based on free labor and universal civil rights (DuBois 1935). The task was entrusted to the Freedmen's Bureau under the authority of General Oliver Otis Howard (1830–1909), a religiously devout Maine-born former abolitionist (McFeely 1968). As custodian of the land and financial assets confiscated from defeated rebels, the bureau had vast resources to bring to the task (Pierce 1904). What it lacked was personnel with the ability to teach former slaves to read and write, to support themselves, and to effectively exercise their political rights.

As an evangelical with years of experience in the voluntary associations these Protestants used to advance their reform agendas, Howard understood the possibilities of a voluntary workforce. He invited northern volunteers (dubbed "Gideonites") to work with the Freedmen's Bureau to carry out its policies (Swint 1967). As the Gideonites poured into the South, the profound differences between those who embraced traditional, religiously grounded conceptions of charity and those who favored more utilitarian approaches became evident. The latter, many of whom had worked with the Sanitary Commission during the war, saw Reconstruction as an opportunity to reorganize the conquered South as an open, multiracial, religiously diverse New England–style civil society (Butchart 1980; Richardson 1986). The former, identified with the Christian Commission, viewed the economic and educational aspects of Reconstruction as subsidiary to the opportunities it afforded to proselytize.

Reconstruction would eventually fail, falling victim to resistance by white southerners (who used voluntary associations such as the Ku Klux Klan to murder and terrorize free blacks), bickering among the volunteer workforce of the Freedmen's Bureau, and the political opportunism of northern politicians who were more interested in the votes of southern whites than in fundamental social and economic reform (Chalmers 1987). After the end of military government in the South in 1876, blacks were quickly pushed out of public life and, in many instances, into plantation peonage. Racial segregation was established by state and federal law, and the exclusion of blacks from public facilities, from schools, and from exercising their political rights was enforced by lynch law. Between the end of the Civil War and the start of World War I, thousands of black men, women, and children were brutally murdered by southern mobs, often with the enthusiastic complicity of public authorities (Dray 2002).

Fleeing the South, hundreds of thousands of blacks moved to northern cities, beginning as a trickle but becoming a flood by the 1920s. In northern cities, urban blacks would create vital communities rich in churches, voluntary associations, and charitable institutions (Giddings 1988; Higginbotham 1993; Gamble 1995; Reed 1997; Cash 2001). Although they suffered discrimination, northern blacks were generally not excluded from politics. By the early twentieth century, black communities were electing their own leaders to municipal and state offices and were joining forces with white humanitarians to fight racism through such national advocacy groups as the National Association for the Advancement of Colored People (NAACP), organized in 1909.

The failure of Reconstruction and the brutal political and economic repression of blacks in both the North and the South proved to be a powerful impetus for voluntary and philanthropic responses among Americans who still embraced democratic values. The earliest foundations—the Peabody Fund (1868), the John F. Slater Fund (1882), and the General Education Board (1903)—would be created by wealthy northern philanthropists to provide education to free blacks (Curry 1898; Curti and Nash 1965; Anderson 1999). A variety of activist groups arose to oppose lynching, to defend the civil rights of blacks, and to call international attention to the racial situation in the United States (Dray 2002). A group of southern institutions—Howard University, the Tuskegee Institute, Fisk University, and others—would not only enjoy the continuing support of northern donors but also work energetically to promote racial understanding through fund-raising tours of musical groups, such as the Fisk Jubilee Singers (Ward 2000).

The rise of racism in America after the Civil War promoted the expansion of black churches. Barred from the mainstream of economic and political life, black people turned to the church for solace and consolation. Church also offered opportunities for community building and civic engagement, and one of the few avenues of professional advancement available to ambitious blacks (Lincoln and Mamiya 1990). Although generally not politically active as institutions, black churches often served as platforms for political initiatives, and black clergies would prove to be reliable sources of political leadership. The civil rights movement of the 1950s and 1960s would draw on these sources of strength.

The Institutional Response to Immigration and Urbanization

Post–Civil War racism was a component of a broader response by native-born whites to deep changes in American life in the decades between the Civil War and 1920. In response to opportunities created by industrialization and to economic conditions and political and religious repression in their homelands, the flood of immigration that had begun in the 1830s continued unabated. The Germans and Irish who had predominated before the war were joined by Italians and Eastern Europeans. By 1890 in many cities, native-born citizens were actually in the minority.

It was not the mere demographic presence of the foreign-born that so alarmed native-born Americans. It was their increasingly powerful political and institutional presence. In many cities, political machines based on patronage and the votes of the foreign-born dominated municipal life and gave rise to extraordinary levels of political corruption. With swelling numbers of adherents, the Roman Catholic Church became an enormously important institutional presence, not only erecting impressive church edifices but also building parochial schools, hospitals, and social welfare institutions that demanded and in many places received significant government support (Dolan 1985, 1987; Oates, 1995).

Perhaps more disturbing was the growing Jewish presence. Whereas Catholics challenged native-born Protestants institutionally and politically, Jews challenged them as competitors on their own ground—in higher education, commerce, and their professions. By the turn of the century, the elite private universities were limiting the admission of Jews and Catholics and such professions as law and medicine were raising educational standards for admission to the bar and to hospital privileges in order to exclude non-Protestants (Oren 2001; Auerbach 1976). In response to the rise of institutional anti-Semitism, Jews established their own philanthropies, hospitals, social agencies, and clubs (Morris and Freund 1966; Linenthal 1990; Soyer 1997).

The impact of these changes on Protestants was dramatic. Despite their differences over Reconstruction and urban charity, they drew together to form a united front against the immigrants. Led by such nondenominational evangelists as Dwight L. Moody (1837–1899), huge revival meetings were held in cities across the country. New federated Protestant organizations such as the Christian Workers established chapters in cities and towns throughout the United States and Canada (Butler 1997). Moody himself was an active institution builder who founded the Northfield–Mt. Hermon School (a leading private boarding school) and Chicago's Moody Church and Moody Bible Institute.

Among the most important outcomes of this Protestant/nativist revival was a powerful effort to reform urban charities led by Protestant clergy and laity (Gurteen 1882; Watson 1922). Based on practices originally developed in Scotland in the 1860s and 1870s, the charity reform movement sought to systematize and render more efficient and effective poor relief by eliminating "mendacity" (claims for relief by the undeserving), duplication of services, and political influence on the distribution of charity. These professed high purposes actually masked a more sinister agenda. The charity reformers sought to register all applicants for poor relief, oversee their activities, and, whenever possible, ensure that no relief was given unless in exchange for work. Eliminating all forms of publicly provided relief—in order to cut the tie between relief and patronage and thus to break the political power of the urban bosses—was high on the charity reformers' list of priorities. From its start in Buffalo in 1879, the movement spread rapidly. By 1890 charity reform organizations were operating in two dozen American cities (National Conference 1881).

Charity reformers worked closely with other Protestant political and social reformers in taking on urban political machines and advocating for civil service systems locally and nationally. The temperance and prohibition movements were revived during this period and now focused less on the inherent evils of alcohol than on the problem of the saloon as the chief social and political center of immigrant communities. The reformers also worked with groups urging compulsory school attendance (as a way of "Americanizing" immigrants' children) and child labor laws (to remove children from parental control and place them in settings where they could be subjected to proper influences; Pozzetta 1991).

The harsh methods of the charity reformers generated resistance not only in the ethnic communities toward which they directed their efforts but also among many Protestants. In the late 1880s, Jane Addams (1860–1935) and other Americans who had spent time at London's Toynbee Hall, a Christian community of middle-class students and professionals located in the city's slums, brought back an alternative method of addressing urban poverty—the settlement house (Addams 1938; Davis 1984; Linn 2000; Elshtain 2002). At the same time, from within Protestant ranks, preachers such as Nebraska Congregationalist Charles Sheldon (1857–1946) challenged their congregations to address the problem of poverty as Christians. "What would Jesus do in solving the problems of political social and economic life?" Sheldon asked in his best-selling novel *In His Steps* (1899).

By the 1890s, a sufficient number of Americans were devoting themselves to problems of poverty and dependency as a full-time occupation to dispel many of the myths and class-interested assertions about the causes of poverty and the ways in which social welfare policy and practice could address them (Warner 1894; Lubove 1965; Chambers 1963; Bremner 1991). As this happened the focus of charity began to shift from reforming the morals of the poor to changing the conditions that created poverty. The founding of the National Conference of Charities and Correction in 1892 marked the emergence of a growing cadre of secular social welfare professionals and the development of academic social sciences addressing pressing public problems.

Despite this, religion remained an important element in the private provision of social services (Huggins 1971; Smith-Rosenberg 1971; Hopkins 1982). The Salvation Army, an evangelical group founded in England, established rescue missions throughout the United States in the last years of the nineteenth century (Winston 1999). By the early years of the twentieth century, seminaries and divinity schools were training students in social ministry and in the beliefs associated with the "social gospel." Religiously based organizations such as Phillips Brooks House at Harvard and Dwight Hall at Yale sent students out into the community to work with public and private social agencies, while urban churches expanded their social ministries to serve the poor.

Women proved to be an important element in the new activism that emerged between the wars. Increasingly well-educated but deprived of opportunities for careers in most fields, many middle-class women found outlets for their energies in reformist activism of many kinds (Scott 1991; Waugh 1997). Inspired by the antislavery movement, some women worked to promote political equality for women (Minkoff 1995; Murolo 1997). Others became active in moral reform causes. The Women's Christian Temperance Union, founded in 1874, commanded the loyalty of more than a million members by the beginning of the twentieth century. The organizational and advocacy efforts of women resulted in the enactment of the Eighteenth Amendment (prohibition) and Nineteenth Amendment (women's suffrage) to the U.S. Constitution. Their success was testament to the growing political power of special interest groups working through nationally federated associations.

Associational activism helped to open new career paths for women. Nursing, social work, teaching, and other careers in the "helping professions" were more likely to flourish in nonprofit settings, where women often sat on governing boards and held staff positions, than in business or government, which continued to be male dominated (McCarthy 1982, 1991).

All of these forces played a role in the creation of one of the earliest modern foundations, the Russell Sage Foundation. It was founded in 1907 on a gift of $10 million from Margaret Olivia Sage (1828–1918), the widow of financier Russell Sage, "for the improvement of social and living conditions in the United States of America" (see Glenn, Brandt, and Andrews 1947; Hammack and Wheeler 1994; and Crocker 2002). The foundation, she instructed, "should preferably not undertake to do that which is now being done or is likely to be effectively done by other individuals or by other agencies. It should be its aim to take up the larger and more difficult problems, and to take them up so far as possible in such a manner as to secure co-operation and aid in their solution" (Sage 1907).

Sage's gift, in a very real way, brought together all the strands of American philanthropy and voluntarism as it had developed since the early nineteenth century. A product of a New England evangelical household, she had been educated at Emma Willard's Troy Female Seminary, an evangelical institution. At her graduation in 1847, she presented an oration on those "who spend their wealth in deeds of charity" (Crocker 2002:202). Sage was involved in the whole range of post–Civil War urban reform movements: she was an active supporter of religious causes, and she served on the board of the New York Women's Hospital and the New York Gospel Mission, as well as the New York Exchange for Women's Work and the Women's Municipal League, "a political organization that aimed to unseat Tammany and bring more women into public life" (Crocker 2002:201). She was deeply involved in charity reform movement activities and was a generous benefactor of such Protestant groups as the YMCA and the Women's Seamen's Friend Society.

The Russell Sage Foundation anticipated both the think tanks and the grant-making foundations that would become so central to the modern American state. Its importance as a policy research institution cannot be underestimated. Such projects as the Pittsburgh Survey (1909–1914), which reviewed conditions of work and life among that city's working class, set standards for careful and thorough empirical social research as a basis for philanthropic and government action. The foundation also did pioneering work on living costs that became the basis for government policies. Most important, the foundation's programs signaled a shift toward a genuinely scientific philanthropy directed to identifying and solving the root causes of social problems rather than treating their symptoms.

The Rise of the Private Research University

Central to the transformation of American institutional life between the Civil War and World War I was the development of the private research university (Geiger 1986; Graham and Diamond 1997). It became the most important locus of basic research in the social, life, and physical sciences, and the chief source of the experts, professionals, and executives who staffed the corporate and government bureaucracies that would be the distinguishing feature of twentieth-century life.

The American research university was not an imitation of foreign models nor was it modeled on its institutional predecessor, the sectarian college. Intentionally crafted to serve the needs of a people engaged in nation building and a rapidly growing industrial economy, it was distinctively secular in orientation, independent of government in ways the earlier colleges had not been, and dependent on the wealth of the new industrial elite. The private research university was a capitalist institution in every sense of the word: it sought to amass *intellectual capital,* by hiring faculty internationally and making huge investments in the libraries, museums, and laboratories essential to carrying out pathbreaking research; *financial capital,* through aggressive fund-raising, adroit financial management, and the systematic cultivation of relationships with the nation's wealthiest men; and *human capital,* by issuing degrees that were nationally and internationally recognized and nurturing continuing relationships among alumni after graduation. Perhaps most important of all, the private research university sought to create *institutional capital,* by placing itself in the center of a network of powerful entities essential to national economic, political, social, and cultural integration.

No individual was more responsible for the creation of the private research university than Charles W. Eliot (1834–1926), the young president of Harvard who, in 1869, proclaimed that the nation was "fighting a wilderness, moral and physical" that could be conquered only if Americans were trained and armed for battle by private institutions (Eliot 1869:203). Eliot had little patience for traditional forms of politics or voluntarist sentimentality. "As a people," he declared in his inaugural address, "we have but a halting faith in special training for high professional employments. The vulgar conceit that a Yankee can turn his hand to anything we insensibly carry into high places where it is preposterous and criminal. . . . Only after years of the bitterest experience, did we come to believe the professional training of a soldier to be of value in war" (Eliot 1898:12). Combining postwar elite triumphalism with new social ideas extrapolated from Darwinism, Eliot reconceptualized the role of elites from social groups whose authority was grounded in tradition to functional elites whose authority was based on public-serving scientific expertise.

Having spent the war years abroad studying European educational systems and their relation to economic development, Eliot added to these social ideas a keen appreciation for the relationship between specialization and the achievement of large-scale collective tasks. "The civilization of a people may be inferred from the variety of its tools," he declared in his inaugural address. "There are thousands of years between the stone hatchet and the machine shop. As tools multiply, each is more ingeniously adapted to its own exclusive purpose. So with the men that make the State. For the individual, concentration, and the highest development of his own peculiar faculty, is the only prudence. But for the State, it is variety, not uniformity, of intellectual product, which is needful" (Eliot 1898:12–13). Eliot's ideas made sense to the business elite, whom the war had awakened to the possibilities of production and marketing on a hitherto unimaginable scale. With their generous backing, Eliot set about the task of transforming Harvard College into America's first great research university—an institution that both nurtured every domain of knowledge, from the physical and social sciences to literature and philosophy, and sought to recruit its students nationally and its scholars internationally (Buck 1965; Hawkins 1972).

In the years between 1870 and 1920, business wealth poured into Harvard and other private universities, including a host of new institutions—Cornell (1865), Johns Hopkins (1876), Stanford (1891), and the University of Chicago (1891). Public institutions, particularly the universities of Michigan, Wisconsin, and California, emulated the private university model, though they would not be able to fully realize their possibilities until after World War II, when the federal government began providing significant financial aid to higher education (Geiger 1993).

In the closing years of the nineteenth century, higher education institutions became embedded in an increasingly dense and complex network of organizations including business corporations, charitable and cultural institutions dependent on them for technology and expertise, professional and scholarly societies and book and periodical publishers that disseminated the scholarship of their faculties, and trade associations and groups advocating social and economic reform that translated scholarship into policy.

The increasing absorption of higher education by big business was not unopposed. When New York businessmen and professionals tried to wrest control of Yale from the Connecticut Congregational clergymen who had governed it for nearly two centuries, the clergy fought back with compelling critiques of the shortcomings of the market mentality, especially as applied to higher learning (Porter 1870; Veblen 1918). But the clergy and other opponents—notably the defenders of the "genteel culture"—could do no more than delay the inevitable. Temporarily thwarted, Yale's business alumni withheld their contributions until 1899, when the corporation finally elected a railroad economist as president and placed the university's future in the hands of the avatars of the New York Central Railroad and the Standard Oil Company (Hall 2000).

The ascendancy of business in politics, society, and culture at the end of the nineteenth century was not a simple matter of heavy-handed conquest. The business leaders of the Gilded Age of the 1870s, many of them rough-hewn, self-made men, were being replaced by young men who had university educations, who identified with the nationalist and bureaucratic ideals articulated by Eliot and others, and who were enthusiastic participants in the dense networks of professional, political, and social associations. Herbert Croly (1869–1930), a member of the Harvard class of 1889 and author of *The Promise of American Life* (1909), a volume generally regarded as the bible of the progressive movement, spoke for the new generation of American leaders when he declared that an individual who "makes himself a better instrument for the practice of some serviceable art" could "scarcely avoid becoming also a better instrument for the fulfillment of the American national Promise" (Levy 1985). Such individuals would, "in the service of their fellow-countrymen . . . reorganize their country's economic, political, and social institutions and ideas" (Croly 1909:438–439).

Why were key members of the older generation of business individualists—such as Carnegie, Morgan, and Rockefeller—willing to make way for a new generation of university-trained professionals and managers who were far more collectivist in their orientation? If Andrew Carnegie (1835–1919), perhaps the most articulate business leader of his time, can be believed, it stemmed from their recognition that the conditions that had made it possible for them to accumulate their fortunes would, if unchecked, lead to the destruction of the capitalist system itself. Saving capitalism would require changing it.

Viewing the labor violence of the mid-1880s through the lenses of social Darwinism, Carnegie came to believe that inequality was the inevitable concomitant of industrial progress (Carnegie 1886a, 1886b). Vast enterprises required "men with a genius for affairs" to organize them, men who would inevitably wield more power and reap greater rewards than the mass of employees who labored in them. As a man of humble origins, Carnegie did not believe that the "genius for affairs" that created great fortunes was likely to be passed on to the heirs of men like himself, and he worried that large inherited fortunes would "sap the root of enterprise", curtailing opportunities for the talented and industrious on whom dynamic capitalism depended (Carnegie 1889:645).

In 1889, Carnegie published an essay on wealth, in which he endeavored to reconcile the inequality resulting from industrial progress with equality needed for continuing social and economic progress. He urged his fellow millionaires to use the same genius for affairs that they had used in building their enterprises to distribute their fortunes. Traditional charity would not suffice because it merely encouraged "the slothful, the drunken, and the unworthy." Instead, Carnegie argued that "the best means of benefiting the community is to place within its reach the ladders on which the aspiring can rise"—in effect, replacing traditional equality of condition with equality of opportunity. Carnegie went well beyond encouraging his wealthy counterparts to administer their wealth wisely as stewards for the progress of the human race; he urged that those who failed to do so should be subject to confiscatory estate taxation that would forcibly redistribute private fortunes.

Carnegie offered his readers a long list of worthy objects for their generosity, but as originally formulated the roster still enumerated conventional institutions—libraries, churches, parks, museums, and universities. By the turn of the century, he and his contemporaries were beginning to think more boldly, envisioning an entirely new kind of charitable vehicle—the grant-making foundation, a permanent endowment with broad purposes (such as the "good of mankind") administered by experts.

The Modernization of Charities Law and the Emergence of Grant-Making Foundations

There were formidable legal and political obstacles to the creation of such institutions. New York State, where America's greatest fortunes were increasingly concentrated, had shown a pronounced hostility to private philanthropy. In the late 1880s, a major bequest to Cornell was held invalid on grounds that it exceeded the amount of property the university was permitted to hold by its charter, and a multimillion dollar bequest by former presidential candidate Samuel Tilden for charitable purposes to be determined by his trustees was held invalid on technical grounds (*Cornell University v. Fiske* 1890; *Tilden v. Green* 1891). With organized labor and farmers uniting under the banner of populism to demand an income tax and government control of the banks and railroads, the political climate for the creation of foundations in the 1890s was insalubrious. Working behind the scenes, legal scholars, reformers, and the benevolently wealthy waged a successful campaign to liberalize New York's charity laws, with counterparts in other industrial urban states ("American Millionaires" 1893; Stead 1893; Ames 1913; Katz, Sullivan, and Beach 1985; Hall and Marcus 1998).

The defeat of populism and the rise of political progressivism in both Republican and Democratic parties in the new century created new opportunities for innovative philanthropists, who could now link their benevolence to reformist causes. The first modern grant-making foundations were all chartered in New York, both because it was the nation's economic center and because its laws were particularly friendly to innovative philanthropy. In the first eleven years of the century, Carnegie established three foundations—the Foundation for the Advancement of Teaching (1905), the Endowment for International Peace (1910), and the Carnegie Corporation of New York (1911)—that were progressively more open-ended in intention and in the discretion granted their trustees (Lagemann 1992a, 1992b). The first genuinely modern foundation, which combined grant making with active involvement in the fields it proposed to subsidize, was the Russell Sage Foundation established in 1907. John D. Rockefeller (1839–1937), by then the wealthiest American, moved from narrowly focused educational (University of Chicago, Baptist Education Society), medical (Rockefeller Medical Institute), and religious philanthropy to more broad-ranging initiatives such as the General Education Board (1905), which helped to underwrite the modernization of higher education and provide support for black colleges and universities (Fosdick 1952, 1962; Corner 1964; Brown 1979; Ettling 1981; Jonas 1989).

While this kind of large-scale benevolence helped Americans accept the idea that wealth could be something other than predatory and self-serving, the furor that greeted Rockefeller's effort to obtain a congressional charter for a $100 million open-ended grant-making foundation—whose mandate was "to promote the well being of mankind"—suggested that Americans' hostility toward large institutions and their creators had not been entirely dispelled. In spite of his close ties to big business, Progressive presidential candidate Theodore Roosevelt opposed the effort, claiming that "no amount of charity in spending such fortunes [as Rockefeller's] can compensate in any way for the misconduct in acquiring them." The conservative Republican candidate, William Howard Taft denounced the effort as "a bill to incorporate Mr. Rockefeller." Samuel Gompers, president of the American Federation of Labor, sneered that "the one thing that the world would gratefully accept from Mr. Rockefeller now would be the establishment of a great endowment of research and education to help other people see in time how they can keep from being like him" (Collier and Horowitz 1976:64). Nothing Rockefeller could do to counter charges that the foundation would serve his private interests—including an offer to make the appointment of the foundation's trustees subject to government approval—was sufficient to quell the uproar. The Rockefeller Foundation was eventually chartered by the New York legislature (see Gates 1977; Fosdick 1952; Harr and Johnson 1988; and Chernow 1998).

The new foundations, particularly Russell Sage and Rockefeller, were unusual not only in the broad discretion granted their trustees but also in their explicit goals of reforming social, economic, and political life. These lofty ends were to be achieved not by direct political action but by studying conditions, making findings available to influential citizens, and mobilizing public opinion to bring about change. This relationship between academic experts, professional bodies, business, and government would become the paradigm of a new kind of political process—one based on policy rather than partisan politics.

It was precisely this emerging relationship between industrial wealth and public life that underlay the 1910–1913 controversy over the chartering of the Rockefeller Foundation and the 1915–1916 hearings of the Senate Commission on Industrial Relations (U.S. Senate 1916). In a general sense, the fears of those who opposed the foundations were not ungrounded. The foundations, through their ability to channel huge amounts of money toward charitable objects at will, could have become major instruments through which "the interests" could influence public policy and the teaching and research agendas of colleges and universities (Laski 1930; Karl and Katz 1981, 1985, 1987; Stanfield 1985; Colwell 1993; Sealander 1997). But the fierce controversy over their existence served to make philanthropists extraordinarily cautious. While a few foundations, such as Russell Sage, the Brookings Institution (1916), and the Twentieth Century Fund (1919), would focus directly on public policy matters, most acted with greater circumspection, either by funding relatively noncontroversial activities such as health care and education or by indirectly influencing public policy through grants to such intermediary organizations as the National Research Council, the Social Science Research Council, the American Council of Learned Societies, and the National Bureau of Economic Research. Foundation grants to intermediary organizations and to universities had a profound impact on universities' research priorities and on the growth of new disciplines, particularly the social sciences (Fisher 1993). Foundation initiatives, such as the Carnegie Corporation–sponsored *Medical Education in the United States and Canada* (better known as the Flexner Report; Flexner 1910) helped to transform not only the training of physicians but the entire field of health care (Starr 1982; Wheatley 1988; Bonner 2002). In the 1940s, sociologist Gunnar Myrdal's Carnegie-funded study of American race relations, *An American Dilemma: The Negro Problem and Modern Democracy* (1944), helped call the attention of policy makers and the public to a central contradiction in American public life.

By the eve of World War I, a constellation of foundations, universities, policy-making bodies, and progressively tilted trade associations such as the National Industrial Conference Board were becoming the basis for a national "establishment" of progressive institutions and individuals. American entry into the war would mobilize this establishment, completing the economic, political, and cultural task of nation building. While subcultures, backwaters, and centers of resistance to the new order persisted—as events such as the Scopes trial and the resurgence of the Ku Klux Klan demonstrated—the new integrated, institutionally based bureaucratic order emerged triumphant after the war to proclaim the birth of a new "business civilization."

WELFARE CAPITALISM, SCIENTIFIC MANAGEMENT, AND THE "ASSOCIATIVE STATE," 1920–1945

By the turn of the century, almost all Americans had embraced some version of the progressive ideal—the belief that defects of their economic, social, and political institutions could be remedied by the application of scientific principles, compassion, and expertise. Most, however, were averse to governmental solutions, though even for the most conservative, government had a legitimate and central role to play in public life. The period between the world wars was one in which virtually all major social actors strove to find ways of balancing the possibilities of free economic enterprise—which was seen as the ultimate source of innovation and general prosperity—against shared beliefs in democratic governance and economic justice. Philanthropically supported institutions would play key roles in both moderating the excesses of capitalism and at the same time expanding its reach into every aspect of public and private life (Cyphers 2002).

The belief that making economic, political, and social institutions more efficient would also make them more just was a central pillar of the progressive faith (Alchon 1985). This belief originated in the business community, not only in the thinking of such leaders as Carnegie, who justified improvements in working conditions on economic grounds, but in the writings of engineers who, as early as the 1880s, had begun studying and experimenting with the interrelationships of tools, materials, labor processes, compensation schemes, the organization of the workplace, productivity, and profitability. By the turn of the century, these engineer-economists had developed methods that increased efficiency and profitability and linked these with economic empowerment of the workforce. This encouraged the convergence of the professionalization of management and broader programs of political and social reform. Frederick Winslow Taylor (1856–1915) promoted the best known of these "scientific management" schemes (Taylor 1911; Kanigel 1997). Based on these ideas, progressive managers implemented ambitious "welfare capitalist" programs that provided workers with education, health, housing, and other services in order to boost their productivity and discourage them from joining unions (Brandes 1976; Brody 1980; Jacoby 1985).

Fordism: The Corporation as Social Enterprise

Pioneer automobile manufacturer Henry Ford (1863–1947) took these ideas a step further, using new assembly line techniques to reduce manufacturing costs and the prices of his products, while raising his employees' wages to enable them to purchase the products they produced. "Fordism" expanded the reach of the ideal of efficiency beyond the internal arrangements of the industrial plant into society itself: low-priced automobiles, credit purchasing, aggressive advertising, and a national distribution system based on dealer-owned franchises offered a paradigm for a self-sustaining economy based on consumer purchasing power. While Ford sneered at traditional kinds of philanthropy, his investments in product development and the welfare of his workers were sufficiently large to prompt a stockholder lawsuit in 1915, in which he was accused of diverting profits for humanitarian purposes instead of distributing them as dividends (Nevins 1957). Though Ford declared as his ambition a desire to "employ still more men, to spread the benefits of this industrial system to the greatest possible number, to help them build up their lives and their homes," the court, in a decision that would restrict corporate philanthropy for decades to come, ruled that because "a business corporation is organized and carried on primarily for the profit of the stockholders," companies could not legally divert profits in order to devote them to philanthropic purposes unrelated to the business (*Dodge v. Ford* 1919).

Despite such efforts to restrict social initiatives by business, many major corporations during the 1920s, guided by top executives who closely identified with the progressive social agenda, used compensation schemes, pricing, product lines, and advertising not only to provide goods and services but to transform society (see Loth 1958; Heald 1970; Sklar 1988). Before the war, these companies had produced expensive products primarily for other businesses. After the war, they shifted their efforts to building mass markets of households and individual consumers. Consumer-based markets offered not only opportunities for profits based on high-volume sales of relatively low-price products but also unparalleled opportunities for shaping consumer preferences in ways that brought efficiency into homes and communities (Ewen 1976). These firms invested not only in advertising but in education—underwriting the development of home economics and shop courses that familiarized millions with new products and domestic technologies (Rose 1995). In doing so, they were able to achieve many of the progressives' public health goals, since improved nutrition and sanitation required the domestic appliances and brand-name products they produced. At the same time their executives assumed leadership roles on the boards of grant-making foundations and universities, where they promoted the ideals of corporate citizenship.

Business leaders continued to press for changes that would permit more generous corporate contributions. In the mid-1930s, they successfully lobbied Congress to make corporate philanthropic contributions tax deductible. After World War II, a group of top corporate executives mounted a successful challenge to legal strictures on corporate contributions. In a 1952 test case involving a stockholder suit against a company's donation to Princeton University, the New Jersey Supreme Court was persuaded by the executives' argument that the survival of free enterprise depended on the vitality of charitable and educational institutions. The elimination of legal barriers, combined with an aggressive campaign to promote corporate philanthropy, led to the emergence of company foundations and corporate contribution programs as a significant source of nonprofit revenues (*A. P. Smith Manufacturing Co. v. Barlow* 1952; Andrews 1952; Ruml 1952; Curti and Nash 1965; Hall 1989a; Himmelstein 1997).

Business and the Emergence of New Philanthropic Vehicles

The democratization of consumption was accompanied by the invention of new kinds of philanthropic organizations that encouraged middle- and working-class Americans to become more civically engaged. The Community Chest, invented by members of the Cleveland Chamber of Commerce, was a fund-raising mechanism that sought to make charitable fund-raising more efficient by preventing duplication of fund-raising appeals, ensuring that funds went to worthy organizations, broadening the donor base, and ensuring the alignment of charitable and business agendas (Seeley et al. 1957; Cutlip 1965; Brilliant 1990; Hutchinson 1996). (Today's United Way is a descendant of the Community Chest.) The community foundation, another Cleveland philanthropic innovation, also sought to democratize philanthropy by encouraging small donors to establish charitable trusts and to place them under common management (Hall 1989b; Hammack 1989; Magat 1989a, 1989b). Spearheading drives for hospitals, for the Red Cross, and for an assortment of national health charities, professional fund-raising firms applied business expertise, including hard-sell advertising techniques, to generate mass-based support for charitable enterprises. Taken together, these innovations represented a shift of organized charity away from the moralizing amateurism of the charity organization movement and toward business models and methods.

Because they were often dominated by Protestants, Catholics and Jews often resisted cooptation by these civic initiatives. Instead, they organized parallel federated fund-raising organizations (Catholic Charities, the United Jewish Appeal) to generate support for their own benevolent institutions (Oates 1995).

Business, Philanthropy, and the Associative State

Mobilization for World War I intensified cooperation between business, philanthropy, and government (Cuff 1973; Galambos and Pratt 1988). Even before American entry into the war, a privately supported preparedness movement was training elite businessmen and professionals as officers, while the Red Cross, the American Friends Service Committee, and other nongovernmental groups were operating ambulance corps to assist the British, Canadian, and French armies (Curti 1965; Clifford 1972). Once the United States entered the war, industrial production, transportation, food, finance, and other crucial domains were coordinated by quasi-public bodies staffed by volunteers from big businesses. The war provided the impetus for national fund-raising efforts: the Community Chest was transformed from a midwestern oddity into a national charitable force, while the Red Cross energetically solicited private corporations and individuals.

One of these "dollar-a-year" men, millionaire-businessman Herbert Hoover (1874–1964), both articulated the ideals of the progressive business civilization of the 1920s and helped to implement them during his terms as secretary of commerce under Harding and Coolidge and during his own presidency (Hawley 1974). Hoover's 1922 book *American Individualism* envisioned a society self-governed by dense networks of associations working in partnership with government to advance public welfare by combining the pursuit of profit with the higher values of cooperation and public service.

Hoover's efforts in the housing field embodied his conception of the possibilities of such an "associative state." After the end of World War I, Hoover used the Building and Housing Division of the Department of Commerce to address the problems of unemployment and substandard housing by stabilizing the construction industry, building new markets by overcoming resistance to mass production and standardization, fostering city planning and zoning activities, and promoting the "spiritual values" (and economic stimulus) inherent in widespread home ownership. To do this, the Housing Division worked through an organization known as Better Homes in America. Originally a promotional activity initiated by a household magazine, the *Deliniator,* Better Homes was reorganized as a public service corporation in 1923. Operating as a "collateral arm" of the Commerce Department, Better Homes "secured operating funds from private foundations, persuaded James Ford, a professor of social ethics at Harvard, to serve as executive director, and secured the enterprise's ties to the Housing Division by having directors of the agency serve as officers in the new nonprofit corporation." Working through some 3,600 local committees and a host of affiliated businesses, trade associations, and schools, Better Homes carried on massive advertising and educational campaigns "to provide exhibits of model homes, foster better 'household management,' promote research in the housing field, and generate a greater, steadier, and more discriminating demand for 'improved dwellings,' especially for families with 'small incomes'" (Hawley 1974:142–143). By 1932, Hoover boasted that these initiatives had led to the construction of 15 million "new and better homes" (Hoover 1938:7).

The impact of Hoover's associationalism was as much local as national. The national association form perfected by religious denominations and fraternal and sororal organizations was adapted to economic and political purposes through trade associations, service clubs (such as Rotary and Kiwanis), character-building groups (Boy Scouts), veterans' groups (American Legion), and professional societies (American Society of Civil Engineers) (Naylor 1921; Galambos 1966; Charles 1993; Macleod 1983; Murray 1937; Rumer 1990). From their national headquarters, local civic groups learned how to organize community chests and community foundations, and about city planning, education reform, and the benefits of organized recreation and leisure.

Hoover's promotion of voluntary associations as mechanisms for civic betterment rather than mutual benefit helped to transform Americans' attitudes toward nonprofit organizations and helped to socialize a generation of citizens—Robert Putnam's "long civic generation"—who gave, volunteered, and participated at unprecedented levels (Putnam 2000).

The New Deal and the Expansion of Public-Private Partnership

Though Hoover himself was discredited by his failure to deal effectively with the Great Depression, his ideas formed the basis for the first phase of the New Deal; the National Recovery Administration (NRA), the centerpiece of Franklin Roosevelt's 100 Days, was little more than a formalization of the cooperative relationships between business, charity, and government that Hoover had promoted during the 1920s (Himmelberg 1976). This is hardly surprising, given the dependence of Roosevelt's "brain trust" on private think tanks such as the Brookings Institution and on foundation-funded academic expertise (Critchlow 1985; Smith 1991a, 1991b; Rich 2004).

Intended to revive the economy through stimulating consumer demand, the NRA and other early New Deal programs were a continuation of older ideas of public-private partnership rather than bold statist initiatives. Unlike its economic management initiatives, the federal government's wholesale assumption of responsibility for social insurance—old age pensions, unemployment compensation, and disability payments—was a major departure from the past. While the federal government had provided for veterans, workers involved in interstate commerce, and certain other special classes of citizens, until the establishment of Social Security in 1935, social insurance had been largely a private enterprise, much of it provided through national fraternal and sororal organizations (Skocpol 1992; Beito 2000; Kaufman 2002). The New Deal did not entirely bypass private social insurance; its labor legislation, in strengthening the legal and political position of unions, established the basis for contracts that not only covered wages and working conditions but required employers to provide pensions, health insurance, and other benefits (Jacoby 1997).

The New Deal in its various phases never articulated a coherent or comprehensive program of economic management. It was, rather, a series of experiments and expedients—all predicated on the assumption that economic recovery would permit a reduction of government activism. It is important to recognize that government activism is not the same as "big government." Although Americans learned to look to the president and the federal government for leadership during the 1930s, Roosevelt preferred to work through state and local governments and private entities, rather than creating the kind of vast central state bureaucracies that were emerging in other advanced industrial nations. The NRA, for example, though a national program, was based on a decentralized system of code enforcement, and the Works Progress Administration (WPA), though it employed hundreds of thousands of people nationwide, was based on state and local organizations which poured millions of dollars into counties and municipalities. Roosevelt's expansion of tax preferences (such as the corporate charitable deduction) encouraged greater business support for private charities by permitting firms to use contributions to write down their tax liabilities. Further, by making taxation of personal income steeply progressive, he gave added impetus to charitable giving by the wealthy (Webber and Wildavsky 1986; Howard 1997).

While the Depression underscored the limited capacities of state and local governments, businesses, and private charities to deal effectively with widespread unemployment and social and economic dislocation, New Deal policies affirmed rather than diminished the importance of voluntary organizations and philanthropy. Not only did federal tax policies encourage private support for charitable institutions, but government at all levels depended on the private organizational infrastructure both for policy expertise and to provide services at the community level. In addition, the recognition of organized labor, mandated under the Wagner-Connery Act of 1935, helped to restore many of the welfare capitalist programs of the 1920s, as corporations negotiated agreements that included health and other social insurance benefits (Jacoby 1997).

Perhaps the most compelling evidence for the growing interdependence of public and private initiatives in this period is the vast number of buildings constructed by the Public Works Administration (PWA), which provided venues for the activities of nonprofit groups. The Civic Center in Hammond, Indiana, completed in 1938, included not only a 5,000-seat auditorium for performances and public programs but also offices and meeting spaces for "Boy and Girl Scout headquarters, camera clubs, practice rooms for drama, . . . and a complete layout for the activities of local teams and athletic clubs" (Short and Stanley-Brown 1939:93). In addition to municipal auditoriums and civic centers, the PWA built art and natural history museums, libraries, dormitories, stadiums, and classroom buildings for private colleges and universities.

THE WELFARE STATE AND THE INVENTION OF THE NONPROFIT SECTOR, 1945–2000

While many conservatives feared—and many liberals hoped—that the lessons of World War II would lead the nation toward the kind of social democratic regimes being embraced by Western European nations, the political and administrative foundations laid by the New Deal ensured that postwar policies would be devolutionary and privatizing rather than centralizing and collectivist. To be sure, American governments in the postwar decades faced unprecedented challenges: never before had the nation been required to bear sustained international responsibilities. As leader of the free world in a period of continuing international tension, the United States would have to be able to respond effectively to international crises. This would require capacities not only for military and economic mobilization but also for maintaining domestic economic and political stability (see U.S. Department of Commerce 1954:27–29).

Though there never seems to have been any comprehensive articulation of the form that the postwar polity would take, the writings of policy experts in and outside of government clearly identify national goals and the tools of economic and political management that would be needed to realize them. Two things proved to be crucial to realizing these goals: universal income taxation, enacted in 1943, which gave the federal government a virtually unlimited source of revenue, and innovations in public finance economics and systems for gathering and interpreting economic and social data that gave planners and policy makers a basis for developing fiscal practices consistent with government's enlarged role (Webber and Wildavsky 1986:453; see also Donahue 1989).

This transformation of the politics of public finance played a key role in fueling the proliferation of nonprofits, which became increasingly important both as providers of government-funded services and as advocates seeking to influence government policies. As the nation assumed its responsibilities as leader of the free world, the emphasis in budgeting and spending shifted from balancing revenues and expenditures (and other attempts to limit government spending) to meeting strategic and policy objectives. As Carolyn Webber and Aaron Wildavsky explain it, "The process of budgeting became introspective rather than critical. The question of 'How much?' was transmuted into 'What for?'" (1986:478). With the virtually unlimited revenues available through universalized income taxation and deficit spending (indeed, the government's borrowing capacity itself became an important economic management tool), budgeting ceased to be a zero-sum game in which one agency's gain was another's loss.

Despite increasingly sophisticated oversight capacities and the creation of new policy-making and monitoring bodies (the Council of Economic Advisors, the Office of Management and Budget), the budgetary process became less—rather than more—centralized. Because most federal policies were implemented not by the federal government itself but by an assortment of agencies that interfaced with the states, localities, and private sector actors that actually carried out these policies, each area of activity developed its own internal and external constituencies: agency officials pushing to expand their resources and prerogatives, congressional and other elected officials who stood to gain from spending and hiring by government agencies, and organized beneficiary groups—"special interests" operating as nonprofits—which lobbied Congress, contributed to electoral campaigns, mobilized voters, and sought to influence public opinion through advertising and journalism (Wildavksy 1992).

In the decades following World War II, federal social, tax, and spending policies transformed the overlapping domains of nonproprietary associational, charitable, and philanthropic entities. Steeply progressive taxes on personal income and estates, combined with high corporate tax rates, created powerful incentives for tax avoidance—incentives that could be engineered to direct the flow of private resources into state and local governments (via investments in tax-exempt bonds) and other areas in which the government was interested, such as cultural, educational, health, and welfare services. High estate and corporate taxation also provided incentives for the wealthy to establish foundations, which became major sources of funding for entities designated as charitable and tax-exempt by the government. Government further encouraged the growth and proliferation of nongovernmental, nonproprietary entities through direct and indirect subsidies, such as the Hill-Burton Act (1946), which provided funding for the expansion of public and nonprofit hospitals; grants from such bodies as the National Science Foundation and the National Institutes of Health, which flowed disproportionately to private institutions; and the G.I. Bill, which created a system of tuition vouchers that transformed American higher education.

Fueled by these incentives, the number of nonproprietary entities, charitable and noncharitable, began to grow dramatically: between 1939 and 1950, the number of fully or partially exempt entities more than doubled, and between 1950 and 1968, the number of charitable tax-exempts increased more than twentyfold, from 12,500 to more than a quarter million (table 2.1). While some of this growth can be accounted for by the conversion of proprietary entities into nonprofits, the vast majority were new establishments, more often than not firms established to take advantage of direct and indirect federal funding and to serve as private agencies for implementing government policies.

Nonprofits and Social Movements

As the United States assumed undisputed leadership of the free world after the Iron Curtain descended over Europe in the late 1940s, the policies of public and private institutions that subjugated racial and religious minorities and women became increasingly difficult to defend. Although the seniority of southern congressmen ensured that no significant civil rights legislation was enacted by the federal government until 1964, nonprofit advocacy groups, funded by foundations, worked tirelessly to change public opinion on civil rights issues and to pressure political leaders to change their votes.

One of the great legacies of twenty years of Democratic control of the White House and Congress was a liberal activist federal judiciary. Two significant legal innovations enacted by these jurists transformed litigation into an important instrument of policy making and turned nonprofits into major agents of policy change.

The first was the adoption of the doctrine of incorporation by the U.S. Supreme Court beginning in the late 1930s (Friedman 2002:203–207). The incorporation doctrine derives from the Fourteenth Amendment, which declares that no state can deprive a person of life, liberty, or property

TABLE 2.1. POPULATION OF CHARITABLE AND NONCHARITABLE NONPROFIT ORGANIZATIONS AND RELIGIOUS CONGREGATIONS, 1936–1996

Year	Total NPOs and congregations	Total NPOs	Noncharitables	Charitables	Congregations
1936					179,742
1939				12,500	
1943		80,250	62,800	17,450	
1946		93,458	65,958	27,500	
1950				32,000	
1967		309,000			
1968		358,000			
1969		416,000	278,000	138,000	
1972		535,000			
1973		630,000			
1974	1,005,000	673,000			332,000
1975		692,000			
1976		763,000	503,000	260,000	
1977	1,123,000	790,000	514,000	276,000	333,000
1978		810,000	516,000	294,000	
1979		825,000	521,000	304,000	
1980	1,182,000	846,000	526,000	320,000	336,000
1981		851,000	523,000	328,000	
1982		841,000	518,000	323,000	
1983		845,000	509,000	336,000	
1984	1,209,000	871,000	518,000	353,000	338,000
1985		887,000	521,000	366,000	
1986		897,424	409,817	487,183	
1987	1,285,105	939,105	416,354	522,751	346,000
1988	1,318,177	969,177	502,609	489,952	349,000
1989	1,343,561	992,561	502,432	490,129	351,000
1990		1,024,766	540,766	484,000	
1991		1,055,545	407,006	512,551	
1992	1,481,206	1,085,206	554,614	530,592	396,000
1993		1,118,131	575,162	542,969	
1994		1,138,598	616,598	522,000	
1995		1,164,789	604,732	560,057	
1996		1,188,510	615,245	573,265	

Source: Hall and Burke 2006.
Note: Blank cells indicate no available data.

without "due process of law." In a series of cases, the Supreme Court held that these words "incorporated" the Bill of Rights in such a way as to make them applicable to the states. This meant that states that routinely deprived nonwhites of rights guaranteed by the U.S. Constitution—such as the right to vote—were subject to the jurisdiction of the federal courts.

The second innovation was a change in the federal rules of civil procedure—the code that defines the kinds of legal action permissible in the federal courts. In 1966, the U.S. Supreme Court, which enacts these rules, changed the rule governing who had standing to initiate litigation to permit "claims by unorganized groups" to be presented "as if they were those of organizations" (Friedman 2002:255). The impact of this rules change was dramatic. As legal historian Lawrence Friedman writes, "Litigation in late-twentieth century America became a political and economic instrument, a tool, a locus for strategic behavior. The class action was an important way to involve courts in battles over civil rights, corporate governance, protecting the environment, and consumer protection. And class action is central in the society of 'local justice.' Class actions depend on quirks and accidents of procedural history and the peculiarities of the American legal order—many legal systems have no such beast as the class action at all. But the class action has long since transcended its origins. It grew fat on the fodder of twentieth-century culture" (Friedman 2002:255).

Civil rights organizations such as the NAACP were quick to recognize the opportunities offered by these changes. The NAACP's landmark 1954 litigation over school segregation in Topeka, Kansas, *Brown v. Board of Education,* was based on the ability of its litigators to persuade the court that separate educational facilities were inherently unequal and, as such, violated the Fourteenth Amendment, which guarantees all citizens "equal protection of the laws." This and other federal court decisions based on it compelled a reluctant federal government to initiate the process of intervening in states that excluded nonwhites from public schools, public transportation, restaurants, and other public accommodations.

Southern resistance to court-ordered desegregation gave rise to the civil rights movement of the 1950s and 1960s in which a variety of nonprofits—churches, advocacy organizations (the Southern Christian Leadership Conference, the NAACP, the Student Non-violent Coordinating Committee, and others), and foundations—worked together to mobilize demonstrators and voters to fight segregation (Jenkins and Ekert 1986; Jenkins 1987). When the movement shifted its focus to northern practices of de facto segregation, resistance by political leaders grew, particularly among ethnic urban bosses whose power was undermined by drives to register black voters; it produced demands for the curtailment of political activities by nonprofits.

The logic and methods of constitutionalizing the civil disabilities associated with racial segregation were soon embraced by other groups—women, the physically and mentally disabled, the aged, and gays and lesbians (Lauritsen and Thorstad 1995; Berkeley 1999; Barnartt and Scotch 2001; Fleischer and Zames 2001; Marcus 2002; Minton 2002; Rimmerman 2002). Litigation and political action by these groups, organized as social movements through Washington-based nonprofits, transformed American politics in the second half of the twentieth century. Federal civil rights legislation of the 1960s addressed both racial and gender issues, challenging not only discriminatory state and municipal ordinances but also the practices of private institutions that excluded participation on the basis of race, gender, and religion. Suits challenging the treatment of the mentally disabled led to the court-ordered dismantling of state mental institutions and training schools and the rise of a huge government-funded nonprofit group home industry (Rothman and Rothman 1984). Rights-oriented and class action litigation launched by national nonprofit groups changed public opinion and public policy regarding consumer safety, the environment, smoking, drunken driving, child abuse, and other issues. These kinds of advocacy-oriented social movement activity made nonprofits an increasingly central part of political life.

Tax Reform

Between 1947 and 1954, Congress labored to introduce some order into a tax system that had become a patchwork of amendments since it was originally enacted in 1916 (U.S. House of Representatives 1948; Seidman 1954; Feingold 1960; Internal Revenue Service 1963; "Macaroni Monopoly" 1968; Gilbert 1983; Witte 1985). An important part of this effort was a rationalization of the tax and regulatory treatment of exempt entities. Under the original Internal Revenue Code, exempt entities had been covered by a catch-all category, section 101, which included everything from foundations and fraternal orders through mutual savings banks and insurance companies. After protracted inquiries into exempt entities, including two high-profile congressional investigations of the political inclinations of "foundations and other tax-exempt entities," tax writers forged section 501(c) as part of the 1954 Internal Revenue Code. Section 501(c) promulgated an elaborate classificatory scheme that accorded different kinds of tax privileges and degrees of regulatory oversight to the various types of nonproprietary entities (U.S. House of Representatives 1953a, 1953b, 1954).

What Congress had done, in effect, was to bring together the various types of nonproprietary entities—nonstock and mutual benefit corporations, charitable trusts, voluntary associations, cooperatives—and place them in a common regulatory framework. The IRS code and its regulatory provisions transformed individual and corporate charitable giving into a tax-driven activity, with gifts and bequests carefully calculated to provide donors with the greatest possible financial benefits. When John D. Rockefeller gave $100 million to establish the Rockefeller Foundation in 1913, he derived no financial benefit from the transaction. In contrast, when Henry Ford established the Ford Foundation as part of his estate plan, his family was able to transfer ownership of one of the nation's largest industrial enterprises and private fortunes from one generation to another without paying any significant estate taxes (MacDonald 1956). In the decades after the enactment of postwar tax reforms, lawyers, accountants, and consultants specializing in estate and tax planning flourished. Tax reforms, combined with direct and indirect government subsidies, also impacted organizations that stood to benefit from the increased scope, scale, and focus of philanthropic giving. In industries such as health care and education, proprietary entities rushed to convert to nonprofit ownership (see, for example, Friedman 1990:158–166).

As nonprofits became increasingly favored as recipients of direct and indirect subsidies, they took on increasingly active roles in formulating and advocating particular policies (Jenkins and Halcli 1999). Advocacy activities that in the past would have been carried on through trade associations now came to be the province of national mass membership associations with 501(c)(3) status (such as the National Audubon Society, the Sierra Club, and the American Association of Retired Persons; see Putnam 2000). Not only did charitable tax-exempt status cloak the causes these entities promoted in an aura of disinterested public service, but also, because donations to them were deductible, it made them attractive to foundations, corporations, and individual donors large and small. Though classed as membership organizations, these new entities little resembled the national associations of the prewar decades (fraternal and sororal, veterans', and patriotic groups) (Skocpol 1999c). The postwar associations had no social dimension: members seldom if ever met face-to-face, individually or collectively. Membership became a political and financial act, not a social commitment (Putnam 2000:148–180).

More importantly, in terms of its political role, the emergent charitable tax-exempt universe of the postwar era differed dramatically from its associational domain of earlier decades. In the past, when national associations, foundations, think tanks, and other philanthropically supported entities sought to influence government, they generally did so as outsiders. In the postwar decades, associations, now enjoying the benefits of charitable tax-exempt status, increasingly became—if not extensions of government itself—an intrinsic part of the *organizational field* of public governance. The relationship between the Brookings Institution and the government which produced the Social Security Act in the 1930s was exceptional. By the late 1950s, such relationships were becoming routinized not only on the institutional level (with government contracting with think tanks for all manner of policy and technical services) but on the individual level, as professional careers moved individuals from universities to grant-making foundations or from business corporations to government agencies and congressional staffs—and sometimes to elective office (Jenkins 1987).

The most remarkable aspect of the postwar elaboration of federal power was the extent to which it acted through the private sector and states and localities—a fact powerfully demonstrated by table 2.2, which shows federal civilian employment in the period 1951–1999 remaining virtually unchanged while the number of state government employees increased sharply, from 4.3 million to 14.7 million, and employment in the nonprofit sector increased from 5.6 million in 1977 to 9.7 million in 1994. During this period, the flow of direct federal subsidies to nonprofits also increased dramatically from about $30 billion in 1974 to just under $160 billion in 1994.

As noted, the reinvention of American government that took place in the decades following World War II did not follow a master plan. It appears, rather, to have been the outcome of a process of incremental decision making in which deeply embedded prejudices against big government accommodated themselves to the necessities of global leadership. Because the process was incremental, legislators and policy makers remained largely unaware of the extent of the changes they had wrought until forced by circumstances—such as the astonishing proliferation of nonprofit entities—to make sense of them (Donahue 1989).

By the late 1950s, journalists and politicians had begun to call attention to the inequities of the tax code, particularly the extraordinary favors—"loopholes"—from which the very wealthy benefited (Vogel 1989:59–64, 1996). In 1959, in response to efforts to liberalize the tax treatment of charitable contributions by large donors, a vocal minority on the Senate Finance Committee wrote a sharply worded minority report which criticized the proposal. "The tax base is being dangerously eroded by many forces, among them tax-exempt trusts and foundations," the senators declared. "Not only is the tax base being eroded, but even more harmful social and political consequences may result from concentrating and holding in a few hands and in perpetuity, control over large fortunes and business enterprises" (U.S. Senate 1961).

In May 1961, Texas congressman Wright Patman issued the first of a series of highly publicized reports criticizing foundation abuses (see Andrews 1969). The Kennedy administration evidently shared these concerns, appointing Harvard Law School professor Stanley Surry—a noted critic of tax code inequities—as assistant secretary of treasury for tax policy.

Inflation and tax increases heightened tax sensitivity during the 1960s—a sensitivity to which politicians were responsive. In the closing days of the Johnson administration, retiring secretary of the treasury Joseph Barr warned of a taxpayer revolt if tax inequities were not addressed. Barr claimed that middle-income taxpayers were bearing the brunt of taxation while millionaires who took advantage of loopholes with the advice of lawyers and accountants paid nothing. Over the coming year, the House Ways and Means Committee held exhaustive hearings covering every aspect of the tax code and its favorable treatment of particular groups and industries, including foundations (Vogel 1989:62).

The hearings on foundations were particularly acrimonious, with members of Congress focusing not only on financial abuses, but also on the ways in which some foundations, such as the Ford Foundation, used their resources for political rather than philanthropic purposes. Foundation leaders stonewalled Congress, defending philanthropy as quintessentially American and challenging the government's right to limit its prerogatives. But echoing Tocqueville in an era when tax policy makers thought in terms of public finance economics proved futile. The Tax Reform Act of 1969 signed by President Nixon included provisions to limit self-dealing and donor control, regulate investment practices and payout, and require the annual filing of financial reports.

TABLE 2.2. FEDERAL CIVILIAN, STATE GOVERNMENT, AND NONPROFIT EMPLOYMENT (IN MILLIONS), 1951–1999

Year	Federal civilian employees	State employees	Nonprofit employees
1951	2.5	4.3	
1956	2.4	5.2	
1961	2.5	10.2	
1966	2.9	8.5	
1971	2.8	10.2	
1977			5.6
1981	3	13.4	
1982			6.5
1983	2.9	13.2	
1987			7.4
1992	3.1	13.4	9.1
1994			9.7
1999	2.8	14.7	

Source: Hall and Burke 2006.
Note: Blank cells indicate no available data.

Inventing the Nonprofit Sector

John D. Rockefeller 3rd (1906–1978) had admitted to Congress, almost alone among philanthropic leaders, that big philanthropy needed to change its ways. Although deploring many aspects of the 1969 Tax Reform Act, he understood that dampening further outbreaks of regulatory enthusiasm would require foundations and other tax-exempt entities not only to eliminate abuses that attract unfavorable attention from the press and politicians but also to come up with a coherent and compelling rationale for the existence of nonprofits and the privileges they enjoyed. He organized the Commission on Private Philanthropy and Public Needs (better known as the Filer Commission), a privately funded group operating under the sponsorship of the Department of the Treasury that sponsored exhaustive research on tax-exempt organizations and issued a report which, among other things, recommended the establishment of a permanent "bureau of philanthropy" in the Treasury Department (see Hall 1992 and Brilliant 2000). The commission's most enduring contribution was its suggestion that all tax-exempt entities—donor and donee institutions alike—composed a distinctive "third," "nonprofit," or "independent" sector whose welfare was essential to the future of democracy.

Rockefeller's hopes that the Treasury Department would establish a philanthropy bureau were dashed with the election of Jimmy Carter. Reluctant to abandon the achievements of the Filer Commission, Rockefeller and his associates established Independent Sector, a nonprofit umbrella organization that convened donor and donee organizations and encouraged them to identify their common interests. He also provided initial funding for the first academic research center devoted to the study of philanthropy and nonprofits, Yale's Program on Non-Profit Organizations (PONPO).

These efforts represented a new phase in the process of imposing legibility on what had begun in the early 1950s, with congressional attempts to make sense of the rapidly growing and changing domain of "foundations and other exempt entities." Earlier efforts by policy makers, legislators, and scholars had focused on *what* voluntary associations, charitable trusts, eleemosynary corporations, cooperatives, religious bodies, and other nonproprietary entities and activities did. With the concept of ownership form as the framework for enquiry, focus shifted to *how* such institutions functioned and to their relationship to government and business.

This new approach greatly simplified things. What mattered was not the murky issues of charitable intent and altruistic motivation but the awesome diversity of a domain of organizations involved with virtually every kind of activity, organizations that ranged in scale from charitable endowments controlled by a single trustee to private universities and hospitals employing thousands. The sectoral approach focused not on the diversity of organizations within the sector but on their commonalities—on the characteristics of the nonstock corporation, the impact of the nondistribution constraint, and the treatment of these entities by tax and regulatory authorities.

The new approach was not without its critics. One irate foundation executive, on hearing of the establishment of the Filer Commission, privately asked a colleague, "Has charity become all law? Is it irrecoverably committed to lawyers instead of its traditional practitioners?" (Goheen 1974). Later, as scholarship on the new nonprofit sector began to appear, critics worried that the sanitized language of law and economics obscured important aspects of these organizations, particularly their relationship to wealth and power (Karl and Katz 1987; Hall 1992).

The Nonprofit Sector and the Conservative Revolution

For most of the twentieth century, political conservatives viewed the growth of foundation philanthropy and its nonprofit offshoots with suspicion. This was not surprising, given the generally liberal domestic and international policies favored by foundations and the tendency of nonprofits to locate themselves on the front line of struggles for social and economic justice. After the defeat of Barry Goldwater in 1964, however, conservative strategists began to recognize that decisively swaying public opinion in their favor would require more than political agitation. Flush with new wealth from the South and West, conservatives embraced nonprofits, intent on creating a counter-establishment based on policy research institutes, foundations, and advocacy groups sympathetic to their views. These would be important to efforts by conservatives to formulate credible alternatives to dominant liberal policies.

In contrast to Goldwater's ideological posturing, Ronald Reagan, the Republican's candidate in the 1980 presidential election, offered a far more reasoned and grounded set of proposals, including major cutbacks in government spending, which he believed would empower community groups and private initiatives. Breaking with traditional conservatism, Reagan encouraged individual and corporate philanthropy, establishing the Task Force on Private Sector Initiatives, which was directed by Burt Knauft, who had served on the staff of the Filer Commission.

Reagan's policies forced scholars and policy makers—who, until then, had been describing nonprofits as private, donation-supported, voluntary entities—to reexamine their assumptions about relations between nonprofits and government. An important series of studies by political scientists Lester Salamon, Alan Abramson, and others called attention to the extent of the sector's dependence on government subsidy, pointing out that in many industries federal funding composed between a third and three-quarters of organizational revenues (Salamon and Abramson 1982; Salamon 1987). Suggesting that the American welfare state represented a kind of "third-party government" in which federal programs were largely carried out through nongovernmental actors, they predicted that federal spending cuts would cripple nonprofits, rather than empower them.

Contrary to those predictions, Reagan's budget cuts appear to have both stimulated the continuing proliferation of nonprofits (the number of charitable tax-exempt entities increased by more than 30 percent between Reagan's first and last years in office) and enhanced the sophistication with which they were managed. Unlike nonprofit scholars, who were largely occupied with churning out rhetorical justifications for the existence of the sector, practitioners recognized the range of possibilities in a complex funding environment that offered opportunities for supporting organizations with a mix of earned revenues, donations, foundation and government grants, and contracts with governments and business. In the closing decades of the twentieth century, nonprofits would become increasingly entrepreneurial under the guidance of executives trained as management professionals.

The growth of the group-home industry in the 1980s offers an illuminating example of the kinds of innovative nonprofit entrepreneurship that began to emerge in the Reagan era. As part of a broad process of extending civil rights law to such areas as education and health, the federal courts issued a series of decisions ordering that the mentally disabled be deinstitutionalized and placed in small community-based facilities (Rothman and Rothman 1984; Hall 1996). Unable or unwilling to create and operate such facilities themselves, the states encouraged private groups to provide residential, educational, and rehabilitative services to the retarded and mentally ill. Within a very short period of time, thousands of nonprofit and for-profit firms were established, and they in turn, using millions of state and federal dollars, purchased and renovated residential properties as group homes. Because such a decentralized system was expensive to operate, group-home operators sought economies of scale through various forms of cooperation. In many states, nonprofit holding companies supplied financial and property management services and lobbied and litigated on behalf of the industry. Eventually many providers merged into national companies with huge budgets and impressive political clout.

Human-services contracting proved especially attractive to entrepreneurs because of its physically decentralized character and the variety and richness of its resource base. The complexity of contracting regimes, involving revenues from federal, state, and local governments, as well as donations and grants from private sources, made government regulation and oversight nearly impossible (Smith and Lipsky 1993; Grønbjerg 1993). The closure of state institutions and the placement of hundreds of thousands of clients in nonprofit group homes was accompanied by rising levels of concern about deteriorating care, abuse and neglect, and outright fraud.

With the presidential campaign of Reagan's successor, George H. W. Bush, nonprofits moved to center stage politically. In his 1988 speech accepting the Republican presidential nomination, Bush denounced big government and enthused about the possibilities of replacing the existing system of social welfare provision with "a thousand points of light," each representing a voluntary, community-based initiative serving the dependent and disabled.

Behind the front lines of electoral politics, conservative policy scientists and journalists were devising both the ideas and the programs that would, they claimed, "end welfare as we know it" through aggressive privatization of human services and devolution of government responsibilities to states and localities. Ironically, neither the triumphant conservatives, who took over both houses of Congress in 1994, nor the embattled liberals, who watched in disbelief as the social programs of the past century were dismantled, understood that the much vaunted "Republican revolution" was little more than a continuation and intensification of privatizing and devolutionary dynamics that had been unfolding since the late 1940s. The major innovations were philosophical and rhetorical: the liberal version of third-party government had been based on the belief that alleviating poverty required changes in social and economic conditions; the conservative version was predicated on the notion that changing social and economic conditions required changes in the values and behavior of individuals.

Perhaps the issue that best illuminated the general failure of political imagination in the 1990s was the debate over "charitable choice," the section of the 1994 welfare reform package that promised to remove obstacles to government subsidizing of faith-based human-service provision. Conservatives had enacted the legislation in the belief that there were significant legal obstacles to government support of religiously tied organizations. Liberals reacted to the proposal with alarm, proclaiming that such aid would breach the "wall of separation" between church and state. Neither seems to have been aware that governments had, for decades, been contracting with religious bodies (such as the Salvation Army) and church-controlled secular corporations (such as Catholic Charities and Lutheran Social Services), or that no significant legal obstacles stood in the way of the practice.

The one positive accomplishment of the charitable choice debate was the extent to which it kindled a new appreciation for the importance of religion in public life. For decades, academics and policy makers had acted on the assumption that secularization was an inevitable concomitant of modernity and that religion had long ceased to wield any significant public influence. The astonishing political mobilization of Christian conservatives in the 1980s, which had largely made possible the conservative revolution, challenged these assumptions (see Hodgson 1996). They were further challenged by the failure of efforts to establish market democracies after the fall of the Iron Curtain—which made evident the extent to which the viability of economies and governments depended on the values and informal social networks that bound citizens together and enabled them to act collectively (Putnam 1994, 1995, 2000; Fukuyama 1995). Religious institutions, it turned out, were centrally important as settings in which citizens acquired the values and skills needed to be economically and politically effective (Verba, Schlozman, and Brady 1995).

By the 1990s, religion and religious institutions were generally understood, by conservatives and liberals alike, to be important components of the nonprofit sector—a fitting conclusion, given the fact that religious entities composed 20 percent of America's nonproprietary organizations and represented nearly 60 percent of the sector's revenues.

The charitable choice debate also raised some important questions about the actual impact of efforts to dismantle big government. Religious bodies, even when providing services under government contract, had been largely free of the monitoring and oversight to which secular entities were subjected. As religious leaders contemplated charitable choice, they became aware that increased volumes of government revenue might be accompanied by public demands for accountability and compliance with industry standards. A backward glance at the ways in which the secular charities had been transformed into quasi-governmental "nonprofits" in the decades following World War II was hardly reassuring. More than anything else, it raised the question of whether "privatization" meant the dismantling of big government—or an unprecedented expansion of government into new domains of activity. Recognizing the extent to which dependence on government funding might compromise their capacity to "speak truth to power," many religious bodies declined to avail themselves of the opportunities offered by charitable choice initiatives.

THE FUTURE OF THE NONPROFIT SECTOR

This chapter began with a description of the difficulty of constructing a historical account of the nonprofit sector—a synoptic conception that had not, until thirty years ago, been considered to be a coherent domain of institutions, organizations, and activities. Speculating about the future of the nonprofit sector is no less problematic, because accelerating changes in public policy and in organizational practices defy any effort to capture the essence of nonprofit enterprise.

Nonprofits were once constrained by legal definitions of charity that required them to serve a fairly narrow range of charitable, educational, or religious purposes; today all that the law requires of nonprofits is that they not distribute their surpluses (if any) in the form of dividends and that their beneficiaries be a general class of persons rather than specific individuals. As a result, nonprofits can now be found providing every sort of good and service.

The formal organizational characteristics have become similarly protean. In addition to traditional types of membership and nonmembership organizations, incorporated and unincorporated associations, freestanding charitable trusts and aggregations of trusts under common administration (community foundations), and freestanding and federated/franchise form nonprofits, there are organizational hybrids in which for-profit and nonprofit units are nested in various ways. In the health-care industry, for example, it is not uncommon to have nonprofit hospitals operated by for-profit companies or to have for-profits in control of nonprofit subsidiaries. Many nonprofit universities own the investment firms that manage their endowments. Some for-profit companies, such as Newman's Own, donate all their profits to charity. The for-profit financial services firm, Fidelity Investments, has become one of the major managers of charitable funds, rivaling community foundations in the size of its assets. The range of variations is seemingly endless.

Government-nonprofit hybrids have also become increasingly common. Publicly controlled nonprofit corporations, such as the Port Authority of New York and New Jersey, have for decades been among the largest and most powerful entities in many American cities. Municipalities have frequently delegated economic development, housing, and urban revitalization tasks to nonprofits. Government-nonprofit hybridization has been given further impetus by the privatization of a wide range of public services.

Despite the trend toward formal elaboration among many nonprofits, the realm of informal nonprofits has grown dramatically. Alcoholics Anonymous and other self-help groups which are unincorporated and which have no formal structure command the loyalty of millions both here and abroad. These loosely federated small groups, usually clustered around formally incorporated general-service organizations that provide publications and technical assistance to members, are a relatively new organizational form, which only began to emerge in the 1930s.

The religious domain has produced as many organizational variations as the secular realm. Over the past half century, there has been a huge proliferation of freestanding nondenominational congregations, as well as faith communities that eschew traditional congregational forms. After years of litigating with the Church of Scientology over its eligibility for tax exemption, the IRS finally conceded that it could not come up with a definition of "religious organization" that did not violate the Constitution's Establishment Clause, which states that "Congress shall make no law respecting an establishment of religion, or prohibiting the free exercise thereof." Today virtually any organization can qualify for exemption as a religious organization as long as it conforms to the general requirements imposed on all nonprofits.

The resource base of nonprofits has become diverse as well. While there are still many organizations supported by donations and endowment income, they have been joined by entities that are wholly dependent on the sale of goods and services, grants, contracts, and government vouchers. Once wholly dependent on contributions to defray capital costs, today nonprofits not uncommonly finance physical expansion through the sale of government-guaranteed tax-exempt bonds.

As Evelyn Brody notes in this volume, American charities law has become singularly nonprescriptive about the substance of charitable activities, concerning itself almost entirely with formal issues of fiduciary behavior. As a result, the range of purposes for which nonprofits are created is virtually unlimited. (There are exceptions, such as Pennsylvania law, which has made tax exemption contingent on specific standards of charitableness and public benefit—but no other state has followed its lead.)

The body of law relating to nonprofits continues to grow and change, responding not only to the shifting political inclinations of voters, legislators, and the judiciary but also to ongoing innovations in organizational form, role, and function. For much of the twentieth century, law and policy treated nonprofits as quasi-public entities, subject to regulatory accountability and compliance with civil rights legislation. In recent years, with such decisions as the U.S. Supreme Court's 2003 decision in *Boy Scouts of America v. Dale,* the pendulum has begun to swing back toward treating nonprofits as private associations. In its ruling, the court held that the Scouts enjoyed a "right of intimate association" that permitted them to exclude homosexuals, atheists, and others who did not embrace their beliefs. This right has been used as the basis for permitting faith-based charities receiving government funds to practice employment discrimination.

Regulatory modalities are changing as well. After a succession of scandals involving such high-profile nonprofits as the United Way, Covenant House, the New Era Foundation, and the Red Cross, conventional forms of accountability based on filing periodic reports with the IRS and other agencies are being replaced by mandated public disclosure of pertinent financial information. Rather than subjecting nonprofits to scrutiny by often toothless regulatory bodies, this new regime empowers the general public to make informed judgments about whether organizations are worthy of its support and often provides the information needed to spark journalistic exposés and initiate civil litigation.

The forces shaping the future of American nonprofits do not originate solely within the United States. In recent years, a variety of new kinds of nongovernmental organizations have emerged which operate globally. Some of these are domestically based entities that provide services abroad. Others are genuinely transnational, involving cooperative and collaborative relationships among advocates, funders, and service providers operating across national borders. Many of these pursue broad humanitarian agendas, promoting sustainable development, human rights, economic and environmental justice, and other causes that seek to advance the well-being of humanity in general rather than that of particular nations.

Another manifestation of globalization that is significant for nonprofits is the growing presence in the United States of communities of foreign workers and refugees from developing and transitional countries. Ineligible for public services because of their alien status, the task of providing for their educational, health, and welfare needs is falling to nonprofit agencies, often religious congregations and other faith-based organizations from outside the Judeo-Christian tradition. As labor markets become more globalized and the labor force more mobile, these communities are likely to grow in ways that will both challenge existing religious and secular agencies and introduce new charitable players (such as transnational Islamic, Hindu, and Buddhist organizations) to the American scene.

Given the variety of forces and actors involved, it seems inevitable that the nonprofits of the future will be as kaleidoscopically varied and complex as those of the past, and that their changing forms and functions will continue to defy the efforts of scholars and lawmakers to measure them against any abstract standard of charitableness, public benefit, or voluntariness.

REFERENCES

"An Act Concerning Associations for Religious, Charitable, Educational, and Other Purposes." 1874. *Acts and Resolves Passed by the General Court of Massachusetts in the Year 1874.* Boston: Wright and Potter.

Addams, J. 1938. *Twenty Years at Hull House: With Autobiographical Notes.* New York: New American Library.

Alchon, G. 1985. *The Invisible Hand of Planning: Capitalism, Social Science, and the State in the 1920s.* Princeton, NJ: Princeton University Press.

"American Millionaires and Their Public Gifts." 1893. *Review of Reviews* 7 (37): 48–60.

Ames, J. B. 1913. "The Failure of the Tilden Trust." In *Essays in Legal History and Miscellaneous Legal Essays.* Cambridge, MA: Harvard University Press, 285–97.

Anderson, E. 1999. *Dangerous Donations: Northern Philanthropy and Southern Black Education, 1902–1930.* Columbia: University of Missouri Press.

Andrews, F. E. 1952. *Corporation Giving.* New York: Russell Sage Foundation.

———. 1969. *Patman and the Foundations: Review and Assessment.* Occasional Paper No. 3. New York: Foundation Center.

A. P. Smith Manufacturing Company v. Barlow. 98 A.2d 581 (N.J. 1953).

Auerbach, J. S. 1976. *Unequal Justice: Lawyers and Social Change in Modern America.* New York: Oxford University Press.

Bacon, L. 1847. "Responsibility in the Management of Societies." In *The New Englander* 5: 1, 28–41.

Bailyn, B. 1970. *The Apologia of Robert Keayne.* Gloucester, MA: Peter Smith.

Baltzell, E. D. 1996. *Puritan Boston and Quaker Philadelphia: Two Protestant Ethics and the Spirit of Class Authority and Leadership.* New Brunswick, NJ: Transaction.

Banner, S. 1996. "Written Law and Unwritten Norms in Colonial St. Louis." *Law and History Review* 14 (Spring): 33–80.

Barnartt, S. N., and Scotch, Richard. 2002. *Disability Protests: Contentious Politics, 1790–1999.* Washington, DC: Gallaudet University Press.

Beito, D. T. 2000. *From Mutual Aid to the Welfare State: Fraternal Societies and Social Services, 1890–1967.* Chapel Hill: University of North Carolina Press.

Bender, T. 1987. *New York Intellect: A History of Intellectual Life in New York City.* New York: Alfred A. Knopf.

Berkeley, K. C. 1999. *The Women's Liberation Movement in America.* Westport, CT: Greenwood Press, 1999.

Bestor, A. E. 1971. *Backwoods Utopias: The Sectarian Origins and the Owenite Phase of Communitarian Socialism in America, 1663–1829.* Philadelphia: University of Pennsylvania Press.

Beyan, A. J. 1991. *The American Colonization Society and the Creation of the Liberian State: A Historical Perspective, 1822–1900.* Lanham, MD: University Press of America.

Billias, G. A. 1965. *Law and Authority in Colonial America.* New York: Dover Books.

Blair, K. J. 1989. *The History of American Women's Voluntary Organizations, 1810–1960: A Guide to Sources.* Boston, MA: G. K. Hall.

Bledstein, B. 1976. *The Culture of Professionalism: The Middle Class and the Development of Higher Education in America.* New York: W. W. Norton.

Bonner, T. N. 2002. *Iconoclast: Abraham Flexner and a Life in Learning.* Baltimore, MD: Johns Hopkins University Press.

Bowditch, C. P. 1889. *An Account of the Trust Administered by the Trustees of the Charity of Edward Hopkins.* Cambridge, MA: Harvard University.

Bowen, W. G., et al. 1994. *The Charitable Nonprofits: An Analysis of Institutional Dynamics and Characteristics.* San Francisco, CA: Jossey-Bass.

Boy Scouts of America v. Dale. 530 U.S. 640 (2000).

Brandes, S. 1976. *American Welfare Capitalism.* Chicago: University of Chicago Press.

Bremner, R. H. 1991. *From the Depths: The Discovery of Poverty in the United States.* New Brunswick, NJ: Transaction.

Brilliant, E. L. 1990. *The United Way: Dilemmas of Organized Charity.* New York: Columbia University Press.

———. 2000. *Private Charity and Public Inquiry: A History of the Filer and Peterson Commissions.* Bloomington: Indiana University Press.

Brint, S. 1994. *In an Age of Experts: The Changing Role of Professionals in Politics and Public Life.* Princeton, NJ: Princeton University Press.

Brody, D. 1980. "The Rise and Decline of American Welfare Capitalism." In D. Brody (ed.), *Workers in Industrial America.* New York: Oxford University Press, 48–81.

Brown v. Board of Education. 347 U.S. 483 (1954).

Brown, E. R. 1979. *Rockefeller Medicine Men: Medicine and Capitalism in America.* Berkeley: University of California Press.

Buck, P. S. (ed.). 1965. *The Social Sciences at Harvard, 1860–1920: From Inculcation to the Open Mind.* Cambridge, MA: Harvard University Press.

Bushman, R. L. 1967. *From Puritan to Yankee: Character and the Social Order in Connecticut, 1690–1765.* Cambridge, MA: Harvard University Press.

Butchart, R. E. 1980. *Northern Schools, Southern Blacks, and Reconstruction, 1862–1875.* Westport, CT: Greenwood Press, 1980.

Butler, J. 1997. "Protestant Success in the American City, 1870–1920: The Anxious Secrets of Re. Walter Laidlaw, Ph.D." In Harry S. Stout and D. G. Hart (eds.), *New Directions in American Religious History.* New York: Oxford University Press, 296–333.

Calhoun, D. H. 1965. *Professional Lives in America: Structure and Aspiration, 1750–1850.* Cambridge, MA: Harvard University Press.

Carnegie, A. 1886a. "An Employer's View of the Labor Question." *Forum* 1:114–125.

———. 1886b. "Results of the Labor Struggle." *Forum* 1:538–551.

———. 1889. "Wealth." *North American Review* 148:653–664; 149:682–698.

Cash, F. L. B. 2001. *African American Women and Social Action: The Clubwomen and Volunteerism from Jim Crow to the New Deal, 1896–1936.* Westport, CT: Greenwood Press.

Chalmers, D. M. 1987. *Hooded Americanism: The History of the Ku Klux Klan.* Durham, NC: Duke University Press.

Chambers, Clarke A. 1963. *Seedtime of Reform: American Social Service and Social Action, 1918–1933.* Repr., Westport, CT: Greenwood Press, 1980.

Chandler, A. D. 1952. *Henry Varnum Poor. Business Editor, Analyst, and Reformer.* Cambridge, MA: Harvard University Press.

Charles, J. 1993. *Service Clubs in American Society.* Champaign: University of Illinois Press.

Chernow, R. 1998. *Titan: The Life of John D. Rockefeller, Sr.* New York: Random House.

Cherry, C. 1996. *Hurrying toward Zion: Universities, Divinity Schools, and American Protestantism.* Bloomington: Indiana University Press.

Clawson, M. A. 1989. *Constructing Brotherhood: Class, Gender, and Fraternalism.* Princeton, NJ: Princeton University Press.

Clifford, J. G. 1972. *The Citizen Soldiers: The Plattsburg Training Camp Movement, 1913–1920.* Lexington: University Press of Kentucky.

Collier, P., and Horowitz, D. 1976. *The Rockefellers: An American Dynasty.* New York: Holt, Rinehart and Winston.

Colwell, M. A. C. 1993. *Private Foundations and Public Policy: The Political Role of Philanthropy.* New York: Garland.

Cornell University v. Fiske. 136 U.S. 152, 10 S. Ct. 75 (1890).

Corner, G. W. 1964. *A History of the Rockefeller Institute, 1901–1953: Origins and Growth.* New York: Rockefeller Institute Press.

Critchlow, D. T. 1985. *The Brookings Institution, 1916–1952: Expertise and the Public Interest in a Democratic Society.* De Kalb: Northern Illinois University Press.

Crocker, R. 2002. "From Gift to Foundation: The Philanthropic Lives of Mrs. Russell Sage." In Lawrence J. Friedman and Mark D. McHarvie (eds.), *Charity, Philanthropy, and Civility in American History.* New York: Cambridge University Press, 188–216.

Croly, H. 1909. *The Promise of American Life.* New York: MacMillan.

Cuff, R. D. 1973. *The War Industries Board: Business-Government Relations during World War I.* Baltimore, MD: Johns Hopkins University Press.

Curran, W. L. 1951. "The Struggle for Equity Jurisdiction in Massachusetts." *Boston University Law Review* 31:269–296.

Curry, J. L. M. 1898. *A Brief Sketch of George Peabody and a History of the Peabody Education Fund through Thirty Years.* Cambridge, MA: Harvard University Press.

Curti, M. 1965. *American Philanthropy Abroad.* New Brunswick, NJ: Rutgers University Press.

Curti, M., and Nash, R. 1965. *Philanthropy and the Shaping of*

American Higher Education. New Brunswick, NJ: Rutgers University Press.

Cutlip, S. M. 1965. *Fund Raising in the United States: Its Role in America's Philanthropy.* New Brunswick, NJ: Rutgers University Press.

Cyphers, C. J. 2002. *The National Civic Federation and the Making of a New Liberalism, 1900–1915.* Westport, CT: Praeger.

Davis, A. F. 1984. *Spearheads for Reform: The Social Settlements and the Progressive Movement, 1890–1914.* New Brunswick, NJ: Rutgers University Press.

Davis, J. S. 1917. *Essays in the Earlier History of American Corporations.* Cambridge, MA: Harvard University Press.

DiMaggio, P. J. 1986. "Cultural Entrepreneurship in Nineteenth Century Boston." In P. J. DiMaggio (ed.), *Nonprofit Enterprise in the Arts.* New York: Oxford University Press.

Dodge v. Ford Motor Company. 204 Mich. 459, 170 (1919).

Dolan, J. P. 1985. *The American Catholic Experience: A History from Colonial Times to the Present.* Garden City, NY: Doubleday.

———. 1987. *The American Catholic Parish: A History from 1850 to the Present.* New York: Paulist Press.

Donahue, J. D. 1989. *The Privatization Decision: Public Ends, Private Means.* New York: Basic Books.

Dray, P. 2002. *At the Hands of Persons Unknown: The Lynching of Black America.* New York: Random House.

Du Bois, W. E. B. 1935. *Black Reconstruction: An Essay toward a History of the Part which Black Folk Played in the Attempt to Reconstruct Democracy in America, 1860–1880.* New York: Harcourt, Brace.

Dumenil, L. 1984. *Freemasonry and American Culture, 1880–1939.* Princeton, NJ: Princeton University Press.

Dunlavy, Colleen A. 2000. "From Partners to Plutocrats: Nineteenth-Century Shareholder Voting Rights and Theories of the Corporation." Paper presented at the Conference on the Corporation as a Cultural Project, Kennedy School of Government, Harvard University.

Eliot, C. W. 1869. "The New Education." *Atlantic Monthly* 23:203–220, 358–367.

———. 1898. "Inaugural Address as President of Harvard." In *Educational Reform: Essays and Addresses.* New York: Century.

Eliot, S. A. 1845. "Public and Private Charities of Boston." *North American Review* 56 (July): 135–159.

Ellis, J. T. (ed.). 1987. *Documents of American Catholic History.* 3 vols. Wilmington, DE: Michael Glazier.

Elshtain, J. B. 2002. *Jane Addams and the Dream of American Democracy: A Life.* New York: Basic Books.

Episcopal Academy v. Philadelphia et al., Appellants. 150 Pa. 565, 25 A. 55 (1892).

Ettling, J. 1981. *The Germ of Laziness: Rockefeller Philanthropy and Public Health in the New South.* Cambridge, MA: Harvard University Press.

Ewen, S. 1976. *Captains of Consciousness: Advertising and the Social Roots of Consumer Culture.* New York: McGraw-Hill.

Feingold, E. N. 1960. "The Internal Revenue Act of 1954: Policy and Politics." PhD diss., Princeton University.

Finke, R., and Stark, R. 1992. *The Churching of America, 1776–1990: Winners and Losers in Our Religious Economy.* New Brunswick, NJ: Rutgers University Press.

Fischer, D. H. 1994. *Paul Revere's Ride.* New York: Oxford University Press.

Fisher, D. 1993. *Fundamental Development of the Social Sciences: Rockefeller Philanthropy and the United States Social Science Research Council.* Ann Arbor: University of Michigan Press.

Fleischer, D. Z., and Zames, F. 2001. *The Disability Rights Movement: From Charity to Confrontation.* Philadelphia, PA: Temple University Press.

Fleming, W. L. (ed.). 1906. *Documentary History of Reconstruction: Political, Military, Social, Religious, Educational and Industrial, 1865 to the Present Time.* Cleveland, OH: Arthur H. Clark.

Flexner, Abraham. 1910. *Medical Education in the United States and Canada.* New York: Carnegie Foundation for the Advancement of Teaching.

Fosdick, R. B. 1952. *The Story of the Rockefeller Foundation.* New York: Harper and Row.

———. 1962. *Adventure in Giving: The Story of the General Education Board, a Foundation Established by John D. Rockefeller.* New York: Harper and Row.

Foster, C. I. 1960. *An Errand of Mercy: The Evangelical United Front, 1890–1837.*

Foster, M. S. 1962. *"Out of Smalle Beginnings . . .": An Economic History of Harvard College in the Puritan Period, 1636–1712.* Cambridge, MA: Harvard University Press.

Fox, D. M. 1963. *Engines of Culture: Philanthropy and Art Museums.* Madison: State Historical Society of Wisconsin.

Fox, E. L. 1919. *The American Colonization Society, 1817–1840.* Baltimore, MD: Johns Hopkins Press.

Francois Fenelon Vidal et al. v. The Mayor, Aldermen, and Citizens of Philadelphia, et al. 43 U.S. 127 (1844).

Franklin, B. 1961. *Benjamin Franklin: The Autobiography and Other Writings.* New York: New American Library.

Frederickson, G. M. 1965. *The Inner Civil War: Northern Intellectuals and the Crisis of the Union.* New York: HarperCollins.

Friedman, L. J. 1990. *Menninger: The Family and the Clinic.* New York: Alfred A. Knopf.

Friedman, L. M. 2002. *American Law in the Twentieth Century.* New Haven: Yale University Press.

Fukuyama, F. 1995. *Trust: The Social Virtues and the Creation of Prosperity.* New York: Free Press.

Galambos, L. 1966. *Competition and Cooperation: The Rise of a National Trade Association.* Baltimore, MD: Johns Hopkins University Press.

———. 1977. "The Emerging Organizational Synthesis in Modern American History." In E. J. Perkins (ed.), *Men and Organizations.* New York: G. P. Putnam's Sons, 3–15.

———. 1983. "Technology, Political Economy, and Professionalization: Central Themes in the Organizational Synthesis." *Business History Review* 35:471–493.

Galambos, L., and Pratt, J. 1988. *The Rise of the Corporate Commonwealth: United States Business and Public Policy in the Twentieth Century.* New York: Basic Books.

Gamble, V. N. 1995. *Making a Place for Ourselves: The Black*

Hospital Movement, 1920–1945. New York: Oxford University Press.

Gates, F. T. 1977. *Chapter in My Life.* New York: Free Press.

Geiger, R. L. 1986. *To Advance Knowledge: The Growth of American Research Universities, 1900–1940.* New York: Oxford University Press.

———. 1993. *Research and Relevant Knowledge: American Research Universities since World War II.* New York: Oxford University Press.

Giddings, P. 1988. *In Search of Sisterhood: Delta Sigma Theta and the Challenge of the Black Sorority Movement.* New York: William Morrow.

Giesberg, J. A. 2000. *Civil War Sisterhood: The U.S. Sanitary Commission and Women's Politics in Transition.* Boston, MA: Northeastern University Press.

Gilbert, J. D. 1983. *The U.S. Internal Revenue Service and the Income Tax: A Chronological History.* Monticello, IL: Vance Bibliographies.

Ginzberg, L. D. 1990. *Women and the Work of Benevolence: Morality, Politics, and Class in the Nineteenth-Century United States.* New Haven: Yale University Press.

Glenn, J. M., Brandt, L., and Andrews, F. E. 1947. *The Russell Sage Foundation, 1907–1947.* New York: Russell Sage Foundation.

Goheen, R. F. 1974. Memorandum to Eugene Struckhoff. Rockefeller Archive Center, Council on Foundations Files, box 3, Agency File, 8/73–4/74.

Goode, G. B. 1897. *The Smithsonian Institution: The History of Its First Half Century.* Washington, DC: Smithsonian Institution.

Graham, H. D., and Diamond, N. 1997. *The Rise of American Research Universities.* Baltimore, MD: Johns Hopkins University Press.

Grønbjerg, K. 1993. *Understanding Nonprofit Funding.* San Francisco, CA: Jossey-Bass.

Gurteen, S. H. 1882. *A Handbook of Charity Organization.* Buffalo, NY: Published by the author.

Hall, P. D. 1974. "The Model of Boston Charity: A Theory of Charitable Benevolence and Class Development." *Science and Society* 38 (4): 464–477.

———. 1989a. "Business Giving and Social Investment in the United States." In R. Magat (ed.), *Philanthropic Giving: Studies in Varieties and Goals.* New York: Oxford University Press.

———. 1989b. "The Community Foundation in America." In R. Magat (ed.), *Philanthropic Giving: Studies in Varieties and Goals.* New York: Oxford University Press.

———. 1992. *Inventing the Nonprofit Sector and Other Essays on Philanthropy, Voluntarism, and Nonprofit Organizations.* Baltimore, MD: Johns Hopkins University Press.

———. 1996. "There's No Place Like Home: Contracting Human Services in Connecticut, 1970–1995." PONPO Working Paper 234, Program on Non-Profit Organizations, Yale University.

———. 2000. "Noah Porter Writ Large: Reflections on the Modernization of American Education and Its Critics, 1866–1916." In R. L. Geiger (ed.), *The American College in the Nineteenth Century.* Nashville, TN: Vanderbilt University Press.

Hall, P. D., and C. B. Burke. 2006. *Historical Statistics of the United States: Millennial Edition.* New York: Cambridge University Press.

Hall, P. D., and Marcus, G. E. 1998. "Why Should Men Leave Great Fortunes to Their Children? Class, Dynasty, and Inheritance in America." In R. K. Miller and S. J. McNamee (eds.), *Inheritance and Wealth in America.* New York: Plenum Press.

Hammack, D. C. 1989. "Community Foundations: The Delicate Question of Purpose." In R. Magat (ed.), *An Agile Servant.* New York: Foundation Center, 23–50.

Hammack, D. C., and Wheeler, S. 1994. *Social Science in the Making: Essays on the Russell Sage Foundation, 1907–1972.* New York: Russell Sage Foundation, 1994.

Harr, J. E., and Johnson, P. J. 1988. *The Rockefeller Century.* New York: Charles Scribner's Sons.

Harris, S. 1970. *The Economics of Harvard.* New York: McGraw-Hill.

Haskell, T. L. 1977. *The Emergence of Professional Social Science: The American Social Science Association and the Nineteenth-Century Crisis of Authority.* Urbana: University of Illinois Press.

——— (ed.). 1984. *The Authority of Experts: Studies in History and Theory.* Bloomington: Indiana University Press.

Hatch, N. O. (ed.). 1988. *The Professions in American History.* Notre Dame, IN: University of Notre Dame Press.

Higginbotham, E. B. 1993. *Righteous Discontent: The Women's Movement in the Black Baptist Church, 1880–1920.* Cambridge, MA: Harvard University Press.

Hawkins, H. 1972. *Between Harvard and America: The Educational Leadership of Charles W. Eliot.* New York: Oxford University Press.

Hawley, E. W. 1974. *Herbert Hoover as Secretary of Commerce: Studies in New Era Thought and Practice.* Iowa City: University of Iowa Press.

Heald, M. 1970. *The Social Responsibilities of Business: Company and Community, 1900–1960.* Cleveland, OH: Case Western University Press.

Himmelberg, R. F. 1976. *The Origins of the National Recovery Administration: Business, Government, and the Trade Association Issue.* New York: Fordham University Press.

Himmelstein, J. L. 1997. *Looking Good and Doing Good: Corporate Philanthropy and Corporate Power.* Bloomington: Indiana University Press.

Hirchler, E. S. 1939. "A Survey of Charitable Trusts in Virginia." *Virginia Law Review* 23:109–116.

Hodgson, G. 1996. *The World Turned Right Side Up: A History of the Conservative Ascendancy in America.* Boston: Houghton-Mifflin.

Hoover, H. 1922. *American Individualism.* Garden City, NY: Doubleday, Page.

———. 1938. *Addresses upon the American Road.* New York: Charles Scribner's Sons.

Hopkins, C. H. 1982. *The Rise of the Social Gospel in American Protestantism, 1865–1915.* New York: AMS Press.

Horowitz, H. L. 1976. *Culture and the City: Cultural Philanthropy in Chicago, 1880–1917.* Chicago: University of Chicago Press.

Horowitz, M. 1977. *The Transformation of American Law, 1774–1869.* Cambridge, MA: Harvard University Press.

Howard, C. 1997. *The Hidden Welfare State: Tax Expenditures and Social Policy in the United States.* Princeton, NJ: Princeton University Press.

Huggins, N. 1971. *Protestants against Poverty: Boston's Charities, 1870–1900.* Westport, CT: Greenwood Press.

Hutchinson, J. F. 1996. *Champions of Charity: War and the Rise of the Red Cross.* Boulder, CO: Westview Press.

Internal Revenue Service. 1963. *Income Taxes, 1862–1962: A History of the Internal Revenue Service.* Washington, DC: Government Printing Office.

Jacoby, S. M. 1985. *Employing Bureaucracy: Managers, Unions, and the Transformation of Work in American Industry, 1900–1945.* New York: Columbia University Press, 1985.

———. 1997. *Modern Manors: Welfare Capitalism since the New Deal.* Princeton, NJ: Princeton University Press.

Jefferson, T. 1856. Thomas Jefferson to William Plumer, July 21, 1816. In W. Plumer, Jr., *The Life of William Plumer, by His Son, William Plumer, Jr, Edited, with a Sketch of the Author's Life, by A. P. Peabody.* Boston: Phillips, Sampson.

Jenkins, J. C. 1987. "Nonprofit Organizations and Policy Advocacy." In W. W. Powell (ed.), *The Nonprofit Sector: A Research Handbook,* 1st ed. New Haven: Yale University Press.

Jenkins, J. C., and Eckert, C. 1986. "Channeling Black Insurgency: Elite Patronage and the Development of the Civil Rights Movement." *American Sociological Review* 51:812–830.

Jenkins, J. C., and Halcli, A. L. 1999. "Grassrooting the System? The Development and Impact of Social Movement Philanthropy, 1953–1990." In E. C. Lagemann (ed.), *Philanthropic Foundations: New Scholarship, New Possibilities.* Bloomington: Indiana University Press, 229–256.

Jonas, G. 1989. *The Circuit Riders: Rockefeller Money and the Rise of Modern Science.* New York: W. W. Norton.

Jordan, W. K. 1960. *The Charities of London, 1480–1660.* London: Allen and Unwin.

Kanigel, R. 1997. *The One Best Way: Frederick Winslow Taylor and the Enigma of Efficiency.* New York: Viking Press.

Kanter, R. M. 1972. *Commitment and Community: Communes and Utopias in Sociological Perspective.* Cambridge, MA: Harvard University Press.

Karl, B. D., and Katz, S. N. 1981. "The American Private Foundation and the Public Sphere, 1890–1930." *Minerva* 19:236–270.

———. 1985. "Grantmaking and Research in the US, 1933–1983." In *Proceedings of the American Philosophical Society* 129 (1): 1–19.

———. 1987. "Foundations and Ruling Class Elites." *Daedalus* 116 (1): 1–40.

Katz, M. J. 1996. *In the Shadow of the Poorhouse: A Social History of Welfare in America.* New York: Basic Books.

Katz, S. N. 1971. "The Politics of Law in Colonial America: Controversies over Chancery Courts and Equity Law in the Eighteenth Century." In D. Fleming and B. Bailyn (eds.), *Law in American History.* Boston: Little, Brown, 257–288.

Katz, S. N., Sullivan, B., and Beach, C. P. 1985. "Legal Change and Legal Autonomy: Charitable Trusts in New York, 1777–1893." *Law and History Review* 3:51–89.

Kaufman, J. 2002. *For the Common Good? American Civic Life and the Golden Age of Fraternity.* New York: Oxford University Press.

Kimball, B. A. 1995. *The "True Professional Ideal" in America: A History.* Lanham, MD: Rowman and Littlefield.

Lagemann, E. C. 1992a. *The Politics of Knowledge: The Carnegie Corporation, Philanthropy, and Public Policy.* Chicago: University of Chicago Press.

———. 1992b. *Private Power for the Public Good: A History of the Carnegie Foundation for the Advancement of Teaching.* New York: College Entrance Examination Board.

——— (ed.). 1999. *Philanthropic Foundations: New Scholarship, New Possibilities.* Bloomington: Indiana University Press.

Laski, H. J. 1930. "Foundations, Universities, and Research." In *The Dangers of Obedience and Other Essays.* New York: Harper and Brothers.

Lauritsen, J., and Thorstad, D. 1995. *The Early Homosexual Rights Movement, 1864–1935.* Ojai, CA: Times Change Press.

Levy, D. W. 1985. *Herbert Croly of the New Republic: The Life and Thought of an American Progressive.* Princeton, NJ: Princeton University Press.

Lincoln, C. E., and Mamiya, L. H. 1990. *The Black Church in the African American Experience.* Durham, NC: Duke University Press.

Linenthal, A. J. 1990. *First a Dream: The History of Boston's Jewish Hospitals, 1896–1928.* Boston: Beth Israel Hospital in association with the Francis A. Countway Library of Medicine.

Linn, J. W. 2000. *Jane Addams: Biography.* Urbana: University of Illinois Press.

Liverant, S. 1933. "A History of Equity in Pennsylvania." *Dickinson Law Review* 37:156–183.

Loth, D. 1958. *Swope of G.E.* New York: Simon and Schuster.

Lubove, R. 1965. *The Professional Altruist: The Emergence of Social Work as a Career, 1880–1930.* Cambridge, MA: Harvard University Press.

"Macaroni Monopoly: The Developing Concept of Unrelated Business Income of Exempt Organizations." 1968. *Harvard Law Review* 81:1280–1294.

MacDonald, D. 1956. *The Ford Foundation: The Men and the Millions.* New York: Reynal.

Macleod, D. I. 1983. *Building Character in the American Boy: The Boy Scouts, YMCA, and Their Forerunners, 1870–1920.* Madison: University of Wisconsin Press.

Magat, R. (ed.). 1989a. *An Agile Servant: Community Leadership by Community Foundations.* New York: Foundation Center.

——— (ed.). 1989b. *Philanthropic Giving: Studies in Varieties and Goals.* New York: Oxford University Press.

Marcus, E. 2002. *Making Gay History: The Half-Century Fight for Lesbian and Gay Equal Rights.* New York: Perennial.

Marshall, H. E. 1937. *Dorothea Dix: Forgotten Samaritan.* Chapel Hill: University of North Carolina Press.

Mather, C. 1710. *Bonifacius: An Essay upon the Good, That Is to Be Devised and Designed, by Those Who Desire to Answer the Great End of Life, and to Do Good while They Live. . . .* Boston: B. Green.

McCarthy, K. D. 1982. *Noblesse Oblige: Charity and Cultural Philanthropy in Chicago, 1849–1929.* Chicago: University of Chicago Press.

———. 1991. *Women's Culture: American Philanthropy and Art, 1830–1930.* Chicago: University of Chicago Press.

McFeely, W. S. 1968. *Yankee Stepfather: General O. O. Howard and the Freedmen.* New Haven: Yale University Press.

McKinney, H. J. 1995. *The Development of Local Public Services, 1650–1850: Lessons from Middletown, Connecticut.* Westport, CT: Greenwood Press.

Miller, H. S. 1961. *The Legal Foundations of American Philanthropy.* Madison: Historical Society of Wisconsin.

Minkoff, D. C. 1995. *Organizing for Equality: The Evolution of Women's and Racial-Ethnic Organizations in America, 1955–1985.* New Brunswick, NJ: Rutgers University Press.

Minton, H. L. 2002. *Departing from Deviance: A History of Homosexual Rights and Emancipatory Science in America.* Chicago: University of Chicago Press, 2002.

Morris, R, and Freund, M. (eds.). 1966. *Trends and Issues in Jewish Social Welfare in the United States, 1899–1952: The History of American Jewish Social Welfare, Seen through the Proceedings and Reports of the National Conference of Jewish Communal Service.* Philadelphia, PA: Jewish Publication Society of America.

Moss, L. 1868. *Annals of the United States Christian Commission.* Philadelphia, PA: J. B. Lippincott.

Murolo, P. 1997. *The Common Ground of Womanhood: Class, Gender, and Working Girls' Clubs, 1884–1928.* Urbana: University of Illinois Press.

Murray, W. D. 1937. *The History of the Boy Scouts of America.* New York: Boy Scouts of America.

Myrdal, G. 1944. *An American Dilemma: The Negro Problem and Modern Democracy.* New York: Harper and Brothers.

National Conference of Charities and Correction. 1881. *Charity Organization Societies as Presented by the Committee on Organization of Charities in Cities at the National Conference of Charities and Correction, Boston, July 26, 1881.* Boston: National Conference of Charities and Correction.

Naylor, E. H. 1921. *Trade Associations: Their Organization and Management.* New York: Ronald Press.

Nelson, W. E. 1975. *The Americanization of the Common Law: The Impact of Legal Change on Massachusetts Society, 1760–1830.* Cambridge, MA: Harvard University Press.

Nevins, A. 1957. *Ford: Expansion and Challenge, 1915–1933.* New York: Charles Scribner's Sons.

New Haven Council of Social Agencies. 1932. *Directory of Social and Civic Agencies Serving New Haven, Connecticut and Vicinity.* New Haven, CT: New Haven Council of Social Agencies.

Noyes, John Humphrey. 1870. *History of American Socialisms.* Philadelphia, PA: J. B. Lippincott.

Oates, M. J. 1995. *The Catholic Philanthropic Tradition in America.* Bloomington: University of Indiana Press.

Oren, D. A. 2001. *Joining the Club: A History of Jews and Yale.* New Haven: Yale University Press.

Philadelphia Baptist Association v. Hart's Executors. 4 *Wheaton's Reports* 518 (1819).

Pierce, F. 1854. "Veto Message, May 3, 1854." In James D. Richardson (1898), *A Compilation of the Messages and Papers of the Presidents, 1789–1897,* vol. 5. Washington, DC: Published by the authority of Congress, 201.

Pierce, P. S. 1904. *The Freedmen's Bureau: A Chapter in the History of Reconstruction.* Iowa City: University of Iowa.

Pierson, G. W. 1983. *A Yale Book of Numbers: Historical Statistics of the College and University, 1701–1976.* New Haven: Yale University.

Porter, N. 1870. *The American Colleges and the American Public: With After-Thoughts on College and School Education.* New York: Charles Scribner's Sons.

Pozzetta, G. E. (ed.). 1991. *Americanization, Social Control, and Philanthropy.* New York: Garland.

Prescott v. Tarbell. 1 *Massachusetts Reports* 1804.

Putnam, R. D. 1994. *Making Democracy Work: Civic Traditions in Modern Italy.* Princeton, NJ: Princeton University Press.

———. 1995. "Bowling Alone: America's Declining Social Capital." *Journal of Democracy* 6 (1): 65–78.

———. 2000. *Bowling Alone: The Collapse and Revival of American Community.* New York: Simon and Schuster.

Putnam, R. D., and Gamm, G. 1999. "The Growth of Voluntary Associations in America, 1840–1940," *Journal of Interdisciplinary History* 29:511–557.

Reed, C. R. 1997. *The Chicago NAACP and the Rise of Black Professional Leadership, 1910–1966.* Bloomington: Indiana University Press.

Rhees, W. J. 1859. *An Account of the Smithsonian Institution, Its Founder, Building, Operations, Etc., Prepared from the Reports of Prof. Henry to the Regents, and Other Authentic Sources.* Washington, DC: Thomas McGill.

Rich, A. 2004. *Think Tanks, Public Policy, and the Politics of Expertise.* New York: Cambridge University Press.

Richardson, J. M. 1986. *Christian Reconstruction: The American Missionary Society and Southern Blacks, 1861–1890.* Athens: University of Georgia Press.

Rimmerman, C. A. 2002. *From Identity to Politics: The Lesbian and Gay Movements in the United States.* Philadelphia, PA: Temple University Press.

Rose, M. H. 1995. *Cities of Heat and Light: Domesticating Gas and Electricity in Early America.* University Park: Pennsylvania State University Press.

Rosen, D. A. 2001. "Acoma v. Laguna and the Transition from Spanish Colonial Law to American Civil Procedure in New Mexico." *Law and History Review* 19 (Fall): 513–546.

Rothman, D. J. 1971. *The Discovery of the Asylum: Social Order and Disorder in the New Republic.* Boston: Little, Brown.

Rothman, D. M., and Rothman, S. 1984. *Willowbrook Wars.* New York: Simon and Schuster.

Rumer, T. A. 1990. *The American Legion: An Official History.* New York: M. Evans.

Ruml, B. 1952. *The Manual of Corporate Giving.* Washington, DC: National Planning Association.

Sage, M. O. 1907. "Letter of Gift." Available online at http://www.russellsage.org/about/history/letter.

Salamon, L. M. 1987. "Partners in Public Service: The Scope and Theory of Government-Nonprofit Relations." In W. W. Powell (ed.), *The Nonprofit Sector: A Research Handbook,* 1st ed. New Haven: Yale University Press, 99–117.

Salamon, L. M., and Abramson, A. J. 1982. *The Federal Budget and the Nonprofit Sector.* Washington, DC: Urban Institute.

Sander, K. W. 1998. *The Business of Charity: The Women's Exchange Movement, 1832–1900.* Urbana: University of Illinois Press.

Saunders, M. K. 1995. "California Legal History: A Review of Spanish and Mexican Legal Institutions." *Law Library Journal* 37 (Summer): 487–510.

———. 1998. "The California Constitution of 1849." *Law Library Journal* 90 (Summer): 447–480.

Schneider, J. C. 1996. "Philanthropic Styles in the United States: Toward a Theory of Regional Differences." *Nonprofit and Voluntary Sector Quarterly* 25 (2): 190–209.

Scott, A. F. 1991. *Natural Allies: Women's Associations in American History.* Urbana: University of Illinois Press.

Scott, D. M. 1978. *From Office to Profession: The New England Ministry, 1750–1850.* Philadelphia: University of Pennsylvania Press.

Sealander, J. 1997. *Private Wealth and Public Life: Foundation Philanthropy and the Reshaping of American Social Policy from the Progressive Era to the New Deal.* Baltimore, MD: Johns Hopkins University Press.

Sears, J. B. 1922. *Philanthropy in the Shaping of American Higher Education.* Washington, DC: U.S. Bureau of Education, Department of the Interior.

Seeley, J. R., et al. 1957. *Community Chest: A Case Study in Philanthropy.* Toronto, ON: University of Toronto Press.

Seidman, J. S. 1954. *Seidman's Legislative History of Federal Income and Excess Profits Tax Laws, 1953–1939.* New York: Prentice-Hall.

Sheldon, C. 1899. *In His Steps: "What Would Jesus Do?"* New York: H. M. Caldwell.

Short, C. W., and Stanley-Brown, R. 1939. *Public Buildings: Architecture under the Public Works Administration, 1933–39.* Washington, DC: Public Works Administration.

Sklar, M. J. 1988. *The Corporate Reconstruction of American Capitalism, 1890–1916: The Market, the Law, and Politics.* New York: Cambridge University Press.

Skocpol, T. 1992. *Protecting Soldiers and Mothers: The Political Origins of Social Policy in the United States.* Cambridge, MA: Belknap Press of Harvard University Press.

———. 1999a. "Making Sense of the Civic Engagement Debate." In T. Skocpol and M. Fiorina (eds.), *Civic Engagement in American Democracy.* Washington, DC: Brookings Institution Press, 1–26.

———. 1999b. "How Americans Became Civic." In T. Skocpol and M. Fiorina (eds.), *Civic Engagement in American Democracy.* Washington, DC: Brookings Institution Press, 27–80.

———. 1999c. "Advocates without Members: The Recent Transformation of American Civic Life." In T. Skocpol and M. Fiorina (eds.), *Civic Engagement in American Democracy.* Washington, DC: Brookings Institution Press, 461–510.

Smith, D. H. 2000. *Grassroots Associations.* Thousand Oaks, CA: Sage.

Smith, J. A. 1991a. *The Idea Brokers: Think Tanks and the Rise of the New Policy Elite.* New York: Free Press.

———. 1991b. *Brookings at Seventy-five.* Washington, DC: Brookings Institution.

Smith, J. D. (ed.). 1993. *The American Colonization Society and Emigration.* New York: Garland.

Smith, S. R., and Lipsky, M. 1993. *Nonprofits for Hire: The Welfare State in the Age of Contracting.* Cambridge, MA: Harvard University Press.

Smith-Rosenberg, C. 1971. *Religion and the Rise of the American City: The New York City Mission Movement, 1812–1870.* Ithaca, NY: Cornell University Press.

Snyder, C. A. 1975. *The Lady and the President: The Letters of Dorothea Dix and Millard Fillmore.* Lexington: University of Kentucky Press.

Soyer, D. 1997. *Jewish Immigrant Associations and American Identity in New York, 1880–1939.* Cambridge, MA: Harvard University Press.

Stanfield, J. H. 1985. *Philanthropy and Jim Crow in American Social Science.* Westport, CT: Greenwood Press.

Starr, Paul. 1982. *The Social Transformation of American Medicine.* New York: Basic Books.

Stead, W. T. 1893. "Jay Gould: A Character Sketch." *The Review of Reviews* 7:37.

Story, R. 1980. *The Forging of an Aristocracy: Harvard and Boston's Upper Class, 1800–1870.* Middletown, CT: Wesleyan University Press.

Sullivan, J. A. 1803. "Opinion of the Attorney General of Massachusetts on the Life of the Corporation." In O. Handlin and M. F. Handlin (1969), *Commonwealth: A Study of the Role of Government in the American Economy—Massachusetts, 1774–1861.* Cambridge, MA: Harvard University Press.

Swint, H. L. 1967. *The Northern Teacher in the South, 1862–1870.* New York: Octagon Books.

Taylor, F. W. 1911. *The Principles of Scientific Management.* New York: Harper and Brothers.

Terrett v. Taylor et al. 13 *United States Reports* 43 (1815).

Tilden v. Green. 130 *New York Reports* 29 (1891).

Tocqueville, A. de. 1945. *Democracy in America.* Trans. Henry Reeve. New York: Alfred A. Knopf.

———. 1988. *The Ancien Regime.* Trans. John Bonner. London: Dent.

Trattner, W. I. 1979. *From Poor Law to Welfare State: A History of Social Welfare in America.* New York: Free Press.

Trustees of Dartmouth College v. William H. Woodward. New Hampshire Superior Court of Appeals, November 1817.

Trustees of Dartmouth College v. William H. Woodward. 17 *United States Reports* 518, 4 L. Ed. 629 (1819).

U.S. Department of Commerce. 1954. *National Income, 1954 Edition: A Supplement to the Survey of Current Business.* Washington, DC: Government Printing Office.

U.S. House of Representatives. Committee on Ways and Means. 1948. *Revenue Revisions, 1947–48: Hearings before the Committee on Ways and Means; Tax Exempt Organizations Other than Cooperatives.* 80th Cong., 1st sess. Committee Print.

U.S. House of Representatives. 1953a. *Final Report of the Select Committee to Investigate Foundations and Other Orga-*

nizations. 82nd Cong., 2nd sess. Washington, DC: Government Printing Office.

———. 1953b. *Hearings before the Select Committee to Investigate Tax-Exempt Foundations.* 82nd Cong., 2nd sess. Washington, DC: Government Printing Office.

———. 1954. *Hearings before the Special Committee to Investigate Tax-Exempt Foundations and Comparable Organizations.* 83rd Cong., 2nd sess. Washington, DC: Government Printing Office.

U.S. Senate. 1916. *Industrial Relations: Final Report and Testimony Submitted to Congress by the Commission on Industrial Relations.* 64th Cong., 1st sess., S. Doc. 154. Washington, DC: Government Printing Office.

———. Finance Committee. 1961. *Limitation on Deduction in Case of Contributions by Individuals for Benefit of Churches, Educational Organizations, and Hospitals—Report Together with Minority and Supplemental Views.* 87th Cong., 1st sess., S. Rep. 585 (July 20). Washington, DC: Government Printing Office.

Veblen, T. 1918. *The Higher Learning in America: A Memorandum on the Conduct of Universities by Business Men.* New York: B. W. Huebsch.

Verba, S., Schlozman, K. L., and Brady, H. 1995. *Voice and Equality: Civic Voluntarism in American Politics.* Cambridge, MA: Harvard University Press.

Vogel, D. 1989. *Fluctuating Fortunes: The Political Power of Business in America.* New York: Basic Books.

———. 1996. *Kindred Strangers: The Uneasy Relationship between Business and Politics in America.* Princeton, NJ: Princeton University Press.

Ward, Andrew. 2000. *Dark Midnight When I Rise: The Story of the Jubilee Singers, Who Introduced the World to the Music of Black America.* New York: Farrar, Straus, and Giroux.

Warner, A. G. 1894. *American Charities: A Study in Philanthropy and Economics.* New York: Thomas Y. Crowell.

Washington, G. 1796. Farewell Address. In S. Commins (ed.) (1948), *Basic Writings of George Washington.* New York: Random House, 608–616.

Watson, F. D. 1922. *The Charity Organization Movement in the United States: A Study in American Philanthropy.* New York: Macmillan.

Waugh, J. 1997. *Unsentimental Reformer: The Life of Josephine Shaw Lowell.* Cambridge, MA: Harvard University Press.

Webber, C., and Wildavsky, A. 1986. *A History of Taxation and Expenditure in the Western World.* New York: Simon and Schuster.

Wheatley, S. C. 1988. *The Politics of Philanthropy: Abraham Flexner and Medical Education.* Madison: University of Wisconsin Press.

White, G. T. 1955. *The Massachusetts Hospital Life Insurance Company.* Cambridge, MA: Harvard University Press.

———. 1957. *History of the Massachusetts Hospital Life Insurance Company.* Cambridge, MA: Harvard University Press.

Whitehead, J. S. 1973. *The Separation of College and State.* New Haven: Yale University Press.

Wiebe, Robert M. 1967. *The Search for Order.* New York: Hill and Wang.

Wildavsky, A. 1992. *The New Politics of the Budgetary Process.* New York: HarperCollins.

Wilson, D. C. 1975. *Stranger and Traveler: The Story of Dorothea Dix, American Reformer.* Boston: Little, Brown.

Winston, D. H. 1999. *Red-Hot and Righteous: The Urban Religion of the Salvation Army.* Cambridge, MA: Harvard University Press.

Witte, J. F. 1985. *The Politics and Development of the Federal Income Tax.* Madison: University of Wisconsin Press.

Wooten, J. A. 1990. "The Emergence of Nonprofit Legal Education in New York: A Case Study of the Economic Theory of Nonprofit Organizations." PONPO Working Paper 154, Program on Non-Profit Organizations, Yale University.

Wosh, P. J. 1994. *Spreading the Word: The Bible Business in Nineteenth-Century America.* Ithaca, NY: Cornell University Press.

Wright, C. E. 1994. *The Transformation of Charity in Postrevolutionary New England.* Boston: Northeastern University Press.

Wyllie, I. G. 1959. "The Search for an American Law of Charity." *Mississippi Valley Historical Review* 46 (2): 203–221.

Zollmann, Carl. 1924. *American Law of Charities.* Milwaukee, WI: Bruce.

3

Scope and Dimensions of the Nonprofit Sector

ELIZABETH T. BORIS
C. EUGENE STEUERLE

The nonprofit sector comprises a large and, by most measures, growing share of the U.S. economy. The sector is also extremely diverse. It includes religious congregations, universities, hospitals, museums, homeless shelters, civil rights groups, labor unions, political parties, and environmental organizations, among others. Nonprofits play a variety of social, economic, and political roles in society. They provide services as well as educate, advocate, and engage people in civic and social life. Given this diversity, conclusions about one type of nonprofit organization do not translate easily to other types. For example, large hospitals are complex organizations with a disproportionate share of the sector's assets, while other types of health and human service organizations tend to be small and close to community life. Memorial Sloan-Kettering Cancer Center had more than $1 billion in revenues in 2000, while Rainbows and Moonbeams, a facility for children with fetal alcohol syndrome, had revenues of less than $133,000. Educational organizations are also quite varied, ranging from Harvard University with close to $6 billion in revenues in 2000 to Treasure Island Christian School with less than $265,000.

Why try to explore the scope and dimensions of such a diverse nonprofit sector? For the same reasons that we measure the dimensions of the business and government sectors and compile data on national income, business profits, tax collection, and the costs of defense and social welfare. The nonprofit sector influences our lives in so many ways through its impact on the economy, on communities, and on us as citizens and individuals.

The scope and dimensions of nonprofits must be interpreted carefully because although the data become the basis for many decisions, they can easily be misconstrued. Public officials, for instance, are interested in whether nonprofit organizations are able to meet various public needs, as well as whether particular organizations use their resources to serve public or private interests. A common misperception—largely dispelled by the data—is that the nonprofit sector is mainly concerned with charity and depends upon donations and volunteers for most of its resources. In fact, many parts of this varied sector are not engaged in serving the poor, depend little or not at all on contributions, and pay wages, sometimes substantial, to individuals. The data reveal a vibrant sector, but not one solely concerned with social welfare and civic engagement.

This chapter provides an overview of the nonprofit sector, primarily from an organizational perspective, including information on organizational types, finances, and roles within the U.S. economy. Other chapters in this volume examine in much more detail particular aspects of the nonprofit sector, such as contributions and volunteers, as well as particular subsectors, such as health organizations.

Attempts to map and study the nonprofit sector are relatively new. The pioneering research of Burton Weisbrod (1977) for the Commission on Private Philanthropy and Public Needs (also known as the Filer Commission) is among the earliest systematic work. Chapters by Gabriel Rudney and Lester Salamon in the first edition of *The Nonprofit Sector: A Research Handbook* (Powell 1987), along with the comprehensive coverage of Virginia Hodgkinson and Murray Weitzman's *Nonprofit Almanac: Dimensions of the Independent Sector, 1992–1993* (1992), and Boris and Steuerle's *Nonprofits and Government* (1999), further developed, refined, and discussed measures of the nonprofit sector.

An accurate mapping of the nonprofit sector is limited by several factors. For instance:

- Estimates of the size and scope depend on extrapolations of data from multiple sources that use varied definitions and classifications. Limited information exists on organizations not subject to government filing requirements, and some organizations fail to file or file incomplete or erroneous information.[1]
- Separation of nonprofit organizations from other organizations in government statistics is difficult, especially for service industries.
- Government data on employment exclude most organizations with fewer than four employees.

Further development and improvement of basic data remains a priority for those concerned with understanding, monitoring, and influencing the future of the nonprofit sector.

DEFINING AND MEASURING THE NONPROFIT SECTOR: AN OVERVIEW

We define the nonprofit sector as those entities that are organized for public purposes, are self-governed, and do not distribute surplus revenues as profits. Nonprofit organizations are independent of government and business, although they may be closely related to both. The National Taxonomy of Exempt Entities (NTEE), the nonprofit classification system developed by the National Center for Charitable Statistics (NCCS) and used by the IRS, organizes nonprofits into the following major categories: arts, culture, and humanities; education; environment and animals; health; human services; international and foreign affairs; civic and public benefit (including philanthropic foundations); and religion.[2]

Nonprofits are only a sliver of the national organizational picture. Of the estimated 27.7 million formal organizations in the United States in 1998, 1.6 million (5.9 percent) were nonprofits (including religious congregations). Businesses make up approximately 94 percent of all entities, and government only 0.3 percent (Weitzman et al. 2002).

The U.S. tax code defines nonprofit organizations in terms of their tax status. They are a subset of those organizations exempted from federal income taxes by virtue of their public purposes.[3] Exempt organizations are additionally prohibited from distributing profits. The largest subset of exempt organizations—known as charitable organizations and described under section 501(c)(3) of the Internal Revenue Code—is composed of nonprofits permitted to receive tax-deductible contributions from individuals and corporations. To receive this deduction, they must be engaged in educational, religious, scientific, or other forms of charitable behavior; for this reason, they are sometimes referred to as "public benefit" organizations. Other nonprofits, such as social clubs and unions, are defined as nonprofits and may be exempt from taxes on the income they generate internally on their assets and sales, but they cannot receive tax-deductible charitable contributions.

Tax-exempt organizations that register and report information to the Internal Revenue Service (IRS) compose the primary universe for financial trend data on the U.S. nonprofit sector. The IRS is responsible for granting tax-exempt status, collecting basic information, and monitoring tax-exempt activities.[4] The IRS requires nonprofit organizations with more than $5,000 in annual gross receipts to register. Organizations with more than $25,000 in gross receipts must complete an annual report on the IRS Form 990 that includes, for example, details on revenues, expenditures, and assets; descriptions of programs; names of board members; and compensation of top staff members. Most of the information on Form 990 must be disclosed to the public.

Religious congregations and related religious organizations are generally considered an integral part of the nonprofit sector. At present there are an estimated 330,350 congregations, 246,562 of which do not register with the IRS.[5] Congregations are granted automatic tax-exempt and charitable status, which means both that they do not pay taxes on their net income (although taxes are due on employees' wages) and that they are eligible to receive tax-deductible contributions. Their automatic status derives from a longstanding tradition of separation of church and state, and does not rely upon other factors such as whether they are member-serving or charitable. Congregations are not required to register with or report to the IRS, although some do choose to register and a few even file an annual Form 990.[6] Most data on religious congregations, therefore, must be estimated from sources other than the IRS.[7]

In 2000, approximately 1.36 million tax-exempt organizations registered with the IRS (table 3.1). This excludes religious congregations that do not register, which would swell the total number of nonprofit organizations in 2000 to more than 1.6 million (table 3.2). Registered charities (501(c)(3) charitable organizations), which numbered 819,000 in 2000, have become the largest group of nonprofit organizations over the past decade.[8] While 79,000 organizations were classified as private foundations in 2000, grantmaking foundations numbered less than 57,000 in 2000, according to the Foundation Center (table 3.3).[9]

Many nonprofit organizations, both informal and incorporated, do not register with the IRS and are not reflected in the statistics. Some should register but do not. Others fall below the minimum requirement of $5,000 in annual gross receipts. Yet they could be considered part of the nonprofit sector and civil society. Little systematic information exists for the multitude of small self-help, civic, and social groups. They are generally created and run by members and volunteers, and rarely have significant budgets. Researchers such as David Horton Smith estimate that these organizations number in the many millions and account for perhaps as much as 90 percent of nonprofit entities (Colwell 1997; Smith 2000).

The nonprofit sector is in constant flux, with new organi-

TABLE 3.1. REGISTERED TAX-EXEMPT ENTITIES IN THE UNITED STATES, 1989 AND 2000

Tax code Section	Type of tax-exempt organization	Number of organizations		Finances of organizations in 2000 BMF (in million $)	
		1989	2000	Income	Assets
Total[a]		992,537	1,355,894	1,391,284	2,185,807
501(c)(1)	Corporations organized under act of Congress	9	20	16	221
501(c)(2)	Titleholding corporations	6,090	7,009	3,143	14,586
501(c)(3)	Religious, charitable, etc.	464,138	819,008	997,022	1,573,635
501(c)(4)	Social welfare	141,238	137,037	68,139	65,782
501(c)(5)	Labor, agriculture organizations	72,689	63,456	23,247	22,418
501(c)(6)	Business leagues	63,951	82,246	31,508	39,221
501(c)(7)	Social and recreational clubs	61,455	67,246	10,437	15,013
501(c)(8)	Fraternal beneficiary societies	99,621	81,980	14,090	65,098
501(c)(9)	Voluntary employees' beneficiary societies	13,228	13,595	173,796	109,516
501(c)(10)	Domestic fraternal beneficiary societies	18,432	23,487	1,162	2,579
501(c)(11)	Teachers' retirement funds	11	15	936	1,431
501(c)(12)	Benevolent life insurance associations	5,783	6,489	26,672	58,450
501(c)(13)	Cemetery companies	8,341	10,132	3,156	7,065
501(c)(14)	State-chartered credit unions	6,438	4,320	15,526	171,096
501(c)(15)	Mutual insurance companies	1,118	1,342	1,824	5,166
501(c)(16)	Corporations to finance crop operations	17	22	28	355
501(c)(17)	Supplemental unemployment benefit trusts	674	501	536	439
501(c)(18)	Employee-funded pension trusts	8	2	1,332	1,748
501(c)(19)	War veterans' organizations	26,495	35,249	2,297	2,315
501(c)(20)	Legal service organizations[b]	200	—	—	—
501(c)(21)	Black lung trusts	22	28	0	0
501(c)(23)	Veterans associations founded prior to 1880	—	2	313	1,902
501(c)(24)	Trusts described in section 4049 of ERISA[c]	—	1	0	0
501(c)(25)	Holding companies for pensions	—	1,192	5,147	23,082
501(c)(26)	State-sponsored high-risk health insurance organizations	—	9	—	—
501(c)(27)	State-sponsored workers' compensation reinsurance organizations	—	7	—	—
501(d)	Religious and apostolic organizations	94	127	—	—
501(e)	Cooperative service organizations	79	41	—	—
501(f)	Cooperatives operating educational organizations	1	1	—	—
521	Farmers' cooperatives	2,405	1,330	10,959	4,689

Source: Numbers of organizations are reported in the IRS *Data Book,* Publication 55B, and internal finances are reported from the May 2000 IRS Business Master File.

Note: Fewer organizations are contained in the Business Master File than are reported in the *Data Book.* Financial records are for the most recent reporting year, circa 1999.

[a] Not all section 501(c)(3) organizations are included because certain organizations, such as congregations, integrated auxiliaries, subordinate units, and conventions or associations of churches, need not apply for recognition of exemption unless they desire a ruling.

[b] The IRS no longer categorizes organizations as 501(c)(20). Organizations with this former ruling have reapplied for alternate rulings.

[c] ERISA: Employee Retirement Income Security Act.

zations forming, some growing, others declining, and many dying (Galaskiewicz and Bielefeld 1998; Twombly 2000). Defunct organizations often fail to notify the IRS, while new organizations (particularly small ones) may not register or file with the IRS or state authorities for several years. Some organizations may never reach the threshold of $25,000 in revenues (annual gross receipts) that triggers required filing of Form 990, or they may reach the threshold one year and fall below it the next year. Still others, for whatever reason, neglect to register or file with the IRS. Several studies reveal the extent to which the IRS files at any point in time lack returns from nonprofits that should have filed (Bielefeld 2000; Dale 1993; Grønbjerg 1989; Haycock 1992). Related studies begin to explore the scope of the broad array of community organizations in different regions (Grønbjerg and Paarlberg 2001a).

DETAILS ON NUMBERS AND TYPES OF TAX-EXEMPT ORGANIZATIONS

Organizations eligible to receive tax-deductible contributions (that is, those registered as 501(c)(3) organizations), including religious congregations, number more than one million and represent approximately two-thirds of all tax-exempt nonprofits. Much of our analysis uses detailed information on tax-exempt organizations derived from Form 990. These data are available to the public and made accessible to researchers through the NCCS (Lampkin and Boris 2001).[10]

Tax-exempt organizations come in all shapes and sizes and serve public purposes in diverse ways. They include, for example, large national organizations like the Metropolitan Museum of Art, the National Audubon Society, and the Boy Scouts of America. They also include small local groups

TABLE 3.2. NUMBER OF TAX-EXEMPT NONPROFIT ORGANIZATIONS, 1989 AND 2000

	1989		2000		
Private nonprofit organizations by IRS reporting status	Number (in thousands)	Percent of total number (%)	Number (in thousands)	Percent of total number (%)	Change from 1989 to 2000 (%)
Total	1,262	100	1,603	100	27
Number of religious congregations not registered with the IRS[a]	269	21	247	15	–8
Nonprofits registered with the IRS[b]	993	79	1,356	85	37
Registered as other than 501(c)(3) or 501(c)(4) organizations	388	31	400	25	3
Registered as 501(c)(4) social welfare organizations	141	11	137	9	−3
Registered as 501(c)(3) charitable organizations[c]	464	37	819	49	77
Private foundations	42	3	79	5	87
Total registered public charities	422	33	741	46	75
Excluded organizations (mainly registered but not reporting on IRS Form 990[d])	285	23	492	31	72
Reporting public charities[e]	137	11	250	16	83
Operating	124	10	225	14	81
Supporting	13	1	25	2	95

Sources: IRS Return Transaction File, 1990–2000, and May 2000 IRS Business Master File as adjusted by the National Center for Charitable Statistics; Stevenson et al. 1997; *Nonprofit Almanac, 1996–1997* as updated by Independent Sector, 1998; *2002 Data Book,* Publication 55B.

[a] Hodgkinson et al. (1992) estimates the number of congregations as 351,000 in 1989. In 2000, Independent Sector estimates 330,350 religious congregations. The figure in the table above was adjusted to exclude the approximately 83.7 thousand religious congregations registered and counted as Section 501(c)(3) charitable organizations in 2000, and the estimated 82,000 that registered in 1989. These organizations do not generally file tax Form 990.

[b] For definitions of all groups see appendix.

[c] Includes public charities and private foundations. All section 501(c)(3) entities are not included because certain organizations, including congregations and conventions or associations of churches, need not apply to the IRS for recognition of their 501(c)(3) status unless they desire a ruling.

[d] Includes organizations not reporting on Form 990, those reporting with gross receipts below $25,000, and foreign/governmental organizations. Also in this category are mutual benefit organizations (category Y of the NTEE-CC classification system) that register under 501(c)(3). (Most mutual benefit organizations register under other sections of the tax code.)

[e] Governmental, foreign, and mutual benefit 501(c)(3) organizations (representing less than 0.4 percent of reporting public charities) are excluded from reporting public charities for this analysis.

like the Helen Tyson Middle School PTA in Springdale, Arkansas; the Tremont String Quartet in Geneseo, New York; Senior Citizens Services of Morrisania in the Bronx; and Save Our Children of Pulaski County, Arkansas.

The remaining one-third of nonprofit organizations (not eligible for tax-deductible charitable donations) include the following:

- social welfare organizations (501(c)(4))—for example, such well-known advocates as the American Civil Liberties Union and the National Rifle Association
- business leagues (501(c)(6))—for example, the Chamber of Commerce
- social and recreation clubs (501(c)(7))—for example, the local private golf club
- state-chartered credit unions, farmers' cooperatives, and others detailed in table 3.1

In many cases, these organizations are eligible for tax exemption because they are cooperative or social in nature, and because they share benefits among members rather than providing profits for shareholders. Some serve public purposes, but they do so through political or electoral activities that are not permissible for groups eligible to receive tax-deductible contributions.[11]

Figure 3.1 shows both the significant scope of religious congregations in this country and the general growth in nonprofit organizations from 1989 to 2000. All nonprofit organizations (including religious congregations) increased by about a quarter, from 1.3 million to more than 1.6 million. Most of this growth was due to the increase in the number of registered charities. They rose by 76 percent, from 464,138 to 819,008, and increased in scope from composing less than half of all nonprofits in 1989 to more than 60 percent by 2000. The number of congregations decreased by about 6 percent, while the number of social welfare organizations

TABLE 3.3. NUMBER, GIVING, ASSETS, AND GIFTS RECEIVED OF GRANT-MAKING FOUNDATIONS

Type of foundation[a]		1989	2000
All foundations	No. of Foundations	31,990	56,582
	Total Giving	$7,911	$27,563
	Total Assets	$137,538	$495,622
	Gifts Received	$5,522	$27,614
Independent	No. of Foundations	28,669	50,532
	Total Giving	$5,992	$21,346
	Total Assets	$117,941	$418,286
	Gifts Received	$3,668	$19,156
Corporate	No. of Foundations	1,587	2,018
	Total Giving	$1,366	$2,985
	Total Assets	$5,727	$15,899
	Gifts Received	$1,112	$2,902
Community[b]	No. of Foundations	282	560
	Total Giving	$427	$2,166
	Total Assets	$6,002	$30,464
	Gifts Received	$554	$3,829
Operating	No. of Foundations	1,452	3,472
	Total Giving	$125	$1,066
	Total Assets	$7,865	$30,973
	Gifts Received	$189	$1,727

Sources: 1989 data are from Renz 1991; 2000 data are from Lawrence, Atienza, and Marino 2003.
Note: Dollars in millions, not adjusted for inflation.
[a] Excludes foundations that do not make grants, including some operating foundations and organizations that are reclassified as foundations because they fail to qualify as public charities.
[b] Technically public charities.

declined by almost 3 percent. Other types of nonprofits showed modest growth of about 3 percent.

501(c)(3) versus 501(c)(4)

Much of the research on nonprofit organizations to date is based on reports to the IRS filed by public charities and private foundations classified as 501(c)(3) organizations. One reason for this focus is practical—the availability of data. Another, however, is that special attention is often paid to the charitable activities of organizations eligible for tax-deductible contributions—essentially the organizations in the nonprofit sector to whom the largest tax subsidy is given. Although 501(c)(3) organizations are allowed to do legislative lobbying, there are a variety of limits, mainly designed to ensure that charitable contributions are used primarily for charitable, rather than political, purposes.

The 501(c)(4) category contains the second largest number of nonprofit organizations. These 137,000 "social welfare" organizations are sometimes identified as public interest advocacy organizations because they are permitted to do unlimited lobbying. But the label can be misleading, as it applies to only some of the groups. Social welfare organizations include environmental, civil rights, and social action groups that do lobby. Examples include the Association for the Advancement of Retired Persons, the Sierra Club, the National Organization for Women, and the National Rifle Association. However, many other 501(c)(4) organizations, such as the Rotary Club, the Lions Club, parent-teacher associations, the Georgia Amateur Wrestling Association, and English First, are not generally considered public interest lobbying organizations. This category includes a mixture of seemingly unrelated organizations that requires further analysis (Krehely and Golladay 2001).

Social welfare organizations sometimes form as affiliated or lobbying arms of parent charitable organizations. Such organizations as Bread for the World and Planned Parenthood create both 501(c)(3) and 501(c)(4) organizations.[12] The dual structure allows these groups to both be politically active and receive charitable donations. When incorporated separately, however, the count of nonprofit organizations increases. Recent research is beginning to document the complex organizational structures that characterize politically active nonprofits (Boris and Krehely 2002; Reid and Kerlin 2002).

Size Estimates Vary

Estimates of the size of the nonprofit sector vary depending on which organizations are included. The two most comprehensive sources deal in depth with only selected parts of the nonprofit universe. The *Nonprofit Almanac,* compiled by Independent Sector and the NCCS, combines charities, religious congregations, and social welfare organizations to create a group called the "independent sector" (Weitzman et al. 2002). The authors adjust the IRS data by omitting "out of scope" organizations such as (1) foreign organizations that are not based in the United States, (2) governmental entities that have registered with the IRS, and (3) organizations such as foundations directly connected with and supporting pub-

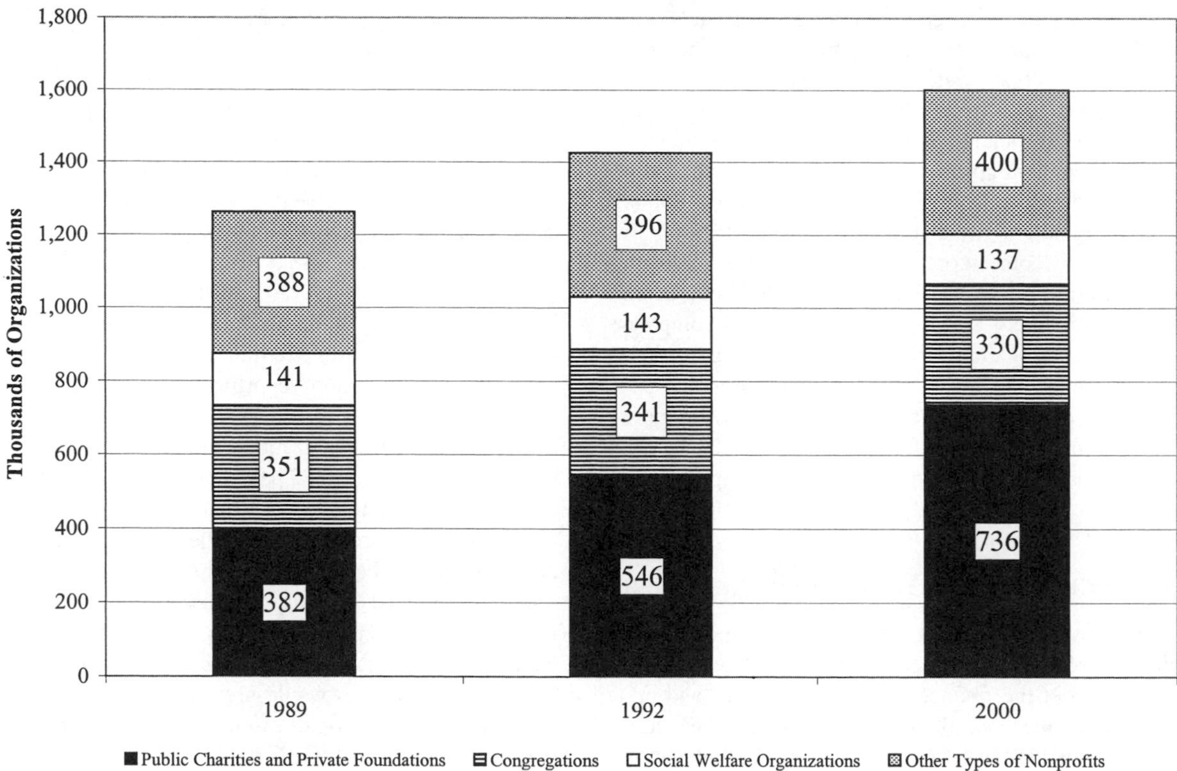

FIGURE 3.1. ESTIMATED DISTRIBUTION OF ORGANIZATIONS IN THE TAX-EXEMPT UNIVERSE

Notes: "Public Charities and Private Foundations" exclude government, foreign, and mutual benefit organizations; see table 3.2, note e. "Congregations" include both registered and nonregistered congregations.

Sources: The Urban Institute, NCCS Core Files, 1990, 1993, 2001; Stevenson et al. 1997; Independent Sector 2001; Hodgkinson et al. 1992.

lic universities. Further, the authors rely on non-IRS data to estimate the number of religious congregations. This independent sector is designed to capture the public-serving, autonomous, and voluntary aspects of the nonprofit sector.

In *America's Nonprofit Sector: A Primer,* 2nd ed. (1999), Lester Salamon divides the nonprofit sector into two groups, public-serving organizations (funders, churches, service providers, action agencies) and member-serving organizations (social and fraternal, business and professional, labor unions, mutual benefit and cooperatives, political). Salamon combines data from the IRS with estimates of religious congregations that do not register with the IRS, and then he adjusts upward by 25 percent, based on survey research he conducted in the 1980s, to account for organizations that do not report to the IRS. His estimates of the size and economic impact of the nonprofit sector are higher than the numbers reported in the *Nonprofit Almanac* or in this chapter.

It is unclear whether Salamon's upward adjustment by 25 percent is appropriate. Several studies do document an undercount of organizations in the IRS files (Bielefeld 2000; Grønbjerg 1989; Haycock 1992; Salamon 1992; Smith 1997; De Vita, Manjarrez, and Twombly 1999). In a study of New York City, however, researchers found almost equal numbers of nonprofits that did not appear in the files and of nonprofits that did appear in the files but could not be found or contacted (Haycock 1992). This suggests both the rapid creation and demise of organizations not captured in the IRS data; proposed legislation would tackle this issue in part by requiring periodic re-registration. A study of Washington, DC, nonprofits found an additional 8 percent of organizations not in the IRS files, but in certain neighborhoods, the researchers found many fewer organizations than appeared in the IRS files (De Vita, Manjarrez, and Twombly 1999).

Studies undertaken by Kirsten Grønbjerg provide more fine-grained estimates of the various types of nonprofits in one state. For selected areas of Indiana, Grønbjerg and colleagues performed exhaustive fieldwork to identify nonprofit organizations and compare those identified with local, state, and federal sources. The IRS files accounted for the greatest number of nonprofits (60 percent), but the researchers found that many organizations are not on IRS or state registration lists even though significant numbers of these organizations appear to fall within federal and state reporting requirements. Grønbjerg's study is still under way, but based on the work so far, Grønbjerg estimates that the total number of nonprofits could be doubled, to perhaps 2.5 million (Grønbjerg 2002:1758).[13]

When completed, the results of the Grønbjerg study are likely to suggest appropriate ways to adjust the IRS data to account for those nonprofits that do not register or file reports even though they are required to do so. The study will also shed light on those small incorporated and unincorporated organizations that are not required to register. Even unregistered nonprofits with modest resources are important for studies of local social capital and community building.

The IRS data on nonprofits have gradually become more accurate and comprehensive (Froelich, Knoepfle, and Pollak 2000) In particular, as the annual Form 990 and 990PF financial reports become more visible to the public through the Web sites of the NCCS, GuideStar, and the Foundation Center, it seems likely that more nonprofits will complete Form 990 in a careful and timely manner.[14] Starting in 2004, electronic filing of Form 990 became available and is expected to ease the burden of reporting and to provide more accurate data in a shorter time frame, for both regulatory and research purposes.[15] The IRS data sources on nonprofits are summarized in the appendix.

THE FINANCES OF REPORTING PUBLIC CHARITIES

Form 990 provides important information on the finances of nonprofit organizations, but it is easier to gather in-depth information about the finances of public charities and private foundations because their information has been digitized and included in the NCCS, GuideStar, and Foundation Center databases. Figure 3.2 shows trends in the finances of 250,000 reporting public charities—that is, those 501(c)(3) organizations, excluding private foundations and most religious groups—that filed a Form 990 with the IRS. From 1989 to 2000, total revenue and expenses of reporting public charities (in real dollars) stayed in roughly similar proportions, although revenues grew slightly faster in the last five years of the period, reflecting the economy. Revenues exceeded expenses usually by about 8 percent.

Expenses

Organizations with over $10 million in annual expenses represent only 3.9 percent of reporting public charities, but they are responsible for over 80 percent of total expenses. At the other extreme, organizations with under $500,000 in expenses represent almost 75 percent of reporting public charities, yet they account for less than 3 percent of aggregate expenses. As figure 3.3 shows, the expenses of reporting charities tend to be highly concentrated, which masks the vitality of this cast of thousands. If we were to include organizations with less than $25,000 in gross receipts in our calculations, the percentage of public charities with less than $100,000 in expenses would greatly exceed 40.7 percent.[16] A similar concentration of resources holds for private foundations (Ganguly and Gluck 2001).

Health organizations, including hospitals, clinics, and med-

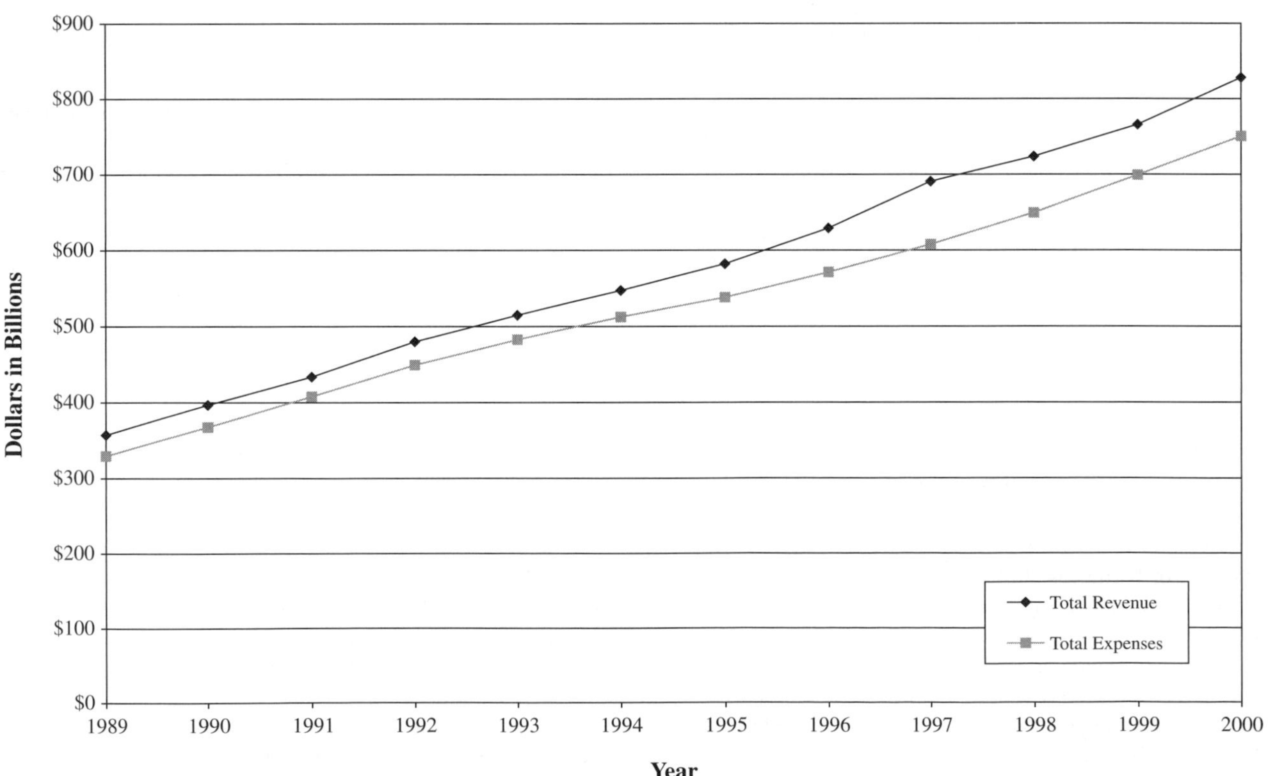

FIGURE 3.2. TRENDS IN REVENUES AND EXPENSES OF REPORTING PUBLIC CHARITIES, CIRCA 1989–2000 (NOT ADJUSTED FOR INFLATION)

Source: The Urban Institute, NCCS Core Files, 1990–2001.

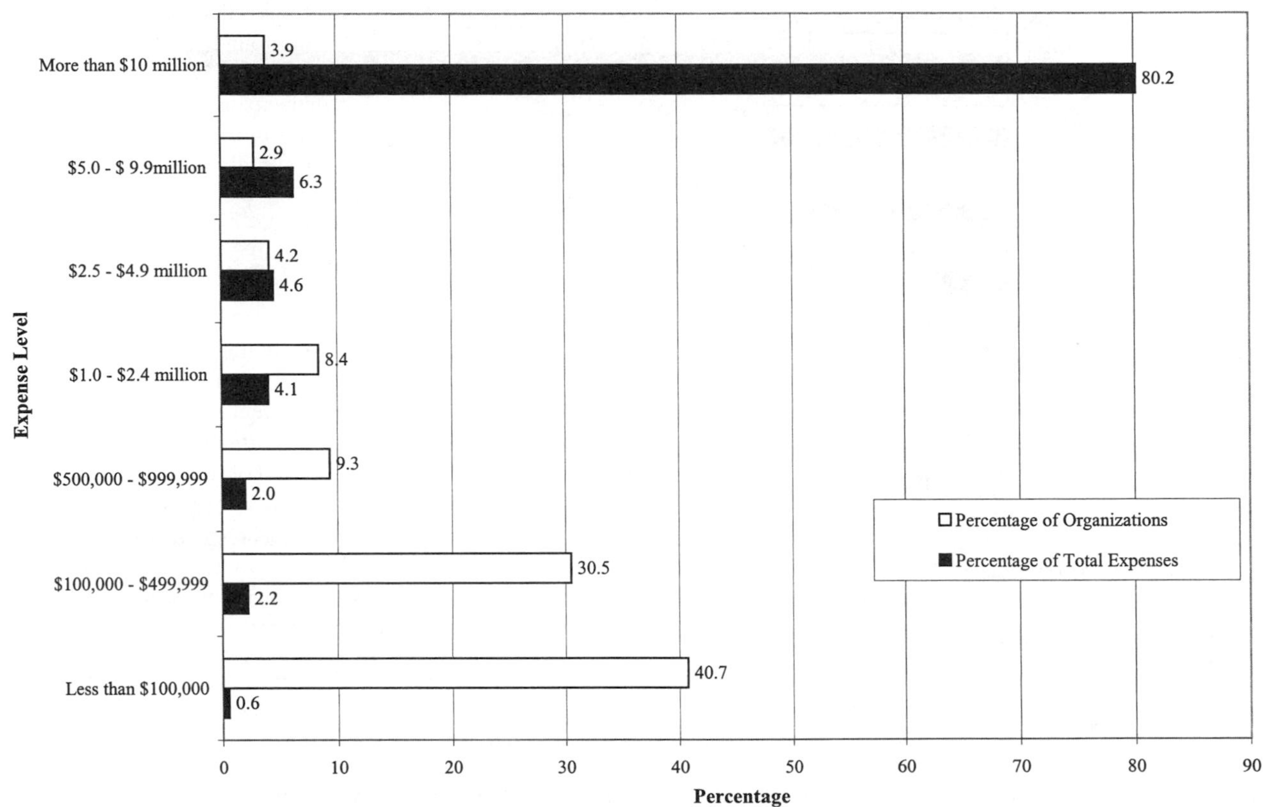

FIGURE 3.3. PERCENTAGE OF REPORTING PUBLIC CHARITIES AND TOTAL EXPENSES BY EXPENSE LEVEL, 2000
Source: The Urban Institute, NCCS/GuideStar National Nonprofit Database, 2000.

ical research organizations, clearly dominate the finances of public charities. They generate almost 60 percent of all expenses of reporting public charities, and hospitals alone generate almost 75 percent of expenses in the health area. Figure 3.4 provides a breakdown of expenses by type of organization. Arts, environmental, human service, societal benefit, or religious organizations that do file tend to be smaller, and so have lower average expenses than, for example, health and educational institutions. Of course, averages are only averages, and there is wide variation within categories and subcategories. The Nature Conservancy, the Art Institute of Chicago, the Save the Children Foundation, and the American Red Cross, for instance, are all large organizations with significant expenses and revenues. And although most religious congregations tend to be modest in size and have lower expenses, there are many substantial religious organizations (Chaves 2002).

Employment is a major expense for nonprofits because many are service organizations that rely heavily on skilled labor. The nonprofit sector's share of total U.S. paid employment was approximately 12 percent in 1998 (Weitzman et al. 2002). Among reporting public charities in 1998, about 46 percent of operating expenses were for salaries and wages. As they grow in size, organizations tend to rely increasingly on staff rather than on volunteers.

Despite a few publicized cases of high executive salaries among nonprofits, the median annual salary for nonprofit chief executives in 1998 was $42,000. But differences in chief executive salaries illustrate the variation among types and sizes of nonprofits. Hospitals and higher educational institutions, for example, tend to report the highest average chief executive salaries at $169,000 and $114,000, respectively (Twombly and Gantz 2001). Generally, the larger the organization's revenues, the higher the chief executive's salary (Preston 2002). Some chief executives, however, receive compensation from more than one affiliated organization, and a few receive compensation through intermediaries (such as consultant organizations), which keeps their total compensation from showing up on any one tax return.

Fundraising and administrative expenses also vary by type and size of organization. Studies have combined IRS data with survey research to delve into this difficult-to-measure area. One 2001 finding is that, on average, the overhead costs of smaller organizations tend to make up a higher percentage of their total costs (Hager, Pollak, and Rooney 2001). This trend varies and is more pronounced in certain types of nonprofits than others, but it certainly points toward a need for caution in using simplistic cost ratios as measures of efficiency. For instance, most organizations start out small, so high cost ratios in one year may not reflect the cost ratio for those same organizations over their lifetimes.

Significant research has focused on the geographical distribution of charities and how expenses vary by region (Bielefeld 2000; Haycock 1992; Stevenson et al. 1997; De

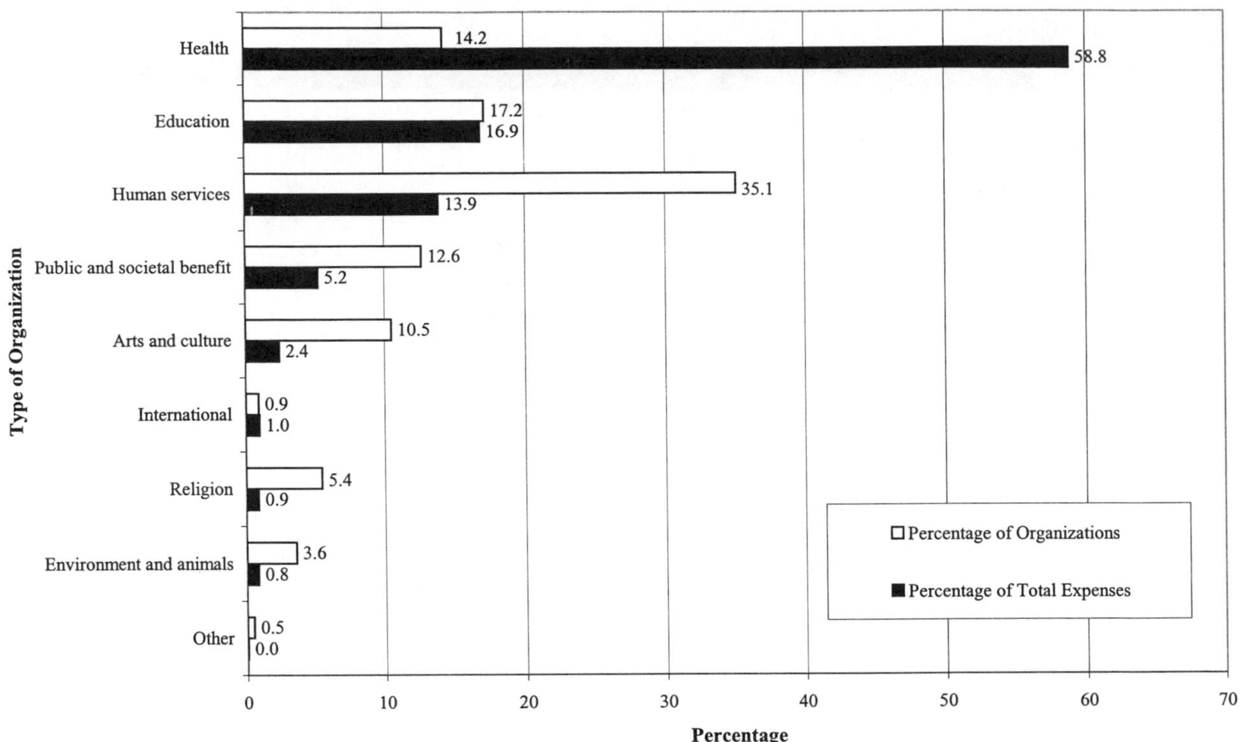

FIGURE 3.4. PERCENTAGE OF REPORTING PUBLIC CHARITIES AND TOTAL EXPENSES BY ORGANIZATIONAL TYPE, 2000
Source: The Urban Institute, NCCS/GuideStar National Nonprofit Database, 2000.

Vita et al. 2004). Figure 3.5 displays the per capita expenses of reporting public charities by state. The highest expense levels are generally in New England and northern central states, where per capita expenses of charities are often more than $3,000. In southern and less-populous western states, expenses of charities are usually less than $2,000 per capita. Again, one must be careful with interpretation. Large national and international organizations with corresponding expenses may be more likely to locate their headquarters in those coastal states where prices tend to be higher. Some of this discrepancy may also reflect simply the length of time a state has been populated, reliance on congregations for human services in the South, or the concentration of large private universities in the Northeast. The chapter by Peter Hall in this volume has an in-depth discussion of regional variations in the nonprofit sector.

There is also considerable variation in the numbers and types of nonprofit organizations in various states, cities, and even neighborhoods (Stevenson et al. 1997; De Vita, Manjarrez, and Twombly 1999; Grønbjerg and Paarlberg 2001b; De Vita and Twombly 2002).[17] These variations in local nonprofit infrastructure have implications for both policy and practice that are just beginning to be recognized and explored. Charities are often located downtown and in better-off neighborhoods (De Vita, Manjarrez, and Twombly 1999). Lack of locally based nonprofits could limit access to services, amenities, and job opportunities for residents in poorer neighborhoods.

Revenues

While nonprofit health organizations rely heavily on fees, many arts organizations rely on private donations. Figure 3.6 demonstrates the various sources of revenues—fees for goods and services, private contributions, government grants, investment income, and others—for the major categories of reporting public charities. Fees also include income from other government and private contracts. Private contributions, which include individual donations and grants from foundations and corporations, are the single most important source of revenues for arts, environment and animals, public benefit, religious, and international organizations. For all major categories of organizations, investment income composes only between 2 percent and 7 percent of revenues.[18]

The total amount of support to charities from government sources is difficult to measure accurately, as it flows to the organizations in many different ways, including governmental transfers, vouchers, tax credits, and access to tax-exempt bonds. Health organizations are heavily dependent upon government-funded Medicare and Medicaid paid out as fees for services. Also, government educational assistance can either flow directly to higher educational institutions or be distributed as grants or subsidies to individuals who then pay the fees to the institutions.

Although government grants totaled $67.0 billion (8 percent of $823.4 billion in revenues for the public charities that reported to the IRS in 2000), government funds gener-

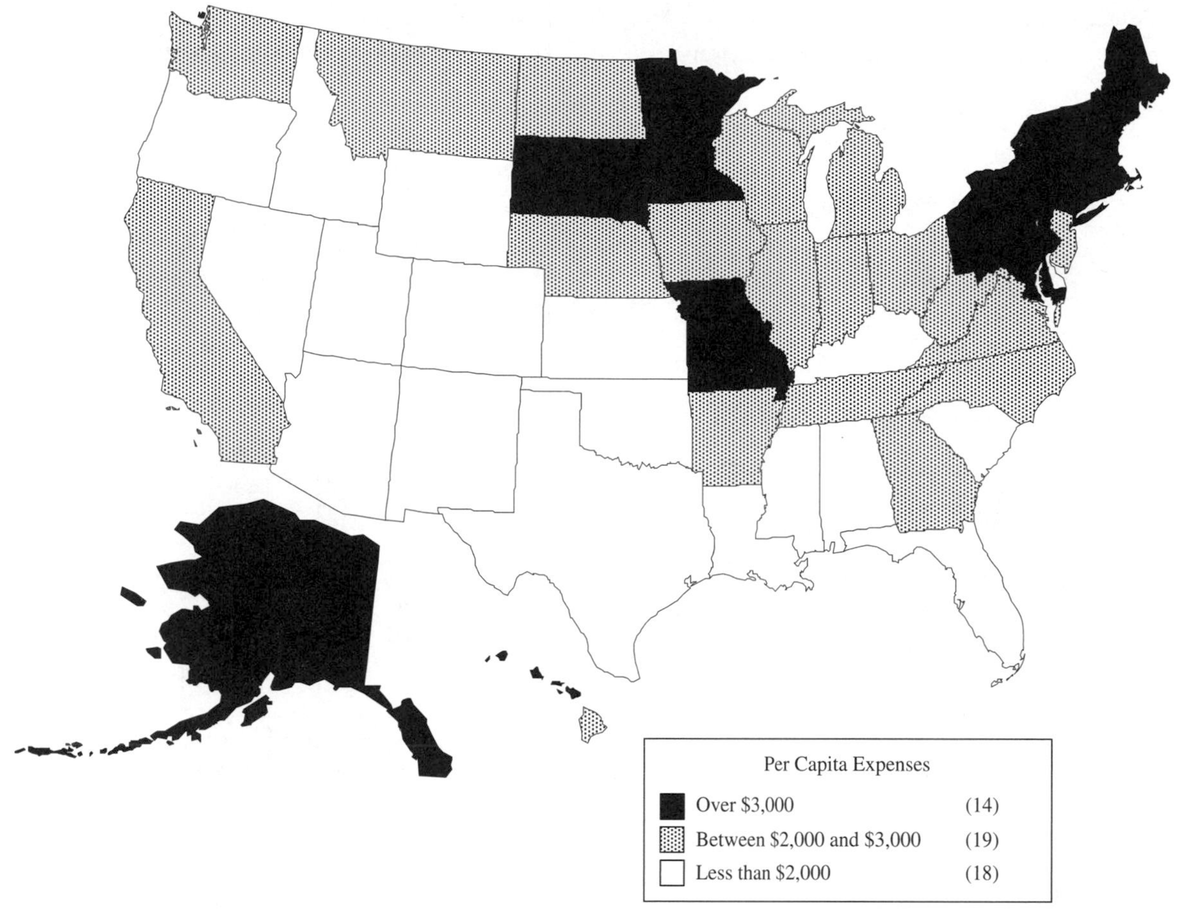

FIGURE 3.5. PER CAPITA EXPENSES OF REPORTING PUBLIC CHARITIES, 2000
Sources: The Urban Institute, NCCS/GuideStar National Nonprofit Database, 2000; U.S. Census Bureau, Census 2000, Summary File 1.

ate considerably more revenues for this sector.[19] Grants only capture direct government support, which is important for human service, international, and public benefit organizations. Program service revenues totaled $539.2 billion, or 65 percent of nonprofit revenues. The distinction between government grants and government fees reported along with other program service fees is somewhat arbitrary. A grant to provide a service to the public, for example, should be reported under "Government contributions (grants)," while a contract to provide a service or good to the government itself should be reported under "Program service revenue." The reliability of reporting on this breakdown of grants and fees is open to question because often the nonprofits cannot identify the source of particular payments.

The *Nonprofit Almanac* and *America's Nonprofit Sector* both attempt to divide fee income into government and private sources. They also estimate total government revenues from grants and contracts for slightly different subsets of the nonprofit universes. In the *New Nonprofit Almanac and Desktop Reference,* the government sector is estimated to have provided 31.3 percent ($207.8 billion) of the total $664.8 billion in revenues for the independent sector in 1997—a proportion that increased from 26.6 percent in 1977 (Weitzman et al. 2002). In *America's Nonprofit Sector,* government revenues are estimated at 36 percent ($185.4 billion) of $515 billion in total revenues in 1996 (Salamon 1999). Both are reasonable estimates and quite close, despite the somewhat different groups and methods used. Until there are better ways to track nonprofit program fees back to government sources (which can be from direct and indirect federal, state, and local payments), estimates will differ moderately in size. For public policy purposes, the information needs to be better documented.

The fees received by the health sector, largely Medicare and Medicaid payments, account for 85 percent ($385.0 billion) of the $450.7 billion in revenues for health-related nonprofits and almost half of the total revenue of all reporting nonprofits ($823.4 billion). While the amounts of government fee revenues paid to nonprofits outside of health-related payments are much smaller, those dollars are more difficult to track.

FOLLOW THE MONEY

Revenues and expenses can be crude measures. For instance, a government grant may be given to a public charity

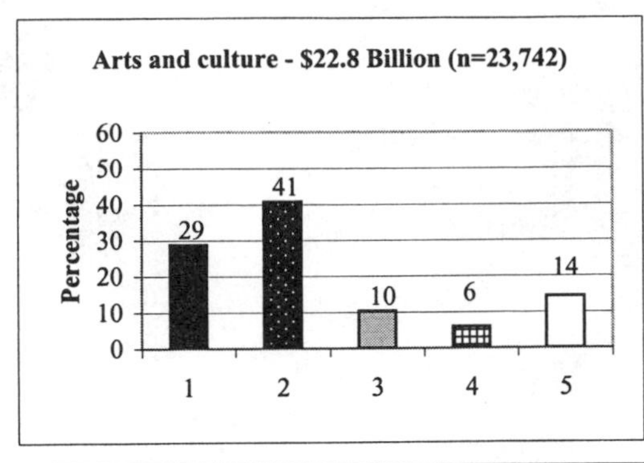

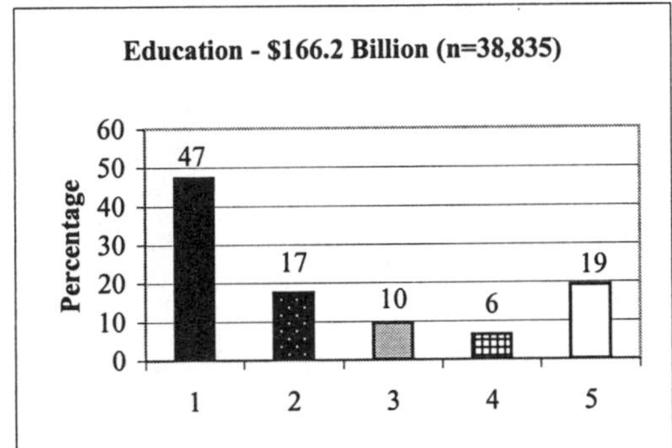

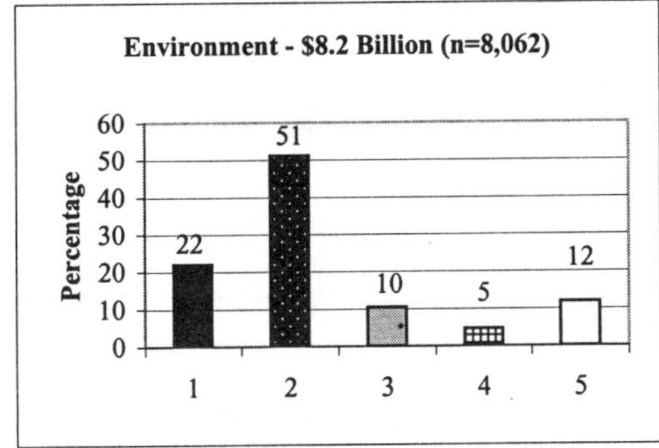

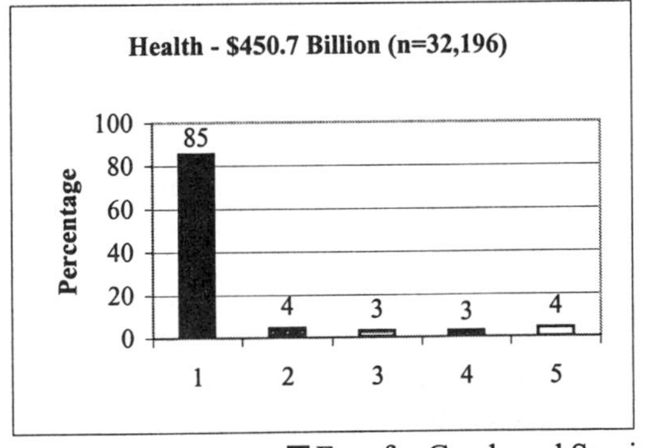

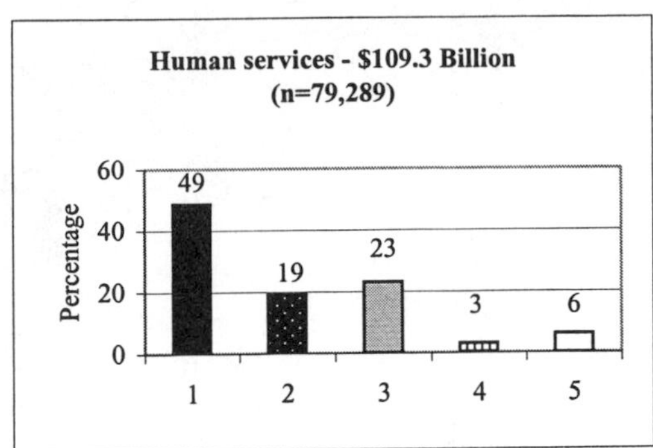

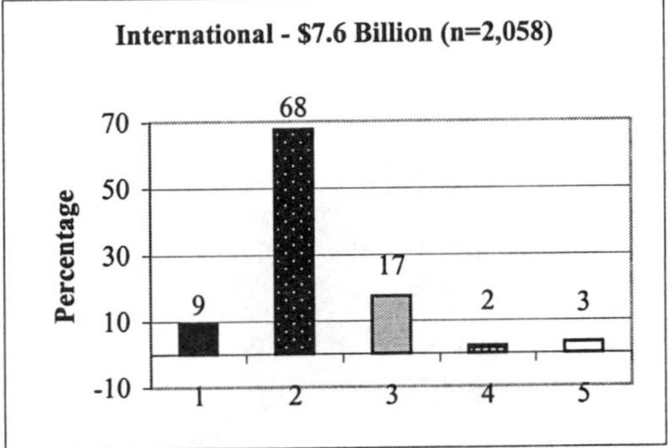

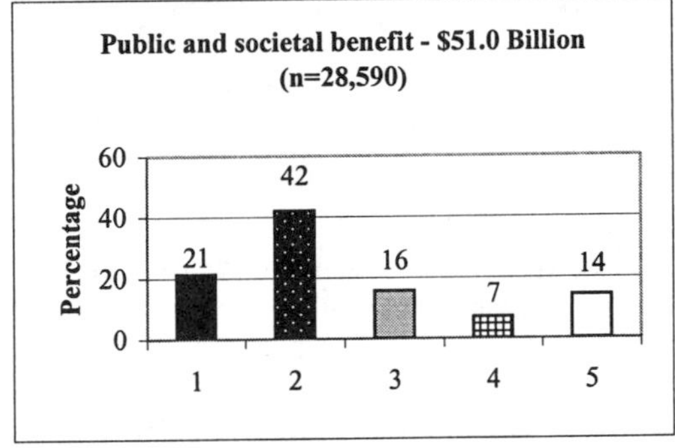

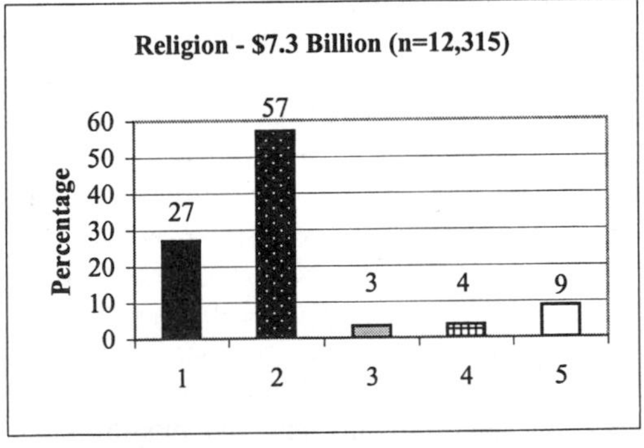

1 ■ Fees for Goods and Services

2 ■ Private Contributions

3 □ Government Grants

4 ⊞ Investment Income

5 □ Other

FIGURE 3.6. SOURCES OF REVENUE FOR REPORTING PUBLIC CHARITIES, 2000
Note: Due to rounding, the totals may not equal 100 percent.
Source: The Urban Institute, NCCS/GuideStar National Nonprofit Database, 2000.

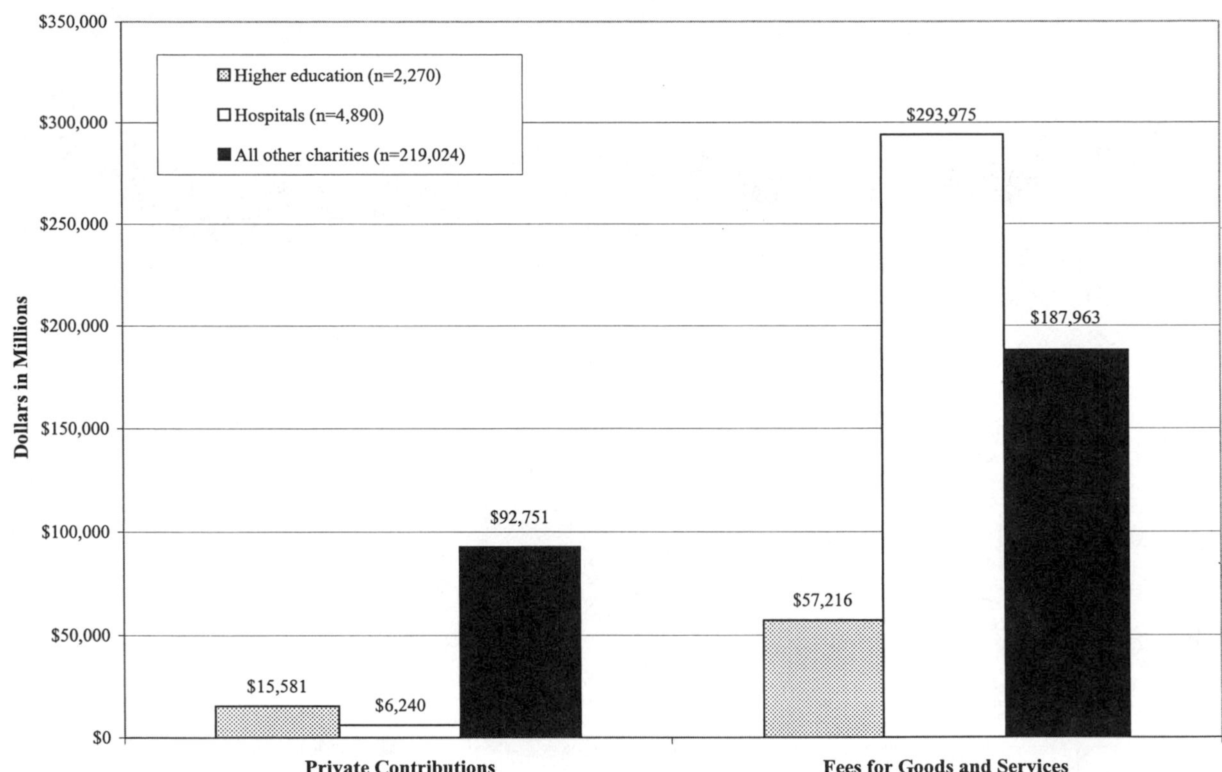

FIGURE 3.7. PRIVATE CONTRIBUTIONS AND FEES FOR GOODS AND SERVICES FOR HIGHER EDUCATION, HOSPITALS, AND ALL OTHER CHARITIES, 2000
Source: The Urban Institute, NCCS/GuideStar National Nonprofit Database, 2000.

that subcontracts through a second charity to have work performed. In this case, the source of funds is the U.S. taxpayer, and most work takes place in the second charity. The first charity may have significant additional revenues and expenses because of this series of transactions but obtain little income from its own donors or internal sources.[20]

Although private charitable contributions are not the primary source of revenues for nonprofits overall, they are major sources of support for five subsectors, including arts (41 percent), environment (51 percent), international (68 percent), public societal benefit (42 percent), and religious (57 percent). Charitable contributions strongly define the character of many nonprofit organizations and reflect the willingness of individuals voluntarily to forgo their own consumption for the good of others. Figure 3.7 breaks down the health and education categories to show how higher education and hospitals, the two dominant sets of organizations in terms of finances and employment, differ from the rest of nonprofits in their limited reliance on private contributions (see also figure 3.6).

Individual lifetime giving is much larger than corporate and bequest giving.[21] Figure 3.8 breaks down contributions from those three major sources as a percentage of gross domestic product (GDP). From 1970 to 1998, combined giving was relatively stable at close to 2 percent of GDP with some modest exceptions. During the 1980s, levels of giving were somewhat higher than in the 1970s, and in the last years of the century, when economic growth rates rose, the levels of giving increased even further. A small spike in giving seems to have occurred around the time of the passage of the Tax Reform Act of 1986, which lowered tax rates and effectively reduced tax subsidies for giving. Individuals made some contributions early at the higher subsidy rate. In the 1980s, corporate giving increased somewhat as a proportion of GDP, but overall it remained low.

Bequests declined after 1972 and did not vary much from then on. While charitable bequests are important to a number of wealthy people, there is little tax incentive for most people to give through their estates, since most estates are exempt from taxation. Giving does, however, go up with wealth—indeed, the very presence of wealth in an estate indicates that consumption, for either oneself or one's posterity, is not the only motivating force in an individual's life. Legislation passed in 2001 reduced the estate tax and would potentially eliminate it after 2010. This change would both reduce tax incentives to give at death and increase the wealth from which heirs could later give.

Individuals also make gifts of money and assets to foundations, which the foundations then invest and use to generate revenue to make grants. Ken Prewitt's chapter in this volume examines foundations in depth, so we touch on them here only briefly. Our goal is to see how their scope and dimensions fit within the broader nonprofit universe. Table 3.3 provides the number of foundations along with the amounts

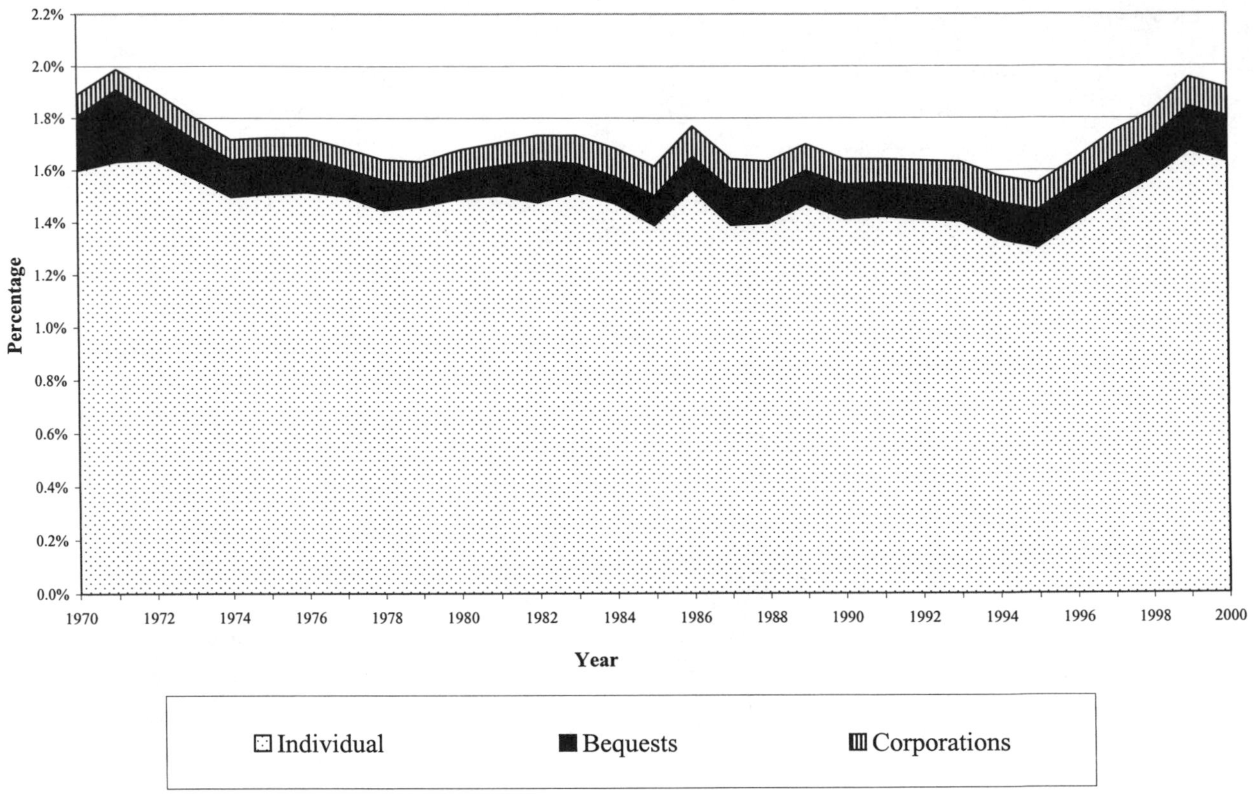

FIGURE 3.8. TRENDS IN GIVING BY SOURCE AS A PERCENTAGE OF GDP, 1970–2000
Sources: AAFRC Trust for Philanthropy 2001; U.S. Office of Management and Budget 2003, table 10.1.

of total giving, total assets, and gifts received for each of the major types of foundations that make grants, including independent, corporate, community, and operating foundations. In addition, there are more than 22,500 organizations classified as private foundations that do not make grants.[22]

Some reports on charitable activity misleadingly double count financial contributions. Foundations, for instance, generally make grants to public charities, while individuals make their contributions to foundations and public charities. Estimates of total giving by the public should not count both giving to foundations (approximately $27.6 billion in 2000) and the later giving of foundations to public charities and others (approximately $27.6 billion in 2000).

Many larger grant-making foundations, such as Gates, Ford, Rockefeller, Carnegie, and Kellogg, are well known to the public, but there were 56,582 grant-making foundations in 2000, approximately 75 percent more than in 1989. An estimated 5,228 new foundations formed in 2001, a record one-year increase (Lawrence, Atienza, and Merino 2003). Like public charities, these foundations come in all sizes and shapes. Some accept solicitations for grants and some do not. Some make thousands of grants and some make only one or two. Private independent (non-operating) foundations dominate the mix of foundations and many are vehicles for family giving. Community foundations, such as the New York Community Trust and the Boston Foundation, number only about 600, but they are growing rapidly and becoming a greater force. Total assets of foundations approximated $495.6 billion by 2000, but growth from 1999 had slowed to 8.4 percent, compared with double-digit growth enjoyed in previous years, a reflection of the decline in the stock market. By 2001 foundation assets decreased to $476.8 billion, the first decline since 1981. A further decline of almost 7 percent occurred in 2002. Half of the top fifty foundations experienced asset losses in 2000. Foundation assets began to increase with the economic expansion and stock market recovery after the 2001 recession (Lawrence, Atienza, and Barve 2005).

Assets and Net Worth

Total assets of reporting public charities have been on an upward trend throughout the 1990s with assets toward the end of that period growing faster than liabilities, undoubtedly due to a robust stock market throughout most of that decade (figure 3.9). Assets and liabilities include bills payable and receivable—items that often tend to grow or decline in tandem. Still, estimates for total assets are likely understated, because some assets, particularly real estate, are often counted at book value rather than market value.

Most of the assets and liabilities of the entire charitable sector reside in higher education and hospitals (figures 3.10 and 3.11). Higher education, which relies heavily on endowment gifts from its donors, has the greatest amount of net as-

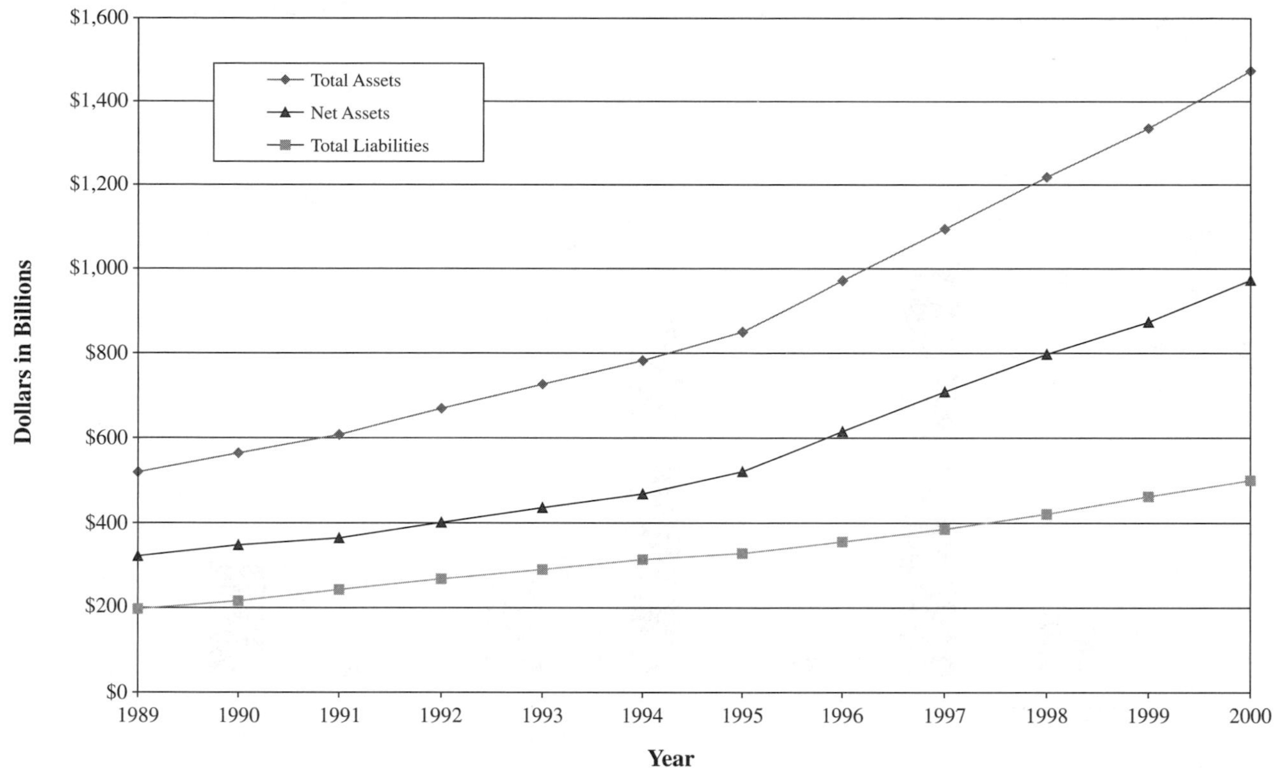

FIGURE 3.9. TRENDS IN ASSETS AND LIABILITIES OF REPORTING PUBLIC CHARITIES, CIRCA 1989–2000 (NOT ADJUSTED FOR INFLATION)

Note: Total assets include real estate, accounts and pledges receivable, grants receivable, inventories, and other assets. Net assets equal total assets minus total liabilities. Total liabilities include accounts and grants payable, deferred revenue, and other liabilities.
Source: The Urban Institute, NCCS Core Files, 1990–2001.

sets. Health care bills, both receivables and payables, contribute to that sector's greater amount of total assets. These two types of institutions also employ a large percentage of nonprofit workers.

Real estate is not the only asset that is often not valued at market prices. Nonprofit assets, such as art collections or zoo animals, receive special treatment and are not subject to requirements of capitalization and depreciation. Therefore, the net assets of organizations such as museums and zoos are, in some sense, understated. Contributions of art must be valued initially if the donor is to receive a tax deduction, but such assets and their appreciation are usually not reflected in asset value unless sold. Under the Tax Reform Act of 1969, artists who donate art to nonprofit organizations receive a deduction only for materials, not for the market value of the art (Bell 1987). Additionally, Financial Accounting Standards Board (FASB) rules, in effect since 1995, require nonprofits to report the value of pledges as income in the year the pledges are made, causing for some an overstatement of income due to pledges never realized.

THE NONPROFIT SECTOR AND THE U.S. ECONOMY

Using a variety of sources, the Bureau of Economic Analysis (BEA; 2001) estimated that the nonprofit sector produced 4.2 percent of GDP in 2000—up from 3.1 percent in 1970 (figure 3.12).[23] By contrast, the government sector produced 10.8 percent in 2000 (down from 13.9 percent in 1970), while the business sector produced 84.9 percent of all goods and services.

Obviously, if one piece of the national pie grows as a share of the total, at least one other piece's share must shrink. In the 1970s, the government's share shrank. But before concluding simply that these changes in national income indicate a decline in the influence of the government sector and an expansion of the nonprofit sector, one must look behind the numbers. From 1970 to 2000, the government sector's participation in the *direct* production of output, primarily in the defense budget, certainly did decline. Increasingly, however, government has taken its revenues and shifted toward making transfers for others to spend (as in social security payments) or contracting out for services. Indeed, declines in government employment for producing goods and services nearly match increases in nonprofit employment, just as declines in government output (mainly from its employees) nearly match increases in nonprofit output (mainly from *its* employees; Steuerle and Hodgkinson 1999). Contracting is examined in more depth in the chapter by Grønbjerg and Smith in this volume; we simply emphasize that the shift in national income and growth in nonprofit

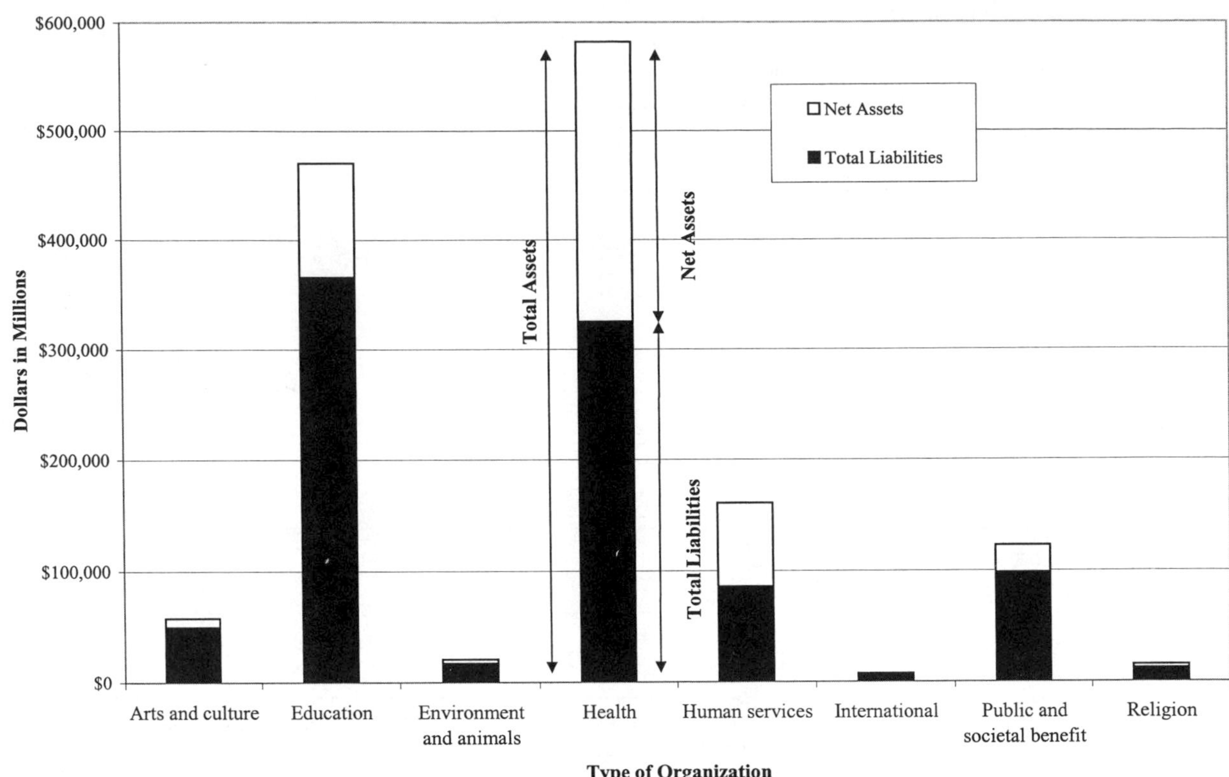

FIGURE 3.10. TOTAL LIABILITIES AND NET ASSETS OF REPORTING PUBLIC CHARITIES BY ORGANIZATIONAL CATEGORY, 2000
Source: The Urban Institute, NCCS/GuideStar National Nonprofit Database, 2000.

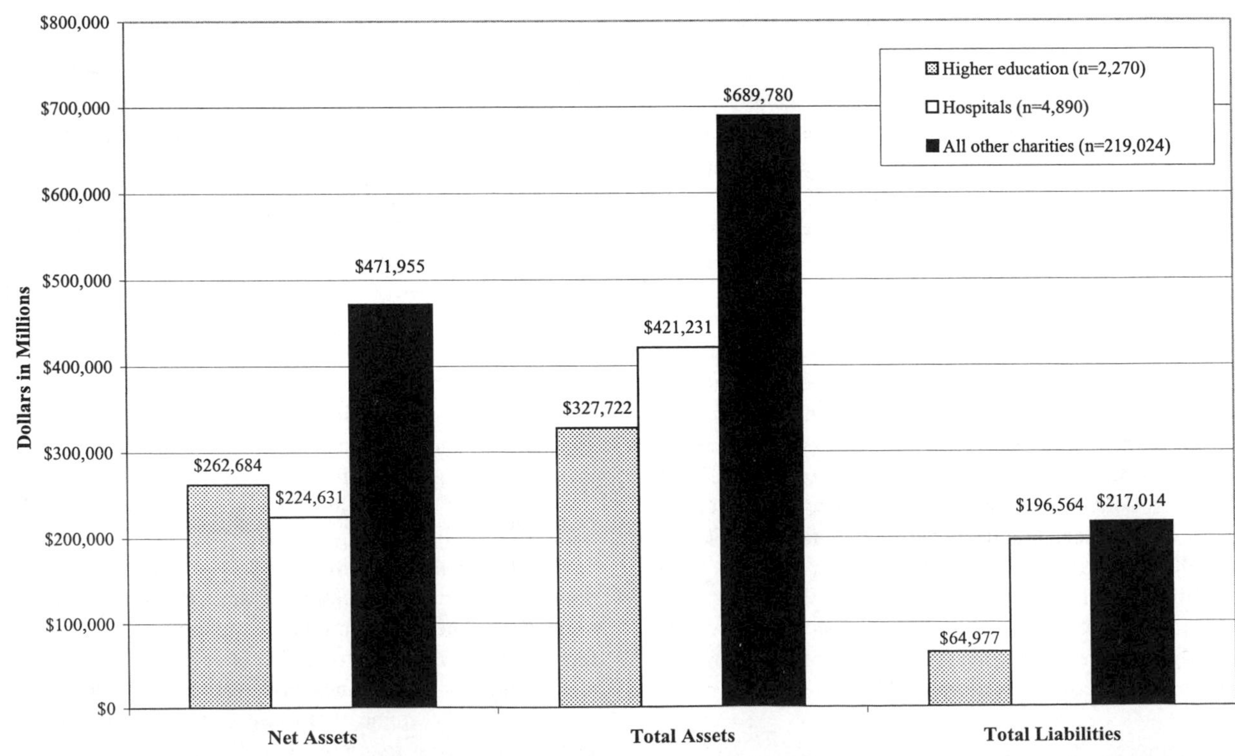

FIGURE 3.11. NET ASSETS, TOTAL LIABILITIES, AND TOTAL ASSETS OF HOSPITALS, HIGHER EDUCATION, AND OTHER TYPES OF PUBLIC CHARITIES, 2000
Source: The Urban Institute, NCCS/GuideStar National Nonprofit Database, 2000.

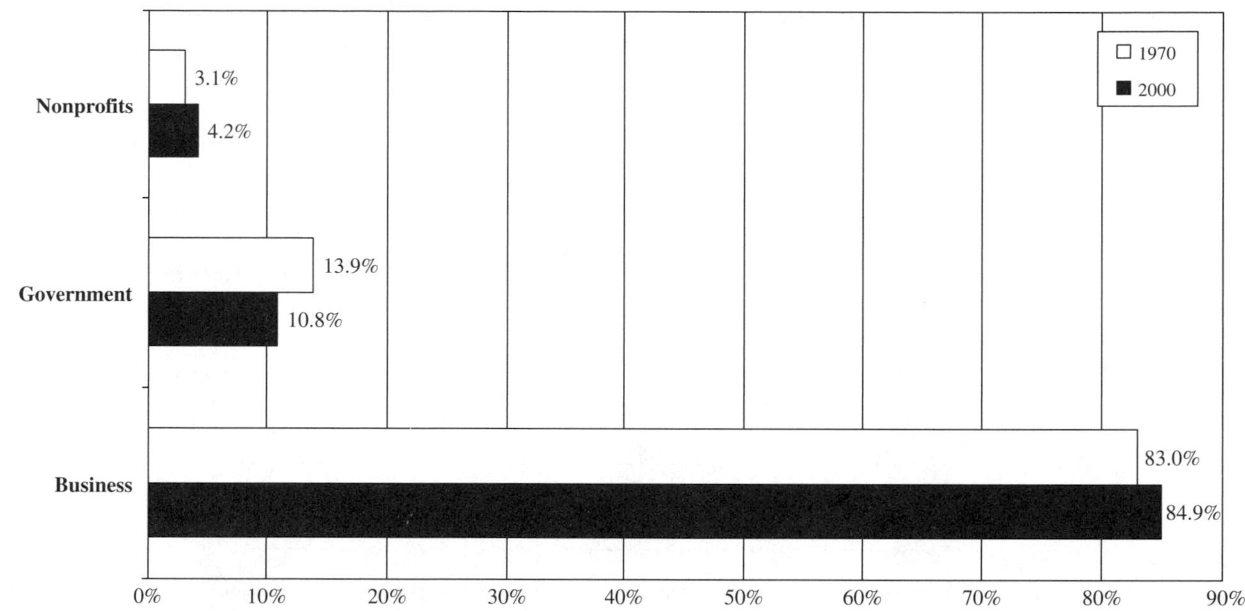

FIGURE 3.12. NATIONAL INCOME BY SECTOR AS A PERCENTAGE OF GDP

Note: BEA defines the nonprofit sector as comprising all tax-exempt entities, and values each on the basis of paid compensation only. Others use alternative methods to calculate the nonprofit sector's share of national income. For example, our estimate includes paid compensation and volunteer time to calculate a national income in 1998 of $7.3 trillion, of which 6.7 percent is attributable to nonprofit organizations (See Independent Sector 2001).

Source: BEA 2001.

output largely reflect the government's contracting out for more services. The primary examples are payments to health-care providers through Medicare and Medicaid.

Government also provides a variety of subsidies that bolster the nonprofit sector. For example, special tax breaks for the purchase of health insurance likely led to an increase in the demand for medical services traditionally provided by nonprofits. At the same time, increased government subsidies or voucher payments, especially through Medicare and Medicaid, have enticed business to compete for these services. The increasing proportion of for-profit health providers like home health care agencies is one example (see Schlesinger and Gray, this volume).[24]

More generally, an increasing share of the national economy involves the types of goods and services that *can* and often do flow through nonprofit providers. For instance, demand for health and information services is growing much faster than demand for steel and cars (Cordes, Steuerle, and Twombly 2004). This remains true whether demand is generated by individuals directly, or through government.

Transfers versus Output

Individuals' contributions of tax dollars to finance government social welfare expenditures (around 20 percent of personal income) are almost ten times larger than individuals' direct charitable contributions (about 2 percent of personal income) (Steuerle and Hodgkinson 1999).[25] Taxation, of course, is compulsory, while contributions are voluntary (Havens, O'Herlihy, and Schervish, this volume).

Regardless of the reason, government dominates spending, particularly through its retirement and health programs such as Social Security, Medicare, and Medicaid. While charitable contributions have remained fairly constant as a share of personal income over the past three decades, government's social welfare function increased significantly in the 1960s and early 1970s before reaching a more constant level of about one-fifth of personal income.

The nonprofit sector's growth as a share of the national economy shown in figure 3.12 corresponds roughly to the increase in operating expenses of the nonprofit sector shown in figure 3.13. The relative consistency in the level of giving as a percentage of personal income demonstrates that the growth in national output was financed not through increased charitable giving but through fees received for services that the nonprofit sector rendered.

What Is Not Measured (or Not Measured Well) in National Income Data

National income estimates of nonprofit activity do not count volunteer labor or work at below-market wages. If we count volunteers, estimates suggest that the output of the nonprofit sector as a percentage of GDP would be about two points higher. Including this estimated value of volunteer labor, nonprofit sector output was 5.5 percent in 1977 and rose to 6.7 percent in 1998.[26] In an attempt to quantify voluntary labor contributions, Virginia Hodgkinson and Murray Weitzman developed a methodology based on survey data of volunteering activities. They have reported estimates of vol-

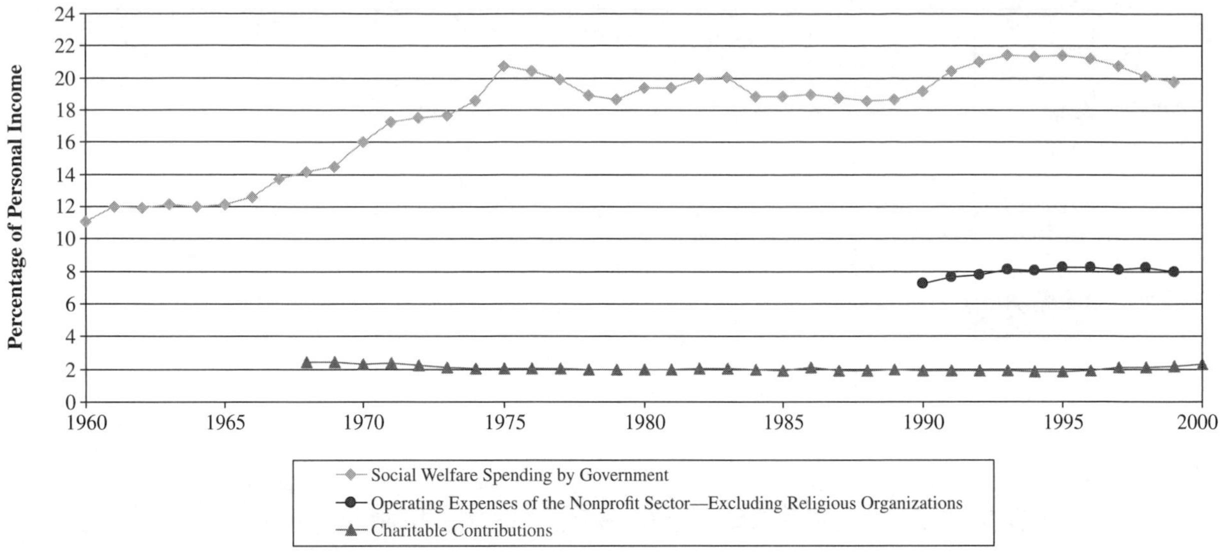

FIGURE 3.13. GOVERNMENT SOCIAL WELFARE SPENDING AND CHARITABLE CONTRIBUTIONS, 1960–1999
Note: Includes federal, state, and local social welfare spending.
Sources: BEA 2001; Social Security Administration, *Annual Statistical Supplement to the Social Security Bulletin,* 2000; AAFRC Trust for Philanthropy 2001; IRS Statistics of Income Exempt Organizations Sample Files, 1990–1999.

unteer output in the *Nonprofit Almanac,* developed by staff at Independent Sector (Hodgkinson, Weitzman, et al., various editions).[27]

A more complicated issue is what value to place on those individuals in the nonprofit sector who might be working at either above- or below-market wages. Some individuals might be paid more when they work for nonprofits if they can capture some of the charitable contribution rather than transferring it to other beneficiaries. Others may work for less, contributing the equivalent of volunteer labor. Yet, again, if the value of their output is lower by the difference between what they are paid and what they could earn elsewhere, then lower pay may indeed reflect lower productivity. For example, the pay differential could be absorbed in more amenities and benefits on the job or a slower work pace. Many individuals in nonprofit organizations, however, work very hard, so a general rule is hard to apply. Within those parts of the sector that deal with issues of poverty or need, in particular, it is generally thought that many employees accept a salary below market wages and are happy to contribute in this way.

What does the empirical evidence say? Weisbrod (1983) found that public interest nonprofit lawyers earned roughly 20 percent less than comparable attorneys in the corporate sector. Others have also reported significantly lower pay in the nonprofit sector compared with the for-profit sector (Johnston and Rudney 1987; Preston 1989). In a study of nonprofit employment in Louisiana, Sarah Dewees and Lester Salamon (2001) report that the weekly wages of nonprofit workers average $482 compared with $522 for business and $598 for government workers.

Yet, in some industries nonprofit wages are higher than comparable for-profit wages. In Louisiana, nonprofit employees engaged in education received weekly wages of $610 compared with $500 for workers in for-profit industries (Dewees and Salamon 2001). Laura Leete (2001) has conducted one of the most comprehensive examinations of nonprofit wage differentials and finds nonprofit pay higher in areas like hospitals and higher education, but lower in areas like primary and secondary education and job training.[28] (See Leete, this volume, for a comprehensive discussion.)

Net Worth of Nonprofit Organizations

The net worth of the nonprofit sector is also significant—about 6 percent ($1.6 trillion) of the total net worth of the household and nonprofit sectors combined (figure 3.14). Note that to avoid double counting, the business sector is not reported separately, since many households own stock or a business as part of their asset portfolios. The nonprofit net worth estimate reported here is fairly accurate when it comes to the major holders of assets—such as foundations, educational institutions, and hospitals—but weak when it comes to churches, which are not required to report to the government.

One might argue that assets held within the nonprofit sector, and enhanced by favorable tax treatment, are more "valuable" than similar assets held within the household sector. Typically, the income is not taxed for the nonprofit holder.[29] Also, nonprofits are usually exempt from paying most property taxes on their real estate assets. Accordingly, one could argue that assets implicitly have a higher after-tax value when held by the nonprofit sector than when held by taxable individuals. This is one reason why the earlier in life an individual makes gifts to a charity, the greater the amount (usually) that is transferred to the charity over time. Still, the is-

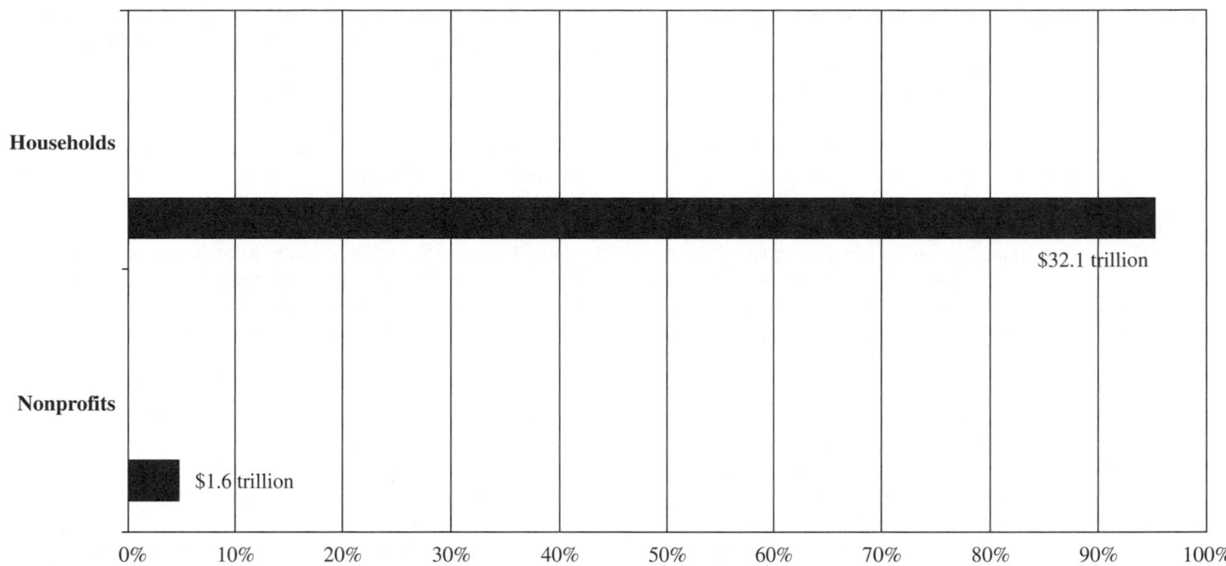

FIGURE 3.14. NET WORTH OF U.S. HOUSEHOLDS AND NONPROFITS IN 2000
Note: The Federal Reserve defines the nonprofit sector to include 501(c)(3) and 501(c)(4) through 501(c)(9) organizations, private foundations, and charitable trusts. This definition does not include religious organizations or those with less than $25,000 in gross annual receipts.
Sources: Board of Governors of the Federal Reserve 2000; Center on Nonprofits and Philanthropy, the Urban Institute, 2001.

sue is complicated, as when the tax advantage subsidizes inefficiency or when the capital (e.g., a church building) is less salable in an open market. Also, taxpayers in aggregate pay the cost of the subsidy in the sense that the revenue transfer to charities means less revenues available for other government expenditures.

Research on the scope and dimensions of the nonprofit sector, however defined, has come a long way since the Filer Commission. While all data must be interpreted with caution, those on the nonprofit sector are becoming more robust and accessible.[30] The available data document the significant and growing nonprofit sector and the increasing economic activity generated by nonprofit organizations. Resources in hospitals and higher education institutions are responsible for much of the economic activity in the sector. That said, aggregate economic data do not reveal the many vital roles nonprofits play in communities. Through nonprofit associations, people connect to one another and to their communities. People give, volunteer, and lend their support to nonprofits that provide formal and informal education and youth development, promote artistic and cultural development, care for the sick, feed and house the poor, and represent interests and values in the broader society and polity. Much of this work is done with minimal resources and a great deal of volunteer and underpaid labor.

The composite picture of the nonprofit sector shows color, variation, and dynamic activity. While not all nonprofits operate in the public interest, most advance some worthwhile purpose beyond the personal needs of founders and the contributors of time and money. That this sector flourishes in the U.S. economy reflects well upon the aspirations and dedication of its citizens. That the sector is as large as it is means that the nation is constantly enriched with new and different sources of ideas and information. Activities of this sector often fill niches that simply cannot be met purely by a business sector devoted to profits or a government sector relying upon compulsory taxation and majority rule to achieve its public ends. Since the nonprofit sector contains so many organizations and is so varied, it gives society a texture and depth that could not be achieved in any other way. Diverse purposes and, at times, inadequate accountability certainly result in some duplication and efficiency costs. Nonetheless, if diversity is a sign of health—and we believe it is—the nonprofit sector demonstrates the robust health of our democratic society.

ACKNOWLEDGMENTS

The authors are grateful for the assistance of Perri Gottlieb, Adam Carasso, Eric Twombly, Cory Fleming, Pho Palmer, Linda Lampkin, Tom Pollak, and Dan Oran in the preparation of this chapter.

NOTES

1. Religious congregations and small nonprofits with less than $5,000 in annual gross receipts are not required to register with the IRS. Organizations with more than $25,000 in annual gross receipts must report financial and program information to the IRS annually on Form 990. All private foundations must report to the IRS annually on Form 990PF.

2. See Stevenson et al. (1997) for a description of the 26 major categories and 645 subgroups. The National Taxonomy of Exempt Entities—Core Codes (NTEE-CC), developed in 1998, includes defini-

tions of the classifications. Updated manuals are posted at www.nccs .urban.org.

3. Some tax-exempt organizations, such as credit unions and some cooperatives, are profit-making for their members. That is, they are not nonprofit.

4. Most state governments monitor nonprofit activities through state charity offices or the state attorney general's office.

5. Estimate projected from *Nonprofit Almanac* (Hodgkinson and Weitzman 1996).

6. Religious congregations are not required to register with the IRS, but NCCS researchers found that significant numbers do. In 2000, approximately 84,000 voluntarily registered with the IRS; most do not file Forms 990 (NCCS analysis of IRS Business Master File, July 2005).

7. Some financial data on religious congregations and their affiliated organizations are available from the National Council of Churches of Christ in the United States of America (*Yearbook of American and Canadian Churches,* 1916–2001). Various surveys have also been conducted—for example, *From Belief to Commitment: The Community Service Activities of Religious Congregations in the United States* (Hodgkinson and Weitzman 1993) and "The National Congregations Study" (Chaves et al. 1999), a comprehensive survey of 1,236 religious congregations nationwide. These studies are beginning to provide better estimates of the numbers and finances of congregations, but no one data source provides a complete picture.

8. Includes approximately 84,000 congregations. See note 5.

9. Table 3.3 is compiled by the Foundation Center and includes only foundations that make grants. Private foundations are created by individuals, families, or corporations, and they have a more stringent regulatory framework than public charities. Donors usually give a sum of money to create an endowment that generates interest used to make grants and operate programs for charitable purposes. Community foundations hold the charitable gifts of many individuals and use them to benefit specific communities. Community foundations are public charities and therefore they do not fall under the private foundation regulations. Operating foundations are private foundations that operate a charitable program such as a residential facility or a research institute, although some may make grants. The data in table 3.2 include all charities classified as private foundations, whether they make grants or not.

10. The NCCS is the national repository of data on nonprofit organizations. Formerly an Independent Sector program, in 1996 the NCCS relocated to the Urban Institute. The NCCS receives IRS files on nonprofits and creates research databases that are accessible to researchers electronically over the Internet and on CD-ROM (www.nccs. urban.org).

11. See Reid (1999) for a discussion of the regulation of nonprofit political and electoral activities.

12. In such an arrangement, the 501(c)(3) organization accepts charitable contributions primarily for research and related public education efforts, while the 501(c)(4) group actively conducts legislative lobbying. Some 501(c)(4) organizations, like the Sierra Club, are also affiliated with political action committees, which are permitted to engage in electoral campaigns (Boris and Krehely 2002).

13. Grønbjerg's analyses so far consider all nonprofits and do not break out public charities.

14. The Web site Quality 990 (www.qual990.org), a collaborative project, promotes a number of projects and activities to improve the accuracy of nonprofit reporting on Form 990; however, some observers suggest that increased visibility of Form 990 will result in less accurate reporting as organizations try to present their finances in the most favorable light.

15. Electronic filing of Form 990 is being pilot tested by the NCCS to facilitate implementation by the IRS.

16. For example, approximately 58 percent of public charities (488,000 of 840,000) listed in the 2003 Business Master File (2001 data) report less than $25,000 in gross receipts.

17. Spatial analyses are in the early stages and still must surmount problems of accounting for organizational headquarters and service locations or mobile services. Accounting for embedded organizations is also problematic. For example, university-based theaters or child care centers and small nonprofits housed in church basements are difficult to identify and map.

18. Note also that this calculation is for the year 2000, when public returns from stock market investment and interest rates were higher than in at least the succeeding couple of years.

19. We have excluded supporting organizations and foundations to avoid double counting.

20. Measures of productivity and outcomes are beyond the scope of this chapter, but there is a growing demand for reliable measures of efficiency and effectiveness, and increased experimentation with concepts like cost-benefit analysis, social return on investment, and others.

21. Individual giving includes giving to private and public foundations but does not include foundation grants.

22. The private foundation category is a residual category under the tax code; tax-exempt organizations that cannot demonstrate sufficient public support are classified as private foundations, a less favorable tax status. Community foundations are classified as public charities. There are, in addition, some private foundations that operate facilities and make no grants.

23. The BEA estimates the nonprofit sector portion of GDP based on compensation only and currently does not consider consumption of fixed capital.

24. In one study of 5,768 hospitals by Needleman, Chollet, and Lamphere (1997), a total of 175 hospitals (6 percent) reported a change in their ownership status between 1980 and 1990. Of these, 110 (63 percent) converted to for-profit status. Gray and Schlesinger (2002) show major growth in the numbers of for-profit rehabilitation hospitals but a decline in the number of for-profit acute care hospitals between the mid-1980s and the late 1990s.

25. Although government social welfare payments are broadly defined, the disparity is even greater because a significant proportion of charitable contributions is given for sacramental religious purposes.

26. Weitzman et al. (2002) add the value of unpaid family business workers to overall employment. They calculate the wage value of unpaid family workers as one-half the average annual earnings of the self-employed multiplied by the number of unpaid family workers estimated by the U.S. Census Bureau. This calculation, in effect, compensates for volunteers to family businesses, in order to create a more complete base of employment for the business sector. However, business "volunteers" should not, as in the case of the nonprofit sector, add to output since that is already reflected in profits which would be lower by the amount of wages, if paid, to the "volunteers."

27. *The New Nonprofit Almanac in Brief: Facts and Figures on the Independent Sector* (Independent Sector 2001) and *The New Nonprofit Almanac and Desk Reference* (Weitzman et al. 2002). Volunteer time is calculated by taking the average hourly wage of nonagricultural employees and increasing it by 12 percent to estimate fringe benefits in 1998. Since individuals volunteer for government and business as well as for nonprofits, this estimate is calculated by first adding volunteer input to the national income and then calculating the proportion that applies to the nonprofit sector based on surveys conducted on behalf of Independent Sector. The 1998 estimate is based on volunteering data indicating that 109.4 million Americans volunteered 19.9 million hours in that year. The calculated value of volunteer time to formal organizations, using the average nonagricultural wage, is approximately $225.9 billion (Independent Sector 2001). See also Hodgkinson and Weitzman, *Giving and Volunteering in the United States* (1999, 2001).

28. See table 6 in Leete (2001).

29. In a technical sense, the issue is whether the future income from assets of a nonprofit should be discounted at the private after-tax interest rate. The stream of income from an asset is higher for the holder of an asset (but not for society) when some of it is not siphoned off to government. Of course, in the case of corporate stock, the underlying corporations still pay corporate tax on their income, so there is no corporate tax advantage, only an individual tax advantage, in shifting the ownership of corporate stock to charities.

30. Further progress will depend to some extent on government taking greater responsibility for developing and maintaining the data sets on nonprofits and doing a better job of including nonprofit organizations as a sector when employment data are gathered and national income is estimated.

REFERENCES

AAFRC Trust for Philanthropy. 2001. *Giving USA: The Annual Report on Philanthropy for the Year 2000.* Indianapolis: AAFRC Trust for Philanthropy.

Bell, Douglas J. 1987. "Changing I.R.C. §170(e)(1)(A): For Art's Sake." *Case Western Reserve Law Review* 37:536–568.

Bielefeld, Wolfgang. 2000. "Metropolitan Nonprofit Sectors: Findings from NCCS Data." *Nonprofit and Voluntary Sector Quarterly* 29(2): 297–314.

Board of Governors of the Federal Reserve. 2000. *Flow of Funds Accounts of the United States.* Washington, DC: Government Printing Office, 2000.

Boris, Elizabeth T. 1999. "The Nonprofit Sector in the 1990s." In *Philanthropy and the Nonprofit Sector in a Changing America,* edited by Charles T. Clotfelter and Thomas Ehrlich. Indianapolis: Indiana University Press.

Boris, Elizabeth T., and Jeff Krehely. 2002. "Civic Participation and Advocacy." In *The State of Nonprofit America,* edited by Lester M. Salamon. Washington, DC: Brookings Institution Press.

Boris, Elizabeth T., and C. Eugene Steuerle, eds. 1999. *Nonprofits and Government: Collaboration and Conflict.* Washington, DC: Urban Institute Press.

Bureau of Economic Analysis (BEA). 2001. National Income and Product Account Tables, Table 1.7: Gross Domestic Product by Sector. Available at http://www.bea.gov/.

Chaves, Mark. 2002. "Religious Congregations." In *The State of Nonprofit America,* edited by Lester M. Salamon. Washington, DC: Brookings Institution Press.

Chaves, Mark, Mary Ellen Konieczny, Kraig Beyerlein, and Emily Barman. 1999. "The National Congregations Study: Background, Methods and Selected Results." *Journal for the Scientific Study of Religion* 38:458–476.

Colwell, Mary Anna Culleton. 1997. "The Potential for Bias When Research on Voluntary Associations Is Limited to 501(c)(3) Organizations." Nonprofit Sector Research Fund Working Paper Series. Washington, DC: Aspen Institute.

Commission on Private Philanthropy and Public Needs. 1975. *Giving in America: Toward a Stronger Voluntary Sector.* Washington, DC: U.S. Department of Treasury.

Cordes, Joseph J., Elizabeth Rowland, and Sarah Wilson. 2000. "The Business of Nonprofits: Investigating the Reliance on Business-Like Sources of Income." Paper presented at the 29th Annual Conference of the Association for Research on Nonprofit Organizations and Voluntary Action, New Orleans.

Cordes, Joseph J., C. Eugene Steuerle, and Eric C. Twombly. 2004. "Dimensions of Nonprofit Entrepreneurship: An Exploratory Essay." In *Public Policy and the Econonmics of Entrepreneurship,* edited by Douglas Holtz-Eakin and Harvey Rosen. Cambridge: MIT Press.

Dale, Harvey. 1993. "On Estimating the Size of the Nonprofit Sector in the U.S. Economy." *Voluntas* 4(2): 183–189.

De Vita, Carol J., Carlos Manjarrez, and Eric C. Twombly. 2000. "Poverty in the District of Columbia—Then and Now." Paper presented at the DC Poverty Summit: Strategies for the New Millennium, sponsored by the United Planning Organization, Washington, DC.

———. 1999. "Organizations and Neighborhood Networks that Strengthen Families in the District of Columbia." Report to the Annie E. Casey Foundation, August.

De Vita, Carol J., and Eric C. Twombly. 2002. "A Comparison of Nonprofit Sectors in Arkansas, Nevada, and Oklahoma." Report to Donald W. Reynolds Foundation, September.

De Vita, Carol J., Eric C. Twombly, Jennifer Auer, and Yuan You. 2004. "Charting Resources of the Pittsburgh Region's Nonprofit Sector." Report to Forbes Fund, September.

Dewees, Sarah, and Lester M. Salamon. 2001. *Louisiana Nonprofit Employment.* Baltimore: Johns Hopkins Center for Civil Society Studies.

Edie, John A. 1987. "Congress and Foundations: Historical Summary." In *America's Wealthy and the Future of Foundations,* edited by Teresa J. Odendahl. New York, Foundation Center.

Froelich, Karen, Terry Knoepfle, and Thomas Pollak. 2000. "Financial Measures in Nonprofit Organization Research: Comparing IRS 990 Return and Audited Financial Statement Data." *Nonprofit and Voluntary Sector Quarterly,* Spring.

Galaskiewicz, Joseph, and Wolfgang Bielefeld. 1998. *Nonprofit*

Organizations in an Age of Uncertainty: A Study of Organizational Change. New York: Aldine de Gruyter.

Ganguly, Dia, and Robin Gluck. 2001. "Foundation Reporting." *Foundations Today Series.* New York: Foundation Center.

Gantz, Marie G., and Nicholas A. J. Stengel. 1999. "Completing the Puzzle: Combining Disparate Datasets to Illuminate the Human Service Sector in Los Angeles County." Paper presented at the 28th Annual Conference of the Association for Research on Nonprofit Organizations and Voluntary Action, Washington, DC.

Gordon, Teresa P., Janet S. Greenlee, and Denise Nitterhouse. 1999. "Tax-Exempt Organization Financial Data: Availability and Limitations." *Accounting Horizons* 13(2): 113–128.

Gray, Bradford, and Mark Schlesinger. 2002. "Health." In *The State of Nonprofit America,* edited by Lester Salamon. Washington, DC: Brookings Institution Press.

Grønbjerg, Kirsten A. 2002. "Evaluating Nonprofit Databases." *American Behavioral Scientist* 45(11): 1741–1777.

———. 1992. "Using NTEE to Classify Nonprofit Organizations: An Assessment of Human Service and Regional Applications." *Voluntas* 5(3): 301–328.

———. 1989. "Developing a Universe of Nonprofit Organizations: Methodological Considerations." *Nonprofit and Voluntary Sector Quarterly* 18(1): 63–80.

Grønbjerg, Kirsten A., and Laurie Paarlberg. 2001a. "Community Variations in the Size and Scope of the Nonprofit Sector: Theory and Preliminary Findings." *Nonprofit and Voluntary Sector Quarterly* 30(4): 684–706.

———. 2001b. "Extent and Nature of Overlap between Two Nonprofit Databases: IRS Tax-Exempt Registration and Nonprofit Incorporation—The Case of Indiana." Paper presented at the 30th Annual Conference of the Association for Research on Nonprofit Organizations and Voluntary Action, Miami, FL.

Hager, Mark A. 2001. "Financial Vulnerability among Arts Organizations: A Test of the Tuckman-Chang Measures." *Nonprofit and Voluntary Sector Quarterly* 30(2): 376–392.

Hager, Mark A., Joseph Galaskiewicz, Wolfgang Bielefeld, and Joel Pins. 1996. "Tales from the Grave: Organizations' Accounts of Their Own Demise." *American Behavioral Scientist* 39(8): 975–994.

Hager, Mark A., Thomas Pollak, and Patrick Rooney. 2001. "Variations in Overhead and Fundraising Efficiency Measures: The Influence of Size, Age, and Subsector." Working paper, Center on Nonprofits and Philanthropy, Urban Institute.

Haycock, Nancy. 1992. *The Nonprofit Sector in New York City.* New York: Nonprofit Coordinating Committee of New York.

Hodgkinson, Virginia A., and Murray S. Weitzman. 1993. *From Belief to Commitment: The Community Service Activities of Religious Congregations in the United States.* Washington, DC: Independent Sector.

———. 1999, 2001. *Giving and Volunteering in the United States.* Washington, DC: Independent Sector.

Hodgkinson, Virginia A. and Murray S. Weitzman, with John A. Abrahams, Eric A. Crutchfield, and David R. Stevenson. 1996. *Nonprofit Almanac, 1996–1997: Dimensions of the Independent Sector.* San Francisco: Jossey-Bass.

Hodgkinson, Virginia A., Murray S. Weitzman, Christopher M. Toppe, and Stephen M. Noga. 1992. *Nonprofit Almanac, 1992–1993: Dimensions of the Independent Sector.* San Francisco: Jossey-Bass.

Independent Sector. 2001. *The New Nonprofit Almanac in Brief: Facts and Figures on the Independent Sector.* Washington, DC: Independent Sector.

Johnston, Denis, and Gabriel Rudney. 1987. "Characteristics of Workers in Nonprofit Organizations." *Monthly Labor Review* 110(7): 28–33.

Krehely, Jeff. 2001. "Assessing the Current Data on 501(c)(3) Advocacy: What IRS Form 990 Can Tell Us." In *Exploring Organizations and Advocacy,* edited by Elizabeth J. Reid and Maria D. Montilla. Washington, DC: Urban Institute Press.

Krehely, Jeff, and Kendall Golladay. 2001. "Understanding 501(c)(4) Social Welfare Advocacy Organizations: Scope, Dimensions, and Policy Advocacy." Paper presented at the 30th Annual Conference of the Association for Research on Nonprofit Organizations and Voluntary Action, Miami, FL.

Lampkin, Linda, and Elizabeth Boris. 2001. "Nonprofit Organization Data: What We Have, What We Need." *American Behavioral Scientist* 45(11): 1675–1715.

Lawrence, Steven, Josefina Atienza, and Asmita Barve. 2005. *Foundation Yearbook: Facts and Figures on Private and Community Foundations.* Foundations Today Series. New York: Foundation Center.

Lawrence, Steven, Josefina Atienza, and Leslie Marino. 2003. *Foundation Yearbook: Facts and Figures on Private and Community Foundations.* Foundations Today Series. New York: Foundation Center.

Lawrence, Steven, and Dia Ganguly. 2002. *Foundation Yearbook: Facts and Figures on Private and Community Foundations.* Foundations Today Series. New York: Foundation Center.

Lawrence, Steven, and Loren Renz. 2003. *Foundation Growth and Giving Estimates: 2002 Preview.* Foundations Today Series. New York: Foundation Center.

Lawrence, Steven, and Loren Renz. 2002. *Foundation Growth and Giving Estimates: 2001 Preview.* Foundations Today Series. New York: Foundation Center.

Leete, Laura. 2001. "Whither the Nonprofit Wage Differential? Estimates from the 1990 Census." *Journal of Labor Economics* 19(1): 136–170.

National Council of Churches of Christ in the United States of America. Various editions, 1916–2001. *Yearbook of American and Canadian Churches.* Nashville, TN: National Council of Churches of Christ in the United States of America.

Needleman, Jack, Deborah J. Chollet, and JoAnn Lamphere. 1997. "Hospital Conversion Trends." *Health Affairs* 16(2): 187–195.

Powell, Walter, ed. 1987. *The Nonprofit Sector: A Research Handbook,* 1st ed. New Haven: Yale University Press.

Preston, Anne. 2002. "Compensation in Nonprofit Organizations." Task Force Report, National Center for Nonprofit Enterprise.

———. 1989. "The Nonprofit Worker in a For-Profit World." *Journal of Labor Economics* 7:438–463.

Reid, Elizabeth J. 1999. "Nonprofit Advocacy and Political Participation." In *Nonprofits and Government: Collaboration and Conflict,* edited by Elizabeth T. Boris and C. Eugene Steuerle. Washington, DC: Urban Institute Press.

Reid, Elizabeth J., and Janelle Kerlin. 2002. "Complex Organizational Structures in the Nonprofit Sector: Political Influence and Public Accountability." Paper presented at the 24th Annual Research Conference of the Association for Public Policy Analysis and Management, Dallas, TX.

Renz, Loren. 1991. *Foundation Giving: Yearbook of Facts and Figures on Private Corporate and Community Foundations.* New York: Foundation Center.

Rudney, Gabriel. 1987. "The Scope and Dimensions of Nonprofit Activity." In *The Nonprofit Sector: A Research Handbook,* 1st ed., edited by Walter W. Powell. New Haven: Yale University Press.

Salamon, Lester M. 1999. *America's Nonprofit Sector: A Primer.* 2nd ed. New York: Foundation Center.

———. 1992. *America's Nonprofit Sector: A Primer.* New York: Foundation Center.

Smith, David Horton. 2000. *Grassroots Associations.* Thousand Oaks, CA: Sage.

———. 1997. "The Rest of the Nonprofit Sector: Grassroots Associations as the Dark Matter Ignored in Prevailing 'Flat Earth' Maps of the Sector." *Nonprofit and Voluntary Sector Quarterly* 26(2): 114–131.

Steuerle, C. Eugene, and Virginia A. Hodgkinson. 1999. "Meeting Social Needs: Comparing the Resources of the Independent Sector and Government." *Nonprofits and Government: Collaboration and Conflict,* edited by Elizabeth T. Boris and C. Eugene Steuerle. Washington, DC: Urban Institute Press.

Stevenson, David R., Thomas H. Pollak, and Linda M. Lampkin, with Nicholas A. J. Stengel and Katherine L. S. Pettit. 1997. *State Nonprofit Almanac, 1997: Profiles of Charitable Organizations.* Washington, DC: Urban Institute Press.

Twombly, Eric C., and Marie Gantz. 2001. "Executive Compensation in the Nonprofit Sector: New Findings and Policy Implications." Policy Brief No. 11, Charting Civil Society series, Center on Nonprofits and Philanthropy. Washington, DC: Urban Institute.

———. 2000. *Organizational Response in an Era of Welfare Reform: Exit and Entry Patterns of Nonprofit Human Service Providers.* PhD diss., George Washington University.

U.S. Office of Management and Budget. 2003. *Budget of the United States Government: Fiscal Year 2003.* Washington, DC: Government Printing Office, 2003.

Weisbrod, Burton A. 1983. "Nonprofit and Proprietary Sector Behavior: Wage Differentials among Lawyers." *Journal of Labor Economics* 1(3): 246–263.

Weisbrod, Burton A., with S. Long. 1977. "The Size of the Voluntary Non-Profit Sector: Concepts and Measures." Research paper sponsored by the Commission on Private Philanthropy and Public Needs. Washington, DC: Government Printing Office.

Weitzman, Murray S., Nadine Tai Jalandoni, Linda L. Lampkin, and Thomas H. Pollak. 2002. *The New Nonprofit Almanac and Desktop Reference.* San Francisco: Jossey-Bass.

Wolpert, Julian, and T. Reiner. 1985. "The Not-for-Profit Sector in Stable and Growing Metropolitan Regions." *Urban Affairs Quarterly* 20(4): 487–510.

APPENDIX: IRS NONPROFIT DATA SOURCES

IRS Business Master File

The IRS Business Master File (BMF) is a cumulative list of all active nonprofit organizations that have registered with the IRS and obtained recognition of their tax-exempt status. The BMF is updated monthly and available from both the IRS and NCCS. It contains identifying information such as name, address, and exempt purpose, and two financial variables, total assets and gross receipts. As the most comprehensive list of nonprofit organizations available, it is often used to determine if an organization is eligible for tax-deductible contributions. Much of the information is from the date that the organization received its tax exemption. Every few years it is further updated following a process that includes mailing postcards to organizations to verify that they still exist. The BMF lists many inactive organizations for years after they cease operation. The BMF is useful for analysis of the organizational makeup of the nonprofit sector. The financial variables are of limited utility.

IRS Statistics of Income Sample File

The Statistics of Income (SOI) Division of the IRS annually creates data sets of 501(c) organizations filing in a given calendar year; the data are available from both the IRS and NCCS. The SOI Sample File for 501(c)(3) entities includes 14,000 organizations. It includes those with \$30 million or more in assets and over a third of all organizations with \$10 million to \$30 million in assets, plus a random sample of smaller organizations stratified and weighted by asset level. Another data set includes about 10,000 organizations that are tax exempt under section 501(c)(4) through (9). Information from Form 990-PF, filed by all private foundations, is used to create a foundation data set. SOI files include over 300 financial and programmatic variables from Form 990. These are high-quality research data sets that are valuable for economic analyses but not for geographic or subsector analyses.

NCCS Core Files

NCCS annually creates a research Core File by combining the descriptive information (name and address plus various codes) from the BMF and financial variables from the Return Transaction File. The Return Transaction File is an administrative database created by the IRS from Forms 990 filed by nonprofit organizations. NCCS conducts standardized checks on the financial information, flagging mistakes, and correcting them where possible. Data are cross-checked with the SOI Sample data where possible. NCCS enhances the file by adding the NTEE classification codes of the organizations and by classifying any organizations that have not received NTEE codes. Checks for missing organizations and duplicates are conducted. NCCS adds a zip code–to–county cross-check that assigns Federal Information Processing Standards (FIPS) codes for state and county jurisdictions to aid in geographic analysis and calculates several financial variables including gross receipts, total revenue, expenses, and assets.

The Urban Institute, NCCS/GuideStar National Nonprofit Database

NCCS and GuideStar, in collaboration with the IRS, have scanned Forms 990 and digitized the data to create an electronic database of more than 400 items. Variables cover sources of revenues, areas of expenses, types of assets, salaries, and descriptions of programs and expenses. Data for the years 1998, 1999, and 2000 are available to researchers. The NCCS research version of the database (NCCS/GuideStar National Nonprofit Database) includes the NTEE organizational classifications and is checked for omissions, duplicates, amended returns, and other problems.

4

The Nonprofit Sector in Comparative Perspective

HELMUT K. ANHEIER
LESTER M. SALAMON

In 1987, in the first edition of this *Handbook,* Estelle James (1987:398–399) noted in her seminal chapter, "The Nonprofit Sector in Comparative Perspective," that "little has been written analytically about the role of the indigenous nonprofit sector . . . cutting across industries and/or countries and attempting to relate these facts to the theoretical paradigms of nonprofit growth and behavior." She found that "data on the size of the nonprofit sector are not available for a large number of countries" and that these organizations tended to be overlooked in policy and academic debates. This made it difficult, she suggested, to take on the true challenge of research in the field: to draw on international experience to question and test the "conventional wisdom" of nonprofit theories derived from the American context.

Twenty years later, to what extent is James's assessment still valid? What is the state of knowledge about the nonprofit sector internationally and what theoretical insights does the current state of knowledge hold for our understanding of this field more generally?

The purpose of this chapter is to answer these central questions. Needless to say, given the vastness of the subject there is no way to do this comprehensively. Our objective, therefore, is to identify some of the most salient features of this sector as we have come to understand them, to underline the implications that this understanding holds for some of the major lines of theorizing in this field, and to identify some of the more promising theoretical perspectives that have surfaced in recent years. More specifically, we call attention to five major observations that seem to flow from a review of the current state of knowledge about the nonprofit sector globally:

- First, the field of comparative nonprofit sector studies has grown from one of widespread neglect to one of extensive contestation, with multiple definitions and concepts of what the field encompasses competing for attention.
- Second, nonprofit organizations have moved closer to the center of policy concern. Policy makers in a wide assortment of different settings have discovered the nonprofit sector and made it a focus of policy initiatives and policy debates.
- Third, partly as a consequence, and partly as a cause, of this increased policy interest, the scope and scale of this sector have grown massively. Indeed, a veritable "global associational revolution" seems to be under way throughout the world, a significant upsurge of organized private voluntary activity in virtually every corner of the globe—in the developed market economies; in the transition countries of Central and Eastern Europe; and in the developing regions of Latin America, Africa, the Middle East, and South Asia (Salamon 1994).
- Fourth, as attention has come to focus more heavily on these organizations, significant improvements have been made in the basic data available on them. In addition, a broader research agenda has opened up as scholars have increasingly discovered the nonprofit sector at the international level as a focus for research and analysis.
- Finally, even though the research agenda has expanded significantly over the last decade, our understanding of the role of these institutions is still limited, and data coverage frequently remains patchy. What is more, despite some significant breakthroughs, the theoretical challenges remain

quite severe and no single theory has come to dominate the field. Indeed, one of the major consequences of the growth in knowledge has been to cast doubts on many of the prior theories, which emerged in the context of Western market economies.

A CONTESTED ARENA

In her treatment of the international nonprofit sector in the first edition of this *Handbook,* Estelle James was able to settle relatively quickly on a terminology and a definition of nonprofit organizations that focused essentially on providers of social-welfare services (mostly education, but to some extent also health and social services) that operate under the constraint that they do not distribute profits to their owners. No such consensus exists at the present time, however, about the scope, nature, and composition of the set of institutions that composes the nonprofit sector cross-nationally. There is even dispute, as we will see, over whether the definition should be restricted to "institutions" or "organizations" at all, or extended as well to embrace spontaneous citizen activity in the "public space." Contestation about what the field contains, as well as about what it should be called, has, in fact, become one of the central features of the comparative nonprofit landscape. This doubtless reflects the ambiguity of the basic concepts that have long characterized this field (see Salamon and Anheier 1997; Deakin 2001). But it also reflects quite different societal traditions and patterns as well as ideologies (Fowler 2002). Indeed, the field of nonprofit studies has become a revealing vantage point from which to observe a wide variety of social, economic, religious, and cultural differences among countries (Salamon and Anheier 1998).

Thus, for example, Anheier and Seibel (2001) compared the United States to Germany and identified critical differences in the roles of the nonprofit sector historically that continue to affect state-society relations. In nineteenth-century America, voluntarism and associational life evolved as a compromise between individualism and collective responsibility. This Tocquevillian pattern (greatly simplified here for purposes of comparison) evolved into the system of third-party government and the patchy welfare state that we see today (Salamon 1995). By contrast, in Germany, three quite different principles combined to shape the country's state-society relations and its nonprofit sector well into the late twentieth century:

- The *principle of self-administration,* or self-governance, originating from the nineteenth-century conflict between state and citizens, allowed parts of the nonprofit sector to emerge and develop in an autocratic society, where the freedom of association had only partially been granted (see Schuppert 1981, 2003). It also allowed for a specific civil society development in Germany that emphasized the role of the state as grantor of political privilege and freedom instead of spontaneous self-organization.
- The *principle of subsidiarity,* originally formulated in the work of the Jesuit scholar Nell-Breuning (1976), sought to provide a framework for settling secular-religious frictions and, after World War II, developed into a policy prescription that prioritized nonprofit over public provision of social services (Sachße 1994). This fostered the creation of a set of six nonprofit conglomerates that today rank among the largest nonprofit organizations worldwide (Boeßenecker 1995; Backhaus-Maul and Olk 1994).
- The *principle of Gemeinwirtschaft* (communal economics) was based on the search for an alternative to both capitalism and socialism, and linked to the worker's movement. It led to the cooperative movement and the establishment of mutual associations in banking, insurance, and housing (see Thiemayer 1970).

Even among countries with similar levels of economic development, important differences exist in the nature of what we here call the "nonprofit sector." Taking Europe as an example, we thus have the following:

- The French notion of the "economie sociale," which emphasizes mutualism and the communal economy. It groups nonprofit associations together with cooperatives and mutual organizations, thereby combining the underlying notions of social participation, solidarity, and mutuality as a contrast to the capitalist, for-profit economy (see Archambault 1996; Deforny and Develtere 1999).
- The Italian notion of associationalism, which is seen as a countervailing force against both church and state powers at the local level (Barbetta 1997).
- The German tradition of subsidiarity, described above, and its close counterpart, the concept of "pillarization" in the Netherlands, both of which place primary responsibility for the delivery of social-welfare services in the hands of private, nonprofit organizations, but with extensive state subsidies (Sachße 1994; Kramer 1981; Anheier and Seibel 2001).
- The Swedish model of broadly based social movements whose demands are picked up by the state and incorporated into social legislation (Lundstrøm and Wijkstrøm 1997).
- The British tradition of charity and voluntary action, which delineates a sphere of private institutions and individual social responsibilities running parallel to those of the state (Kendall and Knapp 1996).

Even more striking differences separate the social, cultural, religious, and economic contexts of nonprofit sector realities among developing nations. Thus, the tribal traditions of Africa differ markedly from the plantation culture of much of Latin America, and individualistic Hinduism differs strikingly from the communal and service-oriented philosophy of Islam (Anheier and Salamon 1998b; Landim 1998; Kandil 1998).

What this demonstrates is the importance of sensitivity to the different traditions, patterns, and cultures of nonprofits and philanthropy. While there may be "nonprofit organizations" and "nonprofit sectors" throughout the world, they nonetheless exist in very different contexts and are linked to distinct histories, cultures, and political traditions.

Adding to the growing disputation in this field internationally is the confusion between form and function that has crept into the debate and the related problem of differentiating between function and intent. This often gives the discussion a heavy ideological tenor. Part of the problem here results from the fact that nonprofit or civil society organizations play different roles, some of which are considered more legitimate than others in the eyes of various observers. Thus, for example, third-sector organizations often deliver various services, such as health care, education, or relief from poverty. By relieving the symptoms of social distress, however, these organizations intentionally or unintentionally support the status quo by easing pressures for more basic change. Other third-sector organizations focus less on services and more on empowering the disadvantaged. Whether both sets of organizations should be considered part of the same "sector" and described with the same term thus becomes a matter of fierce ideological dispute (see, for example, Plowden 2001).

These complexities have given rise to at least four different "concepts" for characterizing the social space between the market and the state internationally. Each of these has become associated, moreover, whether fairly or unfairly, with a particular term or set of terms and often a particular part of the world.

Charitable, Nonprofit, or Voluntary Sector

Perhaps the oldest concept in this field has its roots in the Elizabethan Poor Law of 1601 and focuses on a set of services that are considered inherently "charitable." An illustrative list of these services was incorporated into the Statute of Charitable Uses, but these have since been extended and refined in the English common law tradition and modified as this tradition was extended to other countries. The central concept emphasizes organizations that deliver services to benefit the disadvantaged, the general public, or an appreciable segment of the public, and not merely those who own or operate the organization (Kendall and Knapp 1996). This has been reflected in legal provisions in many places prohibiting such organizations from distributing profits to their directors or members and in the use of terms such as *charitable, nonprofit,* or *voluntary* to depict this range of organizations.

Social Economy

A somewhat different concept of the nonprofit sector focuses less on the services that these organizations provide than on the ethos or philosophy that suffuses their operation. Of particular focus here has been the ethos of solidarity or mutuality emphasized in the concept of *social economy.* This concept of the nonprofit sector, which has had a particular following in continental Europe, especially those parts imbued with Catholic social doctrines, identifies the nonprofit sector as "all economic activities conducted by enterprises, primarily co-operatives, associations, and mutual societies, whose ethics convey the following principles: (1) placing service to its members or to the community ahead of profit; (2) autonomous management; (3) a democratic decision-making process; (4) the primacy of people and work over capital in the distribution of revenues" (Defourny, Develtere, and Fonteneau 1999:18). Unlike the nonprofit concept noted above, it embraces cooperative and mutual enterprises within the nonprofit sector even though these organizations distribute their profits to the organizations' members. Unlike for-profit firms, however, the distribution is based on membership rather than contributed capital.

Nongovernmental Organizations (NGOs)

A considerably different concept of the nonprofit sector is evident among those who begin from a conflict model of society and who see the nonprofit sector as the organized vehicle of citizen protest against dominant elites in both political and economic life. In this view, the nonprofit sector is preeminently a set of institutions designed to empower the disadvantaged and thereby alter the balance of social power (Korten 1990; Fisher 1993). This is thus a narrower concept of the nonprofit sector than that depicted by the term *nonprofit organization.* Indeed, it views many nonprofit service organizations as instruments of social control designed to alleviate the worst symptoms of unequal social conditions while keeping the sources of inequality intact. This concept is most common in treatment of the nonprofit sector in the developing world and tends to use the term *nongovernmental organization* (NGO) to depict the entities on which it focuses.

Civil Society

More recently, a somewhat different version of the conflict model of the nonprofit sector has taken hold. Embodied in the term *civil society* that gained prominence during the Central European struggle to overthrow state socialism in the 1980s and early 1990s, this concept extends the nonprofit sector beyond its organizational boundaries to encompass spontaneous citizen action designed to break the hold of dominant elites and social institutions (see, for example, Darcy de Oliveira and Tandon 1994). This formulation implies a critique even of NGOs, which themselves have come to be viewed in certain quarters as instruments of northern domination or sources of southern corruption (Hulme and Edwards 1997:7–11). In this view, only the people, the citizens, can speak for themselves. Nonprofit organizations, NGOs, governments, and the market are all subject to their own forms of repression and mission drift. Civil society, the space of citizen action, must therefore be kept open to serve as a control on these other institutions.

Clearly, given this degree of conceptual diversity and conflict, the development of a coherent research agenda for the nonprofit sector internationally has become a treacherous minefield. Scholars differ fundamentally about what the appropriate focus for research should be, let alone about what the empirical features of the field so defined might be. This is especially the case since at least some of the definitions require assessments not only of organizational structure and form but also of organizational intentions and performance. This naturally raises the danger of serious tautologies since it treats as "true" nonprofit organizations only the entities performing the functions that the particular observer considers appropriate. This makes it logically impossible, of course, to find nonprofit organizations that do not perform the specified functions. The "problem" of nonprofit sector performance therefore disappears by definition.

INCREASED POLICY SALIENCE

One possible reason for the growing contestation within the field of nonprofit sector studies is that this field has recently become more consequential as a result of shifts in the broader policy environment within which the field exists. These shifts have thrust nonprofit sector institutions into unaccustomed prominence near the center of contemporary policy debates. Three impulses in particular have played a role in this development: first, the emergence of a "new public management"; second, the growing popularity of the concept of "social capital"; and third, globalization.

The New Public Management

A central impetus for the changed policy position of the nonprofit sector internationally has been the growing political attractiveness of neoliberal public policies heralded by the election in the 1980s of Margaret Thatcher in the United Kingdom and Ronald Reagan in the United States. The centerpiece of this political perspective is an assault on the modern welfare state, on the concept of the state as the protector of human welfare (Palmer and Sawhill 1982). Needing an explanation for how social-welfare problems would be dealt with once government spending was cut and government social-welfare protections eliminated, Reagan and Thatcher pointed to the nonprofit sector and philanthropy as the answer, thus increasing the visibility and policy relevance of these long-neglected institutions (Salamon and Abramson 1982b).

Although the initial thrust of this neoliberal agenda was to dismantle the welfare state and shift its functions to the private sector, subsequent formulations embodied a broader notion of engaging the market in the solution of public problems through a combination of outsourcing and reliance on market-based incentives. These changes were advanced as ways to incentivize improved performance on the part of public employees and to restructure the state's relationships with those it serves. Thus was born a "new public management" inspired by "public choice" economic theories and dedicated to increasing citizen "choice" and improving the efficiency and effectiveness of public action (Tullock 1965; Schultze 1977; Osborne and Gaebler 1992; Terry 1998; Kettl 1997, 2000; LeGrand 1999).

Largely overlooked both in the neoliberal rhetoric and in the "new public management" enthusiasm it helped to feed was the extent to which key features of the new dispensation were already built into existing government operations. Certainly in the United States by the 1970s, behind the rhetoric of the welfare state lay an elaborate system of "third-party government" characterized by extensive government reliance on nonprofit and for-profit institutions to deliver publicly financed services in such fields as health, social services, and scientific research (Salamon and Abramson 1982a; Salamon 1987, 1995; Wolch 1990; Smith and Lipsky 1993). And similar patterns operated elsewhere as well (Salamon and Anheier 1994; Kramer 1981; James 1987; Anheier and Seibel 2001; Knapp, Hardy, and Forder 2001; Archambault 1996). What is more, research increasingly demonstrated that the management of the resulting systems of indirect government was every bit as difficult, and perhaps more so, than traditional public management (Kettl 1993; Salamon 2002).

Nevertheless, the rise of neoliberalism and the new public management thrust third-sector institutions into the middle of the public debate over the appropriate role of government in the latter part of the twentieth century. In the process, private, nonprofit organizations came to be seen as essential partners in making the new public management work. This led to experimentation with new contracting models (Ferlie 1996; McLaughlin, Osborne, and Ferlie 2002), new forms of "constructed markets" and "managed competition" (LeGrand 1999), and efforts to systematize the terms of engagement between the nonprofit sector and the state, such as New Labour's "Compact" in the United Kingdom (Mulgan 1999; Plowden 2001) or François Mitterand's policy of "insertion" to cope with the problems of long-term unemployment in France (Archambault 1996). More generally, activists across the political spectrum came to view cooperation with third-sector institutions as a critical part of a middle, or "third," way between sole reliance on the market and sole reliance on the state to cope with public problems (Giddens 1998).

These developments have affected the policy position of nonprofit sector organizations not only in advanced market economies. Similar shifts are also evident in the developing world, where they have been encouraged by structural adjustment policies pursued by the World Bank and northern aid agencies as well as by widespread frustrations on the part of development experts with top-down development policies pursued by corrupt or ineffective governments. This has led to a new emphasis on "assisted self-reliance" and "participatory development" (Uphoff 1988), and a "new policy agenda" stressing increased support for the private sector, both for-profit and nonprofit, to promote economic advance and governmental reform (Clarke 2003; UNDP 2002).

In short, thanks to the new public management and associated neoliberal economic policies, nonprofits are no longer seen as the poor cousin of the state or as some outmoded organizational form complementing state provision on the margins by meeting limited special demands for quasi-public goods (see Weisbrod 1977; Quadagno 1987; Esping-Anderson 1990). Rather, they have moved to the center of the policy debate and have come to be viewed as central instruments of development and welfare state reform.

TABLE 4.1. LEVEL OF INTERPERSONAL TRUST BY MEMBERSHIP IN VOLUNTARY ASSOCIATIONS

	Percentage of respondents who agree		
Number of memberships	"Most people can be trusted"	"One cannot be too careful"	Number of respondents (N = 36,321)
None	23	77	18,661 (100%)
One	30	70	9,114 (100%)
Two	40	60	4,056 (100%)
Three or more	51	49	4,930 (100%)

Source: European Value Survey, 2000, cited in Halman 2001.

The Social Capital Persuasion

If neoliberal economic policies and accompanying new public management approaches are one source of the new policy salience of third-sector organizations, recent concerns about the contributions these organizations make to "social capital" constitute a second. Where the former focuses on the service role of third-sector institutions, the latter focuses on their social-integrative and participatory function and the contribution they make to community building.

According to this line of thinking, economic growth and democratic government depend critically on the presence of social capital, on the existence of bonds of trust and norms of reciprocity that can facilitate social interaction (Coleman 1990:300–321; Putnam, Leonardi, and Nanetti 1993; Putnam 2000; Fukuyama 1995). Without such norms, contracts cannot be enforced or compromises sustained. Hence markets and democratic institutions cannot easily develop or flourish.

This line of argument was powerfully validated through an analysis of the progress of governmental decentralization in Italy by political scientist Robert Putnam and associates (1993). They found that the regions with high levels of trust and civic engagement were also the regions that exhibited the highest levels of political stability, governmental effectiveness, and economic growth. Most important for our purposes, Putnam and his colleagues traced the higher levels of trust in northern Italy compared to southern Italy to the far denser networks of voluntary associations in the northern region, confirming a conclusion reached nearly 170 years earlier by the French political philosopher Alexis de Tocqueville in his study of the United States.

This relationship between voluntary association and trust has since been validated further by the 1999–2000 wave of the European Value Survey.[1] According to this survey, for twenty-eight of the thirty-two participating countries, a positive and significant relationship holds between the number of associational memberships a person holds and that person's level of interpersonal trust (Anheier and Kendall 2002).[2] Respondents with three or more memberships were twice as likely to state that they trust people than those holding no memberships (table 4.1). Overall, there is an almost linear relationship between increases in membership and the likelihood of trusting people.

A similar survey in the United States reached a similar conclusion: nearly half (46 percent) of respondents with no memberships felt that people would try to take advantage of them as opposed to only 29 percent of those with five and more memberships (World Values Survey 2000). Participation in voluntary associations, it appears, creates greater opportunities for repeated "trust-building" encounters among individuals, an experience that is subsequently generalized to other situations.

This neo-Tocquevillian line of argument has created an additional rationale for serious attention to the state of "civil society" in both developed and developing societies, and policy makers have seized on it with relish, perhaps because it assigns responsibility for a wide range of social ills not to underlying inequalities of power or economic opportunity but to the lack of supportive social ties among the disadvantaged. This line of argument has provided a convenient explanation for rising levels of crime and poverty in the developed countries (Putnam 2000). It has had great appeal in the developing world as well where it offers an explanation for widespread poverty and underdevelopment that focuses on shortcomings among the people of the less developed regions rather than on unequal terms of trade, globalization, or the power of entrenched elites (Edwards 1999; Tarrow 1996; Howell and Pearce 2001).

A somewhat different version of the social capital line of argument has been embraced by some on the left, but for different reasons. In this formulation, civil society is viewed not as a vehicle for promoting solidarity, but as a set of mechanisms for mobilizing popular pressures for a more radical project of empowerment and change. Here the inspiration is not Tocqueville, but the Italian Marxist Antonio Gramsci, who viewed civil society as a legitimizing agent for challenging existing structures of power. This alternative conception finds reflection in David Korten's image of third- and fourth-generation civil society organizations that mobilize grassroots political power to produce systemic change at both the national and international levels, and in the work of other civil society activists as well (Korten 1990:120–128; Howell and Pearce 2001:33–36; Darcy de Oliveira and Tandon 1994; Fisher 1993).

Whichever line of argument is embraced, the social capital/civil society focus has contributed importantly to the growing policy salience of the nonprofit sector throughout the world (see Anheier 2004). Through it both conservatives and radicals have found common ground for investing in the development and growth of civil society institutions even though they may expect quite different consequences from their investments—the one greater social harmony and the other very likely just the opposite.

Globalization

A third impulse helping to move the nonprofit sector to the center of policy discourse in countries throughout the world has been the pervasive influence of "globalization," the growing international connectedness of people and institutions. Globalization has traditionally been seen as a force that is weakening the power of nation-states and increasing the influence of global corporations (Korten 1995; Friedman 2000). But many of the same developments that have helped create the global corporation have also opened the way for a global civil society, an extensive network of organizations operating at the transnational level and interacting with national governments, international organizations, and global corporations to shape public and private action (Boli and Thomas 1997; Keck and Sikkink 1998; Florini 2000; Clark 2001; Edwards 1999; Kriesberg 1997; Anheier, Glasius, and Kaldor 2001).

Among the more important of these developments have been the end of the Cold War and the rise of a multipolar world nominally dominated by a superpower committed to a minimalist, liberal state; the resulting growing importance of international forums organized by the United Nations system and others, which have provided opportunities for NGO participation and interaction (Kriesberg 1997; Kaldor, Anheier, and Glasius 2003a); the major expansion of democracy across many parts of the world, which has opened channels of political expression and sanctioned the growth of associations (Huntington 1991; Linz and Stepan 1996; Diamond 1997); the "thickening" of the international rule of law since the 1970s, which has facilitated the growth of human rights and environmental organizations such as Amnesty International, Human Rights Watch, and Greenpeace (Keck and Sikkink 1998); the general economic prosperity in the major world economies since the late 1940s, which fostered a broad value change emphasizing human rights, individual freedoms, environmental protection, and related lifestyle issues (Inglehart 1990; Berry 1999); and the enormous changes in telecommunications, which not only opened the way for the creation of the new global economy but also made global corporations more vulnerable in their home markets to charges of misconduct in far-off lands and significantly reduced the costs of organizing and achieving cross-national coordination (Salamon 1994; Clark 2001; Naughton 2001).

Taken together, these developments have opened an increasingly global "organizational space" for civil society organizations. Emerging civil society networks have effectively taken advantage of this space to mobilize popular pressures for greater environmental protection, for the elimination of land mines, for the expansion of human rights, and for fair labor practices on the part of multinational corporations. Their efforts have been legitimated, moreover, by international organizations, by nation-states desirous of promoting greater openness and a level playing field for their own businesses in far-off lands, and by corporations eager to forge partnerships with responsible civil society organizations to protect their own "reputational capital." All of this, again, has worked to advantage the policy agendas of third-sector organizations and increase their salience in the global policy debate.

A SIGNIFICANT PRESENCE: THE SCOPE AND STRUCTURE OF THE GLOBAL NONPROFIT SECTOR

Fortunately, the growing policy relevance of the nonprofit sector and the increased contestation over its nature and role have helped to trigger a considerable growth in basic knowledge about this set of institutions. To be sure, important gaps in this base of knowledge remain. Yet the data situation that Estelle James confronted twenty years ago when she undertook her survey of the international nonprofit sector has improved considerably in the intervening years.

In part, this has been due to early work by individual researchers on the United States (e.g., Rudney 1987; Salamon and Abramson 1982a), Germany (Goll 1991), France (Archambault 1984), and other countries (James 1982, 1984, 1987), and to the investment in basic data gathering made by nonprofit umbrella groups such as Independent Sector in the United States (Hodgkinson and Weizman 1982, 1993) and the National Council for Voluntary Organizations in England (Jas et al. 2002). It was not until the large-scale collaborative research undertaken through the Johns Hopkins Comparative Nonprofit Sector Project in some forty countries throughout the world, however, that major progress was made in generating a systematic body of comparative data on the nonprofit sector (Salamon and Anheier 1994; Salamon et al. 1999; Salamon, Sokolowski, and Associates 2004).

Toward an Operational Definition

A central challenge in this work, as James rightly observed, was "to redefine terms and categories in a way that is meaningful in other countries as well as the United States" (1987:398). To cope with this challenge, the Johns Hopkins Project adopted an inductive approach, building up its definition of the nonprofit sector from the actual experiences of the broad range of countries that the project covered. This involved a three-step process: first, the identification by researchers in participating countries of the kinds of entities that lie outside the market and the state and the different terms used locally to denote them; second, the creation of a grid comparing these various local pictures to each other, and the identification of the operational features shared by the largest portion of them; and finally, an in-country review of the extent to which these common features adequately

Box 4.1. The Structural-Operational Definition of the Nonprofit Sector

1. *Organized—i.e., institutionalized to some extent.* What is important is that the organization has some institutional reality to it. This is signified by some degree of internal organizational structure, relative persistence of goals, structure and activities, or meaningful organizational boundaries (e.g., some recognized difference between members and nonmembers). Purely ad hoc and temporary gatherings of people with no real structure or organizational identity are excluded.
2. *Private—i.e., institutionally separate from government.* Nonprofit organizations are not part of the apparatus of government. They are "nongovernmental" in the sense of being structurally separate from the instrumentality of government, and they do not exercise governmental authority, though they may receive significant public-sector funding.
3. *Self-governing—i.e., equipped to control their own activities.* Some organizations that are private and nongovernmental may nevertheless be so tightly controlled either by governmental agencies or private businesses that they essentially function as parts of these other institutions even though they are structurally separate. To meet this criterion, organizations must control their own activities to a significant extent, have their own internal governance procedures, and be able to cease operations on their own authority.
4. *Non-profit-distributing—i.e., not returning profits generated to their owners or directors.* Nonprofit organizations may accumulate profits in a given year, but the profits must be plowed back into the basic mission of the agency, not distributed to the organizations' owners, members, founders, or governing board.
5. *Non-compulsory—i.e., involving some meaningful degree of voluntary participation.* Participation in the organization must be based on free choice and not be mandated by law or accident of birth.

Source: Salamon and Anheier 1997; Salamon, Sokolowski, and Associates 2004

captured the nonprofit sector locally and an identification of any gaps or gray areas that might result from using these features to depict the third-sector scene in each site (Salamon and Anheier 1997).

Out of this process emerged a consensus on five structural and operational features that defined the nonprofit sector for the purposes of this project (box 4.1). This definition embraces within the nonprofit sector a broad set of institutions—educational institutions, hospitals, clinics, soup kitchens, advocacy groups, professional associations, business organizations, religious congregations, NGOs, cultural institutions, sports clubs, and many more. Moreover, since it uses an operational definition rather than a legal one, it embraces informal organizations that lack legal status as well as more formally constituted and registered organizations. The definition does not assume that any particular country will have all of these different types of entities, or even that the entities will take the same exact form in every locale. To the contrary, it is precisely in order to highlight the differences that result from differing social, political, and cultural traditions that a common definition is so necessary.

Scope and Structure of the Nonprofit Sector Cross-Nationally

Armed with this definition, researchers associated with the Hopkins project have made considerable headway in generating a systematic body of empirical data on the nonprofit sector in a broad assortment of countries, including fourteen advanced industrial countries, five transition countries in Central and Eastern Europe, and sixteen developing countries in Latin America, Africa, the Middle East, and South Asia.[3] In the process, a number of crucial dimensions of the nonprofit sector have come into much clearer focus (Salamon et al. 1999; Salamon and Anheier 1999; Salamon and Sokolowski 2004).

Size

In the first place, this research has documented the enormous size of the nonprofit sector. This is evident most clearly in the human resources that this set of organizations mobilizes in its work. In the thirty-five countries for which data were available when this chapter was prepared, the nonprofit sector accounted for a cumulative total of 39.5 million full-time workers, or an average of 4.4 percent of the economically active population in these countries. To put these figures into context, if the nonprofit sector in these countries were a separate national economy, its expenditures would make it the seventh largest economy in the world, ahead of Italy, Brazil, Russia, Spain, and Canada and just behind France and the United Kingdom.

While the nonprofit sector is a sizable force in these countries, there are considerable differences in size of the nonprofit sector from country to country. The nonprofit sector workforce—both paid and volunteer—thus varies from a high of 14 percent of the economically active population in the Netherlands to a low of 0.4 percent in Mexico (fig-

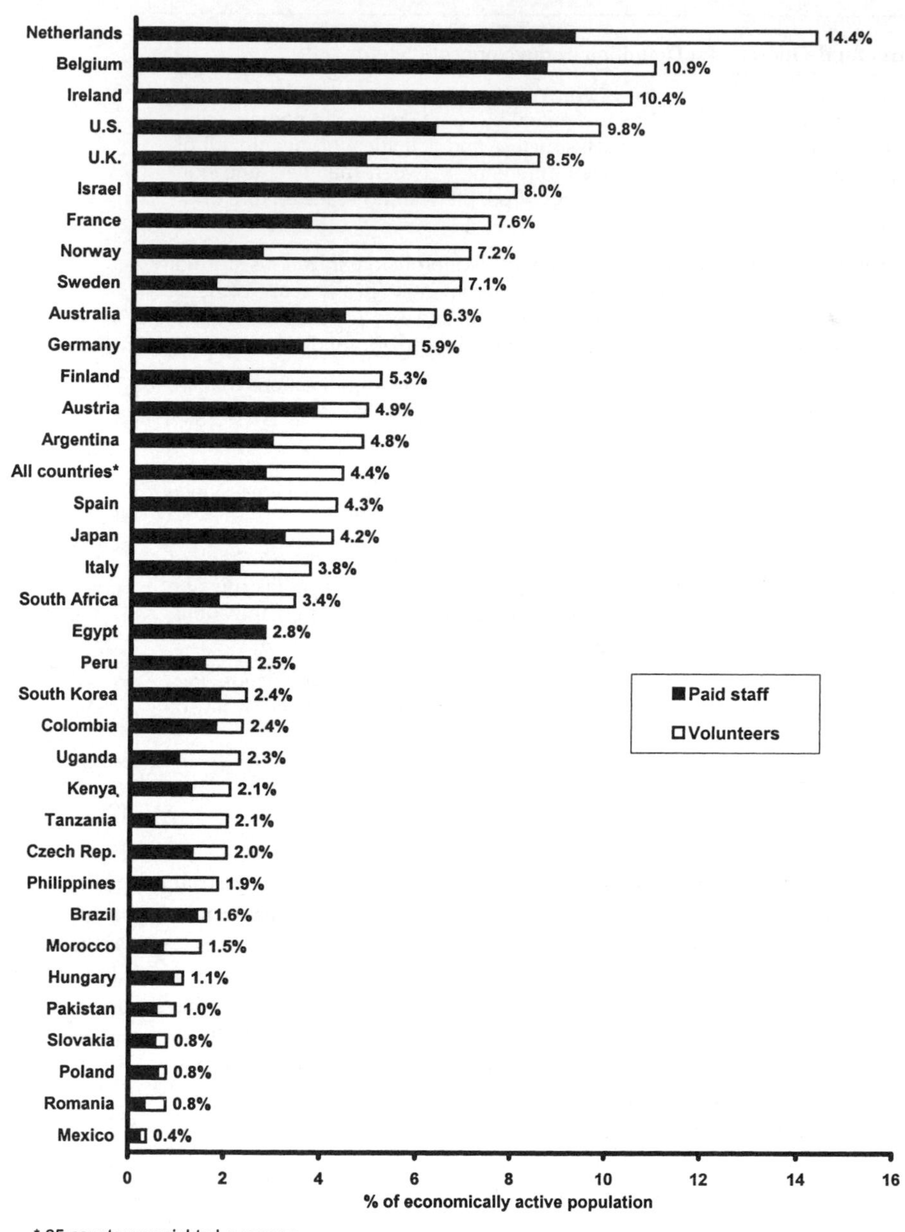

FIGURE 4.1. NONPROFIT WORKFORCE AS PERCENTAGE OF ECONOMICALLY ACTIVE POPULATION BY COUNTRY

ure 4.1). Interestingly, when measured as a share of the workforce, the United States does not have the largest nonprofit workforce in the world, as is commonly assumed. Indeed, three other countries of the thirty-five examined record proportionately larger nonprofit sector workforces, and all of these are in Western Europe.

A closer look at figure 4.1 also shows that the nonprofit sector is relatively larger in the more developed countries than in the less developed and transition countries, even when account is taken of volunteer effort. In fact, the nonprofit workforce in the developed countries averages proportionally more than four times larger than that in the developing countries (7.4 percent versus 1.7 percent of the economically active population).[4] This does not mean, of course, that the scale of the nonprofit sector is uniform even in the developed countries. To the contrary, there are intriguing variations in the scale of nonprofit activity there as well.

Composition

Nonprofit organizations are not simply places of work, whether paid or volunteer, of course. What makes them significant are the functions they perform, and these functions are multiple, as we have seen (Salamon 1999; Kramer 1981). What is more, many organizations engage in a variety of activities, making it especially difficult to provide a fully comprehensive picture of what this set of organizations does. Nevertheless, figure 4.2 provides a rough approximation of the composition of this set of organizations by grouping organizations according to their principal activity and then assessing the level of effort each such activity absorbs.[5] As this chart shows, nearly two-thirds of nonprofit activities are concentrated in essentially service functions, chiefly the traditional social-welfare services of education (23 percent of the workforce), social services (19 percent), and health (14 percent) (Salamon, Sokolowski, and List 2004; Salamon and Sokolowski 2004). At the same time, about one-third of the effort is concentrated in the sector's more expressive activities such as culture and recreation (19 percent), professional and business representation (7 percent), and civic advocacy and environmental protection (6 percent). If the organizations engaged in "development" work are counted as part of the expressive functions rather than the service functions (on the ground that they involve empowerment activities and not simply service delivery), the expressive functions swell to 40 percent of the effort and the service functions shrink to 56 percent.

While the dominance of service functions seems to hold for most countries, it is by no means uniform. For example, development work absorbs a substantially higher proportion of nonprofit activities in the developing countries than in the developed ones (16 percent versus 5 percent), and in the African countries this figure reaches 25 percent of the nonprofit workforce. This suggests an especially marked grassroots component of the nonprofit sector in these developing

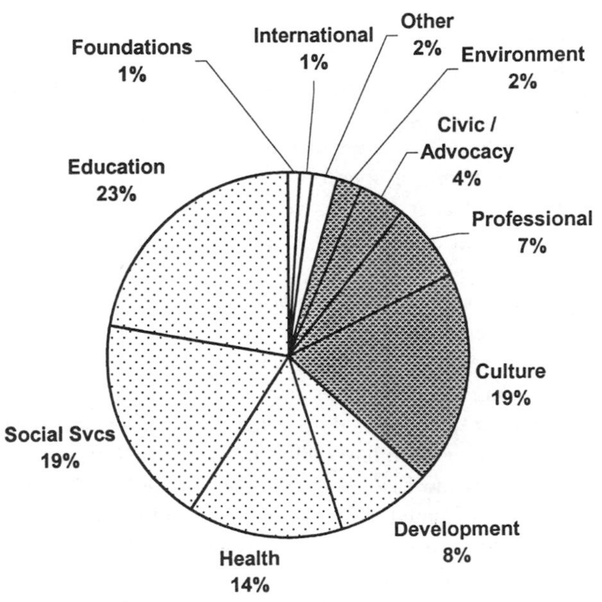

FIGURE 4.2. NONPROFIT WORKFORCE BY FIELD AND TYPE OF ACTIVITY

regions, particularly in Africa, and underlines again the distinction between the NGO-type organizations in these areas and the more assistance-oriented nonprofit service agencies. Even among the developed countries, moreover, significant differences are apparent. Thus, social services are especially prominent among the service offerings of nonprofit organizations in Western Europe, whereas health services are more prominent in the United States, Japan, Australia, and Israel. And in the Nordic countries and in Central Europe the expressive functions of the nonprofit sector are far more prominent than the service ones. This likely reflects the far more dominant role of the state in providing human services in these countries and, in the Scandinavian context, the vibrant heritage of citizen-based social movements and citizen engagement in advocacy, sports, and related expressive fields. Clearly, different societies have made different choices about how they handle crucial social functions, which makes the nonprofit sector an instructive vantage point from which to observe broader social realities.

Volunteer Inputs

Not only do countries vary in the size and role of their nonprofit sectors, but they also vary in the extent to which these organizations rely on paid as opposed to volunteer labor. This reflects in part the important variations that exist across countries in notions of what a volunteer is, which are closely related to aspects of culture and history. In Australia or the United Kingdom, volunteering is closely related to the concept of a voluntary sector—a part of society seen as separate from both the business sector and the statutory sector of government and public administration. This notion of voluntarism has its roots in the Lockean concept of a self-organizing society outside the confines of the state, a concept that created a strong association between voluntarism and democracy in the Anglo-Saxon countries. In other countries, however, the notion of volunteering is different, emphasizing communal service to the public good rather than democracy. The German term *Ehrenamt* (honorary office) comes closest to this tradition. In the nineteenth century, the modernization of public administration and the development of an efficient, professional civil service within an autocratic state under the reformer Lorenz von Stein allocated a specific role to voluntarism. Voluntary office in the sense of trusteeship of associations and foundations attracted the growing urban middle class (Pankoke 1994; Anheier and Seibel 2001). A vast network of associations and foundations emerged in the middle and late nineteenth century, frequently involving paid staff but run and managed by volunteers. But unlike in the United States, the German notion of voluntarism as a system of "honorary officers" developed in a still basically autocratic society where local and national democratic institutions remained underdeveloped. This trusteeship aspect of voluntarism came to be seen as separate from other voluntary service activities such as caring for the poor, visiting the sick, or assisting at schools, which remained the domain of the church and, increasingly, of the emerging workers' movement during the industrialization period.

Systematic information and knowledge about volunteering in non-Western countries is still sketchy, although it seems clear that the liberal, individualistic concept of voluntary, uncoerced action for the public good is historically bound to a very few countries such as the United States, the United Kingdom, Scandinavia, and the Netherlands, though Western notions of volunteering are gaining currency in countries as diverse as South Korea, Armenia, and Brazil, and at the international level as well. For South Korea, Chang-Ho (2002) reports that despite the long-standing historical roots of voluntarism, the concept became a fixture in the country's social and political scene only after the Asian Games of 1986 and the introduction of corporate volunteer programs. In Japan, it was the Kobe earthquake of 1995 that provided the impetus for a growth of voluntarism (Yamamoto 1997). For Armenia, Grigoryan (2002) suggests that while volunteering remains uncommon as a formal activity, spontaneous volunteer efforts appear more frequently. In the case of Brazil, DeLaMar (2000) shows the success of the Programa Voluntarios, created in 1995 as part of a larger effort to establish local councils that enlist different stakeholders from civil rights activists to business leaders, to engage in community problem solving. Finally, the United Nations, with its proclamation of 2001 as the International Year of the Volunteer, lent additional political weight to the increasingly global spread of voluntarism in the Western sense (Rhule 2001).

One of the few explicit studies of volunteering in Europe, conducted in 1995, found that 27 percent of the adult population in the nine countries studied (Belgium, Bulgaria, Denmark, Germany, Great Britain, Ireland, Netherlands, Slovakia, and Sweden) volunteered in the previous year (Gaskin and Smith 1997).[6] The level of volunteering among the adult population in the nine countries varied significantly, from a low of 12 percent in Slovakia to a high of 43 percent in the Netherlands. The most common area of volunteering was sports and recreation (28 percent of all volunteers), followed by social services (17 percent) (Gaskin and Smith 1997:28–31).

A more widely comparable measure of volunteer activity is available from the Johns Hopkins Comparative Nonprofit Sector Project, which gathered information for each field not only on the number of volunteers but also on the number of hours volunteered (Salamon, Sokolowski, and List 2004). It was thus possible to express volunteer time in terms of the full-time equivalent workers that it represented. Of the 39.5 million full-time equivalent nonprofit jobs identified by the Hopkins research teams, therefore, over 40 percent—16.8 million full-time equivalent workers—were volunteers.[7] This demonstrates the ability of nonprofit organizations to mobilize sizable amounts of volunteer effort.

While over 40 percent of the combined nonprofit workforce in the thirty-five countries for which data are available were volunteers, the percentages varied from a high of more than 75 percent in Sweden to a low of less than 3 percent in Egypt. Moreover, contrary to widespread beliefs, paid staff do not seem to displace volunteers. Rather, research by Salamon and Sokolowski (2003) shows a general tendency for volunteer involvement to *increase* as paid staff involvement increases (figure 4.3). This may reflect the fact that volunteering is not just an individual act but a social one: people volunteer at least in part to join together with others. What is more, volunteers must be mobilized and their involvement structured to be most effective, and this often requires permanent staff. This may also help to explain why the overall scale of volunteering tends to be higher in the developed countries (2.7 percent of the economically active population) than in the developing ones (0.7 percent). As figure 4.3 also shows, however, this pattern is by no means universal. The major deviations are the Nordic countries, where volunteering is exceptionally high despite the relatively limited scale of paid nonprofit employment. As already noted, this reflects the strong social movement tradition that helped to produce the Nordic welfare state.

Not only does the level of volunteer effort vary among countries, but also it varies among different functions. Thus, as a general rule paid staff are even more heavily involved in the service functions of the nonprofit sector than are the volunteers (72 percent versus 52 percent, respectively). Particularly noticeable is the role that volunteers play in cultural, recreational, civic, and environmental protection activity. Even in their service functions, volunteers appear to concentrate their efforts in different fields than do paid staff. In particular, volunteers focus disproportionately on social service and development activities. In fact, nearly half of all the work effort in these two fields is supplied by volunteers.

Revenue Structure

Recent work has also helped to clarify the revenue structure of the nonprofit sector at the international level. In her 1987 overview, James already noted the striking presence of government support for nonprofit service provision (1987:407). With the broader perspective now available through the Hopkins project, it is clear that heavy reliance on government support is particularly a feature of the Western European pattern of nonprofit sector development, whereas fees and commercial sources play a much larger role elsewhere. For the thirty-two developed and developing countries on which comparable revenue data were available at the time this chapter was prepared, over half of all revenue on average came from such fees and charges (figure 4.4; Salamon, Sokolowski, and List 2004). By comparison, public sector payments amounted to 35 percent of the total, while private philanthropy—from individuals, corporations, and foundations combined—accounted for a much smaller 12 percent.

Fee income is a particularly important source of nonprofit sector revenue in Latin America, Africa, and Central and Eastern Europe, as well as in the United States, Australia, and Japan. By contrast, public sector support is the most important source of income for the nonprofit sector in Western Europe. South Africa is the only developing country

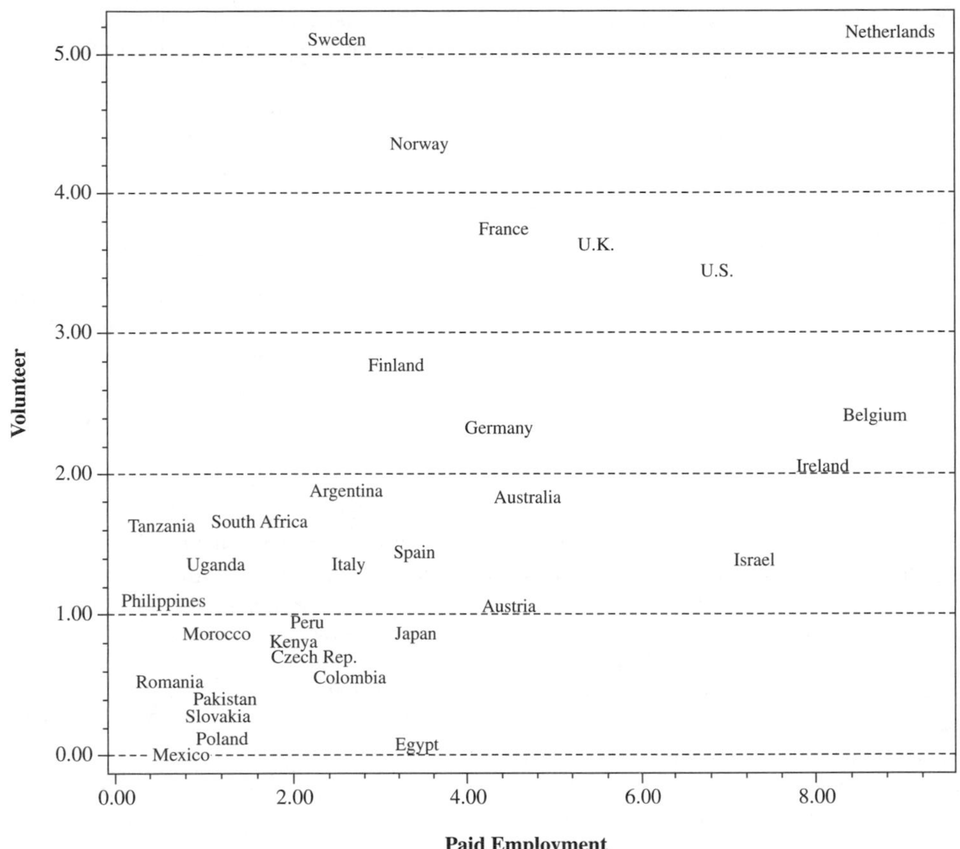

FIGURE 4.3. RELATIONSHIP BETWEEN SIZE OF PAID NONPROFIT EMPLOYMENT AND VOLUNTEER INPUT (AS PERCENTAGE OF ECONOMICALLY ACTIVE POPULATION)

where fee income is less important than government funding, reflecting the post-apartheid policy of supporting nonprofit institutions as a means of strengthening civil society.

This picture of nonprofit sector finance changes significantly, however, when volunteer time is factored into the equation and counted as a part of philanthropy. When this is done, philanthropy's share of total nonprofit sector support increases from 12 percent to 30 percent, edging government out of second place as a source of nonprofit sector revenue (Salamon, Sokolowski, and List 2004). This demonstrates how much more important contributions of time are to the support base of third-sector institutions as compared with contributions of money. This is particularly true in less developed regions, where monetary resources are limited. But it also holds in the Nordic countries as well, where volunteer work is particularly widespread.

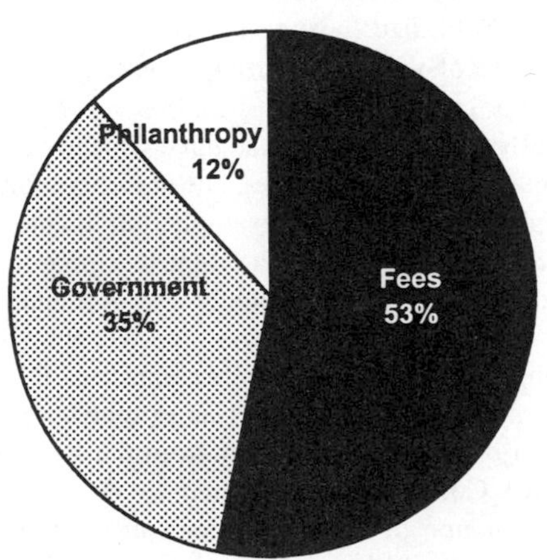

FIGURE 4.4. SOURCES OF REVENUE FOR NONPROFIT SECTOR, 32-COUNTRY AVERAGE

Recent Trends

Not only is the nonprofit sector quite immense in a significant range of countries around the world, but also its scale and presence appear to be expanding substantially. One sign of this is the growth in the number of such organizations. The number of associations formed in France, for example, increased from approximately 10,000 per year in the 1960s and early 1970s to 40,000–50,000 per year in the 1980s and 1990s (Archambault 1996). Similar striking growth was recorded in the number of nonprofit sector institutions in Italy in the 1980s, as new forms of "social cooperatives" took shape to supplement strained state social-welfare institutions (Barbetta 1997). Developments in Central and Eastern Europe and in much of the developing world were even more dramatic since they often started from a smaller base (see, for example, Landim 1998; Fisher 1993; Ritchey-Vance 1991:28–31).

The number of organizations is a notoriously imperfect variable through which to gauge the growth of this sector, however, since organizations vary so fundamentally in size and complexity. What is more, the apparent growth in numbers of organizations may really reflect a change in legal procedures for registering entities that previously existed in a more informal state.

Regrettably, however, reliable time-series data on the more tangible dimensions of the nonprofit sector have been lacking for all but a handful of countries, though such data may become more generally available as a consequence of the 2003 issuance by the United Nations Statistics Division of a new *Handbook on Nonprofit Institutions in the System of National Accounts.* This *Handbook* calls on national statistical offices to prepare a "satellite account" on the nonprofit sector as part of their regular economic data gathering and reporting (Salamon and Tice 2003). Already as of this writing nineteen countries have adopted this *Handbook* and have produced or plan to produce such satellite accounts.

Even without these more comprehensive data, however, initial investigation through the Johns Hopkins Comparative Nonprofit Sector Project documented a striking increase in the scale of the nonprofit sector in the early 1990s. Focusing on seven countries for which time-series data could be assembled for 1990 and 1995 on a consistent range of organizations, researchers within the Hopkins project found that employment within the nonprofit sector increased from an average of 3.5 percent of nonagricultural employment in 1990 to 4.5 percent in 1995 (table 4.2; Salamon et al. 1999). Put somewhat differently, employment in the nonprofit sector grew by an average of 29 percent in these seven countries between 1990 and 1995, whereas overall employment grew by only 8 percent. At the same time, volunteering and membership rates expanded as well. In fact, despite the attention generated by political scientist Robert Putnam's assertion that Americans and others are increasingly "bowling alone," all seven countries reported increases in volunteering and membership affiliation rates.

TABLE 4.2. INDICATORS OF NONPROFIT SECTOR GROWTH, 1990–1995

	Indicator					
	Total paid employment (%)		Percentage of population volunteering		Percentage of population holding memberships	
Country	1990	1995	1990	1995	1990	1995
Hungary	0.8	1.3	5	7	44	N/A
Japan	2.5	3.5	12	N/A	27	46
Sweden	2.5	2.6	36	51	84	91
Germany	3.7	4.9	13	26	64	77
U.K.	4.0	6.2	34	48	47	53
France	4.2	4.9	19	23	36	43
U.S.	6.9	7.8	37	49	59	79
Average	3.5	4.5	24	29	53	65

Source: Johns Hopkins Comparative Nonprofit Sector Project.

A Multidimensional Phenomenon

From what has been said, it should be clear that the nonprofit sector is a multidimensional phenomenon that cannot be captured fully by any single measure. This is consistent with the insight of neo-institutionalism, which emphasizes that organizational structures and forms are rooted in the context in which they operate (Powell and DiMaggio 1991). As these contexts vary substantially, so do the patterns of nonprofit sector development that result.

This multidimensionality of the nonprofit sector is clearly evident in figure 4.5, which compares the "shape" of the nonprofit sector in a number of countries along three different dimensions:

- the number of full-time equivalent *employees* in the nonprofit sector per 1,000 people in the labor force (economic measure)
- the number of people *volunteering* as a percent of the total adult population (participation measure)
- the number of people holding *membership* in nonprofit organizations and voluntary associations as a percent of the adult population (social capital measure)

Combining these measures yields three-dimensional representations of the nonprofit sector that vary in terms of their overall size and their individual dimensions (see figure 4.5).

First, in terms of "volume," or size, there are smaller cubes for Hungary, Italy, and Japan, and larger ones for Sweden, the United Kingdom, and the United States, with Germany and France ranking in between. Among the countries included here, Sweden, which ranks low in terms of nonprofit employment, nevertheless ranks second largest in overall nonprofit size (next to the United States) once account is taken of volunteer participation and organizational membership.

Second, in some countries, the three dimensions are about equal, whereas in other countries, one or two dominate. Thus, in the United Kingdom, for example, employment, volunteering, and membership data suggest a nonprofit sector rooted both in the service economy *and* in social participation. The overall result is a relatively perfect cube-like structure. Hungary represents the other extreme. Its nonprofit sector in the early 1990s was based primarily on membership, much of which carried over from the socialist period (Kuti 1996). Consequently, the three-dimensional representation of its nonprofit sector has a long and narrow shape.

Third, the overall shape or proportionality of the three dimensions appears more similar among some countries than others. France and Germany are more similar to each other

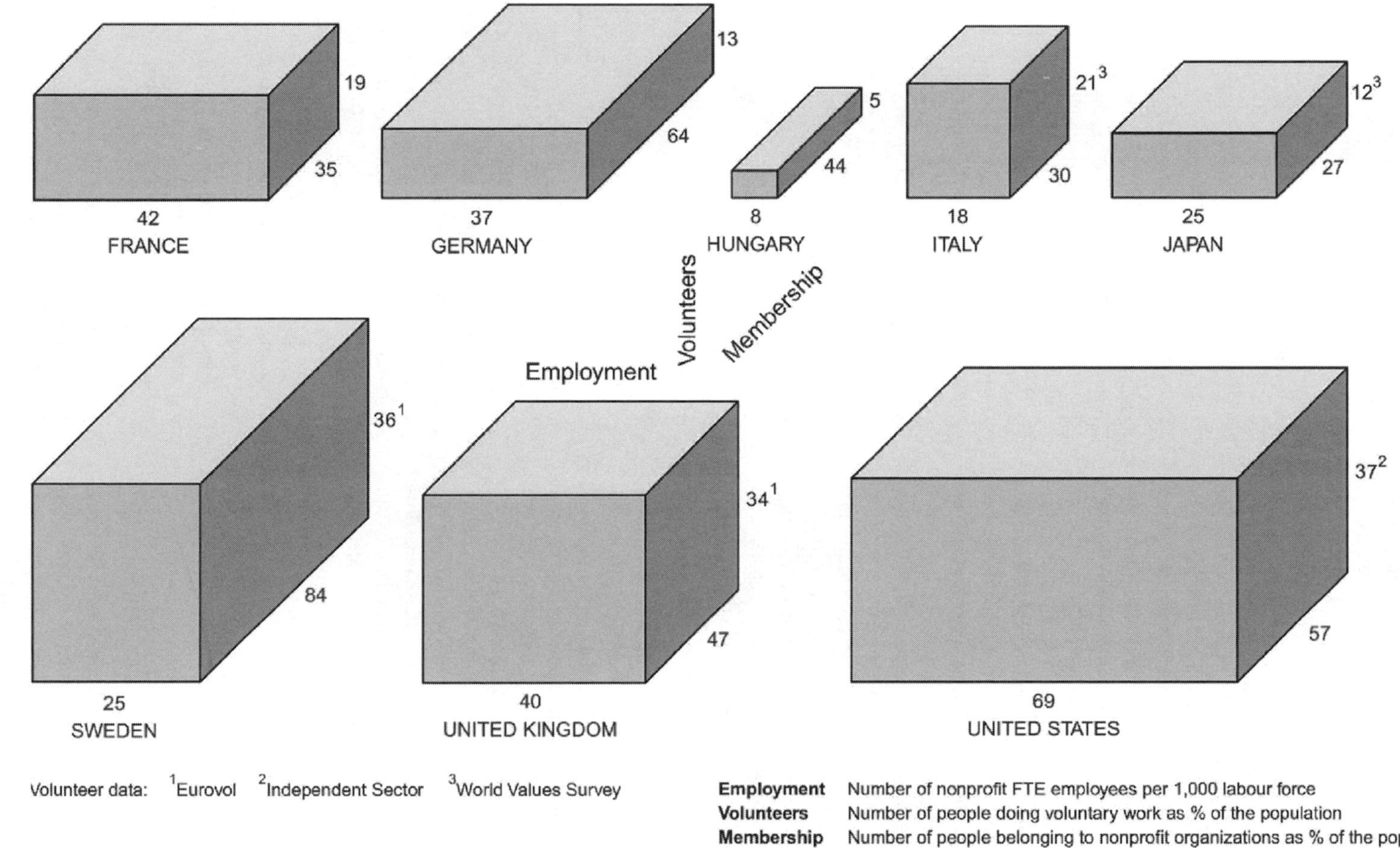

FIGURE 4.5. DIMENSIONS OF THE NONPROFIT SECTOR IN EIGHT COUNTRIES

than to any of the other countries in figure 4.5. The same holds for the United Kingdom and the United States, and for Hungary and Sweden, with membership being the characteristic feature for the latter pair. Japan and Italy are exceptions; the former resembles both France and the United States, the latter resembles the United Kingdom and Sweden.

Fourth, and related to the previous point, some countries are similar to each other along some dimensions but diverge along others. France and Germany, for example, are similar in that their nonprofit sectors rank fairly high in terms of employment and lower in terms of volunteering. They differ, however, in membership, with Germany's nonprofit sector far more membership-oriented than its French counterpart. Sweden and the United States are similar in the social dimensions of their nonprofit sectors: high levels of membership combined with high levels of volunteering. They differ dramatically in the direct economic importance of the sector, with the Swedish employment figures well below the American ones.

These patterns suggest the need for a complex matrix in order to compare and contrast the nonprofit sector from place to place. One potentially fruitful approach to this task is suggested in Salamon and Sokolowski's work (2004) in formulating a composite index of civil society development based on three different dimensions—capacity, sustainability, and impact—each of which, in turn, embodies a number of different measures. Thus, the capacity dimension measures the nonprofit sector's employment level, the diversification of its employment, its mobilization of volunteers, and its stimulation of charitable resources. The sustainability dimension measures the sector's financial base, its level of popular support (as reflected in memberships and share of population volunteering), and the supportiveness of the legal environment in which it operates. The impact dimension measures the share of various services (e.g., health, education) the nonprofit sector provides and the sector's involvement in expressive functions. By combining these measures, Salamon and Sokolowski were able to construct a composite index that locates various countries in relation to each other in terms not of a single dimension but of the multiple dimensions along which it is appropriate to measure this complex set of institutions (table 4.3).

TABLE 4.3. CIVIL SOCIETY ORGANIZATION INDEX (PRELIMINARY)

Country	Dimension			Composite score
	Capacity	Sustainability	Impact	
Netherlands	81	97	91	90
Belgium	68	90	82	80
US	88	68	63	73
Sweden	73	63	80	72
Israel	79	72	60	70
Ireland	69	65	74	69
Norway	65	63	72	67
UK	75	57	64	65
Finland	55	65	57	59
Australia	58	56	55	57
Germany	51	60	54	55
France	61	48	55	55
Argentina	50	47	64	54
Spain	57	41	49	49
Japan	44	47	55	49
Austria	43	54	42	47
Tanzania	51	36	51	46
South Korea	36	52	50	46
South Africa	47	34	48	43
Italy	39	45	44	43
Kenya	48	40	40	42
Brazil	34	38	46	40
Hungary	41	45	32	39
Czech Rep.	39	39	37	39
Colombia	41	30	39	37
Philippines	31	33	41	35
Slovakia	35	31	33	33
Peru	36	30	33	33
Romania	30	38	31	33
Poland	34	34	31	33
Mexico	26	39	27	31
Country average	51	50	52	51

Source: Johns Hopkins Comparative Nonprofit Sector Project, cited in Salamon and Sokolowski 2004

Transnational Civil Society

Apart from its varying national manifestations, the nonprofit sector is also increasingly a transnational presence, and this dimension, too, has recently come into better focus (see Boli, this volume; Boli and Thomas 1997; Keck and Sikkink 1998; Florini 2000; Anheier and Themudo 2002). For one thing, we have come to understand better the scale and complexity of individual transnational civil society organizations. Examples include Amnesty International, with more than one million members, subscribers, and regular donors in more than 140 countries and territories; Friends of the Earth Federation, which combines about 5,000 local groups and one million members; and the Climate Action Network, which has established partners and national coalitions engaged in advocacy campaigns and public education in nearly 40 countries. Similarly, Care International is now an organization with over 10,000 professional staff. Its U.S. affiliate alone has income of around $450 million. The International Union for the Conservation of Nature brings together 735 NGOs, 35 affiliates, 78 states, 112 government agencies, and some 10,000 scientists and experts from 181 countries in a unique worldwide partnership.

The number of international NGOs (INGOs) has also expanded dramatically, beginning in the 1970s and accelerating after 1990 (figure 4.6). What is more, formal organizational links between INGOs and international organizations like the United Nations Development Program (UNDP), the World Health Organization (WHO), and the World Bank have also increased (Glasius, Kaldor, and Anheier 2002:330).

This growth in INGOs reflects the significant opening of the international environment for civil society organizations that has resulted from the end of the Cold War, growing popular concerns about human rights and environmental protection, and the emergence of international forums such as the succession of special United Nations conferences through

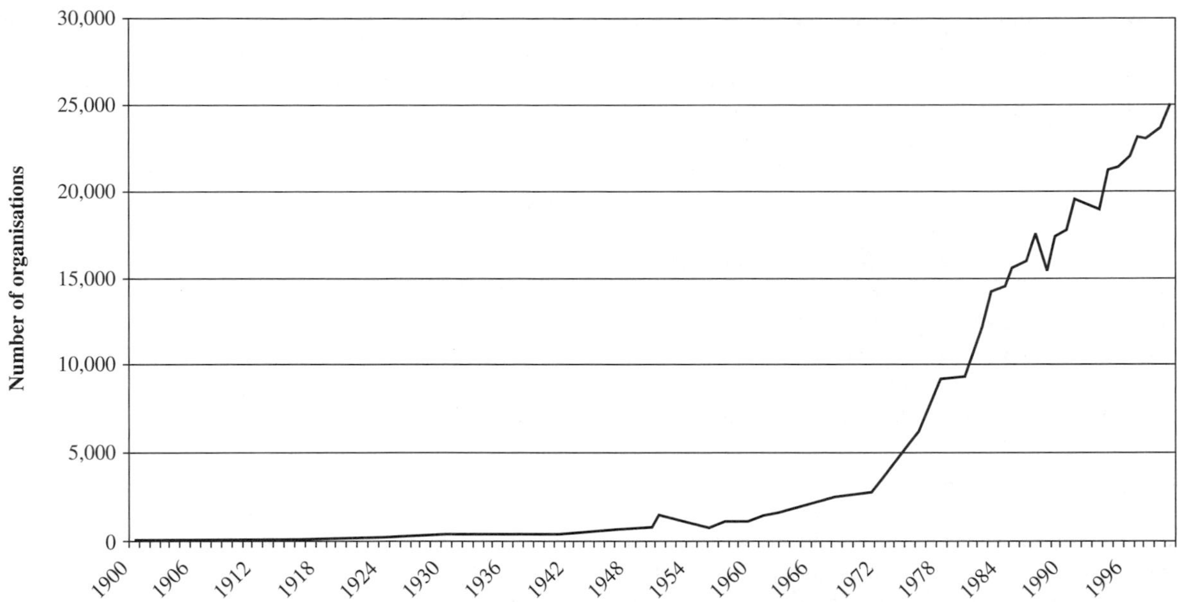

FIGURE 4.6. GROWTH IN INTERNATIONAL NONGOVERNMENTAL ORGANIZATIONS, 1900–2000 (ALL ACTIVE ORGANIZATIONS)
Source: Union of International Associations, cited in Anheier, Glasius, and Kaldor 2001b, and Kaldor, Anheier, and Glasius 2003b.

which INGOs can exert influence and demonstrate their worth (Keck and Sikkink, 1998; Clark 2001, 2003; Edwards 1999; Lindenberg and Bryant 2001; Kriesberg 1997; Edwards and Hulme 1996). Whatever the causes, this opening of a transnational and increasingly global "organizational space" and the greater recognition of cross-border needs (e.g., environmental protection, human rights) have provided an extraordinary opportunity for nonprofit development and growth at the transnational level.

EXPLAINING THE PATTERNS OF NONPROFIT SECTOR DEVELOPMENT

Considerable progress has thus been achieved on the "data front" in the struggle to comprehend the nonprofit sector cross-nationally. But can we say the same for our progress in the theoretical realm? To what extent have the economic models that have long dominated conceptual work in this field been confirmed or challenged by researchers? What new theoretical perspectives have been brought to bear and with what results? Clearly, it is even more difficult to summarize developments here. Nevertheless, several lines of theoretical evolution are evident.

The Growing Awareness of Multidimensionality

Perhaps the most significant development in the evolution of theoretical comprehension of the world's nonprofit sector has been the growing recognition of its multidimensional character. In fact, this has been one of the direct outgrowths of the greater empirical study of the sector in a broad cross section of countries. In a sense, the more we have learned about the nonprofit sector in different countries, the more aware we have become of the cross-national differences. This outcome may seem paradoxical at first since systematic cross-national research has to start with a common understanding of the phenomenon to be studied. Far from dictating a common conclusion about the shape of this phenomenon from place to place, however, this is the only way to document, and hence highlight, its variations. And that is just what the research reported above has done.

What this underscores, however, is the need for theory that can account not just for one dimension of the nonprofit sector, but for multiple dimensions. Whether any single theory can do this is obviously doubtful. At the least, it is unlikely that any monocausal theory will suffice. The empirical findings have thus complicated the task of theory-building. With more to explain, it is inevitable that the more elegant theories will find it harder to account for the known facts.

Elaborations on the Economic Theories

This growing complexity of the nonprofit sector theoretical debate is clearly evident in the efforts to apply many of the early economic theories formulated in the United States to cross-national variations. At their core, these theories sought to reconcile the presence of nonprofit institutions in market democracies with the central precepts of classical economics. They therefore had the luxury of holding constant many of the things that vary fundamentally in cross-national settings—cultural norms, the presence of a market, democratic forms of governance, basic economic relationships and property rights, religious traditions, and general levels of economic development. Perhaps because of this, they tended to focus on the service functions of the nonprofit sector since other functions were assumed to be handled by other institutions, such as democratic governments. The presence or absence of nonprofit institutions in these theories was thus attributed to variations in the demand for, and supply of, public and quasi-public goods. Work by Weisbrod (1977, 1988), Hansmann (1987), Rose-Ackerman (1996), Anheier and Ben-Ner (1997), and Ben-Ner and Gui (2003) thus identified several demand and supply conditions that favor the establishment of nonprofit organizations relative to public agencies and/or for-profit firms. For example, the presence of differentiated demand for public and quasi-public goods was hypothesized to increase the demand for nonprofit institutions because democratic governments can only respond to the demands for such goods that enjoy majority support, leaving significant "unsatisfied" demand that nonprofits can fill. Similarly, significant information asymmetries make it dangerous to rely on profit-seeking enterprises in fields where the consumer of services is not the purchaser (e.g., nursing-home care), since such firms have an incentive to take advantage of ill-informed purchasers. Because nonprofits are prohibited from distributing their profits they are more trustworthy providers in such circumstances.

In her 1987 assessment of the theoretical basis for cross-national variations in nonprofit scale, James already identified a number of limitations of these prevailing theories for explaining cross-national differences and offered a number of elaborations that helped account for the apparent anomalies. For one thing, she acknowledged that the "differentiated demand" explanations of nonprofit development might apply better to developed than developing countries and suggested a supplementary "excess demand" argument to explain the presence and structure of the nonprofit sector in the developing world (James 1987:401). Beyond this, James formulated an additional "supply-side theory" that called attention to variations not only in the demand for nonprofit services but also in the supply of entrepreneurs willing to come forward to meet this demand, and to meet it by forming nonprofit as opposed to for-profit institutions. This latter, she argued, was closely related to the religious traditions at work in different countries, and particularly to the degree of religious competition, since the incentive to form nonprofit organizations was closely tied to efforts to win converts and adherents to one's religious tradition. In addition, James acknowledged the substantial presence of public funding of nonprofit activity in many developed countries, something largely overlooked or treated as an aberration in the prevailing demand-side theories, which assumed that substantial nonprofit sectors would develop mainly where governmental involvement was lacking. To explain the coexistence of nonprofit provision and government funding, James formulated a separate set of explanations for why governments might prefer nonprofit over pure public production of public goods.

Suggestive though these insights were, however, they were not integrated into either a full-scale critique of the prevailing theories or a fully developed alternative theory. As James (1987:405) noted, such integration and theory testing had to await the development of more comprehensive data on the scope and scale of this sector in different national settings and on the many other variables identified as important in the existing theories. Fortunately, such data have become more plentiful, and considerable further theoretical progress has been made.

Empirical Testing of the Economic Theories

Perhaps most fundamentally, with the increased availability of systematic cross-national data, it has been possible to subject the prevailing economic theories to more rigorous empirical testing. To be sure, the significant practical barrier to such testing cited by James remains: many of the core explanatory variables cited by these theories—such as the degree of cultural heterogeneity, the presence or absence of religious conflict, and hence the potential motivations for the appearance of nonprofit entrepreneurs—are extremely difficult to measure.

Nevertheless, Salamon and Anheier (1998) and Salamon and Sokolowski (2002) have made considerable progress in testing these economic theories against the data generated by the Johns Hopkins Comparative Nonprofit Sector Project, focusing on cross-national variations in the size and financing of the nonprofit sector. More specifically:

- Demand heterogeneity was measured directly in terms of ethno-linguistic diversity and indirectly in terms of the scale of government social-welfare spending, since the demand heterogeneity argument predicts that popular support for government provision of public goods will be more limited, and hence the demand for nonprofit services greater, where considerable population diversity exists (Weisbrod 1977, 1988).
- The supply side theory was tested with a measure of religious diversity, since this theory predicts that religiously inspired individuals are the most common source of nonprofit entrepreneurs and that they are most likely to come forward to form nonprofit institutions where they are in competition for adherents (James 1987).
- Trust theory was tested using a measure of a country's degree of trust in business, since this theory predicts that nonprofits are likely to emerge where the non-profit-distribution constraint is needed to generate confidence that services will be provided adequately because information asymmetries give for-profit businesses an opportunity to take advantage of consumers (Hansmann 1987).

The results of these tests raise significant questions about the validity of these theories cross-nationally. While a significant relationship was discovered between the size of the nonprofit sector and demand heterogeneity, the crucial relation with government social-welfare spending was the opposite of what the demand heterogeneity argument suggested: instead of decreasing as government social-welfare spending rises, the size of the nonprofit sector *increases*. Beyond this, the data did not confirm the expectation of the demand heterogeneity theory that the size of the nonprofit sector is positively related to the level of private philanthropic support. To the contrary, the more dependent the nonprofit sector of a country is on private philanthropy the smaller the sector is, a finding that confirms James's observation about the importance of public funding to the growth of nonprofit institutions (1987).

The results with respect to the supply side theory were more consistent. The scale of the nonprofit sector cross-nationally does seem to vary directly with the extent of religious diversity, as the supply side theory would predict. Curiously, however, this relationship failed to hold in the education field, the one where James predicted it would be in clearest evidence.

Nor did the trust theory find much support in the evidence. No measurable relationship was found between a country's relative degree of trust in nonprofits (as opposed to business) and either the size of its nonprofit sector or the extent of nonprofit reliance on fees to support their activities.

To be sure, the measures so far available to test these various theories are far from perfect. What is more, the fact that these theories do not explain cross-national patterns of nonprofit development does not mean that they lack power to explain micro-level variations within countries or macro variations among subsets of countries. After all, many of these theories were developed in the context of liberal democratic market societies and it is perhaps not surprising that they would not work as well in other settings.

At the same time, the empirical tests of the existing economic theories, though far from perfect, nevertheless suggest strongly the need for additional theoretical perspectives to explain the overall growth and cross-national variations in nonprofit sector size, composition, and financing from place to place.

Macro Theories

One such alternative line of theoretical development focuses on various macro explanations of nonprofit sector evolution. These theories seek to explain the overall patterns of the nonprofit sector around the world in terms of broad social, economic, or cultural developments. To the extent that they account for variations in growth from place to place or region to region, they do so in terms of the relative presence or absence of the factors thought to be propelling the worldwide developments.

One such body of theory traces the growth of the third sector to the emergence of a "world polity" and an integrating global culture emphasizing universalism, individualism, rational voluntary authority, a particular view of progress, and world citizenship (Boli and Thomas 1997:180–182). According to this line of theory, this set of values has gained ascendance on the world stage through the work of a particular subset of nonprofit organizations—namely a new class of transnational nongovernmental organizations—whose "primary concern" is "enacting, codifying, modifying, and propagating world-cultural structures" (Boli and Thomas 1997:174). These transnational organizations have, in turn, prompted the creation of counterpart organizations in particular nations as societies struggle to keep pace with an evolving set of international norms. The growth of civil society organizations within various countries is thus seen, from this perspective, as the unfolding of a global cultural narrative propagated by a particular set of international organizations.

A more virulent version of this same line of argument attributes the growth of at least some types of civil society organizations not just to universalism and individualism but to a particular ideology and set of global actors—namely global corporations and their ideology of market capitalism. The promotion of philanthropy, voluntarism, and nonprofit service organizations is viewed from this perspective as part of a broader neoliberal project aimed at undercutting traditional social institutions that might offer potential resistance to powerful market forces and at weakening support for state institutions that might tax capital on behalf of the disadvantaged (Howell and Pearce 2001). Western notions of civil society are thus viewed as "biased" by failing to distinguish adequately between citizen-based action and assistance-oriented nonprofit organizations that function as instruments of domination rather than liberation (Fowler 2002).

In between these more abstract explanations lies a middle range of theories that attribute the international growth of the nonprofit sector to a variety of more concrete factors. Salamon (1994), for example, identifies "four crises" and "two revolutions" that have come together in the period since the early 1970s to propel the emergence of nonprofit organizations throughout the world. The four crises—including the crisis of the welfare state, the crisis of development, the crisis of the market, and the crisis of state socialism—underlined the inability of either the state or the market to cope on their own with the serious public challenges facing humanity in the late twentieth century. They occasioned a search for alternative forms of response, alternatives that in many cases involved enlisting grassroots energies and popular initiative through civil society organizations. These demand factors coincided, moreover, with two revolutions that helped guarantee that such organizations would be formed—the revolution in communications technology, and the revolution of rising expectations among a new class of educated elites frustrated by the lack of political and economic opportunities in their societies and eager for new opportunities. Combined with the support of outside actors such as the Catholic Church in Latin America and Western foundations and development agencies, which found it advantageous to provide resources to new types of nongovernmental organizations dedicated to fostering development, organizing the poor, or enhancing the environment in developed or transitional countries, the result was a striking surge in the formation of civil society organizations in disparate parts of the world, as well as the forging of growing connections among these organizations.

Social Origins Theory

Finally, Salamon and Anheier (1998) and Salamon and Sokolowski (2002, 2003a) have sought to reconcile the evidence of general growth of the nonprofit sector with the equally striking reality of significant variations in the scope, scale, composition, and revenue base of the nonprofit sector through an application of the "social origins" perspective originally formulated by Barrington Moore, Jr. (1966). This perspective emphasizes the embeddedness of the nonprofit sector in the cultural, religious, political, and economic realities of different countries. It thus views decisions about whether to rely on the market, the nonprofit sector, or the state for the provision of key services as not simply open to choice by individual consumers in an open market (as advocates of the economic theories seem to suggest). Rather, it views these choices as heavily constrained by prior patterns of historical development and by the relative power of various social groupings that have significant stakes in the outcomes of these decisions.

According to the social origins theory, therefore, the size and character of the nonprofit sector in any society is "path-dependent": it reflects not only current pressures and developments but also historical patterns of social and economic evolution that make certain outcomes far more likely than others (Salamon and Sokolowski 2002). Of particular importance according to this body of theory is the relative influence of a particular constellation of actors: landed elites, urban middle-class elements, the rural peasantry, the urban working class, the state, organized religion, and external actors such as colonial powers (Moore 1966; see also Rueschemeyer, Stephens, and Stephens 1992). To understand the current nature of the nonprofit sector, it is therefore necessary to delve into this sector's "social origins," the pattern of relations among these various actors that have influenced the role that this sector plays. According to this social origins theory, moreover, while these patterns are in some respects unique to particular countries, they are not infinitely varied or sui generis. Rather, certain uniformities can be detected in the broad contours of evolution, if not in the specific events and actors in each country. The challenge of theory-building in this field is thus to identify these uniformities and the links between them and nonprofit sector development.

While far from fully elaborated, this set of concepts has already yielded some rich insights into the historical factors that explain a number of significant features of nonprofit sector evolution. More specifically, Salamon and Anheier (1998) have suggested a fourfold division of "nonprofit regime types"—liberal, social democratic, statist, and corporatist—building on a typology of welfare regimes originally developed by Esping-Andersen (1990). Each of these regime types is characterized by a particular combination of state and nonprofit roles and by a particular structure, composition, and financing of the nonprofit sector. More importantly, each can be traced to a particular constellation of social forces. Table 4.4 differentiates these regimes in terms of two of their key dimensions—first, the extent of government social-welfare spending, and second, the scale of their nonprofit sector.

TABLE 4.4. THIRD SECTOR REGIME TYPES

Public social-welfare spending as percentage of GDP	Civil society employment as percentage of economically active population	
	Low	High
Low	Statist	Liberal
High	Social Democratic	Corporatist

The *liberal model* is characterized by a relatively low level of government social-welfare spending and a relatively large nonprofit sector. This is the pattern predicted by the economic theories of the nonprofit sector in societies with substantial social heterogeneity. The social origins theory attributes this result, rather, to a more complex set of social circumstances associated with a strong commercial middle class that has effectively neutralized both landed elites and the working class, and that is consequently able to resist demands for expanded government social-welfare benefits. Where these circumstances coexist with religious influences stressing individualism and with religious communities that place a premium on institutionalization (e.g., Christianity and Judaism as contrasted with Hinduism), the result is likely to be relatively limited public social-welfare provision and extensive reliance instead on a private nonprofit sector financed extensively by private charity.

The *social democratic model,* by contrast, is characterized by extensive state-sponsored and state-delivered social-welfare protections and a relatively limited service-providing private nonprofit sector. This is the pattern that the economic theories attribute to circumstances of cultural homogeneity, where demands for public goods are fairly uniform and where majorities can consequently be mustered in support of public provision of them. The social origins theory traces the roots of this pattern to a more complex set of historical circumstances—that is, situations where working-class elements are able to mobilize effective political power in a context of limited church influence and a weakened landed upper class. Where these circumstances exist, middle-class elements can be persuaded to accept widespread governmentally financed and delivered social-welfare services. While the upshot is a limited service-providing nonprofit sector, the social origins theory is able to explain what turns out to be a sizable expressive nonprofit sector in such settings. Indeed, it is precisely the presence of strong nonprofit organizations that explains the existence of the social democratic welfare state.

In between these two models are two additional ones that have tended to be overlooked in the prevailing economic theories, but which turn out to be among the most common at the international level. One of these, the *corporatist model,* is characterized by sizable government social-welfare spending *and* a sizable nonprofit sector. Prevailing economic theories have no clear explanation for this model, and James (1987) was only able to account for it by supplementing the prevailing theories with a theory of public sector preferences for private over public provision of state-financed services. The social origins theory sees the roots of this pattern, rather, in the same kinds of factors used to explain the other observed patterns: namely, the relations among social classes, organized religion, and state institutions in the period of industrialization. Unlike the liberal or social democratic patterns, however, the corporatist pattern emerges where landed elites retain a significant power base during the process of industrialization and make common cause with state organs and organized religion to contain working-class pressures for expanded social-welfare protections. The result is a partnership between the state and religiously affiliated nonprofit organizations to deliver increased social-welfare protections, but through the "premodern" institutions of religious nonprofits, thus preempting more radical demands for state-delivered social welfare and maintaining a greater degree of social control.

The final pattern, which the social origins theory terms the *statist model,* is characterized by both limited public social-welfare protections and limited nonprofit development. This outcome is likely where landed elites retain considerable power, where industrialization is limited and significant portions of the population remain on the land, where the urban middle and working classes consequently remain weak, and where external colonial influences are strong. In such circumstances, the resources for expanded public social-welfare spending remain limited, and the pressures for such spending are easily brushed aside. Moreover, the development of private nonprofit organizations independent of state control is stymied to preempt possible challenges to the state's hegemony. As a result, the legacy of the statist regime is limited social-welfare protections and a small nonprofit sector.

According to the social origins theory, these nonprofit regime types are heuristic devices intended to demarcate broad tendencies. The particular constellations of social, economic, and historical developments that lead to the different regimes can therefore vary from place to place. Thus, middle-class elements can be weak because of a strong state or because of powerful landed elements that keep them under control. Whichever the case, however, the prospects for a liberal model are not good. A corporatist or statist outcome is more likely, depending on a variety of other social and historical circumstances (e.g., the extent of industrialization, the strength of working-class protest, the nature and role of religious institutions, and the presence or absence of colonial influences). What is more, the social origins theory treats these development paths not as predetermined outcomes but as likely contingencies: developments in one epoch are viewed as stacking the cards in favor of a particular line of evolution, but discontinuities can occur that change the course of events. The value of this line of theorizing is thus to establish a set of expectations against which actual developments can be compared and a guide to the facets of social reality that may hold the clues to any unexpected outcomes.

Because of the complexity and relative amorphousness of the factors it identifies as important, the social origins theory is even more difficult to test empirically than the other theories discussed here. It lacks the parsimony of economic theories and calls for difficult qualitative judgments about the relative power of broad social groupings such as the commercial middle class or landed elites. Even then, such judgments establish only "propensities" and "likelihoods" rather than fully determined results (Steinberg and Young 1998; Ragin 1998). What is more, the four patterns identified by this theory are archetypes, so that many of the actual cases may be hybrids that encompass features from more than one pattern.

Despite this, the social origins theory has been examined against the available data on the scope and structure of the nonprofit sector and found to be quite helpful in unraveling a number of anomalies left behind by the other theoretical approaches. Examples of all four regime types reflected in this theory could be found among the countries for which data have been generated, and the explanations suggested by the theory seem confirmed by the historical records of the respective countries.

Thus, for example, the United States, Australia, and the United Kingdom exhibit the social conditions that the social origins theory posits should be associated with a liberal nonprofit regime—namely a sizable urban middle class that effectively disrupted (or, in the cases of the United States and Australia, never really confronted) a landed upper class while holding urban working-class elements at bay. The upshot has historically been relatively limited government social-welfare spending and a relatively large private nonprofit sector. The U.S. and Australian cases exhibit these features more strongly than the British, most probably because the middle classes in these countries were much more successful at fending off working-class pressures than their counterparts in the United Kingdom—in part because the United States and Australia never really had an entrenched landed elite to unseat, and in part because ethnic and racial diversity in these countries kept the working classes more highly splintered. This may explain why the United Kingdom deviated more sharply from this liberal pattern in the aftermath of World War II, when a surge of working-class pressures led to the creation of at least some features of the social democratic pattern there, especially in the field of health care. The United Kingdom thus emerged as a mixture of the liberal and social democratic models.

The social democratic pattern is more fully apparent in the cases of Sweden, Norway, Finland, and, to a lesser extent, Italy, all of which are characterized by relatively high levels of government social-welfare spending and relatively small nonprofit sectors, at least as measured in terms of paid employment. In all of these cases, moreover, the social conditions that the social origins theory suggests would lead to this pattern are in evidence. This is particularly true in Sweden, where working-class political parties gained extensive power early in the twentieth century and managed to push for extensive state-guaranteed social-welfare benefits in a context characterized by a weakened, state-dominated church and a limited monarchy. In Italy, the same social outcome was produced through a slightly different route. With Catholic Church–dominated social-welfare institutions placed firmly under state control beginning in the mid-nineteenth century as part of the effort to achieve national unification, the Fascist regime was able to move in the 1920s to establish a state-centered system of social-welfare protections that was then extended by the democratic governments of the postwar era. The upshot was a strong tradition of state-provided welfare assistance with little room (until recently) for an independent nonprofit sector. In the cases of Sweden, Norway, and Finland, moreover, it is clear that a small nonprofit sector in terms of employment does not necessarily mean a small nonprofit sector overall. To the contrary, the very social conditions that produced the welfare state in these countries—namely a strong tradition of working-class social movements—have left behind a strong residue of grassroots voluntary organizations engaged in advocacy and expressive functions.

Beyond these two widely accepted models, the available data also validate the existence of the two other models identified in the social origins theory. The corporatist model is represented by Germany, Belgium, the Netherlands, and several other countries, including, in more recent times, France. In these countries the state has been either forced or induced to make common cause with nonprofit organizations, albeit for different historical reasons. In Germany, the state, backed by powerful landed elements and in cooperation with a relatively weak urban middle class, responded to the threat of worker radicalism by forging an agreement with the major churches beginning in the latter nineteenth century to create a state-dominated social-welfare system that nevertheless maintained a sizable church—and hence nonprofit—presence. This agreement was ultimately embodied in the concept of "subsidiarity" as the guiding principle of social policy (Nell-Breuning 1976; Anheier and Seibel 2001). The upshot has been a close working relationship between the state and voluntary organizations—both secular and religious—and the coexistence of extensive government social-welfare spending and a sizable nonprofit sector.

In the Netherlands, a rather different sequence led to a similar result. There, tensions between the secular and religious segments of society ultimately were resolved through a political compromise early in the twentieth century under which public and private (denominational) schools were recognized as parts of a universal system of education and were given equal rights to public sector support. The resulting pattern of publicly financed–privately provided services was then replicated in numerous other fields, producing a pattern known as "pillarization" (Kramer 1981).

France reached a similar outcome through yet a different route—a period of hostility to civil society organizations in the wake of the French Revolution, followed by the growth of a substantial state-centered social-welfare system in the twentieth century, and finally, in the 1980s, a rapprochement between state and civil society when a socialist government reached out to civil society to assist in the extension of social-welfare benefits (Archambault 1996; Ullman 1998).

Finally, the cases of Japan, Brazil, and much of the developing world fit the statist model, with low levels of government social-welfare spending accompanied by a relatively small nonprofit sector. For Japan, this reflects a tradition of state dominance established during the Meiji Restoration of 1868 that, in the absence of effective urban middle-class or working-class movements, has allowed the state apparatus to retain considerable autonomous power. Combined with extensive corporate welfare, the result has been a relatively low level of government social-welfare protection without a corresponding growth of independent nonprofit activity. Similarly, in much of Latin America and elsewhere in the developing world, dominant social classes have allied with colonial powers to limit the growth of either state-provided social welfare or sizable nonprofit sectors. Combined with a religious apparatus firmly allied with the conservative elites or those holding governmental power, and limited or nonexistent working-class power or peasant mobilization, the result has been a classic statist outcome, though a variety of internal and external pressures have recently produced important pressures for change (see Anheier and Salamon 1998a).

Not only has the social origins theory helped unravel some of the variations in nonprofit size and composition, but also it has helped account for some of the apparent anomalies in nonprofit finance. Thus, this theory leads us to expect a higher level of private philanthropic support for nonprofit organizations in the liberal regimes than in the corporatist ones, and a higher level of public funding in the corporatist regimes, and this is exactly what we find. Similarly, this theory predicts a greater reliance on fees in the statist regimes, and here again the data support the expectation. The one deviation is the case of the social democratic regimes, where the social origins theory would predict that private philanthropy would be especially prominent but where fee income is especially prominent instead. However, once the value of volunteer time is considered, the prediction holds for the social democratic countries as well.

The social origins theory thus suggests that the nonprofit sector is rooted in long-standing patterns of nonprofit-government and nonprofit-society relations. But does this mean that these long-established patterns are impervious to change? The answer suggested by the social origins theory is that contemporary pressures will have different effects in different nonprofit "regimes."

In the liberal regime, where nonprofit organizations rely less on public sector payments, the pressures to seek additional and alternative revenue in the "private market" are strongest (see Salamon 1995, 2002). Observers point to the commercialization of the nonprofit sector, a trend that is particularly acute in the United States, as the health-care industry is changed by the increased presence of for-profit health providers (Weisbrod 1998). At the same time, popular political programs such as the 1997 welfare reform and the 2001 faith-based initiative emphasize the importance of private business and private charity in solving the social problems of a rapidly changing society.

The situation in the United Kingdom is similar when it comes to commercialization pressures, but it differs in terms of the "moving force" behind it. In the United States the moving force is the penetration by the for-profit sector into nonprofit domains like health and education, and the resulting internalization of market-like ideologies among nonprofit managers. In the United Kingdom, however, what seems to have happened in recent years is a systematic and highly centralized government attempt to enlist the voluntary sector in social service delivery while reducing public sector provision (Plowden 2001). One result of this policy is the emergence of competitive contract schemes and engineered quasi-markets, which are leading to an expansion of the U.K. nonprofit sector via larger flows of both public sector funds and commercial income.

The situation in social democratic countries such as Sweden is very different. A broad public consensus continues to support state provision of basic health care, social services, and education (Lundstrøm and Wijkstrøm 1997). At the same time, the role of nonprofit organizations in service provision is likely to increase, though typically in close cooperation with government, leading to the emergence of public-private partnerships and innovative organizational models to reduce the burden of the welfare state.

The situation in corporatist countries is ambivalent. Throughout the 1990s, the French government channeled massive sums of public sector funds to the nonprofit sector to help reduce youth unemployment and other pressing social issues while keeping some of the same restrictive laws in place that make it difficult for nonprofit organizations to operate more independently from government finance (Archambault 1996). In Germany, too, the nonprofit sector continues to be a vehicle for implementing government policies, not only in the area of unemployment and social services but also more generally in the process of unification, with a massive institution-building effort to establish a "ready-made" nonprofit sector in the eastern part of the country based on the West German model (Anheier and Seibel 2001). Yet increased strains on public budgets will most likely result in greater flexibility in how the subsidiarity principle is applied, shifting its focus away from the provider of the service and more toward the consumer, thereby introducing market elements in an otherwise still rigid corporatist system. The first moves in this direction have become apparent since the late 1990s, and it is likely that the German nonprofit sector will rely more on private fees and charges in the future (Zimmer and Priller 2001).

Finally, in statist countries like Japan, there may be the first signs of change in the government's posture toward the nonprofit sector. Today, the Japanese government speaks more favorably about the role of nonprofit organizations and grudgingly acknowledges the nonprofit sector's abilities in addressing emerging issues that confront Japan, such as the influx of foreign labor, an aging society, and environmental problems. In general, the state retains a highly instrumental policy posture: if the state shares a common interest with a particular nonprofit, it will provide financial support, but it will also exert great control over the organization. By contrast, if the state does not share a common interest with a nonprofit, the nonprofit may be ignored, denied legal status, not considered for grants or subsidies, and not given favorable tax treatment. In other words, Japan's nonprofit sector has undergone incremental changes but not a fundamental shift (Yamamoto 1997).

The nonprofit sector internationally has emerged over the past decade and a half as an arena of increased contestation, but also of increased focus and concern. Contemporary policy debates over the appropriate roles for public and private action in coping with societal problems, over the adequacy and importance of "social capital" in promoting democracy and development, and over the dynamics and consequences of globalization as a force for improving the quality of human life now regularly turn on the capacity and role of nonprofit institutions.

Inevitably, this increased focus has enveloped the nonprofit sector in a heavy ideological overlay. The sector is regularly invoked as an abstract idea intended to justify policies being pursued for other purposes rather than as a concrete reality to be measured and assessed. Nevertheless, important progress has been made on the empirical front, and this progress has challenged some of the favorite ideological conceptions as well as much of the prevailing theoretical baggage in the field. The nonprofit sector thus turns out to be a much larger force in countries throughout the world than formerly assumed, including many countries where prevailing theories pictured a dominant "welfare state" that had displaced voluntary organizations. Similarly, the role of philanthropy in the financial base of this sector turns out to be much smaller than many assumed, and the role of government much larger.

The notion of the nonprofit sector as a substitute for the state thus stands revealed as a romantic ideal at best. Beyond this, the theories portraying the nonprofit sector as the mute vehicle for meeting social demands left behind by the limitations of other societal institutions or as the expression of purely altruistic impulses have been supplemented by alternative conceptions that view the nonprofit sector as the reflection of broader power relationships among social classes and social institutions. In the process, the nonprofit sector, and the wide civil society of which it is a part, has come to be seen both as a force for social control and as a base for social empowerment, an arena where "power relationships not only are reproduced but also challenged [and] where the possibilities and hopes for change reside" (Howell and Pearce 2001:3).

Despite the significant empirical and conceptual progress that has been made, however, much remains to be done.

Hopefully, the discussion here has demonstrated the rich terrain for theory-building and policy discourse that the global nonprofit sector now represents and thus will spur others to join in the exploration of it.

ACKNOWLEDGMENTS

We would like to thank Estelle James and John Boli for providing very helpful comments and suggestions on earlier versions of this chapter.

NOTES

1. The European Value Survey covers the following countries: Britain, France, Germany, Austria, Italy, Spain, the Netherlands, Belgium, Denmark, Sweden, Iceland, Northern Ireland, Ireland, Estonia, Latvia, Lithuania, Poland, Czech Republic, Slovakia, Hungary, Romania, Bulgaria, Croatia, Greece, Russia, Malta, Luxembourg, Slovenia, Ukraine, Belarus, and the United States. The countries where the positive relationship between trust and memberships in voluntary associations either does not exist or is weak are Romania, Russia, Ukraine, and Belarus (see Halman 2001).

2. This includes memberships in health and social welfare associations, religious/church organizations, education, arts, music or cultural associations, trade unions and professional associations, local community groups and social clubs, environmental and human rights groups, youth clubs, women's groups, political parties, peace groups, and sports and recreational clubs, among others. Interpersonal trust was measured by the following question: "Generally speaking, would you say that most people can be trusted or that you need to be very careful when dealing with people?"

3. Since this chapter was drafted, data have become available on three other countries—Canada, Portugal, and Chile. However, data on these countries are not reflected in the discussion here.

4. The distinction between developed and developing countries here is based on per capita gross domestic product. Of the thirty-five countries covered, sixteen fall into the developed category and nineteen into the developing and transitional category.

5. For this purpose, an International Classification of Nonprofit Organizations was developed based on the International Standard Industrial Classification but with additional detail to accommodate the range of activities in which nonprofit organizations are typically involved. For further detail, see Salamon and Anheier (1997).

6. Reported percentages are weighted averages based on the response distribution in each country. The study was coordinated by the National Centre for Volunteering in Britain and involved population surveys as part of a larger omnibus questionnaire survey, using either telephone or face-to-face interviews. Each national team used a standard set of questions but somewhat different sampling approaches, including quota sampling (Belgium, Ireland), random location (Netherlands), random location combined with quota controls (Great Britain), and multistage cluster sampling (Bulgaria, Denmark, Germany, Slovakia, and Sweden). Sample sizes ranged from 870 in Belgium to 1,843 in Denmark. Unfortunately, this study neglected to ask questions about the *amount* of volunteering (Gaskin and Smith, 1997:115–117).

7. This is a weighted average considering the aggregate number of paid and volunteer workers. The unweighted average differs slightly because the countries with the larger nonprofit sectors also tend to have higher numbers of volunteers. The unweighted average volunteer share of nonprofit employment is thus 38 percent.

REFERENCES

Anheier, H. K. (1991). "Employment and Earnings in the German Nonprofit Sector: Structure and Trends." *Annals of Public and Cooperative Economics* 62 (4): 673–694.

———. (2004). *Civil Society: Measurement, Evaluation, Policy.* London: Earthscan.

Anheier, H. K., and Ben-Ner, A. (1997). "The Shifting Boundaries: Long-term Changes in the Size of the For-profit, Nonprofit, Cooperative and Government Sectors." *Annals of Public and Cooperative Economics* 68 (3): 335–354.

Anheier, H. K., Glasius, M., and Kaldor, M. (2001). "Introducing Global Civil Society." In H. K. Anheier, M. Glasius, and M. Kaldor (eds.), *Global Civil Society 2001.* Oxford: Oxford University Press.

Anheier, H. K., and Kendall, J. (2002). "Interpersonal Trust and Voluntary Associations: Examining Three Approaches." *British Journal of Sociology* 53 (3): 343–362.

Anheier, H. K., and Salamon, L. M. (1998a). "Nonprofit Institutions and the Household Sector." In United Nations Statistics Division (ed.), *The Household Sector.* New York: United Nations, 315–341.

———. (1998b). "Introduction: The Nonprofit Sector in the Developing World." In H. K. Anheier and L. M. Salamon (eds.), *The Nonprofit Sector in the Developing World.* Johns Hopkins Nonprofit Sector Series, ed. L. M. Salamon and H. K. Anheier. Manchester: Manchester University Press, 1–52.

Anheier, H. K., and Seibel, W. (2001). *The Nonprofit Sector in Germany.* Manchester: Manchester University Press.

Anheier, H. K., and Themudo, N. (2002). "On the Governance and Management of International Membership Organisation." Global Civil Society Working Paper, Centre for Civil Society, London School of Economics.

Archambault, E. (1984). "Les associations en chiffres." *Revue des Etudes Cooperative* 12:11–46.

———. (1996). *The Nonprofit Sector in France.* Johns Hopkins Nonprofit Sector Series, ed. L. M. Salamon and H. K. Anheier. Manchester: Manchester University Press.

Backhaus-Maul, H., and Olk, T. (1994). "Von Subsidiarität zu 'outcontracting': Zum Wandel der Beziehungen von Staat und Wohlfahrtsverbänden in der Sozialpolitik." In W. Streeck (ed.), *Staat und Verbände.* Opladen: Westdeutscher Verlag, 100–135.

Barbetta, P. (1997). *The Nonprofit Sector in Italy.* Johns Hopkins Nonprofit Sector Series, ed. L. M. Salamon and H. K. Anheier. Manchester: Manchester University Press.

Ben-Ner, A., and Gui, B. (eds.) (1993). *The Non-Profit Sector in the Mixed Economy.* Ann Arbor: University of Michigan Press.

———. (2003). "The Theory of Nonprofit Organizations Revisited." In H. K. Anheier and A. Ben-Ner (eds.), *The Study of the Nonprofit Enterprise.* New York: Plenum/Kluwer, 27–52.

Berry, J. (1999). *The New Liberalism: The Rising Power of Citizen Groups.* Washington: Brookings Institution Press.

Boeßenecker, K. H. (1995). *Spitzenverbände der Freien Wohlfahrtspflege in der BRD.* Münster: Votum.

Boli, J., and Thomas, G. M. (1997). "World Culture in the World Polity: A Century of International Non-governmental Organization." *American Sociological Review* 62 (April): 171–190.

Chang-Ho, L. (2002). "Volunteerism in Korea." *Journal of Volunteer Administration* 20 (3): 10–11.

Clark, J. (2001). "Trans-National Civil Society: Issues of Governance and Organisation." Paper prepared as background for the Seminar on Transnational Civil Society, London School of Economics, June 1–2.

———. (2003). *Worlds Apart: Civil Society and the Battle for Ethical Globalization.* Bloomfield, CT: Kumarian Press.

Coleman, J. (1990). *Foundations of Social Theory.* Cambridge, MA: Harvard University Press.

Darcy de Oliveira, M., and Tandon, R. (1994). "An Emerging Global Civil Society." In *Citizens: Strengthening Global Civil Society,* Washington, DC: CIVICUS.

Deakin, N. (2001). *In Search of Civil Society.* Basingstoke, Eng.: Palgrave.

DeFourny, J. P., and Develtere, P. (1999). *The Social Economy: The Worldwide Making of a Third Sector.* Liège, Bel.: Centre d'Economie Sociale.

DeFourny, J. P., Develtere, P., and Fonteneau, B. (1999). *L'economie sociale au Nord et au Sud.* Paris: De Boeck Université.

DeLaMar, R. (2000). "Volunteerism in Brazil: A Society Redefines Its Concept of Service." *Volunteer Leadership* (Spring): 26–28.

Diamond, L. (ed.) (1997). *Consolidating the Third Wave Democracies: Themes and Perspectives.* Baltimore, MD: Johns Hopkins University Press.

Edwards, M. (1999). "Legitimacy and Values in NGOs and Voluntary Organizations: Some Sceptical Thoughts." In D. J. Lewis (ed.), *International Perspectives on Voluntary Action: Reshaping the Third Sector.* London: Earthscan.

Edwards, M., and Hulme, D. (eds.) (1996). *Beyond the Magic Bullet: NGO Performance and Accountability in the Post–Cold War World.* London: Macmillan.

Esping-Andersen, G. (1990). *The Three Worlds of Welfare Capitalism.* Princeton, NJ: Princeton University Press.

Ferlie, E. (ed.) (1996). *The New Public Management in Action.* Oxford: Oxford University Press.

Fisher, J. (1993). *The Road from Rio: Sustainable Development and the Nongovernmental Movement in the Third World.* Westport, CT: Praeger.

Florini, A. (2000). *The Third Force: The Rise of Transnational Civil Society.* Washington, DC and Tokyo: Carnegie Endowment for International Peace and Japan Center for International Exchange.

Fowler, A. (2002). "Civil Society Research Funding from a Global Perspective: A Case for Redressing Bias, Asymmetry, and Bifurcation." *Voluntas: International Journal of Voluntary and Nonprofit Organizations* 13:14.

Friedman, T. (2000). *The Lexus and the Olive Tree.* New York: Anchor Books.

Fukuyama, F. (1995). *Trust: Social Virtues and the Creation of Prosperity.* New York: Simon and Schuster.

Gaskin, K., and Smith, J. D. (1997). *A New Civic Europe?* 3rd ed. London: Volunteer Centre.

Giddens, A. (1998). *The Third Way: The Renewal of Social Democracy.* Cambridge, Eng.: Polity Press.

Glasius, M., Kaldor, M., and Anheier, H. K. (eds.) (2002). *Global Civil Society 2002.* Oxford: Oxford University Press.

Goll, E. (1991). *Die freie Wohlfahrtspflege als eigener Wirtschaftssektor: Theorie und Empirie ihrer Verbände und Einrichtungen.* Baden-Baden: Nomos.

Grigoryan, S. (2002). "Volunteering and Volunteer Management in Armenia." *Journal of Volunteer Administration* 20 (3): 12–13.

Halman, L. (2001). *The European Values Study: A Third Wave: Source Book of the 1999/2000 European Values Study Surveys.* Tilburg, Neth.: Tilburg University Press.

Hansmann, H. (1987). "Economic Theories of Nonprofit Organizations." In W. W. Powell (ed.), *The Nonprofit Sector: A Research Handbook,* 1st ed. New Haven: Yale University Press.

Hodgkinson, V. A., and M. Weizman. (1982). *Dimensions of the Independent Sector.* Washington, DC: Independent Sector.

———. (1993). *Nonprofit Almanac: Dimensions of the Independent Sector.* Washington, DC: Independent Sector.

Howell, J., and Pearce, J. (2001). *Civil Society and Development: A Critical Exploration.* Denver, CO: Lynne Rienner.

Hulme, D., and Edwards, M. (1997). *NGOs, States, and Donors: Too Close for Comfort?* London: Macmillan, in association with Save the Children.

Huntington, S. P. (1991). *The Third Wave: Democratization in the Late Twentieth Century.* Norman: University of Oklahoma Press.

Inglehart, R. (1990). *Culture Shift in Advanced Industrial Society.* Princeton, NJ: Princeton University Press.

James, E. (1982). *The Private Provision of Public Services: A Comparison of Holland and Sweden.* Working Paper 60, Program on Non-Profit Organizations, Yale University.

———. (1984). "Benefits and Costs of Privatized Public Services: Lessons from the Dutch Educational System." *Comparative Education Review* 28:605–625.

———. (1987). "The Nonprofit Sector in Comparative Perspective." In W. W. Powell (ed.), *The Nonprofit Sector: A Research Handbook,* 1st ed. New Haven: Yale University Press.

Jas, P., Wilding, K., Wainwright, S., Passey, A., and Hems, L. (2002). *United Kingdom Voluntary Sector Almanac 2002.* London: National Council for Voluntary Organizations.

Kaldor, M., Anheier, H. K., and Glasius, M. (eds.) (2003a). *Global Civil Society 2003.* Oxford: Oxford University Press.

Kaldor, M., Anheier, H. K., and Glasius, M. (2003b). "Global Civil Society in an Era of Regressive Globalisation." In M. Kaldor, H. K. Anheier, and M. Glasius (eds.), *Global Civil Society 2003.* Oxford: Oxford University Press.

Kandil, A. (1998). "The Nonprofit Sector in Egypt." In H. K. Anheier and L. M. Salamon (eds.), *The Nonprofit Sector in the Developing World.* Manchester: Manchester University Press, 122–157.

Keck, M., and Sikkink, K. (1998). *Activists beyond Borders: Advocacy Networks in International Politics.* Ithaca: Cornell University Press.

Kendall, J., and Knapp, M. (1996). *The Voluntary Sector in the UK.* Johns Hopkins Nonprofit Sector Series, ed. L. M. Salamon and H. K. Anheier. Manchester: Manchester University Press.

Kettl, D. F. (1993). *Sharing Power: Public Governance and Private Markets.* Washington, DC: Brookings Institution Press.

———. (1997). "The Global Revolution in Public Management: Driving Themes and Missing Links." *Journal of Policy Analysis and Management* 16 (3): 446–462.

———. (2000). *The Global Public Management Revolution: A Report on the Transformation of Governance.* Washington, DC: Brookings Institution Press.

Knapp, M., Hardy, B., and Forder, J. (2001). "Commissioning for Quality: Ten Years of Social Care Markets in England." *Journal of Social Policy* 30 (2): 283–306.

Korten, D. (1990). *Getting to the 21st Century: Voluntary Action and the Global Agenda.* West Hartford, CT: Kumarian Press.

———. (1995). *When Corporations Rule the World.* West Hartford, CT: Kumarian Press.

Kramer, R. (1981). *Voluntary Agencies in the Welfare State.* Berkeley, CA: University of California Press.

Kriesberg, L. (1997). "Social Movements and Global Transformation." In J. Smith, C. Chatfield, and R. Pagnucco (eds.), *Transnational Social Movements and Global Politics: Solidarity beyond the State.* Syracuse, NY: Syracuse University Press.

Kuti, E. (1996). *The Nonprofit Sector in Hungary.* Johns Hopkins Nonprofit Sector Series, ed. L. M. Salamon and H. K. Anheier. Manchester: Manchester University Press.

Landim, L. (1998). "The Nonprofit Sector in Brazil." In H. K. Anheier and L. M. Salamon (eds.), *The Nonprofit Sector in the Developing World.* Manchester: Manchester University Press, 53–121.

LeGrand, J. (1999). "Competition, Collaboration or Control? Tales from the British National Health Service." *Health Affairs* 18:27–37.

Lindenberg, M., and Bryant, C. (2001). *Going Global: Transforming Relief and Development NGOs.* Bloomfield, CT: Kumerian Press.

Linz, J. J., and Stepan, A. (1996). *Problems of Democratic Transition and Consolidation.* Baltimore, MD: Johns Hopkins University Press.

Lundstrøm, T., and Wijkstrøm, F. (1997). *The Nonprofit Sector in Sweden.* Johns Hopkins Nonprofit Sector Series, ed. L. M. Salamon and H. K. Anheier. Manchester: Manchester University Press.

McLaughlin, K., Osborne, S. P., and Ferlie, E. (eds.) (2002). *New Public Management: Current Trends and Future Prospects.* London: Routledge.

Moore, B., Jr. (1966). *Social Origins of Dictatorship and Democracy: Lord and Peasant in the Making of the Modern World.* Boston: Beacon Press.

Mulgan, G. (1999). "Government and the Third Sector: Building a More Equal Partnership." In H. K. Anheier (ed.), *Third Way: Third Sector, Report No. 1.* London: Centre for Civil Society, London School of Economics, 17–22.

Naughton, J. (2001). "Contested Space: The Internet and Global Civil Society." In H. K. Anheier, M. Glasius, and M. Kaldor (eds.), *Global Civil Society 2001.* Oxford: Oxford University Press, 147–168.

Nell-Breuning, O. (1976). "Das Subsidiaritätsprinzip." *Theorie und Praxis der sozialen Arbeit* 27:6–17.

Osborne, D., and Gaebler, T. (1992). *Reinventing Government: How the Entrepreneurial Spirit Is Transforming the Public Sector.* Reading, MA: Addison-Wesley.

Palmer, J., and Sawhill, I. (eds.) (1982). *The Reagan Experiment: An Examination of Economic and Social Policies under the Reagan Administration.* Washington, DC: Urban Institute Press.

Pankoke, E. (1994). "Zwischen Enthusiasmus und Dilletantismus: Gesellschaftlicher Wandel freien Engagements." In L. Vogt and A. Zwingerle (eds.), *Ehre.* Frankfurt: Suhrkamp, 151–171.

Plowden, W. (2001). *Next Steps in Voluntary Action.* London: Centre for Civil Society, London School of Economics and National Council for Voluntary Organizations.

Powell, W. W., and DiMaggio, P. (1991). *The New Institutionalism in Organizational Analysis.* Chicago: University of Chicago Press.

Putnam, R. (2000). *Bowling Alone: The Collapse and Revival of American Community.* New York: Simon and Schuster.

Putnam, R., Leonardi, R., and Nanetti, R. (1993). *Making Democracy Work: Civic Traditions in Modern Italy.* Princeton, NJ: Princeton University Press.

Quadagno, J. (1987). "Theories of the Welfare State." *Annual Review of Sociology* 13:109–128.

Ragin, C. C. (1998). "Comments on 'Social Origins of Civil Society.'" *Voluntas: International Journal of Voluntary and Nonprofit Organizations* 9:10.

Ritchey-Vance, M. (1991). *The Art of Association: NGOs and Civil Society in Brazil.* Arlington, VA: Inter-American Foundation.

Rose-Ackerman, S. (1996). "Altruism, Non-Profits and Economic Theory." In *Journal of Economic Literature* 34 (2): 701–728.

Rudney, G. (1987). "The Scope and Dimensions of Nonprofit Activity." In W. W. Powell (ed.), *The Nonprofit Sector: A Research Handbook,* 1st ed. New Haven: Yale University Press.

Rueschemeyer, D., Stephens, E. H., and Stephens, J. D. (1992). *Capitalist Development and Democracy.* Chicago: University of Chicago Press.

Rhule, P. (2001). "Global Celebration: Countries Gear Up for the International Year of Volunteers." *Volunteer Leadership* (Winter): 26–27.

Sachße, C. (1994). "Subsidiarität: Zur Karriere eines sozialpolitischen Ordnungsbegriffes." *Zeitschrift für Sozialreform* 40 (1): 717–731.

Salamon, L. M. (1987). "Partners in Public Service: The Scope and Theory of Government-Nonprofit Relations." In W. W. Powell (ed.), *The Nonprofit Sector: A Research Handbook,* 1st ed. New Haven: Yale University Press, 99–117.

———. (1994). "The Rise of the Nonprofit Sector." *Foreign Affairs* 73 (3): 111–124.

———. (1995). *Partners in Public Service: Government-Nonprofit Relations in the Modern Welfare State.* Baltimore, MD: Johns Hopkins University Press.

———. (1999). *America's Nonprofit Sector: A Primer.* New York: Foundation Center.

———. (2002). *The Tools of Government: A Guide to the New Governance.* New York: Oxford University Press.

Salamon, L. M., and Abramson, A. (1982a). *The Federal Budget and the Nonprofit Sector.* Washington, DC: Urban Institute Press.

———. (1982b). "The Nonprofit Sector." In J. Palmer and I. Sawhill (eds.), *The Reagan Experiment: An Examination of Economic and Social Policies under the Reagan Administration.* Washington, DC: Urban Institute Press, 219–243.

Salamon, L. M., and Anheier, H. K. (1994). *The Emerging Nonprofit Sector.* Johns Hopkins Nonprofit Sector Series, ed. L. M. Salamon and H. K. Anheier. Manchester: Manchester University Press.

———. (eds.) (1997). *Defining the Nonprofit Sector: A Cross-National Analysis.* Johns Hopkins Nonprofit Sector Series, ed. L. M. Salamon and H. K. Anheier. Manchester: Manchester University Press.

———. (1998). "Social Origins of Civil Society: Explaining the Nonprofit Sector Cross-Nationally." *Voluntas: International Journal of Voluntary and Nonprofit Organizations* 9 (3): 213–247.

———. (1999). "Civil Society in Comparative Perspective." In L. M. Salamon, H. K. Anheier, R. List, S. Toepler, S. W. Sokolowski, and Associates, *Global Civil Society: Dimensions of the Nonprofit Sector,* vol. 1. Baltimore, MD: Johns Hopkins Center for Civil Society Studies, 3–39.

Salamon, L. M., Anheier, H. K., List, R., Toepler, S., Sokolowski, S. W., and Associates (1999). *Global Civil Society: Dimensions of the Nonprofit Sector.* Baltimore, MD: Johns Hopkins Center for Civil Society Studies.

Salamon, L. M., and Sokolowski, S. W. (2002). "Economic Rationality, Power, and Path Dependence: Explaining the Nonprofit Sector Cross-Nationally." Paper presented at the Annual Conference of the American Sociological Association, Chicago, August 16–19.

———. (2003). "Institutional Roots of Volunteering: Toward a Macro-Structural Theory of Individual Voluntary Action." In P. Dekker and L. Halman (eds.), *The Values of Volunteering: Cross Cultural Perspectives.* New York: Kluwer/Plenum, 71–90.

———. (2004). "Toward a Global Civil Society Index." In L. M. Salamon, S. W. Sokolowski, and Associates, *Global Civil Society: Dimensions of the Nonprofit Sector,* vol. 2. Bloomfield, CT: Kumarian Press.

Salamon, L. M., Sokolowski, S. W., and Associates (2004). *Global Civil Society: Dimensions of the Nonprofit Sector,* vol. 2. Bloomfield, CT: Kumarian Press.

Salamon, L. M., Sokolowski, S. W., and List, R. (2004). "Global Civil Society: An Overview." In L. M. Salamon, S. W. Sokolowski, and Associates, *Global Civil Society: Dimensions of the Nonprofit Sector,* vol. 2. Bloomfield, CT: Kumarian Press.

Salamon, L. M., and Tice, H. (2003). "Measuring Nonprofit Institutions in National Accounts." *OECD Statistics Newsletter* (April).

Schultze, C. (1977). *The Public Use of Private Interest.* Washington, DC: Brookings Institution Press.

Schuppert, G. F. (1981). *Die Erfüllung öffentlicher Aufgaben durch verselbständigte Verwaltungseinheiten.* Göttingen, Ger.: Schwartz.

———. (2003). "Gemeinwohlverantwortung und Staatsverständnis." In H. K. Anheier and V. Then (eds.), *Zwischen Eigennutz und Gemeinwohl: Neue Formen und Wege der Gemeinnützigkeit.* Gütersloh, Ger.: Bertelsmann.

Siriani, C., and Friedland, L. (2000). *Civic Innovation in America: Community Empowerment, Public Policy, and the Movement for Civic Renewal.* Berkeley, CA: University of California Press.

Smith, S. R., and Lipksy, M. (1993). *Nonprofits for Hire: The Welfare State in the Age of Contracting.* Cambridge, MA: Harvard University Press.

Steinberg, R., and Young, D. R. (1998). "A Comment on Salamon and Anheier's 'Social Origins of Civil Society.'" *Voluntas: International Journal of Voluntary and Nonprofit Organizations* 9:12.

Strategy Unit (2002). *Private Action, Public Benefit: A Review of Charities and the Wider Not-For-Profit Sector.* London: Cabinet Office.

Tarrow, S. (1996). "Making Social Science Work across Space and Time: A Critical Reflection on Robert Putnam's Making Democracy Work." *American Political Science Review* 90 (2): 389–397.

Terry, L. D. (1998). "Administrative Leadership, New Managerialism, and the Public Management Movement." *Public Administration Review* 58 (3): 194–200.

Thiemayer, Theo. 1970. *Gemeinwirtschaftlichkeit als Ordnungsprinzip.* Berlin: Dunker und Humblot.

Tullock, G. (1965). *The Politics of Bureaucracy.* Washington, DC: Public Affairs Press.

Ullman, C. F. (1998). "Partners in Reform: Nonprofit Organizations and the Welfare State in France." In W. W. Powell and E. S. Clemens (eds.), *Private Action and the Public Good.* New Haven: Yale University Press, 163–176.

United Nations Development Programme (UNDP). (2002). *Human Development Report.* New York: United Nations.

United Nations Statistics Division (1993). *System of National Accounts, 1993.* Published jointly by the Commission of the European Communities, the International Monetary Fund, the Organisation for Economic Co-operation and Development, and the United Nations.

———. (2003). *Handbook on Nonprofit Institutions in the System of National Accounts.* New York: United Nations Statistics Division.

Uphoff, N. (1988). "Assisted Self-Reliance: Working with, rather than for, the Poor." In J. P. Lewis et al., *Strengthening the Poor: What Have We Learned?* New Brunswick, NJ: Transaction Books, 47–60.

Weisbrod, B. A. (1977). *The Voluntary Non-profit Sector.* Lexington, MA: DC Heath.

———. (1988). *The Non-profit Economy.* Cambridge, MA: Harvard University Press.

———. (1998). *To Profit or Not to Profit: The Commercial Transformation of the Nonprofit Sector.* Cambridge: Cambridge University Press.

Wolch, Jennifer R. (1990). *The Shadow State: Government and Voluntary Sector in Transition.* New York: Foundation Center.

World Values Study Group. (2000). *World Values Survey.* Ann Arbor, MI: Institute for Social Research, Interuniversity Consortium for Political and Social Research.

Yamamoto, T. (1997). *The Nonprofit Sector in Japan.* Johns Hopkins Nonprofit Sector Series, ed. L. M. Salamon and H. K. Anheier. Manchester: Manchester University Press.

Zimmer, A., and Priller, E. (2001). "Der Dritte Sektor in Deutschland: Wachstum und Wandel." *Gegenwartskunde* 1:121–147.

II

NONPROFITS AND THE MARKETPLACE

5

Economic Theories of Nonprofit Organizations

RICHARD STEINBERG

Those unfamiliar with economics, nonprofit organizations, or both may wonder what one subject has to do with the other. Economics does not, of course, provide the reader with everything he or she ought to know but it does provide insight on virtually every problem relating to the role, behavior, management, and regulation of the nonprofit sector. In turn, economics has become a richer discipline for confronting the special challenges posed by analysis of nonprofit organizations.

Economics is the study of choices under scarcity. This goes far beyond the study of things bought and sold and far beyond the financial consequences of decision-making. When consumers decide whether to spend all their limited money on goods and services for themselves or donate some of that money to nonprofit organizations, they are choosing how to allocate a scarce resource. When consumers choose to spend some of their scarce time as volunteers rather than laborers or leisure-takers, they are making an economic decision. When socially conscious entrepreneurs ponder whether to form a new organization, support an existing organization, or lobby government to meet some societal need, they are choosing how to allocate their time and other scarce resources at their command. When financially strapped nonprofit organizations decide to charge their indigent clients a little something rather than eliminate programs, they are making an economic decision forced by scarcity.

Economics as a discipline does not rule out study of the sector, but many simplified models studied by economists divert attention from philanthropic and nonprofit issues. Economists assume that each individual pursues his or her self-interest as they see it. In practice, this is often simplified as the assumption that each cares only about his or her personal consumption of goods and services. However, self-interest encompasses helping others one cares about, and individual perceptions of self-interest can be socially determined. The charitable behavior of donors and volunteers reminds economists that more complicated models are necessary, paying back the analyst with insights that go far beyond understanding charity. In like fashion, economic models typically assume that for-profit firms maximize profits because that is what the owners want to do. Framed in this way, departures from profit maximization appear as "market failures" due to "agency problems" cured by providing the proper financial incentives. Nonprofit organizations cannot be analyzed from the same starting point. These organizations may indeed maximize their "profits" (or financial surplus or endowment) under some circumstances. However, this is a result that must be shown and its significance must be interpreted anew. Thus, for example, Slivinski (2002) shows that a mixture of financial and non-financial incentives is the best way to motivate nonprofit employees in specified circumstances.

This chapter provides an overview on the economics of nonprofit organizations. Many later chapters provide far more detail on the decisions to give or volunteer (Havens, O'Herlihy, and Schervish; Vesterlund; and Leete), the economic relations among the sectors (Brown and Slivinski; Smith and Grønbjerg; Galaskiewicz and Colman; Tuckman and Chang), cross-sectoral comparisons of organizational behavior in specific industries (Kendall, Knapp, and Forder; Schlesinger and Gray) and selected public policy issues (Brody; Simon, Dale, and Chisolm). Here, I survey the big picture and fill some holes left by the collection of other chapters.

In the next section, I provide definitions and distinctions used for the economic approach. Later I discuss an older set of theories, known as the "three-failures theory," regarding the distinctive role of nonprofit organizations in the broader economy. Then, I argue for development of a more comprehensive and integrated theory, lay out the parameters of such a theory, and discuss progress to date in carrying out these ideas. I conclude by illustrating how economic theory provides insight for those designing appropriate public policy for the sector.

DEFINITIONS AND DISTINCTIONS

Many definitions abound in discussion of "the sector," but in this chapter I use Hansmann's (1980) idea: A nonprofit organization is one precluded from distributing, in financial form, its surplus resources to those in control of the organization. By this definition, nonprofit organizations can earn and retain financial surplus ("profits") provided they do not pay dividend checks or their equivalent to the board of directors or top managers. Instead, the surplus is either retained (as endowment, reserves, or temporarily restricted funds), reinvested (in organizational expansion or the provision of charitable services), or given to other nonprofit organizations (as grants). Some nonprofit organizations derive all their resources from commercial operations, and in this sense are just as much "for profits" as any for-profit firm. The distinction is that they must retain or reinvest their profits.

Hansmann (1980) called this prohibition on profit distribution the "nondistribution constraint," and made it central to his theories of nonprofit behavior. As we will see, the nondistribution constraint is an essential part of other economic theories. The constraint provides a clear distinction that affects how the organization obtains resources, how it is controlled, how it behaves in the marketplace, how it is perceived by donors and clients, and how its employees are motivated. Hansmann also defined the companion "fair compensation constraint" that applies nondistribution to executive compensation.

This definition of nonprofit organization excludes consumer cooperatives and worker-owned firms, but includes mutual savings banks. All three distribute their profits to consumers or workers; however, members of the banks' boards of directors do not receive distributions and those receiving distributions have no rights of control. Some organizations are legally incorporated as nonprofits but secretly distribute their profits to those in control, the so-called for-profits-in-disguise. Nonprofits-in-disguise, the opposite phenomenon, are rare but do exist. For example, medical insurance providers in Puerto Rico are required to incorporate under the statutes governing for-profit corporations, but one has nonetheless written nondistribution into its articles of incorporation and bylaws.

The owners (governing board) of a nonprofit organization do not enjoy all the usual rights of ownership. Ben-Ner and Jones (1995) detail three components of property rights: the right to control the use of an asset, the right to retain any financial surpluses generated from that use, and the right to sell the first two rights to a new owner. Nonprofit owners have "attenuated property rights," meaning they are allowed to control the organizational assets and transfer that control, but not allowed to profit financially from using their other rights. If the organization is sold or converted to a for-profit firm, the owners obtain fair market value for the organization's assets, then donate this value to another nonprofit (typically a "conversion foundation" that makes charitable grants). If the owners derive any benefits from control of the organization, they must be in nonfinancial form. These benefits may help only the owners (for example, the organization can have an opulent headquarters, hold board meetings at vacation resorts, and employ attractive but not especially productive staff) or may be enjoyed jointly by the owners (who like using their position of control to make the world a better place) and members of society at large.

Despite sharing a nondistribution constraint, nonprofits differ from one another in a variety of economically meaningful ways. First, some nonprofits deliver services whereas others (such as united fundraising organizations, foundations, and donor-advised funds) make grants and program-related loans to other nonprofits. Second, some nonprofits rely mostly on donations (gifts, grants, and volunteers), others on membership dues, and others on commercial activity (sales to the public or contractual provision of service to the government). Third, nonprofits differ in the way their governing boards are selected. Fourth, nonprofits differ in the services they provide. These services are enumerated in various industrial classification codes (like the North American Industry Classification System) or in taxonomies specific to the nonprofit sector (like the National Taxonomy of Exempt Organizations or the International Classification of Nonprofit Organizations).

Hansmann (1980) emphasized some of these distinctions in his four-way classification of nonprofit firms, summarized in table 5.1. The financing dimension of this classification simply asks whether most of the organizational resources come from donations or other sources. The governance dimension distinguishes mutual nonprofits (where the power to elect the board is in the hands of donors and customers) from entrepreneurial nonprofits (where boards are self-perpetuating or appointed). Hansmann proposes these distinctions as ideal types (real-world nonprofits may straddle the boundaries) and asks whether these types behave differently. Subsequent literature has focused on differences between donative and commercial nonprofits, but work to date has

TABLE 5.1. A FOUR-WAY CATEGORIZATION OF NONPROFIT FIRMS

	Mutual	Entrepreneurial
Donative	Common cause National Audubon Society Political clubs	CARE March of Dimes Art museums
Commercial	American Automobile Assoc. Consumers Union Country clubs	National Geographic Society Educational Testing Service Hospitals Nursing homes

Source: Hansmann 1980, as adapted in Hansmann 1987a.

not analyzed the impact of the governance distinction. This is an unfortunate gap in the literature as political dynamics no doubt explain the role, objectives, performance, and life cycle of nonprofit organizations.

THREE FAILURES: AN EARLY SUCCESS

Before Weisbrod's pathbreaking work in 1975, economists typically viewed nonprofit organizations in isolation (for example, Tullock 1966; Newhouse 1970; Feldstein 1971; Pauly and Redisch 1973). Suppose, they would start, a nonprofit organization was supplying a particular good or service. They would then ask how that nonprofit's behavior would differ from that of a for-profit firm. For example, Newhouse characterized the behavior of a nonprofit hospital that cared about both the quality and quantity of health services it delivered. This was a useful starting point, but it was never clear why nonprofits were supplying the service in question, and not some other kind of organization. Why did organizations with quantity/quality objectives emerge in the hospital industry, but not in automobile manufacturing or accounting services? Given that nonprofit hospitals did arise, why is the hospital industry also populated by for-profit and government hospitals? Would the nonprofit presence in the hospital industry end if special tax advantages were removed, if Medicare shifted to a prospective payment system, if the population aged, or if technology improved?

Weisbrod (1975) began the process of searching for a distinctive set of roles that nonprofit organizations could play in a mixed economy. He catalogued the known virtues of for-profit firms and governmental action, finding a role for nonprofits when these two other sectors are expected to fail (due to "market failure" and "government failure"). In brief, markets fail to provide adequate quantities of collective goods, governments provide these goods in accord with the wishes of the electorate, and those who want higher levels of service than government provides support nonprofit organizations. Hansmann (1980) added an additional shortcoming of markets to the mix: contract failure. In cases where the quantity or quality of service cannot be verified, markets take advantage of informational asymmetries. Organizations that cannot distribute profits, including private nonprofits and government agencies, provide a more trustworthy alternative. Salamon (1987) turned the process around, cataloguing the virtues of nonprofit organizations and finding a role for the other two sectors when nonprofits are expected to fail ("voluntary failure"). In conjunction, these three approaches began the stream of literature that has become known as "three-failures theory." Next, I discuss each of these failures in more detail, showing how each sector responds to failures by others. Then I summarize some empirical evidence and conclude with the limitations of the three-failures approach.

Figure 5.1 illustrates how the pieces of three-failures theory fit together. I cover these topics row by row, first discussing market success and three sources of market failure (the first two rows). Then, I discuss how government responds to each of these failures and why, in turn, government fails to completely address the problems (rows three and four). Nonprofits respond to the three sources of market and government failure (row five), but their response is not completely adequate either (row six). In addition, nonprofits generate their own failures (row seven), and markets and governments respond to these (the feedback loop from the bottom to the top and third rows).

Market Failure

Market failure is the best understood of the three failures, and concerns inefficiencies resulting from for-profit provision of goods and services. The term *inefficiency* as used here and elsewhere by economists has a very broad definition. Markets can be inefficient because they waste resources by using the wrong production processes (productive inefficiency), but they can also be inefficient because they waste resources by producing the wrong mixture of goods and services (allocative inefficiency). Allocative efficiency requires an output mixture that properly balances the relative benefits to consumers against the relative costs of production.[1] For-profit firms are, at least in theory, productively efficient but often produce the wrong mixture of outputs in three ways: some worthwhile goods are underprovided, access to some goods is overrestricted, and the quantity or quality of some delivered goods is different from what the consumer or client was promised.

Adam Smith, in exploring the virtues of for-profit markets through his famous "invisible hand," laid the groundwork for the theory of market failure. In more modern terms, this idea circulates as the first fundamental theorem of welfare economics, which asserts that when all goods are traded in perfectly competitive markets, equilibrium outcomes are efficient. As used in the theorem, a "good" is anything that consumers value either positively (goods) or negatively (bads), including services and tangible objects; "perfectly competitive markets" are those in which no individual buyer or seller believes they can affect market prices; "equilibrium" refers to a set of prices such that the amount of each good that consumers would like to buy exactly equals the amount producers would like to sell; and "efficient" is used in the broad economic sense. The first fundamental theorem does not say that free markets are efficient in all circumstances, only that they would be efficient in an imaginary world quite different from the real world. Subsequent work by Pigou (1932) and others established that equilibrium is generally inefficient if some goods are not traded at all, or are traded in imperfectly competitive markets. This failure limits the role of markets and defines a potential role for governments and nonprofit organizations.

Samuelson (1954) analyzed "pure public goods," defined as goods or services that are both nonrival (consumption by one person does not diminish any other person's consumption of that good) and nonexcludable (keeping some individuals from consuming the good is costly or impossible once it has been produced). A defensive militia provides a pure

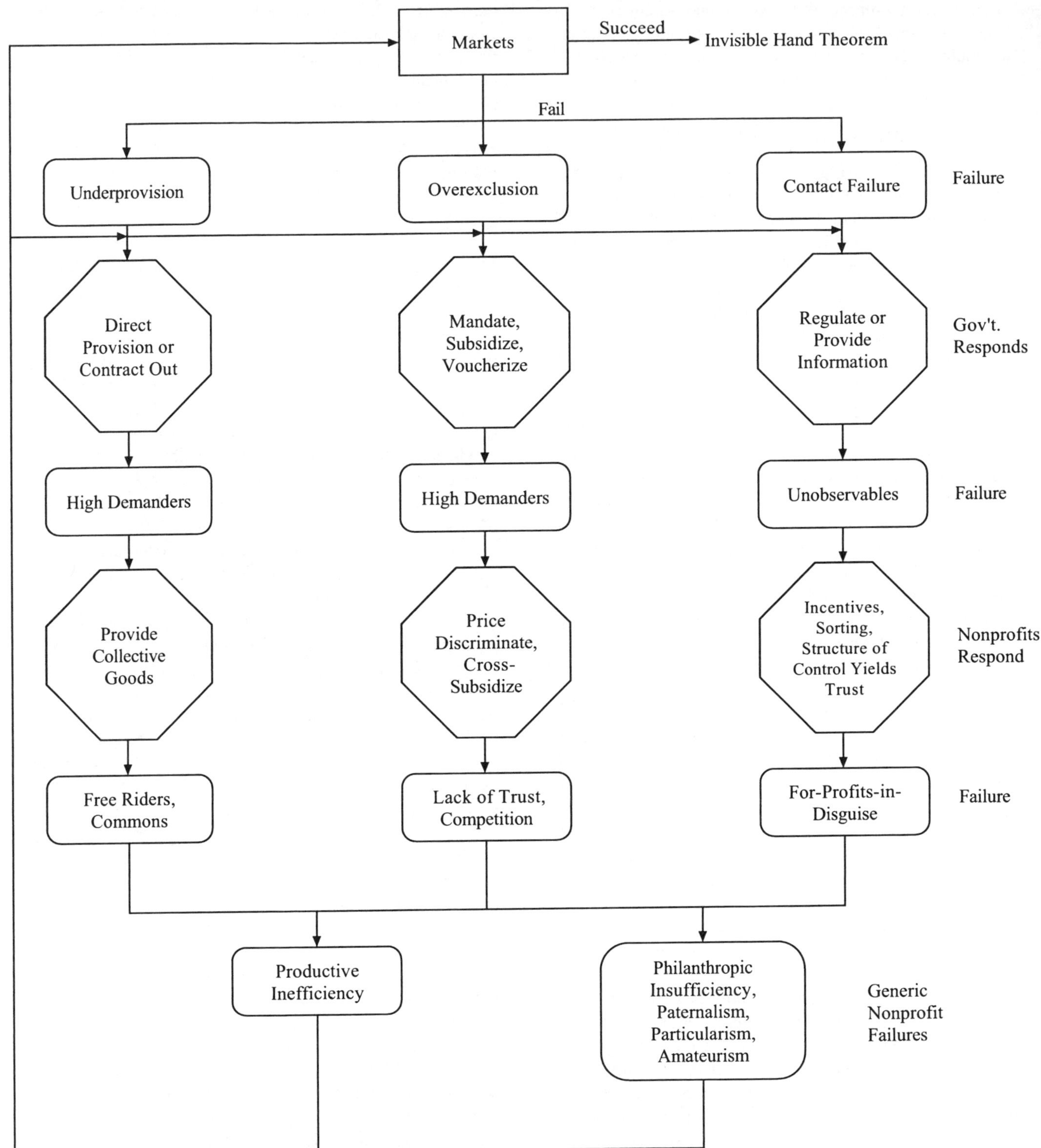

FIGURE 5.1. SCHEMATIC OF THREE-FAILURES THEORY

public good—birth of a new citizen does not diminish the quantity of protection enjoyed by other citizens (nonrivalry), and excluding any citizen from the protection provided by this army would be difficult (nonexcludability). For-profit firms do not produce pure public goods because consumers have the motive and opportunity to consume them without paying. This sort of market failure justifies governmental provision of national defense, hence the name "public goods." However, some "public goods" are produced by private nonprofits, so it has become increasingly popular to call them collective, rather than public, goods.

Some collective goods, like the performing arts, are excludable though still nonrival. Keeping nonpaying customers from enjoying a performance is possible, but once the performance is staged, it does not diminish the enjoyment of existing consumers to let an additional person enjoy the show. Markets for excludable collective goods fail in a different way—although the market may provide the good, it limits consumption to paying customers. However, excluding borderline nonpurchasers (those who would enjoy the show but are not willing or able to pay the required entrance fee) is inefficient. Letting them attend would help them, hurt no one, and consume no additional scarce resources. Nonetheless, for-profit firms fear loss of revenue from paying customers if they let the borderline nonpurchasers in, resulting in an overexclusion market failure. Excludable collective goods may also suffer from the underprovision problem, although this is not our primary focus here.

A private good (for example, a surgical procedure) is the opposite of a pure public good—consumption is rival (no one but the patient is cured of appendicitis when the appendix is removed) and nonpayers can be kept from consuming it. Markets fail to provide the right mixture of private goods in certain cases of asymmetric information, where the seller of services knows more about the quantity or quality of delivered services than the buyer does. Hansmann (1980) extended the original insights of Nelson and Krashinsky (1973) as the theory of "contract failure." Contract failure exists when: "Owing either to the circumstances under which a service is purchased or consumed or to the nature of the service itself, consumers feel unable to evaluate accurately the quality or quantity of the service a firm produces for them. In such circumstances, a for-profit firm has both the incentive and the opportunity to take advantage of customers by providing less service to them than was promised and paid for" (Hansmann 1987a:29).

Contract failure arises when truthful information about the quality or quantity of delivered services cannot be purchased. Consider three cases where contract failure arises. First, suppose that instead of donating a sum of money to a nonprofit and asking it to feed the hungry in some foreign land, the prospective donor tries to purchase the same service from a for-profit. That customer is paying so that additional hungry people will be fed. The customer cannot easily observe whether they are fed, but could hire someone to find out how many people were being fed by the company in question. Still, perhaps some of these people are being fed because of another customer's purchase of food aid. The customer cannot learn whether his or her purchase *added* to the sum of people being fed, so that any explicit or implicit contract to buy food this way would fail.

The second example is a long-term care facility such as a nursing home. Weisbrod and Schlesinger (1986) noted that nursing homes, and services more generally, are bundles of easy-to-observe (type I) and hard-to-observe (type II) characteristics. Although for-profit firms can be trusted to provide the promised level of type I characteristics (room size, presence of medical staff), contract failure is likely for type II characteristics (whether residents are treated with due respect; whether sedatives are administered properly). Two other factors also contribute to contract failure here—the fact that the purchaser of services (often the adult children) is not the consumer of services (the resident) and the fact that if experience proves that contract failure is present in a particular facility, switching to another health provider is difficult for medical, social, and financial reasons.[2] These factors also affect other types of services such as day care for children and inpatient psychiatric care.

The third example comes when governments contract with private agencies to provide social services. Social services are complex and include many type II characteristics that matter to government contractors (e.g., Paulson 1988). For example, it is hard to tell whether foster home placements represent the best available match between caregivers and children. It is also difficult to figure out whether difficult-to-treat clients are steered toward other providers to cut costs or misclassified to reap higher contractual payments.

Governmental Responses to Market Failure

I detailed three sources of market failure above: underprovision of collective goods, overexclusion from excludable public goods, and contract failure. Each of these provides roles for the other two sectors,[3] and here I detail the governmental response. Governments solve the underprovision problem by either producing collective goods or paying a private-sector organization to produce them (contracting out). In effect, government payments complete the market, allowing trading for the collective of beneficiaries. For example, governments directly provide transportation infrastructure (highways and airports), collective recreational and conservation activities (parks), and reduction in the risk of theft or bodily harm (police). Periodically, government privatization efforts have led to the contracting-out of garbage collection, prison facilities, postwar reconstruction, and even public primary and secondary education.

Governments also address the market failure of overexclusion from excludable public goods in a variety of ways. First, when government produces the excludable public good, it sets the terms of exclusion. Many museums and zoos do not require payment of an admission fee, offer fee-free days periodically, or exempt favored groups (such as schoolchildren) from fee requirements. Second, government regulates for-profit providers, sometimes mandating that nonpayers retain access to the collective good (for example, emergency phone service). Third, government gives selected groups special subsidies that enable them to compete for access to excludable public goods (such as housing vouchers for the indigent or work-study positions for eligible college attendees).

Governments address contract failure in a variety of ways. First, governments facilitate the enforcement of contracts, reducing the number of markets that fail in this way. Second, governments regulate the representations that firms make to the public through truth-in-advertising and fraud laws, labeling requirements, and the like. Third, governments limit entry into markets that suffer from asymmetric information problems through licensing and bonding requirements. Finally, government warns consumers of particular abuses and teaches consumers how to detect mistreatment. When government is the contractor, it deals with contract failure by monitoring for-profit providers more intensely (Ferris and Graddy 1991) and by negotiating longer, more detailed, and more complicated contracts (DeHoog 1984).

Government Failure

Subjecting government to the same formal scrutiny as markets, one uncovers a variety of sources of "government failure" (e.g., Wolf 1993). Many disciplines have contributed to the theory of government failure, which includes both efficiency and other considerations. I focus here on those government failures germane to three-failures theory.

Alternative models of political decision-making can be used to predict the levels of collective goods provided (or paid for) by government. Whatever the form of government, one result pervades—some citizens will be dissatisfied with the level, quality, or style of collective goods provided publicly. Tastes, tax burdens, and income differ, creating differing opinions on the ideal level of government spending. For private goods, differences in opinion are easily satisfied—consumers simply buy different amounts. For collective goods, what one person consumes is automatically consumed by everyone else, so that it is technically impossible to adapt to diversity of opinions in this way. Erik Lindahl developed a solution to this problem, today called Lindahl pricing in his honor, whereby each consumer is charged an individualized price for the collective good based on the intensity of their preference for it. Those who, all else equal, would like to buy a large amount of the collective good are charged a high price, those that would like to buy a little receive a low price. At the Lindahl prices, everyone would like to buy the same quantity and diversity in preferences is fully adapted to. The problem is that Lindahl prices are impractical and rarely used in the real world.[4]

Weisbrod (1975) focused on this sort of government failure in developing his theory of the role of the nonprofit sector. The word *failure* is used in a different sense here, to say that governments fail to provide collective goods at the level "high demanders" (those who would like to see the largest quantity or highest quality) would like. Whether or not government provision is efficient in the broad economic sense,[5] it will usually fail to meet the desires of some consumers. In particular, one theory suggests that public good provision in a democracy will be at the level the median-preference voter prefers.[6] Then, half the voters would like to see more provided, half less, and only the middle guy is completely satisfied with the government's choice.

Diversity of opinions leads to unsatisfied demand for collective goods by high demanders. However, the problem is reduced by the interplay of two factors—multi-level governments and migration. Some collective goods are consumed by everyone everywhere (a breathable atmosphere); others, like fire protection, are "local collective goods." Everyone in the United States consumes the same level of national defense, but the quality of fire protection, schooling, streets and roads, and public picnic areas is decided locally in accord with local preferences. To the extent that those who prefer differing levels of collective goods locate in different communities, voter dissatisfaction with governmental provision levels is reduced. Tiebout (1956) considered the logical extreme, with costless migration between an infinity of jurisdictions that provide local collective goods. In this limiting case ("Tiebout equilibrium"), dissatisfied voters move to a community of like-minded voters, and everyone is satisfied with the level of collective goods provided by their local government. Tiebout equilibrium describes some features of the real world, where families with children pick communities with good schools and childless couples pick communities with lower property taxes, but as a practical matter, some dissatisfaction with government always remains.

The market underprovision problem arises because consumers have both the incentive and opportunity to consume collective goods without paying. Government can solve this problem by coercing payments as current taxes (or future taxes if deficit spending is used), but this causes two types of failure absent from markets. First, individual payments are no longer voluntary as they are in markets. The ballot box provides a collective check on tax rules, but individual voters would rarely pay their full tax obligations if payment were not mandatory. Second, individual payments are not linked to either the amount of the collective good consumed or the individual consumer's willingness to pay for that good. Those with and without schoolchildren pay for the schools. The amount they pay is determined by the value of local property owned, income, or purchases of taxable goods rather than anything directly connected to their benefit from local public schools.

A second problem is that government cannot regulate abuses it cannot detect. Government is impotent precisely when contract failure is at its worst. This problem affects government regulation of for-profit sales of goods and services to the public and also affects sales to the government, as when government contracts with for-profits to provide social services.

Another limitation on government is self-imposed through constitutional restrictions on government action. When the government is prohibited from responding to majority demands for particular goods and services (most prominently religious services in the United States) even the median-preference voter will be dissatisfied. Conversely, sometimes the government prohibits other sectors from responding to consumer demands for particular goods and services (James 1989). Then, the government role is too large compared with the unconstrained optimum.

Nonprofit Responses to Market and Government Failure

Markets fail and governments are only partly successful in addressing this failure. The twin failures in each of the three areas discussed above provide the basis for three theories of the role of nonprofit organizations in a multisector economy. Weisbrod (1975) put all this together for collective goods, Hansmann (1981a) for excludable collective goods, and Hansmann (1980) for contract failure. In this section I discuss each in turn, then the failures of nonprofit organizations that lead to roles for the other two sectors.

Weisbrod (1975) observed that nonprofits in almost every nonprofit industry, especially donative nonprofits, provide collective goods. Consider first those nonprofits that help the needy. At first glance, this seems to be a private good—soup is consumed by one individual, and nobody else can be nourished unless more soup is made. Soup is indeed a private good, but "helping the needy" can be enjoyed by everyone who cares about this group of people. Other altruists enjoy the fact that anyone has helped these people. If, in addition, helping the needy reduces crime rates, selfish individuals would also consume this collective good.

Consider next medical research. If a nonprofit organization finds a medicinal cure for cancer, the medicine itself would be a private good—pills cannot be collectively consumed in any useful manner. However, the knowledge that produced that cure is a collective good—the knowledge is not used up by anyone's pill consumption. A patent system makes that collective good excludable, and so we do see for-profit medical research firms. However, for-profits practice overexclusion that public health systems are only partly successful in countering.

The performing arts provide another example of an excludable collective good. Most of the costs of an opera or concert presentation are bound up in rehearsals, sets, costumes, and hall rental. If the hall is not full, an additional consumer can enjoy the show at no cost to existing consumers. Zoos and museums are similar in this respect.

Education produces both collective and private benefits. A good education enhances lifetime earnings—a private benefit. Education also improves the quality of democratic decisions and provides a common language and set of understandings that helps business and social interactions. Health care is another industry that produces mostly private benefits, but the treatment and prevention of contagious diseases provides a collective benefit for those who have not yet suffered from them. Advocacy is simultaneously about collective benefits for the advocating group and collective costs for their opponents.

Many forms of nonprofits, particularly those governed by members or in the religion and education industries, nurture repeated interactions among stakeholders. This is hardly unique to nonprofits, but Ben-Ner and Gui (2003) argue that nonprofit organizations create better personal relationships among stakeholders than for-profits. Thus, nonprofits often serve as creators of the collective good "social capital," a network of relations that facilitates joint action. Religious and other nonprofits complement these relational contributors to social capital by nurturing moral codes and behaviors.

After observing that nonprofits commonly provide collective goods, that government provision of these goods is limited, and that Lindahl prices are not available in the real world, Weisbrod (1975) suggested that high demanders who are dissatisfied with government turn to the nonprofit sector to meet their desires for higher levels of service provision. Governments meet majority demands, and nonprofits meet those demands that do not yet or will never obtain majority support. Sometimes, the service in question is innovative, and the majority is reluctant to support it due to its newness. Then, nonprofits pioneer the idea, and government takes over funding or provision after the idea is proven (as in the Head Start program of early childhood education for disadvantaged groups). Sometimes, the disagreement is only over the size or quality of the collective good, and then nonprofit funding will persist. Sometimes the disagreement is fierce on both sides of the issue, such as on public funding of family planning clinics that discuss the abortion option. Then advocacy groups will be supported separately by high demanders for public funding (pro-choice) and low demanders (pro-life). Sometimes the disagreement is over ideological or cultural attributes (as in the arts [Steinberg 1990b] or primary and secondary education), where there is no clear way to arrange citizens as high and low demanders but there is a majority opinion and a set of private alternatives representing the various minority-support approaches (religious schools, Montessori academies, military schools, and so on).

Migration adds a few twists to the Weisbrod story. James's (1989) discussion points out that the nonprofit option is preferred when assembling dispersed communities of interest is easier than assembling stratified communities satisfied with local government provision. In the basic Weisbrod story, high demanders can supplement public spending on collective goods but low demanders are stuck. Wolpert (1977) noted that low demanders can migrate to a community that has lower taxes and expenditures on the collective good. This means that over time, the average preference for the collective good will increase. At some point, the difference between the preferences of the median voter and the preferences of the high demanders may shrink sufficiently that the nonprofit organization shifts from donative finance to government provision-of-service contracts.

High demanders pay for the supplement to public provision of collective goods with their donations. Unlike taxes, these payments are voluntary, and so in this sense nonprofits provide a superior alternative to governments.[7] However, donations suffer from the same disconnection between consumption and enjoyment of the collective good and amount of payments that taxes do. Perhaps, because the payments are voluntary, the disconnection is less severe, but notions of obligation, patronage, fairness, and competition for prestige may structure voluntary payments on other bases.

Why do high demanders choose the nonprofit recipient rather than donating to the other sectors? Weisbrod did not explicitly model this decision, but his insights are formally developed in later work by Hansmann (1981a) and Bilodeau and Slivinksi (1998). Donations to for-profits are rare because of contract failure.[8] Donations to government are rare for a similar reason—donors fear that governments react to their donation by cutting their own tax-financed support for the collective good in question. However, this same fear seems to affect donations to nonprofit organizations. In response to one's donation, other donors might reduce their contributions or government might reduce its grants and contracts with the recipient organization. Bilodeau and Slivinski (1998) point out that the nondistribution constraint keeps previous donors (notably the founding entrepreneur) from withdrawing their contributions in response to contributions by others, but the problem remains for those who donate contemporaneously. No doubt the repeated structure of interaction that fosters social capital helps, but this would not seem to explain, say, one-time donations to a nonmembership organization. Vesterlund's chapter in this volume explores these questions in greater depth, but puzzles remain whenever we try to make our intuitions on these matters explicit.

How do nonprofits deal with the overexclusion problem? First, we need to understand the market failure a bit better. If for-profit firms knew the maximum amount each consumer was willing to pay and had the power to charge a different price for each attendee ("perfect price discrimination") then overexclusion would not occur. Those willing to pay a penny would be charged a penny, those willing to pay a million dollars would be charged a million dollars, and everyone who enjoyed the excludable collective good in the slightest amount would voluntarily pay the entry fee. However, for-profits do not know enough about consumer willingness-to-pay to practice this strategy. Consumers would not reveal this information to a for-profit firm because it would be used against them. Profit maximizers would collect more than is necessary to provide the collective good in order to maximize their distribution of profits. Ben-Ner (1986) argues that the same does not apply to nonprofits, because of both the nondistribution constraint and the typical structure of nonprofit governance. Consumers might reveal their willingness-to-pay directly, enabling the nonprofit to establish more effective sliding-scale fee structures or financial aid to college students, or they might reveal this information implicitly through the donations they make on top of their purchase. Thus, Hansmann (1981a) refers to donations for excludable collective goods as "voluntary price discrimination."

Hansmann (1981a) analyzes how nonprofits respond to the combined problem of underprovision and overexclusion affecting high-cultural organizations in the performing arts such as opera companies, symphony orchestras, and dance troupes. When, as often happens, most of the costs of production do not depend on the number of performances and consumer demand is moderately high, we have a good that is socially beneficial but won't be provided at all by markets. No single price will attract enough consumers to cover the costs of production, and for-profits cannot successfully practice price discrimination for two reasons. First, as I noted above, Ben-Ner found that consumers would not trust for-profits with the necessary information. Second, tickets can be resold. Nobody would buy tickets directly if they were charged more than others for the same quality seat. Instead, they would ask someone charged a lower price to buy extra tickets for them. Voluntary price discrimination is needed, and that can be provided only by a nonprofit.

Another way that nonprofits deal with the overexclusion problem is to use cross-subsidization (James 1983, 1998; Weisbrod 1998). Here, rather than charge different consumers different prices for the same product, the nonprofit charges higher prices for some products to generate financial surplus that can be used to lower the price, and so reduce exclusion, for other services. For example, zoos and aquariums use profits from gift shops and other concessions to finance an average admission fee that is far below the profit-maximizing level (Cain and Meritt 1998). Cross-subsidization is done for many reasons, of which one is to reduce exclusion from collective goods, and is discussed further in the chapters in this volume by Brown and Slivinski and by Tuckman and Chang.

Nonprofits help to solve contract failure in five ways. First, the nondistribution of profits reduces (or eliminates, depending upon the details of enforcement) the financial benefits from delivering less than the promised quality or quantity of services. Second, the nondistribution constraint affects the rewards of founding and controlling a nonprofit rather than another kind of organization. A process of "entrepreneurial sorting" takes place, and those residing in the nonprofit sector will have different personal objectives regarding what they want to accomplish in their role. Hansmann (1980) wrote about both these arguments, speculating that the sorting would enhance the trustworthiness of nonprofit firms. As we will see in later sections, this is not necessarily the case, although sorting is likely to be important.

Third, nonprofits are often managed by "demand-side stakeholders" (Ben-Ner 1986), those who care about the organizational output quantity or quality and not just their financial returns. Donors, members, and clients are demand-side stakeholders, who presumably want the organization to offer higher quality than others charging the same price and lower prices than others producing the same quality. This is in contrast with for-profit organizations, controlled by "supply-side stakeholders" (stock and debt holders) who want high prices (given the quality) and low quality (given the price). Nonprofit organizations and consumer cooperatives (which are owned by the consumers of the organization's output and receive profits as member dividends) are the two kinds of "patron-controlled organizations" in Ben-Ner's terminology. Both are more trustworthy than for-profits. As he points out, it is good to have your child in a nonprofit day-care center but even better if the center-owner's children are also customers.

Fourth, nonprofit organizations are immune from financially based takeover bids as they do not have shares of stock that can be traded for profit. Thus, the dedication of the founding entrepreneurs to trustworthy behavior is not endangered by organizational transformation. This argument and its limitations have not, to my knowledge, been much explored in the existing literature.

Finally, the existence of some trustworthy nonprofits can have spillover benefits on the trustworthiness of competitors. Hirth (1999) develops a formal model of contract failure in which two types of nonprofit firms (trustworthy and opportunistic), one type of for-profit firm (opportunistic), and two types of consumers (informed and uninformed) are present. Informed consumers can detect contract failure when it occurs, whereas uninformed cannot. Opportunistic nonprofits are "for-profits-in-disguise," organizations that claim to be nonprofits and have received approval for all the tax and other benefits that accompany this status but secretly distribute their profits. The relative proportion of trustworthy and opportunistic nonprofits depends upon enforcement of the nondistribution constraint. Hirth shows that, depending upon the proportions of each type and enforcement, a market consisting of only nonprofits is often trustworthy whereas a market consisting only of for-profits is often not trustworthy. His most interesting result stems from the sorting, not of entrepreneurs, but of consumers. When for-profits and nonprofits compete with each other in the same market, they may both be trustworthy. Uninformed consumers, knowing their inability to detect contract failure, will patronize nonprofit organizations exclusively. This means that the for-profit's pool of customers contains a higher-than-average share of informed consumers, and so it will no longer pay to try to cheat them. The presence of a nonprofit organization creates a spillover benefit, making competing for-profits equally trustworthy.

Voluntary Failure

The third failure in the three-failures theory is by nonprofit organizations. Again, nonprofit organizations fail for many reasons, only some of which concern economic efficiency or the issues discussed here. Salamon (1987) was the first to organize four of these ideas as his theory of "voluntary failure," although we will use this label to include additional arguments. His four sources of failure included philanthropic insufficiency, philanthropic particularism, philanthropic paternalism (or, as I prefer, "parentalism"), and philanthropic amateurism.

Philanthropic insufficiency suggests reasons why nonprofit organizations have difficulty addressing the underprovision of collective goods, particularly in recessions, when the need is greatest. Voluntary action faces the "free-riding problem," discussed in more detail in Vesterlund (this volume). This includes several interrelated issues. First, as discussed above, donors might fear that rather than adding to total provision of some collective good, their donations would enable governments or other donors to withdraw their own contributions. Second, potential donors enjoy the collective good whether or not they contribute. Third, donors may not consider the external benefits they confer on others when they contribute, weighing only their own enjoyment of the collective good in their tabulation of the costs and benefits of their donation. My summary of this literature is that philanthropic insufficiency is a problem, but it is not as severe a problem as the simplest economic theories would suggest. In any case, nonprofit organizations can take many specific actions to reduce the importance of this problem.

Philanthropic particularism refers to the tendency of nonprofit organizations to focus on particular ethnic, religious, geographic, or ideologic groups, leading to duplication in some cases and gaps in coverage in others. To some extent, particularism is a natural consequence of fighting philanthropic insufficiency—it is easier to solve the free-rider problem in a community of similar individuals that repeatedly interact. Paternalism refers to the tendency of those who choose to work or volunteer for nonprofit organizations to treat problems as they perceive them, rather than as the clients perceive them. This is unlike government action, where clients have at least some small say through the ballot box. Amateurism refers to the tendency to rely less on credentialed workers, perhaps appropriate if client needs stem from moral problems rather than societal and technical factors. All these issues are discussed further in the chapters by Clemens and by Grønbjerg and Smith in this volume and by Douglas (1987).

How do nonprofit organizations fall short of curing the three market failures we have discussed? With respect to the underprovision problem, philanthropic insufficiency obviously limits the nonprofit ability to respond. In addition, when too many organizations representing too many causes compete for scarce donations, this causes problems. One organization's solicitation efforts can increase the costs of fundraising at other organizations (and so decrease the net funds available for collective good provision). This "commons externality" was first highlighted by Rose-Ackerman (1982) and is discussed further in Brown and Slivinski (this volume).

Nonprofit ability to solve the overexclusion problem depends upon whether consumers really trust the nonprofits enough to reveal their willingness to pay. Without such trust, nonprofits cannot charge high prices to high demanders, and so absent other sources of finance (such as government grants) they cannot subsidize prices below costs for the low demanders. In addition, there must be limited competition for high demanders. If, for example, a competing for-profit firm picked a price (or set of prices) only modestly above costs, the nonprofit could not set a higher price than its same-quality competitor. This would reduce the nonprofit's ability to subsidize prices for low demanders (Steinberg and Weisbrod 2005).

Nonprofits differ in their ability to combat contract failure for a variety of reasons. First, governments rarely devote substantial resources to monitoring and enforcing the nondistribution constraint. Second, when governments do enforce the constraint, detecting covert distributions is difficult. Nonetheless, it may be easier to detect distributions than shortfalls in output quantity or quality. Weisbrod (1988:22–23) concisely summarized the argument and its limitations: "We regulate what we can monitor easily, and we monitor what we can gauge usefully and inexpensively. If and when regulation of nonprofits per se is easier than direct regulation of outputs, production processes, or the distribution of output, the nonprofit form of institution is attractive."

Thus, nonprofit markets will contain mixtures of genuine nonprofits, which do not distribute, and for-profits-in-disguise, which do.

In the basic contract-failure story, nonprofits do not cut corners and so have higher costs of production. They nonetheless break even because consumers are willing to pay more for the presumably higher-quality nonprofit outputs. However, if consumers believe that some "nonprofits" are actually for-profits-in-disguise, they will no longer be willing to pay such a large premium for products certified by the nonprofit label. Then, the bad drives out the good. Nonprofits that wish to provide the promised quantity or quality at the market price will have increasing trouble breaking even, and may compromise on quality or leave the market to the for-profits-in-disguise. Depending on the assumed details of entry, enforcement ability, and other subsidies granted to organizations that purport to be nonprofit, four outcomes are possible. First, as detailed above in the discussion of Hirth (1999), the honest nonprofits might force the opportunistic ones to behave well. Second, nonprofits and for-profits may occupy different niches, with nonprofits selling high quality at a high price, for-profits selling lower quality at a lower price, and no contract failure. This possibility is discussed in an alternative model in Hirth (1999). Third, honest nonprofits and for-profits-in-disguise may coexist over time, with average trustworthiness higher than it would be without some honest nonprofits and lower than it would be without some for-profits-in-disguise. Finally, for-profits-in-disguise can eliminate honest nonprofits, and so the nonprofit label becomes useless in solving contract failure (Steinberg 1993b).

Third, patron control does not work well when contract failure occurs for a private good (Ben-Ner 1986, 1987). We do not see nonprofit auto-repair shops because the manager can shortchange other consumers to improve the quality of the repair services he or she consumes. Patron control works best when important elements of product quality are jointly consumed by the manager/consumer and all other consumers.

Fourth, although the nondistribution constraint removes one incentive to shortchange donors and consumers, it does not remove other incentives. The organizational mission might differ from what the donor most desires. For example, donors might want to support increased student aid, whereas university administrators want to support increased faculty research. Restricting their gifts in a formal legal sense is relatively easy for donors, but difficult in a more relevant economic sense because budgets can be reallocated to account for actual and likely gifts. Knowing that donors will support financial aid, the university can budget less of its other discretionary resources to the task, so that in effect the donations support additional research rather than additional aid.

At least some collective good is being provided in the preceding example. This does not have to be the case. Nonprofit managers may use donations and profits from sales to give themselves perks that do not help accomplish the organizational mission but are nonetheless legal forms of distribution. For example, nonprofits may locate in prestigious high-rent districts where they build magnificent headquarters. Nonprofit executives may travel first-class to conferences in exotic locations. Alternatively, incompetence, inattention, and indolence can flourish, protected from market competition by the donations, subsidies, and higher consumer willingness-to-pay that accompany the nonprofit label. In all these ways, well-meaning nonprofits can have the same erosive effects on trustworthiness as for-profits-in-disguise. Thus, whether nonprofits are trustworthy depends as well on the dedication of the board to the organizational mission and its vigilance in monitoring the managerial chain of authority (see Ostrower and Stone, this volume, for further discussion).

Finally, the nonprofit label cannot signal trustworthiness or elicit the financial support necessary to act trustworthily if consumers and donors are unaware of it. Surveys find that consumers do not always know whether the organizations they deal with are nonprofit or for-profit (Permut 1981; Mauser 1993). However, consumers may be aware of organizational characteristics associated with nonprofit status that serve as signals of trustworthiness (such as the religious affiliation of a day-care center). The mechanism Hirth (1999) suggests can still work if only some uninformed consumers are unaware of whether they are dealing with nonprofit or for-profit providers. Finally, regulators are certainly aware of sector, and often choose more stringent regulations for for-profit providers (Hansmann 2003). Further discussion of all these challenges to contract failure theory can be found in the chapters by Brody and by Schlesinger and Gray in this volume, Ortmann and Schlesinger (2003), and Hansmann (2003).

Productive and allocative inefficiencies provide additional forms of voluntary failure. The idea, which I have previously labeled the "property rights approach" (Steinberg 1987), is that the attenuated ownership structure of nonprofit organizations reduces owner incentives to care about things that the for-profit market does well. Productive inefficiency arises because the owners do not get to keep a share of financial residuals and so do not labor to keep costs down. As noted above, nonprofit managers may choose higher-cost perk-laden means of production, although here the emphasis is on social costs that occur whether or not consumers are misinformed.[9] The owners would not benefit financially from lower costs, and there are no hostile takeover bids to force them to pay attention. Whether and to what extent this form of inefficiency occurs is quite controversial. The reader should see the chapters by Brown and Slivinski and by Schlesinger and Gray in this volume for further discussion.

Second, attenuated ownership raises the cost of capital, all else equal. Nonprofit organizations cannot sell meaningful shares of stock to raise capital, and so must rely more heavily on debt. Hansmann (1981b) argues that this raises the cost of capital, although the exemption of U.S. nonprofits from the corporate income tax serves as a crude corrective. Higher capital costs lead to an inefficient mix of inputs and inadequate or slow response to increases in demand for outputs. This creates both productive and allocative inefficiency. Again, this form of voluntary failure is controversial, and the reader should see Brown and Slivinski (this volume) and Bilodeau and Steinberg (forthcoming) for further details.

Third, attenuated ownership means that owners who follow changing consumer tastes and demands and innovate accordingly are not rewarded for this attention. Sometimes, nonprofit organizations are proud of their failures here, as in higher education. Nonprofit universities are proud to provide, paternalistically, what they think their students need rather than what they shortsightedly want. However, the pressures of competition with new for-profit universities and less-paternalistic universities are eroding this difference. The definition of economic efficiency does not allow for paternalism, so whether one regards these differences as good or bad, they show up as a form of inefficiency.

Closing the Circle: Reacting to Voluntary Failure

Three-failures theory does not presume that any sector is "first" and the other sectors react to its failures. Rather, the approach arranges the three sectors around a circle, with each reacting to the failures of its two neighbors. Weisbrod's (1975) exposition, followed here, has nonprofits responding to failures by the other two sectors, which allows the argument to proceed linearly but perhaps falls short in developing our intuition about the whole circle. Salamon (1987) recognized this shortcoming, and began his exposition with nonprofits as the first sector, whose failures are addressed by government and for-profits. This brought the new insights regarding voluntary failure. Regardless, we need now to specify how the other two sectors respond to this voluntary failure.

Historically, the Salamon approach may be more accurate, although it is a bit hard to tell because the definitions of the respective sectors have been even fuzzier in the past. In modern times, it is often (but not universally) the nonprofit sector that is the first to respond to a natural disaster or the first to carry out a social innovation because of the natural inertia in government action. Salamon (1987) noted that governmental action requires, in order, public arousal, information gathering, passage of laws, and establishment of a bureaucracy to carry out those laws. Some of these steps are carried out in advance for response to natural disasters, so it remains an open question whether one expects nonprofits to be the first responders. Regardless, voluntary failure limits that response and government supplies additional resources in a less particularistic and more credentialed way.

Salamon did not address how for-profits close the circle. Other literature makes clear that for-profits respond well to productive inefficiency wherever it occurs and to allocative inefficiency in markets for private and some excludable collective goods. Low-cost production, innovation, and attention to consumer demands are the hallmarks of the sector because the owners benefit and because these actions eliminate the takeover threat. When for-profits and nonprofits coexist, competition forces nonprofits to respond likewise or go out of business. This competition is limited because of a variety of "cushions"—subsidies, tax exemptions, and the like provided to nonprofits but not their for-profit competitors—that allow nonprofits to function distinctively (Steinberg 1991, 1993b).

Empirical Evidence

Evidence supports many propositions discussed above. Clearly, nonprofits provide collective goods, but Weisbrod's model suggests that we can predict the relative roles of government and nonprofits in financing these goods. Specifically, he argues that the more heterogeneous a society is, the more dissatisfaction there will be with government provision levels and therefore nonprofit financing of collective goods will be larger. Note that he is not talking about the size of the nonprofit sector, which is largely paid for with government money as grants and contracts, but only about the donatively financed portion of nonprofit expenditures. Thus, the result of Salamon and Anheier (1998) that the nonprofit sector is smaller in more heterogeneous countries is not quite on point (Steinberg and Young 1998). In contrast, James (1993) finds that after controlling for government subsidies to private education, more heterogeneous countries rely more heavily on nonprofit primary and secondary education institutions. She tests various measures of heterogeneity. Religious heterogeneity has the largest effect, and measures of linguistic heterogeneity and income diversity have smaller and less-statistically significant effects. Feigenbaum (1980) used variation over time to explain state spending on income redistribution and total donations in the United States. She finds no statistically significant impacts of heterogeneity on government spending, but a very significant positive correlation between heterogeneity in age and donations. Finally, Chang and Tuckman (1996) find that nonprofits in racially diverse communities rely on donations for a greater share of their revenues.

Many other chapters in this volume present evidence on contract failure (especially Brown and Slivinski; Schlesinger and Gray; and Kendall, Knapp, and Forder), so I will present only an overview here. It is extremely hard to test contract failure theory because it concerns unobservables.

If the author of any study could reliably detect differences in the trustworthiness of organizations, presumably governments could too and they would directly regulate the behavior in question, rather than merely reducing the temptation to cheat. Faced with this dilemma, five strategies have been employed, with the greatest volume of studies testing contract failure in the health-care, day-care, and nursing-home industries. First, some studies look for differences in characteristics that will be observable by some consumers (the informed) but not all. This strategy is particularly effective where the unobservable characteristic is valued differently by different consumers, so that uniform government regulations would reduce desirable diversity in the marketplace. Second, some studies have used indirect tests based on the number of complaints filed with the government determined to be nonactionable because they concerned matters on which regulations had not been set. Third, some studies have used indirect tests based on how the respective sectoral market shares have changed when technological improvements have reduced the cost of monitoring or when state regulations have been changed. Fourth, studies have compared the experiences of different types of consumers—those who search extensively for a provider versus those who do not, or those who are deemed to be at special risk for exploitation versus those who are not. Finally, some studies have simply asked consumers or government contractors why they make the sectoral choices they do.

On balance, it is my opinion that the evidence supports the predictions of contract failure theory, but others have looked at the same studies and come to a different conclusion. The importance of contract failure versus various sorts of voluntary failure has not, to date, been well assessed, so the case for systematically preferring nonprofit providers is, at best, incomplete. The importance of contract failure likely varies across nonprofit industries, and changes with shifts in technology and governmental regulation.

Hundreds of studies attempt to test for efficiency differences between nonprofit and for-profit organizations, and many of these are reviewed in other chapters in this volume (notably Schlesinger and Gray; Kendall, Knapp, and Forder). Most consider the competition between generic nonprofits and for-profits, but some distinguish types within each sector (secular versus religiously affiliated, chain versus independent). A majority of studies conclude that nonprofits are less efficient, but many studies find either no difference or a difference in the opposite direction. I remain skeptical of the conclusions drawn by these studies because of methodological difficulties noted in these chapters and elsewhere. My biggest worry is that organizations produce a multiplicity of outputs, some of which are excluded from available data and some of which are, by their nature, impossible to measure objectively. To the extent that nonprofits produce more unmeasured outputs, the costs of the measured outputs will be overstated and nonprofits will seem less efficient. For example, hospitals produce a collective benefit that is typically omitted from empirical studies—the assurance that in case of a sudden increase in demand due to epidemics or disasters, they will have the capacity to treat everyone (Holtmann 1983). Are unused hospital beds evidence of productive inefficiency, or of the efficient production of capacity insurance, an output excluded from empirical studies?

A related strand of literature assumes that nonprofit inefficiency is limited by competition with for-profit providers. Thus, for example, many studies (summarized and evaluated in more detail in Steinberg 1987) compare the cost per claim processed by nonprofit and for-profit health insurance firms. The studies find that nonprofit costs are higher by an amount that varies with the size of the tax breaks given to nonprofits but not their for-profit competitors. The authors of these studies argue that the two sectors are doing the same thing, one at higher costs, so that higher costs represent productive inefficiency. However, claims processing can be done carefully, with every valid claim approved and every fraudulent claim disapproved, or less carefully to cut costs or increase revenues. Without measuring the quality of claims processing by the two sectors, we cannot tell whether nonprofits are inefficient.

A third strand of literature focuses on the reaction of both sectors to changes in demand. Steinwald and Neuhauser (1970) and Hansmann (1987b) find that the nonprofit market share is lower in markets that are rapidly expanding, which is consistent with either a failure to pay attention, lack of capital for expansion, or paternalistic preferences. Hansmann (1996) argues that nonprofits are less likely to exit markets when demand for services decreases; a later article provides modest supporting evidence (Hansmann, Kessler, and McClellan 2003).

Shortcomings of the Three-Failures Theory

Three-failures theory, at least in my exposition, is incomplete.[10] The various pieces explain why consumers would want to buy from and donors donate to nonprofits, but do not explain why nonprofits are there for them to use. What is needed is a theory of the supply of this organizational form to complement the theories of demand. Unless we know why and when nonprofit organizations will be created, it is hard to assess whether they can play the roles we have discussed. Predicting the objectives and behavior of individual organizations is also hard. How will they respond to changes in public policy, competition, the economy, or technology? Understanding the coexistence of providers from each sector in the same service industry is also difficult. If nonprofits are more trustworthy, why do they not drive their competitors out of business? If nonprofits are less efficient, do they survive only because of subsidies? If they have counterbalancing trust advantages and efficiency disadvantage, is the nonprofit market share entirely arbitrary or do economic theories have more to say on the matter?

The second problem with three-failures theory is its excessive focus on efficiency, in the broad economic sense. Efficiency is certainly important, but it leaves out much and the other sorts of roles that nonprofit organizations can play in a mixed-sector economy are ignored by this literature. Efficiency concerns the size of the economic pie—whether the most-valued mixture of outputs is produced. It says nothing about how the pie is shared by consumers, about distributional justice. The fair distribution of income is a much more controversial matter, but one where arguably for-profits fail and governmental redistribution is limited. Nonprofit missions talk of helping the indigent, of providing affordable housing, of assuring that nobody is denied medical care because of insufficient income, and the other sectors leave room for nonprofits to play this role. The literature has made only the barest of starts in understanding this nonprofit role (e.g., Clotfelter 1992; Steinberg and Weisbrod 1998), but it rests well within, if not exclusively within, the economists' toolbox.

Efficiency is defined with respect to preexisting consumer preferences. These preferences determine the value placed on various goods and services for use in determining the value-maximizing mix. Yet, the stated mission of many nonprofits is to change those preferences—to make people want to enjoy a habit of lifetime learning, worship God, preserve the environment, stop child abuse, or respect the decisions made by gun owners. Advertising, social marketing, and advocacy play a role in market efficiency, but I believe persuasion involves more than just informing those with preexisting preferences. Governments and for-profits also play roles in seeking to change preferences. Much more research should be conducted on the distinctive roles best played by each sector. Perhaps economists are not the best ones to conduct this sort of research, but the work that economists do should not blind us to the importance of these other roles.

Three-failures theory also leaves out other roles for the sector. For example, Mason (1996) talks of the instrumental, expressive, and affiliative roles of the sector. Economists study the instrumental role—the use of nonprofits to obtain stated objectives such as finding job placements or feeding and housing the indigent. However, work in the nonprofit sector is not just about doing. It is about making statements and being with others. Philanthropic amateurism and particularism may seem like failures when viewed through the instrumental lens, but they are valued roles for the sector when viewed through the expressive and affiliative lenses. Nonprofits play many additional roles, omitted here because they are best discussed by sociologists and political scientists (see the chapters in this volume by Grønbjerg and Smith and by Clemens). Nonetheless, these roles should always be kept in mind.

TOWARD A COMPLETE THEORY

Three-failures theory is incomplete, omitting the supply side and focusing on the efficiency roles of the sector to the relative exclusion of other roles. In this section, I address some of these holes. However, just filling the holes is not enough—the supply side interacts with the demand side so that, for example, whether nonprofits deal with the under-provision problem depends on which theory of supply we adopt. We need an integrated approach, where all the various pieces are mutually consistent and jointly establish the respective roles of each sector. I begin this section by laying out the framework of a complete theory, then discuss the various supplements and partially integrated theories offered to date.

The theory of long-run supply by for-profit firms is well established. Every firm wants to maximize its profits. If demand increases, more firms enter the market, but each of these new entrants also wants to maximize profits. There is a logical separability between the number of firms and their respective objectives. This is sensible since for-profit firms that did not want to maximize their profits would not survive as such due to competition and the market for takeover bids. The situation is more complicated in the nonprofit sector, because no overwhelming force automatically makes new entrants have the same objectives as existing ones. Thus, I argue in my 1993a paper, a satisfactory model of nonprofit supply should simultaneously explain the decision to enter and the objectives of those who do enter. This aspect of theory integration leads to a clearer understanding, as the following example illustrates. A partial theory based on Hirth (1999) would conclude that under specified circumstances, nonprofit organizations would remain trustworthy despite the presence of a few for-profits-in-disguise. Another partial theory would say that if a trustworthy nonprofit organization receives a government subsidy, it would expand and the market would function better. Putting these two theories together without any explanation for where organizational objectives come from would lead to the conclusion that government subsidies to nonprofits improve the efficiency of the market. However, Hirth actually has an integrated theory with respect to this example, where an increase in government subsidies would attract more for-profits-in-disguise into the market. In turn, competition with for-profits-in-disguise makes it more difficult for legitimate nonprofits to remain trustworthy and survive. Subsidies can make contract failure worse. The theory that combines objectives and entry gets a different, and more accurate, conclusion than the theory that separates the two.

Some progress is made if, like the first models of nonprofits, one simply asserts some specific organizational objective and explores the consequences of having that objective. Much more progress is made if the theory includes those factors that determine which organizational objectives are likely to emerge and thrive. Then we can better understand why nonprofit organizations play different roles in different countries, at different points in time, or following a change in public policy. Nonprofits first respond to the changing conditions, using their preexisting objectives, and then their objectives evolve, provoking further response.

Figure 5.2 provides a schematic diagram to aid our thinking about complete and integrated theories.[11] The supply decision is made by those who are tempted to found a new nonprofit organization or those who might want to maintain or transform existing nonprofits. For convenience, I refer to

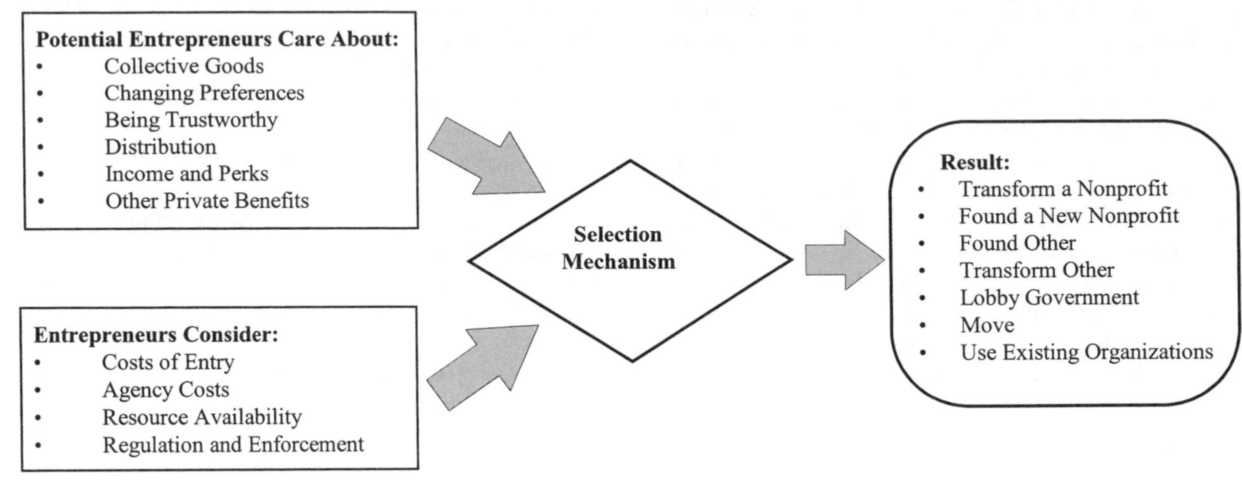

FIGURE 5.2. SCHEMATIC OF A COMPLETE THEORY

both kinds of actors as "entrepreneurs." Defined this way, entrepreneurs are a logical construct encompassing founders and agents of change, rather than specified persons.

The top left part of the figure tells us what potential entrepreneurs care about. Potential entrepreneurs consider how best to obtain their objective—by founding a new nonprofit, transforming the behavior of existing nonprofits, preserving the mission against pressures to change, founding or transforming a different kind of organization (for-profit, consumer cooperative, labor-managed firm, and so on), or working to change the decisions of government agencies. Alternatively, they take a nonentrepreneurial role—supporting existing organizations as donors, volunteers, and customers or moving to a location where existing organizations meet their needs. They decide by considering their own objectives and the various factors that make those objectives easier to achieve if they pick the nonprofit form. The factors that determine whether objectives can be accomplished through nonprofit entrepreneurship (founding or transforming) appear on the bottom left, and the possible outcomes of entrepreneurial decision-making appear on the right of figure 5.2.

Once each potential entrepreneur has pondered what to do if granted control of the organization, a selection mechanism or internal political process determines who is given that control and nonprofit behavior flows from this choice. The same process of decision-making leads to the emergence, or nonemergence, of competing organizations and simultaneously determines the objectives of competitors.

This approach is clearly inspired and influenced by a paper and later book by Young (1981, 1983). He argues that the objectives of nonprofit organizations are determined by the objectives of their entrepreneurs, who establish the organizational culture and/or write the articles of incorporation and the bylaws. He lists a variety of pure entrepreneurial types, garnered from the management literature, and speculates on the factors that led some types to prefer to work in the different sectors and in different industries. This began the "entrepreneurial sorting" approach, which, I think, has yet to bear its fullest fruit. It is also inspired and influenced by Ben-Ner and Van Hoomissen (1991). Both will be discussed in context below.

Alternative Objectives

In the first part of figure 5.2, I list six categories of entrepreneurial objectives. Entrepreneurs might care about collective goods, either because, as a consumer, they want to guarantee that someone makes them available (as in Bilodeau and Slivinski 1996, 1997, 1998) or because they get a special warm glow from playing a personal role in providing them to the community (as in Eckel and Steinberg 1993; Steinberg and Eckel 1994; or Roomkin and Weisbrod 1999).

The second category of objectives involves changing the preferences or consumption behavior of others. This includes a variety of missions—conversion of others to one's faith or ideology (James 1982, 1986, 1989; James and Rose-Ackerman 1986), cultivation of tastes for the arts (Throsby and Withers 1979; Hansmann 1981a), and various forms of social engineering, such as encouraging people to stop smoking, enjoy safe sex, use their seat belts, or exercise more. Strong believers would have sufficient motivation to incur the substantial costs required of entrepreneurs, and may prefer the nonprofit form if doing so signals a sincerity that facilitates the conversion of others.

Third, some entrepreneurs care about not abusing the trust consumers and donors place in them. Thus, some models of nonprofit behavior include trustworthy entrepreneurs among the set of potential founders and managers (such as Schiff and Weisbrod 1991). Fourth, potential entrepreneurs may care about the distribution of income, either directly or about changes in that distribution that they can take credit for (Steinberg and Weisbrod 2005).

The fifth category is income plus perquisites. This objective is used in the property rights literature (e.g., Frech 1976) but also appears in Preston 1988; Gassler 1989; Schiff and Weisbrod 1991; Eckel and Steinberg 1993; Steinberg and Eckel 1994; and Glaeser and Shleifer 2001. By perquisites, I refer here to job attributes other than monetary compensation that are valued by the entrepreneur but not by others, including first-class travel, fancy offices, and on-the-job leisure. In a sense, the warm glow from providing public goods is also a perquisite. This is a job attribute the entrepreneur might value, but it also provides benefits to others so, for example, Steinberg and Eckel (1994) call this a "public-benefit perk."

The last category is a catchall, intended to remind us of all the benefits that economists typically leave out of their models. This includes desires for power, control, expression, affiliation, legitimation, and the like. Many entrepreneurial types listed in Young's (1981) original typology belong here, including "artists" (who value the creative act in reshuffling organizational blocks or creating a whole representing their vision), professionals (who value the pursuit and development of new ideas), searchers (out to prove themselves), independents (who want to avoid sharing authority and decision-making), conservers (loyalists who innovate only during crises), and power seekers (who either like to control the individuals that work for them or want a larger stage to wield power from).

My classification of entrepreneurial motives does not necessarily show the motives and behavior of the organization for three reasons. First, many entrepreneurs will have multiple motives. This idea is exploited in Eckel and Steinberg (1993) and Steinberg and Eckel (1994), where potential entrepreneurs care about varying mixtures of collective goods and private-benefit perks. Second, other factors (such as the dependence of resources on the nonprofit output mix, contractual stipulations, and public regulation) may force entrepreneurs with one objective to pursue alternative goals. For example, Preston's (1988) entrepreneurs care only about their own income, but donors reward those entrepreneurs that provide collective goods with higher incomes. Finally, the internal political dynamics of the organization may cause the organizational objectives to stray from those of the original entrepreneurs.

Many existing models of nonprofit organizations postulate an organizational objective consistent with mixtures of these entrepreneurial motivations. For example, Newhouse's (1970) nonprofits maximize a mixture of the quantity and quality of their output. He does not explicitly incorporate entrepreneurs. However, this organizational objective could stem from entrepreneurs that care to change the preference and consumption of others (refining their tastes so that they appreciate a "higher quality" of artistic expression). Alternatively, it could result from those that want to be trustworthy (and so provide the promised high level of quality despite opportunities to do otherwise), from those that value provision of an excludable collective good (who deal with the overexclusion problem through quantity maximization), or from those that care about prestige (an element of the catch-all category). Tullock (1966) and Niskanen (1971) postulated that some nonprofits care about maximizing the budget under their control. This organizational preference might stem from entrepreneurs that care about prestige or income (which are generally higher the larger the organization). Lee (1971), Pauly and Redisch (1973), and Feigenbaum (1987) have nonprofits that care about their use of preferred inputs, which can be doctors, high-tech equipment, or disabled employees. Finally, Malani, Philipson, and David (2003) provide a general model, where three of the hybrid motivations provided in other literature are special cases. Unfortunately, none of these models start with entrepreneurial preferences or otherwise incorporate a model of how and when organizational objectives would change.

Factors Hindering or Aiding Accomplishment of Objectives through the Nonprofit Form

The theory of market failure already tells us why entrepreneurs who want to provide collective goods or operate trustily would prefer the nonprofit form. True, a for-profit firm could donate all its profits to charity, but especially for publicly held firms (where shares of stock are openly traded), the threat of a takeover bid limits such behavior. Nonprofit organizations are different. Nonprofits that want to provide collective goods are immune from takeover and any initial investment by the entrepreneur is supplemented by the donations of others. This bit of foreshadowing suggests that we enumerate the factors that promote or hinder the entrepreneur's ability to accomplish his objectives through the nonprofit organizational form.

First, there are costs of entry (or of transforming the mission of an existing nonprofit). Ben-Ner and Van Hoomissen (1991) detail these costs as including: (a) identifying and assembling a collection of willing stakeholders; (b) determining whether collective demand is sufficient to cover costs; (c) organizing production decisions; (d) inducing stakeholders to truthfully reveal their preferences; and (e) establishing a governance mechanism to ensure stakeholder control against free-riding, internal incentive problems, and the like. A new organization is formed if the expected flow of net benefits exceeds the flow of net benefits from the next best alternative.[12] Thus, for collective goods, the entrepreneur compares the expected net benefits from current governmentally supported provision with those if a new organization is created and makes his choice accordingly. If government is not supporting the entrepreneurial cause at all, the entrepreneur compares the expected net benefits from creating a nonprofit with the net benefits from lobbying government to meet the need. In this calculation, the entrepreneur recalls Salamon's (1987) list of the transactions costs of governmental action: public arousal, information gathering, passage of laws, and establishment of a bureaucracy to carry out those laws.

Most of the costs of founding a nonprofit are reduced if the founder is a member of a group of like-minded individuals who repeatedly interact with each other and so gain mutual trust. This happens through clubs, alumni groups, and most importantly religious congregations, so it is not surprising that many nonprofits are founded through a seed organization like a congregation.[13] In contrast, the costs are increased if the pool of potential stakeholders is diverse. Although all might be high-demanders, if they thoroughly disagree among themselves about what expenditure level on collective goods would be optimal, they might not agree to mutually form a new organization to meet their high demands. This suggests a revision of Weisbrod's theory—preferences for the collective good must be heterogeneous (otherwise government suffices) but lumpy, with a cluster of agreeable high-demanders willing and able to work together (Ben-Ner and Van Hoomissen 1991).

Agency costs result whenever the entrepreneur (the principal) requires the assistance of others (agents) whose objectives are not thoroughly aligned with his own. The principal uses costly mechanisms that realign the agent's incentives (such as profit-sharing plans), monitors the performance of agents, and accepts that some failure will remain after incentives and monitoring are carried out. Agency costs are likely to differ with the prospective choices that an entrepreneur makes. Profit-sharing plans are somewhat restricted in the nonprofit sector by the nondistribution constraint, but to the extent nonprofit workers are motivated by accomplishment of the nonprofit mission, they receive a distribution in kind that plays a similar role (Slivinski 2002; see also Brown and Slivinski, this volume, and Bilodeau and Steinberg, forthcoming).

One agency cost recognizes the finite duration of entrepreneurial control. Entrepreneurs can lose control during their lifetime if their for-profit firm is taken over or if their nonprofit board moves in a different direction, and certainly lose control after their deaths. Closely held corporations, with dynastic control, reduce this problem in the for-profit world, but for at least some purposes, establishment of a charitable trust or corporation provides a better solution.

The availability of resources also determines entrepreneurial choice. In the for-profit sector, entrepreneurs can obtain capital by issuing shares of stock or obtaining loans. Nonprofits can do only the latter, and because any loans are not backed by at-risk shareholder investments, the cost of debt is higher for nonprofits (Hansmann 1981b). However, nonprofits can use grants and donations, volunteer labor, and (depending upon local laws) tax-exempt bonds to obtain capital, and can accumulate retained earnings for investment more quickly if they are exempt from corporate income taxes. Resources from sales or from fundraising depend, in part, on competition from other organizations, so that entrepreneurs should also consider the likely evolution of competitors over the lifetime of their mission.

Finally, the way in which organizations in the various sectors are regulated, and the quality of enforcement of those regulations, determines where the entrepreneurial objective can be best accomplished. We have already seen how these factors affect the emergence of for-profits-in-disguise; the other ways they matter are numerous and self-evident.

The integrated approach I advocate assumes that the entrepreneur picks the organizational form that best accomplishes his objectives. That said, nonprofits arise in situations where it is very difficult to accomplish objectives using any kind of organization. The correspondence between organizational behavior and entrepreneurial objectives need not be very close, as entrepreneurs are hindered in this "least-worst" situation by transactions costs, agency costs, resource dependencies, and governmental regulations that make it hard to transform objectives into results.

Fitting the Pieces Together

There are many ways to fit these various pieces together correctly and gain deep insight into the role of the nonprofit sector. The literature has only begun this process. Perhaps the best effort to date is found in a series of papers by Bilodeau and Slivinski (1996, 1997, 1998) and by Bilodeau (2000), employing variations on a common structure. In all these models, a group of individuals cares about a collective good. Comparing the benefits of founding a new nonprofit or for-profit to provide that good with those from supporting organizations founded by another member of the group, one of them chooses to be the entrepreneur. She invests an initial sum of money toward providing that good, adds any resources obtainable through donations by others, and then devotes the total amount to the collective good. If the entrepreneur picks the for-profit form, she is allowed to withdraw some of the initial investment after seeing how much other people donate, but if she picks the nonprofit form, any such withdrawal would violate the nondistribution constraint.

One puzzle for any theory of supply is why the founder would choose to permanently constrain her future option to receive profits. Dividends can always be donated, and it would seem that the entrepreneur would like to retain the right to keep some dividends if the venture proves more than profitable enough to support the collective good. Bilodeau and Slivinski provide an answer to this puzzle: other donors consider the organization's sector in making their decisions. If they knew that the entrepreneur could withdraw part or all of her initial investment in response to their donation, they would be reluctant to give. Thus, those entrepreneurs that need the donations of others to accomplish their goal would want to give up the right to receive dividends.[14] The various papers by Bilodeau and Slivinski extend this approach to explain how nonprofits compete with each other or form a united campaign, how they compete in commercial markets also populated by for-profits, and how enforcement of the fair compensation constraint affects performance.

Several papers tackle aspects of entrepreneurial sorting. In Bilodeau and Slivinski (1996), potential entrepreneurs differ in entrepreneurial costs and the value they place on the collective good, but they focus on who emerges as a nonprofit founder without considering other entrepreneurial options across the sectors. Gassler (1989) and Schiff and Weisbrod (1991) assume that entrepreneurs are of two types (those valuing only profits, and those valuing other things). These types sort perfectly across the for-profit and nonprofit sectors respectively. Steinberg and Eckel (1994) assume that potential entrepreneurs value three things: income, private-benefit perks, and public-benefit perks, varying in the relative importance placed on the last two factors. They show both short-run effects of competition and tax policy (responses by preexisting nonprofits) and long-run effects (due to changes in the type of entrepreneur who locates in each sector). It is unclear at this time how much their results will generalize.

Evidence

What evidence is available on the prevalence of various entrepreneurial and organizational objectives? One could simply ask those in control what they are trying to do, or collect and analyze organizational mission statements. I am not aware of any studies that systematically survey founders, managers, and board members or that categorize mission statements according to the set of objectives detailed above,[15] and doing so would be worthwhile. However, this approach is problematic. Mission statements specify multiple, often competing, objectives without detailing how one objective is weighed against another. Mission statements are intentionally vague, as too much specificity risks alienating selected groups of stakeholders. The stated mission of a nonprofit organization will sometimes differ from its real objectives.

Instead of surveying the stated objectives of organizations, researchers have analyzed nonprofit behaviors to detect the "revealed objectives" of the organization—those objectives which organizations act as if they are trying to achieve. For example, Steinberg (1986) examines whether organizations act as if they want to maximize their net resources available for service provision (contributions minus fundraising costs) or their total budget (contributions) when they conduct fundraising campaigns. Service maximizers spend until the last dollar of fundraising expenditure brings in one dollar of added donations (with every previous dollar generating net resources), whereas budget maximizers spend until the last dollar brings in no additional donations. Steinberg finds that "welfare" organizations act like service maximizers; "education," "arts," and "research" organizations spend less on fundraising than they would if they were service maximizers, and "health" organizations act like budget maximizers. Other studies using similar methods challenge his results and the question remains open.[16]

Steinberg's study illustrates both the merits and drawbacks of the revealed objectives approach. Mismatches between stated and revealed objectives can be due to inaccurate statements, resource dependencies or regulations that impinge on behaviors, managerial errors or lack of knowledge, or the inability to control the actions of employees, subcontractors, and volunteers. For example, those in control of arts organizations may want to maximize the net returns from their fundraising campaign but lack up-front capital to do so. Still, behavior counts. Those in control of health organizations may have no intention of maximizing their budget, but the fact that they appear to act like budget maximizers is important.

Lowry (1997) generalizes this approach to include the effect of other sorts of nonprofit expenditure on total revenues and to broaden the class of objectives studied. He theorizes, like James (1983), that nonprofit managers have favored, neutral, and disfavored activities. Managers may care about revenues for their own sake (as in budget maximization), for their ability to support increased provision of favored activities, or both. He then analyzes a panel of citizen environmental groups and finds that they spend too little on fundraising (suggesting either that they are capital-constrained service maximizers or that they view fund-raising as a disfavored activity) and too much on collective goods (suggesting that the provision of collective goods is a favored activity) compared with the surplus-maximizing expenditure levels. He also finds that spending on selective incentives and information (loosely, member benefits) is excessive, suggesting that this too is a favored activity. A similar approach is taken by Vitaliano (2003), who compared religious nonprofit, secular nonprofit, and government nursing homes in New York State. Twenty-one percent of these homes extended the quality and quantity of care beyond their estimated profit-maximizing level, suggesting the organizations acted as if they had quality and quantity objectives. The same share of each kind of organization departed from profit maximization. The remainder of the organizations acted like "for-profits-in-disguise," although Vitaliano concedes this could be due to insufficient revenues to do anything else rather than duplicity.

Other papers infer the organizational objectives from the structure of managerial compensation. For example, Ballou and Weisbrod (2003) examine bonuses paid to hospital executives in secular nonprofit, religious nonprofit, and government hospitals. Controlling for many factors, they find that government hospitals are least likely to pay a bonus based on the quality of care, secular nonprofits are somewhat more likely, and religious nonprofits are much more likely to do so. They conclude that secular and religious nonprofit hospitals have different objectives, but that government hospitals face different constraints so it is not clear whether the behavioral difference is due to objectives or constraints. Related studies (Roomkin and Weisbrod 1999; Erus and Weisbrod 2003) come to similar conclusions. Finally, Ehrenberg et al. (2000) look at contractual bonuses given to university presidents when they meet academic, research, and performance goals.

A variety of other approaches for uncovering objectives have been tried. Eldenburg et al. (2004) examine the factors that determine the composition of hospital boards, board turnover, and CEO turnover to uncover objectives with respect to providing uncompensated care, generating excess revenues, and administrative costs. They find that for-profit, secular nonprofit, teaching nonprofit, religious nonprofit, government, and district hospitals place different weights on these three objectives. That said, uncovering the exact form of objectives from evidence of high turnover related to each factor is hard. Deneffe and Masson (2002) look at the response of hospital prices for private patients to changes in the Medicare, Medicaid, and charity caseload. They find that hospitals consider both profits and output as objectives. Lastly, Kapur and Weisbrod (2000) examine whether government and private nonprofit nursing homes and facilities for the mentally handicapped differ in their use of waiting lists and consumer satisfaction levels. Finding significant differences, they note that one explanation is that government pursues a supplier-of-last-resort objective function.

IMPLICATIONS FOR PUBLIC POLICY

Economic theories about the role of the nonprofit sector have much to contribute to the public policy debates that swirl around the sector. Rather than treat any policy comprehensively (a task left to other chapters in this volume), I end this chapter by illustrating the ways in which economic theory can be used here.

How should we design nonprofit corporation statutes, and how should we enforce the nondistribution constraint? The theory of contract failure suggests that our decisions here affect the trustworthiness of the sector, and this is one of the first published policy applications (Hansmann 1981c). From the trust perspective, the value of the nonprofit label applies equally well to purely commercial ventures as to traditional charities. Nondistribution policy also affects the ease with which nonprofits can obtain capital, and so interacts with the plethora of other statutes that exempt nonprofits from corporate taxation and allow them to benefit from tax-exempt bonds. The manner in which nondistribution is applied to takeovers and conversions affects whether entrepreneurs will choose the nonprofit form in order to restrict changes in mission. Finally, the way in which the fair compensation constraint is applied to board and executive compensation is critical. If the constraint is set too high, it does nothing to stop distributions. If the constraint is too low, entrepreneurs who value collective goods will prefer to found for-profit firms (Bilodeau 2000).

How should we treat nonprofit monopolies? Combinations in restraint of trade are restricted by antitrust legislation, with few allowances made for differences among the sectors. This is perhaps unfortunate, as there are real differences in the roles played by the respective sectors and the manner in which they will use their monopoly profits (Steinberg 1993a; Eckel and Steinberg 1993). Regardless of sector, monopoly power results in underprovision of the monopolized good, a market failure that antitrust law seeks to address. For-profit monopolies distribute their profits to owners, but nonprofit monopolies may use those profits to fix a different market failure (underprovision of collective goods or overexclusion from excludable public goods) or to supply redistributive financial aid. They may also waste those profits on private-benefit perks. Depending on the balance of these factors, nonprofit monopolies can be efficiency-enhancing or efficiency-diminishing, and ideally public policy should take account of this. Differences in the structure of control also change the motivation for merger and the suspicion with which authorities should view this activity. Patron-controlled nonprofits are more likely to be motivated by cost savings, whereas for-profits are more likely to be motivated by increased revenues resulting from underprovision.

When governments contract out for provision of social services, should they employ competitive bidding? Should they seek both nonprofit and for-profit bidders? Steinberg (1997) takes a first stab at these questions, noting that contract failure can make nonprofits a better option, but their productive inefficiency works in the opposite direction. Competitive bidding might help solve the latter problem, but reduces the ability of nonprofits to be trustworthy and still offer a winning bid, resulting perhaps in more for-profits-in-disguise.

Should we exempt nonprofit organizations from income, sales, value-added, and property taxes? Exemption gives nonprofits more resources, but this is hardly the most efficient way to deal with market failures. Direct subsidies for providing collective goods can be offered to organizations in both sectors (as in the U.S. tax credit for historic preservation), or government can provide the collective good itself. Nonprofit exemption from the corporate income tax rewards organizations in proportion to their capital stock, exemption from sales or value-added tax rewards them in proportion to commercial activities, and exemption from property taxes rewards them in proportion to the value of their property. None of these are particularly good at fostering the distinctive roles we have noted for the nonprofit sector.[17]

ACKNOWLEDGMENTS

I am grateful to Wolfgang Bielefeld, Marc Bilodeau, Kirsten Grønbjerg, Estelle James, Patrick Rooney, and Richard Turner for helpful comments and Barry Harvey for his help with the diagrams.

NOTES

1. More precisely, an economy is a list of the quantities of each good affecting each person. An economy is efficient (syn. "Pareto-efficient") if it is feasible, and any alternative economy that at least one person ranks higher and no person ranks lower is not feasible. In general, there are an infinite number of efficient economies, differing in their distribution of income. Efficiency is socially desirable in a limited sense, necessary but not sufficient. Some specific inefficient economies might be socially preferred to other efficient economies. However, if we accept the mild judgment that one economy is better than another if everyone (weakly) prefers that economy, then there is always at least one efficient economy that would be preferred to any specific inefficient

one. Atkinson and Stiglitz (1980: chapter 11) provide a fine introduction to the subtleties of this topic.

2. If there is no lock-in effect, then contract failure does not arise. For-profit firms solve the problem by offering money-back guarantees.

3. There are other causes of market failure (such as monopoly) that are not discussed here because nonprofits do not seem to play a role in coping with them. Ben-Ner and Gui (2003) provide an alternative but more comprehensive discussion of the demand for nonprofit organizations in situations of market failure.

4. To use Lindahl prices, the government must know each person's preferences. However, consumers would have an incentive to misrepresent their preferences to secure a lower price.

5. If, as suggested below, the median preference voter is decisive and the warm-glow motivation (Vesterlund, this volume) is inoperative, then governmental provision is efficient if and only if the distribution of most-preferred provision levels is symmetric about the mean.

6. This result, known as the "median voter theorem," was proved by Bowen (1943) for direct democracy and by Hotelling (1929) and later Downs (1957) for representative democracy. For the former, the proof involves showing that a referendum proposing the median preference voter's most-preferred level of provision will defeat any alternative by a majority of voters; for the latter, that vote-maximizing politicians would select as their platform the median voter's ideal. Both proofs make restrictive assumptions, but the median voter theorem is a useful starting point for analysis.

7. Sometimes, tax laws are so poorly enforced that payment of taxes is almost purely voluntary. Conversely, sometimes social pressures to make donations are so strong that payment is almost coerced. Nonetheless it is often reasonable to view the nonprofit alternative as less coercive than government.

8. Contract failure is less important for certain types of volunteering than for donations of money (e.g., Steinberg 1990a). Volunteers observe and help decide how their labor is used, allowing them to obtain the incremental output they want. Thus, parents donate their time to for-profit day-care centers and adult children donate their time to for-profit hospitals and nursing homes to provide recreational, educational, and social services that would otherwise be lacking.

9. Provision of perks is not, by itself, inefficient (Schlesinger 1985). Nonprofit managers are efficiently producing a mixture of mission-related outputs and perks; they have no desire to produce perks inefficiently. The problem is really an allocative inefficiency, where (a) managerial compensation takes the form of a mixture of money and perquisites that, owing to the nondistribution constraint, is higher cost than the optimal mixture and (b) when nonprofits compete with for-profits but enjoy otherwise lower costs because of tax subsidies, these subsidies can be applied to perk production. The higher social cost of nonprofit production is not reflected in prices due to the subsidy, and so the market produces a mixture that includes relatively too much high-social-cost nonprofit output and too little low-social-cost for-profit output. Nonetheless, because these inefficiencies show up as higher cost, the literature has errantly labeled this a form of productive inefficiency, a tradition we repeat here for consistency with the literature.

10. The solution to this problem lies in adding more to the three-failures theory. As a result, some received conclusions will change, but the three failures will remain a part of the story. Whether to call the result an enhanced three-failures theory or another name is entirely a matter of taste and semantics.

11. In private conversation, Wolfgang Bielefeld suggested a further broadening of the modeling agenda, creating a "blended" theory that would embed economic theories within a world shaped by political, sociologic, historical, and cultural factors. Thus, both the preferences of entrepreneurs and the factors affecting their decisions would be determined by the social structure, networks, history, and the like. In turn, the behaviors of nonprofit organizations at any point in time helps to determine the future evolution of networks, government regulations, and even cultural norms. This approach would integrate the distributional, preference-shaping, affiliative, and expressive roles of nonprofit organizations into the analysis. This approach would also help us understand the evolution of the roles played by the various sectors, and so seems well worthy of further development.

12. More precisely, Ben-Ner and Van Hoomissen argue that a self-provision coalition is formed if the expected flow of net benefits exceeds the next best alternative. This coalition can take the form of founding a nonprofit or a consumer cooperative, with additional factors skipped here governing that choice.

13. James (1982, 1986, 1989) observes that most secular nonprofits are founded out of such groups, especially religious congregations, but explains this as an attempt to gain converts.

14. More precisely, they show that the decision to incorporate as a nonprofit solves a moral hazard problem between the entrepreneur and other donors by acting as a commitment device in a three-stage game of perfect information. Donations still suffer from the free-rider problem, but they do not also suffer from this problem of moral hazard.

15. Tuckman and Chang (this volume) analyze selected mission statements to see what they reveal about nonprofit commercial activities. This is a start, but a more systematic and broad-ranging effort would be interesting.

16. See Weisbrod and Dominguez (1986), Posnett and Sandler (1989), Khanna, Posnett, and Sandler (1995), Okten and Weisbrod (2000), Khanna and Sandler (2000), Hewitt and Brown (2000), and Tinkelman 2004. These studies challenge Steinberg's (1986) specific findings, but do not agree on which charitable industries act like budget or service maximizers.

17. In the interests of space, I am leaving out many more economic arguments on both sides of the tax exemption question, as well as the noneconomic arguments. Personally, I am more supportive of exemption than my brief summary here might suggest. See Simon, Dale, and Chisolm (this volume), Steinberg (1991), and Steinberg and Bilodeau (1999) for a more balanced and comprehensive perspective.

REFERENCES

Atkinson, Anthony B., and Joseph E. Stiglitz. 1980. *Lectures on Public Economics.* New York: McGraw Hill.

Ballou, Jeffrey, and Burton A. Weisbrod. 2003. "Managerial Rewards and the Behavior of For-Profit, Governmental, and Nonprofit Organizations: Evidence from the Hospital Industry." *Journal of Public Economics.* 87:1895–1920.

Ben-Ner, Avner. 1986. "Nonprofit Organizations: Why Do They Exist in Market Economies?" Pages 94–113 in *The Economics of Nonprofit Institutions,* edited by Susan Rose-Ackerman. New York: Oxford University Press.

———. 1987. "Birth, Death, and Bureaucratization in Nonprofit Organizations: An Economic Analysis." Mimeo, University of Minnesota.

Ben-Ner, Avner, and Benedetto Gui. 2003. "The Theory of Nonprofit Organizations Revisited." Pages 3–26 in *The Study of Nonprofit Enterprise: Theories and Approaches,* edited by Helmut Anheier and Avner Ben-Ner. New York: Kluwer Academic/Plenum Publishers.

Ben-Ner, Avner, and Derek Jones. 1995. "Employee Participation, Ownership, and Productivity: A Theoretical Framework." *Industrial Relations* 34:532–554.

Ben-Ner, Avner, and Theresa Van Hoomissen. 1991. "Nonprofit Organizations in the Mixed Economy: A Demand and Supply Analysis." *Annals of Public and Cooperative Economics,* 62:519–550.

Bilodeau, Marc. 2000. "Profitable Nonprofit Firms." Department of Economics Working Paper, IUPUI, Indianapolis, Ind.

Bilodeau, Marc, and Al Slivinski. 1996. "Volunteering Nonprofit Entrepreneurial Services." *Journal of Economic Behavior and Organization.* 31:117–127.

———. 1997. "Rival Charities." *Journal of Public Economics.* 66:449–467.

———. 1998. "Rational Nonprofit Entrepreneurship." *Journal of Economics and Management Strategy* 7:551–571.

Bilodeau, Marc, and Richard Steinberg (1997). "Ransom of the Opera." Department of Economics Working Paper, IUPUI, Indianapolis, Ind.

———. Forthcoming. "Donative Nonprofit Organizations." In *Handbook on the Economics of Giving, Reciprocity, and Altruism,* edited by S.-C. Kolm and J. Mercier Ythier. New York: Elsevier/North Holland.

Bowen, Howard R. 1943. "The Interpretation of Voting in the Allocation of Economic Resources." *Quarterly Journal of Economics* 58:27–48.

Cain, Louis, and Dennis Meritt, Jr. 1998. "Zoos and Aquariums." Pages 217–232 in *To Profit or Not to Profit: The Commercial Transformation of the Nonprofit Sector,* edited by Burton A. Weisbrod. Cambridge, U.K.: Cambridge University Press.

Chang, Cyril F., and Howard P. Tuckman. 1996. "The Goods Produced by Nonprofit Organizations." *Public Finance Quarterly* 24:25–43.

Clotfelter, Charles T., ed. 1992. *Who Benefits from the Nonprofit Sector?* Chicago: University of Chicago Press.

DeHoog, Ruth. 1984. *Contracting Out for Human Services: Economic, Political and Organization Perspectives.* Albany, N.Y.: State University of New York Press.

Deneffe, Daniel, and Robert T. Masson. 2002. "What Do Not-For-Profit Hospitals Maximize?" *International Journal of Industrial Organization* 20:461–492.

Douglas, James. 1987. "Political Theories of Nonprofit Organizations." Pages 43–54 in *The Nonprofit Sector: A Research Handbook,* edited by Walter W. Powell. New Haven, Conn.: Yale University Press.

Downs, Anthony. 1957. *An Economic Theory of Democracy.* New York: Harper and Row.

Eckel, Catherine C., and Richard Steinberg. 1993. "Competition, Performance, and Public Policy Towards Nonprofits." Pages 57–81 in *Nonprofit Organizations in a Market Economy,* edited by David Hammack and Dennis R. Young. San Francisco: Jossey-Bass.

Ehrenberg, Ronald, John Cheslock, and Julia Epifantseva. 2000. "Paying Our Presidents: What Do Trustees Value?" Cambridge, Mass.: NBER Working Paper 7886.

Eldenburg, Leslie, Benjamin E. Hermalin, Michael S. Weisbach, and Marta Wosinska. 2004. "Governance, Performance Objectives, and Organizational Form: Evidence from Hospitals." *Journal of Corporate Finance* 10:527–548.

Erus, Burcay, and Burton A. Weisbrod. 2003. "Inferring Nonprofit Organization Objective Function from Compensation Structure: The 'Mixed' Hospital Industry." Pages 117–142 in *The Governance of Not-For-Profit Firms,* edited by Edward Glaeser. Chicago: University of Chicago Press.

Feigenbaum, Susan. 1980. "The Case of Income Redistribution: A Theory of Government and Private Provision of Collective Goods." *Public Finance Quarterly* 8:3–22.

———. 1987. "Competition and Performance in the Nonprofit Sector: The Case of US Medical Research Charities." *Journal of Industrial Economics* 35:241–253.

Feldstein, Martin. 1971. "Hospital Price Inflation: A Study of Nonprofit Price Dynamics." *American Economic Review* 61:853–72.

Ferris, James, and Elizabeth Graddy. 1991. "Production Costs, Transaction Costs, and Local Government Contractor Choice." *Economic Inquiry* 29:541–554.

Frech, H. E., III. 1976. "The Property Rights Theory of the Firm: Empirical Results from a Natural Experiment." *Journal of Political Economy* 84:143–152.

Gassler, Robert Scott. 1989. "The Economics of the Nonprofit Motive: A Suggested Formulation of Objectives and Constraints for Firms and Nonprofit Enterprises." Vesalius College Working Paper. Vrije Universiteit Brussel, Brussels, Belgium.

Glaeser, Edward L., and Andrei Schleifer (2001). "Not-For-

Profit Entrepreneurs." *Journal of Public Economics* 81:99–116.

Hansmann, Henry. 1980. "The Role of Nonprofit Enterprise." *Yale Law Journal* 89:835–901.

———. 1981a. "Nonprofit Enterprise in the Performing Arts." *Bell Journal of Economics* 12:341–361.

———. 1981b. "The Rationale for Exempting Nonprofit Corporations from the Corporate Income Tax." *Yale Law Journal* 91:45–100.

———. 1981c. "Reforming Nonprofit Corporation Law." *University of Pennsylvania Law Review* 129:497–623.

———. 1987a. "Economic Theories of Nonprofit Organization." Pages 27–42 in *The Nonprofit Sector: A Research Handbook,* edited by Walter W. Powell. New Haven, Conn.: Yale University Press.

———. 1987b. "The Effect of Tax Exemption and Other Factors on the Market Share of Nonprofit Versus For-Profit Firms." *National Tax Journal* 40:71–82.

———. 1996. "The Changing Roles of Public, Private, and Nonprofit Enterprise in Education, Health Care, and Other Human Services." Pages 245–275 in *Individual and Social Responsibility: Child Care, Education, Medical Care, and Long-Term Care in America,* edited by Victor Fuchs. Chicago: University of Chicago Press.

———. 2003. "The Role of Trust in Nonprofit Enterprise." Pages 115–124 in *The Study of the Nonprofit Enterprise: Theories and Approaches,* edited by Helmut Anheier and Avner Ben-Ner. New York: Kluwer/Plenum.

Hansmann, Henry, Daniel Kessler, and Mark McClellan. 2003. "Ownership Form and Trapped Capital in the Hospital Industry." Pages 45–70 in *The Governance of Not-for-Profit Organizations,* edited by Edward L. Glaeser. Chicago: University of Chicago Press.

Hewitt, Julie A., and Daniel K. Brown. 2000. "Agency Costs in Environmental Not-For-Profits." *Public Choice* 103:163–183.

Hirth, Richard A. 1999. "Consumer Information and Competition Between Nonprofit and For-Profit Nursing Homes." *Journal of Health Economics* 18:219–240.

Holtmann, Alphonse G. 1983. "A Theory of Non-Profit Firms." *Economica* 50:439–449.

Hotelling, Harold. 1929. "Stability in Competition." *Economic Journal* 39:41–57.

James, Estelle. 1982. "The Nonprofit Sector in International Perspective: The Case of Sri Lanka." *Journal of Comparative Economics* 6:99–129.

———. 1983. "How Nonprofits Grow: A Model." *Journal of Policy Analysis and Management.* 2:350–365.

———. 1986. "The Nonprofit Sector in Comparative Perspective." Pages 397–415 in *The Nonprofit Sector: A Research Handbook,* edited by Walter W. Powell. New Haven, Conn.: Yale University Press.

———. 1989. "Introduction." Pages 3–30 in *The Nonprofit Sector in International Perspective: Studies in Comparative Culture and Policy,* edited by Estelle James. New York: Oxford University Press.

———. 1993. "Why Do Different Countries Choose a Different Public-Private Mix of Educational Services?" *Journal of Human Resources* 28:571–592.

———. 1998. "Commercialism Among Nonprofits: Objectives, Opportunities, and Constraints." Pages 271–286 in *To Profit or Not to Profit: The Commercial Transformation of the Nonprofit Sector,* edited by Burton A. Weisbrod. Cambridge, U.K.: Cambridge University Press.

James, Estelle, and Susan Rose-Ackerman. 1986. *The Nonprofit Enterprise in Market Economies,* a monograph in the series Fundamentals of Pure and Applied Economics and Encyclopedia of Economics, edited by J. Lesourne and H. Sonnenschein. London: Harwood Academic Publishers.

Kapur, Kanika, and Burton A. Weisbrod. 2000. "The Roles of Government and Nonprofit Suppliers in Mixed Industries." *Public Finance Review* 28:275–308.

Khanna, Jyoti, John Posnett, and Todd Sandler. 1995. "Charity Donations in the U.K.: New Evidence Based on Panel Data." *Journal of Public Economics* 56:257–272.

Khanna, Jyoti, and Todd Sandler. 2000. "Partners in Giving: The Crowding-In Effects of UK Government Grants." *European Economic Review* 44:1543–1556.

Lee, M. 1971. "A Conspicuous Consumption Theory of Hospital Behavior." *Southern Economics Journal* 38:48–58.

Lowry, Robert C. 1997. "The Private Production of Public Goods: Organizational Maintenance, Managers' Objectives, and Collective Goals." *American Political Science Review* 91:308–323.

Malani, Anup, Tomas Philipson, and Guy David. 2003. "Theories of Firm Behavior in the Non-Profit Sector: A Synthesis and Empirical Evaluation." In *The Governance of Not-for-Profit Organizations,* edited by Edward L. Glaeser. Chicago: University of Chicago Press.

Mason, David E. 1996. *Leading and Managing the Expressive Dimension: Harnessing the Hidden Power Source of the Nonprofit Sector.* San Francisco: Jossey-Bass.

Mauser, Elizabeth. 1993. "Is Organizational Form Important to Consumers and Managers?: An Application to the Day-Care Industry." Unpublished Ph.D. dissertation in Economics. Madison, Wisc.: University of Wisconsin.

Nelson, Richard, and Michael Krashinsky. 1973. "Two Major Issues of Public Policy: Public Policy and the Organization of Supply." Pages 47–69 in *Public Subsidy for Day Care of Young Children,* edited by Richard Nelson and Dennis Young. Lexington, Mass.: D.C. Heath.

Newhouse, Joseph. 1970. "Toward a Theory of Non-Profit Institutions: An Economic Model of a Hospital." *American Economic Review* 60:64–74.

Niskanen, William A., Jr. 1971. *Bureaucracy and Representative Government.* Chicago: Aldine-Atherton.

Okten, Cagla, and Burton Weisbrod. 2000. "Determinants of Donations in Private Nonprofit Markets." *Journal of Public Economics* 75:255–272.

Ortmann, Andreas, and Mark Schlesinger. 2003. "Trust, Repute, and the Role of Nonprofit Enterprise." Pages 77–114 in *The Study of the Nonprofit Enterprise: Theories and Approaches,* edited by Helmut Anheier and Avner Ben-Ner. New York: Kluwer/Plenum.

Paulson, Robert W. 1988. "People and Garbage Are Not the Same: Issues in Contracting for Public Mental Health Services." *Community Mental Health Journal.* 24:91–102.

Pauly, Mark P., and Michael R. Redisch. 1973. "The Not-for-Profit Hospital as a Physicians' Cooperative." *American Economic Review* 63:87–99.

Permut, Steven. 1981. "Consumer Perceptions of Nonprofit Enterprise: A Comment on Hansmann." *Yale Law Journal* 90:1623–1632.

Pigou, Arthur C. 1932. *The Economics of Welfare,* 4th ed. London: Macmillan.

Posnett, John, and Todd Sandler. 1989. "Demand for Charity Donations in Private Non-Profit Markets: The Case of the U.K." *Journal of Public Economics* 40:187–200.

Preston, Anne E. 1988. "The Nonprofit Firm: A Potential Solution to Inherent Market Failures." *Economic Inquiry* 26:493–506.

Roomkin, Myron, and Burton Weisbrod. 1999. "Managerial Compensation and Incentives in For-Profit and Nonprofit Hospitals." *Journal of Law, Economics and Organizations* 15:750–781.

Rose-Ackerman, Susan. 1982. "Charitable Giving and Excessive Fundraising." *Quarterly Journal of Economics* 97:193–212.

Salamon, Lester M. 1987. "Partners in Public Service: The Scope and Theory of Government-Nonprofit Relations." Pages 99–117 in *The Nonprofit Sector: A Research Handbook,* edited by Walter W. Powell. New Haven, Conn.: Yale University.

Salamon, Lester M., and Helmut K. Anheier. 1998. "Social Origins of Civil Society: Explaining the Nonprofit Sector Cross-Nationally." *Voluntas* 9:213–248.

Samuelson, Paul A. 1954. "The Pure Theory of Public Expenditure." *Review of Economics and Statistics* 36:387–389.

Schiff, Jerald, and Burton A. Weisbrod. 1991. "Competition Between For-Profit and Nonprofit Organizations in Commercial Activities." *Annals of Public and Cooperative Economics* 62:619–640.

Schlesinger, Mark. 1985. "Economic Models of Nonprofit Organizations: A Reappraisal of the Property Rights Approach." Working Paper, JFK School, Harvard University. Cambridge, Mass.

Slivinski, Al. 2002. "Team Incentives and Organizational Form." *Journal of Public Economic Theory* 4:185–206.

Spiegel, Menachim. 1995. "Charity Without Altruism." *Economic Inquiry* 33:625–639.

Steinberg, Richard. 1986. "The Revealed Objective Functions of Nonprofit Firms." *Rand Journal of Economics* 17:508–526.

———. 1987. "Nonprofits and the Market." Pages 118–138 in *The Nonprofit Sector: A Research Handbook,* edited by Walter W. Powell. New Haven, Conn.: Yale University Press.

———. 1990a. "Labor Economics and the Nonprofit Sector: A Literature Review." *Nonprofit and Voluntary Sector Quarterly* 19(2):151–170.

———. 1990b. "Morality and Diversity: A Comment on Lipman." *Society* (September/October): 12–14.

———. 1991. "'Unfair Competition' by Nonprofits and Tax Policy." *National Tax Journal* 44: 351–364.

———. 1993a. "How Should Antitrust Laws Apply to Nonprofit Organizations?" Pages 279–305 in *Governing, Leading, and Managing Nonprofit Organizations,* edited by Dennis R. Young, Robert M. Hollister, Virginia A. Hodgkinson, and associates. San Francisco: Jossey-Bass.

———. 1993b. "Public Policy and the Performance of Nonprofit Organizations: A General Framework." *Nonprofit and Voluntary Sector Quarterly* 22:13–32.

———. 1997. "Competition in Contracted Markets." Pages 161–180 in *The Contract Culture in Public Services,* edited by Perri 6 and Jeremy Kendall. Brookfield, Vt.: Ashgate.

Steinberg, Richard, and Marc Bilodeau. 1999. *Should Nonprofit Organizations Pay Sales and Property Taxes.* Washington, D.C.: National Council of Nonprofit Associations.

Steinberg, Richard, and Catherine C. Eckel. 1994. "Tax Policy and the Objectives of Nonprofit Organizations in a Mixed-Sector Duopoly." Indiana University Center on Philanthropy Working Paper, IUPUI, Indianapolis, Ind.

Steinberg, Richard, and Burton A. Weisbrod. 1998. "Pricing and Rationing by Nonprofit Organizations with Distributional Objectives." Pages 65–82 in *To Profit or Not to Profit: The Commercial Transformation of the Nonprofit Sector,* edited by Burton A. Weisbrod. Cambridge, U.K.: Cambridge University Press.

———. 2005. "Nonprofits with Distributional Objectives: Price Discrimination and Corner Solutions." *Journal of Public Economics* 89:2205–2230.

Steinberg, Richard, and Dennis R. Young. 1998. "A Comment on Salamon and Anheier's 'Social Origins of Civil Society.'" *Voluntas* 9:249–260.

Steinwald, Bruce, and Duncan Neuhauser. 1970. "The Role of the Proprietary Hospital." *Law and Contemporary Problems* 35:817–838.

Throsby, C. D., and G. A. Withers. 1979. *The Economics of the Performing Arts.* New York: St. Martin's Press.

Tiebout, Charles. 1956. "A Pure Theory of Local Expenditures." *Journal of Political Economy* 64:416–424.

Tinkelman, Daniel. 2004. "Using Nonprofit Organization-Level Financial Data to Infer Managers' Fund-Raising Strategies." *Journal of Public Economics* 28:2181–2192.

Tullock, Gordon. 1966. "Information Without Profit," *Papers on Non-Market Decision Making* 1:141–159.

Vitaliano, Donald F. 2003. "Do Not-For-Profit Firms Maximize Profit?" *Quarterly Review of Economics and Finance* 43:75–87.

Weisbrod, Burton A. 1975. "Toward a Theory of the Voluntary Non-Profit Sector in a Three-Sector Economy." Pages 171–195 in *Altruism, Morality, and Economic Theory,* edited by Edmund Phelps. New York: Russell Sage.

———. 1988. *The Nonprofit Economy,* Cambridge, Mass.: Harvard University Press.

———. 1998. "Modeling the Nonprofit Organization as a Multiproduct Firm: A Framework for Choice." Pages 47–64 in *To Profit or Not to Profit: The Commercial Transformation of the Nonprofit Sector,* edited by Burton A. Weisbrod. Cambridge, U.K.: Cambridge University Press.

Weisbrod, Burton A., and Nestor Dominguez. 1986. "Demand for Collective Goods in Private Nonprofit Markets: Can Fund Raising Expenditures Help Overcome Free-Rider Behavior?" *Journal of Public Economics* 30:83–95.

Weisbrod, Burton A., and Mark Schlesinger. 1986. "Public, Private, Nonprofit Ownership and the Response to Asymmetric Information: The Case of Nursing Homes." Pages 133–151 in *The Economics of Nonprofit Institutions: Studies in Structure and Policy,* edited by Susan Rose-Ackerman. New York: Oxford University Press.

Wolf, Jr., Charles. 1993. *Markets or Governments: Choosing Between Imperfect Alternatives, Second Edition.* Cambridge, Mass.: MIT Press.

Wolpert, Julian. 1977. "Social Income and the Voluntary Sector. *Papers, Regional Science Association,* 39:217–229.

Young, Dennis R. 1981. "Entrepreneurship and the Behavior of Nonprofit Organizations: Elements of a Theory." Pages 135–162 in *Nonprofit Firms in a Three-Sector Economy,* edited by Michelle White. Washington, D.C.: Urban Institute Press.

———. 1983. *If Not for Profit, for What?* Lexington, Mass.: D. C. Heath.

6

Nonprofit Organizations and the Market

ELEANOR BROWN
AL SLIVINSKI

Economists think about markets by thinking about the behavior of the people and firms who populate them. These consumers and producers are modeled as rational agents who assess their circumstances and act to advance their own interests. For-profit firms are assumed to behave so as to maximize profit, while politicians and those working in government agencies are viewed as responding optimally to the incentives of their political environments. This chapter reviews what economists have learned about the behavior of nonprofit organizations, viewing them too as rational optimizers responding to the incentives of the marketplace.

One distinctive feature of nonprofit firms is that they are unlikely to set out simply to maximize profit. They have been granted nonprofit status because of their proclaimed public purpose, and have foresworn the opportunity to distribute profits to owners. Throughout this chapter, we assume that nonprofits are rational optimizers pursuing objectives—call them their "missions"—related to at least some of the economic activities they undertake and in which their public purpose resides.

In this chapter, we look at the various markets in which nonprofits operate, laying out the research questions that have been raised in the literature and the range of answers that have been offered up. We deal extensively with the behavior of nonprofit firms in the markets for the services they provide. We explore their behavior in markets in which they "demand" rather than "supply"; these include labor markets, the markets for physical and financial capital, and the "market" for grants and charitable donations. This multiplicity of markets is considered because each market affects the functioning of the nonprofit firm, and because conditions in one market may affect the firm's behavior in another. Due to our emphasis on the behavior of nonprofits as suppliers and demanders of goods and services, we limit our attention to operating nonprofits; for a discussion of nonprofit foundations, see the chapter in this volume by Prewitt. The presence of a mission is what makes it important for economists and others who study any market to address in their analyses the special circumstances of the nonprofit firm, and we often contrast the behavior of mission-driven nonprofit firms with the behavior of their profit-maximizing counterparts. More generally, our strategy in this chapter is to present the predictions that emerge from economic modeling of nonprofit behavior, and to use empirical studies to illustrate occasions on which these predictions match, or tellingly fail to match, observed behavior. Given the wealth of empirical literature that addresses the market behavior of nonprofit firms, we cannot provide an exhaustive review of empirical studies; we settle for choosing examples that inform the economic theories and their place in our understanding of nonprofit behavior.

THE IMPORTANCE OF MISSION IN UNDERSTANDING THE MARKET BEHAVIOR OF NONPROFITS

It is hard to overstate the importance of mission in shaping the economic study of nonprofits. Mission attracts entrepreneurs, employees, donors, and volunteers. Mission leads governments to exempt from taxation nonprofits' revenues raised in mission-related activities. Mission can lead to struggles among stakeholders who differ in the details of their preferred conceptualizations of a nonprofit firm's goals.

Much of the richness of economic models of the behavior of nonprofits stems from the frequency with which nonprofits' missions are of interest to a broader set of constituents than are the profits of a profit-maximizing firm. That is, individuals outside any particular nonprofit may care about the extent and quality of its activities. While the demand for the services of a for-profit firm is summed up in the willingness to pay of its customers, the "demand side" of the market comprises many more players in the case of a nonprofit firm. Donors may care about the services provided by the nonprofit; their willingness to pay is then part of the demand for the firm's output. Similarly, private foundations and governmental agencies may be willing to subsidize the activities undertaken by nonprofit firms precisely because they view its services as serving a larger public purpose. Employees who embrace the nonprofit's mission may accept lower wages than they could command elsewhere. All of these stakeholders, along with paying customers, combine to constitute the demand side of the market(s) in which nonprofits provide goods and services.

With this multiplicity of stakeholders may come a multiplicity of conceptions of the mission of the nonprofit. Donors, granting agencies, and the entrepreneurs who run nonprofits may have different preferred missions for the firm. One set of tradeoffs facing a nonprofit organization is between mission purity and the extensiveness of their operations. For example, government contracts may allow nonprofit social services providers to serve more clients but at the same time restrict their ability to select exactly the clientele they most wish to serve. These considerations add to models of the nonprofit firm a complexity that is largely absent in models of for-profit firms, where decisions are assumed to be based on profit maximization.[1]

The differences in the tax and statutory treatment of nonprofits exist precisely because of a presumption that nonprofits have a mission that is of general public interest. Some purposes receive greater government support than others; the nonprofits that qualify as 501(c) (3) organizations under U.S. tax law must serve charitable, religious, educational, scientific, or literary purposes, and donations to these and only these nonprofits are tax deductible.

Finally, we note that the choice by the founder of any organization to seek nonprofit status is a voluntary one, and it need not be coincident with having a mission that differs from profit maximization. There may be cases in which profit-maximizing firms find it advantageous to choose the nonprofit form, due to tax exemptions, for example. Conversely, some mission-driven entrepreneurs may find that the nondistribution constraint is too restrictive and their mission can be better pursued while organized as a for-profit firm. Although we link mission-driven firms with the nonprofit form and profit-maximization with the profit-taking form, we acknowledge that this is a simplifying assumption.

We turn our attention first to the markets in which nonprofits acquire the resources necessary for production. We focus in turn on labor, land and physical capital, and donations. We then consider the markets in which nonprofits provide services, where we first survey work concerned with the quality of the services nonprofits provide. We then move on to the literature on nonprofit decision-making regarding what menu of services to provide, and how to price them to clients. Much of the analysis in this section involves comparisons with the behavior of for-profit firms, and this leads us to a section on research directed at understanding those markets in which nonprofit and for-profit organizations coexist.

INPUT MARKETS

Labor

The nonprofit labor force is covered at length in the chapter in this volume by Leete, including a comprehensive survey of theories and evidence on the conditions under which nonprofit labor is cheaper or costlier than the labor hired by for-profit firms. Here, we review the impact on the labor market of two distinctive features of nonprofit enterprise: first, their management is not accountable to shareholders; second, the mission or other attributes of the nonprofit setting may lead workers to offer their services at discounted wages. These special circumstances of nonprofit organizations can lead them to combine labor with other resources in distinctive ways, even if they have access to the same technological choices for production as do for-profit firms, and can affect the levels of service nonprofits can provide.

One avenue through which labor differentially affects performance in the nonprofit sector springs from the lesser accountability of nonprofit managers who, although they answer to a board of directors, do not answer either to current stockholders or to potential stockholders who might take over a loosely run operation. If nonprofit managers are less driven to optimize they may, through inattentiveness or a disposition to share scarcity rents with their workers, end up paying higher wages than do their for-profit counterparts. For nonprofits whose missions involve providing as great a level of service as their budgets allow, lax budgeting affects performance by raising costs and, as a result, reducing the levels of service provided.

A countervailing force stems from the existence of a nonprofit mission, which carries with it the potential that workers care about that mission. This in turn implies that otherwise identical workers may be willing to work in a nonprofit at a lower wage than they would in a similar for-profit firm.[2] An obvious example of this is to be found in volunteer labor, most of which is supplied to nonprofits.[3] A second important class of examples is highly paid professionals, such as doctors and lawyers, who by accepting lower-than-market rates of compensation can belong to firms that serve populations with limited abilities to pay for generally expensive services. Francois (2001) and Slivinski (2002) develop models that predict that nonprofit organizations are able to motivate their workers at lower cost than could an otherwise identical profit-taking firm. This holds only if workers care about the effect of their effort on the quantity or quality of the enterprise's output.

It is an empirical question which of the many hypothesized links between nonprofit form and employee wages, including greater motivation and lesser oversight, has the greatest impact on wages and, thereby, on production in the nonprofit sector. Leete (2001) uses U.S. Census data on more than four million employees and finds an overall wage differential between nonprofit and for-profit sectors of roughly zero, with significant differentials, both positive and negative, at the level of particular occupations and industries. Controlling for other factors, employment in the nonprofit sector is associated with a small but statistically significant reduction in wages for managerial and professional workers relative to wages in the for-profit sector, and statistically significantly higher wages in the nonprofit sector for precision, craft, and repair workers, for operators, fabricators, and laborers, and for technical, sales, and administrative workers. Of ninety-one industries containing both for-profit and nonprofit firms, thirty-four showed significant wage differentials; within industries with a significant wage differential and in which the nonprofit sector accounted for at least 5 percent of employment, about half the differentials were positive and half negative. The relationship between nonprofit form and wages varies across occupations and industries; consequently, the impact of labor markets on nonprofit organizations' delivery of goods and services, relative to the performance of firms in other sectors, will vary from case to case.[4]

When mission leads workers to accept lower ("donative") wages, will nonprofits save money not only through direct payroll savings but also to some extent by substituting cheap labor for land and capital?[5] As we see in the next section, the nonprofit sector also enjoys certain cost advantages in markets for land and physical capital, making it difficult to predict whether nonprofits will in general use a mix of inputs in producing their goods and services that differs from the mix chosen by for-profit firms.

Land and Physical Capital

While one can imagine nonprofit missions that affect certain nonprofits' behavior in labor markets—they might hire the physically handicapped, prison parolees, or persons of a particular faith, for example—there is no obvious reason for the existence of a nonprofit mission to affect behavior in the markets for land and physical capital (buildings, equipment, etc.). However, there are predicted differences in the behavior of for-profit and nonprofit firms that arise as a result of the regulatory and tax treatment of nonprofit organizations. Nonprofits in the United States, for example, typically enjoy exemption from property, sales, and corporation income taxes and these advantages suggest that nonprofits will make greater use of land and equipment than do similar for-profit firms.

Economists find that real estate values reflect property taxes (as well as many other factors, of course). Property buyers realize that they are purchasing both the right to use land and a tax obligation, and the tax obligation reduces the price they are willing to pay for the property accordingly. For nonprofit firms that don't have to pay them, property taxes depress the purchase price of land without imposing an offsetting tax liability.

This gives nonprofit firms a cost advantage in the purchase of land and structures. It also gives nonprofit organizations an incentive to locate in jurisdictions with high property taxes. McEachern (1981) notes that this is potentially problematic for high-property-tax jurisdictions, who might be forced to raise property taxes still higher as nonprofits move in and their taxable property tax base shrinks; the hike in tax rates would then invite further entry by tax-exempt firms, displacing still more property-taxpayers.

The exemption of nonprofit firms from paying corporation income taxes reinforces this tendency for the nonprofit sector to work with more capital than we see in the incorporated for-profit sector. When the owners of a firm have money tied up in machines, buildings, and other forms of capital, the return on this investment is part of the firm's net income. When the corporation income tax reduces the rate of return to capital in for-profit corporations by taxing part of the return away, economists predict that some capital will be moved out of the taxed part of the economy and into other parts where its return is not diminished by the tax.

Because hospitals use a great deal of land, buildings, and equipment, the hospital industry is a natural focus for empirical research on the practical importance of the tax advantages accorded to nonprofits. Using state-level data on the U.S. hospital industry from 1967 through 1987, Gulley and Santerre (1993) find that the nonprofit share of the hospital market is statistically significantly higher when corporate income or property tax rates are higher. Their estimates suggest that eliminating the property tax would cause the nonprofit share of the hospital market to fall from 70.7 percent to 69 percent; alternatively, eliminating the corporation income tax would lower it to 67.8 percent; and eliminating both sources of tax advantage would reduce the nonprofit share of the hospital market to 66.1 percent.[6]

Such studies address the question of whether the property tax exemption lowers nonprofit costs and thus gives them a larger market share than they would otherwise have when competing with for-profits. The question of whether they also utilize relatively more property and structures than do their for-profit counterparts seems a worthy area for further research.

We note that the incentive for nonprofits to use more capital than their profit-taking counterparts does not necessarily imply that they will own more capital. Depreciable capital equipment may be more profitably owned in the for-profit sector, where generous depreciation allowances can be used to reduce corporate tax liabilities. When the tax law allows profit-taking corporations to depreciate assets quickly, nonprofit firms may find that for-profit firms are willing to lease equipment to them at prices that make leasing an attractive option.[7]

In those cases in which nonprofits can hire labor at below-market wages, it is clear that nonprofit organizations may pay lower effective prices for land, labor, and equipment than do for-profits. Other things the same, economists expect such cost advantages to lead to an expanded nonprofit sector; in subsectors in which nonprofits compete with for-profit entities (see our discussion of such competition below), this expansion can come at the expense of the for-profit sector. As we see later in this chapter, one countervailing advantage of the for-profit sector lies in its ability to sell stock in order to raise the funds needed to purchase land, equipment, and labor services.

Donations

In recent decades, private donations have accounted for roughly one-fifth of the revenues of the nonprofit sector in the United States (Weizman et al. 2002). These donations come from corporations, foundations, and individuals and their estates. They tend to represent a greater fraction of revenues for nonprofit organizations providing collective consumption goods, for which it is difficult to charge consumers, than for nonprofits such as universities and hospitals that provide goods with a significant component of private consumption (Weisbrod 1980). Although nonprofit firms must decide how much to pursue each of these funding sources, our emphasis here is on the biggest of them, donations from individuals. The strategic behavior of donors themselves is covered in the chapter by Vesterlund in this volume, and we consider it here only to the extent that it influences the behavior of firms.

In modeling the relationship between nonprofit firms and their donors, scholars often conceive of donors as interested third parties whose demand for an organization's services is on behalf of a client base to which they do not themselves belong. This is a reasonable approach for a wide range of nonprofits, including those seeking funds for programs for the needy or for international causes. For nonprofits in other areas, notably in the arts, donors are likely to enjoy the firm's output directly as customers. The literature reviewed in this section generally ignores the fact that donors are also sometimes customers; we return to the issues raised by this dual role in the section on nonprofit pricing of services.

Whether or not donors consume the services produced by the nonprofits they support, they are likely to have opinions about how nonprofits should view their missions and conduct their affairs. That is, donors may care about the quantities of services provided, the specific attributes of those services (for example, the inclusion of a religious message), or the mix of services provided (for example, drug-rehabilitation clinics differ in the mixes of medication, counseling, and occupational therapy they employ in treating clients). The extent to which the preferences of donors and nonprofit managers coincide on such matters will vary across organizations. Further, nonprofit organizations must take into account how potential donors react to levels of fundraising activity, and whether private donations are positively or negatively influenced by the organization's success in attracting funding from other sources, such as government grants.

A key determinant of the extent to which donor preferences influence the behavior of nonprofit organizations is the level of competition among nonprofits vying for donor support. An organization facing few competitors loses fewer donations by ignoring donor preferences than does one that has many competitors offering what donors see as close substitutes for its activities and services. It follows from this that the ease of entry into the provision of services is important, since more entry increases the likelihood donors will have such close substitutes available to which to donate.

How do nonprofits attract the attention of potential donors? Firms use advertising to attract customers; in the nonprofit world, firms use fundraising to attract patrons. The analogy between advertising and fundraising as strategies to enhance the demand for an organization's product is an informative one. Rose-Ackerman (1982) exploits this parallel in a series of behavioral models of nonprofit organizations and potential donors. Fundraising itself is viewed in this work as simply "asking," and potential donors do not give unless they are asked. The framework recalls the standard economic notion of monopolistic competition: there are many nonprofit establishments competing for donations via fundraising, each of them producing a distinct mix of services determined by the preferences of the nonprofit's owner-manager, in a market with no barriers to entry.

It is assumed that nonprofit managers have a most-preferred service mix that incorporates their ideology surrounding the firm's mission, and that it is the manager's ideology that determines how the organization's mission is carried out. Donors are assumed to have a most-preferred service mix also, and each gives to that soliciting organization whose ideology they find most appealing. Managers are assumed to wish to maximize donations received, net of fundraising expenditures. A new nonprofit will begin operation any time its owner-manager's ideology is such that it can expect positive net donations, and it is assumed that there exist potential owner-managers representing a wide variety of ideologies.

In the most completely elaborated of the models, donors pay no attention to whether their dollars are spent on the provision of services or on fundraising. This model predicts that nonprofits enter until there is no way for another entrant to attract donations in excess of fundraising costs. In such a world, nonprofit organizations provide a variety of service mixes, with the extent of that variety reflecting donors' ideologies. Nonprofits also engage in extensive fundraising, much of which may serve to redirect donors' dollars from one organization to another rather than bringing new donations to the group.

This result suggests that consolidation of fundraising efforts through a federated fund (such as United Way) campaign might allow nonprofits to raise a given amount of revenue at a lower cost, although perhaps at the cost of a reduction in the variety of services funded. Analyses of the behavior of federated funds and of their consequences for variety can be found in Rose-Ackerman (1980), Bilodeau (1992), and Bilodeau and Slivinski (1997).

Rose-Ackerman (1987) develops the analysis of conflicting preferences between nonprofits and their donors by allowing the ideologically motivated nonprofit manager to deviate from his or her preferred ideology in order to attract more donations. Potential donors have preferred ideologies and donate more as nonprofit services more closely conform to their own preferences. The manager sees deviations from his or her own preferred ideology as costly, and at the margin will weigh the benefits of added donations from more satisfied donors against the costs of having to do business in a modified way. In this model, there is no entry by new organizations, and grantmakers offer grants that do not demand ideological concessions. These unrestricted grants are taken to be governmental, but they could also come from foundations that were interested in service provision and indifferent to ideology.

It follows that the receipt by a nonprofit of an unrestricted grant allows its manager to devote fewer resources to costly fundraising and to pay less attention to the preferences of potential donors. The model thus generates an important prediction: an increase in unrestricted grants to any nonprofit implies that it will do less fundraising and therefore will earn less in private donations. In this sense, government grants that do not interfere with the organization's ideology partially "crowd out" private donations from supporters whose ideologies differ from those of the nonprofit. This is, however, only one of the ways in which grants may influence donations; as will be seen below, there are also reasons to expect grants to increase private donations, as noted in Rose-Ackerman (1981).[8]

The two models just discussed illustrate the importance of taking entry into account when analyzing the effects of government support for nonprofit organizations. If, as in the 1982 paper, there is truly free entry into an area of nonprofit activity, then a sprinkling of seed grants into the sector by the government will increase the number of organizations. The greater variety provided by the larger number of firms will bring about a closer match on average between the service mix that donors want and what is provided. If, on the other hand, there is no entry and hence a fixed number of nonprofits, as in the 1987 paper, those same government grants allow established nonprofits to more readily ignore donor preferences, and the alignment between donors' preferences and the design of nonprofit services deteriorates.

Do firms have to consider whether donors have preferences over the fraction of their revenues devoted to fundraising? One possibility is that an organization's donors respond to the "price" they pay—that is, to the out-of-pocket cost to donors of generating a dollar's worth of services provided by the organization—and fundraising, by diverting revenue from service provision, raises that price. When donations are tax deductible, donors might estimate this price as $p = (1 - t)/[1 - F - A]$, where t is the marginal tax rate faced by a donor, and F and A are the fractions of the revenues of the recipient organization devoted to expenditures on fundraising and administration, respectively.[9] The donor's tax rate t is relevant only if donations are tax deductible, in which case the taxpayer's gift of one dollar generates a tax saving of t dollars, implying that a dollar gift costs the taxpayer only $(1 - t)$ dollars, as represented in the numerator of the expression for p. The denominator gives the fraction of the firm's revenues devoted to service provision rather than fundraising or administrative costs.

A shortcoming of this formulation is that the denominator reflects what happens to an average dollar donated to the firm, whereas a donor might reasonably care about how the firm will spend the extra (marginal) dollars from his or her contemplated gift. Steinberg (1986c:361) provides theoretical arguments that this measure of price is "essentially unrelated" to the actual cost to a donor of eliciting another dollar's worth of service provision. Donors might nonetheless consider it to be the best available estimate of how their money might be spent, a conviction reinforced by the attention paid by nonprofit watchdog organizations to average fundraising shares (Rose-Ackerman 1982). If there were little variation across nonprofits in the fractions of their revenues represented by administrative and fundraising costs, donors would have little to gain from investigating variations in the price of giving to different organizations. In a sample of 35,244 organizations, however, Hager et al. (2001) find considerable variation in this price of giving in different nonprofit subsectors.[10]

It remains an empirical question, then, whether potential donors will respond to this imperfect signal of the efficacy with which their donations will be used. Using IRS Form 990 data on nonprofits in four metropolitan areas during 1974–1976, Steinberg (1986c) finds no evidence that the level of donations is affected by the value of this price measure. Weisbrod and Dominguez (1986) test the significance of the price variable on a broader set of 990 data from essentially the same time period (adding 1973), however, and find that the average price variable has a negative effect on donations in all seven areas of nonprofit activity considered, with all but donations to "supplying goods to the poor and aged" achieving statistical significance. Using a large and long panel data set based on IRS Form 990 files from 1982 to 1994, Okten and Weisbrod (2000) find negative and significant effects at the industry level. Khanna and Sandler (2000), using a panel of data on 159 charities in the United Kingdom, find negative price effects on donations that are statistically significant in the case of overseas charities and marginally significant (at the 10 percent level) in the case of social welfare charities.

Two concerns arise from empirical evidence that donors react to the price of eliciting another unit of output from the nonprofit organization. First, because fundraising diverts resources from the immediate production of output, the nonprofit's decision of how much fundraising to undertake will optimally take into account the depressive effect of fundraising's share of revenues on the volume of donations received. Second, reaction to the price of additional output gives information about just what donors are interested in when they make a donation. For example, if donors' motives are principally expressive, they may receive a "warm glow" from the number of dollars they transfer to a worthy nonprofit and be concerned with the "price" set by the tax system for making such a donation, but not be concerned with the price of output. Concern with the price of output is consistent with a warm-glow motive centered on inducing output rather than simply donating dollars; it is also consistent, however, with a view of donors as concerned with the level of output of the firm (or of the industry as a whole). Some patrons of the opera, for example, might donate in hopes of securing a high-quality opera season and be inclined to give less to the opera if the gifts of others suffice to ensure a satisfactory program. Donor interest in the level of output raises the question of whether private donations are crowded out in this fashion by other sources of nonprofit revenue, such as governmental grants. We address these two issues in turn.

Given that fundraising encourages donations through an effect similar to that of advertising, and discourages donations by diverting funds from their immediate application to the mission, how do nonprofit firms decide how much fundraising is enough? One plausible behavioral assumption is that nonprofits solicit donations up to the point at which they maximize donations net of fundraising costs, thereby maximizing the amount of money available for service provision.[11] An alternative goal is the maximization of total donations gross of fundraising costs. This strategy will appeal to managers whose chief concern is the size of the budget they control, or the power or control it gives them.

Steinberg (1986b) finds that nonprofit firms in welfare, education, and the arts seem to maximize net donations, whereas firms in the health industry look more like gross-donations maximizers. Straub (2003) finds that half the public radio stations in his sample could increase net donations by spending less on fundraising. Weisbrod and Dominguez (1986) find evidence that changes in total fundraising have no total impact on donations in all seven industries considered, thus suggesting that these nonprofits engage in fundraising to the point at which additional fundraising expenditure would result in no increase in total donations. In other words, nonprofits are maximizing the total donations received, gross of fundraising expenses.

Okten and Weisbrod (2000) find evidence that nonprofits stop short of the level of fundraising that maximizes gross revenues in the case of libraries, and possibly in the case of hospitals; in other industries, nonprofits devote money to fundraising up to the point where no additional donations would be raised through further efforts. By contrast, Khanna and Sandler (2000) find evidence that U.K. religious charities behave so as to maximize *net* donations, and that other U.K. charities do too little fundraising, in the sense that they stop short of maximizing net donations.

Donors' concern with the price they face in eliciting increased output is consistent with the view that donors are concerned with the level of services provided by the firm. If this is the case, will donors be less inclined to give if the nonprofit increases its capacity through the receipt of grants from government or other sources? A literature focused on the optimizing behavior of donors (see, for example, Posnett and Sandler [1989], Kingma [1989], Khanna et al. [1995], Payne [1998], and Khanna and Sandler [2000]) has looked for this type of crowd-out within specific areas of nonprofit activity, as discussed in the chapter by Vesterlund.

Several recent papers investigate the interaction within nonprofits among the many ways of generating revenues. Andreoni and Payne (2003) examine the effect of government grants on fundraising efforts in a model that owes much to Rose-Ackerman's work. Fundraising by nonprofits is modeled as costly advertising, which may or may not make contact with any particular potential donor. Spending more increases the probability of such contact, and the amount donated by any contacted donor depends on the service mix produced by the organizations whose ads are seen, since donors care about this mix. The model predicts, as in Rose-Ackerman (1987), that government grants reduce fundraising effort by the recipient organization, resulting in reduced private donations. The key empirical finding is that increases in government grants do in fact cause nonprofit organizations to do less fundraising, a result that reinforces the inverse relationship between government and donor support of nonprofit activity.

Raising funds is an activity in which nonprofits compete with one another, and a recent literature attempts to understand the details of the fundraising strategies that arise in this competition. For example, many fundraising campaigns begin by soliciting a select group of individuals and then announcing the total donated by that group, before moving on to a more general solicitation of funds. Andreoni (1998, 2002), Vesterlund (2003), and Romano and Yildirim (2001) address this phenomenon in various ways. Andreoni (1998) considers the problem of raising funds for a large capital project, such as a new hospital wing, that cannot be undertaken unless the level of donations reaches a certain threshold. He shows that inducing a small group of "leaders" to make binding pledges of donations can be effective in eliciting sufficient contributions in situations in which the threshold might otherwise not be reached.

Vesterlund (2003) and Romano and Yildirim (2001) tackle a related question: What is the rationale for the practice of soliciting potential donors over time and announcing each donation or pledge as it is given, before moving on to solicit further donors? Vesterlund shows that if there is uncertainty among donors about the amount of public benefit a project will generate, then it can be that the sequential solicitation and announcement strategy will indeed generate greater donations. Romano and Yildirim demonstrate that even when there is no "quality uncertainty," if donors are motivated partly by something other than generating public benefits, such as "warm glow" or the desire to join others in supporting a cause (the so-called bandwagon effect), this sequential announcement strategy can again result in greater donations than a simultaneous announcement of totals donated.[12]

In other work on fundraising practices, Harbaugh (1998b) considers the possibility that donors are motivated partly by the prestige that comes from having others know how much they give. When they are, fundraisers can get greater donations by committing to publicize them and by following the common practice of reporting donations as falling into preset categories. Harbaugh (1998a) uses data on gifts to a law school that reported donations by categories to test the extent to which donors are motivated by prestige, and estimates that from 20 percent to 25 percent of the donations the school received could be attributed to the prestige motive. Glazer and Konrad (1996) develop a model based on the similar notion that announced donations provide a socially sanctioned means for donors to signal to others how much wealth they have accumulated. This assumption has similar predictions for donor and nonprofit behavior, particularly with regard to announcements and the use of gift categories.

Another observed fact about nonprofit fundraising is that the methods used vary considerably across organizations. One source of this variation is the decision to contract with a professional fundraiser rather than to hire employees or to utilize volunteers to raise funds. Further, when an organization does contract with an outside professional, the contract the two parties enter into can vary in many ways. Greenlee and Gordon (1998) looked at a large set of contracts between nonprofits and professional fundraisers and found that charities using professionals tended to be larger than average, and that professional fundraising contracts were most prevalent among advocacy, disease/disorder, and public-safety organizations. The contracts in the sample were categorized as to whether the professional solicitor was paid a fixed fee, a percentage of the donations generated, or some combination. It was found that solicitors who were paid only a fixed fee garnered greater total funds, on average, and returned a larger proportion of the total raised to the charities that employed them. These findings are consistent with the fundraising model of Steinberg (1986a), who first pointed out that if donors are aware of the nature of the contract, paying a commission to a solicitor raises the price to donors of generating a dollar's worth of services from the charity, and hence may be inferior to a fixed fee, which leaves that price at a dollar.

When nonprofits and for-profit firms compete with each other in output markets that are so competitive that even profit-maximizing firms earn zero profit, donations can allow nonprofits to deviate from profit-maximizing behavior, emphasizing quality, quantity, or some other dimension of service that advances the mission of the firm, without being run out of business. In the next section of this chapter, we look at the behavior of nonprofit firms in their output markets.

THE MARKET FOR SERVICES: QUALITY, PRODUCT MIX, AND PRICING DECISIONS

The provision of services puts nonprofits squarely in the role of market participants. Even when their missions can be pursued without recourse to market transactions (serving a clientele who do not pay for services, for example), nonprofits must make decisions about quality, quantity, and prices charged for ancillary services. They have choices to make about the provision of mission-related services to mission-extraneous clients (as by a health clinic designed to serve the poor but open to all) and of other services that can generate net revenue to subsidize mission-fulfilling activities. In this section we consider in turn issues of the quality of service provided, the mix of services produced, and the pricing strategies adopted by nonprofit firms. Within industries populated by both for-profit and nonprofit firms, each of these dimensions of market behavior provides the theoretical grounding for empirical work that seeks to document behavioral differences between nonprofit firms and their for-profit counterparts.

Selling both mission-related and unrelated services, nonprofits derive a large portion of their revenues from dues, fees, and charges. In many large subsectors in many countries, revenue from sales is the dominant source of income for nonprofit firms (see the chapters in this volume by Boris and Steuerle and by Salamon et al. for details).[13]

The importance of sales revenue to nonprofit organizations underscores that while "charity" is a common mission among nonprofits, charging at least some clients for at least some services is an effective way to generate funds to support targeted populations. Such cross-subsidization can be effected by charging different prices for the same service, such as when universities selectively offer scholarships and hospitals provide uncompensated care, or by undertaking commercial activities, such as museum gift shops, for the express purpose of generating revenues for mission-based activities.

Further, the importance of revenue reminds us that there are many reasons besides charity for the existence of nonprofit firms. In theorizing about what mission-related products and services nonprofits will produce, economists generally view nonprofit organizations as the economy's third sector. Economists take as a starting point the production decisions made by the for-profit and government sectors (and, implicitly, nonmarket production within households), and think of the nonprofit sector as stepping in to modify the resource allocation that results.[14] From this perspective, there are several categories of services nonprofits can usefully provide. For a more detailed presentation of the several rationales for nonprofit service provision than we present here, see the chapter by Steinberg in this volume.

As discussed by Weisbrod (1998b, chapter 3), the consumption of some goods and services is *collective,* or *public.* An example is a radio broadcast: once it is produced, the same broadcast can be enjoyed by many people, and one person's tuning in does not interfere with another's "consumption" of the same broadcast. Some collective consumption goods can be produced for profit because there are easy ways to exclude nonpaying customers; an example is a movie shown in a movie theater. Others are privately produced because they are tied to excludable services; there are for-profit radio stations not because customers are charged but because advertising time is provided only to businesses that pay for it. Other collective consumption goods are what economists refer to as *nonexcludable:* it is very costly to exclude anyone from enjoying the benefits of such collective services, once they are provided. Basic research is a classic example of this kind of public good. Nonexcludable collective goods are seldom produced in the for-profit sector, although there are examples in which the benefits to one consumer are great enough to induce that consumer to provide the good for the benefit of all; an example would be a large maritime shipping company that paid for the construction of a lighthouse. The nonprofit sector is active in the production of collective consumption goods, such as basic research in private universities. It also produces collective consumption goods neglected by the government, such as those exalting religious ideals, for instance a public performance by a Salvation Army band.

Other mission-related services are *private,* and they are by nature *excludable.* For example, one person's occupancy of a bed in a nursing home precludes another's use of it (its consumption is private rather than collective), and the nursing home controls access to its beds (exclusion is straightforward). Although many such goods and services are produced in the for-profit sector, there are several reasons a mission-driven nonprofit firm might produce them as well. First, the consumption of some goods gives rise to benefits for persons other than the consumer.[15] Education is a prime example: while the person pursuing an education receives direct benefits, fellow citizens enjoy the results of better-informed voting, lower probabilities of criminal behavior, and so on. These beneficial side effects are known as *externalities.* Sports leagues for youth are an example of a private good (a spot on a sports team) with externalities (a youth culture with an appreciation of athletic participation and accomplishment) provided largely by the nonprofit sector. Education is another important industry in which the production of externalities (e.g., leadership and the promotion of liberal or religious ideals) lies at the heart of the mission of nonprofit firms.

Other private goods that might be provided by nonprofit firms are those for which it is costly for consumers to observe quality. Profit-minded firms might cut corners rather than produce costly but unobservable quality, while nonprofit firms, lacking a profit motive to cheat on quality, might respond less opportunistically to this or similar *information problems.* Nursing homes and child day-care centers are examples of nonprofits providing *trust goods* in markets in which quality is an important dimension of care not fully observed by potential consumers.

Finally, the nonprofit sector sometimes acts to increase the access of certain groups to particular goods and services. People's ability to pay may not be sufficient to elicit for-profit production of certain goods that nonprofits would like to see made available. Examples include the provision of food and shelter to the poor and the provision of expensive cultural services such as art museums and opera performances for the rich. Alternatively, quite apart from the incomes of potential consumers and the costs of producing certain goods, there may be goods that excite missionary zeal because of some perceived intrinsic merit that is underappreciated in people's preferences. Nonprofit organizations may spring up in order to promote the consumption of *merit goods,* encouraging us to forsake alcohol, to embrace celibacy, to enjoy folk art, or to follow more closely God's teachings.

In summary, economics explains mission-related nonprofit activity as a response to goods that are underprovided because of their collective consumption nature, externalities, incomplete information, inability of potential clients to pay market prices, and a disparity between what people choose and what others think is in their best interest. Beyond this mission-driven activity, at least since the work of James (1983) there has been the recognition that nonprofits may sell some services purely as a means of generating net revenue. The provision of these services is not seen as part of the organizational mission except as they generate net revenue to subsidize mission-related activity. We make this distinction by referring to mission-related versus commercial services. We note that the possibility of generating net revenue may exist in markets for mission-related services as well as commercially motivated ones, and in either case the market may attract competition from profit-taking firms. We address issues of direct competition between for-profit and nonprofit firms in the provision of services later in this chapter.

Service Quality

Discussions of the quality of service provided by nonprofits can be broken into two strains. The first strain focuses on conflicts among stakeholders whose preferred quality choices do not coincide. Service quality, in other words, is an important application of the models of ideological tension between managers and donors discussed earlier. In this literature, quality, though valued differently by different stakeholders, is readily observed by all parties. The second strain of literature examines the nonprofit response to informational asymmetries when service quality is not costlessly observed.

The full-information literature on service quality choice suggests a caveat for interpretations of empirical findings of quality differentials between the services of for-profit and nonprofit firms. Typically, individuals differ in their preferences for quality of service. Even when services are provided solely by for-profits, there is variation across firms in the level of quality provided. The clothing sold by Wal-Mart is of lower quality than that sold by Neiman Marcus, and this is not taken as evidence that Wal-Mart is behaving badly, or that it would be better for consumers if Wal-Mart were a nonprofit establishment. It is not obvious a priori that differences in quality of care across, for example, child-care centers reflect anything other than differences in the choice of which market niche to inhabit. If quality is found to vary systematically with the choice of organizational form, it may be because nonprofits are less tempted to exploit their informational advantage, but it may also be that the nonprofit form is somehow better suited to the provision of a particular quality of care even when clients are well informed about quality and so cannot be taken advantage of.

The lesson of this logic for interpreting empirical work on the effect of ownership form on product quality is this: Quality differentiation is not itself evidence of an information problem that might be solved by the introduction of nonprofit firms. Any of the other economic motives for nonprofit provision of services can motivate a level of quality different from the profit-maximizing one. Nonprofit opera companies may produce higher-quality opera, as adjudged by opera aficionados, because donations allow them to avoid pandering to a broad audience with less rarified tastes. Here, a merit-good argument underlies a quality differential. Similarly, nonprofit institutions of higher education may be more strongly devoted to imparting to their students an appreciation of cultural diversity and tolerance of others than are for-profit institutions of higher education; such positive externalities are internalized by the broader mission of the nonprofit college. It is important to document the information problem that arises in a market before concluding that quality differentials result from it.

In the strand of literature that focuses on incomplete information as a determinant of service quality, it is observed that for some services those who produce them are better informed about service quality than any outsider, including potential consumers. This informational advantage can be exploited by producers. Hansmann (1980) first extended to nonprofits in general a point that had been made previously about specific nonprofits (see Nelson and Krashinsky [1974] and Arrow [1969]). He argued that the nondistribution constraint provides a reason to expect that nonprofits have less incentive to cheat on the quality of service they provide than do for-profits, when service quality is difficult for clients or donors to monitor.

This follows from the fact that the nondistribution constraint reduces the advantage to managers of nonprofits from saving costs by reducing service quality in hard-to-detect ways. Glaeser and Schleifer (2001) develop a theoretical model in which entrepreneurs can enter an industry by starting up either a for-profit or nonprofit organization. The distinction in their model between organizational forms lies in their assumption that net revenues generated by a nonprofit entity accrue to the entrepreneur as "perquisites" that come with the job of managing the firm, which are assumed to be less valuable to the entrepreneur than cash.[16] The service provided by any organization is of unknown quality before purchase, and after purchase the buyer cannot sue for fraud or misrepresentation of quality, because quality is assumed to be unverifiable by a third party, such as a court of law.[17] Their model predicts that for-profit firms charge lower prices and provide lower-quality service.

There is a substantial literature that seeks to determine in various ways whether predictions about the relative provision of hard-to-observe quality of service holds true, and the results are mixed. The chapters on health care, social care, and culture in this volume contain many references to literature on the links between nonprofit provision and the quality of services provided.

One organization well suited to a study of the question of nonprofit quality differentials based on hard-to-observe quality differences is the kidney dialysis clinic. First, because most of the cost of dialysis is borne by Medicare through its End Stage Renal Disease Program, whose $11.7 billion budget in 1999 represented annual expenditures of more than $47,000 per patient, patients are unlikely to be budget-mindedly seeking low-quality dialysis. Quality variation in this market, then, is unlikely to reflect variation in patients' willingness to pay. Second, suppliers of dialysis services have greater information about the quality of care they provide than the patient can readily observe. As described in greater detail by Ford and Kaserman (2000), a patient's dialysis session typically lasts two to five hours, and a longer treatment, other things equal, means cleaner blood and better health. While a patient can easily observe treatment duration, the appropriate duration for any one patient depends on many factors, including the patient's muscle mass, the rate of blood flow the patient can tolerate, and the filtering capacity of a particular dialysis filter, so that it is difficult for a patient to assess quality. Third, Medicare reimbursement for kidney dialysis treatments is a fixed fee per treatment session. Since dialysis is both costly and labor-intensive, the costs of each session increase significantly with its duration, creating a clear tradeoff between quality and profit. Finally, freestanding dialysis clinics are operated under a variety of ownership forms, including nonprofit, owner-operated, and stockholder-owned forms.

Using data from 1992 on 2,389 dialysis patients, of whom 40 percent received their treatment in nonprofit clinics, 7 percent in physician-owned clinics, and the remainder in for-profit incorporated clinics, Ford and Kaserman investigate the effect of ownership form on session duration. Controlling for relevant factors, they find that both nonprofit and physician-owned clinics provided significantly longer treatment sessions than did corporate-owned dialysis clinics. Garg et al. (1999) document further that patients of nonprofit dialysis clinics experience lower mortality rates and higher rates of referral for kidney transplants, further indicators of higher-quality care in the nonprofit sector.

Hard-to-observe quality plays a major role in other, more complicated settings as well. Many health-care markets, including hospital care, nursing homes, and psychiatric hospitals (see Weisbrod [1988] and the chapter by Schlesinger and Gray in this volume), are plagued with information problems and vexed additionally with multiple dimensions along which quality might be assessed.

An important and similarly vexed example outside the health-care industry is child care. Using a national sample of 2,089 child-care centers collected as part of the Profile of Child Care Settings Study, Mauser (1998) finds that quality is higher in both religious nonprofits and other nonprofits than in for-profit centers, and the variability in quality is lower in religious nonprofit centers. Parents who find it hard to observe important characteristics of care, such as the extent of individual attention paid to each child and the developmental value of activities, and who live in child-care markets large enough to make information gathering especially costly, are less likely to choose for-profit child-care providers. Hagy (1998), employing the same data set, finds that, after accounting for observable dimensions of quality, parents pay a premium of $0.18 per hour at independently operated nonprofit centers, perhaps because they trust these centers to provide higher levels of hard-to-observe quality.

Other scholars, using other data, obtain different results on the relationships between quality and ownership form in the child-care industry. Using the Cost, Quality, and Child Outcomes in Child Care Centers data set, in which hard-to-observe quality was assessed by teams of child-care specialists who spent a day in each classroom included in the study, Mocan (2001) documents the difficulty parents have in interpreting available signals of hard-to-observe quality in child day care. Because parents (and especially parents with limited educational attainment) cannot easily assess quality, he asserts that the market for center-based child care is likely to be a lemons market in which informational asymmetries keep quality low. Based on his empirical analysis, he concludes that nonprofit firms do not solve the information problem. Parents do not interpret nonprofit status as a signal of quality, even though the observations of outside evaluators suggest that it is. Further, some nonprofit firms themselves take advantage of customer ignorance, for example by providing a sparkling clean reception area while skimping on other, hard-to-observe dimensions of quality. The possibility of inefficiently low levels of quality obtaining in such a market suggests a potential role for government action in setting minimum standards for day-care centers. Morris and Helburn (2000) use the same data set and find that in North Carolina, a state with lax licensing requirements, for-profit child-care centers skimp on hard-to-observe dimensions of quality relative to easily observed dimensions of quality. This was not found in states with stricter licensing requirements; in those cases, easily observed measures of quality were good predictors of hard-to-observe quality and nonprofit status added no further information.[18]

Service Mix

Much of the work on nonprofit behavior in service provision since James (1983) has assumed the provision of an array of services. If a nonprofit can potentially provide such an array, then an immediate question is: what determines the actual "mix" of services provided?

Many nonprofits provide services that have little to do with their mission. They provide (and sometimes charge for) parking, they provide cafeteria meals to clients and non-clients, they sell gifts in shops that may not even be located on the organization's premises, and they run lotteries. If these services are produced completely independently of the mission-related services of the organization, and if managers and donors have no ideological preferences regarding the provision of commercial services, then nonprofits are predicted to participate in these markets in order to generate net revenues that can be diverted to the production of mission-oriented services. In markets that are unrelated to mission, nonprofits should maximize profit. James (1983) and Schiff and Weisbrod (1991) consider the possibility that nonprofit managers actively dislike providing some commercial services. In this case, nonprofits will not act like for-profit firms in producing these commercial services. James assumes there exist three types of services: those that give the nonprofit manager positive utility (i.e., those consistent with mission), those that generate net revenue and have no direct impact, aside from revenue generation, on utility (i.e., they are unrelated to mission), and those services that generate negative utility (detracting from mission) along with positive revenue. As long as the production of the second class of services, those that are purely commercial and unrelated to mission, has no impact on the cost of producing other services, these activities should be undertaken at the levels that maximize the net revenue they generate. This prediction allows us to test for the presence of the third class of services, commercial services that the nonprofit manager would rather not engage in. When budgets are tightened, say because donations fall, managers will be driven to increase their reliance on distasteful commercial activities. By contrast, they will not step up their production of unrelated commercial activities, since these were being pursued at the profit-maximizing level to begin with. Similarly, this model allows us to test whether nonprofits are really "for-profits-in-disguise." A nonprofit will react to any unanticipated windfall in donations by increasing the production of mission-consistent services and relying less on distasteful mission-compromising services; neither of these changes would be observed in a profit-maximizing firm.

An extension of James's model asks whether managers personally dislike certain commercial activities, or alternatively whether they are reacting strategically to donors' dislike of those activities. If potential donors dislike seeing a nonprofit engage in commercial activities, any organization that does so imperils its donor support. Segal and Weisbrod (1998) assemble a panel of the 2,697 nonprofits with assets over $50 million that filed IRS 990s from 1985 through 1993. They find a negative relationship between donations and revenue from sales. This suggests that nonprofit managers do indeed dislike commercial activity; otherwise, they would conduct it at its profit-maximizing level at all times, rather than resort to it only when donations are scarce. Tests for the direction of causation suggest that commercial activity increases in response to reductions in available donations, but that donations do not respond to the firm's level of commercial activity. This suggests that nonprofit managers' distaste for commercial undertakings is not purely a strategic response to the attitudes of donors, since donors seem not to care.[19]

Finally, it may be that the production of commercial services reduces a nonprofit organization's ability to produce mission-related services, for purely technological reasons. This can occur when the cost of producing mission-related services is affected by the production of commercial services. For example, a nonprofit university will be able to educate fewer undergraduates if its faculty and facilities are engaged in providing consulting services to private firms or governments for a fee. In this case, too, a nonprofit will not be expected to engage in the commercial activity to the same extent as would a profit-taking firm. From a longer perspective, however, a prior decision to provide nonmission services could result in the building of greater capacity (i.e., larger or more numerous classrooms) with a concomitantly greater provision of mission-related services than if no commercial activities are contemplated.[20]

Beyond considerations of cost and capacity, deciding to engage in commercial activities can involve fundamental changes in personnel and organizational structure, including the membership of the board of trustees. The chapter by Tuckman and Chang in this volume deals explicitly with whether undertaking commercial activities to raise revenue is harmful to the mission of nonprofits; see also the chapter by Minkoff and Powell.

When many mission-related services are provided, the mix of services must be decided on, and we expect nonprofit managers, founders, trustees, donors, and clients will have preferences regarding this mix. One empirical strategy is to infer the net impact of stakeholder preferences on the mix of services provided by contrasting nonprofits' behavior with that of profit-maximizing firms. Luksetich, Edwards, and Carroll (2000) study Minnesota nursing homes, for example, and their finding that nonprofit homes spend more per patient-day on nursing care and less on general and administrative expenses than do for-profit homes suggests that nursing care is a preferred activity among nonprofit stakeholders.

The Pricing and Provision of Mission-Related Services

Any nonprofit providing a service must decide who is eligible to receive it, and at what price. The organization may offer its service free to all comers (and adopt any of a variety of rationing mechanisms if the quantity demanded exceeds the quantity supplied), it may charge a fee, or it may devise a more elaborate fee structure. It may also use various devices other than fees, such as waiting lists, to target the set of individuals who ultimately receive its services.

In some instances, a nonprofit's mission will have direct implications for its pricing scheme. Programs designed to feed the hungry generally provide services free of charge and use nonprice mechanisms, such as the modest quality of prepared food in a soup kitchen or long lines and eligibility requirements at a food bank, to direct services to their preferred client base. Private colleges pursue a diverse and talented pool of students by setting a fee structure that pegs price to ability to pay; among high-priced private colleges offering a four-year degree in 1993, well over a third of them selectively offered average discounts off the full tuition rate, via student aid packages, of 30 percent or more (Davis 1997).

McCready (1988) discovers that some social service agencies set the prices of their services to disadvantaged clients equal to the prices at which similar services are available to the broader population. The mission of such agencies can be interpreted as one of "leveling the playing field" by ignoring the higher costs involved in serving disadvantaged populations. For example, the price charged a physically handicapped person for customized transportation might ignore the costs of providing the service; instead, the service might be priced at the cost of a municipal bus ticket, equalizing the price of "transportation" for handicapped and nonhandicapped persons.

One mission frequently attributed to nonprofits is that they wish to maximize output, subject to avoiding bankruptcy. This may arise because the service they provide is a merit good in the eyes of the nonprofit manager or founder, or simply because it is a public good that is viewed as being otherwise underprovided.

If nonprofit firms must finance some of the cost of their service through fees, and if they can identify distinct subgroups among their potential clientele, economics predicts that different groups of customers will be charged different prices. Those clients who would be most deterred by high prices will face low prices, because the organization does not wish to deter consumption. A nonprofit family-planning clinic, for example, might have a fee schedule that varies directly with income, recognizing that low-income clients might not come forward if they were charged a fee while middle-income clients are undeterred by reasonable charges. Steinberg and Weisbrod (1998) cite several industries in which nonprofits use this type of sliding scale. They also point out that while a profit-taking firm will never sell a service to any client at a price below the cost of producing the incremental amount, a nonprofit might do so, using profits earned on other sales to subsidize the resulting net losses.

When a nonprofit seeks to maximize output, or indeed when it pursues any mission different from profit maximization, its prices will generally vary with market conditions in ways that distinguish its behavior from that of a profit-maximizing firm. Pricing behavior, then, gives us another way to test whether nonprofits behave differently from for-profit firms. Jacobs and Wilder (1984), for example, examine the pricing behavior of Red Cross blood centers. They find that these blood centers respond to output-invariant subsidies by reducing the price of whole blood supplied to hospitals. This behavior is predicted by the output maximization model, and is inconsistent with profit maximization. Weisbrod (1998a) finds that nonprofit nursing homes and facilities for the mentally handicapped price their outputs closer to average per-unit production cost than do their for-profit counterparts.

Lynk (1995) argues that if nonprofit hospitals do not simply maximize profits, then a change in market concentration should have a greater effect on the prices charged by for-profit hospitals than on those charged by nonprofit hospitals. Using price data for the ten most common diagnostic-related groups from a large sample of California hospitals in 1988, he finds that mergers between for-profit hospitals led to greater price increases than did mergers between nonprofits. The policy implication of this work is that antitrust law enforcement should consider ownership form when evaluating the desirability of proposed hospital mergers.[21]

If nonprofit firms interpret their public benefit role as including a mandate to be mindful of economic efficiency,[22] we might again expect to see price schedules in which prices are higher for customers who are less deterred by high prices. McCready (1988) fails to find any evidence of price-setting behavior that reflects clients' price sensitivity among a set of social services agencies in Ontario, Canada. Indeed, he finds little pricing at all, with most of the organizations surveyed either waiving fees or providing services free of charge.

Nonprofits that choose to provide their services free of charge or at greatly subsidized rates may need to ration access to those services. They may face capacity or budget constraints that limit output and their mission may target specific groups of clients. It surely matters to the operators of homeless shelters, for example, that the people they take in lack better housing options. Like their for-profit counterparts, nonprofits provide services using many allocative mechanisms that are more elaborate than simply setting a uniform fee. Steinberg and Weisbrod (1998) discuss many such mechanisms used by nonprofits. They also provide us with a promising beginning in the task of determining the differences in the ways in which these two types of organizations use sophisticated pricing and rationing mechanisms.

One pricing strategy used by some for-profit firms is to require would-be customers to pay an access fee before they are allowed to purchase the firm's service. Country clubs, for example, charge a membership fee and then sell dinners and rounds of golf to their members. While this two-part pricing strategy is not strictly analogous to the observed practices of such nonprofits as symphonies and opera companies who extract (voluntary) donations from (many but not all of) their ticket-buyers, the similarity has been exploited in modeling the impact on the quantity, quality, and price of these nonprofit services when customers are also donors. Bilodeau and Steinberg (1999) model this practice by nonprofits, building on the earlier insights of Hansmann (1981) and Ben-Ner (1986). Their model predicts greater output under two-part pricing, and a usage fee that is below the average cost per unit of producing the service and is lower than the usage fee that would result without donations.

Spiegel (1995) considers a similar case in which lower-income and higher-income patrons differ in their willingness to pay for product quality. Voluntary donations offer a way for the high-income patrons to pay more than a proportionate share of the cost of an increase in quality. High-income patrons can cooperatively pledge a certain level of donations in order to raise product quality. If they control the pricing decision of the nonprofit (perhaps through their influence on the board of trustees), the nonprofit will then raise ticket prices by as much as the lower-income patrons will tolerate for the higher-quality product, shifting as much of the cost of the quality increase to the non-donor customers as they will bear. In this case, the presence of voluntary donations by a class of customers is associated with higher product quality and higher product price. With a smaller price increase, all customers could be better off in the equilibrium with voluntary donations by the high-income patrons.

If symphonies and opera companies are plausibly described by this model, in which well-heeled patrons and nonprofit management coordinate their donations, quality, and pricing decisions, are there other nonprofits described by another case considered by Spiegel, one in which the nonprofit's pricing decision is in the hands of the non-contributing, lower-income patrons? Imagine a church-run child-care center that attracts both high-income and lower-income patrons who value the religious training (in which the center has a local monopoly) but have differing willingness to pay for child-care quality. The wealthier parents value quality highly enough to make voluntary contributions to the center. If the less-wealthy patrons constitute a substantial majority of the customer base, or if their well-being is the concern of the child-care manager, the child-care center might react to the receipt of these contributions by lowering the price charged for child care. This is essentially an instance of crowding out: the donations suddenly allow lower-income patrons a higher standard of living than they had before, and they want to spread this affluence across their consumption of other goods besides quality child care. They do this by getting the nonprofit to lower the price they pay for child care, leaving them more money to spend elsewhere.

Some nonprofits also use waiting lists. A basic question of interest is whether for-profit and nonprofit firms use nonprice rationing devices like waiting lists, or non-uniform fees, to a different extent, or in different circumstances. Looking at nursing homes and facilities for the mentally handicapped, Weisbrod (1998a) finds that in each industry the use of waiting lists is significantly more prevalent in church-run facilities than in for-profit ones, with secular nonprofits falling in between.

It is worth noting that these complex allocation mechanisms arise in markets in which the nonprofit has some protection from competition: there is not a second opera company skimming off the wealthier patrons, nor another child-care center espousing the same religious views, nor an equally caring nursing home to absorb the customers on the waiting list. This suggests that the theoretical and empirical modeling of nonprofits' production and pricing decisions will vary with the competitiveness of the environment in which they operate. In more competitive markets, the models often face the further challenge of explaining the coexistence of for-profit and nonprofit firms.

COMPETITION WITH FOR-PROFIT FIRMS

In many markets, nonprofit providers of services function alongside for-profit and/or government providers. In the United States, child day-care centers are roughly 60 percent nonprofit and 40 percent for-profit, with the nonprofit numbers containing a small number of publicly run centers (Morris and Helburn 2000). Measured in terms of the number of acute-care hospital beds, the hospital industry in the United States in 1995 was 65 percent nonprofit, 11 percent for-profit, and 24 percent public (Cutler 2000). In the performing arts, again in the United States, for-profit firms dominate the market for circuses (representing 80 percent of the firms and garnering 93 percent of the revenues), split the market for theater companies (representing 48 percent of the companies and 68 percent of the revenues), and barely make their presence known among symphony orchestras and chamber music groups (13 percent of the ensembles but only 4 percent of revenues) (U.S. Department of Commerce 2000).[23]

Confronting this coexistence of organizational forms within markets, Rose-Ackerman (1996:718) asks the economist's first questions: "How can we explain the persistence of mixed service sectors? Why doesn't one form drive out the others?" One can easily add a corollary question, "When industries are mixed, what determines the market shares of production by nonprofit, for-profit, and public enterprises?" The existence of tax advantages for nonprofits does not, on its own, explain the varied presence of nonprofits across industries, since nonprofits' tax advantage is omnipresent and nonprofit dominance is not. The same is true for the for-profit sector's generally advantageous access to equity markets. With these considerations in mind, we survey the literature that attempts to understand markets in which both for-profit and nonprofit firms operate.

Research that seeks to explain variation in nonprofit share across locations and industries has looked either at variations in the importance of the financial advantages (tax breaks) and disadvantages (lack of access to equity markets) that attend the nonprofit organizational form or at variations in the strength of the underlying forces (externalities, public goods, information asymmetries, etc.) that motivate nonprofit production. Although tax breaks for nonprofits are ubiquitous, they vary in magnitude across jurisdictions, and it is reasonable to think this may induce variations in their market share when both types of firm operate. Hansmann (1987) takes an empirical look at the importance of tax breaks and, indirectly, access to capital markets in explaining variations in the market shares of nonprofit firms in different states. Some states impose higher taxes on for-profit firms than do others; the advantages to nonprofit status are larger and one might see a larger market share of nonprofits in states in which their tax exemptions give them a greater advantage over their for-profit counterparts. Some states experience faster population growth than others; expanding markets have been seen as advantaging the for-profit sector with its ability to raise financial capital in equity markets. Looking at nursing homes, hospitals, and schools, Hansmann finds that the combined tax advantages from property tax exemption, sales tax exemption for purchased inputs, and corporate tax exemption explain significant and substantial amounts of the variation in market shares, with the nonprofit share higher in states offering greater tax advantages. He also finds that market growth reduces the nonprofit share, which is consistent with the notion that access to capital markets allows profit-taking firms to enter growing markets more quickly.

Ben-Ner and Van Hoomissen (1991) explore the conditions under which costly information evokes a greater or lesser nonprofit presence in a market. They incorporate the idea in Weisbrod (1975) that for-profit and government-sector behavior may leave some demand unsatisfied, and add that some demand-side stakeholders may find it worthwhile to form a nonprofit firm as a means of gaining control over the quantity and quality of services supplied. Thus, there is both a demand for and a supply of nonprofit provision of services that ultimately determines the representation of nonprofits in any industry. Consider, for example, services with hard-to-observe quality; the larger the market, the greater the costs of gathering costly information and the greater the return to having a firm controlled by demand-side stakeholders. For trust goods, then, the nonprofit share of the market increases with market size. Similarly, well-educated consumers can more easily identify trustworthy for-profit providers; the nonprofit share of trust-good markets should fall as education levels rise.[24]

Addressing the question of how coexistence comes about in the first place, there is a strand of literature that focuses on heterogeneity in the motivations of entrepreneurs to explain the coexistence of nonprofit and for-profit firms in some markets. Schiff and Weisbrod (1991) analyze competition in the provision of commercial services by adapting the James (1983) model of a multiservice nonprofit to analyze entry into a market and competition with for-profits. They assume the nonprofit can produce both a mission-related service and a commercial service, and that it is run by a manager who likes producing the mission-related service and is at best indifferent about producing the other, perhaps even disliking it.

For-profit competition is introduced by specifying the existence of firms that produce only the commercial service, run by managers who get no personal payoff from producing the mission-related service. The key question, then, is: under what conditions does this model predict that the nonprofits that remain also operate in the commercial market, producing both services? The key to the answer lies in the following argument. If for-profits enter this market until their economic profit is zero, then they are earning a competitive rate of return for the owner-managers of the firms. In the absence of any distaste for it, the commercial service doesn't have to yield as great a return to the nonprofit entrepreneur-manager, because the nonprofit entrepreneur-manager is simultaneously receiving some utility directly from the production of the mission-related service. Such an individual will, in addition to producing the mission-related good, produce the commercial service in the face of for-profit competitive entry if the net monetary return from doing so allows for sufficient subsidy of the mission-related service to compensate for any distaste attached to producing the commercial service. Thus, if the entrepreneurial distaste for the commercial activity is not too great (or if there are sufficient cost or demand complementarities between the commercial and mission-related activity), the nonprofit firm will compete in the market for the commercial activity.

The James-Schiff-Weisbrod model of a mixed industry applies to those nonprofit organizations that compete with for-profits in commercial activities. Lakdawalla and Philipson (2002) have developed an alternative model based on entrepreneurial preferences in which firms produce only a single service, and may also receive donations from noncustomers. Any competition between the two organizational forms must be in the market for this single service. They assume that entrepreneurs care about profits and, to varying degrees, about the level and/or quality of output their firm produces. Entrepreneurs who do care about service levels directly are said to have "profit-deviating preferences." Each entrepreneur can choose to enter the market by starting up either a for-profit firm or a nonprofit. Choosing nonprofit status implies the imposition of a nondistribution constraint, which here is modeled as an upper limit (possibly zero) on the profits the organization can earn.[25] A key feature of the Lakdawalla-Philipson model is that it implies that when there is free entry into the industry, the two types of firms can coexist only if there is a scarcity of entrepreneurs with "profit-deviating preferences"; otherwise, the nonprofit firms would be the only producers by virtue of the assumption that nonprofit status implies lower costs, due to tax advantages. The model therefore implies that for-profit firms are the "marginal firms" in any mixed industry; adjustments in the market are generally accomplished via changes in their numbers. One testable implication of the marginal nature of the for-profit firms is that in a mixed industry with government service providers as well as for-profit and nonprofit firms, expansions (or contractions) of the government presence should crowd out (or in) the for-profit firms and not the nonprofit firms. Using a U.S. panel data set on the nursing-home industry broken down by states, Lakdawalla and Philipson find empirical evidence that the for-profit market share is crowded out by public-sector provision, while the nonprofit sector is not. This supports the important prediction of their model that an increase in government provision of services will increase the share of output that comes from the nonprofit sector relative to the for-profit sector.[26]

The models above adopt what is an essentially "competitive" view of mixed industries. That is, they assume that establishments, whether for-profit or nonprofit, believe that they cannot influence the price at which their services are sold, and that there are many firms producing homogeneous services. The relative advantages of nonprofit and for-profit organizational form have been explored in less-competitive settings as well. In markets that will be dominated by a single service provider, such as a small city with only one hospital, these relative advantages determine whether the monopoly is organized as a for-profit or a nonprofit entity. Bilodeau (2002) develops a model of entry into the provision of a service by a monopoly establishment and relates the initial choice of organizational form to various market and regulatory parameters.

Intermediate to these models of competitive markets and monopoly markets are those characterized by organizations selling differentiated services. The models of Rose-Ackerman (1982, 1987), for example, have a number of nonprofit organizations providing similar but not identical services. These nonprofits do not earn revenue from sales, explicitly, but that is not a difficult feature to add, with the demand for each nonprofit's service varying inversely with the number and similarity of service of other nonprofit organizations in the market. Although competition with for-profits is not explicitly modeled, one can also add to her model a "for-profit fringe" of firms whose product characteristics are dictated by the tastes of paying customers with no influence from (nonexistent) donors and (indifferent) entrepreneurs. The preponderance of for-profit firms would depend on the prevalence of customer willingness to pay for varieties that are not of interest to nonprofit entrepreneurs. As in Lakdawalla-Philipson, for-profits could not successfully compete with nonprofits for any variety that is of interest to donors, since donors will subsidize production by nonprofits but not by for-profit firms (who might appropriate donations in the form of profits to stockholders). Preston (1988) also develops a monopolistic competition model of mixed nonprofit and profit-taking industries in which the services produced by various firms differ in terms of how much public benefit they provide. The model predicts that if both types of firms produce, the nonprofits produce services with higher public benefits.

One of the oldest arguments for the existence of nonprofit firms is the Arrow-Hansmann idea that they represent a solution to the "contract failure" that arises in markets in which consumers are at an informational disadvantage regarding the quality of service provided by firms. (This line of argument is laid out in detail in the chapter by Steinberg in this volume.) Hirth (1999) develops a model of the coexistence of nonprofit and for-profit firms that uses this idea. The model assumes that consumers vary in how well informed they are, that entrepreneurs vary in their level of honesty, and that entrepreneurs can choose which type of firm to operate. It also allows for the nondistribution constraint to be enforced in varying degrees. The result most germane to the present discussion shows that if there are enough badly informed consumers and if enforcement of the nondistribution constraint is sufficiently stringent, nonprofits will enter and compete with for-profits, drive out any firms behaving as "nonprofits-in-disguise," and raise the quality of service being provided in the market. Further, the nonprofit firms charge higher prices for the services they provide. Glaeser and Schleifer (2001) develop a model in which heterogeneity in customers' tastes supports the coexistence of for-profit and nonprofit firms whose outputs are differentiated by quality. Entrepreneurs choose an organizational form, knowing that as managers of nonprofit firms they accrue net revenues only as perquisites that they value less than they would the cash itself. When quality is observed only after purchase and only by the consumer, they find that it is possible to have an equilibrium in which the two types of firms coexist. When both types of firms do produce, the nonprofits charge higher prices and provide higher quality than do the for-profit firms.[27] Most behavioral models, such as those presented above, predict that nonprofit and for-profit firms behave differently within any market in which they do coexist. Rose-Ackerman (1996) and Weisbrod (1998a) provide overviews of research on differences in firm behavior within mixed industries, including nursing homes, day care, and education. It is a fair characterization of this empirical literature that most studies find that organizations of different forms that operate in mixed industries behave differently in at least some (measured) dimensions. It also seems to be generally true that the *level of competitiveness* (measured by the total number of competing firms, or number of competing nonprofits) is found to have a significant effect on the extent to which the two types of firms behave differently.[28]

The conversion of nonprofit organizations to for-profit status (and in some cases vice versa), especially in the health-care and insurance industries, has attracted a good deal of attention in recent decades. At least four reasons have been put forward for such conversions. In the hospital market, conversion has variously been viewed (see, for example, Cutler [2000] and Cutler and Horwitz [2000]) to be: a survival strategy employed by marginally viable firms, a strategy for taking advantage of the potentially high profitability of some nonprofits, a way to gain access to relatively inexpensive working capital through equity markets in order to expand or to finance debt, and a response to the perceived increase in risk that came with running hospitals under changeable federal regulations and reimbursement strategies, leaving relatively risk-averse nonprofit managers less eager to run hospitals than their for-profit counterparts.

There is room in the conversions literature for further research that pays attention to both explicit behavioral modeling and institutional details such as the workings of debt and capital markets in the hospital industry. Further discussion of hospital conversions can be found in Goodeeris and Weisbrod (1998), Sloan (1998), and the chapter in this volume by Gray and Schlesinger.

Given economists' experience and expertise in modeling the market behavior of profit-taking firms, it is not surprising that some of the most fully developed models in the economics of nonprofit firms deal with interactions between nonprofit and profit-taking firms, addressing issues of the competitive advantages accruing to each organizational form, their coexistence within markets, and conversions from one form to the other. Further research in this area should strive to combine the rigor of existing models with a more nuanced understanding of the particular industries in which nonprofits thrive.

CONCLUDING REMARKS

Economists think of nonprofit organizations as rational optimizers that respond strategically to market incentives and statutory constraints. If their objective were to maximize net revenue—what for-profit firms experience as profit—the economists' task in studying nonprofits would be simple. We would not expect them to behave identically with for-profits, because they operate under a different set of constraints. Rather, observed differences in behavior between for-profit and nonprofit firms would be attributable to the differences in constraints, and the chosen organizational form would be that which allowed greater profit.

Although the economic study of nonprofits seldom takes this observation as its starting point, it seems clear that nonprofits behave differently from for-profit firms, and the differences are not those that would be predicted merely as a consequence of their regulatory environments. Evidence on the quality of nonprofit firms' services, on the industries in which they are concentrated, their pricing strategies, and the differences in their product mixes suggests that nonprofits do indeed pursue objectives different from profit maximization. Nonprofit firms are not, in general, for-profits in disguise.

Neither are nonprofits easily categorized as muddleheaded bastions of ideology that, freed from stockholder oversight, waste resources with flagrant disregard for market signals of value and scarcity. Deviations from profit-maximizing behavior are generally consistent with plausible optimization based on objectives that differ from profit-maximization, such as providing quality and increasing quantities consumed by targeted clienteles. This behavior can indeed be seen, in some circumstances, as providing corrections for market and government failures, internalizing externalities, or responding to heterogeneous tastes.

As Steinberg (1987) wrote in the version of this chapter appearing in the first edition of this book, "Thus, the market structure paradigm seems invaluable for understanding the functioning and performance of nonprofit organizations." In confirmation of this view, the past two decades have seen an explosion of research on the market behavior of nonprofit firms, and many fruitful lines of research invite further inquiry. We summarize some of the most salient ones here.

While nonprofit wage differentials relative to the for-profit sector have been studied extensively, differences in the use of labor relative to other inputs, such as capital equipment and real estate, have not. There is also much to be learned about differences in the forms of compensation adopted within nonprofits.

There is a long-standing belief that nonprofits are characterized by sloppy management, due to a lack of any market for nonprofit control, such as equity markets provide in the for-profit world. However, if mission really matters to individuals outside a nonprofit, and those individuals have resources that give them the ability to "bribe" their way onto a board of trustees with a large donation, then it seems this might play a similar role. Further development of economic models of board behavior, as well as empirical work on board structure and turnover, is needed to understand whether this phenomenon is a real one, and the extent to which it provides a means to discipline nonprofit management.

The economic study of the interaction of fundraising, grant-seeking, and nonprofit service mix has made recent advances; these models are ready for analytical refinement and empirical confirmation. The fundraising activity of nonprofits, including their use of hired professional fundraisers, has been controversial; further study of the contracts between nonprofits and fundraising firms seems particularly critical here.

A large empirical literature already exists on nonprofit/for-profit quality differentials in service provision. As shown in the paper by Hirth, Hansmann's original identification of the importance of contract failure remains the point of departure for theoretical work in this area. Similarly, the James-Schiff-Weisbrod formulation of the behavior of nonprofits engaged in providing multiple services provides a solid jumping-off point for public policy debates on the commercial activities of nonprofits.

Steinberg and Weisbrod (1998) have provided a laudable agenda for further analysis of sophisticated pricing strategies and other allocative mechanisms used by nonprofits.

Finally, there have been recurring public debates over the impact on for-profit firms of competition from their tax-exempt nonprofit counterparts. Behavioral modeling of competition in mixed markets is a recent development, and empirical work designed to sort out which models are most relevant will add to our understanding of markets in which multiple organizational forms coexist.

NOTES

1. There are, of course, other conflicts of interest that arise in for-profit firms—managers enjoy perquisites, workers enjoy slacking off—and an extensive economics literature addresses them.

2. It also implies that they must be paid *more* if they find that mission odious. An example of a local labor market that might be dominated by a nonprofit with a mission that could be found to be objectionable to some employees is a city whose only hospital has a religious affiliation that affects the nature and/or scope of the services it provides.

3. In the United States, 10 percent of volunteer labor is supplied to the for-profit sector (Weitzman et al. 2002). The fact that the nonprofit sector as a whole attracts more volunteers than does the for-profit sector does not guarantee that nonprofits have greater access to volunteers *within* an industry. One industry for which there exist data to allow such a comparison is child day care. There is evidence that nonprofit child-care centers do in fact use more volunteer labor than their for-profit counterparts. The Cost, Quality, and Child Outcomes in Child Care Centers data set examines two hundred for-profit and two hundred nonprofit centers in four states. In this data set, nonprofit centers use significantly more monthly volunteer hours per child than do for-profit centers. We are grateful to Naci Mocan and Kaj Gittings for providing us with this comparison.

4. All of these considerations deal with differences in the *level* of compensation received in the two types of firms. Nonprofit status may also affect the *form* in which nonprofit employees are compensated. Modern thinking about firm behavior suggests for-profit employees tend to be compensated in ways that induce them to behave so as to maximize the firm's profits. Making stock options part of for-profit managers' overall compensation is one obvious example of this, and one not available to nonprofits. Leete (this volume) contains a survey of empirical studies on nonprofit executive compensation, including evidence that nonprofit hospital managers have higher base pay and lower bonuses than do their counterparts in for-profit hospitals (Roomkin and Weisbrod 1999) and that the sensitivity of CEO and board turnover to various service level and other performance indicators differs between for-profit and nonprofit hospitals in California (Eldenberg et al. 2001).

5. Among theories that predict higher wages in nonprofit firms, not all predict unambiguously more labor-intensive production. For example, if lax oversight leads to lax management, this laxity may extend to the purchase of inputs other than labor. If nonprofit firms pay higher wages because they wish to attract higher-quality workers as they skimp less than for-profit firms in producing hard-to-observe product quality, they may be paying more for similarly high-quality nonlabor inputs as well.

6. Earlier studies based on cross-sectional data yielded mixed results. Hansmann (1987) looks at nonprofits' share among private hospitals only (treating government share as exogenous) and finds no effects at the state level, but finds in a sample of large cities that the nonprofit share of the hospital market increases with corporation income tax rates. Chang and Tuckman (1990) look at counties in Tennessee and find the nonprofit hospital share of the total market, including public hospitals, is *lower* in jurisdictions with higher property tax rates.

7. In the United States, the federal tax code generally prohibits accelerated depreciation of property that is leased to tax-exempt entities under leases of more than three years (five years for certain forms of technology), including options to renew the lease. (For details, see the Internal Revenue Code, Subtitle A, Chapter 1, Subchapter B, Part VI, Sec. 168(g)–(i).) As Brody (1998:613) chronicles, these restrictions were put into place in reaction to some creative "sale-leaseback" arrangements between tax-exempt and for-profit organizations: "In the early 1980's a tax abuse arose from sale-leasebacks. . . . Exempt organizations could not use depreciation deductions and investment tax credits. As a result, Bennington College arranged to sell its campus to its alumni and lease it back. When the Navy began doing the same with its battleships, Congress enacted rules providing that property used by a tax-exempt entity (including a government) is not eligible either for accelerated depreciation or the investment tax credit."

8. Posnett and Sandler (1989) and Khanna et al. (1995) find that increases in government grants do not reduce private donations—there is no crowding out. Indeed, some studies have found instances in which such grants lead to an increase in private donations, a phenomenon known as "crowding in"; see, for example, Okten and Weisbrod (2000) and Payne (2001).

9. This is the formulation used in Weisbrod and Dominguez (1986), following a similar one in Rose-Ackerman (1982).

10. Hager et al. (2001) note that some of this variation in price may reflect variation in accounting practices.

11. Some analyses cast this distinction in terms of the present value of the stream of net or gross donations.

12. Andreoni (2002) investigates a related question: which of a set of potential donors will pay the cost of determining the quality of a charity? The answer is that more wealthy potential donors are likely to do so, other things equal.

13. In the United States, as in many countries, dues, fees, and charges make up the nonprofit sector's single largest revenue source. In 1997, they accounted for 37.5 percent of U.S. nonprofit sector revenue (Weitzman et al. 2002). Within the nonprofit sector, some industries are far more reliant on commercial revenues than others. Segal and Weisbrod (1998) cite a high of 89 percent of revenue from sales in the health industry and a low of 11 percent in community improvement.

14. This line of thinking is developed in detail in Weisbrod (1975).

15. Cornes and Sandler (1984) formulate a theory of demand for goods having both private consumption and public characteristics.

16. Many previous authors, notably Migué and Belanger (1974), have incorporated these two methods of compensating managers into models of managerial behavior.

17. This same assumption rules out the use of "quality guarantees" to deal with the asymmetry of information about quality between providers and consumers.

18. Interpretations of the effect of organizational form on quality in the market for child care are complicated by diverse notions of quality care. Church-run centers on average provide low quality as measured by child development experts but may very well be providing high-quality care in terms of religious sensibilities. For-profit centers may be providing convenience by locating near parents' places of work or along their commuting routes.

19. Further evidence that volunteers and donors are unconcerned by a nonprofit's level of commercial activities is found in a case study based on individual survey data collected and analyzed by Herman and Rendina (2001).

20. There are in fact many reasons to expect that revenues from commercial activities affect and are affected by donations, and a number of authors have developed behavioral models of some variant of this phenomenon. In some of these models, commercial revenues respond as nonprofit managers adjust the prices they charge rather than the quantities they provide in response to fluctuations in the level of support provided through donations (see, e.g., Jacobs and Wilder [1984]—discussed further below—and Kingma [1995]).

21. See Lynk and Neumann (1999) for a discussion of the debate spawned by Lynk (1995).

22. At least one textbook on economics for nonprofit managers promotes this perspective; see Young and Steinberg (1995).

23. For industry mix by ownership form in several other U.S. industries, see Rose-Ackerman (1996).

24. Ben-Ner and Van Hoomissen (1992) is an attempt to measure some of these effects using county-level data from four service industries in New York State, with limited success.

25. The nondistribution constraint is typically taken to limit the ways in which profit can be distributed, rather than the amount earned. Since the authors here assume there is only one place for profits to go—into the pockets of the entrepreneur—it can be argued that this formulation is equivalent.

26. A direct comparison with the predictions of Ben-Ner and Van Hoomissen (1991) is not possible, since their model does not encompass nonprofit production of completely private services, which is what is produced in the Lakdawalla-Philipson model.

27. For further work in which the existence of mixed industries centers on differences within the client population in the ability to detect or deal with quality variation, see Weisbrod and Schlesinger (1986), Weisbrod (1988), and Holtmann and Ullmann (1991), as well as the articles cited in the section of this chapter dealing with the quality of nonprofit service provision.

28. Duggan (2000) is a recent example. None of this work, or any other of which we are aware, looks at organizational-form-driven differences in the provision of purely commercial services, however. For example, do nonprofit hospitals charge differently for visitor parking than do for-profits?

REFERENCES

Andreoni, J. 1998. "Toward a Theory of Charitable Fundraising." *Journal of Political Economy* 106:1186–1213.

Andreoni, J. 2002. "Leadership Giving in Charitable Fund-Raising." Typescript, University of Wisconsin-Madison.

Andreoni, J., and A. Payne. 2003. "Do Government Grants to Private Charities Crowd Out Giving or Fundraising?" *The American Economic Review* 93:793–812.

Arrow, K. 1969. "Uncertainty and the Welfare Economics of Medical Care." *American Economic Review* 53:941–973.

Ben-Ner, A. 1986. "Nonprofit Organizations: Why Do They Exist in Market Economies?" In S. Rose-Ackerman, ed., *The Economics of Nonprofit Institutions: Studies in Structure and Policy.* New York, Oxford University Press.

Ben-Ner, A., and T. Van Hoomissen. 1991. "Nonprofit Organizations in the Mixed Economy: A Demand and Supply Analysis." *Annals of Public and Cooperative Economics* 62:519–550.

———. 1992. "An Empirical Investigation of the Joint Determination of the Size of the For-Profit, Nonprofit and Government Sectors." *Annals of Public and Cooperative Economics* 63:391–415.

Bilodeau, M. 1992. "Voluntary Contributions to United Charities." *Journal of Public Economics* 48:119–133.

———. 2002. "Profitable Nonprofit Firms." Typescript.

Bilodeau, M., and A. Slivinski. 1997. "Rival Charities." *Journal of Public Economics* 66:449–467.

Bilodeau, M., and R. Steinberg. 1999. "Ransom of the Opera." Typescript, Indiana University and Purdue University at Indianapolis.

Brody, E. 1998. "Of Sovereignty and Subsidy: Conceptualizing the Charity Tax Exemption." *Journal of Corporation Law* 23:585–629.

Chang, C., and H. Tuckman. 1990. "Do Higher Tax Rates Increase the Market Share of Nonprofit Hospitals?" *National Tax Journal* 43:175–187.

Cornes, R., and T. Sandler. 1984. "Easy Riders, Joint Production, and Public Goods." *Economic Journal* 94:580–598.

Cutler, D. M. 2000. "Introduction." In Cutler, David M., ed., *The Changing Hospital Industry: Comparing Not-for-Profit and For-Profit Institutions.* Chicago, University of Chicago Press.

Cutler, D. M., and J. Horwitz. 2000. "Converting Hospitals from Not-for-Profit to For-Profit Status: Why and What Effects?" In Cutler, David M., ed., *The Changing Hospital Industry: Comparing Not-for-Profit and For-Profit Institutions.* Chicago, University of Chicago Press.

Davis, Jerry. 1997. "College Affordability: A Closer Look at the Crisis." Washington, D.C., Sallie Mae Education Institution.

Duggan, M. 2000. "Hospital Market Structure and the Behavior of Not-For-Profit Hospitals: Evidence from Responses to California's Disproportionate Share Program." NBER Working Paper 7966.

Eldenberg, L., B. Hermalin, M. Weisbach, and M. Wosinka. 2001. "Hospital Governance, Performance Objectives, and Organizational Form." NBER Working Paper 8201.

Ford, J., and D. Kaserman. 2000. "Ownership Structure and the Quality of Medical Care: Evidence from the Dialysis Industry." *Journal of Economic Behavior and Organization* 43:279–293.

Francois, P. 2001. "Employee Care and the Role of Nonprofit Organizations." *Journal of Institutional and Theoretical Economics* 157:443–464.

Garg, P., K. Frick, M. Diener-West, and N. Powe. 1999. "Effect of Ownership of Dialysis Facilities on Patients: Survival and Referral for Transplantation." *New England Journal of Medicine* 341(22):1653–1660.

Glaeser, E., and A. Schleifer. 2001. "Not-for-Profit Entrepreneurs." *Journal of Public Economics* 81:99–116.

Glazer, A., and K. Konrad. 1996. "A Signaling Explanation for Charity." *American Economic Review* 86:1019–1028.

Goodeeris, H., and B. Weisbrod. 1998. "Conversion from Nonprofit to For-Profit Status: Why Does It Happen and Should Anyone Care?" In B. Weisbrod, ed., *To Profit or Not to Profit: The Commercial Transformation of the Nonprofit Sector.* Cambridge, Cambridge University Press.

Greenlee, J., and T. Gordon. 1998. "The Impact of Professional Solicitors on Fund Raising in Charitable Organizations." *Nonprofit and Voluntary Sector Quarterly* 27, no. 3 (September): 277–299.

Gulley, O. D., and R. Santerre. 1993. "The Effect of Tax Exemption on the Market Share of Nonprofit Hospitals." *National Tax Journal* 46(4):477–486.

Hager, M., T. Pollak, and P. Rooney. 2001. "Variations in Overhead and Fundraising Efficiency." Manuscript, March.

Hagy, A. P. 1998. "The Demand for Child Care Quality: An Hedonic Price Theory Approach." *Journal of Human Resources* 33(3):683–710.

Hansmann, H. 1980. "The Role of Nonprofit Enterprise." *Yale Law Journal* 89:835–898.

———. 1981. "Nonprofit Enterprise in the Performing Arts." *Bell Journal of Economics* 12:341–361.

———. 1987. "The Effect of Tax Exemption and Other Factors on the Market Share of Nonprofit Versus For-Profit Firms." *National Tax Journal* 40:71–82.

Harbaugh, W. 1998a. "The Prestige Motive for Making Charitable Transfers." *American Economic Review, Papers and Proceedings* 88:277–282.

———. 1998b. "What Do Donations Buy? A Model of Philanthropy Based on Prestige and Warm-Glow." *Journal of Public Economics* 67:269–284.

Herman, R., and D. Rendina. 2001. "Donor Reactions to Commercial Activities of Nonprofit Organizations: An American Case Study." *Voluntas* 12(2):157–169.

Hirth, R. A. 1999. "Consumer Information and Competition Between Nonprofit and For-Profit Nursing Homes." *Journal of Health Economics* 18:219–240.

Holtmann, A., and S. Ullmann. 1991. "Transaction Costs, Uncertainty, and Not-for-Profit Organizations: The Case of Nursing Homes." In A. Ben-Ner and B. Gui B., eds., *The Nonprofit Sector in the Mixed Economy,* Ann Arbor, University of Michigan Press.

Jacobs, P., and R. Wilder. 1984. "Pricing Behavior of Non-Profit Agencies: The Case of Blood Products." *Journal of Health Economics* 3:49–61.

James, E. 1983. "How Nonprofits Grow: A Model." *Journal of Policy Analysis and Management* 2:350–365.

Khanna, J., J. Posnett and T. Sandler. 1995. "Charity Donations in the U.K.: New Evidence Based on Panel Data." *Journal of Public Economics* 56:257–272.

Khanna, J., and T. Sandler. 2000. "Partners in Giving: The Crowding-in Effects of U.K. Government Grants." *European Economic Review* 44:1543–1556.

Kingma, B. 1989. "An Accurate Measurement of the Crowd-Out Effect, Income Effect and Price Effect for Charitable Contributions." *Journal of Political Economy* 97:1197–1207.

———. 1995. "Do Profits Crowd Out Donations or Vice Versa? The Impact of Revenues from Sales on Donations to Local Chapters of the Red Cross." *Nonprofit Management and Leadership* 6:21–38.

Lakdawalla, D., and T. Philipson. 2002. "The Nonprofit Sector and Industry Performance." Typescript.

Leete, L. 2001. "Whither the Nonprofit Wage Differential? New Estimates from the 1990 Census." *Journal of Labor Economics* 19:136–170.

Luksetich, W., M. Edwards, and T. Carroll. 2000. "Organizational Form and Nursing Home Behavior." *Nonprofit and Voluntary Sector Quarterly* 29:255–279.

Lynk, W. 1995. "NFP Hospital Mergers and the Exercise of Market Power." *Journal of Law and Economics* 38:437–461.

Lynk, W., and L. Neumann. 1999. "Price and Profit." *Journal of Health Economics* 18:99–116.

Mauser, E. 1998. "The Importance of Organizational Form: Parent Perceptions Versus Reality in the Day Care Industry." In W. W. Powell and E. Clemens, *Private Action and the Public Good.* New Haven, Conn., Yale University Press.

McCready, D. 1988. "Ramsey Pricing: A Method for Setting Fees in Social Service Organizations." *American Journal of Economics and Sociology* 47, no. 1 (January): 97–110.

McEachern, W. A. 1981. "Tax-Exempt Property, Tax Capitalization, and the Cumulative-Urban-Decay Hypothesis." *National Tax Journal* 34:185–192.

Migué, J.-L., and G. Belanger. 1974. "Toward a General Theory of Managerial Discretion." *Public Choice* 17:27–47.

Mocan, N. 2001. "Can Consumers Detect Lemons? Information Asymmetry in the Market for Child Care." NBER Working Paper 8291.

Morris, J., and S. Helburn. 2000. "Child Care Quality Differences: The Role of Profit Status, Client Preferences, and Trust." *Nonprofit and Voluntary Sector Quarterly* 29:377–399.

Nelson, R., and M. Krashinsky. 1974. "Public Control and Economic Organization of Day Care for Children." *Public Policy* 22:53–75.

Okten, C., and B. Weisbrod. 2000, "Determinants of Donations in Private Nonprofit Markets." *Journal of Public Economics* 75:255–272.

Payne, A. 1998. "Does the Government Crowd Out Private Donations? New Evidence from a Sample of Nonprofit Firms." *Journal of Public Economics* 69:323–345.

———. 2001. "Measuring the Effect of Federal Research Funding on Private Donations at Research Universities: Is Federal Research Funding More Than a Substitute for Private Donations?" *International Tax and Public Finance* 8:731–751.

Posnett, J., and T. Sandler. 1989. "Demand for Charity Donations in Private Non-profit Markets: The Case of the U.K." *Journal of Public Economics* 40:187–200.

Preston, A. 1988. "The Nonprofit Firm: A Potential Solution to Inherent Market Failures." *Economic Inquiry* 26:493–506.

Romano, R., and H. Yildirim. 2001, "Why Charities Announce Donations: A Positive Perspective." *Journal of Public Economics* 81:423–448.

Roomkin, M., and B. Weisbrod. 1999. "Managerial Compensation and Incentives in For-Profit and Nonprofit Hospitals." *Journal of Law, Economics, and Organization* 15:750–781.

Rose-Ackerman, S. 1980. "United Charities: An Economic Analysis." *Public Policy* 28:323–348.

———. 1981. "Do Government Grants to Charity Reduce Private Donations?" In Michelle White, ed., *Nonprofit Firms in a Three-Sector Economy.* Washington, D.C., The Urban Institute.

———. 1982. "Charitable Giving and Excessive Fundraising." *Quarterly Journal of Economics* 97:193–212.

———. 1987. "Ideals Versus Dollars: Donors, Charity Managers, and Government Grants." *Journal of Political Economy* 95:810–823.

———. 1996. "Altruism, Nonprofits, and Economic Theory." *Journal of Economic Literature* 34:701–728.

Schiff, G., and B. Weisbrod. 1991. "Competition Between For-profit and Non-profit Organizations in Commercial Markets." *Annals of Public and Cooperative Economics* 62:619–640.

Segal, B., and B. Weisbrod. 1998. "Interdependence of Commercial and Donative Revenues." In B. Weisbrod, ed., *To Profit or Not to Profit: The Commercial Transformation of the Nonprofit Sector.* Cambridge, New York, and Melbourne: Cambridge University Press.

Slivinski, A. 2002. "Team Incentives and Organizational Form." *Journal of Public Economic Theory* 4:185–206.

Sloan, F. 1998. "Commercialism in Nonprofit Hospitals." *Journal of Policy Analysis and Management* 17:234–252.

Spiegel, M. 1995. "Charity Without Altruism." *Economic Inquiry* 33:625–639.

Steinberg, R. 1986a. "Optimal Contracts Need Not Be Contingent: The Case of Nonprofit Firms." In Hyman and Parkum, eds., *Models of Health and Human Services in the Nonprofit Sector.* Harrisburg, Penn., Association of Voluntary Action Scholars.

———. 1986b. "The Revealed Objective Functions of Nonprofit Firms." *Rand Journal of Economics* 17:508–526.

———. 1986c. "Should Donors Care About Fundraising?" in S. Rose-Ackerman, ed., *The Economics of Nonprofit Institutions: Studies in Structure and Policy.* New York, Oxford University Press.

———. 1987. "Nonprofit Organizations and the Market." Pages 118–138 in W. Powell, ed., *The Nonprofit Sector: A Research Handbook.* New Haven, Conn., Yale University Press.

Steinberg, R., and B. Weisbrod. 1998. "Pricing and Rationing by Nonprofit Organizations with Distributional Objectives." In B. Weisbrod, ed., *To Profit or Not to Profit: The Commercial Transformation of the Nonprofit Sector.* B. Weisbrod, ed., Cambridge, New York, and Melbourne, Cambridge University Press.

Straub, J. 2003. "Fundraising and Government Crowd-Out of Charitable Contributions: New Evidence from Contributions to Public Radio." Typescript, College Station, Texas A&M University.

U.S. Department of Commerce, Census Bureau, 2000. *Establishment and Firm Size (Including Legal Form of Organization). 1997 Economic Census, Health Care, and Social Assistance and Arts, Entertainment, and Recreation.* Subject Series, October.

Vesterlund, L. 2003, "The Informational Value of Sequential Fundraising." *Journal of Public Economics* 87:627–657.

Wedig, G., M. Hassan, and M. Morrisey. "Tax-Exempt Debt and the Capital Structure of Nonprofit Organizations: An Application to Hospitals." *Journal of Finance* 51, no. 4 (September 1996): 1247–1283.

Weisbrod, B. 1975. "Toward a Theory of the Voluntary Nonprofit Sector in a Three-Sector Economy." In E. Phelps, ed., *Altruism, Morality, and Economic Theory.* New York, Russell Sage Foundation.

———. 1980. "Private Goods, Collective Goods: The Role of the Nonprofit Sector." In K. Clarkson and D. Martin, eds., *The Economics of Nonproprietary Organizations Research in Law and Economic Supplement 1,* Greenwich, Conn., JAI Press.

———. 1988. *The Nonprofit Economy.* Cambridge, Mass., Harvard University Press.

———. 1998a. "Institutional Form and Organizational Behavior." In W. W. Powell and E. Clemens, eds., *Private Action and the Public Good.* New Haven, Conn., Yale University Press.

———. 1998b. *To Profit or Not to Profit: The Commercial Transformation of the Nonprofit Sector.* Cambridge, Cambridge University Press.

Weisbrod, B., and N. Dominguez 1986. "Demand for Collective Goods in Private Nonprofit Markets: Can Fundraising Expenditures Help Overcome Free-Rider Behavior?" *Journal of Public Economics* 30:83–96.

Weisbrod, B., and M. Schlesinger. 1986. "Public, Private, Nonprofit Ownership and the Response to Asymmetric Information: The Case of Nursing Homes." In S. Rose-Ackerman, ed., *The Nonprofit Sector: Economic Theory and Public Policy.* Fairlawn, N.J., Oxford University Press.

Weitzmann, M., N. Jalandoni, L. Lampkin, and T. Pollak. 2002. *The New Nonprofit Almanac and Desk Reference.* San Francisco, Jossey-Bass.

Young, D. and R. Steinberg. 1995. *Economics for Nonprofit Managers.* New York, The Foundation Center.

7

Work in the Nonprofit Sector

LAURA LEETE

As world income and manufacturing productivity has risen and as the information economy has expanded, the service sector has come to dominate employment in the United States and other advanced industrialized nations. Because nonprofit entities are typically service sector organizations, they increasingly account for both a significant and a growing share of employment. Furthermore, the policy relevance of questions relating to the nonprofit labor force is growing. Changes in government policy in recent decades, in the United States and elsewhere, have increasingly shifted the burden of maintaining social safety nets to nonprofit workers, paid and unpaid.

Along with the growing importance of the topic, the literature on the paid and volunteer nonprofit labor force has mushroomed in recent years. Many authors have recognized that the differences between nonprofit and for-profit organizations extend, to varying degrees, to their reasons for existence, organizational goals and methods, products produced, and constituencies served. An increasingly organized literature is emerging that examines whether these factors translate into differences across sectors in pay, working conditions, and quality of work for paid workers, as well as the management and motivation of volunteers.

In this chapter, I review the status of the literature on the nonprofit labor force and summarize its primary contributions. I cover numerous aspects including: the measurement of the size of the labor force, determination of the level and distribution of compensation (for both workers in general, and for CEOs), patterns of career mobility, theories of volunteer motivation, and the relationship between donations of time and money to the sector.

Much of the work highlighted here draws on explicit comparisons between conditions in the nonprofit and for-profit sectors. It draws from multiple disciplines in the social sciences, ranging from economics and management to anthropology, sociology, political science, and social work, and is based on a variety of theoretical, quantitative, and qualitative methodologies. Taken together, this work contributes to a developing picture of the important and unique aspects of nonprofit enterprise. From this we can learn not only about the nonprofit sector, but also about how industrialized societies can best organize themselves to produce those goods, and particularly services, that will not be satisfactorily supplied by for-profit entities. Public policy implications of this work range from optimal tax policy to employment discrimination policy to work/family considerations.

PAID LABOR

Data on paid employment in the nonprofit sector in the United States are now available from a number of sources. Information on individuals who are specifically identified as employees of nonprofit organizations is available from a number of disparate surveys at various points in time.[1] The only ongoing source of estimates of total nonprofit employment and payroll is the organization Independent Sector (IS), which derives the estimates from publicly disclosed information from the U.S. Internal Revenue Source Form 990 nonprofit tax return (e.g., Hodgkinson and Weitzman 1996).

Consistent differences exist in the definition of the nonprofit sector associated with these two types of data sources. Survey data composed of individual responses generally rely on self-reporting of the sector of employment. In this case, the nonprofit sector is generally taken to be made up of all organizations incorporated as nonprofit entities, regardless of type (e.g., educational, charitable, or religious). Significant reporting error in these data is likely, as many individual workers are less than cognizant of their employer's tax status. The misreporting of nonprofit status is likely to blur the measurement of any distinctions between the sectors that actually exist.[2] In contrast, the Independent Sector analysis of Form 990 data is limited to those "philanthropic" agencies organized under IRS code sections 501(c)(3) or 501(c)(4), and religious congregations, and excludes private

TABLE 7.1. NONPROFIT SECTOR EMPLOYMENT IN THE UNITED STATES, 1972–2001

Year	Nonprofit sector employment[a],*	U.S. civilian employment**	Percent nonprofit employment
1972	4,576,000	82,153,000	5.6
1977	5,519,500	92,017,000	6.0
1982	6,500,000	99,526,000	6.5
1987	7,400,000	112,440,000	6.6
1992	9,100,000	118,492,000	7.7
1997	10,600,000	129,558,000	8.2
1998	10,900,000	131,463,000	8.3
2001	11,700,000	136,933,000	8.5

[a] Defined here as the philanthropic organizations, registered as 501(c)(3) and 501(c)(4) for tax code purposes, as well as religious congregations.

**Sources:* 1972—Rudney and Weitzman (1984); 1977—Hodgkinson and Weitzman (1996); 1982–1998—Independent Sector and the Urban Institute (2002); 2001—Independent Sector (undated).

***Source: U.S. Economic Report of the President* (U.S. Government Printing Office, 2005), Table B-36.

nonprofit commercial enterprises and membership groups. The latter group includes social clubs, fraternal organizations, labor unions, chambers of commerce, trade associations and business leagues, organizations that are tax exempt under federal law but may not receive tax-deductible donations. While these data provide for a very accurate assessment of the organizations that are covered, they limit how expansively one can define the nonprofit sector.

Based on the most recent estimates from Independent Sector, there were 11.7 million individuals employed in the U.S. nonprofit sector in 2001, representing 8.5 percent of U.S. civilian employment. As seen in table 7.1, this proportion has been rising steadily over time, up from 5.6 percent in 1972. Table 7.2 shows the distribution of nonprofit-sector employment across different sectors. In 2001, 41.9 percent of nonprofit employment was devoted to health services, 21.9 percent to education or research organizations, 11.8 percent to religious organizations (including congregations), 18.3 to legal and social services, with the remainder in foundations, arts and culture, and civic, fraternal, and social organizations. As seen in table 7.2, these proportions have been relatively stable over time, with the exception of a significant drop in the proportion of employment in religious organizations and congregations in the 1970s, and a steady rise over time in legal and social services. In the 1980s there was an increase in the proportion in health services that reversed itself in the 1990s.

Outside the United States, the size and scope of employment in the nonprofit sector is less well documented, with the exception of a recent comparative multinational effort to assess the size and scope of the nonprofit sector internationally (the Johns Hopkins University Comparative Nonprofit Sector Project),[3] work in the United Kingdom by Almond and Kendall (2000a, 2000b), and work on Japan by Kamimura and Yamauchi (2002).[4] Anheier and Salamon (this volume) report the share of employment in the nonprofit sector as a share of the economically active population for thirty-five countries (see figure 4.1). Several European countries have employment shares exceeding 7 percent (the Netherlands, Ireland, and Belgium), while 6.3 percent of U.S. employment is classified as nonprofit by the definitions used here. In contrast, nonprofit employment drops to less than 1 percent of total activity in many other countries, including Slovakia, Romania, and Mexico.

Many authors have documented systematic differences between nonprofit and for-profit workers in the United States. The comparison in table 7.3, derived from individual-level 1990 U.S. Census data, shows that a larger proportion of nonprofit than for-profit employees are women, speak fluent English, and have higher levels of education, with only small differences in racial composition. A number of other researchers (working with a variety of other data sets and time periods) have found similar results for the United States (e.g., Mirvis and Hackett 1983; Preston 1989; Mirvis 1992; Ruhm and Borkoski 2003). Findings of Almond and Kendall (2000a, 2000b) and Kamimura and Yamauchi (2002) in the United Kingdom and Japan, respec-

TABLE 7.2. DISTRIBUTION OF NONPROFIT[a] (PHILANTHROPIC) EMPLOYMENT ACROSS DIFFERENT TYPES OF ORGANIZATIONS IN THE UNITED STATES, 1972–2001

Year	Health services	Education/ research	Religious organizations	Social and legal services	Civic, social, and fraternal organizations	Arts and culture	Foundations
1972	42.2	21.1	19.0	10.2	6.1	1.9	0.3
1977	44.5	23.2	12.3	13.0	5.5	1.2	0.3
1982	47.0	22.1	10.6	14.1	4.7	1.4	0.3
1987	45.6	22.5	8.8	16.2	5.0	1.6	0.3
1992	46.6	20.6	10.5	15.6	4.6	1.8	0.3
1997	43.5	21.6	11.4	17.2	4.2	1.9	0.3
1998	42.9	21.6	11.6	17.5	4.2	1.9	0.3
2001	41.9	21.9	11.8	18.3	3.9	1.9	0.3

Sources: 1972—Rudney (1987); 1977—Hodgkinson and Weitzman (1996); 1982–1998—Independent Sector and Urban Institute (2002); 2001—Independent Sector (undated).

[a] Defined here as the philanthropic organizations, registered as 501(c)(3) and 501(c)(4) for tax code purposes, as well as religious congregations.

TABLE 7.3. CHARACTERISTICS OF U.S. NONPROFIT AND FOR-PROFIT SECTOR WORKERS, 1989 (NOT DISABLED AND NOT ENROLLED IN SCHOOL)

	For-profit	Nonprofit
Female	43.9	66.6
Not fluent in English	3.1	1.3
Race		
White	81.5	83.8
African American	9.4	9.5
Hispanic	3.4	2.5
Asian	2.6	2.4
Other race	3.2	1.9
Education level		
Eighth grade or less	5.6	2.7
Some high school, no degree	13.6	6.5
High school graduate or GED	35.2	21.7
Some college	20.5	17.6
Associate's degree	6.7	9.4
Bachelor's degree	13.5	22.6
Graduate degree	4.9	19.4

Source: Leete 2001.

tively, echo the same broad patterns. In addition, there is a higher concentration of part-time work in the nonprofit sector in both the United States and the United Kingdom. Leete (2001) reports that in the United States, 16.5 percent of nonprofit workers worked fewer than twenty-five hours per week in 1989, as compared to only 9.8 percent of their for-profit counterparts. Using pooled data for the United States for 1994–1998, Ruhm and Borkoski (2003) also report lower mean weekly work hours among nonprofit workers. Almond and Kendall (2000a) report that 35.3 percent of U.K. nonprofit employees work part-time as compared to 22.1 percent of for-profit employees.[5] They also note a higher proportion of temporary employment in the nonprofit sector as well. These differences in worker and job characteristics are largely presumed to be a function of the concentration of nonprofit organizations in the service sector. Service sector employment, in contrast with the manufacturing sector, has traditionally had lower wages, a higher percentage of women, and more part-time and temporary work (perhaps in part because of less history of unionization).[6]

The Nonprofit Wage Level

The simplest comparisons between the wage levels of nonprofit and for-profit workers have been made without taking into account differences in distribution of occupations, industries, or worker characteristics between the sectors noted above (e.g., Mirvis and Hackett 1983; Johnston and Rudney 1987). In the United States, comparisons of this type typically show that nonprofit wages are significantly lower than those earned in other sectors. Ruhm and Borkoski (2003) report average weekly earnings of $621, $573, and $557 in the government, for-profit, and nonprofit sectors, respectively. In the United Kingdom, Almond and Kendall (2000b) report a somewhat different ranking of pay. Overall, mean gross hourly pay is highest among public sector workers (£8.7), and slightly higher among nonprofit than for-profit sector workers (£7.6 versus £7.4). Among professional workers, however, they report significantly lower pay for nonprofit than for-profit workers.

Simple economic theory suggests that wages should vary among workers with different skills who are performing different kinds of work. According to the theory of compensating differentials (with roots in Smith [1776] 1976), workers with skills that are more difficult or more expensive to learn, or those working in less desirable working conditions, will be paid more. Workers with more readily learnable skills and those working in better working conditions will be paid less. Thus, differences in the nature and level of skill and differences in working conditions will be reflected in differences in wage levels across different jobs.

Because each sector of the economy (nonprofit, for-profit, and government) is composed of a different mix of occupations and industries (each of which embodies different distributions of skills and working conditions) one should expect different earnings levels in each sector. Furthermore, we may also observe differences in pay that are attributable to the differential effects of organizational structure, mission, and constraints across sectors. While those studying pay differences between the sectors have often considered these factors distinctly separate causal forces, one might also entertain the possibility that ultimately they are entwined. At a level yet to be formally modeled, the industry, occupation, and skill mix in a sector may be determined by or jointly determined along with the factors that determine organizational structure and mission.

In the theoretical literature to date relating to sectoral pay differences, explanations for differences fall into two broad categories. In the first category, broadly referred to here as the donative labor hypothesis, nonprofit firms produce a different good or a different quality of good than their for-profit counterparts in the same (measured) industries and occupations. Due to the nature of the good or service produced by nonprofits, nonprofit workers derive well-being from participating in the enterprise, and are thus willing to accept a lower wage. For example, teachers at a religious school may be devoted to the principle of the education they are producing and willing to work there for lower pay than they would accept in a secular setting.

The second set of explanations accounts for differences in pay between nonprofit and for-profit organizations that are producing otherwise identical products. In this case, pay differences are attributed to a variety of either observable or unobservable differences in the characteristics of nonprofit and for-profit firms, workers, or their jobs. In these cases, nonprofit wages could be either higher or lower than for-profit wages for comparable workers, depending on the nature of the differences being pinpointed.

The donative labor hypothesis covers the cases in which the goods produced by nonprofit and for-profit workers have different properties. These ideas are attributable to the work of Hansmann (1980), Preston (1989), Rose-Ackerman (1996), and Frank (1996). While each author offers a slightly different rationale and formulation, in each case individuals accept lower pay from a nonprofit organization in return for assisting with production in which the worker finds intrinsic value. According to Preston, this lower pay is equivalent to a monetary donation to an organization producing public goods. Frank views it as a compensating differential in return for work that is more morally palatable. Alternately, Rose-Ackerman notes that ideologues may accept lower pay in return for the guarantee that their efforts are helping to achieve their idealistic goals and are not lining the pockets of for-profit stockholders. Hansmann suggests that it is a result of a sorting mechanism through which employees more interested in the production of quality services than in financial gain signal this to nonprofit organizations. Handy and Katz (1998) elaborate on these same themes. These variants are particularly applicable to the case in which nonprofit organizations are formed due to information asymmetries and consumers take nonprofit status as an indicator of either product quality or integrity along ideological lines. For these hypotheses to explain nonprofit/for-profit wage differences *within* the same (measured) industry classification, nonprofit and for-profit firms must produce either *different* products or, as emphasized by Hansmann, a *different quality* of product.

The second class of explanations of nonprofit/for-profit wage differences explains differences in pay between nonprofit and for-profit firms that are producing identical outputs. Under these conditions, pay differences are theorized to result from different conditions that prevail in the two sectors. These differences may or may not be inherent in nonprofit status and could be either positive or negative. A number of authors suggest reasons why nonprofit wages might be higher than comparable for-profit wages: Rose-Ackerman (1996:218) points out that in industries in which nonprofit and for-profit organizations compete (hospitals, skilled nursing facilities, day-care centers, and social-service organizations, among others), nonprofit organizations are generally larger. Larger organizations typically pay higher wages, perhaps due to their ability to exploit economies of scale (Brown and Medoff 1989). In the same vein, nonprofit organizations might sometimes be characterized by "philanthropic amateurism" (Salamon 1987), a lack of professionalism, or small-scale operations, or be subject to the uncertainties of a competitive funding environment. These conditions in turn would lead to lower rates of pay than would otherwise be expected (Cunningham 2000; Almond and Kendall 2000b). Alternately, a positive or negative nonprofit wage differential could result from unobservable (to the researcher) differences in working conditions, worker characteristics, or both. Firm and worker differences may be correlated if different work environments or corporate cultures cause workers with different traits to self-select differentially into the two sectors.

Feldstein (1971), Shackett and Trapani (1987), Borjas, Frech, and Ginsburg (1983), and Preston (1989) have all suggested that freedom from tax, regulatory, or profit-maximizing pressures may increase the resources available to pay workers in the nonprofit sector. Feldstein suggests that nonprofits offer high pay as a charitable act of their own. Borjas et al. argue that because nonprofits are constrained from accumulating a surplus, there is less incentive for them to minimize costs. Preston notes that nonprofit managers, who are not subject to profit-maximizing pressures, may receive utility from paying higher wages to themselves or their workers.

Werner, Konopaske, and Gemeinhardt (2000) propose a variation of this theme in applying agency theory (Jensen and Meckling 1976, among others) to nonprofit organizations. They argue that nonprofit *or* for-profit managers who are not effectively monitored by organization owners or stakeholders may operate in their own self-interest, paying themselves, their employees, and their coworkers higher salaries. In this view, nonprofit and for-profit salary levels could diverge if, for instance, monitoring of managers were consistently less vigilant in one sector than the other. If, in comparison with for-profit managers, nonprofit managers are more intrinsically motivated and their interests are better aligned with organization stakeholders, then they may be less inclined to "overpay" themselves and their workers. This would result in higher pay for for-profit managers and workers, and lower pay for nonprofit managers and workers. This resembles outcomes expected under the donative labor hypothesis but has different theoretical underpinnings. Finally, Ito and Domain (1987) suggest an application of the efficiency wage hypothesis (Yellen 1984) to the nonprofit sector that could fall into either class of explanations offered above. They argue that efficiency wages—wages that exceed the market clearing level for the purpose of eliciting higher effort levels—might be more prevalent in nonprofit settings due to the nature of the output in the sector and the difficulty of monitoring worker effort there.

There are still relatively few studies measuring nonprofit and for-profit wage differences that control for a significant number of measurable characteristics. Preston (1989) estimated nonprofit/for-profit wage differences of −15.2 percent for managerial and professional workers and of −6.1 percent for clerical and sales workers in the United States, without controlling for industry of employment or more detailed occupational categorizations. Leete (2001) found that the introduction of 206 detailed industry and 226 occupational categorizations eliminated the estimated differences for managerial and professional and clerical and sales workers, as well as yielding an economy-wide nonprofit/for-profit wage difference of close to zero. With the inclusion of limited industry and occupational controls (six and seven categories, respectively), Ruhm and Borkoski (2003) estimate an overall nonprofit differential of −3.6 percent.[7] Using panel data, they also estimate that movements from nonprofit to for-profit jobs increase relative wages by 4 percent, suggesting that nonprofit employment is associated with a modestly lower wage.

Taking these results together, it is apparent that the size of estimated nonprofit/for-profit differences depends importantly on the level of detail of occupation and industry controls included in the estimation. One interpretation is that after controlling for all relevant job characteristics, nonprofit workers are paid roughly on par with their for-profit counterparts. This might be taken to refute any of the above theories that suggest either positive or negative sectoral wage differences. A second interpretation, however, is that when industry controls are highly disaggregated, an industry may be dominated (sometimes exclusively) by either for-profit or nonprofit organizations. In this case, pay differences attributable to industry and pay differences attributable to sector will be indistinguishable. Seen one way, the low level of nonprofit pay that is generally observed may be attributable to the concentration of nonprofit firms in low-paying industries. Seen another way, those same industries may be low paying precisely because they are engaged in activities to which workers, nonprofit *or* for-profit, are willing to make "donative" contributions. Thus, "industry" pay differences and the "donative" pay differences could be one and the same. The nature of the industry's production and its relation to the nonprofit form of organization then becomes an interesting question in its own right.

A third interpretation depends on a disaggregation of the economy-wide averages that have been estimated. Leete (2001) estimates nonprofit wage differentials separately for individual occupations and industries and finds a wide range of both positive and negative effects (which cancel one another out in aggregate). This suggests that many of the factors discussed above could be in play, affecting nonprofit wages with different force in different parts of the sector. This view is entirely consistent with the diversity of what is included under the rubric of nonprofit (in the United States and elsewhere). Along these lines, a few authors have looked closely at the nonprofit wage differentials for very specific industry and occupation groups using specialized survey data with information on worker qualifications, working conditions, and the organizational structure of particular occupations and industries. They find interesting and disparate results that are consistent with several of the theories posed earlier.

Borjas, Frech, and Ginsburg (1983) found that relative to for-profit providers, government-owned nursing homes paid significantly higher wages and church-owned facilities paid significantly lower wages. They found little difference between the pay of workers in other (non-church) nonprofit nursing homes and their for-profit counterparts. Weisbrod (1983) found 20 percent lower pay among lawyers practicing public-interest law as compared with those in for-profit practice. These findings disappeared, however, when Goddeeris (1988) analyzed the same data set accounting for the self-selection of lawyers into their sector of work. Preston (1988) found that workers in nonprofit day-care centers earned 5 to 10 percent more than their for-profit counterparts. More recently, Mocan and Tekin (2003) find similar results for nonprofit day-care workers with a rich survey data set collected on day-care center employers and employees. Despite the overall positive differentials they find for nonprofit workers, they are also able to conduct a relatively direct test of the donative labor hypothesis—asking workers whether they think their job is "an important job that somebody needs to do." Those nonprofit workers who agree with this statement earn 2 to 5 percent less than others, controlling for all other factors.

In an interesting study of within nonprofit-sector wage differences, Werner, Konopaske, and Gemeinhardt (2000) use survey data on 1,811 workers in 69 U.S. nonprofit organizations in one metropolitan area to examine the differences in workers' salaries in United Way and non–United Way organizations. They find that, after controlling for basic worker and organization characteristics, those with United Way membership pay higher salaries to their employees. This refuted their original hypothesis that United Way member organizations might be subject to higher levels of reporting and monitoring that would lead to lower wages via agency theory. Instead, they argue that the favorable budget conditions of being United Way members are bestowed only on higher-quality organizations.

Executive Compensation

In the 1990s, the question of how compensation practices in the nonprofit sector do or should diverge from those in the for-profit sector came to the forefront of public discourse, along with the more specific question of how nonprofit executive pay should be structured. This focus resulted from the confluence of three factors: the rapid rise of for-profit executive compensation in the United States and elsewhere in the late 1980s and the 1990s, the shift of for-profit executive compensation toward performance-based packages, and the public prominence of the "Aramony scandal" in the early 1990s, in which the president of United Way of America was convicted of misappropriating funds for his personal use. A rash of commentary followed, discussing how much and in what fashion nonprofit executives should be compensated.

Most literature on for-profit executive compensation focuses on the methods used to link executive compensation to firm performance in order to better align the interests of managers and shareholders. The conundrum for many nonprofits, of course, is that it can be difficult to develop both easily quantifiable and meaningful measures of organizational goals and performance. In addition, performance-based pay structures may give rise to questions as to whether a nonprofit is entering the territory of excessive compensation that is legally prohibited by the nondistribution constraint. Furthermore, the general public, nonprofit customers, and donors all can care deeply about both the level and structure of nonprofit executive compensation. Pay levels and structures that would be interpreted as an appropriate return to skill and performance levels in the for-profit sector may be taken as an indicator of fraud and waste or of a lack of intrinsic motivation on the part of nonprofit managers

(Oster 1998). Finally, the donative labor hypothesis (discussed above) suggests that nonprofit workers may accept lower pay as a "donation" toward the production of goods and services that they perceive as having public benefit. This hypothesis is most likely to hold for the higher-level workers (executives and managers) in an organization who most directly perceive and control the social impact of their work. Taken together, these considerations suggest that executive compensation in nonprofits should be lower than in comparable for-profit organizations and less likely to incorporate performance-based elements (Frumkin and Keating 2001).

Using a variety of data sources on nonprofit executive pay in the United States, Oster shows that the use of performance-based pay for executives in nonprofits is limited. Roomkin and Weisbrod (1999) and Ballou and Weisbrod (2003) draw similar conclusions using compensation survey data of top management in nonprofit and for-profit hospitals. They find that despite similar levels of job complexity and responsibility across the two sectors, top managers in nonprofit hospitals receive lower total compensation and that a smaller share of their compensation package is devoted to performance bonuses. These differences eroded over the period 1992–1997, however. As health-care cost containment put downward pressure on hospital revenues, executive compensation packages of secular (nonreligious) nonprofit hospitals have come to more closely resemble those of their for-profit counterparts.

The most recent developments in this literature come from the use of data from the IRS Form 990 tax filings of nonprofit organizations (e.g., Frumkin and Keating 2001; Twombly and Gantz 2001; Hallock 2002). These data shed previously unavailable light on the pay of nonprofit executives. It covers a representative sample of (501(c)(3)) nonprofit organizations in operation in the United States, and sample sizes are considerable. Organization-level data from the tax filings include information on the industry of operation, the level and structure of managerial compensation, the compensation of board members, and revenue sources.

Using the Form 990 data, Frumkin and Keating (2001) report that nonprofit CEOs are paid more in industry subsectors with freer cash flows (as measured by commercial revenues, liquid assets, and investment portfolios). Hallock (2002) and Twombly and Gantz (2001) also note a significant reliance of nonprofit compensation on benefit plans and expense accounts. All three articles report a significant relationship between organization size and CEO pay. However, using comparable data for for-profit CEOs (derived from Standard and Poor's EXECUCOMP), Hallock (2002) estimates that the relationship between firm size (measured as assets) and CEO pay is five times *stronger* among for-profit firms than among nonprofit firms. He also notes that after controlling for organizational effects there is no relation between size of government grants received and executive pay, and that the larger the number of paid board members, the lower the managerial pay. The latter suggests that paid boards might substitute for managerial talent. Taken all together, these results suggest that much of what we expected about executive pay in nonprofits is in fact true—nonprofit managers make less than their for-profit counterparts and are less likely to have a performance-based pay structure. However, there is still significant variation in the ways that executive compensation in nonprofits reflects the competing pressures of mission, performance incentives, nondistribution, and the market for managerial talent.

The Distribution of Wages

If differences in the mission, motivation, and products produced by nonprofit and for-profit organizations can lead to differences in the level and the structure of pay in those organizations, they might also lead to differences in the distribution of pay within nonprofit and for-profit firms. A growing literature suggests that employee perceptions of employer fairness may be important to developing and maintaining employee motivation. Wage equity—a relative narrowing of the difference between the highest and lowest pay levels in an organization—is an important element of that perceived fairness (e.g., Rabin 1998). Furthermore, as discussed above, nonprofit employers may be more likely than their for-profit counterparts to rely on intrinsically motivated employees (those who are motivated to work by the nature of the work itself). Leete (2000) argues that if both of these conditions hold, one would expect nonprofit organizations to exhibit more wage equity (measured as a reduced variance in pay or as a low ratio of high to low pay levels) than for-profit organizations.

There are a number of places to look for evidence connecting nonprofit status and the nature of worker motivation. Weisbrod (1988:32) discusses evidence of the sorting of nonprofit and for-profit managers by goals and personality type. Mirvis and Hackett (1983:7–9) analyze Quality of Employment Survey data for 1977 by sector of employment and find that nonprofit employees are more likely (than government or for-profit sector employees) to report that "their work is more important to them than the money they earn" (7). In a comparison of matched samples, they also find that nonprofit employees reported the most variety and challenge in their jobs, the most autonomy (defined as freedom and responsibility to decide what to do and when), and the least extent of "overeducation." Furthermore, nonprofit workers were also less likely to report "that their jobs sometimes go against their conscience" (9) and reported higher levels of intrinsic rewards from the job, such as feelings of accomplishment and self-respect when they do their jobs well. Newman and Wallender (1978) report that nonprofit workers develop a "mystique" about their organization.

Using 1990 Census data, Leete (2000) finds lower wage dispersion among employees of nonprofit organizations than among those of for-profit organizations. The lower dispersion holds for nominal wages, for the measured returns to particular worker and job characteristics, and for the residual wage.[8] Interestingly, the findings are strongest among white-collar executive and managerial employees. This fact is consistent with the theoretical expectation that differences in motivational requirements among different types of organizations are most significant at the managerial and white-collar level.

Nonprofit Employment and Discrimination

While an extensive literature has examined all aspects of labor market discrimination against women and minorities past and present, little has been written explicitly about discrimination in nonprofit organizations. In conjunction with findings of reduced wage dispersion in the nonprofit sector, Leete (2000) found lower levels of unexplained wage differences in nonprofit organizations between white men, women, and racial minorities. In every case, race and gender wage differences are diminished in the nonprofit sector as compared with the for-profit sector. Using the 1977 Quality of Employment Survey, Preston (1990, 1994) found similar results for men and women. Furthermore, Preston found that the reduced male/female pay differential, along with better opportunities to engage in work that leads to more skill development (opportunities that were not available to women in the for-profit sector) were important factors in explaining the disproportionate representation of women in nonprofits.

This reduction in race and gender discrimination might simply be a by-product of a nonprofit wage compression that works to bolster the intrinsic motivation of workers in that sector. However, while Preston's (1990) findings of better skill development opportunities are suggestive of a more fundamental reduction in discriminatory attitudes in nonprofits, Gibelman's (2000) findings of "glass ceiling" barriers to women's career advancement in nonprofit organizations suggest otherwise. Ultimately, however, since much of Preston's work relies on data from 1977, at the cusp of women's advancement into traditionally male high-profile careers in the for-profit sector, it is difficult to know whether the nonprofit sector continues to offer opportunities for women that are unavailable elsewhere, even if it once did.

Non-Wage Compensation and Quality of Work

The literature on nonprofit compensation discussed thus far focuses almost exclusively on the wages paid to nonprofit and for-profit workers. However, as long ago as Adam Smith ([1776] 1976), economists recognized that jobs were composed of a bundle of both monetary and nonmonetary characteristics. Non-wage compensation (or "benefits") frequently includes an employer contribution to an employee's health plan and retirement fund, as well as paid leave and other possible benefits such as parking, transportation, or health club subsidies. Furthermore, the nonmonetary conditions of work include the ethos of a workplace (e.g., cooperative or competitive), the degree of flexibility in scheduling work, the implementation of family-friendly policies, the stability of employment, and the degree to which a workplace affords upward career mobility. For many workers, these latter characteristics of a job can be an equally important part of the remuneration they perceive themselves as receiving.

For lack of data, nonmonetary benefits and job characteristics have been left out of virtually all comparisons of nonprofit and for-profit compensation. If non-wage and wage compensation are positively correlated in both the nonprofit and for-profit sectors (i.e., higher-paying jobs have better benefits packages and working conditions, and vice versa), then the pattern of differences in nonprofit and for-profit total compensation would parallel those found in wage compensation alone. As Almond and Kendall (2000b) point out, Hansmann's (1980) observation that nonprofit managers may accept lower pay for work they find meaningful might just as well apply to other non-wage job characteristics. However, the economic theory of wages known as compensating differentials (discussed above) would suggest just the opposite. High pay should compensate for poor benefits and working conditions, and vice versa. If pay in nonprofits is limited by the nondistribution constraint, nonprofit workers may be "compensated" by better working conditions or nonmonetary benefits. Almond and Kendall (2000b:12) note other possible underpinnings for the same type of compensation mix: "A low wage-high non-wage remuneration combination could be a deliberate 'screening strategy' by third sector organizations seeking to attract the right type of managers under conditions of information asymmetry (Handy and Katz, 1998). In addition, Preston (1990, p. 564) suggests that, while third sector employers must keep pay down in order to avoid alienating private givers (who could object if salary levels were 'too high'), they may compensate for this with nonfinancial advantages."

Similarly, Preston (1990:564) notes that if nonprofits provide services that depend importantly on the quality and effort put forth by the employee, they "may adopt a compensation structure which attracts and rewards workers who are motivated by service provision rather than income." If any of these arguments hold, then the inclusion of non-wage compensation and job characteristics in any of the above analyses could significantly alter the findings based on monetary compensation alone.

While rigorous studies of nonprofit monetary compensation have yet to include direct measures of nonmonetary compensation, a number of descriptive works characterize the nature and quality of nonprofit employment. Some studies focus on fairly objective measures of working conditions, while others rely more on psychological measures of worker perceptions of the nature of their work and working conditions. In the latter group of studies, it is sometimes difficult to disentangle the characteristics of nonprofit work and the characteristics of the individuals who are attracted to nonprofit work.

Almond and Kendall (2000b) provide a comprehensive review of nonmonetary aspects of employment quality, using objective measures of job characteristics. In simple descriptive analyses comparing nonprofit, for-profit, and government sector workers in the United Kingdom, nonprofit workers appear to: have somewhat more unpaid overtime than their counterparts in government or for-profit organizations, have a higher degree of flexibility in work arrangements than government workers, receive significantly higher levels of training than for-profit and government workers, and have levels of job tenure similar to the for-profit labor force but below those of government workers. Reporting on the United States with data from the 1977 Quality of Employment Survey, Preston (1990) found that women in the nonprofit sector had more schedule flexibility (paid sick leave and the ability to take time off for personal matters) and were more likely to report that their work promoted skill development, was less repetitive, and offered more chances for promotion. Along the same lines, Hohl (1996) found that 85 percent of 156 nonprofit organizations surveyed offered one or more of eight different flexible work arrangements (arrangements such as flex-time, part-time work, or telecommuting meant to provide more flexibility for the employee). This figure is slightly lower than that found in a similar survey of large for-profit firms (Christensen 1989), but higher than the comparable economy-wide figure estimated by the U.S. Bureau of Labor Statistics (1992). Preston (1990) makes the point that these job characteristics, which are more difficult for women to come by in the for-profit sector, are important in explaining the overrepresentation of women in the nonprofit sector.

A number of other studies evaluate the working conditions in the nonprofit sector, but do so with a focus on individual perceptions. In a survey of Australian nonprofit workers, Onyx and Maclean (1996) confirm that nonprofit workers choose their sector of work in part due to the opportunities for interesting and challenging work, opportunities to work independently and to develop one's own skills, the quality of colleagues, and the opportunities for social action. However, there are no comparable data for for-profit workers. Mirvis and Hackett (1983), and later Mirvis (1992), draw on surveys of 1,000 or more working adults in the United States at two points in time. Similar to Onyx and Maclean, they find that nonprofit employees gain more satisfaction from their jobs than other kinds of workers, and are more likely to be satisfied with their pay, benefits, and job security.

Another element of the quality of employment in a sector is the longitudinal aspects of employment, in particular the opportunities for upward career mobility within the sector.[9] There is, as yet, no comprehensive documentation of career patterns that delineates nonprofit and for-profit careers (or the relation between them). Such documentation would require the collection of comprehensive longitudinal data on individual careers (that included the identification of sector of employment) with large enough sample sizes to effectively represent the nonprofit sector.

A few authors have gained insight into career movements within limited subpopulations in the nonprofit sector. In studying scientists and engineers in the United States, Preston (1993) found sectoral exit was higher for those working in the nonprofit sector, where they were paid considerably less. This was especially true among those with low levels of experience. Her results suggest that workers (in these occupations) are sensitive to sectoral wage differentials, and support the idea that young scientists and engineers use the nonprofit sector as a training ground before they go on to more lucrative careers in the for-profit sector. Gibelman (2000) examines occupational distributions in nonprofit human-services organizations with an explicit eye toward opportunities for career advancement for women. She finds that women are overrepresented in direct service positions and increasingly underrepresented as one moves up the management career ladder, which might be taken as evidence of "glass ceiling" barriers to women's career advancement in nonprofit organizations, that perhaps parallel those in for-profit organizations. Finally, Onyx and Maclean (1996) examine the career orientation of nonprofit-sector workers in Australia and find work patterns and attitudes that are more consistent with a "spiral" model of career mobility (Driver 1980) than with a more conventional linear view of career mobility. Nonprofit sector workers commonly make lateral job changes and shift between part-time and full-time work. They also express strong preferences for work that is personally challenging, socially meaningful, and (especially among women) that allows for work–family life balance.

UNPAID LABOR

That nonprofit employees are perhaps more satisfied and gratified by their work than their for-profit counterparts should come as no surprise if one considers that they are sometimes working side by side with volunteers who are willing to do similar work for no pay. While volunteer work is often treated as a result of a distinctly different process than paid work, this sharp distinction may not be merited. Instead, volunteer labor might be viewed as the extreme case of the donative labor hypothesis—the case where workers have "donated" back their entire wage. And it is likely that the intrinsic motivation of workers, paid and unpaid alike, is important to the basic functioning of many nonprofit organizations. That said, there is also a multiplicity of ways that volunteer work must be considered to be distinct from paid work in the nonprofit sector.[10] For most people, volunteer work is far less of an imperative than paid work. And because it is unpaid, volunteering must impart something of value to its participants above and beyond the benefits that paid workers perceive from their work. Furthermore, volunteer work is most likely the result of a sequential decision-making process, and is chosen only after primary decisions about paid labor force participation have been made and other time commitments (to one's family and children, for instance) have been met. Thus, volunteer efforts vary more over the life cycle than paid work and may hang more delicately from a complex web of motivations. These factors give rise to much of the discussion summarized here.

It has long been understood that while volunteers are unpaid, they are not free. In using volunteers, organizations will make expenditures on training, supplies, insurance, and management (Weinberg 1980; Lovelock and Weinberg 1984; Schiff 1984). Furthermore, the presence of volunteers may complicate the management and motivation of paid staff. While Brudney (1995:327) focuses on volunteers in public agencies, his discussion is pertinent to the nonprofit context as well. He notes that paid staff "may come to view volunteers as competitors—for organizational resources, clients, positions—rather than as collaborators in attaining agency goals." As Young (1984) found, the management of nonprofit volunteers can also be made difficult if some have familial or political connections with trustees of the organization, enabling them to disregard a certain degree of management control.

The nonprofit sector is unique in receiving the lion's share of donations of unpaid labor. Independent Sector reports that 83.9 million adults volunteered their time in the United States in 2000. Of these, approximately 67 percent did so in nonprofit organizations. Comparing the number of volunteers with the estimated number of paid workers in the nonprofit sector (from table 7.1), there are nearly six volunteers for every paid worker in the nonprofit sector in the United States. While the hourly commitments of the two groups are very different (see discussion below for figures on average hours per volunteer), at a minimum one can conclude that volunteers play an important role in the nonprofit sector, making a significant and often unmeasured contribution to GDP.

There are varying definitions of what it means to volunteer, some quite broad and others with more narrow strictures or requirements. Numerous authors have elaborated on the nuances (Wilson 2000). Shure (1991), for instance, defines a volunteer as a person offering him- or herself for a service without obligation to do so, willingly and without pay. Some limit the idea of volunteering to service that is done for formal organizations (e.g., National Association of Counties 1990); some specify precisely what types of organizations can benefit from the efforts of volunteers (e.g., Jenner 1982). Other scholars expand the definition of volunteering to include informal help provided to friends, family, or neighbors (Wilson 2000).

Further requirements can be imposed relating to the underlying motivations of volunteers. For example, Smith (1982) notes that volunteers should expect to receive psychic benefits, and Ellis and Noyes (1990:4) suggest that volunteering be done "in recognition of a need, with an attitude of social responsibility . . . going beyond one's basic obligations." Some authors distinguish between volunteerism and activism, volunteerism focusing on ameliorating individual problems while social activists are oriented to broader social change. Furthermore, some definitions of volunteering are also inclusive of those working for pay lower than they could earn elsewhere ("quasi-volunteers"; Smith 1982). Cnaan, Handy, and Wadsworth (1996) capture these various notions in identifying four dimensions along which activity can be ranked: (1) freedom of choosing participation, (2) extent of remuneration, (3) extent to which action is structured versus informal, and (4) extent to which beneficiaries are distanced from the volunteer's personal sphere. Finally, Freeman (1997) suggests that perhaps much volunteerism is not voluntary at all, but something that many individuals do out of perceived social obligation when they are asked.

For the purposes of the discussion in this section, we adopt the definition provided by the President's Task Force on Private Sector Initiatives (1982:4), "the voluntary giving of time and talents to deliver services or perform tasks with no direct financial compensation expected." This definition casts a wide net and avoids many of the restrictions noted above. Freeman's contention of "involuntary" volunteerism will be discussed as well. However, we do not include any discussion of "quasi-volunteers," considering it to fall into the context of the donative labor hypothesis and paid labor discussed above. It should be noted that the restriction that volunteers do not receive monetary compensation does not imply that volunteers may not benefit in any way from their service. As will be discussed below, the opposite is frequently the case.

We also restrict the discussion here in two important ways. We only consider formal volunteer labor (eliminating from the discussion informal services and favors done by friends and family) and we will only be discussing the use of volunteer labor by nonprofit organizations. While the nonprofit sector receives the majority of the hours spent volunteering, 26 percent of voluntary labor accrues to the public sector, and 7 percent to the for-profit sector (Hodgkinson and Weitzman 1996). Examples of public-sector volunteers include those working in the Peace Corp, VISTA, volunteer firefighting, public schools, public health, parks, recreation and tourism programs, and in all kinds of advisory and governance capacities at the local, state, and federal levels of government.[11] Volunteering in the for-profit sector is more unusual, but includes activities such as work-related volunteerism and donations of time to for-profit health-care institutions ("pink ladies" in for-profit hospitals).[12] To date, studies of volunteerism in the for-profit and government sectors are insufficient to indicate whether the nature of volunteering in those sectors is fundamentally different from that in the nonprofit sector.[13]

WHO VOLUNTEERS AND HOW MUCH

Methodology for Quantifying Volunteerism

While the value of a monetary gift is often proudly reported by donors and recipients alike and tracked for the purposes of claiming tax deductions, the amount of time donated to nonprofit organizations can be virtually invisible. In the United States, because nonprofit organizations are not required to report on the amount or type of contributions of *time* they receive, there is no official source of data on these matters. Instead, researchers rely on any number of privately commissioned and financed surveys.

Two survey methodologies are commonly used—retrospective surveys and time-diary studies. Most commonly, retrospective surveys inquire about an individual's recent history of volunteering (e.g., the past year, the past week, in a typical week). These surveys suffer the same problems of recall and reporting bias that plague many other types of self-reported or retrospectively gathered information. The most comprehensive of these surveys was conducted by Gallup polls for Independent Sector. This random survey of the U.S. population was conducted biennially from 1988–2002 (see, for example, Independent Sector and the Urban Institute 2002).[14] In addition, questions regarding volunteer motivation (taken from Volunteer Function Inventory, developed by Clary and colleagues; see below) were included as an addendum to this survey in 1992.

A new and potentially important source of data on volunteerism (and philanthropic behavior more generally) comes in the form of a supplemental survey appended to the Panel Survey of Income Dynamics (PSID), a high-quality, long-running longitudinal survey of 7,400 households. The Center on Philanthropy's (Indiana University, Purdue University, Indianapolis) Panel Study was conducted in 2001, 2003, and 2005, and may be administered on an ongoing basis. The PSID has surveyed a sample of families regularly for more than thirty years. Linking questions on philanthropic behavior to the information available in this panel will allow for exploration of a huge range of topics that relate volunteering and giving to family histories, intergenerational transmission, and the state of the local economy, among other things.

Several other national surveys have also collected information on the volunteering behavior of Americans. Hayghe (1991) and Freeman (1997) both use information gathered in a supplement to the May 1989 U.S. Current Population Survey (CPS). Supplements to the May 1965 and 1974 CPS also collected such information. Goss (1999) reports on proprietary data collected annually since 1975 as part of a national survey commissioned by an advertising firm. This survey included questions about the frequency of volunteering, along with a whole host of social, demographic, and attitudinal questions.

The second methodology generally employed to measure voluntary activity is the use of time-diary data. Time diaries are studies in which participants record in five-minute intervals on a real-time basis (over a typical week or weekend day, for instance) the activities in which they are engaged. Because this method of recording activity does not suffer from recall bias it is considered to be a more accurate accounting of time (Juster and Stafford 1991). The most widely used and temporally consistent examples of time-diary data collected in the United States are the surveys conducted in 1965, 1975, 1985, and 1993 by Juster and Stafford and colleagues, generally known as the Michigan and Maryland Time-Use Studies. Studies of volunteerism by Carlin (2000) and Tiehen (2000) both rely on one or more of these data sets.

Despite the existence of a number of surveys relating to volunteer activity, the same ambiguities in the definition of volunteer efforts that were discussed at the beginning of this section lead to difficulties in interpreting the data. In particular, there is no uniform understanding either among researchers or in the general public about exactly what kind of activities for which organizations constitute volunteering. The Gallup/IS surveys include informal volunteering (that not performed on behalf of any organization or institution) as one example of volunteer work that respondents might report, whereas the May 1989 CPS supplement inquired only about unpaid work for "hospitals, churches, civic, political and other organizations." In part due to these wording differences, and in part due to other differences in the way that the surveys were administered,[15] the 1989 CPS and the 1990 Gallup/IS survey for the same year yielded vastly different estimates of the percent of U.S. adults who volunteered in a year. The CPS reported that 20 percent of the population aged sixteen and over had volunteered in the past year; the Gallup/IS poll reported that 54 percent of those aged eighteen and over had (Hayghe 1991; Freeman 1997). In a survey measuring volunteerism in Indiana, Steinberg, Rooney, and Chin (2002) demonstrate that the longer and more detailed the survey module used, the higher the reported incidence and hours of volunteerism.

How Much Time Is Volunteered?

The Gallup/IS surveys provide information on giving and volunteering over the period 1987–1998 and, using a new methodology, for 2000. These surveys provide measures of the number and percent of Americans who volunteer in a given year and the average and aggregate number of hours that they contribute in a given week and year. These are reported in table 7.4. They demonstrate that consistently over time about half of adults perform some volunteer work in a given year, and that the average volunteer contributes about four hours per week (estimates ranging from 3.5 to 4.7 hours per week). In sum, these contributions are estimated to have added 15.5 billion hours of labor to the U.S. economy in the year 2000. Compared with the approximately 235 billion hours worked in the United States in that year by paid labor,[16] this figure represents an additional 6.6 percent hours worked that are officially unaccounted for.

These figures are consistent with those reported by other authors. Using proprietary marketing survey data, Goss (1999) reports that the percent of adults volunteering in a given year hovers around 50 percent from 1975 to 1990 and then fluctuates around 55 percent during the 1990s. Using time-diary data of married women in 1975–1976, Carlin (2000) estimates that a typical volunteer spends 170 hours per year on volunteer activity, implying an average of 3.2 hours per volunteer per week, a figure somewhat lower than but not entirely inconsistent with the range reported from the Gallup/IS survey for the period 1987–2000.

There are, however, any number of inconsistencies between the IS results and those derived from other methodologies. As noted above, the volunteer participation rates recorded by Independent Sector and recorded in the CPS

TABLE 7.4. MEASURES OF VOLUNTEER EFFORTS IN THE UNITED STATES, 1965–2000

	Independent sector survey of giving and volunteering[a]				Time-diary data[b]
	Percent of adults volunteering in year	Total number of volunteers (in millions)	Average weekly hours per volunteer	Total annual hours volunteered (in billions)	Total annual hours volunteered (in billions)
1965					24.12
1975					25.37
1985					23.02
1987	45.3	80.0	4.7	19.6	
1989	54.4	98.4	4.0	20.5	
1991	51.1	94.2	4.2	20.5	
1993	47.7	89.2	4.2	19.5	28.36
1995	48.8	93.0	4.2	20.3	
1998	55.5	109.4	3.5	19.9	
2000*	44.0	83.9	3.6	15.5	

[a] *Source:* Independent Sector (2001).
[b] *Source:* Tiehan 2000.
*Data collected for 2000 reflect significant changes in survey methodology and are not directly comparable to data collected in previous years. These changes included a change from in-person to telephone interviews, exclusion from the sample of 18–20-year-olds, and changes in wording of questions.

supplements on volunteering are quite different. Furthermore, the most recent survey figures from Independent Sector imply that adults (ages eighteen and over) contributed approximately 19.5 billion hours of volunteer work in the United States in 1993. In contrast, Tiehen (2000), using the Michigan time-use diary data, estimates a higher level of aggregate volunteer involvement, reporting figures ranging from 23.0 to 28.4 billion hours annually for years from 1965 to 1993. Steinberg (1990) reported on seven previous studies covering years between 1964 and 1984 that estimate aggregate volunteer hours to be anywhere from 2.6 billion in 1965 to 11.2 billion in 1984. While aggregate volunteer hours should be expected to have risen with population growth over the years covered by these studies, the various studies still yield disparate results. Thus, it is difficult to ascertain for sure just how much volunteer labor has been supplied in the United States, past or present.

The Value of Volunteer Activity

Once one has ascertained *how much* labor is volunteered in an economy, a second and perhaps more difficult set of methodological questions surrounds the issue of how to value that labor. Few researchers have made this calculation, which is problematic both conceptually and practically, and yet estimates suggest that the value of donated time in the U.S. economy is on par with the value of donated money (Brown 1999). While the value produced by paid labor is generally measured by the wage that is paid, this metric is unavailable for measuring the value of unpaid labor. Moreover, goods and services produced by volunteers are frequently not sold at market prices and so their value is also not easily quantified. Alternate approaches include measuring the wages of those doing comparable work or the wages that volunteers themselves earn (or could earn) in the market for paid labor. Because many studies of volunteer motivation imply that value accrues to the volunteer as well as to the recipient receiving the good or service, a social welfare accounting approach dictates that both of these sources of value be counted when valuing volunteer output.

Using data collected in their survey, Independent Sector values volunteer labor at the average hourly wage of nonagricultural workers in the United States, increasing that by 12 percent to incorporate the value of fringe benefits that are also paid to the average worker. In 2000, they estimate a total value of $239.2 billion (Independent Sector and Urban Institute 2002). If it had been included in national income accounts, this would have constituted a 2.4 percent increase in U.S. GDP for that year.[17] Brown (1999) makes a more complex set of estimates, taking into account both the market valuation of a volunteer's skills and the utility to the volunteer of the activity itself. Her estimates for 1996 range from $203 billion to $410 billion. Of that, $146 billion to $208 billion accrue to the recipients of volunteer services, and the remainder accrues to the volunteers in the form of social interaction, skill accrual, and or other nonmonetary benefits.[18]

Who Volunteers

A number of researchers have looked at *who* volunteers and most find consistent patterns across a variety of data sets. Goss (1999), Hayghe (1991), Freeman (1997), and others have all reported that women, whites, married persons, and those with higher educational attainment and income are more likely to volunteer; that volunteering peaks among those aged thirty-five to fifty-four; and that employed persons are more likely to volunteer than those who are not employed, but those who work part-time are likely to contribute more hours. In addition, Tiehen (2000) and Carlin (2000) both find that the presence of preschool children somewhat deters volunteer participation among women, but that the presence of children ages six to twelve enhances it.

Trends in Volunteerism

In recent years, the work of Putnam (1995a, 2000) has sparked much debate and discussion regarding trends in civic engagement—meaningful social involvement in one's community. Putnam argues that America has suffered a decades-long decline in civic engagement and the associated social capital that it affords. He points to declines in activities ranging from voting, to newspaper reading, to participation in community organizations, to socializing with neighbors; declines that have undermined our social and community well-being and even the underpinnings of democracy.[19] The sources of this decline could be as far-ranging as the increased labor force participation of women, increased geographic mobility, suburbanization, television, and the rise of the welfare state (Putnam 1995b). While Putnam cites declines in organizational membership, meeting attendance, and the number of bowling leagues, among other things, embedded within this discussion is the question of whether volunteerism has shown a similar trend (Greeley 1997). Somewhat conflicting forces could be at work. On the one hand, one might expect the increased participation of women in the paid labor market to have cut the amount of time available for volunteering (e.g., Clotfelter 1985). And, because a significant amount of volunteering is done by parents in association with the school and recreational activities of their children, one might expect that delayed childbearing and smaller families in recent years had taken its toll as well. On the other hand, as Goss (1999) points out, rising incomes, education, and employment levels should all be associated with higher rates of volunteerism, as all three characteristics are known to be related to the propensity to volunteer.

The fact that much of the data on volunteerism have not been collected consistently over time hinders the analysis. There are, however, two sources of information on volunteerism that span longer time periods in the United States: they are the Gallup/IS survey of giving and volunteering from 1988 to 2000 and Goss's (1999) study of proprietary survey data for the period 1975 to 1999.[20] Goss (1999) finds that the propensity to volunteer is relatively steady during this period, holding close to 50 percent and rising slightly in the 1990s. The IS data (shown in table 7.4) show volunteerism of approximately the same magnitude. While this data exhibits more year-to-year variation, there does not appear to be a particular trend over time.

Goss (1999) conducts an in-depth analysis of volunteerism over time as well. In addition to the relatively stable trend in the propensity to volunteer, she also finds that the median number of volunteer activities is fairly steady at about 2, but that the average number of volunteer activities has risen dramatically, from 6 to 7.5. Taken together, these two factors suggest some shift in the distribution of volunteer activities over time. Following a very detailed cohort analysis, she concludes that while cohorts born since 1930 have followed a familiar life-cycle pattern—increasing volunteer participation in early to middle adulthood and decreasing participation after middle age—those born prior to 1930 defy this pattern. This group has experienced ever-increasing volunteer involvement during the period 1975–1999—years during which they age from forty-five and over, to seventy and over. Thus, seniors are responsible for nearly all the observed increase in the number of voluntary activities. In a multivariate regression analysis of senior volunteer activity, Goss finds that after accounting for variables such as economic security, social capital, health status, and belief in the importance of private charities, there is something special about those born before 1930, but a stronger unexplained time trend, with volunteer episodes rising over time. She suggests that possible explanations could include a changing social view of retirement (with a shift in emphasis from leisure to activity) and an increase in the number of senior-oriented nonprofit organizations (for instance, those dealing with Alzheimer's and cancer prevention) calling on their members for contributions of time.

Why People Volunteer

Volunteerism is clearly an important resource for the nonprofit sector and to the economy more generally. Thus, the determinants of this resource flow are important underpinnings of the ability of nonprofits (and, to a lesser extent, other types of organizations) to supply a whole range of goods and services. Researchers from a variety of disciplines have written on people's reasons for volunteering, identifying factors that range from the purely altruistic to the completely self-interested to the rationally economic. Whether one or all of these classes of motivation (or one of a number of others) is in play can have significant implications for the maintenance of volunteer labor supply in the face of a changing economic, social, demographic, or policy environment.

If volunteerism is closely tied to life-cycle considerations, as some have suggested, then major demographic shifts (such as the imminent aging of the baby boom generation into retirement) could have dramatic effects on rates of volunteerism. Alternatively, efforts to recruit volunteers and programs to manage them might be designed differently for those who are altruistically motivated than for those seeking self-improvement through work experience. If individuals make decisions based on an explicit tradeoff between donations of time and money, the changes in the tax treatment of donations or income could significantly alter the contribution mix. Furthermore, Segal and Weisbrod (2002) make the point that the motivation for and benefits from volunteering vary across different industries in the nonprofit sector. Thus, changes in factors that underlie volunteer motivation may have very different implications for the supply of volunteer labor in different industries, and the policy and management implications of different volunteer motivations are as wide-ranging as the theories of motivation themselves.

Because volunteer work is often composed of the same or similar tasks that many individuals perform in the context of paid work, and because paid work is often assumed to have some disutility associated with it, it is reasonable to assume that some disutility can be associated with volunteer activities. According to Clary, Snyder, and Stukas (1996:485) volunteer work "is effortful, it is work . . . it is time-consuming, and it involves interaction with strangers. . . . Finally, some volunteers engage in work that is clearly trying." Thus, a basic question posed by researchers is: Why do people seek out opportunities and overcome substantial obstacles in order to do such unpaid work? Implicit in this question and in most of the work on volunteerism (with the exception of Freeman 1997, discussed below) is the assumption that volunteers do so voluntarily. The presumption that guides all discussions of volunteer motivation is that the benefits (psychic, social, or otherwise) that accrue to volunteers outweigh any costs. The discussion that follows provides taxonomy of the possible sources of volunteerism and volunteer motivation as discussed in the literature. An illustration of this taxonomy is presented in figure 7.1.

The literature on the motivation of volunteers focuses on identifying the nature of the benefits of volunteering to volunteers. Extrinsic benefits accrue *as a result of* the work accomplished, whether they are monetary, psychic, or social. Intrinsic benefits are satisfactions resulting simply from engagement in the activity itself. Most arguments put forth can be broadly categorized into those that focus on one or the other of these types of benefits; Cappellari and Turati (2004) are unique in building a model of volunteer motivation that incorporates both.

Interestingly, while the intrinsic motivation of workers and managers has long held an important place in the literature on paid employment in the nonprofit sector (discussed above), less has been written about its role relative to volunteerism. Much of what has been written has come out of the context of leisure studies (Henderson 1981, 1984), where extrinsically (or goal-) oriented activity is often defined to be "work," and intrinsically oriented activity is often defined to be "leisure." Along these lines, Henderson argues that the categorization of volunteer activity as "work" is too limiting, as many volunteers are highly intrinsically motivated. In the same vein, Brown (1999) echoes the theme in the literature on paid nonprofit workers, noting that volunteers may especially be recruited to do tasks for which a demonstration of intrinsic motivation is important (fundraising or hospice care, for example) because their devotion is more credible than that of someone being paid.

The remaining discussions of the benefits accruing to volunteers speak to a variety of extrinsic motivations. The theories espoused can be grouped into four categories: those that emphasize the desire on the part of volunteers to accomplish certain outcomes; those that rely on psychological motivations or self-understanding; those that emphasize human capital and individual and household utility maximization; and those that focus on organizational connections and social capital (Wilson 2000). The psychological factors are often broken down into those that emphasize helping others (altruism) and helping oneself (egoism) (Stebbins 1996:213).[21]

The first category of motivations is those that are explicitly instrumental. Volunteers will donate their time in order to increase the supply of public goods. In the same vein, leaders and celebrities will sometimes leverage their volunteerism, using it as a catalyst and encouraging others to contribute to a cause as well (Havrilesky, Schweitzer, and Wright 1973). Another kind of instrumentalism may be displayed by prospective monetary donors who may choose to spend time volunteering within the organization in order to gather more information prior to making a donation (Schiff 1984).

Within the second category of motivations for volunteers, the literature emphasizing psychological factors often identifies one or more of the following themes. Here individuals engage in volunteer work in order to: express or act upon values that are important to them (including altruism), increase their understanding of the world, engage in their own psychological development and enhance their self-esteem, or cope with inner anxieties or conflicts (Clary, Snyder, and Stukas 1996).

Within the third category of explanations, the literature written from the human-capital and rational-choice perspective often addresses the connection between human capital and both the costs *and* the benefits of volunteering. On the cost side, this literature emphasizes that some costs (albeit not opportunity costs) of volunteering are lower for those with more education because education boosts awareness of problems, empathy, and self-confidence, as well as bringing any number of skills into play. On the benefits side, this literature emphasizes unpaid work that allows the volunteer to enhance, for instance, their skills or marketability in the paid labor market, their career advancement, or their status within their profession (Day and Devlin 1998).

More generally, the economics literature derived from a rational-choice and utility-maximization model primarily focuses on the tradeoffs between gifts of money and time and between paid and unpaid work that are implied by strict economic calculus. These theories imply that as the opportunity cost of volunteering rises (with an individual's market wage), the amount of time an individual donates will decline. The same approach suggests that households will allocate time according to the law of comparative advantage—with the highest earners in a household working more hours in the paid labor market and volunteering less, and the lower-wage earners working fewer hours for pay but contributing more time to volunteering.[22]

Finally, a fourth branch of the literature focuses on the importance of volunteerism in developing and maintaining social resources and connections. It is observed that social

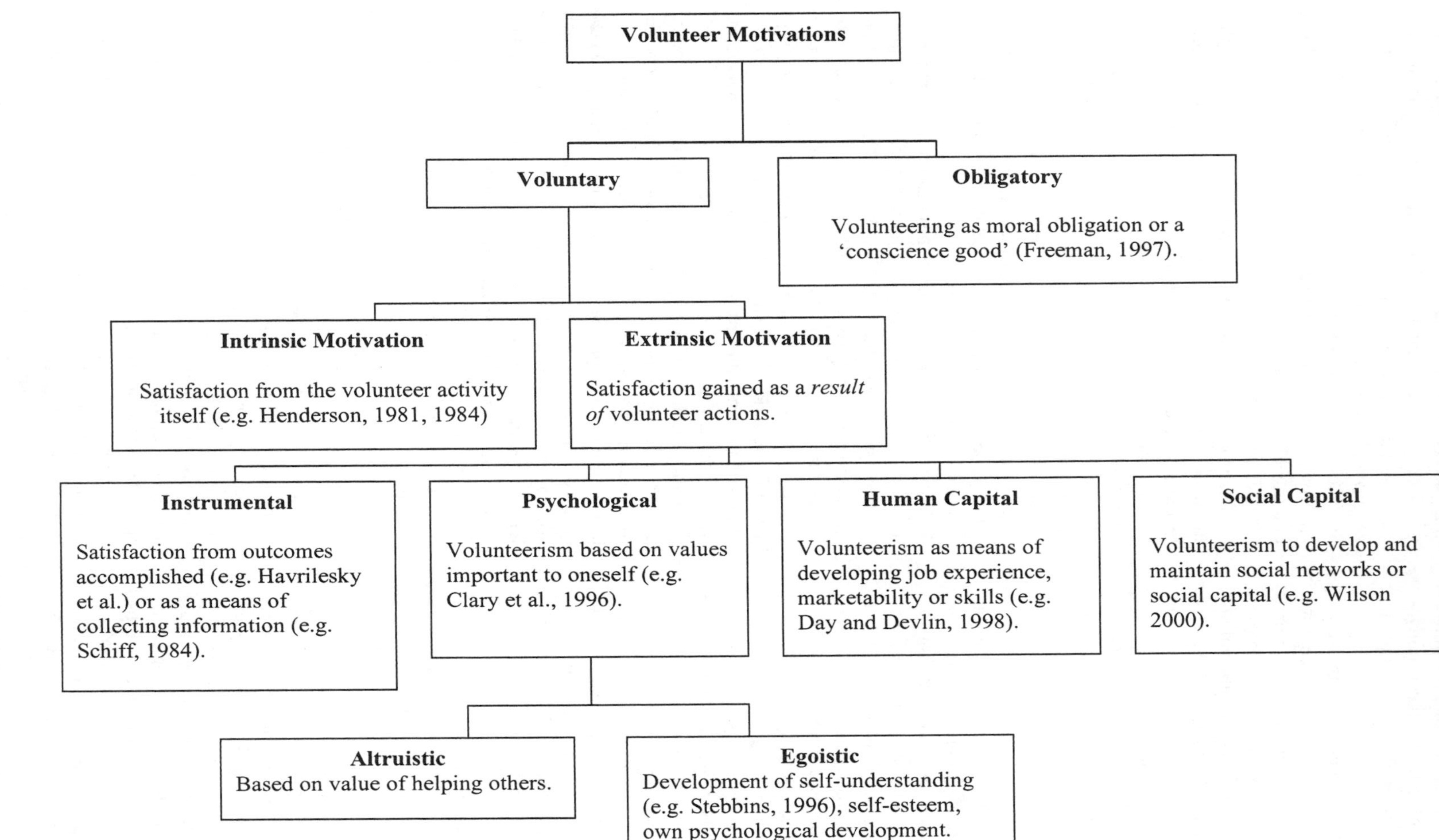

FIGURE 7.1. TAXONOMY OF THEORIES OF VOLUNTEER MOTIVATION

networks, organizational memberships, prior volunteer experience, personal connections, and any other activities that increase social solidarity in a community all play a crucial role in involving individuals and motivating them to volunteer. Much as in the human-capital view, these social ties both lower the costs of volunteering (for example, via prior knowledge of organizations and tasks or the provision of more and better opportunities) and increase the benefits of volunteering (through an enhanced sense of community, strengthening of personal ties, or the increased esteem of friends, families, and neighbors).

The discussion thus far has focused on literature that is based on the premise that volunteering is undertaken voluntarily. Freeman (1997:s140) is alone in positing an explanation that falls somewhat outside this framework. He suggests that instead of being truly voluntary, volunteer work "is a 'conscience good or activity'—something that people feel morally obligated to do when asked, but which they would just as soon let someone else do," thereby free-riding on the public good production that takes place. In this context, one might consider an individual to still be operating within a cost-benefit calculus, but the terms of engagement have changed. Now the primary benefit to the individual agreeing to volunteer is *avoiding* the social stigma associated with refusing the request. In this case, the stronger the social ties to the person or organization (or their social network) making the request, the more likely the request will be met.

Evidence to support the theories discussed above has been offered at a number of levels. At the first level, authors have tried to establish support for the idea that volunteers do in fact accrue some nonmonetary benefit through their activity. Brown (1999) makes an interesting and insightful observation that supports this idea. She notes that it is frequently observed that volunteers who have higher-than-average education and wage levels will perform volunteer work equivalent to that performed by workers earning below-average wages. If volunteers cared solely about maximizing the help they provided to nonprofit organizations, this would not happen. Instead, volunteers with high earning potential would choose to work extra hours at their paid job and donate the cash to the organization, who in turn could "get more for their money" by hiring lower-paid labor. The fact that they do not can be attributed to an inability to increase hours of work in the paid labor market or some kind of nonmonetary benefit that accrues to the volunteer or the organization. Similarly, Wilson (2000:222) summarizes more evidence that cost-benefit assessments do motivate volunteers, including the fact that parents are more likely to volunteer in their own children's schools than in other schools, that the stigma associated with certain volunteer jobs makes it harder to recruit for them, and that volunteers are not indifferent to recognition of their efforts and may quit if they do not receive it.

At the next level, numerous authors have searched the available data for patterns consistent with any number of the theories discussed above. This work should be understood in the context of two particular caveats. First, many of these theories of volunteer motivation are overlapping in the sense that any one individual can be simultaneously motivated by any number of factors. Ultimately their behavior will reflect the net sum of all the costs and benefits that they perceive to be associated with a particular decision. The more complex this calculation, the more difficult it will be to relate observed behavior to any particular underlying motivation. Second, even if operating in isolation, some of these theories may be observationally equivalent to one another, at least at the level at which data have been gathered. Any one example of a behavior could be accounted for by any number of theories. For example, one frequently cited pattern of volunteer behavior is that of parents who increase their volunteer effort in the context of their school-age children's educational, athletic, religious, or social activities. This pattern is often noted as an explanation of the higher-than-average incidence of volunteerism among thirty- to forty-four-year-olds. This phenomenon could be accommodated by any number of the theories discussed here. First, among extrinsic motivators, this pattern could reflect pure altruism. Parents are motivated to help out as their experiences expose them to pockets of need. It could be a self-interested altruism from which parents offer their help in ways that benefit their own children. It could be a "tit-for-tat" altruism in which parents help out to the benefit of their own and others' children with the expectation that other parents will do the same in the future. Social networks could come into play as parents become enmeshed in a variety of community and social institutions via their children, participating in order to fulfill their role in these networks. Or, in the context of Freeman's argument, parents of school-age children may be increasingly exposed to the implicit social coercion of being asked to volunteer. All those extrinsic motivations belie the fact that some parents could be intrinsically motivated by a pleasure they find in engaging in activities with their own children. Distinguishing among these possible explanations requires moving beyond the identification of basic economic and demographic patterns of volunteering (with or without the controls of multivariate regression analysis) and requires direct information on what individuals perceive as the costs and benefits of their behavior. At present, this kind of information is available only in the addendum to the Gallup/IS poll done in conjunction with work by Clary and colleagues (see below).

Thus, while Wilson (2000) argues that the social-capital perspective helps explain the connections between volunteering, socioeconomic status, and education, he fails to note that these relationships can also be explained from any number of other perspectives as well. The same can be said of Freeman (1997). Using data from the Gallup/IS poll, Freeman shows that among those who were asked to do so in the past year, 89 percent volunteered, as compared with only 29 percent who were not asked. In a multivariate regression analysis, being asked to volunteer is a strong predictor of volunteerism. While this may support the idea that social pressure or obligation is a primary motivator for volunteerism, it is also consistent with the view that being asked to volunteer reduces any social barriers and transactions costs associated with actually doing so. Day and Devlin (1996) use Canadian survey data to demonstrate a positive relation between some types of volunteering and current earnings; they suggest that this is evidence that volunteering can be an investment in one's own earning capacity. The data are insufficient to rule out reverse causality, however. Higher-income people might be more inclined to volunteer in certain capacities.

Clary, Snyder, and Stukas (1996) probe interesting territory by analyzing survey data designed to relate volunteer behavior directly to six specific motivational categories. The 1992 implementation of the Gallup/IS survey asked respondents about twenty different reasons for volunteering (of which thirteen were drawn directly from Clary et al.'s Volunteer Functions Inventory). They found consistent differences in the answers of volunteers and non-volunteers to these questions. Furthermore, they found differences in underlying motivations for those with different degrees of volunteer experience and commitment, and differences in underlying motivations among volunteers working in different fields. Their evidence is more direct than most, and is consistent with the view that people engage in volunteering in order to satisfy important social and psychological needs and goals, and that these psychological factors appear to be related to whether and how much individuals volunteer and what type of volunteer work they pursue. Furthermore, they find that many individuals are apparently pursuing more than one set of goals through their volunteer activity. In the same vein, Cappellari and Turati (2004) use data derived from a survey of Italian workers to identify separate effects of proxies for both extrinsic and intrinsic psychological orientations. Controlling for other factors, they find that intrinsically oriented individuals volunteer more and extrinsically oriented individuals volunteer less.[23]

Because it is primarily focused on tradeoffs between donations of money and time—more easily measured concepts than human motivation—the evidence relating to the rational choice literature is somewhat more straightforward. Nevertheless, it has still yielded numerous conflicting conclusions. Authors have estimated the relationship between the value of an individual's time (typically measured as the wage they earn in the paid labor market) and the extent to which they donate their time to volunteering. The measurement of this effect is formalized in the calculation of the wage elasticity of volunteer labor supply—the percentage change in the hours of volunteer labor provided resulting from a 1 percent increase in one's own wages. Estimates of this elasticity have ranged from −0.8 (Andreoni, Gale, and Scholz 1995), to −0.4 (Menchik and Weisbrod 1987), to 0 (Brown and Lankford 1992). The differences in these estimates may be a result of a number of factors, including differences in time periods covered (from the 1970s to the 1990s), differences in the proportions of men and women, and married and single individuals included (all of whom are supposed to have different propensities to volunteer), or in the case of Menchik and Weisbrod, in the use of imputed rather than actual wages.

The negative results are consistent with the theoretical expectation that when their time becomes more valuable, people will donate less of it. However, Brown and Lankford's finding suggests that wages do not influence the supply of volunteer labor at all. Instead, they find a correlation between the time available for volunteering and the actual number of hours volunteered. Similarly, Freeman (1997) finds that higher-wage individuals and those who work full-time volunteer more, not less. And Carlin (2000), studying married women only, finds a positive effect of wages on their volunteer labor supply and a positive (although statistically insignificant) effect of time available on hours spent volunteering. These results support the idea that a sequential (rather than a simultaneous) model of time allocation is called for and that women's volunteering behavior is different from men's. Carlin, who used data from the 1990s, suggests that his results may be a function of both the increasing presence of women in professional or managerial careers in recent decades (where both opportunities for and career rewards of volunteering are more prevalent) and the desire of high-wage women to maintain their human capital by volunteering while temporarily out of the labor force raising children.

Donations of Time and Money

Thus far, I have discussed the rational-choice approach to volunteering only as it relates to the determinants of the supply of volunteer labor. In fact, because it recognizes a basic economic tradeoff between time and money, the rational-choice approach extends to a consideration of the contributions of time *and* money, and the relation between them. Duncan (1999) highlights that such models must be correctly specified with regard to an individual's underlying motivation for giving. If an individual is making contributions in order to increase the production of a public good then, Duncan argues, this suggests substitutability between donations of time and money. Alternatively, if an individual is making contributions because of the well-being he or she gets from the act of contributing itself, what Duncan calls the private-consumption model, then donations of time and money will be complementary. Whether contributions of money and time are substitutes or complements is significant for tax policies as they relate to the taxation of income and to the tax treatment of contributions. If donations of time and money are substitutes, then tax policy that encourages gifts of money may discourage gifts of time. Alternatively, if donations of time and money are complements, then any policy that encourages one might encourage the other. Similarly, an understanding of the relative importance of substitutability and complementarity should be significant to those in the business of soliciting donations of either money or time.[24]

Much of the empirical evidence on this issue has indicated a complementarity between donations of time and money. Carlin (2000) finds that contributions of money and volunteer participation appear to be complements. Brown and Lankford (1992) and Menchik and Weisbrod (1987) found that as the after-tax cost of monetary charitable contributions went up, people spent less time volunteering, again suggesting a complementarity.[25] Duncan (1999) argues, however, that these results are predicated on an underlying "private consumption" model of donation and that estimates that incorporate the public-goods aspect of donating time and money imply substitutability between donations of time and donations of money.

The literature on the nonprofit labor force, paid and unpaid, is far richer and more nuanced today than it was twenty, ten, or even five years ago. In some areas, a clear framework for analysis has been constructed. Nevertheless, there is still little that is thoroughly understood about this topic. In particular, the potential role of intrinsic motivation to all efforts in the nonprofit sector deserves far more attention than it has received. It may provide an important common thread running through our understanding of the utilization of both paid and unpaid labor in the nonprofit sector.

With regard to paid labor, there are a number of aspects about which we know virtually nothing. There has been no discussion of the relationship between sectoral status and cyclical or structural job security. One might surmise that nonprofit employment is more stable over the business cycle than for-profit employment, by virtue of being largely concentrated in the service sector. But within a given industry, we have no idea if nonprofit organizations are more or less resilient than their for-profit counterparts in the face of an economic downturn. For instance, out of altruistic or mission-related concerns for their employees, nonprofit organizations might go to greater lengths than for-profit organizations to avoid layoffs during economic downturns. Different levels of job security in different sectors may have profound implications for employees. And while there are hints that labor-market discrimination might be less apparent in the nonprofit sector, there is virtually no commentary directed at this. Labor-market discrimination along the lines of race and gender has plagued many societies for eons. A finding that a particular institutional form helps minimize its manifestation would be significant indeed.

Methodological quandaries found in other research on the nonprofit sector are also troublesome here. In the work on paid labor there is still little agreement on how to best identify the sector of employment of individuals. A complete understanding of the relationships between worker characteristics, job characteristics, and nonprofit status will ultimately hinge on having industry classifications that group work in more meaningful ways. We also lack a systematic methodology for quantifying, or even classifying, the many nonmonetary benefits of employment. The work by Almond and Kendall (2000b) is one step in this direction. Nonmonetary factors may ultimately prove to be key in helping us determine the relative benefits of for-profit and nonprofit employment.

Similarly, the contributions of volunteering, to individual organizations, to the economy, and to society as a whole, are still barely quantified and are poorly understood. The study of volunteerism lacks its own dedicated concepts, theories, and data collection (Cnaan and Goldberg-Glen 1991). Wilson (2000) notes that volunteer activity captures a huge array of activities that people conduct for any number of complex reasons that cannot possibly be explained with one theory. A meaningful taxonomy for describing volunteer activity is needed. Among other things, future work on volunteerism should research the careers of volunteers—examine how one set of volunteer activities progresses to another, delve into the relationships between the volunteer contributions of different household members, and look more carefully at intrinsic motivations. Freeman's (1997) contention that much volunteering is not exactly voluntary warrants further investigation. Both Cnaan and Goldberg-Glen (1991) and Gidron (1984) note that existing research virtually ignores the distinction between what first motivates volunteers and what motivates them to remain committed later.[26] Interestingly, while the literature on motivations has attempted to understand the benefits that motivate volunteers to do their work, little attempt has been made to itemize or quantify the costs, which are presumed to be significant but surmountable.

Perhaps most critical for policy purposes is a better understanding of volunteer motivation, how it relates to specific fields and types of activities, and how it relates to the costly and time-consuming processes of volunteer recruitment and retention. In the same vein, it will be important to understand the role of intrinsic motivation for volunteers and their effectiveness. This connection is perhaps one of the most poorly understood aspects of volunteerism.

Amid these unanswered questions, one bright note is that future work will soon be enhanced with the availability of a new and systematically collected data series on time use. In January 2003, the U.S. Bureau of Labor Statistics began fielding the American Time Use Survey. This time-diary study will provide another source of information on how Americans use their time relative to volunteer activities. The first data became available in 2004.

Research on paid and unpaid work in the nonprofit sector will enrich the contents of a number of academic disciplines, but particularly that of labor economics. The continuum of work and donation that is apparent in the nonprofit sector should challenge economists to think beyond the traditional tradeoff associated with labor and leisure. Instead there would appear to be a range of motivations that spur people to action, paid and unpaid. Nowhere is it more apparent than in the nonprofit sector that jobs are a bundle of monetary, nonmonetary, and psychic characteristics. An understanding of those characteristics and their relative importance to employees has implications far beyond nonprofits. This understanding could lead to inroads relative to family-work policy, worker productivity, and job-stabilization policy, among other things. Finally, the importance of understanding how labor-market discrimination does or does not manifest itself in the nonprofit sector cannot be overstated. If differences among organizational forms exist, then economists and others cannot be too quick in incorporating that understanding into policy efforts to combat discrimination.

NOTES

1. Sources include the 1977 Quality of Employment Survey; the 1980 Worker Assessment of Jobs' Nonmonetary Characteristics, a 1990 survey reported in Mirvis (1992); the 1990 and 2000 U.S. Censuses; and the 1994–1998 Current Population Survey Outgoing Rotation Groups.

2. With misreporting, nonprofit workers with associated characteristics will appear in data sets to be for-profit workers and vice versa. See Hodgkinson et al. (undated) and Leete (2001) for further discussion of the implications of reporting errors.

3. See http://www.jhu.edu/~cnp, Salamon and Anheier (1996), and Salamon and Anheier et al. (1996, 1998).

4. Almond and Kendall (2000a) provide a comprehensive discussion of the current status of nonprofit employment data collection in the international context. They note that recent data-collection efforts, while groundbreaking, are hampered by reliance on the secondary manipulation of data collected for other purposes, low survey response rates, limited information on the sociodemographic profile of the nonprofit sector workforce, and the reliance on surveys of organizations instead of individuals.

5. Differences between the sectors in the incidence of part-time work could be attributable to the overrepresentation of women in the nonprofit sector and the fact that, economy-wide, women are more likely to work part-time than men. Preston (1994) reports about equal rates of part-time work for women in the nonprofit and the for-profit sectors in 1991. Neither Leete (2001) nor Almond and Kendall (2000b) further disaggregate the data.

6. See Ruhm and Borkoski (2003) and Almond and Kendall (2000a, 2000b) for the most recent data on occupational distributions in the United States and the United Kingdom, respectively.

7. Ruhm and Borkoski (2003) also estimate nonprofit differentials separately for men and women, those with and without a college education, and for whites, blacks, and Hispanics.

8. The residual wage is that portion that remains after removing the portion of the wage structure that is "explained" by available worker and job characteristics.

9. Another longitudinal aspect of employment is the degree of job stability offered. While there has been economy-wide research on job stability and job fluctuations for any number of countries, with distinctions sometimes made between public and private sector employment, to date there has been no work on this subject that exclusively focuses on these characteristics of jobs in the nonprofit sector.

10. While volunteers and paid workers may have much in common in the nonprofit sector, they often stand on very different legal footing. Irish and Simon (2002) give an expansive overview of the legal issues that affect volunteers in virtually all countries. This includes ambiguities regarding the application of minimum wage law, child labor laws, Social Security and tax policy to volunteers, as well as questions regarding the liabilities of volunteers and liabilities caused by volunteers.

11. See Brudney (1999) for a descriptive overview of volunteerism in the public sector.

12. Brudney (1999:222) notes: "Volunteering to profit-making firms does occur, but its legal status is debatable," raising concerns regarding possible violations of the Fair Labor Standards Act.

13. See Brudney (1992, 1999) for some of the only cross-sectoral consideration issues relating to volunteer management.

14. However, it should be noted that the figures for the year 2000 reflect significant methodological changes and are not directly comparable to the figures collected in previous years. In particular, they changed the sample, covering adults in the U.S. population from ages eighteen and over, to ages twenty-one and over.

15. In particular, the CPS allowed the respondent to report on volunteer activities for all other members of the household, while the Gallup/IS survey asked respondents only about their own volunteer activities.

16. U.S. Department of Commerce, Bureau of Economic Analysis, National Income and Product Accounts Tables, table 6.9c (http://www.bea.doc.gov/bea/dn/nipaweb/SelectTable.asp?Selected=N).

17. Calculated using total GDP for 2000. U.S. Department of Commerce, Bureau of Economic Analysis, National Income and Product Accounts Tables, table 1.1 (http://www.bea.doc.gov/bea/dn/nipaweb/SelectTable.asp?Selected=N).

18. Steinberg (1990) also reports a variety of estimates of the value of volunteer labor for years ranging from 1964 to 1984.

19. Others have noted that conditions that breed social capital also have a downside. Portes and Landolt (1996), for instance, argue that the same small, tightly knit communities that give rise to social capital also exclude outsiders and smother individuality and initiative.

20. While Tiehen (2000) also reports volunteer participation rates from the available time-diary data for the years 1965, 1975, 1985, and 1993, changes in sample composition from year to year in that data make interpretation of any time trends problematic.

21. Other researchers have proposed any number of other ways to classify motivation to volunteer. In particular, Cnaan and Golberg-Glen (1991) review twenty-seven different studies that contribute twenty-eight different items to a list of motivations relevant to direct service volunteers in the human-services field. These studies offer models two-, three-, and multi-category models of motivation, while other studies that they cite suggest that motivation is a unidimensional concept centered on altruism alone.

22. Implicit in much of the discussion about the relationship between paid and unpaid work is an assumption that the decision to devote hours to each activity is made simultaneously and incrementally. Brown and Lankford (1992), however, argue for a sequential model of decision-making about the allocation of time to either volunteer or paid work. They argue that because there is less flexibility in choosing the number of hours one works in the paid labor market, workers select the conditions of their market work first, and then volunteer time is allocated out of the remaining hours available.

23. Their analysis explicitly takes account of measurement error and the endogeneity of motivations.

24. Studies also look at the crowding-out of time donations by government spending, finding that volunteering and government spending are variably treated as either complements or substitutes, depending on the type of government spending involved (Menchik and Weisbrod 1987; Day and Devlin 1996; Duncan 1999).

25. Since monetary contributions to many kinds of nonprofit organizations are tax deductible, the net cost to the donor of a contribution is the after-tax value (or tax price). This is equal to the contribution itself minus any reduction in the donor's tax bill that results from the contribution.

26. Two exceptions are: Clary, Snyder, Copeland, and French (1994), who examine differences in the effectiveness of messages in recruiting and retaining volunteers; and Vaillancourt (1994), who distinguishes between determinants of satisfaction with volunteer work and of length of service.

REFERENCES

Almond, Stephen, and Jeremy Kendall. 2000a. "Taking the Employees' Perspective Seriously: An Initial United Kingdom Cross-Sectoral Comparison." *Nonprofit and Voluntary Sector Quarterly* 29(2):205–231.

———. 2000b. "The Quality of U.K. Third Sector Employment in Comparative Perspective." Paper prepared for the annual meeting of ARNOVA.

Andreoni, James, William G. Gale, and John K. Scholz. 1995. "Charitable Contributions of Time and Money." Unpublished manuscript, University of Wisconsin-Madison, Department of Economics.

Ballou, Jeffrey P., and Burton A. Weisbrod. 2003. "Managerial Rewards and the Behavior of For-Profit, Governmental and Nonprofit Organizations: Evidence from the Hospital Industry." *Journal of Public Economics* 87:1895–1920.

Borjas, George, H. E. Frech III, and Paul B. Ginsburg. 1983. "Property Rights and Wages: The Case of Nursing Homes." *Journal of Human Resources* 18:231–246.

Brown, Charles, and James Medoff. 1989. "The Employer Size—Wage Effect." *Journal of Political Economy* 97:1027–1059.

Brown, Eleanor. 1999. "Assessing the Value of Volunteer Activity." *Nonprofit and Voluntary Sector Quarterly* 28:3–17.

Brown, Eleanor, and Hamilton Lankford. 1992. "Gifts of Money and Gifts of Time: Estimating the Effects of Tax Prices and Available Time." *Journal of Public Economics* 47:321–341.

Brudney, Jeffrey. 1992. "Administrators of Volunteer Services: Their Needs for Training and Research." *Nonprofit Management and Leadership* 2:271–282.

———. 1995. "The Involvement of Volunteers in the Delivery of Services: Myth and Management." In *Public Personnel Administration: Problems and Prospects,* 3rd ed., Steven W. Hays and Richard C. Kearney, eds. Englewood Cliffs, N.J.: Prentice Hall.

———. 1999. "The Effective Use of Volunteers: Best Practices for the Public Sector." *Law and Contemporary Problems* 62:219–255.

Cappellari, Lorenzo, and Turati, Gilberto, 2004. "Volunteer Labour Supply: The Role of Workers' Motivations." *Annals of Public and Cooperative Economics* 75:619–643.

Carlin, Paul S. 2000. "Evidence on the Volunteer Labor Supply of Married Women." *Southern Economics Journal* 67:801–824.

Christensen, Kathleen. 1989. *Flexible Staffing and Scheduling in U.S. Corporations,* New York: Conference Board.

Clary, E. G., M. Snyder, J. T. Copeland, and S. A. French. 1994. "Promoting Volunteerism: An Empirical Examination of the Appeal of Persuasive Messages." *Nonprofit and Voluntary Sector Quarterly* 23:265–280.

Clary, E., Mark Snyder, and Arthur A. Stukas. 1996. "Volunteers' Motivations: Findings from a National Survey." *Nonprofit and Voluntary Sector Quarterly* 25:485–505.

Clotfelter, Charles T. 1985. *Federal Tax Policy and Charitable Giving.* Chicago: University of Chicago Press.

Cnaan, Ram A., and Robin S. Goldberg-Glen. 1991. "Measuring Motivation to Volunteer in Human Services." *Journal of Applied Behavioral Science* 27:269–284.

Cnaan, Ram A., Femida Handy, and Margaret Wadsworth. 1996. "Defining Who Is a Volunteer: Conceptual and Empirical Considerations." *Nonprofit and Voluntary Sector Quarterly* 25:364–383.

Cunningham, Ian. 2000. "Prospects for Union Growth in the U.K. Voluntary Sector—The Impact of Fairness at Work." *Industrial Relations Journal* 34:192–205.

Day, Kathleen M., and Rose Anne Devlin. 1996. "Volunteerism and Crowding Out: Canadian Econometric Evidence." *Canadian Journal of Economics* 29:37–53.

———. 1998. "The Payoff to Work Without Pay: Volunteer Work as an Investment in Human Capital." *Canadian Journal of Economics* 31:1179–1191.

Driver, M. 1980. "Career Concepts and Organizational Change." In C. Derr, ed., *Work, Family, and the Career.* New York: Praeger.

Duncan, Brian. 1999. "Modeling Charitable Contributions of Time and Money." *Journal of Public Economics* 72:213–242.

Ellis, S. J., and K. H. Noyes. 1990. *By the People.* San Francisco: Jossey-Bass.

Feldstein, Martin S. 1971. *Rising Cost of Hospital Care.* Washington, D.C.: Information Resources Press.

Frank, Robert. 1996. "What Price the High Moral Ground?" *Southern Economic Journal* 63:1–17.

Freeman, Richard B. 1997. "Working for Nothing: The Supply of Volunteer Labor." *Journal of Labor Economics* 15:s140–s166.

Frumkin, Peter, and Elizabeth Keating. 2001. The Price of Doing Good: Executive Compensation in Nonprofit Organizations. Working paper no. 8, Hauser Center for Nonprofit Organizations, Harvard University.

Gibelman, Margaret. 2000. "The Nonprofit Sector and Gender Discrimination: A Preliminary Investigation into the Glass Ceiling." *Nonprofit Management and Leadership* 10:251–269.

Gidron, B. 1984. "Predictors of Retention and Turnover Among Service Volunteer Workers." *Journal of Social Service Research* 8:1–16.

Goddeeris, John H. 1988. "Compensating Differentials and Self-Selection: An Application to Lawyers." *Journal of Political Economy* 96:411–428.

Goss, Kristin. 1999. "Volunteering and the Long Civic Generation." *Nonprofit and Voluntary Sector Quarterly* 28:378–415.

Greeley, Andrew. 1997. "Religion and Social Capital." *The American Prospect* 8(32).

Hallock, Kevin F. 2002. "Managerial Pay and Governance in American Nonprofits." *Industrial Relations* 41:377–406.

Handy, Femida, and Eliakim Katz. 1998. "The Wage Differential Between Nonprofit Institutions and Corporations: Getting More by Paying Less?" *Journal of Comparative Economics* 26:246–261.

Hansmann, Henry B. 1980. "The Role of Nonprofit Enterprise." *Yale Law Journal,* 89:835–901.

Havrilesky, Thomas, Robert Schweitzer, and Scheffel Wright. 1973. "The Supply of and Demand for Voluntary Labor in Behalf of Environmental Quality." Proceedings of the Business and Economics Statistics Section of the American Statistical Association, 170–179.

Hayghe, Howard V. 1991. "Volunteers in the U.S.: Who Donates the Time?" *Monthly Labor Review* 114(2):17–23.

Henderson, K. A. 1981. "Motivations and Perceptions of Volunteerism as a Leisure Activity," *Journal of Leisure Research* 13:208–218.

———. 1984. "Volunteerism as Leisure." *Journal of Voluntary Action Research* 13:55–63.

Hodgkinson, Virginia A., and Murray Weitzman. 1996. *Nonprofit Almanac, 1996–1997.* The Independent Sector.

Hodgkinson, Virginia A., Murray S. Weitzman, Steve M. Noga, and Heather A. Gorski. Undated. *National Summary: Not-For-Profit Employment from the 1990 Census of Population and Housing.* The Independent Sector.

Hohl, Karen L. 1996. "The Effects of Flexible Work Arrangements," *Nonprofit Management and Leadership* 7:69–86.

Independent Sector. 2001. *Giving and Volunteering in the United States.* Washington, D.C.: Author.

———. Undated. *Nonprofit Almanac: Facts and Findings—Employment in the Nonprofit Sector.* Mimeo. Washington, D.C.: Author. (http://www.independentsector.org/PDFs/npemployment.pdf, accessed April 11, 2005)

Independent Sector and the Urban Institute. 2002. *The New Nonprofit Almanac and Desk Reference.* Washington, D.C.: Authors.

Irish, Leon E., and Karla W. Simon. 2002. "Legal Issues Affecting Volunteers." Presented at the Fifth International Conference of the International Society for Third-Sector Research.

Ito, Takatoshi, and Dale Domain. 1987. "A Musical Note on the Efficiency Wage Hypothesis—Programmings, Wages and Budgets of American Symphony Orchestras." *Economics Letters* 25:95–99.

Jenner, J. R. 1982. "Participation, Leadership, and the Role of Volunteerism Among Selected Women Volunteers." *Journal of Action Research* 11(4):27–38.

Jensen, Michael C., and William H. Meckling. 1976. "The Theory of the Firm: Managerial Behavior, Agency Costs and Ownership Structure." *Journal of Financial Economics* 3:305–360.

Johns Hopkins University, Center for Civil Society Studies. Undated. *Global Civil Society At-a-Glance: Major Findings of the Johns Hopkins Comparative Nonprofit Sector Project.* Mimeo.

Johnston, Dennis, and Gabriel Rudney. 1987. "Characteristics of Workers in Nonprofit Organizations." *Monthly Labor Review* 110:28–33.

Juster, F. Thomas, and Frank P. Stafford. 1991. "The Allocation of Time: Empirical Findings, Behavioral Models and Problems of Measurement." *Journal of Economic Literature* 29:471–522.

Kamimura, Kiyoko, and Naoto Yamauchi. 2002. "The Nonprofit Labor Market in Japan: Findings from New Survey Data." Presented at the Fifth International Conference of the International Society for Third-Sector Research.

Leete, Laura. 2000. "Wage Equity and Employee Motivation in Nonprofit and For-Profit Organizations." *Journal of Economic Behavior and Organizations* 43:423–446.

———. 2001. "Whither the Nonprofit Wage Differential? Estimates from the 1990 Census." *Journal of Labor Economics* 19:136–170.

Lovelock, Christopher H., and Charles Weinberg. 1984. *Marketing for Public and Nonprofit Managers.* New York: Wiley.

Menchik, Paul L., and Burton A. Weisbrod. 1987. "Volunteer Labor Supply." *Journal of Public Economics* 32:159–183.

Mirvis, Philip H. 1992. "The Quality of Employment in the Nonprofit Sector: An Update on Employee Attitudes in Nonprofits Versus Business and Government." *Nonprofit Management and Leadership,* 3:23–41.

Mirvis, Philip, and Edward Hackett. 1983. "Work and Work Force Characteristics in the Nonprofit Sector." *Monthly Labor Review* 106(4):3–12.

Mocan, H. Naci, and Erdal Tekin, 2003. "An Analysis of Employer-Employee Matched Data of Child Care Workers." *Review of Economics and Statistics* 85:38–50.

National Association of Counties. 1990. *The Volunteer ToolBox.* Washington, D.C.: Author.

Newman, W. H., and Wallender, H. W. 1978. "Managing Not-for-Profit Enterprises." *Academy of Management Review* 3:24–31.

Onyx, Jenny, and Maclean, Madi. 1996. "Careers in the Third Sector." *Nonprofit Management and Leadership* 6:331–345.

Oster, Sharon. 1998. "Executive Compensation in the Nonprofit Sector," *Nonprofit Management and Leadership,* 8:207–221.

Portes, Alejandro, and Landolt, Patricia. 1996. "Unsolved Mysteries: The Tocqueville Files II." *The American Prospect* 7(26).

President's Task Force on Private Sector Initiatives. 1982. *Volunteers: A Valuable Resource.* Washington, D.C.: Author.

Preston, Anne E. 1988. "The Effects of Property Rights on Labor Costs of Nonprofit Firms: An Application to the Day Care Industry." *Journal of Industrial Economics* 36:337–350.

———. 1989. "The Nonprofit Worker in a For-Profit World." *Journal of Labor Economics* 7:438–463.

———. 1990. "Women in the White-Collar Nonprofit Sector: The Best Option or the Only Option?" *Review of Economics and Statistics* 72:560–568.

———. 1993. "The Market for Human Resources: Comparing Professional Career Paths in the Public, Private, Nonprofit Sector." In *Nonprofit Organizations in a Market Economy: Understanding New Roles, Issues and Trends,* David C. Hammack and Dennis R. Young, eds. San Francisco: Jossey-Bass.

———. 1994. "Women in the Nonprofit Labor Market." In *Women and Power in the Nonprofit Sector,* Teresa Odendahl, and Michael O'Neill, eds. San Francisco: Jossey-Bass.

Putnam, Robert D. 1995a. "Bowling Alone: America's Declining Social Capital." *Journal of Democracy* 6:65–78.

———. 1995b. "The 1995 Ithiel de Sola Pool Lecture: Tuning In, Tuning Out: The Strange Disappearance of Social Capital in America." *Political Science and Politics* 28:664–683.

———. 2000. *Bowling Alone: The Collapse and Revival of American Community.* New York: Simon and Schuster.

Rabin, Matthew. 1998. "Psychology and Economics." *Journal of Economic Literature* 36:11–46.

Rose-Ackerman, Susan. 1996. "Altruism, Nonprofits, and Economic Theory." *Journal of Economic Literature* 34:701–728.

Roomkin, Myron, and Burton Weisbrod. 1999. "Managerial Compensation in Incentives in For-Profit and Nonprofit Hospitals." *Journal of Law, Economics and Organizations* 15:750–781.

Rudney, Gabriel. 1987. "The Scope and Dimensions of Nonprofit Activity." In *The Nonprofit Sector: A Research Handbook,* Walter W. Powell, ed. New Haven, Conn.: Yale University Press.

Rudney, Gabriel, and Murray Weitzman. 1984. "Trends in Employment and Earnings in the Philanthropic Sector." *Monthly Labor Review* 107(9):16–20.

Ruhm, Christopher, and Carey Borkoski. 2003. "Compensation in the Nonprofit Sector." *Journal of Human Resources* 38:992–1021.

Salamon, Lester M. 1987. "Partners in Public Service: The Scope and Theory of Government-Nonprofit Relations." In *The Nonprofit Sector: A Research Handbook,* Walter W. Powell, ed. New Haven, Conn.: Yale University Press.

Salamon, Lester M., and Helmut K. Anheier. 1996. *The Emerging Nonprofit Sector.* New York City: St. Martin's.

Salamon, Lester, M., Helmut K. Anheier, and Associates. 1996. *The Emerging Sector: A Statistical Supplement.* Baltimore, Md.: Institute of Policy Studies.

———. 1998. *The Emerging Sector Revisited.* Baltimore, Md.: Institute of Policy Studies.

Schiff, Jerald. 1984. *Charitable Contributions of Money and Time: The Role of Government Policies.* Ph.D. dissertation, University of Wisconsin, Madison.

Segal, Lewis M., and Burton A. Weisbrod. 2002. "Volunteer Labor Sorting Across Industries," *Journal of Policy Analysis and Management* 21:427–447.

Shackett, Joyce R., and John M. Trapani. 1987. "Earnings Differentials and Market Structure." *Journal of Human Resources* 22:518–531.

Shure, Richard S. 1991. "Volunteering: Continuing Expansion of the Definition and a Practical Application of Altruistic Motivation." *Journal of Volunteer Administration* 9:36–41.

Smith, Adam. [1776] 1976. *An Inquiry into the Nature and Causes of The Wealth of Nations.* Reprint ed. Indianapolis: Liberty Classics.

Smith, D. 1982. "Altruism, Volunteers, and Volunteerism." In *Volunteerism in the Eighties,* J. Harman, ed. Washington, D.C.: University Press of America. 23–44.

Stebbins, Robert. 1996. "Volunteering: A Serious Leisure Perspective." *Nonprofit and Voluntary Sector Quarterly* 25:211–224.

Steinberg, Kathryn S., Patrick M. Rooney, and William Chin. 2002. "Measurement of Volunteering: A Methodological Study Using Indiana as a Test Case." *Nonprofit and Voluntary Sector Quarterly* 31:484–501.

Steinberg, Richard. 1990. "Profits and Incentive Compensation in Nonprofit Firms." *Nonprofit Management and Leadership* 1:137–151.

Tiehen, Laura. 2000. "Has Working Caused More Married Women to Volunteer Less? Evidence from Time Diary Data, 1965 to 1993." *Nonprofit and Voluntary Sector Quarterly* 29:505–529.

Twombly, Eric C., and Marie G. Gantz. 2001. "Executive Compensation in the Nonprofit Sector: New Findings and Policy Implications." Issue Brief: *Charting Civil Society Series,* no. 11, Center on Nonprofits and Philanthropy, The Urban Institute. http://www.urban.org/template.cfm?navmenuid=554&Template=/TaggedContent/CivilSociety.cfm.

U.S. Bureau of Labor Statistics. 1992. Workers on Flexible and Shift Schedules, *U.S. Department of Labor Publication No. 92–491.* Washington, D.C.: Government Printing Office.

U.S. Government Printing Office. 2005. *Economic Report of the President.* Washington, D.C.

Vaillancourt, F. 1994. "To Volunteer or Not: Canada, 1987." *Canadian Journal of Economics* 27:813–826.

Weinberg, Charles. 1980. "Marketing Mix Decision Rules for Nonprofit Organizations." *Research in Marketing* 3:191–234.

Weisbrod, Burton A. 1983. "Nonprofit and Proprietary Sector Behavior: Wage Differentials Among Lawyers." *Journal of Labor Economics* 1:246–263.

———. 1988. *The Nonprofit Economy.* Cambridge, Mass.: Harvard University Press.

Werner, Steve, Robert Konopaske, and Gretchen Gemeinhardt. 2000. "The Effects of United Way Membership on Employee Pay in Nonprofit Organizations." *Nonprofit Management and Leadership* 11:35–48.

Wilson, John. 2000. "Volunteering." *Annual Review of Sociology* 26:215–240.

Yellen, Janet L. 1984. "Efficiency Wage Models of Unemployment." *American Economic Review.* 74:200–205.

Young, Dennis. 1984. Performance and Reward in Nonprofit Organizations: Evaluation, Compensation and Personnel Incentives. Working Paper No. 79, Program on Nonprofit Organizations, Yale University.

8

Collaboration between Corporations and Nonprofit Organizations

JOSEPH GALASKIEWICZ
MICHELLE SINCLAIR COLMAN

In the United States nonprofit organizations and businesses have long been in collaboration. Collaboration has ranged from efforts to advance public welfare to simply making money for both parties. Even so, philanthropic partnerships are seldom purely altruistic, and commercial partnerships often have an element of altruism. This has been the case for well over a hundred years, and we suspect that it will continue. Since one type of organization has the goal to earn money for owners even as they are trying to do good, and the other to advance social welfare even as they are trying to increase revenues, it is inevitable that there will be tension and contradictions as well as synergy.

Hall (1989, 1997) and Karl (1991) documented the early history of business and charity collaborations. Andrews's (1952) book presented an overview of company giving up to 1950 and a detailed analysis of business giving at mid-century. Heald (1970) looked at business social responsibility from the nineteenth century up to 1960. H. Smith (1983) provided a description of corporate giving from 1936 up through the 1970s. Useem's (1987) chapter in the first edition of *The Nonprofit Sector: A Research Handbook* provided an overview of giving in the 1970s and 1980s. This was followed by Galaskiewicz (1989) and H. Smith (1993). Knauer (1994) and Kahn (1997) provided a review of the legal environment surrounding corporate contributions. In 1997 the *New York Law School Law Review* (NYLSLR) published a two-issue volume on topics related to corporate/nonprofit relations, and in 1999 the Conference Board published a report that documented the history of corporate giving to the present (Muirhead 1999). A year later Sagawa and Segal (2000) published a useful practice-oriented overview of philanthropic, marketing, and operational exchanges between businesses and nonprofits. More recently Kotler and Lee (2005) published a volume for practitioners, which draws on the extant research, making the case for corporate social responsibility. They also present numerous case examples. We encourage interested readers to seek out these and other sources for more information and insights on business/nonprofit collaborations.

This chapter updates the Useem one with ideas we introduced in an article written for the *NYLSLR* volume (Sinclair and Galaskiewicz 1997). Nonprofits can relate to businesses in a variety of ways, for example, as subcontractors, competitors, adversaries, owners, suppliers, customers, as well as collaborators (Abzug and Webb 1999). We focus only on collaboration but recognize that businesses and nonprofits are linked in a number of ways.

We describe four types of business/nonprofit collaborations: philanthropic, strategic, commercial, and political. Philanthropic collaborations advance social welfare by facilitating the delivery of nonprofits' mission-related services. They typically entail a unilateral transfer payment from the company to the nonprofit, but in many cases companies cooperate extensively with nonprofits in providing services. A major problem with philanthropic collaborations is that it is often difficult to assess results and the benefits to either party or the larger society. After reviewing the statistics on giving, we examine management issues, companies' motives, and the nonprofit beneficiaries of corporate largesse. The purpose of strategic collaborations is to realize exclusive benefits for the firm while advancing social welfare through the activities of the nonprofit. Sometimes this is called social investing or strategic philanthropy. Measurement is still a problem, but business partners typically have better information on how the collaboration benefits them. We focus on sponsorships and donations of equipment and products. The purpose of commercial collaborations is to increase revenues for both the company and the nonprofit. Social welfare is only of secondary importance, and the benefits for both are relatively easy to measure. We examine cause-related marketing, the licensing of names and logos of nonprofits, and scientific collaborations. Political collaborations aim at reproducing or changing institutional arrangements. Sometimes the purpose is to change corporate practices. The company and the nonprofit may have the same agenda, but they could be in conflict and work together to find a mutually satisfying solution to a problem. Rather than being motivated by immediate financial gains, companies often participate in these collaborations to improve business conditions or out of fear of negative publicity and investor and/or customer disaffection. We examine political collaborations within the United States and in the international context.

BACKGROUND

Collaborations among businesses and charities have a long and storied history in the United States. Although it was not uncommon for businesses to give money to charity in the nineteenth century (Hall 1989), it was not until the 1920s that states began to authorize philanthropic contributions although with restrictions (Kahn 1997:596–97). In 1935 Congress declared a federal income tax deduction for corporate charitable contributions, and after World War II legislatures further liberalized state philanthropy laws. The New Jersey court ruling in *A. P. Smith Manufacturing Co. v. Barlow* (1953), and the Supreme Court's refusal to review the decision, affirmed the corporation's right to make donations that did not directly benefit the firm. While direct benefit was still a legitimate reason to give, the court now formally recognized that philanthropic giving was legitimate as well. In the 1980s and 1990s every administration—both Democratic and Republican—called upon businesses to take a greater role in solving societal problems, reaffirming the legitimacy of this practice.

The debate continues over whether direct benefit or social welfare should be a motive for company giving. In the 1930s Adolf A. Berle, Jr. (1931), and E. Merrick Dodd, Jr. (1932), debated the issue in the *Harvard Law Review,* and Friedman's (1963) admonition that the business of business is business echoes in the ears of many today. In the 1980s many raised the issue of shareholders' rights and shareholder groups have called for full disclosure of charitable activities to keep corporations accountable. In the wake of shareholder activism, mergers, acquisitions, and restructuring in the 1980s and 1990s, the issue of direct benefit went center stage. It is then not surprising that in the late 1980s and 1990s consultants advised companies to make "social investments" and give strategically when making charitable contributions, thus fulfilling their fiduciary obligations to their shareholders (C. Smith 1994b; Weeden 1998).

Strategic philanthropy has become so dominant a rationale for giving that some critics have called for reform. As illustrated in Weisbrod (1998b), companies and nonprofits are actively engaged in business collaborations that generate significant commercial income for both but do little to advance social welfare. Some have even called for the repeal of the corporate charitable deduction under Section 170 of the Internal Revenue Code, because of the self-serving nature of many corporate gifts (Knauer 1994). "While profit-maximizing charitable contributions are uncontroversial from the perspective of corporate law, they are highly controversial as a general theoretical matter, and from the perspective of tax policy analysis" (Kahn 1997:663–64). It would be easier to disallow companies from making charitable contributions and taking the tax deduction, but that would reverse much of U.S. history and many in the corporate and nonprofit communities would fight it.

Because of the complexity of the law and the futility of drawing clear distinctions between corporate self-interest and social welfare, we doubt that the debate over the nature of corporate ends and corporate/nonprofit collaboration will end soon (see, for example, Margolis and Walsh 2003). That many collaborations have political overtones complicates the situation further. In this chapter we draw the distinction between philanthropic, strategic, commercial, and political collaborations. However, it will soon become clear that the differences among the various types of alliances are not that hard and fast.

TYPES OF COLLABORATION BETWEEN CORPORATIONS AND NONPROFITS

Philanthropic Collaborations

Philanthropic partnerships usually entail companies giving money or products to public charities with few or no conditions and no expectation of direct, measurable benefit. The charity, in turn, is expected to use the donations to pursue its tax-exempt purpose. Donations include unrestricted gifts to the operating budgets of theaters, schools, orphanages, and social-service agencies, restricted gifts for endowments or the construction of buildings, matching gifts to employees' designated charities, and the like. The gifts supposedly benefit third parties, but it is often difficult to measure the impact of one's contributions (see Alperson 1996). While these gifts may produce latent benefits for the firm—for example, a better-educated workforce or goodwill—what makes them distinct, according to Lombardo (1995), is that donors do not expect a quid pro quo. These gifts are typically deducted as charitable contributions under Section 170 of the Internal Revenue Code.[1]

Philanthropic partnerships often entail more than check writing or equipment donations. Employees can get involved as volunteers, firms sometimes share their marketing or information systems expertise, company representatives will participate in planning and policy sessions, and a company will often adopt the project as if it were its own.[2] Often many different partners are involved, and there are high coordination costs. Corporations' partnerships with nonprofits, governments, and communities in the area of community/economic development began in the mid-1980s (Muirhead 1999:43; see also Alperson 1998). Companies also formed partnerships with elementary and secondary schools in the 1980s, and these have proliferated over the years (see Brothers 1992; Longoria 1999). More recently, attention has turned to collaborations surrounding public safety (M. Whiting 1999) and welfare to work on the heels of the Personal Responsibility and Work Opportunity Reconciliation Act of 1996 (see Perlmutter 1997; Parkinson 2000; and Stone 2000). This was partly in response to privatization initiated by the Reagan administration, but many other factors—for example—changes in the tax laws and corporate culture, contributed to this as well.

Numerical Overview

Donations are in the form of grants, company products and/or property, and matching gifts. In their survey of larger firms the Conference Board found that 49 percent of the dollar value of corporate gifts in 2003 was in the form of company products, up from 35 percent in 2002, but this varied greatly by industry (Muirhead 2004:10; see also Greene and Williams 2002:7). The Conference Board also claimed that "more than 6,000 companies and corporate foundations in the United States currently match their employees' gifts to nonprofit organizations" (Muirhead 1999:25). However, it is difficult to ascertain the exact dollar amount.

Looking at the numbers—which include all three types of donations—there is no sign that companies have lost interest in making tax-deductible contributions to charity. Table 8.1 and figure 8.1 show that current dollar and inflation-adjusted charitable contributions rose steadily from 1970 to 2004. Despite recessionary periods, growth through the

TABLE 8.1. THE VALUE OF CORPORATE GIFTS AND GIFTS AS A PERCENTAGE OF PRETAX INCOME 1970–2004 ($ IN BILLIONS)

Year	Value of gifts (current dollars)	Value of gifts (2004 dollars)	Pretax net income (2004 dollars)	Gifts as percentage of pretax net income
1970	0.82	3.99	394.31	1.0
1971	0.85	3.96	433.13	0.9
1972	0.97	4.38	487.17	0.9
1973	1.06	4.51	573.83	0.8
1974	1.10	4.21	566.13	0.7
1975	1.15	4.04	511.03	0.8
1976	1.33	4.42	596.62	0.7
1977	1.54	4.80	655.90	0.7
1978	1.70	4.92	713.02	0.7
1979	2.05	5.33	707.57	0.8
1980	2.25	5.16	581.15	0.9
1981	2.64	5.49	506.53	1.1
1982	3.11	6.09	388.61	1.6
1983	3.67	6.96	443.58	1.6
1984	4.13	7.51	488.38	1.5
1985	4.63	8.13	451.96	1.8
1986	5.03	8.67	423.92	2.0
1987	5.21	8.66	528.11	1.6
1988	5.34	8.53	616.43	1.4
1989	5.46	8.32	584.62	1.4
1990	5.46	7.89	591.88	1.3
1991	5.25	7.28	586.67	1.2
1992	5.91	7.96	620.81	1.3
1993	6.47	8.46	675.95	1.3
1994	6.98	8.90	735.58	1.2
1995	7.35	9.11	835.77	1.1
1996	7.51	9.04	882.54	1.0
1997	8.62	10.14	939.34	1.1
1998	8.46	9.80	832.39	1.2
1999	10.23	11.60	879.78	1.3
2000	10.74	11.78	848.40	1.4
2001	11.66	12.44	755.10	1.6
2002	10.79	11.33	795.91	1.4
2003	11.18	11.48	897.72	1.3
2004	12.00	12.00	985.30	1.2

Source: Giving USA Foundation 2005.

FIGURE 8.1. CORPORATE GIVING IN BILLIONS, 1970–2004
Source: Giving USA Foundation 2005.

1970s and 1980s was steady with a marked increase in giving in the mid-1980s. The increase in contributions in 1986 was probably due both to the 1981 Economic Recovery Tax Act, effective in 1982, which increased the value of company products donated for scientific research and raised the limit on charitable contributions from 5 percent to 10 percent, and the Tax Reform Act of 1986, which took effect in 1987 and dropped the marginal tax rate for corporations from 46 percent to 34 percent (Morgan 1997:779). Contributions continued upward during the 1990s and into the twenty-first century. In 2004 total corporate giving was an estimated $12.0 billion up from the estimated $11.2 billion in 2003 and $10.8 billion in 2002 (in current dollars) (Giving USA Foundation 2005). The number for 2001 was greater, $11.7 billion, because of the terrorist attacks on September 11, 2001. The Foundation Center reported that 543 corporations and corporate foundations pledged or donated $621.5 million to 9/11 causes with some of the money coming from donations budgets and some from other corporate funds (Renz 2002b:3; see also Renz 2002a).

Table 8.1 also shows that charitable contributions as a percentage of pretax income stayed between 0.7 percent and 1.0 percent in the 1970s. Contributions as a percentage of pretax income increased in the 1980s and peaked at 2.0 percent in 1986. From 1990 to 1999 the percentage fluctuated between 1.0 percent and 1.3 percent. Because of lower corporate earnings and 9/11 giving, in 2000, 2001, and 2002 the percentage went to 1.4 percent, 1.6 percent, and 1.4 percent. It was back at 1.3 percent in 2003 and 1.2 percent in 2004, which are comparable to percentages for the 1990s. Corporate charitable contributions constituted 4.8 percent of total giving in 2004 (Giving USA Foundation 2005). This figure is very close to the forty-year average of 5.0 percent, which is also the figure Andrews (1952:19) reported at mid-century. In sum, company philanthropic giving over the past thirty-four years has proven to be resilient and popular among companies in both good times and bad.[3]

Although American companies' influence abroad has increased dramatically since World War II, U.S. corporate giving abroad is quite meager.[4] While there are no exact figures on direct cash and product contributions abroad, the Foundation Center (Renz and Martin 2000:2) reported that between 1994 and 1998 "international giving by corporate foundations more than doubled to $57 million." Furthermore, "international giving by corporate foundations nearly doubled from $57 million in 1998 to $108 million in 2001 while overall corporate foundation grant dollars grew by 56 percent" (Renz and Atienza, 2003:2). Still Renz and Atienza (2003) reported that corporate foundation giving made up only a little more than 3 percent of all international foundation giving in 2001. The Foundation Center (2003:65) estimated that giving for international affairs and development constituted only 1.4 percent of corporate foundation giving in 2001.[5] While international contributions are increasing, they are still concentrated in Western democracies (Muirhead 1999:53).

Management Issues

The management of corporate-nonprofit collaborations has become more complex as ties between companies and nonprofits have expanded. The traditional way of disbursing contributions was for the CEO and his secretary or another corporate officer to review requests and then write a check from his office funds. This is still the practice at many smaller, family businesses (Burlingame and Frishkoff

1996:92). Another strategy is to delegate decision-making to a corporate contributions program, the community affairs/relations department, the public relations department, the communications department, or the human resources department (Tillman 1997:39). A staff member might give a preliminary review but the decision-making would be delegated to a committee of mid-level managers or senior-level executives. A few companies have experimented with committees that have employees from across the firm; however, this is a problem if facilities are widely scattered across the globe. Often in branches or local plants responsibility for small grants is delegated to local managers (Tillman 1997:45).

A popular strategy among larger firms is to create a corporate foundation (see Webb 1996a for an overview). Corporate foundations were not that common until the 1950s, when a number of new foundations were created. They continued to proliferate in the 1970s and early 1980s, were the victims of retrenchment, mergers, and acquisitions in the late 1980s and early 1990s, and rebounded somewhat in the 1990s as new foundations were established accompanying the new wealth of that decade (Hall 1989:236; Webb 1994:44–45). In their 2003 survey of large firms the Conference Board found that 75 percent had a corporate foundation (Muirhead 2004:11). The Foundation Center (Renz and Lawrence 2004:4) reported that 2,362 corporate foundations disbursed $3.46 billion in grants in 2002; they estimated that corporate foundations gave $3.40 billion in 2003, a decline of 2 percent. Of course, if only cash gifts were included, foundations would be administering a higher percentage of corporate giving. The law prohibits foundations from making donations that can benefit the parent company directly (Tillman 1997:14). This puts foundations in an awkward position when companies try to extract *direct* benefit from contributions. Often, questionable expenditures will be charged against operating expenses so as to avoid compromising the foundation.

Corporate foundations have several financial advantages. A common strategy is for companies to make tax-deductible contributions to their foundation from company profits in good times, which then enables them to make donations when profits sag (Muirhead 1999:33). Another strategy is to increase giving to corporate foundations when the tax rate is high or is likely to fall in the near future. This ensures that the firm is able to minimize its taxes, while total disbursements (direct giving plus foundation grants) remain "smooth" over time (Webb 1994; see also Webb 1996b, which extends this discussion). Recently it appears that companies are giving more company stock to their foundations, thus enabling them to make disbursements from dividends or the sale of stock. In the late 1990s, the Foundation Center (Renz and Lawrence 2001:5) found that corporate foundations were paying out less than companies were paying in, resulting in a growth in assets. Previously, corporate foundations had very few assets and were mainly flow-through devices. Webb (1996a) notes that there are considerable tax benefits for doing this.

Relations between corporate giving and foundation staff and other corporate managers are not always harmonious. Himmelstein (1997) studied fifty-five of the largest company giving programs in the United States and found that giving officers in particular had a strong commitment to do something genuinely worthwhile for the communities in which their firms operated. Yet, doing good was difficult to defend in companies that were under attack by disgruntled shareholders, embroiled in cutthroat competition, or vulnerable to crises beyond their control. Because the function often did not directly contribute to the "bottom line," to survive it had to have the support of the CEO or chairman of the board or it had to speak to the strategic interests of the firm. Yet, to ensure its integrity the giving program had to guard against becoming a "plaything" of senior executives or an arm of the marketing/personnel/public relations departments. This is often a difficult tightrope to walk.

Measurement issues are at the center of the controversy. If giving is to be strategic, then managers should be able to measure the results. The Conference Board (Alperson 1996) did one of the few studies to look at these issues. They surveyed contributions and community relations managers and found that "just 44 percent of respondents do some form of measurement or evaluation of their corporate contributions and community programs, while 56 percent report that they benchmark them. Among these, about one-third say they both evaluate and benchmark their programs, while another third say they do not measure at all. Companies that have such evaluation and benchmarking programs report mixed levels of satisfaction with the results" (p. 6). Some of the firms performed these functions themselves; others subcontracted the work to consultants. Recently, the Council on Foundations (2000) published a "tool kit" developed by Walker Information, Inc., to help companies measure the business value of corporate philanthropy by measuring stakeholders' perceptions and intentions. Yet, managers still have difficulty measuring the impact of contributions on the achievement of business goals or the solution of societal problems.

It then comes as no surprise that managers' personal values often matter in making contributions decisions. Buchholtz, Amason, and Rutherford (1999) found that managers' values regarding social responsibility partially mediated the relation between firm resources and giving; Campbell, Gulas, and Gruca (1999), Lerner and Fryxell (1994), and Thompson and Hood (1993) also found that managerial values mattered. Thus while companies have tried to rationalize the process, philanthropic grant making is still highly dependent on managers' values and interests. It is also not surprising that Himmelstein (1997) found a transcorporate network of executives and contribution officers who communicated with each other, embraced a common set of beliefs and language, and consulted with each other on common problems. Because of the uncertainty surrounding donations and the lack of measurement, giving officers and foundation staff often relied on the evaluations and gifts of peers to come to funding decisions and thus the preferences of peers were reflected in who the firm funded (Galaskiewicz and Wasserman 1989; Galaskiewicz and Burt 1991).

There are special problems in managing international philanthropy. Griffiths (1992) argued that corporations need to be open about their activities to diffuse any suspicions some have of corporate involvement in social welfare provision. In many countries government has the primary responsibility for these matters. The Conference Board (Gornitsky 1996) noted that companies often have difficulty identifying reliable nonprofit donees in countries where the nonprofit sector and grant seeking is not as institutionalized (see also Flaherty 1992). Proposals are written more informally and often companies have to translate them into English. Grants need to be made in local currencies. From the perspective of the donor, expectations are often excessive. Tax laws differ across countries so that certain types of gifts in certain countries are not considered "charity." According to U.S. tax law, a direct contribution to a foreign charitable organization is not deductible under Section 170 of the Internal Revenue Code (Lashbrooke 1985:225; Internal Revenue Service 2001a). There are also conditions on foundation grants to foreign nonprofits that have discouraged many from giving. Although some have been liberalized (Schwinn 2001:40), post-9/11 sentiment may restrict foundation activity, especially in the Arab world. Many companies solved these problems by having country managers administer funds in a decentralized manner and report them as ordinary business expenses. Others simply funded U.S.-based 501(c)(3) nonprofit organizations working in relevant countries overseas (Gornitsky 1996:15) or used gift brokers such as United Way International (Blum 1999:12).

Motives

In this section we review the literature on why companies engage in philanthropic partnerships. There is more disagreement than agreement. Researchers cannot agree on the motives, and commentators cannot agree on what ought to motivate philanthropic collaborations. To complicate matters, one often finds different motives in the same firm, and sometimes in the same executives.

Increase Profits and Improve Financial Performance. In the 1980s and 1990s many management theorists argued that companies should give to further their business interests and enhance corporate performance.[6] Stendardi (1992) and C. Smith (1994b) argued that contributions should be used to market products and services, boost employee productivity, overcome regulatory obstacles, and so on. They called for companies to use all their assets to maximize their earnings (see also Mescon and Tilson 1987; Zetlin 1990; Stevenson 1993; C. Smith 1994a). The Conference Board further legitimated the "new corporate philanthropy," surveying company giving managers on how they were finding more synergy with other company departments, aligning giving to company business goals, developing ways to measure program results, and spreading around ownership of the function (Alperson 1995:9; see also Garone 1996).

The most common strategy is to use philanthropic contributions to enhance the firm's (or the industry's) image and generate "good will" among stakeholders. The latter includes customers, employees, investors, regulators, or the communities in which firms operate. Webb and Farmer (1996:32–33) argue that a good image can either increase product demand or help reduce operating costs. Managers seem drawn to this rationale. In Marx's (1999:190) study a "favorable company image" was the second most important goal cited by giving officers in strategic giving programs. By "doing good" the company is seen as more public-regarding and less selfish. Supposedly this translates into a reputation for being more honest and trustworthy, which should make the firm a more attractive business partner. "The goal is to become known as a good corporate citizen . . . then, somewhere, somehow, your good image pays off" (Henricks 1991:31). Using data for 2003, Cone, Inc. (2003), found that 89 percent of those surveyed said that in light of the Enron collapse and WorldCom financial situation, it is more important than ever for companies to be socially responsible. Furthermore, a company's commitment to social issues would affect which companies people want to see doing business in their community (84 percent), where they want to work (77 percent), and which stocks or mutual funds they want to invest in (66 percent). Firms regarded as good corporate citizens could realize increased sales, have fewer labor problems, secure favorable legislation, or be given the "benefit of the doubt" in difficult situations. One cannot "bank" one's image or know when one's image "pays off," but it is potentially a valuable corporate asset (Fombrun 1996).

To test the reputational benefits argument, researchers typically identify firms that might realize some reputational gain from giving and then see if they are more likely to be donors. For the most part they have been successful. Burt (1983:197–221) found that industries with a larger percentage of sales to households made greater contributions measured in absolute dollars, per capita dollars, or as a proportion of profits. However, Galaskiewicz (1985, 1997), in his study of Twin Cities firms, found no effect of consumer sales on giving using firm-level data. Several researchers found an association between expenditures on advertising, contributions, and market position. For example, Fry, Keim, and Meiners (1982), Levy and Shatto (1978), Levy and Shatto (1980), and Navarro (1988) all found positive correlations between advertising budgets and corporate giving levels.

Researchers have also studied the relation between firms' personnel needs and company giving. Here the evidence is more mixed. The Council on Foundations reported that 60 percent of the CEOs they surveyed said that contributions to charity helped to attract good people to the community and company (Daniel Yankelovich Group 1988:41). Approximately 80 percent of the larger firms cited this as one of their rationales for giving (see also McElroy and Siegfried 1986 and Yankelovich, Skelly, and White 1982). Nelson (1970) found that an industry with 10 percent more employees gave 2.7 percent more in contributions, when controlling for sales, profits, and officers' compensation. More recently, Fry et al. (1982) and Navarro (1988) found positive correlations between labor intensities and marginal changes in contributions. However, Siegfried, McElroy, and Biernot-Fawkes (1983) and Galaskiewicz (1985) found no effect of labor intensities on giving and Galaskiewicz (1997) found a negative effect.

Research has also looked at the effect of negative public relations on giving. In an early study Ermann (1978) found that firms that were particularly vulnerable to public criticism—oil companies and firms that recently increased their profits—were among the biggest contributors to the Public Broadcasting System. Miles (1982) described how the tobacco industry, when challenged by the Sloan-Kettering Commission and the Surgeon General's report on smoking's health hazards, responded by giving millions of dollars to universities and research institutes that did work on cancer-related topics. This put the tobacco companies in touch with research that was of immediate interest to them but the contributions also signaled the public that the industry wanted to support "objective" research on the effects of cigarette smoking. More recently, Werbel and Wortman (2000) studied 163 companies between 1988 and 1993 and found that giving to educational institutions increased following negative media exposure of the company. King (2001) interpreted the National Football League's Real Men Wear Pink partnership with the Susan G. Komen Foundation (a breast cancer charity) as a way to counteract players' alleged propensity for criminal activity with images of their community service and caring behavior.

Stakeholder research shows that corporate citizenship and contributions do enhance company reputations. Galaskiewicz (1985) and Fombrun and Shanley (1990) found that companies that gave more to charities were regarded by constituencies outside the firm as being especially generous and more socially responsible (see also Haley 1991 and White 1980). In his study of Minneapolis–St. Paul firms Galaskiewicz (1985) also found that companies that gave more to charity were regarded by business leaders as more successful business enterprises. Sen and Bhattacharya (2001) found that corporate social responsibility initiatives improved consumers' evaluations of firms. Turban and Greening (1997) found that firms' corporate social performance made them attractive employers to prospective employees; Albinger and Freeman (2000) found the same results but only for prospective employees who had high levels of job choice. In a fascinating study Williams and Barrett (2000) found an interaction among criminal citations (for OSHA and EPA violations), giving, and corporate reputations—that is, firms that gave more to philanthropic causes experienced less negative image fallout from criminal citations than those that gave less.[7]

Although many claim that philanthropic contributions can benefit the bottom line, the evidence showing a relation between indicators of corporate social responsibility (a construct that often includes contributions but measures much more) and financial performance is weak or unclear. Sturdivant and Ginter (1977), Wokutch and Spencer (1987), McGuire, Sundgren, and Schneeweis (1988), Lewin and Sabater (1996), and Waddock and Graves (1997) show a positive association, while Abbott and Monsen (1979), Cochran and Wood (1984), Aupperle, Carroll, and Hatfield (1985), Berman, Wicks, Kotha, and Jones (1999), and McWilliams and Siegel (2000) found little relation between the two. Reviewing research from the 1970s, Arlow and Gannon (1982:235) concluded that the relation among social responsiveness, corporate citizenship, and financial performance was inconclusive. After reviewing the literature in the 1980s and 1990s, Burlingame (1994), Wood and Jones (1996), as well as the Conference Board (Garone 1999) came to a similar conclusion. Reviewing studies from 1972 to 2002, Margolis and Walsh (2003) found either a positive or no effect of corporate social performance on financial performance and only rarely a negative effect.[8]

Advance Managerial Utility. A second explanation for charitable contributions is that they are a form of executive perquisite and serve managerial utility. Drawing on Oliver Williamson's (1964) model of discretionary behavior, one could argue that some managers prefer corporate contributions as well as after-tax profits. Managers may be motivated by religious commitments, political beliefs, personal interests in a nonprofit, or access to elite social circles. In any event, executives may use corporate contributions to further their own interests, thus making contributions a form of executive compensation.

Economists argue that if both profits and contributions are important to managers, fluctuations in tax rates should affect contributions, but if contributions are driven only by profits, tax rates should have no effect on contributions (Clotfelter 1985b:188–93). The higher the tax rate, the lower the cost of an additional dollar of contributions and the greater the incentive to contribute, although this comes at the price of lower profits. Most researchers have looked at the complement of the marginal tax rate or the average tax rate; they call this the "price" of a contribution.[9] Currently, firms can deduct charitable gifts up to 10 percent of pretax net income (in 1981 this increased from 5 percent), and this sets a ceiling on giving; this is seldom reached, however. Researchers found that changes in the tax rate do affect company contributions, although the price effect for corporate giving appears to be considerably smaller than for individual contributions (Clotfelter 1985b, 1985a:203). Schwartz (1968) examined data extending from 1936 through 1961, analyzing industrial groups together and then nine separate industry categories. Controlling for the average after-tax income and then for cash flows, the complement of the average tax rate consistently had a negative effect on contributions. Nelson (1970) looked at industry-level data between 1936 and 1963 and analyzed aggregate after-tax corporation income, the complement of the marginal tax rate, and aggregate contributions of corporations. He, too, found a price effect, but his analysis produced a lower price-elasticity coefficient. Levy and Shatto (1978) and Clotfelter (1985b) had similar findings on the relation between the complement of the marginal tax rate and giving; Navarro (1988) found no tax effect; and Boatsman and Gupta (1996) found a negative relation between firm-level estimated marginal tax rates and contributions. In general, these findings suggest that giving may very well be driven by managerial utility.

Others argue that if contributions are managerial perks, firms disciplined by tight principal control should give less to charity. In contrast, firms with more diffuse ownership and stronger insider control—and thus greater managerial autonomy—are free to give more. Because of the weak coupling of charitable giving to company performance, managers who are accountable to powerful owning interests (families, individuals, or corporate investors) are less likely to make contributions. Owners will prefer to make their own gifts without the help of managers (unless they can reduce executive compensation by substituting "perks" for pay). Only when managers are free of ownership supervision are they free to make contributions, if that's their preference. Whether or not they choose to do so is another matter and may depend on exogenous factors (see also Shaw and Post 1993; Kahn 1997).

Empirical work on ownership control has been suggestive. Atkinson and Galaskiewicz (1988) found that Twin Cities companies gave less to charity if the CEO owned a greater percentage of stock or there was someone other than the CEO who owned more than 5 percent of the company's stock. In a reanalysis of the data, Galaskiewicz (1997) found that the effect of peer pressure on contributions was weaker if the firm came under the control of large outside investors. In their studies of corporate boards and contributions, Wang and Coffey (1992; see also Coffey and Wang 1998) found that as the ratio of insiders to outsiders increased, charitable contributions increased. This supports the agency hypothesis, since "a higher proportion of outsiders on a board can better monitor and control the opportunistic behavior of the incumbent management" (p. 771). They also found that the percentage of stock owned by inside directors, a measure of managerial control, was positively related to firms' charitable contributions. Bartkus, Morris, and Seifert (2002:332) found that large donors had significantly fewer large blockholders than small donors and large donors had a significantly lower percentage of stock owned by institutional investors than small donors. On the other hand, Navarro (1988) found no relation between managerial control and contributions.

Another body of work examines the role that social acceptance or status plays in motivating contributions. Firms and their executives do not operate in a social vacuum, but are subject to various social pressures to make charitable contributions. This pressure can come from executives at peer institutions, customers, business and civic leaders, or friends and neighbors. While self-aggrandizement may be a motive, business people also know that making contributions to the right nonprofits can earn the company new business and/or keep old business contacts happy. Thus finding a social context effect does not necessarily mean that executives are using company funds to increase their social status.

Several studies have found that other firms, CEOs, and business leaders influence company contributions. Useem (1991) found that broader local business support of the arts resulted in greater individual company giving to the arts, and giving to the arts increased even more if companies reported that their giving program was highly responsive to outside business pressures (see also Useem and Kutner 1986). Navarro (1988) found that firms in cities with tithing clubs were giving at much higher rates than firms in cities without these clubs, and McElroy and Siegfried (1986) found that a firm increased its contributions if other firms in their city had higher contributions. The authors attributed this to "expectations" and suggested that a great deal of corporate giving was motivated by the desire to be responsive to respected peers in the business community.

In a study of U.S. and U.K. firms Useem (1984) showed that an "inner circle" of business elites and peer pressure was an important factor in motivating corporate community service. Companies with more "inner circle" directors on their boards were larger contributors in general and more likely to be recognized as generous contributors to the arts or members of arts or educational organizations (pp. 126–27). In his study of Minneapolis–St. Paul companies Galaskiewicz (1985, 1997) found that companies gave more if their CEO, top executives, or board members moved in the social circles of local business and civic leaders who promoted corporate giving. In open-ended interviews executives and local leaders reported that peer pressure was an important factor in motivating company contributions (1985:72–75). In a study of 160 corporate foundations Werbel and Carter (2002) found that giving was greater if the CEO was a member of many nonprofits and she or he sat on the foundation's board of trustees. Eckstein (2001) described how small businesses in an Italian working-class suburb were pressured into giving by local leaders and groups. Although social acceptance was a factor, merchants knew that business success in these neighborhoods depended on their being good corporate citizens. Besser (1998) found that business owners in thirty Iowa communities were more likely to assume leadership roles (but not more likely to give support to the community) if they thought their community exhibited high levels of collective action and expected that they would participate.

At a macro level Kirchberg (1995) studied eleven metropolitan areas between 1977 and 1991 and found that increases in service-sector income, decreases in manufacturing-sector income, and increases in the population's educational attainment were positively correlated with changes in corporate arts support. Wolpert (1993), in a secondary analysis of local generosity that included corporate giving as a dependent variable, found that giving was greater where larger corporations were prominent, income was greater, unemployment was lower, and the welfare ideology was more liberal. Both authors interpreted their findings in terms of "local attitudes and regional climates of corporate giving" (Kirchberg 1995:316).

Further Social Welfare. Many companies genuinely seek to advance social welfare with their contributions. *Smith vs. Barlow* was important because it legitimated giving that was for the collective good. The theme of social responsibility and moral obligation emerged in Himmelstein's (1997) study. Here "doing good" was as important as "looking well." Reynold Levy (1999), the former president of the AT&T Foundation, echoed this theme. Marx's (1999) nationwide study of 194 strategic philanthropy programs in 1993 found that corporate contribution managers said that "high-quality community life" (96.4 percent), "improved community services" (93.8 percent), and "racial harmony" (83.5 percent) were important or extremely important goals of their giving programs (p. 190). Galaskiewicz (1985, 1997) found similar sentiments in the Minneapolis–St. Paul business community.

What is behind this interest in social welfare? Some firms have a strong sense of corporate social responsibility. Davis (1973:312) defined corporate social responsibility as "the firms' consideration of, and response to, issues beyond the narrow economic, technical, and legal requirements of the firm . . . [to] accomplish social benefits along with the traditional economic gains which the firm seeks." Wood (1991) points out that there is a strong sense of obligation or duty among some firms and managers to help solve problems they create or problems related to their activities. Shaw and Post (1993) simply say firms have a moral obligation to behave in a socially responsible manner. This viewpoint became popular in the 1970s as business was considering how to react to urban unrest in the United States (Hall 1997). More recently, the social-responsibility theme has resurfaced in discussions of sustainable development and social justice (Whiting and Bennett 2001).

Some companies believe that their own future depends on the long-term survival and prosperity of society. Firms recognize the importance of physical and societal infrastructure. Recognizing that a "healthy corporation cannot exist in a sick community" (Stendardi 1992:22), corporations should tend to the infrastructure that will ensure their long-term success—for example, supporting environmental efforts helps to ensure that there will be natural resources in the future, supporting K-12 education ensures a talented workforce for the future, and so on. While companies have an eye on the benefits they might realize, they must also understand that others will be free-riding on their generosity. Thus giving to benefit social welfare at best serves firms' "enlightened self interest" (Baumol 1970).

Other companies believe that social welfare can best be served if social institutions would emulate the "business model." Thus firms should either become dominant partners with nonprofits or compete aggressively against nonprofits and government in providing services, thus showing them how to be efficient and effective. In the mid-1980s many businesses became involved in social welfare, education, and other human services, because, it was thought, they could do a better job "fixing" society than either the public or not-for-profit sectors. Control Data Corporation's efforts in the 1980s to use computer-based technology for education and job training were reflective of President William Norris's belief that many of society's social, educational, and welfare problems could better be solved using a business approach (Worthy 1987). Galaskiewicz and Bielefeld (1998: Chapter 2) reported that during the 1980s business executives in the Twin Cities went one step further and pushed for several social innovations ranging from health-maintenance organizations to school vouchers and charter schools. Dees (1998) says that by the 1990s "a new pro-business zeitgeist has made for-profit initiatives more acceptable in the nonprofit world" (p. 56). The idea was to make solving society's problems somehow profitable, or, if that was not possible, to expose sleepy nonprofits and bloated government bureaucracies to business culture and practices through partnerships or other means. This belief in the value of the business model was an important development because it provided a rationale for businesses to look for profits in health care, education, or the social welfare arena. Self-interested investment becomes almost a form of public service, because doing things in a businesslike manner supposedly furthered the collective good (Dienhart 1988).

Cui Bono: Who Benefits?

It is difficult to assess who benefits and what it means. Researchers will use different categories of recipients, making comparisons across studies and over time difficult. When compiling numbers researchers have used the most readily available data—for example, from convenience samples, for the largest firms, or from IRS 990-PFs (for corporate foundations). Missing data are significant and few researchers attempt to address this problem. Researchers have coded only grants over a certain amount of money, and, although the recipient's name is available, coders have not always known how the grant was used. By looking at who benefits, we are tempted to infer motives. Gifts to higher education could be construed as more profit-oriented or strategic; gifts to arts and culture as serving managerial utility; donations to the United Way as more public-regarding; and money to public policy advocates as ideologically motivated. However, such assumptions are dangerous since peer solicitation is an important tactic of United Way; matching gifts are important in corporate giving to colleges and universities; gifts to theaters and orchestras can be used to expose product and company name to upscale audiences; and donations to public interest groups may be for the services they provide (e.g., family planning) rather than the positions they advocate (e.g., abortion rights). Given these problems, we should proceed cautiously.

The Conference Board provides information on to whom large companies contribute. In table 8.2 we present figures for 2001, 2002, and 2003 (Muirhead 2004:31).[10] We see an increase in the percentage going to health and human services and a decline in the percentage going to education.

TABLE 8.2. DISTRIBUTION OF THE CONTRIBUTIONS OF LARGE CORPORATIONS, 2001–2003

Area	2001 (N=183)	2002 (N=205)	2003 (N=232)
Health and human services	31.6%	37.9%	40.9%
Education	31.9%	29.3%	21.5%
Culture and art	8.0%	8.3%	5.5%
Civic and community activities	12.0%	12.3%	10.2%
Environment	[a]	1.3%	1.9%
Other and unknown	16.5%	10.9%	20.0%
Total	100.0%	100.0%	100.0%

Sources: Muirhead 2004:31.
[a] Previously included in civic and community activities

The percentages going to civic and community activities and culture and art have decreased slightly, although partly this was due to environmental grants being reallocated to their own category.[11] These numbers are comparable to Helland and Smith's (2003) analysis of cash contributions among a sample of 262 Fortune 500 firms (and their foundations) in 1998. They found that 26.6 percent of the total went to education; 27.7 percent went to health, social services, and social science; 8.7 percent went to the arts; and 1.1 percent went to environmental causes.

Higher education and arts and culture are often viewed as the big beneficiaries of corporate largesse. Earlier we noted that corporate contributions were estimated at 5.6 percent of total contributions in 2003. The Council for Aid to Education (2004: Table 1) reported that corporate giving accounted for 18.0 percent of all donations to higher education in 2003, the same as in 1998 and 2002. The Theatre Communications Group (2004:23) reported that corporate donations accounted for 13.2 percent of contributions to 214 nonprofit theaters surveyed in 2003, up from 11.1 percent of contributions to 190 nonprofit theaters in 2002 (Theatre Communications Group 2003:17). The American Symphony Orchestra League (2005) reported that business and corporate foundation giving accounted for 15.6 percent of total support in 2003 and 15.2 percent in 2002. This was based on a survey of 192 U.S. League members that participated in the League's 2002–3 Orchestra Statistical Report survey and is extrapolated to America's 1,200 adult orchestras. Although these institutions are heavily dependent upon corporate donors for gifts, they have many other sources of revenue. Corporate donations accounted for only 1.4 percent of higher education expenditures in 2003 (Council for Aid to Education 2004), 5.7 percent of all theater expenditures in 2003 (Theatre Communications Group 2004:24), and 6.5 percent of all orchestras' expenses in 2003 (American Symphony Orchestra League 2005).

Several interest groups, such as the Capital Research Center (CRC) and the National Committee for Responsive Philanthropy (NCRP), have done research on the political orientations of nonprofits supported by corporations. CRC (Yablonski 2001) focuses on the grants by *Forbes* magazine's 250 largest publicly held firms to political advocacy organizations. They coded grant recipients on the basis of their Left or Right leanings. Based on their coding of these organizations and calculations, the forty-five corporations that gave $250,000 or more to public affairs groups in 1997 contributed $4.41 to tax-exempt groups that were sympathetic to the Left for every $1.00 they gave to conservative and free-market-oriented nonprofits (p. 3). NCRP (Paprocki 2000) reported on the grant-making of leading companies in fifteen selected industries in 1995; 124 of 217 firms participated. Their overall grants totaled $1.3 billion, 17 percent of all grant-making from American corporations (p. 6). They found that although racial and ethnic minorities constitute 29 percent of the U.S. population, only 14 percent of corporate giving went to programs where racial/ethnic minorities were the primary beneficiaries (p. 17). Insurance, gas/oil, and banking were the most generous industries that gave to racial/ethnic communities; the least generous were media and entertainment, personal care products, health and pharmaceuticals, and computers and related products (p. 20).

Other researchers have studied who gives to whom in different communities. In the three southern California communities he studied, Nevarez (2000) found that entertainment firms funded environmental groups that were more Leftist-leaning, while software and entertainment firms funded higher education, which was a partner in developing information technology and training programs. Firms that were dependent upon the local infrastructure—for example, banks and the hospitality industry—supported more-traditional charities like the United Way and Boys and Girls Clubs. Nevarez argued that economic restructuring may be leading to a weakening of the political hegemony of local businesses (the "growth machine") and the emergence of coalitions between newer industries and local nonprofits. Studies in Minneapolis–St. Paul showed that status and networks played a big role in explaining which nonprofits corporate donors supported. Galaskiewicz and Rauschenbach (1989) found that corporations were more likely to give to cultural organizations that had their executives sitting on the board of directors or a more prestigious reputation. Studying a broader range of nonprofits, Galaskiewicz (1985) found that nonprofits received more corporate funding if more full-time giving officers among local firms recognized and thought highly of the nonprofit, and Galaskiewicz and Wasserman (1989) found that nonprofits were more likely to receive a donation from a firm if either they were well regarded by local elites, their own board had interlocks with nonprofits that received funding from that donor in the past, or they received funding in the past from donors who had ties to the donor.

Strategic Collaborations

Strategic collaborations are a second type of corporate-nonprofit partnership. We consider event sponsorships and donations of product/equipment to nonprofits. Here the company is hoping to realize direct, exclusive benefits from giving cash or products to nonprofits, but often firms have a social welfare purpose as well. On the one hand, these collaborations are quasi-charitable, because in most instances expenditures can be deducted as charitable contributions (Kahn 1997:669; Knauer 1994:67–71), and they further the missions of the nonprofit partners. On the other hand, they are quasi-commercial, because the firm is seeking direct benefit. Marketing departments often handle sponsorships and equipment donations, and giving is often decentralized; for example, each division has its own marketing department and sponsorships often happen at the plant or store level, but it is not uncommon for marketing, community relations, and foundation staff to work together on projects.

Corporate spending on sponsorships of all kinds is considerable, although it is difficult to know exactly how much is spent on nonprofits. IEG, Inc. (2003), a research and consulting firm, estimated that the value of sponsorships in North America may reach $11.1 billion and worldwide $28.0 billion in 2004. They also presented a chart on the likely distribution of sponsorship spending in North America in 2004. Sixty-nine percent should go to sports, 10 percent to entertainment tours and attractions, 7 percent to festivals, fairs, and annual events, 9 percent to cause marketing, and 5 percent to the arts. A company example is General Motors' ten-year sponsorship of the Olympics, worth roughly $900 million (Meredith 1999). An example on the nonprofit side is the Roundabout Theatre Company in New York, which sold the naming rights to its new theater to American Airlines for $8.5 million and to its lounge to Nabisco for $500,000 (Pogrebin 2000).

In event sponsorships, typically the company pays an amount of money to the nonprofit in exchange for the right to display its name, logo, or products at some event, on the premises, or in conjunction with some program of the not-for-profit. Sponsorships can range from paying for a theater season or concert series, purchasing naming rights to buildings, buying "tents" at golf tournaments, funding mega-events such as the Olympics, to supporting Little League baseball (see Caesar 1986 for other examples). Nonprofits can treat sponsorships as contributions if they only give the sponsor visibility and do not actively promote the company or its product (Internal Revenue Service 2001b; U.S. Department of Treasury 2002). In her study of media sponsorships, Bryan (1991) showed that companies seek to gain credibility by borrowing legitimacy from the event or cause. Thus firms are careful that the event and nonprofit fit with the firm, controversy is avoided, and audiences see the sponsorship. The focus is usually on the event—which is supposed to be fun—rather than on the problem that, in most cases, is serious.

Not all sponsorships go smoothly for corporations. For example, sponsors can lose control over the event, which results in negative publicity. In their case study of Hands Across America (which happened on May 25, 1986), Post and Waddock (1989) described how there was considerable criticism in the media in the weeks following the event, although it raised more than $25 million and netted $16 million. Critics focused on how slowly the money was distributed, how regions and locales were getting less back than they donated, and how none of this really reduced hunger or homelessness. The authors speculated that this may have been due partly to the huge business marketing presence that gave the event more of a commercial flavor than a social cause and raised suspicions among many.

A second type of strategic partnership is the donation of product or equipment to nonprofits in such a way that prospective customers are exposed to the product while it is being utilized for related purposes. Numbers on product donations are difficult to come by and not all have marketing implications. The *Chronicle of Philanthropy* (Greene and Williams 2002:7) reported product giving of $377 million, $288 million, and $283 million by Pfizer, Bristol-Myers Squibb, and Merck and Company in 2001. Microsoft and IBM gave away $179 million and $92 million, and Safeway and Kroger Company gave away $60 million and $52 million respectively. In a comparative study of large manufacturers the Conference Board found that pharmaceuticals, chemicals, and printing, publishing, and media were, by far, the largest donors of non-cash gifts in 2003 (Muirhead 2004).

Why the large number of product contributions? Partly this is due to changes in the law. Under the Economic Recovery Tax Act of 1981, manufacturers could deduct as charitable contributions the cost of the equipment donated plus half of the difference between the cost and selling price of the equipment, if they give the equipment to educational institutions and the latter uses it as scientific equipment or apparatus (Useem 1987:352). Several computer companies, for example, IBM, AT&T, Apple, and Hewlett-Packard, took this opportunity to donate considerable inventory to colleges and universities. In 1997 corporations that made computer technology or equipment could also get an expanded deduction for gifts to elementary or secondary schools (Greene and Williams 2002:16). A similar deduction is available for those wishing to make contributions to nonprofits that benefit infants, the needy, and the ill (Useem 1987:352), which applies to in-kind donations of pharmaceutical firms and food companies especially.

While computer companies rationalized these gifts as part of their philanthropic commitment to higher education, Joyce (1987) argued that in reality there were many direct benefits that they hoped to realize, for example, access to leading-edge researchers and prospective employees and opportunities to experiment with new operating systems and software, cultivate relations with prospective institutional customers, and wean future individual customers on their products. A decade later the *Chronicle of Higher Education* made similar observations about the benefits of Microsoft's product donations to colleges and universities (Guernsey 1998). When five drug companies pledged to donate millions of dollars' worth of medicine, health services, and other support to poorer countries (including Africa) hit hard by the AIDS pandemic, critics charged that this was a way to deflect world criticism and avoid cutting prices or allowing wider use of generic copies of their drugs (Blum 2000b:10).

Few doubt that many product donations are expected to produce direct benefit to the firm; however, others, for example, donations of unsold food to food banks, probably do not.

One recurring problem with sponsorships and product/equipment giveaways is that it is difficult to measure direct benefit. How do managers assess value? Is brand recognition enough, or does one measure sales? An issue of the *Journal of Advertising Research* (Kover 2001) addressed these questions and showed how to measure success or failure of event sponsorships, looking at changes in stock prices (or returns) and responses to survey questionnaires. Yet Dean (1999) argues that the link between the sponsor and the event and the sponsor's product and the event is often not obvious to the consumer. For example, in his research he found that sponsorships affected only consumers' perception of the firm's citizenship, but had little effect on perceptions of product quality and uniqueness or brand esteem. The difficulty of measuring effects is reflected in a survey of nearly 200 leading sponsorships' decision-makers in March of 2001. The IEG (2001) found that "72 percent reported they allocate either nothing or no more than 1 percent of their sponsorship budget to concurrent or post-event research. . . . more than three-quarters spend $5,000 or less per deal on external research prior to making sponsorships decisions" (pp. 1, 4). Sponsors relied heavily on the organizations they sponsored for information on demographics, psychographics, attendance figures, and growth trends, but these data do not tell if people's attitudes toward the brand were affected or if they intend to buy the product.

There are many other varieties of strategic partnerships, but the one thing they all have in common is that there are mixed motives. For example, Kotler and Lee (2005) describe "corporate social marketing" where firms will partner with nonprofits and/or governments on a campaign to change behavior that will have larger welfare benefits, for example, water conservation or a reduction in tooth decay. The firm utilizes its marketing power to bring about a change in behavior, but this directly helps to promote one or more of its product lines, for example, water-saving devices or toothpaste. There is also "venture philanthropy" where donors/investors (often high-tech entrepreneurs) will target nonprofits for support and help them to launch businesses or other revenue-generating programs. Sometimes the transfers are in the form of low- or no-interest loans that the fund expects to be repaid; sometimes they are grants. Many seek a seat on the board of directors and demand measurable indicators of progress, but it is not clear if venture philanthropists make money off the deal (for examples, see Billiterri 2000; see also Letts, Ryan, and Grossman 1997; Frumkin 2003). Dees (1994, 1998) describes "social enterprises"—which could be nonprofit or for-profit organizations—that seek to accrue revenues through commercial ventures but also have an interest in making society better. The social enterprise authors argue that serving society and the bottom line are equal for many for-profits and nonprofits, and partnering in commercial ventures is an excellent way for these organizations to live up to their dual mission. Again, in all these examples, motives are mixed. Companies have an immediate interest in their "bottom line," but they also are interested in furthering the mission of the nonprofits they collaborate with.

Commercial Collaborations

Commercial collaborations are a third type of corporate-nonprofit partnership. We focus on cause-related marketing, licensing of names and logos, and scientific collaboration, but there are many other examples (see Weisbrod 1998b; Weeden 1998; Pankratz and Gibson 1999; Austin 2000a, 2000b; Schwinn 2000; Guthrie and McQuarrie 2003). In these partnerships companies again are looking for direct and exclusive benefits, but now benefits are relatively easy to measure and there is little expressed concern about social welfare. The nonprofit partner hopes to use the funds from these commercial enterprises to subsidize its related program service activities, but the activity itself is unrelated to the mission. Thus it is relatively easy for the nonprofit partner to measure benefits as well. This type of partnership has garnered a great deal of attention recently, because of the scope of the dollars involved and the forms that it is now taking in practice. Often partners form new joint ventures that are for-profit legal entities that sell ownership shares and enjoy limited liability, yet each partner—and its respective mission—remains intact. Weisbrod (1998b:2, 6) describes multimillion-dollar deals between the American Medical Association and Sunbeam, Chicago's Field Museum of Natural History and McDonald's and the Walt Disney Company, and the University of Michigan and Nike. Weeden (1998:3–4) described deals between the American Red Cross and Primestar, the Jane Goodall Institute and HBO, the American Society for the Prevention of Cruelty to Animals and the Walt Disney Company, Save the Children and Denny's, and the All Kids Foundation and Tyco.

In cause-related marketing, a company chooses a cause, charity, or nonprofit organization to adjoin itself to and advertises this newly formed partnership (Varadarajan and Menon 1988; Andreasen 1996). Both parties benefit, because typically the firm gives a percentage of sales to the nonprofit, and the company increases sales because of its association with a credible nonprofit (Garrison 1990). That some charity receives a percentage of the sales supposedly induces the customer to patronize the vendor. A variant on this is the affinity card program. Here a bank offers a credit card with a nonprofit's name and logo on it and then markets the card to the organization's members. The organization is promised a percentage of the total sales as the customers use the cards (Williams 1999:49). Leder (2002:8) reports that more than 1,000 colleges and universities offer affinity cards and MBNA, the leading provider, has three million alumni from 700 schools carrying their card. Some schools have expanded their programs, offering special rates on checking accounts, mortgages, and insurance to alumni.

Another variant is the shopping Web site, for example, 4Charity.com. Here a company creates online shopping sites that may allow shoppers to designate a portion of their purchases for charity, for example, food to hunger organizations. Sometimes the retailer will promise to match the donation. In almost all cases the Web company will split the affiliate fees it receives from retailers with participating charities (see Moore and Williams 1999; Fix 2001). Varadarajan and Menon (1988) found that companies they surveyed paid for cause marketing from advertising or sales promotion budgets (see also Andreasen 1996). More recently, a survey of 211 companies released by Cone, Inc., found that in most firms the majority of the money spent on cause-related programs came from the corporate giving program or corporate foundation (Blum 2000a). On the nonprofits' side the income is generally exempt from unrelated business income tax.[12]

Several case studies and surveys have demonstrated that cause-related marketing works well for both parties. The American Express Corporation's partnership with the Statue of Liberty in 1984 was the most visible example. Card usage increased 28 percent over the previous year, the number of new cards issued rose 45 percent, and the Statue of Liberty restoration fund received $1.7 million from American Express (Wall 1984). Other research has shown that cause-related marketing increases public awareness of the cause (Garrison 1990), expands the organization's base of support, and generates a more positive image of the nonprofit among the public. Hemphill (1996) describes how environmental groups have formed a number of successful marketing partnerships with businesses. Cone, Inc. (2000), released a five-year study done by Roper-Starch Worldwide that showed that by 1998, 74 percent of consumers thought that cause programs were an acceptable business practice (up from 66 percent in 1993), 83 percent had a more positive image of companies who supported a cause they cared about (compared to 84 percent in 1993), 65 percent said they would switch brands and 61 percent retailers, in order to be associated with a good cause (compared to 66 percent and 62 percent in 1993), and 87 percent of employees at companies with a cause program felt a strong sense of loyalty to their employer as opposed to 67 percent of those whose employers did not have such a program.

Not all cause-related campaigns are successful. In their study of medium-size firms that gave to the arts, File and Prince (1995) found that less than a third of those that had developed cause-related marketing programs described themselves as very satisfied with the outcomes (see also File and Prince 2000). Mescon and Tilson (1987) warned that firms and their causes become highly dependent upon and accountable to one another in a joint marketing initiative. Worse still, at the turn of the century many dot-com companies that hoped to make money by partnering with nonprofits on online shopping malls have gone out of business, and returns to nonprofits have been far lower than expected (Fix 2001).

The licensing of the names and logos of nonprofits is a second type of commercial partnership and has been the most controversial.[13] As described by the New York Attorneys General (1999:3), "The nonprofit organization agrees to sell the right to use its name and logo in the promotion of the commercial sponsor's products. In return, the commercial sponsor pays the nonprofit organizations substantial amounts of money for the use of the nonprofit's name and logo in product advertising and through its marketing campaign provides significant publicity for the nonprofit and its message." The same Attorneys General report said that in 1998, businesses paid more than $535 million to nonprofit groups alone for the use of their name or logo in advertising products (1999:7). Much of the activity is carried out in the health-care sector with the American Medical Association's proposed agreement with the Sunbeam Corporation in 1997 as the prototype of how controversial these arrangements can get. In this case the AMA agreed to have its name mentioned in Sunbeam marketing materials and ads for various products and its seal was to appear in advertising and on product packaging, but it had not tested or evaluated any of the products involved and thus was not in a position to say that Sunbeam products were superior to others. Because of the outcry surrounding the announcement of the deal, the AMA reneged on its contract and ended up paying Sunbeam $9.9 million for damages and expenses (pp. 18–19). Yet since then numerous health organizations have endorsed company products, most with exclusive agreements (see New York Attorneys General 1999:8).

The Attorneys General have concerns, because advertisements like these can lead the consumer to believe that the product has been endorsed and/or tested by the nonprofit and was shown to be superior, when only the nonprofit's name is somehow identified with the product in the ad but no product testing has been done nor has it been endorsed by the nonprofit. Also, consumers can be led to believe that, like in cause-related marketing, the advertiser will make a contribution to the nonprofit if the consumer buys the product, but there is often no agreement to that effect. There is also the issue that the advertiser seldom mentions in the ad that it paid the nonprofit for the use of its name and logo and that the nonprofit has agreed not to enter into a similar agreement with a competitor (p. 1). The Attorneys General warn that companies and nonprofits should ensure that they address these issues or risk being in violation of state consumer laws (p. 4).

Scientific collaboration is another type of commercial partnership. One form that this takes is the research park (or science park or technology park) or technology incubator. Companies become tenants of the park with the expectation that close proximity to a university, its people, and resources and other high-tech firms will ease technology transfer (see Klein 1992 for specific examples). Research or technology parks can be nonprofit or for-profit, owned by a university or a university-related entity, or owned by a non-university entity but have contractual relationships with a university (Association of University Related Research Parks 1991: iv). In technology incubators the emphasis is on small, entrepreneurial businesses who are in close proximity to a university or research institute and share support services—for example, financing, marketing, and management. The success of these partnerships depends upon the faculty working with tenants on research of common interest and business's ability to turn scientific knowledge into marketable products.

Another form of scientific collaboration is the joint venture or limited partnership.[14] Universities are now able to claim exclusive commercial rights to their discoveries and to sell or license the patent to those discoveries to companies for further development (Merrifield 1992:56). The company pays for the rights to the patent, and sometimes this is accompanied by a contribution.[15] In exchange the university (and/or faculty) obtains royalties and at times an equity position in the firm (Merrifield 1992:56). The *Chronicle of Higher Education* (Blumenstyk 2003) reported that 142 institutions of higher learning earned more than $827 million in royalties and other payments from licenses on inventions developed by researchers at their universities in 2001. This amount was lower than the $1 billion earned in 2000 but greater than the $641 million earned in 1999. In 2001 Columbia led the pack with $129 million in royalties, followed by MIT with more than $73 million in revenues.

In response to the growing collaboration between universities and industry, legislation was passed that legitimated and encouraged the leasing and eventually the selling of patents by universities and other nonprofits to commercial enterprises. Powell and Owen-Smith (1998:171) cited the 1980 Patent and Trademark Amendments (Public Law 96–517, also known as the Bayh-Dole Act). This was followed by Public Law 98–620, which allowed universities to sell their property rights to others, the Stevenson-Wydler Act of 1980 and its 1986 amendments, the Cooperative Research Act of 1986, the National Competitiveness Technology Transfer Act of 1989, and the 1993 "defense conversion initiative" that opened defense-related research to commercialization (p. 172). While firms do not treat fees to acquire licenses or dividends paid to nonprofit equity partners as charitable contributions, Congress explicitly excludes this form of income to universities from the tax on unrelated business income (Internal Revenue Service 2000:9).

Political Collaborations

While most of the recent literature on nonprofit/for-profit collaboration has focused on strategic philanthropy and economic benefits, many of the partnerships between firms and nonprofits, both domestically and in the international arena, have important political meaning. Many observers are uneasy with this. Friedman's (1963) admonition that the business of business is business was based on his understanding that corporate social responsibility puts firms in an awkward position. "If businessmen do have a social responsibility other than making maximum profits for stockholders, how are they to know what it is? Can self-selected private individuals decide what the social interest is?" (p. 133). Clearly, deciding on the "social interest" is a political decision that takes business beyond business. Any community relations officer who was enmeshed in the Planned Parenthood controversy in the late 1980s and early 1990s or was attacked by the Capital Research Center or the National Committee for Responsive Philanthropy or the target of a corporate campaign by a union or non-governmental organization (NGO) will acknowledge the broader political significance of their work (see David 1993; Himmelstein 1997; Levy 1999; Manheim 2001). Nonprofits are involved in the political process in a number of different ways and, by implication, so are their funders.

Often, in the course of supporting nonprofit organizations, companies seek to further their own political agendas. Haley (1991) argued that as "corporate masques," corporate contributions are often politically proactive, strategic, and instrumental (pp. 486–87). Managers use contributions to capture the attention of key stakeholders, mime messages by symbolically transmitting corporate interests to other stakeholders, and vend values by institutionalizing them in society (p. 487). This not only can help to assure audiences and legitimate the firm, as Kamens (1985) argues, but can also alert audiences to corporate power. The messages can be business- or industry-specific (e.g., the case of the tobacco industry), or they can articulate politically charged, ideological positions. Political conservatives in the 1970s, such as Irving Kristol and William E. Simon, encouraged companies to support nonprofits that were pro-business and abandon those that pursued anti-business agendas (National Chamber Foundation 1978). The Capital Research Group voiced similar views in the 1990s and 2000s.

C. Smith (1994b) labeled this approach to giving "policy marketing." For example, companies will mix lobbying funds with donations to garner grassroots support for various social and political causes or to support nonprofits with different political agendas. Smith cites the case of Binney & Smith (p. 111), the maker of Crayola crayons, who advocated for state funding of arts in education, bike manufacturers donating to nonprofits pushing for more bike trails, and insurers who contribute to public-interest coalitions pushing for the liberalization of industry controls. Policy marketing would also include contributions to educational nonprofits that have thinly veiled political agendas. Many 501(c)(3)s that have "education" as their purpose often engage in advocacy and lobbying.[16] In the 1990s there were also "politicized philanthropies," for example, Newt Gingrich's Progress and Freedom Foundation, which funders supported in an effort to curry political favors (Kahn 1997:645). Policy marketing also includes support of public policy institutes that do research and formulate policies that affect business interests, for example, The American Enterprise Institute, The Brookings Institute, The Heritage Foundation, The Urban Institute, and The Progressive Policy Institute.

Himmelstein (1997) offers a somewhat different view on policy marketing. Rather than viewing it as an exercise in naked political influence, he saw this kind of philanthropy as a tactic that companies used to establish relationships with various social institutions rather than a strategy to intimidate or push a specific agenda. Rather than being vehicles to further conservative or liberal ideologies, these gifts are to provide access to think tanks, politicians, advocacy groups, and other potential "players." As in the case of PAC contributions (Clawson, Neustadtl, and Scott 1992), many companies view philanthropic contributions as a tactic to become credible and ensure that the firm and its interests are taken into account when policies are formulated or decisions are made. Instead of pushing an ideological position, giving is a political tactic to gain access to decision-makers.

The political significance of business/nonprofit collaborations is perhaps most clear in the international arena. According to the Conference Board (Kulik 1999), corporate citizenship at the global level has begun to move beyond simple philanthropy to such concerns as sustainable development, human rights, and the quality of life within host countries. In the wake of the September 11th terrorist attacks, the Conference Board (Vogl 2002) raised the question of whether today's multinationals have a role to play in ending world hunger, seeking social justice, and redistributing wealth. Corporations were not responsible for the attack, but they probably contributed to the anger and frustration around the world at how globalization was playing itself out. While one might applaud the Conference Board for chastising U.S. companies to be more socially responsible, critics have long argued that multinational corporations (MNCs) have done a great deal to destabilize the global community and need to recognize their broader responsibilities.

The pressure on firms to engage in global citizenship initiatives actually began in the 1990s, well before 9/11 (Waddock, Bodwell, and Graves 2002). Corporate executives, especially in Europe, had begun to recognize that they were partly the cause and partly the solution to social welfare, environmental, and political problems at home and globally. As a result, many businesses began partnering with the United Nations, governments, and civil society organizations in constructive ways (Nelson 2002). With the increasing global scope of environmental and human rights activists, the popularity of the "global citizen," global business dependencies, distrust of business abroad, and global media coverage, companies had to go beyond just avoiding corrupt and exploitive behavior and move toward reconsidering their responsibility to stakeholders. Corporate disasters, such as Union Carbide's gas leak in Bhopal, and political scandals; Shell's Nigerian crisis and Unocal involvement in Myanmar, and labor practices; Nike's below-living-wage issues in Indonesia; and the Kathie Lee/Wal-Mart sweatshop debacle in Honduras (Schwartz and Gibb 1999; Herbert 1997), are no longer localized. Corporate images suffer not only in the countries directly harmed but also among consumers internationally. Thus, being part of the solution becomes an essential part of corporate strategy.

As NGOs have evolved on the international scene, from serving solely as disaster and welfare relief organizations to promoting self-reliance and eventually becoming "catalytic facilitators" (Bendall 2000), NGOs and MNCs have at times become collaborators. NGOs do not only serve as the "watchdogs of globalization" (Roddick 2000) on the international level, but also act as facilitators, consultants, and information channels that open dialogues between corporations and the local communities. Many NGOs see the potential benefits of partnering with MNCs and view them as potential levers for promoting global human rights (Rodman 1998; Winston 2002). NGOs can also be very useful to companies. MNCs operating in host countries will rely on NGOs to help them build intellectual, social, and reputation capital and subsequently increase their legitimacy in the local environment and reduce their corporate risk (Bendall 2000). The best partnerships bring about meaningful institutional change and reverse corporate abuses. For example, Bartley (2003) described how this cooperation helped to create private regulatory regimes in the apparel and food products fields. In essence NGOs certify companies based on their social or environmental performance and thus contribute to human rights and sustainable development.

Yet often NGOs are adversaries as well as partners. Rodman (1998) cites examples of how human rights groups' activities in Burma (the Free Burma Campaign pressure against PepsiCo) and Nigeria (activists' pressure against Royal Dutch Shell sparked by the execution of Ken Saro-Wiwa) directly reformed corporate behavior through moral shaming, boycott and divestment, and shareholder activism. With their growing power, NGOs can strongly influence corporate behavior through both positive and negative relations. As global watchdogs, through cooperative and associational relations (Rodgers 2000) and using their powerful transnational advocacy networks (Keck and Sikkink 1998), NGOs have developed ways to get the attention of corporate executives. NGOs are establishing and disseminating benchmarks, standards, and codes of conduct for corporate behavior and putting pressure on MNCs to choose whether they will lead or follow in their international business practices (Rappaport and Flaherty 1992). They pressure MNCs through activities such as auditing MNCs and mobilizing shareholders, organizing boycotts, pushing for divestment, and moral shaming (Winston 2002). NGOs cannot legally enforce or command specific standards, since they do not have the power of nation-states, but they can rely on *inducements* by "creating penalties for socially irresponsible behavior that cause firms to redefine what they consider to be profitable" (Rodman 1998:38). NGOs do not have to make the choice of either in either positive or negative reinforcement modes, but rather their activities can fall on a continuum somewhere between the two ends of the spectrum (Turcott 1995; Winston 2002).

Companies will not abandon the "bottom line" or strategic philanthropy, but they will be called upon to take a leadership role in solving social and environmental problems, to be transparent and reveal to others their environmental and social performance, and to live by an accepted standard of corporate social performance and accountability that does not exploit power advantages (Muirhead 1999:49–56). As American multinationals enter the new millennium, in the wake of phenomenal growth and success followed by recession, 9/11, and a wave of corporate accounting scandals, they are once again examining their social responsibility and citizenship roles. We do not expect that companies will enthusiastically embrace an active citizenship role, especially in the international arena, since it draws them into real politics, which is fraught with uncertainty and danger. Nevertheless, business's stakeholders expect—indeed demand—that firms behave in a moral and ethical manner and will pressure them to act accordingly.

The purpose of the chapter was to describe and understand four different types of corporate-nonprofit collaborations. Specifically, we focused on philanthropic, strategic, commercial, and political collaborations. From all indications there is considerable enthusiasm—on both sides—for all four types of partnerships. It is safe to predict that all four types of collaboration will continue to flourish into the twenty-first century.

Economics alone does not explain companies' participation in these partnerships. Nonprofits are expected to pursue activities that benefit the collective good or further the public interest, but firms are also doing things that affect social welfare. Regardless of the pressure on firms to measure results and prove direct benefit, companies engage in collaborative efforts for which there is little measurable return and that have strong moral overtones. For some this is heartening; for others it is frightening. Being involved in social welfare or the public realm is a political act, and some feel that companies have too much political power already. At the same time, nonprofits are seeing corporations as prospective business partners, and not just donors, who can help them upgrade their operations and earn greater revenues. Companies are not simply well-heeled benefactors. Before we conclude, we want to point to some unresolved issues that cut across all four types of collaboration and that researchers as well as interested citizens should be paying attention to.

First, collaborations are fraught with organizational problems and do not always succeed. The more integrative the collaboration becomes—that is, when nonprofits and businesses jointly engage in activities that involve personnel and resources of both partners (Austin 2000a:26)—the more difficult the collaboration. Austin (2000a) described the ways that fifteen for-profit/nonprofit integrative collaborations came about and evolved over time, and Berger, Cunningham, and Drumwright (2004) studied eleven close relationships among for-profits and nonprofits (see also Sagawa and Segal 2000 and London and Rondinelli 2003 for a discussion of partnering problems). The authors cited several issues that need to be addressed. The partners often have different ends (Austin 2000a). Also, partners must try to mobilize the resources of the other actor to jointly create value for both, and this is often difficult. Austin and Berger and associates agreed that partnerships, where partners' values and structures are congruent, are more likely to be successful. Berger and colleagues also noted that nonprofits and for-profits have many misconceptions of one another, styles of decision-making are often different, often there are feelings of inequity, sometimes partners misuse their power, and mistrust can undermine collaboration. Austin claimed that the personal involvement of top leaders was important in creating interorganizational trust and communication. He also suggested there need to be management structures in place that specify the duties and responsibilities of partners and ways of keeping partners accountable. Both studies agreed that organizational learning was essential and that without efforts to renew the partnership, failure was likely.

Second, we need to know more about the benefits and costs of collaborations for nonprofit partners. There is little or no theory in the nonprofits literature that tells nonprofit managers when it would be strategically advantageous to enter into one type of collaboration or another. For example, the nonprofit KaBOOM!, whose purpose is to build and renovate playgrounds for children, engaged in philanthropic, strategic, and commercial collaborations. KaBOOM! received grants from a wide variety of corporations through their philanthropic partnerships; KaBOOM! also had strategic philanthropy partnerships with numerous corporations, such as Home Depot, whose activities ranged from sponsoring events, making in-kind donations for playground building materials, and promoting and supporting their employees' involvement in volunteering their time to build the playground; and finally, KaBOOM! was also involved in commercial partnerships with companies, such as Ben and Jerry's, who had created the ice cream flavor "Kaberry KaBOOM!" from which a percentage of the proceeds were donated to KaBOOM!. KaBOOM! made no effort to downplay their corporate partnerships and, in fact, went so far as to promote cause-related marketing and their corporate sponsors on their Web site (www.kaboom.org). Yet should we conclude that "the more the merrier"? At what point do collaborations result in diminishing returns to nonprofits?

Indeed, nonprofits can realize many benefits from these collaborations. Cause-related marketing, licensing names and logos, licensing patents to firms, subcontracting with for-profits, and collaborations produce revenues that nonprofits can use to subsidize their related program service activities. There is also the possibility of technology transfer, and for-profits' investment in nonprofits' infrastructure can greatly strengthen the capacity of the nonprofit partners. These partnerships can also enhance human capital. In their research on the effects of industry-university relations in the field of biotechnology, Blumenthal et al. (1986:13) found that "Biotechnology researchers with industrial support publish at higher rates, patent more frequently, participate in more administrative and professional activities and earn more than colleagues without such support."

There are potential costs as well, not the least of which is mission drift (see Young 2001). In the course of the collaboration nonprofits may come to emulate the management style and the goals of the for-profit partner. The transformation may come about because the nonprofit partner is trying to show that it is worthy of an "investment" or asks consultants or trustees to help the organization solve some problem, or the board pressures the organization to change. With prominent managerial gurus such as Philip Kotler (Kotler and Andreasen 1996) and Michael Porter (Porter and Kramer

1999) and the Peter F. Drucker Foundation for Nonprofit Management advocating that nonprofits adopt the best practices and strategies of the for-profit sector, many nonprofits feel pressured to adopt the business model. While this can be beneficial, it can also result in mission drift where the organization loses sight of its tax-exempt purpose and focuses on commercial activities and cost-saving measures.

Although empirical work has not looked much at the relation among collaboration, managerial style, and mission drift, there is evidence that the business model can create problems for nonprofits.[17] Powell and Owen-Smith (1998:189–90) talked about the close ties between universities and industry and the resulting conflicts between faculty and universities over control over research results and changes in university culture. Bowie (1994) described the ethical issues surrounding commercial partnerships between universities and industry. Hall (1990) described the conflict between board members who tried to make a social-service nonprofit more businesslike and staff that tried to protect the mission. Galaskiewicz and Bielefeld (1998) found that over time nonprofits that utilized more managerial tactics tended to have more disagreements internally.

One source of these problems is the different cultures within for-profits and nonprofits. Weisbrod (1998a) pointed out that for-profits and nonprofits operate under different legal rules and the privileges accorded to nonprofits are based on the assumption that they are "different" from for-profits. Firms are characteristically profit maximizers and do things to enhance profits; nonprofits typically are bonoficers and engage in activities that have some socially desirable end (p. 74). Albert and Whetten (1985) argued that the identities (or cultures) as well as the goals of utilitarian (for-profit) and normative (nonprofit) organizations are different. Decisions are legitimated using different criteria, information and ideology play different roles, and members want different things from the organizations. Brower and Shrader (2000) studied nonprofit and for-profit boards of directors and found little difference in moral reasoning but very different ethical climates: more egoism in for-profits, more benevolence in nonprofits. If business culture threatens nonprofit culture, conflict is surely to arise as the latter fends off the threat.

There are other potential costs associated with business/nonprofit partnerships. For example, collaborations dramatically increase environmental uncertainty and complexity, and decisions made at the level of the collaboration can be very disruptive for the nonprofit (Stone 2000:110–11; see also O'Regan and Oster 2000). In university-business partnerships boundary spanning personnel (e.g., a director of technology transfers) are often necessary to monitor the relations with industry and anticipate contingencies (e.g., product liability, sublicensing, further product development by the licensee, and so on) (see Montgomery 1992). Weisbrod (1998b:2) cites examples of cross-sector partnerships where they undermined nonprofits' legitimacy—for example, the American Medical Association's proposed endorsement of Sunbeam Corporation products in exchange for royalties tied to product sales. The Attorneys General report warns that commercial-nonprofit marketing alliances could jeopardize nonprofits' most important assets—the integrity of their names and reputations—and the trust that people have in these organizations (NYAG 1999:4).

There are also possible social costs associated with for-profit/nonprofit collaboration. For example, collaboration based on gaining commercial advantage is different from collaboration aimed at finding solutions to common community problems. The nonprofit, in collaboration with a for-profit partner, selects problems to address that are potentially profitable but may not be critical to the community. That is, problems that have no potential monetary payoff are ignored. Many authors raised this issue with respect to cause-related or joint venture marketing (Barnes 1991; Caesar 1986; Mescon and Tilson 1987). Furthermore, Marx (1997) found that companies that engaged in strategic philanthropy (i.e., linking giving to the strategic goals of the firm) tended to give a lower percentage of their total direct company contributions to United Way, a community-wide cause, because the UW does not allow donors to target their giving and thus further corporate business goals. Krimsky, Ennis, and Weissman (1991:283) suggested that scientific communication may be impeded when many different firms are represented within one university or within a single department (see also Blumenthal, Gluck, Louis, Stoto, and Wise 1986). Krimsky et al. (1991: 284–85) also cautioned that commercial ties could put a strain on peer reviewership (where scientists are on their honor not to pilfer new ideas) and undermine the current system of science. At a more macro community level, extensive involvement of business executives in local nonprofits may increase support of the nonprofit sector—and may even help it grow—but it may also reduce the likelihood of others volunteering or participating in civic affairs (Marquis and Davis 2003).

In conclusion, it is safe to say that since Useem's (1987) review, there has been a blurring of the boundaries across sectors and an expansion of the interface between nonprofits and business. Companies and nonprofits are doing much more than traditional philanthropy. They have strategic, commercial, and political partnerships, which entail both benefits and costs for both parties and for the society as a whole. The lines separating the sectors appear to be blurred as nonprofits openly engage in commercial activities, and companies are drawn into quasi-political roles. The power differences between companies and their partners are still significant, yet even these differences are being neutralized as NGOs learn more effective tactics to bring pressure to bear on companies. From a research perspective, the blurring of boundaries makes studying corporate-nonprofit relations much more challenging inasmuch as the collaboration among the sectors is more complex, and one now needs to study donor, donee, government, and a host of third parties in order to have a complete understanding of the phenomenon.

ACKNOWLEDGMENTS

We would like to thank Richard Steinberg, Natalie J. Webb, James Austin, Jerome Himmelstein, Evelyn Brody, Howard Tuckman, Woody Powell, Kelley Porter, and Alan R. Andreasen for their useful comments on the paper, Kieran Healy for some useful references, George Hobor, Jeff Larson, and Beth Duckles for checking references, and Steve Corral and Olga Mayorova for finding references. We would also like to thank Jan Wilson and Ann E. Kaplan for help finding data for the final revision. Of course, any omissions or errors are the responsibility of the authors.

NOTES

1. See Knauer (1994) for an extended discussion of what qualifies as a charitable deduction under Section 170.

2. Although executive and employee volunteerism is extensive, we will not review the research on this topic. The chapter by Leete in this volume reviews the research on volunteers, and Korngold and Voudouris (1996) provide a review of the limited empirical work on corporate volunteerism and practice (see also Wild 1993 and Troy 1997).

3. It is important to remember that large companies dominate the discussion of corporate contributions. Examining the research results of Andrews (1952), McElroy and Siegfried (1985), and Morgan (1997), we learn that (1) smaller firms are much less likely to take charitable deductions, (2) among firms that take deductions, the ratio of contributions to pretax net income tends to be higher for medium-size firms, and (3) not surprisingly, large companies account for the bulk of corporate giving. Part of the reason for this is that in smaller, privately held firms the owner (or partners) will often make charitable donations out of their household income instead of corporate income for tax purposes (Thompson, Smith, and Hood 1993:48). Although the total amounts given by small firms are much smaller than the total amounts given by large firms, the involvement of small businesses in local community affairs is considerable and makes an enormous impact on neighborhoods, towns, and rural communities (see Besser 1998; Eckstein 2001).

4. For the sake of brevity, we focus on U.S.-based corporations doing philanthropy abroad, but we recognize the literature on Japanese philanthropy at home and in the United States (e.g., London 1991), British company philanthropy (Adams and Hardwick 1998; Campbell, Moore, and Metzger 2002), and studies of company giving to local causes by firms in other countries (e.g., Bennett 1998; Sánchez 2000; Sundar 2000; Brooks 2002).

5. It is important to keep in mind that product donations do not come from the foundation and the value of gifts of medicine, computer hardware and software, and food to causes outside the United States are therefore not counted in these figures.

6. Kristol (1982), Brion (1983), and Ostergard (1994) discuss some of the reasons for the emphasis in the 1980s on direct return.

7. Firms can also become slaves to their reputation. Silver (2001) showed that Chicago companies realized reputational gains from their support of the Chicago Initiatives (an effort to provide inner-city youth with summer recreation and employment), but community organizations, which legitimated the companies' claims of social responsibility, later forced firms to support broader poverty reforms by threatening to invalidate these claims.

8. The discussion of corporate philanthropic giving, profits, and performance is plagued by a number of methodological problems and design issues. Many of the authors cited above note these problems (see also Griffin and Mahon 1997; McWilliams, Siegel, and Teoh 1999; McWilliams and Siegel 2000). What constitutes long- and short-term benefits needs to be resolved, across studies different indicators of social responsibility are used, and corporate philanthropic contributions are only one indicator of social performance. Nonetheless, enough good studies have been done for us to question the link between firms' socially responsible behavior and financial performance.

9. The complement of the marginal tax rate is the price of a contribution because it represents the after-tax cost to the company of providing an additional dollar to the charity.

10. We had hoped to compare the Conference Board data that Useem (1987) presented (from Troy 1984), but the Conference Board reassigned recipients to different categories in 1999 thus making comparisons invalid (Kao 2001).

11. According to Muirhead (2004:41–42), "Civic and Community Activities" included community development, justice and law, housing and urban renewal, the YMCA/YWCAs and other neighborhood or community-based groups, state or local government agencies, regional clubs, and fraternal orders. The "Other and Unknown" category included U.S.-based international organizations (e.g., Care), sponsorships of special events other than cultural and arts events (e.g., the Olympics) and public broadcasting and media, public policy research organizations, faith-based groups, economic and business-related organizations, and donees that did not fall into the other categories. In a separate study, however, Hruby (2001:33) found very little corporate money going to faith-based groups as did Helland and Smith (2003:28).

12. See Knauer (1994:65) for a discussion of revenues from cause marketing. The IRS has attempted several times to make charities pay UBIT on revenues from affinity card programs, but, as of the writing of this chapter, the courts have rejected the IRS's argument and the revenues remain tax free (Ruth and Barnett 2003).

13. The Attorneys General of sixteen states and the District of Columbia Corporation Counsel published a special report on the New York Attorneys General (NYAG) (1999) Web site from which we draw much of our material.

14. Some of the better-researched examples of industry-university collaboration have been in the area of biotechnology. For a description and analysis of partnerships in this industry see Barley, Freeman, and Hybels (1992), Powell and Brantley (1992), Powell, Koput, and Smith-Doerr (1996), and Powell and Owen-Smith (1998).

15. Campbell (1996) showed that firms that had license agreements with universities were more likely to make charitable contributions to universities as well. He interpreted the charitable contribution as the "grease" that helped smooth over the rough edges of licensing contracts. Also, contributions were a way in which firms ensured that they had an inside track on developments at the university, e.g., pre-publication review of articles or reports.

16. Kahn (1997:654) notes that some nonprofits have created what she calls the "c3/c4 split." Legally two organizations exist—one exempt under 501(c)(3) and one under 501(c)(4)—however, in fact there is only one entity with the same offices, staff, and infrastructure. The only difference is that contributions to the former are tax deductible as charitable contributions, while donations to the latter are not. However, the latter is free to engage in unlimited lobbying activity.

17. Cause-related marketing is a prime candidate for such a study, but little empirical research has been done and there is only speculation on how cause-related marketing can create problems for nonprofit partners (e.g., Garrison 1990 and Andreasen 1996).

REFERENCES

Abbott, Walter F., and R. Joseph Monsen. 1979. "On the Measurement of Corporate Social Responsibility: Self-Reported Disclosures as a Method of Measuring Corporate Social Involvement." *Academy of Management Journal* 22:501–15.

Abzug, Rikki, and Natalie Webb. 1999. "Relationships Between Nonprofit and For-Profit Organizations: A Stakeholder Perspective." *Nonprofit and Voluntary Sector Quarterly* 28(4):416–31.

Adams, Mike, and Philip Hardwick. 1998. "An Analysis of Corporate Donations: United Kingdom Evidence." *Journal of Management Studies* 35(5):641–54.

Albert, Stuart, and David A. Whetten. 1985. "Organizational Identity." Pages 263–95 in *Research in Organizational Behavior,* vol., edited by Barry M. Staw and Larry L. Cummings. Greenwich, Conn.: JAI Press.

Albinger, Heather Schmidt, and Sarah J. Freeman. 2000. "Corporate Social Performance and Attractiveness as an Employer to Different Job Seeking Populations." *Journal of Business Ethics* 28:243–53.

Alperson, Myra. 1995. *Corporate Giving Strategies that Add Business Value: A Research Report.* New York: The Conference Board, Inc., Report 1126.

———. 1996. *Measuring Corporate Community Involvement: A Research Report.* New York: The Conference Board, Inc., Report 1169.

———. 1998. *Building the Corporate Community Economic Development Teams.* New York: The Conference Board, Inc., Report 1205.

American Symphony Orchestra League. 2005. Personal communication, April 5.

Andreasen, Alan R. 1996. "Profits for Nonprofits: Find a Corporate Partner." *Harvard Business Review* (November–December): 47–50, 55–59.

Andrews, F. Emerson. 1952. *Corporation Giving.* New York: Russell Sage Foundation.

Arenson, Karen W. 2000. "Columbia Leads Academic Pack in Turning Profit from Research." *New York Times,* August 2, p. 1A.

Arlow, Peter, and Martin Gannon. 1982. "Social Responsiveness, Corporate Structure, and Economic Performance." *Academy of Management Review* 7:235–41.

Association of University Related Research Parks. 1991. *Membership Directory.* Tempe, Az.: AURRP.

Atkinson, Lisa, and Joseph Galaskiewicz. 1988. "Stock Ownership and Company Contributions to Charity." *Administrative Science Quarterly* 33 (March):82–100.

Aupperle, Kenneth E., Archie B. Carroll, and John D. Hatfield. 1985. "An Empirical Examination of the Relationship Between Corporate Social Responsibility and Profitability." *Academy of Management Journal* 28 (2):446–63.

Austin, James E. 2000a. *The Collaboration Challenge: How Nonprofits and Businesses Succeed Through Strategic Alliances.* San Francisco: Jossey-Bass.

———. 2000b. "Strategic Collaboration Between Nonprofits and Businesses." *Nonprofit and Voluntary Sector Quarterly* 29(1):69–97.

Barley, Stephen R., John Freeman, and Ralph C. Hybels. 1992. "Strategic Alliances in Commercial Biotechnology." Pages 311–347 in *Networks and Organizations: Structure, Form, and Action,* edited by Nitin Nohria and Robert G. Eccles. Boston: Harvard Business School Press.

Barnes, N. 1991. "Joint Venture Marketing: A Strategy for the 1990s." *Health Marketing Quarterly* 9(1–2):23–26.

Bartkus, Barbara R., Sara A. Morris, and Bruce Seifert. 2002. "Governance and Corporate Philanthropy: Restraining Robin Hood?" *Business and Society* 41(3):319–44.

Bartley, Tim. 2003. "Certifying Forests and Factories: States, Social Movements, and the Rise of Private Regulation in the Apparel and Forest Products Fields." *Politics and Society* 31(3):433–64.

Baumol, William J. 1970. "Enlightened Self-Interest and Corporate Philanthropy." Pages 3–19 in *A New Rationale for Corporate Social Policy,* by William J. Baumol, Rensis Likert, Henry C. Wallich, and John J. McGowan. Lexington, Mass.: Heath Lexington Books.

Bendall, Jem. 2000. Pages 96–110 in *Terms for Endearment: Business, NGOs and Sustainable Development,* edited by Jim Bendell. Sheffield: Greenleaf.

Bennett, Roger. 1998. "Corporate Philanthropy in France, Germany and the U.K.: International Comparisons of Commercial Orientation towards Company Giving in European Nations." *International Marketing Review* 15(6):458+.

Berger, Ida E., Peggy H. Cunningham and Minette E. Drumwright. 2004. "Social Alliances: Company/Nonprofit Collaboration." *California Management Review* 47 (1): 58–89.

Berle, Adolf A. Jr. 1931. "Corporate Powers as Powers in Trust." *Harvard Law Review* 44:1049.

Berman, Shawn L., Andrew C. Wicks, Suresh Kotha, and Thomas M. Jones. 1999. "Does Stakeholder Orientation Matter? The Relationship Between Stakeholder Management Models and Firm Financial Performance." *Academy of Management Journal* 42(5):488–506.

Besser, Terry L. 1998. "The Significance of Community to Business Social Responsibility." *Rural Sociology* 63(3):412–31.

Billitteri, Thomas J. 2000. "Venturing a Bet on Giving." *Chronicle of Philanthropy* 12(16):1, 7, 10, 12.

Blum, Debra E. 1999. "Companies' Charitable Gifts Follow Their Revenue and Go Overseas." *Chronicle of Philanthropy* 11(18):12.

———. 2000a. "9 of 10 Companies Have Charity Marketing Deals." *Chronicle of Philanthropy* 12(17):39.

———. 2000b. "Companies' Plans to Donate AIDS Drugs to Africa Draw Mixed Response." *Chronicle of Philanthropy* 12(19):10.

Blumenstyk, Goldie. 2003. "Colleges Report $827 Million in 2001 Royalties." *Chronicle of Higher Education* 49(39):A28.

Blumenthal, David M., Michael Gluck, Karen Seashore Louis,

Michael A. Stoto, and David Wise. 1986. "University-Industry Research Relationships in Biotechnology: Implications for the University." *Science* 232:1361–66.

Boatsman, James R., and Sanjya Gupta. 1996. "Taxes and Corporate Charity: Empirical Evidence from Micro-Level Panel Data." *National Tax Journal* 49(2):193–213.

Bowie, Norman E. 1994. *University-Business Partnerships: An Assessment.* Lanham, Md.: Rowman and Littlefield.

Brion, John P. 1983. "Recession Threatens Corporate Philanthropy." *Journal of Commerce and Commercial* 355:4a.

Brooks, Arthur C. 2002. "Charitable Giving in Transition Economies: Evidence from Russia." *National Tax Journal* 55(4):743–53.

Brothers, T. 1992. *School Reform: Business, Education and Government as Partners.* New York: The Conference Board, Inc., Report 1011.

Brower, Holly H., and Charles B. Shrader. 2000. "Moral Reasoning and Ethical Climate: Not-for-Profit vs. For-Profit Boards of Directors." *Journal of Business Ethics* 26:147–67.

Bryan, Kate. 1991. "Corporate and Media Sponsorship of Nonprofit Events in a Marketing-Oriented Society." Master's project, School of Journalism and Mass Communication, University of Minnesota, Minneapolis.

Buchholtz, Ann K., Allen C. Amason, and Matthew A. Rutherford. 1999. "Beyond Resources: The Mediating Effect of Top Management Discretion and Values on Corporate Philanthropy." *Business and Society* 38(2):167–87.

Burlingame, Dwight F. 1994. "Empirical Research on Corporate Social Responsibility: What Does It Tell Us?" *Nonprofit Management and Leadership* 4(4):473–80.

Burlingame, Dwight F., and Patricia A. Frishkoff. 1996. "How Does Firm Size Affect Corporate Philanthropy?" Pages 86–104 in *Corporate Philanthropy at the Crossroads,* edited by Dwight F. Burlingame and Dennis R. Young. Bloomington: Indiana University Press.

Burt, Ronald. 1983. "Corporate Philanthropy as a Cooptive Relation." *Social Forces* 62(2): 419–49.

Caesar, Patricia. 1986. "Cause-Related Marketing: The New Face of Corporate Philanthropy." *Business and Society Review* (Fall): 15–19.

Campbell, David, Geoff Moore, and Matthias Metzger. 2002. "Corporate Philanthropy in the U.K., 1985–2000: Some Empirical Findings." *Journal of Business Ethics* 39:29–41.

Campbell, Eric G. 1996. "Philanthropy and Self-Interest: Academic-Industry Research Relationships." Ph.D. thesis, University of Minnesota, Minneapolis.

Campbell, Leland, Charles S. Gulas, and Thomas S. Gruca. 1999. "Corporate Giving Behavior and Decision-Maker Social Consciousness." *Journal of Business Ethics* 19:375–83.

Clawson, Dan, Alan Neustadtl, and Denise Scott. 1992. *Money Talks: Corporate PACs and Political Influence.* New York: Basic Books.

Clotfelter, Charles T. 1985a. "Charitable Giving and Tax Legislation in the Reagan Era." *Law and Contemporary Problems* 48(4):197–212.

———. 1985b. *Federal Tax Policy and Charitable Giving.* Chicago: University of Chicago Press.

Cochran, Philip L., and Robert A. Wood. 1984. "Corporate Social Responsibility and Financial Performance." *Academy of Management Journal* 27(1):42–56.

Coffey, Betty S., and Jia Wang. 1998. "Board Diversity and Managerial Control as Predictors of Corporate Social Performance." *Journal of Business Ethics* 17:1595–1603.

Cone, Inc. 2000. "1999 Cone/Roper Trends Report: The Evolution of Cause Branding." Executive summary (www.coneinc.com/crm/report.htm), accessed July 20, 2001.

———. 2003. "2002 Cone Corporate Citizenship Study." Press release, (www.coneinc.com/Pages/pr_13.html), accessed October 18, 2003.

Council for Aid to Education. 2001. *Voluntary Support of Education 2000.* New York: Council for Aid to Education.

———. 2004. *2003 Voluntary Support of Education.* New York: Council for Aid to Education.

Council on Foundations. 2000. *Measuring the Business Value of Corporate Philanthropy: Tool Kit.* New York: Council on Foundations.

Daniel Yankelovich Group. 1988. *The Climate for Giving: The Outlook of Current and Future CEOs.* Washington, D.C.: Council on Foundations.

David, Gregory E. 1993. "Of Grants and Grief: Trying to Do Good Can Sometimes Keep a Company from Doing Well." *Financial World* (August 3):64–65.

Davis, K. 1973. "The Case for and Against Business Assumption of Social Responsibilities." *Academy of Management Journal* 16:312–322.

Dean, Dwane Hal. 1999. "Brand Endorsement, Popularity, and Event Sponsorship as Advertising Cues Affecting Consumer Pre-Purchase Attitudes." *Journal of Advertising* 28:1–12.

Dees, J. Gregory. 1994. "Social Enterprise: Private Initiatives for the Common Good." Harvard Business School, November 30. Boston, Mass.: Harvard Business School Press.

———. 1998. "Enterprising Nonprofits." *Harvard Business Review* (January–February): 55–58, 60, 62–67.

Dienhart, John. 1988. "Charitable Investments: A Strategy for Improving the Business Environment." *Journal of Business Ethics* 7(1–2): 63–71.

Dodd, E. Merrick, Jr. 1932. "For Whom Are Corporate Managers Trustees?" *Harvard Law Review* 45:1145.

Eckstein, Susan. 2001. "Community as Gift-Giving: Collectivistic Roots of Volunteerism." *American Sociological Review* 66 (December): 829–51.

Ermann, David M. 1978. "The Operative Goals of Corporate Philanthropy: Contributions to the Public Broadcasting Service, 1972–1975." *Social Problems* 25:504–14.

File, Karen Maru, and Russ Alan Prince. 1995. "Cause-Related Marketing, Philanthropy, and the Arts." *Nonprofit Management and Leadership* 5(3):249–60.

———. 2000. "Cause-Related Marketing and Corporate Philanthropy in the Privately Held Enterprise." *Journal of Business Ethics* 17:1529–39.

Fix, Janet L. 2001. "Nonvirtual Reality Hits Giving Sites." *Chronicle of Philanthropy* 13(17):9, 12, 13.

Flaherty, Susan. 1992. "Philanthropy Without Borders: U.S. Private Foundation Activity in Eastern Europe." *Voluntas* 3(3):335–50.

Fombrun, Charles. 1996. *Reputation: Realizing Value from the Corporate Image.* Boston: Harvard Business School Press.

Fombrun, Charles, and Mark Shanley. 1990. "What's in a Name? Reputation Building and Corporate Strategy." *Academy of Management Journal* 33:233–58.

Foundation Center. 2003. *Foundation Giving Trends,* 2003 edition. New York: Foundation Center.

Friedman, Milton. 1963. *Capitalism and Freedom.* Chicago: University of Chicago Press.

Frumkin, Peter. 2003. "Inside Venture Philanthropy." *Society* 40(4): 7, 9.

Fry, Louis W., Gerald D. Keim, and Roger E. Meiners. 1982. "Corporate Contributions: Altruistic or For-Profit?" *Academy of Management Journal* 25(1):94–106.

Galaskiewicz, Joseph. 1985. *Social Organization of an Urban Grants Economy.* Orlando, Fla.: Academic Press.

———. 1989. "Corporate Contributions to Charity: Nothing More than a Marketing Strategy?" Pages 246–60 in *Philanthropic Giving: Studies in Varieties and Goals,* edited by Richard Magat. New York: Oxford University Press.

———. 1997. "An Urban Grants Economy Revisited: Corporate Charitable Contributions in the Twin Cities, 1979–81, 1987–89." *Administrative Science Quarterly* 42:445–71.

Galaskiewicz, Joseph, and Wolfgang Bielefeld. 1998. *Nonprofit Organizations in an Age of Uncertainty: A Study of Organizational Change.* New York: Aldine de Gruyter.

Galaskiewicz, Joseph, and Ronald S. Burt. 1991. "Interorganization Contagion in Corporate Philanthropy." *Administrative Science Quarterly* 36:88–105.

Galaskiewicz, Joseph, and Barbara Rauschenbach. 1989. "The Corporation-Culture Connection: A Test of Interorganizational Theories." Pages 119–35 in *Community Organizations: Studies in Resource Mobilization and Exchange,* edited by Carl Milofsky. New York: Oxford University Press.

Galaskiewicz, Joseph, and Stanley Wasserman. 1989. "Mimetic Processes Within an Interorganizational Field: An Empirical Test." *Administrative Science Quarterly* 34 (September):454–79.

Garone, Stephen J. 1996. *Strategic Opportunities in Corporate Community Activity: A Conference Report.* New York: The Conference Board, Inc., Report 1144.

———. 1999. *The Link Between Corporate Citizenship and Financial Performance.* New York: The Conference Board, Inc., Report 1234.

Garrison, J. 1990. "A New Twist to Cause Marketing." *Fund Raising Management* 20(12):40–44.

Giving USA Foundation. 2005. *Giving USA 2005.* Indianapolis: Giving USA Foundation, AAFRC Trust for Philanthropy.

Gornitsky, Linda B. 1996. *Benchmarking Corporate International Contributions: A Research Report.* New York: The Conference Board, Inc., Report 1163.

Greene, Stephen G., and Grant Williams. 2002. "Getting the Goods: Tax Incentives Spur Boom in Donations of Products." *Chronicle of Philanthropy,* July 25, pp. 7, 16, 18.

Griffin, Jennifer J., and John F. Mahon. 1997. "The Corporate Social Performance and Corporate Financial Performance Debate: Twenty-Five Years of Incomparable Research." *Business and Society* 36(1):5–31.

Griffiths, John. 1992. "Company Giving in Europe: What Are the Policy Issues for the European Commission?" *Voluntas* 3(3):375–82.

Guernsey, Lisa. 1998. "Corporate Largesse: Philanthropy or Self-Interest?" *Chronicle of Higher Education,* April 24.

Guthrie, Doug, and Michael McQuarrie. 2003. "Corporate Investment in Local Communities: The Political Economy of Organizational Networks and the Case of Low Income Housing." Working paper, Department of Sociology, New York University.

Haley, Usha C. 1991. "Corporate Contributions as Managerial Masques: Reframing Corporate Contributions as Strategies to Influence Society." *Journal of Management Studies* 28(5):485–509.

Hall, Peter D. 1989. "Business Giving and Social Investment in the United States." Pages 221–245 in *Philanthropic Giving: Studies in Varieties and Goals,* edited by Richard Magat. New York: Oxford University Press.

———. 1990. "Conflicting Managerial Cultures in Nonprofit Organizations." *Nonprofit Management and Leadership* 1:153–65.

———. 1997. "Business Giving and Social Investment in the United States, 1790–1995." *New York Law School Law Review* 41(3–4):789–817.

Hansmann, Henry. 1996. *The Ownership of Enterprise.* Cambridge, Mass.: Belknap Press of Harvard University Press.

Heald, Morrell. 1970. *The Social Responsibilities of Business: Company and Community, 1900–1960.* Cleveland, Ohio: The Press of Case Western Reserve University.

Helland, Eric, and Janet Kiholm Smith. 2003. "Corporate Philanthropy." Social Science Research Network, ID=472161.

Hemphill, Thomas A. 1996. "Cause-Related Marketing, Fundraising, and Environmental Nonprofit Organizations." *Nonprofit Management and Leadership* 6(4):403–18.

Henricks, Mark. 1991. "Doing Well While Doing Good." *Small Business Reports* 11:28–38.

Herbert, Bob. 1997. "In America," *New York Times,* April 14 (www.nlcnet.org/Press/Newsclip/scan7.htm).

Himmelstein, Jerome L. 1997. *Looking Good and Doing Good: Corporate Philanthropy and Corporate Power.* Bloomington: Indiana Press.

Hruby, Laura. 2001. "Bush Decries Level of Corporate Giving to Faith Groups." *Chronicle of Philanthropy* 13(16):33, 35.

IEG, Inc. 2001. "Performance Research/IEG Study Highlights What Sponsors Want." *IEG Sponsorship Report,* sample issue (www.sponship.com).

———. 2003. *IEG Sponsorship Report,* vol.22, no. 24, December 22 (www.sponsorship.com/_prodImgs/sr_2003_12_22.pdf).

Internal Revenue Service. 2000. "Tax on Unrelated Business Taxable Income of Exempt Organizations." Publication 598 (revised March 2000). Washington, D.C.: Department of the Treasury.

———. 2001a. "Contributions You Cannot Deduct." *The Digital Daily* (www.irs.gov/formspubs/display/0,,i1=50&genericId=11064,00.html).

———. 2001b. "Excluded Trade or Business Activities." The Digital Daily (www.irs.gov/formspubs/display/0,,i1%3D50%26genericId%3D12668,00.html).

Joyce, Ed. 1987. "Corporate Dollars on Campus: Who Profits?" *Datamation* 33(8):64–68.

Kahn, Faith S. 1997. "Pandora's Box: Managerial Discretion and the Problem of Corporate Philanthropy." *UCLA Law Review* 44(3):579–676.

Kamens, David H. 1985. "A Theory of Corporate Civic Giving." *Sociological Perspectives* 28:29–50.

Kao, Amy. 2001. *Corporate Contributions in 2000.* New York: The Conference Board. Research Report R-1308–01-RR.

Karl, Barry D. 1991. "The Evolution of Corporate Grantmaking in America." Pages 20–34 in *The Corporate Contributions Handbook: Devoting Private Means to Public Needs,* edited by James B. Shannon. San Francisco: Jossey-Bass.

Keck, Margaret E., and Kathryn Sikkink. 1998. *Activists Beyond Borders: Advocacy Networks in International Politics.* Ithaca, N.Y.: Cornell University Press.

King, Samantha. 2001. "An All-Consuming Cause: Breast Cancer, Corporate Philanthropy, and the Market for Generosity." *Social Text* 19(4):115–43.

Kirchberg, Volker. 1995. "Arts Sponsorship and the State of the City: The Impact of Local Socio-Economic Conditions on Corporate Arts Support." *Journal of Cultural Economics* 19:305–20.

Klein, Eva. 1992. "Technology Parks and Incubators: A Nexus Between University Science and Industrial Research and Development." Pages 11–48 in *Innovative Models for University Research,* edited by C. R. Haden and J. R. Brink. Amsterdam: Elsevier Science.

Knauer, Nancy J. 1994. "The Paradox of Corporate Giving," *DePaul Law Review* 44(1):1–97.

Korngold, Alice, and Elizabeth Voudouris. 1996. "Corporate Volunteerism: Strategic Community Involvement." Pages 23–40 in *Corporate Philanthropy at the Crossroads,* edited by Dwight F. Burlingame and Dennis R. Young. Bloomington: Indiana University Press.

Kotler, Philip, and Alan R. Andreasen. 1996. *Strategic Marketing for Nonprofit Organizations.* Upper Saddle River, N.J.: Prentice-Hall.

Kotler, Philip, and Nancy Lee. 2005. *Corporate Social Responsibility: Doing the Most Good for Your Company and Your Cause.* Hoboken, N.J.: John Wiley & Sons.

Kover, Arthur. 2001. "The Sponsorship Issue." *Journal of Advertising Research* 41(1):5–65.

Krimsky, Sheldon, James G. Ennis, and Robert Weissman. 1991. "Academic-Corporate Ties in Biotechnology: A Quantitative Study." *Science, Technology, and Human Values* 16(3):275–87.

Kristol, Irving. 1982. "Charity and Business Shouldn't Mix." *New York Times,* October 17, p. F2.

Kulik, Todd. 1999. *The Expanding Parameters of Global Corporate Citizenship.* New York: The Conference Board, Inc., Report 1246.

Lashbrooke, E. C., Jr. 1985. *Tax Exempt Organizations.* Westport, Conn.: Quorum Books.

Leder, Michelle. 2002. "Your Alma Mater Wants to Become Your Bank." *New York Times,* August 25, p. B8.

Lerner, L. D., and G. E. Fryxell. 1994. "CEO Stakeholder Attitudes and Corporate Social Activity in the Fortune 500." *Business and Society* 33(1):58–81.

Letts, Christine, William Ryan, and Allen Grossman. 1997. "Virtuous Capital: What Foundations Can Learn from Venture Capitalists." *Harvard Business Review* (March–April):36–39, 41–44.

Levy, Ferdinand K., and Gloria M. Shatto. 1978. "The Evaluation of Corporate Contributions." *Public Choice* 33:19–28.

———. 1980. "Social Responsibility in Large Electric Utility Firms: The Case for Philanthropy." Pages 237–49 in *Research in Corporate Social Performance and Policy,* vol. 2, edited by Lee E. Preston. Greenwich, Conn.: JAI Press.

Levy, Reynold. 1999. *Give and Take: A Candid Account of Corporate Philanthropy.* Boston, Mass.: Harvard Business School Press.

Lewin, David, and J. M. Sabater. 1996. "Corporate Philanthropy and Business Performance." Pages 105–26 in *Corporate Philanthropy at the Crossroads,* edited by Dwight F. Burlingame and Dennis R. Young. Bloomington: Indiana University Press.

Lombardo, Barbara. 1995. "Corporate Philanthropy: Gift or Business Transaction?" *Nonprofit Management and Leadership* 5(3):291–301.

London, Nancy R. 1991. *Japanese Corporate Philanthropy.* New York: Oxford University Press.

London, Ted, and Dennis Rondinelli. 2003. "Managing Tensions in Nonprofit-Corporate Partnerships." *Stanford Social Innovation Review* 1(3):28–35.

Longoria, Thomas, Jr. 1999. "The Distribution of Public-Private Partnership: Targeting of Voluntary Efforts to Improve Urban Education." *Nonprofit and Voluntary Sector Quarterly* 28:315–29.

Margolis, Joshua D., and James P. Walsh. 2003. "Misery Loves Companies: Rethinking Social Initiatives by Business." *Administrative Science Quarterly* 48:268–305.

Manheim, Jarol B. 2001. The Death of a Thousand Cuts: Corporate Campaigns and the Attack on the Corporation. Mahwah, N.J.: Lawrence Erlbaum Associates.

Marquis, Christopher, and Gerald F. Davis. 2003. "Golfing Alone? Elite Cohesion and Community Social Capital, 1986–98." Working paper, Department of Organizational Behavior and Human Resource Management, University of Michigan.

Marx, Jerry D. 1997. "Corporate Philanthropy and United Way: Challenges for the Year 2000." *Nonprofit Management and Leadership* 8(1):19–30.

———. 1999. "Corporate Philanthropy: What Is the Strategy?" *Nonprofit and Voluntary Sector Quarterly* 28(2):185–198.

McElroy, Katherine Maddox, and John J. Siegfried. 1985. "The Effect of Firm Size on Corporate Philanthropy." *Quarterly Review of Economics and Business* 25(2):18–26.

———. 1986. "The Community Influence on Corporate Contributions." *Public Finance Quarterly* 14(4):394–414.

McGuire, Jean B., Alison Sundgren, and Thomas Schneeweis. 1988. "Corporate Social Responsibility and Firm Financial Performance." *Academy of Management Journal* 31(4):854–72.

McWilliams, Abagail, and Donald Siegel. 2000. "Corporate Social Responsibility and Financial Performance: Correlation or Misspecification?" *Strategic Management Journal* 21:603–9.

McWilliams, Abagail, Donald Siegel, and Siew Hong Teoh. 1999. "Issues in the Use of the Event Study Methodology:

A Critical Analysis of Corporate Social Responsibility Studies," *Organizational Research Methods* 2(4):340–65.

Meredith, Robyn. 1999. "Despite a Bribery Scandal, General Motors Is Committing Big Money to an Olympics Campaign." *New York Times,* May 12, p. 6+.

Merrifield, D. Bruce. 1992. "Research Consortia: The Concurrent Management of Innovation." Pages 49–62 in *Innovative Models for University Research,* edited by C. R. Haden and J. R. Brink. Amsterdam: Elsevier Science.

Mescon, Timothy, and Donn Tilson. 1987. "Corporate Philanthropy: A Strategic Approach to the Bottom-Line." *California Management Review* 29(2): 49–61.

Miles, Robert. 1982. *Coffin Nails and Corporate Strategies.* Englewood Cliffs, N.J.: Prentice-Hall.

Montgomery, Anthony J. 1992. "Technology Transfer from Universities: Elements of Success." Pages 63–72 in *Innovative Models for University Research,* edited by C. R. Haden and J. R. Brink. Amsterdam: Elsevier Science.

Moore, Jennifer, and Grant Williams. 1999. "Ringing Up a New Way to Give." *Chronicle of Philanthropy* 12(5):1, 23, 25.

Morgan, David R. 1997. "Trends in Corporate Charitable Contributions." *New York Law School Law Review* 41(3–4):771–87.

Muirhead, Sophia A. 1999. *Corporate Contributions: The View from 50 Years.* New York: The Conference Board, Inc., Research Report 1249.

———. 2004. *The 2004 Corporate Contributions Report.* New York: The Conference Board, Inc., Research Report 1355–04–88.

National Chamber Foundation. 1978. *What Direction? Corporate Philanthropy.* Washington, D.C.: National Chamber Foundation.

Navarro, Peter. 1988. "Why Do Corporations Give to Charities?" *Journal of Business* 61(1):65–93.

Nelson, Jane. 2002. *Building Partnerships: Cooperation Between the United Nations System and the Private Sector.* New York: United Nations Publications.

Nelson, Ralph L. 1970. *Economic Factors in the Growth of Corporation Giving.* New York: National Bureau of Economic Research and Russell Sage Foundation.

Nevarez, Leonard. 2000. "Corporate Philanthropy in the New Urban Economy: The Role of Business-Nonprofit Realignment in Regime Politics." *Urban Affairs Review* 36(2):197–227.

New York Attorneys General. 1999. "What's in a Nonprofit's Name? Public Trust, Profit and the Potential for Public Deception" (www.oag.state.ny.us/press/reports/nonprofit/full_text.html/full_text.html), accessed July 9, 2001.

O'Regan, Katherine, and Sharon M. Oster. 2000. "Nonprofit and For-Profit Partnerships: Rationale and Challenges of Cross-Sector Contracting." *Nonprofit and Voluntary Sector Quarterly* 29(1):120–40.

Ostergard, Paul M. 1994. "Fasten Your Seat Belts!" *Fund Raising Management* 25:36–38.

Pankratz, David B., and Sandra Gibson. 1999. "The Not-for-Profit and For-Profit Arts: Current Collaborations and Future Prospects." *Journal of Arts Management, Law and Society* 29(2):75–141.

Paprocki, Steven L. 2000. *Grants: Corporate Grantmaking for Racial and Ethnic Communities.* Wakefield, R.I.: Moyer-Bell.

Parkinson, Deborah. 2000. *Innovative Public-Private Partnerships: Easing the Path from Welfare to Work.* New York: The Conference Board, Inc., Report 1277–00-RR.

Perlmutter, Felice D. 1997. *From Welfare to Work: Corporate Initiatives and Welfare Reform.* New York: Oxford University Press.

Pogrebin, Robin. 2000. "Roundabout Journey to the Top." *New York Times,* July 27, p. B8+.

Porter, Michael E., and Mark R. Kramer. 1999. "Philanthropy's New Agenda: Creating Value." *Harvard Business Review* (November–December): 121–30.

Post, James E., and Sandra A. Waddock. 1989. "Social Cause Partnerships and the 'Mega-Event': Hunger, Homelessness, and Hands Across America." Pages 181–205 in *Research in Corporate Social Performance and Policy,* vol. 11, edited by James E. Post. Greenwich, Conn.: JAI Press.

Powell, Walter W., and Peter Brantley. 1992. "Competitive Cooperation in Biotechnology: Learning Through Networks?" Pages 366–94 in *Networks and Organizations: Structure, Form, and Action,* edited by Nitin Nohria and Robert G. Eccles. Boston: Harvard Business School Press.

Powell, Walter W., Kenneth Koput, and Laurel Smith-Doerr. 1996. "Inter-Organizational Collaboration and the Locus of Innovation: Networks of Learning in Biotechnology." *Administrative Science Quarterly* 41:116–45.

Powell, Walter W., and Jason Owen-Smith. 1998. "Universities as Creators and Retailers of Intellectual Property: Life-Sciences Research and Commercial Development." Pages 169–93 in *To Profit or Not: The Commercial Transformation of the Nonprofit Sector,* edited by Burton A. Weisbrod. New York: Cambridge University Press.

Rappaport, Ann, and Margaret Fresher Flaherty. 1992. *Corporate Responses to Environmental Challenges: Initiatives by Multinational Management.* New York: Quorum Books.

Renz, Loren. 2001. "Foundation Center Announces Estimates for 2000 Foundation Giving." News Release from the Foundation Center, March 27.

———. 2002a. *Assessing the Post-9/11 Funding Environment: Grantmakers' Perspectives.* New York: Foundation Center.

———. 2002b. *Giving in the Aftermath of 9/11: Foundations and Corporations Respond.* New York: Foundation Center.

Renz, Loren, and Josefina Atienza. 2003. *International Grantmaking Update.* New York: Foundation Center.

Renz, Loren, and Steven Lawrence. 2001. *Foundation Growth and Giving Estimates, 2000 Preview.* New York: Foundation Center.

———. 2004. *Foundation Growth and Giving Estimates, 2003 Preview.* New York: Foundation Center.

Renz, Loren, and Jeff Martin. 2000. "New Study Reports $639 Million Jump in International Giving by U.S. Foundations." Press release by the Foundation Center, December.

Roddick, Anita. 2000. "Foreword." Pages 8–9 in *Terms for Endearment: Business, NGOs and Sustainable Development,* edited by Jim Bendell. Sheffield: Greenleaf.

Rodgers, Cheryl. 2000. Pages 40–48 in *Terms for Endearment: Business, NGOs and Sustainable Development,* edited by Jim Bendell. Sheffield: Greenleaf.

Rodman, Kenneth A. 1998. "'Think Globally, Punish Locally': Nonstate Actors, Multinational Corporations, and Human Rights Sanctions." *Ethics and International Affairs* 12:19–41.

Ruth, Susan, and Charles Barrett. 2003. "UBIT: Current Developments." Internal Revenue Service (www.irs.gov/pub/irs-tege/topicn.pdf).

Sagawa, Shirley, and Eli Segal. 2000. *Common Interest, Common Good: Creating Value through Business and Social Sector Partnerships.* Boston, Mass.: Harvard Business School Press.

Sánchez, Carol M. 2000. "Motives for Corporate Philanthropy in El Salvador: Altruism and Political Legitimacy." *Journal of Business Ethics* 27:363–75.

Schwartz, Peter, and Blair Gibb. 1999. *When Good Companies Do Bad Things: Responsibility and Risk in an Age of Globalization.* New York: John Wiley & Sons.

Schwartz, R. A. 1968. "Corporate Philanthropic Contributions." *Journal of Finance* 23:479–97.

Schwinn, Elizabeth. 2000. "Click and Easy: Online Marketing Deals Can Reap Big Benefits, but Questions Remain." *Chronicle of Philanthropy* 13(5):27–29.

———. 2001. "IRS Acts to Ease Overseas Grant Making." *Chronicle of Philanthropy* 13(16):40.

Sen, Sankar, and C. B. Bhattacharya. 2001. "Does Doing Good Always Lead to Doing Better? Consumer Reactions to Corporate Social Responsibility." *Journal of Marketing* 38:225–43.

Shaw, Bill, and Frederick R. Post. 1993. "A Moral Basis for Corporate Philanthropy." *Journal of Business Ethics* 12(7):745–51.

Siegfried, John J., Katherine Maddox McElroy, and Diane Biernot-Fawkes. 1983. "The Management of Corporate Contributions." Pages 87–102 in *Research in Corporate Social Performance and Policy,* vol. 5, edited by Lee Preston. Greenwich, Conn.: JAI Press.

Silver, Ira. 2001. "Strategically Legitimizing Philanthropists' Identity Claims: Community Organizations as Key Players in the Making of Corporate Social Responsibility." *Sociological Perspectives* 44(2):233–53.

Sinclair, Michelle, and Joseph Galaskiewicz. 1997. "Corporate-Nonprofit Partnerships: Varieties and Covariates." *New York Law School Law Review* 41(3–4):1059–90.

Smith, Craig. 1994a. "Corporate Giving: From Responsibility to Opportunity." *Fund Raising Management* 25:34–36.

———. 1994b. "The New Corporate Philanthropy." Harvard Business Review 72(1):105–16.

Smith, Hayden W. 1983. *A Profile of Corporate Contributions.* New York: Council for Financial Aid to Education.

———. 1993. "The Maturity of Corporate Giving and Its Long-Term Consequences." *Nonprofit Management and Leadership* 4(2):215–28.

Stendardi, Edward, J. 1992. "Corporate Philanthropy: The Redefinition of Enlightened Self-Interest." *Social Science Journal* 29(1): 21–30.

Stevenson, Mark. 1993. "What's in It for Me?" *Canadian Business* 66:54–57.

Stone, Melissa M. 2000. "Exploring the Effects of Collaborations on Member Organizations: Washington County's Welfare-to-Work Partnership." *Nonprofit and Voluntary Sector Quarterly* 29(1):98–119.

Sturdivant, Frederick, and James L. Ginter. 1977. "Corporate Social Responsiveness: Management's Attitudes and Economic Performance." *California Management Review* 19 (Spring): 30–39.

Sundar, Pushpa. 2000. *Beyond Business: From Merchant Charity to Corporate Citizenship: Indian Business Philanthropy Through the Ages.* New Delhi: Tata McGraw-Hill.

Thompson, Judith K., and Jacqueline N. Hood. 1993. "The Practice of Corporate Social Performance in Minority vs. Nonminority-owned Small Businesses." *Journal of Business Ethics* 12(3):197–206.

Thompson, Judith K., Howard L. Smith, and Jacqueline N. Hood. 1993. "Charitable Contributions by Small Businesses." *Journal of Small Business Management* 31(3):35–51.

Theatre Communications Group. 2003. "Theatre Facts 2002" (www.tcg.org/programs/files/theatrefacts_2002.pdf), accessed October 18, 2003.

———. 2004. "Theatre Facts 2003" (www.tcg.org/frames/programs/fs_mp_facts.htm), accessed March 6, 2005.

Tillman, Audris D. 1997. *The Corporate Contributions Plan: From Strategy to Budget: A Research Report.* New York: The Conference Board, Inc., Report 1192.

Tolbert, Charles M., Thomas A. Lyson, and Michael D. Irwin. 1998. "Local Capitalism, Civic Engagement, and Socioeconomic Well-Being." *Social Forces* 77(2):401–27.

Troy, Kathryn. 1984. *Annual Survey of Corporate Contributions, 1984 Edition.* New York: The Conference Board, Inc., Report 848.

———. 1997. *Corporate Volunteerism: How Families Make a Difference.* New York: The Conference Board, Inc., Report 1189–97.

Tuckman, Howard P. 1998. "Competition, Commercialization, and the Evolution of Nonprofit Organizational Structures." Pages 25–45 in *To Profit or Not to Profit: The Commercial Transformation of the Nonprofit Sector,* edited by Burton A. Weisbrod. New York: Cambridge University Press.

Turban, Daniel B., and Daniel W. Greening. 1997. "Corporate Social Performance and Organizational Attractiveness to Prospective Employees." *Academy of Management Journal* 40(3):658–72.

Turcott, Marie-France. 1995. "Conflict and Collaboration: The Interfaces Between Environmental Organizations and Business Firms." *Research in Corporate Social Performance,* Supplement 1, 195–229.

United States Department of the Treasury. 2002. "Treasury Issues Guidance that Helps Charities with Corporate Sponsorships Payments" (www.ustreas.gov/press/releases/p03038.htm), accessed October 18, 2003.

Useem, Michael. 1984. *The Inner Circle: Large Corporations and the Rise of Business Political Activity in the U.S. and U.K.* New York: Oxford University Press.

———. 1987. "Corporate Philanthropy." Pages 340–59 in *The Nonprofit Sector: A Research Handbook,* edited by Walter W. Powell. New Haven, Conn.: Yale University Press.

———. 1991. "Organizational and Managerial Factors in the Shaping of Corporate Social and Political Action." Pages 63–

92 in *Research in Corporate Social Performance and Policy,* vol. 12, edited by James E. Post. Greenwich, Conn.: JAI Press.

Useem, Michael, and Stephen I. Kutner. 1986. "Corporate Contributions to Culture and the Arts: The Organization of Giving and the Influence of the Chief Executive Officer and of Other Firms on Company Giving in Massachusetts." Pages 93–112 in *Nonprofit Enterprise in the Arts: Studies in Mission and Constraint,* edited by Paul J. DiMaggio. New York: Oxford University Press.

Varadarajan, P. Rajan, and Anil Menon. 1988. "Cause-Related Marketing: A Coalignment of Marketing Strategy and Corporate Philanthropy." *Journal of Marketing* 52:58–73.

Vogl, A. J., ed. 2002. "Below the Bottom Line." *Across the Board* 39(1):20–32.

Waddock, Sandra A., Charles Bodwell, and Samuel B. Graves. 2002. "Responsibility: The New Business Imperative." *Academy of Management Executive* 16:132–47.

Waddock, Sandra A., and Samuel B. Graves. 1997. "The Corporate Social Performance-Financial Performance Link." *Strategic Management Journal* 18(4):303–19.

Wall, Wendy L. 1984. "Companies Change the Ways They Make Charitable Donations." *Wall Street Journal,* June 21, pp. 1ff.

Wang, Jia, and Betty S. Coffey. 1992. "Board Composition and Corporate Philanthropy." *Journal of Business Ethics* 11:771–78.

Warner, W. Lloyd. 1963. *Yankee City.* New Haven, Conn.: Yale University Press.

Webb, Natalie J. 1994. "Tax and Government Policy Implications for Corporate Foundation Giving." *Nonprofit and Voluntary Sector Quarterly* 23(1):41–67.

———. 1996a. "Corporate Profits and Social Responsibility: Subsidization of Corporate Income Under Charitable Giving Tax Laws." *Journal of Economics and Business* 48:401–21.

———. 1996b. "Tax Incentives for Corporate Giving Programs: What Measures Increase Funds Available?" *Administration in Social Work* 20(3):39–56.

Webb, Natalie J., and Amy Farmer. 1996. "Corporate Goodwill: A Game Theoretic Approach to the Effect of Corporate Charitable Expenditures on Firm Behavior." *Annals of Public and Cooperative Economics* 67:29–50.

Weeden, Curt. 1998. *Corporate Social Investing: The Breakthrough Strategy for Giving and Getting Corporate Contributions.* San Francisco: Berrett-Koehler.

Weisbrod, Burton A. 1998a. "Institutional Form and Organizational Behavior." Pages 69–84 in *Private Action and the Public Good,* edited by Walter W. Powell and Elisabeth S. Clemens. New Haven, Conn.: Yale University Press.

———. 1998b. "The Nonprofit Mission and Its Financing: Growing Links Between Nonprofits and the Rest of the Economy." Pages 1–22 in *To Profit or Not: The Commercial Transformation of the Nonprofit Sector,* edited by Burton A. Weisbrod. New York: Cambridge University Press.

Werbel, James D., and Suzanne M. Carter. 2002. "The CEO's Influence on Corporate Foundation Giving." *Journal of Business Ethics* 40:47–60.

Werbel, James D., and Max S. Wortman, Jr. 2000. "Strategic Philanthropy: Responding to Negative Portrayals of Corporate Social Responsibility." *Corporate Reputation Review* 3:124–36.

White, Arthur H. 1980. "Corporate Philanthropy: Impact on Public Attitudes." In *Corporate Philanthropy in the Eighties.* Washington, D.C.: National Chamber Foundation.

Whiting, Charles. 1996. "Other Cities' Stadium Lessons." *Minneapolis Star-Tribune,* August 25, p. A21.

Whiting, Meredith A. 1999. *Innovative Public-Private Partnerships: Public Safety Initiatives.* New York: The Conference Board, Inc., Report 1253.

Whiting, Meredith A., and Charles J. Bennett. 2001. *The Road to Sustainability: Business' First Steps.* The Conference Board, Research Report R-1309–01-RR.

Wild, Cathleen. 1993. *Corporate Volunteer Programs: Benefits to Business.* New York: The Conference Board, Inc., Report 1029.

Williams, Grant. 1999. "'Affinity Card' Revenue Isn't Taxable, Court Rules." *Chronicle of Philanthropy* (October 21): 49.

Williams, Robert J., and J. Douglas Barrett. 2000. "Corporate Philanthropy, Criminal Activity, and Firm Reputation: Is There a Link?" *Journal of Business Ethics* 26:341–50.

Williamson, Oliver. 1964. *The Economics of Discretionary Behavior: Managerial Objectives in a Theory of the Firm.* Englewood Cliffs, N.J.: Prentice-Hall.

Winston, Morton. 2002. "NGOs Strategies for Promoting Corporate Social Responsibility." *Ethics and International Affairs* 16(1):71–88.

Wokutch, Richard E., and Barbara A. Spencer. 1987. "Corporate Saints and Sinners: The Effects of Philanthropic and Illegal Activity on Organizational Performance." *California Management Review* 29(2):62–77.

Wolpert, Julian. 1993. *Patterns of Generosity in America: Who's Holding the Safety Net?* New York: The Twentieth Fund.

Wood, Donna J. 1991. "Corporate Social Performance Revisited." *Academy of Management Review* 16:691–718.

Wood, Donna J., and Raymond E. Jones. 1996. "Research in Corporate Social Performance: What Have We Learned?" Pages 41–85 in *Corporate Philanthropy at the Crossroads,* edited by Dwight F. Burlingame and Dennis R. Young. Bloomington: Indiana University Press.

Worthy, James C. 1987. *William C. Norris: Portrait of a Maverick.* Cambridge, Mass.: Ballinger.

Yablonski, Christopher. 2001. "Patterns of Corporate Philanthropy: A Mandate for Reform." Capital Research Center (www.capitalresearch.org/misc/pcpXIII.pdf), accessed July 17, 2002.

Yankelovich, Skelly, White, Inc. 1982. *Corporate Giving: The Views of Chief Executive Officers of Major American Corporations.* Washington, D.C.: Council on Foundations.

Young, Dennis R. 2001. "The Influence of Business on Nonprofit Organizations and the Complexity of Nonprofit Accountability." *American Review of Public Administration* 32(1):3–19.

Zetlin, Minda. 1990. "Companies Find Profit in Corporate Giving." *Management Review* 79:10–15.

NONPROFITS AND THE POLITY

9

The Constitution of Citizens: Political Theories of Nonprofit Organizations

ELISABETH S. CLEMENS

From the perspective of political theory, associations and organizations are problematic as well as potent. Incorporated or not, associations are potential sites and resources for political activity outside of formal political institutions. Whether or not they are operated for profit, corporations are political creations (Novak 2001). These creations are endowed with rights—of legal existence and property holding—but are not strictly accountable to the sovereigns or legislatures that bestow these rights.[1] Such organizations are political constructions but are not part of the formal political system. Consequently, analyses of voluntary associations and nonprofit organizations frequently develop at the margins of political theory and are deeply colored by the core concerns of those theories. Rather than "a political theory of nonprofits," different theories of politics lead to widely varying questions and claims about nonprofit organizations and associations.

To date, one theory of politics has claimed pride of place as *the* political theory of nonprofit organizations: a market model of democracy (following Buchanan and Tullock 1962; Dahl 1982; Olsen 1971). As articulated by James Douglas in the first edition of this handbook (Douglas 1987), this theory built on an image of individual citizens holding distinctive preferences for public services as well as votes (or opinions in polls) with which to express those preferences. Public services or goods that gain support from a majority of constituents will be provided by public agencies; those that are more controversial or preferred by only a minority will be provided by nonprofits (albeit often subsidized by public funds; see Salamon and Abramson 1982; Smith and Lipsky 1993:27). This approach has been developed to explain patterns of public-private partnership; its core logic is consistent with both economic models of nonprofit organization (e.g., Weisbrod 1988) and demographic or "entrepreneurial" models (e.g., James 1987). Deploying the imagery of choice that is central to much of contemporary economics and political science (March and Olsen 1989), these arguments use the traits and preferences of citizens to explain the development of nonprofit sectors and the distribution of activities across states, markets, households, and the variously defined "third sector."

Market models of democracy, however, do not exhaust the field of political theory. A range of political theories and theories of state development make important claims about the role of nonprofit organizations and associations, although their terminology may diverge from the conventions of nonprofit research. Most notably, political theories of nonprofit organizations are increasingly entwined with broad debates over civil society, social capital, and the rights of association within a liberal polity. Rather than assuming citizens with preferences already well defined, these approaches problematize the constitution of citizens and constituencies, as well as their capacities for political action.

Tocqueville's classic *Democracy in America* (1835–1840) is a touchstone for an alternative vision in which associational activities are constitutive of citizens as actors, of preferences and interests, and of the capacity to make effective demands on government (Frumkin 2002: ch. 2). Particularly in the research literature on the United States, this theoretical imagery informs studies of political culture or socialization that conceptualize associations as "schools of citizenship," locations where identities and interests are formed rather than organizations whose existence reflects some prior distribution of citizen preferences (Putnam 2000; Verba, Schlozman, and Brady 1995). From this vantage point, associations are understood to generate a capacity for collective or political action that may be exercised as an extension of elite power (Hall 1992), as a vehicle for the mobilization of disadvantaged or disgruntled constituencies (Clemens 1997; McCarthy 2003), or as an expression of the diversity of commitments in a pluralist society (Walzer 1984). Despite their many differences, these arguments concur in viewing the role of associations and formal politics as complementing one another in a democratic polity.

As this line of argument has gained prominence through the "civic engagement" debates of the 1990s (Putnam 2000; Skocpol and Fiorina 1999), critical voices and cautions have multiplied. Not all participatory organizations sustain values consistent with democracy nor are all voluntary associations or nonprofit organizations participatory in the degree assumed by many celebrations of Tocqueville (Chambers and Kopstein 2001; Eliasoph 1998; Gutmann 1998; Kaufman 2002; Skocpol 2003). In combination, transformations of government that increase the influence of organized groups (Crenson and Ginsberg 2002) and lower levels of participation within these groups (due to professionalization and formalization) may actually reverse the presumed relationship of associational participation and democratic values, leading to extremism and gridlock (Fiorina 1999).

For political science and sociology, much of the recent interest in voluntary associations and nonprofit organizations has been fueled by these concerns with the "input" side of democracy: citizenship, participation, and influence. For theorists concerned with governmental services, however, different questions have generated interest in the relations of privately governed associations and public institutions. As with civic participation, these concerns have a Tocquevillian lineage, echoing his claim that the capacity for local citizens to solve problems through associated action forestalls the extension of government responsibility (Tocqueville 1969:515). Whereas this may lead to an understanding of charities and nonprofit organizations as substitutes for government action (Douglas 1983), other arguments highlight complementarities and collaborations (see Grønbjerg and Smith, this volume). State expansion may take the form of borrowing capacity from nonprofit organizations (Smith and Lipsky 1993; Ullman 1998) or states may actively sponsor the formation and growth of nonprofit entities that then implement policy (Salamon 1987), accommodating to and potentially transforming the local communities in which they operate (Evans 1997; Schorr 1997). This line of argument illuminates another role for nonprofit organizations on the "input" side, as sources of experimentation (Douglas 1987), innovation (Frumkin 2002), and policy models that may then feed back into deliberations over future public programs (Dorf and Sabel 1998; Sirianni and Friedland 2001). Here too, however, there is a "dark side" variant of the argument. The increasing delivery of publicly funded programs through nonprofit organizations may obscure relationships of accountability, distort citizens' understandings of how tax revenues are spent, and allow governments to displace the risks of downsizing and policy shifts onto nongovernmental entities (Pierson 1994).

Even within the context of the advanced industrialized democracies and within the United States in particular, there are diverse and conflicting claims about the implications of nonprofit organizations and voluntary associations for the quality of democracy as well as for the efficacy of government. Whereas Douglas's initial formulation drew on market models of democracy to ask "why are some services provided by governments and others by nonprofit organizations?," these broader theoretical debates ask about the consequences for democracy of participation in voluntary associations or production through nonprofit organizations. The divergent arguments about the place of nonprofits and voluntary associations in democratic polities are increasingly relevant as these organizational models are exported to developing nations and formerly socialist states.

Basic questions lie at the core of these debates. Do voluntary associations and nonprofit organizations generate greater democratic participation? Are these organizational forms effective and legitimate vehicles for political engagement? Does reliance on or collaboration with nonprofits improve the efficiency of publicly funded services or generate innovative programs and new solutions to policy problems? In sum, are voluntary associations and nonprofit organizations a necessary or even desirable component of democratic polities? While eluding definitive answers thus far, these questions have fueled renewed attention to the complex social terrain that is neither purely market nor purely state.

POLITICAL SOCIALIZATION AND SOCIAL CAPITAL

Much of the interest of political theory in associations and nonprofit organizations stems from the presumption that associations are, or should be, embodiments of the constitutional forms, organizational skills, and political virtues required by a liberal democracy.[2] Eagerly appropriating the mantle of Tocqueville, such arguments contend that a wide range of formal and informal associations socialize citizens for democratic participation (Fleischacker 1998; Putnam et al. 1993; Wuthnow 1991, 1998) or that this capacity for democratic socialization should guide the legal regulation of associations (for a critical discussion, see Rosenblum 1998a). Empirical studies lend support to the connection between internal democracy and individual commitment to associations (Knoke and Wood 1981). Nonpolitical voluntary associations—along with workplaces and religious organizations—are settings in which citizens may practice skills such as letter-writing, planning meetings, and making speeches (Verba, Schlozman, and Brady 1995:310–20).

Through a commitment to internal democratic governance, such associations ideally sustain a sphere of relative equality decoupled from the structures of privilege that organize other social domains (Walzer 1983). For such arguments, associations are foundational to democracy insofar as they are sites for the cultivation of democratic values and skills. This contention is captured by the argument's theoretical imagery: associations are "schools of citizenship."

The role of associations in political socialization is amply documented—and still more frequently asserted—in historical research on the United States, beginning with Tocqueville's own *Democracy in America* (1969). A burgeoning literature amply documents the "golden age of associationalism" during the nineteenth century, when fraternal lodges and voluntary associations multiplied in cities and towns throughout the nation (Clawson 1989; Dumenil 1984; Gamm and Putnam 1999; Skocpol 1997; Skocpol et al. 2000; for a critical discussion, see Kaufman 2002). In addition to providing arenas for political socialization that could then be expressed through parties and elections, these associations actively collaborated in the provision of public goods (Baker 1983; Beito 2000) and served as vehicles for political mobilization outside of the parties themselves (Clemens 1997; Skocpol 2003). In nondemocratic polities, by way of comparison, rights of association have typically been tightly restricted or regulated. The Roman emperor Trajan, for example, forbade the formation of a fire brigade in a particularly flammable city in Asia Minor, explaining that "this sort of society has greatly disturbed the peace. . . . Whatever name we give them, and for whatever purposes they may be founded, they will not fail to form themselves into dangerous assemblies" (quoted in Mann 1986:324). As Peter Hall (this volume) documents, in the decades after independence, many Americans shared the emperor's suspicions of assemblies (see also McCarthy 2003:23–29).

Where associations are permitted and even encouraged, their capacity to generate political socialization appropriate for a democratic polity depends on a series of organizational features. As the legal framework for association developed in the United States, organizational constitutions often required democratic practices such as the election of officers; as associations were increasingly incorporated and regulated by state governments, these political arrangements were required for all but religious associations (on the "corporation sole," see Dane 1998) and benevolent corporations governed by appointed or self-perpetuating trustees. Material conditions also often encouraged participatory governance; low budgets, low reserves, and little or no professional staff tended to forestall the logic of Michels's "iron law of oligarchy." Instead, membership served as a political apprenticeship instilling mastery of skills such as public speaking and the intricacies of Robert's Rules of Order (Doyle 1977). The widespread cultivation of these skills sustained the circulation of citizens through large voluntary associations: "In huge membership federations, regional or state plus local chapters were widespread, full of intermediate leaders and members seeking to recruit others. Hundreds of thousands of local and supralocal leaders had to be elected and appointed every year. . . . Classic membership federations built two-way bridges across classes and places and between local and translocal affairs" (Skocpol 2003:226).

Fueled by recent claims about the contributions of social capital to democracy (Putnam et al. 1993; Putnam 2000; for a critical review, see Portes 1998), a new wave of research is addressing the role of associations in political socialization. Historical overviews trace the decline of the participatory organizations that were central to the Tocquevillian imagery of American democracy. The large voluntary associations that dominated the organizational landscape from the nineteenth through the mid-twentieth centuries have increasingly given way to professionally managed advocacy groups that tend to privilege the already-educated and already-politicized, rather than serving as schools of citizenship (Skocpol 2003:211–15).

Against the background of this large-scale shift in American civic life, considerable heterogeneity remains in the organizations in which individuals may become politically socialized. Many groups continue to provide opportunities for individuals to acquire civic skills, including most obviously organizations that are explicitly committed to participatory governance (Polletta 2002). Among adolescents, participation in extracurricular activities is associated with increased political involvement during adulthood (Jennings 1981; Glanville 1999). But political skills are also cultivated in less obvious settings. Religious organizations may be incubators of political capacities or provide imageries for political action (for historical reviews, see Hall, this volume; McCarthy 2003, chs. 3 and 5; Morone 2003; M. Young 2002) and may compensate for the obstacles to participation for the poor, minority groups, and women. Thus the *peregrenacion* provided a template for protest mobilization among migrant farmworkers in the 1960s (Ganz 2000) and, through the linking of Catholic parishes to the Industrial Areas Foundation, Latinas in Texas have been transformed into effective community leaders (M. E. Warren 2001). These case studies illuminate a puzzling feature of American democracy: "although the democratic polity is the domain of human endeavor founded upon the quality of all citizens, the religious domain is in fact a more democratic arena of activity. . . . Participation in religious institutions is much less structured by income, race or ethnicity than is political activity. Belonging to a church is even less stratified by income than is having a job" and women are more likely than men to engage in many kinds of religious activities (Verba, Schlozman, and Brady 1995:317).

Comparisons of participation across religious organizations underscore the importance of organizational structure—and denominational commitments—for political socialization. Mainline Protestant, Evangelical, and Catholic associations differ consistently in the extent to which religious participation is associated with political participation and skills (also see Cadge and Wuthnow, this volume). Protestantism of either variety is more likely to be associated with increased skills and participation, but only mainline Protestantism is linked with increased participation in *nonreligious* associations (Verba, Schlozman, and Brady 1995; Wuthnow 1999).

In important respects, this literature extends a longstanding concern in comparative politics for the cultural foundations of democracy. Classic works such as Almond and Verba's *Civic Culture* (1963) addressed the importance of adult socialization in generating the values and practices that sustain democratic polities; associations, not surprisingly, are demonstrated to be important sites of socialization. In an analysis of comparative political stability, Eckstein (1966) argued that *congruence* between the forms of authority that prevailed within families or associations and the system of formal political authority was critical. The closer the fit, the more stable the regime. More recently, Putnam et al. (1993) contributed to the revival of interest in the social foundations of democratic governance—and economic development—in his collaborative study of regional government in Italy.

Although discussions sometimes equate nonprofit organizations with voluntary associations, a closer consideration of this line of research identifies key organizational features that are generative of democratic skills and a propensity to participate. The effects attributed to participatory associations cannot be assumed for nonprofit organizations in general. For nonprofit scholars, the key question is whether the "associations" featured in these political analyses are equivalent—and in what way—to nonprofit organizations. Here, research on the links between religious participation and political socialization is intriguing. Recall that involvement in Catholic associations has weaker political effects than participation in Protestant organizations; this difference, it is argued, reflects the more hierarchical character of Catholic associations and the likelihood that clergy rather than laypeople will be in charge (Verba, Schlozman, and Brady 1995:245; see also Hall, this volume). By extension, one might predict that as nonprofits become more "catholic"—more hierarchical, less likely to engage in participatory governance—they will become less powerful sources of democratic political socialization. As Skocpol has argued (2003:234) the decline of large membership-based voluntary associations and the proliferation of more professionalized organizations has transformed the relations between civic associations and political participation: "Recent civic reorganizations have thus created a mutually reinforcing—and deleterious—interlocking of professionally managed associational and electoral activities. . . . Civic leaders now selectively target carefully delimited slices of the population identified (by expert studies) as already primed to respond to their particular appeals. Large numbers of Americans can easily be ignored if they are part of groups not seen as likely to give money or turn out to vote for particular causes." Thus as nonprofit organizations become increasingly professionalized (Brint and Levy 1999; Hall 1999)—and thus both organizationally distinct from participatory voluntary associations and more likely to survive (Minkoff 1993)—we should not expect them to generate the same levels and socio-economic distribution of democratic political socialization.

Evidence of these connections among organizational structure, resources, and participation can be found throughout the research literature on nonprofit organizations. As nonprofits become more dependent on external funding, they tend to become more bureaucratic and professionalized (Smith and Lipsky 1993:100–108; Grønbjerg 1993:169–98); recent calls for new models of outcomes-based assessment evince a hope that this connection can be broken (Frumkin 2000; Salamon 1987: 113–15; Schorr 1997: ch. 4). In a study of advocacy organizations in the peace movement,[3] Edwards (1994:317) found that larger organizations were "more likely than small to be formally organized, have higher levels of procedural formality, prefer to elect their leaders, and have more centralized financial decision making." Smaller peace organizations were "more likely than large to have higher rates of member participation, to prefer to operate without formally designated leaders, and make decisions by consensus." Among small organizations, the likelihood of formal organization increased with the amount of money handled (1994:327). In a study of nonprofit incorporation among organizations of the homeless, Cress (1997) found that adoption of the form was associated with either increases in resources or concerns for organizational legitimacy.

As a general rule, the larger and richer and more formalized the organization, the fewer the opportunities for participatory governance and democratic socialization of members (to the extent that they exist at all). The implications of this general rule for an evaluation of democratic socialization in the United States are, however, not obvious since most nonprofit organizations (including congregations) remain small in membership or below the $25,000 threshold for filing with the Internal Revenue Service, but a majority of the money (and membership) is concentrated in the large organizations and congregations (Salamon 2003:8; Chaves 2003:276). Thus the opportunities for participation and leadership may be greatest in those organizations with the fewest resources—in members or money—to harness to civic causes. Successful participatory movement organizations have discovered distinctive internal structures that combine some of the advantages of centralization with a commitment to continuous engagement with local activities and leaders (Ganz 2000; M. R. Warren 2001) or falter as organizational growth outstrips the capacities to practice direct democracy within a movement (Polletta 2002).

The central role of participation in accounting for the contribution of associations to political socialization has been underscored by a growing body of literature on democratization in the former socialist nations (Osa 2003) and in the developing world (Fox 1997). The years and months and weeks of protest that led to the fall of state socialist regimes in eastern Europe generated a tremendous interest in the capacity of civil society—the array of associations, clubs, unions, and churches—to sustain and mobilize political opposition under authoritarian rule. This explanatory model has also inspired philanthropic practice. Funded by both foundations and governments, civic education projects have sought to cultivate the practices and attitudes central to theories of democratic socialization. Evaluations of these programs demonstrate the importance of participatory practices—role playing, mock elections, and so forth—to subsequent political participation. In the absence of such exercises, the inculcation of values and information about political institutions has less impact (Finkel 2000; Bratton

1999). Research on the role of associations in development projects leads to similar conclusions, at both the individual and the organizational level. The findings from this literature resonate with the evidence on organizational hierarchy and professionalism in studies of nonprofit organizations in the industrial democracies. Whether as a consequence of organizational size and resources or as the outcome of conscious program design, participation matters for democratic socialization.

To the extent that nongovernmental associations can cultivate political capacities among relatively disadvantaged groups within developing nations or the global economy, this may have important consequences for the balance of power and processes of decision-making. Brown (1998; Brown and Tandon 1993) argues that nongovernmental organizations have the potential to serve as "bridges" among parties with varying power and distinctive interests (see also Ostrom 1997). Local nongovernmental organizations may even give rise to transnationally effective coalitions, engaging in decision-making with national governments and intergovernmental organizations (Brown et al. 2000:276). By establishing ties with different parties prior to initiating interorganizational collaboration, such NGOs may foster the "experience of cooperation among organizations from different sectors, especially organizations that are unequal in power, status, and resources, [which] is rare in many of these settings, and participation in cooperative problem solving that persists over time and produces outcomes in the interest of all the parties may have effects on attitudes, practices, and institutions that reverberate beyond the immediate problem solutions" (Brown 1998:236). Note, however, that these outcomes are not necessary consequences of the "nongovernmental" status of the organizations but reflect particular features of program design.

Despite the tremendous allure of democratic socialization for advocates of the nonprofit sector, these studies suggest that this claim cannot be easily and automatically sustained for all nonprofits or voluntary associations. To the extent that nonprofit organizations are highly professionalized, have large budgets and staffs, or work within the constraints of government programs, they are far less likely to promote the kind of adult political socialization long attributed to participation in voluntary associations. These large and professionalized nonprofits may advance the interests of the disadvantaged or of the public good through their *advocacy* work (Boris and Krehely 2003), but advocacy for others raises a host of issues about legitimate representation (Dovi 2002) that are elided in the process of *self-representation* through participatory governance.

INCIVILITY AND APATHY: CRITICAL REFLECTIONS ON ASSOCIATIONALISM

If organizational structure shapes political socialization, then it is dangerous to export claims that participation generates democratic socialization to the entire field of nonprofit organizations regardless of governance, size, or professionalization. Yet increasingly critics of the optimistic accounts of political socialization go still further, contending that even participatory organizations may fail to generate the skills necessary for democratic participation or that they may cultivate values that are actually hostile to liberal democracy. The more neutral variant of this critique asserts that the simple absence of formal organizational structure and professionalization does not guarantee that participation will nurture political socialization. In a comparative ethnography of local organizations, Eliasoph documents that organizations of volunteers, country-western dancers, and even environmental activists may be infused with "etiquettes" of participation that contribute to "political evaporation," the suppression of conversation around value commitments, public issues, and political challenges (1998:6–7). Community volunteering, "the hegemonic image of good citizenship" (1998:25), actually frustrated efforts to engage in the political conversations that are central to models of participatory democracy (Polletta 2002). Instead, individual volunteers often spent considerable time alone, on preset activities that they themselves had not participated in planning. When conversation did occur, Eliasoph observed that the volunteers kept the conversation focused closely on what was local and practical: "Volunteer work embodied, above all, an effort aimed at convincing themselves and others that the world makes sense and that regular people really can make a difference. . . . Community-spirited citizens judged that by avoiding 'big' problems, they could better buoy their optimism. But by excluding politics from their group concerns, they kept their enormous, overflowing reservoir of concern and empathy, compassion and altruism, out of circulation, limiting its contribution to the common good" (1998:63). Even among activists mobilized around local toxic-waste problems, the cultivation of practices of public political conversation took both time and the discovery of new "audiences" in a statewide network of other environmental organizations. Not even speaking to the media would succeed as politics, since reporters insistently selected women to interview and then steered them into declarations of "mandatory Mom-ism"—a highly personal rather than explicitly political expression of concern for one's own children (1998:246–48). So where arguments about social capital often invite an extrapolation from playing cards with the neighbors to democratic participation (Putnam 2000), Eliasoph demonstrates how social, even civic, engagement may actually cultivate political apathy.

Other revisionist arguments go much further, arguing that voluntary associations may serve as vehicles for the cultivation of separatism, intergroup hostility, and even antidemocratic values. Revisiting the "golden age of fraternity" in late nineteenth-century America, Kaufman (2002) argues that the rich array of Masonic, Pythian, and other lodges cultivated identities grounded in racial, ethnic, and gender separateness. This culture of organization, he argues, undermined support for more universal public programs and fostered an atmosphere of group conflict. The Klan, the Nazi party, hate organizations—all have been held up as potent counter-organizations to the facile equation of participation with democratic values (Fiorina 1999; Rosenblum 1998b; Skocpol 1999:69). Whereas nonprofit scholars have long been attuned to problems of "philanthropic particularism" and the large proportion of charitable donations that sustain cultural activities of interest to those with the income to donate (Salamon 1987:111–12), these critical reflections go beyond the absence of genuine altruism to raise the possibility that voluntary and nonprofit organizations may nurture intolerance and damaging exclusion. As with arguments for democratic socialization, associations are understood to constitute political actors, but not necessarily democratic citizens: "Organized racism is more than the aggregation of individual racist sentiments. It is a social milieu in which venomous ideas . . . take shape. Through networks of groups and activists, it channels personal sentiments of hatred into collective racist acts" (Blee 2002:3). To what extent can a democracy tolerate—much less encourage—associations that cultivate divisiveness and intolerance among citizens? This is a central debate among theorists of liberalism (e.g., Barry 2001:112–93; Rosenblum 1998b) and one that signals the dangers of assuming that all associational participation nurtures civic skills and values.

Associations that practice internal self-governance may also be problematic insofar as they restrict some citizens from membership. The tension between free association and detrimental restrictions on membership has also been central to judicial reflections on the place of voluntary associations in a democratic polity, turning on the "conflict between the values of free association and those of nondiscrimination" (Gutmann 1998:6–11). Recent decisions concerning the Jaycees and the Boy Scouts of America delineate "intimate associations" from groups legitimately subject to requirements of open accommodation and nondiscrimination. As Nancy Rosenblum has argued, expectations of political liberalization do "not attach as spontaneously or confidently to religious associations or to flourishing new phenomena such as residential homeowners' associations or fellowship and support groups as it does to these secular, quasi-civic associations. The onus for cultivating the moral dispositions of liberal democratic citizens falls heavily on voluntary groups such as the Jaycees and their myriad counterparts. So does the demand for congruence and nondiscriminatory policies of admission, with the paradoxical result that the classic voluntary association is denied the core right of freedom of association—the ability to set restrictive membership criteria and to admit only wanted members" (1998b:76).

For liberal theorists, the "dark side" of participation poses a particular problem, demanding a balancing of individual liberties to join associations with concerns for the preservation of core liberal commitments. Chambers and Kopstein contend that the balance may be established around the requirement for reciprocity, "the recognition of other citizens, even those with whom one has deep disagreement, as moral agents deserving civility" (2001:839). In debates over the relation of multiculturalism and liberalism (Barry 2001; I. M. Young 1990), theorists contest the proper relation of deference to distinctive group values and adherence to core liberal principles. Similar questions are provoked by nonprofit status—particularly standing as a "public charity"—with its expectation that legal privileges recognize the provision of some public good or service to some social value. Whether challenged by the presence of "nonprofits in disguise" or by nonprofit organizations promoting controversial as well as illiberal values, the automatic equation of nonprofit status with civic virtues is undermined.

As with the positive claims for the role of voluntary associations in cultivating democratic values and practices, this critical view resonates beyond the advanced industrialized democracies. In the field of international development, international nongovernmental organizations may act to preserve authoritarian government or advance market penetration by firms in the donor country (B. H. Smith 1998). Whereas some projects may be designed to promote civic participation and cultivate democratic skills (Brown and Tandon 2003), other models of intervention may constitute an "anti-politics machine." As James Ferguson has written of a development project in Lesotho: "By uncompromisingly reducing poverty to a technical problem, and by promising technical solutions to the sufferings of powerless and oppressed people, the hegemonic problematic of 'development' is the principal means through which the question of poverty is depoliticized in the world today. At the same time, by making the intentional blueprints for 'development' so highly visible, a 'development' project can end up performing extremely sensitive political operations involving the entrenchment and expansion of institutional state power almost invisibly, under cover of a neutral, technical mission to which no one can object" (1994:256).

Here, the optimistic reading of Tocqueville is countered with insights from Foucault on the operation of power (and depoliticization) through seemingly neutral practices and expert discourses. The consequences of organizational auspice for democratic practices and values are shaped not only by internal organizational structure or values but also by the relation of organizations to broader structures of power. The "anti-politics machine" of technocratic implementation is one possibility; the "Velvet Revolution" of eastern Europe in 1989 another. Thus, voluntary associations and nonprofit organizations matter not only as potential sites of political socialization for individuals but also as vehicles for social regulation.

POLITICAL ENGAGEMENT

The causal chain from participation to political outcomes is not complete with individual socialization and acquisition of civic skills (or even uncivil values). As Tocqueville contended, associations contribute to democracy by articulating interests, by providing a framework for the careers of those in the political opposition and a "center for action" where "they form something like a separate nation within the nation and a government within the government" (1969:190; see also Walzer 1984). Thus any assessment of the political consequences of voluntary associations and nonprofit organizations must directly address the forms of engagement between these private entities and formal political institutions.

This connection is shaped by the direct regulation of political participation. Many arguments for the contribution of associationalism to democracy presume that the skills and values cultivated in associations are easily transposed to formal politics by way of individual behavior, but the legal decoupling of "charitable" nonprofits from significant political engagement disrupts this presumed connection (Berry and Arons 2003:47–65; Boris and Krehely 2003; Wolch 1990:62–74). In combination with the particularism that characterizes many sites of association,[4] these observations demand caveats to claims that participation and membership per se generate democratic skills and values.

Throughout history, rulers have been wary of "privately held public power." The long history of restrictions on association reminds us that voluntary organizations may be potent forces of change (whether or not current elites like the direction of that change) (McCarthy 2003). Given their potential as vehicles for political conflict, we should expect access to political arenas itself to be the object of contestation. If at least some voluntary associations or nonprofit organizations are sites for democratic socialization and mobilization, such organizations are not necessarily equally available to all social groups or for all causes. In addressing these issues, research has become somewhat bifurcated between charities, foundations, and philanthropies that are generally recognized as core concerns for nonprofit research and more politically engaged voluntary associations such as labor unions that are more frequently treated in other research literatures.[5] And, in general, the political or advocacy activities of nonprofit organizations are treated with care—not least by the organizational informants themselves—insofar as "politics" has been held to invalidate nonprofit standing in the context of U.S. politics (but see Berry and Arons 2003; Boris and Krehely 2003; Wolch 1990:62–76) or to prompt challenges to the "public interest" that the organizations seek to advance (Jenkins, this volume). Although Douglas's chapter in the first edition of this book included a discussion of mutual benefit associations and pressure groups (1987:51–53), much of the literature on nonprofits has focused on the "charitable" nonprofits and human service delivery organizations. This division of labor has made it difficult to think comparatively about the ways in which nonprofit organizations serve as vehicles for either elite control or the mobilization of social or ideological minorities.[6]

In a very fundamental sense, the lineage of the nonprofit organization may be traced to efforts by elites to craft a means to extend their wishes in time (beyond the limits of their own mortal existence) and in scale (beyond the capacities of single individuals). As laid out in the Elizabethan Statute of 1601, the law of charities enabled durable and/or collective forms of activity beyond the bounds of the state, so long as that activity was dedicated to purposes approved by the state (Ware 1989). These efforts were initially viewed with suspicion; indeed, many states revoked English law in the wake of the Revolution leaving such efforts without the foundation of the Elizabethan Statute of Charities (Zollman 1924). As Peter Dobkin Hall (1992, this volume) has documented in his studies of what would come to be recognized as "nonprofit organizations" in American history, through the nineteenth century this organizational form represented a controversial but effective vehicle for nationalizing projects of northeastern elites. Well into the twentieth century, the activities and resources of these publicly chartered yet privately governed entities raised political suspicion. State legislation repeatedly enacted tradeoffs of permission or subsidy of private activities for increases in government oversight (Clemens, forthcoming; Novak 2001). The suspicion of resources controlled by private associations persisted in laws limiting the property that could be held.

In the United States, this period of innovation and expansion on the part of elite philanthropy and foundations was accompanied by important changes in the organization of popular voluntary associations. As Tocqueville observed, early nineteenth-century American society was unusual in the extent of voluntary activity[7] and by the second half of the century many of these organizations had large memberships and were national in scope (Skocpol 2003). Mobilizing farmers, workers, women, and other constituencies, these voluntary associations served as vehicles for large-scale political engagement that deeply changed American political institutions (Clemens 1997; Sanders 1999). To many observers, these developments confirmed suspicions of private association outside of formal political institutions. Unions, not surprisingly, bore the brunt of this suspicion. The persistence of master-servant principals and criminal conspiracy in nineteenth-century law meant that the very existence of a labor association could be taken as evidence of future wrongdoing (Hattam 1993). Regulation of other kinds of association—incorporated or not—was more benign, but the linkage of associations to political activity remained problematic. In the 1910s, state courts disagreed as to whether associations dedicated to securing legal change through legal means were properly understood as "charitable" and therefore eligible for exemptions from taxation of property and bequests (Zollman 1924:209).

These early disagreements foreshadowed a history of legislative oversight in which excessive political activity by foundations or nonprofit organizations triggered threats to the exempt status and legal standing of these organizations (Jenkins 1998; Reid 1999:310–21; Wolch 1992:62–69; D. Young 1999:56–61). In the United States, as federal intervention in community and social issues expanded from the 1960s onward, existing community associations and social movement organizations were torn between the appeal of new resources and the perceived threat that engagement with public programs would in time curb their political activities (Andrews 2001; Castells 1983: ch. 13). Similar concerns were prompted by grants from foundations committed to social change (Jenkins 1998:212–15). Tensions also rose between these politically engaged movement organizations and preexisting voluntary and service agencies that had expectations of greater control over new sources of public largesse (Castells 1983:116). By the end of the decade, both social service and environmental organizations had experienced hostile bouts of regulation in reaction to their advocacy activities (Wolch 1990:63–67).

Through their tax-exempt status and receipt of public funds, both advocacy and service organizations remain vulnerable to political efforts to use the leverage of these economic advantages to channel or choke off political activity. In the early 1990s, the U.S. Congress repeatedly considered—and defeated—a proposal from Congressman Istook "to curtail advocacy by nonprofit groups receiving grants" (Reid 1999:316; see also Berry and Arons 2003:66–92). Although these proposals failed, they suggest the durable tension between contestation and collaboration as imageries of the relation of governments to nonprofit organizations and voluntary associations more generally. Research has repeatedly demonstrated that nonprofits spend fewer funds on political activities than are allowed by law and express considerable wariness and uncertainty about the extent of allowable activity. As Jeffrey Berry observes, "the interest group sector with the strongest disincentive to lobby is 501c3 nonprofits. It is the only interest group sector to whom the government says 'you really shouldn't'" (2003:27; Boris and Krehely 2003). Thus even if nonprofits are organized to cultivate civic skills among their members, they are constrained in their capacity to serve as vehicles for this new political capacity. As with the specter of "bad civil society" (Chambers and Kopstein 2001), this history of enforced disengagement from politics—at least on the input side—must qualify any easy assumption of a necessary or complementary relationship between voluntary associations or nonprofit organizations and democracy. This decoupling of nonprofit associations and political activity has become still more problematic as nonprofits become ever more active in the delivery of publicly funded services.

THE POLITICS OF PARTNERSHIP

If the role of nonprofits and associations in political mobilization has been carefully policed, the activity of these organizations in the provision of services has also been a topic of concern, perhaps the central topic in nonprofit scholarship. In the first edition of this handbook, James Douglas turned to democratic theory to address the question of why some services are provided by nonprofit organizations rather than by government agencies. His answer emphasized the "demand structure" for services (e.g., majority vs. minority in democratic polities) as well as the capacity of nonprofits to maintain diversity and to provide a corrective to bureaucratic inflexibility. The object of this influential essay (1987:43) was to develop a political analogue to the economic theories of nonprofit organizations surveyed by Hansmann (1987) in the same volume (see also Weisbrod 1988). Drawing parallels with the economic concept of "market failure," Douglas asks, "why, given the extensive range of services provided by the public (or government) sector, we need to supplement them by private endeavors that are not accountable through the same political channels" (1987:44; for critical discussions see DiMaggio and Anheier 1990:140–41; Ware 1989: ch. 1). Thus voters with clear preferences are assumed by the argument, eliding important questions about how the establishment of such partnerships in the delivery of services may transform processes of political socialization and the constitution of interests.

The explanatory logic emphasizes choice rather than the feedback of policies to recognized preferences (Pierson 1994). If a majority desires some form of social provision, those preferences will support government provision of services. In cases where a minority desires a service, nonprofit organizations represent an alternative vehicle for provision. Consequently, governments may facilitate the formation of nonprofit organizations in order to increase the level of satisfaction with the overall mix of services. Such a "combination of public provision and voluntary provision for public purposes makes it possible to accommodate the views and preferences of a greater range of the community than could public provision alone" (Douglas 1987:45). The resulting argument offers both an explanation for existing distributions of activities across organizational forms and a guide to future decisions over when services should be provided by public agencies *or* nonprofit organizations. If the existing mix meets the preferences of citizens, it should be maintained; if not, policy should be altered to match those preferences.

This conceptualization of public and nonprofit provision as mutually exclusive alternatives—discrete choices—has been challenged by a growing body of empirical research on the role of nonprofit organizations in modern welfare states. Whereas Douglas's argument conceptualizes nonprofit activities as *alternatives* to government provision, Salamon documents that in the United States the nonprofit sector has grown as a *complement* to government programs. Further, rather than viewing nonprofit organizations as a consequence of the absence of majority support for public provision, Salamon contends that the expansion of government programs is better understood as a consequence of *voluntary failure* (2003:33–49; for an overview see D. R. Young 1999).[8]

As an analytic lens, concern for collaboration highlights the division of labor between governments and nonprofit organizations while obscuring issues central to analyses of political socialization and group contestation discussed above. In contrast to studies of political socialization and participatory governance, research on the division of labor between nonprofits and government often rests on a decidedly thin sense of the distribution of preferences and the exercise of choice within democratic polities. Diverging from imageries of conflict and contestation, these arguments assume political actors as individuals with existing preferences for services rather than as already-organized communities and claimants. Consequently, this approach to the division of labor between government agencies and nonprofit organizations obscures the political process by which partnerships are constituted and politics are remade.

Under what conditions do states turn from predominantly

public forms of social provision to more extensive collaboration with nonprofit organizations? And what are the implications of such delegation for democratic governance and the legitimacy of public programs? Douglas (1987) provided a clear answer to the first of these questions: governments will collaborate with nonprofits—rather than providing services directly—insofar as those services are preferred by less than a majority of citizens or where the "categorical constraint" of uniformity and equity is not met. Recent scholarship, however, has tended to develop more dynamic or processual accounts of the turn of welfare states toward greater reliance on or collaboration with nonprofit organizations. This turn from relatively ahistorical economic models has highlighted how policy makes politics, and thus how the expanding partnership between government and nonprofits has reconstructed the political roles of each. During the War on Poverty, for example, the U.S. federal government adopted a "contracting regime" intended to promote innovation and participation as well as to allow a rapid expansion of organizational capacity (Smith and Lipsky 1993; Smith and Grønbjerg, this volume). The resulting growth of government funding of nonprofit activities led, in turn, to a perception of those nonprofits as interest groups lobbying selfishly for increased funding (Berry and Arons 2003:79–85) and calls—most notably in the oft-defeated Istook amendment—to forbid lobbying activity on the part of nonprofit organizations receiving public funds (although existing legislation already forbade the use of federal funds to support such political activities). Thus the expansion of government-nonprofit partnerships has led to the increasing politicization of nonprofits as providers of public services, even as they are increasingly wary of engaging as political actors.

Where the expansion of the welfare state took place primarily through public agencies, support for increased partnerships with nonprofits could be advanced as solutions to the "crisis" of the welfare state. In Europe, well-developed welfare states have turned to expanded collaborations with nonprofits in the face of fiscal crises and "crises of technique" in which traditional bureaucratic methods prove ill suited to policy problems (Ullman 1998). In the late 1990s, Britain's "New Labour" adopted an essentially communitarian endorsement of government collaboration with nonprofits in part as a means of rejecting the Conservatives' exaltation of the market without requiring New Labour to return to the state-centered policies of their predecessors (Kendall 2000). Studies of welfare reform suggest how the use of nonprofit organizations to provide services provides cover for downsizing programs and shifts risk from public authorities (Austin 2003; Pierson 1994). Rather than the distribution of citizen preferences at a particular moment, all these studies emphasize the role of political and policy entrepreneurs, as well as the initiatives and capacities of state bureaucracies, in explaining when and why governments turn to nonprofits.

Insofar as governments turn to extensive collaboration with nonprofit entities, what are the implications for governance and legitimacy? As Milward and Provan (2000) argue, principal-agent theory helps to clarify what is at stake. In democratic polities, voters or citizens may be understood as the principals, elected officials and public bureaucrats as agents. In systems of service provision, however, those officials and bureaucrats take the role of principal contracting out to nonprofit and for-profit entities that deliver services. Whereas such decentralization may be driven by the perception that large—and particularly federal—bureaucracies are too distant from and unresponsive to the public, decentralization itself produces a much more complex terrain of accountability. As Smith and Lipsky observe, "Government accountability to citizens is undermined when responsibility for admission, treatment, and outcomes seems to be in the hands of private organizations" (1993:209). One response is to heighten formal accountability requirements for contracting nonprofits (1993:79–81; on outcome-based evaluations, see also Schorr 1997: ch. 4).

More effective structuring of the principal-agent relation between government and nonprofits may alleviate the second component of the accountability challenge (Milward and Provan 2000), but the issue of accountability to citizens and the perceived legitimacy of public provision remain. Insofar as nongovernmental entities are increasingly visible as the providers of social services, the legitimacy of public provision—increasingly restricted to funding rather than implementation—may be undermined. In the early 1980s, surprise greeted studies by Lester Salamon and Alan Abramson (1982) that documented the extent to which nonprofit organizations were dependent on public funding. In an era when the case for delegation and decentralization is routinely joined to a stylized critique of public bureaucracies as necessarily ineffective (e.g., Chubb and Moe 1990:38–39; Chubb and Peterson 1989: ch. 1; Schorr 1997: ch. 3), evidence of the efficacy of nonprofit organizations—and increasingly "faith-based" programs—is contrasted to the purported failure of public programs. Some commentators argue that such contrasts feed the stream of anti-statism in American political culture (Block 1996; Weisberg 1996), at the same time that others see decentralization of policy provision as a path to the revitalization of democratic participation at the local level (Putnam 2000).

The questions raised by contracting out are rather different when viewed from the perspective of constituting citizens with distinct political interests and capacities for participation. To the extent that publicly funded services are delivered by nongovernmental organizations, it becomes more difficult for citizens to answer the question of "what are my tax dollars doing?" and easier to misrecognize public services as private benefits: "In the United States, when people need help beyond cash assistance, they go to nonprofits and do not interact directly with government. Although many receiving services are not unaware that some of the funding for the nonprofit comes from government, the face of compassion, care, and concern they see is the face of private caregivers and community organizations, not bureaucrats and government agencies" (Berry and Arons 2003:15). This raises the possibility that as publicly funded services are increasingly mistaken for—or at least experienced as—

private and charitable, this will undermine political support for continued public spending on these services. A second concern invokes the problems of patronage politics: will increased government-nonprofit partnerships facilitate the cooptation of these "schools of citizenship" by elected officials? With the transnational turn to privatization and devolution, the answers to these explicitly political questions are not yet clear, but the asking of them is obscured when we consider such partnerships only from the perspective of the quality of service delivery. If voluntary associations and nonprofit organizations are valued, in part, because of their capacity to constitute citizens, then the increasing ties of nonprofits to the states signal an important shift in the relations that constitute democratic polities.

BEYOND PARTICIPATION AND PROVISION

The proliferation of claims for the political salience of voluntary associations or nonprofit organizations underscores how ambiguity about organizational forms pervades research and theorizing on nonprofit entities (see the editors' introduction). For the majority of these claims, the "not-for-profit" status of organizations is less relevant than other traits assumed to be linked to this status: participatory governance and voluntarism; control by a delimited social group and some autonomy from formal political institutions; connections to broader social networks and orientation to particular values; flexibility and diversity. Given the potential for confusion generated by these diverse claims, an assessment of the political salience of nonprofits must avoid attributing traits or consequences to nonprofit organizations simply by virtue of their formal organizational status or auspice.

From the perspective of political theory, nonprofits matter not simply as providers of services but also as potential sites for the constitution of citizens and vehicles for the expression of articulated interests and values. The capacity of nonprofit organizations to serve these functions depends on features of organizational structure: the degree of formal hierarchy and professionalism, the opportunities for practicing participation. But, as those wary of "bad civil society" have argued, even the most participatory organizational structure is not a guarantee that the values and practices advanced by the organization will be consistent with any given understanding of democracy. Consequently, the status of nonprofit organizations and voluntary associations will continue to be fundamentally contested as democratic polities strive to find balance between concerns for freedom of expression and limits on intolerance or exclusion.

While the delineation of freedom of association in a democratic polity is a fundamental issue for liberal theory (Gutman 1998), it is also an ongoing policy question as nonprofit organizations become ever more entwined in the governance and provision of public services. Just as the increase in the size and professionalism of nonprofits should prompt reconsideration of their role in political socialization, so the increasing ties between these nongovernmental—as well as not-for-profit—entities and the state raise important questions about the changing relations of the components of civic society to the formal institutions of representation and rule. In the place of a "political theory of nonprofits," the current moment requires close attention to the implication of nonprofit organizations in diverse projects of state-building and political mobilization. If "policy makes politics," the increasingly complex web of relations among government agencies and nonprofit organizations will not lead to a simple—or singular—political outcome.

NOTES

1. For a historical overview of nonprofit corporations in the United States, see Hall, this volume. On sovereignty versus subsidiary concepts of nonprofit organizations, see Brody and Cordes (1999).

2. These arguments often combine a number of distinct claims: that participation in associations contributes to the development or maintenance of a sense of community, to the preservation of freedom, or to the capacity for self-governance (M. E. Warren 2001:17).

3. For an extended discussion of local or grassroots associations, see Smith (2000).

4. For example, Wuthnow (1999:341–46) demonstrates that the effect of church attendance on participation in nonreligious organizations is consistently significant only for mainline Protestants when compared to Catholics and evangelical Protestants.

5. The study of social movement philanthropy (Jenkins 1998, this volume; Ostrander 1995) represents an important exception to this generalization. For example, in the post-Reconstruction South, money from the Rosenwald Fund aided disenfranchised blacks in "leveraging the state" to expand public education for black children (Strong et al. 2000). Community associations and self-help organizations are also central to the nonprofit literature, another exception to this generalization.

6. The complex taxonomies of organizational form also plague efforts to integrate research on social movements with the study of formal political institutions—the discontinuity between the two is often exacerbated by the use of distinctive analytic vocabularies (Burstein 1998).

7. Although recent research questions these estimates of the level of voluntary activity, the basic comparative insight into the differences with European societies of the time stands. A 1981 survey of associational membership in twelve industrialized democracies found the highest level in the United States (76 percent), followed by Northern Ireland (66 percent), with the lowest levels reported in Italy (26 percent) (reported in Verba, Schlozman, and Brady 1995: 80).

8. Other scholars retain Douglas's causal order—some limitation on government activities generates a turn to nonprofit or voluntary provision—while invoking mechanisms other than majoritarian rule. In a comparative-historical study of Britain and the United States, Ware (1989) argues that the association of nonprofit organizations with particular domains of activity is best understood as an institutional legacy. Mutual and cooperative associations took root in what were once marginal economic areas, serving as savings banks and providing home loans. The characteristic organizational forms persisted even as the scale and importance of these economic activities grew. Thus, Ware argues, the distribution of economic activities across public, for-profit, and not-for-profit entities cannot be attributed to contemporary distributions of preferences within the electorate.

REFERENCES

Almond, Gabriel A., and Sidney Verba. 1963. *The Civic Culture.* Princeton, N.J.: Princeton University Press.

Andrews, Kenneth T. 2001. "Social Movements and Policy Implementation: The Mississippi Civil Rights Movement and the War on Poverty, 1965–1971." *American Sociological Review* 66:71–95.

Austin, Michael J. 2003. "The Changing Relationship Between Nonprofit Organizations and Public Social Service Agencies in the Era of Welfare Reform." *Nonprofit and Voluntary Sector Quarterly* 32(1):97–114.

Baker, Paula. 1983. "The Domestication of Politics: Women and American Political Society, 1780–1920." *American Historical Review* 89(3):620–47.

Barry, Brian. 2001. *Culture and Equality: An Egalitarian Critique of Multiculturalism.* Cambridge, Mass.: Harvard University Press.

Beito, David T. 2000. *From Mutual Aid to the Welfare State: Fraternal Societies and Social Services, 1890–1967.* Chapel Hill: University of North Carolina Press.

Berry, Jeffrey M., with David F. Arons. 2003. *A Voice for Nonprofits.* Washington, D.C.: Brookings Institution Press.

Blee, Kathleen M. 2002. *Inside Organized Racism: Women in the Hate Movement.* Berkeley and Los Angeles: University of California Press.

Block, Fred L. 1996. *The Vampire State: And Other Myths and Fallacies about the U.S. Economy.* New York: The New Press.

Boris, Elizabeth T., and Jeff Krehely. 2003. "Civic Participation and Advocacy." In Lester Salamon, ed., *The State of Nonprofit America.* Washington, D.C.: Brookings Institution Press.

Boris, Elizabeth T., and C. Eugene Steuerle, eds. 1999. *Nonprofits and Government: Collaboration and Conflict.* Washington, D.C.: The Urban Institute.

Bratton, Michael. 1999. "Political Participation in a New Democracy: Institutional Considerations from Zambia." *Comparative Political Studies* 32:549–88.

Brint, Steven, and Charles S. Levy. 1999. "Professions and Civic Engagement: Trends in Rhetoric and Practice, 1875–1995." In Skocpol and Fiorina, eds., *Civic Engagement in American Democracy.*

Brody, Evelyn, and Joseph J. Cordes. 1999. "Tax Treatment of Nonprofit Organizations: A Two-Edged Sword?" In E. T. Boris and C. E. Steurle, eds., *Nonprofits and Government.*

Brown, L. David. 1998. "Creating Social Capital: Nongovernmental Development Organizations and Intersectoral Problem Solving." In W. W. Powell and E. S. Clemens, eds., *Private Action and the Public Good.*

Brown, L. David, Sanjeev Khagram, Mark H. Moore, and Peter Frumkin. 2000. "Globalization, NGOs, and Multisectoral Relations." In Joseph S. Nye and John D. Donahue, eds. *Governance in a Globalizing World.* Washington, D.C.: Brookings Institution Press.

Brown, L. David, and R. Tandon. 1993. *Multiparty Collaboration for Development in Asia.* New York: United Nations Development Programme.

Buchanan, James M., and Gordon Tullock. 1962. *The Calculus of Consent.* Ann Arbor: University of Michigan Press.

Burstein, Paul. 1998. "Interest Organizations, Political Parties, and the Study of Democratic Politics." In A. N. Costain and A. S. McFarland, eds., *Social Movements and American Political Institutions.* New York: Rowman and Littlefield.

Castells, Manuel. 1983. *The City and the Grassroots: A Cross-Cultural Theory of Urban Social Movements.* Berkeley and Los Angeles: University of California Press.

Chambers, Simone, and Jeffrey Kopstein. 2001. "Bad Civil Society." *Political Theory* 29(6):837–65.

Chaves, Mark. 2003. "Religious Congregations." In Lester Salamon, ed., *The State of Nonprofit America.* Washington, D.C.: Brookings Institution Press.

Chubb, John E., and Terry M. Moe. 1990. *Politics, Markets, and America's Schools.* Washington, D.C.: The Brookings Institution.

Chubb, John E., and Paul E. Peterson, eds. 1989. *Can the Government Govern?* Washington, D.C.: The Brookings Institution.

Clawson, Mary Ann. 1989. *Constructing Brotherhood: Class, Gender, and Fraternalism.* Princeton, N.J.: Princeton University Press.

Clemens, Elisabeth S. 1997. *The People's Lobby: Organizational Innovation and the Rise of Interest Group Politics in the United States, 1890–1925.* Chicago: University of Chicago Press.

———. Forthcoming. "Lineages of the Rube Goldberg State: Public Finance and Private Governance, 1900–1940." Stephen Skowronek, ed., *Crafting and Operating Institutions.* New York: New York University Press.

Crenson, Matthew A., and Benjamin Ginsberg. 2002. *Downsizing Democracy: How America Sidelined Its Citizens and Privatized Its Public.* Baltimore: Johns Hopkins University Press.

Cress, Daniel M. 1997. "Nonprofit Incorporation Among Movements of the Poor: Pathways and Consequences for Homeless Social Movement Organizations." *Sociological Quarterly* 38(2):343–60.

Dahl, Robert A. 1982. *Dilemmas of Pluralist Democracy.* New Haven, Conn.: Yale University Press.

Dane, Perry. 1998. "The Corporation Sole and the Encounter of Law and Church." In N. Jay Demerath et al., eds., *Sacred Companies.* New York: Oxford University Press.

DiMaggio, Paul J., and Helmut K. Anheier. 1990. "The Sociology of Nonprofit Organizations and Sectors," *Annual Review of Sociology* 16:137–59.

Dorf, Michael C., and Charles F. Sabel. 1998. "A Constitution of Democratic Experimentalism." *Columbia Law Review* 98:267–473.

Douglas, James. 1983. *Why Charity?* Beverly Hills, Calif.: Sage.

———. 1987. "Political Theories of Nonprofit Organization." In Powell, ed., *The Nonprofit Sector.*

Dovi, Suzanne. 2002. "Preferable Descriptive Representatives: Will Just Any Woman, Black, or Latino Do?" *American Political Science Review* 96:729–43.

Doyle, Don H. 1977. "The Social Functions of Voluntary Associations in a Nineteenth-Century American Town." *Social Science History* 1(3):333–55.

Dumenil, Lynn. 1984. *Freemasonry and American Culture, 1880–1939.* Princeton, N.J.: Princeton University Press.

Eckstein, Harry. 1966. *Division and Cohesion in Democracy: A Study of Norway.* Princeton, N.J.: Princeton University Press.

Edwards, Bob. 1994. "Semiformal Organizational Structure Among Social Movement Organizations: An Analysis of the U.S. Peace Movement." *Nonprofit and Voluntary Sector Quarterly* 23(4):309–33.

Eliasoph, Nina. 1998. *Avoiding Politics: How Americans Produce Apathy in Everyday Life.* New York: Cambridge University Press.

Evans, Peter, ed. 1997. *State-Society Synergy: Government and Social Capital in Development.* International and Area Studies Research Series, 94. Berkeley: University of California.

Ferguson, James. 1994. *The Anti-Politics Machine: Development, Depoliticization, and Bureaucratic Power in Lesotho.* Minneapolis: University of Minnesota Press.

Finkel, Steven E. 2000. "Civic Engagement and the Mobilization of Participation in Developing Democracies." Paper presented at Political Participation: Building a Research Agenda. Princeton University, October.

Fiorina, Morris P. 1999. "Extreme Voices: A Dark Side of Civic Engagement." In Skocpol and Fiorina eds., *Civic Engagement in American Democracy.*

Fleischacker, Sam. 1998. "Insignificant Communities." In Gutmann, ed., *Freedom of Association.*

Foley, Michael W., and Bob Edwards. 1996. "The Paradox of Civil Society." *Journal of Democracy* 7(3):38–52.

Fox, Jonathan. 1997. "How Does Civil Society Thicken? The Political Construction of Social Capital in Rural Mexico." In Peter Evans, ed., *State-Society Synergy.*

Frumkin, Peter. 2000. "After Partnership: Rethinking Public-Nonprofit Relations." In Mary Jo Bane, Brent Coffin, and Ronald Thiemann, eds., *Who Provides? Religion and the Future of Social Welfare in American Democracy.* Boulder, Colo.: Westview Press.

———. 2002. *On Being Nonprofit: A Conceptual and Policy Primer.* Cambridge, Mass.: Harvard University Press.

Gamm, Gerald, and Robert D. Putnam. 1999. "The Growth of Voluntary Associations in America, 1840–1940." *Journal of Interdisciplinary History* 29(4):511–58.

Ganz, Marshall. 2000. "Resources and Resourcefulness: Strategic Capacity in the Unionization of California Agriculture, 1959–1966." *American Journal of Sociology* 105(4):1003–62.

Gidron, Benjamin, Ralph M. Kramer, and Lester M. Salamon, eds. 1992. *Government and the Third Sector: Emerging Relationships in Welfare States.* San Francisco: Jossey-Bass.

Glanville, Jennifer L. 1999. "Political Socialization or Selection? Adolescent Extracurricular Participation and Political Activity in Early Adulthood." *Social Science Quarterly* 80(2):279–91.

Grønbjerg, Kirsten A. 1993. *Understanding Nonprofit Funding: Managing Revenues in Social Services and Community Development Organizations.* San Francisco: Jossey-Bass.

Gutmann, Amy, ed. 1998. *Freedom of Association.* Princeton, N.J.: Princeton University Press.

Hall, Peter Dobkin. 1992. *Inventing the Nonprofit Sector and Other Essays on Philanthropy, Voluntarism, and Nonprofit Organizations.* Baltimore, Md.: Johns Hopkins University Press.

———. 1999. "Vital Signs: Organizational Population Trends and Civic Engagement in New Haven, Connecticut, 1850–1998." In Skocpol and Fiorina, eds., *Civic Engagement in American Democracy.*

Hansmann, Henry. 1987. "Economic Theories of Nonprofit Organization." In Powell, ed., *The Nonprofit Sector.*

Hattam, Victoria. 1993. *Labor Visions and State Power: The Origins of Business Unionism in the United States.* Princeton, N.J.: Princeton University Press.

Heimer, Carol A. 1999. "Competing Institutions: Law, Medicine, and Family in Neonatal Intensive Care." *Law and Society Review* 33(1):17–66.

James, Estelle. 1987. "The Nonprofit Sector in Comparative Perspective." In Powell, ed., *The Nonprofit Sector.*

Jenkins, J. Craig. 1998. "Channelling Social Protest: Foundation Patronage of Contemporary Social Movements." In Powell and Clemens, eds., *Private Action and the Public Good.*

Jennings, M. Kent. 1981. *Generational Politics: A Panel Study of Young Adults and Their Parents.* Princeton, N.J.: Princeton University Press.

Kaufman, Jason. 2002. *For the Common Good? American Civic Life and the Golden Age of Fraternity.* New York: Oxford University Press.

Kendall, Jeremy. 2000. "The Mainstreaming of the Third Sector into Public Policy in England in the Late 1990s: Whys and Wherefores." *Policy and Politics* 28(4):541–62.

Kendall, Jeremy, and Martin Knapp. 2000. "Measuring the Performance of Voluntary Organizations." *Public Management* 2(1):105–32.

Knoke, David, and James R. Wood. 1981. *Organized for Action: Commitment in Voluntary Associations.* New Brunswick, N.J.: Rutgers University Press.

Kuhnle, Stein, and Per Selle. 1992. "The Historical Precedent for Government-Nonprofit Cooperation in Norway." In Gidron et al., eds., *Government and the Third Sector.*

Mann, Michael. 1986. *The Sources of Social Power,* vol. 1. New York: Cambridge University Press.

March, James G., and Johan P. Olsen. 1989. *Rediscovering Institutions: The Organizational Basis of Politics.* New York: Free Press.

McCarthy, Kathleen D. 2003. *American Creed: Philanthropy and the Rise of Civil Society, 1700–1865.* Chicago: University of Chicago Press.

Milofsky, Carl. 1988. "Scarcity and Community: A Resource Allocation Theory of Community and Mass Society Organizations." In C. Milofsky, ed., *Community Organizations:*

Studies in Resource Mobilization and Power. New York: Oxford University Press.

Milward, H. Brint, and Keith G. Provan. 2000. "Governing the Hollow State." *Journal of Public Administration Research and Theory* 10(2):359–79.

Minkoff, Debra C. 1993. "The Organization of Survival: Women's and Racial-Ethnic Voluntarist and Activist Organizations, 1955–85." *Social Forces* 71(4):887–908.

Morone, James A. 2003. *Hellfire Nation: The Politics of Sin in American History.* New Haven, Conn.: Yale University Press.

Novak, William J. 2001. "The American Law of Association: The Legal-Political Construction of Civil Society." *Studies in American Political Development* 15:163–188.

Olsen, Macur. 1971. *The Logic of Collective Action.* Cambridge, Mass.: Harvard University Press.

Osa, Maryjane. 2003. *Solidarity and Contention: Networks of Polish Opposition.* Minneapolis: University of Minnesota Press.

Osborne, S. P. 1998. *Voluntary Organisations and Innovation in Public Services.* London: Routledge.

Ostrander, Susan A. 1995. *Money for Change: Social Movement Philanthropy at Haymarket People's Fund.* Philadelphia: Temple University Press.

Ostrom, Elinor. 1997. "Crossing the Great Divide: Coproduction, Synergy, and Development." In Peter Evans, ed., *State-Society Synergy.*

Pierson, Paul. 1994. *Dismantling the Welfare State? Reagan, Thatcher and the Politics of Retrenchment.* New York: Cambridge University Press.

Polletta, Francesca. 2002. *Freedom Is an Endless Meeting: Democracy in American Social Movements.* Chicago: University of Chicago Press.

Portes, Alejandro. 1998. "Social Capital: Its Origins and Applications in Modern Sociology." *Annual Review of Sociology* 24:1–24.

Powell, Walter W. 1987. *The Nonprofit Sector: A Research Handbook.* First ed. New Haven, Conn.: Yale University Press.

Powell, Walter W., and Elisabeth S. Clemens, eds. 1998. *Private Action and the Public Good.* New Haven, Conn.: Yale University Press.

Putnam, Robert D. 2000. *Bowling Alone: The Collapse and Revival of American Community.* New York: Simon and Schuster.

Putnam, Robert D., with Roberto Leonardi and Raffaela Y. Nanetti. 1993. *Making Democracy Work: Civic Traditions in Modern Italy.* Princeton, N.J.: Princeton University Press.

Reid, Elizabeth J. 1999. "Nonprofit Advocacy and Political Participation." In Boris and Steuerle, eds., *Nonprofits and Government.*

Rein, Martin. 1989. "The Social Structure of Institutions: Neither Public nor Profit." In Sheila B. Kamerman and Alfred J. Kahn, eds., *Privatization and the Welfare State.* Princeton, N.J.: Princeton University Press.

Rosenblum, Nancy L. 1998a. "Compelled Association: Public Standing, Self-Respect, and the Dynamic of Exclusion." In Gutmann, ed., *Freedom of Association.*

———. 1998b. *Membership and Morals: The Personal Uses of Pluralism in America.* Princeton, N.J.: Princeton University Press.

Salamon, Lester M. 1987. "Partners in Public Service: The Scope and Theory of Government-Nonprofit Relations." In Powell, ed., *The Nonprofit Sector.*

———. 2003. "The Resilient Sector: The State of Nonprofit America." In Lester Salamon, ed. *The State of Nonprofit America.* Washington, D.C.: Brookings Institution Press.

Salamon, Lester M., and Alan J. Abramson. 1982. *The Federal Budget and the Nonprofit Sector.* Washington, D.C.: Urban Institute Press.

Sanders, Elizabeth. 1999. *Roots of Reform: Farmers, Workers, and the American State, 1877–1917.* Chicago: University of Chicago Press.

Schorr, Lisbeth. 1997. *Common Purpose: Strengthening Families and Neighborhoods to Rebuild America.* New York: Anchor Books.

Sirianni, Carmen, and Lewis Friedland. 2001. *Civic Innovation in America: Community Empowerment, Public Policy, and the Movement for Civic Renewal.* Berkeley and Los Angeles: University of California Press.

Skocpol, Theda. 1997. "The Tocqueville Problem: Civic Engagement in American Democracy." *Social Science History* 21(4):455–80.

———. 1999. "How Americans Became Civic." In Skocpol and Fiorina, eds., *Civic Engagement in American Democracy.*

———. 2003. *Diminished Democracy: From Membership to Management in American Civic Life.* Norman: University of Oklahoma Press.

Skocpol, Theda, and Morris P. Fiorina, eds. 1999. *Civic Engagement in American Democracy.* Washington, D.C.: Brookings Institution Press.

Skocpol, Theda, Marshall Ganz, and Ziad Munson. 2000. "A Nation of Organizers: The Institutional Origins of Civic Voluntarism in the United States." *American Political Science Review* 94(3):527–46.

Smith, Brian H. 1998. "Nonprofit Organizations in International Development: Agents of Empowerment or Preservers of Stability?" In Powell and Clemens, eds., *Private Action and the Public Good.*

Smith, David Horton. 2000. *Grassroots Associations.* Thousand Oaks, Calif.: Sage.

Smith, Steven Rathgeb, and Michael Lipsky. 1993. *Nonprofits for Hire: The Welfare State in the Age of Contracting.* Cambridge, Mass.: Harvard University Press.

Strong, David, Pamela Barnhouse Walters, Brian Driscoll, and Scott Rosenberg. 2000. "Leveraging the State: Private Money and the Development of Public Education for Blacks." *American Sociological Review* 65:658–81.

Tocqueville, Alexis de. 1969. *Democracy in America.* New York: Anchor Books.

Ullman, Claire F. 1998. *The Welfare State's Other Crisis: Explaining the New Partnership Between Nonprofit Organizations and the State in France.* Bloomington: Indiana University Press, 1998.

Verba, Sidney, Kay Lehman Schlozman, and Henry E. Brady. 1995. *Voice and Equality: Civic Voluntarism in American Politics.* Cambridge, Mass.: Harvard University Press.

Wagner, Antonin. 1992. "The Interrelationship Between the Public and Voluntary Sectors in Switzerland: Unmixing the Mixed-Up Economy." In Gidron et al., eds., *Government and the Third Sector.*

Walzer, Michael. 1983. *Spheres of Justice: A Defense of Pluralism and Equality.* New York: Basic Books.

———. 1984. "Liberalism and the Art of Separation." *Political Theory* 12(3):315–30.

Ware, Alan. 1989. *Between Profit and State: Intermediate Organizations in Britain and the United States.* Princeton, N.J.: Princeton University Press.

Warren, Mark E. 2001. *Democracy and Association.* Princeton, N.J.: Princeton University Press.

Warren, Mark R. 2001. *Dry Bones Rattling: Community Building to Revitalize American Democracy.* Princeton, N.J.: Princeton University Press.

Weisberg, Jacob. 1996. *In Defense of Government: The Fall and Rise of Public Trust.* New York: Scribner.

Weisbrod, Burton A. 1988. *The Nonprofit Economy.* Cambridge, Mass.: Harvard University Press.

———. 1998. "Institutional Form and Organizational Behavior." In Powell and Clemens, eds., *Private Action and the Public Good.*

Wolch, Jennifer R. 1990. *The Shadow State: Government and Voluntary Sector in Transition.* New York: The Foundation Center.

Wuthnow, Robert. 1991. *Between States and Markets: The Voluntary Sector in Comparative Perspective.* Princeton, N.J.: Princeton University Press.

———. 1998. *Loose Connections: Joining Together in America's Fragmented Communities.* Cambridge, Mass.: Harvard University Press.

———. 1999. "Mobilizing Civic Engagement: The Changing Impact of Religious Involvement." In Skocpol and Fiorina, eds., *Civic Engagement in American Democracy.*

Young, Dennis R. 1999. "Complementary, Supplementary, or Adversarial? A Theoretical and Historical Examination of Nonprofit-Government Relations in the United States." In Boris and Steuerle, eds., *Nonprofits and Government.*

Young, Iris Marion. 1990. *Justice and the Politics of Difference.* Princeton, N.J.: Princeton University Press.

Young, Michael P. 2002. "Confessional Protest: The Religious Birth of U.S. National Social Movements." *American Sociological Review* 67:660–88.

Zollman, Carl. 1924. *American Law of Charities.* Milwaukee, Wisc.: Bruce.

10

Scope and Theory of Government-Nonprofit Relations

STEVEN RATHGEB SMITH
KIRSTEN A. GRØNBJERG

INTRODUCTION

Government-nonprofit relations—in the United States and most everywhere else—are complex and dynamic. As other chapters in this volume demonstrate, they include exchanges of financial and other resources as well as efforts to influence one another through regulatory activities or political mobilization. As such, they both reflect and shape the nature of civic engagement. Moreover, they vary across time, space, and fields of activities. Nor do they occur in isolation, but are conditioned by economic and market structures and by activities carried out informally in households or local communities.

The links between government and the nonprofit sector are evident across several dimensions—in the legal framework under which nonprofits operate, in the role they play in the delivery of a wide range of valued services, and in the efforts they make to influence the agenda for government action. Our analysis focuses mainly on the latter two dimensions, although we note that both are conditioned by and intertwined with the development of legal frameworks over time.

Service System Role

The extent and nature of government-nonprofit relations are perhaps most evident and concrete in the mix of auspices under which a wide range of common goods and services are delivered. Where government services are privatized so that private entities deliver services financed by government through line-item subsidies, grants, contracts, or fee-for-service arrangements, and where the bulk of service providers are nonprofits (e.g., human services in the United States), government-nonprofit relations involve complex interdependencies and substantial transaction benefits—and costs—to both parties. These types of relationships expanded dramatically in the United States during the post-1960s period, accounting for a significant proportion of the growth in the nonprofit sector itself (Grønbjerg and Smith 1999).

Where the bulk of government services are delivered directly by government (e.g., state religion, public elementary education), the relationship is likely to become one of competition between government and nonprofit institutions. However, it is most likely a lopsided competition that government dominates because of its better access to resources. Where individuals purchase services directly in the marketplace, with or without state subsidy, the state may foster direct competition among nonprofit and commercial entities (Steinberg, this volume).

The mix of delivery systems through which government-supported services are carried out varies among nation-states (James 1987; Salamon 2002a) and policy fields. Moreover, considerable evidence exists that these so-called tools of government action have diversified in recent years both in the United States (Salamon 2002b; S. R. Smith 2002) and elsewhere. Indeed, many government programs that traditionally provided the bulk of funding for nonprofit activity in the United States have declined in both absolute and constant dollars (except for health), while other public funding sources have grown (Grønbjerg and Smith 1999; S. R. Smith 2002; Grønbjerg and Salamon 2002). Thus the form of government support is shifting from producer- to consumer-side subsidies, including growing use of tax-expenditure vehicles and voucher systems. The result is a corresponding shift in the locus of decision-making and greater competition among service providers across all sectors.

Policy Role

During the past fifty to one hundred years, government has deepened its engagement across a wider scope of policy arenas in many societies and now affects broader segments of the population and in more profound ways. For example, government is now more extensively involved in efforts to regulate economic cycles, stimulate growth, support families, protect health and safety, and invest in human capital than fifty years ago. Although this particular tide recently has turned somewhat in many developed economies, over the long term the result has been to create powerful incentives for various groups and associations to seek control over the public agenda, or at the very least to influence the public agenda in ways compatible with their own policy priorities and goals.

In the United States, organized interest groups have grown in number and size. They dominate politics and the political agenda because of their enormous financial support for political candidates and increasingly sophisticated lobbying activities. At the same time, advocacy groups have flourished to the point that they collectively have come to constitute a virtual political smorgasbord—allowing individuals to pick and choose a portfolio of issues to support that fit their particular interests (Elinor Ostrom, personal communication).

While the underlying dynamics may still be somewhat murky, Walker (1991) and Salisbury (1984) show that the growth of the state is intimately linked to the growth of a variety of advocacy organizations. And these groups appear to be influential in setting and implementing policy initiatives (Skocpol and Fiorina 1999). Similarly, Skocpol's (1999) data from the nineteenth century show how the structures of government and civic associations came to resemble one another as the growing numbers of civic associations very quickly developed a structure parallel to that of government in the United States.

THEORY OF GOVERNMENT-NONPROFIT RELATIONS

Not surprisingly, a wealth of conceptual perspectives is available by which one may seek to disentangle these complexities of government-nonprofit relations. We review several of these approaches in the remainder of this chapter, but we have necessarily had to be selective and have chosen to use as our primary point of departure the extent to which the nonprofit sector is deeply embedded in, indeed inseparable from, the political economy. We argue that it is impossible to understand one without the other. Changes in the scope of government activities, in the mechanisms by which government carries out policies, or in the organization of the economy itself (e.g., competitive market vs. centrally planned) are likely to have significant implications for government-nonprofit relations. Indeed, changes in government-nonprofit relations provide a strategic window through which to understand the nature of political regimes and vice versa.

By the same token, government-nonprofit relations are deeply immersed in political ideologies about the proper role of government, preference for market structures, and priorities accorded to values of fairness, equity, equality, choice, and/or opportunities. As a result, the mechanisms of political decision-making are revealed by the role nonprofits play in shaping public policies compared to other private actors (e.g., the military, wealthy elites, or major corporations). It is also evident in the relative influence of different types of nonprofits and the constituency groups they represent—social movements, grassroots civic associations, nonprofit service providers, religious institutions, labor unions, trade associations, or corporate political action committees. Such features reveal a great deal about how power and political influence are structured in a given society (Clemens, this volume).

Three Models

We examine three broad frameworks evident in the theoretical literature in order to more fully conceptualize the relation between the government and nonprofit sectors. What we refer to as the demand/supply model focuses on ways in which government and nonprofits complement or compensate for one another's weaknesses in meeting the need for particular types of goods and services (also referred to as the "three-failures theory"; see Steinberg, this volume). It is rooted in the conception of nonprofits as akin to firms where demand and supply play a critical role. Perhaps not surprisingly, this model presupposes the presence of a dominant market economy supported by democratic institutions. However, most of the theorists associated with the model have paid little attention to the complex political interactions between government and nonprofits beyond those required to manage transactions.

The civil society/social movement model, our second model, to some extent complements the demand/supply model but focuses more explicitly on the multidimensional relations between government and nonprofits. This model considers how social, economic, and political structures combine to create complex dynamics in the relations between government and nonprofits—relations that evolve over time as first one and then another political issue captures public attention and as new ways to mobilize interests or groups gain prominence. These dynamics may also spread from one society to another, reflecting structures of international dominance and control. Compared with the demand/supply model, the civil society/social movement model allows us to consider a broader range of political economies as the context for understanding government-nonprofit relations. This model also places more emphasis on such diverse societal goals as pluralism, civic participation, and voluntarism.

Our third model, the regime or neo-institutional model, is explicitly comparative in nature. It reflects efforts to understand the processes by which social structures—including nonprofit organizations—become institutionalized over time and the conditions under which governmental structures take on particular forms. While initial conceptualizations of this model tended to ignore the nonprofit sector almost entirely, some more recent approaches have given prominent roles to nonprofit institutions.

Underlying Assumptions

This brief synopsis of the three models alludes to several underlying structures that we discuss in greater detail below. We highlight them here in order to set the stage for that analysis. First, the *nature of institutional relations*—that is, which institutions are dominant and how these institutions operate and maintain their dominance—determines whether the nonprofit sector takes on visible and formalized functions, including special recognition within the legal structure.

For example, societies dominated by large bureaucratic institutions may favor a nonprofit sector that operates with similar structures (DiMaggio and Powell 1983) but may also provide organizational space for those that serve to mediate between the individual and those other impersonal, formal structures (Berger and Neuhaus 1977; D. H. Smith 1973; Van Til 2004; Walzer 1995). By contrast, the role of nonprofits, if they exist at all in a formal sense, will be very different in societies dominated by more intimate social institutions and primary relationships, such as those found in tribal groups or village societies (Woolcock and Narayan 2000).

A second underlying structure shaping government-nonprofit relations concerns the *nature of the economy*. Wealthy, developed, diversified economies provide a very different context for the nonprofit sector than that of developing societies dominated by subsistence agriculture and barter exchanges. Similarly, market economies with their specialized institutions to manage or facilitate market transactions (e.g., credit systems, banks, enforceable contracts, stock exchanges) provide a distinctive context compared with that of centrally planned economies concerned with coordination and enforcement of production goals.

The *nature of the political structure* is also important. A society characterized by high inequality and dominated by a power elite protecting its own interests will provide a very different framework for government-nonprofit relations than one in which multiple, well-defined, counterbalanced groups represent the full spectrum of interests in the policy-making process (Esping-Andersen 1990; Walzer 1995; Titmuss 1969). Thus authoritarian regimes can destroy civil society by greatly reducing the ability and willingness of individuals to organize for mutual benefit or political purposes (J. C. Scott 1998). Further, societies with very centralized political structures such as France or the United Kingdom will have very different government-nonprofit sector relations than countries with decentralized political systems such as the United States. We turn now to a description of the three models.

MODEL I: DEMAND AND SUPPLY PERSPECTIVES

We examine two variations on the demand/supply model of government-nonprofit relations—a market niche model and a transaction model. Both conceive of the relationship as fundamentally structured around the demand for and supply of particular types of economic goods and services within the broader context of rational choice.[1] While complementary, the two models differ in how they conceive of the relation between the government and nonprofit suppliers of goods and services—as relatively independent actors driven by the invisible hand of competitive market forces in a given market niche, or as contractors engaged in complex transactions with a host of associated costs and benefits.

Market Niche Model

The simplest and perhaps most clearly articulated model of government-nonprofit relations emerged out of a straight market model. We refer to it as the market niche model to emphasize the ways in which nonprofits are seen as occupying special niches in the market. As conceived by the property rights school of economics, nonprofits do not belong in the market at all, since the absence of a profit motive leaves them floundering toward the abyss of inefficiency.

However, economists such as Weisbrod (1977), Rose-Ackerman (1996), Hansmann (1980, 1996), and James (1983) argue that a closer look at the nature of demand and supply structures reveals that nonprofits are uniquely suited to supply particular types of goods and services. In this view, nonprofits arise in response to particular demand structures that cannot be adequately met by private firms or government. They can meet these demands because they have access to special advantages and resources. The two major theoretical chapters in the first edition of this volume (Hansmann 1987; Douglas 1987) articulate this model, and several chapters in this edition (Steinberg; Brown and Slivinski) provide additional details and updated analysis.

Sources of demand for nonprofit activities. Theories of contract, market, and government failure all suggest that nonprofits arise to meet demands for particular types of goods and services that cannot be adequately met by the market or government sectors. This may occur if the products do not lend themselves to contractual or political transactions. Nonprofits may also serve to meet demands when tastes or preferences are too diverse to constitute a large enough aggregate demand to interest political entrepreneurs. For instance, immigrant groups often create nonprofit organizations to represent their interest and offer services to their communities. Many religious denominations have also created affiliated service organizations; Catholic Charities and Lutheran Social Services are two such examples. We would add that they may serve a similar function for market entrepreneurs, as suggested by the role of nonprofits in pioneering third-party health insurance, kidney dialysis, health-maintenance organizations, or hospice programs (Gray and Schlesinger 2002).

As discussed by Steinberg and by Brown and Slivinski (both this volume), theories of *contract failure* refer to imperfections in the system of market transactions for private goods so that trust in the provider, rather than known product quality, guides purchase decisions. Here government or nonprofit entities emerge as preferred providers because they give purchasers leverage or confidence that their interests will ultimately be served, not those of a profit-maximizing owner. In the case of nonprofits, the prohibition against distributing profits for private gain and systems of patron control serve to ensure such trust (Hansmann 1980, 1996; Ben-Ner 1987). Thus, a nonprofit theater troupe may reassure donors and the public that it is dedicated to quality programming and the broader community because donors know that the board and staff cannot divert organizational funds to their own personal benefit.

Theories of *market failure* concern themselves with an equally fundamental problem of market exchange systems—that is, that markets fail to operate efficiently when the product is a public good for which an appropriate price cannot be established in the private marketplace. In this case, the purchaser would pay for goods that, while of personal utility, also benefit others who do not pay—the so-called free riders. Under such conditions, the private market would not produce the goods in sufficient quantity to meet demand or maximize overall economic welfare. Consequently, nonmarket mechanisms, such as government, must step in to provide the public goods, at least those that are highly valued. Government can do so because its power of taxation forces everyone to share in the costs.

Theories of *government failure* focus on the different ways in which government and nonprofits respond to the challenges of market and contract failure and suggest that nonprofits step in to provide goods and services when the political process prevents government from doing so. Thus Weisbrod (1977, 1988) argues that government responds to the demands of the "majority" or the median voter, leaving special needs or those affecting small minorities or powerless groups unsatisfied. That happens because government cannot easily meet the conflicting demands of diverse populations, if it is to maintain political consensus. It must also select one policy from multiple options.

Douglas (1987) argues more broadly that government is constrained in its capacity to deliver certain public goods and services due to the limits of the political system and concerns of social justice. He argues that government cannot easily implement untested procedures because lack of knowledge about benefits and costs makes it difficult to present rational justifications and generate majority support for the use of public funds. The political costs of failed initiatives may be significant, since opponents may point to those to weaken the position of proponents. Moreover, government finds it difficult to experiment, since that indicates policies are not uniform and therefore not equitable.

Nor can government bypass demands for public accountability with impunity. Persons subjected to the policy may not be able to exit but can express their voice and opinions. Government must therefore demonstrate that it has followed legal mandates and acted fairly and equitably in carrying out authorized activities if it is to maintain broad public support. To do so, government must document its actions and will find it useful to establish administrative rules to facilitate that process—in other words, it will gravitate toward bureaucratic procedures and red tape (Blau and Meyer 1987; Wilson 1967; Lipsky 1980; Moe 1990).

Nonprofits do not face these particular constraints, or at least not nearly to the same extent, and can therefore compensate for these types of government failures. For example, nonprofits can carve out special niches for themselves and address the needs of minorities or the interests of small segments of the general public. By supplementing the one policy option that government must choose, nonprofits thus help address a central problem of democracy—how to meet diverse needs (James 1987).

Moreover, nonprofits are not beholden to an elected political body or the general public but are self-governing, usually by a relatively small, self-perpetuating board. They can therefore take risks as long as this small group of decision-makers agrees that the costs are worth the risk—if they consider the risks at all.[2] This is why it is plausible to celebrate nonprofits as the major source of social innovation (while private firms are celebrated for their technological and management innovations). It is less clear whether nonprofits (other than perhaps social movement organizations) actually do serve that function (Prewitt 2004).[3]

Limited external accountability also means that nonprofits do not need to document their activities or demonstrate their equity and fairness to nearly the same extent as government. After all, those receiving the services can choose to go elsewhere if they so desire. And nonprofits tend to be small organizations. Both features alleviate the need for extensive—and defensive—documentation and allow nonprofits to be flexible and considerate of special, individual circumstances and therefore more responsive to their particular constituents (Smith and Lipsky 1993). But having to raise funds to subsidize services likely offsets in part (or full) nonprofits' savings from reduced bureaucracy.

Overall, these advantages mean that nonprofits may meet demands for certain public goods sufficiently well to alleviate the need for alternative provisions by government, perhaps even to the point of preventing the emergence of a political consensus to vest public resources in addressing those needs (Wilensky and Lebeaux 1965; Esping-Anderson 1990). By compensating for a variety of contract, market, and government failures in these ways, nonprofits play a critical role in creating a division of labor—for example, market niches in which one of the three sectors (market, nonprofit, government) is uniquely suited to meet particular demands.

Nonprofit supply structures. Nonprofits can meet special

niche demands because they have access to particular types of resources or supply structures (James 1987, 1992). They can solicit and obtain voluntary contributions or membership dues to subsidize the provision of services to those unable or unwilling to pay the full costs. In the case of IRS-recognized charities in the United States, the tax deductibility of donations means that they can confer tax advantages on the majority of taxpayers (e.g., business firms or individuals that itemize their deductions), thereby enhancing incentives for donors to provide subsidies. The legal prohibition against private inurement through the nondistribution constraint allays suspicions that nonprofits will misuse such resources deliberately (Hansmann 1980). However, that particular advantage may be at least partially offset by the lingering suspicions, especially from the business community, that nonprofits do not have incentives to operate as efficiently as possible.

Nonprofits also have access to moral entrepreneurs motivated by religious (James 1987; Chaves 1998; Hammack 1998) or ideological commitments (Young 1983) to take on the tasks of providing goods in the absence of personal financial or political rewards. As Lohmann (1992) argues, nonprofits produce "common" goods that reflect the particular shared (i.e., common) values or interests of a group of individuals and that may benefit that group more or less exclusively. Similarly, Smith and Lipsky (1993) argue that nonprofits emerge to serve the needs of particular communities of like-minded individuals. This is, of course, why nonprofits can address demands of minorities and mobilize shared interests, commitments, repertoires, and other group resources to produce such goods.

To mobilize these resources, however, nonprofits must identify and articulate problems and solutions that resonate with potential constituency groups. Such capacity is at least in part a function of whether there are competing interpretations also seeking to mobilize constituency groups—too many such messages make it difficult to be heard above the din. Alternatively, the opportunity to fine-tune a message against the backdrop of competing interpretations may sharpen it and make it more effective.

Thus Finke and Starke (1992) note that religious competition promotes religious participation and fosters stronger, more active congregations. Similarly, Hammack (1998) shows that religious competition has been a major driving force in the development of the nonprofit sector in the United States, while James (1987) and Salamon and Anheier (1998) argue that religious competition should also be related to larger nonprofit sectors cross-nationally. Finally, Wiewel and Hunter (1985) demonstrate that the presence of similar organizations in a community forces new arrivals to more clearly define their mission, specialize, and focus their activities on a specialized niche in order to increase their prospects for survival.

As we argue below, the ability of nonprofits to mobilize moral entrepreneurs, and thus access the resources such individuals bring, also depends on the level and nature of civic and social engagement present in that society (Putnam 1993a, 1993b, 2000; Guterbock and Fries 1997; Skocpol, Ganz, and Munson 2000; Skocpol 1999) and on the prevalence of interest and stakeholder groups (Tschirhart, this volume; Clemens, this volume). Nonprofits will thus be more likely to raise donations, attract and retain volunteers, and more generally sustain themselves in communities with higher levels of social capital.

Transaction Model

We turn now to a more complex version of the supply/demand model that overcomes some of its limitations. The transaction model focuses squarely on the ability of nonprofits to compensate for government failures but also on the opportunities this creates for direct exchanges between government and nonprofits. If nonprofits compensate for government failure, then they are likely to have services to sell that government needs or wants for its own purposes. At the same time, the ability of government to extract taxes means that it has the resources to buy goods and services from nonprofits. Rather than competing with one another as alternative mechanisms for delivering a particular portfolio of public goods to consumers, government and nonprofits engage in exchange relationships with one another, including formal contracts that spell out how they will cooperate in making the goods available.

The basic elements of the transaction model are articulated by Salamon (1987) in the first edition of this volume, although he refers to it as a theory of government-nonprofit partnership. Salamon lays out an analytical framework that focuses squarely on that relation, drawing on his work to assess the impact of the Reagan budget cuts on the nonprofit sector in the early 1980s and the failure of that initiative to recognize the interdependencies of government and nonprofits. Although Salamon accepts the concept of government failure as a major driving force, he argues that nonprofits, not government, initiate the delivery of public goods. However, nonprofits encounter "failures" of their own—insufficiency, amateurism, particularism, and paternalism—that government is able to address.

The failure of *insufficiency* reflects the fact that nonprofits depend on donations from those able and willing to make contributions. However, the demand for nonprofit public goods most likely exceeds the available donative resources, especially during economic downturns. This sets the stage for tapping government revenues to support nonprofit activities. Nonprofits also face problems of *amateurism* because they may rely on staff and volunteers without extensive professional training and/or supervision or cannot properly professionalize and expand their operations with their own internal resources. Government resources and regulations help nonprofits professionalize (allowing expansion) and meet the demand for public goods.

The charge of *particularism* pertains to the roots of nonprofits in a particular community of interest such as a neighborhood, ethnic group, or cause (Salamon 1987; Kramer 1987). Particularistic emphases allow nonprofits to be responsive to their community of interest (Smith and Lipsky 1993), but that may directly conflict with broader societal interests in making access to public goods equitable and fair—the particularism of individual nonprofits inevitably leaves gaps in the overall service structure. Salamon argues that government funding and regulation of nonprofits make it possible to plug at least some of these holes, while still allowing nonprofits to maintain distinctive goals. For example, without public funding, many nonprofits would not be able to offer programs to the disadvantaged or the poor. With government funding, a nonprofit dance troupe can offer programs to low-income people or a nonprofit child welfare agency can serve children with special needs.

Finally, Salamon argues, nonprofits suffer from *paternalism*—that is, their definition of community problems is driven by the visions and preferences of those who control them, not the community at large (see also Clotfelter 1992; Friedman and McGarvie 2003). Nonprofits do not, individually or collectively, represent the general population, nor do the majority of them have mechanisms in place to monitor interests beyond those of their own specified mission, and even so only to a limited extent. Rather, they tend to be governed by small, self-perpetuating boards, disproportionately selected from the community elite, and they pay close attention to the wishes and interests of major donors (Ostrower 1995; Odendahl 1990; Ostrander 1995; Galaskiewicz 1985; Abzug 1994; James; 1992).

As long as nonprofits depend on elite resources, services favored by the wealthy (e.g., high culture) may be promoted, while those desired by the poor or low-status minority groups (e.g., good housing) may get lip service at best. And when the interests of the latter are considered, the thrust may be more that of social control than self-determination and empowerment. Government, by contrast, is ultimately subject to democratic control; the availability of government funding thus serves to democratize nonprofits.

These offsetting "failures" of government and nonprofits create the basis for an exchange relation between them, Salamon argues, and encourage government and nonprofits to enter into partnerships. The result has been the creation of a structure of third-party government operating through the mechanisms of government grants and contracts to nonprofit service providers.

This argument is closely related to an extensive literature in sociology, political science, and public administration on how government delegates particular responsibilities to other bodies (Williams 1980; Lowi 1979; Drucker 1967). There has also been prior documentation of the importance of government funding to nonprofits (Greenstone and Peterson 1973; Kramer 1981, 1993; Brown 1941; Johnson 1931; Werner 1961). However, Salamon was among the first to draw explicit attention to the significant exchange relationships between government and charitable nonprofits—not just exchanges among different levels of government (in the form of intergovernmental relations) or between government and special-interest or other explicitly political groups seeking to influence public policy.

Despite the important contributions of Salamon to our understanding of government-nonprofit relations, the theory is incomplete. He tells us why transactions between government and nonprofits should develop, not the conditions under which they will develop or how they will manifest themselves. For example, governments routinely overcome the problem of addressing minority demand for public goods through logrolling, suggesting that government does not need nonprofits to address particularistic interests. Similarly, U.S. government funding of nonprofit organizations on an extensive scale has occurred only since the late 1960s. Presumably, philanthropic insufficiencies were common for decades prior to that. Also, arts organizations in particular have obtained large-scale government support in the past forty years, especially at the local level. But arts organizations are patronized primarily by the wealthy, which seems to be a poor fit with the notion that government helps nonprofits address the problem of philanthropic paternalism.

The nature of transactions. Transactions involve exchanges among actors (in this case organizational actors) who make more or less rational decisions about whether the benefits of a particular exchange outweigh the costs of establishing the exchange and of monitoring whether the other party lives up to agreed-upon conditions. Over the past twenty-five years, a considerable literature has emerged on the scope of government grants and contracts to nonprofits and on the nature of the contracting relations in the United States and other national contexts (Gutch 1992; Lewis 1999; Considine 2000). Informed by models of political power, organizational behavior and decision-making, resource dependency (Pfeffer and Salancik 1978), and transaction theory (Williamson 1981), this literature has examined transactions in some detail and outlined the complex set of costs and benefits that accrue to both parties. A significant portion of that literature has focused on government-nonprofit transactions (DeHoog 1984; Smith and Lipsky 1993; Grønbjerg 1993; Hartogs and Weber 1978; Saidel 1991; Perri 6 and Kendall 1997; Ferris and Graddy 1998; DeHoog and Salamon 2002). Indeed, most of the papers in the "industry" section of this volume, as well as those in Salamon (2002b), contain descriptions and assessments of how those patterns play themselves out across various policy fields. While the exact nature of these costs and benefits is not easily determined, several broad categories are evident (Smith and Lipsky 1993; Grønbjerg 1993; Saidel 1991; DeHoog 1984).

The transactions between government and nonprofit organizations have also become increasingly diversified, going well beyond the direct grants and contracts common just twenty years ago. As noted by Salamon (2002a), S. R. Smith (2002), and others, the tools of government have become increasingly diversified. Thus, government support for nonprofit organizations can take many forms. For instance, an art museum might be built on city land and city bonds may be used to help with the capital expenses; a direct government grant might fund an exhibit; the municipal art commission might give a grant to the local school district so that it can bring students to the art museum for an art class; and donations to the art museum are tax deductible and thus subsidized by the federal government (and in some cases state and local government). In sum, the transaction framework is very useful in calling attention to the government-nonprofit relationship. Contracting and grants remain the most extensive direct forms of government support, but as this example underscores, nonprofit organizations have multiple and complex exchange relations with government, reflecting the many forms in which they receive government support.

Transaction benefits and costs to nonprofits. For nonprofits, the benefits include most explicitly receiving financial resources with which to carry out activities related to the organization's mission—usually substantial resources over a sustained period of time. Nonprofits also gain considerable management experience and capacity from interacting with bureaucratic government agencies. The receipt of government funding also brings nonprofits formally into the sphere of participating in the delivery of goods deemed important enough to warrant the expenditures of tax revenues. That, along with their enhanced management capacity, conveys considerable legitimacy on nonprofits. Finally, the close interaction with government agencies brings nonprofits into the political process and gives them a voice in the policy-setting debate.

The costs are substantial as well.[4] In some cases, government funding may threaten nonprofit legitimacy, if it comes with such intrusive strings as to raise concerns that the interests of clients or donors may not be served—for example, agencies serving illegal immigrants or nontraditional religious sects. More important, however, the work of simply managing the government grants and contracts system can be enormous and well beyond the capacity of smaller nonprofits or those with little or no previous experience (Grønbjerg 1993). This is one of the reasons why recent efforts to make government funding available to congregations are raising concerns—do congregations have the capacity to manage such funding? If not, how long will it take them to learn and at what costs in terms of overall efficiency and effectiveness?

Managing government grants and contracts includes submitting high-quality proposals in response to requests for proposals, reviewing contract language, processing financial documents, reporting activities, and monitoring performance. It also requires efforts to track the political process in the particular field of activity at all levels of government in order to anticipate future developments (Grønbjerg 1993). In the United States, these efforts have become more demanding and have less predictable outcomes for nonprofits in recent years. This is because government at all levels has switched from a pattern of regularly renewing grants or contracts to one of relying extensively on performance contracts (S. R. Smith 2002; Kettl 2000) where payments are pegged to specified documented service outcomes. The growths in government funding mechanisms that involve subsidies to consumers rather than directly to nonprofit service providers (S. R. Smith 2002; Grønbjerg and Salamon 2002) also pose major challenges.

Both of these shifts in funding mechanisms squeeze nonprofits financially since performance contracts and consumer subsidies rarely allow sufficient "profit" to cover administration and overhead. More importantly, perhaps, they also force nonprofits to market their services to subsidy-bearing clients and to give priority to controlling the costs rather than maximizing the quality of services. It is telling that for-profit firms have entered fields previously dominated by nonprofits because these new funding structures play to their advantages. It is equally telling that they frequently leave the field again because there isn't enough profit to be made (S. R. Smith 2002; Gray and Schlesinger 2002).

Other costs of the transaction systems to nonprofits are less evident, but not trivial. Government funding tends to limit management discretion for nonprofits, since the latter now have to adhere to procedures established by law and administrative rule. Indeed, the increasing predominance of performance contracts and fee-for-service reimbursement policies means that government has even more powerful tools by which to control nonprofits, although not in as bureaucratic a fashion as under traditional purchase-of-service agreements. Government funding also imposes significant opportunity costs by foreclosing other nonprofit activities.

As a result of these types of costs, nonprofits tend to organize themselves internally in ways that facilitate managing the transactions and other relations with government (Ostrower and Stone, this volume; Grønbjerg 1993). Such structures are not necessarily consistent with long-term planning, coordination, and internal communication and may hinder the process of alternative resource development. The attractiveness of government funding and the costs associated with obtaining it may thus present nonprofits with profound dilemmas involving mission and purpose versus sustainability and capacity (Smith and Lipsky 1993).

Transaction benefits and costs to government. There are corresponding transaction benefits and costs to government. The benefits include most explicitly being able to purchase specialized services without having to develop the expertise in-house. This allows government to use competitive processes to reduce costs in ways not possible with internal government production. Contracting out allows government to circumvent civil service restrictions that require complex—and lengthy—hiring procedures and make it difficult to reward performance or shift government employees from one type of position to another. Thus contracting allows government to substantially reduce program startup costs and quickly respond to newly identified needs or the demands of emergent groups.

For example, under pressure to close or greatly reduce reliance on large public state institutions, state governments shifted care for the developmentally disabled and mentally ill from these public facilities to community-based programs operated primarily by nonprofit organizations. By using nonprofits in this way, state governments were able to respond more rapidly to these pressures than if they had to keep all services entirely within the public sector. Similarly, many cities across the country have shifted their zoos from municipal management to nonprofit management (even as they retain ownership of the land and the zoo facilities). This shift, usually to a "Friends of the Zoo" association, allows the city to shift responsibility for zoo staffing to a nonprofit with much more flexible hiring rules. (Typically, the relation between the society and the city is in the form of a complicated contractual agreement that specifies the extent of continuing city subsidy as well as the nonprofit organization's financial and management responsibility.)

Contracting with nonprofits also allows government to tap into well-articulated local knowledge about needs and service models and thus improves the chance for successful outcomes. At the same time, it reduces government's own visible role and responsibility for failures, thereby diluting accountability. Finally, contracting with nonprofits creates constituency groups with vested interests in particular programs, groups that government agencies can mobilize if the programs come under fire (Grønbjerg 1993). For example, recent proposals to expand government contracting to religious congregations means that all major denominations now have a vested interest in whether and how federal contracting systems fund congregations.

The costs to government include most explicitly the need to design and implement selection, funding, and monitoring structures that allow it to be confident that specified activities are carried out appropriately or that agreed-upon levels of performances are achieved. This is the so-called agency problem (Pratt and Zeckhauser 1985; Donahue 1989)—if you need something to be done, and you do not do the work yourself, how do you know that the agent, who agrees to do it for you, does it appropriately? For example, mission-motivated nonprofits may wish to provide services of higher quality or in greater quantity than may government concerned about cutting costs or restricting eligibility. Alternatively, for-profit providers may wish to cream off those easiest to serve, leaving government to deal with the rest and face complaints about meeting its own mandates.

Government also needs to make sure that the overall mix of services contracted for meets specified program priorities and/or changing needs. That may mean special efforts to recruit and train groups to provide particular types of services not available otherwise. These special efforts are likely to create expectations by providers recruited in this manner that the relationship will be ongoing. Indeed, government may need to invest substantial resources in developing stable, reliable partnerships with provider agencies so that a service infrastructure is in place. This may be particularly problematic if the provider system includes large for-profit firms who may decide to pull up stakes and move into other fields or regions if profits fail to meet investor expectations (Gray and Schlesinger 2002).

As a result, transaction costs to government include anticipating and participating in negotiations with providers as well as responding to political overtures and challenges by contractors. These may involve dealing with organized industry associations (e.g., the Day Care Action Council of Illinois) as well as with individual nonprofit (or for-profit) contractors with powerful board members (or owners) able to exert political pressure on government.

Just as the contracting system allows government to minimize the fallout from failed policies, it also makes it difficult for government to take full credit for successful programs. While government may wish to take credit for such programs (recall that gaining access to nonprofit expertise serves as an incentive for government to contract with nonprofits) nonprofits that provide the services will have the easier case to make. After all, they are on the ground with detailed knowledge of client problems and workable solutions. They will also have strong incentives for taking much of the credit for themselves since that strengthens their bargaining position for the next round of contract negotiations. All of these costs also impose opportunity costs on government in that they absorb staff and other financial resources that could otherwise be devoted to alternative activities. Finally, the contract system makes it more difficult for citizens to know that they benefit from government activities (S. R. Smith 1993) and thus undermines the legitimacy of taxes.

Assessing the Demand and Supply Perspectives

Under the earliest and simplest versions of the demand/supply model described here (market niche), the functions and special advantages of nonprofits consist of their ability to compensate for the failures of market and government entities within particular competitive niches. At the aggregate level, these institutions thus complement one another to maximize overall societal welfare, governed only by the invisible hand of market and political competition. Under this model, government-nonprofit relationships are a mix of competition and complementarity among separate and distinct entities (Young 1999). Shifts in the capacities of one sector to address demands or in the preference structures for specific goods and services will directly affect demands encountered by the other sector(s).

This latter assumption—that the three sectors compete as distinct entities—surfaces in concerns about how one sector may infringe upon activities thought to be more appropriately carried out by another. In the United States and other market-celebrating societies, this is evident in widespread worries that government crowds out private initiatives in both the market and nonprofit sectors. That is, government is thought to interfere with market efficiency by depressing the demands for market goods when it provides the goods directly or extracts discretionary income in the form of taxes. The latter also reduces incentives for donations. The dominance of this particular ideology in the United States is evident in the extent to which arguments to privatize government and reduce taxes carry the day in the political discourse and public-opinion polls. The counterargument—that narrow, private self-interests inappropriately crowd out collective goals of equity and fairness—continues to face an uphill battle and surfaces mainly in arguments about campaign finance reform. Overall, we find the market niche model to be quite useful for understanding the reasons for a division of labor in the delivery of public goods and consistent with the legal framework for the nonprofit sector in the United States (Brody, this volume).

The transaction model helps us understand the complex system of interorganizational relationships under which most public goods services are delivered. It can also illuminate the dynamics under which the competitive edge of nonprofits vis-à-vis government grows or declines, and highlights the many complex ways in which government and nonprofits are intertwined and the increasing complexity of this relationship in many countries around the world.

In the final analysis, the transaction model also raises more political questions about the role of competition in the contracting system and about which types of providers, if any, are or should be favored in such systems. For example, do systems of managed care or performance contracting unduly advantage for-profit over nonprofit providers as some, we included, have claimed? We note that contract failure theory strongly suggests that nonprofits would be the more trustworthy agents of government in providing services that are difficult to evaluate. Ultimately, the transaction model may also raise questions about the extent to which government contracting of services effectively amounts to a delegation of government power to providers and whether providers are subject to all the constraints about equity and fairness that apply to government (Kennedy 2001). While the opportunity for government to escape restrictions may indeed constitute a major rationale for contracting services out, and while the transaction model helps raise these questions, the model does not adequately account for nor fully elucidate the political processes by which they are addressed.

MODEL II: CIVIL SOCIETY AND SOCIAL MOVEMENTS

To a large extent, the demand and supply frameworks discussed above are rooted in traditional theories of welfare economics that justify economic and social intervention by government. As such, these theories imply important normative assumptions about the role of government and nonprofit organizations, especially in the provision of public goods. However, market-related perspectives assign no distinctive properties to community organizations and social relations. Instead, these perspectives—which focus on the strategic choices of rational individuals interacting under various time, budgetary, and legal constraints—hold that groups (including commercial firms and nonprofit organizations) exist primarily to lower the transaction costs of exchange.

While nonprofits may exist to provide public goods that cannot be provided by the other sectors, there is nothing necessarily distinctive about the way in which they do so. And since the emphasis of these theories is on the efficiency of exchange rather than the distinctive values and social relations of the nonprofit sector, there is a relative absence of concern about the possible deleterious effects of government on the nonprofit sector or more generally about social relations at the local community level. We turn now to theoretical perspectives that seek to do so very explicitly.

Civil Society/Social Capital Perspectives

In recent years, a tremendous outpouring of scholarly attention has been devoted to the idea of civil society and its contribution to democracy and freedom. Broadly speaking, civil society refers to the network of associations, groups, and informal activities that exists apart from the state and the market. It is the realm of private voluntary activity and civic participation (Walzer 1992; Foley and Edwards 1996; Hasenfeld and Gidron 2002).[5] From a civil society perspective, the nonprofit sector is regarded as the embodiment of certain values that are crucial to democracy and good government. Thus, scholars with this perspective tend to be much less concerned with efficiency and the provision of public goods than they are with other important goals of society such as responsiveness, freedom, cooperation, legitimacy, individual and community responsibility, citizen participation, obligation, and social capital.

One of the earliest and best-known scholars in this civil society tradition is Alexis de Tocqueville (1835–1840), who forcefully argued that America's democracy rested on its extensive network of voluntary associations. In his view, voluntary associations were vital because they served as an intermediate body between the individual and the state; thus they helped foster individual freedom since they could help protect individuals from the temptation of the state to restrict individual freedom. Voluntary associations were also important because they provided a vehicle for individuals to come together to influence government policy. To Tocqueville, voluntary associations were inherently positive for democracy; the more voluntary associations, the healthier are civil society and government performance.

In the twentieth century, this Tocquevillian perspective was the basis for renewed attention by scholars and policymakers. Hayek (1960), the Austrian social theorist, argued throughout his long life and career that the growth of the welfare state was inimical to freedom and liberty. To him, government was a direct threat to those values. Nisbet, a political theorist, also propounded a variant of this view in his influential book *The Quest for Community* (1953). Quoting extensively from Tocqueville, Nisbet contended that "Most of the tendencies in contemporary society toward the erosion of cultural differences and the standardization of cultural tastes, beliefs and activities, which are so often charged, mistakenly, against technology and science, are the product of a centralization of authority and function and a desiccation of local and cultural associations" (p. 267).

The implication of Nisbet's views was quite far-reaching: government and voluntary associations had opposing agendas and values and the growth of government would threaten community. Whether it was the arts or social services, the growth of government provision would undermine voluntary provision and other local forms of service. Government was a threat to creativity, innovation, and pluralism.

This Tocquevillian perspective also served as the foundation for Berger and Neuhaus's widely read 1977 book, *To Empower People.* They argued that voluntary organizations are crucial mediating institutions between the individual and government, protecting individual freedom and enhancing community responsibility for social problems. Other scholars, including Woodson (1981), Meyer (1982), and Glazer (1989), followed with books articulating similar perspectives. Glazer, for example, suggested that we, as a society, should move toward a "self-service society" with voluntary associations, community groups, and individuals addressing social problems rather than government. The image of the government-nonprofit relation here is one not of partnership or exchange but of inherent tension, with government as a coercive force undermining local and community responsibility and reducing the effectiveness of social programs.

More recently, the image of government as an oppressive force undermining community and voluntary associations has been invoked in the ongoing debate about the charitable choice amendment to the welfare reform legislation of 1996 and the Bush administration's Office of Faith-Based and Community Initiatives. Thus opponents of charitable choice have expressed deep concerns about how government funding will subvert the ability of faith-based organizations to serve as sites where individuals can come together freely to express their views, practice their faith, and participate in community and public affairs without having to account to government for such activities. Indeed, many congregations have decided not to participate in the program for exactly those reasons. At the same time, many supporters of charitable choice have argued that government has discriminated against faith-based organizations when seeking to contract with nonprofit agencies to deliver services and therefore undermined faith, voluntarism, and faith-based community organizations (White House Office of Faith-Based and Community Initiatives 2003).

Two other important variants of this Tocquevillian civil society perspective deserve mention—communitarianism and social capital. The former emerged in the 1980s and 1990s and centers on how to enhance individual responsibility and obligation to the community. To achieve these goals, communitarians are very supportive of community institutions like nonprofit organizations since these can help promote the new social norms. However, in contrast to Berger and Neuhaus, communitarians generally endorse government efforts to promote participation in community organizations as well as to strengthen individual responsibility. For instance, Barber (1984), Etzioni (1993), and many others argue that mandatory community service by young people in nonprofit organizations could greatly help increase civic participation and a sense of personal obligation toward fellow citizens.

The communitarian perspective deliberately contrasts with more individualist, rational choice perspectives on politics and society. Communitarians offer a view of citizens as tied together in a community where voluntary associations and government play important supportive roles. Moreover, nonprofits play an explicit political role when they foster participation that directly challenges or changes how government carries out its responsibility. This view thus differs from how market-based models conceive of the government-nonprofit relation as one where their respective roles are determined by the aggregation of individual decisions.

Communitarians, such as Barber, also suggest that involvement with nonprofits can help transform essentially private goods into public goods supported indirectly or directly by government. For example, government-supported community service in nonprofit community organizations can help individuals rethink public priorities, thereby fostering demands for new programs and services. Communitarian scholars thus view nonprofits as playing important roles in mobilizing demands for policy changes—a mechanism that is largely missing from market-based models.

A final important variant of this broad civil society perspective centers on social capital and focuses more explicitly on the ways that civil society institutions both promote and benefit from networks of interpersonal relationships. Adapting a concept originally developed by Coleman (1988) and others, Putnam argues in *Making Democracy Work* (1993a) that voluntary associations were critical to building "social capital"—networks of cooperation and collaboration that exist in a community or region.

Putnam's research suggests that areas with higher densities of voluntary associations also had more satisfied citizenry, more effective government programs, and higher levels of economic development. Participation in voluntary associations helped build social capital, he argued, by bringing people together, including some who previously may not have known one another. The mechanism by which social capital translates into improved government is presumed to be an indirect one, in which social capital both facilitates and promotes collective action for the common good so that citizens come to demand and expect more from government officials. Putnam (1993a, 1995, 2000) is especially concerned with voluntary organizations that rely on volunteers and serve to bring diverse people together, since social capital is built through the interaction of these volunteers. Examples include the local PTA chapter, choral society, or soccer club.

However, Putnam remains skeptical of the many nonprofit service agencies and national advocacy organizations that have emerged in the past thirty years. As he, Skocpol (1999), and others have noted, many service and advocacy organizations do not have volunteers or members and are therefore not well positioned to build social capital. Putnam's argument, then, raises the possibility that nonprofit organizations may not necessarily contribute to the overall well-being of the community. His work also suggests that many volunteer-driven nonprofits, such as sports clubs or choral societies, may not be providing public goods as conventionally understood but serve as a mechanism for like-minded individuals to jointly address an issue of mutual concern or offer programs that serve their own interest. Voluntary associations then play a key role in contributing to pluralism.

Putnam (1993b) also argues that government can have both positive and negative effects on nonprofit organizations and their ability to create social capital. For example, inappropriate regulations or unstable funding can undermine the health of local community organizations, especially the smaller agencies and associations with close linkages to the community. Government can also help nurture the nonprofit infrastructure through favorable regulations and incentives for people and agencies to collaborate at the local level. Like Barber and others, Putnam endorses community service programs like Americorps, since they bring together people of diverse backgrounds and promote the building of cooperative social networks.

Although some scholars have challenged the validity of Putnam's arguments and evidence, his perspective has gained popular acceptance with far-reaching effects on public policy, the relation between government and nonprofit organizations, and nonprofit views of themselves and their relation to the community. Widespread interest in building social capital has helped fuel public and private support for voluntary organizations and groups. In many developing countries (including the newly democratizing countries of eastern and central Europe), governments have been strongly encouraged by international organizations like the World Bank as well as by the United States and the European Union to revise their laws, regulations, and funding policies to promote the formation of voluntary associations and their sustainability. In many advanced industrial countries, like the United States, the United Kingdom, and Australia, government has actively strived to encourage citizen participation through voluntary groups and organizations. The creation of social capital through participation in voluntary associations is believed to have a number of benefits for government and public policy. First, voluntary organizations can promote transparency and accountability in government and thus improve the quality and effectiveness of government services (World Bank 2003). Second, voluntary groups can offer government an alternative organizational vehicle for providing public services, enhancing consumer choice and the diversity of services. Third, participation in voluntary associations is regarded as facilitating greater civic engagement more generally, thus leading potentially to a more active participation by individuals in public life.[6]

Many scholars also stress that local voluntary organizations thrive when the state actively encourages participation—the thrust of Tendler's findings (1997) on NGOs and the state in Brazil. Pressman (1975) reached similar conclusions from his work on urban reform in the United States. He found that ineffective local governments can drastically undermine local citizen participation. More recently, Putnam (Putnam and Feldstein 2003) noted that government, especially at the local level, can play a very important role in fostering the growth of social capital. Comparative cross-national studies of development have also concluded that rampant corruption, ineffective bureaucracies, vast inequalities, and lack of property rights make it very difficult for citizens to create cooperative social networks and sustainable voluntary organizations (Woolcock and Narayan 2000).

This extensive research suggests many different practical strategies for governments to adopt to support the development of social capital, including seed grants to neighborhood associations, more transparency in government to encourage greater citizen participation, and financial support for volunteers. Nonprofits can also restructure their boards to build their community connections or diversify their programming to promote greater engagement by the public. Regarding the latter, many arts museums have transformed themselves into the central cultural institution in their communities.

Putnam's work on social capital tends to emphasize, almost by definition, collaborative social networks and forging cooperative networks between government and voluntary associations. Social capital also tends to be created in nonpolitical organizations such as sports clubs and choral societies. As a consequence, this perspective has difficulty explaining relatively rapid change in government policy or the widespread emergence of new groups and voluntary associations.

Social Movement Perspectives

In contrast to civil society/social capital models, social movement perspectives attribute a central role to political activity and political associations. For example, Tarrow (1994:3–4) defines social movements as "collective challenges by people with common purposes and solidarity in sustained interaction with elites, opponents and authorities" (as quoted in Hasenfeld and Gidron 2002:3). Many social movements, such as the civil rights movement or the women's movement, begin as loosely structured, informal groups without any formal legal status. Eventually many of these formally incorporate as legal entities in order to raise money and enhance their effectiveness, legitimacy, and sustainability.

Implicit in this broad conceptual perspective (with many variants) are three themes with direct relevance to the government-nonprofit relationship. First, nonprofit social movements have a deliberately conflictual relationship with government; indeed, the entire raison d'être of many social movements is to change government policy. Second, the successful transformation of government policy by social movements has contributed significantly to the growth in the nonprofit sector over the past thirty years. For instance, the women's movement has successfully pressed the establishment of domestic violence shelters, rape crisis centers, and women's health clinics. Many political advocacy groups have emerged to call for action by government on women's issues. The civil rights movement worked in part through nonprofit advocacy organizations and locally based nonprofit community action agencies (O'Connor 1999, 2001; Marris and Rein 1982; Morone 1990). The same basic pattern has been repeated in social movements focused on AIDS, developmental disabilities, the mentally ill, the environment, and civil rights.

Indeed, the institutionalization of social movements into established advocacy and service organizations may help explain why many social movements have been supported by nonprofit foundations (Jenkins and Halcli 1999; Raynor 1999; Clemens 1993, this volume). In essence, social movements have provided the organizational and political mechanisms for translating private concerns into public issues. It is this translation process that makes social movement perspectives so critical to understanding the government-nonprofit relationship. They are vehicles of change.

Also, as Clemens (1993, this volume) notes, the success of the women's movement in achieving institutional change is due in part to the adoption of a "repertoire of organizational models"—unions, clubs, associations, and corporations—in order to push for change. The use of nontraditional organizational models disrupts existing patterns of politics and makes institutional change possible, although women's groups did not achieve all of their goals.

The third theme evident in the social movement perspectives concerns the ways in which social movement nonprofits politicize the environment for other nonprofits. Nonprofit art museums have been the targets of conservative movement organizations that complain about obscene or otherwise objectionable art. Nonprofit advocacy groups have successfully sued in court to press for the deinstitutionalization of the developmentally disabled and mentally ill often housed in nonprofit and public institutions. These suits in turn prompted the creation of many new community-based nonprofits to take advantage of the new funding opportunities that resulted, while many existing nonprofit service agencies responded by changing their operations.

Social movements thus challenge the dualist models of government-nonprofit relations that have been so influential since the time of Tocqueville. As noted by Rein and Rainwater (1986) and others, the dualist model is based upon the assumption of distinctly different sectors. But social movements have altered public policy so that what were previously private concerns are now public concerns that in turn are addressed by nonprofits supported by public funds. As a result, the line between public and private becomes very blurry indeed, particularly since many private nonprofits, such as battered women shelters, AIDS service agencies, and art museums, adjust their behavior in response to changes in public policy initiated by social movement organizations.

A focus on social movements also challenges the tendency to examine government-nonprofit relationships mainly within the boundaries of the nation-state, given the rapid growth of transnational social movements (Keck and Sikkink 1998; Fox 2001; Lindenberg 2001; Bryer and Magrath 1999; Tarrow 2002). As Kaul (2001) observes, one by-product of globalization has been to escalate demands for what she terms "global public goods," such as efforts to deal with the growing refugee crisis, environmental degradation, and war (including related issues such as landmines).

Increasingly, transnational NGOs are involved in helping governments and international organizations such as the World Bank, the United Nations (U.N.), and the International Monetary Fund (IMF) to resolve these emergent global issues. The solution may involve new government policies that are in some cases implemented by nonprofit organizations. As Tarrow (2002) notes, transnational NGOs are not identical to transnational social movements: the former are more likely to have routinized interactions with government and international bodies and provide services to individuals. Transnational social movements are directly involved in "contentious politics" and may not include formally organized and incorporated NGOs.

The growth of transnational NGOs and social movements raises important theoretical issues for nonprofit-sector research. These NGOs often operate in a very fluid political environment composed of international institutions (e.g., U.N., IMF, World Bank), large multinational corporations, and individual nation-states. The occasional global conferences on special topics reveal the complexity of this environment and the extent to which the boundary between public and private on such issues as global warming, deforestation, and economic development is frequently much contested. Indeed, NGOs play an increasingly important role in defining this boundary and pushing governments and international institutions to take more assertive, proactive steps to address "global public goods" previously considered private (Bartley 2003; Dalton, Recchia, and Rohrschneider 2003). Their effectiveness is reflected in the creation of a special "NGO Watch" project by the conservative think tank the American Enterprise Institute for Public Policy Research and the Federalist Society for Law and Public Policy Studies, concerned about the "power of the unelected few" (NGO Watch 2005).

One enduring organizational dilemma that affects the political advocacy of transnational NGOs as well as national or local nonprofits is how to secure adequate resources to carry out such activities. Many nonprofits that emerge from social movements have deliberately confrontational missions and purposes that seek to change—sometimes drastically—existing public policies. Often, these organizations begin as informal groups, associations, and networks of professional colleagues without any formal legal status—for example, a neighborhood association that wants to rid its neighborhood of drug abuse. Eventually such a group may obtain formal 501(c)(3) status as a nonprofit charitable entity and obtain grants to fund its activities from foundations or private donors. But startup grants must end and the organization find new sources of support.

Advocacy organizations that seek public funding for their activities may encounter other dilemmas, since such funding is usually reserved for direct service programs—for example, counseling or job training—rather than advocacy. Consequently, nonprofit advocacy organizations may be forced to shift their focus to providing direct services if they want public funds. This can be a problem in developing countries where initial grants to support advocacy organizations tend to come from foreign donors in the United States or Europe. Once the grants end, these organizations have few options to support themselves since their home countries do not have the wealth or tradition of private donations characteristic of industrialized countries.

Second, nonprofits may feel it necessary to change their advocacy when they receive public funds. For instance, a community-based poverty agency may have initially focused on advocating broadly for the health and income needs of the local disadvantaged population. But if the organization accepts sizable government contracts for job training and does not have other significant revenue sources, it may be constrained in its ability to directly criticize government policy regarding the disadvantaged and public job-training programs in particular.

The advocacy role of many nonprofit service agencies is further complicated by small staffs. While such agencies may not have the capacity to engage in significant advocacy on their own, they can participate in umbrella coalitions or associations, such as state or national associations of home-care providers or child welfare agencies. However, umbrella coalitions tend to concentrate their advocacy on issues of most direct relevance to their member organizations—that is, payment rates, funding levels, and contract regulations. They have few incentives to engage in broad-based advocacy work on behalf of clients or the general public (Smith and Lipsky 1993).

Assessing the Civil Society/Social Movement Model

The civil society and social capital movement perspectives on government-nonprofit relationships focus on how nonprofits serve to create solidarity among individuals and strengthen community in a variety of ways. The social movement perspectives draw more explicit attention to the role of nonprofits in mediating the relationship between individuals and government or other institutions. Both perspectives usefully call attention to the importance of the collective and community in informal and formal activity within the nonprofit sector. They also provide a specific model of institutional and policy change. Both perspectives raise important questions about how government-nonprofit relationships emerge and change over time within the framework of a given society. Neither, however, is easily amenable to comparative analyses across nation-states. Nor do they elaborate on macroanalytic frameworks for understanding the relationships over time. Thus, these perspectives, while very valuable, need to be complemented with a more institutionalist perspective that provides insight into differences in the government-nonprofit relationships across countries and within a particular country.

MODEL III: REGIME AND NEO-INSTITUTIONAL PERSPECTIVES

A very diverse and important set of theoretical perspectives has emerged that places the structure and role of state actors at the center of explanations for a wide variety of phenomena, including cross-national differences in social spending, the size of the nonprofit sector, and the success and effectiveness of nonprofit organizations. We focus here on two key conceptual approaches to understanding the government-nonprofit relationship that reflect this focus on state, society, and the nonprofit sector and that have gained momentum in recent years: regime models and neo-institutional theory. They have emerged, respectively, out of cross-national comparisons of state systems and social policies and from efforts to understand how nonprofits relate to overall societal systems.

Regime and Social Origin Perspectives

Most of the early cross-national comparisons of states and social policy were concerned with how economic development and the emergence of democratic political structures influence the development of the state and social policies (Wilensky 1975; Flora and Heidenheimer 1984; Marshall 1964). These studies sought mainly to explain the shift from less- to more-extensive social policies, but paid very little attention—if any—to the role that nonprofits might play, except as organized political actors.

Esping-Anderson's (1990) more sophisticated regime typology, in which he identifies three distinct welfare state systems and elucidates their underlying dynamics, has been the subject of extensive commentary and follow-up analysis. While his research focuses on income maintenance programs and does not address human service programs specifically, he does describe how regimes differ in their preferences for public delivery mechanisms and in the extent to which welfare benefits are structured as commodities that individuals must obtain through some form of market mechanism.

In de-commodified social-democratic systems, such as in Scandinavia, the state serves as the basic distribution system for benefits. Benefits are high and universal or have broad coverage tied to relevant demographic status (such as age for pensions or family status for child allowances). Corporate regimes, such as in Austria, Germany, France, and Italy, are characterized by intermediary levels of commodification in which welfare coverage is broad but fragmented, and benefits unequal and tied to existing social status, such as religion, region, or occupation. While the state is strong, it is subsidiary to these other institutions.

In highly commodified systems (as in the United States, Canada, and Australia), welfare benefits are contingent on the individual's position in the market, because benefits (or services) are purchased—either at full cost or at a subsidized rate, as in the case of housing vouchers in the United

States—or they are part of an implicit or explicit employment contract. In the latter case, only those who work (or have done so) obtain full benefits (e.g., Medicare, private health insurance, and Social Security in the United States versus Medicaid and TANF—Temporary Assistance to Needy Families). The absence of universal entitlements in commodified regimes and the rejection of a strong state make these systems much more compatible with and able to accommodate service systems that give prominent place to nonprofits, and especially for-profit providers, than do regimes in which welfare benefits are treated as universal entitlements and the direct responsibility of the state.

Salamon and Anheier's (1998) social origins theory of the nonprofit sector builds on both Esping-Anderson's welfare regime theory and B. Moore's (1966) analysis of how three distinct political regimes (democracy, communism, and fascism) emerged out of the interaction of the landed elites, rural peasantry, urban middle class, and the state. In their cross-national research on the size, composition, and sources of funding for the nonprofit sector, Salamon and Anheier conclude that the "social origins" of the national nonprofit sector best explain cross-national differences. They identify four regime types: *liberal* types such as the United States and the United Kingdom with low government social spending and a large nonprofit sector; *corporatist* types such as the Netherlands and Germany with high social welfare spending and a large nonprofit sector; *social democratic* types such as Sweden with high social welfare spending and a relatively small nonprofit sector; and *statist* types exemplified by Japan and its relatively low social welfare spending and small nonprofit sector.

In essence, Salamon and Anheier contend that the nature of the nonprofit sector in each country must be understood as an integral part of the historical developments by which political institutions are shaped by social class in each country (hence the term *social origins*). Using the findings and conclusions of Esping-Anderson (1990) and B. Moore (1966), Salamon and Anheier view political groups that are closely linked to social class interests as agents of change. Then, once key policy decisions have been made, these groups shape the further evolution of social programs, most notably the role of the state, and its relationship to civil society, including the nonprofit sector.

Put another way, class power shapes the allocation of state resources, which in turn further reinforce class power. Sweden, for example, has a powerful working class, extensive state programs, and a relatively small nonprofit sector. The United States, by contrast, has a powerful business community with a strong preference for a limited state, for which the sizable nonprofit sector compensates, at least in part.

The social origins approach then has some similarities to social movement theory in that it places emphasis on political mobilization and its impact on state policy as a defining explanatory reason for the character of the nonprofit sector and the government-nonprofit relationship in particular countries. And like social movement theory, the social origins approach places great importance on political movements (in this case class-based movements and parties) in explaining government social welfare policy. But it is distinctive in its emphasis on historical-contextual factors as shaping the evolution of the nonprofit sector in a given society.

However, as L. Moore (2001) observes, great changes may take place in the role nonprofits play in particular fields that are not easily explained through the lens of social origins theory. For instance, the number of nonprofit art museums in the United States increased dramatically in the past thirty years, and the number of nonprofit human service agencies primarily supported by government funds has almost tripled in the past twenty years. In the Netherlands, the government has introduced market competition in health and social services, leading to a consolidation of many nonprofit agencies and an increased reliance on fee income, while Denmark is privatizing some services. As these examples suggest, government-nonprofit relationships in many different types of countries have undergone a profound shift to a more competitive market model; one would not predict such similar developments among countries of very different social origins. Likewise, the extensive network of voluntary sports clubs in Scandinavia and the important contributions of cooperatives, foundations, and associations in many nations do not easily fit with prevailing definitions of nonprofit organizations employed by Salamon and Anheier.

The signal role attributed to historical forces in the social origins model also characterizes a variant of the regime model that focuses on the role of religion in shaping the nonprofit sector. Hall (this volume) makes this argument in his analysis of the historical development of the nonprofit sector in the United States. Moreover, James (1987), also in the first edition of this volume, argues that cross-national differences in the size and structure of the nonprofit sector could be explained in part by the different role of the church in various countries. Her perspective is similar to Weisbrod's (1977) theory about government failure, noted earlier, which suggests that nonprofit organizations are established to meet the demand for public goods by minority interests who are not satisfied with the public goods provided by government.

James's perspective is consistent with Weisbrod's theory in part because she argues that the nonprofit sector will be larger in countries with diverse religious denominations and groups because religious entrepreneurs will compete for adherents by creating nonprofit educational and social organizations as a strategy to increase their membership.[7] However, she incorporates a more state-centered/institutional explanation into her argument by suggesting that religious groups may be politically powerful enough to secure government subsidies for their affiliated service agencies and to promote government restrictions that limit the ability of other types of public and nonprofit service agencies to receive public funds (James 1987:405). Likewise, the disestablishment of church and state that occurred in the United

States at its founding encouraged the proliferation of many different nonprofit organizations.

More recent work on European social policy has stressed the importance of church-state relations (and conflict) in shaping the development of nonprofit service agencies. Alber (1995), for example, points to weaknesses in conventional approaches to explaining cross-national differences in social policies—for example, Esping-Anderson (1990)—because they focus primarily on class politics and on how public policies are shaped by class conflict. He finds this perspective not very effective in explaining social services, which have become increasingly important in advanced industrial countries. His comparison of services to elderly citizens in Denmark, Germany, and the Netherlands finds that religious institutions play a very strong role.

Thus Germany is a religiously mixed country with longstanding conflicts between church and state. Religiously affiliated service associations are linked to churches and have powerful support among political parties that allows them to resist state regulation and oppose efforts to expand services in response to new demand. In contrast, Denmark is a religiously homogeneous country with a state church. Once the ecclesiastical authorities were merged with secular authorities, religiously affiliated voluntary associations had no exit option available and were absorbed by the public sector. Voluntary service agencies of any kind have thus remained a very small part of the Danish social service system.

A comparison of countries such as Germany and the Netherlands—both with a sizable voluntary service sector—reveals that the level of decentralization is central to the capacity of government to adequately fund and regulate voluntary service agencies. The Netherlands, with a more centralized structure and largely national financing of voluntary services, has been able to offer much more extensive services to the elderly than Germany.

Further support for the key role of church-state relations in the government-nonprofit relationship is found in recent work by Morgan (2002), who concludes that contemporary early childhood education programs in France, Sweden, and Germany were profoundly shaped by religious cleavages dating back to the nineteenth century and before. Like Alber, Morgan found that the "partnership of the Lutheran churches and the Nordic states" precluded the development of a competing sector of non-state schools such as in Germany (Morgan 2002:125). Like Alber, Morgan also found that German voluntary associations resist the creation of new early childhood education programs to meet the increased demand partly for ideological reasons and partly because they are so powerful politically that they are not really accountable to public funding authorities. France and Sweden have public educational systems and are able to respond much more quickly to the increased demand for day care and early childhood education spurred by the big jump in labor force participation by women in the 1960s and 1970s. In sum, state-church relations appear to be a major factor in determining the character of the government-nonprofit relationship and the size of the nonprofit sector in particular countries.

Neo-Institutional Perspectives

We turn, finally, to a more systematic approach to linking nonprofits, the state, and societal systems. The neo-institutional model focuses on the ways in which the institutional environment shapes the nonprofit sector. It emerged out of arguments for "bringing the state back in" to social science research. Noting that the state was something more than aggregated class interests, a force in its own right, Evans, Rueschmeyer, and Skocpol (1985) argue that it plays a vital and central role in influencing the structure of society and the actions of political interest groups. This state-centered perspective set the stage for the development and evolution of institutional theory in the 1990s, which in turn draws upon a broad and diverse literature from political science, economics, and sociology (Powell and DiMaggio 1991; Steinmo, Thelan, Longstreth 1992; W. R. Scott 1994, 1995; Peters 2000; Rothstein and Steinmo 2002).

As it pertains to our understanding of the government-nonprofit relationship, the institutional perspective suggests that the prevalence and vitality of nonprofit organizations are largely the product of the political, legal, and institutional environment (see also Woolcock and Narayan 2000). This emphasis is a marked departure from other approaches to the conceptualization of the government-nonprofit relationship. Civil society and social movement approaches tend to regard the prevalence and health of nonprofit organizations as the products of citizen demand and cooperative social networks, with social capital as an independent variable and nonprofit organizations as the dependent variable. Market theories tend to place the emphasis on citizen demand as the independent variable and nonprofit organizations as the dependent variable.

In contrast, institutional theories stress that nonprofit organizations represent the choices of individuals that are in turn shaped by their institutional environment. Weak and ineffective governments, lack of public funding or appropriate tax incentives, and poor public leadership will profoundly affect the nonprofit sector. Oppressive or inappropriate government regulations can in turn undermine nonprofit organizations and directly affect the willingness of citizens to form nonprofit organizations or participate in these organizations as staff and volunteers.

Important variants of this institutional perspective focus on the mutual dependence and synergism of government and nonprofits. Thus Skocpol (1999) argues that voluntary associations thrive in tandem with active government and that government support for voluntary organizations is critical to the growth of the sector. Similarly, Pressman (1975), Walker (1991), and Salisbury (1984) emphasize the important role of government in spurring nonprofit activity and encouraging the formation of nonprofit advocacy and service organizations. James (1987) notes, based on her comparative research on nonprofit organizations, that government funding and nonprofit organizations grow in tandem.

In a sense, these perspectives build upon social movement theory by calling attention to the impact of social movements on public policy and the formation of nonprofit organizations. However, as Skocpol (1999) notes, without an ultimate change in government policy, social movements would not have been able to sustain their momentum. Not only did government funding support many movements directly or indirectly, but the expansion of government involvement in civil rights provided further incentive for the formation of nonprofit advocacy organizations. In short, social movement theory is very helpful in explaining institutional change, but neo-institutional theory helps explain the ways in which government policy and institutions shape social movements and the nonprofit sector over time. It also helps explain cross-national differences.

Tendler's (1997) work underscores another key issue for institutional theory: she found that personnel from NGOs went to work for the central government and vice versa. The success of NGOs in Brazil hinged in part on the networks created by professionals who crossed the "public-private divide" and thereby aligned and reduced differences between government and NGOs. This perspective is very different from the market and civil society approaches to the government-nonprofit relationship, which presume inherent differences between nonprofit organizations and government. While the market and civil society approaches recognize that government may impinge or otherwise undermine the distinctive values of nonprofit organization, fundamentally, nonprofits are seen as different from government. The normative implication is also that society is better served by sectoral differences.

Tendler's work suggests that blurred public-private boundaries may actually improve nonprofit effectiveness by enhancing opportunities for cooperation and resource development. She also calls attention to the point made by Smith and Lipsky (1993) and Rein and Rainwater (1986) that seemingly private behavior may in fact be quite public in nature. The neo-institutional approach suggests that we need to pay heed to *which* specific institutions play a critical role in altering the environment for producing or consuming a public good—and *how* those processes operate. Indeed, this basic argument was initially propounded by Polanyi (1944) in *The Great Transformation,* where he suggested that the development of free markets in the eighteenth and nineteenth centuries was not a natural process but instead the product of political struggle (see also Lifset 1989; Rein 1982). Similarly, the sectoral division among government, nonprofit, and for-profit organizations is directly influenced by government policy, for government policy can affect the incentives for individuals to incorporate as nonprofits and to sustain nonprofit organizations through donations or other support (Smith and Lipsky 1993; Simon, Dale, and Chisolm, this volume).

In short, decisions about which sector to favor or use for what purpose reflect political choices. The decision to incorporate as a commercial theater or a nonprofit one will be directly affected by the existing government policy and legal framework that exists. Similarly, the decision to convert from a nonprofit hospital to a for-profit hospital will inevitably be affected by tax and regulatory considerations. A nonprofit art museum is a function not just of market failure but also of incentives provided by government to incorporate as a nonprofit.

The central role of institutional forces in shaping government-nonprofit relationships has direct implications for the ongoing debate on privatization and devolution. One perspective on privatization, endorsed by conservative think tanks, suggests that reducing the scope of government will allow more space for voluntary action by nonprofit organizations by stimulating donations and volunteer efforts. However, given the extent to which nonprofits depend on government funding to carry out their activities, it is highly unlikely that voluntary action can grow sufficiently to allow nonprofits to maintain service levels, let alone expand services (Salamon 1987; Grønbjerg and Salamon 2002).

Indeed, the work of Skocpol (1999), Smith and Lipsky (1993), and Grønbjerg (1993) suggests that a withering of the public sector will serve only to desiccate the nonprofit sector. Thus as Polanyi (1944) might assert, the public and nonprofit sectors are interdependent and mutually reinforcing. Moreover, the growth of the nonprofit sector—and people's reliance upon it for services—will likely invite public regulation and monitoring. It is for this reason that the Bush administration's Office of Faith-Based and Community Initiatives might actually invite more regulation and intervention by public entities in the affairs of churches and faith-related organizations than ever before.

As noted earlier, government support of the nonprofit sector has become increasingly diversified. Just as neo-institutional theory would predict, this greater complexity reflects the incentives created for public and nonprofit actors by existing government rules and regulations as well as the norms guiding public policy and management. As we noted earlier, many art museums today are complicated public/nonprofit hybrids even if direct government funding is a relatively small percentage of their budget, since these institutions may also depend upon tax incentives, bond money, and grants to partner institutions who then use museum services and provide other indirect support. An art museum created as a for-profit entity would be unable to take advantage of most of these subsidies.

Other aspects of institutional theory incorporate both institutional and social capital/social movement perspectives. For instance, many development theorists emphasize the "dynamic professional alliances and relationships between and within state bureaucracies and various actors in civil society" (Woolcock and Narayan 2000, p. 236). This perspective reflects three key observations. First, neither government nor nonprofits are inherently good or bad at providing collective goods. Second, government, nonprofits, and business do not alone possess the resources and expertise necessary to provide sustainable development programs. Third, the state's role is particularly problematic because it is a provider of public goods and the final arbiter of the rule of law—it must balance nurturing the nonprofit sector in development while also imposing a meaningful and appropriate performance-based accountability system.

Central to this perspective is the idea of complementarity and embeddedness. The former refers to mutually supportive relationships between public and private actors—for example, the nonprofit sector cannot exist without a supportive legal framework. The latter emphasizes the nature and extent of ties between public and nonprofit officials. As Tendler (1997) observed, effective NGOs are embedded with a network of social relations that transcend the public, nonprofit, and for-profit sectors. Alternatively, Russia demonstrates how weak political institutions and deep cleavages between the public sector and civil society organizations can lead to political instability and a fragile, weak nonprofit sector (Rose 1998). In the United States, many federal social programs fail to sustain themselves because of poor political leadership and a lack of cooperative social networks at the local level.

This focus on synergy is especially important in the context of the other theories discussed in this chapter. Market and government failure theories and the social origins theory treat government and the nonprofit sector as distinct sectors. But the concept of embeddedness calls attention to the blurred boundaries between the sectors—what is public and what is private is not always apparent, nor should it be. Private behavior is a function of public policy and nonprofit actors are embedded in social relations that transcend sectoral boundaries.

As Smith and Lipsky (1993) observe, the relationship between government and nonprofit social welfare agencies constitutes a "contracting regime" characterized by regularized interactions and governed by norms regulating behavior. Wagner (2000) concluded that nonprofit organizations should be viewed "not so much as forming a specific institutional sector but as part of a complex network of organizations" (p. 542). Ostrom (1996) reached a similar conclusion in her study of development in Brazil where she found successful projects to be the result of "co-production" in which the public sector "co-produced" an improved sewer system with local citizens who participated through local associations. Hirschman (1984) noted in his study of grassroots organizations in Latin America that the pluralist politics of Colombia, Peru, and the Dominican Republic were reinforced and supported by dense networks of grassroots movements and social activist organizations. More recently, O'Rourke (2002) found that community groups in Vietnam worked with state actors who supported the goals of these community groups to successfully pressure firms to reduce their pollution. The external ties of these community agencies to state actors were critical to effective community mobilization.

Finally, this synergy perspective suggests that substantial internal variation is likely to exist within countries because the specific ties between local nonprofit associations and groups and state actors may vary significantly. Communities without dense social networks among public and private actors will thus be at a disadvantage in effectively mobilizing for social change and reform.

Our analysis has focused primarily on identifying and describing major approaches to understanding the relationship between nonprofits and government. Each of the three models we identify has been subject to some level of empirical analysis, although major gaps remain. In this concluding section of our chapter, we outline some of the major research opportunities.

First, to assess the utility of the market model of government-nonprofit relationships, we need systematic research on how the sectoral composition of market niches shifts over time and on which factors account for these transformations. As the chapters in Part IV of this volume demonstrate, there has been some work along these lines in the fields of health and education (see also S. R. Smith 2002), but several other industries have been subject to much less systematic attention. Careful comparisons of these dynamics across niches or policy fields are essential if we are to determine the applicability and limitations of the model.

Second, it seems clear from the chapters in Part IV of this volume that the nature of government-nonprofit financial transactions has changed in recent years and that a much broader portfolio of funding structures has emerged. We know little about the extent to which these changes reflect broad political ideologies or the actions of particular interest groups, or are modified by the organizational, professional, or institutional structures of the fields of activity. For example, human service organizations are more numerous and less dominated by very large institutions (such as hospitals), and employ much less professionalized staff than the health field. How important are these structural differences for understanding the transformation in government-nonprofit transactions that have occurred in these two fields?

Third, the social and political structure of the United States—and of other societies—continues to evolve. In the United States, economic inequality has increased markedly since the mid-1970s, as has ethnic and religious heterogeneity, while residential patterns continue to diversify. During the same period, voters seem to be increasingly alienated from the political system. Our second model, the civil society/social movement model, posits that these developments should have major implications for the role of social movement organizations, nonprofit advocacy, and the development of social cohesion and civil society more generally. Or put another way, declines in social capital and trust should then undermine the vitality and sustainability of cooperative activity that forms the backbone of voluntary activity at the local level.

Finally, our regime or neo-institutional model virtually begs for careful, comparative analyses. We need much more in-depth assessments of how particular forms of nonprofit-government relationships have emerged across fields of activities and across nation-states. The social origins model outlined by Salamon and Anheier (1998) remains essentially an ex post facto explanation—labels assigned to particular configurations of state and nonprofit scope of activity. We need more research on whether those configurations are indeed key features of state-nonprofit regimes and of whether similar regimes have emerged through similar historical paths. We know little about what those paths are or what roles religion, ethnic diversity, and social class structures play. This is likely to be difficult, but important, work. The empirical work we summarized as part of our discussion of the institutional component of our third model points to the complexity of these historical and societal factors.

ACKNOWLEDGMENTS

This chapter reflects an ongoing collaboration and we alternate the sequence of our names to reflect our joint contributions to these efforts. We are grateful for the detailed and very helpful comments on this chapter provided by the coeditors of the volume as well as Alan Abramson and several cohorts of our students who read and provided feedback on earlier versions. We also acknowledge valuable input and suggestions from attendees at two ARNOVA conferences where we presented drafts in process. All remaining obfuscation, misinterpretations, and vagueness remain our responsibilities entirely.

NOTES

1. Economists use the concept of demand to mean anything that someone desires and supply to mean anything that someone is willing to provide, including social status, "warm glow," and similar intangibles. This is a broader formulation than we use here. We use demand to mean the desire to obtain economic goods and services in exchange for cash or cash-equivalent value and supply to mean the willingness to make such goods and services available for purchase.

2. It is worth noting that similar arguments about the ability of smaller, more local institutions to foster innovation and accommodate diverse preferences were used in the *Federalist Papers* to justify the allocation of responsibilities among federal, state, and local government in the United States (Richard Steinberg, personal communication). Such arguments still surface in current debates about the merits of devolving federal responsibilities to states and localities. Unlike state or local governments, however, nonprofits need not adhere to interests contained within geographic boundaries.

3. Thus Prewitt (2004) argues that while foundations (and by implication, nonprofits more generally) have contributed to important social changes (e.g., the 911 system for emergency calls; the hospice movement; the Pap smear in cancer treatment; public libraries; the polio vaccine; rocket sciences; *Sesame Street;* white lines on highways; the green revolution; and yellow fever vaccine), there is no systematic research to document their role, only case studies, anecdotal evidence, and self-serving claims. As Prewitt notes, "foundations are marginal rather than central actors when it comes to large-scale social change—which results from social-political movements, shifts in political ideology endorsed by the mass electorate, and technology-driven market forces" (p. 13). By extension, social movements are likely to be more important forces for social change than nonprofit service providers or foundations.

4. See Ben-Ner and Van Hoomissen (1991) for a discussion of the transactions costs of various alternative mechanisms for ensuring that a particular portfolio of goods and services is provided.

5. As noted by Foley and Edwards (1996), the prevailing definition of civil society leaves many unanswered definitional questions, especially as to whether local business or public housing and port authorities, even a municipal department of neighborhoods, could be considered part of civil society.

6. Implicit in Putnam's work on social capital is an assumption that social capital building and more generally the formation of nonprofit organizations are "bottoms-up" processes in which individuals come together to participate in voluntary associations at the local level and in the process create social capital. However, Skocpol (1999) contends that the growth of nonprofit organizations in the nineteenth century was due to the expansion of the national state and the emergence of national federated organizations that accompanied this growth. For instance, the Girl Scouts, the American Red Cross, and the Salvation Army were typical of many national nonprofit organizations with local chapters that were supported and nurtured from "the top" rather than growing from local initiatives.

7. James calls her theoretical approach a "supply-side" approach since it rests largely on the idea that the nonprofit sector will vary across countries depending upon the supply of religious entrepreneurs.

REFERENCES

Abzug, Rikki. 1994. "Stewards of Caring: Family Traditions of Trusteeship in Four Cities." New Haven, Conn.: Program on Non-Profit Organizations, Institution for Social and Policy Studies, Yale University.

Alber, Jens. 1995. "A Framework for the Comparative Study of Social Services." *Journal of European Social Policy* 5(2):131–149.

Barber, Benjamin, R. 1984. *Strong Democracy: Participatory Politics for a New Age.* Berkeley: University of California Press.

Bartley, Tim. 2003. "Certifying Forests and Factories." *Politics and Society* 31(3):433–464.

Ben-Ner, Avner. 1987. "Producer Cooperatives: Why Do They Exist in Capitalist Economies?" *The Nonprofit Sector: A Re-*

search Handbook, 1st ed., ed. Walter W. Powell. New Haven, Conn.: Yale University Press. 434–450.

Ben-Ner, Avner, and Theresa Van Hoomissen. 1991."Nonprofit Organizations in the Mixed Economy: A Demand and Supply Analysis." *Annals of Public and Cooperative Economics* 62(4):519–550.

Bennet, Jared C. 2001. "The Legal Framework." *Understanding Nonprofit Organizations: Governance, Leadership and Management,* ed. J. Steve Ott. Boulder, Colo.: Westview Press. 51–60.

Berger, Peter L., and Richard J. Neuhaus. 1977. *To Empower People: The Role of Mediating Institutions in Public Policy.* Washington, D.C.: American Enterprise Institute for Public Policy Research.

Blau, Peter M., and Marshall W. Meyer. 1987. *Bureaucracy in Modern Society.* New York: McGraw-Hill.

Brown, James. 1941. *The History of Public Assistance in Chicago, 1833 to 1893.* Chicago: University of Chicago Press.

Bryer, David, and John Magrath. 1999. "New Dimensions of Global Advocacy." *Nonprofit and Voluntary Sector Quarterly* 28(4) (Supplement): 168–177.

Chaves, Mark. 1998. "The Religious Ethic and the Spirit of Nonprofit Entrepreneurship." *Private Action and the Public Good,* ed. Walter W. Powell and Elisabeth S. Clemens. New Haven, Conn.: Yale University Press. 47–65.

Clemens, Elisabeth S. 1993. "Organizational Repertoires and Institutional Change: Women's Groups and the Transformation of U.S. Politics, 1890–1920," *American Journal of Sociology* 98(4):755–798.

Clotfelter, Charles T. ed. 1992. *Who Benefits from the Nonprofit Sector?* Chicago: University of Chicago Press.

Coleman, James. 1988. "Social Capital in the Creation of Human Capital." *American Journal of Sociology* 94 (Supplement): s95–s120.

Considine, Mark. 2000. "Contract Regimes and Reflexive Governance: Comparing Employment Service Reforms in the United Kingdom, the Netherlands, New Zealand and Australia," *Public Administration* 78(3):613–638.

Dalton, Russell J., Steve Recchia, and Robert Rohrschneider. 2003. "The Environmental Movement and the Modes of Political Action." *Comparative Political Studies* 36:743–771.

DeHoog, Ruth Hoogland. 1984. *Contracting Out for Human Services: Economic, Political, and Organization Perspectives.* Albany: State University of New York Press.

DeHoog, Ruth Hoogland, and Lester M. Salamon. 2002. "Purchase-of-Service." *The Tools of Government: A Guide to the New Governance,* Lester M. Salamon, ed. New York: Oxford University Press. 319–339.

DiMaggio, Paul J., and Walter W. Powell. 1983. "The Iron Cage Revisited: Institutional Isomorphism and Collective Rationality in Organizational Fields." *American Sociological Review* 48 (April): 147–160.

Donahue, John D. 1989. *The Privatization Decision.* New York: Basic Books.

Douglas, James. 1983. *Why Charity: The Case for a Third Sector.* Beverly Hills, Calif.: Sage.

———. 1987. "Political Theories of Nonprofit Organizations." *The Nonprofit Sector: A Research Handbook,* 1st ed., ed. Walter W. Powell. New Haven, Conn.: Yale University Press. 43–54.

Drucker, Peter F. 1967. *The Age of Discontinuity.* New York: Harper and Row.

Esping-Andersen, Gøsta. 1990. *The Three Worlds of Welfare Capitalism.* Princeton, N.J.: Princeton University Press.

Etzioni, Amitai. 1993. *The Spirit of Community: Rights, Responsibilities, and the Communitarian Agenda.* New York: Crown.

Evans, Peter B., Dietrich Rueschmeyer, and Theda Skocpol. 1985. *Bringing the State Back In.* Cambridge: Cambridge University Press.

Ferris, James, and Elizabeth Graddy. 1998. "A Contractual Framework for the New Public Management Theory." *International Public Management Journal* 1(2):225–240.

Finke, Roger, and Rodney Starke. 1992. *The Churching of America, 1776–1990: Winners and Losers in Our Religious Economy.* New Brunswick, N.J.: Rutgers University Press.

Flora, Peter, and Arnold J. Heidenheimer, eds. 1984. *The Development of Welfare States in Europe and America.* New Brunswick, N.J.: Transaction.

Foley, Michael, and Bob Edwards. 1996. "The Paradox of Civil Society." *Journal of Democracy,* 7(3):38–52.

Fox, Jonathan. 2001. "Vertically Integrated Policy Monitoring: A Tool for Civil Society Policy Advocacy." *Nonprofit and Voluntary Sector Quarterly* 30(3):616–627.

Friedman, Lawrence J., and Mark D. McGarvie, eds. 2003. *Charity, Philanthropy, and Civility in American History.* Cambridge: Cambridge University Press.

Galaskiewicz, Joseph. 1985. *Social Organization of an Urban Grants Economy: A Study of Business Philanthropy and Nonprofit Organizations.* Orlando, Fla.: Academic Press.

Glazer, Nathan. 1989. *The Self-Service Society.* Cambridge, Mass.: Harvard University Press.

Gray, Bradford H., and Mark Schlesinger. 2002. "Health." *The State of Nonprofit America, ed. Lester M. Salamon.* Washington, D.C.: Brookings Institution Press. 65–106.

Greenstone, J. David, and Paul E. Peterson eds. 1973. *Race and Authority in Urban Politics: Community Participation and the War on Poverty.* New York: Russell Sage Foundation.

Grønbjerg, Kirsten A. 1993. *Understanding Nonprofit Funding: Managing Revenues in Social Service and Community Development Nonprofits.* San Francisco: Jossey-Bass.

———. 1997. "Transaction Costs in Social Contracting: Lessons from the U.S.A." *The Contract Culture in Public Service: Studies from Britain, Europe and the USA,* ed. Perri 6 and Jeremy Kendall. Aldershot, U.K.: Arena/Ashgate Publishing.

Grønbjerg, Kirsten A., and Lester M. Salamon. 2002. "Devolution, Privatization, and the Changing Shape of Government-Nonprofit Relations." *State of the Nonprofit America,* ed. Lester M. Salamon. Washington, D.C.: Brookings Institution Press. 447–470.

Grønbjerg, Kirsten A., and Steven Rathgeb Smith. 1999. "Nonprofit Organizations and Public Policies in the Delivery of Human Services." *Philanthropy and the Nonprofit Sector in a Changing America,* ed. Charles Clotfelter and Thomas Ehrlich. Bloomington: Indiana University Press. 139–72.

Gutch, Richard. 1992. *Contracting Lessons from the U.S.* London: National Council of Voluntary Organizations.

Guterbock, Thomas M., and John C. Fries. 1997. *Maintaining America's Social Fabric: The AARP Survey of Civic Involvement.* Washington, D.C.: American Association of Retired Persons.

Hall, Peter Dobkin. 1987. "A Historical Overview of the Private Nonprofit Sector." *The Nonprofit Sector: A Research Handbook,* 1st ed., ed. Walter W. Powell. New Haven, Conn.: Yale University Press. 3–26.

Hammack, David C. 1998. *Making the Nonprofit Sector in the United States.* Bloomington: Indiana University Press.

Hansmann, Henry. 1980. "The Role of Non-Profit Enterprise" *Yale Law Journal* 89:835–901.

———. 1987. "Economic Theories of Nonprofit Organization." *The Nonprofit Sector: A Research Handbook,* ed. Walter W. Powell. New Haven, Conn.: Yale University Press. 27–42.

———. 1996. *The Ownership of Enterprise.* Cambridge, Mass.: Belknap Press of Harvard University Press.

Hartogs, Nelly, and Joseph Weber. 1978. *Impact of Government Funding on the Management of Voluntary Agencies.* New York: The Greater New York Fund/United Way.

Hasenfeld, Yeheskel, and Benjamin Gidron. 2002. "Toward the Integration of Civil Society, Social Movement and Third Sector Theories: Lessons from an International Study of Peace/Conflict Resolution Organizations." Unpublished manuscript.

Hayek, Friedrich A. 1960. *The Constitution of Liberty.* Chicago: University of Chicago Press.

Hirschman, Albert O. 1984. *Getting Ahead Collectively: Grassroots Experiences in Latin America.* New York: Pergamon Press.

James, Estelle. 1983. "How Nonprofits Grow: A Model," *Journal of Policy Analysis and Management* 2(3):350–366.

———. 1987. "The Nonprofit Sector in Comparative Perspective." *The Nonprofit Sector: A Research Handbook,* ed. Walter W. Powell. New Haven, Conn.: Yale University Press. 397–415.

———. 1992. "Commentary." *Who Benefits from the Nonprofit Sector?* Charles Clotfelter, ed. Chicago: University of Chicago Press. 244–250.

Jenkins, J. Craig, and Abigail Halcli. 1999. "Grassrooting the System?: The Development and Impact of Social Movement Philanthropy, 1953–1990." *Philanthropic Foundations: New Scholarship, New Possibilities,* ed. Ellen Condliffe Lagemann. Bloomington: Indiana University Press. 229–256.

Johnson, Arlien. 1931. *Public Policy and Private Charities: A Study of Legislation in the United States and of Administration in Illinois.* Chicago: University of Chicago Press.

Kaul, Inge. 2001. "Global Public Goods: What Role for Civil Society." *Nonprofit and Voluntary Sector Quarterly* 30(3):588–602.

Keck, Margaret E., and Kathryn Sikkink. 1998. *Activists Without Borders.* Ithaca, N.Y.: Cornell University Press.

Kennedy, Sheila Suess. 2001. "When Is Private Public? State Action in the Era of Privatization and Public-Private Partnerships." *George Mason University Civil Rights Law Review* 11:203.

Kettl, Donald F. 2000. *The Global Public Management Revolution.* Washington, D.C.: Brookings Institution Press.

Kramer, Ralph. 1981. *Voluntary Agencies in the Welfare State.* Berkeley: University of California Press.

———. 1987. "Voluntary Agencies and the Personal Social Services." *The Nonprofit Sector: A Research Handbook,* 1st ed., ed. Walter W. Powell. New Haven, Conn.: Yale University Press. 240–257.

———. 1993. *Privatization in Four European Countries: Comparative Studies in Government-Third Sector Relationships.* Armonk, N.Y. : M. E. Sharpe.

Lewis, Jane. 1999. "Reviewing the Relationship Between the Voluntary Sector in Britain in the 1990s." *Voluntas* 10(3):255–270.

Lifset, Reid. 1989. "Cash Cows or Sacred Cows: The Politics of the Commercialization Movement." *The Future of the Nonprofit Sector,* ed. Virginia Hodgkinson. San Francisco: Jossey-Bass. 140–166.

Lindenberg, Marc. 2001. "Reaching Beyond the Family: New Nongovernmental Organization Alliances for Global Poverty Alleviation and Emergency Response." *Nonprofit and Voluntary Sector Quarterly* 30(3):603–615.

Lipsky, Michael. 1980. *Street-Level Bureaucracy.* New York: Russell Sage.

Lohmann, Roger A. 1992. *The Commons: New Perspectives on Nonprofit Organizations and Voluntary Action.* San Francisco: Jossey-Bass.

Lowi, Theodore J. 1979. *The End of Liberalism: The Second Republic of the United States.* New York: Norton.

Marris, Peter, and Martin Rein. 1982. *The Dilemmas of Social Reform.* 2nd ed. Chicago: University of Chicago Press.

Marshall, T. H. 1964. *Class, Citizenship, and Social Development: Essays.* Garden City, N.J.: Doubleday.

Meyer, Jack A., ed. 1982. *Meeting Human Needs: Toward a New Public Philosophy.* Washington, D.C.: American Enterprise Institute.

Moe, Terry. 1990. "The Politics of Structural Choice: Toward a Theory of Public Bureaucracy." *Organization Theory: From Chester Barnard to the Present and Beyond,* ed. Oliver E. Williamson. New York: Oxford University Press. 116–155.

Moore, Jr., Barrington. 1966. *Social Origins of Dictatorship and Democracy: Lord and Peasant in the Making of the Modern World.* Boston: Beacon Press.

Moore, Louella. 2001. "Legitimation Issues in the State-Nonprofit Relationship." *Nonprofit and Voluntary Sector Quarterly* 30(4):707–719.

Morgan, Kimberly J. 2002. "Forging the Frontiers Between State, Church, and Family: Religious Cleavages and the Origins of Early Childhood Education and Care Policies in France, Sweden, and Germany." *Politics and Society* 30(1):113–148.

Morone, James. 1990. *The Democratic Wish.* New York: Basic Books.

NGO Watch. 2005. http://www.ngowatch.org/. A Project of The American Enterprise Institute and the Federalist Society. Accessed November 27.

Nisbet, Robert. 1953. *The Quest for Community: A Study in the Ethics of Order and Freedom.* New York: Oxford University Press.

O'Connor, Alice. 1999. "The Ford Foundation and Philanthropic Activism in the 1960s." *Philanthropic Foundations:*

New Scholarship, New Possibilities, ed. Ellen Condliffe Lagemann. Bloomington: Indiana University Press. 169–194.

———. 2001. *Poverty Knowledge: Social Science, Social Policy, and the Poor in Twentieth-Century U.S. History.* Princeton, N.J.: Princeton University Press.

Odendahl, Teresa. 1990. *Charity Begins at Home: Generosity and Self-Interest Among the Philanthropic Elite.* New York: Basic Books.

O'Rourke, Dara. 2002. "Community-Driven Regulation: Towards an Improved Model of Environmental Regulation in Vietnam." *Livable Cities: The Politics of Urban Livelihood and Sustainability,* ed. Peter Evans. Berkeley: University of California Press.

Ostrander, Susan A. 1995. *Money for Change: Social Movement Philanthropy at Haymarket People's Fund.* Philadelphia: Temple University Press.

Ostrower, Francie. 1995. *Why the Wealthy Give: The Culture of Elite Philanthropy.* Princeton, N.J.: Princeton University Press.

Peters, B. Guy. 2000. *Institutional Theory: Problems and Prospects.* Vienna: Institute for Advanced Studies.

Pfeffer, Jeffrey, and Gerald Salancik. 1978. *The External Control of Organizations: A Resource Dependence Perspective.* New York: Harper and Row.

Polanyi, Karl. 1944. *The Great Transformation.* New York: Farrar and Rinehart.

Popielarz, Pamela A., and J. Miller McPherson. 1995. "On the Edge or in Between: Niche Position, Niche Overlap, and the Duration of Voluntary Association Memberships." *American Journal of Sociology* 101(3):698–720.

Powell, Walter W., and Paul J. DiMaggio, eds. 1991. *The New Institutionalism in Organizational Analysis.* Chicago: University of Chicago Press.

Pratt, Jon W., and Richard J. Zeckhauser, eds. 1985. *Principals and Agents: The Structure of Business.* Boston: Harvard Business School Press.

Pressman, Jeffrey. 1975. *Federal Programs and City Politics.* Berkeley: University of California Press.

Prewitt, Kenneth. 2004. "The Foundation and the Liberal Society." Paper prepared for Legitimacy and Functions of Foundations in Europe and the United States, May 27–29, Paris, France, a conference organized by la Fondation Mattei Dogan and the Social Science Research Council.

Putnam, Robert D. 1993a. *Making Democracy Work: Civic Traditions in Modern Italy.* Princeton, N.J.: Princeton University Press.

———. 1993b. "The Prosperous Community: Social Capital and Public Life." *American Prospect* 13 (Spring): 35–42.

———. 1995. "Bowling Alone: America's Declining Social Capital." *Journal of Democracy* 6(1):65–78.

———. 2000. *Bowling Alone: The Collapse and Revival of American Community.* New York: Simon and Schuster.

Putnam, Robert D., and Lewis Feldstein. 2003. *Better Together: Restoring the American Community.* New York: Simon and Schuster.

Raynor, Gregory K. 1999. "The Ford Foundation's War on Poverty: Private Philanthropy and Race Relations in New York City, 1948–1968." *Philanthropic Foundations,* ed. Ellen Condliffe Lagemann. Bloomington: Indiana University Press. 195–228.

Rein, Martin. 1982. "The Social Policy of the Firm." *Policy Sciences* 14:117–35.

Rein, Martin, and Lee Rainwater, eds. 1986. *The Public/Private Interplay in Social Protection: A Comparative Study.* New York: M. E. Sharpe.

Rose, Richard. 1998. "Getting Things Done in an Anti-Modern Society: Social Capital Networks in Russia." Working paper SPP 304, University of Strathclyde, Center for the Study of Public Policy.

Rose-Ackerman, Susan. 1996. "Altruism, Nonprofits, and Economic Theory." *Journal of Economic Literature* 34:701–728.

Rothstein, Bo, and Sven Steinmo, eds. 2002. *Restructuring the Welfare State: Political Institutions and Policy Change.* New York: Palgrave Macmillan.

Saidel, Judith. 1991. "Resource Interdependence: The Relationship Between State Agencies and Nonprofit Organizations." *Public Administration Review* 51:543–553.

Salamon, Lester M. 1987. "Partners in Public Service: The Scope and Theory of Government-Nonprofit Relations." *The Nonprofit Sector: A Research Handbook,* ed. Walter W. Powell. New Haven, Conn.: Yale University Press. 99–117.

———, ed. 2002a. *The Tools of Government: A Guide to the New Governance.* New York: Oxford University Press.

———, ed. 2002b. *The State of Nonprofit America.* Washington, D.C.: Brookings Institution Press.

Salamon, Lester M., and Helmut Anheier. 1998. "Social Origins of Civil Society." *Voluntas* 9(3):213–248.

Salisbury, Robert H. 1984. "Interest Representation: The Dominance of Institutions." *American Political Science Review* 78(1):64–76.

Scott, James C. 1998. *Seeing Like a State: How Certain Schemes to Improve the Human Condition Have Failed.* New Haven, Conn.: Yale University Press.

Scott, W. Richard. 1994. "Institutional Analysis: Variance and Process Theory Approaches." *Institutional Environments and Organizations: Structural Complexity and Individualism,* ed. W. Richard Scott, John W. Meyer, et al. Thousand Oaks, Calif.: Sage. 81–99.

———. 1995. "Introduction: Institutional Theory and Organizations." *The Institutional Construction of Organizations: International and Longitudinal Studies,* ed. W. Richard Scott and Soren Christenson. Thousand Oaks, Calif.: Sage. xi–xxiii.

6, Perri, and Jeremy Kendall, eds. 1997. *The Contract Culture in Public Services: Studies from Britain, Europe and the USA.* Aldershot, U.K.: Ashgate.

Skocpol, Theda. 1999. "How America Became Civic." *Civic Engagement in American Democracy,* ed. Theda Skocpol and Morris P. Fiorina. Washington, D.C.: Brookings Institution Press. 27–80.

Skocpol, Theda, and Morris P. Fiorina, eds. 1999. *Civic Engagement in American Democracy.* Washington, D.C.: Brookings Institution Press.

Skocpol, Theda, Marshall Ganz, and Ziad Munson. 2000. "A Nation of Organizers: The Institutional Origins of Civic Voluntarism in the United States." *American Political Science Review* 94:527–546.

Smith, David Horton. 1973. *Voluntary Action Research.* Lexington, Mass.: Lexington Books.

Smith, Steven Rathgeb. 2002. "Social Services." *The State of the Nonprofit Sector,* ed. Lester M. Salamon. Washington, D.C.: Brookings Institution Press. 149–186.

———. 1993. "The New Politics of Contracting: Citizenship and the Nonprofit Role." *Public Policy for Democracy,* ed. Helen Ingram and Steven Rathgeb Smith. Washington, D.C.: Brookings Institution Press. 198–221.

Smith, Steven Rathgeb and Michael Lipsky. 1993. *Nonprofits for Hire: The Welfare State in the Age of Contracting.* Cambridge, Mass.: Harvard University Press.

Steinmo, Sven, Kathleen Thelan, and Frank Longstreth. 1992. *Structuring Politics: Historical Institutionalism in Comparative Analysis.* New York: Cambridge University Press.

Tarrow, Sidney. 1994. *Power in Movement: Social Movements, Collective Action and Mass Politics in the Modern State.* New York: Cambridge University Press.

———. 2002. "Transnational Politics: Contention and Institutions in International Politics." Unpublished paper.

Tendler, Judith. 1997. *Good Government in the Tropics.* Baltimore: Johns Hopkins University Press.

Titmuss, Richard M. 1969. *Essays on "The Welfare State."* Boston: Beacon Press.

Tocqueville, Alexis de. 1835–1840. *Democracy in America.* Reprint edition. Ed. and trans. Harvey C. Mansfield and Delba Winthrop. Chicago: University of Chicago Press, 2000.

Van Til, Jon. 2004. "Nonprofit Organizations and Social Institutions." *The Jossey-Bass Handbook of Nonprofit Leadership and Management,* 2nd ed., ed. Robert D. Herman et al. San Francisco: Jossey-Bass. 44–64.

Wagner, Antonin. 2000. "Reframing 'Social Origins' Theory: The Structural Transformation of the Public Sphere." *Nonprofit and Voluntary Sector Quarterly* 29(4):541–553.

Walker, Jack. L. 1991. "Interests, Political Parties, and Policy Formation in the American Democracy." *Federal Social Policy: The Historical Dimension,* ed. D. T. Critchlow and Ellis W. Hawley. University Park: Pennsylvania State University Press.

Walzer, Michael. 1992. *Spheres of Justice.* New York: Basic Books.

———. 1995. "The Concept of Civil Society." *Toward A Global Civil Society,* ed. Michael Waltzer. Providence: Berghahn Books. 7–27.

Weisbrod, Burton. 1977. *The Voluntary Nonprofit Sector.* Lexington, Mass.: Lexington Books.

———. 1988. *The Nonprofit Economy.* Cambridge, Mass.: Harvard University Press.

Werner, Ruth. 1961. *Public Financing of Voluntary Agency Foster Care.* New York: Child Welfare League of America.

White House Office of Faith-Based and Community Initiatives. 2003. *President Bush's Faith-Based and Community Initiative.* www.whitehouse.gov/government/fbci/mission.html.

Wiewel, Wim, and Albert Hunter. 1985. "The Interorganizational Network as a Resource." *Administrative Science Quarterly* 30(4):482–496.

Wilensky, Harold L. 1975. *The Welfare State and Equality: Structural and Ideological Roots of Public Expenditures.* Berkeley: University of California Press.

Wilensky, Harold L., and Charles N. Lebeaux. 1965. *Industrial Society and Social Welfare: The Impact of Industrialization on the Supply and Organization of Social Welfare Services in the United States,* 1st ed. New York: Free Press.

Williams, Walter. 1980. *Government by Agency: Lessons from the Social Program Grants-in-Aid Experience.* New York: Academic Press.

Williamson, Oliver E. 1981. "The Economics of Organization: The Transaction Cost Approach." *American Journal of Sociology* 87:548–577.

Wilson, James Q. 1967. "The Bureaucracy Problem." *Public Interest* 6:3–9.

Woodson, Robert L. 1981. *A Summons to Life: Mediating Structures and the Prevention of Youth Crime.* Cambridge, Mass.: Ballinger.

Woolcock, Michael, and Deepa Narayan. 2000. "Social Capital: Implications for Development Theory, Research and Policy." *World Bank Research Observer* 15(2):225–249.

World Bank. 2003. *World Bank Development Report 2004: Making Services Work for Poor People.* Washington, D.C.: World Bank.

Young, Dennis R. 1983. *If Not for Profit, for What? A Behavioral Theory of the Nonprofit Sector Based on Entrepreneurship.* Lexington, Mass.: Lexington Books.

———. 1999. "Complementary, Supplementary, or Adversarial? A Theoretical and Historical Examination of Nonprofit-Government Relations in the United States." *Nonprofits and Government: Collaboration and Conflict,* ed. Elizabeth T. Boris and C. Eugene Steuerle. Washington, D.C.: Urban Institute. 31–67.

11

The Legal Framework for Nonprofit Organizations

EVELYN BRODY

Anglo-American philanthropy recently marked the 400th anniversary of the Statute of Charitable Uses (43 Eliz. ch. 4). The 1601 Statute of Elizabeth is celebrated for its preamble enumerating a long list of charitable purposes, ranging from "relief of aged, impotent and poor people" and "supportation, aid and help of young tradesmen, handicraftsmen, and persons decayed" to "maintenance of . . . schools of learning" and "repair of bridges, ports, havens, causeways, churches, sea-banks, and highways." The Elizabethans also began the modern, secular legal system for overseeing charity. Unfortunately, the enforcement mechanism in the Statute of Elizabeth proved difficult to carry out, and fell into disuse. To this day and in the United States, the law provides at best an incomplete solution to problems of nonprofit governance and the protection of the public interest.

In America, the law is a relatively weak force in the realm of charity operations. Within broadly bounded charitable purposes, and subject only to a general proscription against insider self-dealing, no laws tell the entity or its managers how to "do" charity. The American legal structure excels at establishing or requiring processes in which individuals may make substantive decisions, and falters at dictating results. Nor, despite the absence of private shareholders to monitor charities, do we find close state regulation of charitable activities. Weak enforcement is a symptom, however, rather than a cause of the independence of the charitable sector: as a basic premise, we do not want the state to run charities.

This laissez-faire structure leaves several important policy questions unaddressed, or answered only indirectly. To society as a whole, the most important question is, "How private is private philanthropy?" In answer, we find that the law endows a charity's board with full governance authority, and generally grants only the state attorney general with standing to sue for a board's breach of fiduciary duty. Subject only to donor-intent limitations, the law defers to boards to make decisions over charity purposes and operations. Some might believe that "there oughta be a law" governing many areas of nonprofit behavior, but no law requires charities to serve only the poor, prohibits charities from charging for their services, bars charities from paying (reasonable) high salaries, or requires charities to be democratically run.

In fact, as discussed elsewhere in this volume (Boris and Steuerle), only a small percentage of charities devote themselves to poverty relief. Market transactions dominate: donations make up less than 20 percent of the sector's total receipts (less than 10 percent excluding churches), and most workers are paid (volunteers represent only 40 percent of total labor). Most charities have no members, and in that small minority of charities with members, membership is often only ceremonial, resulting in self-perpetuating boards. No law imposes term limits on either the life of a charity (most are perpetual) or the service of a board member; nor does the law mandate including members of the beneficiary class or the community on the board, or prohibit nepotism (family members frequently serve on foundation boards).[1]

The law retains jurisdiction in cases of misfeasance and malfeasance by nonprofit fiduciaries. Unfortunately, it is impossible to determine how big a problem this is, and how well government is doing to address it. Charity regulators themselves generally operate in secrecy (to the extent they act at all). Whether you regard the press as watchdog, sensationalist, or part of the prevailing social network, we know essentially the negative anecdotes we read in the newspaper (Fremont-Smith and Kosaras 2003; Fremont-Smith 2004b; Boston Globe Staff 2003). As charity operations gone wrong constantly make front-page news, however, we need to ask ourselves whether the proper response is a change in the law. After all, to seek a legal remedy is to raise yet another question: Who decides? On the private side, candidates include the board, donors, beneficiaries, the community, and the public at large; on the public side, we have the attorney general (and other administrators), the legislature, and the courts. Each of these possible loci of authority has advantages and disadvantages, depending on our view of the appropriate control over the assets, structure, and activities of nonprofit organizations.

Currently, few additional legal checks and balances exist to oversee the classic "board governs, attorney general enforces" structure described above. As we will see, this leads to the twin weaknesses of the charitable sector: the lack of energy and initiative on the part of many nonprofit managers, and the lack of resources and zeal in enforcing the public's interest on the part of many charity regulators. Occasionally, though, we find the reverse problem: a board trying to do the right thing, but thwarted by an overreaching regulator. Sometimes, too, cooperation between a board and an attorney general can produce unwarranted results.

This chapter covers the legal issues relating to the formation, operation, and dissolution of nonprofit organizations, as well as to monitoring and enforcement. Because nonprofits lacking voting members present the greatest challenges to the law, the discussion focuses primarily on the typical charity rather than mutual-benefit organizations. (Indeed, this chapter sometimes uses the terms *nonprofit* and *charity* interchangeably.) Tax rules appear in Simon, Dale, and Chisolm (this volume), although the role of the Internal Revenue Service as a regulator of tax-exempt organizations is also covered here. Finally, no discussion of nonprofit law would be complete without acknowledging the limits of the law. Philanthropy is private precisely because society prefers reasonable discretion exercised by different participants under different conditions to the uniformity of government-directed action. Misguided legal "reform" could make the existing regulatory structure worse for compliant organizations while missing the wayward targets. Accordingly, this chapter concludes with an overview of peer and self-regulatory efforts by charity watchdog and nonprofit groups to improve charity governance and operations.

SOURCES OF LAW

Comparatively little authoritative law exists applicable specifically to nonprofit organizations, despite nonprofits' long history and prominence in American life. Under the decentralized U.S. federal system, substantive nonprofit law is a state concern, with differences occurring across states. Generally, the common law of charity develops on those rare occasions when a testator leaves property to a purported charity, and the disappointed heirs seek to defeat the will; or when a state attorney general is faced with a charity scandal that cannot be ignored. Issues implicating the federal constitution rarely arise; two of the most important U.S. Supreme Court decisions dealing with nonprofit organizations appeared 180 years apart, *Dartmouth College v. Woodward* in 1819 and *Boy Scouts of America v. Dale* in 2000, augmented most recently by a series of cases affirming the free-speech limits on state regulation of charitable solicitations. The most complete and thought-through legal treatment can be found under federal tax law.[2]

However, compared with the law governing business corporations—which is more fully developed because of numerous suits by shareholders—it is not easy to say what "the law" is in the nonprofit sector. While legal standards offer a laissez-faire structure, law as actually practiced by charity fiduciaries, their advisers, and regulators might function at a higher level; the herd behavior of similarly trained professionals leads to relatively consistent and (legally) noncontroversial activities (DiMaggio and Powell 1991).

Even where enforcement action might be occurring, few cases involving nonprofit fiduciary issues have reached the courts. Generally, the charity regulator prefers reform to punishment, in order to improve charity performance and to avoid embarrassment to well-intentioned charity managers. Settlements can be quite detailed, often spelling out changes in governance and future operations, but settlements commonly remain secret.[3] Increasingly, though, regulators are requiring disclosure where the transgression reflects more than a minor infraction by a single bad actor.[4] This invisibility at the informal end of the regulatory spectrum makes it hard to judge the level and the effectiveness of regulators in influencing charity behavior—and whether regulators are motivated by their own or the public's interest. However, the courts have the last word, and so can offer relief if the charity wants to litigate a position taken by the attorney general; by the same token, though, courts are not bound to accept a settlement reached by the attorney general (but there might be no private party with standing to complain).

Most challenging, there is no single "law of nonprofit organizations." Much of the common law of charity, property, and wills and trusts has found its way into state statutes. We find state laws on nonprofit corporations, federal and state tax laws, and state (and sometimes local) laws on charitable solicitations. Like businesses, many nonprofits worry about laws (sometimes with special rules for nonprofits) on contracting, labor and employment, torts and insurance, employee benefits, antitrust, bankruptcy, and political activity, as well as laws that govern specific industries such as hospitals and day care.

Of final importance are several sources that are not themselves law but that influence legal development. The American Law Institute (ALI) published the *Restatement (Second) of the Law of Trusts* in 1959, and has published two portions so far of the *Restatement (Third) of the Law of Trusts* (the first, issued in 1992, covers prudent investing; the second, issued in 2003, addresses, among other topics, the definition of charity and the *cy pres* doctrine). Also in 1992 the ALI produced the *Principles of Corporate Governance,* relating to business corporations, and in 2001 opened a project on "Principles of the Law of Nonprofit Organizations," for which this author is Reporter. The American Bar Association's 1987 Revised Model Nonprofit Corporation Act (the "Model Act") has been enacted (sometimes with variation) in more than two dozen states; the ABA's prior version was adopted in thirty-nine states. The National Conference of Commissioners on Uniform State Laws (NCCUSL) in 1972 adopted the Uniform Management of Institutional Funds Act (UMIFA), enacted (sometimes with minor variation) in forty-eight jurisdictions; a major revision of UMIFA had its first of two required readings in 2003. NCCUSL also approved a uniform trust code in August 2000, and states are beginning to adopt it.[5] In discussions below, for simplicity we usually refer to the ABA's Model Act, UMIFA, the Uniform Trust Code, and the various ALI projects in lieu of specific state laws. Finally, an increasing amount of secondary legal guidance is being produced (see, for example, the very helpful ABA Section of Business Law 1993; Siegel 2006).

NONPROFIT FORMATION, OPERATION, AND DISSOLUTION

Constitutional Protections

Private philanthropy and the nonprofit sector rest on the fundamental constitutional guarantees of private property, liberty of contract, and freedom of worship and expression.[6] These rights are not absolute, however: the government retains the power to regulate the use of property short of a "taking" before having to pay just compensation under the Fifth Amendment. The government can infringe on the First Amendment right of expression if it has a compelling state interest and neutrally applies the least restrictive regulatory means. Less familiar constitutional protections include the contracts clause (*Dartmouth College v. Woodward,* 17 U.S. (4 Wheat.) 518 (1819)) and the commerce clause (*Camps Newfound/Owatonna, Inc. v. Town of Harrison,* 520 U.S. 564 (1997) (Brody 1997b). The U.S. Supreme Court rarely agrees to hear a case dealing with state law that raises no federal constitutional issue.

In *Dartmouth College,* the Supreme Court construed a New Hampshire charter granted to a private college to be a contract between the founder and the state, protected by the contracts clause from legislative interference in the appointment of the board.[7] By contrast, the Supreme Court upheld the forfeiture of the Mormon Church's charter for sanctioning polygamy, a criminal act. See *Late Corporation of the Church of Jesus Christ of the Latter-Day Saints v. United States,* 136 U.S. 1 (1890), modified, 140 U.S. 665 (1891).[8]

The establishment clause of the First Amendment prohibits the government from singling out churches for exemption from laws of general application. In 1997 the Supreme Court struck down the federal Religious Freedom Restoration Act of 1993 (as it applies to the States) (*Boerne v. Flores,* 521 U.S. 507 (1997)).[9] In the tax context, the Supreme Court voided a state sales tax exemption granted to religious publications but not to secular publications. *Texas Monthly, Inc., v. Bullock,* 489 U.S. 1 (1989) (See Simon, Dale, and Chisolm, this volume, which also covers the seminal case *Walz v. Tax Commission,* 397 U.S. 664 (1970), upholding a general nonprofit property-tax exemption scheme that included churches.) The line between the free exercise clause and the establishment clause recently shifted further in favor of churches. In *Mitchell v. Helms,* 530 U.S. 793 (2000), the Court terminated an eroding doctrine when it held that a state could provide financing directly to parochial schools to buy computer equipment. The decision was supported by six justices, although no opinion of the Court attracted more than four votes. Apparently, the government can fund a secular activity so long as churches are not singled out for the benefit, and no diversion of the public funds to a religious activity occurs (see also Wuthnow and Cadge, this volume).

Contrary to popular belief, there is no blanket constitutional "freedom of association" (Emerson 1964; Soifer 1995). Rather, the Supreme Court has recognized "a right to associate for the purpose of engaging in those activities protected by the First Amendment—speech, assembly, petition for the redress of grievances, and the exercise of religion" (*Roberts v. United States Jaycees,* 468 U.S. 609, 618 (1984)). Of course, one person's freedom of association could be another's freedom from association, and discriminatory membership practices sometimes lead to a clash between private and public interests. The Supreme Court has held that "expressive" association is protected from regulation unless the government can show "compelling state interests, unrelated to the suppression of ideas that cannot be achieved through means significantly less restrictive of associational freedoms" (*Roberts v. United States Jaycees,* 468 U.S. 609, 623 (1984)). ("Intimate" association, such as in marital choices and small private clubs, is also protected.)

Thus, as held in *Roberts,* a Minnesota antidiscrimination statute applicable to "public accommodations" could require the Jaycees to admit women as members: the state's goal of eliminating sex discrimination is a compelling state interest unrelated to the suppression of ideas, and Minnesota's law is the least restrictive means of achieving that interest. This decision was unconvincing at the time—after all, the Court also held that the state cannot compel the organization to change its purposes (in this case, advancing the interests of young men), but requiring the group to open up its membership to women would seem to change the group's message as well as its voice (see, e.g., Rosenblum 1998a, 1998b; Gutmann 1998).

The Court expanded the boundaries of expressive association in *Boy Scouts of America v. Dale,* 530 U.S. 640 (2000). The New Jersey Supreme Court had unanimously interpreted New Jersey's Law Against Discrimination to find the Boy Scouts to be a "public accommodation" because it was open to all boys; accordingly, the Boy Scouts could not dismiss a troop leader on the basis of his sexual orientation.[10] Because the Supreme Court cannot reverse a high state court's interpretation of its own state law, when the Supreme

Court agreed to hear the Boy Scout's case, it could only mean that the Court was prepared to visit the constitutional issue. Not only was this bad news for James Dale, the expelled gay troop leader, but it also put the nonprofit sector in a difficult position: strategically, charities did not want to support the type of discrimination engaged in by the Boy Scouts; tactically, however, they feared that if they did not weigh in on the Boy Scouts' side, the pluralism of the sector could be jeopardized.[11]

Holding that "an association need not associate for the purpose of disseminating a certain message in order to be protected, but must merely engage in expressive activity that could be impaired," the Court upheld the Boy Scouts' First Amendment right to assert that a gay troop leader clouds the group's message that "morally straight" and "clean" means heterosexual. The court further found simply: "The state interests embodied in New Jersey's public accommodations law do not justify such a severe intrusion on the freedom of expressive association." Unlike the unanimous decision in *Roberts,* the *Dale* Court split five to four, and coalition-building among the justices can result in odd opinions. Still, Justice Rehnquist's opinion for the Court seems both result-oriented—almost tailored to achieve victory for the Boy Scouts—and so broad that the limits of the holding are difficult to assess. *Dale* will either dramatically change the associational jurisprudence or be quickly limited to its facts (Brody 2002b).

While private parties can constitutionally engage in some forms of discrimination that are foreclosed to government, courts have worried that enforcing discriminatory terms in private agreements results in state action that violates the equal protection clauses of the Fifth and Fourteenth Amendments. In most cases, though, this is not an impediment. For example, in *In the Matter of Association for the Preservation of Freedom of Choice, Inc.,* 188 N.Y.S.2d 885 (1959), the trial judge had rejected the certificate of incorporation of a hate group, ruling: "Our system of government can only be maintained by the free and untrammeled collision of ideas, but when those ideas run counter to the mores or policies of our laws, no group should be permitted to organize in corporate form with the sanction of the State to espouse such ideas." The New York high court reversed, 174 N.E.2d 487 (N.Y. 1961),[12] declaring: "[Agitating] for the repeal or modification of any law . . . , provided such agitation is not coupled with the advocacy of force and violence[,] . . . is not against public policy whether indulged in by an individual or a membership corporation, but of course approval of a corporate charter devoted to such a purpose does not imply approval of the views of its sponsors. It simply means that their expression is lawful, and their sponsors entitled to a vehicle for such expression under a statute which cannot constitutionally be made available only to those who are in harmony with the majority viewpoint."[13]

Of final, but not least, constitutional importance, the Supreme Court repeatedly affirmed the free-speech rights of charities soliciting for contributions, by invalidating state and municipal requirements that capped payments to fundraisers and certain other measures (see the discussion of state regulation of charitable solicitations below).

Purpose

In general, state organizational law takes a laissez-faire attitude toward nonprofit purposes. Nonprofit corporation statutes generally permit "any lawful purpose," and charitable trust law can accommodate a broadly construed public purpose.[14] Both corporate and trust regimes prohibit insiders from enjoying inappropriate financial benefits—indeed, what has come to be known as the "nondistribution constraint" often operates as the sole limit of nonprofit status (Hansmann 1980). To some, the constraint against distributing profits both explains the existence of the nonprofit sector and keeps it honest, ensuring the dedication of assets and effort toward performing good deeds.[15] However, accepting nonprofit status as a signal of trustworthiness results in the law bestowing a "halo" on any nonprofit organization regardless of merit (Brody 1996a; Steinberg, this volume).

Recognizing an organization as entitled to legal status (as a charitable trust or a nonprofit corporation), however, is separate from whether the nonprofit form should enjoy state favoritism, including tax privileges. State property-tax and sales-tax exemptions are limited, in general, to the subset of nonprofits classified as charities. Similarly, the Internal Revenue Code contains about thirty different categories of income-tax exemption, but generally only the charitable category also offers deductibility for contributions. As a practical matter, tax exemption under Internal Revenue Code section 501(c)(3) is so valuable that charities will routinely adopt appropriate purpose language in their articles of incorporation or charitable trust documents. We should not overstate the distinction, however: the tax definition of charity (under which the nondistribution constraint is termed the "prohibition on private inurement") is barely tighter than the status definition (Simon, Dale, and Chisolm, this volume).

Choice of Form

Creators of a new charity can generally choose between two basic regimes: the nonprofit corporation and the charitable trust.[16] (Informal or other unincorporated voluntary associations, which traditionally function under the laws of agency and partnership, could expose the participants to personal liability.) State nonprofit corporation statutes vary. For example, New York State provides rules for four different types of "not-for-profit" corporations; states following the ABA's Model Act differentiate between "public benefit," "mutual benefit," and "religious" corporations (as does California, whose law inspired the ABA); and Delaware and Kansas have a single statute covering both business and nonprofit corporations. Additionally, some states have enacted statutes for, among others, "unincorporated associations" (granting members limited liability), homeowners associations, cooperatives, health-care corporations, and mutual-benefit insurance companies. Finally, many states, again with variation, have codified the common law of charitable trusts, and adopted such specific statutes as UMIFA (Fisch et al. 1974; Bogert and Bogert 2000; Fremont-Smith 2004a). American advisers routinely recommend the nonprofit corporate form, although the trust form might be particularly appropriate for a charity (such as a grant-making foundation) that manages a fund of money and makes distributions.

Standards of fiduciary behavior. Fiduciaries—whether trustees of a charitable trust or directors of a nonprofit corporation—owe the entity they govern the twin duties of loyalty and care.[17] Traditionally, the charitable trust standards of fiduciary law have been stricter than the nonprofit corporate standards, but recent years have brought a liberalization of the trust rules. Moreover, as described below, differences can be minimized at the creation stage. The American Law Institute's project on Principles of the Law of Nonprofit Organizations is endeavoring, to the extent possible, to express uniform duties and standards for fiduciaries regardless of the organizational form of the charity (American Law Institute 2005a and 2005b).

Duty of loyalty. Recognizing that no man can serve two masters, the duty of loyalty aspires to requiring the fiduciary to place the interests of the organization above his or her own. In practice, of course, conflicts of interest abound—indeed, a person's ability to provide certain goods or services might be the very reason that that person makes a desirable member of a charitable board. For trusts, the duty of loyalty absolutely prohibits self-dealing and other conflict-of-interest transactions, but the law permits the creator of the trust (the "settlor") to waive this limitation. In the absence of such a waiver, a trustee who breaches the duty of loyalty can be compelled to make restitution to the entity, even if the transaction was fair. For corporations, the duty of loyalty evolved past absolute bans on self-dealing. The ABA's Model Act blesses an interested transaction that either was fair when entered into or was approved in advance, after full disclosure of the material facts and of the director's interest, by disinterested members of the board acting in good faith on the reasonable belief that the transaction is fair to the charity. Alternatively, under the Model Act, the attorney general or a court may approve the transaction, either before or after it occurs. As a separate matter, additional conflict-of-interest restrictions can be imposed by the articles of incorporation, bylaws, or board resolution; employment contracts; grants or contracts; or professional association rules—with varying sanctions.

Duty of care. The duty of care adopts a "prudent person" standard: the fiduciary must exercise such attention to the affairs of the organization (what to do and how to do it) as would a prudent person in managing his or her own affairs. For trusts, an "ordinary negligence" standard traditionally has applied, requiring the trustee to exercise "reasonable" care, but the trust instrument typically relieves the trustees of legal duties to the maximum extent permitted; this generally results in a lenient standard like that imposed on corporate directors. The default rules in recent trust-law reforms are also moving in this direction. For corporations, nonprofit directors who are informed, exercise independent judgment, and act in good faith are protected under a court-created standard of review called the "business judgment rule." As a result, a director can be found liable for breaching the duty of care only by committing gross negligence (basically, acting recklessly).[18]

In practice, it is not always so easy to separate the twin obligations of loyalty and care. For example, a conflict-of-interest transaction between the organization and a director can implicate both the duty of loyalty and the duty of care: the loyalty of the conflicted director and the care exercised by the other directors in approving the transaction.[19] In general, Peter Swords and Harriet Bograd have found a consensus among the more experienced state charity officials that "inadequate board governance also creates the conditions that make embezzlement, misappropriation of funds and self-dealing possible. The case of the domineering executive director and the weak board seems to be quite typical across the country"[20] (Swords and Bograd 1996). Moreover, regulators and the courts seem more willing to listen to duty-of-care complaints if the transaction is tainted by duty-of-loyalty implications.[21]

For many years, without success, numerous commentators have urged that instead of following organizational form, the law should follow function and adopt a uniform law for charity fiduciaries, both trustees and directors (see, e.g., Karst 1960; Fremont-Smith 1965; Hansmann 1981; Fishman 1985; Fremont-Smith 2004a). Under current law, the well-advised charity founder's choice of form bestows on or denies the public particular rights of state supervision and fiduciary obligations. Many yearn for a structure of trust fiduciary duties for all charity managers, be they legally trustees or directors. Indeed, as described below, some administrators and courts fill gaps in nonprofit corporate law by invoking charitable trust principles when asserting attorney general jurisdiction or applying *cy pres* standards. However, in the area of standards of fiduciary liability, the general trend, while indeed toward conformity, is in the opposite direction: to the corporate standard. Courts prefer to defer to the business judgment of charity managers; legislatures relax the investment duties of institutional fund managers; and Congress bows to the determination of independent board members of public charities in setting compensation and other benefits.

In setting the charity-fiduciary legal standard of care, legislators, regulators, and judges find themselves trying to balance the attractiveness of service against exacting requirements. All parties implicitly recognize changes in the size and behavior of the charitable sector itself, and the need of thousands of new charities to reach beyond traditional populations to fill their boards (Hall 1992:138). Many organizations in today's nonprofit sector operate enterprises subject to the management demands of a complex business, where corporate fiduciary standards seem appropriate. At the same time, even "commercial" charities like nonprofit universities and hospitals must generally supervise endowments and restricted gifts under charitable trust standards. Current corporate standards, observed Michael Hone (the reporter of the ABA's Revised Model Act), allow volunteer directors "to almost be asleep at the gate"; but if the traditional, absolute trust standard were "adopted by the Act, very few sensible people would serve on the boards of nonprofit organizations" (Hone 1988–89:771–72).

Ironically, tightening the standards for nonprofit fiduciaries could worsen the situation. The tension between theory and practice plays out in a somewhat contradictory way. In theory, it is no defense that a director was voluntary and uncompensated. In theory, "D&O" (director and officer) insurance policies and state limits on the extent to which nonprofits can indemnify their fiduciaries remain important concerns of fiduciaries. In theory, then, the fear of potentially high monetary liability discourages good directors from serving. At the same time, in practice, the desire to save directors from financial ruin leads regulators and courts to degrade the legal standards by avoiding findings of liability.[22] In practice, moreover, even where the fiduciary violates the duty of care, lenient enforcement or light punishment nearly always follows. Accordingly, in practice, D&O policies are inexpensive (and might cover the fiduciaries' attorney's fees even in situations of bad faith).[23]

This laxity might change. The existence of a D&O policy now offers all the parties except the insurance company a tempting way to redress the financial harm to the charity. (Of course, as one editorial observed, "You cannot buy a policy that will insure against loss of public confidence" [Columbus Dispatch 2000]). Evidently, attorneys general keep an eye on policy limits in negotiating a settlement. Notably, in October 2000 the attorney general of Hawaii announced a settlement in the case against the highly compensated former trustees of the Bishop Estate for $25 million—the limit of the D&O policy. (Half of the amount went to cover attorney's fees for all parties, including the attorney general's office, with the rest going to the charity.)[24]

Most spectacularly, early 2002 brought a resolution of the civil wrongdoing claims in the largest nonprofit bankruptcy in history. The Allegheny Health, Education and Research Foundation (AHERF), which supported a Pennsylvania-wide umbrella system of health-care institutions, left $1.5 billion in unpaid bills. The state and the parties settled for an agreed total of almost $94 million, of which $24.5 million went to the charity. About $56 million of this total was paid by AHERF's D&O policy, which had already paid at least $12 million for the litigation.[25] If high-dollar investigations and settlements proliferate, D&O insurance companies could be forced to engage in underwriting, and to base lower premiums on improvements in governance practices. Such a market solution could lead to a strengthening of fiduciary standards, akin to the consequences of repealing charity immunity laws (discussed under "Torts," below).

As a policy matter, we would not want to allow caps or waivers of liability for breaches of the duty of loyalty; by contrast, specifying the worst monetary harm a fiduciary could suffer for breaches of the duty of care could be salutary. A voluntary "liability shield," if included in the articles of incorporation and approved by shareholders, is available under many business corporation laws, and the ABA's Revised Model Nonprofit Corporation Act includes it as an option for legislatures. A few state statutes (including Delaware's combined stock and nonstock statute) permit such charter amendments by their nonprofit corporations. With a cap or waiver, the financial risk would be low enough to both continue attracting directors and make attorneys general and courts more willing to find breaches, yet high enough to induce fiduciaries to take their tasks more seriously. This approach preserves the standard of care, while leaving directors at monetary risk for breaches of their duty of loyalty and for failures to exercise care in good faith. Moreover, an attorney general could always seek equitable remedies, such as injunctions and removal of directors or trustees (and other reputational sanctions).

Structural Control

Charitable trusts and nonprofit corporations appear to have radically different structures for control. Trustees of charitable trust are bound by the instructions of its creator, the settlor; any departure requires court approval. By contrast, resort to a court is not generally required for the directors of a nonprofit corporation who are replacing a director or amending the articles of incorporation.[26] However, the trust regime allows for tailoring that minimizes the differences in legal form: a charitable trust instrument would rarely be drafted today without giving broad discretionary powers to the trustees, and the trustees themselves can appoint successors if the instrument provides for self-perpetuation.

State corporate and other enabling statutes generally provide only for the barest of structures for organizational formation and operation, leaving the parties to work out and provide for any additional desired governance restrictions and protections of members, if any. Nonprofit corporations may, but are not required to, have members with rights to elect the board of directors and to exercise other extraordinary powers set forth in the statute or the articles of incorporation, such as approving the board's decision to amend the articles of incorporation or sell substantially all of its assets, merge, or dissolve. If such members do exist, they are entitled to be appropriately informed, and enjoy other procedural rights. Voting membership is more common in the mutual nonprofit: labor organizations, social clubs, and business leagues. For national charities with local affiliates, the affiliates, rather than individuals, might be the formal members. Most charities have no members, or have only ceremonial members. In the absence of "ex officio" or other directors designated in the articles, a memberless nonprofit corporation has a self-perpetuating board of directors.

Avner Ben-Ner has proposed that *all* charities be required to be run by active members, who would acquire their interests in proportion to "contributions," which he defined as monetary donations, purchases, and volunteer time. Specifically, he urged that states grant "stakeholders" the powers to elect the board, to see financial and programmatic information, and to sue the board "for making undisclosed programmatic changes"; in cases of extremely low stakeholder participation, a state agency would elect the board (Ben-Ner and Van Hoomissen 1994:408–10; Ben-Ner 1994). Some might dispute the practicality of mandating active oversight; in any case, courts will not adjudicate disputes over a group's doctrine, and will enforce only due process or property rights granted internally or by statute or public policy (e.g., in the case of expulsion from a professional society).[27] Cruel as the result can be, a member unhappy with a group's policy, and whose power of voice proves fruitless, can always exercise the power of exit and form another group; compare the power of a dissatisfied donor to withhold future contributions (Brody 2002b). As a "somewhat less severe, but still substantial, remedy" to the loss of social benefits that attend membership-structured nonprofit organizations, Dana Brakman Reiser suggests that "nonprofits with and without members could be treated differently, based on their differing contributions to civil society and to a lesser extent their differential ability to make mission-maximizing decisions and to self-monitor. . . . These differences in treatment could halt and perhaps partially reverse the trend away from members" (Brakman Reiser 2003:832, 890).

To some degree, a founding donor can more easily control a charitable trust than a nonprofit corporation. A living donor can be the sole trustee, whereas most states require a nonprofit corporation to have at least three directors. While a donor could set up the charity as a membership corporation with herself as the sole member, even directors elected by members must exercise independent judgment under their duty of care (see, e.g., *Solomon v. Hall-Brooke Foundation, Inc.,* 619 A.2d 863, 866 (Conn. App. Ct. 1993); Clark and Troost 1989:32–34). The sole-corporate-member structure became common with the restructuring of nonprofit hospital systems. Brakman Reiser (2001) discusses the fiduciary duties of a sole corporate member.

The law generally refrains from dictating how a board should carry out its duties of setting policy and engaging and supervising officers. However, reformers usually recommend separating the identity of those who provide governance and those who provide management. For example, California limits charity managers to 49 percent of the board positions.[28] The new standards used by the Better Business Bureau (BBB) Wise Giving Alliance to rate charities recommend that no more than one person who directly or indirectly receives compensation from the charity should serve as a voting member of the board—and should not serve as chairman or treasurer.[29] In 2002, responding to the corporate governance scandals, Congress enacted Sarbanes-Oxley legislation applicable to publicly traded companies. Notable provisions relate to executive certification of financial results, independent audit committees, and whistle-blower protections. The desirability of extending some of these reforms to the nonprofit sector is a subject of much debate, and could influence the choice of form (as trust or corporation), as well as the choice of state of organization.[30]

REGULATION AND ENFORCEMENT

Nonprofit organizations and their fiduciaries are subject to multiple levels of governmental supervision and scrutiny. State attorneys general have achieved important successes in educating the public about fraudulent fundraising and challenging wrongdoing; educating fiduciaries and staffs in meeting their legal obligations and improving charity governance; rectifying self-dealing and other breaches of fiduciary duty by charity insiders; and assisting charities that have lost their way to restructure or dissolve. The "biggest problem" of top state charity officials (according to a survey in which thirty-eight states responded) relates to charitable solicitations, and whether charities spend their money as represented to donors (Mehegan et al. 1994). The Internal Revenue Service also functions as a regulator—often the only effective regulator.

Just a few states fund and actively engage in charity enforcement (Fremont-Smith 2004a). However, the effective coverage is greater than it sounds: a disproportionate percentage of charitable assets is concentrated in a few states with active charity regulation, and, for the many charities operating across state borders, the inactive states can free-ride on the enforcement efforts of the few. To a large degree, legislatures are coming to view sunshine as the best disinfectant, and Congress and the states are increasing nonprofit or tax-exempt disclosure requirements to allow a better-informed public to provide oversight—although private parties cannot generally enforce nonprofit laws in court.

Depending on regulators to enforce charitable duties brings challenges of its own. While attorneys general have long complained about their lack of resources for this function, at some point we must concede that the public might not want to pay for more (or different) oversight than is occurring.[31] Moreover, even with regard to nonprofit organizations, the attorney general remains an inherently political creature. The incentives of this nearly universally elective office impel the incumbent to ignore cases that are politically dangerous and to jump into matters that are politically irresistible but implicate only "business" decisions of charity managers.[32] Ironically, though, the very lack of state involvement with the organization and operation of nonprofit entities might explain how legislatures, attorneys general, and even courts can sometimes misconstrue their proper roles in the regulation of charities and other nonprofits.[33]

Parochialism is a particular concern in charity law enforcement (Brody 2004).[34] Consider two examples, one involving investment assets and the other operating assets. The 2002 Hershey Trust case amounts to a trifecta—eventually all three branches of Pennsylvania government combined to pressure the Milton Hershey School Trust to abandon plans for selling its controlling interest in Hershey Foods (in order to diversify an investment worth more than $5 billion), thereby preserving the local operations of the publicly traded company. The attorney general, who was running for governor, had won a preliminary injunction against the sale. Shortly after losing the gubernatorial election, the attorney general participated in a shakeup of the board that restored local control. The outgoing governor signed a bill that would require the trust to obtain court approval, with attorney general and community input, before any sale.

In the case of the Illinois-based Terra Foundation for the Arts,[35] the board of the financially troubled museum, under pressure from the attorney general, abandoned an exploration of moving to Washington, D.C. The attorney general had sought to read into the purposes of the corporation the desire to benefit primarily "the people of Illinois." A settlement followed when a majority of directors voted to obligate all current board members to step down; to require, for at least twenty-five years, a majority of the board to be residents of Illinois; and to prohibit the assets from leaving the state for fifty years.[36] Terra closed its museum and placed its major pieces on long-term loan to the Art Institute of Chicago.

In some cases when a court is asked to approve the outcome, availability of court review can curb inappropriate regulator zeal[37]—or willingness to compromise.[38] But again, restrictions against private standing might mean no one can challenge attorney general decisions (discussed further below). Moreover, many open questions remain regarding an attorney general's authority over the activities of a charity doing business in-state but incorporated elsewhere.

State-Level Enforcement

Nonprofit corporations obtain their certificate of incorporation from, generally, the state secretary of state's office, and, like other corporations, must file an annual report that is usually quite perfunctory. Charitable trusts and unincorporated associations do not generally file their organizational documents with the state, although wills get filed with a probate or similar court. However, a charity, regardless of organizational form, that applies for recognition of federal tax exemption must provide the Internal Revenue Service with its organizing documents. As mentioned below, an exempt organization must make its application, including these organizing documents, available to the public on request.

A state official, usually the attorney general, can investigate charges of improper charitable activities, view books and records, and subpoena witnesses. The courts, on motion of the attorney general or on their own, can "enjoin[] wrongful conduct, rescind[] or cancel[] a transfer of property, appointment of a receiver, replacement of a fiduciary, compel[] an accounting, redress of a breach or performance of fiduciary duties" (Fisch et al. 1974, §712:549–50), dissolve a corporation, enforce restrictions in gifts, supervise indemnification awards, and surcharge fiduciaries for improperly received benefits (Fishman and Schwarz 2000:255–56).

The other primary focus of state interest relates to statutes governing charitable solicitations, to prevent fraud on donors and the diversion or waste of donated funds.[39] The flood of charitable giving after the September 11, 2001, terrorist attacks on the United States led to a spectacular demonstration of both the legal and political pressures to enforce asserted donor expectations over the use of contributed funds. More than 250 new nonprofit organizations were formed to handle the outpouring of contributions, and obtained expedited federal tax exemption. Yet these new organizations—along with existing major charities like the Red Cross and the Salvation Army—found themselves tripping over each other, unable to ensure that the more than $1.5 billion in contributions was being distributed responsibly.

Most visibly, the American Red Cross chief succeeded in attracting most of the dollars—almost a billion dollars—into a separate "Liberty Fund," a large portion of which, it later transpired, the Red Cross wished to devote to improving its infrastructure, for overhead, and to address the needs of future terrorist events. The adverse public reaction led to charges that the charity was misleading donors, and forced the board of the Red Cross to demand its chief executive's resignation. A congressional body held hearings into the performance of September 11 philanthropy. The Red Cross then promised to spend the balance of the principal of the Liberty Fund on the victims and their families. This position led to reports, however, that the Red Cross to some degree was throwing its money at those who might not need charitable assistance, raising the question of whether the attorney general focused more on his role of protecting donors' expectations and less on his role of ensuring the wise use of charitable resources (see Katz 2003).[40]

In the 1960s and 1970s, the desire to protect charities from "wasting" resources on fundraising led a total of twenty-eight states and countless municipalities to impose ceilings on the percentage of annual revenues that could be spent on fundraising expenses (Hopkins 1996). In the 1980s, however, a trio of Supreme Court decisions blocked these restrictions, on First Amendment free-speech grounds. (*Riley v. National Federation of the Blind of North Carolina, Inc.,* 487 U.S. 781 (1988); *Maryland v. Joseph H. Munson Co.,* 467 U.S. 947 (1984); *Village of Schaumburg v. Citizens for a Better Environment,* 444 U.S. 620 (1980)). To the Court, procrustean percentage limits on fundraising disproportionately impact new charities (with low name recognition and no established donor base) and unpopular causes (which require a greater expenditure to raise a dollar). States may punish fraudulent fundraising speech after the fact, but, as the Court recently confirmed, regulatory approaches seeking to equate fraud with efficiency are invalid (*Madigan v. Telemarketing Associates, Inc.,* 538 U.S. 600 (2003)).[41]

Can nothing be done to address state (and IRS) concerns over excessive fundraising costs? It can be in any given charity's interest to raise another dollar for every $99 pocketed by the fundraiser—not only for a startup charity (whose expenses might even exceed revenues) but also for the desperate charity that perhaps should expire.[42] If the pool of donative dollars is finite, how can the state prevent a tragedy of the commons in promoting the efficient allocation of donative dollars? As a separate question, publicized fundraising excesses by one charity can cause a general decline in confidence in all charities.

The state's desire to eliminate "harmful" competition between charities might evoke sympathy but, in the end, proves futile and misguided. Superficially, one can appreciate the sentiment once expressed by a New York judge: "I do not believe the public should have numerous groups soliciting funds when one well-recognized and well-operated organization is [already] seeking their contributions."[43] However, a solution to these problems that is both efficient and constitutional is not obvious (Steinberg 1997). The marketplace for contributions remains an important check on existing institutions. The regulator still can play an important role in seeking to ensure the efficient use of charitable resources: the New York attorney general prodded the September 11 charities into coordinating their relief efforts by creating a combined database of resources and needs.

While conceding fundraising limits, the states have further concentrated their efforts on requiring charities to increase public disclosure using standardized forms. The majority of states require registration and sometimes annual filings, usually with the attorney general, for charitable trusts and nonprofit corporations that solicit charitable contributions. Most laws also cover professional fundraisers, advisors, and co-venturers. (Thirteen states, though, require no charitable filings.) Statutes commonly exempt small entities, educational institutions, hospitals, and churches—and membership organizations—but variations abound. A charity soliciting in many states will welcome the Uniform Registration Statement accepted in most states requiring registration.[44] However, a number of *localities* also regulate solicitations, sometimes prompting court challenges from overburdened charities and their advisers. (Fishman and Schwarz [2000:304] characterize the multitude of charitable filing requirements as "horrifyingly elaborate"; see generally Fremont-Smith 2004a.)

When the law cannot impose restrictions, voluntary certification can be the solution, as discussed below. However, to some extent nonprofit rating bodies encourage the public to focus overly much on fundraising and overhead percentages.

Federal-Level Enforcement

Federal enforcement over nonprofit activity is primarily confined to the Internal Revenue Service. In general, the Federal Trade Commission has jurisdiction over interstate charitable solicitations only if engaged in by for-profit solicitors, although the FTC does have jurisdiction over a nonprofit used as a shell for the direct private gain of its members.[45] A proposal was introduced in 1990 to bring nonprofit organizations (other than political parties) within the FTC's reach and to define deceptive charitable fundraising as a deceptive trade practice (and preempt state law) (for an earlier proposal, see Yarmolinsky and Fremont-Smith 1977). Some federal enforcement activity against fraud can be credited to the U.S. Postal Service. The Treasury Department has begun to focus on the use of charities to further international terrorist activities (U.S. Treasury Department 2005). Of course, federal regulation, like state regulation, of charitable solicitation is bound by charities' constitutional rights, as described above.

Disclosures. Federal tax law obligates a charity to furnish its exemption application and last three tax returns (Form 990) to any person, no questions asked, upon request. Education and tightened penalties have brought increased compliance by charities, which are often reluctant to disclose the salaries and other compensation paid to their top executives and independent contractors. Moreover, third parties have begun to post information on the Internet that will enable donors and other interested parties to compare charities online (see the path-breaking database at www.guidestar.org).

The staff of the Joint Committee on Taxation issued a congressionally mandated study of the disclosure rules that apply to exempt organizations under the Internal Revenue Code (Joint Committee on Taxation 2000). The staff recommended expanding disclosure to: private letter rulings and audit memoranda without "redaction" of identifying information; business tax returns of exempt organizations and their taxable affiliates; and a description of lobbying activities, including amounts spent on self-defense lobbying and on nonpartisan research and analysis that include a limited "call to action." The staff asserted that such disclosure not only allows increased public oversight but "also allows the public to determine whether the organizations should be supported—either through continued tax benefits or contributions of donors—and whether changes in the laws regarding such organizations are needed" (5). Many of these recommendations have attracted strong criticism by nonprofits asserting privacy rights in information that they are willing to file with the tax collector, but not disclose to the public (Williams 2000). It should be appreciated, though, that the charity itself can always release identifying information, and so prospective donors remain free to withhold contributions until satisfied with information obtained from the charity.[46]

Charities that resist increased standardized disclosure worry about releasing a tax form that the public will misunderstand or misinterpret. Today's charity faces competition from a myriad of other charities, as well as high fundraising and administrative costs. The public fails to appreciate the productive demands and fiscal needs of charities, and often expresses surprise that nonprofit managers are paid at all (Brody 1996b). The solution to this problem, though, is more disclosure—nothing prevents an organization from providing a more positive narrative of its goals and accomplishments. Importantly, the voluntary disclosure of information also serves charities that do not solicit donations. The Joint Committee staff's rationale suggests that even a charity totally funded with income from investments and the performance of services cannot necessarily keep its activities to itself.

The IRS as enforcement agency, and federal-state coordination. Like substantive nonprofit law, the tax rules generally address problems of self-dealing (termed *private inurement* by the Internal Revenue Code) rather than weak management. Moreover, until "intermediate sanctions" legislation in 1996, the only sanction for private inurement was loss of the charity's tax exemption, and the wrongdoer went unpunished. Now the IRS can instead impose a penalty tax of 25 percent on the "excess benefits" portion of a transaction between an insider and the charity (a smaller penalty applies to fiduciaries who knowingly approved), and require restitution to the charity (Simon, Dale, and Chisolm, this volume). The intermediate-sanctions regime, however, does not reach other breaches of fiduciary duty. Thus, short of revoking exemption under the poorly understood prohibition against "private benefit," the IRS cannot statutorily address such inadequacies of governance as running an indifferent charitable program, accumulating excess income, or paying insufficient attention to investment returns.[47]

As a practical matter, though, the Service has been able to achieve sometimes fundamental management reforms through negotiation. For example, the IRS can threaten revocation of recognition of exemption in order to bring the charity to the bargaining table, and then settle for a "closing agreement" that spells out detailed governance changes.[48] Such a power is not statutory, however, and I have argued that the new intermediate sanctions legislation undercuts the IRS's ability to claim de facto full equity powers by demanding broad management changes via closing agreements (Brody 1999).

A charity that violates the private inurement proscription also violates state nonprofit law. Depending on the resources and inclinations of the state attorney general's office, the charity might be facing investigations on two fronts. Under current privacy law applying to exempt organizations, the state can share information with the IRS, but the IRS cannot share information about its investigation short of notifying the state of revocation of exemption. However, because this final determination might "not be made for a number of years, a tax-exempt organization may have exhausted its assets through illicit transactions or disposed of its assets or changed its operations in a way which can no longer be corrected by the time the IRS is permitted" to inform the state (Joint Committee on Taxation 2000:103, citing Lyon 1996, at §5.04).

To address these concerns, the Joint Committee staff's disclosure study contained one well-received suggestion: that Congress would require the IRS to inform the appropriate state of the progress of an exempt-organization investigation. To prevent overreliance by states on the IRS, the recommendation would allow such disclosure in only two situations: (1) when the state has made a specific referral of an organization to the IRS before a denial or revocation of tax exemption; or (2) with state officials who regularly share information with the IRS, when the IRS determines that such disclosure may facilitate the resolution of cases. The Tax Relief Act of 2005, passed by the Senate as S. 2020, contains a provision that, in general, would permit the IRS to inform the appropriate state official of a proposed denial of exemption or a proposed revocation of exemption (151 Congressional Record S13137 (amendment 2670), Nov. 17, 2005). In any case when both federal and state investigations are proceeding, principles of federalism suggest that the IRS should have to defer to the state, or at least stay its hand until the proceedings conclude, to protect the charity from inconsistent mandated governance changes.

Senate Finance Committee staff proposals. In June 2004, the staff of the Senate Finance Committee issued a "discussion draft" containing numerous proposals relating to nonprofit governance (Senate Finance Committee 2004). Some of the proposals have a clear tax focus (e.g., extending the private foundation self-dealing prohibitions to insiders of public charities). Other proposals have less of a traditional federal tax focus (e.g., giving the Tax Court the authority to impose equitable remedies for breach of fiduciary duty). Time will tell whether these and the other proposals will lead to legislation, but they signal growing national frustration with perceived abuses by those entrusted with governing charities, and the nonprofit sector is taking the discussion draft very seriously. Notably, at the Committee's request, the Independent Sector organized a Panel on the Nonprofit Sector, which issued a report addressing those reforms appropriate for legislative change, IRS adoption, and consideration as voluntary best practice by the sector itself (Independent Sector Panel 2005).[49]

Nonprofit Derivative Suits and the Issue of Private "Standing"

Traditionally, private parties—including donors—have no legal authority to sue to enforce charitable duties. "Despite the fact that the organization is legally bound by specific terms of the gift; *legally* it is not the donor's concern. It is *society's* concern, to be pursued (or not) by society's representative, the attorney general" (Chisolm 1995:147, emphasis in original). The reason for disabling the donor might be to recognize the completeness of the gift for public purposes, but the rule applies even when the donor is not seeking a return of the gift—indeed, a donor who retains a "right of reverter" in the case of failure of the gift does have standing to sue for its return. In practice, where, as is most likely, the donor wants to make an irrevocable gift to charity, a "gift over" provision can be useful. Thus, when a gift is made "to charity *X*, but if the terms of the gift are not carried out, then to Charity *Y*," the alternate charity can sue to claim the gift. This direct oversight and prospect of loss would concentrate the mind of the initial donee—but so would granting standing to the donor, a mechanism that might better carry out the donor's original charitable intent.

Nor, except in rare cases, do individual beneficiaries have standing to sue charity trustees or directors, either directly or derivatively on behalf of the charity, because "the human beings who are favorably affected by the execution of the trust are merely the media through whom the social advantages flow to the public" (Bogert 1954:663; see generally Blasko et al. 1993). Courts will grant standing to a director or trustee who is charging the others with breach of fiduciary duty, although this practice is more appropriately limited to breaches of the duty of loyalty; in an ordinary suit for breach of the duty of care, outvoted fiduciaries cannot reargue the board's business decision in court.

To minimize the risk of vexatious and multiple lawsuits but to take advantage of the oversight provided by appropriate private parties, a few modern statutes grant standing to an expanded class of private persons to sue fiduciaries, with any monetary recovery going to the nonprofit.[50] Even without statutory authorization, courts will, on rare occasion, grant standing to those with a "special interest" (Fremont-Smith 1997). One commentary also found: "If a court determines that the attorney general is substantially ineffective, the probability increases that a private party will be allowed to represent, in litigation, the public's beneficial interest in a charity" (Blasko 1993:69). In the case of trusts, section 405(c) of the new Uniform Trust Code allows the settlor "of a charitable trust . . . [to] maintain a proceeding to enforce the trust" (Chester 2003). My draft for the American Law Institute's *Principles of the Law of Nonprofit Organizations,* however, generally denies donor standing to enforce a gift restriction in the absence of a provision to the contrary in the gift instrument (American Law Institute 2005a; see also Brody 2005b).[51]

LEGAL ISSUES AFFECTING INVESTMENTS, OPERATIONS, AND CHANGE OF PURPOSE

Enduring Donor Control

The absolute discretion of a donor to give or withhold making a charitable gift—with whatever conditions the donor imposes—is, to some, the essence of private philanthropy. (The charity also has the right not to accept the gift as restricted, but we will assume that the charity desires the gift.)[52] Once a gift has been made or pledged, however, the arrangements could veer from plan. A charity might not use a contribution as the donor directed (or as the charity promised in soliciting the gift). A donor might not fulfill a pledge. Less simply, a charity might shift its initial mission. Or the charity might maintain its mission, but shift its methods of implementation, to the detriment of current beneficiaries.

Traditionally, the law did not accommodate a donor who later regretted or was willing to alter gift restrictions. For the past thirty years, the Uniform Management of Institutional Funds Act has provided a mechanism for releasing donor restrictions: if written consent cannot be obtained because of the donor's death, disability, unavailability, or impossibility of identification, then the charity may apply to court for release of the restriction. Moreover, the draft 2005 revision of UMIFA would liberalize this regime, and confirm that the charity can always petition the court for relief (even without consulting with the donor, or if the donor objects).

The cy pres *doctrine.* Despite the donor's lack of standing, a charity is legally bound to honor donor restrictions (Peregrine and Schwartz 2000a), no matter how confident are the parties that a better use could be made of the funds. No mortal, however, has perfect foresight, so if the donor's dictates cannot be carried out, a court will consider a *cy pres* petition to modify the restriction.[53] Both the 2003 *Restatement (Third) of Trusts* and the 2000 Uniform Trust Code enlarge the *cy pres* threshold test to embrace charitable purposes that have become not only impossible, impracticable, or unlawful but also "wasteful"—an as-yet-undefined term.[54] Once the threshold is met, the court, purporting to determine what the donor would have wanted had he or she known of the unanticipated circumstance, traditionally applied the doctrine by departing as minimally as possible from the original purpose; as the doctrine has been liberalized by Section 67 of the *Third Restatement,* "the court will direct application of the property or appropriate portion thereof to a charitable purpose that reasonably approximates the designated purpose."

States vary in the degree to which they are willing to grant *cy pres* relief. The Buck Trust is the most notorious American *cy pres* case. To simplify, in 1975 Beryl Buck bequeathed $10 million worth of oil company stock to a trust for the benefit of Marin County, California, one of the richest areas in the country. Ten years later, when the stock had ballooned in value to $400 million, the trustee possessing distribution powers sought court approval to spend some of the income to benefit the greater San Francisco Bay area. The attorney general opposed on the ground that the original restriction was not impossible to carry out. The court agreed, and denied *cy pres* relief; the trustee resigned and was replaced (Simon 1987).

Some reformers believe that in a *cy pres* situation, the charity should have absolute discretion to choose a new charitable use for the funds (Atkinson 1993, 1998), but the prospect of unfettered discretion by "philanthropoids" alarms conservative scholars and advisors. Less radically, the draft *Principles on the Law of Nonprofit Organizations* endorses, "without departing from donor intent as a guide . . . a legal framework in which charities bring suit to modify outmoded restrictions; attorneys general support an increased desire by fiduciaries to respond to current needs; and courts grant reasonable relief sought in good faith" (American Law Institute 2005a, §440, General Comments).

Sometimes charity trustees fail to go to court first, but rather act on their own in applying trust assets to purposes different from those specified by the donor, or in deviating from other restrictions (such as investment restrictions). If the trustee is called to account, and the court agrees that the original purpose has failed, no liability will result, but one wonders if a lesser standard is applied in these cases to avoid surcharging the trustees.[55] Worse, trustees might simply let trust funds languish, accumulating income (perhaps enough to cover fees) rather than seeking relief. Section 66 of the *Restatement (Third) of Trusts* imposes an affirmative duty on a trustee "to petition the court for appropriate modification of or deviation from the terms of the trust," in order to keep the trust productive (see also Fremont-Smith 1966:1058).

Technically, a nonprofit corporation does not hold its assets subject to the trust rules; a corporation owns its assets outright, and the same person cannot be both trustee and beneficiary. Moreover, only a small percentage by value of the typical charity can be traced to donations. We should take care, though, to distinguish between terminology and effect. Corporate donees must still obey any restrictions in a gift, and the modification rules in the draft *Principles on the Law of Nonprofit Organizations* "generally appl[y] in any case where it is appropriate to modify (or release) a restriction on a charitable gift, regardless of whether the property is held in trust or by a corporate charity" (American Law Institute 2005a, §440, General Comments). More broadly, the *cy pres* doctrine exerts its pull on regulators and courts throughout the life of all charities, trust and corporate.

Perpetuities and endowments. Many, if not most, major (and not so major) donors expect immortality of their gift. A donor-imposed prohibition on spending the gift currently is termed an endowment by the common law and by UMIFA. Donors use various expressions to convey perpetuity, such as "to endowment" or "to spend income only" or "to preserve principal intact." The charity enjoys a degree of investment and spending flexibility within such a restriction.

As a separate matter, the attraction of perpetual life induces some donors to start a charity with a small fund whose income, its founder intends, is to accumulate until the principal grows to a certain amount. The law cooperates with such a plan by permitting the accumulation of income for long periods of dormancy if for an eventual charitable purpose.[56] For example, courts upheld the accumulation provisions in Benjamin Franklin's bequest to trusts for the benefit of Boston and Philadelphia, although the diligent trustees resorted time and again to the courts to alter outmoded restrictions (see Simes 1955:129–31, 173 [Appendix]). Today, funds classified as private foundations under federal tax law are subject to an annual 5 percent minimum payout rule.

Importantly, only a donor can impose a legally binding income-only restriction. A charity's self-imposed restriction to maintain principal cannot be enforced. Sometimes charities classify free assets as endowment in order to look more needy to potential donors. In 1993, the Financial Accounting Standards Board adopted the controversial Statement No. 117, requiring charities to categorize their assets as "endowment," "quasi-endowment" (self-imposed), or "current fund" (freely spendable or restricted) (see generally Brody 1997a).

The breaching donor. From the other side, what happens when donors fail to perform as promised? States will typically enforce a charitable pledge, even though the charity provides no "consideration" in the traditional contract sense, if the charity has relied on the promise to its detriment or if the pledge induced others to give (Butig et al. 1992). We are starting to see lawsuits by charities against donors who default on their (major) pledges—often when the donor dies, and the will makes no mention of the promise. Charities seem uneasy about their rights and obligations in such a case, worried about the bad publicity and its effects on prospective donors. Some charities have been told they *must* sue, because of the accounting rules that required them to book the pledge up front (Strosnider 1998). While the law does not impose such an obligation, a board that fails to consider the benefits as well as the costs of suing has not exercised its duty of care (American Law Institute 2005a, §470).

As a separate matter, in light of the recent corporate governance scandals that have snared well-known philanthropists, if a major donor is later charged with a crime, can the charity keep the money but remove the donor's name from a building he or she has funded?[57] Charities hesitate to make gifts look too contractual, but specification in the gift documents could forestall trips to court for application of the doctrine of equitable deviation.

Prudent investment. To counter the perceived conservatism of charity fiduciaries who focused on "income"-paying investments, UMIFA (National Conference of Commissioners 1972) permits charity fiduciaries to make such an investment as "deemed advisable by the governing board, whether or not it produces a current return." About the same time, the U.S. Treasury Department's regulations on "jeopardy investments" by private foundations also blessed such a "total-return" approach, as well as a policy of examining investment decisions in the context of the entire portfolio. Congress adopted this flexible approach in the 1974 federal legislation governing pension trustees.[58] Similar reforms later appeared in the American Law Institute's 1992 *Restatement (Third) of Trusts: The Prudent Investor,* devoted exclusively to this topic.

Charities sometimes face program conflicts when managing their endowments. The *Third Restatement* permits a charity to take "social considerations" into account only if consistent with its charitable mission, "financially or operationally." "Program-related investments" are made to advance a charitable purpose rather than to earn a financial return. At the other extreme, a charity might wish to divest or shun holdings in corporations whose activities clash with its charitable purpose—recall the 1980s divestment in companies doing business in South Africa, echoed today for tobacco stocks. George Bernard Shaw embodied this attitude in Salvation Army Major Barbara, who cringed at accepting "tainted money" from a wealthy distiller and arms merchant.[59]

A donor may direct a charity to retain an investment for personal reasons, such as stock in the donor's business (see, e.g., *In re McCune,* 705 A.2d 861 (Pa. Super. 1997)). As described in Simon, Dale, and Chisolm (this volume), federal tax laws prohibit a "private foundation"—but not other charities, including "supporting organizations"—from owning, generally, more than 20 percent of a business. Moreover, this rule ignores any ownership interest not exceeding 2 percent of the company. Thus, a foundation can be 100 percent invested in a very large company without running afoul of the "excess business holdings" rule. An undiversified portfolio might constitute a "jeopardy investment" subject to another private foundation tax, but the regulations ignore investments gratuitously received. Many of the top foundations hold exclusively a single stock, some with disastrous results (Brody 1998; Dundjerski 2000; Bank 2001).

Importantly, not all foundations with concentrated holdings are limited by their organizing documents to invest in the founder's company. Perhaps diversification would be an unthinkable sign of disloyalty by the trustees, who—if not themselves family members—are probably close advisers to the donor's family or executives in the family business. Generally, state nonprofit law should affirmatively require diversification for all charities, regardless of organizational form, within a reasonable period of time following acquisition. An unusual case in which the regulator obtained the right result through negotiation involved seven "supporting organizations" established by *Reader's Digest* founders DeWitt and Lila Wallace and funded with nonvoting stock of the company for the benefit of the Metropolitan Museum of Art, Lincoln Center, and eleven other charities. Because of their designated public-charity beneficiaries, these supporting organizations were not classified as private foundations under the tax rules. In the 1990s, *Reader's Digest* stock plummeted and slashed its dividends; meanwhile, company executives dominated the supporting organizations' boards. The New York attorney general succeeded in obtaining the dissolution of the organizations; the beneficiary charities are now free to reinvest these holdings (Blumenthal 2001).

In recent years, all investors, including nonprofits, became more conscious of asset allocation. In the mid-1990s, the bull market drew in the smallest charity; foundations, due to their payout requirement, were particularly sensitive to their net worth. Subsequently, posting their first losses after years of positive investment returns, charities seemed to be struggling to maintain their endowments—perhaps overly struggling. As of June 30, 2001, the Art Institute of Chicago had invested nearly $400 million of its $650 million endowment in lightly regulated "hedge funds," only to discover in the fall of that year that a $23 million investment had nearly vanished, and another $20 million was at similar risk. In a lawsuit, the museum complained that the fund in which the loss occurred had promised that the museum "could not lose any of [its] investment, even in a declining market, unless the particular stocks in which the fund assets were invested fell in value by more than 30 percent," but that the fund could not divulge details of its "highly proprietary trading strategy" (Rose 2001). The museum's finance committee included, among others, department-store heir Marshall Field, the chief executive of the Chicago Board of Trade, and a former chairman of Sears, Roebuck; a former chairman of Sara Lee Corporation and the current chairman of Hyatt Hotels Corporation also sat on the board. Commented trustee Field: "This is the risk of the game. And we lost. So what?" (Dugan et al. 2002:A8).

Change of purpose, sale, merger, liquidation, and bankruptcy. Where business corporation statutes require shareholder approval of such extraordinary events as merger or dissolution, nonprofit statutes often require the approval of members. What check, then, applies to fundamental decisions by the fiduciaries of a charity lacking members? Attorneys general can become involved in such extraordinary events as merger, sale of substantially all of the assets, or dissolutions, or application to court to alter the restricted use of assets under the *cy pres* doctrine. A charity cannot, of course, distribute its assets to private individuals. (By contrast, mutual nonprofits, such as social clubs, may, depending on state law, make liquidating distributions to members.) Importantly, charity assets are not inalienable—that is, they can be sold—but then the cash realized on sale is permanently dedicated to charitable use.

Drafters of the ABA's revised Model Act worried about whether a corporate charity (unlike a trust) can alter its purposes without applying to court for *cy pres* relief, quoting *Attorney General v. Hahnemann Hospital,* 494 N.E.2d 1011, 1021 n.18 (Mass. 1986): "Those who give to a home for abandoned animals do not anticipate a future board amending the charity's purpose to become research vivisectionists." Some states apply "quasi–*cy pres* principles" to a charitable corporation's amendment of its purposes; such a court proceeding accords deference to the board's determination instead of permitting the judge to substitute his or her judgment (see, e.g., dictum in *Alco Gravure, Inc. v. Knapp Foundation,* 479 N.E.2d 752, 753 (N.Y. 1985)). The new-purposes problem is often avoided by adopting in the initial articles of incorporation a statement that the charity is formed "for any charitable purpose" or similar broad expression.

Daniel Kurtz (1988) finds a third duty of nonprofit fiduciaries: the "duty of obedience" to the organization's original mission.[60] At some point, though, obedience to mission can cloud the rational use of nonprofit corporate assets. Consider the case of a college suffering declining applications, but whose alumni and students do not want it to close (King 1981; Beh 1998). Henry Hansmann describes how regulatory structures—and the combination of history and culture that he calls "institutional inertia"—already lock assets into the nonprofit sector (Hansmann 1996:295–96). Mandating the application of the *cy pres* doctrine to a reevaluation of corporate mission furthers the expectation that charity managers must honor the original purposes of the charity through thick and thin.

The better principle would be that rather than having a duty of obedience to a particular mission, the members of the governing board have a duty to keep the purpose of the charity current and useful. Some commentators would, moreover, differentiate between shifting purposes within the same field or expanding the charitable class, on the one hand, and substantial changes of purpose (as in the anti-vivisectionist example), on the other hand. Changes of purpose in the latter category might be made subject to greater public oversight or an elevated standard of review (Goldschmid 1998; Fishman 1998). Thus, a college—whether financially healthy or struggling—might be permitted to close a department without resort to the attorney general and courts, but liquidation or merger might require notice and approval.

Following a change of purpose, gifts made with explicit restrictions must continue to be used for the designated purpose, but courts are split on whether the charity may use operating income and general gifts for the post-amendment purpose. The standard for reforming a charitable purpose relates to the question of the uses to which the pre-amendment assets may be put. After all, the more liberally a corporate charity may alter its purposes, the more it might be appropriate to impose restrictions on the post-amendment use of previously acquired assets. By contrast, if the standard for amending purpose is the *cy pres* standard then almost by definition the old assets will have to be redirected somewhere—either to the new purpose of the original charity, or transferred to another charity with the same purpose as the old one (American Law Institute 2005a, draft §§240 and 245).

For the nonprofit industry with the most assets, the rules on change of purpose have largely been superseded by the recent wave of "nonprofit hospital conversion statutes." These statutes, though, can make it even harder for a struggling nonprofit hospital to liquidate its assets and redeploy the proceeds to a more socially useful purpose. A few early, poorly supervised conversions led to the sale of nonprofit assets to hospital insiders at favorable prices. The conversion statutes typically require, among other things, public notice and the right of the attorney general to intervene in a proposed sale of assets by a nonprofit hospital corporation to a for-profit (but usually not nonprofit) buyer. Nevertheless, these statutes seem designed less to ensure the highest price for the assets—and thus the largest fund for the resulting "conversion foundation"—and more to provide an opportunity for "the community" to participate in the decision to sell (Hyman 1998). Once the deal is allowed to proceed, the *cy pres* constraint continues: the resulting funds must be used for "health-care purposes" in the community that the hospital served (Fremont-Smith and Lever 2000). In the absence of such a statute, not all trustees have hewn to the original charity's path. One conversion foundation determined that federal and state programs adequately meet the needs of most uninsured patients, and so shifted its focus to education.

Occasionally, a charity "borrows" from the principal of an endowment in order to cover operations.[61] Legally, such a transaction is analyzed as an investment of endowment assets: if such a loan is not prohibited by the gift document, would it be prudent for the charity to invest these funds this way, taking into account the security of the investment and the expected financial return? (Putting the question this way suggests that the answer would often be no.) One might expect, moreover, that these situations arise where the transaction is motivated by financial distress, and so if donor-designated purposes could be jeopardized, court permission might be required.[62]

An extreme version of this issue arose in the tangled proceedings of the AHERF bankruptcy, described above. The attorney general of Pennsylvania obtained an unprecedented *criminal* indictment against the former chief executive officer, chief financial officer, and general counsel. The indictment charged that the officers invaded the endowments and restricted charitable gifts in order to maintain general charitable operations, and by so doing they committed "Theft by Failure to Make Required Disposition of Funds Received" (a felony); "Misapplication of Entrusted Funds" (a misdemeanor); and conspiracy among them. After a preliminary hearing that lasted for months, the judge narrowed the charges to several hundred allegedly misapplied restricted gifts (apparently some $50 million), and dismissed all charges against the former chief financial officer and the former general counsel (Becker 2002). The former chief executive officer pleaded no contest to a single misdemeanor of misapplication of entrusted funds,[63] and served three months of his sentence of eleven-and-a-half to twenty-three months (Becker 2003).

Can general creditors reach donor-restricted funds? Technically, the creditors of a nonprofit organization cannot force the entity into involuntary bankruptcy, but as a practical matter, a troubled charity would have difficulty obtaining goods and services and so might voluntarily file for bankruptcy. Bankruptcy protection extends to the principal of income-only endowment funds of nonprofit organizations. Evidently, though, creditors can reach donations given outright for a charitable purpose of the organization, and not restricted to a specific purpose (see Brody 2005a).

Legal Issues Raised by Commercial Activities

This section provides a few brief comments about how commercial activities ("related" or "unrelated" to the nonprofit purpose) might implicate legal regimes in addition to the fiduciary and tax laws described above and in the Simon, Dale, and Chisolm chapter of this volume.

Antitrust. Antitrust laws, which bar restraints on trade and attempts to monopolize a product in a market, apply not only to such mutual-benefit nonprofits as labor unions, trade associations, amateur athletic associations, and professional regulatory associations, but also to commercial charities (notably nonprofit hospitals) and universities (e.g., *California Dental Association v. Federal Trade Commission,* 526 U.S. 756 (1999)). The NCAA can impose its eligibility requirements on student athletes, but was held to have improperly restricted the salaries of coaches (who accepted a $54.5 million settlement) (Fishman and Schwarz 2000:1026–27). The American Bar Association—whose law-school accreditations are usually required for applicants to state bars—signed a consent decree with the Justice Department; as one result, the ABA dropped its ban on proprietary law schools. Eckel and Steinberg (1993) discuss additional issues surrounding the antitrust treatment of nonprofit organizations.[64]

Labor. Universities that long tolerated textbook royalties going to the faculty author are now contending that the (hopefully) more lucrative profits from distance-learning programs belong to the university under the "work for hire" doctrine. Universities face union-organizing lawsuits from graduate students in their roles as teaching assistants. The organizing activities of doctors would affect nonprofit health maintenance organizations. Harvard and Yale have been under pressure from students and other constituencies to pay a "living wage" to service employees.

Torts. Charities (but not other nonprofits) in many states formerly enjoyed immunity from tort liability. In the modern era of insurance, however, such a shifting of risk to injured parties came to be viewed as unfair and inefficient, and charitable immunity has all but vanished (e.g., *President and Directors of Georgetown College v. Hughes,* 130 F.2d 810 (D.C. 1942)). More recently, though, an increasing number of tort suits have been filed against individual charity personnel—or at least the perception of liability has grown—leading to state and federal "Volunteer Protection Acts" (Tremper 1991; Light 2001). These statutes are triggered when harm befalls a third party, and do not, by contrast, protect volunteer trustees or directors from suits by or on behalf of the charity, or by the attorney general, for breaches of fiduciary duty. The boundaries of tort law are now being tested by the proliferation of suits arising out of the pedophile scandals in the Catholic Church (e.g., *Archdiocese of Milwaukee v. Superior Court,* 5 Cal. Rptr. 3d 154 (Cal. App. 2003), ruling that the Roman Catholic Archdiocese of Milwaukee is subject to specific personal jurisdiction in California, because, by covering up the pedophile conviction of a transferred priest, it engaged in conduct expressly aimed at California and knew its conduct would cause harm in California, *cert. denied* 124 S. Ct. 2874 (2004)).

Government contracting. Nonprofits that contract with the government are subject to government review of their performance and cost allocations. In addition, governments often condition grants on compliance with government personnel standards, such as affirmative action requirements. Other contract conditions can blur the distinction between public and private[65]: for example, San Francisco adopted an ordinance requiring any nonprofit organization that receives more than $250,000 in city contracts to allow the public to attend one board meeting a year (Stehle 1998). At what point do government contracting requirements result in "unconstitutional conditions"? An amendment proposed in the 1990s by Congressman Ernest Istook would have barred charitable contract recipients from engaging in lobbying and certain other advocacy activities with their own funds.

SELF-REGULATION AND LEGAL REGULATORY REFORM

Self-Regulation

Private regulation takes many forms, which vary in their degree of voluntariness or compulsion, and attendant sanction: at the individual organization level, the demands of funders or of government contracts; at the industry or professional level, the requirements of accreditation bodies; and at the sector level, trade association best-practices guides and even certification (see generally Brody 2002a).

One longtime charity watchdog, the donor-focused BBB Wise Giving Alliance, published the standards it uses in responding to public requests about specific charities. (www.give.org/standards/). These standards cover board membership, activity and policies, accuracy of public information such as solicitations and Web sites, openness about relationships with commercial entities, use of funds, annual report, budget, and, for established charities, whether the organization spends more than a certain percent on fundraising and other administrative costs. Rating systems that employ formulas or grades are the most controversial. More systematically, state nonprofit associations began to design variously named "accountability codes" and "standards of practice."[66] Two of the most thorough—adopted by the Maryland Association of Nonprofit Organizations and by the Minnesota Council of Nonprofits in substantially similar form—cover mission and program evaluation, governance, human resources, financial management, fundraising, public accountability and communications, and public policy and advocacy. (Indeed, these "best practices" might be too prescriptive for some.) The "intermediate sanctions" tax law is inducing more charities to adopt conflict-of-interest policies, and these private guidelines explain what the documents should require. Finally, the Maryland association offers peer-review certification for nonprofits seeking to demonstrate that they abide by its principles.

Private regulation has advantages and disadvantages compared with the compulsory, but minimal, public regulation. A charity has some discretion in orienting itself toward particular validating private authorities having varying requirements. For example, a member-funded private body generally relies on voluntarily supplied and unverified information. On the other hand, standards could be inappropriate in a given case, and a proliferation of tests could either unnecessarily burden compliant charities, or cause small charities lacking the sophistication or resources to conform to appear unworthy of donor support. The relationship between the private regulator and regulated can become just as complicated as in the public sector, with concerns of "capture" and protection of elite, vested interests (Meek 1977:2842–44).

The real test of the effectiveness of private regulation comes when the nonprofit body is faced with having to expel or impose other sanctions against a nonconforming nonprofit. The process sends not just a signal of trustworthiness, but also a credible and legitimate signal.

State or Federal Oversight Board?

Attorneys general do not want to run charities. While attorneys general have recently become more active with respect to troubled nonprofit hospitals, one study found that the directors of the charity offices in New York, Connecticut, and Massachusetts generally believe they "should not get involved when a group is having financial troubles unless illegal conduct is alleged, nor should they intervene in the internal battles of a group with active participants" (Bograd 1994:5–6). In short, they "do not view themselves as the 'ultimate owners' of the underlying assets of all charitable organizations, though they do represent the public, donors, and beneficiaries in certain legal proceedings."

Nevertheless, proposals have emerged from time to time

to create a variously conceived "charities board," either at the state level (Karst 1960; Ben-Ner 1994) or at the federal level (Filer Commission 1977; Ginsburg, Marks, and Wertheim 1977:2640–44; Yarmolinsky and Fremont-Smith 1977:2857; Herzlinger 1996). Joel Fleishman (1999:185) revisited this debate by urging: "For the long-run good of the sector, we cannot continue to rely on an inadequately staffed and insufficiently powerful IRS, the vagaries of inadequately staffed and usually not-very-interested offices of state attorneys general which, in any event, have difficulty in policing a sector which routinely crosses state and national boundaries many times a day, the limited scope and vision of voluntary watchdog agencies, the new information-providing organizations, and the investigatory, inflammatory press."

Fleishman would leave the nonprofit sector to address "unwise, injudicious, or careless—but not illegal—patterns of actions by bona fide not-for-profit organizations," while confining government enforcement action to fraudulent behavior by those acting "under cover of a fake not-for-profit mask" (186). He then advocates for joint efforts by the sector and government. If these two strategies fail, as a last resort he would adopt a new federal agency (subordinate to state enforcement): "Great pains should be taken to ensure that its powers are narrowly focused, that its charter is restricted to 'the rules of the game' whereby not-for-profits function, that it be prohibited from dealing with the substance or content of the programs of not-for-profits, and that all of its actions be subject to court review by the standards of strict scrutiny required when First Amendment interests are at stake" (187–88).

Society continually debates the question of "how private is private philanthropy?" Nonprofits are subject to conflicting demands from their various stakeholders and from the public at large. In addressing these tensions, we need to distinguish between necessary legal reform and desirable private remedies.

For charities, different legal regimes can apply to charitable trusts and to nonprofit corporations. The law is being reexamined to consider when (and why) these regimes should be conformed. Reform would clarify attorney general jurisdiction, application of the *cy pres* doctrine (and address a possible "duty of obedience"), and availability of the "business judgment" standard for review of fiduciaries' exercise of the duty of care. Congress could usefully delineate the roles of the Internal Revenue Service and state attorneys general in investigating fiduciary wrongdoing. Proposals to increase the disclosure of exempt-organization tax information bear close watching.

As currently framed, regulated, and enforced, the law basically treats charitable trusts, nonprofit corporations, and voluntary associations as legally inviolable in the absence of fiduciary self-dealing or gross mismanagement. Donors and beneficiaries (but not voting members) typically lack "standing" to complain about nonprofit decisions. Performance could best be improved through self-regulation from the nonprofit sector itself. Recently published ethical standards and best-practices guidelines make a useful start. Any tightening of the legal duty of care (as opposed to loyalty), however, risks the practical result that regulators and courts would likely avoid findings of liability, or impose light sanctions in order to avoid penalizing voluntary service. A greater use of reputational sanctions (such as removal from the board) might be salutary in encouraging more attentive board service.

ACKNOWLEDGMENTS

I am grateful for comments and suggestions on earlier drafts from Marion Fremont-Smith and Richard Steinberg, as well as from Kristen Goss, Peter Dobkin Hall, Henry Hansmann, Jill Horwitz, Jack Siegel, John Simon, and participants at fall 2000 workshops at the Program on Non-Profit Organizations, Yale University; the Hauser Center on Nonprofit Organizations, John F. Kennedy School, Harvard University; and the annual meeting of the Association for Research on Nonprofit Organizations and Voluntary Action.

NOTES

1. Moreover, the nonprofit universe is broader than those religious, charitable, and educational entities customarily collected under the name "charities." Even less regulated is that host of other types functioning as "mutual-benefit" nonprofits, including labor unions, trade associations, social clubs, fraternal associations, health-maintenance organizations and other mutual insurance entities, and homeowners associations.

2. As described in Simon, Dale, and Chisolm, chapter 12 of this volume, the U.S. Supreme Court has decided numerous important cases under the Internal Revenue Code.

3. By contrast, prosecutions for embezzlement and other crimes are very public affairs. See, for example, the New York attorney general's press release announcing a seventy-two-count indictment against Lorraine Hale, the self-dealing former executive director of Hale House, a home for the children of drug-addicted mothers. Separate from these counts of falsifying business records, forgery, grand larceny, and tax evasion, the attorney general brought a civil forfeiture action seeking restitution of more than $1 million. An investigation by a newly appointed board of directors found that Hale created a phony board (including a fictitious board member), falsified board minutes, and forged signatures (Pristin and Bernstein 2002). "We've got to get some living people on this board," Hale was reported to have once commented (Evans and Saltonstall 2001). Pleading guilty to a single count of larceny, Hale agreed to forfeit about $118,000 worth of assets to Hale House, and to have judgments entered against her and her husband for the balance stolen. See New York Attorney General Press Release, "Former Hale House Director Pleads Guilty to Felony Charges Involving the Misappropriation of Charitable Funds" (July 3, 2002), available at www.oag.state.ny.us/press/2002/jul/jul03a_02.html. Lorraine Hale was sentenced to five years' probation.

4. Notably, regulators conditioned settlement on disclosure by Boston University (Massachusetts), Adelphi University (New York), and the Kamehameha Schools/Bishop Estate (Internal Revenue Service). See, too, the numerous press releases on the New York attorney general's Web site, at www.oag.state.ny.us/charities/press.

5. As of December 2005, the Uniform Trust Code was enacted in fifteen jurisdictions.

6. In the twentieth century the Supreme Court gradually "incorpo-

rated" the Bill of Rights (originally binding only the federal government) into the Fourteenth Amendment's due process protection from the states.

7. Legislatures, however, quickly adopted concurring Justice Story's suggestion to insert "reservation clauses" into charters and later general nonprofit corporation statutes, ensuring that future legislatures could enact statutory amendments to the corporation laws that would apply to existing corporations.

8. This case also approved the transfer of the Mormon Church's property to another charitable purpose under the *cy pres* doctrine as then applied. See Fremont-Smith and Horwitz (2003:16) attributing this aberrational application of "prerogative" *cy pres* to Utah's status as a federal territory.

9. Congress tried again, enacting the Religious Land Use and Institutionalized Persons Act of 2000 (RLUIPA). The more targeted RLUIPA bars governments from implementing a zoning or landmark law in a manner that substantially burdens religious exercise, unless it is the least restrictive means to further a compelling governmental interest. In addition, the statute bars governments from totally excluding religious assemblies from a jurisdiction or "unreasonably" limiting religious assemblies, institutions, or structures within a jurisdiction. Court challenges have begun, with opposite outcomes. See discussion in *Westchester Day School v. Village of Mamaroneck,* 280 F. Supp. 2d 230 (S.D.N.Y. 2003), *vacated and remanded by* 386 F.3d 183 (2d Cir. 2004).

10. By contrast, the California Supreme Court held that the Boy Scouts are not a "public accommodation" under the state's Unruh Civil Rights Act. *Curran v. Mount Diablo Council of the Boy Scouts of America,* 952 P.2d 218 (Cal. 1998) (Boy Scouts denied a homosexual the right to be a troop leader); *Randall v. Orange County Council of the Boy Scouts of America,* 952 P.2d 261 (Cal. 1998) (Boy Scouts denied membership for refusing to affirm a belief in God).

11. In the end, thirty-seven nonprofits joined in "friend of the court" briefs on behalf of James Dale; forty-three nonprofits joined in on briefs for the Boy Scouts. Different organizations of Methodists—the largest sponsors of Boy Scout troops—filed on *each* side.

12. Tax exemption under Internal Revenue Code section 501(c)(3) is a separate matter. See *The Nationalist Movement v. Commissioner of Internal Revenue,* 102 T.C. 558, *aff'd per curiam* 37 F.3d 216 (5th Cir. 1994) (denying section 501(c)(3) status to a white supremacist organization chartered under Mississippi law as "a non-profit charitable, educational and fraternal organization dedicated to advancing American freedom, American democracy and American nationalism"). See generally Simon, Dale, and Chisolm (this volume).

13. One U.S. Supreme Court decision allowed property donated for a municipal park "for whites only" to revert to the family after the fall of Jim Crow laws, ruling that the Georgia courts neutrally applied the *cy pres* doctrine to find that the testator lacked a general charitable intent. *Evans v. Abney,* 396 U.S. 435 (1970). Compare Stephen Girard's will, which created a school for white boys. The Pennsylvania Orphan's Court, on its own, had removed the trustees for refusing to enforce the racial restriction. A federal court found this act to constitute improper state action "which transcended mere testamentary supervision." *Pennsylvania v. Brown,* 270 F. Supp. 782 (E.D. Pa.), *aff'd* 392 F.2d 120 (3d Cir. 1967), *cert. denied* 391 U.S. 921 (1968). Somewhat surprisingly, in 2002, the high court of Maryland unanimously refused to enforce an "illegal racially discriminatory condition by ordering that the proceeds [of a gift for a nursing home benefiting aged white men] be paid to the alternative beneficiary, the University of Maryland Hospital"—although the court assumed for purposes of argument that "judicial enforcement of the racially discriminatory condition, by awarding the proceeds to University Hospital, will not violate the United States Constitution, federal statutes, or the Maryland Constitution." *Home for Incurables of Baltimore City v. University of Maryland Medical System Corporations* 20, 797 A.2d 746, 747 & 750–51 (Md. 2002).

14. Because nonprofit corporations embrace mutual-benefit organizations as well as charities, nonprofit incorporation is permitted for purposes that would not necessarily qualify for charitable trust status.

A charitable trust may not have purposes or provisions that are unlawful or contrary to public policy, but these terms are not self-defining. See section 28 of the *Restatement (Third) of Trusts;* besides finding a prohibition on "invidious" discrimination, as described above, the American Law Institute comments: "A trust for the dissemination of beliefs or doctrines may be charitable although the views are out of harmony with those of a majority of the public. . . . A trust, however, for the dissemination of beliefs or doctrines that are irrational or apparently so foolish as to be of no significant interest to members of the community is not a charitable trust, even though the dissemination is not illegal. A trust to provide instruction in the performance of a criminal act or to induce the commission of such acts is not charitable, although a trust to support the dissemination of literature advocating or explaining the nature and societal benefits of conduct or procedures that are illegal in the state (e.g., assisted suicide) would ordinarily be an educational and thus charitable purpose" (American Law Institute 2003, §28, Comment *h*).

15. Hansmann's compelling construct has even caught the attention of the United States Supreme Court. See *Austin v. Michigan State Chamber of Commerce,* 494 U.S. 652, 675 n.6 (1990) (Brennan, J., concurring) (citations to Hansmann omitted): "The nondistribution constraint helps overcome contractual failure in situations where the activities of the corporation are difficult to monitor, by removing the 'profit motive' and assuring those who contribute to, and contract with, the corporation that the nonprofit's managers will not exploit informational deficiencies to pursue their own private interests. Hence, Justice Kennedy's proposed reliance on a nonprofit's donors to monitor and police the corporation's activities overlooks the raison d'etre of the nonprofit form."

16. From the earliest days of Anglo-American charity, a charity could take either of two legal forms, one court-defined (common law) and the other legislative (statutory). Traditionally, the trust could be created wholly in the private sphere: a settlor makes an agreement with a trustee for the management and disposition of a fund of money or property. If the beneficiaries are indefinite and the trust has a charitable purpose, the trust may exist in perpetuity. A corporation, by contrast, requires the grant of a legislative charter in order to obtain such characteristics as perpetual life. The overwhelming American preference for the corporate form results from historical accident and a combination of institutional forces. As described below, the technical differences between the trust and corporate form for charity are, in practice, minimized by action by the creators and by the existence of charity regulation that applies regardless of organizational form. (See Zollmann 1924; Fremont-Smith 1965; Fremont-Smith 2004a.)

17. The concept of *fiduciary* permeates the law. The word derives from the Latin word for faithfulness. In the nonprofit context, we use the term to refer to trustees of charitable trusts and directors of nonprofit corporations.

18. Practitioner Michael Peregrine and former California charity official James Schwartz distinguish "'passive' errors in judgment"—which courts would not likely find constitute gross negligence—from "consistent and significant failures to exercise board oversight" (Peregrine and Schwartz 2000b:471). They observe that a variety of factors for which nonprofit boards are often criticized will present difficult issues for the courts: "The (unproven and potentially unjust) criticisms typically made against directors in situations involving troubled operations are somewhat uniform, including (a) failure to insist upon timely and understandable reports from management; (b) failure to comprehend (or ask questions regarding) material transactions; (c) failure to insist upon effective internal and external audit functions; (d) over-reliance upon 'dependent' rather than 'independent' advisors; and (e) failure to challenge questionable executive compensation arrangements."

19. For example, the New York State Board of Regents removed

and replaced eighteen of Adelphi University's nineteen trustees for acting "blindly, recklessly and heedlessly" in setting the unreasonable compensation paid to university president Peter Diamandopoulos. Panel of New York State Board of Regents, Report and Recommendations After a Hearing to the Full Board of Regents, *in* The Committee to Save Adelphi, *et al.* v. Diamandopoulos, *et al.* at 26–33 (Albany, N.Y.: Feb. 5, 1997). The Regents also found that several trustees had conflicts of interest, and violated their duty of loyalty. *Id.* at 33–46. As described in note 24 below, in settlement of the subsequent enforcement action brought by the New York attorney general, the former trustees agreed to reimburse the university about $1.6 million it paid in legal fees and other costs.

20. The state charity officials also cited the "self-employment syndrome," where a charity "was created primarily for the benefit of its formerly unemployed executive, and the board, staff, vendors, and contractors include many friends and relatives of the executive."

21. But see *Lynch v. Redfield Foundation,* 9 Cal. App. 3d 293 (1970) (surcharging squabbling directors for permitting funds to accumulate in a non-interest-bearing account for five years).

22. Specifically, under the duty of care, the normative standard of conduct is reasonableness, but the judicial standard of review is more lenient: under the business judgment rule, "a director will not be held liable for a decision—even one that is unreasonable—that results in a loss to the corporation, so long as the decision is rational" (Allen, Jacobs, and Strine 2001:1296). These authors, who have all served on the chancery court in Delaware, defend the result of insulating director conduct from judicial scrutiny on social utility grounds and "to reduce the likelihood of erroneous judicial decisions that might deter director risk-taking."

23. Typifying—if not parodying—the current standard is the notorious Sibley Hospital decision (*Stern v. Lucy Webb Hayes National Training School for Deaconesses and Missionaries,* 381 F. Supp. 1003, 1021 (D.D.C. 1974) (mem.)), where the court found fiduciary breaches, but generally required only that each director read the court's opinion! See Peregrine and Schwartz (2000:464), suggesting that under similar circumstances today, "removal and/or surcharge of the responsible directors would be ordered (or at least certainly sought by the Attorney General)."

24. Compare, though, the settlement between the New York attorney general and the ousted trustees of Adelphi University, who, without admitting wrongdoing, agreed to pay Adelphi $1.23 million and assume more than $400,000 in legal bills. The attorney general purportedly prohibited the D&O policy from being the source of payment (Halbfinger 1998). Unfortunately, the settlement document merely recites the aggregate amounts owed, providing no specific guidance on how the trustees were surcharged. Compare Allen, Jacobs, and Strine (2001:1318): "In cases where the transaction cannot be undone, the court must conduct a director-by-director inquiry into which specific directors actually engaged in a breach of fiduciary duty sufficient to justify monetary liability."

25. AHERF had typically carried $50 million in D&O insurance, but in the months immediately prior to its bankruptcy filing had purchased four times that coverage; the insurance companies asserted that the later policies were fraudulent (Becker 2002).

26. Reportedly, the Bishop Estate considered moving its state of incorporation in order to escape the oversight of the Hawaii attorney general—indeed, it contemplated moving to an American Indian reservation to get out from IRS jurisdiction as well—but, as a trust, hesitated because of the necessity of obtaining court approval.

27. See, e.g., *Fitzgerald v. National Rifle Association,* 383 F. Supp. 162 (D.N.J. 1974) (requiring the NRA's magazine to accept an advertisement about Fitzgerald's candidacy for the board, but not requiring the NRA to allow his ad to solicit for contributions). The ABA's Model Act grants members a right to inspect and copy an organization's membership list if the request is made in good faith and for a proper purpose. See also *Bernstein v. Alameda-Contra Costa Medical Association,* 293 P.2d 862 (Cal. App. 1956) (additional protections for expulsion from professional association). As to religious organizations, see e.g., *Watson v. Jones,* 80 U.S. 679 (1871) (comparing different organizational structures for churches); *Serbian Eastern Orthodox Diocese for the United States of America and Canada v. Milivojevich,* 426 U.S. 696, 710 (1976) (civil courts have no authority to resolve church disputes turning on church doctrine, practice, polity, or administration); *Jones v. Wolf,* 443 U.S. 595 (1979) (applying a test of neutrality). See generally Chafee 1930; Ellman 1981; O'Melinn 2000.

28. Cal. Corp. Code §5227. Mandating a majority of disinterested directors, though, might simply lead to dummy outside directors (see Fishman 1987:448). The ABA's Model Act offers such a provision as optional section 8.13, commenting: "This section is optional as many members of the Subcommittee . . . felt that its provisions would be ineffective in preventing intentional abuses, while presenting a burdensome or inconvenient requirement. . . . Legitimate public benefit corporations might have difficulty in finding active and competent directors who had no financial interest in the corporation."

29. See "BBB Wise Giving Alliance Standards for Charity Accountability" (effective March 3, 2003), and "Implementation Guide to the BBB Wise Giving Alliance Standards for Charity Accountability," available at www.give.org/standards/.

30. For example, on September 30, 2004, the governor of California signed SB 1262, the Charity Integrity Act. Primarily directed to charitable solicitations, SB 1262 also contains some governance provisions. In general, the board or trustee of charities having at least $2 million in annual revenues must: obtain audited financial statements, and make these publicly available; "if it is a corporation, have an audit committee appointed by the board of directors"; and "review and approve the compensation, including benefits, of the president or chief executive officer and the treasurer or chief financial officer to assure that it is just and reasonable." In early 2005 the New York attorney general released a set of legislative proposals to amend the Not-for-Profit Corporation Law. (The four separate bills are available at www.oag.state.ny.us/charities/legislation.html.) One proposal purports to mandate executive committees for organizations with more than twenty-five board members, and audits committees would be required for organizations having audited financial statements or more than $2 million of revenue. The proposal, however, permits any not-for-profit corporation to opt out of these requirements by appropriately amending its articles of incorporation (see generally Brakman Reiser 2005). Note that Drexel University made headlines by voluntarily adopting many of the requirements of Sarbanes-Oxley (see the March 10, 2003, memo from its general counsel to the National Association of College and University Attorneys, with links to board documents, at www.nacua.org/documents/Drexel_Sarbanes-Oxley_Memo.doc.)

31. In defending New York State's delay in discovering and exposing the looting of Hale House (a children's shelter that attracted millions of dollars in donations) by its longtime executive director, "[attorney general] Mr. Spitzer said the charities bureau in his office was charged with helping charities comply with state requirements, rather than aggressively policing them. The bureau has only six accountants to oversee 40,000 charities, he said, and it still must rely on information kept on 3-by-5 index cards to track the organizations. Requests for the money to computerize the operation have been repeatedly rejected" (Bernstein 2002). Moreover, Hale House's founder was the executive director's mother, who "was elevated to sainthood" by Ronald Reagan and popular with other politicians (*Bernstein 2002,* quoting the senior vice president for agency services at United Way).

32. Peregrine and Schwartz (2002) cite the "increasing use [by attorneys general] of charitable trust laws to effect remedies that are unavailable under nonprofit law," resistance to applying the business

judgment rule in the nonprofit context, and even asserting "waste" of corporate assets. Moreover, in the absence of a statute, a state attorney general usually has no enforcement authority over a nonprofit corporation other than a charity.

33. Separately, attorney general action might reflect a rivalry between a state's regulatory agencies: depending on the industry in which it operates, a given nonprofit organization might be regulated by such other agencies as the insurance commissioner, the department of health, education, or commerce, or the corporations commission. In some states, the attorney general's *parens patriae* power is exercised by the district attorney.

34. All of these factors are combining to present particular difficulties for multi-state nonprofit hospital systems seeking to consolidate their assets.

35. I was retained as an adviser to the Terra Foundation defendants in July 2001.

36. See *Joint Press Release re Buntrock, et al. v. Terra Foundation, et al.*, PR Newswire, July 26, 2001.

37. See, e.g., *Nathan Littauer Hospital v. Spitzer,* 734 N.Y.S.2d 671 (N.Y. App. 2001). In this case, a hospital wanted to restructure to create a sole member that, in turn, would adhere to directives for Catholic health care. Abortion rights groups protested and the attorney general asserted approval powers over the disposition of nonprofit corporate assets. The court ruled that the attorney general "has failed to offer any persuasive authority in support of the proposition that a change in the composition of Littauer's membership is the functional equivalent of a sale, lease, exchange or other disposition of corporate assets."

38. See, e.g., *In the Matter of the Trust under the Will of Caroline Weld Fuller,* 636 N.E.2d 1333 (Mass. 1994) (rejecting automatic approval of the attorney general's monetary settlement with the fiduciaries), discussed in Fremont-Smith (1997:15).

39. The Internet revolution highlights the long-standing problems of state charity regulators faced with the interstate activities of both look-alike and legitimate charities. Where is Internet charitable solicitation taking place for legal purposes, and who can regulate it (Monaghan 1996)? The National Association of Attorneys General/National Association of State Charities Officials (NAAG/NASCO) released a proposal on this topic—called the "Charleston Principles" after the conference at which it was developed—in September 2000 (www.nasconet.com).

40. The trust law mechanism of *cy pres,* discussed below, is available when more money is donated for a cause than turns out to be needed; with court approval, the surplus can be redirected to a similar purpose.

41. *Schaumburg* invalidated a municipal ordinance prohibiting the solicitation of contributions by charitable organizations that did not use at least 75 percent of their receipts for "charitable purposes." *Munson* invalidated a statute that forbade contracts between charities and professional fundraisers if, after costs, the fundraiser retained more than 25 percent of collections. *Riley* barred a state from, among other things, requiring professional fundraisers to disclose to potential donors the percentage of prior contributions retained as fees. *Madigan,* which involved a charity whose fundraising contract called for 85 percent of amounts collected to be retained by the professional fundraiser, allowed the Illinois attorney general's suit against the telemarketer to proceed because "the gravamen of the fraud action in this case is not high costs or fees; it is particular representations made with intent to mislead" (123 S. Ct. at 1841).

42. See also the discussion of *United Cancer Council v. Commissioner,* 165 F.3d 1173 (7th Cir. 1999), in Simon, Dale, and Chisolm (this volume). Judge Richard Posner rejected the IRS's assertion that a fundraiser unrelated to the charity became an insider for purposes of the prohibition on private inurement in Internal Revenue Code section 501(c)(3) by negotiating a "one-sided" contract. However, the court remanded the case to see whether the contract resulted in so much private benefit that the charity no longer operated for an exempt purpose. This "private benefit" doctrine is still relatively novel and its boundaries untested; the parties settled before the Tax Court could rule on the issue.

43. *In re Waldemar Cancer Research Ass'n, Inc.,* 130 N.Y.S.2d 426, 426–27 (Sup. Ct. 1954). For a discussion of this and other examples, see Silber (2001:62–63 and accompanying notes).

44. Version v3.00 (September 2004) supports thirty-five jurisdictions (thirty-four states and the District of Columbia), and includes supplemental forms required by six states (www.multistatefiling.org). This form resulted from a joint project of the National Association of State Charities Officials, the National Association of Attorneys General, and the Multi-State Filer Program, a consortium of nonprofits.

45. The post–September 11, 2001, U.S. Patriot Act extended the FTC's authority over charitable-solicitation telemarketing activities. U.S.A. Patriot Act, Public Law No. 107–56, 115 Stat. 272, §1011 ("Crimes against Charitable Americans") (2001), www.ftc.gov/bcp/conline/edcams/charityfraud/index.html.

46. This discussion assumes that donors care about how effectively the charity uses the funds—which could be called "instrumental giving." Giving can also occur for other (or additional) reasons—such as identification with a group, erection of a building, or maintenance of another expressive purpose. Now that disclosure is becoming widespread, we should be able to learn more about the extent to which donors care about the financial position of potential donees. In particular, we can see whether charities with large endowments and other surpluses will change their practices in order to continue attracting contributions.

47. For charities defined as "private foundations," Congress enacted specific penalty taxes for failure to distribute a minimum payout for charitable purposes, maintenance of excess business holdings, and jeopardy investments, as well as self-dealing.

48. See the Kamehameha Schools/Bishop Estate closing agreement, which the IRS insisted be placed on the Web (www.ksbe.edu/newsroom/filings/toc.html#closing). This agreement required, in addition to a payment from KSBE to the IRS of $9 million plus interest (for a total of about $14 million), the permanent removal of the incumbent trustees; the reorganization of KSBE around a chief executive officer to carry out the policy decisions of the board of trustees; the adoption of an investment policy and a spending policy focused on education; adoption of a conflicts-of-interest policy and adherence to the probate court's directive for setting trustee compensation; a ban on hiring any governmental employee or official until three years after termination of governmental service; and the Internet posting of the final closing agreement and of KSBE financial statements for the next five years. Like state settlements, IRS closing agreements usually remain confidential.

49. I was appointed to serve as a member of the Panel's Expert Advisory Group.

50. In a statutory mechanism based on a venerable common law practice, California permits suit by anyone granted "relator" status by the attorney general. "The relator generally takes an active part in the proceeding and is responsible for court costs, but the attorney general retains control of the action and can withdraw, dismiss or compromise it at any time" (Blasko et al. 1993, at 49 [footnote omitted]; see also Fishman [1985:674] urging that successful relators be granted costs and attorney's fees).

51. New York, however, offers a recent contrast. To the surprise and strong criticism of legal scholars, an appellate court in New York granted standing to a donor's widow—as a court-appointed representative of her husband's estate—to challenge the use of his restricted gift, despite an alternative arrangement approved by the attorney general. *Smithers v. St. Luke's-Roosevelt Hospital Center,* 723 N.Y.S.2d 426 (App. Div. 2001). The three-judge majority opinion declared: "We conclude that the distinct but related interests of the donor and the Attorney General are best served by continuing to accord standing to donors

to enforce the terms of their own gifts concurrent with the Attorney General's standing to enforce such gifts on behalf of the beneficiaries thereof."

The lone dissenting judge reviewed the traditional standing rules, distinguishing between any rights that might be held by the donor, the donor's estate, and the donor's heirs. The dissent lamented the effect of the holding in this case on the attorney general's authority to regulate charities: "By determining that the plaintiff may pursue the instant action, the majority necessarily concludes that a decedent's estate, which has no interest in a gift, may prevent the New York State Attorney General from exercising his discretion in determining how to prosecute alleged violations of the law."

52. See, for example, the Association of Fundraising Professionals' November/December 2000 essay on the emerging issue of "How Much Donor Involvement Is Too Much?" at www.afpnet.org/ethics, describing how restrictions might violate a nonprofit's mission statement or conflicts-of-interest policy, as well as public-benefit legal requirements.

53. More frequently applied is the relatively liberal doctrine of equitable deviation, which focuses on means rather than ends. For example, a donor might have specified that the donated building be retained, but if the property is later destroyed or condemned, the resulting insurance or condemnation proceeds would, upon court approval, be re-employed for the original purpose.

54. The *Third Restatement* comments: "The term 'wasteful' is used here neither in the sense of common-law waste nor to suggest that a lesser standard of merely 'better use' will suffice" (American Law Institute 2003, §67, Comment *c(1)*).

As a prerequisite to *cy pres* modification, the donor traditionally must have had a "general charitable intent"; otherwise, on the failure of the charitable purpose, the gift would revert to the donor or his or her successors in interest. Under section 413 of the Uniform Trust Code, a presumption in favor of a general charitable intent exists; moreover, a reversion to a person other than a charity would be permitted only if "(1) the trust property is to revert to the settlor and the settlor is still living; or (2) fewer than 21 years have elapsed since the date of the trust's creation."

55. The *Restatement (Third) of Trusts* comments: "If . . . a trustee (e.g., a recipient institution or community foundation), without prior court authorization, applies property to a purpose other than that designated in the terms of the trust, the trustee is subject to liability for breach of trust. If, however, the application made by the trustee is such as the court would have directed, the court may approve the application, and such approval will be as effective as though the court had authorized the application before it was made" (American Law Institute 2003, §67, Comment *d*). See also Fremont-Smith (1966:1044): "a trustee may be relieved from personal liability for failure to perform a duty or for overstepping the limits of his power but may yet be forced by a court to adhere to that duty in his future conduct."

56. See Fisch et al. 1974, at §119. Courts sometimes exercise equity powers to require that accumulations be reasonable in light of the donor's charitable purpose and public policy. For example, the will in *James' Estate,* 199 A.2d 275 (Pa. 1964) (trust income to accumulate until vesting in the Masons in 400 years). The court stated: "We are reluctant to ascribe to testator the paramount desire merely to turn an approximately $50,000 trust fund into a final gift of almost $15,000,000 at the expense of immediate social needs." Making the gift available immediately to the beneficiary in the absence of evidence that the donor had a specific project in mind, the court observed: "Shifting and advanced social concepts, programs and concerns emphasize the hazards of seeking to correct or alleviate social problems so distantly removed from testator's generation."

57. One college took the donor's money to build a building yet refused to put the donor's name on it. It transpired that when the college's board of regents was voting to accept the gift and name the wing, "unknown to them, appellant had for years been secretly mailing anonymous letters to families and individuals of mixed race and religion. These letters denounced mixed marriages, professed a viewpoint based on racial purity, and, according to some recipients, produced fear in them." Nevertheless, the court noted: "Appellant does not argue that his extracurricular activities did not give Augsburg College a legitimate reason to change its mind to not memorialize his name by naming an important wing of a new building after him. What appellant can claim is that once Augsburg changed its mind, it had a legal obligation to return his money, as the specific reason for giving the $500,000 no longer existed." *Stock v. Augsburg College,* 2002 Minn. App. LEXIS 421, at n.2 (Apr. 16, 2002) (unpublished). Evidently no trend is developing for universities to remove the names of donors now tainted by financial scandal. Compare Hanley (2002) and Pulley (2003).

58. The Employee Retirement Income Security Act (ERISA) also adopted the corporate standard of care and prudence.

59. See Shaw (1906:25–26): "[The Salvation Army] would take money from the devil himself and be only too glad to get it out of his hands and into God's. . . . The notion that you can earmark certain coins as tainted is an unpractical individualist superstition."

60. A New York court recently upheld the attorney general's objection to the sale of assets by one nonprofit hospital to another, invoking such a duty of obedience. The court observed: "Embarkation upon a course of conduct which turns it away from the charity's central and well-understood mission should be a carefully chosen option of last resort. Otherwise, a Board facing difficult financial straits might find sale of its assets, and 'reprioritization' of its mission to be an attractive option, rather than taking all reasonable efforts to preserve the mission which has been the object of its stewardship." *Matter of the Manhattan Eye, Ear & Throat Hospital v. Spitzer,* 715 N.Y.S.2d 575, 595 (1999). Other commentators view the traditional duties of loyalty and care as subsuming a faithfulness to mission, but perhaps with more flexibility.

61. An indirect version of such a transaction can be quite profitable: when the charity can earn a market return on its endowment but borrow from the public by issuing tax-exempt bonds, the charity benefits from the spread. The charity must take care that it does not secure the bonds with its endowment, or else the Internal Revenue Code would require the charity to refund the "arbitrage" profits to the federal government. In practice, a charity will seek a favorable bond rating by granting a security interest, either in real estate or in the income stream from the real estate (see Brody 1997a).

62. In *In the Matter of Estate of Othmer,* 710 N.Y.S.2d 848 (Surrogate's Court of New York, 2000), the court applied *cy pres* to permit a hospital to use a sufficient portion of an income-only fund to secure nearly $90 million in new debt that would implement strategic capital projects and provide working capital. The court cited dramatic changes in the health-care industry since 1995 (notably the growth in managed care, the deregulation of the private sector hospital rate-setting system, the reduction in Medicare reimbursements, and the shift from higher-paying inpatient care to lower-paying ambulatory care). The hospital's bankruptcy and closure, concluded the judge, would frustrate the general charitable purpose of the donors, while the income on the funds was not sufficient to fund long-term operations. The judge cited both the changed circumstances and the "exponential growth" of the donors' assets in approving the recovery plan.

63. A week earlier, the attorney general's press release acknowledges, the court had "dismissed felony theft charges against [former CEO] Abdelhak, saying he did not use the endowment money for his own personal gain." [Pennsylvania] Office of Attorney General Mike Fisher, press release: "AG Fisher: Former AHERF Official Pleads to Raiding Endowments; CEO Sentenced to 11 to 23 Months," August 29, 2002, available at www.attorneygeneral.gov/press/pr.cfm.

64. The Justice Department charged several Ivy League schools and MIT (the "Ivy Overlap Group") with agreeing not to compete over scholarship awards to commonly accepted students. In *United States v. Brown University,* 5 F.3d 658 (3d. Cir. 1993), the court suggested that a

nonprofit might be able to establish a public benefit in order to avoid liability, but the parties settled before the lower court could make findings. In 1994 Congress codified the settlement in a temporary antitrust exception, allowing institutions of higher education awarding need-based student aid to adopt general principles for determining need (but prohibiting agreements on awards to specific students); in 2001, Congress extended the exemption through 2008 and directed the General Accounting Office to study and assess current practices. Need-Based Educational Aid Act of 2001, Public Law 107–72, 115 Stat. 648 (Nov. 29, 2001). With the extension, asserted Congressman James Sensenbrenner, "there will be more money to go around to more good students and to open the doors to these well-endowed, prestigious private colleges and universities to more people to be able to go there." 147 Cong. Record (Nov. 6, 2001): H7731. To Senator Herb Kohl, however, "Our antitrust laws guarantee competition, and competition means lower prices and higher quality for consumers—including students purchasing a college education, but the colleges and universities using the exemption believe that the market functions differently in this case. I am therefore willing to extend the exemption for another seven years but believe that any further activity in this area must be coupled with hard objective data proving that his line exemption does indeed benefit students and their families." 147 Cong. Record (Nov. 3, 2001): S10252.

65. Technology-transfer laws, on the other hand, are allowing researchers to keep more profits.

66. For management-focused membership groups, see the Evangelical Council for Financial Accountability, *Seven Standards of Responsible Stewardship,* at www.ecfa.org; the Maryland Association of Nonprofit Organizations, *Standards for Excellence: An Ethics and Accountability Code for the Nonprofit Sector,* II.B.6 (1998), available at www.mdnonprofit.org/ethicbook.htm; the Minnesota Council of Nonprofits, *Principles & Practices for Nonprofit Excellence* (1998), available at www.mncn.org/pnp_doc.htm#intro; and the Association of Fundraising Professionals (formerly the National Society of Fund Raising Executives), which requires those applying for certification to adhere to its *Code of Ethics and Standards of Professional Practice* in addition to its *Donor Bill of Rights,* available at www.nsfre.org/about/certification/about_certification.html.

REFERENCES

Allen, William T., Jack B. Jacobs, and Leo E. Strine, Jr. 2001. Function over Form: A Reassessment of Standards of Review in Delaware Corporation Law. *Business Lawyer* 56: 1287–1321.

American Bar Association. 1987 (pub. 1988). *Revised Model Nonprofit Corporation Act.* Chicago.

ABA Section of Business Law. 1993. *Guidebook for Directors of Nonprofit Corporations.* Chicago: American Bar Association.

American Law Institute. 1959. *Restatement (Second) of the Law of Trusts.* Philadelphia: American Law Institute.

———. 1992a. *Principles of Corporate Governance: Analysis and Recommendations.* Philadelphia: American Law Institute.

———. 1992b. *Restatement (Third) of the Law of Trusts: The Prudent Investor Rule.* Philadelphia: American Law Institute.

———. 2003. *Restatement (Third) of the Law of Trusts.* Philadelphia: American Law Institute.

———. 2005a. *Principles of the Law of Nonprofit Organizations—Preliminary Draft No. 3.* Philadelphia: American Law Institute. May 12.

———. 2005b. *Principles of the Law of Nonprofit Organizations—Council Draft No. 3.* Philadelphia: American Law Institute. September 22.

Atkinson, Rob. 1993. Reforming Cy Pres Reform. *Hastings Law Journal* 44: 1111–58.

———. 1998. Unsettled Standing: Who (Else) Should Enforce the Duties of Charitable Fiduciaries? *Journal of Corporation Law* 23:655–99.

Bank, David. 2001. H-P Case Illustrates Clout of Foundation Holders. *Wall Street Journal,* December 24, at C1.

Becker, Cinda. 2002. Settling Down; AHERF to Pay $93.7 Million to Creditors, Trusts. *Modern Healthcare,* January 21, at 14.

———. 2003. Early Release: Abdelhak Wins Parole After Serving Three Months. *Modern Healthcare.* February 3, at 18.

Beh, Hazel G. 1998. Downsizing Higher Education and Derailing Student Educational Objectives: When Should Student Claims for Program Closures Succeed? *University of Georgia Law Review* 33:155–210.

Ben-Ner, Avner. 1994. Book Review: Who Benefits from the Nonprofit Sector? Reforming Law and Public Policy Towards Nonprofit Organizations. *Yale Law Journal* 104:731–62.

Ben-Ner, Avner, and Theresa Van Hoomissen. 1994. The Governance of Nonprofit Organizations: Law and Public Policy. *Nonprofit Management and Leadership* 4:393–414.

Bernstein, Nina. 2002. Officials Overlooked Dire Signs at Charity. *New York Times,* Feb. 7.

Blasko, Mary Grace, Curt S. Crossley, and David Lloyd. 1993. Standing to Sue in the Charitable Sector. *University of San Francisco Law Review* 28:37–84.

Blumenthal, Ralph. 2001. 13 Institutions Obtain Control of Vast Bequest. *New York Times,* May 4, at A1.

Bogert, George G. 1954. Proposed Legislation Regarding State Supervision of Charities. *Michigan Law Review* 52:633–58.

Bogert, George G., and George T. Bogert. 2000. *The Law of Trusts and Trustees* (3rd ed.). St. Paul, Minn.: West Group.

Bograd, Harriet. 1994. *The Role of State Attorneys General in Relation to Troubled Nonprofits.* Yale University Program on Non-Profit Organizations, Working Paper No. 206, August.

Boston Globe Staff. 2003. Spotlight: Some Officers of Charities Steer Assets to Themselves. *Boston Globe,* Oct. 9, at 1.

Brakman Reiser, Dana. 2001. Decision-Makers Without Duties: Defining the Duties of Parent Corporations Acting as Sole Corporate Members in Nonprofit Health Care Systems. *Rutgers Law Review* 53(4):979–1026.

———. 2003. Dismembering Civil Society: The Social Cost of Internally Undemocratic Nonprofits. *Oregon Law Review* 82:829–900.

———. 2005. There Ought to Be a Law, The Disclosure Focus of Recent Legislative Proposals for Nonprofit Reform. *Chicago-Kent Law Review* 80:559–612.

Brody, Evelyn. 1996a. Agents Without Principals: The Economic Convergence of the Nonprofit and For-Profit Organizational Forms. *New York Law School Law Review* 40:457–536.

———. 1996b. Institutional Dissonance in the Nonprofit Sector. *Villanova Law Review* 41:433–504.

———. 1997a. Charitable Endowments and the Democratization of Dynasty. *Arizona Law Review* 39:873–948.

———. 1997b. Hocking the Halo: Implications of the Charities' Winning Briefs in Camps Newfound/Owatonna, Inc. *Stetson Law Review* 27(2) (Howard Oleck Memorial Nonprofit Symposium Issue): 433–56.

———. 1998. The Limits of Charity Fiduciary Law. *Maryland Law Review* 57:1400–1501.

———. 1999. A Taxing Time for the Bishop Estate: What Is the I.R.S. Role in Charity Governance? *University of Hawaii Law Review* 21(2) (Symposium Issue on the Bishop Estate Controversy): 537–91.

———. 2002a. Accountability and Public Trust. Pages 471–98 in *The State of Nonprofit America,* ed. Lester M. Salamon. Washington, D.C.: Brookings Institution Press and The Aspen Institute.

———. 2002b. Entrance, Voice and Exit: The Constitutional Bounds of the Right of Association. *University of California at Davis Law Review* 35(4):821–901.

———. 2004. Whose Public? Parochialism and Paternalism in State Charity Law Enforcement. *Indiana Law Journal* 79(4):937–1036.

———. 2005a. The Charity in Bankruptcy and Ghosts of Donors Past, Present, and Future. *Seton Hall Legislative Journal* 29(2):471–530 (Symposium Issue on Bankruptcy in the Religious Non-Profit Context).

———. 2005b. "From the Dead Hand to the Living Dead: The Conundrum of Charitable-Donor Standing." Presented at New York University School of Law, National Center on Philanthropy and Law, Conference on Grasping the Nettle—Respecting Donor Intent and Avoiding the "Dead Hand."

Butig, Mary Frances, Gordon T. Butler, and Lynne M. Murphy. 1992. Pledges to Nonprofit Organizations: Are They Enforceable and Must They Be Enforced? *University of San Francisco Law Review* 27:47–147.

Chafee, Jr., Zechariah. 1930. The Internal Affairs of Associations Not for Profit. *Harvard Law Review* 43:993–1029.

Chester, Ronald. 2003. Grantor Standing to Enforce Charitable Transfers Under Section 405(c) of the Uniform Trust Code and Related Law: How Important Is It and How Extensive Should It Be? *Real Property, Probate and Trust Journal* 37:611–25.

Chisolm, Laura B. 1995. Accountability of Nonprofit Organizations and Those Who Control Them: The Legal Framework. *Nonprofit Management and Leadership* 6 (Winter): 141–56.

Clark, Carolyn C., and Glenn M. Troost. 1989. Forming a Foundation: Trust vs. Corporation. *Probate and Property [Journal]* (May–June): 32–34.

Columbus Dispatch, The. 2000. A Cancer Within Crime Against Charity Will Leave Deep Scars (editorial). June 11, at 2B.

DiMaggio, Paul J., and Walter F. Powell. 1991. The Iron Cage Revisited: Institutional Isomorphism and Collective Rationality in Organizational Fields. Pages 63–82 in *The New Institutionalism in Organizational Analysis,* ed. Walter Powell and Paul DiMaggio. Chicago: University of Chicago Press.

Dugan, Ianthe Jeanne, Thomas M. Vurton, and Carrick Mollenkamp. 2002. Chicago Art Institute Learns Tough Lesson About Hedge Funds. *Wall Street Journal,* Feb. 1, at A1.

Dundjerski, Marina. 2000. Billion-Dollar Growth at Big Funds. *Chronicle of Philanthropy.* February 24, at 1.

Eckel, Catherine C., and Richard Steinberg. 1993. Competition, Performance, and Public Policy Towards Nonprofits. Pages 57–81 in *Nonprofit Organizations in a Market Economy,* ed. David C. Hammack and Dennis R. Young. San Francisco: Jossey-Bass.

Ellman, Ira Mark. 1981. Driven from the Tribunal: Judicial Resolution of Internal Church Disputes. *California Law Review* 69:1378–1444.

Emerson, Thomas. 1964. Freedom of Association and Freedom of Expression. *Yale Law Journal* 74:1–35.

Evans, Heidi, and Dave Saltonstall. 2001. Lorraine Hale's $1.3 Million Slush Fund. *Daily News.* Aug. 8, at News, at 2.

Filer Commission (Commission on Private Philanthropy and Public Needs). 1977. Commentary on Commission Recommendations. In *Filer Commission Research Papers* 1:38. Washington, D.C.: U.S. Treasury Department.

Fisch, Edith L., Doris Jonas Freed, and Esther R. Schachter. 1974. *Charities and Charitable Foundations.* Pomona, N.Y.: Lond Publications.

Fishman, James J. 1985. The Development of Nonprofit Corporation Law and an Agenda for Reform, *Emory Law Journal* 34:617–68.

———. 1987. Standards of Conduct for Directors of Nonprofit Corporations. *Pace Law Review.* 7:389–462.

———. 1998. Checkpoints on the Conversion Highway: Some Trouble Spots in the Conversion of Nonprofit Health Care Organizations to For-Profit Status. *Journal of Corporation Law* 23:701–40.

———. 2003. Improving Charitable Accountability. *Maryland Law Review* 62:218–97.

Fishman, James J., and Stephen Schwarz. 2000. *Nonprofit Organizations: Cases and Materials,* 2nd ed. New York: Foundation Press.

Fleishman, Joel L. 1999. Philanthropy and Outcomes: Dilemmas in the Quest for Accountability. Pages 172–97 in *Philanthropy and the Nonprofit Sector in a Changing America,* ed. Charles T. Clotfelter and Thomas Ehrlich. Bloomington: Indiana University Press.

Fremont-Smith, Marion R. 1965. *Foundations and Government.* New York: Russell Sage Foundation.

———. 1966. Duties and Powers of Charitable Fiduciaries: The Law of Trusts and the Correction of Abuses. *UCLA Law Review* 14:1041–59.

———. 1997. "Enforceability and Sanctions." Presented at New York University School of Law, National Center on Philanthropy and Law, Conference on Governance of Nonprofit Organizations.

———. 2004a. *Governing Nonprofit Organizations: State and Federal Law and Regulation.* Cambridge, Mass.: Belknap Press of the Harvard University Press.

———. 2004b. Pillaging of Charitable Assets: Embezzlement and Fraud. *Exempt Organization Tax Review* 46:333–46.

Fremont-Smith, Marion R., and Jill Horwitz. 2003. The Power of the Legislature: Insurer Conversions and Charitable Funds. Hauser Center on Nonprofit Organizations, Harvard University, Working Paper.

Fremont-Smith, Marion R., and Andras Kosaras. 2003. Wrongdoing by Officers and Directors of Charities: A Survey of Press Reports, 1995–2002. *Exempt Organization Tax Review* 42:25–59.

Fremont-Smith, Marion R., and Jonathan A. Lever. 2000. State Regulation of Health Care Conversions and Conversion Foundations. *B.N.A. Health Law Reporter* 9(19):714–20.

Ginsburg, David, Lee R. Marks, and Ronald P. Wertheim. 1977. Federal Oversight of Private Philanthropy. In *Filer Commission Research Papers* 5:2575–2696. Washington, D.C.: U.S. Treasury Department.

["Giving USA"] American Association of Fund-Raising Counsel Trust for Philanthropy. 2000. Giving USA.

Goldschmid, Harvey J. 1998. The Fiduciary Problems of Nonprofit Directors and Officers: Paradoxes, Problems, and Proposed Reforms. *Journal of Corporation Law* 23:631–53.

Gutmann, Amy. 1998. Freedom of Association: An Introductory Essay. Pages 3–32 in *Freedom of Association,* ed. Amy Gutmann. Princeton, N.J.: Princeton University Press.

Halbfinger, David M. 1998. Lawsuits over Ouster of Adelphi Chief Are Settled. *New York Times,* November 18, at B1.

Hall, Peter Dobkin. 1992. *Inventing the Nonprofit Sector.* Baltimore: Johns Hopkins University Press.

Hanley, Robert. 2002. Seton Hall Removes Name of Benefactor Now in Prison. *New York Times,* Dec. 14, at B3.

Hansmann, Henry. 1980. The Role of Nonprofit Enterprise. *Yale Law Journal* 89:835–901.

———. 1981. Reforming Nonprofit Corporation Law. *University of Pennsylvania Law Review* 129:497–623.

———. 1996. *Ownership of Enterprise.* Cambridge, Mass.: Belknap Press of Harvard University Press.

Herzlinger, Regina E. 1996. Can Public Trust in Nonprofits and Governments Be Restored? *Harvard Business Review* 74(2):97–107.

Hone, Michael. 1988–89. Aristotle and Lyndon Baines Johnson: Thirteen Ways of Looking at Blackbirds and Nonprofit Organizations: The American Bar Association's Revised Model Nonprofit Corporation Act. *Case Western Reserve Law Review* 39:751–63.

Hopkins, Bruce. 1996. *The Law of Fund-Raising.* 2nd ed. New York: John Wiley & Sons.

Hyman, David A. 1998. Hospital Conversions: Fact, Fantasy, and Regulatory Follies. *Journal of Corporation Law* 23:741–78.

Katz, Robert A. 2003. A Pig in a Python: How the Charitable Response to September 11 Overwhelmed the Law of Disaster Relief. *Indiana Law Review* 36:251–333.

Independent Sector's Panel on the Nonprofit Sector. 2005. *Strengthening Transparency, Governance, [and] Accountability of Charitable Organizations* (at www.nonprofitpanel.org/final/Panel_Final_Report.pdf).

Internal Revenue Service. 2003. Announcement 2003–29, International Grant-making and International Activities by Domestic 501(c)(3) Organizations: Request for Comments Regarding Possible Changes. *Internal Revenue Bulletin* 2003–20: 928–29 (at www.irs.gov/pub/irs-irbs/irb03-20.pdf).

Joint Committee on Taxation, Staff of [U.S. Congress]. 2000. Study of Present-Law Taxpayer Confidentiality and Disclosure Provisions as Required by Section 3802 of the Internal Revenue Service Restructuring and Reform Act of 1998, Volume 2: Study of Disclosure Provisions Relating to Exempt Organizations (JCS-1–00, Jan. 28) (at www.house.gov/jct).

Karst, Kenneth L. 1960. The Efficiency of the Charitable Dollar: An Unfulfilled State Responsibility. *Harvard Law Review* 73:433–83.

King, Harriet M. 1981. The Voluntary Closing of a Private College: A Decision for the Board of Trustees? *South Carolina Law Review* 32:547–84.

Kurtz, Daniel L. 1988. *Board Liability: Guide for Nonprofit Directors.* Mt. Kisco, N.Y.: Moyer Bell Limited.

Light, Alfred R. 2000. Conscripting State Law to Protect Volunteers: The Odd Formulation of Federalism in "Opt-out" Preemption. *Seton Hall Journal of Sports Law* 10:9–64.

Lyon, James B. 1996. The Supervision of Charities in the United States by the State Attorneys General (and Other State Agencies) and the Internal Revenue Service. Chapter 5 in *New York University 24th Conference on Tax Planning for 501(c)(3) Organizations.*

Meek, Peter G. 1977. Self-Regulation in Private Philanthropy. In *Filer Commission Research Papers* 5:2781–2855. Washington, D.C.: U.S. Treasury Department.

Mehegan, Sean, Betsy Bush, and Sharon Nacson. 1994. Charity Regulation Today: How the States See It. *NonProfit Times,* March, at 1.

Monaghan, Paul E., Jr. 1996. "Charitable Solicitation Over the Internet and State-Law Restrictions," available at www.charitychannel.com/forums/cyb-acc/resources/monaghan.html.

National Conference of Commissioners on Uniform State Laws. 1972. *Uniform Management of Institutional Funds Act.* Chicago. For the November 2005 draft revision, go to www.nccusl.org.

———. 2000. *Uniform Trust Code.* Chicago.

O'Melinn, Liam Séamus. 2000. The Sanctity of Association: The Corporation and Individualism in American Life. *San Diego Law Review* 37(1):101–65.

Peregrine, Michael W., and James R. Schwartz. 2000a. A General Counsel's Guide to Accessing Restricted Gifts. *Exempt Organization Tax Review* 29(1):27–34.

———. 2000b. The Business Judgment Rule and Other Protections for the Conduct of Not-for-Profit Directors. *Journal of Health Law* 33:455–84.

———. 2002. Key Nonprofit Corporate Law Developments in 2001. *Health Law Reporter* 11:272(February 14).

Pristin, Terry, and Nina Bernstein. 2002. Ex-Head of Hale House and Husband Charged with Theft. *New York Times,* February 6, at B1.

Pulley, John L. 2003. Tainted Gifts. *Chronicle of Higher Education,* Jan. 2, at A32.

Rose, Barbara. 2001. Museum Defends Investing Strategy. *Chicago Tribune,* Dec. 12, Business section, at 1.

Rosenblum, Nancy L. 1998a. Membership and Voice. Pages 191–238 in *Membership and Morals: The Personal Uses of Pluralism in America.* Princeton, N.J.: Princeton University Press.

———. 1998b. Compelled Association: Public Standing, Self-Respect, and the Dynamic of Exclusion. Pages 75–108 in *Freedom of Association,* ed. Amy Gutmann. Princeton: Princeton University Press.

Senate Finance Committee, Staff of [U.S. Congress]. 2004. "Discussion Draft, Tax Exempt Governance Proposals." June 22 (available at www.finance.senate.gov/hearings/testimony/2004test/062204stfdis.pdf).

Shaw, George Bernard. 1906. Preface. *Major Barbara* (Penguin 1957).

Siegel, Jack B. 2006. *A Desktop Guide for Nonprofit Directors, Officers, and Advisors: Avoiding Trouble While Doing Good.* Hoboken, NJ: John Wiley and Sons.

Silber, Norman I. 2001. *A Corporate Form of Freedom: The Emergence of the Nonprofit Sector.* Boulder, Colo.: Westview Press.

Simes, Lewis M. 1955. *Public Policy and the Dead Hand.* Ann Arbor: University of Michigan Law School.

Simon, John G. 1987. American Philanthropy and the Buck Trust. *University of San Francisco Law Review* 21:641–79.

Soifer, Aviam. 1995. *Law and the Company We Keep.* Cambridge, Mass.: Harvard University Press.

Stehle, Vince. 1998. San Francisco Passes "Sunshine" Law, but Critics Say It Shines Little Light. *Chronicle of Philanthropy,* June 18.

———. 1997. On the Regulation of Fundraising. Pages 234–46 in *Critical Issues in Fund Raising, ed. Dwight Burlingame.* New York: John Wiley and Sons.

Strosnider, Kim. 1998. Colleges Face Prickly Dilemma When Donors or Their Heirs Renege on Promised Gifts. *Chronicle of Higher Education,* June 26, at A35.

Swords, Peter, and Harriet Bograd. 1996. "Accountability in the Nonprofit Sector: What Problems Are Addressed by State Regulators?" (at www.charitychannel.com/forums/cyb-acc/resources/ag_prob.htm).

Tremper, Charles Robert. 1991. Compensation for Harm for Charitable Activity. *Cornell Law Review* 76:401–75.

U.S. Congress, Joint Committee on Taxation. See Joint Committee on Taxation.

Williams, Grant. 2000. Tax Report Shakes Up Charities. *Chronicle of Philanthropy,* March 9.

Yarmolinsky, Adam, and Marion R. Fremont-Smith. 1977. Preserving the Private Voluntary Sector: A Proposal for a Public Advisory Commission on Philanthropy. In *Filer Commission Research Papers* 5: 2857–68. Washington, D.C.: U.S. Treasury Department.

U.S. Treasury Department. 2005. *Anti-Terrorist Financing Guidelines: Voluntary Best Practices for U.S. Based Charities.* Dec. 5. (amended version of Guidelines published in November 2002) (at http://www.treasury.gov/offices/enforcement/key-issues/protecting/docs/guidelines_charities.pdf).

Zollmann, Carl. 1924. *American Law of Charities.* Milwaukee, Wisc.: Bruce.

12

The Federal Tax Treatment of Charitable Organizations

JOHN SIMON
HARVEY DALE
LAURA CHISOLM

In a society suffused with taxes and reliant on them as engines of social and economic policy, the union of charity and taxes is in reality indissoluble—and controversy therefore inevitable. Charity[1] seems destined to be enmeshed in tax policy debate not only because that is the fate in America of so much human activity, but also because, over the years, we have come to entrust to the tax system a central role in the nourishment and regulation of the charitable sector.

It is a role that, for better or for worse, is unmatched in other lands. Legislation in other societies often provides a measure of exemption from various taxes and, less frequently, entitles charitable donors to deduct their gifts from their taxes (Salamon 1997; Silk 1999). Yet none of these provisions is as robust and comprehensive in the tax relief it offers to charity—or remotely as complicated—as the U.S. federal tax regime. That contrast reflects, in part, the salience of taxation in American public policy; in part, the high level of tax compliance in this country (exemption and deductibility are less compelling in a tax-evading culture); and, in part, the extraordinary—probably unique—centrality of the nonprofit sector in American social and economic life.

In its extensive and intensive engagement with the world of charity, the federal tax system pursues a number of policy goals, which may be grouped under the following four headings:

1. To encourage, through relief from tax, the continuation and expansion of the nonprofit sector. We call this the *support* function.

2. To bring about, through exemption and deductibility rules, a degree of fairness or redistribution of resources and opportunities, or at least a discouragement of unacceptable forms of discrimination. We call this the *equity* function.

3. To regulate through tax mechanisms the fiduciary behavior of nonprofit managers. We call this the *regulatory* function.

4. To constrain through tax mechanisms the capacity of charitable organizations to operate in the business and public sectors in a way that unduly competes with, controls, or influences the behavior of commercial or governmental entities. We call this the *border patrol* function.

Each of these functions is a major focus of tax policy, and each, in turn, will be analyzed in this chapter, along with a summary of the research—both empirical and theoretical—that has been done, or needs to be done, under each heading. Before carrying out this analysis, however, we first provide (in the next section) an overview of the nonprofit sector and its legal species and of the ways in which each of these species is treated under the federal tax system. Although this *tour d'horizon* focuses, as does this entire chapter, on federal tax treatment of the charitable part of the nonprofit sector and its subspecies, our taxonomy will also refer briefly to the treatment of the noncharitable species within the nonprofit sector and to nonfederal (state and local) tax policies affecting charitable organizations.

Our policy analysis of the federal tax treatment of charity is prefaced by a canvas of two clusters of threshold issues that cut across many of the other sections of this chapter. These are the issue of federal tax jurisdiction—what is the permissible and appropriate reach of the federal tax system in supporting and regulating American charities?—and the issue of boundaries between public and private purpose—what is the permissible and appropriate blend of public gain and private advantage in various charity law contexts?

The next four sections analyze the way the federal tax system seeks to advance the four functions listed above. In each case we seek to summarize the pertinent legal controversies and policy dilemmas, to examine the theoretical and empirical material that bears on these controversies and dilemmas, and to point out areas for further inquiry.[2] The same approach characterizes our exploration (in the next-to-last section) of the special case of churches, which, in some important ways, are treated quite differently from other charitable organizations, thus generating substantial issues of public policy. A concluding section offers some general thoughts about the challenges and difficulties confronting those who seek to understand the ways in which the federal tax system treats American charity.

AN OVERVIEW OF THE FEDERAL TAX TREATMENT OF CHARITABLE ORGANIZATIONS

A Federal Tax Taxonomy

The tax treatment of charitable organizations can best be understood by looking at the big picture—the larger universe of nonprofit entities of which the charitable sector is a major part. Viewing the nonprofit sector as a whole, one realizes that there is not a single federal tax treatment but instead many separate treatments. With some minor exceptions, however, what all of the inhabitants of this sector have in common is, first, the "nondistribution constraint" (Hansmann 1980): they are entitled to make profits but are forbidden to distribute these profits to any person or entity (other than another nonprofit organization)—they have, in conventional terms, no "owners"—and, second, exemption from the federal income tax imposed on non-nonprofit corporations, unincorporated associations, or trusts under the principal exemption statute, §501 of the Internal Revenue Code of 1986, as amended (which we will usually refer to simply as "the code"). There are two major sets of nonprofit organizations:

(1) What we will refer to as "charitable organizations" or "charities"—organizations described in §501(c)(3) as "organized and operated exclusively for religious, charitable, scientific, testing for public safety, literary, or educational purposes."[3] The shorthand "charitable" or "charity" is used for these groups, even though it is only one of several adjectives used in §501(c)(3), partly because "charitable" is the residual category used to classify these groups when they do not fit under any of the other adjectives, and partly because the Supreme Court has held that all §501(c)(3) groups must conform to certain fundamental common-law charitable criteria. (*Bob Jones University v. United States,* 461 U.S. 574 [1983]). In that case, "charity" as used in §501(c)(3) or in the legal argot, it may be noted, does not correspond with the usages of yesteryear, when the word had a meaning largely confined to aid for the poor and the sick (Fremont-Smith 2004; J. Simon 2002).

(2) What we will refer to as "noncharitable nonprofits"—organizations listed in §§501(c)(4)–(25). Here we have social welfare organizations, social clubs, veterans' organizations, labor unions, burial societies, chambers of commerce, marketing cooperatives, and other associations that may roughly be described as carrying forward the private interests of the members.[4]

The distinctions between these two sets of exempt organizations have been expressed not only in the shorthand terms "charitable" and "noncharitable" but also (1) by describing the (c)(3)s as "public benefit" organizations and the other exempt groups as "mutual benefit" entities (Bittker and Rahdert 1976) or (2) by stating that the (c)(3)s tend, more than the other exempt groups, to provide "collective goods" (Weisbrod 1980), often referred to as "public goods"—goods and services whose benefits cannot be captured by any one individual to the exclusion of others.[5] Each of these generalizations is largely accurate, but none is error-free. Thus, many (c)(4) "social welfare" groups would easily meet a "charitable," "public benefit," or "public goods" test but fail to qualify for (c)(3) status for other reasons. And many (c)(3)s fail to meet lay understandings of "charity" (opera companies, for example, that charge $50 for the cheapest seats), act very much like "mutual benefit" organizations (the most exclusive prep schools, for example, or churches that conduct largely social "retreats"), or appear to produce few public goods (very expensive nursing homes, for example).

We find, within the charitable set, two major subsets that are distinctly—one might say dramatically—different legal species: the private foundations and the charities that are not private foundations. Among professionals in the nonprofit field, private foundations are often referred to as "foundations" and the nonfoundations as "public charities"—usages we will follow in this chapter. The foundations are further divided, as we shall see, into the "operating" and "nonoperating" categories.

Before proceeding with our account of these §501(c) sets and subsets, we must note that it is somewhat reductionist. There are several tax-exempt species that lie outside the §501(c) categories (e.g., pension funds, consumer and farmer cooperatives, and political organizations of various kinds). Moreover, each of the categories contains some outliers—organizations (e.g., churches) subject to rules that partly differ from the rules applicable to other entities in the same category. In addition, there are entities—community foundations—that resemble nonoperating foundations but are treated as public charities, and other entities—"exempt operating foundations"—that seem like operating foundations but are subject to different (and lighter) rules. Finally, the expression "federal tax treatment" masks the fact that there are four principal federal taxes—individual income tax, corporate income tax, estate tax, and gift tax—whose provisions relating to the nonprofit sector do not fully overlap.

Consequences of Charitable vs. Noncharitable Status

Focusing on the §501(c) categories, we first consider the consequences of charitable versus noncharitable status. The most celebrated result has to do with deductibility. While all §501(c) organizations are exempt from taxation on their income, there is a dramatic difference in their eligibility for contributions that are deductible by the donors. Contributions of cash or property (but not services) to §501(c)(3) charities generally are deductible by individuals and corporations for income tax purposes (§170) and are also deductible for estate and gift tax purposes (§§2055, 2522). Gifts to noncharitable nonprofits generally are not deductible, except for contributions to veterans' groups, nonprofit cemetery companies, and fraternal benefit organizations that use the gifts for charitable purposes (§170(c)).

An organization's charitable-versus-noncharitable status also determines the regime of regulatory, equity, and border patrol rules to which the organization will be subject. In general, the noncharitable groups are not constrained by a number of the provisions that apply to charities. On the other hand, charities enjoy other benefits not available to the other nonprofits. Some relate to eligibility for various forms of favorable federal tax treatment other than exemption and deductibility. Thus, charities can create retirement plans and make payments into them that are tax-sheltered for the employees—without the elaborate and expensive apparatus of a "qualified pension plan" (§403(b)); charities have a greater capacity to derive capital from municipal bond financing (§145(a)(1)); and only charities are exempt from the Federal Unemployment Tax Act (§§3301–11) and the federal gambling tax (§4421(2)(b)).

Other favorable consequences of a group's charitable status relate to federal nontax provisions. Although preferential nonprofit postal rates are not expressly based on an organization's tax status, the postal regulations use criteria so similar to the tax exemption criteria (39 C.F.R. §111.1 [1990]) that one can safely say that these preferential rates are available to charities but not to the other nonprofits. In addition, the charitable groups—but not the other nonprofits—are exempt from involuntary bankruptcy proceedings (11 U.S.C. §303(a) [1988]), from buyer liability under the Robinson-Patman Act (15 U.S.C. §13c), and, for most purposes, from the securities regulation laws (15 U.S. §§77c(a)(4), 80a-3(c)(10) [1988]).[6]

Distinctions within the Charitable World

Starting in 1954, and more ambitiously in 1969, Congress made distinctions—created a class system, some would say (Bittker 1973)—within the §501(c)(3) charitable world. The charity world was first divided into two parts referred to earlier: the private foundations and the public charities. The private foundations were defined as constituting all groups that flunked certain tests set up by §509 of the tax code. To pass these tests, a group must be a school, a church, a hospital (or hospital-related research entity), a state college or university support entity, a group that meets one of two alternative (and fairly complicated) definitions of a "publicly supported" organization, or an entity that qualifies (under one of three alternative tests) as a "supporting organization" of a public charity. Organizations meeting these tests (and certain variations upon them) obtain public charity classification. This subdivision was meant to separate donor-controlled or otherwise "closely held" grant-making organizations (e.g., the Ford Foundation and lesser dispensers) from operating charities with relatively broad-based donor or beneficiary constituencies—and to accord preferred treatment to the latter group, the public charities. It was in the foundation camp that more fiscal abuses were thought to lie, more political activism, and more "unaccountable" wealth; in any event, it was thought that dollars given to grant-making foundations entered the stream of active charitable use more slowly than gifts to operating charities (J. Simon 2000).

In the midst of the 1969 congressional deliberations, however, it was discovered that the private foundation category, as pending legislation defined it, included all kinds of non–grant-making bodies that did not happen to be schools, churches, hospitals, or publicly supported organizations. Many research institutions, social action groups, museums, and other nonprofits would fall outside the public charity definitions. Congress could have moved them into public charity status, but instead it subdivided the foundation world into the operating foundations and the nonoperating foundations (the grant-making ones). Probably the most important legal feature of the operating foundation is that it spends 85 percent of its income on the active conduct of its charitable program, as opposed to grant making (§4942(j)(3) and related regulations).[7]

Foundations are charity's least-favored branch. Under each of the four functions of nonprofit tax law—support, equity, regulatory, and border patrol—the tax code (largely as a result of the Tax Reform Act of 1969) disadvantages private foundations as compared with other §501(c)(3) entities.[8] This difference in treatment under the code has been generally accepted by the foundation and legal communities. Over the years since 1969 there have been efforts, usually successful, to achieve congressional or administrative moderation of some features of the overall regime. Congress enacted partial—in some cases gossamer—reductions of the tax on investment income, of the payout requirements, of the excess business holdings deadlines, and of the self-dealing provisions (Edie 1987:43–64). And the IRS "provided a mild form of interpretive deregulation" of the antilobbying and jeopardizing investment rules (J. Simon 2000:69). But the basic framework remains intact and—although criticized by some academic commentators (J. Simon 2000)—has not been seriously questioned by the foundations or their legal or associational representatives.

THRESHOLD ISSUES

Two issues that haunt the discussion of all four of the functions covered in this chapter deserve to be identified at the outset. One is a jurisdictional puzzle—why is federal tax policy one of the tools chosen to accomplish support, regulatory, equity, and border-patrol objectives? What is the permissible and appropriate role of the federal tax system in the oversight of charity? The other is the continuing effort to deal with the distinction between public benefit and private benefit.

The Jurisdictional Puzzle

Historically, overseeing the functions of charity and enforcing the fiduciary obligations of those who control and manage charitable organizations have been the concerns of state attorneys general and state courts, successors to the English chancellors in equity who regulated the fiduciary conduct of private trustees. The federal tax system, in contrast, is designed primarily to raise revenue, not to regulate. Increasingly, however, taxation has been used as a major regulatory tool. This chapter illustrates, in one context after another, the prevalence of tax code–based oversight of the charitable sector. What are the source and the scope of the federal government's authority to use tax exemption law as a vehicle for regulating the behavior of American charities? Perhaps more difficult and ultimately more important, what is the appropriate—even optimal—use of the tax system as a tool for oversight of charities and, beyond policing, for the pursuit of non–tax-related social policies?

Congressional Authority

The source of Congress's power to act in this arena is Article I, Section 8, of the U.S. Constitution, which broadly empowers Congress to tax and to spend. A necessary concomitant to decisions about what and whom to tax is identification of entities not subject to taxation. Similarly, when Congress acts to spend public money, it must make choices about what to spend for.[9] Although the Constitution does not grant Congress broad "police power" to regulate in pursuit of the general welfare (this power is reserved to the states by the Tenth Amendment), Congress's authority to use the tax laws as a vehicle for regulation is almost certainly sufficiently far-reaching to support nearly any kind of regulatory overlay it might want to insert into the code.[10] Congress is constrained, however, by other constitutional provisions. Limitations linked to tax exemption, analyzed either as direct prohibitions or as potentially unconstitutional conditions imposed on the "subsidy" provided by exemption and deductibility, must not run afoul of, for example, the Fourteenth Amendment equal protection clause or the establishment, free exercise, or free speech clauses of the First Amendment.

Federal Role as a Matter of Policy

No matter how wide-reaching Congress's constitutional authority to provide support and to regulate through the tax code, the more difficult question—one deserving of far more scholarly work—asks how far Congress *ought* to go. What is the appropriate division of labor between the federal and state governments in supporting and regulating charities? Why should federal tax exemption be used to support activities that may have a decidedly local impact? Why should federal exemption be accompanied by regulation of an organization's structure and activities, or of the behavior of the people who run it?

Some have proposed more federal oversight in the form of expanded Internal Revenue Service attention. A 2004 Senate Finance Committee staff report suggested a variety of additional regulatory powers for the IRS, including, for example, the ability to oust misfeasant and nonfeasant nonprofit board members (U.S. Senate Finance Committee 2004). The argument for such increased federal power has often been that most states are notoriously lacking in the resources, staff, and, sometimes, zeal or interest to do the job well. Others have argued that the IRS is the appropriate locus of significant regulatory activity, because "the Code should promote the same policies as other laws" (Hatfield, Milgram, and Monticciolo 2000:6), or because conditions on tax exemption supply a way for government to avoid encouraging certain activities while stopping short of outright legal prohibition, thereby "preserving continuous and articulate debate about the content of the public good" (Galston 1984:309). Some arguments in favor of a strong federal, Internal Revenue Code–based role are distinctly pragmatic. Sugin (1999:473) has argued that Congress's broad spending and taxing authority is "one of the few vessels that can still be legitimately filled with federal policy." Swords (1997) has noted that despite significant defects in their accuracy and timeliness, the wide and easy availability of Form 990s through Internet posting makes tax exemption–related reporting an increasingly useful tool for direct public accountability for misdirection of charitable funds, although it is far less useful for calling attention to ineffective, though well-meaning, efforts at doing charity.

Other observers have been less enthusiastic about the prospect of an expanding federal role. The Internal Revenue Service is hampered by resource challenges not unlike those faced by state regulators (McGovern 1996). J. Simon (2000, 1995, 1973) has cautioned against easy acquiescence to broad federal intrusion into the traditionally state-based arena of charitable oversight, urging that "a decent respect for principles of federalism should make us wary of relying on the national tax system to perform tasks that might, with help, be handled by state authorities" (J. Simon 2000:75; see also Brody 1996, 1998b, 1999b; Kurtz 2004). Some observers have suggested a solution involving neither the IRS nor the states—assigning supervisory responsibility to a special (non-IRS) unit within the Treasury Department or creating a new, specialized federal agency for charitable supervision based somewhat on the British model (Ginsburg, Marks, and Wertheim 1977; Carson and Hodson 1973). Fleishman (1999) has proposed a variety of alternative regulatory models that involve collaboration and coordination among federal, state, and nongovernmental regulatory bodies. Fremont-Smith (1965) once suggested that the collaboration could take the form of federal subsidies for state enforcement programs that meet minimum uniform standards, although she no longer advocates this approach (Fremont-Smith 2004:xiii).

The Public Benefit–Private Benefit Distinction

Another threshold issue cutting across virtually every aspect of charitable tax exemption and deductibility is the distinction between public and private benefit, along with the related, although not identical, concept of the dividing line between public purpose and private purpose. Both of these distinctions are central to "charity" as a legal construct. The concepts are most clearly embodied in the "no private inurement" language of §501(c)(3) and in the regulations that require that a §501(c)(3) organization "[serve] a public rather than a private interest." (Treas. Reg. §1.501(c)(3)-1(d)(1)(ii)). But the distinctions permeate IRS interpretations and case law across the full spectrum of exemption issues, arising not only when the central question is one of private inurement or excess benefit, but also in questions about commercial activities, advocacy activities (Colvin 2000), private foundation regulation, and other matters.

Although being on the public side of the boundary between public and private benefit is a vital component of "charity," nowhere is the boundary clearly defined (Atkinson 1994:15-8). While there is no question but that a charitable organization may compensate (and thereby benefit) unconnected private individuals and noncharitable entities for providing goods and services that go into producing the organization's charitable output, the questions of whether there are outer limits to this kind of private benefit and, if so, how those limits should be defined, are relatively unexplored. Are there circumstances under which the magnitude of those expenditures ought to be regarded as putting the organization on the wrong side of the public-private boundary?

Apart from private gain issues, the question of which purposes are sufficiently in service of broad public benefit is also, at the margins, a difficult one and deserving of further scrutiny. Are causes that most of the public would agree are frivolous, fruitless, or even distasteful thereby inherently not in pursuit of the public interest and, therefore, not charitable? While charitable trust law has always drawn the line at futility (so that support of the Flat Earth Society, for example, would not likely qualify as a charitable purpose [Fishman and Schwarz 2000:105]), one very important characteristic of the universe of charitable organizations is that its institutions themselves are not, in fact, public but distinctly private. Thus, the process for determining the meaning of public benefit in this context, and the array of sometimes nonmainstream, even idiosyncratic, answers that result, are quite different from the generally majoritarian processes that define the public interest in the public arena.

THE SUPPORT FUNCTION OF CHARITABLE TAX LAW

The assistance provided by the federal tax system is widely perceived to be an important part of the explanation for America's robust nonprofit sector. The basic components of this federal support system are exemption from tax on the organization's income, deductibility of contributions from the donor's income tax, and deductibility of contributions for estate and gift tax purposes. How do these support mechanisms work in practice? What are the theoretical bases—the rationales—for these provisions? These questions—along with the policy issues that they generate—are canvassed in this section.

The Support Function in Practice

The United States has exempted the income of charitable organizations from federal taxation since the enactment of the federal income tax in 1913 (and even in a nineteenth-century precursor statute, the Revenue Act of 1884, ch. 39, 322, 28 Stat. 556), and it has allowed an income tax deduction to individual and corporate donors[11] to charitable organizations since 1917 (War Revenue Act, ch. 63, §1201(2), 40 Stat. 300, 330 [1917]). In outlining the support function in practice, we start with the legal framework, followed by some estimates of the impact of exemption and deductibility on the federal fisc (i.e., revenue losses) and on the charitable sector (i.e., revenue gains attributable to exemption and deductibility).

Legal Framework

Earlier in this chapter we described the basic elements of the legal framework: the exemption from federal income tax of income received by a §501(c)(3) or other exempt nonprofits, and the deductibility of gifts by individuals (for income, gift, and estate tax purposes) or corporations (for income tax purposes) to most but not all §501(c)(3) and a few non-§501(c)(3) organizations. These generalizations are subject to many additional qualifications, of which four major ones deserve mention here:

1. Under exemption, the unrelated business income received by a nonprofit is not spared from taxation under §§511 et seq.

2. Under deductibility, in the typical case—a donation of cash or property to a public charity—the donor may deduct the amount of cash or the fair market value of property donated. For income tax purposes, however, the amount of the deduction generally may not exceed (1) in the case of an indi-

vidual, 50 percent of the individual's "contribution base" (§170(b)(1)(A)),[12] or (2) in the case of a corporation, 10 percent of its taxable income (§170(b)(2)); no such cap applies to gift or estate tax deductions (§2055).[13] The fair-market-value deductibility of property gifts is itself highly controversial—condemned by most tax scholars and cherished by most recipients of appreciated property gifts; we return to it later in this section, in connection with theories of deductibility.

3. Under deductibility, no income tax charitable contributions deduction is allowed unless the charitable donee is organized within the United States.[14] This limitation (which does not apply to gift or estate tax deductions) is subject to two important qualifications. First, eligible U.S. charitable donees may use their funds abroad for charitable purposes. Second, a donor may donate to a U.S. charity that, in turn, donates to a foreign charity (Examples 4 and 5, Rev. Rul. 63–252, 1963–2 C.B. 101). However, the IRS has denied deductions in such a case if the intermediate U.S. charity is a mere conduit, that is, if "the domestic organization is only nominally the donee" but "the real donee is the ultimate foreign recipient" (Examples 1, 2, and 3, Rev. Rul. 63–252, 1963–2 C.B. 101). The deduction nevertheless may be allowed even if the intermediate U.S. donee gives funds only to a particular named foreign entity (Rev. Rul. 66–79, 1966–1 C.B. 48; cf. Rev. Rul. 74–229, 1974–1 C.B. 142); such U.S. intermediate entities are sometimes called "friends-of" organizations because they are frequently so named (see, e.g., Ballan 1994). Although the rationale for this water's-edge policy may be thought to reflect "policing" worries or the notion that U.S. taxpayers should not be subsidizing foreign charities, Congress has never provided a satisfactory explanation for a rule that, at least on gross examination, has an isolationist scent and that is, on the other hand, easily bypassed (Dale 1995:659–63; Blanchard 1993:726).

4. Under both exemption and deductibility, private foundations receive less support than the public charity §501(c)(3) groups. The 2 percent (under some circumstances 1 percent) excise tax on foundation investment income (§4940) represents a departure from the exemption enjoyed by other charities. And deductibility is more limited by reason of two rules: one denies market-value deduction for gifts (except pass-through gifts) of appreciated property to foundations, where that property is not publicly traded or represents more than 10 percent of the issuer's equity (§§170(e)(1)(B)(ii), 170(e)(5)); the other imposes a percentage-of-adjusted-income cap on deductibility of gifts to foundations that is lower than the cap on gifts to public charities (§170(b)(1)(B)). These support limitations are a subset of what some (e.g., Bittker 1973) refer to as the "second-class" status of foundations in the tax law of charity; other aspects are discussed below.

Impact of Exemption and Deductibility

The exemption of approximately $693 billion of revenue received by charitable organizations in 1998 (Independent Sector 2002:124) resulted in a tax revenue loss that is not easy to determine (J. Simon 1987) because of uncertainty about how much of the expenses of these organizations would have been offset against gross receipts for purposes of calculating the taxable income of a taxable business entity (Bittker and Rahdert 1976). However, Brody and Cordes (1999) have estimated that public charities enjoyed nearly $14 billion in income tax savings in 1996 because of exemption—an admittedly crude estimate of the federal revenue loss.

On the deductibility side, total charitable gifts in the United States were estimated to exceed $190 billion in 1999, of which nearly $144 billion came from living individuals, a further almost $16 billion represented testamentary gifts, nearly $20 billion was given by private foundations, and approximately $11 billion came from corporations (AAFRC Trust for Philanthropy 2000:18; see also Independent Sector 2002:52–89). The U.S. budget for fiscal year 2001 estimated the revenue loss occasioned by the §170 charitable deduction in 2001 to be $26.5 billion and the projected cost of the deduction over the 2001–2005 five-year period to be $145 billion (Colombo 2001:658).

How much of this revenue loss resulted in a gain to the charitable sector? With respect to exemption, we assume that the federal revenue loss was equal to the charities' gain. The case is more complicated when it comes to deductibility. There is uncertainty about how much the income tax deduction for charitable giving affects amounts given to charity.[15] Economists analyze this relationship in terms of "price elasticity," the extent to which a reduction in the "price" of giving—resulting, for example, from an increase in the tax rate against which a donor takes a charitable deduction—increases such giving. There is general agreement that the lower the price of giving, the more is given to charity, but quantifying this effect has proved to be extremely difficult.[16] Price elasticities may differ for large donors and small donors. Many analysts believe that the price elasticity is lower for lower-income donors, including the great majority of taxpayers who elect to use the standard deduction in lieu of itemizing deductions (Eaton 2001; Duquette 1999; Clotfelter and Steuerle 1981; but see Dunbar and Phillips 1997); indeed, donors using the standard deduction get no price reduction at all.

Brody and Cordes (1999) estimated the benefit that deductibility confers on charities. They started with an analysis of the impact of replacing the current income tax scheme with a flat tax, projecting that charitable contributions would decline by nearly one-third (Price Waterhouse 1997). Applying that estimate to Hodgkinson and Weitzman's (1996:146) data on 1996 private contributions to charitable organizations, Brody and Cordes estimated that the incentive provided by deductibility accounted for $37.7 billion of the total $117.9 billion in gifts to charitable organizations that year.

Turning from this brief survey of the support function in practice, we now ask: What is the rationale for this tax largesse, and what arguments surround it?

The Support Function in Theory: Search for a Rationale

A search for a rationale (or rationales) for exemption and deductibility can be descriptive—what evidence can be found of congressional intention?—or normative—what is the justification, in terms of tax theory or social policy, for exemption and deductibility? Such a justification or rationale would help us to understand why the law confers exemption and deductibility benefits on some entities and not others, why the tax system is the chosen vehicle for accomplishing the support function, why a deduction is available only for transfers to organized charity and not for transfers to needy individuals, and—assuming the support function is carried out through the tax code—why deduction, rather than exclusion or tax credit, is the appropriate mechanism. These and other issues discussed below cannot fully be addressed without investigating the underlying rationale—or, more accurately, the alternative rationales—for exemption and deductibility.

These explanations or rationales sort into two camps (Atkinson 1990, 1994). *Tax-base-defining rationales* assert that exemption and deductibility necessarily follow from a proper definition of income for tax purposes. *Subsidy rationales* assert that exemption and deductibility can be explained only as a decision to provide indirect public subsidy to favored organizations.[17]

The Tax-Base-Defining Rationales

Some tax scholars, while acknowledging that tax exemption and deductibility nourish nonprofit organizations, deny that support is the point of these provisions. They contend instead that an accurate and internally consistent definition of taxable income for federal purposes, or of taxable property for state purposes, explains exemption and deductibility; a support or subsidy rationale is neither needed nor accurate. In other words, if an item of revenue or property is not a proper part of the tax base in the first place, then the nontaxable treatment of that item should not be characterized or explained as a subsidy to the nonprofit sector.

The descriptive (i.e., historical) basis for the tax-base-defining rationales is not supported by any conclusive evidence, but there are several historical supports for a tax-base-defining theory underlying exemption. One basis for exemption of church property was that "it ceased to be under human control when it was devoted to God" (Stimpson 1934:416)—the property was no longer part of any human tax base. A statutory antecedent to the modern income tax, the Civil War income tax statute, specified the organizations subject to taxation without including charitable entities, thus implying that the income of charities was not thought to be part of the tax base. Rusk suggests that "exemption" language was included in the 1894 general income tax "just to be sure," and that therefore "the notion of exemption is something of an accident of legislative drafting convenience" (1961:10–11). And the draftsman of the 1913 Revenue Act "argued in Congress against an explicit expansion of its exemption clauses to embrace 'benevolent' and 'scientific' organizations, on the ground that the statutory reference to 'net income' automatically excluded all non-profit organizations" (Bittker and Rahdert 1976:303). We are aware of no comparable historical support for the tax-base-defining rationales when it comes to deductibility.

Turning to normative rationales, the progenitors of the tax-base-defining justification for exemption are Boris Bittker and George Rahdert. Writing in 1976, they argued that for charitable nonprofits, the exemption from federal income tax at the entity level arises from (1) the fact that the income tax focuses on business and other activities pursued for personal gain—an underlying objective that does not apply to charitable entities, and (2) the fact that we cannot properly calculate the tax that would be imposed on these organizations. With respect to the latter point, the tax system does not tell us which expenditures made by charities would be offsets to gross income, and we therefore cannot properly calculate taxable income. Moreover, our ignorance of the tax posture of the ultimate charitable beneficiaries makes it impossible to calculate the tax rate that ought to be imposed on the charitable entity that is supposed to be the surrogate for these beneficiaries. Thus, whatever rate we might apply would probably be too high, because the beneficiaries of charitable activities are likely to be in the lowest tax brackets.[18]

In the context of deductibility of contributions, the base-defining rationale is grounded on the widely accepted Haig-Simons definition of the proper tax base: income for any period is the sum of (1) amounts spent by the taxpayer on personal consumption during the period, and (2) the change in the taxpayer's net worth during the period (Simons 1938:50). Because amounts given to charity no longer appear in the taxpayer's net worth, the question becomes whether such giving should be viewed as personal consumption. William Andrews and Boris Bittker have argued that amounts expended for the benefit of those other than the taxpayer, his family, friends, or household personnel do not constitute consumption (Andrews 1972; Bittker 1972). If a charitable gift is not consumption, deductibility is an appropriate method for defining net income subject to tax and should not be viewed as a subsidy (Andrews 1972; Gergen 1988; Weidenbeck 1985).

J. Simon (1987:74) has offered a comparable tax-base-defining rationale for the estate tax deduction:

> Just as income is based on consumption and accumulation and the [income-defining] rationale asserts that this consumption is the private consumption of non-"public" . . . goods and services, we can perhaps say that the definition of personal wealth for estate tax purposes should refer to those assets available for the private accumulation or consumption of non-"public" goods and services. A testamentary charitable contribution reduces the amount of assets available for such private consumption and accumulation;

hence, under this analysis, it is logical to exclude these contributions from the definition of wealth for purposes of the estate tax.[19]

The tax-base-defining rationales have not been widely embraced (see, e.g., Surrey 1973). Some aspects of these rationales appear to be inconsistent with long-standing tax doctrines. For example, the concept that federal income tax and estate tax exemptions are tax-base-defining rather than subsidies depends in part on viewing "charitable organizations as conduit-type entities, a perspective which requires us to look at the beneficiaries of the nonprofit organizations—and their ability to pay" (Yale University Program on Non-Profit Organizations 1982:6). Standard tax doctrine, however, resists the conduit characterization of a corporation (Bittker and Lokken 1999:2–23).[20]

More generally, Hansmann (1981) has argued that taxing the income of charitable organizations would be neither technically incompatible with basic precepts of tax law nor regressive in impact. For example, contributions to a charitable organization could be treated as income and the cost of performing its charitable functions as deductible business expenses. Atkinson (1990, 1994) and Shaviro (1997) generally agree. Shaviro notes that "taxing the organization, net of its expenses, could be thought a reasonable proxy for taxing its beneficiaries directly, despite the conceded impossibility . . . of taxing them at the right rate" and that "the difficulty of picking the precisely correct proxy tax rate hardly necessitates choosing a rate of zero" (1997:1005 and n23).

Likewise, the income- and estate-defining theories of deductibility "bump into a countervailing theme in tax law: the ability to control the disposition of assets has often seemed to be a touchstone of taxability. . . . When one makes a gift to charity, this very act controls the disposition of assets—a fact that may therefore seem inconsistent with the notion that these same gifts reduce the . . . taxpayer's income or estate" (J. Simon 1987:75; see also Colombo 2001). It may also be argued that the no-consumption theme is undermined by the fact that no deduction is allowed for gifts to individuals, as compared to organizations, outside of the family or household. It is hard to see why a gift to a stranger, poor or rich, is consumption, whereas a gift to a charity is not.[21]

Even if the base-defining rationale is accepted, allowing a deduction for the appreciation in value of property donated to charity—without including that increase in the income of the donor—cannot be so justified.[22] To that extent, it must be supported, if at all, on the grounds that it is an incentive or subsidy for giving. If it were thought desirable to preserve the deduction generally but to eliminate the harder-to-justify deduction for appreciation in value of property donated, three routes to achieve this result could be followed: (1) the deduction could be limited to the adjusted basis of the property donated, that is, the deduction for the unrealized appreciation in value could be denied; (2) the deduction could be allowed for the full fair market value of the property donated, but the gain inherent in the property could be included in the donor's income at the time of the gift; or (3) a deduction could be permitted for the full fair market value of the property donated, but the charitable donee could be required to pay tax on the unrealized appreciation in value at any later time when it sells or disposes of the property.

The first route would resemble some provisions already in the code for certain types of charitable gifts;[23] the second and third would be novel in that context.[24] The second approach would require donors to pay tax even though they do not receive any cash or property in exchange for the donated property. The third route would not only defer, perhaps indefinitely, the imposition of any tax on the unrealized appreciation in value, but also would subject it to tax, upon later disposition of the property, at the tax rates of the donee rather than those of the donor. Consideration might be given to making the first route the default rule, but allowing donors to elect to apply the second or (with the consent of the donee) the third route in lieu of the first.

Subsidy Theories

Competing with the tax-base-defining rationale is the view that exemption and deductibility represent a decision to provide indirect public subsidy to the organizations that benefit from them. A good deal of descriptive (historical) evidence supports the subsidy account. The charitable exemption has been defended in Congress as providing support to charities because of what they offer to the larger community: public benefit or reduction of government burden (Diamond 1991). Deductibility, when first enacted in 1917, was explained in subsidy terms. Senator Henry Hollis, one of the authors of the charitable deduction provision, contended that the imposition of heavy World War I taxes would hurt charitable institutions by tempting "wealthy men . . . to economize. . . . They will say, 'Charity begins at home'" (Commission on Private Philanthropy and Public Needs 1975:106).

The most traditional of the normative arguments for a subsidy theory holds that exemption and deductibility are needed to promote the provision of certain kinds of benefits to the public. Public subsidy is warranted when normal market operations result in a less than socially optimal supply of a good or service that yields external benefits to the larger society. This typically occurs when the good or service is, in whole or part, what economists call a "public good," the benefits of which cannot be captured by any one user to the exclusion of others (Weisbrod 1998; Steinberg, this volume), or when a significant redistributive function is involved (Atkinson 1994).

Traditional subsidy theory also recognizes secondary benefits—such as innovation, experimentation, efficiency, and initiative—that are said to arise from the very fact that goods and services are provided by organizations that are not constrained by the usual market forces or electoral accountability (Simon 1987; Sacks 1960). The virtue of the nonprofit sector that is perhaps most often put forth as a secondary benefit worthy of support is pluralism (Douglas 1983:157; Hopkins 2003:11–19; Belknap 1977; Fremont-Smith 1965; Jenkins, this volume). A system that provides for diverse, decentralized decision making about which visions of public benefit merit support is well suited to a heterogeneous society, where many citizens prefer a supply of public goods—like culture, health, welfare, and protection of civil rights and the environment—that exceeds what majoritarian political processes will provide (Weisbrod 1975).

The charitable deduction is further explained in subsidy theory as a reward to individuals who choose to support socially valued undertakings (Bittker 1972) or as a correction for the free-rider problem that inheres in provision of public goods and services (Gergen 1988). Individuals who choose to finance those endeavors are assisted by the subsidy, and nonsupportive individuals are indirectly charged for their free ride by bearing a somewhat higher level of taxation. McConnell (1976) views the deduction as an "alternative tax": although a traditional tax is forgiven as a result of the charitable deduction, the taxpayer's gift resembles an alternative tax because it supports a chosen public interest activity in place of activities selected by the central government. Levmore (1998) offers a related view: that the deduction is a mechanism by which taxpayers "vote" for government subsidy to be directed to particular organizations and functions.

Critics of traditional subsidy theory find the rationale lacking a reliable limiting principle. Some have looked to economics to supply a principle for sorting that which merits subsidy from that which does not. Hansmann (1981) focused on the inefficiency that arises in the case of some nonprofits whose lack of access to equity capital renders them unable to expand rapidly to optimal size; tax exemption addresses this inefficiency. Hall and Colombo (1991) agree with Hansmann that the appropriate goal of the exemption subsidy is to correct market inefficiency; they find that this inefficiency exists when goods and services are donatively financed (consumed by individuals other than those who are paying for them). Donative financing is plagued by free riding, because an individual's desire for redistribution can be satisfied by others' contributions as well as his own. The consequence is a chronic undersupply of donatively financed goods and services. Hall and Colombo propose that tax exemption ought to be reserved for the correction of this market inefficiency and not extended to organizations that sell goods and services to their patrons (see also Bennett and Rudney 1987:1097–98). Finally, why structure the subsidies as supply-side mechanisms, rather than demand-side assistance?[25] Brannon and Strnad (1977) argue for a voucher system that permits consumers to take advantage of government subsidies, in order to avoid the donative misallocations resulting from high-powered fund-raising. On the other hand, Crimm (1998) suggests that exemption provides a government-financed "risk premium" as compensation to nonprofit firms for engaging in projects—the provision of public goods—that virtually guarantee lack of economic return. Atkinson (1990, 1994, 1997) proposes that the element of altruism is the secondary benefit that warrants the subsidy of tax exemption, and finds that element present "whenever an organization with the potential to return profit to its founders is set up on a nonprofit basis" (1994:15–17).

Implications of the Theories

Whether exemption and deductibility are subsidies or whether they are functions of an accurately defined tax base, Congress surely must specify which entities are taxed and which are not. Under the subsidy view, the definitional provisions express what Congress has chosen to "spend" for; under the tax-base-defining approach, the definitional provisions describe entities or revenues that lie outside the congressionally designed tax framework. In either case, it is often difficult to distinguish where definition ends and regulation in pursuit of other socially desirable goals begins. Within a tax-base-defining construct, the process of identifying the ideal tax base is neither easy nor value-neutral.[26] But once the definitional line is set, additional features of the tax exemption law are properly characterized as regulatory overlays—and must be based not on fidelity to the definitions but on some other justification for federal intervention. Under subsidy theory, the line between definition and regulation becomes even more difficult. Accordingly, under both sets of rationales the exemption and deductibility provisions inevitably enter upon regulatory terrain. As a result, we are brought back to the jurisdictional puzzle.

Policy Issues

Our understanding of the rationale underlying exemption tends to shape the mindset we bring to the formulation of policy with regard to exempt organizations. The increasingly casual assertion, as though indisputable, that exemption and deductibility are properly characterized as "subsidies" or "tax expenditures" makes it easy to assume that the fact of tax exemption, particularly under §501(c)(3), justifies federal regulation of almost any kind. Characterizing exemption and deductibility as subsidies, even if the characterization is correct, invites (although it does not command) a somewhat cavalier approach to policy formulation. It is less convenient to justify a federal regulatory role under a tax-base-defining role when it comes, for example, to lobbying restrictions or, for that matter, to other federal constraints, such as the percentage-of-income limits on deductibility by individuals and corporations (§170(b)).[27] The question takes on increased intensity when it comes to the federal regulation imposed on foundations—for example, the assertion of control over the fiduciary conduct of their managers relating to self-dealing, investment prudence, or corporate control.

Constitutional Issues

The divide between the subsidy and tax-base-defining rationales affects the analysis of federal tax power not only from a policy perspective but also as a constitutional matter. If exemption and deductibility are functions of a properly defined tax base, then government is, in theory, not using its spending power to subsidize such exempt-organization activity as religious activity or race- or gender-based discrimination. At the same time, any exemption-related constraints that are *not* necessary to arrive at an accurate measure of the tax base are subject to the same constitutional standards as any direct regulation or prohibition. On the other hand, if exemption and deductibility are "subsidies," then the exemption of religious organizations raises an obvious problem: how can government spend in support of religion? In light of recent equal protection cases (for example, *United States v. Virginia,* 518 U.S. 515 [1996], and *Gratz v. Bollinger,* 539 U.S. 244 [2003]), might Congress and the IRS be constitutionally bound to deny exemption to organizations and programs that promote affirmative action or single-sex education? And, if "subsidies" are involved, then limitations on those subsidies—constraints on exempt organizations' behavior, such as those that limit political advocacy—must be analyzed under the doctrine of unconstitutional conditions.[28]

Unconstitutional Conditions

Because of tax exemption and deductibility, nonprofit organizations generally and charities in particular will always be especially vulnerable to government restrictions or conditions imposed on their very status. The direct government funding received by many organizations in the form of grants or other program support also invites restrictions on how the recipient entities conduct their activities and implicates the doctrine of unconstitutional conditions.[29]

It is generally permissible for government either to fund or to decline to fund an activity. It is also generally permissible for government to impose conditions on its funding of an activity it chooses to support. It is, nevertheless, not permissible for government to impose a condition on its funding if the condition violates the constitutional rights of the recipient of the funds.[30]

Various attempts have been made by courts and commentators to explain when and why some, but not all, governmental conditions on funding will be invalidated as unconstitutional. The attempted line drawing has not been successful in providing sufficient clarity to enable accurate predictions of how courts will act in future cases. Bearing in mind, then, that this area is in need of—and no doubt will receive—further judicial and scholarly attention, some of the articulated factors or distinctions are:

- *Government versus private speech:* The Supreme Court has said that the government may constitutionally place conditions on the use of funds it provides to private recipients for the purpose of disseminating the *government's* message, but is more constrained in restricting the speech of recipients of government funding intended to support the recipient's *own* speech. On this basis, the Court has upheld rules preventing abortion counseling by recipients of government funding for the provision of medical advice on family planning (*Rust v. Sullivan,* 500 U.S. 173 [1991]),[31] while invalidating rules prohibiting government-funded Legal Services attorneys from challenging welfare legislation (*Legal Services Corp. v. Velazquez,* 531 U.S. 533 [2001]). The former were deemed to be consistent with stating the government's own message, whereas the latter were viewed as interfering with the private speech of attorneys.[32]
- *Scope and coerciveness:* If the proffered government benefit is relatively modest in scope (e.g., it will affect or be accepted only by a small subset of relevant organizations), governmental conditions on the benefit may be viewed as less coercive than if the benefit is widely distributed and is viewed as of great importance by most of the affected organizations.[33]
- *Alternative channel:* If the organization subject to governmental restrictions can avoid those restrictions through the use of an alternative, readily available structure (e.g., a legally separate organization under common control), the restrictions may be more likely to be upheld. *Regan v. Taxation with Representation of Washington* (461 U.S. 540 [1983]), discussed in the "Government Border" section of this chapter, is the classic citation for this point.[34]
- *Content versus viewpoint neutrality:* Restrictions on discussing a particular subject matter are more likely to be sustained than restrictions on presenting a particular viewpoint (*Rust v. Sullivan,* 500 U.S. 173, 193 [1991]).

Because governmental conditions on benefits may reach further than direct government proscriptions, and because any level of government—federal, state, or local—may impose them, the much-needed further clarification of the parameters of the unconstitutional conditions doctrine is likely to require years if not decades of additional litigation and scholarship.

THE EQUITY FUNCTION OF CHARITABLE TAX LAW

Service to a wide spectrum of the public—including, and maybe especially, its least advantaged members—is a venerable and transcendent theme in the history of charity. It has roots in ancient Egypt (Gladstone 1982), in the Old and New Testaments (Isa. 61:1; Luke 4:17), and in the 1601 English statute that still dominates Anglo-American charity law (Statute of Charitable Uses, 43 Eliz. I ch. 4 [1601];[35] Gladstone 1982:56–57). It has long been urged that the tax treatment of nonprofits should reinforce this notion of "equity" (as the word is often used in this context), or at least not undermine it. These equity claims, however, sometimes seem to contravene other values that charity seeks to serve—such as the encouragement, in the name of pluralism, of new cultural traditions and the preservation of old ones—interests that may not have high priority for many disadvantaged citizens.

The equity imperative raises three broad categories of policy questions:

1. How much should nonprofit tax policy insist on service to the poor, or, more generally, how much must it incorporate a redistributional ethic? (Redistribution, of course, need not benefit only the poor; it takes place when a middle-class music lover visits the Metropolitan Opera.)

2. Does the allocative power enjoyed by donors as a result of tax policy—the power to direct the flow of charitable dollars—conform to taxation principles of vertical and horizontal equity?

3. To what extent is discrimination or preference based on the race, gender, religion, or ethnicity of the beneficiaries acceptable as a matter of tax exemption policy?

The Redistributional Issue

The redistributional question arises at two levels. At the entity level, the puzzle is whether and how exemption or other beneficial treatment in the tax law should be conditioned on redistribution (particularly, redistribution to the poor). At the individual taxpayer level, the challenge is to specify when an individual's gift to a charitable organization is sufficiently dedicated to the benefit of others instead of self to qualify as a deductible charitable gift.

Redistribution as a Requirement for Exemption

Those who seek an explicit link between the legal criteria for tax-blessed charitable activity and assistance to the poor will only occasionally be able to find it. From time to time, proposals are made to limit the charitable exemption to organizations that directly serve the least advantaged, or at least to reward such organizations with tax benefits beyond those enjoyed by other §501(c)(3) organizations. For example, Halstead and Lind (2001) have proposed "distinguishing between two types of tax-exempt organizations: the minority (like the Salvation Army or a church soup kitchen), which are entirely dedicated to providing direct care to the neediest, and the majority (like most religious institutions, universities, membership organizations, or the opera), which do serve the public interest but not as directly" and favoring the former with deductibility for the donor at 150 percent of the amount of the contribution. However, neither American nor British legislative bodies have adopted the premise that redistribution is a sine qua non of charitable exemption. Historically, the delivery of certain kinds of goods and services—for example, education, religion, and the arts—to anyone has been presumed to be good for the public in general and therefore "charitable," even absent any redistributive component (Atkinson 1990, 1994).

Thus, educational institutions need not meet any redistribution test under federal law or under many state property tax laws (J. Simon 2002). And cultural institutions (so long as they aim to make artistic works widely available and avoid "commercial" modes of operation) qualify for §501(c)(3) status without redistributive objection from the IRS (based, for example, on ticket pricing); nor has this issue attracted significant interest in legislative, judicial, or academic forums considering federal tax issues.[36]

On the other hand, the IRS has sometimes required some service to the poor as a condition of exemption for less traditionally charitable organizations whose activities resemble those often conducted by for-profit firms. For example, providing affordable housing primarily for low-income individuals is charitable, but housing aid to moderate-income individuals generally is not (Hopkins 2003:139), and the IRS has conditioned §501(c)(3) exemption for Internet service providers on providing below-cost service to low-income individuals and charitable organizations (Tech. Adv. Mem. 200203069 [11 June 2001]).

Most of the discussion about whether redistribution ought to be central to exemption has taken place within the context of health care. Treasury regulations once required that hospitals offer free or reduced-cost services, within the limits of financial feasibility, in order to enjoy §501(c)(3) status, but the IRS relaxed this rule in 1969. The IRS recognized in Revenue Ruling 69–545 (1969–2 C.B. 117) that hospitals may provide exemption-worthy "community benefit" in ways other than delivering uncompensated care, and that evidence of such community benefit could be found in an open medical staff, a community-based board, an emergency room open to all regardless of ability to pay, and acceptance of Medicare and Medicaid patients.[37]

This shift in standards has not been without controversy. The early 1990s saw serious efforts in Congress to impose a charity care requirement for hospital exemption (Rubenstein 1997:399–403; Flynn 1992; Hall and Colombo 1991; Seay 1992). Several writers, however, have taken issue with this initiative. Rubenstein (1997:420) asserts that such a move would lead ultimately to less charity care overall, and Flynn (1992) states that it would impose relatively uniform standards on very different kinds of hospitals. Several writers agree that something more than nonprofit structure ought to be required for hospital tax exemption, but they have different ideas about what that something might be: donative financing (Hall and Colombo 1991), a governance process aimed at assessing community needs (Seay 1992), far-reaching research (Rubenstein 1997), or "enhanced access" (Colombo 2005).

The relief-of-poverty aspect of qualification for §501(c)(3) exemption is not entirely gone from the broader health-care context (Colombo 2004). For example, the IRS has begun to insist on provision of indigent charity care as a requisite to exemption for health-care joint ventures (Louthian 2001). Nursing homes seeking exemption must provide services "at the lowest feasible cost" and retain residents who, after being admitted, thereafter "become unable to pay their regular charges" (Hopkins 2003:151). In addition, the IRS has attempted to extrapolate the community benefit criteria of Revenue Ruling 69–545 from hospitals to other health-care entities such as health maintenance organizations, nursing homes, pharmacies, physician practice plans for medical school faculty, and sophisticated integrated delivery systems (an effort described and criticized by Colombo 1994 and Mancino 2005).

The relationship of redistribution to exemption was

brought into sharp focus by disaster relief efforts following the 1995 bombing of the Oklahoma City federal building and, most dramatically, by the events of September 11, 2001. Faced with the almost immediate contribution of more than $1 billion to charities after the unprecedented disaster of September 11, the IRS had to address quickly the questions of what kind of aid to whom by whom constitutes "charity" for purposes of §501(c)(3). In a publication issued shortly after the disaster, the IRS stated that some kinds of services may be provided regardless of financial need because the recipients are "distressed" irrespective of financial condition, but it also took the position that, for cash aid, organizations were bound to make some assessment of financial need—"charitable funds cannot be distributed to individuals merely because they are victims of a disaster" (Internal Revenue Service 2002:7). Congress followed with the Victims of Terrorism Tax Relief Act of 2001 (Pub. L. No. 107–134, 115 Stat. 2427), which provided that payments made by an organization as a result of September 11 would be treated as related to the exempt purposes of the organization "if such payments are made in good faith using a reasonable and objective formula which is consistently applied." Victims and their families are deemed to be a charitable class without taking account of financial need, so long as aid distribution formulas are not designed to favor those who are financially better off. Korman (2002) proposes that this solution be extended to disaster relief more generally, in order to permit charities to respond promptly and effectively.[38] In fact, the IRS and Congress have followed this approach in the wake of the Indian Ocean tsunami in December 2004 and Hurricane Katrina in August 2005, albeit on an after-the-fact, case-specific basis.

It is little wonder that taxing authorities and courts have not consistently required that claimants of charitable tax status demonstrate service to the poor (Persons, Osborn, and Feldman 1977). If such a requirement were proposed for application across the spectrum of §501(c)(3) organizations, it would surely be met with the objection that modern-day charity and modern-day charitable tax law serve other important values. Weighing this objection would take us back to basics—to the search for a rationale for exemption or deductibility, or indeed to even more fundamental issues relating to the primacy of redistributional norms in American law.

Redistribution as a Requirement for Deductibility of Charitable Gifts

Another aspect of redistribution (although here we use the word in a less conventional sense) embodied in tax law turns on the requirement that, in order to be deductible as a charitable contribution, a transfer from taxpayer to charity must not be a quid-pro-quo transaction. Thus, a charitable contributions deduction is allowed for payments when goods or services are received in exchange only to the extent that the payments to the charity are intended to, and in fact do, exceed the fair market value of any goods or services received in exchange by the donor (Treas. Reg. §1.170A-1(h)(1); Kahn and Kahn 2003:512, 525). For these purposes, the value of certain small items provided to the donor may be ignored (Treas. Reg. §1.170A-13(f)(8)(i), intangible religious benefits are not taken into account (§6115(b)),[39] and recognition, praise, and even naming opportunities are disregarded (Rev. Rul. 68–432, 1968–2 C.B. 104; Rev. Rul. 73–407, 1973–2 C.B. 383; Rev. Rul. 77–367, 1977–2 C.B. 193), even though these return benefits might be thought to be inconsistent with concepts of charitable selflessness.

Perhaps the most important controversy about charitable contributions and quid-pro-quo amounts involved the Church of Scientology, which provides its donors, in exchange for their donations, "auditing," "training," and "processing" courses and other services. The IRS ruled in 1978 that no deduction was available in these circumstances (Rev. Rul. 78–189, 1978–1 C.B. 68); after lengthy litigation, the IRS's position denying deductions to some Scientology donors was sustained by the Supreme Court (*Hernandez v. Commissioner,* 490 U.S. 680 [1989]). For reasons not yet revealed, however, in 1993 the IRS issued a ruling that set aside the 1978 ruling that had started the entire process (Rev. Rul. 93–73, 1993–2 C.B. 75). On 31 December 1997 the alleged text of the 1 October 1993 closing agreement between the Scientology organizations and the IRS was made public.[40] The lengthy (over fifty-page) agreement imposes strict restraints on the governance and operations of the Scientology organizations, but nothing in the closing agreement explains the IRS's change of stance vis-à-vis the deductibility of gifts to the church in exchange for auditing, training, and processing courses and other services. How much and what kind of private benefit defeats a charitable deduction, therefore, remains a not fully answered question, nor has it received full scholarly scrutiny.[41] Litigation on these issues continues (see, e.g., *Sklar v. Commissioner,* 282 F.3d 610 [9th Cir. 2002], discussed in Samansky 2004 and Hildenbrand 2002).

Allocative Power Issues

Here we examine two sets of assertions: (1) that the deductibility system itself violates equity principles by giving private persons, rather than majoritarian processes, the power to allocate public funds; and (2) that the current structure of deductibility of charitable contributions violates "vertical equity" by favoring the wealthy and violates "horizontal equity" by favoring itemizers over nonitemizers and some itemizers over other itemizers.

The Charitable Deduction Itself

If exemption and deductibility do function as subsidies, then "while the assistance to philanthropy comes from the federal government, its allocation is privately directed—the government funds are paid to particular institutions at the direction of private persons. Moreover, the assistance is blanket, automatic, no-strings-attached, open-ended aid" (Surrey 1970:385). Much of what the sector provides (religion aside) is a supplement to or substitute for what government might otherwise provide. It can be argued, then, that the capacity of donors to decide how the lost tax revenues will be spent, "without regard to the will of the majority as manifested through Congress," is, in effect, privatization of government power (Galston 1993:1315; Kelman 1979; Gergen 1988).[42] Yet it is plausible to contend that what some perceive as the evil of privatization is the necessary corollary of a decision to leave some judgment about what constitutes the public interest to a robust, independent, and pluralistic charitable sector instead of committing all such determinations to the majoritarian processes of government (J. Simon 2000:73). In the words of Justice Powell, concurring in *Bob Jones University v. United States* (461 U.S. 574, 609 [1983]), "the provision of tax exemptions to nonprofit groups is one indispensable means of limiting the influence of government orthodoxy in important areas of community life."

The objection to privatized power, however, is heightened by the role of wealth in this process, for persons of substantial wealth account for a disproportionate share of all charitable gifts, and an even more disproportionate share of charitable bequests (Auten, Clotfelter, and Schmalbeck 2000:393). This aspect of the allocative power issue is highlighted in the case of private foundations, often closely controlled or at least influenced, dynastically, by wealthy creators (J. Simon 1978). Concern about these foundations—said to be unaccountable "shadow governments" (Hart 1973)—was clearly on the minds of the several congressional committees that appraised foundations in the years leading to the 1969 enactment of the private foundation rules (J. Simon 2000:72; Fishman and Schwarz 2000:612–17).[43] Yet the fact that affluent persons, acting with or without a foundation, have outsized influence is only one illustration of the wealth-power relationship in public and private life—not a phenomenon that can be ended or seriously curtailed by abolishing the charitable tax deduction. Nevertheless, the role of wealth in the philanthropic arena is probably exacerbated by the structure of the charitable contribution deduction.

The Structure of the Charitable Deduction

Vertical Equity

Some critics of the present system, viewing the deduction as a government matching program, note that the government offers a higher match to wealthier, higher-income taxpayers than to lower-income, lower-bracket taxpayers (McDaniel 1972). For example, if a donor who itemizes deductions and whose top marginal tax bracket is 35 percent makes a $100 gift to charity and deducts that amount from his income, the net cost or "price" of the gift is $65.[44] The government, from this viewpoint, is making a $35 matching grant to the charity chosen by the donor. The same gift's cost to a lower-income taxpayer whose top marginal tax bracket is 15 percent is $85, and the government's share is just $15. The late Stanley Surrey (1973:229–30) attacked this process as one that subsidized the wealthy in a "bizarre upside-down fashion" (see also McDaniel 1977; Good and Wildavsky 1977).

One answer to this challenge lies in the tax-base-defining rationales. As noted earlier, if these rationales are accepted, the notion of a subsidy drops out and so does the claim that the deduction subsidizes the rich. Even apart from the subsidy issue, these tax-base theories provide a possible rebuttal to the notion that the deduction reduces the "after-tax cost . . . for the rich" (J. Simon 1978:24). If the donated funds are viewed as never having been part of the contributor's income subject to taxation, then the after-tax cost is the same for rich and poor. However, J. Simon has suggested that this reasoning reflects an "excessively strenuous application" of the tax-base rationales (1978:24n42). Another perhaps more robust answer to the vertical equity or "regressivity" complaint is that it is simply an artifact of the fact that we have progressive income and estate tax systems: all deductions—and all items of income—are symmetrically treated, along the same rate structure; they are all ruled by the same progressivity curve.[45]

If it were thought desirable to eliminate this regressivity, a credit could be provided in lieu of a deduction.[46] The amount of the credit could be calculated, at least approximately, so as to involve any chosen amount of revenue loss and to simulate an equivalent deduction at any selected target tax rate. While this would eliminate the regressivity (because the government's "matching grant" would then be the same at all income levels), it would not be possible to justify a credit of this sort under a tax-base-defining rationale.[47]

Horizontal Equity: Itemizers versus Nonitemizers

Another equity issue is generated by the unavailability of the income tax deduction to nonitemizers. Taxpayers may elect either to itemize their deductions or to take a standard deduction instead (§63(e)). Most—more than 70 percent—choose the standard deduction.[48] As a result, they cannot claim an itemized charitable contributions deduction, and they are entitled instead to the simpler, and at least sometimes more generous, standard deduction. Because the amount of the standard deduction does not vary with actual charitable donations, it provides no incentive to make charitable gifts, and it treats equally—without recognizing differences in sacrifice or generosity—those nonitemizers who donate to charity and those who do not. There is an unavoidable policy tension here between simplification of taxpayer compliance burdens, on the one hand, and a desire for improved incentives and horizontal equity among taxpayers, on the other.[49]

From 1982 to 1986 a nonitemizer charitable contributions deduction was allowed, phasing in during the earlier years until fully effective in 1986. It terminated after 1986 and later was completely repealed. Restoration of the nonitemizer charitable contributions deduction has since been a favorite goal of charitable organizations. Designing a sound nonitemizer deduction requires confronting and balancing inconsistent policies—a task thoughtfully addressed by Steuerle (2000a, 2000b, 2000c) and Aprill (2001).

Horizontal Equity: Itemizers versus Other Itemizers

Another concern has been raised about the §68 limitation on all itemized deductions, which exerts a special impact on charitable deductions. An individual's itemized income tax deductions, including those for charitable donations, must be reduced by the lesser of 3 percent of the excess of adjusted gross income over the "applicable amount," or 80 percent of itemized deductions (§68(a)). The "applicable amount," subject to inflation adjustments, was $137,300 for calendar year 2002 and $145,950 in 2005.

This provision is not evenhanded—taxpayers in different states or with different housing arrangements may be affected differently. That is because the affected itemized deductions, in addition to the charitable contributions deduction, include those for mortgage interest and for state and local taxes. Homeowners making payments on mortgages and persons living in states with income taxes often will incur such expenses in excess of the deduction limitation. Because such payments are not discretionary, the deduction limitation, from one point of view, will not adversely affect these taxpayers' charitable donations deduction. In contrast, people living in rented housing or in states with low or no income taxes may experience this deduction limitation primarily against their charitable gifts.[50]

The Discrimination or Preference Issue

The past half century has witnessed periodic and often heated debate in the discrimination-preference area, triggered—in the years following *Brown v. Board of Education*—by the controversy over IRS denial of tax-exempt status to "segregation academies" in the South and the congressional response thereto (Schwarz and Hutton 1984). The prolonged Bob Jones University litigation, which culminated with the Supreme Court's upholding the denial of exempt status on grounds of racial discrimination (*Bob Jones University v. United States,* 461 U.S. 574 [1983]), put a spotlight on this issue.

Early scholarly attention to tax exemption for racially discriminatory groups considered whether the "support" entailed in exemption and deductibility made the actions of an exempt §501(c)(3) organization "state action" for purposes of the equal protection and due process clauses of the U.S. Constitution. The Supreme Court found it unnecessary to address this question head-on in *Bob Jones,* employing instead a nonconstitutional approach based on §501(c)(3).[51] The Court reasoned that Congress intended to incorporate the common law concept of "charity" into §501(c)(3), that the common law concept of charity excludes purposes and activities that violate "fundamental" public policy, and that racial discrimination in education is clearly counter to strong public values and policies that had evolved in the twentieth century. Therefore, the Court concluded, Congress intended that the §501(c)(3) exemption not be available to schools, such as Bob Jones University, that discriminated on the basis of race.

The *Bob Jones* majority opinion was criticized on three grounds:

- It was considered by some critics to be an example of bad statutory interpretation technique. Justice Rehnquist, for example, argued in his dissent that although Congress certainly could, and probably should, condition exempt status on racial nondiscrimination, in §501(c)(3), as written, it has not.
- The Court rather open-endedly handed off to the IRS the authority to deny exemption on the basis of inconsistency with some "fundamental public policy" that could be discovered outside the duly enacted law of the land (Brennen 2000; Galvin and Devins 1983). Justice Powell expressed discomfort in his concurring opinion (461 U.S. at 611) with the idea that "the Internal Revenue Service is invested with authority to decide which public policies are sufficiently fundamental" to require denial of tax exemption.
- The Court further stated that groups with values "at odds with the common community conscience"—that are not "in harmony with the public interest"—fail to confer public benefit and are not, therefore, within the common law definition of charity or worthy of tax exemption (461 U.S. at 592). Justice Powell was particularly disturbed by this aspect of the majority opinion, noting that this "view . . . ignores the important role played by tax exemptions in encouraging diverse, indeed often sharply conflicting, activities and viewpoints" (609). Commentators writing when the case was fresh noted that the Court's expansive approach could invite IRS determinations that unpopular or unorthodox groups confer no public benefit or are not "in harmony with the public interest," and therefore are not worthy of the §501(c)(3) exemption (K. Simon 1981; Galston 1984).

Twenty years after the *Bob Jones* opinion, it seems clear that the IRS has taken to heart the Court's admonition that, despite its open-ended language, only the most clearly established public policies have a place in exemption determinations (Dale 1990b). The resulting dearth of IRS action in this field has left the bounds of the *Bob Jones* principle largely untested, although they have been explored in the abstract by some writers (e.g., Hatfield, Milgram, and Monticciolo 2000).

Some of the remaining questions—and a brief summary of the discourse to date—are these:

- Is the *Bob Jones* principle applicable outside the context of schools? The IRS has applied *Bob Jones* outside of education, ruling (Private Letter Ruling 8910001 [10 March 1989]) that a fund to aid "worthy and deserving white persons over the age of sixty years" was not charitable. The IRS has not, however, committed to any precedential form the view expressed in that ruling that the *Bob Jones* principle "extends . . . to any activity violating a clear public policy."

- Is *Bob Jones* applicable only to invidious discrimination affecting members of historically disadvantaged groups, or to *all* distinctions based on race? The IRS has only informally expressed the position that the racial discrimination that is inconsistent with §501(c)(3) is the invidious sort, and does not demand color blindness in all situations (Internal Revenue Service 1994; Gen. Couns. Mem. 37462 [17 March 1978]; Gen. Couns. Mem. 39082 [30 November 1983]). Commentators have noted the vulnerability of this position. Brennen has suggested that, given recent executive and judicial attitudes toward affirmative action—more recently exemplified in *Gratz v. Bollinger,* 539 U.S. 244 (2003)—it is entirely possible that the IRS could decide that an organization that uses race-conscious policies to ameliorate the effects of pervasive societal discrimination is not in harmony with established public policy (2001:191).
- Is the *Bob Jones* principle applicable to discrimination on grounds other than race? For example, might single-sex schools find their exemptions at risk (Sugin 1999:453–454; Zelinsky 1998:383–87; Brennen 2000)? Some writers support the IRS's inaction in the gender discrimination arena (Mawdsley 1994; Goldman 1976), others are critical (Hatfield, Milgram, and Monticciolo 2000:40; Hopkins 2003:1124–25; Bittker and Kaufman 1972). Chief Justice Rehnquist, dissenting in *United States v. Virginia,* 518 U.S. 515 (1996), in which the Court found Virginia's funding of the male-only Virginia Military Academy to violate the equal protection clause, noted that "it is certainly not beyond the Court that rendered today's decision to hold that a donation to single-sex colleges should be deemed contrary to public policy and therefore not deductible if the college discriminates on the basis of sex" (518 U.S. 515 at 598).
- What is the framework for identifying those public policies that are sufficiently established and sufficiently "fundamental"? For example, what happens when state and local policies outpace (or pull in a different direction from) federal policy—as in the Supreme Court ruling that the Boy Scouts of America's constitutional right to freedom of association precluded application of the New Jersey public accommodations statute's provision against discrimination on the basis of sexual orientation (*Boy Scouts of America v. Dale,* 530 U.S. 640 [2000]).
- More broadly, is the *Bob Jones* principle applicable to public policies other than discrimination? Brennen notes that a broad reading of the *Bob Jones* public policy test could be used to challenge the exemption of an organization operating a needle-exchange program (2001:784).

Concrete answers to these questions will likely be developed slowly, if at all, because the only way the limits will be tested is by IRS denials of exemption and organizations' challenges of those denials. Although the IRS has indicated that it stands ready to act on the basis of public policy, it has done so only in a limited way to date. When the IRS chooses *not* to deny exemption, those who believe the agency has been too generous nearly always lack standing to raise the issue for judicial resolution (Blasko, Crossley, and Lloyd 1993).

THE REGULATORY FUNCTION OF CHARITABLE TAX LAW

While many other sections of this chapter discuss the tax code regulation of charities, this section focuses on the oversight of the conduct of charitable fiduciaries—an aspect of regulation that commands a central and historic place in the law of charity. We start with a brief survey of fiduciary oversight through the tax system, followed by a closer look at a key aspect of that oversight—the policing of private benefit through three related but distinct avenues, followed by a look at the special fiduciary rules applicable to private foundations. The section closes with a note that deals not with fiduciary behavior, but with some other potential uses of the code to regulate charities.

Fiduciary Regulation in General

Traditionally and historically, fiduciary enforcement—that is, the regulation of the behavior of those who manage and control charitable organizations—has been assigned to state attorneys general and state courts (Fremont-Smith 2004; Brody, this volume; Crimm 2004). In modern times, however, the tax code has assumed a significant regulatory role. Brody (1998a) and Fremont-Smith (2004) provide an extensive catalog of code provisions that regulate the behavior of charitable fiduciaries.

These provisions perhaps can be categorized under the two main duties imposed on charitable fiduciaries under state law: the duty of loyalty and the duty of care. Thus the §501(c)(3) proscriptions against private inurement and against more-than-incidental private benefit and the §4958 rules imposing sanctions on "excess benefit" transactions parallel the state-based *duty of loyalty* rules that regulate and punish fiduciaries' self-dealing and diversion of a charity's financial assets to themselves. The loyalty principle also motivates the §4941 self-dealing provisions imposed on private foundations (reviewed later in this section), applying elaborate prophylactic rules and imposing stiff penalties for their breach; §4941 encompasses not only behavior that would breach state-based duty of loyalty standards but also much self-dealing that would pass muster under those standards.

With respect to the *duty of care,*[52] the most closely related tax code sanctions apply to private foundations and their managers, subjecting them to elaborate requirements and penalties that mirror various components of this duty. The §4944 rules dealing with investment prudence are the most notable of these; other foundation rules described below also overlap certain aspects of the duty of care. Public charities are less constrained by duty-of-care sanctions under the code. No overt parallel to the duty of care is built into §501(c)(3) itself, nor are there explicit reflections of this duty in other provisions applicable to public charities. From time to time the IRS has ventured into duty-of-care territory, albeit usually under some formulation more widely acknowledged to be a part of its assigned turf. Brody describes one of these forays—the IRS's insistence on resignation of the Bishop Estate's incumbent trustees, backed by threatened revocation of tax-exempt status—as a usurpation of state prerogative, unsupported by any evidence that Congress "has empowered the IRS to act as plenary regulator to fill any perceived supervisory vacuums left by the administration of state charity laws" (1999b:577). Another instance was the IRS's revocation of the United Cancer Council's exemption. While the issue was cast by the Tax Court as one of "private inurement," on appeal to the 7th Circuit, Judge Posner quite correctly characterized the issue as implicating a possible failure of duty of care. Judge Posner's instruction to the Tax Court to consider on remand the question, among others, of whether "tax law has a role to play in assuring the prudent management of charities" was never fulfilled, because the case was settled before the Tax Court took up the issue (*United Cancer Council, Inc. v. Commissioner,* 165 F.3d 1173, 1179 [7th Cir. 1999]). Although there is at least indirect evidence that Congress has consciously declined to build duty-of-care obligations into the tax code,[53] recent proposals by the staff of the U.S. Senate Finance Committee (2004) would explicitly assign the IRS a number of duty-of-care duties and powers (including the power to remove charitable trustees for certain breaches). The debate on these ideas has begun (see, e.g., Crimm 2005).

Policing Private Benefit: Three Avenues

Although the charitable tax exemption provisions deal in many ways with the distinction between public and private benefit, the attempt to limit private benefit—and to implement the duty of loyalty—is principally implemented through three distinct but closely related tax code approaches. All concern charities described in §501(c)(3), but two also affect other types of tax-exempt organizations.[54] Two are creatures of the statute;[55] the other is a child of the Treasury regulations.[56] Taken together, they police the quintessential characteristic of charities: that they operate for the public benefit and do not permit their assets or activities to profit persons other than their intended beneficiaries. The three doctrines are: (1) the proscription against inurement, (2) the proscription against more-than-incidental private benefit, and (3) the rules imposing excise taxes on excess-benefit transactions. As will be discussed below, the first and last prevent inappropriate benefits, no matter how minor, from going to persons in control of the exempt organization; the second applies if inappropriate benefits flow to any person, but only if those benefits are more than "incidental."

Inurement

The template for all the inurement provisions was designed in 1909. Section 38 of the 1909 legislation[57] imposed a "special excise tax" on corporations.[58] Several types of organization were excepted, including "any corporation or association organized and operated exclusively for religious, charitable, or educational purposes, *no part of the net income of which inures to the benefit of any private stockholder or individual*" (Pub. L. No. 61–5, §38, 36 Stat. 11, 115 [1909]) (emphasis added). Although the purpose of this language presumably was to differentiate between for-profit entities (taxed) and nonprofit entities (not taxed), the genesis of the specific phraseology is obscure. Furthermore, the words—if taken literally—would pose a number of significant puzzles and problems.[59] For example, it is perfectly clear that the inurement ban does not prohibit the conferring of *any* benefit on an insider: all authorities agree that "the inurement proscription does not prevent the payment of reasonable compensation for goods or services" (Gen. Couns. Mem. 39862 [21 November 1991]).

Given this opaque history, the anti-inurement language should be treated as evocative rather than precise. Reference should be to other sources—such as case law and IRS pronouncements—to determine the scope and content of the proscription. Although it is outside the scope of this chapter to analyze the precedents,[60] several observations are in order:

- The determination of what constitutes proscribed inurement is inherently fact specific.
- Despite a fairly large number of precedents, helpful guidance is scarce.[61]
- It is often easy to decide what is and what is not prohibited, even though it is daunting to try to describe the test.[62]
- The scope of the inurement proscription has been and will be significantly affected by the adoption of §4958, discussed below.

Private Benefit

The limitation on private benefit stems from the Treasury regulations rather than the code.[63] Precedent interprets them as creating a separate test—the more-than-incidental-private-benefit test—for tax-exempt charitable status.[64] Until the late 1980s, there was little guidance on the differences between the inurement and private-benefit doctrines; many earlier precedents are muddled on this point, and the lines drawn, if any, seem indistinct and confused. More recently, however, various IRS pronouncements and court cases have sharpened the edges of the distinctions between the two.

In 1991 the IRS (Gen. Couns. Mem. 39862 [21 November 1991]) helpfully set forth two distinctions: First, while the inurement proscription applies only to benefits received by "insiders," the private-benefit proscription applies to benefits received by anyone, including wholly disinterested persons.[65] Second, the receipt of *any* benefit by an "insider," no matter how trivial, is prohibited,[66] whereas purely "incidental" benefits received by others will not violate the private-benefit restriction.[67]

It is therefore critical to determine whether the benefited

person is an "insider." More than the mere receipt of even abundant benefits from a charity is required to characterize the recipient as an "insider," as the 7th Circuit Court of Appeals has held. In *United Cancer Council,*[68] the charity's outside fund-raiser received $26.5 million as compensation out of a gross amount of $28.8 million raised for the charity. The appellate court declined to accept the Tax Court's view that this situation constituted prohibited inurement, holding that the fund-raiser "did not, by reason of being able to drive a hard bargain, become an insider. . . ."[69] Perhaps the most useful statement of what should be the relevant "insider" test comes from the later-adopted excess-benefit provision—discussed below—which defines a "disqualified person" as "any person who was . . . in a position to exercise substantial influence over the affairs of the organization" (§4958(f)(1)(A). See generally Treas. Reg. §53.4958–3).

Excess Benefit Transactions

Prior to 1969, the only sanction for a tax-exempt organization's serious transgressions was termination of tax-exempt status. As early as 1965, one state bar association commented that an "all or nothing sanction" could lead to a "breakdown of enforcement" because the harshness of the remedy could deter the IRS from invoking it and the courts from decreeing it (Special Committee on Exempt Organizations 1965). The 1969 legislation affecting private foundations put in place, for the first time, a more measured regimen of sanctions: tiers of excise taxes to be imposed on various sorts of sins. It applied, however, only to private foundations, thus leaving other charitable organizations largely under the preexisting all-or-nothing system.[70]

Following 1993 congressional hearings about these concerns, and with the enthusiastic support of most major umbrella groups of nonprofit organizations, the tax code was amended by the enactment in 1996 of §4958, setting forth the so-called intermediate sanctions rules. These new rules represent the most significant legislative change in the federal regulation of charities in the last three decades.

The rules provide for significant penalty excise taxes to be imposed on any insider who receives an "excess benefit" from a public charity (or a §501(c)(4) social welfare organization)[71]—and on any "organization manager" who knowingly participates in the transaction. As noted above, an insider (a "disqualified person") is one who can "exercise substantial influence" over the organization. An "excess benefit" arises from any transaction in which the organization provides an economic benefit to an insider if the value of the benefit exceeds the value of the consideration received by the organization. There is a form of safe-harbor protection: a presumption of reasonableness—albeit subject to rebuttal—may cover a transaction if (1) it is approved by the board of directors or a committee, (2) the approving body is composed entirely of independent individuals, (3) the approval relied on "appropriate comparability data," and (4) the approval is "adequately documented" (Treas. Reg. §53.4958–6(a)).

Notably, the excess benefits statute imposes no excise tax on the organization itself. Thus, the intermediate-sanctions regime, unlike the anti-inurement doctrine, punishes the insiders and responsible managers rather than the charity.

Both the legislative history[72] and early court decisions (see *Caracci v. Commissioner,* 118 T.C. 379, 417–18 [2002]) confirm the view that §4958 should be interpreted so far as possible to be precisely congruent with the scope of the inurement proscription (to the extent that judicial or administrative rulings have given contours to that inscrutable language). Whenever prohibited inurement can occur without violating §4958, the only sanction continues to be revocation of tax-exempt status. It was exactly that undesirable situation that led to the enactment of intermediate sanctions.

At least two policy issues persist in the wake of the new excess benefits legislation. First, what kinds of comparability data can be used when assessing reasonable compensation? Can the compensation of a president of one of the largest foundations be set by reference to the president of one of the largest business corporations? These comparability issues require additional deliberation.[73] Second, to return to the jurisdictional puzzle discussed above, is the federal tax system the most appropriate body to regulate this aspect of the conduct of charitable fiduciaries?

Regulation of Private Foundations

When it comes to the regulation of fiduciary conduct, tax regulation bears more heavily on foundations than on public charities, in several ways:

1. The "self-dealing" rules (§4941) impose outright prohibitions on certain kinds of transactions between a foundation and its fiduciaries or donors, whether or not the transactions are unfair to the foundation—as compared with the standards applicable to public charities, where the test is fairness: would the transaction have resulted from arm's-length bargaining between strangers?

2. The "payout" rule (§4942), which requires annual distributions equaling 5 percent of investment assets, can affect fiduciary behavior by inducing foundation managers to make investment assets more productive of current income in order to reach the required distribution level. Public charities operate under no comparable strictures, although an excessively stingy payout policy might lead to attack under the "operated exclusively" clause.

3. The "jeopardizing investment" rule (§4944) regulates the investment practices of foundation managers. Even though the Treasury regulations call for a "whole portfolio" approach rather than scrutiny of each individual investment (Reg. §53.4944–1(a)(2)), the constraints on speculation or nondiversification appear to be greater than those applying to public charities under §501(c)(3)'s "operated exclusively for . . . charitable . . . purposes" clause (Bittker 1973).

4. The "excess business holding" rule (§4943), which effectively precludes foundation or joint foundation/donor control of a business corporation (briefly noted below), represents another

form of regulation not imposed on public charities. Some, but not all, of the objections to foundation/donor corporate control are framed in terms of breach of fiduciary duty.

The 1969 act policed other foundation practices not related to fiduciary duty. Two such provisions regulate a foundation's granting of travel-study funds to individuals and require a foundation to exercise "expenditure responsibility" over its grants to nonpublic charities (§§4945(d)(3), (4)(B)). The 1969 act also imposes an absolute prohibition on legislative lobbying by foundations (§4945(e)(1)) and considerable constraints on the ability of foundations to fund voter registration activity (§4945(f))—matters briefly covered below.

Not only does the 1969 law impose a more detailed and stringent set of substantive rules on foundations than on public charities; it sets up a more assiduous enforcement system. More detailed annual reporting is required of foundations. More important is the difference in sanctions. Public charities accused of fiduciary misconduct risk loss of exemption. Although draconian, this result does not derive from a deliberate congressional sanctioning decision but is the natural consequence of an IRS determination that the organization no longer meets the §501(c)(3) test of "operated exclusively for . . . charitable purposes." In order to avoid this all-or-nothing approach, discussed earlier in connection with intermediate-sanctions legislation, Congress in 1969 created a special set of sanctions: penalty taxes imposed on the foundations or on the managers or donors involved in the transaction.

The regulatory controls imposed on private foundations—and other foundation rules referred to elsewhere in this chapter—have led one of the present authors (Simon) to refer to private foundations as a "regulated industry" and to offer a number of criticisms of that regime (J. Simon 2000). He questioned the need for this regulatory apparatus; contended that this regulatory regime also failed to comply with certain "norms that characterize, or should characterize, the legislative process"; suggested that the result may have been a loss of resources for the charitable sector and, at least for a time and perhaps even presently—for the largest foundations—a declining foundation birth rate. Several of these criticisms have been rebutted (see, e.g., Troyer 2000), and as Simon conceded, all of them require more empirical investigation and policy analysis than has taken place—a fairly challenging research agenda. That agenda will become even more consequential if and when there is a renewal of earlier efforts to impose the foundation regulatory system on public charities (as discussed in Kurtz 2004).

Other Regulation of Charities through the Tax Code

From time to time, proposals are made to use the tax code to regulate other aspects of the management and governance of charities. These initiatives take us back to fundamental questions of the appropriate role for the federal tax system in governing the charitable sector. For example, are regulation of fund-raising practices, administrative costs, or board composition legitimate subjects of tax exemption–related rules? A similar question is prompted by the U.S. Senate Finance Committee Staff's (2004) proposal to give the IRS authority to remove misbehaving board members and to require, through the tax code, the seating of "independent" directors on the boards of large charities. These are powers heretofore within the jurisdiction—indeed at the limits of the jurisdiction—of state equity courts, not the federal government. The jurisdictional puzzle set forth early in this chapter surely remains to be solved.

THE BORDER PATROL FUNCTION OF CHARITABLE TAX LAW

The Government Border

Active engagement in public affairs has long been touted as a vital and noble function of the third sector, and equally long decried as incursion into territory where exempt organizations—particularly charitable organizations—have no business straying. Constraints imposed by the tax code on the advocacy activities of exempt organizations are generally described either as unfortunate obstacles to a politics that includes the voices of the underrepresented, or as essential though imperfect safeguards against blatant abuse of the nonprofit, tax-exempt form and its privileges to undermine the rules of political fair play. This form of "border patrol" controversy remains salient because of the dynamic nature of the context in which it arises—public policymaking and the selection of policymakers—and neither the technical puzzles nor the deeper issues have yet been resolved.

The Restraints on Charitable Organizations' Political Activities

Exempt organizations, including charitable organizations, are free to educate the populace on issues of public importance, even to the point of taking a distinct stance on controversial issues. So long as the presentation is "reasoned," it need not be "neutral" (Treas. Reg. §1.501(c)(3)-1(d)(3)(i); Rev. Proc. 86–43, 1986–2 C.B. 729; Lu 2004; Thompson 1985). The interpretation and application of this standard at the margins have occasionally been the subjects of some controversy (see *Big Mama Rag, Inc. v. United States,* 631 F.2d 1030 [D.C. Cir. 1980]; *National Alliance v. United States,* 710 F.2d 868 [D.C. Cir. 1983]; *The Nationalist Movement v. Commissioner,* 102 T.C. 558, *aff'd* 37 F.2d 216 [5th Cir. 1994]; Rev. Rul. 78–305, 1978–2 C.B. 172), but, for the most part, have not slowed charitable organizations' efforts to persuade and mobilize the public. The code's constraints on efforts to influence legislation and to elect like-minded candidates to public office, on the other hand, are highly significant to organizations that desire to pursue their charitable missions through involvement in public policy arenas.

The Lobbying Limitations. Section 501(c)(3) and related provisions impose explicit and fairly narrow limits on the lobbying activities of §501(c)(3) public charities. Since 1934, qualification for the §501(c)(3) exemption has required that "no substantial part" of a charitable organization's activities be directed toward influencing legislation.[74]

Private foundations are even more tightly limited, as noted below.

For public charities, the constraints have been relaxed over the past three decades. In 1976 Congress enacted §§501(h) and 4911, which provide an alternative definition of lobbying limits, available as a safe harbor to any §501(c)(3) public charity other than a church. Section 501(h) electively permits the use of a percentage-of-expenditures test instead of the prior and fuzzier "substantiality" limitation on lobbying activities.[75] The 1976 amendments also replace the all-or-none loss of exemption with a scaled system of penalties for exceeding the limits of permissible lobbying.[76] Perhaps the most important feature of these provisions—and the 1990 Treasury regulations that implement them—is their definition of key terms that, for organizations still operating under the "no substantial part" standard, are subject to intrusive and inconsistent application. The total effect is that the §501(h) rules are both more predictable and more generous in their treatment of advocacy efforts than the older "no substantial part" standard.

Election Campaign Intervention. In addition to the constraints it imposes on lobbying, §501(c)(3) denies exemption to organizations that "participate in, or intervene in (including the publishing or distributing of statements), any political campaign on behalf of (or in opposition to) any candidate for public office."[77] The election campaign intervention prohibition is expressed in absolute terms, and even a relatively small infraction can lead to loss of the §501(c)(3) charitable exemption. In addition to the revocation sanction, since 1987 §4955 has imposed excise tax penalties on organizations and their managers for some election-related expenditures.

Although public charities may engage in neutral voter education activities, any explicit or implicit endorsement or disapproval of candidates, even on the basis of principled, considered, nonpartisan evaluation, violates the prohibition (*Association of the Bar of the City of New York v. Commissioner,* 858 F.2d 876 [2d Cir. 1988]).[78] Accordingly, an organization that provided a party-neutral forum and process for citizens to engage in thoughtful investigation of issues and exploration of candidate positions on those issues was found to have violated the campaign participation prohibition because the process resulted ultimately in participants' rating of candidates (Technical Advice Memorandum 9635003 [30 August 1996]).

The Sibling Option. For public charities, a form of relief from the lobbying and, to a lesser extent, electoral campaign constraints may be found in the ability to structure related entities through which to engage in more extensive advocacy activities. This "sibling" option results from the fact that the restrictive regime for charitable organizations stands in sharp contrast to the rules for noncharitable nonprofits. Nothing in the tax code places limits on the lobbying or electoral activities of these latter organizations beyond the requirement that they be organized and operated primarily for purposes that match their classification.[79] Of particular interest to §501(c)(3) organizations is that §501(c)(4) organizations are able to lobby without limit, so long as their efforts are not primarily in pursuit of ends other than "social welfare."[80] Furthermore, so long as engagement in electoral campaigns is not a 501(c)(4) organization's primary purpose,[81] it may pursue that avenue as well (Revenue Ruling 67–293, 1967–2 C.B. 185; Revenue Ruling 81–95, 1981–1 C.B. 332).

Accordingly, a §501(c)(3) organization that finds even the §501(h) safe-harbor limits on legislative advocacy too constraining has the additional option of establishing a sibling organization under §501(c)(4). The §501(c)(4) lobbying affiliate became a comfortable choice in 1983, with the U.S. Supreme Court's decision in *Regan v. Taxation with Representation of Washington* (461 U.S. 540 [1983]). In that case, the Court rejected a free-speech challenge to the constraints on §501(c)(3) lobbying, holding that the limitations reflect a constitutionally permitted policy of not "subsidizing" substantial legislative activity, rather than an unconstitutional penalty on the exercise of free speech. This conclusion depended in part on the fact that an organization wishing to lobby without limit can simply organize and control a legally separate and fiscally separate §501(c)(4) affiliate—tax exempt, but not eligible to receive deductible contributions—through which to channel its legislative activity.

Similarly, the sibling (c)(3)–(c)(4) arrangement may permit the charity to coordinate its nonelectoral activity with the electoral work of a (c)(4), so long as the (c)(3) does not provide a penny's worth of subvention. Indeed, the sibling (c)(4) may then go on to establish a connected §527 political action committee (PAC) through which to carry out election-related activities.[82] This double-sibling structure was approved in *Branch Ministries v. Rossotti,* 211 F.3d 137, 143 (D.C. Cir. 2000).

The Rules for Private Foundations. Private foundations do not have the option of making a §501(h) election and are effectively barred from engaging in any direct or grassroots lobbying or election campaign intervention by a system of steep excise taxes imposed on any such activities by §4945, added to the code in 1969. The line between taxable lobbying activities and permitted educational activities is set by regulations promulgated shortly after the 1969 legislation and modified in 1990 to align the private foundation regime—in this limited respect—with the scheme for public charities. In addition, private foundations are subject to a rigorous restriction on conduct or support of voter registration activities, including a requirement that the voter program be conducted on a multistate basis (§4945(d)(2)). Because they are a subset of §501(c)(3) organizations, private foundations may avail themselves of the sibling organization options but must scrupulously avoid the transfer of any foundation assets to the sibling, as the limit on foundation lobbying begins with the first dollar.

Explaining the Restraints

It is generally agreed that no cogent, consistent rationale for the various restrictions on political activity found in §501(c)(3) and related provisions can be unearthed in the legislative record of their enactment. Rather, the constraints were adopted piecemeal, often with little discussion, and, in the case of the campaigning ban, as an apparently ad hoc response to a perceived affront to the lawmakers who sponsored the bill.[83]

An exception to this pattern of ad hoc construction of the rules was the addition in 1976 of §§501(h) and 4911 to provide a quantified alternative to the "no substantial part" lobbying rule. That enactment was the culmination of a long process of deliberation motivated by a desire to liberalize and clarify the much criticized rule. Even here, however, the legislative history reveals a focus on pragmatic concerns about the inadequacies of the existing rules rather than exploration of the underlying rationales for limiting the political activities of exempt organizations (Chisolm 1990b:621).

Rationales for (and Arguments against) the Restraints on Lobbying by Charities

The standard starting place for evaluating tax-related rules concerning political advocacy is "neutrality" (Galston 1993; Chisolm 1987–88; Boehm 1967). This postulate is derived in part from Judge Learned Hand's pronouncement that "political agitation as such is outside the statute; . . . controversies of that sort must be conducted without public subvention; the Treasury stands aside from them" (*Slee v. Commissioner,* 42 F.2d 184, 185 [2d Cir. 1930]) and from the Supreme Court's later equation of that concept with Congress's "determination . . . that since purchased publicity can influence the fate of legislation which will affect, directly or indirectly, all in the community, everyone in the community should stand on the same footing as regards its purchase so far as the Treasury of the United States is concerned" (*Cammarano v. United States,* 358 U.S. 498 [1958]). Considered from this perspective, the question becomes one of technical tax policy: do the restrictions contribute to maintaining a level playing field with respect to the tax treatment of dollars spent on political activity, no matter who is doing the spending?

Galston (1993) concludes that neutrality is not well served by the existing regime of restrictions on lobbying by §501(c)(3) organizations. The scheme imposes different limits on large and small charities, charities and other exempt organizations, and private foundations and public charities. Similarly, Chisolm (1994) finds that, whereas the rules concerning the tax treatment of election-related expenditures are roughly neutral among categories of exempt and nonexempt organizations, the lobbying rules are not. Nondeductibility of lobbying expenses for individuals and businesses raises the after-tax cost of lobbying to the taxpayer, whereas taxpayers can claim deductions for gifts to charities that lobby. Nevertheless, the legal constraints that apply to such lobbying—even with the liberalized rules of 501(h) and the sibling option—can silence an organization or even cost it its exemption and perhaps its ability to survive (Chisolm 1987–88:241–46; Chisolm 1994:52–54). The degree to which these constraints actually affect the behavior of nonprofits is another matter; empirical explorations have led to no clear consensus on this important question.[84]

A number of arguments beyond neutrality have been offered to support the contention that exempt status and activist stance are inconsistent, and that any organization desiring to assume one of the two should forgo the other. These arguments are generally (but not always) premised upon an implicit assumption that exemption and deductibility are subsidies, and are offered to make the case against "spending" to support legislative advocacy.

- *Lobbying is inherently inconsistent with the historical definition of charity.* This argument rests in part on the fact that the list of charitable purposes set forth in the "starting point of the modern law of charities" (Keeton 1962:10)—the English Statute of Charitable Uses of 1601—contains no suggestion "that it is a charitable purpose to . . . attempt to change the law" (J. Simon 1973:67). Several authors, however, have contended that the common law of charitable trusts in the United States "does not reveal a tradition of reasoned or even intentional opposition to charitable involvement in public policy formulation" (J. Simon 1973:68; see Clark 1960; Lehrfeld 1969; Thompson 1985).
- *Legislative advocacy diverts the nonprofit sector's attention from its more central functions.* Some claim that the social activism of legislative advocacy distorts and demeans the charitable mission (Hart 1973; Graetz and Jeffries 1977). But many others have described efforts to influence public policy as nothing more than one of many legitimate strategies for pursuing charitable mission (Carey 1977; Jordan 1983; Reid 2000; Boris and Krehely 2002). The alleviation of hunger, for example, may be addressed both by serving soup and by urging the legislature to modify unemployment benefits.

  Some argue that lobbying is particularly legitimate as a strategy for religious organizations, because of a long tradition of linking theology to social policy or because of a belief that faith-based perspectives are qualitatively different from otherwise-motivated political positions (Lee 2000; Sneed 1997; Tesdahl 1991; Halloran 1992). This position is sometimes coupled with the separate assertion that religious organizations have a stronger entitlement than other organizations to participate unimpeded, because of the mandates of the free exercise and establishment clauses of the First Amendment (Ablin 1999; Sneed 1997). Courts have not been receptive to these constitutional claims, and Lupu (2000:442) argues that "whatever special treatment religious organizations may be able to claim in other contexts, the area of political activity is one in which the claim to constitutional uniqueness of religion is unusually weak, and the claim to equal participation by all is uniquely strong."
- *Legislative advocacy by charitable organizations is socially inefficient.* Some have argued that legislative advocacy on the part of charitable organizations is wasteful and counterproductive (and therefore unworthy of "support"). A paper prepared by Pepper, Hamilton, and Sheetz (1997) for the Filer Commission asserted that lobbying by charities is likely to be directed toward increased expenditure of public funds, thus adding to rather than relieving government bur-

dens (and thus undermining, in the authors' eyes, the justification for exemption and deductibility). Chisolm (1987–88:248–49) and Galston (1993:1325–29) have questioned the accuracy and the logic of this assertion. It is, however, almost impossible to fashion a complete and accurate picture of which organizations are lobbying how much, to what end, and with what effect (Boris and Mosher-Williams 1998).

- *Lobbying by charities simply amplifies the voices of those who are already heard.* Galston (1993) describes the "countermajoritarian objection" to charities in general and to lobbying by charities in particular. The concern is that those who fund and manage charities will use the charities' legislative advocacy as instruments to promote their own particular visions of the public interest. Since that vision is not subject to the accountability imposed by electoral or market forces, and since the benefits of the tax exemption and deduction "expenditures" are available largely to the better-off members of the populace, allowing charities to lobby simply amplifies the voices of those who are already well represented in the arenas of public policymaking. A number of scholars, however, have offered counterarguments to this point. J. Simon (1973:64) has argued for a "presumption in favor of full participation by all individuals and groups in society, in all of the processes by which our public policies are formulated." Charitable organizations have a long history of giving voice to the interests of the disadvantaged (Couto 1999; Horton-Smith 1990; Bremner 1988) and have "mobilized groups previously underrepresented in the public policymaking process" (Berry 1999:7). Salamon (1995) observes that legal services groups and multiservice social service organizations (which generally serve the traditional objects of "charity") are more likely to engage in policy advocacy than are arts and cultural organizations (which tend to be supported by the well-to-do). And several commentators have observed that politically engaged charitable organizations play a significant facilitative role in the self-actualization of individuals as participants in civic life (Berry 1999; Frumkin and Andre-Clark 2000:29; Boris and Mosher-Williams 1998; Chong 1991; Berger and Neuhaus 1977; Sunstein 1988; West 1985; Reid 1999:291).

Rationales for (and Arguments against) the Campaign Intervention Prohibition

While the most vigorous disapproval of legislative involvement by charities seems to have eased over the last decade or so, attention to election-related activity seems to have intensified. This development can likely be explained, at least in part, by the increasingly creative—some would say aggressive—use of various kinds of exempt organizations by individuals who were (or were perceived to be) aspiring to public office (Chisolm 1990b; Hill 1999).[85]

The policy arguments offered in support of the campaign intervention constraints are the same as those offered in support of the lobbying restrictions, but they tend to encounter less opposition in the electoral context. It is arguable that the connection between election or defeat of particular candidates and an organization's charitable goals is more attenuated than the connection between those goals and a group's legislative efforts.[86] Moreover, campaign intervention by a §501(c)(3) organization, using §501(c)(3) funds, raises private benefit dangers far more acutely than does legislative advocacy (Hill 1997a; Fei 2000; Colvin 2000). And although there is no clear historical support for the idea that politically partisan activities in pursuit of charitable purposes are inherently off limits (Chisolm 1990a), it is hard to argue against the intuitive appeal of keeping charity out of electoral politics and guarding "the nonpartisan integrity [of the charitable sector] from internal and external erosion" (Colvin 2000:67). Finally, unlike lobbying, which is subject to nominal but largely toothless regulation outside of the tax code, campaign intervention is subject to an elaborate if imperfect system of regulation that evidences Congress's desire to monitor and control the flow of money into election campaigns; it is reasonable to expect that the tax exemption rules should not work at cross-purposes to that system.

Providing empirical support to some of these policy arguments, commentators have described an array of relationships between politicians and exempt organizations that suggest the misappropriation of the benefits of the charitable exemption, evasion of campaign finance regulation, and misuse and manipulation of the exempt form for political purposes or personal gain (Chisolm 1990b; Owens 2001; Cohen and Matlack 1989; Hill 1997b, 2001). Even under existing law, Hill believes that §§501(c)(3) and 501(c)(4) are easily used as vehicles for avoiding campaign finance regulation—sometimes with deductibility for the contributor (Hill 1997a, 2001).

The near consensus that keeping §501(c)(3) funds out of elections is good policy does not mean that the rules as now written and implemented have drawn no criticism. For example, Fei (2000), Hill (1999), Colvin (2000), and Trister and Schadler (2002) have explored the practical difficulties occasioned by the substantial mismatch between the tax exemption–related rules concerning election-related activity and the nontax rules found in the Federal Election Campaign Act (2 U.S.C. §§431–55). Several authors have further observed that §§501(c)(3), 501(c)(4), and 527, taken together, create an incomplete and sometimes inconsistent scheme of tax exemption requirements and limits on the wide range of political activities of exempt organizations, with unintended ripple effects (Hill 1999; Fei 2000; Colvin 2002). The passage of the Bipartisan Campaign Reform Act (BCRA) of 2002 (Public Law 107–155, 116 Stat. 81, amending Federal Election Campaign Act of 1971, 86 Stat. 11, as amended, 2 U.S.C. §431 et seq.) adds to the complexity of the relationships between tax and election law. BCRA limits the "electioneering communications" of corporations (including most nonprofit corporations) and requires increased disclosure of contributions and expenditures. Electioneering communications include some activities that tax exemption law permits to §501(c)(3) charities, as well as some §501(c)(4) and §527 activity. The major provisions of BCRA have been upheld by the U.S. Supreme Court in *McConnell v. Federal Election Commission,* 540 U.S. 93 (2003). An excellent analysis of that case and its impact on exempt organizations is found in Hill (2004). The Federal Election Commission is in the process of generating regulations to implement the provisions of BCRA; the particulars of these regulations may well have a significant impact on the design of exempt-organization advocacy activities (see Notice of Proposed Rulemaking on Political Committee Status, 69 Federal Register 11736 [11 March 2004] and subsequent developments available at http://www.fec.gov).

Another objection to the constraints as they now exist is that the rules are enforced unevenly and that, even if applied consistently, they would have an uneven impact, raising the real possibility of skewing the political process (Chisolm 1990a; Carroll 1992; Ablin 1999; Bird 2000). A long-standing pattern of overlooking election-related activities of mainstream churches may have put rival perspectives at a disadvantage. This pattern has begun to shift (Chisolm 1994), but Carroll (1992) and Ablin (1999) have commented on uneven enforcement among religious organizations—whether politically motivated (as Bird [2000] suggests) or not (Staff of the Joint Committee on Taxation 2000).

Some writers have argued that, while the ban on direct election intervention with 501(c)(3) deductible dollars makes good sense, limits on the ability of §501(c)(3) organizations to create and control separately funded organizations constituted especially for political intervention does not (Chisolm 1990a, 1994; Carroll 1992). One argument is constitutional: In order for the prohibition on direct intervention to hold up to unconstitutional conditions analysis, §501(c)(3) organizations must have available a relatively easy alternative channel for unimpeded political speech. Further, even if restraints on alternative vehicles do not violate constitutional free-speech guarantees, they are offensive to first amendment free-speech values (Chisolm 1990a; Carroll 1992).

Another argument is pragmatic, and rooted in a policy preference for fair distribution of access. The inability of charities to trade in the currency that matters to elected policymakers—the prospect of election support or opposition—may undermine the effectiveness of the legislative advocacy of charities (Chisolm 1990a). For diverse views on this question, compare Hill (2001) and Roady (1999) with Berry (1999). These empirical controversies and others noted in this section deserve further pursuit, as do the underlying issues about the role of exempt organizations in civic life.

The Business Border

Turning from the nonprofit–government border to the nonprofit–business border, we find that the federal tax law has erected fences—or at least guard rails—that constrain *commercial activity* by nonprofit entities acting on their own, and *business transactions with for-profit firms,* involving conversions, joint ventures, creation of subsidiaries, and corporate control.

Commercial Activity by Nonprofits Acting on Their Own

The commercial activity issue came increasingly to the fore in the 1980s as voluntary organizations of all kinds scrambled to cope with the combined impact of government reductions in the rate of social service and cultural spending (thus thrusting greater burdens on the nonprofits), government reductions in the rate of grant and contract support for the nonprofits themselves, and charitable giving levels that did not increase fast enough to make up the gap (Urban Institute 1983). These adverse pressures continued in the 1990s and beyond, producing, predictably enough, a rush toward earned income—increased reliance on fees for services, entry into new or expanded forms of commercial operations (whether or not related to the nonprofit's charter purposes), and acquisition of revenue-producing assets distinct from traditional passive investment holdings (Boris and Steuerle 1999; Crimmins and Keil 1983; Young and Salamon 2002; Tuckman and Chang, this volume). During the 1990s, "commercial income," broadly defined, "increased in terms of absolute dollars" (Steuerle 2001:2).[87] The quest for commercial return was foreshadowed in a *New Yorker* cartoon (15 December 1976) depicting Santa Claus saying to his elves: "I've been thinking. This year, instead of *giving* everything away, why don't we charge a little something?"

Earned income activities have been largely responsible, according to Salamon (1987), for the fact that many nonprofits have weathered fiscal storms better than might have been expected. Despite these beneficial effects, however, commercial activity has generated recurrent interest in tax law border patrol. What are the grievances that spur such border guarding?

The Grievances. Perhaps the most prominent grievance is the allegation of "unfair competition" with for-profit firms—a charge that formed the basic rationale for the 1950 legislation enacting the tax on unrelated business income of nonprofit organizations (§§511ff.). The theoretical and empirical justifications for the unfair competition argument are not free from controversy (see Steinberg 1991; Brown and Slivinski, this volume).

The theoretical controversy turns on alternative hypotheses about the impact of tax exemption on competitive fairness. There appears to be general agreement that property tax exemption, because it reduces input costs, assists a nonprofit in a contest with taxable competitors. With respect to the federal income tax, however, opinion is divided. The evident assumption underlying passage of the 1950 legislation was that exemption permits charities to undercut the prices of their taxable competitors and allows expansion with "free" capital—in the form of nontaxed retained earnings—not available to nonexempt rivals. Some economists (for example, Steinberg 1991) call these propositions into question because we do not know enough about nonprofit pricing, determinants of nonprofit entry and exit, and the incidence of the corporate income tax. Similarly, Bittker and Rahdert (1976:319) have questioned "why the price level that had maximized both the pretax and after-tax profits of the enterprise before [acquisition by a tax-exempt organization] would not continue to maximize its profits thereafter." Hansmann (1981:82) contends, however, that the second of these propositions—"free" capital—makes sense if it is interpreted to mean that "exemption from income taxation does permit nonprofit firms to grow faster than they could if they were taxed, and it does give them an incentive to grow, and ultimately perhaps to take markets away from for-profit firms, in a broader range of conditions than would be the case without exemption."

Another perspective comes from Rose-Ackerman (1982), who argues that the relevant unfairness issue raised by exemption does not involve competition between firms in the same industry but rather competition between firms in industries with "tax-favored firms" and firms in those industries without "tax-favored firms." The latter phenomenon, she contends, arises when nonprofits turn from "unrelated" (and therefore taxable) commercial activities to "related" commercial activities in industries whose firms had not previously faced competition from nonprofit, tax-favored enterprises. Steinberg (1991) has provided some qualified support for this analysis, while generally finding claims of unfair competition unpersuasive.

To those who see the nonprofit firm as enjoying competitive tax advantages, the National Human Services Assembly has responded, on behalf of its nonprofit agency members, that small businesses enjoy a congeries of tax advantages of their own, buttressed with Small Business Administration preferences, that at least offset any benefits that accrue to the nonprofits (Wellford and Gallagher 1985). Steinberg (1988:10) has made a similar point: "in a multi-product setting . . . [for-profits] may receive a tax subsidy through offsets which is not available to [nonprofits]. Thus, in some cases, the playing field is tilted in favor of [for-profits]."[88]

Empirical work has not kept pace with the theoretical debate on competition. Hansmann (1982) examined the impact of a variety of state taxes on the relative prevalence of nonprofit and for-profit firms in various jurisdictions, finding, inter alia, that state income taxes made a difference—thus suggesting that federal income tax exemption may give a competitive advantage to nonprofit competitors. Although unfair competition has been alleged to exist in the hospital, physical fitness, and audiovisual and computer software industries (Bennett and DiLorenzo 1989), we are not aware of field investigations of competitive combat—or the behavior of nonprofit and for-profit firms—within these industries in a way that would cast light on the various competitive unfairness theories. Nor in other areas in which such unfairness has been alleged—for example, the research, travel, and stationery industries discussed by Spiro (1979) and the other industries listed by Pires (1985)—do there appear to be detailed case studies that could illuminate the competition issue. Such evidence could also throw light on another tax fairness issue not usually mentioned in the literature: the question of whether the ability of a §501(c)(3) organization to receive deductible contributions and foundation grants provides it with a financing capacity that has competitive consequences distinct from the impact of tax exemption.[89]

Unfair competition is not the only rationale for patrol, via the tax system, of the charity–commerce border. Other concerns may provoke requests that the border be policed: a desire to minimize tax revenue loss through exemption; a fear that if the world of charity, through a process of isomorphism (DiMaggio and Powell 1982), comes to resemble too much the world of business, public support for the nonprofit sector—in terms of funds, volunteering, or legislative support—will weaken; the related apprehension that "if this kind of [commercial] activity increases significantly, it could call into question the tax exemption of certain nonprofit industries,[90] or even the exemption of the entire sector" (Steuerle 2001:5); the prospect of charitable goals and values being abandoned in the rush for revenue; the concern that charities' conduct of commercial enterprises would result in inefficiencies that impair the health of both the enterprises and the charities (Minow 2002:41–43; Hansmann 1989);[91] and, more generally, the possible erosion of a valuable division of labor among the public, for-profit, and nonprofit sectors (Minow 2002:44; Weisbrod 1998; see also Tuckman and Chang, this volume, on "mission drift").

Rebutting these other (non-competition-related) concerns are other policy arguments in favor of commercial activity. Quite apart from the financial benefits derived by struggling nonprofits are other asserted advantages: providing training for disadvantaged persons in a business setting; providing "a real-world laboratory to figure out what really works in helping people get off government rolls and into decent-paying jobs" (Hochberg 2002:36); and using retail facilities to interest the public in the charitable activities of the nonprofit sponsor.[92] Rose-Ackerman (1983) has also suggested that when a nonprofit is providing services to both full-paying customers and charitable beneficiaries, the need to satisfy the former with high-quality performance may also accrue to the benefit of the latter.

Remedies: The UBIT. Those who resolve the foregoing policy debates in favor of tightened border patrol propose various remedies. There have been demands for strengthening of the principal border-patrol instrument: the tax on unrelated business income, known as "UBIT."[93] Originally enacted by Congress in 1950 in the wake of New York University's indirect acquisition of a macaroni company, UBIT is an income tax imposed on otherwise exempt organizations with respect to net revenues of a "trade or business" that is "regularly carried on" by a nonprofit and not "substantially related" to the nonprofit's exempt purposes (aside from the need for funds).[94] As the traffic in nonprofit commerce has grown, the IRS has undertaken new and more controversial UBIT enforcement measures, which have led to litigation over group insurance programs, advertising, sales of mailing lists, and many other income-generating activities (Schwarz and Hutton 1984:681–92). Moreover, small business groups, including a branch of the U.S. Small Business Administration (1984), have sought to cut back on the large number of exceptions that Congress has grafted onto the tax over the years (for example, an exception for nonprofits doing basic scientific research and an exception for work performed by volunteers)—and indeed to tax even the "related" business income of nonprofit organizations. Earlier efforts to expand the coverage of UBIT resulted in a repeal of the special exemption for church groups and in a shrinkage of the exception for rental income

(§512(b)(3)). The more recent efforts to strengthen the tax, however, have not yet overcome opposition from charitable groups.

Remedies: Denial of Exemption. The other major weapon that is used to address commerciality on the part of nonprofits acting on their own is an IRS assault on the charitable exemption of the entity: it is no longer "organized and operated exclusively for religious, charitable, scientific, . . . literary, or educational purposes" (§501(c)(3)).[95] This approach has had less than full success, largely because of the difficulty of coping with the question of the degree to which the quest for nondonative revenue is compatible with §501(c)(3) purposes. Two classes of cases present this question. One involves "unrelated" commercial income where it is alleged that payment of UBIT is not the end of the story—that the amount of such business activity is so great that the tail has wagged the dog and the organization fails the "operated exclusively" test (*Better Business Bureau v. United States,* 326 U.S. 279 [1945]; see Eliasberg 1965). It is not easy to derive from these cases a quantitative measure of when the tail wagging has become fatal for exemption purposes (Gallagher 1984; Spitzer 2002). Indeed, Spitzer argues against such a "per se limit" (2002:1).

The more numerous class of cases involves business activity—prominently including publishing (e.g., *Presbyterian and Reformed Publishing Co. v. Commissioner,* 742 F.2d 148 [3d Cir. 1984])—that qualifies as related but that has a sufficient "commercial hue" to call into question, according to the IRS, the basic charitable purpose of the organization.[96] The "hue" is discerned from the size of profit, or the degree of marketing zeal, or other indicia of "commerciality," or the "inherently" commercial nature of the enterprise, or the degree to which "revenues from such business are used to cross-subsidize charitable activity . . . [an] approach sometimes referred to in IRS rulings as the 'commensurate in scope' doctrine" (Colombo 2002:509–10). The judicial outcomes in the "hue" cases vary widely, if not wildly; prediction is precarious—perhaps a consequence of a shortage of authoritative definitions of §501(c)(3) "purpose."[97] Colombo (2002:505) adds that "purpose" analysis also suffers from the fact that both the courts and the IRS "usually ignore" the question of "whether the commercial activity, even if substantial, is 'in furtherance of' an exempt purpose.'" Spitzer (2002:1, 13) calls for a "more coherent" application by the IRS and courts of certain "enforcement tools" (private inurement, private benefit, "excess benefit," and "exclusively operated" limitations) that should be used to police "related" commercial activity—but without any quantitative limits on that activity.

Remedies: Other Approaches. One further strategy, contemplated by Colombo (2003:345) when a nonprofit provides services "commercially similar" to for-profit providers, is to condition exemption on "whether the organization provides access to services for previously-underserved populations or provides specific services to the majority population that are not provided by the private sector." Another alternative, proposed originally in 1987 (Bennett and Rudney 1987) and revived recently, is to "expand . . . the UBIT to cover all commercial activities," whether or not "related" (Colombo 2002:495). One obstacle to adoption of these reform ideas is the limited state of knowledge, especially empirical information, bearing on the underlying allegations of unfair competition and inefficiency.[98]

The concerns about commercial activity and the rebuttals to them are not confined to the aspect of business border patrol we have just been discussing: commercial activities pursued by nonprofits acting on their own. These and other issues arise with equal force in the context of business transactions with for-profit firms.

Business Transactions with For-Profit Firms

In recent years nonprofits have had several different reasons to enter into an ever-widening range of business alliances and relationships with proprietary businesses: the previously mentioned quest for earned income, the search for capital, the need to recruit talent and expertise, a desire for expanded coverage and outreach, and, more than occasionally, the pecuniary appetite of nonprofit insiders. In consequence, charities have entered energetically into four major categories of transactions with for-profit players: (1) conversions, wherein assets and activities are transferred from nonprofit to for-profit ownership or control; (2) joint ventures, in which a nonprofit and a for-profit enter into a partnership-type relationship; (3) a nonprofit's creation of a for-profit subsidiary; and (4) a nonprofit's possession of voting control of a business corporation.[99]

Conversions. Principally in the health-care field, a rampant phenomenon of past decades—although one that has abated in recent years—has been the process of converting the ownership or control of hospitals, HMOs, and health insurance organizations from nonprofit to for-profit hands (Schlesinger and Gray, this volume; Brown and Slivinski, this volume; Brody, this volume; Donohue 1999). These conversions "typically have been motivated by capital access needs more than any other factor"—access needs heightened by post-1986 restrictions on tax-exempt bond financing and the reduced financial attractiveness of such bonds (Mancino 1997).[100] Conversions take various forms, characterized as "conversions in place," "asset sales," "mergers," and "drop-down conversions" (Mancino 1997), of which the most common variety is the asset sale. Here (to take the case of a hospital), what takes place is an "actual sale or transfer of the nonprofit hospital's assets, name and accounts to a for-profit purchaser for cash, stock, notes or other property" (Donohue 1999); the amount received by the nonprofit seller stays with that entity or is transferred to another nonprofit—typically what is called a "conversion foundation"—and remains dedicated to charitable purposes, albeit not, in most cases, the operation of a hospital. As of 1998, the assets held by the nation's health-related conversion foundations totaled approximately $9 billion (Nelson 1998).

Two of the most prevalent conversion complaints involve valuation and community impact. With respect to valuation, an alleged failure to give the nonprofit seller (or its newly created substitute) a fair price for its assets has characterized many of the past conversion transactions, until state attorneys general and state health regulatory agencies came to the rescue, increasingly backed by legislation providing for just such oversight (Brody, this volume; Fremont-Smith and Lever 2000; Boisture and Varley 1996). But the tax system has a role to play as well, especially when some of the principals of the nonprofit are found as principals (shareholders or executives) of the for-profit. When the for-profit underpays for the nonprofit's assets, that discount may create what the tax code calls an inurement of net earnings for the insiders, imperiling the nonprofit's exempt status under §501(c)(3); several hospital exemption revocations have occurred in these circumstances (Fremont-Smith 1998). Revocation alone, however, is a rather toothless remedy, neither punishing miscreant participants nor restoring funds to the abused nonprofit—indeed, revocation further depletes these resources. The recently enacted excess benefits provision (§4958) likely serves as a more effective disincentive to conversions that represent a bad deal for converters but a good deal for insiders. Here the tax system does not bar the conversion transaction but seeks to make sure that the insiders do not have the last laugh.

A second lament about hospital conversions—one involving community impact—really has two components: first, a concern about the impact of the hospital's change in location or character, under its new ownership, on the community previously served by the hospital; second, a concern about the degree of community benefit flowing from the grants or other expenditures made, after the conversion, by the conversion foundation. Attorneys general and health regulators have frequently used their general or conversion-focused statutory powers to address these issues (Donohue 1999; Brody, this volume). On this front, the federal tax system has not played a role. The IRS might assert that a nonprofit's change of charitable purposes (from hospital care to something else) represents a sufficient departure from the terms of the exemption application to require a new application, but any more robust IRS intervention might well raise hard (but interesting) questions about the scope of the tax system's writ—a "jurisdictional puzzle" briefly considered above.

Joint Ventures. While the conversion "movement" is largely confined to the health-care industry, joint ventures—partnership-like alliances between nonprofit and for-profit entities—have prevailed not only in the health field but also in research (with universities as the nonprofit coventurers), low-income housing, community and economic development (Sanders 2000), and—the area yielding the first court decision on joint ventures—the theater (*Plumstead Theatre Soc., Inc. v. Commissioner,* 675 F.2d 244 [9th Cir. 1982]). "Joint ventures give charitable organizations an opportunity to raise capital beyond individual and corporate giving, give third parties a stake in the enterprise, and create economic efficiencies," as well as bringing the expertise of for-profit coventurers to the enterprise (Sanders 2000:118). In the early days of joint ventures, limited partnerships served as the standard vehicle, but since the advent of the limited liability corporation (LLC), "the LLC has become the entity of choice because it combines the corporate advantage of limited liability with the pass-through tax treatment of partnerships" (Sanders 2000:8); the latter feature permits the for-profit participants to deduct any joint venture losses from their individual and corporate tax liabilities, subject, however, to the severe restrictions on such deductibility imposed by the "passive loss limitation" rules (§469). Some joint venture arrangements represent a "hybrid form of a conversion": a nonprofit hospital transfers its assets to a joint venture partnership or LLC in which the hospital is a stakeholder; with the cash it receives for the transfer, the hospital operates as a conversion foundation (Fremont-Smith 1998).[101]

In contrast with its secondary role in regulating conversion transactions, the IRS has played the leading role in taming joint ventures. Concerned that these arrangements deflect charitable operations and require the nonprofit participants to honor fiduciary obligations to their for-profit partners at the expense of charitable purposes, the IRS at first adopted a per se prohibitory rule to joint ventures (Sanders 2000). After this approach was overruled in *Plumstead Theatre Soc., Inc. v. Commissioner,* the IRS promulgated a two-pronged test to judge the exempt status of joint ventures: "whether the [joint venture] organization is serving a charitable purpose" and "whether the arrangement permits the exempt organization to act exclusively in furtherance of the purposes for which exemption may be granted and not for the benefit of the [for-profit coventurers]" (Sanders 2000:123, quoting Gen. Couns. Mem. 39005 [17 December 1982]). This test has been elaborated in rulings (Rev. Rul. 98–15, 1998–1 C.B. 718; Rev. Rul. 2004–51, 2001–22 I.R.B. 974) and has been implicitly approved by the Ninth Circuit Court of Appeals (*Redlands Surgical Services v. Commissioner,* 242 F.3d 904 [9th Cir. 2001]), and by the Fifth Circuit Court of Appeals (*St. David's Health Care System v. United States,* 349 F.3d 232 [5th Cir. 2003]), although St. David's retained its exemption.

Until very recently, the IRS and the courts were largely preoccupied with "whole organization joint ventures," in which the nonprofit transfers all of its assets and activities to the joint venture. But these arrangements are "virtually unknown outside the health care arena" (Roady 2005:1). In other fields, the "ancillary joint venture" predominates, involving the transfer of only a small part of the nonprofit's assets and activities. A 2004 Revenue Ruling (Rev. Rul. 2004–51) addresses and provides limited approval of these ancillary arrangements, even where the nonprofit exercises less control over the joint venture than would be required in a "whole organization" plan (Buck and Jedrey 2005).

Scholarly and professional critiques have challenged some of these border-patrol measures relating to joint ventures (Schill 1984; Mancino 1998, 2002) and to sales and leasebacks (Pang 1985). Here, however, as in the competitive unfairness area discussed above, empirical investigation—scrutinizing, for example, the factual basis for IRS concerns about charitable subordination in the joint venture setting—has not been forthcoming. On a more theoretical level, one may ask: In the interest of protecting the third sector from distortion of purpose or from public distrust, should legislative and administrative policymakers build less permeable fences between the nonprofit and the for-profit territories? Or will such barriers have perverse effects on both of these sectors? And, in any event (and harking back to the jurisdictional puzzle once more), are either of these questions properly addressed by the tax system?

Creation of For-Profit Subsidiaries. With increasing frequency, exempt organizations establish their own proprietary offspring for one or more of these reasons: "(1) protection of the charity's tax-exempt status; (2) limitation of liability; (3) access to the capital markets; and (4) protecting the treatment of royalty income. . . . An ancillary consideration may include greater flexibility in structuring compensation for key officers and employees" (Roady 2000). Each of these goals depends on the subsidiary's status as an autonomous entity, and it is the tax system that applies this test of autonomy in order to permit the subsidiary arrangement to achieve the first, third, and fourth of these goals. Hence, the exempt organization must establish that, although it is the parent of the subsidiary, the child has been fully emancipated—"separate from the charitable parent . . . and . . . not a mere arm of the parent" (Roady 2000). IRS rulings have fleshed out this rather rigorous border-patrol measure with detailed criteria for emancipation (e.g., Gen. Couns. Mems. 39776 [6 February 1989], 39626 [30 April 1987], 39598 [23 January 1987], and 33912 [15 August 1968]). In fact, however, prevailing tax doctrines tilt strongly toward finding corporations to be emancipated—independent entities and not agents or shams—and tax practitioners do not encounter an assault on the separate status of a wholly owned for-profit subsidiary absent egregious circumstances.

Foundation Voting Control of a Business Corporation. The nonprofit–business border-patrol measures mentioned so far apply, with some exceptions, to charitable and noncharitable nonprofits. However, here as elsewhere in nonprofit law, foundations are subject to an extra degree of constraint not imposed on the other nonprofits. Public charities can hold corporate control stock, that is, a sufficient number of shares to give the nonprofit, alone or in conjunction with the donor of the stock, working control of the company. Foundations are effectively barred from these investments. The "excess business holdings" provision of the 1969 Tax Reform Act (§4943), crudely summarized (it is a robustly complicated section), requires foundations to divest themselves of business interests that, combined with interests held by donors and other related persons, amount to more than 20 percent of the voting power of a company, unless the foundation's own holdings are less than 2 percent of the voting power. This "excess business holdings" rule has been criticized on various grounds, including the rationale for it (Bittker 1973), its possible effect on foundation birth and growth rates (J. Simon 2000), and the failure to pursue less drastic alternative legislative remedies (J. Simon 2000), but it seems unlikely to be disturbed. It is probably the tallest fence we encounter in this survey of business border-patrol measures.

A SPECIAL CASE: CHURCHES

Floating within the nonprofit universe are several celestial bodies that receive tax-exempt treatment distinctly different from that accorded to most other nonprofit entities. Some of these organizations—pension funds, political parties, and consumer cooperatives, to pick three prominent examples—are not covered by the main set of exemption provisions (§§501(c)(3)–(25)); they cannot be covered within our space constraints. America's 330,350 congregations (Boris and Steuerle, this volume) do find a home within §501(c)(3), but they receive significantly more favorable regulatory treatment than other public charities and therefore receive special-case treatment here.

Before discussing these special-treatment questions, we note that even the nonpreferential status of churches[102]—with respect to exemption and deductibility—is a matter of periodic debate. Since the days of the pharaohs and continuing through the church-state conflicts of the Middle Ages, there have been conflicts, sometimes explosive, over the granting—and termination—of tax relief for religious institutions (Gen. 47:26; Adler 1922; Larson and Lowell 1969). Under modern federal and state taxing regimes, neither the grant nor the termination of tax relief to churches is problematic. It has come to be understood that federal tax exemption and deductibility and state property tax exemption will be accorded to religious organizations. A constitutional attack on the inclusion of churches under New York State's property tax exemption for nonprofit organizations, based on the establishment clause of the First Amendment, was turned back by the U.S. Supreme Court in 1970 (*Walz v. Tax Commissioner,* 397 U.S. 664). The court held that the tax exemption's "benevolent neutrality" toward a wide range of eleemosynary institutions, including churches, neither favored nor disfavored religion—and therefore passed muster.[103] With respect to federal exemption, Fishman and Schwarz (2000:431–32) observe, "Although *Walz* involved a state property tax exemption, the Court suggested that the tax benefits provided by the Internal Revenue Code similarly were immune from a First Amendment challenge, but it declined to rule that religious tax exemptions were constitutionally required."

This last question—whether exemption is *required*—presumably would not arise under federal tax law unless Congress amended the code to delete the word "religious" as an alternative adjectival criterion for exemption and deductibility. Under state law, the question of requirement would arise either in the absence of any exemptions at all where normally exemption is found (e.g., where a state provided for no property tax exemption for any eleemosynary landholders) or in the context of a broad-based tax exemption for charities that excluded churches. If these politically extraordinary circumstances exist somewhere, they do not appear to have prompted a challenge that has reached public attention; in any event, we are not aware of any case law that tests the question left unresolved in the *Walz* decision. We think it possible, perhaps likely, that if a case did arise involving a broad-based tax exemption statute that excluded religious groups, such discrimination would be held to violate the free exercise clause of the First Amendment or the equal protection clause of the Fourteenth Amendment.[104]

Beyond the issues of eligibility for exemption and requirement of exemption lies the question of preferred tax treatment of religious groups. Until 1969 a notable example of preference was the exemption of churches, alone among §501(c)(3) groups, from the unrelated business income tax when it was enacted in 1950—a congressional favor that allowed commercial activities run by the Mormon Church, the Christian Brothers order, and other entrepreneurial church groups to finance their expansion with untaxed business profits. When two mainline religious organizations, the National Council of Churches and the United States Catholic Conference, announced opposition to this exemption on the eve of the 1969 Tax Reform Act, Congress ended the exemption as part of that legislation (Schwarz 1976).

But significant preferences remain. "Churches"—more narrowly defined than "religious organizations" (as noted above)—do not have to apply for recognition as tax-exempt entities, as do all other charities over a certain size (§508(c)(1)(A)). The absence of application information on file at the IRS and available to the public deprives regulators, journalists, and watchdog groups of information with enforcement relevance. To the same effect is the statutory relief of churches from filing the annual information returns (Form 990s) that all other charities over a modest size must submit (§6033(a)(2)(A)(i)). And along the same vector of nonenforceability is the substantial immunity of churches from audit procedures applicable to other charities (§7611). These restrictions must surely impede the work of the IRS (even though its representatives may not feel free to say so publicly or loudly)[105] and may have hampered and delayed the investigation of fraudulent behavior by some televangelists and other church leaders in recent years, probably at considerable cost to the victims of these frauds. These surmises should be tested empirically—if research access can be obtained.

Four other code provisions providing privileged status for churches, catalogued by Hammar (1993), are the ability to opt out of the obligation to pay the employer's share of FICA (Social Security) taxes, when the church is opposed "for religious reasons" to such payments (§§3121(b), 3121(w)); especially favorable rules for computing the tax on unrelated business income (§514(b)(3)(E)); the effective exemption of churches from the Federal Unemployment Tax Act (§3309(b)); and "exemption from nondiscrimination rules applicable to tax-sheltered annuities under I.R.C. §403(b)(2)" (Hammar 1993:72; §§403(b)(1)(D), 403(b)(12)(B)).

These preferential rules, as well as the three procedural exemptions mentioned above, deserve more constitutional inquiry than they have received. It has been contended (Joblove 1980) that the three procedural exemptions exalt the legal position of religion in a way that violates the establishment clause, which, generally speaking, "prohibits the government from singling out churches for exemption from laws of general application" (Brody, this volume). One Supreme Court decision lending support to the establishment clause objection is *Texas Monthly, Inc. v. Bullock,* 489 U.S. 1 (1989), which declared unconstitutional the exemption of religious periodicals, but not secular publications, from a state sales tax—although not all the majority justices crisply articulated that preferential treatment was the gist of the establishment clause objection. From another perspective, however, the code exemptions listed above have been defended as necessary to avoid the kind of church-state "entanglement" held to offend the very same establishment clause (*Lemon v. Kurtzman,* 403 U.S. 602 [1971]).

An inquiry into constitutionality could also examine two other features of the tax treatment of religious groups. First, churches are automatically entitled to "public charity" (nonfoundation) status (§§509(a)(1) and 170(b)(1)(A)) without having to meet formulaic public support tests. An objection to this preference, however, is weakened by the fact that hospitals and schools share this privileged status—suggesting that, for all three institutions, the automatic public charity categorization may be based on an assumption of public support (without resort to formulas), rather than a religious preference. Second, churches, along with foundations, cannot take advantage of a safe-harbor provision (§501(h)) permitting a limited amount of legislative lobbying without worrying about whether or not it is "insubstantial" under §501(c)(3). While this provision superficially appears to be a detriment for churches, they actually sought the provision, apparently because they felt confident in their ability to defeat IRS challenges (if any were to arise) under the insubstantiality standard.

The empirical investigations suggested above will be difficult to implement in the present era. As noted, access to empirical data is not easy to obtain under existing disclosure laws, and Congress has exhibited no appetite for such investigations. Standing-to-sue obstacles make it difficult to test the constitutional issues in the courts. Despite these obstacles, both lines of inquiry are worthy objects of scholarly pursuit.

A CONCLUDING LAMENT

In an earlier (1987) version of this chapter, significant gaps were noted in both the empirical and theoretical materials that were needed for scholarship concerning federal tax policy on charity—and particularly scholarship that could inform the policy choices that continue to confront federal lawmakers and regulators. The intervening years have seen some progress in these directions, but significant shortages remain. Thus, under the "support function" heading, the issue of the incentive effectiveness of tax deductibility and exemption has been only partly addressed. Sophisticated econometric analysis has been valuable, but we have yet to use the underemployed tools of psychology and perhaps other behavioral sciences to get inside the human "black box," in order to know more about the motivational dynamics of charitable giving and volunteering. Under the "regulatory function" heading, consideration of the relative roles that might be assigned to state and federal oversight would be greatly assisted by a more comprehensive assessment of the present and potential regulatory effectiveness of state attorneys general and of the IRS. Under the "equity function" heading, empirical work on the redistributional aspects of the nonprofit sector has come a long way (Clotfelter 1992; Jencks 1987). Yet the impact of tax policy on equity issues—for example, access to health care and cultural resources and the impact of private schooling—demands further attention. With respect to the business-nonprofit "border-patrol function," the competitive unfairness assumptions that underlie past or present limits on commerciality have not been subjected to serious testing and analysis in the context of real-life market situations. And the special case of churches raises empirical questions about the impact of minimal disclosure requirements on less-than-holy conduct and, on the other hand, the degree of "entanglement" that would result from increased disclosure.

Even if these not inconsiderable gaps were repaired, a more daunting difficulty continues to confront policy-related research in this area. The plain truth is that the various controversies that arise in tax policy relating to charity echo deeper and nearly intractable issues of public policy. These "gnarled roots"[106] of public policy are often issues that our society has not fully resolved—a congeries of American dilemmas from which tax policy is only a partial outcropping. The problem with outcroppings is that it is hard to deal with them without knowing more about the gnarled roots that germinate them.

For example, lying behind the "support function" discussion is a major set of controversies about the appropriate division of labor in American society among the public, proprietary, and nonprofit sectors—hardly a set of questions that we could resolve in these (or any other) pages. Under the "equity function," distributional questions relating to charitable tax policy are exceedingly difficult to tackle without some basic assumptions about distributive justice and fairness. As to the government-nonprofit "border-patrol function," questions about the role of nonprofits in electoral and legislative affairs are hard to investigate without some basic assumptions about the nature of participation in democratic institutions. And with respect to the "special case" of churches, the argument about church preferences under the tax code invokes fundamental church-state issues that have been troubling since the early days of the Republic.

An extreme form of the gnarled-roots problem was reported many years ago to one of the authors by a senior member of the Episcopal clergy, who said that he was told in seminary that all contemporary policy problems could be resolved by resorting to one of two alternative views of the Creation. That level of inquiry lies beyond our competence, and we have not in this chapter attempted to deal with any of the gnarled roots that we have just adumbrated. Indeed, we believe that useful and even important research can be done without such deep excavations. But here, in the field of federal tax policy on charity, as in other nontrivial pursuits of scholars and policy analysts, we believe it advisable to acknowledge candidly the fear and thrill of knowing that, to varying degrees, the writers are in over their depth.

ACKNOWLEDGMENTS

The authors are grateful to Marion Fremont-Smith, Stephen Schwarz, and Evelyn Brody for their helpful comments on an earlier draft of this chapter and to Susan Belkin of the National Center on Philanthropy and Law for her help in compiling the references. Harvey Dale gratefully acknowledges the support of the Rockefeller Foundation for giving him a one-month residency at its Bellagio Study and Conference Center, where he was able to research and write a significant portion of his share of the chapter.

NOTES

1. The text reflects the state of the law as of the end of 2005. Subsequent legal developments—by court decision, legislation, or regulation—are not reflected in the text and may be significant. In the next section we explain the contours of "charity" (and "charitable organizations") and of "nonprofit organizations," as used in this chapter.

2. The necessarily summary approach of this chapter precludes both a full discussion of the issues and exhaustive citation of all the relevant literature. Readers seeking more will find the task facilitated by consulting the National Center on Philanthropy and the Law's bibliography, available online at http://ncpl.law.nyu.edu/ncplsearch. A comprehensive treatise on nonprofit tax law is Hill and Mancino (2002).

3. Or to "foster [certain types of] national or international amateur sports competition" or "for the prevention of cruelty to children or animals." Sometimes we use the word "charity" to refer not to one of the §501(c)(3) organizations but, in a more general sense, to the doing of charitable works.

4. In using the terms "charities" and "noncharitable nonprofits," we do not mean to imply that the former are all virtuous or that the latter lack virtue; indeed, we do not use these terms descriptively. They are simply shortcut references to groups the tax code refers to as "charitable" and to groups the code does not refer to as such.

5. The non-(c)(3)s, however, can be characterized as providing "local public goods"—goods that are available to all of the members. See also Weisbrod's (1980) "collective" goods categorization.

6. For a comprehensive review of benefits accruing to nonprofit entities, see Facchina, Showell, and Stone (1993).

7. This somewhat amoebic subdivision repeated itself in August 1984. For the purpose of giving certain operating foundations the benefit of public charity treatment in two respects (relief from the foundation excise tax and from the "expenditure responsibility" requirements), Congress carved out a subset of the operating foundation category and called it the "exempt operating foundation": an operating foundation that has a ten-year history of being publicly supported, and has a board "broadly representative of the general public" and not donor-controlled (§4940(d)).

8. In addition, foundations are subjected to greater reporting requirements than public charities. Unless otherwise indicated, the references in this chapter to "foundations" or "private foundations" apply to nonoperating foundations (roughly speaking, grant-making foundations), not operating foundations. We follow this convention simply because nonoperating foundations are much more numerous—and repre-

sent a vastly higher level of assets and expenditures—than operating foundations (Foundation Center 2002:xii).

9. Whether the exemption provisions rest on the taxing or the spending power depends on whether exemption is a function of a technically accurate definition of the tax base or tantamount to an indirect subsidy.

10. In any case, whether or not the taxing power provides a basis for federal regulation of charities, the commerce clause would almost certainly provide a footing for congressional action in this sphere (see *Camps Newfound/Owatonna v. Town of Harrison,* 520 U.S. 564 [1997]).

11. Donations by partnerships, S corporations, and certain other pass-through entities are allowed to the partners, shareholders, and so on, rather than being allowed to the entity (see, e.g., §§703(a)(2)(C), 702(a)(4), 1366(a)(1)). Charitable donations by trusts or estates are subject to a different regime under §642(c).

12. An individual's "contribution base" is his or her adjusted gross income computed without any net operating loss carrybacks (§170(b)(1)(F)).

13. This account of deductibility rules barely touches on the variety of complex rules that have the potential to change the amount of, or even wholly to deny, the charitable contributions deduction. These rules depend on the form of the gift, the type of property donated, and the nature of the donee organization. Even a moderately succinct description of the way these rules operate, prepared by one of the authors (Dale), necessarily consumed far more space than the present format permits. Accordingly, we offer the account (Dale 2003), entitled "Charitable Contribution Deductions—A Primer," as an electronic appendix to this chapter; it may be consulted at this Web address: http://www.nyu.edu/projects/hdale/.

14. Section 170(c)(2)(A) states that the donee must be "created or organized in the United States or in any possession thereof, or under the law of the United States, any State, the District of Columbia, or any possession of the United States."

15. The estate tax, of course, exerts a price effect on bequests, even though it only reaches fairly large estates. Some simulations have suggested that repeal of the estate tax would reduce testamentary charitable gifts by between 24 percent and 44 percent (Clotfelter and Schmalbeck 1996). Others disagree, believing that the "wealth effect"—the increase in estate assets caused by repeal—would overwhelm the "price effect"—the increase in the after-tax cost of giving (Brody 1999a). Some estimates are set forth in Clotfelter (1997), Steinberg (2003), and Auten, Sieg, and Clotfelter (2002).

16. An April 1999 conference at the Urban Institute convened economics experts who explored this issue. A consensus emerged that there was "much uncertainty" about price elasticity, and that the issue "is far from settled" (Cordes 1999).

17. Brody (1998b) has suggested that the terms in which both sides of the debate have been advanced have "sovereignty overtones." That is, our tendency, conscious or not, to view the charitable sector as quasi-sovereign leads us to stand back from imposing a tax burden, while at the same time imposing constraints designed to avoid allowing the sector and its institutions to become too powerful.

18. Different explanations for the exemption of noncharitable nonprofits (the "mutual benefit" entities) appear in Bittker and Rahdert (1976:358), Atkinson (1994:15–26), and Hansmann (1981:96).

19. Of course, if taxes are imposed not on income or transfers but on some other base, such as consumption (as in certain forms of proposed tax reform), different considerations apply and much of the analysis in this chapter may become less relevant.

20. Congress has explicitly departed from standard doctrine to provide for conduit treatment of certain noncharitable nonprofits—social clubs, homeowners' associations, and political organizations (Hopkins 2003:20–21)—as well as for-profit corporation-partnership hybrids (so-called subchapter S corporations, §§1361–79), but it is not clear that it meant to relax the no-conduit doctrine in the case of charitable corporations.

21. A plausible response to this point is that neither gift is "consumption," and that administrative convenience, not doctrinal muddiness, explains the difference in treatment. It is a way of making it "practical to establish and audit the amount of redistribution from donors to recipients" (Andrews 1972:351). But Colombo (2001:683) has pointed out that some donations to individual recipients, such as bank funds established to aid particular victims of misfortune, would not be difficult to track, and that similar tracking difficulties have not led to similar limitations in other contexts (for example, the business expense deduction).

22. As Andrews puts it, "Whatever its origin, the fair market value rule must now be viewed as a subsidy or artificial inducement, above and beyond mere tax exemption, for philanthropic giving. The magnitude of the subsidy is a function of the amount of unrealized appreciation in relation to the basis of the property and the taxpayer's rates of tax, being greatest for taxpayers in highest brackets and with most appreciation" (1972:372).

23. For example, certain special reduction rules tend to limit the deduction to the adjusted basis of the donated property (§§170(e)(1)(A), 170(e)(1)(B)(i)–(ii)).

24. In other contexts, charitable gifts sometimes trigger gain to the donor. For example, charitable donations of installment obligations accelerate gain to the donor (Rev. Rul. 60–352, 1960–2 C.B. 208; Rev. Rul. 55–157, 1955–1 C.B. 293). Charitable donations of property subject to indebtedness also trigger gain to the donor (Rev. Rul. 81–163, 1981–1 C.B. 443).

25. Brody (1999a:705–13) describes a trend toward demand-side tax subsidies such as tax credits for educational expenses.

26. McIntyre (1980:84–85) likens the process of distinguishing tax expenditure items from deductions necessary to reach an accurate measurement of income to the process of distinguishing a weed—"a plant that has no proper place in a flower garden"—from a nonweed: "part of what makes a weed a weed is an aesthetic judgment that it is out of place where it is. The same is true of a tax expenditure. Since their meanings depend in part on value judgments, their definitions necessarily have soft, fuzzy edges—not the crispness of an itemized list."

27. Michael Krashinsky, however, sees a way to reconcile these limits with the tax-base-defining rationale (J. Simon 1987:74n8).

28. No matter how persuasive base-defining theories may be, however, exemption and deduction benefits are likely to be viewed by courts as subsidies. For example, although the U.S. Supreme Court's majority opinion in *Regan v. Taxation with Representation of Washington* (461 U.S. 540, 461n5 [1983]) does recognize "that exemptions and deductions, on the one hand . . . [and] cash subsidies, on the other . . . [are not] in all respects identical" (citing *Walz v. Tax Commission,* 397 U.S. 664 [1970]), all of the justices accepted the equivalence of the former with the latter for purposes of the case. A leading commentator concludes that "typically, the two may be treated alike" (Sullivan 1989:1425). For further discussion of this issue, see Bittker (1969) and Zelinsky (1998:393–95, 428).

29. For a sampling of the extensive literature analyzing this doctrine, see Sullivan (1989), Cole (1992), L. Baker (1995), and Berman (2001).

30. As one commentator recently wrote, "it is now universally recognized that such conditional offers are sometimes constitutionally permissible and sometimes not" (Berman 2001:3).

31. As the Supreme Court itself has subsequently stated, "The Court in *Rust* did not place explicit reliance on the rationale that the counseling activities of the doctors under Title X amounted to governmental speech; when interpreting the holding in later cases, however, we have explained *Rust* on this understanding" (*Legal Services Corp. v. Velazquez,* 531 U.S. 533, 541 [2001]).

32. In a dissenting opinion, however, four of the nine Supreme Court justices rejected this distinction as "so unpersuasive it hardly

needs response" (*Legal Services Corp. v. Velazquez,* 554 (Scalia, J., dissenting)).

33. Compare, for example, the relatively narrow family planning program in *Rust v. Sullivan* (500 U.S. 173 [1991]) with the lobbying restrictions considered in *Regan v. Taxation with Representation of Washington* (461 U.S. 540 [1983]), affecting all tax-exempt charities—although in both cases the government restrictions were sustained.

34. See also *Branch Ministries v. Commissioner* (211 F.3d 137 [D.C. Cir. 2000] (use of a PAC to participate in political campaigns).

35. Recent developments in the United Kingdom are significant. The 1601 statute, as interpreted most famously by Lord Macnaghten in *Commissioners for Special Purposes of Income Tax v. Pemsel* (1891, A.C. 531), contemplated four divisions of charity. The Prime Minister's Strategy Unit report, "Private Action, Public Benefit," released 25 September 2002 (full text available at http://www.strategy.gov.uk/downloads/su/voluntary/report/downloads/strat-data.pdf), recommended enlarging that to ten categories of charity, and suggested other far-reaching changes to the law. Following months of comments from the nonprofit community, the U.K. government, in July 2003, released its responses to those comments in a report entitled "Charities and Not-for-Profits: A Modern Legal Framework."

36. With respect to action at the state level, in 1971 the New York state legislature gave municipalities the authority to put a subset of charitable organizations (including cultural institutions) back on the property tax rolls (1971 N.Y. Law ch. 414; see Swords 1981:85). Massachusetts once held, for property tax purposes, that an otherwise charitable cultural institution—the Boston Symphony Orchestra—lost its charitable status when it charged admission. See *Boston Symphony Orchestra v. Board of Assessors* (294 Mass. 248 [1936], discussed in Fremont-Smith (1965:70–71).

37. The evolution of the IRS's approach to exemption for hospitals is described in Mancino (1988:1037), Colombo (1990:476–79), and Rubenstein (1997:389–99).

38. For excellent accounts of the charitable response and how legal standards developed in the wake of the 9/11 tragedy, see Bjorklund (2002), Steuerle (2002), and Katz (2003).

39. IRS Pub. No. 1771, "Charitable Contributions—Substantiation and Disclosure Requirements" (2002:5), states: "What are 'intangible religious benefits?' Generally, they are benefits provided by a tax exempt organization operated exclusively for religious purposes, and are not usually sold in commercial transactions outside a donative (gift) context. Examples include admission to a religious ceremony and a de minimis tangible benefit, such as wine used in a religious ceremony. Benefits that are not intangible religious benefits include education leading to a recognized degree, travel services, and consumer goods."

40. The full text of the closing agreement can be found at *Exempt Organization Tax Review* 19 (1998): 227. None of the parties to the closing agreement has authenticated the text, but none has denied its accuracy, either.

41. One other deductibility area that raises "private benefit" issues involves "split-interest" trusts. There are two broad categories of split-interest charitable trusts: charitable lead trusts (in which the charitable beneficiary's interest precedes the interest of noncharitable beneficiaries) and charitable remainder trusts (in which the reverse is true).

42. Under the tax-base-defining rationales, the government never had a claim on the revenues allocated privately by donors; thus there is no issue of private exercise of government power.

43. The allocative power issue may explain the fact that, among operating foundations, a distinction is drawn between donor-controlled and non-donor-controlled organizations, with the former ineligible to take advantage of the more favorable "exempt operating foundation" status introduced in the 1984 Tax Reform Act (§§4940(d), 4945(d)(4)).

44. It is assumed for purposes of this simplified example that no special reduction rules, deduction floors, or other limitations or adjustments are applicable.

45. For example, the same phenomenon occurs when a sole proprietor deducts expenses, such as salaries and rent, incurred in business: a higher-income proprietor gets a greater benefit from those deductions than a lower-income proprietor.

46. The credit would probably have to be refundable if all taxpayers, even those with very low incomes, were to be treated equally.

47. For further discussions of a credit rather than a deduction for charitable giving, see Clotfelter (1985), Gergen (1988), Weidenbeck (1985), and McNulty (1984).

48. "For 2001, an estimated 110.3 million returns, or 72.1 percent of all filers, will utilize the standard deduction, while an estimated 42.7 million returns, or 27.9 percent of all filers, will itemize" (Staff of Joint Committee on Taxation, "Study of the Overall State of the Federal Tax System and Recommendations for Simplification, Pursuant to Section 9022(3)(B) of the Internal Revenue Code of 1986," JCS-3–01, 34 [Comm. Print 2001]).

49. For a thoughtful analysis of the history of, policy considerations affecting, and possible legislative amendments to the nonitemizer charitable contributions deduction, see April (2001). See also Staff of Joint Committee on Taxation, "Description and Analysis of Present Law and Proposals to Expand Federal Tax Incentives for Charitable Giving," JCX-13–01 (Comm. Print 2001).

50. For an insightful discussion of this limitation, see Shuldiner and Shakow (2001).

51. For an illuminating analysis of the "state action" claim in an analogous situation, see Judge Henry Friendly's dissenting opinion in *Jackson v. Statler Foundation,* 496 F.2d 623, 637–40 (2d Cir. 1973).

52. The duty of care encompasses the obligation to be diligent, prudent, and reasonably competent in managing the organization's resources and operations.

53. Brody (1999b) finds the evidence in Congress's failure to extend the private foundation rules to public charities, in its failure to enact 1977 Treasury Department proposals to impose a payout requirement on public charities and to cloak the U.S. District Courts with broad equity powers in connection with enforcement of the tax exemption laws, and in its failure to specify any duty-of-care–related rules when it enacted the intermediate sanctions rules that explicitly incorporate some aspects of the duty of loyalty into the tax code.

54. The private-benefit regulations affect only §501(c)(3) organizations. The inurement proscription applies to many types of organizations described in §501(c), and the excess benefit regime of §4958 covers both §501(c)(3) charities and §501(c)(4) social welfare organizations.

55. The inurement regime is based upon language in §501(c)(3) and several other paragraphs of §501(c), although substantially identical words also appear in Treas. Reg. §1.501(c)(5)-1(a)(1). The excess benefit rules are contained in §4958. Anti-inurement language appears in nine separate paragraphs of §501(c)(3) and at least thirteen other places in the code.

56. The limitation on private benefit stems from Treas. Reg. §1.501(c)(3)-1(d)(1)(ii).

57. The act is entitled "An Act to Provide Revenue, Equalize Duties and Encourage the Industries of the United States, and for Other Purposes" (Pub. L. No. 61–5, 36 Stat. 11 [1909]). It was signed on 5 August 1909.

58. The tax was structured as an excise tax rather than as an income tax because of congressional concerns that an income tax might be unconstitutional under *Pollock v. Farmers' Loan and Trust Co.,* 157 U.S. 601 (1895).

59. A detailed demonstration of this point and an elaboration of many other portions of this section appear in a paper written by one of the authors (Dale), entitled "The Crux of Charity: Inurement, Private Benefit, and Excess Benefit Transactions," available in full text at the following Web site: http://www.law.nyu.edu/ncpl/libframe.html.

60. See Redmond (1996); Hopkins (2003: §§19.1–19.9).

61. As one court put it, more than sixty years after the anti-inurement language first appeared in the code, "there is very little material by way of guidance to this Court in the regulations or in any case law as to the application and meaning of that sentence" (*Universal Church of Scientific Truth v. United States,* 74–1 U.S. Tax Cas. (CCH) §9360, 32 A.F.T.R.2d 73–6122, 6123 [N.D. Ala. 1973]).

62. As the service's then associate chief counsel (for employee benefits and exempt organizations) put it: "In my view, the definition of inurement isn't the problem—most practitioners and most agents know it when they see it." Speech by James McGovern to the American Bar Association's Tax Section, San Diego, 5 February 1993, reprinted in *Exempt Organization Tax Review* 7 (1993): 556.

63. The regulations read: "An organization is not organized or operated exclusively for one or more of the purposes specified in subdivision (i) of this subparagraph unless it serves a public rather than a private interest. Thus, to meet the requirement of this subdivision, it is necessary for an organization to establish that it is not organized or operated for the benefit of private interests such as designated individuals, the creator or his family, shareholders of the organization, or persons controlled, directly or indirectly, by such private interests." Treas. Reg. §1.501(c)(3)-1(d)(1)(ii).

64. For example, the Tax Court stated that "while the prohibitions against private inurement and private benefits share common and often overlapping elements, . . . the two are distinct requirements which must independently be satisfied" (*American Campaign Academy v. Commissioner,* 92 T.C. 1053, 1068 [1989]). Congress has accepted this view; see, for example, H.R. Rep. No. 104–506 (1996), at 53n2: "Even where no prohibited private inurement exists, however, more than incidental private benefits conferred on individuals may result in the organization not being operated 'exclusively' for an exempt purpose. See, e.g., *American Campaign Academy v. Commissioner.* . . ."

65. As the Tax Court agreed, "nonincidental benefits conferred on disinterested persons may serve private interests" (*American Campaign Academy v. Commissioner,* 92 T.C. 1053, 1069 [1989]).

66. As Gen. Couns. Mem. 39862 puts it, "inurement may be found even though the amounts involved are small. . . . There is no de minimis exception to the inurement prohibition."

67. Id.; accord., *American Campaign Academy v. Commissioner,* 92 T.C. 1053, 1068 (1989); Hopkins (2003).

68. United Cancer Council, Inc. v. Commissioner, 165 F.3d 1173 (7th Cir. 1999), *rev'g and remanding* 109 T.C. 326 (1997), referred to earlier in this section. For discussions of the decision, see Ford (2000), Josephs (1999), and Raby and Raby (1999).

69. 165 F.3d at 1178. Judge Posner did agree, however, that the more-than-incidental-private-benefit doctrine might apply, even though the inurement proscription did not, and the case was remanded to the Tax Court to decide that question. Because the parties subsequently settled the case, the Tax Court never ruled on that issue.

70. The "largely" qualifier is because there are two specialized exceptions, §4911 and §4955, that impose excise taxes on excess lobbying expenditures and on certain political campaign expenditures, respectively.

71. The statute expressly excludes from its coverage private foundations—already subject to strict self-dealing rules mentioned later in this section.

72. The report of the House Ways and Means Committee first states that Code §4958 may be applied either "in lieu of (or in addition to) revocation of an organization's tax-exempt status" (H.R. Rep. No. 104–506 [1996], at 59). The accompanying footnote, however, goes on to state: "In general, the intermediate sanctions are the *sole* sanction imposed in those cases in which the excess benefit does not rise to the level where it calls into question whether, on the whole, the organization functions as a charitable or other tax-exempt organization. In practice, revocation of tax-exempt status, with or without the imposition of excise taxes, would occur only when the organization no longer operates as a charitable organization." *Id.,* n15 (emphasis added). Recently published proposed regulations describe factors that would argue for or against revocation in addition to intermediate solutions.

73. For a sampling of the writings on this issue, see Kaufmann (2002); Kuhn (2001); Miller (2001); Schwartzman (1999); Henzke and Davis (1997, 1998); Kurtz and Paul (1997); Crozier (1996); Roady and Ward (1996); Ten Broeck (1994).

74. A more general set of restrictions on both lobbying and electoral activity flows from the §501(c)(3) requirement that the organization be "operated exclusively" for charitable purposes. Treas. Reg. §1.501(c)(3)-1(c)(3) specifies that an organization is not organized and operated exclusively for charitable purposes if it is an "action organization." The regulations go on to define "action organization" to include organizations that engage in more than insubstantial lobbying, organizations that intervene in election campaigns, and organizations that have a "main or primary objective or objectives" that "may be attained only by legislation or defeat of legislation" and that "advocate . . . for the attainment of such . . . objective or objectives." Although these regulations are not deployed by the IRS as frequently as the specific code restrictions, they are occasionally cited as an independent source of limits, and questions about how the two relate to one another have not been fully answered.

75. Those amounts are up to 20 percent of the organization's expenditures for exempt purposes, with declining percentages for larger organizations, and with a limit on grassroots lobbying expenditures of 25 percent of the total amount allowed for lobbying. The CARE Act, passed by the Senate and House in 2004 but not accorded conference committee action, would have done away with the separate grassroots limit.

76. Violations initially result in imposition of a 25 percent excise tax on excess lobbying expenditures. Only when the four-year average of the organization's lobbying expenditures exceeds its limits is the organization subject to revocation of its §501(c)(3) status.

77. For detailed descriptions of the tax-exemption-related provision concerning election campaign intervention, see Cerny and Hill (1996) and Roady (1999).

78. The association lost its §501(c)(3) exemption for rating the qualifications of judicial candidates in a nonpartisan election.

79. Treasury regulations under §170 denying the charitable deduction for contributions to organizations that lobby substantially or intervene in election campaigns do not make an exception for §501(c)(19) veterans' organizations, but they have never been applied to those groups.

80. §501(c)(4) social welfare organizations must be "primarily engaged in promoting in some way the common good and general welfare of the people of the community."

81. Treas. Reg. §1.501(c)(4)-1(a)(2)(ii) provides that support for or in opposition to candidates does not promote social welfare. See also Rev. Rul. 81–95, 1981–1 C.B. 332 (a §501(c)(4) organization may intervene in election campaigns so long as campaign intervention is not its primary activity), and Rev. Rul. 67–3688, 1967–2 C.B. 194 (an organization whose primary activity is election intervention does not qualify for § 501(c)(4) exemption).

82. A §527 political organization is unlimited in its election-related activities, and is not subject to limits on other activities (such as lobbying) beyond the requirement that it be operated "primarily" for the purpose of influencing the selection of individuals to fill elective or appointive office. However, §527 contemplates and encourages an organization more than "primarily" focused on elections. A §527 organization is not taxed on the money it collects and spends on election-related activities, but it does pay tax at the highest corporate rate on other income (such as investment income) and on expenditures that are not intended to influence elections (such as lobbying or nonpartisan voter education). Contributions to a §527 organization are not deductible to the donor. The Full and Fair Political Activity and Disclosure Act of 2000,

Public Law 106–230, 114 Stat. 477, imposes several reporting and disclosure requirements on §527 organizations: an initial notice of political organization status (to be filed within twenty-four hours of establishment), periodic reports of contributions and expenditures, and annual returns, all of which are open to public disclosure. In addition, PACs are subject to extensive regulation via the Federal Election Campaign Act and the Bipartisan Campaign Reform Act of 2002, which operate independently of tax exemption rules.

83. The legislative history of the 1934 lobbying provision is covered in G. Baker (1986), Bucholtz (1998), Chisolm (1987–88), and Galston (1993). The lawmaker referred to in the text was Senator Lyndon Johnson, who offered the 1937 electoral prohibition as a floor amendment; differing interpretations of his motives are found in Hopkins 2003:584 and in *Lobbying and Political Activities of Tax-Exempt Organizations: Hearings before the Subcommittee on Oversight of the Committee on Ways and Means,* 100th Cong., 1st Sess. 124, 144, 148–49, 423, 437, 446–53. The anecdotal nature of the arguments in favor of §4955—which imposes penalty excise taxes on certain electoral activity—is noted in Chisolm (1990b).

84. Compare Weisbrod, Handler, and Komesar (1978:556–57) and Center for Community Change (1996), which find a negative impact of legislative activity, with Berry (1999:17–20) and Berry and Arons (2000), who have found that tax law constraints are not a significant obstacle to organizations that want to lobby.

85. These uses do not always involve the provision of funds *by* an exempt organization to arguably election-related activity, although that is sometimes the complaint. Contributions *to* politician-affiliated organizations by people seeking favor have also been part of the pattern (Chisolm 1990b). A recent news article reported that children's charities associated with House Majority Leader Tom Delay are generously supported by corporations, executives, and lobbyists. "[A] charity linked to Mr. DeLay, Celebrations for Children, was effectively shut in 2003 after criticism of its plans to sponsor fund-raising galas at the Republican National Convention last year. Its organizing committee, which included Mr. DeLay's daughter, said at the time that proceeds from the events, including dinners with Mr. DeLay, Broadway shows and a yacht trip, were intended for the DeLay Foundation" (Shenon and Strom 2005).

86. At least one commentator has argued, however, that election of like-minded candidates is a far more efficient and effective means of influencing public policy than lobbying on an issue-by-issue basis (Tesdahl 1991:1176).

87. "In a panel of 130,000 organizations that filed IRS Form 990 returns in both 1993 and 1998, 66 percent reported an increase in the amount of commercial income. The increase was most prevalent among higher education organizations and hospitals" (Steuerle 2001:2).

88. When the PTL Ministry (run by Jimmy and Tammy Faye Bakker) went bankrupt, the IRS filed a Revenue Agent's Report asserting that the PTL should not qualify as a tax-exempt organization or, in the alternative, that if it was tax exempt it owed tax on its unrelated business income. The tax deficiency claimed on the first theory (that the PTL was fully taxable) was millions of dollars *less* than the tax deficiency claimed on the second theory (that the PTL was tax exempt).

89. The industry studies in Weisbrod (1998) provide valuable information on the commercialism process, but data were not available to the authors that would permit empirical analysis of "competitive unfairness" claims.

90. This reconsideration has already taken place in the nonprofit insurance industry, affecting organizations such as the TIAA-CREF and Blue Cross/Blue Shield entities. See §501(m), repealing exemption for organizations "providing commercial-type insurance [as a] substantial part of [their] activities."

91. See, however, Steinberg's (1991) cautionary note about the state of research bearing on efficiency issues.

92. A survey conducted by the Yale School of Management–Goldman Sachs Foundation Partnership on Nonprofit Ventures found that 80 percent of nonprofit respondents reported that business ventures improved the nonprofit's reputation, and more than two-thirds said that the business ventures improved the nonprofit's delivery of organizational services; one-half pointed to a favorable impact on the ability to attract and retain staff personnel (Hochberg 2002).

93. On UBIT generally, see Dale (1990a).

94. As noted, the legislative history of the tax reflects a congressional desire to avoid "unfair competition" between taxable and nontaxable businesses, although alternative explanations of the tax, not based on competitive considerations, have been developed (Schwarz and Hutton 1984:680).

95. As previously noted, the word "exclusively" in the statute has been transmogrified into "primarily" by the regulations (Treas. Reg. §1.501(c)(3)-1(c)(1)).

96. The history of the "commerciality" doctrine is set forth by Hopkins (1992), who calls the doctrine "an enigma." The doctrine is subjected to detailed analysis in Spitzer (2002) and Colombo (2002). A recent case suggesting the analytical difficulties of applying the doctrine is *Airlie Foundation v. Internal Revenue Service,* 283 F. Supp. 2d 58 (D.D.C. 2003).

97. The court in *Presbyterian and Reformed Publishing Co. v. Commissioner,* 742 F.2d 148 (3d Cir. 1984), lamented the lack of a clear definition of or test for determining "purpose."

98. A note on state tax treatment: Both the claims of unfair competition and the fears of public revenue loss that we encountered in discussing federal tax aspects of commercial activity also arise in connection with state property tax exemption for charities engaged in business endeavors. In other words, the specter of charities enjoying commercial income while occupying tax-exempt real estate can trigger both grievances, often prompting state or local tax officials to revoke property tax exemptions of groups engaging in commercial activity and sometimes leading to state legislative action limiting exemption to "purely charitable" organizations. It should be noted that the issue of competitive unfairness resulting from property tax relief has undergone a degree of theoretical and empirical scrutiny even less searching than similar issues arising under federal taxation (but see Brody 2002).

99. We make no effort here to enter into the immensely technical tax-regulatory thicket that has grown up around these transactions—especially joint ventures and foundation corporate control. Some notion of the complexity of the joint venture rules is conveyed by the fact that the leading treatise on the subject—Sanders's *Joint Ventures Involving Tax-Exempt Organizations* (2000)—runs 618 pages.

100. A more detailed explanation of the motivations for conversion appears in Goddeeris and Weisbrod (1998) and in Cutler and Horwitz (2000), which also discusses the impacts of conversions.

101. A related mechanism once in vogue was the sale and leaseback: here, property owned by a nonprofit—property that could give rise to depreciation allowances, investment tax credits, and other write-offs in the hands of a taxable (for-profit) owner—is sold to such an entity, which then leases it back to the nonprofit under terms that allow the two parties to share in the tax savings enjoyed by the taxable owner (Pang 1985). Extreme versions of this device—for example, the proposed sale and leaseback of the entire Bennington College campus—begot adverse regulation from the IRS and some restrictive legislation (see §168(j)).

102. §3121(w) defines "church" as follows: "For purposes of this section, the term 'church' means a church [usually interpreted to mean a congregation], a convention or association of churches, or an elementary or secondary school which is controlled, operated or principally supported by a church or a convention or association of churches." The expression "church" does not include other religiously affiliated organizations, such as universities, hospitals, or social service organizations.

103. Even though exemption is commonly referred to as a subsidy, subsidy of religion via exemption was and is treated very differently from subsidy via cash grants or other forms of direct support; the lat-

ter—but not the former—is ordinarily judged to violate the establishment clause. In a gray area are forms of indirect subsidy—most prominently, at this time, school vouchers, which in June 2002 received an important (if not the final) measure of constitutional approval from the Supreme Court (*Zelman v. Simmons-Harris,* 536 U.S. 639).

104. There are federal and state cases in which religious organizations claim that they have been denied a tax exemption made available to other groups. However, the courts have denied these claims on the ground that the cause of the groups' taxability was not their religion but their *lack* of religiosity—their "secular" orientation (Fishman and Schwarz 2000:447)—or because the group, albeit religious, "violated one or more requirements that apply to all organizations seeking §501(c)(3) status" (ibid.). See the earlier discussions of the *Bob Jones University* and *Church of Scientology* cases.

105. A recent report by the General Accounting Office to the Senate Finance Committee on "Improvements Possible in Public, IRS, and State Oversight of Charities," based in part on interviews with IRS and Treasury officials, makes no reference to any "oversight" difficulties caused by these statutory exemptions (U.S. General Accounting Office 2002).

106. This phrase is Marvin Chirelstein's way of describing such underlying—often submerged—issues or premises.

REFERENCES

AAFRC Trust for Philanthropy. 2000. *Giving USA 1999.* New York: AAFRC Trust for Philanthropy.

Ablin, Erik J. 1999. "The Price of Not Rendering to Caesar: Restrictions on Church Participation in Political Campaigns." *Notre Dame Journal of Law, Ethics and Public Policy* 13:541–88.

Adler, Phillip. 1922. "Historical Origin of Tax Exemption of Charitable Institutions." Pp. 1–88 in *Tax Exemption on Real Estate—An Increasing Menace, Part I.* Westchester County, N.Y.: Chamber of Commerce.

Andrews, William D. 1972. "Personal Deductions in an Ideal Income Tax." *Harvard Law Review* 86, no. 2 (December): 309–85.

Aprill, Ellen P. 2001. "Churches, Politics, and the Charitable Contribution Deduction." *Boston College Law Review* 42:843–74.

Atkinson, Rob. 1990. "Altruism in Nonprofit Organizations." *Boston College Law Review* 31:501–639.

———. 1994. "Theories of the Special Tax Treatment of Nonprofit Organizations." Pp. 15-1–15-36 in *Federal and State Taxation of Exempt Organizations,* edited by Frances R. Hill and Barbara L. Kirschten. Boston: Warren, Gorham and Lamont.

———. 1997. "Theories of the Federal Income Tax Exemption for Charities: Thesis, Antithesis, and Synthesis." *Stetson Law Review* 27:395–431.

Auten, Gerald E., Charles T. Clotfelter, and Richard L. Schmalbeck. 2000. "Taxes and Philanthropy among the Wealthy." Pp. 392–426 in *Does Atlas Shrug? The Economic Consequences of Taxing the Rich,* edited by Joel B. Slemrod. New York: Russell Sage Foundation; Cambridge, Mass.: Harvard University Press.

Auten, Gerald E., Holger Sieg, and Charles T. Clotfelter. 2002. "Charitable Giving, Income, and Taxes: An Analysis of Panel Data." *American Economic Review* 12 (1): 371–82.

Baker, George. 1986. "Lobbying by Public Charities: Summary of Proposed Regulations." *Tax Notes* 33:1145–50.

Baker, Lynn A. 1995. "Conditional Federal Spending after Lopez." *Columbia Law Review* 95:1911–89.

Ballan, Judith S. 1994. "How to Aid a Foreign Charity." Chap. 4 in *NYU Conference on Tax Planning for Section 501(c) (3) Organizations,* vol. 23. New York: New York University School of Law.

Belknap, Chauncey. 1977. "The Federal Income Tax Treatment of Charitable Organizations: Its Origins and Underlying Policy." Pp. 2025–43 in *Research Papers,* vol. 4, edited by the Commission on Private Philanthropy and Public Needs. Washington, D.C.: Treasury Department.

Bennett, James T., and Thomas J. DiLorenzo. 1989. *Unfair Competition: The Profits of Nonprofits.* Lanham, Md.: Hamilton Press.

Bennett, James T., and Gabriel Rudney. 1987. "A Commerciality Test to Resolve the Commercial Nonprofit Issue." *Tax Notes* 36:1095–98.

Berger, Peter L., and Richard John Neuhaus. 1977. *To Empower People: The Role of Mediating Structures in Public Policy.* Washington, D.C.: American Enterprise Institute for Public Policy Research.

Berman, Mitchell N. 2001. "Coercion without Baselines: Unconstitutional Conditions in Three Dimensions." *Georgetown Law Journal* 90:1–112.

Berry, Jeffrey M. 1999. *The New Liberalism: The Rising Power of Citizen Groups.* Washington, D.C.: Brookings Institution Press.

Berry, Jeffrey M., and David Arons. 2000. "Organizational Capacity and Nonprofit Advocacy." Paper prepared for the annual conference of the Association for Research on Nonprofit Organizations and Voluntary Action, New Orleans, November 1–18.

Bird, Wendell R. 2000. "Political Activities of Exempt Organizations—and of the IRS and Congress." *Journal of Taxation of Exempt Organizations* 11:248–56.

Bittker, Boris I. 1969. "Churches, Taxes and the Constitution." *Yale Law Journal* 78:1285–1310.

———. 1972. "Charitable Contributions: Tax Deductions or Matching Grants?" *Tax Law Review* 28:37–63.

———. 1973. "Should Foundations Be Third-Class Charities?" Pp. 132–62 in *The Future of Foundations,* edited by Fritz F. Heimann. Englewood Cliffs, N.J.: Prentice-Hall.

Bittker, Boris I., and Kenneth M. Kaufman. 1972. "Taxes and Civil Rights: 'Constitutionalizing' the Internal Revenue Code." *Yale Law Journal* 82:51–87.

Bittker, Boris I., and Lawrence Lokken. 1999. *Federal Taxation of Income, Estates and Gifts.* 3rd ed. Boston: Warren, Gorham and Lamont.

Bittker, Boris I., and George K. Rahdert. 1976. "The Exemption of Nonprofit Organizations from Federal Income Taxation." *Yale Law Journal* 85:299–358.

Bjorklund, Victoria. 2002. "Reflections on September 11: Legal Developments." Pp. 11–46 in *Perspectives from the Field of Philanthropy,* edited by the Foundation Center. New York: Foundation Center.

Blanchard, Kimberly S. 1993. "U.S. Taxation of Foreign Charities." *Exempt Organization Tax Review* 8:719–29.

Blasko, Mary Grace, Curt S. Crossley, and David Lloyd. 1993. "Standing to Sue in the Charitable Sector." *University of San Francisco Law Review* 28:37–84.

Boehm, R. T. 1967. "Taxes and Politics." *Tax Law Review* 22:369–438.

Boisture, Robert A., and Douglas N. Varley. 1996. "State Attorneys General's Legal Authority to Police the Sale of Nonprofit Hospitals and HMOs," *Exempt Organization Tax Review* 13:227–32.

Boris, Elizabeth, and Jeff Krehely. 2002. "Civic Participation and Advocacy." Pp. 299–330 in *The State of Nonprofit America,* edited by Lester M. Salamon. Washington, D.C.: Brookings Institution Press.

Boris, Elizabeth, and Rachel Mosher-Williams. 1998. "Nonprofit Advocacy Organizations: Assessing the Definitions, Classifications, and Data." *Nonprofit and Voluntary Sector Quarterly* 27:488–506.

Boris, Elizabeth T., and C. Eugene Steuerle, eds. 1999. *Nonprofits and Government: Collaboration and Conflict.* Washington, D.C.: Urban Institute Press.

Brannon, Gerald, and James F. Strnad II. 1977. "Alternative Approaches to Encouraging Philanthropic Activities." Pp. 2361–88 in *Research Papers,* vol. 4, edited by the Commission on Private Philanthropy and Public Needs. Washington, D.C.: U.S. Treasury.

Bremner, Robert H. 1988. *American Philanthropy.* 2nd ed. Chicago: University of Chicago Press.

Brennen, David A. 2000. "The Power of the Treasury: Racial Discrimination, Public Policy, and 'Charity' in Contemporary Society." *University of California Davis Law Review* 33:389–447.

———. 2001. "Tax Expenditures, Social Justice, and Civil Rights: Expanding the Scope of Civil Rights Laws to Apply to Tax-Exempt Charities." *Brigham Young University Law Review* 2001:167–228.

Brody, Evelyn. 1996. "Institutional Dissonance in the Nonprofit Sector." *Villanova Law Review* 41:433–502.

———. 1998a. "The Limits of Charity Fiduciary Law." *Maryland Law Review* 57:1400–1501.

———. 1998b. "Of Sovereignty and Subsidy: Conceptualizing the Charity Tax Exemption." *Journal of Corporation Law* 23:585–629.

———. 1999a. "Charities in Tax Reform: Threats to Subsidies Overt and Covert." *Tennessee Law Review* 66:687–763.

———. 1999b. "A Taxing Time for the Bishop Estate: What Is the I.R.S. Role in Charity Governance?" *University of Hawaii Law Review* 21:537–91.

———, ed. 2002. *Property Tax Exemption for Charities: Mapping the Battlefield.* Washington, D.C.: Urban Institute Press.

Brody, Evelyn, and Joseph J. Cordes. 1999. "Tax Treatment of Nonprofit Organizations: A Two-Edged Sword?" Pp. 141–75 in *Nonprofits and Government: Collaboration and Conflict,* edited by Elizabeth T. Boris and C. Eugene Steuerle. Washington, D.C.: Urban Institute Press.

Bucholtz, Barbara K. 1998. "Reflections on the Role of Nonprofit Associations in a Representative Democracy." *Cornell Journal of Law and Public Policy* 7:555–603.

Buck, Charles R., and Christopher M. Jedrey. 2005. "Ancillary Joint Ventures of Exempt Health Care Organizations Involving Taxable Partners." *Taxation of Exempts* 16:281–86.

Carroll, Ann B. 1992. "Religion, Politics, and the IRS: Defining the Limits of Tax Law Controls on Political Expression by Churches." *Marquette Law Review* 76:217–63.

Carson, John J., and Henry V. Hodson, eds. 1973. *Philanthropy in the 70's: An Anglo-American Discussion.* New York: Council on Foundations.

Carey, Sarah C. 1977. "Philanthropy and the Powerless." Pp. 1109–64 in *Research Papers,* vol. 2, edited by the Commission on Private Philanthropy and Public Needs. Washington, D.C.: Treasury Department.

Center for Community Change. 1996. *How and Why to Influence Public Policy: An Action Guide for Community Organizations.* Washington, D.C.: Center for Community Change.

Cerny, Milton, and Frances R. Hill. 1996. "The Tax Treatment of Political Organizations." *Tax Notes* 71:651–75.

Chisolm, Laura B. 1987–88. "Exempt Organization Advocacy: Matching the Rules to the Rationales." *Indiana Law Journal* 63:201–99.

———. 1990a. "Politics and Charity: A Proposal for Peaceful Coexistence." *George Washington Law Review* 58:308–67.

———. 1990b. "Sinking the Think Tanks Upstream: The Use and Misuse of Tax Exemption Law to Address the Use and Misuse of Tax-Exempt Organizations by Politicians." *University of Pittsburgh Law Review* 51:577–640.

———. 1994. "Political Advocacy Meets the Internal Revenue Code: 'There's Got to Be a Better Way.'" Paper presented at the Center on Philanthropy and the Law conference; Nonprofit Speech: Lobbying and Political Campaign Activities, New York University School of Law.

Chong, Dennis. 1991. *Collective Action and the Civil Rights Movement.* Chicago: University of Chicago Press.

Clark, Elias. 1960. "The Limitation of Political Activities: A Discordant Note in the Law of Charities." *Virginia Law Review* 46:439–66.

Clotfelter, Charles T. 1985. *Federal Tax Policy and Charitable Giving.* Chicago: University of Chicago Press.

———, ed. 1992. *Who Benefits from the Nonprofit Sector?* Chicago: University of Chicago Press.

———. 1997. "The Economics of Giving." Chap. 4 in *Giving Better, Giving Smarter: Renewing Philanthropy in America,* edited by J. W. Barry and B. V. Manno. National Commission on Philanthropy and Civic Renewal. Available online at http://pcr.hudson.org/article_docs/book_giving_intro.pdf.

Clotfelter, Charles T., and Richard L. Schmalbeck. 1996. "The Impact of Fundamental Tax Reform on Nonprofit Organizations." Pp. 211–43 in *Economic Effects of Fundamental Tax Reform,* edited by Henry J. Aaron and William G. Gale. Washington, D.C.: Brookings Institution Press.

Clotfelter, Charles T., and C. Eugene Steuerle. 1981. "Charitable Contributions." Pp. 403–46 in *How Taxes Affect Economic Behavior,* edited by Henry J. Aaron and Joseph A. Pechman. Washington, D.C.: Brookings Institution Press.

Cohen, Richard E., and Carol Matlack. 1989. "All-Purpose Loophole." *National Journal* 9 December:2980–87.

Cole, David. 1992. "Beyond Unconstitutional Conditions: Charting Spheres of Neutrality in Government-Funded Speech." *New York University Law Review* 67:675–749.

Colombo, John D. 1990. "Are Associations of Doctors Tax-Exempt? Analyzing Inconsistencies in the Taxation of Health Care Providers." *Virginia Tax Review* 9:469–523.

———. 1994. "Health Care Reform and Federal Tax Exemption: Rethinking the Issues." *Wake Forest Law Review* 29:215–71.

———. 2001. "The Marketing of Philanthropy and the Charitable Contributions Deduction." *Wake Forest Law Review* 36:657–703.

———. 2002. "Commercial Activity and Charitable Tax Exemption." *William and Mary Law Review* 44:487–567.

———. 2003. "Regulating Commercial Activity by Exempt Charities: Resurrecting the Commensurate-in-Scope Doctrine." *Exempt Organization Tax Review* 39:341–52.

———. 2004. "The Role of Access in Charitable Tax Exemption." *Washington University Law Quarterly* 82:343–87.

———. 2005. "The Failure of Community Benefit." *Health Matrix: Journal of Law-Medicine* 15:29–65.

Colvin, Gregory L. 2000. "How Well Does the Tax Code Work in Regulating Politics?" *Journal of Taxation of Exempt Organizations* 12:66–72.

———. 2002. "Political and Lobbying Activities: Long-Awaited Clues to IRS Views on Election Rules." *Taxation of Exempts* 14:42–48.

Commission on Private Philanthropy and Public Needs. 1975. *Giving in America.* Washington, D.C.

Cordes, Joseph. 1999. *The Cost of Giving: How Do Changes in Tax Deductions Affect Charitable Contributions?* Emerging Issues in Philanthropy Seminar Series. Washington, D.C.: Urban Institute Press.

Couto, Richard A. 1999. *Making Democracy Work Better: Mediating Structures, Social Capital, and the Democratic Prospect.* Chapel Hill: University of North Carolina Press.

Crimm, Nina J. 1998. "An Explanation of the Federal Income Tax Exemption for Charitable Organizations: A Theory of Risk Compensation." *Florida Law Review* 50:419–62.

———. 2004. "High Alert: The Government's War on the Financing of Terrorism and Its Implications for Donors, Domestic Charitable Organizations, and Global Philanthropy." *William and Mary Law Review* 45:1341–1452.

———. 2005. "Do Fiduciary Duties Contained in Federal Tax Laws Effectively Promote National Health Care Policies and Practices?" *Health Matrix: Journal of Law-Medicine* 15:125–47.

Crimmins, James C., and Mary Keil. 1983. *Enterprise in the Nonprofit Sector.* Washington, D.C.: Partners for Livable Places. New York: Rockefeller Brothers Fund.

Crozier, Brian W. 1996. "Intermediate Sanctions Will Affect Exempt Organizations' Hiring and Compensation Policies." *Journal of Taxation of Exempt Organizations* 8:61–68.

Cutler, David M., and Jill R. Horwitz. 2000. "Converting Hospitals from Not-for-Profit to For-Profit Status: Why and What Effects?" Pp. 45–92 in *The Changing Hospital Industry: Comparing Not-for-Profit and For-Profit Institutions,* edited by David M. Cutler. Chicago: University of Chicago Press.

Dale, Harvey P. 1990a. "About the UBIT . . ." Chap. 9 in *NYU Conference on Tax Planning for 501(c)(3) Organizations,* vol. 18. New York: New York University School of Law.

———. 1990b. "Public Policy Limits on Tax Benefits: *Bob Jones* Revisited." *Tax Forum* 459:15–19.

———. 1990c. "Standing to Challenge Tax-Exempt Status." Pp. 491–541 in *Nonprofit Organizations 1990: Current Issues and Developments.* PLI Tax Law and Estate Planning Course Handbook Series, no. 307. New York: Practising Law Institute.

———. 1995. "Foreign Charities." *Tax Lawyer* 48:655–704.

———. 2003. "Charitable Contribution Deductions—A Primer." Available online at http://www.nyu.edu/projects/hdale.

Diamond, Stephen. 1991. "Of Budgets and Benevolence: Philanthropic Tax Expenditures in Nineteenth-Century America." Paper prepared for the Center on Philanthropy and the Law conference: Rationales for Federal Income Tax Exemption, New York University.

DiMaggio, Paul, and Walter W. Powell. 1982. "The Iron Cage Revisited: Conformity and Diversity in Organizational Fields." Working paper #52, Program on Non-Profit Organizations, Yale University.

Donohue, Kevin F. 1999. "Crossroads in Hospital Conversions—A Survey of Nonprofit Hospital Conversion Legislation." *Annals Health Law* 8:39–96.

Douglas, James. 1983. *Why Charity? The Case for a Third Sector.* Thousand Oaks, Calif.: Sage Publications.

Dunbar, Amy E., and John Phillips. 1997. "The Effect of Tax Policy on Charitable Contributions: The Case of Nonitemizing Taxpayers." *Journal of the American Taxation Association* 19:1–20.

Duquette, Christopher M. 1999. "Is Charitable Giving by Nonitemizers Responsive to Tax Incentives? New Evidence." *National Tax Journal* 52:195–206.

Eaton, David H. 2001. "Charitable Contributions and Tax Price Elasticities for Nonitemizing Taxpayers." *International Advances in Economic Research* 7:431–42.

Edie, John A. 1987. "Congress and Foundations: Historical Summary." Pp. 43–64 in *America's Wealthy and the Future of Foundations,* edited by Teresa J. Odendahl. New York: Foundation Center.

Eliasberg, Kenneth C. 1965. "Charity and Commerce: Section 501(c) (3)—How Much Unrelated Business Activity?" *Tax Law Review* 21:53–101.

Facchina, Bazil, Evan Showell, and Jan E. Stone. 1993. "Privileges and Exemptions Enjoyed by Nonprofit Organizations: A Catalog and Some Thoughts about Nonprofit Policymaking." In *Topics in Philanthropy,* vol. 3. New York: New York University School of Law.

Fei, Rosemary E. 2000. "The Uses of Section 527 Political Organizations." Pp. 23–33 in *Structuring the Inquiry into Advocacy,* vol. 1, Nonprofit Advocacy and the Policy Process: A Seminar Series, edited by Elizabeth J. Reid. Washington, D.C.: Urban Institute Press.

Fishman, James J., and Stephen Schwarz. 2000. *Nonprofit Organizations: Cases and Materials.* 2nd ed. New York: Foundation Press.

Fleishman, Joel L. 1999. "Public Trust in Not-for-Profit Organizations and the Need for Regulatory Reform." Pp. 172–97 in *Philanthropy and the Nonprofit Sector in a Changing America,* edited by Charles T. Clotfelter and Thomas Erlich. Bloomington: Indiana University Press.

Flynn, David M. 1992. "Hospital Charity Care Standards: Reexamining the Grounds for Exempt Status." *Journal of Taxation of Exempt Organizations* 3:13–23.

Ford, Daniel M. 2000. "Insiders and Inurement: The Seventh Circuit's Reversal of the Tax Court in *United Cancer Council v. Commissioner.*" *Case Western Reserve Law Review* 50:909–31.

Foundation Center. 2002. *Foundation Yearbook: Facts and Figures on Private and Community Foundations.* New York: Foundation Center.

Fremont-Smith, Marion R. 1965. *Foundations and Government.* New York: Russell Sage Foundation.

———. 1998. "The Role of Government Regulation in the Creation and Operation of Conversion Foundations." Paper presented at Health Care Conversions meeting, New York Academy of Medicine.

———. 2004. *Governing Nonprofit Organizations: Federal and State Law and Regulation.* Cambridge, Mass.: Harvard University Press, Belknap Press.

Fremont-Smith, Marion R., and J. A. Lever. 2000. "Analysis and Perspective: State Regulation of Health Care Conversions and Conversion Foundations." *Bureau of National Affairs Health Care Reporter* 9:714–20.

Frumkin, Peter, and Alice Andre-Clark. 2000. "When Missions, Markets, and Politics Collide: Values and Strategy in the Nonprofit Human Services." *Nonprofit and Voluntary Sector Quarterly* 29:141–61.

Gallagher, Edward. 1984. "Limits on the Commercial Involvement of Nonprofit Organizations." Paper prepared for Yale Law School seminar.

Galston, Miriam. 1984. "Public Policy Constraints on Charitable Organizations." *Virginia Tax Review* 3:291–322.

———. 1993. "Lobbying and the Public Interest: Rethinking the Internal Revenue Code's Treatment of Legislative Activities." *Texas Law Review* 71:1269–1354.

Galvin, Charles O., and Neal Devins. 1983. "A Tax Policy Analysis of *Bob Jones University v. United States.*" *Vanderbilt Law Review* 36:1353–82.

Gergen, Mark P. 1988. "The Case for a Charitable Contribution Deduction." *Virginia Law Review* 74:1393–1449.

Ginsburg, David, Lee R. Marks, and Ronald P. Wertheim. 1977. "Federal Oversight of Private Philanthropy. Pp. 2575–2696 in *Research Papers,* vol. 5, edited by the Commission on Private Philanthropy and Public Needs. Washington, D.C.: Treasury Department.

Gladstone, Francis. 1982. *Charity, Law, and Social Justice.* London: Bedford Square Press.

Goddeeris, John H., and Burton A. Weisbrod. 1998. "Conversion from Nonprofit to For-Profit Legal Status: Why Does It Happen and Should Anyone Care?" *Journal of Policy Analysis and Management* 17:215–33.

Goldman, Jane V. 1976. "Note: Taxing Sex Discrimination: Revoking Tax Benefits of Organizations which Discriminate on the Basis of Sex." *Arizona State Law Journal* 1976:641–62.

Good, David A., and Aaron Wildavsky. 1977. "A Tax by Any Other Name: The Donor-Directed Automatic Percentage Contribution Bonus." Pp. 2389–2416 in *Research Papers,* vol. 4, edited by the Commission on Private Philanthropy and Public Needs. Washington, D.C.: Treasury Department.

Graetz, Michael J., and John C. Jeffries Jr. 1977. "Limitations on Lobbying by Charitable Organizations." Pp. 2945–71 in *Research Papers,* vol. 5, edited by the Commission on Private Philanthropy and Public Needs. Washington, D.C.: Treasury Department.

Hall, Mark A., and John D. Colombo. 1991. "The Charitable Status of Nonprofit Hospitals: Toward a Donative Theory of Tax Exemption." *Washington Law Review* 66:307–411.

Halloran, Deidre D. 1992. "Reaction to the Tesdahl Proposal for Political Intervention by Religious Organizations." *Exempt Organization Tax Review* 5:217–19.

Halstead, Ted, and Michael Lind. 2001. "Alter the Tax Code to Avert Elder Care Crisis." *Chronicle of Philanthropy.* December.

Hammar, Richard R. 1993. "Federal Income Tax Issues." Paper presented at the Center on Philanthropy and the Law conference; Religious Institutions as Nonprofit Entities: Issues of Access, Special Status and Accountability, New York University School of Law.

Hansmann, Henry B. 1980. "The Role of Nonprofit Enterprise." *Yale Law Journal* 89:835–901.

———. 1981. "The Rationale for Exempting Nonprofit Organizations from Corporate Income Taxation." *Yale Law Journal* 91:54–100.

———. 1982. "The Effect of Tax Exemption and Other Factors on Competition between Nonprofit and For-Profit Enterprise." Working paper #65, Program on Non-Profit Organizations, Yale University.

———. 1989. "Unfair Competition and the Unrelated Business Income Tax." *Virginia Law Review* 75:605–35.

Hart, Jeffrey. 1973. "Foundations and Social Activism: A Critical View." Pp. 43–57 in *The Future of Foundations,* edited by Fritz F. Heimann. Englewood Cliffs, N.J.: Prentice-Hall.

Hatfield, Michael, Anne Milgram, and Michelle Monticciolo.

2000. *Bob Jones University: Defining Violations of Fundamental Public Policy.* New York: National Center on Philanthropy and the Law.

Henzke, Leonard J., Jr., and Julie Davis. 1997. "Assessing the Reasonableness of Compensation under the Intermediate Sanctions." *Journal of Taxation of Exempt Organizations* 9:118–20.

———. 1998. "Avoiding Excise Taxes for Officers and Directors of Exempt Organizations under the Intermediate Sanctions." *Journal of Taxation of Employee Benefits* 5:226–28.

Hildenbrand, H. 2002. "No, You Still Can't Deduct That Payment to Your Child's Private Religious School: An Analysis of the Ninth Circuit Decision in *Sklar v. Commissioner*." *Tax Lawyer* 55:995–1004.

Hill, Frances R. 1997a. "Corporate Philanthropy and Campaign Finance: Exempt Organizations as Corporate-Candidate Conduits." *New York Law School Law Review* 41:881–942.

———. 1997b. "The Role of Intent in Distinguishing between Education and Politics." *Journal of Taxation of Exempt Organizations* 9:9–15.

———. 1999. "Probing the Limits of Section 527 to Design a New Campaign Finance Vehicle." *Exempt Organization Tax Review* 26:205–19.

———. 2001. "Softer Money: Exempt Organizations and Campaign Finance." *Exempt Organization Tax Review* 32:27–53.

———. 2004. "McConnell and the Code: Exempt Organizations and Campaign Finance." *Exempt Organization Tax Review* 45:71–91.

Hill, Frances R., and Douglas M. Mancino. 2002. *Taxation of Exempt Organizations.* Valhalla, N.Y.: Warren, Gorham and Lamont.

Hochberg, E. 2002. "Business Ventures Go beyond the Bottom Line." *Chronicle of Philanthropy.* 8 August.

Hodgkinson, Virginia A., and Murray S. Weitzman, with John A. Abrahams, Eric A. Crutchfield, and David R. Stevenson. 1996. *Independent Sector Nonprofit Almanac 1996–97.* San Francisco: Jossey-Bass.

Hopkins, Bruce R. 1992. "The Most Important Concept in the Law of Tax Exempt Organizations Today: The Commerciality Doctrine." *Exempt Organization Tax Review* 5:459–67.

———. 2003. *The Law of Tax-Exempt Organizations.* 8th ed. Hoboken, N.J.: John Wiley and Sons.

Horton-Smith, David. 1990. "The Impact of the Volunteer Sector on Society." Pp. 347–55 in *The Nonprofit Organization: Essential Readings,* edited by David L. Gies, J. Steven Ott, and Jay M. Shafritz. Pacific Grove, Calif.: Brooks/Cole.

Independent Sector. 2002. *The New Nonprofit Almanac and Desk Reference.* San Francisco: Jossey-Bass.

Internal Revenue Service. 1994. *Examination Guidelines for Colleges and Universities.* IRS Announcement 94–112, 1994–37 I.R.B. 1. Washington, D.C.: Internal Revenue Service.

Internal Revenue Service. 2002. *Disaster Relief: Providing Assistance through Charitable Organizations.* Publication 3833. Washington D.C.: Internal Revenue Service.

Jencks, Christopher. 1987. "Who Gives to What?" Pp. 321–39 in *The Nonprofit Sector: A Research Handbook,* edited by Walter W. Powell. New Haven, Conn.: Yale University Press.

Joblove, Leonard. 1980. "Special Treatment of Churches under the Internal Revenue Code." Working paper #21, Program on Non-Profit Organizations, Yale University.

Jordan, Vernon E., Jr. 1983. "We Cannot Live for Ourselves Alone." Pp. 401–6 in *America's Voluntary Spirit,* edited by Brian O'Connell. New York: Foundation Center.

Josephs, Stuart R. 1999. "No 'Insider' Inurement Finding Reinstates Charitable Exemption." *Tax Adviser* 30:298–99.

Kahn, Douglas A., and Jeffrey H. Kahn. 2003. "Gifts, Gafts, and Gefts: The Income Tax Definition and Treatment of Private and Charitable Gifts and a Principled Policy Justification for the Exclusion of Gifts from Income." *Notre Dame Law Review* 78:441–526.

Katz, Robert A. 2003. "A Pig in a Python: How the Charitable Response to September 11 Overwhelmed the Law of Disaster Relief." *Indiana Law Review* 36:251–333.

Kaufmann, Pamela S. 2002. "Designing Executive Compensation in the Era of Intermediate Sanctions." *Taxation of Exempts* 13:203–18.

Keeton, George W. 1962. *The Modern Law of Charities.* London: Pittman.

Kelman, Mark G. 1979. "Personal Deductions Revisited: Why They Fit Poorly in an 'Ideal' Income Tax and Why They Fit Worse in a Far from Ideal World." *Stanford Law Review* 31:831–83.

Korman, Rochelle. 2002. "Charitable Class and Need: Whom Should Charities Benefit?" Paper presented at the National Center on Philanthropy and the Law conference; Defining Charity: A View from the 21st Century, New York University School of Law.

Kuhn, Nancy Ortmeyer. 2001. "Intermediate Sanctions on NPO Executive: Unreasonable Compensation Can Bring an Unexpected Tax Liability." *Journal of Accountancy* 192:81–86.

Kurtz, Daniel L. 2004. "Sanctions and Enforcement: Federal and State Laws." Paper presented at the National Center on Philanthropy and the Law conference; Diversions of Assets: Crimes and Punishments, New York University School of Law.

Kurtz, Daniel L., and Sarah E. Paul. 1997. "Determining Reasonable Compensation for Nonprofit Executives: Avoiding Private Inurement and the Imposition of Intermediate Sanctions." Chap. 4 in *NYU Conference on Tax Planning for 501(c)(3) Organizations,* vol. 25. New York: New York University School of Law.

Larson, Martin A., and C. Stanley Lowell. 1969. *Praise the Lord for Tax Exemption.* Washington, D.C.: Robert B. Luce.

Lee, Randy. 2000. "When a King Speaks of God; When God Speaks to a King: Faith, Politics, Tax Exempt Status, and the Constitution in the Clinton Administration." *Law and Contemporary Problems* 63:391–436.

Lehrfeld, William. 1969. "The Taxation of Ideology." *Catholic University Law Review* 19:50–73.

Levmore, Saul. 1998. "Taxes and Ballots." *University of Chicago Law Review* 65:387–431.

Louthian, Robert. 2001. "Community Benefit and Charity Care: The De-evolution of the Community Benefit Standard for Health Care Organizations." *Taxation of Exempts* 13:118–20.

Lu, Lynn. 2004. "Flunking the Methodology Test: A Flawed

Tax-Exemption Standard for Educational Organizations that 'Advocate a Particular Position or Viewpoint.'" *NYU Review of Law and Social Change* 29:377–424.

Lupu, Ira C. 2000. "Threading between the Religion Clauses." *Law and Contemporary Problems* 63:439–51.

Mancino, Douglas M. 1988. "The Income Tax Exemption of the Contemporary Nonprofit Hospital." *Saint Louis University Law Journal* 32:1015–74.

———. 1997. "Converting the Status of Exempt Hospitals and Health Care Organizations." *Journal of Taxation of Exempt Organizations* 9:16–27.

———. 1998. "New Ruling Provides Guidance, Raises Questions for Joint Ventures Involving Exempt Organizations." *Journal of Taxation* 88:294–98.

———. 2002. "Exempt Organizations: Planning Joint Ventures with Exempt Organizations after *Redlands Surgical Services*." *Business Entities* 4:12–19.

———. 2005. "The Impact of Federal Tax Exemption Standards on Health Care Policy and Delivery." *Health Matrix: Journal of Law-Medicine* 15:5–27.

Mawdsley, Ralph D. 1994. "Limiting the Right of Religious Educational Institutions to Discriminate on the Basis of Religion." *Education Law Reporter* 94:1123–40.

McConnell, Ann. 1976. "Justifying the Charitable Deduction." Paper prepared for Yale Law School seminar.

McDaniel, Paul. 1972. "Federal Matching Grants for Charitable Contributions: A Substitute for the Income Tax Deduction." *Tax Law Review* 27:377–413.

———. 1977. "Study of Federal Matching Grants for Charitable Contributions." Pp. 2417–2534 in *Research Papers,* vol. 4, edited by the Commission on Private Philanthropy and Public Needs. Washington, D.C.: Treasury Department.

McGovern, James J. 1996. "A Look in the Rearview Mirror: What Does It Tell Us about the Road Ahead?" Speech before the Committee on Exempt Organizations of the American Bar Association Tax Section, 10 May 1996, reprinted in *Exempt Organization Tax Review* 13:937–40.

McIntyre, Michael J. 1980. "A Solution to the Problem of Defining a Tax Expenditure." *University of California at Davis Law Review* 14:79–103.

McNulty, John K. 1984. "Public Policy and Private Charity: A Tax Policy Perspective." *Virginia Tax Review* 3:229–53.

Miller, Steven T. 2001. "Rebuttable Presumption Is Key to Easy Intermediate Sanctions Compliance." *Tax Notes* 91:1735–38.

Minow, Martha. 2002. *Partners, Not Rivals: Privatization and the Public Good.* Boston: Beacon Press.

Nelson, Harry. 1998. "The California Wellness Foundation." Paper presented at Health Care Conversions meeting, New York Academy of Medicine.

Owens, Marcus S. 2001. "Politicians, Nonprofits, and Opportunities for Personal Enrichment." Pp. 27–35 in *Exploring Organizations and Advocacy: Strategies and Finances,* vol. 2, Nonprofit Advocacy and the Policy Process: A Seminar Series, edited by Elizabeth J. Reid and Maria D. Montilla. Washington, D.C.: Urban Institute Press.

Pang, Presley W. 1985. "Restricting Tax Benefits for Property Leased to Nonprofit Entities." Paper prepared for Yale Law School seminar.

Pepper, Hamilton, and Sheetz. 1997. "Legislative Activities of Charitable Organizations Other than Private Foundations." Pp. 2917–44 in *Research Papers,* vol. 5, edited by the Commission on Private Philanthropy and Public Needs. Washington, D.C.: Treasury Department.

Persons, John P., John J. Osborn, and Charles F. Feldman. 1977. "Criteria for Exemption under Section 501(c)(3)." Pp. 1909–2025 in *Research Papers,* vol. 4, edited by the Commission on Private Philanthropy and Public Needs. Washington, D.C.: Treasury Department.

Pires, Sheila. 1985. *Competition between the Nonprofit and For-Profit Sectors.* Washington, D.C.: National Assembly.

Price Waterhouse, L.L.P., and Caplan and Drysdale, Chartered. 1997. "Impact of Restructuring on Tax-Exempt Organizations." Report commissioned by the Council on Foundations and Independent Sector (n.d.; released 28 April 1997). Available in LEXIS, Fedtax Library, TNT file as 97 TNT 83–21 (30 April 1997).

Raby, Burgess J. W., and William L. Raby. 1999. "Private Inurement, Private Benefit, UCC, and Intermediate Sanctions." *Tax Notes* 82:1979–81.

Redmond, Brian H. 1996. "Annotation. Federal Tax Exemption: When Do Earnings of Religious, Charitable, Educational, or Similar Organizations Inure to Benefit of Private Shareholders or Individuals within Meaning of 26 USCS §501(c)(3)?" Pp. 255–96 in *American Law Reports Federal,* vol. 92. Rochester, N.Y.: Lawyers Cooperative; San Francisco: Bancroft-Whitney.

Reid, Elizabeth J. 1999. "Nonprofit Advocacy and Political Participation." Pp. 291–325 in *Nonprofits and Government: Collaboration and Conflict,* edited by Elizabeth Boris and C. Eugene Steuerle. Washington, D.C.: Urban Institute Press.

———. 2000. "Understanding the Word 'Advocacy': Context and Use." Pp. 1–7 in *Structuring the Inquiry into Advocacy,* vol. 1, Nonprofit Advocacy and the Policy Process: A Seminar Series, edited by Elizabeth J. Reid. Washington, D.C.: Urban Institute Press.

Roady, Celia. 1999. "Political Activities of Tax-Exempt Organizations: Federal Income Tax Rules and Restrictions." *Exempt Organization Tax Review* 22:401–19.

———. 2000. "Relationships between Charities and Non-Exempt Entities: Corporate Sponsorships, Licensing, Joint Ventures, Subsidiaries." In *ALI-ABA Course of Study Materials: Tax-Exempt Charitable Organizations.* Philadelphia: American Law Institute–American Bar Association.

———. 2005. Unpublished paper on ancillary joint ventures (on file with the authors of this chapter).

Roady, Celia, and Carolyn Osteen Ward. 1996. "Intermediate Sanctions: A New IRS Weapon against Tax-Exempt Compensation Abuse." *Benefits Law Journal* 9:49–72.

Rose-Ackerman, Susan. 1982. "Unfair Competition and Corporate Income Taxation." *Stanford Law Review* 34:1017–39.

———. 1983. "Social Services and the Market: Paying Customers, Vouchers and Quality Control." *Columbia Law Review* 83:1405–39.

Rubenstein, Helena G. 1997. "Nonprofit Hospitals and the Federal Tax Exemption: A Fresh Prescription." *Health Matrix: Journal of Law-Medicine* 7:381–427.

Rusk, Dean. 1961. *The Role of the Foundation in American Life.* Claremont, Calif.: Claremont University College.

Sacks Albert M. 1960. "The Role of Philanthropy: An Institutional View." *Virginia Law Review* 46:516–38.

Salamon, Lester M. 1987. "Partners in Public Service: The Scope and Theory of Government-Nonprofit Relations." Pp. 99–117 in *The Nonprofit Sector: A Research Handbook,* edited by Walter W. Powell. New Haven, Conn.: Yale University Press.

———. 1995. *Partners in Public Service: Government-Nonprofit Relations in the Modern Welfare State.* Baltimore: Johns Hopkins University Press.

———. 1997. *The International Guide to Nonprofit Law.* New York: John Wiley and Sons.

Samansky, Allen J. 2004. "Deductibility of Contributions to Religious Organizations." *Virginia Tax Review* 24:65–108.

Sanders, Michael I. 2000. *Joint Ventures Involving Tax-Exempt Organizations.* 2nd ed. New York: John Wiley and Sons.

Schill, Michael H. 1984. "The Participation of Charities in Limited Partnerships." *Yale Law Journal* 96:1355–74.

Schwarz, Stephen. 1976. "Limiting Religious Tax Exemptions: When Should the Church Render unto Caesar?" *University of Florida Law Review* 29:50–105.

Schwarz, Stephen, and William T. Hutton. 1984. "Recent Developments in Tax-Exempt Organizations." *University of San Francisco Law Review* 18:649–94.

Schwartzman, Randy A. 1999. "Reasonable Compensation Rules." *Tax Adviser* 30:300–302.

Seay, J. David. 1992. "Tax-Exemption for Hospitals: Towards an Understanding of Community Benefit." *Health Matrix: Journal of Law-Medicine* 2:35–48.

Shaviro, Daniel. 1997. "Assessing the 'Contract Failure' Explanation for Nonprofit Organizations and Their Tax-Exempt Status." *New York Law School Law Review* 41:1001–7.

Shenon, Philip, and Stephanie Strom. 2005 "DeLay Charity for Children Financed by Corporations." *New York Times,* 21 April, p. A16.

Shuldiner, Reed, and David Shakow. 2001. "Lessons from the Limitation on Itemized Deductions." *Tax Notes* 93:673–94.

Silk, Thomas, ed. 1999. *Philanthropy and Law in Asia: A Comparative Study of the Nonprofit Legal Systems in Ten Asia Pacific Countries.* San Francisco: Jossey-Bass.

Simon, John G. 1973. "Foundations and Controversy: An Affirmative View." Pp. 58–100 in *The Future of Foundations,* edited by Fritz F. Heimann. Englewood Cliffs, N.J.: Prentice-Hall.

———. 1978. "Charity and Dynasty under the Federal Tax System." *Probate Lawyer* 5:1–92.

———. 1987. "The Tax Treatment of Nonprofit Organizations: A Review of Federal and State Politics." Pp. 67–98 in *The Nonprofit Sector: A Research Handbook,* edited by Walter W. Powell. New Haven, Conn.: Yale University Press.

———. 1995. "The Regulation of American Foundations: Looking Backward at the Tax Reform Act of 1969." *Voluntas* 6:243–54.

———. 2000. "Private Foundations as a Federally Regulated Industry: Time for a Fresh Look?" *Exempt Organization Tax Review* 27:66–80.

———. 2002. "Is There a Law of Charity?" Paper presented at the Center on Philanthropy and the Law conference; Defining Charity: A View from the 21st Century, New York University School of Law.

Simon, Karla W. 1981. "The Tax-Exempt Status of Racially Discriminatory Religious Schools." *Tax Law Review* 36:477–516.

Simons, Henry. 1938. *Personal Income Taxation.* Chicago: University of Chicago Press.

Sneed, Jason M. 1997. "Note: Regaining Their Political Voices: The Religious Freedom Restoration Act's Promise of Delivering Churches from the Section 501(c)(3) Restrictions on Lobbying and Campaigning." *Journal of Law and Politics* 13:493–511.

Special Committee on Exempt Organizations, New York State Bar Association Tax Section. 1965. "Comment on Treasury Foundation Report." Pp. 710–35 in Committee on Ways and Means, U.S. House, *Additional Written Statements . . . on Treasury Department Report on Private Foundations.* Committee Print.

Spiro, Thomas. 1979. "'Unfair Competition' between Taxable and Tax-Exempt Organizations." Paper prepared for Yale Law School seminar.

Spitzer, Adelbert L. 2002. "Commerciality: How Much Is Too Much?" Paper presented at the Center on Philanthropy and the Law conference; Defining Charity: A View from the 21st Century, New York University School of Law.

Staff of the Joint Committee on Taxation. 2000. "Report of Investigation of Allegations Relating to IRS Handling of Tax-Exempt Organization Matters."

Steinberg, Richard. 1988. "Fairness and Efficiency in the Competition between For-Profit and Nonprofit Firms." Working paper #132, Program on Non-Profit Organizations, Yale University.

———. 1991. "'Unfair' Competition by Nonprofits and Tax Policy. *National Tax Journal* 44:351–64.

———. 2003. "Economic Theories of Nonprofit Organizations: An Evaluation." Pp. 277–310 in *The Study of the Nonprofit Enterprise: Theories and Approaches,* edited by Avner Ben-Ner and Helmut Anheir. New York: Kluwer Academic.

Steuerle, C. Eugene. 2000a. "Charity Deduction for Nonitemizers: Where Do You Draw the Line?" *Tax Notes* 86:1773–74.

———. 2000b. "Nonitemizers' Charitable Deduction: The Administration's Floor Plan." *Tax Notes* 86:1625–26.

———. 2000c. "The Right Way to Extend Charitable Deductions to Nonitemizers." *Tax Notes* 86:1297–98.

———. 2001. *When Nonprofits Conduct Exempt Activities as Taxable Enterprises.* Emerging Issues in Philanthropy Seminar Series. Washington, D.C.: Urban Institute Press.

———. 2002. "Charities and Disaster Relief—Parts 1 and 2." *Exempt Organization Tax Review* 35:49–51.

Stimpson, Claude W. 1934. "The Exemption of Property from Taxation in the United States." *Minnesota Law Review* 18:411–28.

Sugin, Linda. 1999. "Tax Expenditure Analysis and Constitutional Decisions." *Hastings Law Journal* 50:407–74.

Sullivan, Kathleen M. 1989. "Unconstitutional Conditions." *Harvard Law Review* 102:1413–1506.

Sunstein, Cass R. 1988. "The Civic Republican Tradition: Beyond the Republican Revival." *Yale Law Journal* 97:1539–90.

Surrey, Stanley S. 1970. "Federal Income Tax Reform: The Varied Approaches Necessary to Replace Tax Expenditures with Direct Governmental Assistance." *Harvard Law Review* 84:352–408.

———. 1973. *Pathways to Tax Reform: The Concepts of Tax Expenditures.* Cambridge, Mass.: Harvard University Press.

Swords, Peter. 1981. *Charitable Real Property Tax Exemptions in New York State—Menace or Measure of Social Progress?* New York: Association of the Bar of the City of New York.

———. 1997. "The Form 990 as an Accountability Tool." Paper presented at the Center on Philanthropy and the Law conference; Governance of Nonprofit Organizations: Standards and Enforcement, New York University School of Law.

Ten Broeck, Eric. 1994. "Preventing Private Inurement by Measuring the Reasonableness of Compensation for Executives." *Journal of Taxation of Exempt Organizations* 6:21–27.

Tesdahl, D. Benson. 1991. "Intervention in Political Campaigns by Religious Organizations after the Pickle Hearings—A Proposal for the 1990s." *Exempt Organization Tax Review* 4:1165–84.

Thompson, Tommy S. 1985. "The Availability of the Federal Educational Tax Exemption for Propaganda Organizations." *University of California Davis Law Review* 18:487–553.

Trister, Michael B., and Holly Schadler. 2002. "Bipartisan Campaign Reform Act of 2002: How Will It Affect Nonprofits?" *Exempt Organization Tax Review* 36:171–76.

Troyer, Thomas A. 2000. "1969 Private Foundations Law: Historical Perspective on Its Origins and Underpinnings." *Exempt Organization Tax Review* 27:52–65.

Urban Institute. 1983. "Serving Community Needs: The Nonprofit Sector in an Era of Governmental Retrenchment." Nonprofit Sector Project Progress Report no. 3, September.

U.S. General Accounting Office. 2002. *Tax Exempt Organizations: Improvements Possible in Public, IRS and State Oversight of Charities.* Washington, D.C.: U.S. Government Printing Office.

U.S. Senate Finance Committee. 2004. "Senate Finance Committee Discussion Draft of Proposals for Reforms and Best Practices in the Area of Tax-Exempt Organizations." Available online at http://www.finance.senate.gov/hearings/testimony/2004test/062204stfdis.pdf.

U.S. Small Business Administration, Office of Advocacy. 1984. *Unfair Competition by Nonprofit Organizations with Small Business: An Issue for the 1980s.* 3rd ed. Washington D.C.: U.S. Small Business Administration.

Weidenbeck, Peter J. 1985. "Charitable Contributions: A Policy Perspective." *Missouri Law Review* 50:85–137.

Weisbrod, Burton A. 1975. "Toward a Theory of the Voluntary Non-Profit Sector in a Three-Sector Economy." Pp. 171–95 in *Altruism, Morality, and Economic Theory,* edited by Edmund Phelps. New York: Russell Sage Foundation.

———. 1980. "Private Goods, Collective Goods: The Role of the Nonprofit Sector. Pp. 139–69 in *The Economics of Nonproprietary Organizations,* Supp. 1, edited by Kenneth W. Clarkson and Donald L. Martin. Greenwich, Conn.: JAI Press.

———, ed. 1998. *To Profit or Not to Profit: The Commercial Transformation of the Nonprofit Sector.* New York: Cambridge University Press.

Weisbrod, Burton A., Joel F. Handler, and Neil K. Komesar. 1978. *Public Interest Law: An Economic and Institutional Analysis.* Berkeley: University of California Press.

Wellford, Harrison, and Janne G. Gallagher. 1985. *The Myth of Unfair Competition by Nonprofit Organizations: A Review of Government Assistance to Small Business.* Washington, D.C.: National Assembly and Family Service America.

West, Robin L. 1985. "Liberalism Rediscovered: A Definition of the Liberal Pragmatic Vision." *University of Pittsburgh Law Review* 46:673–738.

Yale University, Institution for Social and Policy Studies, Program on Non-Profit Organizations. 1982. "Parsing Property Tax Policy." Pp. 5–7 in *Research Reports,* no. 2.

Young, Dennis R., and Lester M. Salamon. 2002. "Commercialization, Social Ventures, and For-Profit Competition." Pp. 423–46 in *The State of Nonprofit America,* edited by Lester M. Salamon. Washington, D.C.: Brookings Institution Press.

Zelinsky, Edward A. 1998. "Are Tax 'Benefits' Constitutionally Equivalent to Direct Expenditures?" *Harvard Law Review* 112:379–433.

13

Nonprofit Organizations and Political Advocacy

J. CRAIG JENKINS

Echoing James Madison's worries about the "mischief of faction" and Alexis de Tocqueville's diagnosis of America as a "nation of joiners," contemporary analysts have advanced conflicting assessments about the nature of nonprofit political advocacy and its impact on the health of the American political system. Where Madison worried that excessive interest advocacy (i.e., the "mischief of faction") might undermine democratic government and prescribed expanding the cross-checks of broader interest group competition, de Tocqueville's worry was that the "tyranny of the majority" would undermine minority voice and create a stultifying political conformity. These concerns are echoed by contemporary analysts of the "advocacy explosion" in the United States. Some argue that the growth of political advocacy has "overloaded" the American political system, producing political paralysis, weakened authority, political distrust, and economic stagnation (Huntington 1982; M. Olson 1982; Rausch 1994). Nonprofit advocacy is seen as contributing to this political "overload" by promoting "single-issue" positions and political innovations, such as town hall meetings and direct democracy measures, that reduce the autonomy and deliberative power of governmental institutions (Dahl 1994) and create polarized controversies that undermine majority rule (Fiorina 1999). Others counter that nonprofit political advocacy has provided a Madisonian check on the upper-class bias of the interest group system by representing the disadvantaged and the general public and by broadening civic engagement (Berry 1977, 1999; Walker 1991; McFarland 1984, 1992, 1998). Still others contend that Americans are disengaging from civic involvement, "bowling alone" (Putnam 2000) and substituting "checkbook" advocacy by "professional social movements" (Zald and McCarthy 1987) and "protest businesses" (Jordan and Maloney 1997) for direct participation (Skocpol 1999, 2003). By this view, nonprofit advocacy has minimal substantive impact on policy and contributes little to political and civic engagement.

These discussions raise four major questions about nonprofit political advocacy. First, how central are nonprofit organizations to the recent growth in political advocacy? Second, what leads to the formation of new nonprofit advocacy organizations? Third, what accounts for the survival and maintenance of nonprofit advocacy organizations? Fourth, what has been the impact of nonprofit advocacy on public policy and on the health of the American political system? Although nonprofit political advocacy exists in other countries and is central to international relations (see Anheier and Salamon, this volume), this chapter will focus primarily on the U.S. experience, which has generated a large and growing literature. The discussion will focus largely on advocacy by nonprofit social welfare and general citizen organizations, which have received the most attention, in part because they are critical to the "mischief of faction" and "political overload" theses. Lying behind these concerns are general assumptions about the meaning of the public interest and its relationship to nonprofit political advocacy.

NONPROFIT ADVOCACY AND THE PUBLIC INTEREST

Nonprofit political advocates typically argue that they represent the collective interests of the general public and underrepresented groups as opposed to the interests of well-organized powerful groups, especially business, mainstream social institutions, and the elite professions. Thus one rationale for nonprofit advocacy is that it advances the "public interest," defined as the collective or indivisible interests of the general public. Berry (1977:7), for example, defines the nonprofit organizations active in public interest lobbying in terms of their advocacy of "collective good(s), the achievement of which will not selectively and materially benefit the membership or activists of the organization." Similarly, Schuck (1977), in discussing nonprofit public interest law firms, argues that they pursue "collective interests shared by broad publics" as opposed to the narrow private economic interests typically represented by private law firms and professional lobbyists. Tesh (1984:29–31) contrasts "issue groups" with "interest groups" by arguing that the former have an open or nonexclusive membership and base their appeals in terms of "moral convictions about the rightness of policies" as opposed to narrow economic interests. The federal tax code reflects this conception, reserving the nonprofit status for charitable, social welfare, educational, and related civic activities that benefit the general public. In this view, nonprofit political advocacy is a corrective for the "excess of faction" as well as counterbalancing the bias toward privileged groups by advancing the collective interests of the general public and underrepresented groups.

This *public interest* conception of nonprofit advocacy has been challenged on several grounds, the most important being the question of objectivity. Who gets to say what is the public interest? Gone is the optimism of Walter Lippmann (1955:42), who could naively claim that "the public interest may be presumed to be what men [*sic*] would choose if they saw clearly, thought rationally, acted disinterestedly and benevolently." Interests are diverse and inherently subjective. One person's "public good" may be another's "public bad." Those who claim to speak in the name of the general public can claim no privileged insight.

An alternative *procedural conception* defines the public interest in terms of ensuring a "process of open, critical deliberation" (Mansbridge 1997:12) and a decision-making process in which "all significant views are represented" (Jaffe 1976:31), including "groups that have been unable to organize effectively to compete in the marketplace for the services of skilled advocates" (Rabin 1975:207). In other words, the public interest is not any specific policy or viewpoint (i.e., any specific collective good) but rather a set of procedures for ensuring an open, competitive process in which all significant and relevant interests are represented. The public interest is served by ensuring greater pluralism in terms of political and social representation. This might be called a Madisonian solution to the "mischief of faction" and the dominance of narrow well-organized groups, and is endorsed by analysts who define democracy in terms of all-inclusive political participation (e.g., Barber 1984; Habermas 1998). Nonprofit advocacy helps correct imbalanced political representation by ensuring that a broader set of interests are voiced.

This procedural conception, however, is not specific about how these interests are represented. As discussed below, a significant limitation of contemporary nonprofit advocacy is that it is often limited to professionalized advocates. The idea of "strong democracy" (Barber 1984) contends that civic engagement is the key to strong and effective political advocacy. Professionalized advocacy is a weak substitute for broader civic engagement (Skocpol 1999, 2003). Nonprofit advocacy may also contribute to the political overload problem insofar as it increases the number and complexity of the contending voices, leaving all with a sense of diminished power and a political process out of control.

A stronger rationale for nonprofit advocacy combines both arguments. The first or substantive conception of the public interest is useful in emphasizing the importance of collective interests but mistakenly implies that all sectors of society benefit equally from specific collective goods. The second procedural conception provides a counterbalance by pointing out the need for broader representation but is unspecific about how these interests are organized. A fuller conception of the public interest emphasizes the idea of civic participation, both directly in advocating specific decisions and indirectly through expressions of public opinion, and the need for a broader representation of otherwise underrepresented interests.

What is "advocacy"? A narrow conception is "the act of pleading for or against a cause, as well as supporting or recommending a position," along with lobbying in the sense of "addressing legislators with a view to influencing their votes" (Hopkins 1992:32). Boris and Mosher-Williams (1998) call this "rights-based" advocacy, which includes legal advocacy in the courts, program advocacy in terms of monitoring government programs, and participating in the process of defining rules and procedures (Reid 1998). Advocacy, however, also includes "civic involvement" (Boris and Mosher-Williams 1998), such as grassroots lobbying (encouraging others to contact legislators to support or oppose specific legislation), attempts to influence public opinion, and educational efforts designed to encourage community and political participation. Political advocacy in the strict sense focuses on governmental decision makers, while social advocacy attempts to influence public opinion, to encourage civic and political participation, and to influence the policies of private institutions such as corporations, private schools, universities, and other nonprofit organizations (Reid 2000). Environmental groups, for example, often focus on "corporate polluters" as well as governmental agencies and courts. Likewise, the women's movement and their "pro-life" opponents often target universities, churches, and social welfare organizations as well as legislatures, courts, and administrative bodies. While nonprofit advocacy includes the advocacy activities of other 501 organizations, this review focuses primarily on the advocacy of charitable and religious [501(c)(3)] and social welfare organizations [501(c)(4)], which constitute the majority of existing nonprofit organizations (Boris 1999).

How is advocacy done? Most nonprofits rely on the previously mentioned institutionalized actions, but some also engage in protest and unruly politics. Due to the legal regulations on formal lobbying by public charities and considerable confusion within the nonprofit sector about the nature of these restrictions (Simon, Dale, and Chisolm, this volume; Berry and Arons 2003), many nonprofits avoid rights-based advocacy and even avoid using the term "advocacy" to refer to their public educational and representational activities. Nonprofit service organizations are often involved extensively in negotiations over the implementation of governmental service programs as well as in civic advocacy activities without referring to "advocacy." It is also important to keep in mind that advocacy is not the same as actual influence. Advocacy is a question of articulating a position and mobilizing support for it. According to the procedural view of nonprofit advocacy, actual policy influence is less critical than ensuring that a broad set of views are expressed and taken into account. It therefore is useful to distinguish between political advocacy and actual policy *enactment* (the governmental or institutional decision) and *implementation* (putting the decision in place). While most of this chapter's discussion focuses on governmental policy, it is also important to consider the policies of social institutions such as private corporations, universities, and other nonprofit organizations.

Insofar as nonprofit advocacy focuses on collective benefits for otherwise unrepresented groups, there is an overall bias toward promoting governmental growth in terms of regulation and provision of services on behalf of unrepresented groups. Critics often target this liberal bias, contending that the underlying objective is governmental expansion (e.g., Burt 1982; Bennett and DiLorenzo 1985; Nagai, Lerner, and Rothman 1994). But there is also a growing "new right" of nonprofit advocacy that promotes laissez-faire and conservative religious views of government and civil society (Himmelstein 1990; Moen 1992; Guth et al. 1998), indicating that nonprofit advocacy is not necessarily linked to governmental growth.

A NONPROFIT ADVOCACY EXPLOSION?

All observers agree that since the 1960s there has been an "advocacy explosion" in national and state politics in the United States (Walker 1991; Schlozman and Tierney 1986; Petracca 1992; Gray and Lowery 1996; Baumgartner and Leech 1998). There is also a general consensus that private business and the for-profit or elite professions are the best represented, leading to the often quoted claim that "the flaw in the pluralist heaven is that the heavenly chorus sings with a strong upper-class accent" (Schattschneider 1960:35). The disagreement is over whether this bias has persisted, grown, or been reduced.

Four methods have been used to gauge the role of nonprofits in this "advocacy explosion." One has been to survey the national advocacy organizations active in Washington, D.C. The benchmark study is Schlozman and Tierney's (1986) analysis of over 5,000 Washington, D.C., representatives listed in the *Encyclopedia of Associations* and *Washington Representatives* directories for 1981. This study found that 72 percent of these organizations represented corporations or trade and business associations, 8 percent professional associations, and only 20 percent the nonprofit sector (with 5 percent being general citizens' groups, 2 percent representing civil rights and the poor, and 1 percent women, the elderly, and the handicapped). Comparing these data against the 523 Washington, D.C., representatives listed in the *Congressional Quarterly* in 1960, Schlozman and Tierney concluded that, although there has been a major absolute increase in the number of nonprofit advocacy organizations, these groups "do not form a more significant component in the pressure community" and, "if anything, the distribution of organizations within the Washington pressure community is even more heavily weighted in favor of business organizations," leading to a conclusion of "more of the same" (1986:81, 388). Gray and Lowery (1996:86–103) found a similar pattern in their study of lobbyists registered with state governments. While the number of registered state lobbyists increased by over 75 percent between 1975 and 1990, the for-profit versus nonprofit distribution did not change. Industry and trade associations made up over 70 percent of all registered lobbyists, and nonprofit advocates were less than 30 percent. What Gray and Lowery call the "social sector," which comprises rights-based and civic advocacy, constituted between 13 and 16 percent of the total. While nonprofit advocacy increased more rapidly between 1975 and 1980, for-profit advocacy grew more rapidly in the 1980s, reestablishing its numerical dominance.

This research is limited, however, insofar as it focuses on organizations involved largely in rights-based advocacy. Another approach has been to survey national membership organizations, which primarily taps the broader set of social welfare organizations [501(c)(4)]. In two surveys of over 1,000 Washington, D.C., membership organizations in the early 1980s, Walker (1991:62–64) found that citizens' groups grew the most rapidly, increasing by over 50 percent between 1965 and 1983, and made up almost a quarter of all membership organizations in 1983. Traditional nonprofit organizations from the fields of health, social welfare, education, and arts/culture made up another 32.5 percent, with for-profit business and professional associations making up only 37.8 percent. Historically, traditional nonprofits grew the most rapidly during the Progressive Era, business associations during the 1940s and 1950s, and citizens' groups in the post-1960 period. Although Walker's survey was limited to existing organizations and thus might underestimate sector differences in organizational mortality, there was no evidence of differential mortality by sector. The survey focused on membership organizations, which had the virtue of capturing both civic and rights advocacy, but it missed corporate lobbyists and legal representatives, thereby underestimating the representation of the for-profit sector. It also missed advocacy by nonmembership social service organizations, such as the Catholic Charities and advocates for the homeless, which are more involved in civic engagement.

A second approach has been to examine the listings in the *Encyclopedia of Associations,* which attempts to provide a comprehensive picture of public charities, religious, fraternal, sports, and avocational groups, as well as business and trade associations, chambers of commerce, labor unions, and professional societies. Table 13.1 summarizes Baumgartner and Leech's (1998:102–11) analysis of change

TABLE 13.1. THE DISTRIBUTION OF NONPROFIT AND FOR-PROFIT ORGANIZATIONS, 1959–1995

Type	1959	1970	1980	1990	1995	Average annual growth (%)
Public affairs	117	477	1,068	2,249	2,178	48.9
Social welfare	241	458	994	1,705	1,938	19.6
Cultural and educational	563	1,357	2,376	4,178	3,250	13.3
Health and medical	433	834	1,413	2,227	2,426	12.8
Environmental and agriculture	331	504	677	940	1,136	6.8
All for-profits	4,158	6,678	8,198	10,960	12,370	5.5
Total	5,843	10,308	14,726	22,259	23,298	8.3
% Public affairs only	2.0	4.6	7.3	10.1	9.3	
% All nonprofits	28.8	35.2	44.3	50.8	46.9	
% For-profit	71.2	64.8	55.7	49.2	53.1	

Source: Derived from Baumgartner and Leech 1998:103.

in the number of organizations listed in the *Encyclopedia* over time within three broad sectors: (1) public affairs nonprofits (i.e., those involved in rights-based and civic advocacy); (2) traditional nonprofits (i.e., hospitals, educational, and social service agencies); and (3) the for-profit sector. Between 1959 and 1995, public affairs organizations, which include citizens' groups, think tanks, and public education groups, increased by over eighteen times, creating an average annual growth rate of 49.1 percent, with the highest increase between 1959 and 1980. In 1990, public affairs organizations made up 10 percent of all organizations. Traditional nonprofits grew by over 4.5 times, or an annual average of 12.7 percent, while for-profits grew by 1.6 times, or an annual rate of 5.5 percent. Between 1959 and 1980, public affairs and traditional nonprofits grew the most rapidly, increasing from 28.1 to 44.3 percent of all organizations; they made up slightly over half of all organizations in 1990 but then declined slightly in the early 1990s. For-profits grew the slowest, declining from around 70 percent to under half of all organizations in 1990 and then rebounding in the early 1990s. While this analysis misses the for-profit representation by law firms, corporate offices, and lobbying offices, which have grown significantly in the 1980s and 1990s, it suggests that the for-profit sector remains numerically dominant but is increasingly checked by the growth of the nonprofit public affairs sector.

A third and ultimately more accurate research method has been to use Internal Revenue Service (IRS) data to estimate the number and activities of public charities and social welfare organizations. While this approach cannot address the sector balance question, it can inform our assessment of the number of nonprofit advocacy organizations. According to the National Center for Charitable Statistics (Krehely 2001; see also http://www.nccs.urban.org), 246,112 public charities filed reports in 1999 with the IRS, a little less than half of the total number of public charities with a tax exemption. Another 320,000 did not report because their gross receipts were less than $25,000, they were exempt religious organizations, they were inactive, or they simply failed to file. These results are similar to the reporting rates in Grønberg's (1994) community study of nonprofits and in Berry and Arons's (2003) national survey of nonprofits. Very few public charities are involved in rights-based advocacy. Only .7 percent, or 1,779, described themselves as centrally involved in "civil rights, social action and advocacy," and another 1.9 percent, or 4,727, claimed a primary involvement in "environmental quality and protection." The revenues and expenditures of these two categories constituted less than .1 percent of total public charity resources.

A more complete picture is provided by Boris and Mosher-Williams's (1998) analysis of the IRS Business Master File. In 1996–97 they found 8,282 "rights" and 14,994 "civic involvement" public charities. These two categories of public charities made up 5.5 percent of all 501 organizations, slightly smaller than the comparable "public affairs" sector identified by Baumgartner and Leech for 1995. The IRS Return Transaction File identified a slightly smaller number—17,021, or 9 percent of all charitable and religious organizations—primarily involved in civic involvement, and only 1 percent involved in rights activities. The budgets of these advocacy public charities represented a comparable share of all reporting public charities, but their income was much more dependent on direct public support in the form of contributions, grants, gifts, and bequests (29 percent) and government grants (29 percent), reinforcing Walker's (1991) conclusion that institutional patronage is a key financial basis for nonprofit advocacy. Underscoring the small scale of rights advocacy, less than 5 percent of these charitable advocacy organizations reported any legislative lobbying expenses, and these expenses represented less than 1 percent of their total budgets. At the same time, between 1989 and 1996, there was a 40 percent growth in the number of nonprofit organizations (Boris 1999). This evidence reinforces the conclusion that nonprofit advocacy has grown rapidly in recent decades but also underscores the points that: (1) nonprofit advocacy is a small portion of the activities in the nonprofit sector; and (2) rights advocacy is probably less than a quarter of all nonprofit advocacy.

A fourth research method has been to examine advocacy around specific issues such as the environment, minority and women's rights, and the like. The best documented issue area is the environmental movement, which grew steadily from the late nineteenth century through the early 1960s' explosion of a new set of advocacy organizations that has persisted through the 1990s (Dunlap and Mertig 1992; Shaiko 1999; McLaughlin and Khawaja 2000; Brulle 2000; Jenkins, Brulle, et al. 2005). By the mid-1990s several major environmental organizations had annual budgets of $25–40 million (Jordan and Maloney 1997) and assets of $1.5 million or more (Bosso 1995:105; Brulle 2000:244–45), making them comparable in size to some of the larger private corporate law firms. Jordan and Maloney (1997:15) estimate that in the early 1990s environmental advocacy mobilized over $2.9 billion in the United States alone and operated transnationally throughout most of western Europe, Canada, and the United States. Roughly a quarter of this funding has come from private foundations, with the remainder coming from government grants, sales, and membership donations from over twelve million individuals (Jordan and Maloney 1997:14; Brulle 2000:242–43; Mitchell, Mertig, and Dunlap 1992:13; Berry 1997:33). Other studies have indicated similar organizational growth in the women's movement (Gelb and Palley 1996; Costain 1992; McCann 1994; Ferree and Hess 1994); community organizing among the poor, minorities, and the middle class (Boyte 1980; Boyte, Booth, and Max 1986; Delgado 1986; McCarthy and Castelli 1994); public interest legal advocacy (Council for Public Interest Law 1976; Aron 1988); and advocacy for Latinos (E. Carson 1999; Diaz 1999), the disabled (S. Olson 1984), peace (Lofland 1993; Marullo and Lofland 1990; Edwards and Marullo 1995), gay/lesbian rights (Kayal 1993; Rimmerman 1992; Riggle and Tadlock 1999), animal rights (Jasper and Nelkin 1992; Silverstein 1996), and a host of other causes. Likewise, there has been an explosive growth of nationally focused think tanks specializing in policy evaluation and advocacy, which grew steadily from around fifty in the early 1970s to over 200 in 1995, many of which advocate from a "new right" or conservative perspective (Rich and Weaver 1999).

Ultimately, a more complete picture of the organizational growth of nonprofit advocacy is needed. The most promising source is the wealth of information collected by the National Center for Charitable Statistics from IRS data. This can be used to estimate the income, assets, and major categories of expenditures by all nonprofit organizations that file with the IRS (Boris and Mosher-Williams 1998; Boris and Kreheley 2002) and covers the period from 1992 through the present. While it cannot fully address the grand question of the nonprofit/for-profit balance insofar as it cannot estimate the use of for-profit law firms, public relations firms, and private representatives that represent business and the organized professions, it can be used to gauge more clearly the number of nonprofit organizations involved in various types of advocacy activity, the relative share of resources invested in advocacy work, and the specific fields in which this advocacy occurs.

A second priority is cross-national analysis. An emerging body of research supports the contention that economic development, the duration of political democracy, and competition among Christian religious traditions facilitates the growth of nonprofit associations (J. Curtis, Baer, and Grabb 2001; Salamon and Anheier 1999; Paxton 2002). Social democratic and corporatist countries such as Sweden, Norway, Denmark, and the Netherlands have higher membership rates in nonprofit associations, reflecting both a political culture supporting civic duties and governmental subsidies for these associations (especially labor unions), while liberal democratic countries such as the United States, Britain, Canada, and Ireland have higher voluntary labor contributions to these associations, especially the "new social movements" promoting peace, environmental protection, and human and women's rights, suggesting a stronger voluntaristic culture (Janoski 1998; Schofer and Fourcade-Gourinchas 2001). Nonprofit advocacy organizations also contribute to social capital and to political democracy (Minkoff 1997; Paxton 2002).

THE FORMATION OF NONPROFIT ADVOCACY ORGANIZATIONS

Organizational formation means the creation of a formally structured group with a statement of goals, authority, and, in many cases, an IRS tax exemption. In the past, three explanations have been used: (1) "disturbance" or strain ideas; (2) resource mobilization; and (3) political opportunities. Recently these ideas have been extended by (4) organizational ecology theory and (5) social constructionist arguments about the framing of collective grievances and organizational repertoires.

Disturbance theories focus on the strains and social discontinuities that create widespread grievances, prompting groups to form organizations to bring about social and political change (Truman 1951; Kornhauser 1959; Smelser 1963). Wars, depressions, and social disruptions created by mass migration and unemployment create widespread grievances, thereby prompting groups to form organizations to advocate their interests and reduce strains. This is a classic "demand-side" theory, insofar as it puts emphasis on the demand for social and political change. Once strains reach a sufficient scope and intensity, so this argument goes, a relevant organization should spontaneously form. While strains and collective grievances are undoubtedly critical, this approach is unable to address the "collective goods" problem of how such organizations form and control free riding (M. Olson 1968).

Resource mobilization theory takes a "supply-side" approach by arguing that political entrepreneurs are central to developing the goal definitions and incentives that overcome the free-rider problem (M. Olson 1968; Salisbury 1969) and, in an extreme form, takes the view that the supply of entrepreneurs and organizational resources accounts for the expansion of collective grievances and strain definitions (Zald and McCarthy 1987). Resources are defined broadly to include moral resources such as organizational legitimacy; material resources like meeting facilities, means of transportation and communication, and finances; informational resources such as knowledge about how to maintain the organization; and human resources, especially volunteer labor.

The starting point for this discussion is Mancur Olson's (1968) theory of collective goods. Arguing that rational actors will not respond to collective goods per se but will attempt to ride free on the contributions of others, Olson contends that the formation of new organizations requires entrepreneurs who will develop selective incentives such as cheap insurance, discounted drug purchases, or union shop–protected jobs. Selective incentives are "by-products" (Salisbury 1964) in that they are separate and distinct from the collective good itself. Olson also proposes two other solutions. Privileged actors with surplus resources may calculate that their individual gains will be sufficient to warrant creating the collective good for themselves. Second, in small groups, individual benefits (including individual social approval and honors, often called "selective solidarity incentives") may be sufficient to motivate contributions to the collective good.

This argument makes use of the general recognition that creating new organizations is problematic and that only a small percentage of potential supporters is ever mobilized, an issue that anyone who has ever tried to organize collective action is acutely aware of. In this sense, the collective goods problem is central. Olson's theory, however, is premised on the misleading assumption that individuals make decisions in isolation and are not influenced by moral commitments and social pressures (James Wilson 1995; Ferree 1992; Gamson 1992). Empirical studies have found that lack of participation is typically due not to a free-riding calculus but to pessimism about the probability of success, skepticism that one's own contribution will make a difference, weak commitments to the collective good itself, and lack of exposure to organizing attempts (Walsh and Warland 1983; Klandermans and Oegema 1987; Klandermans 1997:chap. 3). Participants are also quite aware of the free-rider problem, which actually works to motivate their contributions. Thus the free-rider problem is not necessarily an obstacle to organizational formation, but it presents significant barriers to groups lacking entrepreneurial resources, co-optable social networks, and strong cultural commitments that favor collective action.

Marwell and Oliver (1993:61) argue that free riding is an option only when individuals respond to a *decelerating production function,* that is, where "each contribution makes others' subsequent contributions less worthwhile, and thus less likely." Central to this calculus is skepticism about the likelihood of success, the importance of one's own individual contribution, and the value of the collective good itself. Successful mobilization follows, in contrast, an *accelerating production function* in which "each contribution makes the next one more worthwhile and thus, more likely" (Marwell and Oliver 1993:63). This dynamic depends on calculations about the probability of success, the likely contributions of others, the value of one's own contribution to a successful outcome, underlying commitments to the collective good itself, and selective incentives. In fact, those who contribute the most are typically the most aware of the free-rider problem and typically act to ensure that others will also contribute. Entrepreneurs are critical because they pay the initial startup costs, devising activities that build solidarity, make commitments to collective goods, and develop goal definitions that clarify the link between individual participation and collective goods (Klandermans 1997:78–87).

Hence a key issue is the supply of entrepreneurs willing to initiate collective action and possessing appropriate organizing skills. The core argument is that the greater the supply of entrepreneurs and organizing resources, the greater the mobilization. Collective action tends to be self-perpetuating, training new entrepreneurs and creating a culture of solidarity that sustains collective action (Fantasia 1988). Zald and McCarthy (1987) point to entrepreneurial supply as key to the growth of social movement organizations during the past three decades, and several studies show that entrepreneurs are often activists in prior organizing efforts (McAdam 1988; Fendrich 1991; Edwards 1994). The general growth of the nonprofit sector as a whole and the establishment of formal training schools for organizers, including programs such as Union Summer by the AFL-CIO, the Industrial Areas Foundation, the Mid-West Organizing Institute, and the like, have created a growing pool of entrepreneurs and new organizing techniques. Entrepreneurial efforts are also facilitated by institutional patronage such as foundation grants and donations from individuals and institutions. Walker (1991:81–83) found that over 80 percent of all national interest organizations received patronage during their initial formation. In this vein, Minkoff (1995:86–89) found that aggregate foundation giving and the supply of educated women and minorities were associated with an increased rate of founding new women's and minority advocacy organizations.

Political opportunity theory argues that the more favorable the political environment in terms of reduced repression and elite tolerance, the greater the foundings of new advocacy organizations and the growth of their activities. McAdam (1999) argues that the formation of new African American civil rights organizations in the 1950s and early 1960s was facilitated by urban migration and the decline of lynching, which weakened the traditional repressive Jim Crow racial order, and by increased elite tolerance and support for civil rights reforms. Early movement victories such as the Supreme Court ruling in *Brown v. Board of Education* and the Montgomery bus boycott spurred the creation of new organizations such as the Southern Christian Leadership Conference (SCLC) and the Student Nonviolent Coordinating Committee (SNCC). Jenkins, Jacobs, and Agnone (2003) show how these political opportunities and those associated with the political power of northern Democrats in Congress with access to a Democratic president facilitated the growth of civil rights protests in the 1950s and 1960s. Minkoff (1995:87–88) found that Democratic presidents have boosted the founding of women's and minority advocacy organizations and encouraged advocacy organizations to adopt protest strategies (Minkoff 1998). In a similar vein, comparative research has shown that elites in constitutionally decentralized states (such as the United States or Germany) are likely to follow an inclusionary strategy for dealing with new groups and issues, and thereby have experienced greater "new social movement" mobilization (Kriesi et al. 1995). Further, the duration of political democracy contributes to the general growth of nonprofit associations (J. Curtis, Baer, and Grabb 2001; Paxton 2002). In this argument, reduced organizing costs and the promise of success are major spurs to forming new advocacy organizations. Critics, however, point out that opportunities have to be perceived to be acted upon, which depends on the construction of meanings that favor the collective perception of opportunities and/or threats (Gamson and Meyer 1996), and that repression and mixed opportunities (Eisinger 1973; Opp and Ruehl 1990), including the imposition of "suddenly imposed grievances" in the form of crises and major disruptions (Walsh and Warland 1983), are often more relevant. Thus resource arguments need to be complemented by these ideas.

The fourth argument—organizational ecology theory—expands on the discussion of resources by focusing on how organizational density (or population size) both legitimizes and constrains the founding of new organizations. The core thesis is that organizational density at low to moderate levels increases the legitimacy or organizational standing of specific organizational forms, giving them a taken-for-granted quality and thus encouraging their founding. But, as the form of organization becomes established, competitive pressures take over, and the founding of new organizations declines and organizational mortality increases (Hannan and Freeman 1989). This view suggests that organizational density has a curvilinear effect on the formation of organizations over time, contributing positively at first but then reducing it later. Organizational density also raises organizational mortality by putting greater competitive pressure on existing organizations.

Several social movement studies support these ideas. "Early riser" movement organizations initially legitimize the goals and activities of "late riser" groups, facilitating the creation of new groups and applying an organizing strategy to new constituencies and issues (Tarrow 1998:142–50). The density of African American organizations increased the organizational foundings of women's, Asian American, and Hispanic American organizations, but at higher densities these organizations competed against one another, lowering the organizational founding rate (Minkoff 1995:110–15). There are also positive spillover effects across organizational repertoires. The older type of advocacy organization—the nonprofit service organizations (like the Urban League and the YMCA)—boost the founding of the newer protest and advocacy organizations (like the Student Nonviolent Coordinating Committee and the Southern Christian Leadership Conference), while these newer protest and advocacy organizations both legitimize and compete against each other (Minkoff 1994). Similarly, service organizations have contributed to the rise of new hybrid organizations that combine advocacy with services, often partnering nonprofits with 501(c)(3) and (c)(4) status, thereby reinforcing the resources and legitimacy of these new identity-based organizations (Minkoff 2002).

Organizational ecology is limited, however, in that it presents a passive view of organizations, emphasizing ecological selection and assuming that legitimacy is due simply to organizational density (Zucker 1989; Baum and Powell 1995). Organizations are also strategic (Scott 1992), and legitimacy has to be constructed (partly through publicity), which depends on the skills of entrepreneurs, their social networks, and existing cultural resources (Powell and DiMaggio 1991). These observations point to the need to analyze the constructive activities of entrepreneurs and their networks and resources.

Social construction theory argues that the formation of new advocacy organizations requires the development of a charter for the organization, a conception of the social problems that it addresses, and a convincing method for bringing about change. Focusing on social movement organizations, Snow et al. (1986) coin the term "social injustice frames" to refer to the constructive activity that identifies "what was previously seen as an unfortunate but tolerable situation . . . as inexcusable, unjust or immoral." Snow and Benford (1988) refer to "frame alignment" as the interpretive interaction between movement entrepreneurs and potential participants that creates (or fails to create) congruence between individual and organizational claims about the causes of grievances as "injustices" and the development of a strategy for altering these conditions.

A central part of frame alignment is developing an organizational repertoire that defines how to organize social change efforts. Although entrepreneurs are important, significant mobilization requires a larger group of organizational activists—which Marwell and Oliver (1993) refer to as the "critical mass." Ganz (2000) shows how the diverse skills, cultural understandings, and interpersonal networks of the organizing cadre for the United Farm Workers Union provided for effective mobilization in a setting where other organizing efforts had failed. Clemens (1997) shows how the Progressive Era labor, agrarian, and women's movements constructed an organizational repertoire for nonpartisan citizen politics that framed the central problem as corrupt political parties and argued the need for nonpartisan advocacy based on expertise and public opinion. In a similar fashion, neoprogressives in the 1960s and 1970s developed a similar organizational repertoire for public interest advocacy by contending that the core problem was the "capture" of government agencies by powerful interest groups and claiming that this could be countered by nonprofit political advocacy focused on governmental accountability and procedural inclusiveness (Pertschuk 1982; McCann 1986). The importance of frame construction to organizational foundings is also illustrated by the environmental movement, which has long depended on the constructive efforts of lawyers, policy experts, and scientists. Gauging framing activity from the number of new environmental books listed in the Library of Congress from 1895 to 1994, McLaughlin and Khawaja (2000) find a curvilinear "rise-and-decline" impact of the number of newly published environmental books on the foundings of new environmental organizations.

As should be evident, these theories need to be synthesized. Most existing studies are case analyses and so cannot control for multiple factors. They may also be biased in their case selection. What is needed are large sample studies controlling for multiple theories. What exists are limited studies of specific samples. One of the better samples is Berry's (1977:23–44) study of public interest organizations, which found that two-thirds of the organizations originated from entrepreneurial efforts and a third from disturbances. Even those stemming from disturbances included entrepreneurship at some point in their formation, indicating that these are not exclusive arguments. Zald and McCarthy (1987) advance what they call the "extreme" argument that entrepreneurs can manufacture grievances, while the opposite idea that major social disturbances attract the attentions of entrepreneurs is equally plausible. Neither hypothesis has been examined systematically. McAdam (1999) argues that increasing political opportunities stimulate a "cognitive liberation" in which conditions are redefined as mutable and unjust and therefore "disturbing." This concept does not, however, explain how framing occurs. Similarly, ecological spillover and selection operate within the broad constraints of resource distribution but cannot account for the constructive activities of entrepreneurs and organizers.

How might these theories be fruitfully synthesized? In another context, Gamson, Fireman, and Rytina (1982) suggest a useful approach that might be adapted to this situation. In their study of collective rebellions, they found that a combination of five distinct factors had to be present. Singly, each factor was necessary but not sufficient; only the combination was sufficient. Each factor had to reach a minimum threshold value, but increments beyond that were not important. Surpluses in one factor compensated for deficits in others. Extending this general logic to our concern, disturbances, resources, new political opportunities, legitimacy, competitive selection, and social construction can all be considered critical to the formation of new advocacy organizations. Each must be present at a minimal threshold level, and surpluses in one might compensate for others. In any particular setting, one or more of these theories may be most relevant depending on the other factors present. Ultimately, multivariate analyses with significant samples of advocacy organizations are needed to fully assess these explanations.

Existing studies highlight the central importance of entrepreneurship, constructive efforts, and new opportunities, especially institutional patronage. Crises and various disturbances stimulate nonprofit advocacy among relatively resourceful groups, but many of the groups represented by nonprofit advocacy lack resources and are initially disorganized. Entrepreneurs are crucial because they solve the free-rider problem, but, more important, they define injustice frames and develop organizational repertoires. Opportunities in the form of external patronage that provides legitimacy as well as tangible resources are often critical. Nonprofit advocacy often focuses on the interests of disorganized groups that not only confront the free-rider problem but also need entrepreneurs to develop a favorable "accelerating production function."

Take consumers, for example. The free-rider problem is clear. The stake of any individual consumer is vastly outweighed by the costs of collective action. Even more important, there are few social networks through which consumers can be organized. While there may be a strong cultural framework for consumer rights, it is not strong enough alone to mobilize consumers. Entrepreneurial efforts, often combined with institutional patronage, were key to the formation in the 1930s of the Consumers Union, which was sponsored by trade unions and wealthy donors. Most recently, Ralph Nader's entrepreneurial activities were decisive in launching the consumer movement (Pertschuk 1982); a particular benchmark was his donation of the proceeds from an out-of-court settlement with General Motors to create the Center for Auto Safety. Also critical was the sponsorship of the Consumer Federation, which provided initial office space and credibility, and the financial patronage of several wealthy individuals and private foundations (McCarry 1972; Gorey 1975). The Consumer Advisory Council in the Kennedy and Johnson administrations also helped by bringing consumer activists together, creating a critical mass of organizers and legitimacy for the problem (Creighton 1976), allowing for the development of a general frame for consumer rights.

A similar picture is provided by the creation of the Environmental Defense Fund, which was launched in 1967 by a group of wildlife biologists concerned about the effects of DDT poisoning on birds. Drawing on funding from the Rachel Carson Fund of the Audubon Society, they framed the problem of environmental risks to wildlife and, by securing foundation grants and a direct-mail membership of over 200,000, built one of the largest environmental public interest law firms. Likewise, the Natural Resources Defense Council was created in the late 1960s when the Ford Foundation brought together a group of wealthy individuals attempting to block construction of the Storm King power plant on the Hudson River with a group of Yale law students inspired by the idea of public interest law (Adams 1974). Still another example is the creation of the National Organization for Women (NOW), which drew on the entrepreneurial efforts of former civil rights and labor activists who had participated in the White House–sponsored National Conference on the Status of Women. Building on office space, legitimacy, and small funding from the United Auto Workers union and the Institute for Policy Studies, they proceeded to create an "NAACP for women" that grew to over 250,000 members and mobilized early organizational support from private foundations and wealthy benefactors (Freeman 1975:52–56; Gelb and Palley 1996).

There are multiple explanations of patronage for nonprofit advocacy. M. Olson (1968) argues that patronage is due to surplus wealth, which lowers the cost of producing collective goods so that individual benefits outweigh them.

While this interpretation may help explain the political donations of multimillionaires, such as Doris Day's support for the animal rights activism of the People for the Ethical Treatment of Animals (PETA) or Robert Redford's support for the environmental movement, it oversimplifies the motives. How does one put a price on the ethical imperative of protecting defenseless animals? Cultural commitments, however explained, are critical.

A second explanation is social control. Drawing on the civil rights experience, McAdam (1999) argues that, during the 1960s, the political threat of indigenous protest and the urban riots created elite fears about broader instability, spurring private foundations to fund moderate advocates to blunt the potential impact of militants. Haines (1988) documents a strong "radical flank effect," with most of the foundation funding going reactively to the moderate civil rights organizations that were competing against militant black groups. Jenkins and Eckert (1986) concur that most of the funding was reactive, spurred by the major civil rights protests and legal victories. In addition to strengthening the moderates, this funding also responded to the promise that civil rights legal victories would be institutionalized, ensuring that African Americans would gain voting and other civil rights. In this vein, the Kennedy administration pressured several foundations to create the Voter Education Project and encouraged the American Bar Association to create the Lawyers' Committee for Civil Rights Under Law (Navasky 1977; Wolford 1992), hoping to channel the conflict into institutional routines and to strengthen Democratic voter support. But it is also important to recognize that some foundations had funded the SCLC and SNCC long before the protests and court victories. In the mid-1930s the National Association for the Advancement of Colored People (NAACP) had created a legal office for challenging Jim Crow racism with funding from the Garland Fund (Krueger 1972; Rabin 1975), and the Stern Fund and Field Foundation of Chicago were supporting SCLC and the NAACP in the early 1950s (Jenkins 1989, 1998; Jenkins and Halcli 1999).

This history suggests a third interpretation of patronage stimulated by "conscience." In the early 1960s the National Council of Churches (NCC) sponsored a range of protest movements, ranging from SCLC and Saul Alinsky's Industrial Areas Foundation to the United Farm Workers and the National Welfare Rights Organization (Jenkins 1977, 1985; West 1981). The autonomy of the professional NCC staff allowed them to pursue the "social gospel" by sponsoring a range of nonprofit advocacy groups involved in civil rights, community organizing, and welfare rights on behalf of the poor. The underlying motive was a moral commitment to empower excluded groups and create a more inclusive political process. Similarly, highlighting their moral commitment to countering the power disparity between the wealthy and the disadvantaged, several public charities have banded together to form the Funding Exchange, which promotes the idea that community activists should have control over at least some of the grants that are allocated, thereby narrowing the gap between the donors and the donees (Ostrander 1995; Jenkins 1998, 2001).

These moral commitments are often constrained by political interests. Patrons are more supportive of initiatives that reinforce their own power and prestige. In the 1960s the Kennedy and Johnson administrations promoted the creation of the Voter Education Project as well as the consumer movement (Nadel 1971), the women's movement (Freeman 1975), and the "gray lobby" (Pratt 1977), calculating that these movements would reinforce their own political power and social recognition for doing good works. In the 1980s the Reagan White House provided seed funding for Mothers Against Drunk Drivers (MADD), seeing it as a way to advance its conservative social issues agenda (McCarthy and Wolfson 1992). Conscience donations, therefore, are often genuine but are also constrained by political and status interests.

The U.S. tax code regulates institutional patronage and the organization of political advocacy. As discussed elsewhere (Simon, Dale, and Chisolm, this volume), private foundations and individuals can make tax-deductible gifts to 501(c)(3) organizations, but these organizations are banned from "substantial political activity." Contributions to social welfare organizations [501(c)(4)] are not tax-deductible, but these organizations are free to engage in unlimited political activity. These and related tax incentives encourage advocacy groups to incorporate as public charities and to take on more professional and formal organization. It also discourages them from engaging in direct political activity, especially rights advocacy (Cress 1997; McCarthy, Britt, and Wolfson 1991; Berry and Arons 2003). The legal meaning of "political activity" has varied over time. In 1930 the U.S. courts denied the tax-exempt status of Margaret Sanger's American Birth Control League on the grounds that legislative lobbying for change in access to birth control constituted a public subsidy for political advocacy (*Slee v. Commissioner,* 42 F. 2d 184 [2d Cir. 1930]). In the 1950s conservative southern congressional representatives, piqued by the *Brown v. Board of Education* decision, got the Justice Department to reevaluate the tax-exempt status of the NAACP Legal Defense and Education Fund, Inc., which had been incorporated in the 1930s as a 501(c)(3) charitable organization. The Justice Department eventually allowed the Legal Defense Fund to be chartered as a 501(c)(3) but with a governing board fully separate from the NAACP, which was then reorganized as a 501(c)(4) (Kluger 1976). Although this certified the legality of tax-exempt legal advocacy, it also limited the political advocacy of 501(c)(3) organizations. In 1966 the IRS revoked the 501(c)(3) status of the Sierra Club because it took out full-page ads in the *New York Times* and several national magazines, opposing federal plans to build a dam that would have flooded part of the Grand Canyon and other projects (Berry and Arons 2003:73–76).

In the Tax Reform Act of 1969, Congress defined "politics" narrowly as direct endorsements in electoral campaigns and attempts to directly influence decisions made by Congress and the executive branch. Appearances before Congress or administrative bodies were unregulated if they were "educational"—that is, factual and solicited by the governmental body in question. Grassroots lobbying, such as the Sierra Club ads, were defined as legal so long as they did not directly endorse a specific electoral candidate or specific pending legislation. Voter registration was deductible so long as it was nonpartisan (i.e., independent of campaign organizations) and general (i.e., covering a five-state area). These distinctions are reinforced by Federal Elections Commission rules that define "express advocacy" in terms of advocating the election or defeat of a candidate by instructing voters to vote for or against a specific candidate. In the 1976 Tax Reform Act (further clarified by IRS administrative rules), Congress further defined "substantial political activity" to mean costs in excess of 20 percent of the first $500,000 of a charity's budget, with declining percentages above that.

There have also been several highly visible political disputes over tax-exempt status. In general the IRS has followed a lenient policy, requiring little more than a general statement of purpose that fits "religious, educational, charitable, scientific, or literary" activities. In 1969 the IRS initially refused to grant 501(c)(3) status to the Natural Resources Defense Council and the Project on Corporate Responsibility, claiming that public interest advocacy lacked a legally defensible constituency. After extensive controversy and the resignation of the IRS commissioner, the exemptions were approved with regulations requiring public interest legal organizations to decline client fees and to file annual reports documenting the "public interests" served by their activities (Halperin and Cunningham 1971; Adams 1974). During the Reagan administration, the IRS conducted punitive audits of several progressive foundations and charitable organizations, including the Foundation for National Progress, publisher of *Mother Jones* magazine, and the Rosenberg Foundation, but did not succeed in revoking any tax exemptions or securing broader restrictions on nonprofit advocacy (MacKenzie 1981; Greve 1987; Shear 1995). Nonetheless, many public charities refrain from any significant advocacy out of fear of appearing too political and inviting IRS audits. Highly publicized audits and the counsel of accountants and attorneys fearful of IRS scrutiny have discouraged advocacy by public charities (Berry and Arons 2003). At the same time, many public charities involved in service programs are involved in administrative lobbying over the details of governmental programs, claiming that these activities do not constitute advocacy.

THE STRUCTURE OF NONPROFIT ADVOCACY ORGANIZATIONS

Like any formal organizations, nonprofit advocacy groups need structures for defining goals, making decisions, mobilizing resources, and directing resources toward goals. Organizational structures condition the impact of advocacy on policy change, as well as the broader questions of procedural representativeness and civic engagement. Analysts have typically drawn in varying degrees on two general approaches to organizational structure: a *closed system* approach that treats organizations as able to control all the relevant variables, and a *natural system* approach in which organizations search for the most satisfactory strategy given resource and institutional constraints (Scott 1992). The first focuses on how goals inform organizational structures and the latter on how technological and institutional constraints shape structures.

The major debate has been over the advantages and effectiveness of decentralized versus bureaucratic organization. Responding to the democratic and humanitarian values associated with nonprofit advocacy, several argue on normative grounds that nonprofit advocacy organizations should be decentralized participatory organizations with minimal formal structure, relying on consensus or majority voting to reach major decisions and focusing on developing a strong sense of community, an egalitarian division of labor, and minimal role differentiation. Also called "collectivist" organizations (Rothschild-Whitt 1979), these decentralized groups embody democratic values and maximize the impact on civic involvement (Pateman 1970; Breines 1982; Rosenthal and Schwartz 1989). Proponents of this view take heart from Gerlach and Hine's (1970) contention that social movements are typically segmental, polycephalous, and reticulate and that this decentralized structure has survival advantages. Organized informally around a large number of loosely connected cells or affinity groups (segmental), social movements typically have many competing leaders vying for attention and support (polycephalous), and are loosely integrated by multiple diffuse networks, "traveling evangelists," and common ideology (reticulate). This decentralized structure maximizes access points for proselytization, the motivating effectiveness of solidarity and purposive incentives, promotes tactical innovations and the escalation of action through competitive diffusion, and reduces the risk of repression. Echoing Michels's (1962) classic "iron law of oligarchy" thesis that bureaucratization creates centralized control and conservative goal change, Piven and Cloward (1977) argue that, at least for resource-poor constituencies, developing permanent membership organizations diverts resources and compromises the major strategic option available to the poor, namely, their ability to engage in mass defiance.

Others question the advantages of decentralized organizations and the inevitability of conservative goal change. In addition to problems with inefficient decision making, coordinating large numbers, and reconciling strong minority sentiments with majority rule (Mansbridge 1982), decentralized structures have resource limits. Freeman (1973) warns against the "tyranny of structurelessness" experienced by the early women's "consciousness-raising" groups. Lack of formal structure and central leadership prevented growth by limiting organizing to socially homogeneous middle-class women. It also prevented these groups from engaging in effective institutional advocacy. Others argue that there is no imperative that organizational rationalization must lead to conservative goal change. Zald and Ash (1966) argue that this outcome depends on inclusive membership rules that allow leaders to change constituencies. Jenkins (1977) contends that professionalization may in fact lead to "radical oligarchies" that pursue more social change values.

A related argument is Zald and McCarthy's (1987) thesis that the contemporary trend is toward professionalized advocacy, especially by professional movement organizations. Professional movement organizations maintain full-time professional staffs that mobilize resources from a "conscience constituency" through direct mail, media appeals, and soliciting foundation grants; have small or nonexistent "paper" memberships; and attempt to "speak for" rather than organize beneficiary constituencies. The discretionary time schedules of professionals and college students, the discretionary resources of private foundations and social welfare institutions, and the growth of the mass media make these organizations possible. A related argument is that centralized advocacy organizations have greater "combat readiness" in terms of tactical flexibility and control over resources, and that formalization reduces internal factionalism and enhances coordination, contributing to organizational survival as well as strategic effectiveness (Gamson 1990).

The professionalization thesis has been criticized for overstating the prominence of professional movement organizations. Analyzing the civil rights movement, Jenkins and Eckert (1986) show that professional movement organizations were secondary and depended on indigenous mobilization, which gave their claims legitimacy. However, there are major issues and constituencies for which professional advocacy is the only realistic possibility, such as the children's and disabled rights movements (S. Olson 1984), and these organizations have clear technical and legitimacy advantages in conducting rights advocacy before governmental bodies (Bosso 1995, 1999).

The general debate about decentralized versus centralized organization has been clouded by several confusions. First, both types of organization have advantages that are often overlooked by their critics. Decentralized organizations maximize participation and personal change outcomes, while bureaucracy is best at organizational survival and institutional change (R. Curtis and Zurcher 1974; Staggenborg 1989). Second, these structures are not so much "chosen" as reflecting the resources and organization of different constituencies. The pro-life movement is rooted in a rich network of local churches, which has led to a decentralized structure, while the pro-choice movement lacks a comparable social infrastructure, forcing it to rely largely on professional advocacy (McCarthy 1987). Third, these organizational models are ideal types, which means that actual organizations typically mix these structures. Most national membership associations, such as the NAACP, the Sierra Club, and the American Civil Liberties Union (ACLU), are federalized organizations with decentralized local chapters and a centralized national office. It is also possible to combine decentralized networks with central structure. The SCLC was centralized around the person of Martin Luther King Jr. but reached out through a large network of informal "bridge leaders" who stood at nodal points in the informal networks of the African American community (Robnett 1996). Similarly, the environmental movement consists of a loose multi-organizational field populated by multiple organizational types (Diani 1995). The YMCA was originally a federation of local informal groups that later developed a central structure for organizing new units (Zald 1970). Most political issue areas are also characterized by a "multi-organizational field" (R. Curtis and Zurcher 1973) in which multiple organizations with variable structures compete and cooperate toward common goals. Fourth, some analysts have often confused their own normative preferences for direct democracy with the task of explaining organizational structure. Adhering to the normative argument that participatory democracy is desirable is not the same as arguing that it is typical or more effective at institutional change.

The first three points are underscored by Bordt's (1997) study of ninety-five women's advocacy and service organizations in New York City. Women's nonprofits are an ideal testing ground because of the long-standing ideological debates about their organization. Significantly, Bordt found that the majority were hybrids that combined bureaucratic and collectivistic structures. Collectivist organizations were the least frequent (8 percent), with the most common being pragmatic collectives with little differentiation and decentralized authority but reliance on material incentives and little emphasis on shared beliefs (45 percent). Professional organizations were next (27 percent), combining collectivistic decision making with a common ethos but displaying a moderate division of labor. Bureaucracies made up 19 percent, with centralized authority, high differentiation, and an emphasis on material incentives and little emphasis on shared beliefs.

What accounts for these organizational structures? In Bordt's study, age, size, and task (or organizational technology) were key, along with ideological commitments. Older organizations with more employees and volunteers and routine tasks are more likely to be bureaucratic, supporting both organizational life-cycle and contingency theories about the constraints of routine technology (Perrow 1970). Pragmatic collectives are typically associated with radical feminism, suggesting that they adapt collectivistic ideology to their work constraints. Yet most of the collectivistic organizations identify as "nonfeminist," and one radical feminist organization is bureaucratic. In interviews, most responded that ideological debates about organization were passé and that their organization "just happened" or "emerged from the work" (Bordt 1997). This pattern suggests the impact of institutional traditions and organizational technology. The professional organizations are dominated by social-service professionals, reflecting their professional identities and nonroutine tasks. Pragmatic collectives are centrally involved in interorganizational and community networking activities, making this an effective form of organization for sustaining multiorganizational ties. Similar evidence comes from

Minkoff's (1998) study of minority and women's nonprofits, which supports a "fluidity of aging" thesis that older organizations and those with greater staff size and professionalization exhibit greater strategic flexibility, including the ability to respond to a favorable political environment by adopting more militant protest tactics.

The existence of "multi-organizational fields" (R. Curtis and Zurcher 1973) suggests that multiple types of organization may be active in the same issue area, complementing one another. The southern civil rights movement was a network of "local movement centers" organized around churches and student groups that mobilized "direct action" protests coordinated by professional cadre organizations, most notably the SCLC and SNCC (Morris 1984). The women's movement was initially ideologically divided between a decentralized "radical feminist" wing and a centralized "liberal feminist" wing (Freeman 1975, 1979), but, with the development of hybrid structures and the collapse of several organizations, these wings gradually merged, creating an organizationally diverse multiorganizational field (Ferree and Hess 1994:208–12; Gelb and Palley 1996:xix–xxi). While ideological debate over organization persists (see Ferree and Martin 1997), this organizational diversity has been a source of strength by sustaining innovation and multiple types of efforts. Lune and Oberstein (1999) describe a similar interorganizational synergy among the nonprofits responding to the AIDS crisis in New York during the 1980s. Bureaucratic organizations provided routine services, a decentralized cadre organization (ACT UP/NY) staged dramatic protests that pressured governmental elites to respond to new issues, and professional research organizations conducted relevant policy research and engaged in administrative lobbying. Addressing the AIDS crisis entailed cooperation from all three, despite recurrent disputes over agenda and strategy.

A remaining question is organizational democracy. A mid-1990s survey by the National Center for Nonprofit Boards found that almost three-fourths of all nonprofit boards were self-perpetuating and only 19 percent had elected boards or chapters (Moyers and Enright 1997). Brulle (2000:249) classified 61 percent of the national environmental organizations as oligarchies, with the membership having no formal power over the board. Almost a third of the boards do, however, share decision making with members through formal consultation and polling. In his study of the public interest movement, Berry (1977:196–98) found that two-thirds were staff-dominated and less than 10 percent significantly consulted members. A different picture is provided by Foley and Edwards's (2002) national survey of over 7,700 peace organizations. While most of the large national advocacy organizations were oligarchic, the majority of the smaller organizations active outside the Beltway were at least semi-democratic, and less than a quarter were professional movement organizations with only "checkbook" members.

Advocates of decentralization typically argue that democracy is best ensured by minimizing formalization and avoiding central control, a permanent staff, and a fixed division of labor (Rothschild-Whitt 1979). This strategy, however, entails costs in terms of organizational growth, survival, and effectiveness. An alternative is polyarchy, that is, regular competitive elections with organized factions and open communication, which can be combined with bureaucratic and professional structures. Polyarchy provided significant member control in the International Typographic Union (Lipset, Trow, and Coleman 1956) and characterizes over half of U.S. trade unions (Edelstein and Warner 1979). Member control often depends on more than competitive elections. McFarland (1984) found that leadership commitments to accountability are as important in Common Cause as formal structures. The staff also keeps in touch with member sentiments through regular consultations with volunteer activists plus routine polling. To encourage diversity on the board, nominations are designed to ensure that handpicked nominees do not consistently win and to represent a diverse cross-section of the membership. In several instances, nonrenewal of memberships has led the staff to alter Common Cause policies.

Contrary to the "iron law of oligarchy" thesis, centralized control does not inevitably lead to conservative goal transformation. During the 1960s, the staff of the National Council of Churches transformed the organization from a "home mission" program into an "aligned movement" that sponsored civil rights, farm worker unionization, and community organizing (Jenkins 1977). Although this change precipitated an internal fight that led several conservative denominations to withdraw, the staff preserved the policy. Similarly, the president and staff of the Sierra Club prodded the organization into more aggressive political advocacy during the 1960s, leading to the previously mentioned loss of its 501(c)(3) status. Although this eventually led to David Brower's resignation and his creation of Friends of the Earth (Fox 1981), the Sierra Club has remained active in political advocacy, creating a political action committee and a new 501(c)(3) to raise funds for advocacy. Zald and Ash (1966) argue that organizations that rely on material incentives for participation and have inclusive membership rules are more vulnerable to goal transformation. Inclusiveness means that new members with new ideas are continually entering the organization, pressing for change in strategies. A focus on providing material benefits to members encourages an emphasis on organizational maintenance.

A final question is the organizational impact of institutional patronage. Several case studies link oligarchy and conservative goal change to foundation and governmental support. In the late 1960s the Woodlawn Organization was an Alinsky-style community organization that protested city hall's and the University of Chicago's neglect of the largely African American neighborhood surrounding the campus. Due to a centralized structure, the staff was able to quickly transform the organization into a community development corporation that restored dilapidated buildings and created new businesses, while curtailing protest and community organizing (Fish 1973). Oligarchy facilitated the transformation of Mobilization for Youth, which was the model for the War on Poverty Community Action Program, from a contentious protest organization organizing rent strikes and antidiscrimination protests into a noncontentious social service organization (Helfgot 1981). Yet Cress and Snow (1996) found that the churches and community organizations that served as long-term patrons of the homeless movement, which the authors call "benefactors," endorsed contentious politics. Similarly, Minkoff (1998) found no evidence that foundation support leads to conservative strategic change among minority and women's groups. Organizational change needs to be treated as a series of contingencies with multiple relevant factors, pointing toward the need to integrate these various theories instead of playing them off as mutually exclusive rival explanations.

THE "CARE AND FEEDING" OF ADVOCACY ORGANIZATIONS

James Q. Wilson (1995:30) defines the problem of organizational maintenance in terms of "not only survival but also . . . producing and sustaining cooperative effort." How does a nonprofit advocacy organization sustain participation? The usual starting point for this discussion is the debate over M. Olson's (1968) collective action theory, especially the selective incentives argument. As noted earlier, analysts have largely rejected Olson's theory by bringing in "soft selective incentives," such as solidarity and moral satisfaction (Moe 1980), and the collective incentives of moral commitments and collective solidarity (Fireman and Gamson 1979; Ferree 1992; Rothenberg 1992; Marwell and Oliver 1993). In Clark and Wilson's (1961) theory of organizational incentives, organizational participation is motivated by purposive incentives (i.e., moral commitments to the collective good itself) and solidary incentives (i.e., emotional rewards and punishments). Purposive incentives are inherently collective, based on commitment to a moral vision. One gains only with the realization of the collective good itself. Solidarity may be selective, such as individual honors and the penalties of ostracism, as well as collective, such as collective recognition for a cause or group. All three types coupled with selective material incentives may help sustain participation. The United Farm Workers Union developed stronger farm worker support because it mixed narrow material appeals to a community benefit program with broad moral appeals to worker rights, workplace protection, and challenging racial discrimination, as well as appealing to the religious and ethnic loyalties of its supporters. It also initially focused organizing among the more stable farm worker communities; only later did it attempt to organize the more ethnically diverse migrant and seasonal workers (Jenkins 1985, 1999).

How do advocacy organizations sustain participation? Klandermans (1997:78–86) argues that social movements rely on three methods: (1) emphasizing the importance of specific action goals; (2) creating positive "success expectations"; and (3) providing selective incentives. Advocacy organizations need to enlist both sympathizers and bystanders by creating positive attitudes about the legitimacy and benefits of specific actions. In general, it is easier to mobilize support to defend a threatened right, such as environmental security, than support for innovations, such as new laws or government programs. Not only is the benefit of an untried innovation unclear, but existing practices have greater legitimacy. Drawing on "prospect theory" (Quattrone and Tversky 1988), some argue on psychological grounds that "negatives" or threats are more motivating than "positives" or gains. Mitchell (1979) argues that the major impetus for environmental mobilization is fear of collective environmental negatives, not future positive gains. Threats to strongly held identities and solidarities stimulate both purposive and solidarity commitments. To create an "accelerating production function" (Marwell and Oliver 1993), organizers also need to create favorable "success expectations," that is, the belief that one's own participation will contribute to the likelihood of success and that enough others will contribute to make the effort successful. Effective mobilization is typically based on small group organizing and informal networks, focusing initially on narrow goals and building on past successes. Participation is often sustained by positive interactions with significant others, especially friends and family members. Studies of recruitment to social movements show that individuals are more readily mobilized who are embedded in co-optable social networks, that is, interpersonal networks involving significant others with similar positive views of movement goals (Snow et al. 1986; McAdam 1988; Opp 1989; Gould 1995). The Clamshell Alliance, which protested the Seabrook nuclear power plant in New England during the 1970s, organized around affinity groups, using small-group decision making to sustain commitment (Barkan 1979).

Advocacy organizing confronts two problems: (1) preventing erosion or the loss of sympathy; and (2) nonconversion, that is, the classic free-rider problem of failing to convert sympathizers into active participants. Social networks, framing of grievances, and organizing efforts are critical to addressing both. In a study of the petition campaign against the basing of U.S. nuclear weapons in the Netherlands during the early 1980s, Klandermans and Oegema (1987) found that erosion was largely due both to preexisting loyalties to political parties that opposed the petition and to the active disapproval of friends and family members. Nonconversion was largely due to communication failure, specifically lack of contacts from petition campaigners and active petition supporters in personal networks. In the Three Mile Island nuclear disaster, nonconversion was largely due to ignorance about events and prior family and work obligations (Walsh and Warland 1983). Framing the problem in terms of legal equity can boost support independent of specific material benefits that contributors might hope to receive, as McCann (1994) found in the women's wage equity campaigns. To sustain mass participation, advocacy organizations must maintain concrete programs with specific goals, frame appeals in broad moral terms that appeal to generally accepted standards, highlight relevant material benefits, continually build new membership contacts, and work through and reinforce existing co-optable networks.

Synthesizing organizational incentive theory with learning arguments, Rothenberg (1992) argues that participation in Common Cause has varied across time, with participants initially attracted by the moral purposes of the organization, in this case fostering governmental accountability and openness. With experience, participants become more knowledgeable about the working of public interest advocacy. A majority drop out or become simply "checkbook" contributors. But a small percentage become more strongly committed and skilled at advocacy work by volunteering their time and assuming leadership roles. Given a 30 to 40 percent annual turnover rate in membership, Common Cause has found it necessary to keep the membership dues and requirements low, so as to encourage new memberships, and to use direct mail and mass advertising as well as informal network appeals to recruit broadly. A small portion of those contacted go on to become volunteers, sustaining the organization with direct participation. Other advocacy organizations using "direct mail" to prospect for members have similar 1 to 2 percent positive response rates and significant turnover in renewals (Johnson 1999).

Social groups differ in their receptiveness to organizational incentives. In general, the more educated middle and upper classes are more receptive to moral appeals, reflecting their economic security, while the lower class is more receptive to a mix of material and solidarity (James Wilson 1995:62–67). There is also some evidence that humanistic and social service professionals such as college professors, doctors, and social workers are more receptive to moralistic appeals and more likely to participate in nonprofit advocacy groups (Weisbrod, Handler, and Komesar 1978:109–45; McFarland 1984; Lichter and Rothman 1983; Brint 1985; Jenkins and Wallace 1996). Their occupational cultures emphasize public service, and their affluence and discretionary time schedules facilitate participation. Within the Christian evangelical community, the tradition of "witnessing" one's faith by specific deeds or acts similarly serves as a cultural resource for conservative activists attempting to mobilize support. For low-income groups, combining purposive appeals with material interests and solidarity may be more important. The classic Alinsky (1969, 1972) community organizing model emphasizes the use of direct material issues, such as access to public services and equitable taxation (Horwitt 1989). Studies of rent strikes show that low-income tenants are more concerned about their immediate needs for hot water, heat, and building safety and, at least initially, are largely uninterested in broad social-change goals (Brill 1971; Lawson 1986). Collective incentives may become more important with longer participation. In the welfare rights movement, welfare mothers initially responded to material benefits, like access to special welfare payments, but activists gradually became committed to both the ideology of welfare rights and the solidarity of the group (Bailis 1974; West 1981).

Nonprofit advocacy cannot rely on solidarity alone, if only because people have better alternatives; instead it must combine solidarity with purposive and material appeals. Overreliance on solidarity also runs the risk of goal diversion. In the 1940s the Townsend Movement, which was initially created to press for governmental pensions for the elderly, was transformed into a social club that survived by marketing geriatric products (Messinger 1955). Similarly, activists in the National Welfare Rights Organization, which was formally committed to obtaining guaranteed family-income legislation, forced the resignation of their leader, George Wiley, to campaign against a politically feasible guaranteed-income proposal proposed by the Nixon administration out of fear that the measure would undermine the selective incentives that sustained their organization (Kotz and Kotz 1977; West 1981).

Organizational survival can be critical, facilitating rapid mobilization when mass activism reemerges. Rupp and Taylor (1987) show that the Women's Party served as an abeyance structure, providing ideology and collective identities for the reemergence of "second wave" feminist activism in the 1960s. In addition, many of the factors that influence organizational formation also affect organizational survival. Declining collective grievances and resources, restrictive political opportunities, increased interorganizational competition, and framing encumbrances have all been linked to organizational mortality. Partial movement victories, internal schisms over the "black power" concept that led to the withdrawal of key organizers and patrons, and reduced political opportunities all contributed to the dissolution of several major civil rights organizations (Meier and Rudwick 1973; C. Carson 1982; McAdam 1999). In a historical analysis of the collapse of the Knights of Labor in the nineteenth century, Voss (1996) argues that framing encumbrances in which leaders failed to externalize blame and to develop "fortifying myths" about the inevitability of change contributed to the demise of the organization. Organizational ecology theory posits a liability of "adolescence," with organizations being more likely to fail after a medium period of existence (Singh and House 1990); when initial enthusiasm has waned, foundations and donors who prefer to provide startup funds rather than program maintenance are more likely to withdraw. A final factor is the question of organizational structure. In a study of 53 historical movements active between 1815 and 1945, Gamson (1990) found that centralization and formal structure contribute to organizational survival, reducing the likelihood of internal schisms.

Minkoff's (1995:91–95) study of organizational mortality of women's and racial advocacy groups supports the resource argument, as well as grievance and organizational density arguments. She found that higher mortality was associated with reduced grievances linked to improvements in women's and black's education. Similarly, increases in federal social welfare spending and disposable personal income reduced concerns about these problems, thereby raising mortality. In line with organizational ecology theory, organizational density increases organizational mortality, indicating increased competition for scarce resources. However, increased resources in terms of foundation funding also worked in the opposite direction, increasing organizational mortality because foundations favored new projects over established groups and thereby contributed to higher mortality rates (see also Minkoff 1998).

Further light is shed by Edwards and Marullo's (1995) analysis of 411 peace movement organizations active in the late 1980s. Organizations that had existed from three to eight years were the most likely to dissolve, along with those with narrow goals and weak external legitimacy (in terms of media coverage). Smaller organizations with less than a hundred members and those with minimal formal structure were also more likely to disband. Smaller organizations were more likely to suffer demise due to weak membership mobilization, while large and national organizations were vulnerable to problems of weak external legitimacy and linkages to other peace groups. The content of peacemaking frames had no significance, suggesting that the internal schisms associated with framing activities may be either ubiquitous or not as contentious as typically portrayed. Relying on insider tactics and shunning protest contributed to organizational survival.

In general, these studies show that formal and centralized structures facilitate organizational survival, while decentralized structures contribute to grassroots participation. A hybrid structure that combines elements of both may be optimal. Resources are critical, especially when constraints stem from organizational adolescence, interorganizational competition, short-term institutional patronage, and weak external legitimacy. At the organizational population level, a key problem with organizational ecology theory is the indirect measurement of interorganizational competition. Organizational density does not necessarily tap aggregate resource constraints. Moreover, legitimacy effects may sustain organizations beyond their usefulness. Few studies examine survival probabilities for different types of organizations. Future research on organizational survival needs to show more clearly how legitimacy and resource constraints at the population level shape the survival probabilities of particular types of organizations.

THE IMPACT OF NONPROFIT POLITICAL ADVOCACY

Nonprofit advocates generally present themselves as counteracting the dominance of the "special interests." While this characterization is largely framed in terms of the policy process, it also affects private social institutions, cultural practices, and citizen involvement. In the following section, we focus largely on public policy because this has been the major focus of nonprofit advocacy and has received more analytic attention, but, where relevant, we also discuss the broader institutional and cultural impact of nonprofit advocacy. Influencing the policy process involves four major steps: (1) getting an issue onto the political agenda; (2) securing favorable decisions; (3) ensuring that these decisions are implemented; and (4) making sure that these activities create favorable social outcomes for specific constituencies (Schumaker 1975; Giugni 1998).

Agenda access involves getting authorities to hear the concerns of a group and to take an issue seriously. Of the numerous potential issues, only a fraction are ever organized into the policy process. Disorganization, privatistic values, and institutional procedures "bias the system" and keep many issues off the agenda (Schattschneider 1960; Bachrach and Baratz 1962). The major function of nonprofit advocacy is to define issues and to publicize them so that they gain public attention, especially through mass media coverage, and get onto "the list of items which decision makers have formally accepted for serious consideration" (Cobb, Ross, and Ross 1977:126).

How do nonprofit advocates gain agenda access? Since the mass media constitute the major forum for public debate, media coverage is central. The major function of advocacy leaders is framing issues so that they have broad appeal and gain media coverage. Ralph Nader's talent at converting a technical report on governmental agency abuses into a public issue is legendary, and his reputation for providing "good copy" ensures that the media will cover his press releases. Many nonprofit leaders are institutional personalities in the sense that their reputations for framing issues ensure media access and overshadow the reputations of their particular organizations. The most effective framing appeals to general moral principles of equity and fairness, thereby "socializing conflict" (Schattschneider 1960) by appealing to generally shared cultural norms and mobilizing third parties as well as direct beneficiaries. Despite the general public view that unions are privatistic, Ryan (1990) shows that a Boston hotel and restaurant workers union was able to gain favorable media coverage by appealing to general norms of justice and dignity. As the union president explained: "You can't organize people over money. You have to organize people over ideas. We talk about non-negotiable issues, like dignity, respect on the job, social justice" (Ryan 1990:56). This approach works for both direct beneficiaries as well as the general public. Leaders often use "condensing symbols" (Cobb and Elder 1972:96) that tell a complex story in an emotionally captivating, abbreviated form. In the conflict over the Equal Rights Amendment in the 1980s, opponents used the claim that the amendment would lead to unisex public bathrooms and the conscription of women as frontline military combatants, both of which were erroneous but served as captivating symbols that helped defeat the amendment (Boles 1979; Mansbridge 1986). It is also important to be aware of news routines. Reporters seek "good copy" that will capture viewer or reader interest, they have to meet filing deadlines, and they need to maintain continued access to reliable sources, especially government officials. Not all media are created equal. Large city newspapers and national television news organizations have more educated readers and viewers and are more likely to cover nonprofit advocacy claims (Goldenberg 1975).

A related question is the effectiveness of protest. Some contend that media coverage of protest creates negative images of disruptions, while others argue that it puts issues on the political agenda, increasing public awareness of issues, raising the salience of particular issues, and making elites aware of favorable public opinion. Media coverage is notoriously difficult to control, as Gitlin (1980) shows for the anti–Vietnam war movement in the 1960s. To maintain newsworthiness, movement leaders have to devise innovative, provocative tactics, which run the risk of losing the focus and escalating into violence or outlandish behavior, thereby creating a public opinion backlash. Media coverage tends to focus on the event itself rather than the problem behind the protest, and it can create media celebrities whose existence proves internally divisive and may divert attention from organizing. By maintaining a dignified and disciplined nonviolent stance, the civil rights protestors kept media attention on the justice of their cause and thus mobilized broad public support, eventually pressuring elites to respond. The protestors also benefited indirectly from police repression, which created a media image of disciplined dissent versus out-of-control authorities (Garrow 1978; Barkan 1984). During the protests against the Seabrook nuclear power plant in the late 1970s, media coverage was initially limited until the governor of New Hampshire ordered mass arrests that created daily coverage of the imprisoned protestors, giving the mainstream antinuclear groups, such as the Union of Concerned Scientists, the opportunity to air concerns about the safety of nuclear power (Barkan 1979; Gamson and Modigliani 1989). The impact of protest may in fact be limited to setting the agenda. In their study of anti–Vietnam war protests, Burstein and Freudenburg (1978) conclude that the protests initially heightened public awareness of the issue and congressional awareness of emerging negative public opinion, but that, once the issue was on the political agenda, other issues, such as the human and financial costs of the war, became central to actual policy decisions.

Another avenue for agenda access is to influence the stances of political parties. Parties are aggregative institutions, attempting to compromise the interests of diverse constituencies so as to maximize votes. Nonprofit advocacy organizations are, by contrast, issue maximizers generally committed to specific policies and moral visions. Compromise is often seen as reflecting a lack of principle, which sets up a potential struggle between citizens' groups and parties. Berry and Schildkraut (1998) show that, between 1948 and 1992, over two-thirds of all platform fights in the Democratic and Republican national conventions originated from citizens' groups. Reflecting the new constituencies involved, postmaterialist issues have become increasingly prominent and typically have involved contentious protest. Traditional business, labor, and agricultural groups have gradually lost significance. Reflecting their influence, these new advocacy organizations have forced the parties to adopt controversial stances on "wedge" issues, ranging from gay/lesbian rights to abortion and prayer in the schools, thereby keeping these issues on the national political agenda and undermining the ability of the parties to operate as aggregative institutions.

The second step is actual *policy enactment.* The literature on congressional decision making indicates a general shift away from tightly organized "subgovernments" and "iron triangles" dominated by industry, congressional, and administrative experts toward more fluid "issue networks" with a large number of actors, greater access, and fluid coalitions (Heclo 1978; Heinz et al. 1993). Congressional decentralization, the growth of the mass media, the increasing complexity of administrative regulation, and the advocacy explosion have created greater opportunities for nonprofit advocacy. The strongest support for this claim is Berry's (1999:chap. 4) analysis of congressional decision making. Comparing all congressional decisions on domestic social and economic legislation that received a hearing for the 1963, 1979, and 1991 sessions, liberal nonprofit citizens' groups increased their representation in congressional testimony from 23 to 32 percent of all appearances and their visibility in national press coverage from 28 to 40 percent. Although business was consistently the most frequent winner in terms of win/loss ratios on decisions (3.8, 1.9, and 1.8 for each congressional session), liberal citizens' groups improved their lobbying success (1.0, .9, and 1.4) over time. Despite raising considerable money, the conservative citizens' groups were not highly effective at lobbying but instead invested most of their resources in developing strong ties with the congressional Republican leadership.

Several objections can be made regarding this picture of declining business power and limited "new right" impact. First, many of the liberal victories were defensive measures, such as preventing rollbacks in the Clean Air Act and consumer legislation. It would be useful to distinguish new legislation versus protecting existing statutes and to weigh legislation by its substantive importance. Second, focusing on roll-call votes may underestimate the behind-the-scenes lobbying of business groups and "new right" public interest organizations, which may have influenced the formulation of basic legislation. Third, Berry's study does not cover the period since the 1994 Republican takeover of Congress, which may have altered the influence of different citizens' groups. In any case, this study provides a benchmark for further studies of the policymaking impact of citizens' nonprofit lobbies.

The literature on congressional lobbying argues that the most effective approach is informational lobbying that emphasizes research and insider information, avoids "burning bridges," and creates information dependency (Berry 1997:98–102; Heinz et al. 1993). But nonprofit advocates often single out members of Congress or regulatory bodies by identifying "dirty dozens," organizing media events, staging protests that castigate decision makers, and mounting high-profile lawsuits (Walker 1991). These tactics suggest that, at least for nonprofit advocacy, information lobbying, positive relations, and continued access are less critical than maintaining a clear moral stance, mobilizing constituents, and pressuring elites.

What is the effectiveness of outsider tactics? In Gamson's (1990) historical study of political challengers, unruliness contributed to tangible benefits as well as political acceptance, a conclusion which has been reinforced by several multivariate reanalyses of his data. Other studies argue that protest has little direct effect on policy but may contribute by changing public opinion and interacting with favorable political opportunities. In a study of congressional floor motions on equal employment legislation, Burstein (1985) found that civil rights protests had no direct impact, but they did heighten the salience of the issue among the general public, thereby indirectly contributing to policy adoption. A similar picture is provided by Costain's (1992:132–35, 150–55) structural equation analysis of congressional adoption of women's legislation, in which women's movement actions interactively combined with favorable public opinion toward voting for a female presidential candidate to produce policy adoption. In another study, Costain and Majstorovic (1994) show that this process was mediated by favorable media attention, which kept women's issues on the political agenda.

Combining protest with insider strategies may be the most effective strategy. In their study of the impact of African American and Hispanic political mobilization on city policies, Browning, Marshall, and Tabb (1984) show that protest alone had little effect on policy enactment, whereas combining protest with electoral strategies was effective. This observation can be extended to litigation. Silverstein (1996) shows that the animal rights movement has combined protest with high-profile litigation and media events, creating a double-barreled threat that mobilizes adverse public opinion against targets, as well as imposing costly litigation. McCann (1994) shows that private companies are often concerned about the effects of adverse publicity stemming from protracted lawsuits over gender pay equity, and thus they settle out of court independently of the legal merits of a case. Yet, as a tactic, litigation alone is often limited in that courts are better at blocking actions than at creating positive changes. The environmental movement has found that litigation can block construction projects and penalize polluters but is limited as a tool for bringing about positive compliance with environmental laws (R. Andrews 1976:7–19). Nonetheless, the law has a moral force that, when reinforced by other pressures, often brings about change.

The impact of protest may be mediated by the presence of political allies and other favorable opportunities. In a study of farm worker unionization, Jenkins and Perrow (1977) show that favorable governmental decisions combined with labor and liberal advocacy group support made the United Farm Workers boycotts effective, eventually forcing growers to accept unionization. Civil right victories likewise drew on partisan competition for the black vote and supportive white opinion, as well as the persistent patronage of liberal foundations and advocacy organizations (McAdam 1999). Costain (1992) traces much of the legislative success of the women's movement to the electoral rivalry between Republicans and Democrats, which was fed by the growing gender gap in voting, and the pressure of insider allies in Congress.

The receptiveness of governmental institutions also plays a role. Eisinger (1973) argues that mayor/ward–based city governments are more responsive to urban riots than reformed city governments with at-large councils and city managers. Button (1989) found a similar pattern in his study of the spending and employment policies of four city governments in Florida. Mayor/ward systems facilitate a favorable response to protest and electoral efforts by African Americans. Amenta, Carruthers, and Zylan (1992) coined the term "mediation model" to capture this intervening effect of political institutions on advocacy outcomes. The strength of Townsend clubs contributed to the payments associated with state old-age pensions in the 1940s, with the effects being partially mediated by the favorable opportunities created by reformed political parties, strong voting rights, elite allies, and strong state bureaucracies. Similarly, McCammon et al. (2001) found that the procedural ease of passing new legislation in state legislatures contributed to the state passage of the Nineteenth Amendment granting women suffrage rights.

Yet protest can also have a direct impact on policy. In 1963 the SCLC organized mass protests in Birmingham, Alabama, creating sufficient disruption that the downtown business community and city officials were forced to desegregate and extend voting rights (Morris 1993). Likewise, Santoro (2002) shows that the early civil rights protests operated as independent "dramatic events" that pressured favorable government policies; only later did protest impact depend on favorable public opinion. In a study of urban spending priorities, Jaynes (2002) found that civil rights protest increased the percentage of spending on social programs independent of the form of city government and that, except for boosting spending on police, the mayor versus council form of government was not important. Policy impacts may also vary by the form of protest. McAdam and Su (2002) found that persuasive forms of anti–Vietnam war protest put the issue on the political agenda in terms of the number of congressional roll-call votes but did not affect the outcome of these votes; conversely, disruptive protest contributed to favorable vote outcomes but reduced the number of roll calls. Thus, as in Burstein and Freudenburg (1978), persuasive protests helped set the congressional agenda; but, contrary to the earlier study's findings, McAdam and Su (2002) conclude that disruptive protest was more effective in securing favorable decisions.

A related question is the impact of organization. Here the literature points to the benefits of an interorganizational division of labor between centralized and decentralized organizations, allowing an oscillating mix of both routine and protest tactics. At the peak of the civil rights struggle, the white supremacist attacks on the NAACP created a split between local church groups urging more protest and the legally oriented national organization. "The two approaches—legal action and mass protest—entered into a turbulent but workable marriage" (Morris 1984:39). The abortion conflict has created a similar clash between a decentralized pro-life movement centered in church groups and the decentralized action cells of Operation Rescue versus the more centralized pro-choice advocates (Staggenborg 1991), allowing the pro-life movement to gain restrictions on specific abortion procedures. At the same time, the centralized pro-choice strategy has thus far prevented an overturning of the legality of abortion.

The third policy step is *implementation.* Implementation constitutes a major focus of nonprofit advocacy, monitoring government programs, participating in administrative rule setting, and applying pressure to ensure that statutes are actually enforced. Following the maxim that "the truth lies in the details," environmental advocacy organizations invest well over half of their efforts on monitoring the Environmental Protection Agency and its state surrogates, attending administrative hearings, and responding to technical issues, attempting to strengthen congressional oversight of administrative bodies (Peterson and Walker 1986). Without this monitoring, statutes would go unenforced or be controlled by industries that are supposed to be regulated. Social service nonprofits often become partners of local government, becoming involved in the definition of client problems as well as in devising possible strategies (Berry and Arons 2003:chap. 5). Others claim, in contrast, that public advisory bodies and other participatory mechanisms linked to implementation have minimal impact. Alford and Friedland (1975:455–64) critiqued the citizens' advisory committees associated with the Community Action Program (CAP) in the 1960s as "participation without power": representatives of the poor were selected by city political leaders, and if the representatives displayed independence, they were removed. Rothman (1974) contends that public advisory committees for the Environmental Protection Agency have not affected administrative rulings; administrators select the representatives to be appointed, bringing in those already known to be supportive of prevailing policies. Alexander, Nank, and Strivers (2001:279) argue that local government funding of social service nonprofits has "substantially diminished their capacity to be political" and to advocate on behalf of their clients.

The policy implementation impact of nonprofits probably depends on their organization and advocacy tactics. In a study of the funding for the CAPs in Mississippi during the middle and late 1960s, K. Andrews (2001) shows that strong NAACP chapters and electoral support for the Mississippi Freedom Democratic Party (MFDP) boosted CAP funding at the county level. Although Office of Economic Opportunity (OEO) officials attempted to preempt the local movement groups and to play divide and conquer by favoring the NAACP moderates over the more militant MFDP activists, local groups countered by using a combination of testimony at public hearings, administrative lobbying, and protest to gain control of the local CAP projects. Paralleling the earlier argument about policy enactment, a "double-barreled" approach is thus considered critical to influencing policy implementation. Others have argued that social service nonprofits' most potent weapon is their expertise and sharing of information, making them partners in developing policy (Berry and Arons 2003:chaps. 5 and 6).

Can nonprofit advocates effectively use the courts to influence implementation? As noted earlier, the courts are limited in their resources and willingness to get involved in administrative regulation. Handler (1978) argues that effective litigation depends on the ability to ensure implementation. Only where there is a technically simple solution or where administrative discretion is minimal will litigation work. This argument underscores the importance of clear statutes and the public accessibility of administrative bodies charged with implementing policy (Lowi 1979). Nonetheless, there is considerable evidence that actual and threatened litigation has secured the favorable implementation of policies regarding the environment (McCann 1986), racial discrimination (Burstein and Monaghan 1986; Burstein 2000), gender pay equity (Gelb and Palley 1996; Dobbin et al. 1993), and the rights of the disabled (S. Olson 1984). Take, for example, the Title VII provisions of the Equal Employment Act, which prohibited employment discrimination on the bases of race, sex, national origin, and religion. Statutory definitions of discrimination and affirmative action were initially ambiguous and eventually clarified by the courts in litigation initiated by nonprofit law firms and the Equal Employment Opportunity Commission staff. Court rulings created precedents, which combined with persistent litigation, administrative and conventional lobbying, and protests, have created strong legal tools for reducing employment discrimination (Burstein 1991, 2000). The key questions are the organizational strength of the nonprofit advocates and their use of multiple strategies against relevant targets.

Overall, the literature on nonprofit advocacy policy impacts has been limited in its coverage of multiple types of impact, time sequences, and the range of relevant factors that might condition the effectiveness of nonprofit advocacy. Few studies are multivariate, and few capture the political context that may influence the effectiveness of different types of advocacy work. Most research has focused on legislative lobbying and protest directed at policymakers, ignoring grassroots lobbying and educational work. There has been even less attention to institutional and cultural change, both of which are important targets of nonprofit advocacy. The field clearly would benefit by more comparable multivariate studies that took into account multiple types of advocacy outcomes as well as multiple factors that may contribute to political and social change.

NONPROFIT ADVOCACY AND THE HEALTH OF THE AMERICAN POLITICAL SYSTEM

Nonprofit political advocacy is often presented as a major force for the renewal of American democracy. By creating greater inclusiveness and balance in political representation, nonprofit advocacy is believed to counteract long-standing business dominance. By organizing the unorganized and promoting citizen involvement, nonprofit advocacy is said to create a "stronger democracy" (Barber 1984), in which a broader array of citizens have direct input into major decisions. In contrast, critics contend that nonprofit advocacy has created divisive conflicts that have weakened public authority and majority rule, promoted unnecessary governmental growth, and, by creating "professional social movements" (Zald and McCarthy 1987) and "protest businesses" (Jordan and Maloney 1997), done little to counteract civic disengagement; they may even have contributed to the decline in mass participation (Skocpol 1999, 2003).

The majority of nonprofit advocacy organizations are "neoliberal" in the sense that, while endorsing modern liberal ideas about the benefits of scientific and rational approaches to public policy, they are skeptical of centralized government authority and favor direct citizen access and decentralized authority (McCann 1986). In general, they have accepted Lowi's (1979) critique of interest group liberalism as allowing "big government" to be captured by the "special interests," and have sought statutory and political methods to ensure governmental accountability through direct citizen participation, open access rules, freedom of information, clarity of legal standards, and strong judicial review. These procedures are seen as important for countering the "iron law of decadence" (Lowi 1971), in which narrow organized groups gain effective control over governmental institutions claiming to serve the public interest.

There has also been a significant growth of new conservative nonprofit advocates promoting smaller government, stricter morality, and greater reliance on self-help and market solutions. In large part, this "new right" has modeled its tactics on the neoliberals, using research, litigation, and public education to promote their agenda. If Berry's (1999) evidence is correct, their actual policy influence has been quite limited and their impact restricted to influencing the leadership of the Republican party. Nonetheless, their effect may be quite substantial during periods of Republican control over Congress and the White House, which have increased since the 1970s and 1980s.

A key debate about nonprofit advocacy is the legitimacy of granting tax privileges to organizations that are obviously political. Is the tax exemption for 501(c)(3) organizations a subsidy for the advocacy of particular sectional interests? Several critics have charged that liberal nonprofit advocates are biased toward the interests of the affluent educated middle class and against the general populace and the business community (Lichter and Rothman 1983; Tucker 1982). Public interest advocacy is seen by these critics as advancing the careers of public sector professionals by promoting governmental growth, pressing for aesthetic goals like preserving wilderness areas for affluent backpackers at the expense of jobs for the less affluent, and instituting consumer and environmental protections at the expense of economic well-being.

Although the financial support and membership of many of the liberal nonprofit advocacy organizations are biased toward the educated middle and upper classes, a stronger case can be made that their programmatic bias is toward the interests of the disadvantaged and the general public. Why is the financial and volunteer base skewed toward the middle and upper classes? A first step is to recognize the free-rider problem and the difficulty of mobilizing large dispersed groups that lack cohesive networks and cultural supports for collective action. Insofar as the educated middle and upper classes have discretionary time and income as well as a strong participation ethic, they are more willing to pay the costs. They are also more responsive to moral appeals framed in terms of the public interest and more likely to be contacted by liberal public interest organizations. It is also important to emphasize the indigenous bases of other groups like the NAACP, the Association of Community Organizations for Reform Now (ACORN), and community organizations that mobilize low-income populations and minorities as well as the church bases for the Christian "new right" and pro-life movements. Both left and right organizations derive benefits from the tax subsidy. Overall, the tax exemption ensures the representation of groups and interests that would otherwise go unrepresented. Although there is some disagreement about the degree of business dominance (e.g., Schlozman and Tierney 1986 versus Walker 1991 versus Baumgartner and Leech 1998, summarized in table 13.1), all agree that the for-profit sector is better represented. At the same time, it is also clear that nonprofit advocacy is growing in resources and influence and provides some significant corrective balance. It is also important to recognize the recent growth of conservative nonprofit advocacy, which in some policy arenas has become more influential than the advocacy of older liberal and progressive groups.

A second line of criticism focuses on the uncompromising moralism of nonprofit advocates. While it is clear that nonprofit advocacy organizations mobilize around moral principles and that moralists often find it difficult to strike compromises, it is not clear that the major problems identified by these critics stem from nonprofit advocacy per se. The use and abuse of open records laws, citizen participation requirements, and the like are not primarily due to nonprofit advocacy. These tools are used by conventional political operatives as well as the media to create a politics of scandal. While nonprofit advocacy may contribute to the persistence of weak public confidence in institutions, the primary origins of the "confidence gap" were political disasters and policy mistakes such as the Kennedy assassination, the Vietnam war, and the 1970s oil embargos and subsequent stagflation (Lipset and Schneider 1983). More recent scandals, such as the Iran-contra affair during the Reagan years, the Clinton administration's Monica Lewinsky scandal, and the George W. Bush administration's problematic justification for invading Iraq, are similarly more critical than the nonprofit advocacy around these issues. At most, nonprofit citizens' groups have fed off citizen disillusionment and frustration with political leaders, magnifying the visibility of mistakes, corruption, and problems.

A more telling criticism is that nonprofit advocacy has weakened the political parties, interjecting emotionally charged symbolic issues that make it more difficult for the parties to aggregate interests. Berry and Schildkraut's (1998) evidence on party platform fights points to this interpretation. Yet it is also important to keep in mind that American political parties have traditionally been weak at aggregating interests, focusing on sectional economic interests and achieving only modestly effective results in aggregating broader horizontal conflicts. These nonprofit groups, along with the broader movements that they represent, have promoted new issues that the parties have only partially assimilated.

There is also some truth to the claim that the advocacy explosion has contributed to a general sense of political stalemate. As policy has shifted from "subgovernments" and "iron triangles" to "issue networks" and "hollow cores," organized groups have confronted increased competition and the need to compromise. Yet compromise does not necessarily contribute to the resources of the advocacy group, especially if strident, moralistic images are critical to mobilizing support. The growth of nonprofit advocacy has reinforced this trend, adding new voices to the political process. This has encouraged many observers to conclude that the system is overloaded with interest groups (Huntington 1982; Salisbury 1990). But given the political system's overall bias toward business and existing institutions, the stalemate would seem to be largely due to excessive representation for the better-organized sectors rather than to nonprofit advocacy.

Perhaps the most potent criticism is that, by building "professional social movements" and "protest businesses," nonprofit advocacy has done little to boost civic involvement and may even be counterproductive. While there are no systematic data on the prevalence of these "movements without members," it is clear that they are growing more numerous and that this trend coincides with a decline in national civic organizations and electoral participation (Putnam 2000; Skocpol 1999, 2003). Some have argued that professional movement organizations represent a new type of "corporatism" in which institutional patrons control the representation of interests (Handler 1978; John Wilson 1983). Given their hierarchical structure, these organizations are often criticized for their oligarchic practices and for blunting the edge on conflicting positions (Dowie 1995; Brulle 2000). It is also important to keep in mind that most professional advocacy organizations are focused on broad public interests that confront major free-rider problems. In this setting, professional advocacy may be the most viable option. There is also evidence of market saturation and increased competition among nonprofit advocacy organizations, as well as efforts to reduce their financial dependence on traditional foundation donors. The bottom line, however, is that professional advocacy organizations probably do little to boost civic involvement and, insofar as they satisfy a need for political involvement without imposing significant personal costs, they may actually discourage direct participation. Nonetheless, there is also evidence that, where they are part of a broader coalition that includes membership organizations, they contribute to more effective political advocacy.

The broad picture that emerges from this discussion is of an "imperfect pluralism" in which the growth of nonprofit political advocacy has partially counterbalanced business dominance and provided political voice for a broader set of disadvantaged interests. Pluralist theory erroneously claims that institutional tactics are sufficient for gaining political voice and that the political system is equally permeable to all significant social interests (McFarland 1998; Gamson 1990). Many social interests are organized out of the system due to lack of cohesion, co-optable networks, and proactive cultures and leadership. Business and existing institutions are overrepresented. For underrepresented groups, a scrappy challenge is often the most effective strategy. Nonprofit advocacy provides such groups with greater political voice and a vehicle for creating greater balance in the political system.

ACKNOWLEDGMENTS

This essay benefited from the comments of Mayer Zald, Bob Brulle, Nella van Dyke, Dick Scott, Bob Bothwell, Jeffrey Berry, David Suarez, and Linda Nations and from the research assistance of Steve Boutcher.

REFERENCES

Adams, John H. 1974. "Responsible Militancy: The Anatomy of a Public Interest Law Firm." *Record of the Association of the City of New York* 29:631–45.

Alexander, Jennifer, Renee Nank, and Camille Strivers. 2001. "Implications of Welfare Reform." Pp. 263–89 in *Understanding Nonprofit Organizations,* edited by J. Steven Ott. Boulder, Colo.: Westview Press.

Alford, Robert, and Roger Friedland. 1975. "Political Participation and Public Policy." *Annual Review of Sociology* 1:429–79.

Alinsky, Saul. 1969. *Reveille for Radicals.* New York: Random House.

———. 1972. *Rules for Radicals.* New York: Random House.

Amenta, Edwin, Bruce Carruthers, and Yvonne Zylan. 1992.

"A Hero for the Aged? The Townsend Movement, the Political Mediation Model and U.S. Old Age Policy, 1934–1950." *American Sociological Review* 49:678–702.

Andrews, Kenneth. 2001. "Social Movements and Policy Implementation." *American Sociological Review* 66:71–95.

Andrews, Richard. 1976. *Environmental Policy and Administrative Change.* Lexington, Mass.: Lexington Books.

Aron, Nan. 1988. *Liberty and Justice for All.* Boulder, Colo.: Westview Press.

Bachrach, Peter, and Morton Baratz. 1962. "The Two Faces of Power." *American Political Science Review* 56:947–52.

Bailis, Lawrence. 1974. *Bread or Justice.* Lexington, Mass.: Lexington Books.

Barber, Benjamin. 1984. *Strong Democracy.* Berkeley: University of California Press.

Barkan, Steven E. 1979. "Strategic, Tactical and Organizational Dilemmas of the Protest Movement against Nuclear Power." *Social Problems* 27:19–37.

———. 1984. "Legal Control of the Southern Civil Rights Movement." *American Sociological Review* 49:552–65.

Baum, Joel, and Walter W. Powell. 1995. "Cultivating an Institutional Ecology of Organizations." *American Sociological Review* 60:529–38.

Baumgartner, Frank, and Beth L. Leech. 1998. *Basic Interests.* Princeton, N.J.: Princeton University Press.

Bennett, James T., and Thomas DiLorenzo. 1985. *Destroying Democracy.* Washington, D.C.: Cato Institute.

Berry, Jeffrey M. 1977. *Lobbying for the People.* Princeton, N.J.: Princeton University Press.

———. 1997. *The Interest Group Society.* 3rd ed. New York: Longman.

———. 1999. *The New Liberalism.* Washington, D.C.: Brookings Institution Press.

Berry, Jeffrey M., and David F. Arons. 2003. *A Voice for Nonprofits.* Washington, D.C.: Brookings Institution Press.

Berry, Jeffrey M., and Deborah Schildkraut. 1998. "Citizens Groups, Political Parties and Electoral Coalitions." Pp. 136–56 in *Social Movements and American Political Institutions,* edited by Anne N. Costain and Andrew McFarland. Lanham, Md.: Rowman and Littlefield.

Boles, Janet. 1979. *The Politics of the Equal Rights Amendment.* New York: Longman.

Bordt, Rebecca L. 1997. *The Structure of Women's Nonprofit Organizations.* Bloomington: Indiana University Press.

Boris, Elizabeth. 1999. "Nonprofit Organizations in a Democracy." Pp. 3–29 in *Nonprofits and Government,* edited by Elizabeth Boris and C. Eugene Steuerle. Washington, D.C.: Urban Institute Press.

Boris, Elizabeth, and Jeff Krehely. 2002. "Civic Participation and Advocacy." In *The State of Nonprofit America,* edited by Lester M. Salamon. Washington, D.C.: Brookings Institution Press.

Boris, Elizabeth, and Rachel Mosher-Williams. 1998. "Nonprofit Advocacy Organizations." *Nonprofit and Voluntary Sector Quarterly* 27:488–506.

Bosso, Christopher. 1995. "The Color of Money: Environmental Groups and the Pathologies of Fund Raising." Pp. 101–30 in *Interest Group Politics,* 4th ed., edited by Allan J. Cigler and Burdett M. Loomis. Washington, D.C.: Congressional Quarterly Press.

———. 1999. "Facing the Future: Environmentalists and the New Political Landscape." In *Interest Group Politics,* 5th ed., edited by Allan J. Cigler and Burdett M. Loomis. Washington, D.C.: Congressional Quarterly Press.

Boyte, Harry C. 1980. *The Backyard Revolution.* Philadelphia: Temple University Press.

Boyte, Harry C., Heather Booth, and Steve Max. 1986. *Citizen Action and the New American Populism.* Philadelphia: Temple University Press.

Breines, Wini. 1982. *Community and Organization.* New York: Praeger.

Brill, Harry. 1971. *Why Organizers Fail.* Berkeley: University of California Press.

Brint, Steven. 1985. "The Political Attitudes of Professionals." *Annual Review of Sociology* 11:389–414.

Browning, Rufus, Dale Marshall, and David Tabb. 1984. *Protest Is Not Enough: The Struggle of Blacks and Hispanics for Equality in Urban Politics.* Berkeley: University of California Press.

Brulle, Robert. 2000. *Agency, Democracy and Nature.* Cambridge, Mass.: MIT Press.

Burstein, Paul. 1985. *Discrimination, Jobs and Politics.* Chicago: University of Chicago Press.

———. 1991. "Legal Mobilization as a Social Movement Tactic." *American Journal of Sociology* 96:1201–25.

———. 2000. "The Impact of EEO Law." Pp. 129–59 in *Legacies of the 1964 Civil Rights Act,* edited by Bernard Grofman. Charlottesville: University Press of Virginia.

Burstein, Paul, and William Freudenburg. 1978. "Changing Public Policy: The Impact of Public Opinion, Anti-War Demonstrations and War Costs on Senate Voting on Vietnam War Motions." *American Journal of Sociology* 84:99–122.

Burstein, Paul, and Kathleen Monaghan. 1986. "Equal Opportunity and the Mobilization of the Law." *Law and Society Review* 20:355–88.

Burt, Dan. 1982. *Abuse of Trust.* Chicago: Gateway.

Button, James W. 1989. *Blacks and Social Change.* Princeton, N.J.: Princeton University Press.

Carson, Claybourne. 1982. *In Struggle.* Berkeley: University of California Press.

Carson, Emmett D. 1999. "The Roles of Indigenous and Institutional Philanthropy in Advancing Social Justice." Pp. 248–74 in *Philanthropy and the Nonprofit Sector in a Changing America,* edited by Charles Clotfelter and Thomas Ehrlich. Bloomington: Indiana University Press.

Clark, Peter B., and James Q. Wilson. 1961. "Incentive Systems: A Theory of Organizations." *Administrative Science Quarterly* 6:129–66.

Clemens, Elizabeth. 1997. *The People's Lobby.* Chicago: University of Chicago Press.

Cobb, Roger, and Charles Elder. 1972. *Participation in America.* Boston: Allyn and Bacon.

Cobb, Roger, Jennie Keith Ross, and Marc Howard Ross. 1977. "Agenda Building as a Comparative Political Process." *American Political Science Review* 70:126–38.

Costain, Anne N. 1992. *Inviting Women's Rebellion.* Baltimore: Johns Hopkins University Press.

Costain, Anne N., and Steven Majstorovic. 1994. "Congress, Social Movements and Public Opinion." *Political Research Quarterly* 47:111–35.

Council for Public Interest Law. 1976. *Balancing the Scales of Justice.* Washington, D.C.: Council for Public Interest Law.

Creighton, Lucy Black. 1976. *Pretenders to the Throne.* Lexington, Mass.: Lexington Books.

Cress, Daniel M. 1997. "Nonprofit Incorporation among Movements of the Poor." *Social Problems* 38:343–60.

Cress, Daniel M., and David A. Snow. 1996. "Mobilization at the Margins: Resources, Benefactors, and the Viability of Homeless Social Movement Organizations." *American Sociological Review* 61:1089–1109.

Curtis, James E., Douglas E. Baer, and Edward G. Grabb. 2001. "Nations of Joiners: Explaining Voluntary Association Membership in Democratic Societies." *American Sociological Review* 66:783–850.

Curtis, Russell, and Louis A. Zurcher. 1973. "Stable Resources of Protest Movements: The Multi-Organizational Field." *Social Forces* 52:53–61.

———. 1974. "Social Movements: An Analytical Exploration of Organizational Forms." *Social Problems* 11:356–70.

Dahl, Robert. 1994. *The New American Political (Dis)Order.* Berkeley: Institute of Governmental Studies Press.

Delgado, Gary. 1986. *Organizing the Movement.* Philadelphia: Temple University Press.

Diani, Mario. 1995. *Green Networks.* Edinburgh: Edinburgh University Press.

Diaz, William A. 1999. "Philanthropy and the Case of the Latino Communities in America." Pp. 279–92 in *Philanthropy and the Nonprofit Sector in a Changing America,* edited by Charles Clotfelter and Thomas Ehrlich. Bloomington: Indiana University Press.

Dobbin, Frank, John Sutton, John Meyer, and William R. Scott. 1993. "Equal Opportunity Law and the Construction of Internal Labor Markets." *American Journal of Sociology* 99:396–427.

Dowie, Mark. 1995. *Losing Ground.* Cambridge, Mass.: MIT Press.

Dunlap, Riley, and Angela Mertig. 1992. "The Evolution of the U.S. Environmental Movement from 1970–1990." Pp. 1–10 in *American Environmentalism,* edited by R. E. Dunlap and A. G. Mertig. Philadelphia: Taylor and Francis.

Edelstein, J. David, and Malcolm Warner. 1979. *Comparative Union Democracy.* New Brunswick, N.J.: Transaction.

Edwards, Bob. 1994. "Semiformal Organizational Structure among Social Movement Organizations." *Nonprofit and Voluntary Sector Quarterly* 23:309–33.

Edwards, Bob, and Sam Marullo. 1995. "Organizational Mortality in a Declining Social Movement." *American Sociological Review* 60:908–27.

Eisinger, Peter. 1973. "The Conditions of Protest Behavior in American Cities." *American Political Science Review* 67:11–28.

Fantasia, Rick. 1988. *Cultures of Solidarity.* Berkeley: University of California Press.

Fendrich, James M. 1991. *Ideal Citizens.* Albany: State University of New York Press.

Ferree, Myra. 1992. "The Political Context of Rationality." Pp. 29–52 in *Frontiers in Social Movement Theory,* edited by Aldon Morris and Carol Mueller. New Haven, Conn.: Yale University Press.

Ferree, Myra, and Beth H. Hess. 1994. *Controversy and Coalition.* 2nd ed. New York: Twayne.

Ferree, Myra, and Patricia Yancey Martin. 1997. *Feminist Organizations.* Philadelphia: Temple University Press.

Fiorina, Morris. 1999. "Extreme Voices: The Extreme Side of Civic Engagement." Pp. 395–426 in *Civic Engagement in American Democracy,* edited by Theda Skocpol and Morris Fiorina. Washington, D.C.: Brookings Institution Press.

Fireman, Bruce, and William Gamson. 1979. "Utilitarian Logic in the Resource Mobilization Perspective." Pp. 8–44 in *The Dynamics of Social Movements,* edited by Mayer N. Zald and John D. McCarthy. Cambridge, Mass.: Winthrop.

Fish, F. Hamilton. 1973. *Black Power/White Control.* Princeton, N.J.: Princeton University Press.

Foley, Michael, and Bob Edwards. 2002. "How Do Members Count? Membership Governance and Advocacy in the Nonprofit World." Unpublished paper, Departments of Sociology, Catholic University, Washington, D.C., and East Carolina University, Greenville.

Fox, Stephen. 1981. *John Muir and His Legacy.* Boston: Little, Brown.

Freeman, Jo. 1973. "The Tyranny of Structurelessness." *Ms.* 3:20–25.

———. 1975. *The Politics of Women's Liberation.* New York: David McKay.

———. 1979. "Resource Mobilization and Strategy." Pp. 167–89 in *The Dynamics of Social Movements,* edited by Mayer Zald and John D. McCarthy. Cambridge, Mass.: Winthrop.

Gamson, William. 1990. *The Strategy of Social Protest.* 2nd ed. Homewood, Ill.: Dorsey Press.

———. 1992. "The Social Psychology of Collective Action." Pp. 53–76 in *Frontiers in Social Movement Theory,* edited by Aldon Morris and Carol Mueller. New Haven, Conn.: Yale University Press.

Gamson, William, Bruce Fireman, and Stephen Rytina. 1982. *Encounters with Unjust Authority.* Homewood, Ill.: Dorsey Press.

Gamson, William, and David S. Meyer. 1996. "Framing Political Opportunity." Pp. 275–90 in *Comparative Perspectives on Social Movements,* edited by Doug McAdam, John D. McCarthy, and Mayer N. Zald. New York: Cambridge University Press.

Gamson, William, and Andre Modigliani. 1989. "Media Discourse and Public Opinion on Nuclear Power." *American Journal of Sociology* 95:1–37.

Ganz, Marshall. 2000. "The Paradox of Powerlessness: Leadership, Organization and Strategy in the Unionization of California Agriculture, 1959–1977." *American Journal of Sociology* 105:1003–62.

Garrow, David. 1978. *Protest at Selma.* New Haven, Conn.: Yale University Press.

Gelb, Joyce, and Marian Lief Palley. 1996. *Women and Public Policy.* 2nd ed. Charlottesville: University Press of Virginia.

Gerlach, Luther, and Virginia Hine. 1970. *People, Power and Change.* Indianapolis: Bobbs-Merrill.

Gitlin, Todd. 1980. *The Whole World Is Watching.* Berkeley: University of California Press.

Giugni, Marco. 1998. "How Social Movements Matter." Pp. xii–xxxiii in *How Social Movements Matter,* edited by

Marco Giugni, Doug McAdam, and Charles Tilly. Minneapolis: University of Minnesota Press.

Goldenberg, Edie. 1975. *Making the News.* Lexington, Mass.: Lexington Books.

Gorey, Hays. 1975. *Nader and the Power of Everyman.* New York: Grosset and Dunlap.

Gould, Roger V. 1995. *Insurgent Identities: Class, Community and Protest in Paris from 1848 to the Commune.* Chicago: University of Chicago Press.

Gray, Virginia, and David Lowery. 1996. *The Population Ecology of Interest Representation.* Ann Arbor: University of Michigan Press.

Greve, Michael S. 1987. "Why Defunding the Left Failed." *Public Interest* 89:91–106.

Grønberg, Kirsten. 1994. "Using NTEE to Classify Non-Profit Organizations." *Voluntas* 5:301–28.

Guth, James L., Lyman A. Kellstedt, Corwin E. Smidt, and John C. Green. 1998. "Thunder on the Right? Religious Interest Group Mobilization in the 1996 Election." Pp. 169–92 in *Interest Group Politics,* 4th ed., edited by Allan Cigler and Burdett Loomis. Washington, D.C.: Congressional Quarterly Press.

Habermas, Jürgen. 1998. *On the Pragmatics of Communication.* Cambridge, Mass.: MIT Press.

Haines, Herbert. 1988. *Black Radicals and the Civil Rights Mainstream, 1954–1970.* Knoxville: University of Tennessee Press.

Halperin, Charles, and John Cunningham. 1971. "Reflections on the New Public Interest Law." *Georgetown Law Journal* 59:1095–1126.

Handler, Jack F. 1978. *Social Movements and the Legal System.* New York: Academic Press.

Hannan, Michael, and John Freeman. 1989. *Organizational Ecology.* Cambridge, Mass.: Harvard University Press.

Heclo, Hugh. 1978. "Issue Networks and the Executive Establishment." In *The New American Establishment,* edited by Anthony King. Washington, D.C.: American Enterprise Institute.

Heinz, John P., Edward O. Laumann, Robert L. Nelson, and Robert H. Salisbury. 1993. *The Hollow Core.* Cambridge, Mass.: Harvard University Press.

Helfgot, Joe. 1981. *Professional Reforming.* Lexington, Mass: Lexington Books.

Himmelstein, Jerome. 1990. *To the Right.* Berkeley: University of California Press.

Hopkins, Bruce. 1992. *Charity, Advocacy and the Law.* New York: Wiley.

Horwitt, Sanford D. 1989. *Let Them Call Me Rebel.* New York: Knopf.

Huntington, Samuel P. 1982. *American Politics.* Cambridge, Mass.: Harvard University Press.

Jaffe, Sanford. 1976. *Public Interest Law.* New York: Ford Foundation.

Janoski, Thomas. 1998. *Citizenship and Civil Society.* New York: Cambridge University Press.

Jasper, James M., and Dorothy Nelkin. 1992. *The Animal Rights Crusade.* New York: Free Press.

Jaynes, Arthur. 2002. "Insurgency and Policy Outcomes." *Journal of Political and Military Sociology* 30:90–112.

Jenkins, J. Craig. 1977. "The Radical Transformation of Organizational Goals." *Administrative Science Quarterly* 22:248–67.

———. 1985. *The Politics of Insurgency.* New York: Columbia University Press.

———. 1989. "Social Movement Philanthropy and American Democracy." Pp. 292–314 in *Philanthropic Giving,* edited by Richard Magat. New York: Oxford University Press.

———. 1998. "Channeling Social Protest: Foundation Patronage of Contemporary Social Movements." Pp. 206–16 in *Private Action and the Public Good,* edited by Walter W. Powell and Elizabeth Clemens. New Haven, Conn.: Yale University Press.

———. 1999. "The Transformation of a Constituency into a Movement Revisited: Farm Worker Organizing in California." Pp. 277–302 in *Waves of Protest,* edited by Jo Freeman and Victoria Johnson. Lanham, Md.: Rowman and Littlefield.

———. 2001. "Social Movement Philanthropy and the Growth of Nonprofit Advocacy." Pp. 51–66 in *Exploring Organizations and Advocacy,* edited by Elizabeth J. Reid and Maria D. Montilla. Washington, D.C.: Urban Institute Press.

Jenkins, J. Craig, Robert Brulle, Jason Carmichael, and Liesel Turner. 2005. "The Organizational Development of the U.S. Environment Movement." Paper presented at the annual meeting of the American Sociological Association, Philadelphia. http://www.pages.drexel.edu/~brullerj/Envorgdata.htm.

Jenkins, J. Craig, and Craig M. Eckert. 1986. "Channeling Black Insurgency." *American Sociological Review* 51:812–29.

Jenkins, J. Craig, and Abigail Halcli. 1999. "Grassrooting the System? The Development of Social Movement Philanthropy, 1953–1990." Pp. 227–56 in *Philanthropic Foundations,* edited by Ellen Condliffe Lagemann. Bloomington: Indiana University Press.

Jenkins, J. Craig, David Jacobs, and Jon Agnone. 2003. "Political Opportunities and African-American Protest, 1948–1997." *American Journal of Sociology* 109:277–303.

Jenkins, J. Craig, and Charles Perrow. 1977. "Insurgency of the Powerless: Farm Workers Insurgency, 1946–1972." *American Sociological Review* 42: 249–68.

Jenkins, J. Craig, and Michael Wallace. 1996. "The Generalized Action Potential of Social Movements." *Sociological Forum* 11:183–207.

Johnson, Paul E. 1999. "Interest Group Recruiting: Finding Members and Keeping Them." Pp. 35–62 in *Interest Group Politics,* 5th ed., edited by Allan Cigler and Charles M. Loomis. Washington, D.C.: Congressional Quarterly Press.

Jordan, Grant, and William Maloney. 1997. *The Protest Business? Mobilizing Campaign Groups.* Manchester, U.K.: Manchester University Press.

Kayal, Philip M. 1993. *Bearing Witness: Gay Men's Health Crisis and the Politics of AIDS.* San Francisco: Westview Press.

Klandermans, Bert. 1997. *The Social Psychology of Protest.* Oxford: Blackwell.

Klandermans, Bert, and Dirk Oegema. 1987. "Potentials, Networks, Motivations and Barriers." *American Sociological Review* 52:519–31.

Kluger, Richard. 1976. *Simple Justice.* New York: Random House.

Kornhauser, William. 1959. *The Politics of Mass Society.* Glencoe, Ill.: Free Press.

Kotz, Nick, and Mary Lynn Kotz. 1977. *A Passion for Equality.* New York: Norton.

Krehely, Jeff. 2001. "Assessing the Current Data on 501(c)(3) Advocacy: What IRS Form 990 Can Tell Us." Pp. 37–50 in *Exploring Organizations and Advocacy,* edited by Elizabeth J. Reid and Maria D. Montilla. Washington, D.C.: Urban Institute Press.

Kriesi, Hans Peter, Ruud Koopmans, Jan Willem Duyvendak, and Marco Giugni. 1995. *The New Social Movements of Western Europe.* Minneapolis: University of Minnesota Press.

Krueger, Richard. 1972. *The Trumpet Shall Sound.* Cambridge, Mass.: Harvard University Press.

Lawson, Ron. 1986. *The Tenant Movement in New York City, 1904–1984.* New Brunswick, N.J.: Rutgers University Press.

Lichter Robert, and Stanley Rothman. 1983. "What Interests the Public and What Interests the Public Interests?" *Public Opinion* 14:44–48.

Lippmann, Walter. 1955. *Essays in the Public Philosophy.* Boston: Little, Brown.

Lipset, Seymour Martin, and William Schneider. 1983. *The Confidence Gap.* New York: Free Press.

Lipset, Seymour Martin, Martin Trow, and James Coleman. 1956. *Union Democracy.* Garden City, N.Y.: Doubleday Anchor.

Lofland, John. 1993. *Polite Protestors.* Syracuse, N.Y.: Syracuse University Press.

Lowi, Theodore. 1971. *The Politics of Disorder.* New York: Norton.

———. 1979. *The End of Liberalism.* 2nd ed. New York: Norton.

Lune, Howard, and Hillary Oberstein. 1999. "Embedded Systems: How Location Guides Form in State-Nonprofit Relations." Unpublished paper, National Development and Research Institutes, New York.

MacKenzie, Angus. 1981. "When Auditors Turn Editors." *Columbia Journalism Review* 9:29–34.

Mansbridge, Jane. 1982. *Beyond Adversary Democracy.* New York: Basic Books.

———. 1986. *Why We Lost the ERA.* Chicago: University of Chicago Press.

———. 1997. "On the Contested Nature of the Public Good." Pp. 3–19 in *Private Action and the Public Good,* edited by Walter W. Powell and Elisabeth S. Clemens. New Haven, Conn.: Yale University Press.

Marullo, Sam, and John Lofland. 1990. *Peace Action in the 1980s.* New Brunswick, N.J.: Rutgers University Press.

Marwell, Gerry, and Pam Oliver. 1993. *The Critical Mass.* New York: Cambridge University Press.

McAdam, Doug. 1988. *Freedom Summer.* New York: Oxford University Press.

———. 1999. *Political Process and the Development of Black Insurgency.* 2nd ed. Chicago: University of Chicago Press.

McAdam, Doug, and Yang Su. 2002. "The War at Home: Antiwar Protests and Congressional Voting, 1965 to 1973." *American Sociological Review* 67:696–721.

McCammon, Holly, Ellen M. Granberg, Karen E. Campbell, and Christine Mowery. 2001. "How Movements Win: Gendered Opportunity Structures and U.S. Women's Suffrage Movements, 1866 to 1919." *American Sociological Review* 66:49–70.

McCann, Michael. 1986. *Taking Rights Seriously.* Ithaca, N.Y.: Cornell University Press.

———. 1994. *Rights at Work: Pay Equity Reform and the Politics of Legal Mobilization.* Chicago: University of Chicago Press.

McCarry, Charles. 1972. *Citizen Nader.* New York: Saturday Review Press.

McCarthy, John D. 1987. "Pro-Life and Pro-Choice Mobilization." Pp. 46–69 in *Social Movements in an Organizational Society,* edited by John D. McCarthy and Mayer Zald. New Brunswick, N.J.: Transaction.

McCarthy, John D., David Britt, and Mark Wolfson. 1991. "The Institutional Channeling of Social Movements by the State in the United States." *Research in Social Movements, Conflict and Change* 13:45–76.

McCarthy, John D., and Jim Castelli. 1994. "Working for Justice: The Campaign for Human Development and Poor Empowerment Groups." Washington, D.C.: Life Cycle Institute, Catholic University.

McCarthy, John D., and Mark Wolfson. 1992. "Consensus Movements, Conflict Movements, and the Cooptation of Civic and State Infrastructures." Pp. 273–98 in *Frontiers in Social Movement Theory,* edited by Aldon Morris and Carol Mueller. New Haven, Conn.: Yale University Press.

McFarland, Andrew S. 1984. *Common Cause.* Chatham, N.J.: Chatham House.

———. 1992. "Interest Groups and the Policy Process." Pp. 58–79 in *The Politics of Interests,* edited by Mark P. Petracca. Boulder, Colo.: Westview Press.

———. 1998. "Social Movements and Theories of American Politics." Pp. 7–19 in *Social Movements and American Political Institutions,* edited by Anne N. Costain and Andrew S. McFarland. Lanham, Md.: Rowman and Littlefield.

McLaughlin, Paul, and Marwan Khawaja. 2000. "The Organizational Dynamics of the U.S. Environmental Movement." *Rural Sociology* 65:422–39.

Meier, August, and Elliott Rudwick. 1973. *CORE.* New York: Oxford University Press.

Messinger, Sheldon. 1955. "Organizational Transformation." *American Sociological Review* 20:3–10.

Michels, Robert. 1962. *Political Parties.* New York: Free Press.

Minkoff, Debra C. 1994. "From Service Provision to Institutional Advocacy: The Shifting Legitimacy of Organizational Forms." *Social Forces* 72:943–69.

———. 1995. *Organizing for Equality.* New Brunswick, N.J.: Rutgers University Press.

———. 1997. "Producing Social Capital: National Social Movements and Civil Society." *American Behavioral Scientist* 40:606–19.

———. 1998. "Bending with the Wind: Strategic Change and Adaptation by Women's and Racial Minority Organizations." *American Journal of Sociology* 104:1666–1703.

———. 2002. "The Emergence of Hybrid Organizational

Forms: Combining Identity-Based Service Provision and Political Action." *Nonprofit and Voluntary Sector Quarterly* 31:377–401.

Mitchell, Robert C. 1979. "National Environmental Lobbies and the Apparent Illogic of Collective Action." Pp. 87–135 in *Collective Decision Making,* edited by C. S. Russell. Baltimore: Resources for the Future.

Mitchell, Robert C., Angela E. Mertig, and Riley R. Dunlap. 1992. "Twenty Years of Environmental Mobilization." Pp. 11–22 in *American Environmentalism,* edited by Riley R. Dunlap and Angela E. Mertig. New York: Taylor and Francis.

Moe, Terry. 1980. *The Organization of Interests.* Chicago: University of Chicago Press.

Moen, Matthew C. 1992. *The Transformation of the Christian Right.* Tuscaloosa: University of Alabama Press.

Morris, Aldon. 1984. *The Origins of the Civil Rights Movement.* New York: Free Press.

———. 1993. "Birmingham Confrontation Reconsidered." *American Sociological Review* 58:621–36.

Moyers, Richard L., and Kathleen P. Enright. 1997. *A Snapshot of America's Nonprofit Boards: 1997 Edition.* Washington, D.C.: National Center for Nonprofit Boards.

Nadel, Mark. 1971. *The Politics of Consumer Protection.* Indianapolis: Bobbs-Merrill.

Nagai, Althea K., Robert Lerner, and Stanley Rothman. 1994. *Giving for Social Change.* Westport, Conn.: Praeger.

Navasky, Victor. 1977. *Kennedy Justice.* New York: Atheneum.

Olson, Mancur. 1968. *The Logic of Collective Action.* Cambridge, Mass.: Harvard University Press.

———. 1982. *The Rise and Decline of Nations.* New Haven, Conn.: Yale University Press.

Olson, Susan. 1984. *Clients and Lawyers.* Westport, Conn.: Greenwood Press.

Opp, Karl-Dieter. 1989. *The Rationality of Political Protest.* Boulder, Co.: Westview Press.

Opp, Karl-Dieter, and Wolfgang Ruehl. 1990. "Repression, Micromobilization and Political Protest." *Social Forces* 69:521–47.

Ostrander, Susan. 1995. *Money for Change: Social Movement Philanthropy at Haymarket People's Fund.* Philadelphia: Temple University Press.

Pateman, Carole. 1970. *Participation and Democratic Theory.* New York: Cambridge University Press.

Paxton, Pamela. 2002. "Social Capital and Democracy: An Interdependent Relationship." *American Sociological Review* 67:254–77.

Perrow, Charles. 1970. *Organizational Analysis.* Belmont, Calif.: Wadsworth.

Pertschuk, Michael. 1982. *Revolt against Regulation.* Berkeley: University of California Press.

Peterson, Mark A., and Jack L. Walker. 1986. "Interest Group Response to Partisan Change." Pp. 67–89 in *Interest Group Politics,* 2nd ed., edited by Allan J. Cigler and Burdett A. Loomis. Washington, D.C.: Congressional Quarterly Press.

Petracca, Mark P. 1992. *The Politics of Interests.* Boulder, Co.: Westview Press.

Piven, Frances, and Richard Cloward. 1977. *Poor People's Movements.* New York: Pantheon.

Powell, Walter, and Paul J. DiMaggio. 1991. *The New Institutionalism in Organizational Analysis.* Chicago: University of Chicago Press.

Pratt, Henry. 1977. *The Gray Lobby.* Chicago: University of Chicago Press.

Putnam, Robert. 2000. *Bowling Alone.* New York: Simon and Schuster.

Quattrone, George A., and Amos Tversky. 1988. "Contrasting Rational and Psychological Analysis of Political Choice." *American Political Science Review* 82:719–36.

Rausch, Jonathan. 1994. *Demosclerosis.* New York: New York Times Books.

Rabin, Robert. 1975. "Lawyers for Social Change." *Stanford Law Review* 28:207–61.

Reid, Elizabeth. 1998. "Nonprofit Advocacy and Political Participation." Pp. 291–325 in *Nonprofits and Government: Collaboration and Conflict,* edited by Elizabeth Boris and Eugene Steuerle. Washington, D.C.: Urban Institute Press.

———. 2000. "Understanding the Word 'Advocacy.'" Pp. 1–8 in *Nonprofit Advocacy and the Policy Process.* Vol. 1. Washington, D.C.: Urban Institute Press.

Rich, Andrew, and R. Kent Weaver. 1999. "Advocates and Analysts: Think Tanks and the Politicization of Expertise." Pp. 235–57 in *Interest Group Politics,* 5th ed., edited by Allan Cigler and Burdett Loomis. Washington, D.C.: Congressional Quarterly Press.

Riggle, Ellen D. B., and Barry L. Tadlock. 1999. *Gays and Lesbians in the Democratic Process.* New York: Columbia University Press.

Rimmerman, Craig A. 1992. *From Identity to Politics : The Lesbian and Gay Movements in the United States.* Philadelphia: Temple University Press.

Robnett, Belinda. 1996. "African-American Women in the Civil Rights Movement, 1954–1965." *American Journal of Sociology* 101:1661–93.

Rosenthal, Naomi, and Michael Schwartz. 1989. "Spontaneity and Democracy in Movements." Pp. 33–60 in *Organizing for Social Change,* edited by Bert Klandermans. Greenwich, Conn.: JAI Press.

Rothenberg, Lawrence S. 1992. *Linking Citizens to Government: Interest Group Politics at Common Cause.* New York: Cambridge University Press.

Rothman, Jack. 1974. *Planning and Organizing for Social Change.* New York: Columbia University Press.

Rothschild-Whitt, Joyce. 1979. "The Collectivistic Organization." *American Sociological Review* 44:509–27.

Rupp, Leila, and Verta Taylor. 1987. *Survival in the Doldrums: The Women's Rights Movement, 1945 to the 1960s.* New York: Oxford University Press.

Ryan, Charolette. 1990. *Media Strategies for Organizers.* Boston: South End Press.

Salamon, Lester M., and Helmut K. Anheier. 1999. *Global Civil Society: Dimensions of the Nonprofit Sector.* Baltimore: Johns Hopkins Center for Civil Society Studies.

Salisbury, Robert. 1969. "An Exchange Theory of Interest Groups." *Midwest Journal of Political Science* 13:1–35.

———. 1990. "The Paradox of Interest Groups in Washington: More Groups, Less Clout." Pp. 203–30 in *The New American Political System,* edited by Anthony King. Washington, D.C.: American Enterprise Institute.

Santoro, Wayne. 2002. "The Civil Rights Movement's Struggle

for Equal Employment Rights: A 'Dramatic Events–Conventional Politics' Model." *Social Forces* 81:177–206.

Schattschneider, E. E. 1960. *The Semi-Sovereign People.* New York: Holt, Rinehart and Winston.

Schlozman, Kay Lehman, and John T. Tierney. 1986. *Organized Interests and American Democracy.* New York: Harper and Row.

Schofer, Evan, and Marion Fourcade-Gourinchas. 2001. "The Structural Context of Civic Engagement: Voluntary Association Membership in Comparative Perspective." *American Sociological Review* 66:806–28.

Schuck, Peter. 1977. "Public Interest Groups and the Policy Process." *Public Administration Review* 37:137–49.

Schumaker, Paul. 1975. "Policy Responsiveness to Protest Group Demands." *Journal of Politics* 37:488–521.

Scott, W. Richard. 1992. *Organizations: Rational, Natural and Open Systems.* Englewood Cliffs, N.J.: Prentice-Hall.

Shaiko, Ronald G. 1999. *Voices and Echoes for the Environment.* New York: Columbia University Press.

Shear, Jeff. 1995. "The Ax Files." *National Journal,* 15 April:924–27.

Silverstein, Helen. 1996. *Unleashing Rights: Law, Meaning and the Animal Rights Movement.* Ann Arbor: University of Michigan Press.

Singh, Jitendra V., and Robert J. House. 1990. "Theory and Research in Organizational Ecology." *Annual Review of Sociology* 16:161–95.

Skocpol, Theda. 1999. "Advocates without Members." Pp. 461–510 in *Civic Engagement in American Democracy,* edited by Theda Skocpol and Morris Fiorina. Washington, D.C.: Brookings Institution Press.

———. 2003. *Diminished Democracy.* Norman: University of Oklahoma Press.

Smelser, Neil. 1963. *The Theory of Collective Behavior.* Glencoe, Ill.: Free Press.

Snow, David, and Robert Benford. 1988. "Ideology, Frame Resonance and Participant Mobilization." In *From Structure to Action,* edited by Bert Klandermans, Hans Peter Kriesi, and Sidney Tarrow. Greenwich, Conn.: JAI Press.

Snow, David, Burke Rochford, Steven Worden, and Robert Benford. 1986. "Frame Alignment Processes, Micromobilization, and Movement Participation." *American Sociological Review* 45:787–801.

Staggenborg, Suzanne. 1989. "Stability and Innovation in the Women's Movement." *Social Problems* 36:75–92.

———. 1991. *The Pro-Choice Movement.* New York: Oxford University Press.

Tarrow, Sidney. 1998. *Power in Movement.* 2nd ed. New York: Cambridge University Press.

Tesh, Sylvia. 1984. "In Support of 'Single-Issue' Politics." *Political Science Quarterly* 99:27–44.

Tucker, William. 1982. *Progress and Privilege: America in the Age of Environmentalism.* Garden City, N.Y.: Doubleday.

Truman, David. 1951. *The Governmental Process.* New York: Knopf.

Voss, Kim. 1996. "The Collapse of a Social Movement." Pp. 227–60 in *Comparative Social Movements,* edited by Doug McAdam, John D. McCarthy, and Mayer N. Zald. New York: Cambridge University Press.

Walker, Jack. 1991. *Mobilizing Interest Groups in America.* Ann Arbor: University of Michigan Press.

Walsh, Edward, and Rex H. Warland. 1983. "Social Movement Involvement in the Wake of a Nuclear Accident." *American Sociological Review* 48:764–80.

Weisbrod, Burton, Jack Handler, and Neil Komesar. 1978. *Public Interest Law.* Berkeley: University of California Press.

West, Guida. 1981. *The National Welfare Rights Movement.* New York: Praeger.

Wilson, James Q. 1995. *Political Organizations.* 2nd ed. Princeton, N.J.: Princeton University Press.

Wilson, John. 1983. "Corporatism and the Professionalization of Reform." *Journal of Political and Military Sociology* 11:53–68.

Wolford, Harris. 1992. *Of Kennedys and Kings.* Pittsburgh: University of Pittsburgh Press.

Zald, Mayer. 1970. *Organizational Change.* Chicago: University of Chicago Press.

Zald, Mayer, and Roberta Ash. 1966. "Social Movement Organizations." *Social Forces* 44:327–40.

Zald, Mayer, and John D. McCarthy. 1987. *Social Movements in an Organizational Society.* New Brunswick, N.J.: Transaction.

Zucker, Lynne. 1989. "Combining Institutional Theory and Population Ecology." *American Sociological Review* 54:542–45.

14

International Nongovernmental Organizations

JOHN BOLI

As this volume illustrates, the nonprofit sector is usually associated with national societies. It comprises organizations and associations in the "third sector" that lies "between states and markets" (Wuthnow 1991), that is, outside the business and political realms: service organizations, soup kitchens, recreation clubs, nonprofit hospitals, animal rights groups, private schools, and so on. In world society, an analogous sector operates outside both the global economy (dominated by transnational corporations and managed by such intergovernmental organizations as the International Monetary Fund and the World Trade Organization) and the global interstate system (centered on the United Nations). This global third sector is the realm of international nongovernmental organizations (INGOs), all those voluntary associations, confederations, societies, alliances, councils, conferences, and committees that organize on a transnational basis in pursuit of goals and purposes that transcend the boundaries of national territories and state jurisdictions. INGOs have received much attention over the past decade (Charnovitz 1997; Florini 2000; Keck and Sikkink 1998; Hulme and Edwards 1997; Boli and Thomas 1999; Willetts 1996), and a good many INGOs are widely known: human rights organizations like Amnesty International, Human Rights Watch, and International PEN (Castermans et al. 1991); environmental groups such as the World Wildlife Fund, Greenpeace, and the Rainforest Action Network (Frank et al. 1997; Wapner 1996; Lipschutz 1996); and relief and development organizations such as the Red Cross, Médecins sans frontières, World Vision International, and CARE International.

Despite the recent upsurge of interest in INGOs, this global third sector is poorly understood, and few comprehensive studies of the sector are available (for earlier overviews, see Speeckaert 1957; Feld 1971). It is much more extensive and differentiated than most people realize. Currently, some 6,000 to 7,000 fully transnational INGOs are in operation, along with tens of thousands of transnationally oriented nongovernmental organizations. They span virtually the entire spectrum of organized human endeavor, from electrical engineering to gourmet cooking and from rubber production to studying the philosophy of Spinoza. INGOs also have much deeper historical roots than is commonly recognized. Many discussions of INGOs assume that they suddenly began to flourish only in the 1990s, as a consequence of communism's demise and neoliberalism's global triumph. But the formative period for INGOs was the second half of the nineteenth century, and a large and complex INGO population was in place even before World War I. Similarly, the breadth and importance of INGOs' role in world society are sorely underappreciated, although recent work has begun to rectify this deficiency.

Hence, this chapter has three main purposes:

- to provide a comprehensive overview of the growth of INGOs over the past 150 years;
- to describe the full range of INGO activity with quantitative data that draw attention to types of INGOs that are largely absent from public discussion; and
- to show how INGOs operate in global governance processes, with an emphasis on their relationships with and effects on states, intergovernmental organizations, and transnational corporations.

ORIGINS AND GROWTH SINCE 1850

Table 14.1 summarizes the growth of INGOs between 1909 and 2000, with several categories of organizations shown for more recent years. Category (A) includes federations of INGOs whose members are themselves large INGOs, such as the International Scientific Union, the International Film and Television Council, and the World Federation of Trade Unions. Categories (B) through (D) are INGOs of varying membership dispersion: (B), "universal," includes INGOs with members in at least sixty countries, or at least thirty countries but well-balanced across continents; category (C) INGOs, "intercontinental," have members in many countries on at least two continents but are not as broadly distributed as (B) INGOs; and category (D) encompasses regional bodies with members in one continent or region. The table also shows the total number of active INGOs of all sorts, including a wide variety of internationally oriented organizations such as think tanks, foundations, research centers, and award-granting associations.

The proliferation of INGOs is impressive. Active INGOs have increased from fewer than 400 to more than 25,000 over these ninety years, with the numbers for categories (B) through (D) increasing substantially in the past twenty years.[1] The nonprofit sector has been expanding rapidly and in unbroken fashion at the international and global levels, yielding a dense population of organizations that form an almost bewilderingly complex array of networks concerned with an enormous number of social activities and issues. Note in the lower part of the table that intergovernmental organizations (IGOs) have increased greatly as well, but INGOs outnumber IGOs by a factor of seven to twelve throughout the period.

Definitions and Data

The figures in Table 14.1 are taken from various editions of the *Yearbook of International Organizations* (*YIO*), the premier source of information about international organizations. It is published by the Union of International Associations (UIA), which was founded as the Central Office of International Associations in Brussels in 1907 by Paul Otlet, secretary-general of the International Institute of Bibliography (an INGO), and Henri La Fontaine, a member of the Belgian parliament and president of the Permanent International Peace Bureau in Bern (also an INGO; La Fontaine won the 1913 Nobel Peace Prize for his work, with which Otlet was also engaged). The UIA took its present name at the First World Congress of International Organizations in Brussels in 1910. It lobbied intensively in favor of the founding of the League of Nations and the International Institute of Intellectual Cooperation (the predecessor of UNESCO), and it founded the first international university in the 1920s. The first *YIO* appeared in 1909, with information on about 200 organizations.[2] The UIA gradually emerged as the main repository of information about international organizations, becoming the quasi-official source associated with the United Nations (UN).

The UIA's concept of an INGO is similar to that used to identify domestic nonprofit organizations: any organization that operates on a nonprofit basis and is not a creature of the state. This concept is, however, deceptively simple, and the UIA's current director of communications and research, Anthony Judge, has written extensively on the issue of how best to delineate the INGO population. The definition used by the United National Economic and Social Council (ECOSOC) provides a good starting point: "Any in-

TABLE 14.1. NUMBER OF INGOS AND IGOS, 1909–2000

	1909	1920	1931	1940	1951	1960	1972	1981	1991	2000
International Nongovernmental Organizations										
Total "conventional" INGOs	374	474	801	841	1,307	1,987	2,976	4,265	4,620	6,357
(A) Federations	—	—	—	—	—	—	—	43	39	37
(B) Universal	—	—	—	—	—	—	—	370	427	475
(C) Intercontinental	—	—	—	—	—	—	—	859	773	1,063
(D) Regional	—	—	—	—	—	—	—	2,991	3,381	4,782
Other INGOs	—	—	—	—	—	13	622	5,133	11,493	11,966
Special forms	—	—	—	—	—	—	—	539	2,654	6,946
Currently active INGOs, all types	374	474	801	841	1,307	1,987	2,976	9,937	18,767	25,269
Intergovernmental Organizations										
Total "conventional" IGOs	37	—	—	—	123	154	280	337	297	243
Other IGOs	—	—	—	—	—	—	—	702	1,497	1,593
Special forms	—	—	—	—	—	—	—	—	306	709
Currently active IGOs, all types	37	—	—	—	—	—	—	1,039	2,100	2,545

Source: Union of International Associations, *Yearbook of International Associations,* various years.
Note: Figures for 1909–72 are based on data using founding and dissolution dates from the 1988–89 and 1984–85 *Yearbooks.* Actual totals are underestimated due to missing data.

ternational organization which is not established by intergovernmental agreement shall be considered as a nongovernmental organization for the purpose of these arrangements, including organizations which accept members designated by government authorities, provided that such membership does not interfere with the free expression of views of the organization" (quoted in Judge 2000). This definition does not explicitly rule out profit-oriented companies, but it does suggest the voluntary-associational character of INGOs, and for ECOSOC the term "international organization" excludes business corporations. A more elaborate statement offered by the UN Department of Public Information (2004) stipulates:

> A non-governmental organization (NGO) is a not-for-profit, voluntary citizens' group, which is organized on a local, national or international level to address issues in support of the public good. Task-oriented and made up of people with a common interest, NGOs perform a variety of services and humanitarian functions, bring citizens' concerns to Governments, monitor policies and programme implementation, and encourage political participation of civil society stakeholders at the community level. They provide analysis and expertise, serve as early warning mechanisms and help monitor and implement international agreements.

This definition includes domestic nonprofit organizations that are not explicitly international in structure or membership. Such broad usage of the term "NGO" is common—both practitioners and scholars employ it loosely, without distinguishing between domestic and international or global organizations. The definition also unduly emphasizes the social service and political advocacy aspects of INGO activity; many INGOs have other, very different concerns.

Judge shows that the variety of international organizations that must be considered as possible INGOs is too great to produce a satisfactory abstract definition. Instead, the *YIO*'s editors have developed seven rules to identify an international NGO "in terms of aims, members, structure, officers, finance, autonomy, and activities. The intent has been to include only those bodies oriented to three or more countries" (Judge 2000). The thrust of these rules is that INGOs must be functioning organizations with a high degree of autonomy, a demonstrated international presence or orientation, and ongoing activities oriented to reasonably well-specified goals. Reacting against the term "international" because of its implicit emphasis on interaction between nations, the UIA prefers to refer to INGOs as "transnational associations" that rise above the national level, but that term has not been widely adopted.

The data in the *YIO* are as timely and complete as one could reasonably expect (Boli and Thomas 1999). The UIA maintains regular contact with many thousands of INGOs (the latest figure it mentions is 25,000), and it combs extensive sources of information to identify new INGOs and to keep up with the activities of established organizations. Few new organizations appear immediately in the *YIO,* but most are identified within five years of their establishment. Hence, while any given *Yearbook* underestimates the number of INGOs operating in the years immediately prior to its publication, the UIA database remains the most reliable and comprehensive source of information available.

The Formative Era, 1850–1910: The Ideology of One World

Table 14.1 shows that a dense INGO universe was in operation long before the 1990s, when INGOs rather suddenly began to attract popular and scholarly attention. The first handful of INGOs emerged before 1850; for example, the British and Foreign Anti-Slavery Society (founded in 1839) and the World's Evangelical Alliance (1846). Steadily thereafter, INGOs began to form across a wide range of sectors: the World Alliance of Young Men's Christian Associations (1855); the Société universelle d'ophthalmologie (1861); the International Committee of the Red Cross, the International Working Men's Association (the First International), and the International Geodetic Association (all in 1864); the Association for the Reform and Codification of the Law of Nations (1873); the International Union of Marine Insurance (1874); the World's Woman's Christian Temperance Union (1883); the International Institute of Bibliography (1895); and the International Council of Nurses (1899). Thus we find organizations devoted (respectively) to humanitarian work, political action, science, international law, business, moral issues, knowledge, and the professions among the early INGOs, plus many other types as well.

Another way to appreciate the growth of the INGO population is by considering the number of new INGOs founded in each decade. In 1851–60, only five INGOs were founded; by 1871–80, twenty-two new INGOs appeared. The succeeding two decades then produced thirty-eight and ninety-five new organizations, and 1901–10 added an astonishing 261 new INGOs, indicating an exponential rate of increase.[3] The 1850–1910 period thus represents the first great wave of third-sector internationalism and globalization, alongside the powerful wave of economic internationalism that also occurred at this time.

European powers were dominant in this period, extending their imperialist reach throughout the globe. Correspondingly, most of the INGOs founded by 1910 had European origins, though they drew members from many other parts of the globe, particularly the Americas. However, from the point of view of the geographers, lawyers, industrial workers, women's rights advocates, teetotalers, cyclists, engineers, sugar producers, dentists, photographers, prisoners' relatives, mathematicians, ethicists, vintners, firefighters, Zionists, ice-skaters, insurers, explorers, surveyors, and freethinkers involved—all these groups, and many more, established INGOs in the formative period—these were not European organizations or European issues. Rather, nearly all of the INGOs founded before World War II were explicitly global in their outlook, orientation, aims, and endeavors. They understood the world as a single, comprehensive society embracing all of humanity. In naming their budding organizations, they used not only "international" but also "world," "universal," "federation," and "union" (in the sense of global unification) to describe themselves. "International" normally conveyed the sense of the more recent term "transnational"—these organizations transcended nations and states, addressing problems, organizing knowledge, sponsoring competitions, and seeking rights for oppressed groups throughout the world. They welcomed members from all corners of the globe and hoped to engage as broad a range of individuals and societies as possible. For many early INGOs, in fact, transcending the nation-state and nationalism was an urgent matter because of the catastrophic violence and inequities they blamed on the nation-state system. More, perhaps, than at any time before or since, the ideology of one world—to be organized and governed by all-encompassing bodies promoting peace, harmony, and cooperation among all peoples—reigned in the formative INGO period.

The Interwar Period

The world wars disrupted this powerful globalizing wave, just as they disrupted economic internationalization, in a fierce outburst of nationalism and total conflict. Only thirty-nine INGOs were founded while war raged in Europe between 1914 and 1918, as compared with 134 during the other five years of this decade. But INGO organizing did not go into limbo in the interwar years—far from it. The nationalistic trauma of World War I quickly gave way to a new wave of rapid transnationalization: many more INGOs were established in the 1920s than in the 1900s—almost thirty-eight per year compared with twenty-six—and this rate declined only modestly (to about thirty per year) in the 1930s. The war also prompted more formal state collaboration, foremost in the League of Nations and the International Labour Organization but also in other IGOs (though IGOs would remain rare until after World War II; fewer than 100 were founded before 1940). This wave of internationalism sought above all to prevent future wars and to find ways of consolidating and securing peace, but, as in the prewar period, INGOs of many kinds were founded during the interwar era. Those explicitly concerned with world peace, international law, or international harmony were only a small minority.

Postwar Expansion: Rapid and Sustained Growth

During the World War II years of 1939–45, only fourteen new INGOs were founded per year, dropping to a low of nine organizations in 1944. Even more striking than in the 1920s, however, the INGO rebound after the war was a virtual rocket launch: thirty-five new INGOs in 1945, sixty-eight in 1946, and ninety-one in 1947 (far surpassing the previous high of forty-nine INGOs in 1921). Thereafter, more than 100 INGOs were created almost every year, with the population continuing to expand rapidly through the 1990s, as Table 14.1 shows.

Two trends that have characterized the burgeoning INGO population in the postwar period are noteworthy. The first is the rise of regional INGOs. "Regional" here refers not to geographic dispersion of membership, as in UIA category (D) above, but to an explicit regional focus or range of action, that is, INGOs limiting themselves to some portion of the world rather than a fully global involvement. By the 1960s, roughly half of all new INGOs were of regional rather than global or all-encompassing character. This was a marked departure from the formative and interwar periods, when the vast majority of INGOs—more than 80 percent, and even 90 percent for some social sectors—presented themselves as fully global, that is, addressing issues of universal concern or relevance.

Immediately after World War II, many types of regional organizations emerged. Foremost among these were geographic regional bodies (e.g., the Latin American Confederation of Tourism Organizations from 1957, or the Middle East Neurological Society, founded in 1958), and also many other types of subglobal INGOs: linguistic regions (the Association de psychologie scientifique de langue française, 1950), religious regions (the Muslim World League, 1962), former-empire regions (the Commonwealth Engineers Council, 1946), and so on. Geographic regional INGOs are especially common in Europe, but they have been forming at rapid rates in other areas of the world as well, particularly in Latin America and Asia.

The second new trend has been the knotting of networks among INGOs working in the same or related social sectors. As international communication has become cheaper and faster, INGOs have found it ever easier to maintain regular contact, coordinate their activities, and participate in joint campaigns. Such networks have been most widely discussed in the areas of environmentalism, women's rights, human rights, and development aid (Keck and Sikkink 1998), but they are also common across less visible INGO sectors, particularly in technical, scientific, knowledge, medical, and business domains. The networks extend to other types of global actors, particularly IGOs and transnational corporations, often in antagonistic network relationships, as we shall discuss below.

By the beginning of the twenty-first century, well over 6,000 fully global or transnational INGOs were in operation, covering almost every type of activity or issue imaginable. They are complemented by tens of thousands of other voluntaristic, associational organizations with an international, transnational, or global orientation, as well as hundreds of thousands of domestic bodies (NGOs) that have relationships of varying intensity with INGOs. Many INGOs rank as the peak global governance organizations in their respective social sectors, in much the same way that the World Trade Organization and the Universal Postal Union constitute the dominant state-based global governance structures in their domains. This topic will also be explored below.

The table in the appendix to this chapter provides basic information about a variety of major INGOs across many social sectors. Some are well known around the world, while others are hardly known at all. The table suggests the diversity of INGOs in terms of types of members, global reach, size of budget and staff, and other features.

STRUCTURES AND OPERATIONS

The basic building block for INGOs is the interested individual, whether bridge player or bridge builder, animal rights activist or professional hunter. The great majority of INGOs are voluntary associations of individuals or associations of associations. A small proportion are umbrella federations like the International Scientific Union, which brings together dozens of peak scientific INGOs and is thereby considered capable of speaking for world science as a whole. Business and industry associations differ from most INGOs in that they typically have companies as members. Large companies, usually transnational corporations (TNCs), may be individual members, but in many business INGOs the primary members are associations of companies, usually national industry or trade associations. Very few INGOs admit states or other political units as members; such hybrid organizations as the International Labour Organization (which brings together labor, employers, and states) are rare.

INGO structures generally conform to a standard global model: governance is overseen by a board of directors or advisers; officers, led by a secretary-general, president, or chair, are elected by the members; the office staff consists of employees and volunteers, with volunteers often doing the lion's share of routine work; elected or volunteer committees carry out specialized tasks. Strictly democratic, egalitarian governance is the norm: every member has one vote (even for companies in most business INGOs), all members are eligible to hold office, decisions are made by majority vote (though consensual decision making is frequently preferred), and dissenting or critical voices are to be encouraged.

Variants of this standard model abound. Governing boards may appoint the executive officer; membership may be differentiated between full members and associate or student members, the latter having fewer participatory rights; membership fees may be income-related, particularly in professional and business INGOs, and in the latter voting strength is sometimes proportional to fees paid. Predominantly, though, INGOs posit and promote egalitarian membership, active participation, and openness to initiatives from the rank-and-file members.

Activities

The full range of INGO activities is too extensive to list, but three principal types stand out. First, INGOs gather, produce, and disseminate mountains of information—on environmental problems, bidding systems for bridge games, strengths of building materials, breast cancer treatments, political prisoners, or comet sightings, to mention but a few examples. They publish newsletters, reports, books, and trade magazines. They mail and e-mail calls to action and appeals for support to their members or potential members. They issue press releases, submit newspaper articles, and place advertisements to draw attention to their activities or causes. Second, INGOs sponsor meetings, conferences, conventions, workshops, seminars, competitions, and a host of other gatherings. These range from such peak global events as the Olympic Games, the World Cup, and NGO forums (regarding "parallel summits," see Pianta 2001) at major UN events like the 1992 Conference on Environment and Development in Rio de Janeiro, or the 1975 World Conference of the International Women's Year in Mexico City, to the thousands of annual or biennial international INGO meetings known only to their respective members and supporters. These gatherings dramatize the transnational character of the organizations and their activities, while reinforcing the transnational outlook and orientation of their members. They also strengthen networks among INGOs and domestic NGOs, since many global INGO gatherings include national and local groups from all over the globe.

Third, INGOs attempt to influence other actors in world society. For social movement INGOs, major targets include such IGOs as the World Trade Organization, the International Monetary Fund, the UN Development Programme, and the World Health Organization, as well as individual states (urging them to improve pollution controls, to protect homosexuals, to stop censoring the press, and so on) and particular TNCs (accused of polluting the planet, exploiting less developed countries, and the like). INGOs also target regional and local government units, aiming to bypass national states to achieve specific goals in specific places. Trade and industry groups lobby IGOs and states as well, but, evidently, with quite different aims in mind. For the latter groups, and for technical, scientific, and other less explicitly political INGOs, lobbying is often indirect, through national associations that make up the more encompassing world bodies. Sometimes INGOs even lobby other INGOs; for example, international sports federations woo the International Olympic Committee to get their sports into the Olympics.

Membership Trends

INGOs and INGO members initially were concentrated in Europe and the Americas, but this is less and less the case; the peoples of non-Western countries are increasingly active in INGOs, and many newer INGOs have non-Western origins. Systematic counts of the national origins of INGO members are not available, but for most INGOs the *YIO* lists the countries that have at least one member in each organization. These lists enable us to determine the number of INGOs to which residents of each country belong—for example, the number of INGOs in 1960 to which residents of Kenya, Thailand, and Austria belonged (72, 125, and 656, respectively). We can also study growth in these numbers over time (by 1988, these figures had risen to 603, 661, and 1,773 INGOs, respectively). This measure captures the breadth of participation in INGOs but not the total numbers of people belonging to INGOs.

For the period 1960–88, the number of fully transnational INGOs (categories A–D) for which breadth of membership data are available rose from 1,987 to 4,474, an increase of 125 percent (Boli, Loya, and Loftin 1999). For all countries (or colonies before independence), the mean number of INGOs to which residents belonged jumped from 122 in 1960 to 485 in 1988, an increase of almost 300 percent—far more than the increase in the number of INGOs. The rate of increase in membership breadth was far from uniform, however. Membership increased much faster in the non-Western world than in the West: the percentage of increase was higher for African (676 percent), Pacific-Oceanian (489 percent), and Asian (396 percent) countries than for Europe and the Americas (228 percent and 283 percent). Similarly, breadth of membership grew faster among the poor than among the rich. If we divide all countries into four quartiles by GDP/capita, we find that the poorest two quartiles increased their INGO participation the most (352 percent for the poorest 25 percent of countries, 376 percent for the second quartile), while the third quartile was up 307 percent and the richest quartile increased the least (176 percent). More rapid growth outside the West is also indicated by the facts that newer countries have increased their breadth of participation faster than older countries, and that non-Western civilizational arenas (countries where, for example, Islam or indigenous or folk religions dominate) have increased their INGO participation more rapidly than Protestant or Catholic Christian countries. Thus, while Europeans and Americans (North and South) still belong to more INGOs than residents of non-Western countries, the gap is narrowing rapidly.

The basic message is that people from all over the world have been flocking to INGOs throughout the past several decades, with the non-European, non-Western, and poorer countries' peoples broadening their participation especially rapidly. These general patterns are borne out well by studies of particular INGO sectors, such as Meyer, Frank, et al.'s (1997) work on environmental INGOs and Schofer's (1999) examination of scientific INGOs. As the INGO population expands, more people from more countries are joining an ever wider array of INGOs, and the INGOs themselves are becoming increasingly global (or more fully regional).

Language Use

In contrast with the membership trends, the 1999–2000 *YIO* data on the languages officially employed by INGOs reveal heavy European-language dominance. Of the 10,023 official languages (usually two or three for any given organization), English is by far the most common, used by 4,194 INGOs or almost 42 percent.[4] French follows at 2,298, then German (1,023) and Spanish (914). These four account for 84 percent of all official languages; the next six—Italian (212), Dutch (180), Arabic (190), Portuguese (200), Swedish (136), and Russian (131), only two of which are not European—represent less than 11 percent of the total. Another thirty languages, ranging from Danish (100) to Korean (12) to Creole (1), are used by at least some INGOs and account for 5.5 percent, while one artificial language, Esperanto, makes the list (used by five INGOs). Hence, English remains the official language of the great majority of fully international INGOs, French of well over half, and German and Spanish of about a fifth each. The rapid broadening of INGO participation by peoples outside the West has occurred within a context of heavy reliance on these European tongues, which are still the only languages of broad significance for interaction in world society.

Impact of the Internet

Not least among INGOs themselves, the Internet is routinely described as a great boon to global nongovernmental organizing (Naughton 2001). The typical INGO includes links to numerous compatible organizations on its Web pages and is in frequent contact with such bodies for information, consultation, advice, and shared planning. The Internet has made coordination for massive campaigns possible at a level never seen before, with startling and increasingly well-known results. Most striking was the success of the Campaign to Ban Landmines (one of the unassuming leaders of which, Jody Williams, won the Nobel Peace Prize in 1997). The campaign targeted states, UN agencies, global political leaders, and the public, and in the space of only six years succeeded in generating an international convention prohibiting the production or use of antipersonnel mines, which entered into force in 1999. Other noted campaign efforts in recent years have included vigorous opposition to the Organisation for Economic Co-operation and Development's Multilateral Agreement on Investment, which was eventually abandoned by the OECD; mobilization to protest World Trade Organization policies at the Seattle WTO meeting in 1999; and further efforts aimed at meetings of the WTO, the International Monetary Fund, and the World Economic Forum in the years since.

An interesting Internet wrinkle is what are known as Web rings—organizations linked to one another as if arrayed around a doughnut, without any central body occupying the space of the doughnut hole. A Web ring encourages users to move from organization to organization, learning about the entire linked set of INGOs and thereby gaining a more comprehensive overview of the main issues and endeavors in the particular sector addressed by the ring. Most rings include a "random-jump" facility that takes the user to randomly selected sites in the ring, thereby distributing visitors evenly across the organizations that compose the ring.

SOCIAL SECTORS OF INGO ACTIVITY

Most well-known INGOs focus on the environment, human or women's rights, development, disaster relief, or labor issues, but these sectors constitute only a small portion of the INGO population. Table 14.2 shows the distribution of

TABLE 14.2. SECTORAL DISTRIBUTION OF INGOS FOUNDED IN THREE ERAS (PERCENTAGES)

Social sector	Founded by 1910	Founded 1911–45	Founded 1946–88	INGOs active in 1988
Industry/trade/industrial groups	11.0	14.2	17.7	17.6
Medicine/health	8.6	10.3	13.6	14.9
Sciences/math/knowledge/space	13.8	9.5	12.2	11.6
Sports/hobby/leisure	5.4	6.6	5.7	8.0
Technical/infrastructural communications	6.5	6.7	8.2	7.5
Tertiary economic/finance/tourism	4.2	6.0	7.9	7.2
Individual rights/welfare	5.4	8.8	5.7	6.3
World polity–oriented	10.5	11.2	7.2	6.2
Religion/family/cultural identity	10.3	9.4	6.6	6.0
Labor/professions/public administration	12.4	7.6	5.0	6.0
Education/students	4.7	4.0	5.1	4.2
Humanities/arts/philosophy	4.9	4.0	4.2	3.9
Political ideologies/parties	2.6	1.9	0.9	0.6
Total	100.00	100.00	100.00	100.00
Number of INGOs	429	854	3,673	4,449

Source: Union of International Associations, *Yearbook of International Associations* 1985, 1988–89.

INGOs founded in three eras: by 1910, when the INGO population reached its first peak of expansion; 1911–45, covering the turmoil of the world wars and the interwar period; and 1946–88, when the INGO population exploded and began to differentiate into global and regional organizations.[5] The sectors are ranked by the fourth column, which indicates the distribution of INGOs active in 1988.

Evident in Table 14.2 is the predominance of business, scientific, medical, knowledge-related, technical, infrastructural, and sports and hobby INGOs. These types (the first six categories) accounted for 66.8 percent of the active bodies in 1988, 65.3 percent of those formed after 1945, and 49.5 percent of those founded by 1910. INGOs concerned with rights, the environment, relief, and development fall within the "individual rights/welfare" and "world polity–oriented" categories (the latter including bodies working holistically for global concerns regarding the environment, international law, peace, world government, and so on), which together accounted for only one-eighth of the total in 1988, though somewhat more earlier (20 percent in the 1911–45 period). The great majority of INGOs—entire sectors of the INGO population—have little in common with the INGOs in these two categories, and they almost never catch the public eye. Many of them maintain close relationships with IGOs and deal with other globally important issues: medical and health-care INGOs are involved with the World Health Organization, technical INGOs with the International Telecommunication Union, and scientific and humanistic bodies with UNESCO. Yet only their respective members typically know much about most INGOs, and even powerful business and industry INGOs normally stay below the public radar screen—except for those few that come under attack from other INGOs concerned about the environment, labor issues, social justice, and the like.

Table 14.2 also shows that some sorts of activities have fared rather poorly at the transnational level. Note the declines in labor/professions/public administration, from 12.4 percent of early INGOs to 5.0 percent of those founded after World War II; in political INGOs, from 2.6 percent to 0.9 percent; and in religion/family/cultural identity bodies, from 10.3 percent to 6.6 percent. Labor organizations account for all of the decline in the first of these categories; they fell from 9.3 percent to 2.2 percent of organizations across the three periods, while professional and public administration groups increased modestly, from 3.1 percent to 3.8 percent. For religion/family/cultural identity, the decline was sharp for both religious and family-oriented INGOs, but cultural identity's proportion of all INGOs remained roughly unchanged. It appears, then, that INGOs built around collective units and identities—religions, the family, labor unions—have become relatively less common despite the resurgence of various forms of "traditional" collective identities in the latter part of the 20th century. Transnational political organizations (most of which have been socialist, communist, or broadly leftist in orientation) have always been rather rare.

Given their relative paucity, how can we account for the high global profiles of human rights, environmental, relief, development, and group rights INGOs? The most important factor at work is their direct involvement with states and the responsibilities of states. Rights and environmental INGOs habitually make demands of states, urging conformity with certain standards of conduct and promoting particular social and economic policies. Relief and development organizations step in to make up for the failures of states to maintain internal order or international peace (relief and refugee work) or to stimulate national development (see Rosenau 1997). Many of these prominent INGOs even go so far as to challenge the very existence and legitimacy of states, arguing that states and nations are archaic impediments to the promotion of a peaceful, just, and humane world. Thus, the most prominent INGOs are those that most directly confront states or step into the breach to correct states' failures to meet public welfare obligations.

Many other INGOs—such as sports, hobby, and leisure organizations; scientific, infrastructural, and technical bodies; humanities and literary associations; religious groups;

medical specialists; industry and trade groups; and knowledge-oriented INGOs—operate largely autonomously from states and keep their distance from politics. They therefore are not perceived as directly relevant to the issues that dominate the public realm. A good many such bodies have considerable indirect interaction with states, either via IGOs or through the INGOs' constituent national associations, but under normal circumstances such matters as bridge design, research on surgical techniques, spelunking, library management, and postmodernist philosophy are not considered important arenas of state policy or of much relevance to the struggles for political and economic power that dominate the public realm.

Social Movement Organizations (SMOs)

A special class of INGOs that have become highly prominent in global affairs are social movement organizations, which include many of the rights INGOs and environmental organizations mentioned above, along with organizations concerned with democracy, labor policies, working conditions, child labor, global and regional inequalities, sexual exploitation, and so on. They are the subjects of much recent scholarly work (O'Brien, Goetz, and Scholte 2000; Tarrow 2000; Waterman 1998; Keck and Sikkink 1998; Smith, Pagnucco, and Romeril 1994; Smith, Chatfield, and Pagnucco 1997; Lipschutz 1996; Wapner 1996) and have become central to global discourse about INGOs. These INGOs take it upon themselves to promote views critical of dominant global practices and governance structures on behalf of the poor, the marginalized, the excluded, and the oppressed of world society. Their primary targets are the "big three" governance IGOs of the world economy—the International Monetary Fund, the World Trade Organization, and the World Bank (Scholte and Schnabel 2002; Fox and Brown 1998)—as well as TNCs based in developed countries (especially oil companies, apparel and shoe manufacturers, electronics and computer producers, and toy companies) whose operations in the less developed world they decry as exploitative, supportive of repressive governments, and detrimental to the natural environment. They are also avid participants in UN-sponsored global conferences on such issues as women's rights, the environment, development, and labor, seeking to push both UN agencies and member states to adopt and implement policies to alleviate the problems that give these INGOs their raison d'être (Otto 1996; Pianta 2001). Hence, social movement organizations are in the thick of global politics, and they strive to maintain high profiles because one of their primary sources of leverage with respect to states, IGOs, and TNCs is the diffuse and ineffable construct of "world public opinion" that they claim to represent and are intent on shaping and mobilizing on behalf of their causes.

Research in the past decade has identified "precursors" (Keck and Sikkink 1998) to contemporary INGO-driven global social movements: the establishment of rules of war by the International Committee of the Red Cross (Finnemore 1999), the antislavery movement of the nineteenth century and the anti–foot-binding movement in China early in the twentieth century (Keck and Sikkink 1998), the international women's movement (Berkovitch 1999), and an early version of the environmental conservation movement in the latter part of the nineteenth century (Frank, Hironaka, and Schofer 2000). All these movements had considerable success and paved the way for the explosion of social movement INGOs from the late 1960s onward. By the 1990s, INGO-led global social movements had become so prominent and effective that a backlash began to emerge. States, IGOs, and TNCs began to snipe at INGOs in an effort to delegitimate them, calling them insufficiently transparent, narrow in their single-issue concerns, exaggerated in their claims, and not accountable to the general public through democratic checks and balances (Edwards 2000b).

INGOS, GLOBAL CIVIL SOCIETY, AND GLOBAL GOVERNANCE

Geopolitical conditions and global intellectual culture strongly shape scholarly work. The bipolar world of the postwar era favored ideas and theories emphasizing political and economic conflict against a backdrop of strong state sovereignty and systemic anarchy. States were the only entities that were given much credence by the academic community. As growing global integration and cosmopolitanism fostered conceptualizations of societal problems as global rather than national (Meyer, Boli, et al. 1997), and oil shocks, debt crises, deficit spending, stagflation, and neoliberalism undermined the charisma of the state (Jepperson 2002), politicians and scholars began to perceive a need for global structures that could overcome the problems inherent in the system of squabbling states and even to recognize that some such structures had already emerged in the postwar period. The bias toward states remained strong, though. Scholars began to pay some attention to such economic IGOs as the International Monetary Fund and the World Bank, to General Agreement on Tariffs and Trade (GATT) negotiations, and to the UN, and some even ventured to study specialized IGOs like the International Telecommunication Union (Cowhey 1990), Intelsat (Krasner 1991), or the International Civil Aviation Organization (Sochor 1991), but horizons generally remained narrow. That INGOs could be important in global governance was an entirely foreign notion throughout the 1980s.

The collapse of communism and the end of the Cold War, along with a variety of other factors, partially removed the blinders that had limited scholarly vision. Quite suddenly, "civil society" was rediscovered—or imagined, in places where it was not actually functioning. Organizations outside the state and the formal economy mattered after all. Civil society was even found to have a global dimension (Keane 2001; Anheier, Glasius, and Kaldor 2001; Falk 1993; Kaldor 1999; Otto 1996; Pasha and Blaney 1998; Salamon et al. 1999), organized primarily by INGOs but also involving many domestic NGOs. It became the darling of both left-leaning groups (championing "progressive" social movements and "oppositional" grassroots action) and the neoliberal right (lauding the charitable and social-service activities of voluntary associations in lieu of welfare programs). But these ideological commitments from both sides kept scholarly interest focused on a small subset of all global civil society organizations—social movement INGOs and charity, relief, and development bodies—leaving the great majority of INGO sectors outside the scholarly compass and the popular media as well.

Nevertheless, it is now widely recognized that INGOs act as the chief representatives of and spokespersons for global civil society and play an important role in global governance (Young 1997; Diehl 1996; Charnovitz 1997; Lipschutz 1992, 1996; Weiss and Gordenker 1996; Clark 1995). Put another way, INGOs are the primary medium through which "world citizens" act collectively, typically in voluntary associational form, to organize, shape, and express world opinion in the global public sphere (Boli 1997; Falk 1994; Van Steenbergen 1994; Guidry, Kennedy, and Zald 2001; Edwards and Gaventa 2001) and to foster a "global civic culture" (Boulding 1990). They increasingly coordinate their programs and actions to increase their influence on states, IGOs, and TNCs, often forming important elements of "epistemic communities" (Haas 1992) that assess and shape state and IGO policies. INGO networks provide flexible, largely informal frameworks within which INGOs in particular sectors can present a more or less unified front. Some INGOs concentrate on promoting global civil society as such. Civicus World Alliance for Citizen Participation (2005), for example, works toward a "worldwide community of informed, inspired, committed citizens engaged in confronting the challenges facing humanity," focusing on both substantive issues and the "architecture" of civil society. Other examples include Action without Borders, which serves as an information clearinghouse for global civil society (staying in contact, it claims, with 27,000 organizations in 153 countries), and Ashoka (2002), which supports "social entrepreneurs" who introduce innovative approaches to solving social problems at the grassroots level on five continents.

Global civil society organizations participate in global governance in many ways, some of which have already been mentioned. In many social sectors, INGOs dominate the global governance structures and states and IGOs are only peripherally involved. This is especially true in highly rationalized realms—scientific, medical, engineering, technology, and infrastructure organizations—as well as many global economic sectors, represented by various business, industry, and trade groups (Cutler, Haufler, and Porter 1999; Haufler 2000). In these sectors, the INGOs involved enjoy quasi-official status in world society. They operate as comprehensive and well-legitimated representatives of their constituencies (for example, information managers, biologists, cardiologists, industrial engineers, biomedical technicians, and urban planners, on the one hand; accounting, chemicals, automobile manufacturing, textiles, insurance, shipping, tourism, and food processing companies, on the other), and they routinely engage in formulating rules, principles, and procedures to manage the global dimensions of their respective spheres (Porter 2002). Similar autonomous, rational-voluntaristic authority (Boli 1999) is often exercised by INGOs in the sports, hobby, leisure, humanities, and arts sectors: the International Badminton Federation sets global rules for the game and independently organizes the Thomas and Uber Cups World Team Championships; the International Go Federation determines world champion amateur Go players each year; the International Association of Paper Historians (2002) "coordinates all interests and activities in paper history as an international specialist association" and sets global standards for identifying and registering papers "with or without watermarks." INGOs like these constitute in themselves the global governance structures within their particular domains (sometimes in conjunction with one or two other INGOs), and no other actors (states, TNCs, or IGOs) are involved in or are relevant to the governance structures.

In numerous domains, however, INGOs do not operate with such a high degree of autonomy, because other global and national actors have important or central roles. The most important of these, of course, are states, their associated IGOs, and transnational corporations.

Relationships with States and Intergovernmental Organizations

INGO relationships with states and IGOs have become dense and complex in the past two decades, but even in the formative period, INGO relationships with states were commonplace. The Red Cross arose to induce states to limit harm to civilians during wartime and to improve the survival chances of wounded soldiers (Finnemore 1999). The International Council of Women and the International Women's Suffrage Association lobbied states to demand women's suffrage (Berkovitch 1999). The International Professional Association of Manufactory, Industrial, and Handicraft Workers sought to restructure labor laws to improve working conditions and safety regulations. In these early examples INGOs lobbied individual states, but with the formation of the International Labour Organization (ILO) in 1919, labor, employer, and eventually women's INGOs had a central global focus for their efforts. The ILO was the first IGO with a definite social mandate and broad state participation, and it was soon recognized as a fulcrum by which INGOs could gain leverage over many states at once.

Following World War II, the UN emerged as the center of global governance, and INGOs clustered around the new global institutions to have a say in their direction and priorities. A strong foundation was laid with the establishment in 1948 of the Conference of Non-Governmental Organizations in Consultative Relationships with the United Nations (CONGO), which remains the primary association of INGOs working directly with the UN. The most striking example of INGO engagement with IGOs is ECOSOC, which lists more than 2,000 nongovernmental organizations in consultative status with the organization (United Nations Economic and Social Council 2002).

One little-known feature of the INGO-IGO relationship is the fact that many IGOs originated as the result of INGO activity. For example, UNESCO's roots lie in the International Congress on Intellectual Activities held in 1921, which was convened by the UIA and produced the International Bureau of Education. This body, in turn, stimulated the League of Nations to establish the International Institute of Intellectual Cooperation, which the UN co-opted as UNESCO in 1948. Other prominent IGOs with INGO origins include the International Meteorological Organization, the International Labour Organization, and the World Tourism Organization, among others. Even the contours of the United Nations itself were shaped by INGOs, many of which were represented at the founding conference for the UN and lobbied hard to give the UN a broad social and economic mandate. The most striking recent example of this process was the formation of the International Criminal Court, which was conceived and designed largely by INGOs. The strong global campaign mounted by INGOs since the mid-1990s has been crucial to the creation of the court, the treaty for which entered into force in July 2002 (Coalition for the International Criminal Court 2005).

INGO relationships with states and IGOs are both cooperative and conflictual (Willetts 1996). On the one hand, many INGOs work as partners with IGOs on major global issues (Spiro 1995; Weiss and Gordenker 1996), jointly constituting governance "regimes" that are broadly recognized as the core global structures managing particular domains (Young 1997; Hasenclever, Mayer, and Rittberger 1997; Frank et al. 1997; Nadelmann 1990). Notable examples include the many health and medical INGOs collaborating with UNAIDS to deal with the AIDS epidemic; food, medical, and scientific INGOs working with the Codex Alimentarius Commission of the Food and Agriculture Organization on matters of food hygiene, labeling, and inspection; the International Hotel and Restaurant Association, which works with the World Tourism Organization to reduce child sexual exploitation and with the UN Environment Programme to promote "sustainable tourism"; the International Telecommunication Union, which brings together industry INGOs and states to manage the electromagnetic spectrum, satellite orbits, and telecommunications standardization; and the International Chamber of Commerce, whose codes and rules regulate much of global commerce and often are enforceable in national courts.

On the other hand, many INGOs constantly confront states and IGOs to challenge the rules of global governance, international relations, and the political economy of global capitalism (Florini 2000; Fox and Brown 1998; Mathews 1997; Waterman 1998). A variety of examples here include the Campaign to Ban Landmines, directed at the conduct of war; the campaign against the OECD's Multilateral Agreement on Investment, directed at foreign investment policies; the loosely coordinated efforts to put labor and working conditions, environmental issues, and inequality concerns on the World Trade Organization's agenda (most spectacularly evident at the "battle of Seattle" in 1999); the campaign in opposition to the Three Gorges Dam project on the Yangtze River in China, which convinced the World Bank and the Export-Import Bank of the United States not to help with the dam's financing; and ongoing pressure by environmental INGOs to persuade the International Whaling Commission to ban certain forms of whaling and strictly limit others.

INGOs not only advocate and lobby, they also monitor the actions of IGOs and states. Examples: Earth Summit Watch monitors implementation of the 1992 Rio de Janeiro accords on the environment; Amnesty International watches for human rights violations by states (and other actors, such as rebel forces); WEDO (Women's Environment and Development Organization) tracks the implementation of UN agreements on the environment and women's issues; Social Watch monitors states' efforts to reduce poverty and gender inequality; and the Third World Network's South-North Development Monitor scrutinizes the progress and consequences of development projects organized by states, IGOs, and international development NGOs.

A great deal of INGO criticism and vitriol in recent years has centered on the "big three" global governance IGOs—the International Monetary Fund, the World Trade Organization, and the World Bank (O'Brien, Goetz, and Scholte 2000; Scholte and Schnabel 2002; Edwards and Gaventa 2001)—and on the states, above all the United States, that are most influential within them. Heavy concentration on these organizations has the unintended consequence, however, of leaving most IGOs free to carry on with their global governance activities largely unnoticed. The same observation applies to most global business and industry INGOs, which usually are strong supporters of the World Trade Organization and the International Monetary Fund; only in rare instances are they targeted by environmental, social justice, labor, or other social movement INGOs.

Relationships with Transnational Corporations

Relations between INGOs and global corporations are mostly hostile (except, of course, for business and industry INGOs), the more so as TNCs' global influence appears to have increased in recent decades (Higgott, Underhill, and Bieler 2000). TNCs are often vilified as the sources of many global ills, ranging from inequality and exploitation to environmental degradation, anti-union policies, support of authoritarian regimes, and much else (Korten 2001; Starr 2000). INGOs began targeting TNCs in the 1970s, the first prominent example being the campaign against the Swiss food giant, Nestlē, for its promotion of infant formula in Africa. Following the Bhopal gas poisoning disaster that killed nearly 4,000 people in India in 1984, the global chemical industry came under the gun; the Exxon *Valdez* oil spill in Alaska in 1989 similarly prompted INGO mobilization against the oil industry. Since the 1980s, INGO efforts to demand "socially responsible" behavior by TNCs have multiplied in many directions—drives against Nike and other footwear makers for poor working conditions and low wages in subcontractor factories; against the Gap clothing retailer and similar companies for exploitation in Asian and Latin American manufacturing facilities; against Unocal and Total for a pipeline project in Burma that would prop up the repressive military state; against Freeport McMoRan's huge mining operations in Irian Jaya for the displacement of indigenous peoples and pollution of the land and water with heavy-metal residues. Hundreds of companies have faced the ire of social movement INGOs. U.S.-based companies are especially likely targets, and many European TNCs have come under the gun; on the other hand, most TNCs have largely been ignored. Company responses range from silence to rhetorical defense of their actions to formal measures to "clean up their act," meeting the critics at least halfway so that criticism will be defused and company legitimacy can be restored.

Behavioral and Moral Codes and Their Enforcement

Not content to engage in piecemeal efforts that require inordinate resources to obtain even partial compliance from particular TNCs, a number of INGOs, sometimes in cooperation with the relevant companies and their industry IGOs, have developed codes of conduct or sets of corporate ethics intended to guide companies toward socially responsible behavior. Initial but unsuccessful attempts in this direction came from the UN Center on Transnational Corporations, part of a movement in the 1970s to produce a "new world economic order" that would ameliorate the inequalities produced by global capitalism. The first ethical code to have a substantial impact was the Sullivan Principles, originally presented in 1977 and directed at corporations doing business in South Africa; it was followed by the MacBride Principles of 1984, which targeted corporate activities in Northern Ireland. More recently, comprehensive global business codes of conduct have crystallized. The best known are the CERES Principles, a ten-point code developed by the Coalition for Environmentally Responsible Economies as an elaboration of its Valdez Principles (sparked by the oil tanker disaster). Another code of increasing importance is the Social Accountability 8000 (SA 8000) Standards, developed in 1997 by the Council on Economic Priorities Accreditation Agency (now called Social Accountability International, which accredits firms by conducting audits of manufacturers to evaluate their compliance with SA 8000 standards). The most highly formalized operation in this arena is that of ISO, the International Organization for Standardization, whose ISO 14000 standards for environmental management require companies seeking certification to undergo an extensive process of evaluation and organizational review.

A number of global companies have endorsed such principles generated by "outsider" INGOs, but business INGOs often generate their own voluntary codes of behavior (Cutler, Haufler, and Porter 1999), such as the Caux Round Table Principles for Business (1994) and the International Chamber of Commerce's Business Charter for Sustainable Development: Principles for Environmental Management (1991). Meanwhile, UN Secretary-General Kofi Annan has been promoting his Global Compact for several years, and in 1999 he and Leon Sullivan presented the Global Sullivan Principles of Corporate Social Responsibility as official UN policy.

Professional INGOs habitually prescribe codes of ethics for their members. The International Federation of Accountants has its Code of Ethics for Professional Accountants, dating from 1996; the International Association for Bridge and Structural Engineering its Declaration for Sustainable Development (1996); the World Medical Association its International Code of Medical Ethics (1949, revised repeatedly since); the International Society for Professional Hypnosis its Code of Ethics and Standards (1978). These are voluntary codes but, for professions involving licensing or certification by states, national or local versions of these codes have strong practical implications, since violations can lead to sanctions and even exclusion from the profession.

Voluntary principles and codes hardly guarantee compliance, and many critics argue that companies endorse codes solely to gain legitimacy. As with IGOs and states, INGO watchdog organizations engage in extensive monitoring to make sure that deeds match words. They send investigative teams to production sites, quiz company officials, and sometimes become directly involved in company-funded compliance monitoring. Some notable examples include Corporate Watch (which monitors and critiques general TNC activity), Nike Watch (subcontractor labor practices and working conditions), the Medical Lobby for Appropriate Marketing (advertising by pharmaceutical companies), Privacy International (surveillance by corporations and states), and the CEE Bankwatch Network (actions of international financial institutions).

Moral Exemplars

Some companies have emerged as exemplars of socially responsible corporate behavior and policies. The Body Shop, manufacturer of skin and hair products, loudly opposes animal testing and calls for defending human rights, protecting the planet, and supporting community trade. Levi Strauss, the jeans maker, proclaims that its operations are built on four "core values": empathy, originality, integrity, and courage. In 1991 it became "the first worldwide company to establish a comprehensive ethical code of conduct for manufacturing and finishing contractors." Other exemplars include Max Havelaar (for fair-trade practices), Ben & Jerry's (general social responsibility), and Patagonia (environmental preservation).

INGOs have developed an extensive array of awards to recognize moral exemplars. The most prominent are the Right Livelihood Awards (the "Alternative Nobel Prizes"), from the foundation of the same name, which go to community activists, peace promoters, champions of the environment, and so on. Other examples, among many others, are the Anti-Slavery Medal of Anti-Slavery International (first awarded in 1991) and the World Food Prize, given by a foundation established by agricultural scientist Norman Borlaug to recognize "achievements of individuals who have advanced human development by improving the quality, quantity or availability of food in the world" (World Food Prize Foundation 2005).

INGOs also recognize exemplars of less explicitly moral character, offering an enormous variety of awards for excellence in specific fields or activities. Awards for technical excellence or artistic virtuosity cover virtually the entire spectrum of human endeavor, ranging from the Hans Christian Andersen Awards (from the International Board on Books for Young People, first awarded in 1956) and the International Trombone Association Award (1972) to the Skerman Award for Microbial Taxonomy (from the World Federation for Culture Collections, an association of microbiologists, 1996) and the Bank Insurance Industry Award (from the Financial Institutions Insurance Association, 1998). Thousands of world prizes and awards are now given each year, conferring considerable global status on their winners.

CRITICAL ASSESSMENTS OF INGOS

INGOs are generally considered the "good guys" of world society. They promote respect for human rights, protection of the natural world, relief in times of natural or human disaster, aid to the world's poor and hungry, and other widely lauded goals. They have been called the "conscience of the world" (Willetts 1996), and they are even seen as helping to ease tensions among civilizations (Boulding 1991). Since the mid-1990s, however, as INGOs have become more widely recognized as important players in world issues and as various campaigns directed at specific TNCs and major IGOs drew worldwide attention, a backlash has occurred. Challenges to INGO legitimacy and moral authority have arisen above all from ideological defenders of global capitalism, particularly those associated with major publications such as the *Financial Times, Economist, Forbes,* and the *Wall Street Journal* (George 2001; the most vigorous responses to these attackers tend to come from *Le monde diplomatique*). States, IGOs, and corporations are on the attack as well, resenting the pesky intrusion of INGOs into their normally shielded activities, while other forms of criticism have emerged among the very people whom INGOs intend to help.

Defenders of capitalism, TNCs, and the big global governance IGOs question the representativeness, transparency, and accountability of INGOs (Rieff 1999; Edwards 2000a, 2000b; Bond 2000; Islam 2001). They ask, for example, what constituencies have given the Coalition to Abolish the Fur Trade the right to demand an end to fur trading, why Greenpeace restricts its decision making to a small group of professional activists, and to whom Attac is accountable in its "irresponsible" call for a tax on all currency transactions and its demand that rich countries forgive Third World debts. Such attacks on INGO legitimacy have gained force since 1999, in the wake of numerous incidents of street violence at major IGO conferences and meetings.

At the same time, some intellectuals and activists of the less developed world, as well as critics from the developed countries, criticize INGOs on other grounds. More radical critics decry INGOs as handmaidens of capitalist elites or powerful states, while more moderate analysts worry about Western biases, universalizing tendencies, insufficient concern for local circumstances, and the like (Hulme and Edwards 1997; *Current Issues in Comparative Education* 1998). The most radical critics reject even such widely praised bodies as human rights INGOs, because they see universalistic human rights ideology as violent colonization that undermines authentic local cultures (Esteva and Prakash 1998). The most common themes, though, are the familiar arguments that have been directed against the West for decades: cultural imperialism, ideological domination, promotion of dependency relations, and so on. The most common targets are development INGOs, which are seen as purveyors of Western models of development, American values, or Eurocentric notions of development and civilization. Development INGOs are blamed for projects that are poorly grounded in local situations and circumstances, directed by outsiders, unpredictable in their long-term consequences, and advantageous to the already well-off.

Highly sensitive to these various lines of criticism, many INGOs have undergone intense periods of self-critical soul-searching and tried to adapt appropriately, emphasizing local participation and local priorities while trying to develop better knowledge of local cultures and sociopolitical conditions. One institutional response has been the idea of a "humanitarian ombudsman," which is being considered by a collection of development and relief INGOs (CARE, CARITAS, the Danish Refugee Council, Red Cross/Red Crescent, Oxfam, and World Vision) as a mechanism to monitor humanitarian relief efforts and give those affected a means of being heard when relief organizations are not listening.

CONCLUSION: INGOS AND GLOBAL CHANGE

Given the explosive growth of INGOs and their vigorous efforts to influence other major global actors, a question that constantly arises is, How much do they matter? Do they change the behavior of states, IGOs, and TNCs? Are they truly helping to slow global warming, improve agriculture in poor countries, empower women, end corruption, slow the spread of HIV, and so on?

That INGOs do matter, sometimes a great deal, is clear from numerous studies of particular issues and organizations, many of which have been cited above. Yet systematic evidence of INGO effectiveness is lacking; most of the evidence is based on case studies and compilations of anecdotes. Evaluation research in the development sector, the most thoroughly studied INGO sector of all, is inconclusive:

though development INGOs have become more important as project managers and conduits for official development assistance, they are not clearly succeeding in helping the less developed countries economically or socially (Riddell et al. 1997).

As stated, however, the question of INGO effectiveness is misleading. In many global sectors, the relevant INGOs are effective by definition because there are no other significant actors involved. In other sectors, such as the global standardization sector (Loya and Boli 1999), INGOs dominate and other actors are either incorporated into INGO structures or kept at the margins. In still other sectors, INGOs work intimately with other global actors, and the effectiveness of any single set of actors is impossible to disentangle. Thus it is fair to say that INGO effectiveness is vastly underappreciated and unrecognized, in large part because so many INGO sectors remain mostly unstudied.

On a more theoretical level, it is useful to consider effectiveness in terms of INGOs' role in structuring and propagating world culture (Boli and Thomas 1997). Far more numerous than IGOs, far more focused on global issues, practices, and policies than either states or TNCs, INGOs today constitute the organizational backbone of world culture. They make operational rules for global activities, as when the International Chamber of Commerce sets requirements for a proper bill of lading in international trade (Berman 1988). They define global conceptual schemes, as when the International Astronomical Union formally distinguishes between a planet and a cold dwarf star. They help generate and propagate bodies of universalistic knowledge, as when the International Radiation Protection Association publishes proceedings containing papers by leading researchers in the field. INGOs also express, debate, and shape moral and normative principles (Nadelmann 1990) that are deemed applicable throughout the world (albeit not without controversy), such as the principle that endangered animal species are to be vigorously protected, or that women have the right to control their own bodies, or that TNCs have social obligations that reach well beyond their concerns for profit and efficiency. These general rules, definitions, bodies of knowledge, and moral standards form the world-cultural context in which states, TNCs, individuals, and INGOs themselves are embedded; they thereby shape the identities, goals, operations, and values of these and other actors (Meyer, Boli, et al. 1997).

These manifold processes, involving a highly differentiated INGO population that helps generate and constantly reconstitute the highly differentiated and incoherent world-cultural canopy, are a major source of social change in world society. In a world without INGOs, it is extremely unlikely that so many states would have undertaken many of the new responsibilities they have assumed in recent decades (regarding the role and status of women, safety standards, the rights of homosexuals, pollution control, support for scientific research, and much more). Without INGOs, it is highly doubtful that TNCs would have put so many resources into environmental programs, made equal-opportunity hiring a standard feature of their employment practices, or jumped on the bandwagon of every new organizational management technique that comes along (Management by Walking Around, Total Quality Management, Business Process Reengineering, and so on). Without INGOs, the world economy would be much less integrated and stable, technology would be much less standardized, conceptions of psychological and social problems would be much more varied, and human rights would be violated far more often. By the same token, many forms of disagreement and discord would also be much less evident, for INGOs are especially apt to spring into being around axes of contention and contest in world culture.

Perhaps the best way to sum up the effectiveness of INGOs, and this review of the INGO population as a key segment of the global nonprofit sector, is to conclude that, above all, INGOs make the world far more global than it would otherwise be. As an essential driving force in globalization, INGOs push all the other actors in world society—states, IGOs, TNCs, individuals, and various collectivities—toward greater involvement in and awareness of the global dimensions of everyday life. Such has been the case since their formative period in the nineteenth century, and it is likely to be the case throughout the twenty-first century as well.

NOTES

1. Figures of 40,000 to 50,000 organizations frequently are mentioned in academic and popular publications, but these appear to derive from a careless reading of the *YIO* statistical tables. The 2000 *YIO* (p. 549) lists 50,373 organizations as the "TOTAL ALL TYPES," but this figure should be diminished by the 17,508 "currently inactive nonconventional bodies," 4,023 "dissolved or apparently inactive organizations," 3,370 "national organizations," 2,028 "multilateral treaties and intergovernmental agreements," and a few other categories.

2. The UIA worked closely with the Institut international de la paix of Monaco, which published the *Annuaire de la vie internationale* in 1905, 1906, and 1907. The UIA joined in the effort for the 1908–1909 edition and eventually recast it as the *Yearbook of International Organizations.* See the UIA's Web site (http://www.uia.org/uiaprof/history.php) for further information.

3. The data on foundings are based on the 1984–85 and 1988–89 *YIO,* which were manually coded and analyzed by Boli and Thomas (1999), whose database is the source of many of the figures in this section.

4. Only INGOs in the UIA categories (A)–(D) are included in the language figures provided here, to be consistent with most of the other data in the chapter. The patterns for all organizations in the *YIO* are quite similar to those for this more restricted set of INGOs.

5. Only organizations founded by 1988 are included, drawing again on the database generated by Boli and Thomas (1999).

REFERENCES

Anheier, Helmut, Marlies Glasius, and Mary Kaldor, eds. 2001. *Global Civil Society 2001.* Oxford: Oxford University Press.

Ashoka. 2002. "Ashoka's Mission." http://www.ashoka.org/what_is/mission.cfm.

Berkovitch, Nitza. 1999. *From Motherhood to Citizenship: Women's Rights and International Organizations.* Baltimore: Johns Hopkins University Press.

Berman, Harold J. 1988. "The Law of International Commercial Transactions." *Emory Journal of International Dispute Resolution* 2:235–310.

Boli, John. 1997. "Rights and Rules: Constituting World Citizens." Chap. 14 in *Public Rights, Public Rules: Constituting Citizens in the World Polity and National Policy,* edited by Connie L. McNeely. New York: Garland.

———. 1999. "World Authority Structures and Legitimations." Pp. 249–66 in *Constructing World Culture: International Nongovernmental Organizations since 1875,* edited by John Boli and George M. Thomas. Stanford, Calif.: Stanford University Press.

Boli, John, Thomas A. Loya, and Teresa Loftin. 1999. "National Participation in World-Polity Organization." Pp. 50–77 in *Constructing World Culture: International Nongovernmental Organizations since 1875,* edited by John Boli and George M. Thomas. Stanford, Calif.: Stanford University Press.

Boli, John, and George M. Thomas. 1997. "World Culture in the World Polity: A Century of International Non-Governmental Organization." *American Sociological Review* 62:171–90.

———, eds. 1999. *Constructing World Culture: International Nongovernmental Organizations since 1875.* Stanford, Calif.: Stanford University Press.

Bond, Michael. 2000. "The Backlash against NGOs." *Prospect Magazine.* Available online at http://www.globalpolicy.org/ngos/backlash.htm.

Boulding, Elise. 1990. "Building a Global Civic Culture." *Development* 2:37–40.

———. 1991. "The Old and New Transnationalism: An Evolutionary Perspective." *Human Relations* 44:789–805.

Castermans, Alex Geert, Lydia Schut, Frank Steketee, and Luc Verhey, eds. 1991. *The Role of Non-Governmental Organizations in the Promotion and Protection of Human Rights.* Leiden: Stichtung NJCM-Boekerij.

Charnovitz, Steve. 1997. "Two Centuries of Participation: NGOs and International Governance." *Michigan Journal of International Law* 18:183–286.

Civicus World Alliance for Citizen Participation. 2005. "About CIVICUS." http://www.civicus.org/new/about_civicus.asp?c=00265D%20default.asp.

Clark, Ann Marie. 1995. "Non-Governmental Organizations and Their Influence on International Society." *Journal of International Affairs* 48:507–25.

Coalition for the International Criminal Court. 2005. "Building the Court." http://www.iccnow.org/buildingthecourt.html.

Cowhey, Peter F. 1990. "The International Telecommunications Regime: The Political Roots of Regimes for High Technology." *International Organization* 44:169–99.

Current Issues in Comparative Education. 1998. Special issue, "Are NGOs Overrated?" Vol. 1, no. 1, 15 November.

Cutler, A. Claire, Virginia Haufler, and Tony Porter, eds. 1999. *Private Authority in International Affairs.* Albany: State University of New York Press.

Diehl, Paul F., ed. 1996. *The Politics of Global Governance: International Organizations in an Interdependent World.* Boulder, Colo.: Lynne Rienner.

Edwards, Michael. 2000a. "Time to Put the NGO House in Order." *Financial Times,* 6 June.

———. 2000b. *NGO Rights and Responsibilities: A New Deal for Global Governance.* London: Foreign Policy Centre.

Edwards, Michael, and John Gaventa, eds. 2001. *Global Citizen Action: Perspectives and Challenges.* Boulder: Lynne Rienner.

Esteva, Gustavo, and Madhu Suri Prakash. 1998. *Grassroots Post-Modernism: Remaking the Soil of Cultures.* London: Zed Books.

Falk, Richard. 1993. "The Infancy of Global Civil Society." Pp. 219–34 in *Beyond the Cold War: New Dimensions in International Relations,* edited by Geir Lundestad and Odd Arne Westad. Oslo: Scandinavian University Press.

———. 1994. "The Making of Global Citizenship." Pp. 127–40 in *The Condition of Citizenship,* edited by Bart van Steenbergen. London: Sage Publications.

Feld, W. 1971. "Non-Governmental Entities and the International System: A Preliminary Quantitative Overview." *Orbis* 15:879–922.

Finnemore, Martha. 1999. "Rules of War and Wars of Rules: The International Red Cross and the Restraint of State Violence." Pp. 149–65 in *Constructing World Culture: International Nongovernmental Organizations since 1875,* edited by John Boli and George M. Thomas. Stanford, Calif.: Stanford University Press.

Florini, Ann M., ed. 2000. *The Third Force: The Rise of Transnational Civil Society.* Tokyo: Japan Center for International Exchange; Washington, D.C.: Carnegie Endowment for International Peace.

Fox, Jonathan A., and L. David. Brown, eds. 1998. *The Struggle for Accountability: The World Bank, NGOs, and Grassroots Movements.* Cambridge, Mass.: MIT Press.

Frank, David John, Ann Hironaka, and Evan Schofer. 2000. "The Nation-State and the Natural Environment over the Twentieth Century." *American Sociological Review* 65:96–116.

Frank, David John, John W. Meyer, Evan Schofer, Nancy Tuma, and Ann Hironaka. 1997. "The Structuring of a World Environmental Regime, 1870–1990." *International Organization* 51:623–51.

George, Susan. 2001. "Democracy at the Barricades." *Le monde diplomatique,* August.

Guidry, John A., Michael D. Kennedy, and Mayer N. Zald, eds. 2001. *Globalizations and Social Movements: Culture, Power, and the Transnational Public Sphere.* Ann Arbor: University of Michigan Press.

Haas, Peter M. 1992. "Introduction: Epistemic Communities and International Policy Coordination." *International Organization* 46:1–35.

Hasenclever, Andreas, Peter Mayer, and Volker Rittberger. 1997. *Theories of International Regimes.* Cambridge: Cambridge University Press.

Haufler, Virginia. 2000. "Private Sector International Regimes." Chap. 7 in *Non-State Actors and Authority in the Global System,* edited by Richard A. Higgott, Geoffrey R. D. Underhill, and Andreas Bieler. London: Routledge.

Higgott, Richard A., Geoffrey R D. Underhill, and Andreas Bieler, eds. 2000. *Non-State Actors and Authority in the Global System.* London: Routledge.

Hulme, David, and Michael Edwards. 1997. *NGOs, States and Donors: Too Close for Comfort?* Houndmills, U.K.: Macmillan.

International Association of Paper Historians. 2002. "International Standard for the Registration of Papers with or without Watermarks." Marburg/Lahn, Germany: IAPH. Available online at http://www.paperhistory.org/standard.htm.

Islam, Shada. 2001. "E.U. Ministers Warn Protestors: 'We Are Democratically Elected.'" *Deutsche Presse-Agentur,* 16 July.

Jepperson, Ronald L. 2002. "Political Modernities: Disentangling Two Underlying Dimensions of Institutional Differentiation." *Sociological Theory* 20:61–85.

Judge, Anthony. 2000. "Types of International Organization." Brussels: Union of International Associations. Available online at http://www.uia.org/organizations/orgtypes/orgtypea.php.

Kaldor, Mary. 1999. "The Ideas of 1989: The Origins of the Concept of Global Civil Society." *Transnational Law and Contemporary Problems* 9:475–88.

Keane, John. 2001. "Global Civil Society?" Chap. 2 in *Global Civil Society 2001,* edited by Helmut Anheier, Marlies Glasius, and Mary Kaldor. Oxford: Oxford University Press.

Keck, Margaret E., and Kathryn Sikkink. 1998. *Activists beyond Borders: Advocacy Networks in International Politics.* Ithaca, N.Y.: Cornell University Press.

Korten, David C. 2001. *When Corporations Rule the World.* 2nd ed. Bloomfield, Conn.: Kumarian Press.

Krasner, Stephen D. 1991. "Global Communications and National Power: Life on the Pareto Frontier." *World Politics* 43:336–66.

Lipschutz, Ronnie D. 1992. "Reconstructing World Politics: The Emergence of Global Civil Society." *Millennium: Journal of International Studies* 21:389–420.

Lipschutz, Ronnie D., with Judith Mayer. 1996. *Global Civil Society and Global Environmental Governance: The Politics of Nature from Place to Planet.* Albany: State University of New York Press.

Loya, Thomas A., and John Boli. 1999. "Standardization in the World Polity: Technical Rationalization over Power." Pp. 169–97 in *Constructing World Culture: International Nongovernmental Organizations since 1875,* edited by John Boli and George M. Thomas. Stanford, Calif.: Stanford University Press.

Mathews, Jessica T. 1997. "Power Shift." *Foreign Affairs* 76:50–66.

Meyer, John W., John Boli, George M. Thomas, and Francisco O. Ramirez. 1997. "World Society and the Nation-State." *American Journal of Sociology* 103:144–81.

Meyer, John W., David Frank, Ann Hironaka, Evan Schofer, and Nancy B. Tuma. 1997. "The Rise of an Environmental Sector in World Society." *International Organization* 51:623–51.

Nadelmann, Ethan A. 1990. "Global Prohibition Regimes: The Evolution of Norms in International Society." *International Organization* 44:479–526.

Naughton, John. 2001. "Contested Space: The Internet and Global Civil Society." Chap. 6 in *Global Civil Society 2001,* edited by Helmut Anheier, Marlies Glasius, and Mary Kaldor. Oxford: Oxford University Press.

O'Brien, Robert, Anne Marie Goetz, and Jan Aart Scholte. 2000. *Contesting Global Governance: Multilateral Economic Institutions and Global Social Movements.* Cambridge: Cambridge University Press.

Otto, Dianne. 1996. "Nongovernmental Organizations in the United Nations System: The Emerging Role of International Civil Society." *Human Rights Quarterly* 18:107–41.

Pasha, Mustapha Kamal, and David Blaney. 1998. "Elusive Paradise: The Promise and Peril of Global Civil Society." *Alternatives* 23:417–50.

Pianta, Mario. 2001. "Parallel Summits of Global Civil Society." Chap. 7 in *Global Civil Society 2001,* edited by Helmut Anheier, Marlies Glasius, and Mary Kaldor. Oxford: Oxford University Press.

Porter, Tony. 2002. *Technology, Governance and Political Conflict in International Industries.* London: Routledge.

Riddell, Roger C., Stein-Erik Kruse, Timo Kyllönen, Satu Ojanperä, and Jean-Louis Vielajus. 1997. *Searching for Impact and Methods: NGO Evaluation Synthesis Study. A Report Produced for the OECD/DAC Expert Group on Evaluation.* Helsinki: Department for International Development Cooperation, Finland Ministry of Foreign Affairs.

Rieff, David. 1999. "The False Dawn of Civil Society." *Nation* 268 (7 February): 11–16.

Rosenau, James N. 1997. *Along the Domestic-Foreign Frontier: Exploring Governance in a Turbulent World.* New York: Cambridge University Press.

Salamon, Lester M., Regina List, S. Wojciech Sokolowski and Associates, Stefan Toepler, and Helmut K. Anheier, eds. 1999. *Global Civil Society: Dimensions of the Nonprofit Sector.* Baltimore: Center for Civil Society Studies, Johns Hopkins University.

Schofer, Evan. 1999. "Science Associations in the International Sphere, 1875–1990: The Rationalization of Science and the Scientization of Society." Pp. 249–66 in *Constructing World Culture: International Nongovernmental Organizations since 1875,* edited by John Boli and George M. Thomas. Stanford, Calif.: Stanford University Press.

Scholte, Jan Aart, and Albrecht Schnabel, eds. 2002. *Civil Society and Global Finance.* London: Routledge.

Smith, Jackie, Charles Chatfield, and Ron Pagnucco, eds. 1997.

Transnational Social Movements and World Politics: Solidarity beyond the State. Syracuse, N.Y.: Syracuse University Press.

Smith, Jackie, Ron Pagnucco, and Winnie Romeril. 1994. "Transnational Social Movement Organisations in the Global Political Arena." *Voluntas* 5:121–54.

Sochor, Eugene. 1991. *The Politics of International Aviation.* London: Macmillan.

Speeckaert, Georges Patrick. 1957. "The 1,978 International Organizations Founded since the Congress of Vienna." *Documents for the Study of International Nongovernment Relations,* no. 7. Brussels: Union of International Associations.

Spiro, Peter J. 1995. "New Global Communities: Nongovernmental Organizations in International Decision-Making." *Washington Quarterly* 18:45–56.

Starr, Amory. 2000. *Naming the Enemy: Anti-Corporate Movements Confront Globalization.* London: Zed Books.

Tarrow, Sidney. 2000. "La contestation transnationale." *Cultures et Conflits* 38–39:187–223.

Union of International Associations. 1961–2000. *Yearbook of International Organizations,* vols. 8–37. Munich: K. G. Saur.

United Nations Department of Public Information. 2004. "NGOs and the Department of Public Information: Some Questions and Answers." Available online at http://www.un.org/dpi/ngosection/brochure.htm.

United Nations Economic and Social Council. 2002. "NGOs in Consultative Status with ECOSOC." Paris: UNESCO. Available online at http://www.un.org/esa/coordination/ngo/.

Van Steenbergen, Bart. 1994. "Towards a Global Ecological Citizen." Pp. 141–52 in *The Condition of Citizenship,* edited by Bart van Steenbergen. London: Sage Publications.

Wapner, Paul. 1996. *Environmental Activism and World Civic Politics.* Albany: State University of New York Press.

Waterman, Peter. 1998. *Globalisation, Social Movements and the New Internationalisms.* London: Cassell/Mansell.

Weiss, Thomas G., and Leon Gordenker, eds. 1996. *NGOs, the UN, and Global Governance.* Boulder, Colo.: Lynne Rienner.

Willetts, Peter, ed. 1996. *"The Conscience of the World": The Influence of Non-Governmental Organizations in the UN System.* Washington, D.C.: Brookings Institution Press.

World Food Prize Foundation. 2005. "The World Food Prize." Available online at http://www.worldfoodprize.org/.

Wuthnow, Robert, ed. 1991. *Between States and Markets: The Voluntary Sector in Comparative Perspective.* Princeton, N.J.: Princeton University Press.

Young, Oran, ed. 1997. *Global Governance.* Cambridge, Mass.: MIT Press.

APPENDIX: CHARACTERISTICS OF SELECTED MAJOR INGOS

	Headquarters location	Founded	Members	Countries	Staff	Budget	IGO/INGO ties	Major publication
Business and industry								
International Chamber of Commerce	Paris	1919	89 national committees, individuals	118	130	18 million Euros	7 IGOs, many INGOs	*Documentary Credits* *Insight*
International Hotel and Restaurant Association	Paris	1946	Companies, national associations	155	11	—	7 IGOs, 6 INGOs	*Hotels*
International Air Transport Association	Montreal	1945	220 airline companies	132	1,500	—	9 IGOs, 5 INGOs	*Airlines International*
Development and relief								
CARE	Brussels	1945	12 international and 67 country offices	67	13,000	>$1 billion	7 IGOs, 3 INGOs	*CARE Overseas* *Association Newsletter*
Caritas	Vatican	1950	162 national organizations	151	23[a]	—	11 IGOs, 18 INGOs	*Emergency Calling*
African Women's Development and Communication Network (FEMNET)	Nairobi	1988	Local and national NGOs	48	—	$400,000	2 IGOs, 4 INGOs	*FEMNET News*
World Vision	Monrovia, Calif.	1950	78 national offices	78	4,700	$1.25 billion	7 IGOs, 33 INGOs	*Together Magazine*
Education								
International Association of Universities	Paris	1950	670 institutions of higher education	126	19	1.1 million Euros	10 IGOs, 4+ INGOs	*Higher Education Policy*
International Union of Students	Prague	1946	National student organizations	113	—	—	3 IGOs, 24 INGOs	*World Student News*
Science								
International Council for Science	Paris	1919	103 national scientific bodies, 27 international scientific unions	103	13	5.1 million Euros	14+ IGOs, 1 INGO	*Science International Newsletter*
International Social Science Council	Paris	1952	14 social science associations, 21 science councils	21	2	$400,000	5 IGOs, 1 INGO	*ISSC Newsletter*
Human, women's rights								
Amnesty International	London	1961	Groups and individuals	167	410[a]	£24 million	8 IGOs, 11 INGOs	*Amnesty International Report*
International Council of Women	Singapore	1888	National councils	63	—	—	18 IGOs, 22 INGOs	*ICW Newsletter*

APPENDIX: CHARACTERISTICS OF SELECTED MAJOR INGOS (CONTINUED)

	Headquarters location	Founded	Members	Countries	Staff	Budget	IGO/INGO ties	Major publication
Environment								
Greenpeace International	Amsterdam	1971	38 country offices	38	1,300	163 million Euros	20 IGOs, 11 INGOs	Topical reports
Worldwide Fund for Nature	Gland, Switzerland	1961	49 country offices	>100	4,000	$380 million	—	*Living Planet Report*
EarthAction Network	Amherst, Mass.	1992	1,966 INGOs, NGOs	162	5	—	5 IGOs, 2 INGOs	*Parliamentary Alert*
Labor								
International Confederation of Free Trade Unions	Brussels	1949	231 organizations (= 158 million people)	150	70	ca. $15 million	15 IGOs, 10 INGOs	*Trade Union World*
World Federation of Trade Unions	Prague	1945	Organizations (= 120 million people)	126	38	—	8 IGOs, 3 INGOs	
Medicine and health								
World Medical Association	Ferney–Voltaire, FR	1947	National associations	78	7	—	6 IGOs, 31 INGOs	*World Medical Journal*
World Federation for Mental Health	Alexandria, Va.	1948	136 organizations, 1,300 individuals	91	4	$520,000	5 IGOs, 9 INGOs	*Mental Health Observer*
International Planned Parenthood Foundation	London	1952	National associations	139	223	$73 million	12 IGOs, 37 INGOs	*IPPF Medical Bulletin*
Professions								
International Pharmaceutical Federation	The Hague	1912	National organizations = 500,000 pharmacists	85	8	—	9 IGOs, 9 INGOs	*International Pharmacy Journal*
International Union of Architects	Paris	1948	National, regional sections = 1 million architects	95	7	$500,000	8 IGOs, 3 INGOs	*IUA Newsletter*
Recreation and hobbies								
World Crafts Council	Ioannina, Greece	1964	National, international, regional organizations	81	1	$100,000	9 IGOs, 2 INGOs	*WCC Newsletter*
World Chess Federation	Lausanne	1924	National organizations	162	3	980,000 SwFr	14 INGOs	*Rating List*
Religion								
World Council of Churches	Geneva	1948	344 churches (denominations)	113	215	47 million SwFr	3 IGOs, many INGOs	*Ecumenical News International*
International Association for Religious Freedom	Oxford, U.K.	1900	Groups and individuals	32	—	£572,000	4 IGOs, 4 INGOs	*IARF World*

Sports								
International Olympic Committee	Lausanne	1894	199 national Olympic committees	199	197	51 million SwFr	10 IGOs, 115 INGOs	*Olympic Review*
International Association of Athletics Federations	Monaco	1912	209 national associations	209	55	—	1 IGO, 19 INGOs	*IAAF Magazine*
Technology and standardization								
ISO (International Organization for Standardization)	Geneva	1947	National standards bodies	97	163	27.4 million SwFr	ca. 75 IGOs, 2 INGOs	*ISO Bulletin*
Institute of Electrical and Electronics Engineers	Piscataway, N.J.	1884	335,000 engineers	152	—	$247 million	5 INGOs	*IEEE Technical Activities Guide*
World peace and world law								
International Law Association	London	1873	Regional branches	52	1	—	7 IGOs, 2 INGOs	*ILA Newsletter*
Women's International League for Peace and Freedom	Geneva	1915	Individuals in national sections, groups	50	2	—	9 IGOs, 16 INGOs	*International Peace Update*
Children and youth								
International Save the Children Alliance	London	1979	National NGOs	29	22[a]	$570 million[a]	12 IGOs, 15 INGOs	*Annual Report*
World Organization of the Scout Movement	Geneva	1920	National scouting organizations = 128 million members	151	32[a]	3.5 million SwFr[a]	9 IGOs, 11 INGOs	*World Scouting News*

Sources: Union of International Associations, *Yearbook of International Organizations, 2004–2005* (Brussels: UIA); Individual INGO Web sites.
Note: SwFr = Swiss francs.
[a]Budget and staff figures refer to central office only.

IV

KEY ACTIVITIES IN THE NONPROFIT SECTOR

15

Foundations

KENNETH PREWITT

INTRODUCTION: A PRELIMINARY DEFINITION

Foundations date to antiquity. They have flourished in some regions and been largely absent in others. They have generally been welcomed by the state, but not always and not everywhere, and at times have been prohibited. They have ranged from single-purpose institutions to those active across numerous sectors. Although "grant making"—what we now take to be a defining characteristic of most foundations—occurs early in foundation history, with medieval alms giving, the vast majority of foundations since antiquity have taken direct responsibility for their own programs rather than giving grants to other institutions. For more than two millennia, foundations have funded and managed academies, hospitals, schools, orphanages, cultural institutions, relief agencies, and many other organizations. Today we call these institutions operating foundations to distinguish them from grant-making foundations.

In this chapter passing reference will be made to historical variability in the institutional form and practices of foundations, and in how they have varied in their relations to the state and to the market. The emphasis, however, is on contemporary foundations, especially of a type now prevalent in the United States, expanding across western Europe, and, in many fewer numbers, appearing in Japan, India, and Latin America.

These are commonly called the modern grant-making foundations, which began to acquire their distinguishing traits in the United States toward the end of the nineteenth century. A key feature of the foundation is a permanent endowment, not committed to a particular institution or activity, that provides a grant-making capacity reaching across multiple purposes and into the indefinite future. A permanent endowment attached to a broad, permissive mission is a defining characteristic of present-day foundations. This configuration provides considerable latitude for changing priorities as new conditions emerge and differentiates the foundation from a long tradition of bequests for a narrow purpose or particular institution, though in this—and in any and all generalizations about foundations and philanthropy—there are exceptions. The endowment also sharply distinguishes the foundation from the much larger number of institutions in the nonprofit sector that survive through membership dues, fees for services, government contracts, or product marketing.

AN OVERVIEW

The treatment to follow proceeds under three broad questions. First is an abstract discussion attempting to situate foundations in society at large by asking, why have a nonprofit sector and, more specifically, why have foundations? What do foundations do that cannot just as easily be done by the state or the market?

Second is a more historical, descriptive section that focuses on what in American foundation history is called scientific philanthropy, especially as pioneered in the late nineteenth century. Here the key question is how philanthropy differs from charity. This section also describes the size and characteristics of the foundation sector, primarily in the United States and to a lesser extent in Europe. It merits early acknowledgment that this essay is American-centric, for several reasons. Foundations of the type described here are more prevalent, wealthy, and active in the United States than elsewhere. The historical and descriptive literature is also more developed about American foundations than about those elsewhere. Many of the more general points to be made about foundations come into sharper focus in the United States, though it is hoped that these points are relevant to practices elsewhere

The final section is titled "Thinking Theoretically about Foundations." It offers views on different ways to classify foundations, on the argument that explanation proceeds by making distinctions that then allow for comparison or analysis of historical trends and institutional variability. The section turns to what is arguably the central question for any theory of foundations—the social impact of foundations—before concluding with a discussion of accountability.

THE STATE, THE MARKET, THE NONPROFIT SECTOR, AND FOUNDATIONS

Foundations cannot be understood apart from the sector in which they thrive. We proceed on the basis of the familiar if simple schematic that distinguishes the three broad domains of human organization: the state or public sphere, the market or economic sphere, and the civil society or private sphere. The nonprofit sector is, of course, firmly planted in the third of these domains, in civil society. Nonprofits share with the market that they are structured independently of the state, and share with the state that they are largely unconstrained by the economic criteria of market transactions.

Although the nonprofit sector is both nonstate and nonmarket, it has taken on distinctive obligations that would otherwise belong either to the state or to the market. This observation, as explored below, leads inevitably to the question of why we have a nonprofit sector in the first place.

A Quasi-State Actor

The nonprofit sector is quasi-state in its obligation for the public good. It shares with the state the task of compensating for market failures: for providing goods and services that are in the public interest but are not forthcoming from the normal functioning of the market.

Though assuming responsibilities for the public good, the nonprofit sector does not advance them in the same manner as does the state. The nonprofit sector has no coercive powers. It obtains funds voluntarily rather than through mandatory taxes, and generally tries to persuade the state to allow voluntary gifts to move directly to nonprofits without passing through the tax system. The nonprofit sector cannot legislate to enforce desired behaviors. It cannot regulate the market. Thus, though taking on a central function of the state—protecting and extending the public good—the nonprofit sector carries out this mission through instrumentalities that are decidedly not statelike.

A Quasi-Market Actor

At its core then, the nonprofit sector must rely on persuasion. In this it is similar to the market. It provides services that its members or beneficiaries need or want, or believe they do. But just as nonprofits function without a key resource of the state, they function without a key resource of the market.[1]

Markets satisfy private interests. Relying on the profit motive, market actors attract funds from those whose private well-being is advanced by investing in or purchasing from the market. The profit motive is a powerful asset in supplying organization and motivation to human affairs. It is an asset not available to the nonprofit sector.

Continuing for a moment with this schematic (and therefore simplifying) exercise, the nonprofit sector might be characterized in terms of resources it cannot command. It cannot deploy the coercive power of the state; it cannot rely on the profit motive of the market. If two basic human emotions, fear and greed, are unavailable, how does the nonprofit sector mobilize resources, even in vast amounts, that allow it to do things that neither the state nor the market seem willing or able to do? It relies, of course, on charity, voluntarism, and philanthropy.

For the purposes of this essay, then, the nonprofit sector serves the public good through individual and communal action that is voluntary (not coerced) and charitable (not profitable).

Negotiating Boundaries

Before situating foundations in this definitional space, I emphasize again its schematic character. What makes history interesting is that the borders separating state, market, and society are porous, contested, ever changing. Even the distinctions themselves had very different meanings before the modern nation-state era. The Holy Roman Empire, for example, and contemporary Islam in some of its expressions have blurred boundaries between state and society. Precolonial African cultures would not have recognized a sharp distinction between state and society. Communism attempted to meld state and market into one system. Neoliberalism would shrink the state sector in order to provide more space for the market. More specific to the subject matter of this handbook, the determination to expand civil society reflects an effort to temper state coercion without ceding too much power to the market.

Much of public policy and law involves negotiating what occurs at the borders separating the three sectors.[2] As discussed in greater detail below, this is one reason why private foundations devote so much of their resources to policy analysis and policy advocacy. Through these efforts they hope to influence what ends up where. Can the democratic transitions in central Europe and Latin America reduce the scope of authoritarian state power in favor of a greater role by civil-society actors? Will shifting energy provision from the state to the market protect the public good? Voucher programs that benefit parochial schools or tax funds to faith-based organizations providing social services are not new issues, but they are freshly presented as public policy challenges in today's democracies. The examples are endless, but the point is simple: the size, shape, and functions of a nonprofit sector change across time and across societies in ways necessarily responsive to broad political and economic currents. Private foundations are embedded in the nonprofit sector, and consequently their opportunities for growth and action shift with the broader fortunes of that sector.

The grant-making foundation, managing as it does private funds dedicated to public purposes, channels the majority of its grants to the nonprofit sector.[3] That is, the nonprofit sector is its legal but also its natural home. The few exceptions when grants are made to a government agency or to a profit-making firm are easily explained. A grant to a government agency enables it to do something precluded by its budgetary authority but desired by a foundation—as in co-sponsoring a commission to examine a major social issue. A grant to a for-profit firm might persuade it to operate at odds with market forces—as in funding research and development for a drug or vaccine whose primary users will be too poor to pay market prices.

Foundation grants, then, even where practices of the market or the state are at issue, go overwhelmingly to nonprofit actors. These actors in turn are expected to influence policy or practice in some desired direction, a point to which we will return later. Here we make the introductory point that foundations are linked to the nonprofit sector in a pattern of reciprocal dependency. It follows, from consideration of self-interest as well as more lofty motives, that foundations actively work to expand the scope of the nonprofit sector and to strengthen its functioning. Without a nonprofit sector, foundations would have too few places to spend their funds. They would either become adjuncts of the state, serve as extensions of the market, or simply disappear. As, of course, they largely did under the statist policies following the French Revolution or under communist rule, which was ideologically prevented from imagining that scholarship, policy development, or service delivery could be provided outside the state.

Why Have a Nonprofit Sector?

To answer why there is a nonprofit sector we may draw on scholarly literature that is analytic (Hansmann 1980), comparative (James 1993; Salamon and Anheier 1998), and historical (Hall, this volume). Arguments can be summarized under two headings: the nonprofit sector exists because the state and market allow it to, and because the sector asserts its independent rationale. These explanations start from the assumptions that there are market failures and government failures, and that the nonprofit sector exists as provider of unmet collective goods (Weisbrod 1988; Salamon 1992).

The Space That Is Allowed

The first explanation stipulates that the space occupied by the nonprofit sector expands and contracts in ways not under its own control. Given the vastly superior resources that accrue to the state and to the market, the nonprofit sector must make do without the powerful assets that each of those other sectors controls: respectively, coercion and the profit motive. It must therefore secure its place by proving that it offers what neither the state nor the market provides. Sometimes this requires contesting the always uncertain border separating the civil society from the other sectors—for example, the underground arts and culture in the former Soviet Union or the quiet efforts to secure women's rights in conservative Islamic states. More often, however, the state and/or the market willingly cede particular responsibilities to the nonprofit sector. This is especially true when the nonprofits—churches and charities—serve population groups too poor to purchase from the market and too politically weak to matter to the state (DiMaggio and Anheier 1990; Robbins, this volume).

If, however, the nonprofit sector does less service delivery and more social action, it becomes an alternative power center. History abounds with examples of states becoming uncomfortable with this autonomous sector. France under the sway of postrevolutionary secular doctrine closed down the Catholic foundations. Philanthropy in precolonial Africa was used to establish local authority, and thus disappeared when colonial powers created authority outside the traditional cultures. Congressional committees in the United States have periodically investigated foundations thought to be too political and not sufficiently charitable in their grant making.

Similarly, although the market mostly ignores service sectors in which the nonprofit sector is especially active, this too can change if the market sees profitable opportunities. The fast growth of for-profit higher education services is a case in point (Gumport and Snydman, this volume); millions of students around the world now purchase education from for-profit providers. Another instance is in the information sector. Large public data sets (censuses, for example), long considered a public good and disseminated through nonprofit institutions, are now routinely enhanced and packaged by for-profit vendors. A public good is thus in the process of being privatized, and with this the market expands into an arena previously ceded to the nonprofit sector.

These cursory examples help establish the first premise: the boundaries that provide the space within which a nonprofit sector functions are subject to powerful forces well beyond the control of the nonprofit sector itself. This noted, it does not follow that the nonprofit sector exists only with the forbearance of state and market.

The Space That Is Claimed

The nonprofit sector has resources that belong uniquely to it, and these are advantages it brings to contests over the boundaries that provide an autonomous space for civil society. Three factors are germane: human nature, resistance, and pluralism.

The initial and obvious point is that there is more to human nature than can be explained by fear of the state's coercive powers or the greed that underlies the market's profit-maximizing strategy. While this is not the place to review the enduring inquiries into altruism, charity, empathy, community, faith, and ethics, there is simply too much philanthropy taking too many forms across human history to explain it as solely disguised self-interest.[4]

A space that lies outside the state and outside the market provides a home for something basic to being human. This is a powerful resource on which the nonprofit sector draws as it contests for its own protected space. The most lasting example, of course, is the persistence of the great world religions through periods of persecution and state-sponsored destruction. The Roman Empire came to accept Christianity. The cosmology of the Indians native to America was not destroyed by the wholesale disruption of their cultures and their forced relocation. Secular modernism continues to do battle with Islam, but Islam is expanding numerically and geographically. Communism drove the church underground but did not eliminate it. The refusal of the church to give in to state coercion was illustrated in the cynical question famously put by Stalin, mocking Pope Pius XI: "Just how many divisions does the Pope have?" More, it turned out, than Stalin could ever have imagined.

The nonprofit sector has another, closely related resource. It is the arena from which to mount resistance when the state encroaches too far into the personal sphere or when the market is too indifferent to the public good.[5] Resistance to excessive state control has given rise to all the civil protections we now take for granted in democracies. The nonstate sector offers an arena for asserting that resistance, covertly in totalitarian regimes or overtly in liberal polities. The demand for a space outside the state's control is an independent basis for the civil society in which nonprofit institutions and foundations thrive.

This point can be elaborated by considering the demand for public goods underproduced by market transactions, which gives rise to the state sector in the first place. The state, however, resorts to regulation, taxation, conscription, and eminent domain. Liberal doctrine worries that this process will hamper market flexibility and reduce personal choice. That is, public goods too aggressively produced will threaten liberal values.

The challenge for the liberal society is to have public goods at the least cost to economic and political freedom. A nonprofit sector that does not have to return a profit and that has no coercive power can, so the theory goes, produce public goods at minimal risk to liberal values. Charity, private patronage, and philanthropy establish a realm "where individuals undertake voluntary actions in concert with others to realize their version of the public good" (Ilchman, Katz, and Queen 1998:xiv). The nonprofit sector claims its own space and legitimacy because it can push back if the state becomes too intrusive and yet do so without relinquishing so much space to the market that the public good is ignored.

Pluralism is a further rationale justifying a protected space for the nonprofit sector. Pluralism, following Berlin (1990), is the liberal philosophy that sets itself against the single or universal truth to which all must conform—whether that truth be the Roman Empire, Christianity, communism, the superiority of the Aryan race, or the neoliberalism of a global economy. But pluralism stops short of a subjective relativism that recognizes no common human values. It treats what is common in human experience as emerging from different cultural habits and temperaments. For Berlin, we are human because we have both common values and differences.

A strong nonprofit sector is a necessary and perhaps even sufficient condition for pluralism. It provides a more diverse collection of services, institutions, and opportunities than can the state.[6] The modern state is expected to provide approximately the same services or opportunities for all citizens, or at least all citizens within a category for which the service is provided. Diversity within the nonprofit sector allows for social experimentation, for trying out the odd practice. Foundations are critical here; they offer support to the unusual or the unexpected because they are not beholden to the consensus-forcing expectations placed on the public sector.

The nonprofit sector is also home to unpopular ideas or art forms. Such ideas can be put in practice without imposing them on others, as would be the case were they part of official state doctrine. Publicly funded art is vulnerable to censorship, especially if found offensive by some part of the population. Here again, foundations find justification; they fund the survival of ideas that are too idiosyncratic to attract widespread voter support or to compete in the marketplace.

Of course the market also provides ample opportunity to satisfy idiosyncratic needs—look at the magazine racks of any large retailer or the proliferation of cable channels. But the market fills niches only if there is profit to be made, a survival test from which the nonprofit sector is more or less free. This freedom gives space for designing programs or providing services such as the search for an AIDS vaccine or support for documentary films on subjects of public import but limited market appeal.

The social value of pluralism is, then, a further reason why an independent civil society has been sustained across human history. The space ceded by state and market and the space claimed by the nonprofit sector provide the context within which to focus more specifically on the private foundations.

Why Have Foundations?

We do not usually ask why we have states, because history demonstrates without doubt that there needs to be authoritative regulation of social and economic interactions if there is to be a predictable and just social order. We do not usually ask why we have markets, because history demonstrates that the profit motive generates economic growth and innovation. We have now suggested why we have a nonprofit sector: because human nature spurs us to voluntarily act on behalf of others in need, because we need a place from which to push back if the state encroaches on personal freedom, because there are public goods that the market underproduces, and because a nonprofit sector protects the liberal values of pluralism.

But why foundations?[7] Certainly neither the state nor the market necessarily requires foundations, even though they make use of them. Even the nonprofit sector receives the vast bulk of its funds from membership dues, fees for services, government sources, individual gifts and donations, and investment income. In the United States the revenues of the nonprofit sector easily exceed half a trillion dollars annually. The record-level grant making by foundations in 2000, $27.6 billion, was less than one-half of 1 percent of nonprofit revenues. Charitable giving alone is nearly ten times as large as all foundation grant dollars.

We are left with a puzzle. What is it that modern grantmaking foundations do or represent that earns them public acceptance and legitimacy? Though there is not likely to be a single, satisfactory answer to a question so broadly stated, the question takes its importance from the fact that foundations benefit from favorable tax treatment and from laws that encourage their establishment. Many countries want them and forgo assets that might otherwise come to the government (in taxes) in order to bring them into existence.

Redistribution. One common answer is that foundations, like charity, are redistributive. Money flows from the wealthy to the poor. This answer is especially important where the tax code exempts from taxation the private funds that establish foundations (Simon 1987). Because these funds do in fact come from the wealthy, and because foundation programs do often disproportionately benefit the less-well-off, redistribution presents itself as a plausible explanation for the public encouragement of foundations. This argument also has the merit of continuing a long tradition—dating from Elizabethan England's 1601 Statute of Charitable Uses—that allowed donors to entrust property for eleemosynary purposes.

The empirical evidence on redistribution has been summarized and analytically interpreted in an informative essay by Julian Wolpert (2004), who reports that there are complex, unresolved empirical issues surrounding the measurement of redistribution, making it difficult to be definitive regarding its magnitude. However, the weight of evidence suggests that the benefits of foundation grants do, on balance, flow downward, though less dramatically than foundation claims imply. As another scholar concludes from a study of the nonprofit sector more generally, "there is great diversity within the nonprofit sector, and no overarching conclusions about distributional impact can be made." But there is also no "evidence that benefits are dramatically skewed away from the poor and toward the affluent" (Clotfelter 1992:22). Wolpert adds to this finding a useful distinction between short- and long-term equity effects, suggesting that short-term targeting—even if not immediately redistributive, such as grants to wealthy private universities or to professionally managed pilot projects—can be instrumental in promoting greater long-term equity by removing barriers to upward mobility.

Even if the net flow is redistributive, there remains the question of whether the foundation asset is more redistributive than had it been taxed in the first place. On this issue, Wolpert is persuasive in arguing that, for the United States, the wealth placed in foundations might not otherwise have found its way into the tax stream. This may be less the case in Europe. It is suggestive though hardly conclusive that European countries, with their much smaller foundation sectors, have preserved a strong and redistributive welfare state funded by higher personal and estate taxes than Americans will tolerate.

Cost-effectiveness. A different approach suggests that foundations and the nonprofit organizations they fund have a better ratio of accomplishment to funds spent than does the public sector (Weisbrod 1988). The flexibility and imaginativeness of foundations, at least compared with cumbersome, risk-averse government agencies, are cited as the reasons.

This is a difficult hypothesis to test, and in one important respect it is counterintuitive. The efficient use of resources is presumed to rely on a method that holds those who spend funds accountable for their performance, that is, on a bottom line. The market is believed to have the most reliable bottom line: its products and services are purchased, or they are not; inefficiency is rapidly followed by ruthless punishment in shrinking markets and falling share prices. For government, the softer but still meaningful bottom line is public support. The electoral theory of democracy, for example, rests on the assumption that there are always competitors eager to claim that they can more effectively discharge public responsibilities than can the current power holders. Even the nonprofit sector has its version of the bottom line, for if its services are not cost-effective, there are always competitors trying to attract its membership base, user fees, tuition payments, government contracts, or public acclaim.

The foundation is unusual and perhaps unique in its distance from any such accountability mechanism—no shareholders, no customers, no voters, no dues-paying members, no clients who can withhold contributions or support. Even attempts to hold foundations accountable to the wishes of the original donor turn out to be difficult, for reasons discussed below. Although foundation officers assertively claim to be excellent stewards of funds that would otherwise be taxed, the empirical basis for this assertion has not been forthcoming.

Liberal Doctrine. An alternative approach focuses less on what foundations do than on what they represent. The private foundation is uniquely positioned to reflect liberal doctrine. The liberal society wants public goods at the least cost to economic and political freedoms, and it turns to private foundations as noncoercive funders of public goods. In this argument, the foundation is not necessarily measured by how well it does its job or by whether it is redistributive or capable of bringing about important changes. It is welcomed because of what it represents—directing private wealth to the provision of public goods without encroaching on political and economic freedoms (Prewitt 2004).

Pluralism, Social Change, and Charity. Additional explanations for the ubiquity of foundations and their public acceptance can be found in the arguments about pluralism suggested above and also in the claim that modern foundations are important sources of social change.[8] Such claims have merit. As previously noted, foundations do provide funds for nonprofit organizations to experiment, innovate, advance the unpopular, and protect the idiosyncratic. They are certainly part of the mix that gives the nonprofit sector its distinctive role in social life. How much they contribute to important social change is less clear; this topic is taken up in this chapter's final section.

Throughout the long history of foundations, dating to antiquity, probably their foremost justification has been that foundations are associated with charity. This explanation for why foundations are encouraged, and are now given tax-free status, is complicated by the radical shift in foundation practice that occurred toward the end of the nineteenth century. The modern foundation was self-consciously designed to move beyond charity by adopting scientific philanthropy. In turning to this issue, we shift from the foregoing abstract treatment to material more historically grounded.

THE EMERGENCE OF THE MODERN FOUNDATION

There is neither space nor author inclination to offer a chronological or comprehensive historical account of foundations. It is, however, instructive to note the ways in which the contemporary foundation scene was anticipated in earlier times.[9] The modern foundation blends old practices with new legal and institutional forms.

Foundations in History

Early endowments in both Greece and the Roman Republic established and then sustained academies, libraries, public works, and welfare organizations. There was, as now, a complicated interaction between foundation funds and public taxation. The Greek polis, for example, had no regular taxation and thus depended on subscriptions from wealthy donors to further civic projects. Similarly, in the Roman Republic, public officials and private individuals were expected to cooperate across a wide range of social services, including erecting public monuments: "gifts were made in a social and political context that did not draw sharp distinctions between private philanthropy and public initiatives" (Smith and Borgmann 2001:4). The boundaries separating subscription, taxation, and philanthropy were blurred, and they remain so today. The absence of a sharp distinction between the private and the public is characteristic of other foundation traditions as well. In South Asia "a good King is a generous King"; kings earned allegiance by bestowing their wealth, and "the recipients of the gifts have thus a vested interest in maintaining the status quo" (Anderson 1998:67).

Then as now, the state had to step in to ensure that the donor intent was honored after his or her departure from the scene. This intervention did not happen quickly. Many bequests in ancient Greece presumed perpetuity but depended on trustees transmitting an obligation from one generation to the next. Roman law tightened up this obligation by making legally enforceable the responsibility of successive trustees to honor donor intent or to modify it in a lawful manner.

We also see in early foundations an array of philanthropic motives familiar today. Cicero observed of his times that "most people are generous in their gifts not so much by natural inclination as by reason of the lure of honour—they simply want to be seen as beneficent" (Smith and Borgmann 2001:4). Naming opportunities go back two millennia.

If the desire for public acclaim is ancient, so is the more charitable motivation to relieve the suffering of the less fortunate. Starting in the early centuries after Christ, and based on his behavior as well as his teachings, the biblically based injunction to be charitable became a strong, consistent message. But charity is not only Christian. It appears in Buddhism, Hinduism, and Islam, and in the cosmology of American Indians and the practices of precolonial Africa. The vulnerable members of society needed help, and the wealthy were expected to give generously—including by establishing trusts and other foundation-like instruments.

By the medieval period, Christian teachings on charity had become more elaborated; personal salvation could be earned through charitable giving. In Islam, religious motives are central to giving and again are bound up with personal salvation. Philanthropy thus offers the charitable a way to draw nearer to God.

Stewardship emerged as a theme in the fourth century and was echoed across the centuries in, for example, the writings of Saint Thomas Aquinas and, much later, John Calvin. Andrew Carnegie's famous essay on wealth, discussed below, was anticipated by a sixth-century bishop who argued that all property belonged to God and that wealthy individuals, after caring for basic family needs, should dedicate the rest of their riches to philanthropy. An explicit issue here was redistribution. Foundations were perceived as instruments to shift the wealth of one generation to the poor of the next, although how successfully this worked is not any clearer in the medieval period than in the present.

Of course early foundation giving, as well as that of today, could spring from more than one motive. Leper hospitals were a favored foundation project as early as the eleventh century. That these would care for the suffering was obvious, but certainly they also were an attempt to distance a public health threat. This mixture of motives is present today when Western philanthropy takes up developing-country poverty and disease because, otherwise, civil disorder might disrupt world markets or emergent diseases might cross borders.

Neither is the porous boundary between the market and foundations new to today's entrepreneurial philanthropy. In the fourteenth and fifteenth centuries, Italian banks were offering low-interest loans to the poor and to workers, echoes of which we see today in microcredit lending and the program-related investments (PRIs) favored by many U.S. foundations.

The boundaries between the market and nonprofits, and between the state and nonprofits, came more sharply into view as the modern European state emerged. "Across the continent the boundaries between governmental and philanthropic institutions were redefined. Some states integrated their foundations into the growing governmental sector; others offered them encouragement, protection and a high degree of autonomy; still others subdued and dissolved them" (Smith and Borgmann 2001:22).

Official doubts about foundations are well illustrated in the centralization of power characteristic of France after the

Revolution. Foundations were viewed as an escape from taxation and a potential power center beyond the control of the state. Enlightenment philosophers gave grounds for seeing foundations, even their welfare role, as offensive and as usurping citizens' rights. France was not alone in dismantling foundations; Spain's medieval foundations were dissolved in the early nineteenth century, and constitutionally allowed again only in 1978. Portugal and Belgium followed a similar path.

England differed from its continental neighbors. It created a culture of philanthropy that, by the eighteenth century, included a supportive legal framework as well as workable mechanisms for ensuring accountability. The government "left wide scope for privately run institutions to serve public purposes" (Smith and Borgmann 2001:22). The Nordic countries also continued a long tradition of involving foundations in education, health, and social welfare.

Such variations in foundation history can, of course, be traced to larger political and economic forces. Whether one considers the legacy of revolution and counterrevolution that suppressed foundations in France or the absence of civil struggles in Denmark and Sweden that offered space for a foundation sector, the organizational forms taken by philanthropy, especially the quasi-permanent foundation, have been conditioned by state and market formation. This point is so obvious as to hardly need mention, but it does help explain why, today, one count shows France to have 404 foundations and Belgium even fewer (310), but Great Britain nearly nine thousand and Sweden as many as thirty thousand (Anheier 2001).

Across the sweep of European history, from ancient Greece and Rome to the present, foundations have mostly been operating foundations—whether of hospitals, schools, orphanages, or other welfare institutions. As with any generalization, there have been exceptions. Western European monasteries in the early Middle Ages resembled what today we would call grant-making foundations. Their assets were land and the income from agriculture. With this income, in addition to supporting their own learning, they "pursued public purposes in the form of almsgiving and hospitality, had formal organizational structures shaped typically by either the Benedictine or Augustinian monastic rules, and reflected the pious intentions of individual donors or groups of benefactors" (Smith and Borgmann 2001:22). But taking on wider grant making rather than simply operating an institution has been an exception in the long foundation history of Europe. This pattern holds today. Across continental Europe, operating foundations far outnumber grant-making foundations. The relatively recent growth of the foundation sector in Germany is one reversal of this trend, though it is much too early to assess what patterns might appear elsewhere.

The one European nation in which the grant-making foundation clearly dominates is Great Britain, a consequence of the reform of foundations that followed the Tudor seizure of power from the church. The emphasis on grant making rather than operating foundations has taken on its greatest significance in the United States, and especially in the twentieth century, a story to which we now turn.

Creating the American Foundation

American foundations date to the colonial period, although, much like the European foundations on which they were modeled, these early foundations were trusts or bequests dedicated to a particular institution. We pick up the history of foundations at a later moment, the late nineteenth century.[10] This period generated the wealth that led to modern foundations in the form familiar today.

The United States has been unusually receptive to letting the private sector, in both its for-profit and nonprofit expressions, do what elsewhere is a state responsibility. Born of a revolution against tyrannical state power, the new Republic was based on a political theory of minimal government—"that government is best which governs least." Theorists describe this as the weak-state tradition. Among other things, it led eventually to a tax code hospitable to a robust nonprofit sector and to charitable giving. Of course this tax code functions as an indirect public subsidy to philanthropy and nonprofit institutions. As such, it creates a complicated web of relations that simultaneously separates and yet links the nonprofit sector to the state.

Three persons were particularly influential in the form that the modern American foundation took. Two were men of great industrial wealth: Andrew Carnegie and John D. Rockefeller. Carnegie articulated the rationale for the private foundation, and Rockefeller created the prototypical institutional form. The third, Margaret Olivia Sage, used inherited wealth to establish an innovative foundation that bears the name of her deceased husband, Russell Sage. The literature on Rockefeller and Carnegie is vastly more developed, and it will be used to describe the early period, but Mrs. Sage's contribution was no less significant. She saw clearly the link between (social) science and the institutions and policies necessary to ameliorate the costs to human welfare associated with rapid industrialization and urbanization.

Andrew Carnegie's Gospel of Wealth

Social Darwinian theories favored by late-nineteenth-century industrialists and their apologists played a role in the emergence of the private foundation. These theories justified the acquisition of vast wealth in private hands. An influential statement that specifically linked Darwinian notions to charitable giving is that of Andrew Carnegie's widely circulated essay, *The Gospel of Wealth.* He argued: "We accept and welcome, therefore, as conditions to which we must accommodate ourselves, great inequality of environment; the concentration of business, industrial and commercial, in the hands of the few; and the law of competition between these, as being not only beneficial, but essential to the future progress of the race" (Carnegie 1889, 1:656). He went on to suggest that industrial capitalism was providing more and more benefits to ever greater proportions of the population. This was a good in and of itself, even though the workings of capitalism inevitably generated substantial surplus wealth under control of the few.

What to do about this concentration of wealth? Carnegie was quick to say that it was his Christian obligation to give it away. Max Weber, in *The Protestant Ethic and the Spirit of Capitalism,* gave sociological depth to the idea that getting wealth and giving it away were linked: Protestant asceticism emphasized discipline and deferred gratification, while celebrating the thrifty, hardworking business ethic that shaped modern capitalism. The Protestant ethic smiled on the greatest possible productivity but frowned on luxurious enjoyment of the wealth so earned. If work was to manifest God's glory, the profits of work were to be reinvested in that which was productive and socially beneficial. To do good works in this life were a sign of grace. This was a convenient doctrine for those, Carnegie notably among them, who were both devoutly religious and wealthy beyond easy measure. It was comforting to know that one could dedicate oneself to acquisition and yet be virtuous. Rockefeller put it bluntly: "A man should make all he can and give all he can" (Nevins 1953, 2:191).

These beliefs echoed much earlier chapters in religious philanthropy, and though explicitly religious motives are less often cited in today's secular culture, they lurk in the background. The notion that one is a steward of surplus wealth appears in many explanations of the philanthropic act, as do echoes of the belief that good works in this life signal moral worth. Late-twentieth-century billionaires, when launching foundations that bear their name, continued to speak of an obligation to repay society for having been so good to them.

The social Darwinian environment within which foundations emerged was compatible with another feature of American political culture: the weak-state tradition. In linking private funds to public purpose, the foundation plays its assigned part in this tradition. If wealth is accumulated in an amount too substantial to be consumed or given away in one's lifetime, and thought to be too great to bequeath to family members, there are a limited number of ways to dispose of it. Furthermore, if the political culture as well as law and taxation invite the wealthy to create private institutions that can function as an alternative to the state, there is much satisfaction to be gained by creating a foundation.

There is an irony, perhaps, in the fact that the foundation results from the accumulation of substantial private wealth and yet in instance after instance declares that its mission is to improve the lot of the poor and powerless. It goes about that mission by helping to lower the barriers to upward mobility, by working to ensure basic civil and political rights, or by contributing to education and health for the poor. It does not, however, go about that mission by calling into question the political-economic arrangements that allow for great inequalities in wealth acquisition. This is despite the oft-repeated claim that foundations will find and eliminate the "root causes" of poverty, discrimination, and illness. Capital accumulation in large amounts was not imagined by the wealthy early philanthropists as a root cause of distressing social conditions, though of course it was by the radical reformers of the day.

American foundations that otherwise favor progressive, redistributional policies have not launched study commissions or funded advocacy groups dedicated to, for example, higher inheritance and estate taxation. It would be worth knowing whether such taxes could more radically transfer wealth from the very rich to the very poor than by parking it in tax-exempt foundations with their 5 percent payout policies.

Rockefeller and Scientific Philanthropy

Carnegie had strong feelings about the proper way to spend his wealth. Anticipating what today we reference as "moral hazard," Carnegie wrote: "Indiscriminate charity is one of the serious obstacles to the improvement of our race. It were better for mankind that the millions of the rich were thrown into the sea than so spent as to encourage the slothful, the drunken, and the unworthy. Of every $1,000.00 spent on so-called charity, it is probable that $950.00 is unwisely spent. So spent, indeed, to produce the very evils which it hopes to mitigate or cure" (Carnegie 1889, 1:13–15).

Carnegie would have none of the Victorian morality that commended the charitable act, the gift to the poorhouses, the orphanages, the local hospital, or the Christmas basket. But if not almsgiving, if not charity, what then? It was Rockefeller who most carefully drew the distinction between charity and philanthropy.[11]

In establishing his philanthropies, explained Rockefeller, "I do not believe in giving money to street beggars, but this is not a reason why one should be exempt from doing something to help the situation represented by the street beggar" (Rockefeller 1984:110). Charity is a temporary bandage; philanthropy finds and changes whatever it is that needs the bandage. Charity might feed the hungry, care for the sick, shelter the homeless, and clothe the naked, but it cannot end the flow of those in need. Earthquake relief is charity; the scientific study of plate tectonics that can lead to preventive engineering is tackling the cause. Philanthropy, as viewed by Rockefeller and his colleagues, had a purpose and reach that extended beyond charity. "The best philanthropy," stated Rockefeller, "involves the search for cause, an attempt to cure evils at their source."[12] This was Rockefeller's formulation of the justly famous root-cause metaphor.

The root-cause metaphor was a turning point in American foundation history, though it was prefigured in eighteenth-century European practice (Robbins, this volume). It was also a turning point in Rockefeller's own history. Tithing was part of his Baptist upbringing. If he made a dollar, he gave a dime. Tithing worked in the early years of his successful business career, as he responded to requests from churches, mission organizations, orphanages, and other mostly Baptist-related charities. Soon, however, Rockefeller's wealth began to outpace his capacity to give even 10 percent of it away. Especially difficult was making responsible gifts. Rockefeller had a sharp sense of stewardship, and it troubled him that he could not be certain that a given gift would be spent for the purpose for which it was requested. This was less of a problem when his giving was at modest levels; he could determine that a church did need to rebuild after a fire or that a mission was sending people for its work overseas. As his level of giving increased, however, personal attention was no longer possible. While Rockefeller's wealth grew in the 1870s and 1880s, his charitable giving proportionately declined. His biographers make clear that this was not a withdrawal of his commitment to tithing. It was that such large sums were difficult to dispense with responsibly (Harr and Johnson 1988).

In solving this problem, Rockefeller set in motion a key element of modern philanthropy. He sought out a person experienced in the arena in which his giving was concentrated. This Baptist minister, the Reverend Frederick Gates, had entrepreneurial talents that well equipped him to become the prototype of the professional foundation officer. He straightened out Rockefeller's giving, gave it programmatic focus, and turned it to projects at a scale commensurate with the magnitude of Rockefeller's wealth.

The manner in which Gates transformed Rockefeller's giving established practices that today guide most large-scale foundations. Professional foundation officers do not just award grants. They design an integrated cluster of grants, given over an extended time frame, with a clear goal in mind—eradicating a disease, nurturing a new discipline, advancing an art form, saving a natural resource, resolving a social conflict, and so on. It is the task of the professional officer to seek out institutions that will ensure that this goal is reached, and when such do not exist, to create them. Gates, viewed as the first professional foundation officer, pioneered practices that went far toward shifting Rockefeller's giving from charity to philanthropy.

The search for root causes and professionally directed, strategic grant giving were the building blocks of the modern private foundation. But those building blocks required something else. If wealth was to provide a flexible form of giving into perpetuity, there had to be a way to convert that wealth into an endowment not too tightly associated with a given project or purpose. Prior to this period, major endowments were tied to a single institution, as are many endowment gifts today. It was the desire of Rockefeller and his associates that the Rockefeller wealth not be so limited. Because they firmly (and correctly) believed that the generation which bequeathed the money could not anticipate conditions in the future or be certain which institutions could most intelligently respond, it was necessary to establish trusts, or foundations, able to adopt new program goals and select new grantees as required by the times. In effect this meant a permanent endowment with a permissive mission statement. Those foundations in which the founders attempt to tightly prescribe giving after their departure risk locking their successors into programs of decreasing relevance. The Rockefeller Foundation avoided this danger by declaring its goal in the broadest of terms: to promote the "well-being of mankind around the world."

Three principles—the search for root causes, a professional staff responsible for realizing strategically selected program goals, and a flexible form of giving into perpetuity—are basic to the innovation that marked the beginning of American foundations as we know them today. The idea of scientific philanthropy is, however, broader than these institutional innovations. Karl and Katz present a compelling argument that it must be viewed less within the historical context of a charitable obligation than within the Enlightenment's conception of progress in human affairs. They write: "the modern idea of philanthropy rests on a recognition of progress and choice; it makes the eradication of poverty possible, not through divine intervention but through human endeavor" (Karl and Katz 1987:6). Scientific philanthropy can support this human endeavor through education and research-based knowledge. Rockefeller and his contemporaries had learned that building business on the foundation of science had been enormously profitable; they now intended to place philanthropy on the same footing.

The Critics Respond

The Rockefeller initiative was not without critics. Indeed, the motivations of those who established private trusts to advance public purposes have been questioned throughout the history of the modern foundation. Of Rockefeller it was held by many that he invested in philanthropy as a way to counter the greedy and grasping person he had become in the public imagination. Of Henry Ford it is noted that, though he may have been charitable, it was no accident that the complex way in which the Ford Foundation was chartered protected the family's control over the Ford Motor Company, and in a manner that avoided heavy taxation. Of the Duke Endowment it has been pointed out how its founder, the tobacco and utility magnate James Buchanan Duke, managed to direct its grant making to areas served by the Duke Power Company, thus securing favorable publicity for his business interests.[13]

Tax avoidance in particular has been cited as a motive for the establishment of foundations, though Rockefeller, Carnegie, and others in the late nineteenth century cannot be so charged, since their trusts predated the progressive income tax and estate taxes. But later in the century, tax avoidance became much more pronounced, a motive not limited to American philanthropy. Reinhard Mohn, founder of the Bertelsmann Foundation in Germany, writes of the "burden of inheritance taxation" and notes that the establishment of the foundation derived from "the wish to secure the continuity of the corporation" (Mohn 1997:25).

Vanity is another motive frequently ascribed to those who establish foundations, a claim supported by the fact that foundations, especially in the United States, often carry the name of the original donor: to Rockefeller, Carnegie, and Sage in the early years have now been added Ford, Mellon, MacArthur, Sloan, Duke, Packard, Gates, and many more. In general, however, efforts to assess the differing personal motives of founders—stewardship, charitable impulses, vanity, guilt, business interests, tax avoidance—have mostly been a case of selective quotation and anecdote. It is difficult to be systematic with such an elusive topic.

Much more analytically important than determining personal motives has been questioning whether foundations were designed to advance political-economic goals. This charge, which surfaced early in U.S. foundation history, goes to the core of whether foundations serve the public interest or a narrower, self-interested agenda. It was voiced in the first congressional investigation into private foundations. The Walsh Commission (1915–16), named for its chairman, observed that industry and wealth in the United States had come under the control of a few very wealthy persons.[14] The commission alleged that this small group intended to continue and extend this control by establishing "enormous privately managed funds for indefinite purposes" (U.S. Congress 1916:18). Here is coupled the late-nineteenth-century anxiety about the concentration of economic power with the fear that private foundations would perpetuate the dominance of business interests in American political and social life. (For additional coverage of congressional investigations of foundations, see Hall, this volume.)

It has been a theme repeated often. In the 1930s, for example, a study of the purposes of large private foundations concluded that "philanthropic and business interests are not merely complementary, they are identical. Just as you can't run a steel mill without machine guns, so you can't run a capitalist democracy without pretence of philanthropy" (Coon 1938:276). By the 1980s, the argument that foundations exist to perpetuate American business interests had been extended to account for its overseas grant making. The phrase "cultural imperialism" appears in the title of one work, wherein a Marxian-influenced account is presented of foundations as instruments of capitalist exploitation of third-world countries (Arnove 1980; Berman 1983).

This critique from the political left found its mirror image in a critique from the political right. A mid-century congressional investigation charged foundations not with extending but with undermining capitalism. Congressman B. Carroll Reece was convinced that certain foundations "support efforts to overthrow our government and to undermine our American way of life" (*Congressional Record* 99 [no. 141]: 10188). This critique, which has been echoed in the conservative press down to the present, frequently adds the argument that subsequent generations of trustees and officers have deflected foundations from the purposes intended by their original donors. Cited as evidence is the resignation of Henry Ford II, grandson of the founder of Ford Motor Company, from the foundation that bears his name. Although the Ford Foundation existed only because of capitalism, he said, there was little trace of that fact in anything the foundation was doing.

These critiques of the left and the right share the assumption that foundations intend to perpetuate the system under which huge private wealth is accumulated. The left fears that this nefarious mission is successful, while the right fears that this wholesome mission is thwarted by liberals who have captured the foundation. Both versions are hampered by their resort to conspiracy accounts, where arguments and counterarguments proceed from anecdote to assertion rather than from evidence to conclusion.

Historians offer more nuanced accounts. Karl reminds us that the "modern foundation was created at a point in the history of the Western world when science and technology were beginning to place new burdens on the management of mass industrial societies" (Karl 1997:208). The public question was whether modern technological societies could be governed democratically. The Progressive movement in the United States was pushing for a nonpartisan, apolitical professional class. (For predecessors to this movement, see Hall, this volume.) At issue was how to train and empower a managerial elite consistent with democratic principles. Historians suggest that we should assess the early mission of American foundations with this context in mind. The transition from charity to scientific philanthropy, as noted above, rested on the assumption that the problems of industrialization could be solved. Needed was a system of training designed "to build a society of highly educated men and women who could run a modern democracy effectively" (Karl 1997:211). If these power circles were permeable—if, to use Mosca's term, there was a circulation of elites—effective management need not put democracy at risk. The foundation project could simultaneously protect economic interests from civil violence or class conflict, and also be guided by democratic instincts that would lead to a heavy investment in leadership training as well as public education and enlightenment. Building a modern social science, whose personnel and research could help guide democratic decision making, was a major foundation task consistent with this broad goal (Prewitt 1995).

Karl, reflecting on the tension between democracy and technological advances across the whole of the twentieth century, reaches the conclusion that many of the more troubling features of American democracy have been constructively balanced by the elite professionalism long associated with private philanthropy.[15]

The Foundation Sector Today

Criticisms and challenges notwithstanding, the growth of the U.S. foundation sector throughout the twentieth century was phenomenal. What were once just a half-dozen pioneering institutions trying to sort out their missions and practices has become a large and largely professional operation of nearly seventy thousand foundations. The last quarter of the twentieth century was a period of particularly robust growth—the number of grant-making foundations more than doubled between 1975 and the turn of the century, and total giving across this period (in constant dollars) more than tripled.

Expansion has not been as dramatic elsewhere in the world, but it has not been absent. Although trend data for Europe are not readily available, Anheier (2001:51) estimates eighty to ninety thousand foundations in western Europe. His discussion makes clear that this number represents sharp growth over the past quarter-century. The same is true for central and eastern Europe, where current estimates reach twenty to forty thousand, though many of these are small institutions without endowments.

Given the expansion of the foundation sector in the latter decades of the twentieth century, and its institutionalization in the civil-society sector across much of the world, we would like to have a theoretical account not just of its origins and growth but of its practices and social significance. Theory is still thin in this regard.

THINKING THEORETICALLY ABOUT FOUNDATIONS

Science proceeds by making distinctions, constructing classifications, and then offering theoretically informed explanations for why one class of objects behaves differently from other classes. If we want scientifically grounded explanations of how foundations behave, what they accomplish, how they change, and so on, we should start with a taxonomy that classifies foundations in some meaningful way. We review some possible classifications below, though none are wholly satisfactory.

Legal Distinctions

The most commonly offered classification is based on legal distinctions. In the United States, for example, the approximately sixty thousand foundations are generally classified into four subgroups: independent grant-making foundations (the vast majority, 90 percent), corporate foundations (about 4 percent), operating foundations (about 3 percent), and community foundations (only 1 percent).[16] This classification is based on the law that charters foundations. Similar law-based classifications are made in Europe. In Europe, however, it is common to include the government-created and government-sponsored foundations (Anheier 2001). The United States also has government foundations, some with significant grant-making budgets. The largest are in the sciences: the National Science Foundation and the grant-making programs of the National Institutes of Health. The National Endowment for the Humanities and for the Arts are much smaller. Overviews of U.S. foundations (including this chapter) do not usually include the government foundations.[17]

Community foundations are comparatively small and are structurally tied to the community they serve. Corporate foundations offer grants that, presumably, bring favorable public attention to the company that sponsors them. But their public reporting and legal obligations do not distinguish them from independent foundations. Moreover, grantees make no distinction among community, corporate, and independent foundations—and will seek funds from all three sources. With respect to what foundations do and what groups benefit from their funds, there are few meaningful distinctions to be made among the three types of grant-making foundations.[18]

There is more to be gained theoretically in the distinction between the operating foundation and grant-making foundations. The work of an operating foundation is carried out by its own staff, and operating foundations often house other institutions. Large operating foundations in the United States today include the Getty Foundation, which operates the Getty Museum, and the Howard Hughes Foundation, which directly funds a number of specialized medical research laboratories. In Portugal, the Gulbenkian Foundation encompasses both a museum and a symphony orchestra. The Bertelsmann Foundation in Germany blends practices familiar to both corporate and operating American foundations and also designs programs that, in the United States, would normally be housed in an independent think tank. In Europe it is not unusual to find foundations that combine features of the operating and independent grant-making foundations, harkening back to an earlier period in the United States when Rockefeller and Carnegie blended the two practices.

An ambitious effort to explain foundations in Europe has largely relied on legal distinctions, though in this case comparing legal codes cross-nationally (Schluter, Then, and Walkenhorst 2001:appendix 1). This classification is a backdrop to useful commentary on a range of foundation issues: sources of funds, accountability and public scrutiny, management, and tax relief among them. But in Europe, as in the United States, classifying foundations in terms of legal differences does not lend itself to theoretical explanations of what foundations do and how much impact they have.

Distinctions Based on What Is Funded

An alternative classification might differentiate foundation spending in terms of the areas or sectors in which grants are made. This approach has merit insofar as foundations see themselves and are seen by others in terms of the social conditions engaged. It is plausible to suggest that what and who is funded matters to how we assess foundations and their consequences.

Subject-matter typologies are useful for tracking the sectors to which funds are granted, but are of much less use in distinguishing among different foundations.[19] One difficulty arises from the obvious fact that many foundations are engaged with a number of social sectors, and thus following a subject-matter definition can only lead to describing them as multiple-mission foundations.

Based on the statistics it collects from thousands of private foundations, the New York–based Foundation Center uses a ten-part classification to report grant making by subject matter: arts and culture, education, environment, health, human services, international affairs and development, public/society benefit, science and technology, social science, and religion. The larger foundations offer grants across this array. The Ford Foundation has programs in all ten areas. Kellogg, Pew, MacArthur, Mellon, Rockefeller, or Packard may skip one or two areas, but they have seldom limited themselves to fewer than a half-dozen sectors. Of the large foundations, it is generally the operating foundations that tend to be less dispersed in grant making—the Getty Foundation in the arts and the Howard Hughes Foundation in biomedical research.

One might expect that what is true of the largest foundations would not be true for the smallest, that a small foundation would select one arena in which to be active so as to maximize its influence. But small foundations are normally regional or local foundations. They find it difficult to contribute to the city museum but not the after-school program for disadvantaged children, or to make a grant to the homeless shelter but ignore nature conservation. Small community-based foundations are thus not less likely than larger foundations to pursue multiple purposes.

It is in the midrange that we often encounter "niche foundations," that is, institutions that specialize in one sector. Examples are the Spencer Foundation, which spends exclusively on educational research, and the Russell Sage Foundation (an operating foundation), which is tightly focused on the social sciences. Of course the correlation between size and focus is not perfect. The Robert Wood Johnson Foundation works exclusively in the health sector, and the largest foundation in the United States, the Gates Foundation, focuses heavily on health and education, particularly on technological innovations regarding vaccines and information technology.

This absence of fit between foundation size and number of program areas does not prevent classifying foundations with reference to subject matter. But for many and perhaps a majority of foundations, it is not informative. To say that a foundation's mission is to advance the well-being of mankind by working through arts, culture, environment, health, population, education, human services, and religion is to say little more than that the foundation wants to do good in a large number of ways. And at least over the last decade, the relative importance of the various sectors in U.S. grant making has not shifted much. Although trend data are less available in Europe, cross-national data are. Pinter (2001) uses aggregated spending levels by subject matter in a cross-national comparison.

The geographic focus of a foundation is a further complicating factor. Though smaller foundations tend to concentrate at the community level, the larger foundations operate at regional, national, and, increasingly, international levels. In some respects it tells us more about a foundation to learn that it operates internationally than to learn about its subject-matter emphases. For example, the Ford and Rockefeller foundations maintain a high profile internationally. From this perspective, their missions are similar. In fact, they are more similar than are the missions of the Rockefeller and the Robert Wood Johnson foundations, even though both are heavily engaged with the health sector. But because the health program of the former is (at present) international and that of the latter is (at present) domestic, they share few grantees and grant-making strategies. To classify, then, Ford, Rockefeller, and Robert Wood Johnson in terms of subject matter is less instructive than to know that the former two operate internationally and the latter does not. Incidentally, few foundations elsewhere in the world practice international philanthropy in the way that many U.S. foundations do. We are not surprised to find Ford Foundation offices around the world, or the Gates Foundation to have taken up the cause of immunization in dozens of impoverished countries. We would, however, be surprised to find a Brazilian-based foundation active in India, or an Indian foundation active in Brazil.

Other factors complicate the attempt to use subject matter for classification purposes. Foundations differ sharply in the proportion of their grant dollars that provide general support or that support capital campaigns. The policies of many foundations preclude contributions to building projects, capital campaigns, or even general support, and instead favor program and project grants. Other foundations—Kresge is an example—dedicate practically all their grant dollars to capital projects, usually in a highly leveraged fashion by requiring that matching funds be secured by the grant recipient. Among the largest foundations in the United States, program and project grant making absorbs approximately three of every five grant dollars and capital projects about one of every five dollars. General support is even less popular; not more than 10 percent of grant funds typically are awarded for this purpose. Endowment gifts are even rarer. There is good reason. The typical annual grant expenditure by a foundation is 5 percent of the current market value of its endowment, or a 20:1 ratio of endowment holdings to grant making. If a foundation uses its grant funds to build the endowment of a nonprofit organization (as is often requested), and the nonprofit in turn uses about 5 percent of the value of its endowment for annual expenditures, the initial foundation endowment is now productive at a 400:1 ratio. Only exceptional circumstances justify grants to endowments of other organizations.

The different ways that subject-matter classifications are constructed thus provide only limited usefulness if the task is to devise a theory-derived taxonomy that can address the quality, reach, and impact of foundation grant making. The next section offers a different approach, one that considers different change strategies adopted by foundations.

A Taxonomy Based on Change Strategies

At the core of what nearly all foundations describe as their mission is the intent to make the world a better place, to improve on the current order of things: less poverty, war, sickness, illiteracy, violence, parochialism, hunger; and, conversely, more freedom, art, understanding, opportunity, security, education, health.

Foundations differ in what they include in their "less of" and "more of" lists, but every foundation operates from an implicit if not explicit notion of how their philanthropic dollars can change the underlying conditions—back to the root-cause metaphor—that lead to human suffering and strife. Many of the cliché terms found in foundation materials reflect this concern: "leverage," "go to scale," "make a difference," "risk," "countercyclical," "venture capital," "strategic partnerships," and so on. All these terms are in search of the point of intervention which will increase the odds that foundation funds can bring about desired social change.

This essay employs the social change vocabulary rather than the traditional "root-cause" metaphor or the newer "strategic philanthropy" formulation. Root causes are useful in drawing attention to the distinctions between charity and philanthropy, but they then quickly lose theoretical relevance. How deep do the roots go? Consider the continuum from immediate relief for victims in the aftermath of an earthquake to basic research on plate tectonics that might someday enable earthquake prediction with sufficient lead time to evacuate a population at risk. Between immediate relief (charity) and basic seismological research are many other philanthropic possibilities: early warning systems, as exist for tsunami alerts in the Atlantic; public education on emergency preparedness; policy advocacy for building codes that would minimize loss of life in earthquake-prone regions or coastal areas vulnerable to tsunamis; or funding a school of engineering to study alternative earthquake-resistant construction design. Where along this continuum does a grant, in Rockefeller's terminology, cure an evil at its source—that is, stop being charity and start being philanthropic?

Strategic philanthropy offers an alternative formulation, but it has emerged in conjunction with the entrepreneurial terminology that draws attention to a hands-on, business-oriented set of practices associated with the recent arrival of comparatively young philanthropists from the high-technology industries. The staying power of "entrepreneurial philanthropy" is unclear, and in grant-making power it remains small in comparison with the dominant actors on the American foundation scene.

Focusing on change strategies offers the possibility of a taxonomy that, eventually, could lead to useful theory about foundation behavior and impact.[20] The schema presented here draws sharper distinctions than occur in the actual practice of grant making, and it misses many nuances in foundation practice. But of course these are the limits of any classification system that summarizes a wide range of characteristics or practices under a set of general labels. The more serious limitation of the change-strategy schema is its lack of empirical referent. It is offered as a rough starting point from which to understand foundations from the perspective of their strategic choices.

In this formulation, strategic choices are not about the social conditions that foundations address—peace, justice, health, inequality, arts, and so on. They are about the approach or course of action brought to such conditions. A strategic choice gives operational meaning to the theory of change adopted (even if implicitly) by a foundation. Does the foundation operate on the assumption that ideas drive history, or that technologies do, or social movements, market incentives, government interventions, moral exhortations? If ideas drive history, the foundation should invest in research and intellectual efforts; if government interventions drive history, it should invest in policy analysis and advocacy; if exhortation matters most, it should invest in public education. Grant making seeks the point of leverage judged to be most productive for the social change favored by the foundation.

Foundations are fond of "strategic planning" exercises, in which officers prepare documents for trustees that focus on what the foundation's broad goals should be, how grants should address those goals, and what types of grantees will be favored. A foundation's approach is essentially revealed in the grantees it typically funds: universities and scientific laboratories versus advocacy organizations and grassroots groups versus service delivery agencies.

I do not intend to suggest that a foundation need be guided by just one change strategy. Just as a foundation can be active across a number of subject areas, it can simultaneously pursue a number of approaches or basic strategies. But anecdotal evidence suggests that a promiscuous mixing of too many change strategies can complicate a foundation's management. When some officers are committed to a university-based research agenda and other officers favor activist groups and grassroots philanthropy, senior management (and trustees) find themselves trying to balance competing assumptions about what constitutes foundation effectiveness. The coherence of grant making is easily sacrificed.

Any effort to identify particular strategic choices must accept at the outset that the categories will be imprecise, the boundaries overlapping. These cautions voiced, I offer a six-part taxonomy: new knowledge, applied knowledge, policy analysis, policy advocacy, social movements, and service delivery.

Creating New Knowledge

A deeper understanding is one of the oldest visions of what foundations can accomplish. Major philanthropic gifts in support of scholarship date to ancient Greece. Notable examples include Plato's bequest of land to endow his famed Academy. Epicurus did likewise in endowing a school that survived for six hundred years, and Aristotle's Lyceum was funded through a bequest specified in the will of Theophrastus. The renowned library of Alexandria was funded and sustained by the Ptolemies. The Roman Republic offers further examples, as does medieval philanthropy's support of libraries and monasteries.

Non-Western philanthropy has been equally engaged in the generation and transmission of knowledge. Islamic foundations, or *waqfs,* historically were closely aligned with teaching academies (Arjomand 1998). Basing education on charitable trusts, the waqfs helped ensure equal opportunity and social mobility. Foundation support for Brahmins in Southeast Asia is given in expectation that a learned group of experts will use knowledge to guide social and moral policy (Anderson 1998).

Foundations and universities have been closely linked for centuries. The teaching and research tradition of the famous Hôtel-Dieu in Burgundy was established in 1443, when the benefactor provided a highly valued vineyard that produces vintage burgundies to this day. The University of Uppsala, also established with a gift of land, continues to receive income from this source today. Several major American universities were founded with philanthropic gifts, which by the end of the nineteenth century were more likely to be linked to industrial wealth than to land. Stanford University, though affectionately known as "the Farm," benefited less from Leland Stanford's horse farm than from his profitable Southern Pacific Railroad. Rockefeller's first large gift established the University of Chicago.

Foundations have continued to make major investments in universities and in research institutions, equipment, and personnel, as part of a broad strategy to advance basic human understanding in nearly every field of study imaginable: anthropology, astronomy, biology, chemistry, economics, history, medicine, music, physics, political science, and psychology. These investments have at times been sustained over long periods, illustrated by the Rockefeller Foundation's century-long involvement with medical science (Kohler 1991). And for some foundations for certain periods of their history, the search for new, fundamental knowledge defined what they were about, what they took to be their vocation (Lagemann 1989). The Howard Hughes Foundation (an operating foundation) is focused on basic research in the biomedical fields. The Russell Sage Foundation has, for the social sciences, been closely associated with the search for new knowledge.

New-growth theory in economics offers a deep rationale for philanthropic engagement with advancing knowledge.[21] In its hypothesis that economic growth results from new ideas as much as from the traditional factors of labor, capital, and natural resources, new-growth theory justifies knowledge creation as a powerful point of leverage for foundations interested in social change.

Applying Knowledge

Foundations with a bias toward knowledge generation seldom leave things to chance; new knowledge should be applied in socially beneficial ways. The Rockefeller Foundation has invested in public health professionals and organizations as a means to ensure that discoveries in the biomedical sciences would reach the broadest population possible, especially groups that the market ignores. Similarly, basic knowledge in learning theory has been coupled with school reform efforts, and basic knowledge in plant physiology has been linked with higher-yielding food crops suitable for growing conditions in poorer countries.

Foundations that view the creation of new knowledge as central to their task often commit grant dollars to seeing that it is applied. The reciprocal, however, is not the case. There is a much heavier foundation investment in applying knowledge than in creating it, and the imbalance has grown over the past half-century. This trend largely reflects the heavy investment in basic research by government agencies, supposedly leaving less space for foundation dollars. In some instances this strategy has proven to be shortsighted. AIDS vaccine research, for instance, was long ignored, even by foundations actively involved in developing-country diseases. When it became obvious that government sources were insufficient and pharmaceutical firms indifferent, leadership by private foundations, especially the Gates Foundation, stimulated new interest.

Foundations that define their mission as generating and/or applying new knowledge have been responsible for some of the most impressive of foundation accomplishments. Rockefeller philanthropy comes first to mind—in its establishment of Rockefeller University, its close association with the eradication of hookworm and yellow fever, and its work with the Ford Foundation that led to the Green Revolution. The impact of such basic discoveries in health and agriculture are more easily assessed than that of those in the social sciences, but Rockefeller funds helped establish the professional social sciences in both the United States and Europe, as did funding from the Carnegie Corporation and later the Ford Foundation. Several German foundations—the government-sponsored Alexander von Humboldt Foundation, for example—have also embraced knowledge generation as central to their mission.

In the second half of the twentieth century, however, funding scholarship came increasingly to mean support for the analysis of public policy, to which we next turn.

Policy Analysis

Foundations have had a long, close relation with intellectual work regarding public policy, starting with the ancient Greeks, continuing through the support for the learned classes in Islam, Hinduism, and medieval Christianity, and into the modern era. Late-nineteenth-century foundation support for studies of poverty or child labor prefigured a substantial twentieth-century investment in policy research institutions that now date in the thousands. The independent policy institute and the independent foundation are not only intricately linked in the United States, but also responsive to the same deep strand in the American political culture that prefers the private to the public sector.

Foundation funding of the social sciences, initiated before the turn of the century, was motivated by a search for improved public policy (Prewitt 1995; Sealander 1997). The close relationship between foundation funds and public policy analysis in the United States underscores how privately held philanthropic resources can attempt to advance public purposes. This relationship has been a complicated one, attracting its share of sharp criticism from both the political left and political right in the United States. Foundations have been little deterred by this criticism, and the production of policy analysis remains a central grant-making activity by American foundations.

This philanthropic agenda is becoming increasingly important in European countries. The German-based Bertelsmann Foundation, for example, announces as one of its primary goals the provision of new concepts and models for the social market economy and for public administration. Not surprisingly, as European foundations have turned to policy analysis as a leverage point for grant making, there has been a parallel growth in policy analysis organizations.

Although the emergence of policy analysis as a philanthropic project initially focused exclusively on the laws and policies of the home country, this is no longer the case. In the early years of decolonization, the Ford Foundation engaged in "state building" in dozens of new nations—funding everything from professionalizing the civil service to creating institutes with national development policy as their charge. (The state-building agenda has recently reemerged under the awkward label of "capacity building" in the World Bank and other aid agencies.) Foundations, both American and western European, were quick to fund policy analysis relevant to the emerging economies of eastern Europe and the former Soviet Union. Here the goal of the foundations was to urge policies that would strengthen civil-society organizations. Foundations put resources into where and how the boundaries separating state, market, and society would be drawn, with a strong bias in favor of a larger and more autonomous space for the civil society. The aptly named Open Society Foundation, funded by George Soros, has been the most visible proponent. With mixed success, grant making in China has pursued a similar strategy, though with less public fanfare than accompanied the arrival of Western foundations in eastern and central Europe.

Policy analysis has now moved to the global scene. Significant amounts of American and European foundation funds are focused on global public policies and the international settings in which they are made. Human rights, health and population policies, and climate change are obvious instances. The World Bank, the World Trade Organization, and the World Health Organization have all had their policies scrutinized courtesy of foundation funds. Indeed for some foundations, policy analysis is almost exclusively focused on global policies and international organizations.

Historically, of course, policy analysis has often had government in its sight. Largely this was justified as a way to "go to scale." Foundation dollars were too few to bring about school reform, to solve refugee problems, or to preserve cultural sites. But they would not be too few to make certain that governments or international agencies adopted the "right" policies that in turn would generate the desired outcomes. Insofar as the behaviors of business-sector firms were of interest, the strategy of choice was to affect regulation, taxation, and other public policies to influence market behavior. From the vantage point of the foundations, the public sector was "resource-rich, but supposedly idea-poor," offering the ideal target for philanthropic influence (Lenkowsky 1999).

With the advent of neoliberalism and the shrinking of the state, foundations have begun to ask whether the logic of policy analysis should be turned on market actors. This agenda is undeveloped as yet, but some early victories will further embolden foundations in this direction. The health sector illustrates one early accomplishment: Citing unfavorable market conditions, pharmaceutical manufacturers ignored diseases plaguing poor countries. The consumer base was not there to reward the high research and development costs. But, prodded by foundation-funded policy analysis and advocacy efforts, the drug companies have discovered the merits of tiered pricing, low-cost production, and even selective research-and-development investment in diseases of the poor. Microcredit lending (below-market loans in impoverished areas for small-scale entrepreneurs) has also brought foundations directly into the market, again with success. In this instance, going to scale was accomplished by attracting the World Bank to microcredit lending.

Another commercial sector that has drawn foundation activity is energy, where major corporations are beginning to adopt serious environment-friendly practices such as greater attention to renewable energy sources. Foundation grant dollars from, for example, MacArthur and Pew, can take some credit. More dramatic changes can be expected if foundations are successful in prodding corporations to start pricing the risks of continued global warming. A large German insurance company, Munich Re, has estimated costs as high as $300 billion per year associated with global warming by 2050. These costs are projected in the form of weather damage, agricultural losses, and compliance with regulatory regimes. Environmental activists, with foundation support, are warning that many industries are not publicly stating these potential vulnerabilities. If these costs are included in the accounting on which investors rely to assess long-term profit potential, there is likely to be a stronger movement toward limits on fossil fuel consumption (Cortese 2002).

With the arrival on the foundation scene of young, recently wealthy entrepreneurs from the high-technology industries, market-focused philanthropy has increased. This entrepreneurial or venture-capital philanthropy has also ushered in a preoccupation with performance measures. The degree to which this trend will supplant rather than add to traditional patterns of public policy funding is uncertain, though it is unlikely that foundations will soon exit the long-established field of public policy analysis.

Policy Advocacy

Policy advocacy is to policy analysis what application is to new knowledge. That is, if policy analysis does not of itself change policy, some foundations choose to put pressure on the policymakers by funding advocacy groups. Many twentieth-century foundations did so—supporting a seemingly endless parade of organizations dedicated to fighting for the "right" public policies in human rights, equal opportunity, nuclear disarmament, environmental protection, children's welfare, and so on. Such funding gained special momentum in the post–World War II period as governments became increasingly active in areas long of interest to the philanthropic sector and as the number of public policy institutes dramatically increased (Rich 2004). If foundation funds could pressure government leaders to adopt progressive policies, the impact would be far greater than what could be accomplished with foundation funds alone. It was with this goal in mind that foundation administrators talk of "going to scale."

Stated more abstractly: government, through its regulatory and taxation powers, influences private expenditure patterns; foundations reverse the flow of influence by using private (tax-free) funds on advocacy that will alter government spending priorities. There are, of course, laws that regulate whether a foundation can be political in its activities, but the definition of what is permitted varies widely from country to country.[22] Nowhere are the laws easy to enforce. In the United States, for example, laws prohibit foundations from directly influencing legislation but not from influencing public views about pending legislation, executive branch consideration of policy choice, or legal challenges to existing or proposed laws.[23]

As policy analysis has shifted to the international and global arena, so of course has policy advocacy. The World Bank agencies and the specialized agencies of the United Nations have been so imposed upon by advocacy groups that they have institutionalized forums for policy advice from nongovernmental groups. When such groups are not given privileged access, they establish alternative venues that compete for media attention and otherwise pressure the international agencies. Foundations have provided the funds for these activities. The partnership between foundations and advocacy groups has been especially active in environmental issues, in women's education and health, and more broadly in establishing human rights as a recognized obligation of the world community.

Policy advocacy shades into the next category, social-movement philanthropy, when foundations turn to what is often called, if not very precisely, civil-society funding.

Social Movements and Social Empowerment

Though overlapping policy advocacy, social-movement philanthropy differs because broad-scale social movements encompass more than policy change. In recent decades, foundations have funded social movements organized around equality for women, environmental protection, and civil rights for racial and ethnic minorities. Although each of these social movements originated outside philanthropy, foundation dollars rather quickly helped to stabilize them, often by funding full-time, professional leadership. Support for social movements generally dates from the social activism of the 1960s and particularly connects with the rights-based liberalism that was then gathering momentum (O'Connor 2001). Social-movement grant making has now been internationalized, as worldwide organizations have formed to mobilize around environmental protection, individual rights, or children's welfare. What foundations refer to as support for grassroots organizations or community groups is often an element of social-movement philanthropy. It is frequently described as a "bottom-up" rather than "top-down" change strategy and is self-consciously differentiated from an investment in new knowledge or policy studies.

Closely associated with such funding is an emphasis on social empowerment: the direct empowerment of the powerless or disenfranchised. An example is microcredit lending, which is designed to put resources directly in the hands of the powerless poor. Social-movement and social-empowerment philanthropy are linked in that the former has the dual purpose of empowering its adherents and changing the social landscape. But empowerment in itself need not be part of an effort to create a social movement. The beneficiaries of a microcredit lending program or a women's education strategy are not generally viewed as members of a movement in the same way that environmentalists or feminists are. Social empowerment, of course, is a close cousin to charity—the direct relief of suffering. But it differs from charity insofar as it intends to remove what leads to the suffering for which relief is sought.

Social Service Delivery

The foundation strategy most resembling charity is grant making focused on delivery of social services: youth development, housing, health care, special education, and legal aid. What distinguishes service-delivery philanthropy from charity is that the former, as a foundation project, can be justified as testing a model or promoting an innovation that can then be adopted elsewhere. A large proportion of community foundation grant making falls into the service-delivery category, as does grant making by smaller foundations. In the aggregate, social-service philanthropy accounts for approximately 20 percent of grant activity in the United States.

Service delivery lies the furthest from the scientific philanthropy pioneered by Rockefeller and Carnegie as a way to distinguish their efforts from Victorian-era charity. That it persists is testimony to the power of the human instinct to relieve suffering directly and not just circuitously through knowledge or policy.

Change Strategies and Theory

This rudimentary taxonomy based on change strategies underscores the thinness of our theory of foundation activity. We know much more about how foundations came to be than what they accomplish. The taxonomy suggests that foundations with a common view toward effecting social change are likely to be more alike, even if active in different sectors, than are foundations that fund similar issues or sectors but bring to their grant making different views of how best to leverage funds.

Such a taxonomy, more carefully constructed than what is offered here, could be the beginning point for an accounting of how foundation strategies have varied across time and in response to what external conditions. This is the first step to theorizing. To suggest a few obvious questions: Do foundations adopt different change strategies as the state expands or contracts relative to the market? Does donor intent tend to favor different notions about change than those favored by the professional staff that eventually and inevitably gains influence over the foundation agenda? Are foundations in transitional democracies or emerging economies likely to view their vocation differently from those in more established democracies or mature economies? Questions abound, but answers are in short supply.

Foundation Methods

The notion of a change strategy suggests that foundations might be characterized in terms of their stance toward social improvement. Another alternative is to consider the methods used by foundations; for example, demonstration projects, training programs, public commissions, endowment contributions, and institution building. Though the distinction between strategy and method lacks precision, it helps us see that a given method can be used across different change strategies.

Training, or what is now often called "human capital development," offers a clear example. It is supported by many foundations that otherwise differ widely in what and how they fund. Foundations give grants to advance scientific careers and thus new knowledge, to train leaders for policy advocacy work and social movements, and to offer in-career training opportunities to the staff of social-service organizations. The fact that the same method is used across diverse subject matters and strategies suggests the usefulness of treating it as a separate dimension of foundation practice. The distinction is nevertheless blurred, because certain methods correlate with particular strategies—demonstration projects are usually associated with service-delivery philanthropy; media campaigns are often part of policy advocacy funding; commissions are used to study and report on social problems; and fellowships have long been favored as an instrument to advance knowledge by bringing new talent to a field.

Probably the method that is most common across foundation programs is public enlightenment. There have been countless instances over the past century suggesting that a foundation hoped to correct wrong beliefs and improve misguided public practices. A public inclined to permit inefficient and corrupt partisan politics, for example, might be taught to appreciate the virtues of independent expertise and a professional civil service in government—and thus turn-of-the-century American philanthropy took up this progressive cause. Similarly, a public too given to racial prejudice might be enlightened to the moral worth of racial tolerance—a major philanthropic project throughout the twentieth century. In more recent decades, some foundations have aimed to help the public understand the value of multiculturalism, while other foundations have worried whether multiculturalism undermines a common civic culture.

This same public has, at different moments in the last half-century, been seen as parochial, leading the more cosmopolitan private foundations to launch efforts to create a more internationally conscious civic culture. Other examples multiply easily: the public has been considered inefficient in its use of energy, ignorant of the dangers of population growth, illiterate about its national history, prone to unhealthy eating habits, and, repeatedly, insensitive to the plight of—depending on the times—women, workers, children, the poor, immigrants, minorities, or others from a long list that has changed its emphasis from decade to decade but has never been absent from the philanthropic portfolio. These deficiencies in public knowledge, understanding, or attitude have been targeted for correction through the selective use of foundation resources: introducing new elements into the school curriculum, publishing influential books, developing media campaigns, creating different policy incentives, and helping leaders with new and "better" values to emerge.

It is somewhat arbitrary, of course, to characterize public enlightenment as a foundation method rather than a strategy. What is important is recognizing how pervasively it has endured throughout foundation history in the United States and Europe. This is not surprising. Democracies require an enlightened public; it stands to reason that foundations in democratic nations will promote public understanding of the principles and practices of liberal democracy. To a lesser extent, foundations have promoted public understanding of the principles and practices of a free-market economy, though this has emerged as an active cause primarily for more conservative foundations in recent decades.

What are commonly described as conservative foundations have been exceptionally focused on public education efforts designed to challenge the underlying premises of the welfare state. The more prominent of these foundations—Bradley, Olin, Scaife, and Smith Richardson—have funded policy institutions such as the American Enterprise Institute and the CATO Institute, which began to gain influence with the election of President Reagan in 1980. They have steadily increased their influence by funding major scholars, whose books, often written for the general public, have helped balance the liberal inclinations of the larger and longer-established foundations.

A Historical Model

Classifications based on change strategies or on the methods used by foundations could, in principle, be applied historically to gauge changes in emphases for an individual foundation or for the sector as a whole. The scholar who has come closest to attempting an account of broad-scale shifts in the American foundation sector is James Allen Smith (1999). He offers five stages: the protofoundation era, from 1890 to 1910; the early evolution of the modern grant-making foundation, from 1910 to the early 1930s; a phase from the 1930s until the mid-1940s, in which foundations responded to national economic need and then to the war effort; the postwar era, from the late 1940s to about 1970, which witnessed a renewed self-confidence about the foundation mission; and the most recent period, which starts with the regulatory regime imposed by the Tax Act of 1969 and includes the vast growth of the sector from the assets generated by the technological revolution of the late twentieth century, adding large foundations based on the wealth of Bill Gates, David Packard, William Hewlett, and Gordon Moore.

Smith suggests that a sequence of scientific metaphors characterizing different research phases in the twentieth century might help us understand shifting foundation strategies. He starts with the germ-theory metaphor that gave rise to scientific philanthropy at the turn of the last century. Germ theory focused on a specific cause of a specific disease; eliminate the cause, eliminate the disease. This biomedical concept was adopted by Rockefeller and his colleagues when they announced that "root causes" would be their focus. Later in the century, writes Smith, foundation leaders were more likely to cite metaphors from physics and even psychology, with their emphases on restoring equilibrium to unbalanced systems. For example, during the Depression of the 1930s, the focus was on economic stabilization.[24] In the words of a Rockefeller officer, business cycle fluctuations were "the underlying forces in which much of our physical suffering, illness, mental disorder, family disintegration, crime, political upheaval, and social instability have their origins" (Smith 1999:44–45). Citing the document that shaped the postwar Ford Foundation, Smith suggests that the period from the mid-1940s to 1970 draws from engineering metaphors, with their emphasis on knowledge application and systems analysis. This metaphor, in turn, gave way to a viral metaphor, brought forcefully to attention by the AIDS epidemic. "The HIV assault on the immune system is far more complex than the attack of a germ or parasite and cannot be reduced to a single causal model" (Smith 1999:47–48). This suggests that foundations today have to think differently about cause-and-effect relations, and thus about what might make philanthropic interventions effective.

The usefulness of this attempt to frame foundation history in terms of successive scientific metaphors remains to be determined, but the effort to track shifting emphases across time is an important step toward thinking theoretically about foundation practice and performance.

A Cross-National Model

An alternative and equally useful approach adopted by Anheier (2001) is based on cross-country comparison, using European examples. This analysis classifies European countries into seven groups: social democratic, state-centered, corporatist, liberal, peripheral, Mediterranean, and post-statist. It then compares these country groupings in terms of the importance they place on foundations and the major characteristics of their foundation sectors. In social democratic countries such as Sweden and Norway, there are large operating foundations integrated with the public welfare system as well as many smaller foundations often associated with social movements. In contrast, state-centered countries such as France and Belgium make less use of foundations, supervise them closely, and generally expect them to engage in welfare delivery. The liberal model, illustrated by the United Kingdom, gives prominence to independent grant-making foundations, similar to those in the United States. Ireland and Greece, the "peripheral" examples, tend to have few grant-making foundations and instead rely on foundations as service providers that compensate for the public sector's shortfall (Anheier 2001:68–75).

This effort has the substantial merit of enabling cross-national comparisons; it also is a start toward systematic attention to an issue raised in this chapter's first section: how the boundaries that separate the state, the market, and the nonprofit sector are being renegotiated and what roles foundations are playing in those processes.

None of the theoretical approaches summarized here—legal distinctions, change strategies, foundation methods, historical analyses, cross-national comparisons—are sufficiently developed to offer a general theory of foundation behavior. None, to date, have attempted to answer a question necessarily at the core of any attempt to theorize about foundations: how much impact do they have? With this caution in mind, and at the risk of relying on anecdotes and informed opinion, the final section takes up this question.

Measuring the Impact of Foundations

Foundation funding does matter in ways already suggested: they are a force for pluralism, scientific investigation, policy reform, public education, institution building, social-welfare provision, and much more. If it is safe to claim that foundation funds do nudge social change in desired directions, social scientists would still like to assess the magnitude of that impact in relation to the funds spent. It would be useful to have a metric of impact. None exists, and thus we must fall back on generalizations informed by historical knowledge.

The proposition with which I am most comfortable can be simply put: foundations work at the edges of large-scale social change rather than cause those changes in the first place. The major strategic choices made by foundations—scientific research, policy analysis, policy advocacy, social movements—or their attempts at redistribution or provision of social services are dwarfed by the larger forces generated in the political, social, economic, and technological arenas. What foundations can do, if they catch the wave, is accelerate what is already under way, redirect it to a limited extent, selectively and partially prevent unfortunate side effects, help to institutionalize positive change by giving it professional footing, and bring the results to public attention. These are not trivial achievements.

Foundations themselves are not of much use in assessing these achievements. Self-evaluations, for example, are designed to help a foundation review a particular program, but they do not lead to generalizations that can advance theoretical thinking about social impact. With the exception of a few excellent case studies (Kohler 1991; Lagemann 1989), there is little theory in foundation evaluation.

Of even less use is foundations' rhetoric about their accomplishments. Rare indeed is the foundation that admits to working at the edge of social forces vastly greater than its resources. They too often write as if they can, in fact, eradicate poverty, secure world peace, eliminate diseases, reform public education, provide leadership for the next generation, empower the disenfranchised, and more. The annual reports of most foundations read more like campaign documents than balanced accounts of modest successes, false starts, and even a few failures. We would have a surer sense of what has and can be achieved if foundations' language better matched the realities.

A perspective on foundation impact can be provided by appraising a specific time and a place. Consider the United States in the second half of the twentieth century. Certainly in the modern period no nation was ever so blessed with foundation funds. In the postwar period, the foundation sector had substantial resources, strong leadership, vigorous self-confidence, public support, and ample opportunity to engage the standard repertoire of foundation causes. We ask of this period, what were the significant social changes and what was the role of foundations in shaping them?

The 1950s incubated the civil rights movement, certainly a transforming moment in American history. The civil rights movement led to the dismantling of discriminatory social, political, and economic practices that stretched back to the colonial period and that had effectively denied civic membership not just to slaves and their descendants but also to American Indians, Asians, and Hispanics, while limiting mobility for women. American foundations had long been active in civil rights issues and were certainly involved in the 1950s. But it was a broad-based social movement, organized principally by churches, that forced the major changes. It was not caused or funded by foundations, nor could it have been. Social movements are not planned.

This observation is also clear in the other social movements that have so reshaped American society in recent decades. The antiwar movement, which shaded into far-reaching cultural change, challenged public authority in the name of freedom, gave momentum to notions of participatory democracy, and, perhaps, sanctioned a civic culture that values personal satisfaction over social responsibility and obligation. Both the civil rights and the antiwar movements were bolstered by the earlier victories of the feminist movement that so successfully challenged comfortable assumptions about the proper role of women in society. To these could be added the environmental movement and, somewhat later, the gay and lesbian rights movement.

Foundations played important supportive roles in these developments, but mostly in an attempt to catch up with forces far more powerful than any they could have launched on their own. The feminist movement, for example, found early support from the Ford Foundation, which helped provide professional leadership and academic respectability and in other ways facilitated its legitimacy. Similarly with environmentalism: a century-old concern with the conservation of nature was transformed when it merged with issues ranging across global climate change, ozone depletion, energy inefficiencies, recycling, air and water quality, toxic waste, and sustainable development. Foundation funding played an important role in the expansion and transformation of environmentalism as a social movement and a public preoccupation. But these funds were just one of many factors. Government-funded science and university research were critical to shaping what became the environmental agenda. Membership-based organizations, funded by dues and private contributions, forced policy changes. Public attitudes changed in response to media coverage, to politicians who adopted the environmental cause, and to millions of small-scale civic efforts. There were foundation funds in this mix, but they represented a fraction of the research, advocacy, and public education resources.

Foundations cannot invent a social movement for the simple reason that they cannot operate on behalf of a cause that does not already have organizational underpinnings. Grant dollars have to be sent somewhere. In some instances, under special conditions, a foundation can create institutions for a given purpose, as the Rockefeller Foundation did in establishing schools of public health or Carnegie did in establishing public libraries. But there have to be willing partners—universities in the former case and city governments in the latter. Even if they had the imagination and vision to do so, foundations are not equipped to blaze trails in advance of the grantee institutions on whom they depend for program ideas and implementation.

If foundations, despite their rhetoric, are much more likely to be early followers than leaders in the social arenas they have long favored, the pattern is even more pronounced in the political-economic realm. Consider the social impacts of the broad shifts in public policy associated with the Reagan-Thatcher years. Wealth redistribution was taken off the political agenda; the liberal claim that a regulated economy is a more just economy was successfully challenged; the assumption that the state had responsibilities for the vulnerable gave way to privatization. The political left now espouses a "third way" in which the public good is, apparently, better served under liberal market assumptions. Though a few conservative foundations prepared position papers for the Reagan administration, to believe that foundations caused this seismic shift in political-economic thought and practice is wildly off the mark. Conservative foundations continue to generate studies, books, lectures, and conferences supportive of these shifts in public thinking, and liberal foundations counter as best they can. But the transformation itself did not need foundation support.

Neither, of course, did the most sweeping technological change since the assembly line. High-speed personal computers—with all their implications for how we learn, work, produce, cooperate, mobilize, and play—evolved in a business sector outside of and even unaware of foundations or the much larger nonprofit sector. It has been left to foundations to worry about the digital divide, to explore the promise of distance learning, and to question whether poor countries can propel themselves into the modern era on the back of the information revolution. These are not small concerns, and they are fitting as foundation issues. But, again, foundations have worked at the edges, doing what they can to minimize the harm and maximize the good of large transformations well beyond their control.

We end, thus, where we started. Lacking a general theory

of foundations, and uncertain about how best to classify the multiple ways they try to effect social change, we fall back on informed opinion, anecdotes, or case studies to try to answer the core question: what is the impact of foundations?[25] This, I suggest, is the question that should shape a research agenda for the scholarly community. This research agenda intersects in important ways with a question confronting modern governments that have encouraged a vigorous philanthropic sector: is foundation autonomy compatible with democratic accountability?

THE ACCOUNTABILITY OF FOUNDATIONS

Foundations are frequently subjected to accountability claims (Collins, Rogers, and Garner 2000; Brody 1998). Three general reasons are cited: foundations receive a public subsidy; they project their vision of the public good into the public arena; and they create a state-protected power asymmetry between those with money and those who want it. The foundation sector is, by definition and in law, largely undemocratic, for how else to characterize a wealthy elite who apply tax protected dollars to enact their vision of the public good (Frumkin 2004).

The earlier sections of this chapter noted various rationales given for the substantial autonomy granted to foundations, covering such issues as cost-effectiveness, redistribution, enhancing pluralism, and expressive of liberal doctrine. Hovering over all of these rationales is the assumption that foundations "do good." That is, they meet a consequentialist test. This returns us to the analysis of social change strategies. What are the social conditions that foundations intend to improve? Are they successful in doing so? While the first of these questions can be answered by reading mission statements and program goals, an answer to the second, as we have seen, is more elusive.

By their own testimony, foundations are hugely successful. The U.S. Council on Foundations shares with its members a list of ten foundation achievements that can be used to convince the public that foundations are worthy institutions. It is an interestingly eclectic list: the 911 system for emergency calls; the hospice movement; the Pap smear in cancer treatment; public libraries; the polio vaccine; rocket sciences; PBS's *Sesame Street* series; white lines on highways; the Green Revolution, and yellow fever vaccine. It is no accident that the list tilts toward public health, a generally safe area, and ignores achievements with more political content—such as civil rights funding, environmental causes, prochoice advocacy, or arms control. It is the latter type of grant making that calls forth demands for more accountability, though governments have had little success at imposing limits on the agendas pursued by foundations. Attempting to regulate the areas in which foundations offer grants runs against the notion that foundations are expected to seek out market failures and policy inadequacies—both criticizing and compensating for them.

In recent years, at least in the United States, accountability has been framed less around grant-making portfolios than around issues of transparency, efficiency, and fiscal responsibility (including officer compensation). This strong attention to procedural accountability has focused not just on foundations but on the entire nonprofit sector (Fleishman 1999; Bradley, Jansen, and Silverman 2003). Accountability arrangements for the nonprofit sector tend to stress legal and regulatory mechanisms that mandate particular practices and/or establishing conditions that must be met before funds can be made available. These arrangements can be effective for nonprofits, which do not have the luxury of an endowment that provides protection against, especially, funding conditionalities. But they have had limited impact on foundations, whose endowments leave the government few regulatory options. For example, in 2003, the U.S. Congress focused on the minimum level of distribution—normally 5 percent of a foundation's asset base. The modest contemplated change was to remove foundation administrative expenses from the 5 percent calculation. This proposal immediately generated an extensive and expensive lobbying effort by the foundation sector. (The issue has not been resolved as of this writing, but it is unlikely that there will be a serious change in standing foundation management practices.)

The American foundation sector has been successful in deflecting demands for substantive accountability by expanding in such areas as transparency and professionalism (Frumkin 1999, 2004). Transparency, as Frumkin notes, is less threatening than substantive accountability. Foundations have become adept at generating information about their grant-making criteria and program priorities—often in glossy annual reports and expensive Web sites easily the equal of commercial firms'. Foundations have also turned to self-evaluation. Grants and sometimes entire programs are subjected to extensive retroactive evaluations, using a mixture of in-house staff and outside consultants. Although these evaluations often improve foundation practice, they are also used to deflect external assessments of foundation priorities and accomplishments.

There has been some interest in "peer review" to strengthen the accountability of foundations, modeled on the accreditation systems used by higher education in the United States. Depending on its design, such a system could move closer to substantive accountability—and perhaps for that reason it has remained an issue for discussion in scholarly journals more than an active topic among foundation trustees and officers.

It is likely that the foundation sector will continue to improve its procedural accountability—its treatment of grantees, its financial management, its public reporting. It is certain that foundations will strongly and probably successfully resist accountability of a more substantive type—a review of their program priorities or of the effectiveness with which they accomplish their self-defined missions. In fact, the more developed the procedural accountability, the easier to resist substantive accountability.

We are left with an unresolved and probably irresolvable question: What is the proper balance of autonomy and substantive accountability for the foundation sector? Society grants unique privileges to foundations and in return requires that philanthropic wealth promote the public good. But there is a circularity in this formulation. What emerges as the "public good" is itself the result of private deliberation. There is no effective mechanism by which various interests in society can voice their preferences for what public goods are appropriate as foundation agendas. This would require substantive accountability of a sort that foundations resist and that governments have shown no appetite to impose.

As with the leading analytic question of scholarly research—what is the social impact of the private foundation?—answers are in short supply for the leading political question—should foundations be more substantively accountable? In the meantime, the private foundation sector will continue to expand in numbers and in wealth.

NOTES

1. An extended and more nuanced treatment of these issues appears in Steinberg (1987).

2. Simon (1987) usefully describes how regulatory and tax law influences these borders.

3. This observation is easily confirmed by inspecting *Who Gets Grants* (Foundation Center 1998).

4. The forms are copiously displayed in a survey of philanthropy across the world's religious and cultural traditions in Ilchman, Katz, and Queen (1998). See also Robbins, this volume.

5. Robbins, this volume, offers a useful extension and even correction of this point when he observes that philanthropy can be used by rival factions vying for political power and to unseat the reigning social factions.

6. Anheier, based on an extensive review of foundations across Europe, comes to a similar conclusion. He notes that, in the aggregate, foundations add capacity to what is provided by governments and markets. "In this sense, foundations initiate additional, different 'search procedures' in addressing the social, political, economic and cultural problems of our time" (2001:75).

7. This section draws from Prewitt (1999).

8. Anheier discusses European foundations in these terms and comes to the conclusion that pluralism is promoted by the "aggregate effect of foundations," if not by each individual foundation (2001:75).

9. For European materials in this section, I am indebted to Smith and Borgmann (2001) and to other material collected in Schluter, Then, and Walkenhorst (2001). The best source of historical materials on foundations in other world regions is Ilchman, Katz, and Queen (1998). Robbins, this volume, offers a theoretically informed discussion of traditions of philanthropy in the West.

10. For detailed treatment of the period prior to the late nineteenth century, as well as additional treatment of the modern period, see Hall, this volume.

11. Many have written to this point, though none have been as theoretically informed as Karl and Katz (1987).

12. Cited in Fosdick (1952:22).

13. These examples and others are noted in MacDonald (1956:42–44).

14. Hall (this volume) reminds us that official resistance to philanthropic initiatives predated this period, noting among other examples that President Andrew Jackson questioned the appropriateness of accepting the bequest of British aristocrat James Smithson that established the Smithsonian Institution.

15. Karl writes specifically of the United States when he observes that our government, "uniquely among the major governments of the world, depends on the side of democracy which classical philosophers most feared: instant responsiveness to mass opinion to quell or generate revolution, an often ruthless demagoguery which attracts temporary but insistent majorities, that special form of ignorance which comes from the need of the inexperienced to learn how to do what their publics have elected them to do, and the short span of popular attention" (1997:219).

16. For an overview of these classifications, see Boris (1999). For a detailed review of corporate foundations, see Levy (1999).

17. The Foundation Center is the premier source of data about U.S. foundations, but it does not include in its documentation the grants made by the National Science Foundation, the National Institutes of Health, the National Endowment for the Humanities, or the National Endowment for the Arts. These government agencies are modeled on and behave in ways similar to private foundations.

18. Margo has used the distinction between independent, community, and corporate foundations to compare payout rates, and finds that across nearly three decades the corporate foundations have much higher average payout rates than either community or independent foundations. Corporates have two to three times the payout rates of community foundations, and the community foundations tend to be marginally higher than the independent foundations, with the latter staying close to a 5 percent payout rate (1992:219).

19. Margo (1992:221) uses such distinctions to track change over time, but his analysis is complicated by coding and other changes in the data provided by the Foundation Center.

20. This section's discussion of change strategies is based on a version first published in Prewitt (2001).

21. For a summary of economic growth theory, see Jovanovic (2001).

22. For a discussion of selected European cases, see Drobnig (2001:625–26).

23. See Lenkowsky (1999) for a discussion of the impact on the policy advocacy agenda of the devolution of selected government programs from federal to local governments.

24. Hall, this volume, suggestively titles a section covering this historical period as "Social Engineering: Welfare Capitalism, Scientific Management, and the Associative State."

25. Anheier, for Europe, offers some useful hypotheses comparing postsocialist countries with corporatist, social democratic, and liberal models, positing that foundations may have led to more social change in the former than they have in the latter (2001:74–75).

REFERENCES

Anderson, Leona. 1998. "Contextualizing Philanthropy in South Asia: A Textual Analysis of Sanskrit Sources." Pp. 57–78 in *Philanthropy in the World's Traditions,* edited by Warren F. Ilchman, Stanley N. Katz, and Edward L. Queen. Bloomington: Indiana University Press.

Anheier, Helmut K. 2001 "Foundations in Europe: A Comparative Perspective." Pp. 35–81 in *Foundations in Europe: Society, Management and Law,* edited by Andreas Schluter, Voker Then, and Peter Walkenhorst. London: Directory of Social Change.

Arjomand, Said Amir. 1998. "Philanthropy, the Law, and Public Policy in the Islamic World before the Modern Era." Pp. 109–32 in *Philanthropy in the World's Traditions,* edited by Warren F. Ilchman, Stanley N. Katz, and Edward L. Queen. Bloomington: Indiana University Press.

Arnove, Robert F. 1980. *Philanthropy and Cultural Imperialism: The Foundations at Home and Abroad.* Boston: G. K. Hall.

Berlin, Isaiah. 1990. *The Crooked Timber of Humanity,* edited by Henry Hardy. London: HarperCollins, Fontan Press.

Berman, Edward H. 1983. *The Influence of the Carnegie, Ford, and Rockefeller Foundations on American Foreign Policy: The Ideology of Philanthropy.* Albany: State University of New York Press.

Boris, Elizabeth T. 1999. "The Nonprofit Sector in the 1990s." Pp. 1–33 in *Philanthropy and the Nonprofit Sector in a Changing America,* edited by Charles T. Clotfelter and Thomas Ehrlich. Bloomington: Indiana University Press, 1999.

Bradley, Bill, Paul Jansen, and Les Silverman. 2003. "The Nonprofit Sector's $100 Billion Opportunity." *Harvard Business Review.* May.

Brody, Evelyn. 1998. "Of Sovereignty and Subsidy: Conceptualizing the Charity Tax Exemption." *Journal of Corporation Law* 23:585–629.

Carnegie, Andrew. 1889. "Wealth." *North American Review* 148 (June): 653–64 and 149 (December): 682–98. Reprinted in *The Gospel of Wealth and Other Timely Essays* (New York: Century, 1900).

Clotfelter, Charles T. 1992. "The Distributional Consequences of Nonprofit Activities." Pp. 1–23 in *Who Benefits from the Nonprofit Sector?* edited by Charles T. Clotfelter. Chicago: University of Chicago Press.

Collins, Chuck, and Pam Rogers with Joan P. Garner. 2000. *Robin Hood Was Right: A Guide to Giving Your Money for Social Change.* New York: Norton.

Congressional Record. 1953. Vol. 99, no. 141, 27 July.

Coon, Horace. 1938. *Money to Burn: What the Great American Foundations Do with Their Money.* New York: Longmans, Green.

Cortese, Amy. 2002. "As the Earth Warms, Will Companies Pay?" *New York Times,* 18 August.

DiMaggio, Paul J., and Helmut K. Anheier. 1990. "The Sociology of Nonprofit Organizations and Sectors." *Annual Review of Sociology* 16:137–59.

Drobnig, Ulrich. 2001. "Foundations as Institutionalized Charitable Activity." Pp. 604–26 in *Foundations in Europe: Society, Management and Law,* edited by Andreas Schluter, Voker Then, and Peter Walkenhorst. London: Directory of Social Change.

Fleishman, Joel L., 1999. "Public Trust in Not-for-Profit Organizations and the Need for Regulatory Reform." Pp. 172–97 in *Philanthropy and the Nonprofit Sector in a Changing America,* edited by Charles T. Clotfelter and Thomas Ehrlich. Bloomington: Indiana University Press.

Fosdick, Raymond B. 1952. *The Story of the Rockefeller Foundation: Nineteen Thirteen to Nineteen Fifty.* New York: Harper and Brothers.

Foundation Center. 1998. *Who Gets Grants: Foundation Grants to Nonprofit Organizations.* 5th ed., edited by Rebecca MacLean and Denise McLeod. New York: Foundation Center.

Frumkin, Peter. 1999. "Private Foundations as Public Institutions: Regulation, Professionalization, and the Redefinition of Organized Philanthropy." Pp. 69–100 in *Philanthropic Foundations: New Scholarship, New Possibilities,* edited by Ellen Condliffe Lagemann. Bloomington: Indiana University Press.

———. 2004. "Accountability and Legitimacy in American Foundation Philanthropy." Conference paper for "Legitimacy and Functions of Foundations in Europe and the United States," organized by the Fondation Mattei Dogan and the Social Science Research Council, Paris. To be published in *The Legitimacy of Philanthropic Foundations,* edited by Kenneth Prewitt, Mattei Dogan, Steven Heydemann, and Stefan Toepler. New York: Russell Sage Foundation, 2006.

Hansmann, Henry. 1980. "The Role of Nonprofit Enterprises." *Yale Law Journal* 89:835–901.

Harr, John Ensor, and Peter J. Johnson. 1988. *The Rockefeller Century.* New York: Charles Scribner's Sons.

Ilchman, Warren F., Stanley N. Katz, and Edward L. Queen II. 1998. *Philanthropy in the World's Traditions.* Bloomington: Indiana University Press.

James, Estelle. 1993. "Why Do Different Countries Choose a Different Public-Private Sector Mix of Educational Services?" *Journal of Human Resources* 28:571–92.

Jovanovic, Boyan. 2001. "Economic Growth: Theory." Pp. 4098–4101 in *International Encyclopedia of the Social and Behavioral Sciences,* vol. 6, edited by Neil Smelser and Paul B. Baltes. New York: Elsevier.

Karl, Barry. 1997. "Philanthropy and the Maintenance of Democratic Elites." *Minerva* 35:207–20.

Karl, Barry D., and Stanley N. Katz. 1987. "Foundations and Ruling Class Elites." *Daedalus: Journal of the American Academy of Arts and Sciences* 116:1–40.

Kohler, Robert E. 1991. *Partners in Science: Foundations and*

Natural Scientists, 1900–1945. Chicago: University of Chicago Press.

Lagemann, Ellen Condliffe. 1989. *The Politics of Knowledge: The Carnegie Corporation, Philanthropy, and Public Policy.* Middletown, Conn.: Wesleyan University Press.

Lenkowsky, Leslie. 1999. "Reinventing Philanthropy." Pp. 122–38 in *Philanthropy and the Nonprofit Sector in a Changing America,* edited by Charles T. Clotfelter and Thomas Ehrlich. Bloomington: Indiana University Press.

Levy, Reynold. 1999. "Corporate Philanthropy Comes of Age: Its Size, Its Import, Its Future." Pp. 99–121 in *Philanthropy and the Nonprofit Sector in a Changing America,* edited by Charles T. Clotfelter and Thomas Ehrlich. Bloomington: Indiana University Press.

MacDonald, Dwight. 1956. *The Ford Foundation: The Men and the Millions.* New York: Reynal.

Margo, Robert A. 1992. "Foundations." Pp. 207–34 in *Who Benefits from the Nonprofit Sector?* edited by Charles T. Clotfelter. Chicago: University of Chicago Press.

Mohn, Reinhard. 1997. "Objectives of an Operating Foundation." Pp. 24–32 in *The Work of Operating Foundations: Strategies—Instruments—Perspectives.* Gütersloh, Germany: Bertelsmann Foundation.

Nevins, Allan. 1953. *Study in Power: John D. Rockefeller, Industrialist and Philanthropist.* 2 vols. New York: Scribner.

O'Connor, Alice. 2001. *Poverty Knowledge: Social Science, Social Policy, and the Poor in Twentieth-Century U.S. History.* Princeton, N.J.: Princeton University Press.

Pinter, Francis. 2001. "The Role of Foundations in the Transformation Process in Central and Eastern Europe." Pp. 282–317 in *Foundations in Europe: Society, Management and Law,* edited by Andreas Schluter, Voker Then, and Peter Walkenhorst. London: Directory of Social Change.

Prewitt, Kenneth. 1995. *Social Sciences and Private Philanthropy: The Quest for Social Relevance.* Essays on Philanthropy, no. 15. Bloomington: Indiana University Center on Philanthropy.

———. 1999. "The Importance of Foundations in an Open Society." Pp. 17–30 in *The Future of Foundations in an Open Society,* edited by the Bertelsmann Foundation. Gütersloh, Germany: Bertelsmann Foundation.

———. 2001. "The Foundation Mission: Purpose, Practice, Public Pressures." Pp. 340–71 in *Foundations in Europe: Society, Management and Law,* edited by Andreas Schluter, Voker Then, and Peter Walkenhorst. London: Directory of Social Change.

———. 2004. "Modern Philanthropic Foundations and the Liberal Society." Conference paper for "Legitimacy and Functions of Foundations in Europe and the United States," organized by the Fondation Mattei Dogan and the Social Science Research Council, Paris. To be published in *The Legitimacy of Philanthropic Foundations,* edited by Kenneth Prewitt, Mattei Dogan, Steven Heydemann, and Stefan Toepler. New York: Russell Sage Foundation, 2006.

Rich, Andrew. 2004. *Think Tanks, Public Policy, and the Politics of Expertise.* New York: Cambridge University Press.

Rockefeller, John D. 1984. *Random Reminiscences of Men and Events.* Tarrytown, N.Y.: Rockefeller Archive Center, Sleepy Hollow Press.

Salamon, Lester. 1992. "Social Services." Pp. 134–73 in *Who Benefits from the Nonprofit Sector?* edited by Charles T. Clotfelter. Chicago: University of Chicago Press.

Salamon, Lester, and Helmut K. Anheier. 1998. "Social Origins of Civil Society: Explaining the Nonprofit Sector Cross-Nationally." *Voluntas* 9:213–48.

Schluter, Andreas, Voker Then, and Peter Walkenhorst. 2001. *Foundations in Europe: Society, Management and Law.* London: Directory of Social Change.

Sealander, Judith. 1997. *Private Wealth and Public Life: Foundation Philanthropy and the Reshaping of American Social Policy from the Progressive Era to the New Deal.* Baltimore: John Hopkins University Press.

Simon, John G. 1987. "The Tax Treatment of Nonprofit Organizations: A Review of Federal and State Policies." Pp. 67–98 in *The Nonprofit Sector: A Research Handbook,* edited by Walter W. Powell. 1st ed. New Haven, Conn.: Yale University Press.

Smith, James Allen. 1999. "The Evolving American Foundation." Pp. 34–51 in *Philanthropy and the Nonprofit Sector in a Changing America,* edited by Charles T. Clotfelter and Thomas Ehrlich. Bloomington: Indiana University Press.

Smith, James Allen, and Karsten Borgmann. 2001. "Foundations in Europe: The Historical Context." Pp. 2–34 in *Foundations in Europe: Society, Management and Law,* edited by Andreas Schluter, Voker Then, and Peter Walkenhorst. London: Directory of Social Change.

Steinberg, Richard. 1987. "Nonprofit Organizations and the Market." Pp. 118–38 in *The Nonprofit Sector: A Research Handbook,* edited by Walter W. Powell. 1st ed. New Haven, Conn.: Yale University Press.

U.S. Congress. 1916. Senate Commission on Industrial Relations. *Final Report and Testimony,* vol. 1. 64th Cong., 1st sess., S. Doc. 415. Washington, D.C.: Government Printing Office.

Weisbrod, Burton A. 1988. *The Nonprofit Economy.* Cambridge, Mass.: Harvard University Press.

Wolpert, Julian. 2004. "Redistributional Effects of America's Private Foundations." Conference paper for "Legitimacy and Functions of Foundations in Europe and the United States," organized by the Fondation Mattei Dogan and the Social Science Research Council, Paris. To be published in *The Legitimacy of Philanthropic Foundations,* edited by Kenneth Prewitt, Mattei Dogan, Steven Heydemann, and Stefan Toepler. New York: Russell Sage Foundation, 2006.

16

Nonprofit Organizations and Health Care: Some Paradoxes of Persistent Scrutiny

MARK SCHLESINGER
BRADFORD H. GRAY

Our understanding of nonprofit health care is rife with paradox. Few aspects of American society are as salient for the general public as is medical care. Extensive media coverage of its successes and failures is followed with considerable interest by much of the public (Brodie et al. 2003). People have regular encounters with the health-care system, either for their own care or for the treatment received by their family and friends. From this media exposure and personal experience, many Americans have formed strong opinions about the performance of the health-care system, simultaneously recognizing its remarkable accomplishments and persisting failures (Immerwahr, Johnson, and Kernan-Schloss 1992; Jacobs and Shapiro 1999). Nevertheless, we will argue in this chapter that prevailing public attitudes and beliefs are in some cases sharply at variance with the evidence about the relative performance of nonprofit and for-profit health-care providers.

A similar paradox exists in the academic literature. Empirical research on the implications of ownership for the delivery of medical care is far more extensive than for any other field of nonprofit activity. It has grown dramatically over the past fifteen years: we have identified more than 210 empirical studies comparing performance of for-profit and nonprofit hospitals, nursing homes, and managed-care organizations. All but about forty have been published since 1986.[1] The more recent research is markedly more sophisticated in statistical technique. Simple comparisons of means or matched pairs of facilities have been replaced by complex multivariate statistical models. Despite this burgeoning research, there remains sharp disagreement among researchers about whether ownership "matters" in health care. We will argue that many scholarly reviews inadequately and inaccurately represent the findings that have emerged from these studies.

In short, we contend that the prevailing portrait of nonprofit health care in public discourse, policy debates, and the academic literature often is based on a distorted picture of how ownership actually shapes medical care. Our goal in this chapter is to provide a more accurate, comprehensive, and nuanced reading of the empirical literature. We also have a second, somewhat more ambitious objective: to try to explain *why* contemporary understandings of nonprofit health care have been so inaccurate.

We trace these distortions to several sources. Some false impressions can be linked to characteristics of health care that make it distinctive from other socially valued goods and services. Most strikingly, health care is a field that subsumes a wide variety of different goods and services, shaped to varying degrees by rapid technological change, information asymmetries between purchasers and purveyors of services, and the norms of professional training. The varying nature of the services subsumed within the rubric of health care has created the impression of inconsistencies in the relative performance of nonprofit and for-profit health-care providers. In our assessment, however, this cross-service variation can be more accurately interpreted to explain *how* ownership actually shapes medical care.

Other sources of confusion can be traced to factors that health care shares with other services provided by the nonprofit sector. In health care, as in other fields, ownership form may be inaccurately identified by purchasers of services. Because they then misinterpret their subsequent experiences, these perceptions distort the perceived implications of nonprofit ownership. In health care, as in other fields, researchers may disagree about whether any measurable differences in performance related to ownership are sufficiently large or consistent to be "meaningful." Consequently, how empirical results are interpreted often proves as important as the results of the statistical models. Finally, there is often disagreement about which other factors should be incorporated into the statistical models in order to appropriately isolate the effects of ownership on organizational behavior.

We explore these issues in the remainder of the chapter. We begin by reviewing the prevailing perceptions of the impact of nonprofit ownership in health care. We next summarize what is known about the dynamics of ownership change over the past fifteen years and the magnitude of ownership-related differences in health-care delivery. We then identify factors that may mediate the effects of ownership in medical care, creating different patterns of performance for different health services. We next explore the factors that may have distorted our understanding of nonprofit health care, through either popular impressions or academic assessments. We conclude by identifying some questions that require additional research, and commenting on the relationship between our understanding of nonprofit health care and the public policies that are intended to improve the performance of the health-care system.

PERCEPTIONS OF CHANGE AND PERFORMANCE IN THE NONPROFIT HEALTH-CARE SECTOR

We consider perceptions of the nonprofit health-care sector held by both the American public and academics who have studied its performance. Each of these perspectives shapes policymakers' understanding of the role and importance of ownership in American medicine.

Public Perceptions of Expanding For-Profit Health Care

To many Americans, health care has become dominated by profit-making organizations (Kuttner 1996a, 1996b; J. Bell 1996). In a national survey fielded in early 1998, roughly half of all respondents believed that the majority of hospitals, nursing homes, and insurance plans were operated by for-profit companies (Kaiser Family Foundation 1998).[2] These perceptions have been reinforced by the characterizations offered by some political leaders. For example, during the presidential campaign of 2000, Ralph Nader sought to emphasize his radically reformist stance toward medical care by suggesting that, if he were elected, his policies would "recast our health-care system in a nonprofit mode."

The perception that American medicine is being transformed into a profit-making enterprise makes many people uncomfortable. Depending on the wording of the question, surveys indicate that between 45 and 50 percent of the public believes that the spread of for-profit ownership is bad for the health-care system.[3] In the words of one survey researcher who recently examined this issue, "most people do not think of health care as a business and would prefer health care services to be provided by nonprofits or government. . . . There is little appetite for businesses to run home care, health insurance, nursing homes, hospitals, or medical research."[4] These concerns are reported to affect their choices among health-care providers. In a nationally representative survey of adults conducted in 1995, 46 percent reported that ownership was an important criterion in selecting a health plan and that nonprofit ownership would be their favored choice (Towers Perrin 1995).

But the public's specific expectations about ownership-related behaviors are more complex. Most Americans believe that for-profit health-care facilities provide better care[5] and deliver services more efficiently.[6] These expectations seem quite stable over time, having been replicated in surveys since the mid-1980s. On the other hand, nonprofit facilities are seen by the public as having the comparative advantages of being "more helpful to the community"[7] and charging consumers less for their services.[8]

Some of these perceptions are remarkably accurate. We will document later in this chapter that, although the relative efficiency with which services are provided appears to depend on the nature of the service, for-profit health-care organizations consistently charge purchasers more than do their nonprofit counterparts. There is also consistent evidence that nonprofit health-care providers are both more oriented to the local community and more likely to provide specific services that benefit the community.

But other perceptions are not consistent with the empirical research on ownership in health care. Although the public is convinced that health care has become a largely for-profit business, in fact the growth of for-profit ownership is limited to particular services. For others, nonprofit ownership remains dominant; for some services, the market share of nonprofit providers has increased over the past decade. Although the public is convinced that for-profit ownership is associated with higher-quality care, empirical studies producing this finding are rare. For some services there is evidence that nonprofit providers offer consistently higher quality. For other services the evidence is less consistent, but the modal findings suggest either that ownership does not matter or that nonprofits offer somewhat better care.

Academic Assessments of Ownership-Related Performance

Paradoxically, the burgeoning empirical research has in some ways made it more difficult to determine whether ownership "matters" in medical care. Perhaps because of the diversity of disciplines from which the studies emerge and the academic imperative to make each new publication distinctive from previous work, the accumulating studies use a variety of statistical techniques, measures, and samples. This diversity almost assures that there will be some variation in findings. For virtually every outcome, there are studies that suggest that the behavior of nonprofit organizations does more to foster socially desirable results, studies that find more favorable results in for-profit settings, and studies that find no statistically significant differences at all. Some studies that incorporate multiple measures of performance have results of all three types.

Over the past fifteen years, numerous books and articles have assessed the state of our knowledge about ownership in health care. Some of these have been written by economists (Malani, Philipson, and David 2003; Irvin 2000; Sloan 1998; Hirth 1997; Frank and Salkever 1994; Salkever and Frank 1992; Pauly 1987), others by sociologists (Kramer 2000; Flood 1994; Gray 1992, 1993; DiMaggio and Anheier 1990), and still others by researchers trained in other disciplines (Horwitz 2003; Devereaux et al. 2002; Needleman 2001; Bloche 1998; Davis 1991). The authors all acknowledge the diversity of findings in the literature, but they interpret this diversity in different ways.

Some authors interpret the evidence as showing that ownership is not a meaningful predictor of performance (Malani, Philipson, and David 2003; Kramer 2000; Sloan 1998; Bloche 1998; Davis 1991; Pauly 1987) or is, at best, a predictor whose meaning is deeply contested (Flood 1994). These skeptics fall into two camps. The first group claims that ownership form was never a meaningful distinction. They argue that nonprofit ownership has functioned largely as a facade to disguise the private appropriation of profits by physicians or others affiliated with the organizations (Sloan 1998; Pauly 1987). The second set of skeptics contends that, while ownership may have been a reliable marker of distinctive performance in an earlier era, nonprofit distinctiveness has eroded as competitive pressures have increased in health-care markets, as nonprofit and for-profit facilities have more often affiliated with large national systems, and as regulatory constraints have reduced variability in quality and accessibility of health services (Needleman 2001; Kramer 2000; Flood 1994).

A third critical perspective about the performance of nonprofit health providers questions whether the ownership-related differences that exist are sufficiently large to justify the tax subsidies accorded to nonprofit enterprise (Bloche 1998). One evocative assessment questioned whether there was more than "a dime's worth" of difference in the performance of nonprofit and for-profit hospitals (Sloan et al. 2001).[9] Other critics argue that, even if nonprofit and for-profit health-care providers differ in their *average* performance, many nonprofit firms have shirked in their performance, providing too few community benefits to justify their tax exemptions (Nicholson et al. 2000; Morrisey, Wedig, and Hassan 1996; Friedman, Hattis, and Bogue 1990; U.S. General Accounting Office 1990).

Other scholars have drawn different conclusions from the existing literature. Some argue that inconsistencies in findings are largely a product of methodological variations and inadequacies (Lewin, Eckels, and Miller 1988). One response is to pool studies to detect persisting ownership-related differences that would otherwise be obscured (Devereaux et al. 2002). Others suggest that the variation across studies reflects a meaningful difference, identifying conditions under which ownership will be associated with particular differences in organizational behavior (Hirth 1999; Frank and Salkever 1994). For example, DiMaggio and Anheier observe that the empirical literature appears "vast and inconclusive," but they judge that "given available evidence, one can conclude that legal form *does* make a difference, but the difference it makes depends on the institutional and ecological structures of the industry in question" (1990:150).

Skeptical perspectives have become dominant in the literature on nonprofit health care. But we believe that the conclusion that ownership makes little or no consistent difference inaccurately represents the empirical research. Given a sufficiently large and representative set of empirical studies, it is clear that ownership-related differences cut across all health services. But the way in which the behavior of nonprofits and for-profits differs depends on the nature of the service, the market conditions under which organizations operate, and the external constraints on their behavior. Strikingly, some external factors that have been presumed to produce convergence between nonprofit and for-profit health care have not actually done so; others produce partial convergence, though significant ownership-related differences persist. Whether these differences are sufficiently large or reliable to merit preferential treatment for nonprofit health-care providers is an issue to which we'll return at the end of the chapter.

VARIED PATTERNS OF OWNERSHIP AND PERFORMANCE WITHIN THE HEALTH-CARE FIELD

In the first edition of this handbook, the chapter on health care identified two sources of variation related to ownership (Marmor, Schlesinger, and Smithey 1987). First, the authors documented variability in the market shares of nonprofit and for-profit organizations. Some services, such as acute-care hospitals, health maintenance organizations (HMOs), and home health-care agencies operated largely under nonprofit auspices. Other services—such as nursing homes and blood banks—were delivered primarily by for-profit enterprise.[10] For other services such as residential care, centers for renal dialysis, and health insurance, there was an even balance between nonprofit and for-profit entities. There was no evidence of convergence toward a common ownership mix for all health services.

Second, the authors documented that, although ownership form was associated with performance differences throughout medical care, the nature of these differences varied from one service to the next. This observation was best documented for the two services for which there had been the most extensive empirical research: hospitals and nursing homes. Among nursing homes there was strong evidence that nonprofit ownership was associated with higher costs of care, and suggestive (but more limited) evidence that nonprofit nursing homes provided a higher quality of treatment.

Ownership did not appear to be related to charitable activity among nursing homes. By contrast, evidence from the hospital industry suggested that costs were probably higher in for-profit facilities (and the amounts they charged for services were certainly higher), that quality was not closely related to ownership, and that nonprofits were substantially more willing than for-profit facilities to treat indigent patients.

Fifteen years later, we have additional information about ownership trends and far more extensive documentation about the consequences of ownership in health care. This evidence suggests that, despite changing conditions (growing competition, regulation, and system affiliation), variation continues among different types of health services in the relative presence of nonprofit and for-profit entities and in the nature of ownership-related differences in performance.

Variation in Market Shares across Types of Health Services

We observed previously that much of the American public believes that the health-care system has become dominated by profit-oriented enterprise. Figure 16.1 suggests one possible explanation for this perception: there has been dramatic growth in the market share of for-profit providers for a number of services in which they had previously been scarce. These include services, like HMOs, that were the focus of intense scrutiny by the media, the public, and policymakers during the 1990s (Blendon et al. 1998). Substantial for-profit expansion also occurred in some services, such as home health care, that intimately touch the lives of tens of millions of Americans every year (Stone 2000).

But this visible expansion of for-profit ownership for some services masked persisting diversity in ownership for health care more generally (Gray and Schlesinger 2002). A number of services (e.g., acute hospitals, residential facilities for emotionally disturbed children, hospice programs, and community mental health centers) remained predominantly under private nonprofit auspices. Two services with a substantial for-profit presence experienced a decline in for-profit market share (nursing homes) or a rapid increase followed by a rapid decrease (psychiatric hospitals) over the past fifteen years. Ironically, the domain about which concerns regarding a for-profit transformation have been most frequently expressed—acute-care hospitals (Kuttner 1996a, 1996b; Japsen 1996)—saw little change in ownership mix over this period. Acquisitions of nonprofit hospitals by for-profit companies were offset by continued conversions of other hospitals from for-profit to nonprofit status (Desai, Young, and VanDeusen Lukas 1998), and higher closure rates among for-profit facilities (Gray and Schlesinger 2002).

Notably, one ownership pattern from the 1980s has largely disappeared fifteen years later. In the earlier period, there were several services (e.g., residential care facilities, psychiatric hospitals, health insurance, and dialysis centers) for which nonprofit and for-profit suppliers had approximately equal market shares (Marmor, Schlesinger, and Smithey 1987). By the end of the 1990s, however, the ownership distribution across health services was largely bimodal. Six of the ten services included in figure 16.1 are predominantly for-profit (with a for-profit market share between two and three times that of private nonprofit agencies). For the other four services, nonprofit ownership dominates (with market shares of private nonprofit agencies three

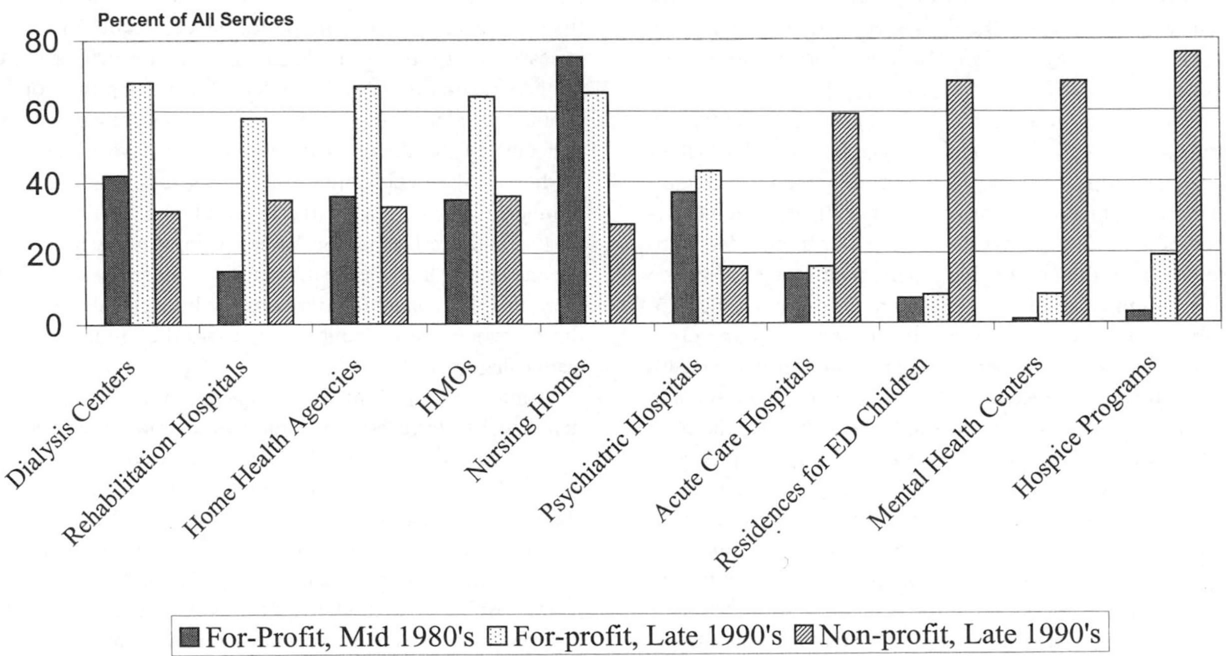

FIGURE 16.1. MARKET SHARES BY OWNERSHIP: SELECTED HEALTH SERVICES, 1980S–1990S

to five times as large as for their for-profit counterparts). This bifurcation of American medicine into predominantly for-profit and nonprofit domains has implications for the continued legitimacy of nonprofit enterprise, which we explore later in this chapter.

Does the expanding market share of for-profit firms for some services presage a time when the nonprofit provision of those services will disappear entirely? The recent history of services in which for-profits have been dominant suggests otherwise. For-profit facilities have been by far the most common form in the nursing-home industry since the 1950s. But as figure 16.1 reveals, their market share has actually decreased substantially over the past fifteen years. The rapid expansion of for-profit ownership among private psychiatric hospitals made this form of ownership the norm among private facilities during the 1980s. But the for-profit market share for psychiatric hospitals peaked in the early 1990s and declined later in that decade (Schlesinger and Gray 1999). Nonprofits appear able to maintain a distinctive niche, even for those services that are primarily provided under for-profit auspices (Gray and Schlesinger 2002).

Variation in Ownership-Related Performance among Health Services

The depth and quality of empirical research on ownership-related differences in medical care has increased considerably over the past fifteen years. Using this more extensive empirical literature, we can (a) revisit the question of whether there are distinctive patterns of ownership-related performance for different health services, (b) explore whether the magnitude of these differences has been reduced by ongoing changes in the markets for medical services, (c) expand our comparison to additional services for which there is now a critical mass of empirical research, and (d) consider additional dimensions of organizational behavior.

We followed several steps in assembling the empirical literature on which these analyses are based and which is summarized in our tables. First, we attempted to be comprehensive in identifying articles that compared the performance of nonprofit and for-profit health-care providers published through the end of 2002. This goal required that we review a number of distinct academic fields, including economics, sociology, business administration (including organizational behavior and accounting), health services, health policy, clinical sciences (including medical and nursing journals), and the journals devoted to research on the nonprofit sector. Second, we screened the studies for quality of empirical analysis. We incorporated into this summary only those studies that identified ownership-related differences in the context of multivariate statistical models that controlled for plausible other factors that might influence organizational performance (including the size and specialization of the facility, characteristics of the local market, and characteristics of the patients being served).[11]

Our objective in this analysis of the literature is to identify broad patterns in ownership-related performance that might be obscured by errors of measurement or variation in methods from one study to the next (we will return to these methodological issues). In this sense, we are providing a form of meta-analysis of the empirical literature. But we have not structured this review as a formal meta-analysis. While formalized ways of combining results across studies can be quite insightful (see, for example, Devereaux et al. 2002), they are most effective when one is combining outcomes that are relatively homogeneous. As will be evident, however, the researchers considered here have used a variety of measures of economic performance, quality, and accessibility of treatment, and the nature of these measures varies across services. The diversity of these measures and their relationship to ownership form is itself informative. Where relevant, we will compare our findings with the more formal meta-analyses that have appeared in the literature.

Old Comparisons with New Evidence

In their earlier review, Marmor, Schlesinger, and Smithey (1987) suggested that the nature of ownership-related performance varied sharply between nursing homes and hospitals. Since that review was completed, an additional ninety-six articles have been published that met our screening criteria for the sophistication of empirical analysis and that also studied the three dimensions of organizational performance that were identified in the first edition of the *Handbook:* economic outcomes, quality of care, and accessibility of services for unprofitable patients.

The findings from our new literature review are summarized in table 16.1. The studies are categorized in the following manner: For both hospitals and nursing homes, the studies are grouped according to the dimension of performance they assess (e.g., economic performance, quality of care, or accessibility for unprofitable patients) and the primary thrust of their results (e.g., whether they favor nonprofits or for-profits or find no statistically significant differences). To further convey the flavor of the results, we have grouped the studies by the dependent variable that was examined. The number following each variable reports the number of studies that had similar findings. When a single study uses multiple measures, and the results fall into more than one category, the study is counted separately in each category. (See the footnotes to the table for the specific studies cited in each category.)

It may be helpful to discuss one set of results in greater detail to illustrate how the findings are presented. For instance, consider one quality measure used frequently in studies of hospitals: the mortality rate for patients after discharge from the hospital.[12] Of the twelve studies using this measure, five found mortality rates were significantly lower in nonprofit facilities than in otherwise comparable for-profit hospitals. Six studies found no statistically significant differences related to ownership, while one found mortality rates to be lower in for-profit facilities. From this overview, one could plausibly conclude that the weight of evidence suggests that nonprofit hospitals have a modest performance advantage in this aspect of quality.[13]

The advantage of a summary of this sort, however, is that it reveals broad patterns in findings, rather than focusing on any particular outcome measure. At this broader level of analysis, one can identify ownership-related differences for both hospitals and nursing homes. As Marmor, Schlesinger, and Smithey had suggested, the patterns of differences are quite distinct for the two services.

The first distinction appears in terms of economic performance. These studies suggest that, while for-profit nursing homes have a consistent advantage over their nonprofit counterparts in terms of expenses incurred in producing services (also known as economic efficiency),[14] this is not true for hospitals, where nonprofit facilities appear to be at least as efficient, and possibly more efficient, as comparable for-profit hospitals. Among nursing homes, every study but one over the past thirty years has found nonprofit ownership to be associated with higher expenditures per day or per stay. By contrast, the studies of hospital expenses have produced mixed findings, with a slight preponderance suggesting that there are higher costs among for-profit facilities. The most sophisticated empirical studies have constructed explicit measures of inefficiency using "frontier" or "efficiency envelope" techniques. The same pattern holds for this work: seven of eight find that for-profit nursing homes are more efficient, but three of six find that nonprofit hospitals are more efficient than for-profits.

There are, however, some dimensions of economic performance for which ownership appears to be more consistently linked with performance. For both nursing homes and hospitals, nonprofit facilities appear to have lower prices and equal or lower administrative costs than do their for-profit counterparts.[15]

The differences in the other two dimensions of performance are equally striking. Consider first measures of quality of care. Among hospitals, studies have produced mixed results, with the preponderance of findings (twenty out of thirty-eight) indicating no significant ownership-related differences. A very different picture emerges for nursing homes: although a handful of studies detected no ownership-related differences (and two favored for-profit facilities), the great preponderance of the empirical research (twenty-five studies using a half-dozen different measures of quality) found quality to be significantly higher under nonprofit ownership, controlling for a variety of other characteristics of the facility and patient population. This pattern is perhaps best illustrated with a quality measure used for both types of services: the frequency of adverse outcomes for patients (other than death). The nine studies of adverse outcomes in hospitals divided fairly evenly among those that found better performance in nonprofit facilities (four), those that found better quality in for-profit settings (three), and those that found no ownership-related differences (two). By contrast, in nine studies of adverse events in nursing homes, eight found significantly better outcomes in nonprofit facilities.

The pattern is reversed for studies of access by unprofitable patients, although this dimension of performance in nursing homes has received relatively little study. Among hospitals, the vast preponderance of evidence finds that private nonprofit institutions provide greater access for unprofitable patients than do comparable for-profit hospitals. This pattern holds for a variety of different measures of accessibility, with the sole exception being treatment for Medicaid patients (who are covered by government-provided insurance that often pays below-market rates). Among nursing homes the ownership-related differences in access favor for-profit facilities.

Comparing Old and New Evidence: Has There Been Convergence in Performance?

As previously noted, skeptical observers have argued that ongoing changes in the market for health-care services have obviated any ownership-related differences that may have historically existed. The specific claims take several different forms. Some suggest that as the federal government enacted programs to pay for indigent clients (most notably Medicaid), it reduced the social value of treating indigent clients and thus the willingness of nonprofit health-care providers to engage in these activities (Kramer 2000). Other observers have predicted that the ability of nonprofit providers to engage in a distinctive mission will diminish as markets become more competitive and more facilities affiliate with large national systems (Sloan 1998). Still other skeptics argue that, as for-profit ownership expands in the delivery of particular services, the nonprofit organizations in that field will start to emulate the commercial practices of their for-profit competitors, a process characterized in the sociological literature as "mimetic isomorphism" (Clarke and Estes 1992).

We will explore the question of convergence in two ways. The first strategy makes use of the findings presented in table 16.1, interpreting them in ways that shed light on this question. The second approach considers specifically those studies that have examined how price competition and system affiliation affect the magnitude of ownership-related differences in performance.

The findings summarized in table 16.1 are relevant to claims about convergence in several ways. Most evidently, they juxtapose one service (hospitals) that has been predominantly nonprofit over the past seventy-five years with another service that has been provided primarily under for-profit auspices for the same period (nursing homes) (Vladeck 1980). If isomorphic pressures produced by an expanding for-profit market share were sufficient to fully "commercialize" the practices of their nonprofit competitors, this ought to have been long since evident among nursing homes. In fact, we observe that there are significant ownership-related differences among nursing homes in terms of efficiency, pricing policies, and quality of care. Of course this observation does not demonstrate that isomorphism is not at work—the ownership-related differences might have been far larger

TABLE 16.1. CATEGORIZING EMPIRICAL FINDINGS COMPARING ORGANIZATIONAL PERFORMANCE BY OWNERSHIP: ACUTE-CARE HOSPITALS VERSUS NURSING HOMES

	Specific measures (number of studies using this measure)		
Direction of findings	Economic performance	Quality of care	Accessibility for unprofitable patients
Studies of Acute-Care Hospitals			
Nonprofit advantage	Administrative overhead (3)[a] Costs per admission (10)[b] Measures of inefficiency (3)[c] Revenues per admission (5)[d]	Postdischarge mortality (5)[e] In-hospital mortality (1)[f] Adverse outcomes (4)[g] Process measures (3)[h] Regulatory violations (1)[i]	Locating in low-income areas (5)[j] Treating uninsured patients (12)[k] Restricting access of uninsured (4)[l] Providing unprofitable services (5)[m] Treating Medicaid patients (2)[n]
No difference	Costs per admission (7)[o] Revenues per admission (2)[p] Measures of inefficiency(2)[q]	Malpractice suits (1)[r] In-hospital mortality (7)[s] Postdischarge mortality (6)[t] Satisfaction with treatment (1)[u] Adverse outcomes (2)[v] Perinatal mortality (1)[w] Process measures (1)[x] Hospital readmissions (1)[y]	Treating uninsured patients (6)[z] Treating Medicaid patients (3)[aa]
For-profit advantage	Costs per admission (5)[bb] Measures of inefficiency (1)[cc]	Adverse outcomes (3)[dd] Postdischarge mortality (1)[ee]	Treating Medicaid patients (1)[ff]

[a] Woolhandler and Himmelstein 1997; Carter, Massa, and Power 1997; Eskoz and Peddecord 1985

[b] Clement and Grazier 2001; Ettner and Hermann 2001; Potter 2001; Menke 1997; Custer and Willke 1991; Lawrence 1990; Register, Sharpe, and Stevans 1988; Grannemann, Brown, and Pauly 1986; Becker and Sloan 1985; Eskoz and Peddecord 1985

[c] Zuckerman, Hadley, and Iezzoni 1994; Ozcan and Luke 1993; Ozcan, Luke, and Haksever 1992

[d] Clement and Grazier 2001; Melnick, Keeler, and Zwanziger 1999; Meurer et al. 1998; Lynk 1995; Eskoz and Peddecord 1985

[e] Yuan et al. 2000; McClellan and Staiger 2000; Kuhn et al. 1994; Al-Haider and Wan 1991; Hartz et al. 1989

[f] Pitterle et al. 1994

[g] Broome 2002; Shen 2001; Lanksa and Kryscio 1998a, 1998b; Kovner and Gergen 1998

[h] Weinstein 1997; Keeler et al. 1992; Placek, Taffel, and Moien 1983

[i] Mark 1996

[j] Clement, White, and Valdmanis 2002; Norton and Staiger 1994; Homer, Bradham, and Rushefsky 1984; Mullner and Hadley 1984; Kushman and Nuckton 1977

[k] Clement, White, and Valdmanis 2002; Sloan, Taylor, and Conover 2000; Wolff and Schlesinger 1998; Schlesinger et al. 1997a; Olfson and Mechanic 1996; Zeckhauser, Patel, and Needleman 1995; Campbell and Ahern 1993; Gray 1991; Seidman and Pollock 1991; Frank, Salkever, and Mullan 1990; Lewin, Eckels, and Miller 1988; Marmor et al. 1987

[l] Wolff and Schlesinger 1998; Schlesinger et al. 1997b; Schlesinger et al. 1996a; Marmor, Schlesinger, and Smithey 1987

[m] Sloan, Taylor, and Conover 2000; Boscarino and Chang 2000; Schlesinger et al. 1997b; Marmor, Schlesinger, and Smithey 1987; Shortell 1985

[n] Lee, Alexander, and Bazzoli 2003; Frank, Salkever, and Mitchell 1990

[o] Potter 2001; Ettner and Hermann 2001; McCue and Thompson 1997; Mark 1996; Vita 1990; Friedman and Shortell 1988; Sloan and Vraciu 1983

[p] Shukla, Pestian, and Clement 1997; McCue and Thompson 1997

[q] Burgess and Wilson 1996; Eakin 1991; Register and Bruning 1986

[r] Gray 1991

[s] Bond et al. 1999; Lanska and Kryscio 1998a; Shortell and Hughes 1988; Gaumer 1986; Bays 1979; Ruchlin, Pointer, and Cannedy 1973; Roemer, Moustafa, and Hopkins 1968

[t] Sloan et al. 2001; Rosenthal et al. 1998; Kuhn et al. 1994; Keeler et al. 1992; Manheim et al. 1992; Gaumer 1986

[u] Weisbrod 1988:213

[v] Sloan et al. 2001; Kovner and Gergen 1998

[w] Spann 1977

[x] Keeler et al. 1992

[y] Ettner and Hermann 2001

[z] Brotman 1995; Buczko 1994; Gruber 1994; Norton and Staiger 1994; Zeckhauser, Patel, and Needleman 1995; Seidman and Pollock 1991

[aa] Gray 1986; Pattison and Katz 1983; Lewin, Derzon, and Margulies 1981

[bb] Carter, Massa, and Power 1997; Ferrier and Valdmanis 1996; Robinson and Luft 1985; Cowing and Holtmann 1983; Bays 1979

[cc] Ferrier and Valdmanis 1996

[dd] Chiu 1999; Anders 1993; Brennan et al. 1991

[ee] Mukamel, Zwanziger, and Tomaszewski 2001

[ff] Bays 1977

TABLE 16.1 (CONTINUED)

	Specific measures (number of studies using this measure)		
Direction of findings	Economic performance	Quality of care	Accessibility for unprofitable patients
Studies of Nursing Homes			
Nonprofit advantage	Administrative overhead (1)[gg] Revenues per admission (4)hh	Malpractice suits (1)[ii] Satisfaction with treatment (2)[jj] Process measures of quality (6)[kk] Regulatory violations (5)[ll] Adverse outcomes (8)[mm] Physical restraints (3)[nn]	Services at reduced charge (1)[oo]
No difference	Administrative overhead (3)[pp] Measures of inefficiency (1)[qq]	Regulatory violations (2)[rr] Functional improvements (3)[ss] Process measures (2)[tt]	Medicaid admissions (1)[uu]
For-profit advantage	Average operating cost (7)[vv] Measures of inefficiency (7)[ww] Average total cost (5)[xx]	Adverse outcomes (1)[yy] Antipsychotic use (1)[zz]	Medicaid admissions (4)[aaa]

[gg] Luksetich, Edwards, and Carroll 2000
[hh] Ballou 2000; Philipson 2000; Koetting 1980; Birnbaum et al. 1981
[ii] Troyer and Thompson 2004
[jj] Weisbrod 1988:213; Riportella-Mueller and Slesinger 1982
[kk] Bradley and Walker 1998; Holtmann and Idson 1991; Nyman and Bricker 1989; Weisbrod 1988:150; Hawes and Phillips 1986; Koetting 1980
[ll] Harrington et al. 2000; Castle 2000; Holmes 1996; Johnson, Cowles, and Simmens 1996; Ullmann 1987
[mm] Chou 2002; Spector, Selden, and Cohen 1998; Mukamel 1997; Aaronson, Zinn, and Rosko 1994; Moseley 1994; Davis 1993; Kayser-Jones, Wiener, and Barbaccia 1989; Lee 1984
[nn] Castle 2000; Mukamel 1997; Aaronson, Zinn, and Rosko 1994
[oo] Marmor, Schlesinger, and Smithey 1987
[pp] Koetting 1980; Spitz and Weeks 1980; Spitz 1980
[qq] Vitaliano and Toren 1994
[rr] Weisbrod and Schlesinger 1986; Riportella-Mueller and Slesinger 1982
[ss] Porrell et al. 1998; Moseley 1994; Bell and Krivich 1990
[tt] Hughes, Lapane, and Mor 2000; Castle and Shea 1998
[uu] Spector, Selden, and Cohen 1998
[vv] Luksetich, Edwards, and Carroll 2000; Davis 1993; Ullmann 1987; Arling, Nordquist, and Capitman 1987; Caswell and Cleverly 1983; Birnbam et al. 1981; Reis and Christensen 1977
[ww] Knox, Blankmeyer, and Stutzman 1999; Anderson, Lewis, and Webb 1999; Chattopadhyay and Ray 1996; Ozcan, Wogen, and Mau 1998; Rosko et al. 1995; Fizel and Nunnikhoven 1992; Nyman and Bricker 1989
[xx] Holmes 1996; Caswell and Cleverly 1983; Frech and Ginsburg 1981; Bishop 1980; Ruchlin and Levey 1972
[yy] Zinn, Aaronson, and Rosko 1993
[zz] Hughes, Lapane, and Mor 2000
[aaa] Johnson, Cowles, and Simmens 1996; Clarke and Estes 1992; Mather 1990; O'Brien 1988

if the nursing-home industry were predominantly nonprofit. But it clearly demonstrates that such isomorphic pressures do not, in themselves, eliminate practices that distinguish nonprofit and for-profit enterprise.

A second take on convergence draws on a comparison of results from more recent empirical research, to determine whether the patterns of results described above have persisted in the contemporary health-care system. These sorts of comparisons are most helpful for hospitals, since the market for hospital services experienced significant increases in both price competition[16] and system affiliation[17] during the 1980s and early 1990s. By restricting our literature review to more recent studies, we can explore whether there have been observable shifts in hospital performance. For ease of comparison, we present only those studies published after 1995 in table 16.2.[18]

The general pattern of ownership-related behavior for hospitals does not appear to have altered in the most recent empirical research. Nonprofit hospitals remain consistently more accessible to indigent and other unprofitable clients. Quality measures predominantly suggest that there are no significant differences between nonprofit and for-profit facilities, but some results show modestly better outcomes in nonprofit settings. Nonprofit hospitals are still less likely than their for-profit counterparts to have high markups on their charges for services. Efficiency in the delivery of hospital care *may* be reflecting a shift toward for-profit advantage.

These findings suggest that neither isomorphic pressures nor recent changes in health-care markets have eliminated differences between nonprofit and for-profit behavior. These same factors may, however, have either reduced or transformed the ownership-related differences that persist. To explore this issue, we turn now to research that has explicitly

TABLE 16.2. EMPIRICAL FINDINGS CATEGORIZING HOSPITAL PERFORMANCE BY OWNERSHIP: STUDIES PUBLISHED SINCE 1995

	Specific measures (number of studies using this measure)		
Direction of findings	Economic performance	Quality of care	Accessibility for unprofitable patients
Nonprofit advantage	Administrative overhead (2) Costs per admission (3) Revenues per admission (4)	Postdischarge mortality (2) Adverse outcomes (2) Regulatory violations (1) Process measures (1)	Locating in low-income areas (1) Treating uninsured patients (5) Restricting access of uninsured (3) Providing unprofitable services (3) Treating Medicaid patients (1)
No difference	Costs per admission (4) Revenues per admission (2) Measures of inefficiency (2)	In-hospital mortality (2) Postdischarge mortality (2) Adverse outcomes (2) Hospital readmissions (1)	Treating uninsured patients (1)
For-profit advantage	Costs per admission (2) Measures of inefficiency (1)	Postdischarge mortality (1) Adverse outcomes (1)	

assessed the differential effects of competition and system affiliation on ownership-related differences in performance. (We later examine studies of isomorphic pressures.)

Does Price Competition Reduce Ownership-Related Differences in Performance?

Nursing homes have always competed on the basis of price, while hospitals, because of health insurance, have long competed on attributes unrelated to price.[19] But the spread of managed-care practices in the mid-1980s brought price competition to the hospital industry. The resulting price cuts, it has been argued, are threatening the traditional mission of nonprofit health-care providers, reducing the resources available to provide various forms of community benefits. Despite a nationwide trend toward greater price competition for hospital services, the intensity of competition varies considerably from one part of the country to the next (Bamezai et al. 1999). This variability has allowed researchers to examine the impact of competition in two ways. The first set of studies compares the relative performance of nonprofit and for-profit hospitals in markets with more or less competitive conditions (we'll refer to these as "cross-sectional studies"). The second set of studies compares ownership-related performance over time, assuming that later years will reflect a more competitive environment (we'll refer to these as "longitudinal studies").

Virtually all the research on this topic has focused on the implications of competition for ownership-related differences in hospitals' treatment of indigent patients. Although one might expect that ownership-related differences in quality would be affected in a similar manner to differences in accessibility, for reasons that will become clear below, these two aspects of organizational performance may respond quite differently to competitive pressures.

Researchers have documented that, as competitive pressures among hospitals have grown over the past fifteen years, both nonprofit and for-profit facilities have responded by cutting prices (Keeler, Melnick, and Zwanziger 1998).[20] Economic theory suggests, however, that the consequences of these price reductions will be quite different in nonprofit and for-profit settings. Among nonprofit organizations, as price cuts lead to smaller surpluses one would expect to observe a reduction in treatment of indigent patients, given the hospitals' more limited ability to subsidize unprofitable activities (Schlesinger et al. 1997a). In contrast, as for-profit providers face increased price competition, theory suggests (if they are maximizing profits) that they will treat *more* uninsured patients as a by-product of efforts to increase volume (e.g., by opening or expanding an emergency department, which is an important source of admissions). Combined, these diverse responses ought to diminish ownership-related differences in the accessibility of hospital services.

Cross-sectional studies generally support these theoretical predictions. In markets with more intense price competition and lower hospital surpluses, nonprofit hospitals do tend to treat fewer indigent patients than in other markets (Schlesinger et al. 1997a; Gruber 1994; Campbell and Ahern 1993). But while some studies document that for-profit hospitals treat more uninsured patients in more competitive markets than they do in less competitive markets (Banks, Paterson, and Wendel 1997; Schlesinger et al. 1997a), others have found the opposite (Clement, White, and Valdmanis 2002). On net, although high-competition markets are associated with smaller differences between nonprofit and for-profit hospitals in their treatment of the uninsured, most studies suggest that an ownership-related difference persists even under the most competitive conditions (Clement, White, and Valdmanis 2002; Banks, Paterson, and Wendel 1997; Campbell and Ahern 1993), though other research finds more (though not total) convergence (Schlesinger 1998). By contrast, for-profit hospitals do appear to be quicker than nonprofit facilities to drop marginally profitable or unprofitable services in the face of increased competitive pressures (Horwitz 2003; Schlesinger et al. 1997a; Shortell 1985). This tendency leads to larger ownership-related differences in access to these less profitable services when nonprofit and for-profit hospitals are under competitive pressure.

Because price competition has been increasing in the hospital industry, one might expect that the longitudinal studies would document a reduction over time in the magnitude of ownership-related differences in treatment of indigent clients. Surprisingly, however, virtually all the studies that have examined changes in the magnitude of ownership-related differences over the past fifteen years find exactly the opposite for the treatment of uninsured patients (Hirth 1997). Nonprofits appear to have maintained their policies and practices of providing access to uninsured patients (Potter 2001); the gap in the amount of indigent care between nonprofit and for-profit facilities actually appears to be growing (Ferris and Graddy 1999; Zeckhauser, Patel, and Needleman 1995; Campbell and Ahern 1993; Frank and Salkever 1991; Sloan, Morrisey, and Valvona 1988).

What might account for this seeming anomaly? One possible explanation involves disaggregating the patient population that is unprofitable for hospitals to treat. It is composed of two quite different groups. The first involves patients who are unable to pay for their care—typically those without medical insurance. The second involves patients—for example, certain complex cases—for whom the costs of treatment may exceed the payments received from insurers. Hospitals seeking to stem losses can adopt policies to reduce the number of uninsured patients treated or to eliminate services for which expenses exceed revenues. One study of psychiatric hospitals found that, before the era of intense competition, private nonprofit facilities had treated both more uninsured patients and a more complex patient mix than did their for-profit counterparts (Wolff and Schlesinger 1998). As competition intensified during the 1980s, however, nonprofit psychiatric hospitals were able to maintain the accessibility of services for the uninsured only by screening out more costly cases, making them more like for-profit hospitals for complex cases but not for the uninsured.

Caring for uninsured patients might be the favored form of community service for nonprofit facilities under financial stress, because this care is more observable by potential donors and community advocates. (This form of community service has also been encouraged by recent changes in state policies intended to establish greater accountability over the nonprofit health sector, a trend explored later in this chapter.) Following the same logic, one might also expect that, as competitive pressures on nonprofit hospitals increase, nonprofits' quality advantages would become increasingly concentrated in the more visible dimensions.

Does System Affiliation Reduce Ownership-Related Differences in Performance?

As more nonprofit and for-profit facilities have become part of large, multifacility systems, some academics have predicted that these connections would reduce or eliminate ownership-related differences in behavior (Kramer 2000; Clarke and Estes 1992). The logic of this claim invokes a second form of isomorphic pressure, typically termed "coercive isomorphism." As both nonprofit and for-profit organizations depend increasingly on a central corporate headquarters for authority, information, and resources, it is hypothesized that the impact of ownership at the level of the individual facility will be supplanted by the bureaucratic practices common to all large organizations.

In contrast to the empirical research on the effects of competition, which has focused on a single outcome (care for indigent clients) in a single industry (hospitals), the empirical studies that have examined the potential convergence of behavior following system affiliation are scattered among a variety of services (hospitals, nursing homes, health plans, and home health agencies) and outcomes (patient satisfaction, efficiency, pricing practices, mortality, adverse outcomes, and access for indigent patients), making it harder to discern a clear pattern of findings. Nonetheless, two patterns appear to be reasonably consistent across these studies. First, system affiliation has a larger effect on performance of for-profit than nonprofit health-care providers. Second, these differential influences are associated with *increases* in the magnitude of ownership-related differences in performance, with the possible exception of economic dimensions of performance.

Studies that have compared the performance of system-affiliated nonprofits, system-affiliated for-profits, unaffiliated nonprofits, and unaffiliated for-profits have generally found that the differences in behavior associated with system affiliation are more pronounced in the for-profit sector. This pattern has been demonstrated for the efficiency (Menke 1997; Ozcan, Luke, and Haksever 1992) and accessibility (Schlesinger et al. 1986) of hospital services; the accessibility of home health care (Clarke and Estes 1992); and the quality of health plans (Schlesinger et al. 2005; Landon et al. 2001). The exception involves nursing homes; some studies show larger system effects in nonprofit homes (Luksetich, Edwards, and Carroll 2000), others in for-profit homes (Hughes, Lapane, and Mor 2000).

These same studies suggest that system affiliation causes a divergence on dimensions of accessibility and quality of care between nonprofit and for-profit facilities (Schlesinger et al. 2005; Landon et al. 2001; Luksetich, Edwards, and Carroll 2000; Hughes, Lapane, and Mor 2000; Schlesinger et al. 1986), although findings related to access in home health agencies run in the opposite direction (Clarke and Estes 1992). By contrast, system affiliation appears to be associated with a convergence of behavior in the economic dimensions of performance, at least in the hospital industry, where it has been most extensively studied (Young, Desai, and Hellinger 2000; Menke 1997; Ozcan, Luke, and Haksever 1992). We offer some possible explanations for this pattern of findings later in the chapter.

Adding New Services to the Comparison

Over the past fifteen years, there has been additional research on the effects of ownership on the delivery of a wide variety of health services.[21] However, for only one of these services—managed-care health plans (sometimes termed health maintenance organizations, or HMOs)—has there been a sufficient accumulation of studies across all three of our dimensions of performance that we can identify patterns in the findings comparable to those in the literature on hospitals and nursing homes.

The earliest of managed-care plans have been in operation since the 1930s (Luft 1981). They combine the functions of a traditional health insurer (that is, they agree to provide medical care to enrollees for a fixed annual premium) with authority over the actual delivery of medical care, selecting the providers of services and monitoring (in some cases proactively authorizing) the care that they provide. These characteristics make the services provided by these plans quite distinct from those delivered by either hospitals or nursing homes.

Managed-care plans also have a second important distinction: they are relatively new as important components of American medicine. Whereas hospitals have been a primary setting for treating serious illness for more than a century (Stevens 1989) and nursing homes the primary setting for long-term care for the elderly and disabled for the past half century (Vladeck 1980), only a few managed-care plans existed until the 1970s. The growth of health plans was encouraged by federal policies adopted in 1973 and by the changing accountability and cost-containment demands of employers and other large purchasers of health care (Schlesinger, Gray, and Bradley 1996). But they have come to play an important role in the delivery of health services only in the last twenty years. These plans thus provide an interesting test case for whether ownership effects exist among health-care providers that do not have deep historic roots in the communities that they serve (Needleman 2001).

Empirical assessments of the implications of ownership among these plans have recently begun to appear in the academic literature. The findings from these studies are summarized in table 16.3. Although this research is still limited, it suggests that substantial ownership-related differences in performance exist here, too. But they take on a pattern different from those found among either hospitals or nursing homes. In terms of economic performance, the impact of ownership in HMOs appears to be most akin to that found among hospitals: findings suggest that the efficiency of nonprofit plans is equal to or greater than otherwise comparable for-profit plans.

In contrast, the patterns of ownership-related differences in quality and accessibility appear more like those identified among nursing homes. A preponderance of studies shows that nonprofit plans deliver a significantly higher quality of care than for-profit plans, controlling for characteristics such as plan age, size, or model type.[22] The only study suggesting that ownership was not related to quality relied on data voluntarily reported by health plans (Born and Simon 2001). Virtually all the worst-ranked for-profit plans withheld their data, skewing the results (Consumers Union 1999). In the one study that attempted to rank health plans according to overall quality, eight of the top ten operated under nonprofit auspices (Consumers Union 1999:28–29). (Approximately 35 percent of all plans are nonprofit.) Nine of the ten worst-ranked plans operated under for-profit auspices.

As with nursing homes, there appears to be a much less consistent linkage between the ownership form of a health plan and its willingness to provide unprofitable services.

TABLE 16.3. CATEGORIZING EMPIRICAL FINDINGS COMPARING ORGANIZATIONAL PERFORMANCE BY OWNERSHIP: MANAGED-CARE HEALTH PLANS (A.K.A. HMOS)

	Specific measures (number of studies using this measure)		
Direction of findings	Economic performance	Quality of care	Accessibility for unprofitable patients
Nonprofit advantage	Total costs (2)[a] Premium charges (1)[b]	Process measures of quality (6)[c] Enrollee satisfaction (3)[d] Disenrollment rates (4)[e] Quality assurance systems (1)[f]	Free or subsidized treatment (1)[g] Community-rated premiums (1)[h] Targeting services to low-income neighborhoods (1)[i]
No difference	Measures of inefficiency (1)[j]	Process measures of quality (1)[k]	Subsidized premiums (1)[l] Enrolling costly cases (1)[m]
For-profit advantage			Medicaid participation (1)[n] Enrolling low-income groups (1)[o]

[a] Patterson 1997; Schlesinger et al. 1986
[b] Schlesinger et al. 1986
[c] Gesten 1999; Greene 1998; Consumers Union 1999; Himmelstein et al. 1999; Tu and Reschovsky 2002; Patterson 1997; Palmiter 1998
[d] Tu and Reschovsky 2002; Landon et al. 2001; Consumers Union 1999; Green 1998
[e] Prospective Payment Assessment Commission 1994; Landon et al 2001; Riley, Ingber, and Tudor 1997; Rossiter et al. 1989
[f] Landon and Epstein 2001
[g] Schlesinger, Mitchell, and Gray 2003
[h] Schlesinger, Mitchell, and Gray 2003
[i] Schlesinger, Mitchell, and Gray 2003
[j] Rosenman, Siddharthan, and Ahern 1997
[k] Born and Simon 2001
[l] Schlesinger, Mitchell, and Gray 2003
[m] Blustein and Hoy 2000
[n] Landon and Epstein 2001
[o] Blustein and Hoy 2000

Nonprofit plans are more likely to target services to low-income neighborhoods and to offer premiums that are community-rated (that is, based on the average costs of medical care in the community, which implicitly subsidizes the premiums of older and sicker residents) (Schlesinger, Mitchell, and Gray 2003). But for-profit plans actually enroll more low-income people and do not appear to be avoiding the most complex cases, which represent potentially high costs and thus unprofitable care (Blustein and Hoy 2000; for a related finding, see Schneider, Zaslavsky, and Epstein 2004). And for-profit plans are just as likely to participate in the Medicaid program, which covers only low-income groups. All told, the accessibility of services appears to be quite similar between nonprofit and for-profit plans.

Adding New Dimensions of Performance: Hidden Quality and Trustworthy Practices

To this point, we have emulated the chapter in the first edition of the *Handbook* by treating "quality of care" as a unidimensional construct. This strategy can encompass a variety of practices and measures of quality. But the literature on the nonprofit sector published since the first edition has introduced a theoretically important distinction related to quality. Weisbrod (1988) distinguished between dimensions of quality that are relatively easy to monitor or assess (Type 1) and dimensions that are difficult to monitor (Type 2). Theories of nonprofit organizations predict that there may be ownership-related differences for either aspect of quality, but they are likely to emerge under different circumstances and have different implications for societal welfare.

One line of analysis suggests that managers of nonprofit enterprises will pursue Type 1 forms of quality to a greater extent than will their counterparts in for-profit firms. The logic is this: since nonprofit administrators are limited in the extent to which they can be rewarded for the organization's financial performance, they will seek instead to maximize other markers of organizational performance, particularly those that carry prestige in the eyes of their peers (Rose-Ackerman 1997; Schlesinger, Gray, and Bradley 1996; Newhouse 1970). Nonpecuniary rewards in the form of prestige and respect substitute for the financial incentives that are more common in for-profit settings. Activities can generate prestige and various forms of community endorsement only if they are visible to outside observers. Type 1 quality is an example (Wolff and Schlesinger 1998; Frank and Salkever 1991).

A second line of analysis suggests that Type 2 forms of quality will also be more pronounced in nonprofit settings. Many services provided by nonprofit agencies involve substantial information asymmetries between the provider and the purchaser of the services (Hansmann 1980). Under circumstances that are common in health services,[23] these informational asymmetries create opportunities to profit by misrepresenting the quality of care that the organization is providing, since buyers will pay more when they are ostensibly receiving better treatment (Pauly 1988; Arrow 1963). Profit-maximizing providers are predicted to exploit information asymmetries (i.e., to misrepresent their behavior) to a greater extent than will nonprofit providers, who cannot garner the monetary benefits from this deception (Gray 1991; Chillemi and Gui 1991; Easley and O'Hara 1988). If consumers recognize the greater trustworthiness of nonprofit agencies, one would expect that those who are aware of their vulnerability to being misled would gravitate to nonprofit settings (Hirth 1997). This in turn produces an important spillover benefit from nonprofit enterprise. If some of the most vulnerable (least informed) patients choose only nonprofit health-care providers, then this reduces the incentives for misrepresentation by for-profit firms, since their clientele is now, on average, better able to detect when providers are making false claims about quality of care.

The literature summarized in tables 16.1 and 16.3 suggests that there are substantial quality differences between nonprofit and for-profit nursing homes and health plans, with more moderate (and less consistent) differences among hospitals. Can we differentiate among the types of quality measures that are summarized in these tables to help determine whether these differences are more closely linked to Type 1 or Type 2 aspects of quality? To some extent, all empirical research that directly measures quality is biased toward measuring Type 1 aspects, since they are by definition those that are more readily measured.

But a useful distinction can be made between those aspects of quality that *can* be measured and those that are measured with sufficient regularity that they become publicly visible. Among hospitals, the most visible measures of quality involve measures of mortality, which, though not perceptible to the average patient, are sometimes compiled and publicized by state or federal agencies. For nursing homes, the more visible measures involve regulatory violations, about which information can be obtained by consumers who are choosing among facilities. For health plans, both satisfaction scores and measures of the process of care are compiled in various "report cards" (produced by the National Committee on Quality Assurance and some consumer organizations) that are available to the public and used by some purchasers.

Focusing on these measures, we can discern ownership-related differences for Type 1 aspects of quality. The distribution of findings is clearest for nursing homes and health plans. Although the findings are a bit less consistent for hospitals, a meta-analysis of these mortality studies revealed significant differences in mortality rates between nonprofit and for-profit hospitals (Devereaux et al. 2002). Since Type 1 aspects of quality could be identified by consumers, the ownership-related differences reflect a propensity for nonprofit providers to deliver quality above the level demanded by informed consumers. (Whether this additional quality is beneficial to society is a matter to which we'll return.)

But how can we identify Type 2 aspects of quality, which, by their nature, are more difficult to measure? Researchers have pursued four broad strategies for dealing with this problem. (A fifth approach, relying on assessments by expert observers, is just beginning to appear in the literature [Schlesinger et al. 2005].) One approach is based on Hansmann's (1980) original observation that if nonprofits are indeed more trustworthy, then less-informed consumers should seek out nonprofit providers, since they are more at risk of exploitation in for-profit settings (Hirth 1997). A second strategy compares the experiences of consumers who are more at risk for exploitation with those who are less vulnerable, assessing the magnitude of ownership-related differences for each group (Schlesinger, Gray, and Bradley 1996). A third strategy assesses the prevalence of actions that would occur if consumers had been misled about quality—that is, if they received lower-quality care than they had expected, given the price that they were willing or able to pay (Weisbrod 1988). A fourth approach compares different aspects of quality provided by a given set of firms, comparing the magnitude of ownership-related differences for aspects of quality that are asserted to have Type 1 or Type 2 attributes (Ortmann and Schlesinger 1997).

Only a handful of published studies have pursued each strategy. Only for nursing homes are there studies that cut across all four categories. And each strategy has some important limitations, which we note below. Nonetheless, viewed as a whole this research offers fairly strong evidence that (a) there are ownership-related differences in Type 2 aspects of quality, (b) differences are larger for Type 2 than for Type 1 aspects of quality, and (c) this pattern of findings holds across a variety of health services.

The first approach to assessing Type 2 quality looks at the distribution of vulnerable consumers in nonprofit versus for-profit settings. Studies of nursing homes suggest that nonprofit facilities are more heavily populated by consumers who are ill-informed or who have characteristics that one would expect to be correlated with reduced consumer information, such as limited education, limited experience with the service in question, or limited support for making decisions (Chou 2002; Hirth 1999; Holtmann and Ullmann 1993). But the same pattern does not hold for institutional purchasers of health plans. Small employers, who are markedly less informed about plan quality than are larger employers (Hargraves and Trude 2002), are no more likely to select a nonprofit plan (Schlesinger, Gray, and Bradley 1996).

This first approach presumes that ill-informed consumers are sufficiently aware of their information deficit to recognize their own vulnerability and sufficiently informed about the meaning of nonprofit ownership to select a provider on the basis of ownership. Our earlier review of public opinion indicated that most people expect quality to be better in for-profit settings, so these assumptions are not entirely plausible. The second strategy for studying Type 2 quality differences avoids these assumptions by focusing on the experiences of vulnerable populations in nonprofit and for-profit plans. Here the evidence is both more consistent and more persuasive. Studies have found that (a) there are no ownership-related differences in quality as reported by relatively healthy enrollees, but for sicker enrollees for-profits provide significantly worse quality of care (Tu and Reschovsky 2002);[24] (b) there were no ownership-related quality differences in nursing homes for residents who had family members to act as their advocates, but residents without these family advocates experienced significantly worse care in for-profit than nonprofit homes (Chou 2002); and (c) there were no differences between nonprofit and for-profit health plans in the dimensions of quality valued by their best-informed consumers, but among the less-informed consumers, those in nonprofit settings were more likely to value Type 2 aspects of quality (Schlesinger, Gray, and Bradley 1996).

The third approach to assessing Type 2 quality relies on consumer responses to being misled about quality. Several studies have examined the prevalence of complaints filed by consumers with state agencies charged with oversight of quality. These have included both nursing-home care (Allen 2001; Weisbrod and Schlesinger 1986; Riportella-Mueller and Slesinger 1982) and treatment in psychiatric hospitals (Mark 1996). Each of the studies found that complaints were more common among clients of for-profit facilities than in otherwise comparable nonprofit organizations. One could view malpractice suits as a similar expression of consumer grievances; here the findings are mixed. Troyer and Thompson (2004) document that consumers were less likely to file legal claims against nonprofit nursing homes than otherwise comparable for-profit facilities.[25] But Gray (1991) found no ownership-related differences in malpractice claims filed against hospitals.

The final approach to detecting differences in hard-to-measure aspects of quality involves comparing the performance of nonprofit and for-profit providers across multiple aspects of quality, to determine how ownership-related differences relate to the measurability of quality. Here again there are only a few studies, but they suggest a consistent pattern in which ownership-related differences are more pronounced for aspects of quality that are more difficult to measure. Two of these studies focused on nursing-home care. Hirth (1999) found that there were no ownership-related differences in the range of services offered by facilities (arguably, a dimension that can be assessed before a facility is selected), but that there were significant differences in the amount of services that residents actually received. Weisbrod and Schlesinger (1986) found no ownership-related differences in regulatory violations in nursing homes (as noted above, information that is made available to consumers), but significantly more complaints about quality were filed by residents of for-profit facilities. Hirth, Chernew, and Orzol (2000) found that, in renal dialysis facilities, for-profits actually scored higher on easy-to-assess "amenities" but lower on measures of "technical quality" that would be harder for consumers to judge.

Adding New Dimensions of Performance: Other Forms of Community Benefit

Regarding charitability, the empirical literature has focused primarily on the provision of treatment to indigent patients. But researchers have identified a variety of other ways in which these organizations might benefit the community,[26] including the provision of public goods (collection or dissemination of information related to health needs; immunization programs), addressing market failures (providing services that have large social benefits that may not be recognized by individual patients or purchasers), improving the performance of the health-care system (e.g., educating health-care professionals), or supporting the infrastructure of the health system in meeting vital local needs (assisting community health centers, social service agencies, homeless shelters, school-based health programs, and so forth) (Needleman 2001; Schlesinger, Gray, and Bradley 1996; Buchmueller and Feldstein 1996).

Although there is only limited research available in these different aspects of community benefit, they generally suggest that all forms are more common among nonprofit organizations. Both nonprofit health plans (Mays, Halverson, and Stevens 2001) and nonprofit hospitals (Proenca, Rosko, and Zinn 2000) are more likely to collaborate with local health departments and health-care agencies to address local needs. Both nonprofit hospitals (Buchmueller and Feldstein 1996) and nonprofit health plans (Schlesinger, Mitchell, and Gray 2003) are more likely to conduct needs assessments of the local community. Both nonprofit health plans (Schlesinger, Mitchell, and Gray 2003) and nonprofit hospitals (Proenca, Rosko, and Zinn 2003; Horwitz 2003) are more likely to provide services that improve the health of the local community, above and beyond the treatment given to their own patients. However, ownership patterns are less consistent in some dimensions of community benefit. Although nonprofit hospitals are more involved than their for-profit counterparts in medical education (Needleman 2001), this difference is not found among health plans (Schlesinger, Mitchell, and Gray 2003).

Summarizing the Findings: Does Ownership Matter for Health Care?

The sheer scope of the literature comparing nonprofit and for-profit health care makes it challenging to synthesize the results in a meaningful manner. But it seems clear that ownership form is associated with significant differences in organizational behavior, albeit in ways that vary strikingly across different types of health services.

This variation is not found in all dimensions of organizational performance. Across the services surveyed here, for-profit organizations appear to consistently mark up their prices more aggressively than do their nonprofit counterparts, suggesting that they are more oriented to maximizing revenues. (This difference, however, appears to be somewhat diminished by the growth of price competition and system affiliation, at least among hospitals.) Nonprofit ownership also appears to be consistently linked with higher levels of quality, particularly for aspects of quality that are difficult for consumers to measure.

But in other dimensions of performance, the forms of ownership-related differences seem more strikingly different for some services than for others. There is a substantial and persisting pattern of greater access to services for nonprofit hospitals in comparison with for-profits, but there appear to be few if any significant differences in access for nursing homes or health plans, fields in which there is little history of charitable fund-raising or service to the uninsured. Ownership-related differences in quality (particularly of Type 1), by contrast, are far more pronounced for health plans and nursing homes than in hospitals. However, the most striking pattern involves costs incurred in providing services. For-profit nursing homes have a distinctive "efficiency" advantage over their nonprofit counterparts. But this advantage in spending less on care of service recipients does not extend to either hospitals or health plans, and it does not translate into savings for the purchasers of services.

This intriguing pattern of ownership-related differences appears to be robust over time and in the face of substantial changes in the delivery of health services, including increased price competition and system affiliations. Ownership clearly matters, but it appears to do so in ways that are contingent on the nature of the services being provided. Even within the health-care domain, the services are sufficiently varied to shape the form of ownership-related differences into distinctive patterns.

These varying consequences of ownership can seem quite confusing. The conclusions that we have drawn from the literature are in sharp contrast with the conclusions that are most often found in the scholarly literature. They also conflict, in certain important ways, with the American public's perceptions about nonprofit health care. We believe that the cross-service variations that we have documented here are themselves an important source of these inaccurate perceptions. But we believe that to more fully understand both why misperceptions arise, and why ownership-related performance differs so strikingly across the domains within health care, we must explore in more detail the factors that are driving this variation in perceptions and performance.

THE ORIGINS OF VARIATION IN BEHAVIOR AND PERCEPTIONS OF NONPROFIT HEALTH CARE

We believe that the confusion in the academic literature and in public perceptions can be attributed in part to the heterogeneous ways in which ownership matters for different health services and in part to persisting distortions in the ways in which ownership is *understood* to matter. We thus begin by exploring the sources of the cross-service variations that we have documented above. We then identify factors that persistently distort our understanding of nonprofit health care.

Sources of Cross-Service Variations in Ownership Mix and Consequences

We have seen that the market shares of nonprofit and for-profit providers vary dramatically across services within health care, that the extent and direction of change in these market shares also vary, and that the consequences of ownership form for the cost, quality, and accessibility of services also vary from one type of service to the next. In our assessment, two key characteristics of contemporary health care account for much of this cross-service variation. The first involves the interplay of technological change and public policy within medical care. The second involves the role of professionals as key decision makers in the delivery of medical care. Neither of these features is unique to health care, but both play a particularly crucial role in this domain. And both factors vary in important ways *within* health care, with implications that we explore below.

Technological Change and a Life-Cycle Perspective on Nonprofits' Role

Scholars agree that the content, form, and cost of medical care are driven to a powerful degree by changing technology (Gelijns, Zivin, and Nelson 2001; Weisbrod 1991). In the first edition of *The Nonprofit Sector,* Marmor, Schlesinger, and Smithey (1987) hypothesized that the roles of nonprofit and for-profit enterprise have varied in a systematic manner depending on the "stage" of technological change and diffusion that was being experienced for each service. This "life-cycle" theory involved four distinct stages, each typified by a different mix of ownership and different factors that influence the balance between nonprofit and for-profit providers. We present here a slightly revised version of this theory to better capture developments of the past fifteen years, as well as the earlier period.

In the first stage, innovative services are first developed, and they are provided primarily under the auspices of nonprofit agencies. The first hospitals in nineteenth-century America were virtually all nonprofit (albeit with subsidies from local government) (Rosenberg 1987; Stevens 1982). Early forms of health insurance operated almost entirely on a nonprofit basis, either as mutual aid societies (Starr 1982) or as state-chartered monopolies (Cunningham and Cunningham 1997; Law 1976). When the treatment of end-stage renal disease first became feasible in the 1960s, treatment was rarely found outside of nonprofit hospitals (Rettig and Levinsky 1991; U.S. Department of Health, Education and Welfare 1977). Most precursors to what are now called HMOs were established as nonprofit or cooperative enterprises (Durso 1992).

The second stage of the life cycle begins when demand starts to increase. This increase is often gradual, as the benefits of the innovation become reasonably well established. Where nonprofits are not meeting the increasing demand (most often in communities with limited civic infrastructure), entrepreneurs with access to capital respond by creating for-profit firms. Because these for-profits are growing mostly in areas in which nonprofits are scarce, competition between nonprofit and for-profit firms is muted in this phase (Vladeck 1980; Kushman and Nuckton 1977; Lave and Lave 1974; Steinwald and Neuhauser 1970; Hamilton 1961). This relatively stable phase can persist for long periods (several decades) unless an external shock occurs.

Two kinds of external shocks can induce the third phase of the life cycle, which is characterized by rapid growth of the for-profit sector. The first is a legislative change that provides insurance coverage or other funding for a service that had not heretofore been covered. The second is a regulatory change that induces major changes in utilization patterns or that removes barriers to for-profit enterprises. We can illustrate each impetus for change with several examples.

The proprietary nursing-home industry developed in the 1930s as a result of the Social Security legislation that put money in the pockets of elderly people who needed assistance, while forbidding funds to be used for housing the elderly in publicly owned facilities. The discontinuation of certain state regulations created the commercial health insurance industry to supplement nonprofit Blue Cross plans in the 1940s. The demand created in 1965 with Medicare and Medicaid funding for the elderly and poor led to the transformation of the proprietary hospital and nursing-home industries into investor-owned fields.[27] In 1972 Medicare coverage was extended to pay for dialysis and other treatment for end-stage renal disease. In 1983 Medicare coverage was expanded again to pay for hospice services for those at the end of life.

All these coverage expansions stimulated the number and market share of for-profit providers (Gray and Schlesinger 2002). Regulatory changes were responsible for the rapid growth of several other types of for-profit providers, including HMOs, rehabilitation hospitals, and home care agencies (ibid.). The fields in which the for-profit share increased substantially were all characterized by large increases in the total number of organizations and little or no decrease in the number of nonprofit service providers. Typically, nonprofit provision was growing as well, simply not as quickly as services provided under for-profit auspices. This pattern signals the importance of the rapid demand increases as forces that transform the ownership composition of fields.

The fourth stage of the life cycle might be termed the "mature" phase of service development. As demand stabilizes, competition intensifies and pressures increase for convergence in behavior between nonprofit and for-profit agencies. Government-financed purchasing programs use their leverage to hold both nonprofit and for-profit firms to common standards of performance. In the face of growing financial and administrative constraints, providers begin to consolidate or to leave markets entirely, a response that is strongest among for-profit providers (Long and Yemane 2005; Needleman 2001; Norton and Staiger 1994; Gray and Schlesinger 2002; Glavin et al. 2002/3). In this fourth phase, the nonprofit share of the marketplace can begin to increase, as occurred during the 1990s among nursing homes, private psychiatric hospitals, and home health agencies.

Different health services embody this technological dynamic to varying degrees and are at different stages in this life cycle. The services witnessing the most extensive growth in for-profit market share (as shown in figure 16.1) all experienced significant increases in demand over the past fifteen years (Gray and Schlesinger 2002). It appears that these more dynamic considerations are the primary explanation for the cross-service variations in the market share of nonprofit and for-profit health-care providers.

Because different health services are at different stages in their technological life cycles, one would also expect that ownership-related distinctions would appear in different aspects of performance. In early stages, the distinctive nonprofit role relates to quality of care as innovative technologies are introduced and refined. In later stages, but prior to the expansion of government subsidies for treatment, accessibility is likely to become the primary way in which ownership-related differences emerge. But as public and private programs that finance care expand, other areas of community benefits or quality are likely to define the major distinctions between nonprofit and for-profit health care.

The (Changing) Interactions of Professionalism and Ownership in Medical Care

Health care is powerfully shaped by the authority and expectations of the medical profession (Schlesinger 2002; Starr 1982). Writing almost twenty years ago, Marmor, Schlesinger, and Smithey suggested that the role of physicians in particular was important in shaping the scope and implications of nonprofit health care. They made two specific claims about this relationship. First, they suggested that the medical profession acted as a buffer against the expansion of profit-making firms: "The services in which doctors play the least important role . . . are those in which proprietary enterprises deliver the largest portion of services" (1987:229). This claim seemed plausible, based on the pattern of ownership that existed across services in the mid-1980s. It was also consistent with the scholarship of that period, which claimed that the objectives of nonprofit organizations were particularly compatible with prevailing norms of professional practice (Gray 1986; Majone 1984). Subsequent events, however, have shown that this barrier either was illusory or had been adulterated by other developments in American medicine.[28] A number of services for which there is active physician involvement experienced a dramatic expansion of for-profit ownership during this period (see figure 16.1). This pattern was most pronounced for HMOs but was also apparent for dialysis centers, psychiatric hospitals, and rehabilitation hospitals.

The second hypothesis developed by Marmor, Schlesinger, and Smithey posited that differences in the role of health-care professionals across various health services influence the forms in which ownership-related differences emerge. Organizations in which physicians have an important role will have similarities that result from the influence of these professional norms. Because these professionals played a much larger role for some services (hospitals, dialysis centers, HMOs) than for others (home health agencies, hospice programs, nursing homes), it was argued that a part of the cross-service variation in ownership-related performance could be explained by the varying influence of professional norms. More specifically, the authors concluded that significant ownership-related differences in performance appeared in organizations in which physicians played only a limited role in the allocation of services, but few if any differences were observed "for those facilities in which physicians control the delivery of care" (1987:232). This pattern was most extensively documented for costs and quality of care, with nursing homes the prime example of a health service for which physicians had modest involvement (Vladeck 1980; Koetting 1980) and hospitals the context in which they were argued to have near-total authority (Harris 1977).

Empirical findings available in the mid-1980s appeared to support this pattern of performance: larger ownership-related differences in nursing homes, modest differences in hospitals. These predictions were consistent with ideas about isomorphism in organizational fields, concepts that were entering the sociological literature at the time (DiMaggio and Powell 1983). Professional norms among physicians were argued to create pressure for "normative isomorphism"—that is, because physicians practicing in either nonprofit or for-profit settings had similar training, their preferences would encourage similar organizational practices, regardless of the ownership of the facility in question.[29]

In one sense, the additional research that has accumulated over the past fifteen years offers a strong validation of the observation by Marmor, Schlesinger, and Smithey that physicians' roles mediate the implications of ownership. Certainly the prevailing pattern of ownership-related differences is quite different for hospitals than for nursing homes. But the simple story of normative isomorphism is not supported by this research—ownership-related differences are not uniformly smaller across all dimensions of behavior for hospitals than for nursing homes. Quality of care is the one dimension in which professional isomorphism may be at work. Certainly ownership-related differences for quality emerge less consistently among hospitals than among nursing homes.[30] The results for quality in managed-care plans initially seem inconsistent. Here physicians play a crucial role in allocating services, yet ownership-related differences in quality appear to be quite pronounced. But this may reflect the ability of managed-care plans to control the autonomy of their clinicians through utilization review and other protocols (Schlesinger, Gray, and Perreira 1997).

Normative isomorphism doesn't appear to be at all useful for understanding other dimensions of organizational performance. It is not surprising that professional norms exert no isomorphic pressures in terms of treating unprofitable patients. Physicians' ethical codes impose no duty for organizations to treat unprofitable patients or even to maintain an "open door" for anyone who might seek treatment (Kultgen 1988). But the ownership-related differences in terms of uncompensated care are much more pronounced for hospitals than for nursing-home care.[31] Other factors must account for these differences in performance across services.

The comparison of ownership-related performance in costs of care (which economists refer to as technical or productive efficiency) poses the most challenging puzzle.

Among nursing homes, one finds quite striking differences in costs; stays in nonprofit homes cost between 10 and 40 percent more than in otherwise comparable for-profit facilities, holding constant various aspects of quality. More sophisticated empirical assessments of technical efficiency find equally striking ownership-related differences among nursing homes. Yet among hospitals, the cost differences are not simply smaller; costs seem to be *lower* in nonprofit facilities. This result has been replicated among the most sophisticated statistical models of technical efficiency in hospital settings (Burgess and Wilson 1996; Zuckerman, Hadley, and Iezzoni 1994; Ozcan and Luke 1993; Ozcan, Luke, and Haksever 1992; Eakin 1991).

The researchers who have documented these differences have struggled to explain them. One hypothesis has been that the perceived incompatibility of professional ethics and profit-making organizations forced for-profit hospitals to spend more on expensive technologies, in order to attract physicians (Ozcan, Luke, and Haksever 1992). But this explanation is not supported by studies of the diffusion of new technologies, which find that the new and most prestigious technologies are more quickly adopted in nonprofit settings (Robinson and Luft 1985; Cromwell and Kanak 1982; Russell 1978). Earlier studies of cost differences in hospitals were discounted because the then-current payment systems were based on reported costs, providing little incentive for efficient production of services. But as we saw above, these efficiency differences have persisted in more recent studies, after virtually all payers had shifted to payment systems based on per-case rates. Nor are higher costs in for-profit hospitals an artifact of proprietary hospitals being poorly managed by their physician-owners—for-profit hospitals owned by large corporations appear to be no more efficient (Valdmanis 1990).

Summarizing the Sources of Cross-Service Variation in Nonprofit Performance

Variations in the life cycle for specific health services and the varying influence of the medical professions can thus account for some, but not all, of the observed cross-service variation in ownership mix and ownership-related outcomes. Although the varying role of professional authority across health services may well mediate the effects of ownership, the medical profession is clearly no longer an effective barrier to the expansion of for-profit health care in the form of corporate medicine. And normative isomorphism appears at best a weak force shaping ownership-related behavior. To the extent that professionalism interacts with ownership in the delivery of medical care, it probably does so in ways more complex than either of these simple stories (Schlesinger 1998). We will return later to this issue.

Factors that Distort the Apparent Influence of Nonprofit Ownership in Health Care

The prevailing misperceptions about nonprofit health care cannot be attributed solely to these complex patterns of service-specific outcomes. Several other factors come into play that lead both the American public and academic researchers to assess the implications of ownership in an incomplete or distorted fashion.

The Fragmentation of the Literature on Nonprofit Health Care

One confounding factor emerges from the very nature of scholarship about nonprofit organizations. As previously noted, the meaning and implications of ownership form in health care have engaged researchers from a range of different disciplines. In the study of health care, the academic enterprise is further fragmented across clinical, health services, and health policy journals. Two other factors compound the problem: tools for searching the literature stop at disciplinary borders, and titles and abstracts of articles do not always convey that a study contains data pertaining to ownership form.

These problems undermine our understanding of nonprofit health care in several ways. First, review articles that purport to summarize the current state of knowledge about ownership in medical care are usually based on empirical research from only one or perhaps two of the different disciplinary literatures. The typical review article cites a few dozen empirical studies. The most comprehensive of these articles cites just fewer than sixty empirical studies. By checking multiple databases and trying numerous search terms, we have been able to identify more than 230 empirical studies of ownership in the literature—roughly 140 using data from hospitals (including psychiatric and rehabilitation facilities), fifty from nursing homes, twenty from managed-care organizations, and another twenty for assorted other forms of medical care. As we have noted, many of the broad patterns in the empirical research on nonprofit health care are apparent only when one has accumulated a substantial number of studies. What first appears simply to be inconsistency of findings resolves itself into a more reliable pattern of ownership-related differences, albeit one mediated by particular characteristics of the services or the context in which those services are delivered.

A second consequence of the disciplinary fragmentation of the literature is that each discipline identifies certain influences on organizational behavior that it considers most critical to assessing the delivery of health services. Economists study most closely the characteristics of local markets. Sociologists attempt to measure the factors thought to encourage isomorphic pressures or the local norms of medical practice. Clinicians introduce more comprehensive measures of the severity of the diseases being treated. Specialists in organizational behavior assess strategic orientations or introduce more sophisticated measures of organizational effectiveness. This diversity of disciplinary perspectives can be a powerful stimulus for enriching the study of ownership in health care. But it guarantees that the empirical models developed from each perspective will include different sets of explanatory variables. These inconsistent methods introduce considerable variation across studies in the measured effects of ownership. This may make it *appear* that ownership is not a reliable marker for organizational performance, when in fact the variation is being introduced by the inconsistent ways in which researchers are statistically assessing that performance. We consider this methodological variation in more detail below.

Misidentification of Ownership

We know remarkably little about the ways in which the American public comprehends nonprofit ownership. What we do know suggests that the public has somewhat inaccurate impressions about the implications of ownership, owing to a limited understanding of the meaning of "nonprofit" as a characteristic of an organization. Perhaps more surprisingly, we believe that academic researchers have also fallen into the practice of misidentifying ownership, though in this case the errors involve for-profit ownership.

Evidence derived from public opinion surveys raises doubts about the ability of most Americans to use ownership to discriminate meaningfully among health-care providers. A survey fielded in 1996 asked a representative sample of the public about their "feelings" toward for-profit health care. Reactions were evenly split between positive and negative responses. More important, for our current considerations, 24 percent of the public reported that they were unfamiliar with the term.[32] The proportion that was unfamiliar with this term climbed to almost 40 percent in some sociodemographic subgroups. In subsequent surveys, the proportion of the public who didn't understand the term "for-profit" ranged from 17 percent to 27 percent (Schlesinger, Mitchell, and Gray 2004).

A second survey revealed how an incomplete understanding about ownership can distort the conclusions that the public draws from its own experiences. In 1997 there were a series of well-publicized scandals involving the Columbia/HCA health-care corporation, an investor-owned company that owned hospitals, home health agencies, and other facilities throughout the country. The company was accused of defrauding the federal government of almost $1 billion in false charges for services that were never delivered or were inappropriate for the patients in question. A survey fielded after several months of media coverage asked respondents how closely they had followed these stories. Almost half claimed that they had followed the coverage "somewhat" or "very" closely. They were then asked whether "the Columbia/HCA hospital chain" was a for-profit or a not-for-profit chain. Thirty-nine percent responded that it was nonprofit; only 12 percent correctly identified it as a for-profit chain. Another 49 percent acknowledged not knowing the answer.[33] If these responses accurately captured Americans' understanding of these events, they suggest that the scandals probably undermined the legitimacy of the *nonprofit* health-care sector during this intensely negative media coverage.

Academic researchers face a different problem of ownership identification. Virtually every study compares the performance of nonprofit providers to a generic category of for-profit firms. However, this approach combines two different types of profit-making enterprises: locally owned proprietary organizations and facilities of investor-owned corporations that own multiple facilities (Gray 1991). This aggregation presumes that both types of organizations are similarly motivated to "maximize profits to be able to at least break even in economic terms" (Hirth, Chernew, and Orzol 2000). In our assessment, however, this aggregation potentially distorts our understanding of the relationship between ownership and organizational performance, since (a) the mix of investor-owned and proprietary ownership has varied across services and over time, and (b) there is some evidence suggesting that the two forms of for-profit enterprise behave in distinctly different ways.

Among the services listed in figure 16.1, the proportion of investor-owned for-profits ranges from a low of 40 percent among hospice programs to a high of 83 percent among dialysis centers (Hirth, Chernew, and Orzol 2000) and 75 percent among hospitals (Ettner and Hermann 2001). This cross-service variation reflects in part where these services are in their life cycle. In early growth stages, the for-profit presence is embodied by proprietary ownership. For example, as the hospital industry developed in the early twentieth century, the numerous for-profit hospitals were owned primarily by individual physicians (Stevens 1989; Bays 1983). The first wave of for-profit nursing homes were literally homes, with couples taking in boarders to supplement their incomes (Vladeck 1980). The early for-profit HMOs started at mid-century were owned by groups of physicians or business entrepreneurs (Luft 1981). The first for-profit renal dialysis facilities were established in the 1970s by individual nephrologists or small groups of clinicians. The first for-profit hospice programs were created as employee-owned corporations in the mid-1980s.

Because the two forms of for-profit enterprise are typically grouped together in empirical studies, we know relatively little about their distinctive patterns of behavior. But the limited evidence that exists suggests that their performance may be quite different. Among nursing homes, for example, for-profit facilities affiliated with publicly traded national corporations have been shown to have consistently higher costs (Luksetich, Edwards, and Carroll 2000; Anderson, Lewis, and Webb 1999) and lower quality of care (Castle 2000; Johnson, Cowles, and Simmens 1996) than do independent for-profit homes. For-profit hospitals affiliated with national corporations appear less willing to treat unprofitable patients than are other for-profit facilities (Schlesinger et al. 1986). Whether these differences reflect diseconomies of scale or distinctive goals for local versus corporate investors remains less clear. The only study that has attempted to expressly measure the influence of investors on organizational behavior drew data from a recent survey of the community-oriented services provided by HMOs (Schlesinger, Mitchell, and Gray 2003). It found that some forms of community benefits provided by for-profit HMOs were distinctly lower when the plan (as reported by the CEO) was strongly influenced by investors (see table 16.4).

Perhaps the most dramatic differences between proprietary and investor ownership involve the dynamics of orga-

TABLE 16.4. IMPACT OF INVESTOR INFLUENCE ON COMMUNITY BENEFITS PROVIDED BY HMOS

	Measure of community benefit		
Ownership form of HMO	Spending per enrollee in community-benefit budget	Spending per enrollee on donations to community	Index of community-benefit activities
Private nonprofit	$5.12	$3.66	2.91
All for-profit plans	$3.25	$1.63	2.07[a]
For-profit plans with strong investor influence	$1.02[a]	$2.71	1.67[a]

Source: Data from Schlesinger, Mitchell, and Gray 2003.
[a]Difference with private nonprofit is statistically significant.

nizational behavior—the ways in which organizations respond to changes in demand or other external influences. The more extensively that for-profit firms use equity markets, the more they must adapt their performance to the preferences of investors. Since the first publicly traded health-care companies were created in the late 1960s, capital has been attracted by growth opportunities. Expanding revenues are interpreted by many investors as a predictor of future profitability (Robinson 2000), giving these companies a strong incentive to achieve growth. The most rapid path is through acquisitions.

This structure of incentives has produced periods of omnivorous growth among the investor-owned health-care corporations, with companies swallowing one another, acquiring any existing proprietary facilities, and seeking nonprofit organizations that can be convinced to sell their assets (Cutler and Horwitz 2000; Goddeeris and Weisbrod 1998; Gray 1997). Maintenance of a high stock price requires continued growth in revenues, which depends on ever-expanding acquisitions. One analyst has likened the process to a Ponzi scheme (Reinhardt 2000) because the dance of expansion looks quite different when the music stops. When opportunities for growth are curtailed by scandal, regulatory changes, or stagnant demand, the stock value of the corporation can decline precipitously (Gray 1991). This increased cost of capital chokes off further growth. Indeed, the company may be forced to sell off assets and may itself become a target for acquisition. This sequence has produced a boom-bust cycle over the past twenty years for virtually every investor-owned corporation in health care, aside from the pharmaceutical industry (Gray and Schlesinger 2002; Schlesinger and Gray 1999; Kuttner 1996a, 1996b).

These dynamic properties also explain why dramatic increases in for-profit market share never lead to the complete demise of nonprofit involvement. For the investor-owned companies, once the opportunities for rapid growth are exhausted, the investor capital fueling the expansion moves elsewhere. But nonprofit capital tends to remain in place: the mirror image of the nonprofit sector's failure to respond rapidly to expanding demand is its stability in the face of unfavorable market conditions (Hansmann, Kessler, and McClellan 2003).

Investor-owned corporations first established a foothold in health care in the late 1960s in companies owning chains of nursing homes. When the chances for profitable acquisitions were curtailed by the mid-1970s (a product of demand saturation and regulatory reform), several of these companies shifted capital to acute-care hospitals. By the mid-1980s, the investor community became enamored with psychiatric hospitals, followed in the 1990s by enthusiasm for investing in rehabilitation facilities. In each case, the surge of for-profit ownership became self-limiting, as the opportunities for rapid growth were fully exploited.

This greater mobility of capital among investor-owned corporations may be seen as either a benefit or a liability from the standpoint of society as a whole (Hansmann, Kessler, and McClellan 2003). On one hand, it ensures that financial resources can be rapidly funneled into aspects of health care with the greatest unmet demands. Consequently, as the benefits of innovative services become established and as new government programs address emerging health needs, an investor-owned health-care system can quickly redirect resources to support an expanded treatment capacity. On the other hand, these rapid shifts in capital can produce excess investment in particular services or localities. For example, when state regulations in Utah were changed to facilitate expansion of hospital capacity in the mid-1980s, large hospital corporations simultaneously built seven psychiatric facilities in Salt Lake City—roughly five more than were needed to treat the residents of that city (Dorwart and Schlesinger 1988). For most services, such a glut would lead in the short run to cut-rate prices (a benefit to consumers) and perhaps the eventual closure of some facilities. For health care, however, excess capacity may induce providers to provide excessive treatment, which may both waste resources and actually harm patients (Wennberg, Fisher, and Skinner 2004).

Highly mobile capital may also be a concern when markets for health services become less profitable. Investor-owned facilities are less "committed to place" than are either nonprofit or proprietary health-care providers (Needleman 2001). When local economies slump or when local markets for health services become unprofitable, the investor-owned firms are the quickest to close their facilities. This pattern has been repeated in the hospital industry, among health plans, and among psychiatric hospitals. Under some circumstances, quick closures are in the public interest. Under other circumstances, they may leave residents of particular communities without geographically accessible medical care, may diminish a region's capacity to respond to dramatic increases in health-care needs, or may disrupt patients' arrangements with their health-care professionals (Glavin et al. 2002/3; Booske, Lynch, and Riley 2002).

Whether one sees the distinctive performance of investor-owned for-profit firms as beneficial or deleterious to society, it is important to recognize that research that conflates investor and proprietary ownership introduces yet another source of extraneous variation to empirical studies of nonprofit health care. Over time, as the share of for-profit agencies owned by investors increases, the standard of performance against which nonprofit organizations are compared implicitly changes. Similarly, the performance of nonprofit hospice providers is being compared to a very different standard than is the performance of nonprofit acute-care hospitals, since investor-owned hospital corporations control twice as large a share of their industry's for-profit sector than is true for hospices.

Misspecification of Statistical Models Identifying the Impact of Ownership on Behavior

As we previously noted, researchers from different disciplines tend to incorporate different variables into the statistical models they use to identify the distinct influence of ownership on organizational behavior. One could debate which of these specifications is the most appropriate. But three issues of model specification have become persistent themes in recent empirical research and merit some analysis. The first involves the risk of "overcontrolling"—of introducing variables that are closely correlated with ownership and thus inappropriately eliminating the statistical relationship between ownership and organizational performance (Weisbrod 1998b). The second issue involves a related question: how researchers should take into account differences in the locational patterns of nonprofit and for-profit health-care providers. The third issue involves how best to measure interactions between the performance of nonprofit and for-profit providers in local markets.

The Problem of Overcontrolling. Several characteristics of health-care providers have been shown both (a) to affect the cost, quality, and accessibility of services and (b) to be closely correlated with nonprofit ownership. The two most commonly identified in the literature are whether the organization has a religious affiliation and whether the organization is engaged in medical education (affiliated with an accredited professional school or training program).[34] These affiliations create several problems for the empirical studies of ownership.

First, these characteristics are incorporated inconsistently into analysts' statistical models, so some studies of ownership effects hold these characteristics constant, while others essentially report the combined effects of ownership, teaching status, and religious affiliation. (Roughly one-fourth of studies have incorporated a variable measuring either religious or teaching affiliations at the facilities under review. Only a handful of studies controlled for both characteristics.) The question is, how ought these factors be taken into account? Most researchers would argue that the appropriate approach would be to include each of these characteristics as additional explanatory variables, along with a dichotomous ownership variable, in regression models explaining various outcomes. The coefficient of the ownership variable itself is then treated as the only measure of the ownership effects.

In our assessment, this reasoning is flawed because of the close correlation of nonprofit ownership with both teaching and religious affiliation. Although programs for training health professionals are found at some for-profit hospitals, major teaching programs are almost all located at nonprofit and public institutions (Keeler et al. 1992). Although there are a small number of for-profit nursing homes with religious affiliations (Bradley and Walker 1998), virtually all hospitals and nursing homes with religious connections are nonprofit (White and Ozcan 1996; Weisbrod and Schlesinger 1986). Under these circumstances, introducing these closely correlated variables into a regression reduces the *apparent* impact of ownership.

To the extent that nonprofit ownership is a necessary precursor (or functionally close to that) for religious or teaching affiliations, one should more appropriately treat these forms of affiliation as *consequences* of nonprofit ownership. Following this rationale, one would therefore estimate the effect of ownership on the delivery of these services by combining the measured effect of ownership itself with the effect associated with religious or teaching affiliation (weighted by the proportion of all nonprofits that have such affiliations). Based on the magnitude of the religion and teaching coefficients that have been estimated in the literature, these combined ownership effects would lead to substantially larger differences between nonprofit and for-profit quality for both hospitals and nursing homes. The consequences for efficiency are more ambiguous: teaching facilities have significantly higher costs, but the implications of religious affiliation are less certain.[35]

The Problem of Location. A related question involves the treatment of locational factors in the empirical assessment of ownership-related performance. The argument that locational differences account for nonprofit hospitals' larger share of uncompensated care dates back to the mid-1980s (Gray 1991). Over the past fifteen years, the study of locational factors has been refined in a number of ways. Norton and Staiger (1994) explored these issues at length in their investigation of access to hospital services for people without health insurance. They found that while nonprofit hospitals, on average, treated more uninsured patients than did for-profit facilities, these differences could be explained by characteristics of the communities within which the hospitals were located. The nonprofit hospitals that treated a disproportionate share of the uninsured were located in inner cities. For-profit hospitals, in contrast, tended to be located in suburban areas where fewer people were uninsured. Nonprofit hospitals located in those same communities also treated only a modest number of patients without insurance.

Do these findings suggest that there are not in fact ownership-related differences in the accessibility of hospital services? Some researchers derive from them precisely this conclusion (Mobley and Bradford 1997). Once again, the implication of the results depends critically on their interpretation. If the location of for-profit hospitals were unrelated to the probability that they would be confronted by uninsured patients, then these findings would suggest that ownership was not an important causal factor in access to care.[36] But there is in fact evidence that the location of for-profit organizations reflects their strategic calculations about the profitability of local markets.

For-profit hospitals, home health agencies, and dialysis centers are significantly more common in states that have enacted programs to provide financial support for these services (Marmor, Schlesinger, and Smithey 1987). For-profit hospitals are more frequently established in states with extensive or particularly generous private insurance coverage (Watt et al. 1986; Mullner and Hadley 1984; Bays 1983). Within states, they tend to avoid counties in which private insurance is less extensive (Clement, White, and Valdmanis 2002; Homer, Bradham, and Rushefsky 1984). This means that the locational patterns of hospitals are themselves a consequence of ownership-related incentives, a reflection of the reduced willingness of for-profit organizations to treat unprofitable patients. To compare the behavior of nonprofit and for-profit hospitals only in those communities in which the for-profits have selectively located is misleading—it is little wonder that nonprofit hospitals treat few indigent clients in communities in which there are few poor residents.

To appropriately incorporate the strategic behaviors underpinning the location of for-profit hospitals, one should explicitly take locational choices into account in the statistical models. One recent study did so by estimating a two-stage model in which the first stage captured the community characteristics in which for-profit hospitals were choosing to locate. Controlling for these selection effects, there were still statistically significant differences in the extent to which for-profit and nonprofit hospitals treated indigent patients (Clement, White, and Valdmanis 2002).

The Problem of Proximity. The convergence of behavior of for-profit and nonprofit health-care providers located in the same community may not simply be a consequence of responding similarly to equivalent community needs. There are several other reasons to expect that the close proximity of for-profit and nonprofit competitors will itself induce a reduction in ownership-related differences in behavior. The first involves isomorphic pressures toward conformity. Prevailing notions about appropriate health care are strongly influenced by local norms of practice (Roos and Roos 1994; Wennberg, Fisher, and Skinner 2004). When individual consumers or collective purchasers choose a provider, their preferences will be shaped by these norms. Consequently, when a for-profit health-care organization enters a market dominated by nonprofit health-care providers, it will tend to emulate their practices in order to gain legitimacy (Marsteller, Bovbjerg, and Nichols 1998; DiMaggio and Powell 1983). Conversely, when for-profit providers dominate a local market, nonprofit facilities in that community will be under pressure to behave in a more "business-like" manner (Schlesinger et al. 1987).

A second factor that may induce greater conformity between nonprofit and for-profit firms competing in the same markets stems from Hirth's hypothesis that the presence of a nonprofit organization in a local market will attract the most vulnerable consumers and thus reduce the incentive for for-profit providers to exploit consumer ignorance (Hirth 1997). One would thus expect the magnitude of ownership-related differences in Type 2 quality to be smaller when nonprofits and for-profit providers share the same communities.

A number of studies have examined the behavioral effects of ownership proximity (Schlesinger et al. 2005; Horwitz 2005; Grabowski and Hirth 2003; Clement, White, and Valdmanis 2002; Duggan 2002; Barro and Chu 2002; Ettner and Hermann 2001; Kessler and McClellan 2001; Silverman and Skinner 2001; Garg et al. 1999; Spector, Selden, and Cohen 1998; Schlesinger et al. 1997a; Hughes and Luft 1990; Schlesinger et al. 1987). Most of these studies have explored the impact of for-profit entry on the behavior of neighboring nonprofit firms. Only a few studies have examined whether entry by nonprofit providers influences the performance of for-profit facilities in the same community. Both sets of studies identify statistically significant market-level effects, albeit in different domains of performance. A larger nonprofit market share appears to enhance quality in for-profit settings (but does not influence practices related to access), whereas a larger for-profit market share appears to influence nonprofit practices related to both access and cost, encouraging nonprofits to be more sensitive to financial considerations.

Evidence suggests that a larger nonprofit presence leads to higher-quality services in for-profit providers, but to no comparable changes involving access to care. Garg and colleagues (1999:1659) found that for-profit dialysis centers that had nonprofit competitors in the same county had significantly lower mortality rates (15 percent versus 29 percent) and higher referral rates (44 percent versus 14 percent) for kidney transplantation (which reduces the number of patients on dialysis and thus the center's future revenue stream) than did other for-profit centers. Similarly, Grabowski and Hirth (2003) found that the larger the share of nonprofit homes in a local market, the higher the quality of care in for-profit nursing homes (and the average quality in local markets). Schlesinger et al. (2005) determined that for-profit health plans were less likely to mislead enrollees or to stint on hard-to-measure dimensions of quality when the local nonprofit market share exceeded 20 percent.

By contrast, Clement, White, and Valdmanis (2002) found that the number of unprofitable patients treated by for-profit hospitals was not influenced by the uncompensated care practices of nonprofit hospitals in the same locale.

Nor is propensity to treat Medicaid patients at for-profit hospitals sensitive to the local market share of nonprofit hospitals (Duggan 2002).

Nine studies have examined the impact of for-profit neighbors on the behavior of nonprofit hospitals.[37] All found significant effects related to the firm's financial bottom line. A larger local for-profit presence encourages nonprofit hospitals to (a) increase revenues by adding more profitable services (Horwitz 2005; Hughes and Luft 1990), altering the diagnostic mix of patients to generate larger revenues (Silverman and Skinner 2001), or otherwise trying to attract profitable patients (Duggan 2002; Barro and Chu 2002); (b) reduce their treatment of unprofitable patients (Schlesinger et al. 1997a), in part by inhibiting admission of uninsured patients (Schlesinger et al. 1987); and (c) reduce resources devoted to treating those patients whom they do admit (Ettner and Hermann 2001; Kessler and McClellan 2001).

Although limited to a small number of services, this research does suggest some convergence of ownership-related performance in local areas that have both nonprofit and for-profit health-care facilities. With the existing studies, we cannot determine whether this convergence is the result of isomorphic pressures or of a sorting of consumers. But the evidence that nonprofit hospitals are less likely to treat unprofitable patients when they have for-profit neighbors seems suggestive of some sort of isomorphic pressures on their behavior.[38] These pressures appear to diminish, but not eliminate, the ownership-related differences that were documented earlier. But in a health-care system in which many services have a mixture of ownership types, the performance of the system seems to be influenced by whether there is a mixture across all communities or whether organizations of different ownership forms are concentrated in distinct locales.

DISCUSSION AND CONCLUSIONS

On the basis of our review of the empirical and theoretical literature, we have concluded that ownership matters for the delivery of medical care, but it does so in ways that vary among the different services that make up the American health-care system. Readers familiar with health-care literature will recognize how much this conclusion differs from the conventional portrayal, particularly in the economics literature. Many reviews of ownership conclude that ownership is largely an irrelevant feature. For example, several recent articles on the hospital industry have suggested that historically meaningful distinctions between nonprofit and for-profit facilities are a thing of the past (Sloan 1998). White (2000:221) concluded that "whereas hospitals once were charitable organizations for the sick and injured, they have gradually adopted characteristics of businesses. For-profit and nonprofit hospitals exhibit similar attributes and espouse similar missions and goals."

In our assessment, these assessments are misleading, reflecting a literature that is fragmented along disciplinary lines and in which empirical models are sometimes specified in ways that obscure rather than illuminate ownership-related differences. Most fundamentally, we believe that these misperceptions reflect researchers' essentially asking the wrong question. Those who see only inconsistency in the empirical literature are asking, sometimes implicitly, whether ownership form "matters" in some fashion that holds for all forms of health care under all local market conditions. From this perspective, if ownership seems to matter for some studies but not others, or appears to produce significant effects on performance for some organizations but not others, then the findings are "inconsistent" and the answer to the question is "no." We believe the quest for such a generalized prediction about the implications of ownership is fundamentally misguided, leading researchers to miss substantial effects of ownership that vary across services.[39]

Once researchers take into account changes over time in the ways in which health care is financed, the intensity of price competition among health-care providers, the extent to which nonprofit and for-profit providers operate in the same local markets, and the prevalence of affiliations with national and regional health-care systems, ownership appears clearly consequential, in predictable ways. The evidence documenting these more complex patterns is relatively robust. Nonetheless, we believe that there remain some important unanswered questions about nonprofit health care that merit further research.

Directions for Future Research

Throughout this review of the theoretical and empirical literature on nonprofit health care, we have identified a number of patterns of performance that merit additional study. These include:

- exploring reasons why public perceptions of nonprofit and for-profit health care diverge from ownership-related behaviors documented in research, especially for quality of care;
- further documenting the differences in the delivery of health care between proprietary and investor-owned for-profit health-care facilities;
- more thorough analyses of the ways in which external constraints (market pressures, community characteristics, regulatory environment) mediate how ownership-related differences translate into concrete performance;
- more research on the ways in which nonprofit and for-profit facilities located in the same community affect one another's behavior; and
- additional study of the ways in which professional norms may mediate ownership-related differences in behavior, as well as the ways in which changing ownership in American medicine may alter the autonomy and authority of the medical profession.

Two additional issues require somewhat greater elaboration. The first involves the unexpected association of nonprofit ownership with apparently greater efficiency in hospitals and managed-care plans. Nonprofits' advantages in property tax exemptions and the cost of capital (because of tax-exempt bond financing) may play a role. We will offer here one additional speculative answer, though its verification will require additional empirical research.

We believe that one plausible explanation involves the relationship between hospitals (or health plans) and the physicians with which they have affiliations. Because physicians strongly influence resource allocation in these settings, efficient organizations encourage their medical staff to practice in a cost-conscious manner.[40] For-profit hospitals can use profit sharing and other financial incentives to pursue such ends (Hyatt and Hopkins 2001). But the effectiveness of profit sharing or ownership incentives weakens as the network of affiliated physicians expands, because in large networks the actions of any one physician can have only a marginal impact on the organization's financial bottom line.

Unlike financial incentives, motivations based on an organization's mission or community commitments are not weakened by having many colleagues. The nonpecuniary rewards of "doing good" are not diminished when shared with others. Although for-profit firms can also make use of nonpecuniary rewards, whenever for-profit firms ask their physicians to conserve resources to boost the hospital's year-end surplus, the physicians must ask themselves what proportion of this surplus will be diverted to stock dividends or other spending that is inconsistent with a charitable mission. In short, physicians must trust that the resources they are saving will be put to good use by the firm. If this "trust-based efficiency" hypothesis is valid, efficiency differences between nonprofit and for-profit organizations should be most evident in large-scale organizations, where the incentives of profit sharing are attenuated. Given this comparative advantage, we would expect to find for-profit ownership concentrated among smaller hospitals and large facilities to be mostly nonprofit.

Historically, this has been exactly the pattern over several decades: nonprofit organizations have tended to be larger than their for-profit counterparts, even those operated by large national corporations (Steinwald and Neuhauser 1970). More recent research that has attempted to measure the optimal scale for efficient operation of nonprofit and for-profit hospitals has found that the latter are most efficient with fewer beds (Burgess and Wilson 1996:12). The two empirical studies that have examined the interactions among ownership, efficiency, and hospital size have in fact found that the efficiency gap between nonprofit and for-profit hospitals is greatest in the largest size range (Ozcan, Luke, and Haksever 1992; Register and Bruning 1986).[41]

A final aspect of ownership-related behavior that merits more exploration involves aspects of trustworthy behavior in organizations' relationships with purchasers as well as consumers of services. Because of the complexity of health services and the inability of debilitated patients to monitor the treatment that they are receiving, payers are vulnerable to fraudulent billings—e.g., being asked to pay for services that are not needed, that are of lesser quality than represented, that are not eligible for payment, or that have not even been provided. Fraudulent billings account for as much as 15 percent of health expenditures in the United States (Sparrow 2000). Substantial instances of fraudulent practices at the organizational level have been documented in both nonprofit and for-profit settings. But the incentives associated with investor ownership appear to have particularly exacerbated pressures on facility administrators to meet ambitious corporate goals for economic performance (Kuttner 1996b; Gray 1991).

Several major episodes of systematic fraudulent behavior were detected among large investor-owned health-care companies in the 1980s (Gray 1991), but the scale of fraudulent episodes seemingly expanded during the 1990s. In 1994 National Medical Enterprises (NME), then the second largest hospital company, paid $379 million in fines and penalties to settle fraud charges with the federal government and twenty-eight states, pleading guilty to six felony counts involving the payment of kickbacks for referrals of patients to its psychiatric facilities.[42] Similar practices were documented in subsequent investigations for two other leading investor-owned psychiatric hospital companies, Community Psychiatric Centers and Charter Medical Corporation (*Modern Healthcare* 1995). In the year 2000, four major federal investigations came to a head:

The federal government submitted a claim for more than $1 billion against the bankrupt nursing home and hospital company Vencor for Medicare fraud involving double billing, overbilling, kickback payments, and other fraudulent payments (Saphir 2000).

Beverly Enterprises, one of the largest nursing-home companies, settled a claim for $170 million (including $5 million on a criminal plea) to settle charges that the company had submitted inflated requests for payment.

Fesenius, the largest provider of dialysis services, agreed to pay $486 million to settle civil and criminal charges that it had defrauded Medicare (Taylor 2000).

Columbia/HCA, the largest for-profit health-care corporation, agreed provisionally to pay the federal government $745 million in partial settlement of a variety of charges involving billing fraud and other matters stemming from investigations in several states (Texas, Florida, North Carolina, and Oklahoma); a final settlement at the end of 2002 raised the total to more than $1.7 billion.

This pattern of apparently large-scale organizational fraud may be an artifact of selective enforcement practices, resulting from regulators' distrust of for-profits. Another possibility is that regulators with limited resources might want to use them to investigate large targets, although the prevailing lore is that large cases actually carry high risk of failure, encouraging enforcement agencies to improve their batting average by going after smaller fish (Gray 1991). Despite these caveats, in our assessment this evidence suggests that (a) fraudulent billing practices are likely to be more common among investor-owned health-care corporations and (b) the magnitude of these ownership-related differences will be most pronounced in the fourth stage of the technological life cycle that we described earlier, as demand stagnates and opportunities for growth are limited. Anecdotal evidence of this sort cannot, of course, prove these claims. It does suggest that they are promising hypotheses that need to be tested through more systematic investigation.[43]

The Policy Relevance of Nonprofit Health Care

As is common in the research literature, much of our discussion of ownership-related differences has been cast in terms of statistical significance. For policy purposes, however, the substantive magnitude of these differences is also relevant. It is here that the preconceptions of researchers become most evident. Those intent on defending the nonprofit sector often interpret modest differences in performance in the most dramatic terms. For example, a study that detected ownership-related differences on the order of 5 percent in various quality measures in HMOs concluded that the results indicated that "the decade-old experiment with market medicine is a failure. The drive for profit is compromising quality of care" (Himmelstein et al. 1999:563). Yet the authors virtually ignored quality differences among models of HMOs as large as 20 to 25 percent.

Similarly, skeptics about the value of nonprofit ownership sometimes discount differences that appear quite substantial. For example, a recent study of postdischarge mortality among patients admitted to for-profit and nonprofit hospitals found that the magnitude of the ownership-related differences had increased significantly between 1985 and 1994 (McClellan and Staiger 2000). Depending on the model specification, the differential grew between two- and eight-fold over that decade. But the authors concluded that nonprofit hospitals performed only "slightly better" and discount the difference that they had documented by immediately noting that "this small average difference masks an enormous amount of variation in hospital quality within for-profit and not-for-profit hospital groups" (ibid.:111). They fail to note that the ownership-related differences in mortality by the mid-1990s were actually larger than those associated with teaching affiliations for hospitals, a characteristic previously demonstrated to have important quality implications for hospital treatment (Keeler et al. 1992).

To avoid falling victim to preconceptions about ownership, it is important to have some clear criteria for what constitutes a meaningfully large difference between nonprofit and for-profit performance. Several standards can be found in the literature, though each is subject to challenge. The first approach compares the impact of ownership-related practices to the magnitude of the "problem" that they address. For example, skeptics of the value of the nonprofit sector have noted that the number of additional patients who are treated as a result of hospitals' nonprofit status represents only a small fraction of the 45 million Americans who lack health insurance (Marmor, Schlesinger, and Smithey 1987). But this does not seem a compelling test of the social value of nonprofit ownership. Implicitly, it suggests that if nonprofit organizations addressed "small" social problems (which they could more completely remedy), they should be considered more worthy than if they addressed problems that are the most daunting for society because they demand substantial resources.

A second standard for substantive differences compares the difference between nonprofit and for-profit outcomes to the performance of some other actor. For example, the treatment of uninsured patients in nonprofit settings is often compared with the number of uninsured patients treated in governmental health-care facilities. One critical review of the nonprofit hospital industry couched its critique in the observation that "there is a greater difference in the provision of uncompensated care [treatment not reimbursed by any source] by public hospitals on the one hand and either type of private hospital on the other" (Sloan 1998:166). But this comparison is also potentially deceptive. Research using a representative national sample of hospitals found that the additional uncompensated care available at private nonprofit hospitals (compared to treatment at for-profit hospitals) accounted for about 2 percent of annual revenue (Frank, Salkever, and Mullan 1990). The "gap" between uncompensated care at private nonprofit and government-run hospitals, in contrast, represented more than 5 percent of annual revenue. This makes the nonprofit contribution seem comparatively small. But taken in aggregate, revenues at private nonprofit acute-care hospitals are approximately two-and-a-half times as large as revenues at government-run hospitals (American Hospital Association 1999). In aggregate, the additional uncompensated care provided by private nonprofit hospitals (above the level provided by their for-profit counterparts) amounts to just as much free care as is provided by all government-run hospitals combined. Certainly this contribution seems socially consequential.

A third standard for assessing community benefits involves comparisons with the monetary value of the tax exemptions accorded to nonprofit health-care facilities. This approach has some obvious difficulties, since it requires monetizing the value of the various community-benefit activities pursued by nonprofit providers, along with the even more difficult challenge of valuing the quality differences such as lower mortality rates for the patients treated in their facilities (Schlesinger et al. 1998; Barnett 1997; Buchmueller and Feldstein 1996). But it nonetheless has been attractive to some state and federal policymakers who have been critical about the performance of some nonprofit health-care providers.

This third standard motivated a series of reports in the early 1990s comparing the provision of uncompensated care with the financial value of tax exemptions among community hospitals. These studies generally concluded that, although nonprofit hospitals in aggregate provided more community benefit than their tax benefits, the community benefits provided by a substantial number of these facilities (ranging from 20 to 71 percent, depending on the measure of community benefit, the location, and the methods used for assessment) had less value than the tax benefits they received.[44]

Although federal initiatives to establish standards for community benefits foundered in the health reform debacle of the early 1990s (Hyatt and Hopkins 2001; Schlesinger, Gray, and Bradley 1996), later in the decade a dozen states adopted policies to better define the expectations of nonprofit health care. Collectively labeled as "community-benefit laws," these initiatives (a) focused primarily on the hospital sector, although some extended their purview to HMOs (e.g., Massachusetts, Minnesota, and Connecticut) or other large agencies (e.g., New Hampshire), and (b) emphasized reporting of community-benefit activities, either to state officials or to the communities in which the nonprofit agencies were located. A few states (Texas, Pennsylvania, and Utah) mandated a minimum level of community-benefit spending, most commonly for the treatment of indigent patients (Sullivan and Karlin 1999).

To date there has been little evaluation of the impact of these laws (Schlesinger, Mitchell, and Gray 2003). But they clearly reflect a changing sentiment about how to assess the performance of nonprofit health care. Claims about the aggregate benefits of nonprofit providers have become less persuasive, with policymakers insisting instead that *all* nonprofit facilities must reach some threshold for community benefits. These laws reflect a narrowed view of the perceived benefits of the nonprofit sector. While most states have defined community benefits quite broadly, some have emphasized only care for indigent patients. And none have incorporated ways to value differences in quality, trustworthiness, or other related aspects of organizational performance.

Final Thoughts

The scope and impact of nonprofit ownership in American medicine have been extensively documented. The findings illuminate a variety of ownership-related differences, though these vary across services in ways that are not fully understood. But this extensive research into the impact of ownership for organizational performance tells us little about the broader role of the nonprofit health sector as a social institution, with voluntary agencies fostering pluralism and participation in American society. There is certainly evidence from both hospitals and health plans that nonprofit providers have greater community involvement than their for-profit counterparts (Schlesinger, Gray, and Gusmano 2004). But it must also be recognized that community involvement does not always readily translate into effective public deliberation or real community control. There are real tensions between the pluralistic conceptions of community-based resource allocations and certain scientific aspirations of the medical professions (Schlesinger 1997; Lomas 1997). How nonprofit ownership might help mediate these tensions remains an open and provocative area for debate.

These topics could also be the focus of additional research. But what happens in the meantime, as policymakers push for greater accountability over nonprofit health care? How can one make the case for a more comprehensive understanding of community benefits, when this broadening requires counting forms of community involvement for which concrete benefits may be very difficult to measure and the relationship with the organization's involvement hard to define?

These are not easy questions to address. But they are no less salient for many other aspects of nonprofit activity than they are for medical care. Indeed, we believe that some of the most important lessons to extract from the study of nonprofit health care involve implications for the broader nonprofit sector in American society. Although health care as a whole is perhaps unique in its heterogeneity, technological dynamic, and salience for the average American, different health services seem to have reasonably close parallels with other forms of commercial nonprofit activities. It does not require a great leap of imagination to see the parallels between hospitals and higher education in terms of the powerful norms of professional autonomy that shape their performance. There are clearly similarities between long-term care or home health care for the elderly and day care for children. The sort of technological life cycle that we have documented for health care may well also apply to other aspects of the nonprofit economy, particularly to institutions involved in the arts.

Finally, and perhaps most important, we believe that the same sort of misperceptions that appear to drive public and academic perceptions of nonprofit health care may also be relevant toward other sorts of nonprofit services. If this presumption is correct, then it is essential to better document the forms that such misperceptions might take, since these perceptions are likely to shape the ways in which policymakers understand the nonprofit sector and design policies to improve its accountability or performance. Unless researchers in this field develop more effective ways of informing the policy process, there is a real possibility that some vital aspects of nonprofit behavior will be lost from the sight of policymakers, who strive only to measure the countable. Valuable activities could also be lost from the mission of nonprofit organizations, as they seek to satisfy the standards that have been established for community-benefit activities.

Ultimately, we return to our earlier observation about the contingent meaning of ownership for organizational performance. The consequences of ownership represent a certain sort of organizational potential. Although we have documented that these ownership-related differences appear rather resilient in the face of changing external circumstances, the impact of public policies on these differences remains only poorly understood. Because the nonprofit sector is so intrinsically connected with notions of the public good in American society, this linkage to public policy and policymakers' expectations remains a vital connection to explore in the future.

NOTES

1. The first academic studies of the impact of ownership form in health care began to appear in journals in the late 1960s and early

1970s. See, for example, Holmberg and Anderson (1968), Steinwald and Neuhauser (1970), Greenwald and Linn (1971), Clarkson (1972), and Ruchlin, Pointer, and Cannedy (1973).

2. The percentages reporting that either "all" or "half" of these services were provided under for-profit auspices were 53 percent, 54 percent, and 49 percent for nursing homes, health plans, and hospitals, respectively. These percentages were significantly higher than the perceived role of profit-making companies for either social services or art museums (Kaiser Family Foundation 1998:2).

3. All unpublished data are available from the Roper Center for Public Opinion at the University of Connecticut (online at http://www.ropercenter.uconn.edu). For specific questions, we provide here the accession number, identifying the question in Roper's iPOLL database. In 1997 Americans were asked on two different surveys whether the conversion of health insurance plans, HMOs, and hospitals "from nonprofit status into for-profit institutions" was "a good thing for health care in this country, a bad thing, or doesn't make much of a difference." Forty-seven percent of the respondents on one poll and 45 percent on the other reported that these conversions were a "bad thing" (accession nos. 0353759 and 0355011). On a 1998 survey, respondents were asked whether "it's wrong for profit-making companies to be involved in certain areas where trying to earn a profit might come into conflict with serving the public interest." The percentage of respondents who reported that for-profit ownership was "wrong" ranged from 43 percent for hospitals and nursing homes to 48 percent for HMOs and managed-care plans (Kaiser Family Foundation 1998).

4. Ironically, the survey in question was fielded by a consortium headed by the *Wall Street Journal,* a publication that is quite supportive of commercial enterprise (Wall Street Journal Online 2003).

5. The earliest surveys, fielded in the mid-1980s, asked about quality of care in hospitals. Most respondents reported that ownership did not matter, or indicated that they did not know its import. Of those who thought that ownership did matter, 60 percent felt that for-profit hospitals would have higher quality (Roper accession no. 0313117). On a 1995 survey about long-term care, 26 percent of respondents reported that for-profit organizations would "provide better long-term care services"; 22 percent felt that nonprofit organizations would provide better services (accession no. 0248507). A report from the Kaiser Family Foundation indicates that, in 1995, a substantial majority (57 percent to 34 percent) felt that for-profit hospitals delivered higher quality, a differential that persisted in a subsequent survey fielded in 1997 (at that time, 55 percent thought for-profit hospitals provided better quality, compared with 32 percent favoring nonprofit hospitals) (Kaiser Family Foundation 1995, 1998). Similar differences were reported for health plans.

6. In 1995, 59 percent saw for-profit hospitals as more efficient (compared with 35 percent who favored nonprofit hospitals); in 1997, the percentage viewing for-profit hospitals as more efficient was 57 percent (Kaiser Family Foundation 1995, 1998). Again, a similar pattern was reported for health insurance plans.

7. Questions about the impact on communities were asked only from the mid-1990s. However, several surveys in the mid-1980s asked respondents whether investor-owned hospitals would be more or less likely than nonprofit hospitals to "care for uninsured people who are unable to afford to pay for the care provided." In 1986, 60 percent of the public reported that investor-owned hospitals would be less likely to provide these services (9 percent thought they would be more likely, 15 percent thought that they'd be about the same, and 17 percent were unwilling to express an opinion) (Roper survey ID: USCAMREP.86OCT.R165). The proportion of the public reporting that nonprofit hospitals would be more helpful to the community ranged from 60 to 65 percent in surveys fielded between 1995 and 1997 (Kaiser Family Foundation 1998), with comparable percentages favoring nonprofit health plans.

8. In surveys in the mid-1980s, most respondents either felt that nonprofit and for-profit hospitals would be about the same in terms of charges (31 percent) or reported that they didn't know how ownership might matter (30 percent). Of those who did expect ownership to matter, the vast majority felt that nonprofit hospitals would be less expensive (Roper survey ID: USCAMREP.86OCT.R163). By the mid-1990s, this perceived distinction was much sharper. Several surveys between 1995 and 1997 reported that more than 70 percent of respondents believed that nonprofit hospitals would "cost you less" as a site for treatment (about 20 percent felt that for-profit hospitals would cost less). Slightly smaller differences were perceived for health plans (Kaiser Family Foundation 1998).

9. They concluded that there was such a difference regarding cost to Medicare but not in quality.

10. As of the early 1980s, the proportion of hospital, HMO, and home health services provided by private nonprofit agencies was 69.6 percent, 84.2 percent, and 64.1 percent, respectively. By contrast, 63.3 percent of the blood banks and 67.6 percent of the nursing homes were operated as for-profit facilities (Marmor, Schlesinger, and Smithey 1987:223).

11. Our quality screen on the research literature eliminated less than 10 percent of the published studies. Studies eliminated were mainly early and relatively primitive studies published in the medical literature.

12. The "window" for measuring deaths after leaving a hospital varies among these studies. Some count only those deaths that occur in the first thirty days after discharge. Others examine mortality rates for sixty or ninety days after discharge. Some studies examine mortality rates for periods as long as one year after hospital treatment, but the authors of this work generally agree that shorter time periods are more likely to reflect the quality of care during hospitalization, as opposed to differences in severity of illness, quality of outpatient treatment, or other factors.

13. Hospital mortality was the topic of a more formal meta-analysis by Devereaux et al. (2002), though this review included studies of both postdischarge and in-hospital mortality. Aggregating across these studies, they found that nonprofit facilities indeed had moderately better performance, with a 2 percent lower mortality rate than found in for-profit hospitals.

14. "Efficiency," in this context, is used by economists to refer to whether resources are being used in the most cost-effective fashion. The empirical studies that attempt to measure efficiency (as opposed to simply comparing costs across facilities) must therefore also measure and statistically control for differences in quality of care across facilities. Because these quality measures are rarely complete, the conclusions derived from these studies are open to question.

15. The failure to observe consistently higher administrative costs in nonprofit settings poses a puzzle for some economists, who predicted that nonprofits would be less efficient because administrators would "slack off" in the absence of financial rewards. Since organizational slack is predicted to raise administrative costs (Alchian and Demsetz 1972; Clarkson 1972), this theory seems a poor fit with observed differences in costs. However, there is some controversy about whether administrative overhead can be measured with sufficient reliability to be a meaningful measure (Altman and Shactman 1997).

16. The extent of price competition varies dramatically across local markets, but it increased sharply beginning in the early 1980s in California, with price competition gradually diffusing to other parts of the country (Bamezai et al. 1999).

17. Between 1979 and 1993, the percentage of hospitals belonging to multihospital systems gradually increased from 26 percent to 36 percent (Cerne 1995). Corporate affiliations subsequently mushroomed, reaching 72 percent of all U.S. hospitals by the end of the century (Bazzoli et al. 1999).

18. The specific cutoff date for this comparison is obviously an arbitrary one. Selecting 1995 (as opposed to 1994 or 1996) does not substantially affect the pattern of results.

19. Historically, nonprofit hospitals have competed with one another for prestige and community support (Frank and Salkever 1991).

This form of competition appears to have stimulated greater quality, at least in terms of a broad array of technological services at each facility (Dranove, Shanley, and Simon 1992; Hughes and Luft 1990). The impact of this form of competition on other socially valued aspects of performance, such as treating indigent patients, appears to be mixed. On one hand, the larger the number of nonprofit hospitals in a community, the fewer uninsured patients that are treated in each nonprofit hospital (Thorpe and Brecher 1987; Frank, Salkever, and Mitchell 1990). But the aggregate amount of care for indigent clients is nonetheless greater where there are more nonprofit facilities. When a new hospital is established, the reductions in uncompensated care at competing facilities are collectively smaller than the additional uncompensated care provided at the newly entering hospital.

20. Studies have found, for example, that for-profit hospitals respond to increased competition by cutting their prices to privately insured patients, while nonprofit hospitals raise their prices (Sharma 1998).

21. These include community mental health centers (Clark, Dorwart, and Epstein 1994), women's health centers (Khoury, Weisman, and Jarjoura 2001), drug treatment facilities (Friedman, Alexander, and D'Aunno 1998), rehabilitation agencies (McCue and Thompson 1997), and renal dialysis facilities (Hirth, Chernew, and Orzol 2000; Frankenfield et al. 2000; McClellan, Soucie, and Flanders 1998; de Lissovoy et al. 1994; Griffiths et al. 1994; Held et al. 1991; Schlesinger, Cleary, and Blumenthal 1989).

22. Model types differ regarding whether physicians are employees of the health plan (versus being self-employed or employed by an organization that contracts with the health plan) and regarding how physicians are paid (e.g., salary versus fee-for-service).

23. The prediction that nonprofit enterprise will, in the long term, prove more trustworthy than for-profit organizations requires several additional assumptions to be fully consistent (Ortmann and Schlesinger 1997). First, one must assume that for-profit firms won't quickly ruin their reputations through misrepresentation. In other words, for-profits must be able to fool some of the people all of the time. If not, ill-informed consumers would learn to avoid for-profit firms, eliminating the incentive to misrepresent. Whether this ancillary assumption is plausible depends on the type of health care in question. For nursing homes, for example, it is unlikely that most consumers will be able to develop an effective picture of quality at different facilities. Decisions to admit a family member are often made on short notice, under difficult emotional circumstances (Vladeck 1980). Because most people are uncomfortable discussing the fact that they are "institutionalizing" a family member, it is difficult to learn from the previous experiences of others. With a constant influx of new and relatively naive consumers, markets for nursing-home care hold considerable potential for consistent, recurrent misrepresentation. Other forms of health care, such as optometry, would seem to have much less potential for untrustworthy practices (Pauly 1988). People repeatedly purchase eyeglasses, often discuss these purchases with friends and family, and can readily ascertain the reputation of any given provider in a local market. Second, those who are at risk for misrepresentation must be sufficiently aware of this threat that they take actions to reduce their risk. If consumers or purchasers are so misinformed that they are unaware that health-care agencies might misrepresent the quality of services, then they would have no motivation to identify nonprofit agencies or prefer nonprofit services. Third, if consumers or purchasers *do* think nonprofits more trustworthy and act on this perception, it creates an incentive for profit-oriented providers to masquerade as nonprofits, exploiting vulnerable patients (Steinberg and Gray 1993). Unless there is effective enforcement of the nondistribution constraint, the entry of "for-profits in disguise" would adulterate the trustworthiness of the purportedly nonprofit sector.

24. More seriously ill enrollees are more vulnerable in these plans, because they are less inclined to switch plans if dissatisfied with performance, particularly if this requires that they sever their connections with the physicians who are currently providing their care (Schlesinger, Druss, and Thomas 1999). Also, in some circumstances, individuals with an existing condition may face barriers in trying to obtain new coverage.

25. In their sample, nonprofit facilities represented 15.8 percent of all nursing homes, but only 7.4 percent of those that faced legal claims and 5.2 percent of those against whom legal claims had been successful pursued.

26. Under Internal Revenue Service policy, for a nonprofit health-care organization to be tax exempt as "charitable," it must provide services that benefit the community, not just individuals. The meaning of "community benefit" has been contested for the past thirty years and has evolved in response to changing conditions in health care and changing IRS policies (Schlesinger, Gray, and Bradley 1996).

27. Because of previous public policies, an ample supply of beds existed in these fields by the time the legislation was passed (Gray and Schlesinger 2002).

28. Both factors likely came into play. On one hand, physicians were clearly losing their capacity to influence health policy and the form of the health-care system (Schlesinger 2002). Writing in the mid-1990s, one sociologist described the decline of medical authority as "the fall of a giant," suggesting that "no profession in our sample has flown quite as high in guild power and control as American medicine, and few have fallen as fast" (Krause 1996:36). On the other hand, physicians were clearly learning that the expansion of for-profit ownership didn't pose that great a threat to their autonomy (Schlesinger, Dorwart, and Epstein 1996; Musacchio et al. 1986; Reynolds and Ohsfeldt 1984). One representative survey of physician attitudes toward for-profit ownership found that three-quarters of all clinicians did not see for-profit ownership of hospitals as threatening physicians' clinical discretion (Gray 1991:176). And, of course, physicians have been investors in some hospital ventures.

29. A similar argument was developed about the same time by the economist Robert Evans (1984), who suggested that professional norms would lead even ostensibly profit-seeking hospitals to behave as "not-only-for-profit" organizations.

30. The pattern of quality in renal dialysis facilities, another service with a strong physician role, is similar to that found in hospitals. Some studies suggest that quality is higher in nonprofit dialysis centers (Hirth, Chernew, and Orzol 2000; Garg et al. 1999; de Lissovoy et al. 1994), but other analyses find no significant ownership related differences (Frankenfield et al. 2000; Held et al. 1991) and a few document better outcomes in for-profit centers (Held, Pauly, and Diamond 1987). On balance, there appear to be modest quality advantages for nonprofit ownership (Devereaux et al. 2002), though these again appear to be smaller than those documented for nursing homes.

31. The need for charitable services is low for nursing-home care because indigence makes one eligible for Medicaid coverage for nursing-home services in a way that does not hold for hospital services.

32. Data from the Roper archives (accession no. 0279764).

33. Data from the Roper archives (accession no. 0355022).

34. Religious affiliations are associated with greater accessibility for indigent patients (White and Begun 1998/99; Gruber 1994; Campbell and Ahern 1993) and lower cost of hospital services (White and Ozcan 1996). Religious affiliation among nursing homes has been shown to improve quality of care (Bradley and Walker 1998; Weisbrod and Schlesinger 1986) and consumer choices (Ballou 2000). Curiously, there's been virtually no study of the impact of religious affiliation on the quality of hospital care or on the efficiency of service provision among nursing homes. The impact of teaching affiliations has been studied only for acute-care hospitals—they've been shown to be associated with lower mortality rates (Kuhn et al. 1994; Keeler et al. 1992), as well as greater accessibility (White and Begun 1998/99; Gruber 1994; Campbell and Ahern 1993; Seidman and Pollock 1991; Frank, Salkever, and Mitchell 1990) and lower cost of hospital services (Ettner and Hermann 2001; Menke 1997; Lawrence 1990). The limited evidence on quality-of-care measures is mixed, although it tends to suggest

that teaching status improves average patient outcomes (Sloan et al. 2001; Keeler et al. 1992).

35. One study found that religiously affiliated hospitals were more efficient (White and Ozcan 1996), but another found no relationship between religious affiliation and efficiency (Eakin 1991).

36. One can construct a story consistent with this interpretation. Past studies have documented that for-profit hospitals are more likely to be established in fast-growing communities (Hansmann 1987; Hoy and Gray 1986; Steinwald and Neuhauser 1970). Because these rapidly growing communities tend to be relatively prosperous, it may just be happenstance that for-profit facilities confront few uninsured patients.

37. These studies examined the impact of the local for-profit market share on the behavior of *all* hospitals in a county. Because the presence of for-profit hospitals is relatively limited for these services, the measured effects should reflect primarily changes in behavior among nonprofit hospitals.

38. Since these studies have independent measures of the intensity of competition, the convergence is not a product of greater competition in the areas in which for-profit hospitals locate (see Hirth 1997 for a discussion of the correlations between for-profit entry and the competitiveness of local markets).

39. DiMaggio and Anheier (1990:149) also suggest that "the quest for generalizable differences among NPOs [nonprofit organizations], proprietaries and public agencies is problematic." Their concerns are more related to the difficulties of measuring ownership-related differences, given the institutional variations that exist among organizations, types of services, and national social structures. Our argument, by contrast, is that such variation should be expected on theoretical grounds, not simply because theoretical predictions are made difficult to assess by complex institutional realities.

40. Most physicians treating patients are neither employees nor owners of the hospital; the interests of the physician and hospital may often diverge (Pauly and Redisch 1973).

41. For example, in the 100- to 349-bed range, Ozcan, Luke, and Haksever (1992:788) found that 42.0 percent of the government-run hospitals were efficient, 33.4 percent of the private nonprofit hospitals were efficient, and 31.7 percent of the for-profit hospitals. In contrast, for hospitals of 350 beds and larger, the percent of efficient facilities in these three forms of ownership were 72.4 percent, 54.7 percent, and 42.2 percent, respectively.

42. The fraud charges included instances in which adolescents had been kept in NME facilities unnecessarily until their insurance benefits expired; billing for false diagnoses; and providing patients with unnecessary services.

43. For a preliminary exploration of these issues related in psychiatric hospitals, see Vandenburgh (1996).

44. One study concluded that only 20 percent of nonprofit hospitals in California failed to provide uncompensated care equivalent to the value of their tax exemption (Morrisey, Wedig, and Hassan 1996). Nonetheless, even more optimistic estimates suggested that a substantial number of facilities were not meeting a strict test for charitable contribution. A study of nationwide scope concluded that, even with the most generous assumptions, a third of nonprofit hospitals provided charity care of less value than their tax exemptions (Kane and Wubbenhorst 2000). Other studies using somewhat different standards reached more pessimistic conclusions (Nicholson et al. 2000).

REFERENCES

Aaronson, William E., Jacqueline S. Zinn, and Michael D. Rosko. 1994. "Do For-Profit and Not-for-Profit Nursing Homes Behave Differently?" *The Gerontologist* 34:775–86.

Alchian, Armen, and Harold Demsetz. 1972. "Production, Information Costs and Economic Organization." *American Economic Review* 62:777–95.

Al-Haider, Abdolmohsin S., and Thomas T. H. Wan. 1991. "Modeling Organizational Determinants of Hospital Mortality." *Health Services Research* 26:303–23.

Allen, Priscilla. 2001. "An Exploration of Complaints Forwarded to the Connecticut Long Term Care Ombudsman Program: What Are the Correlates of Nursing Home Complaints Reported?" Ph.D. dissertation, Fordham University.

Altman, Stuart H., and David Shactman. 1997. "Should We Worry about Hospitals' High Administrative Costs?" *New England Journal of Medicine* 336:798–99.

American Hospital Association. 1999. *Hospital Statistics,* 1999 ed. Chicago: American Hospital Association.

Anders, Robert L. 1993. "Administrative Delays: Is There a Difference between Nonprofit and For-Profit Hospitals?" *Journal of Nursing Administration* 23:42–50.

Anderson, Randy I., Danielle Lewis, and James R. Webb. 1999. "The Efficiency of Nursing Home Chains and the Implications of Non-Profit Status." *Journal of Real Estate Portfolio Management* 5:235–47.

Arling, Greg, Richard Nordquist, and John A. Capitman. 1987. "Nursing Home Cost and Ownership Type: Evidence of Interaction Effects." *Health Services Research* 22:255–69.

Arrow, Kenneth. 1963. "Uncertainty and the Welfare Economics of Medical Care." *American Economic Review* 58:941–69.

Ballou, Jeffrey. 2000. "The Role of the Not-for-Profit Firm in the Mixed Industry: Three Empirical Analyses of the Long-Term Care and Hospital Industries." Ph.D. dissertation, Northwestern University.

Bamezai, A., Jack Zwanziger, Glenn A. Melnick , and J. Mann. 1999. "Price Competition and Hospital Cost Growth in the United States (1989–1994)." *Health Economics* 8:233–43.

Banks, Dwayne A., Mary Paterson, and Jeanne Wendel. 1997. "Uncompensated Hospital Care: Charitable Mission or Profitable Business Decision?" *Health Economics* 6:133–43.

Barnett, Kevin. 1997. *The Future of Community Benefit Programming.* Berkeley, Calif.: Public Health Institute.

Barro, Jason, and Michael Chu. 2002. "HMO Penetration,

Ownership Status, and the Rise of Hospital Advertising." NBER working paper #8899. Cambridge, Mass.: National Bureau of Economic Research.

Bays, Carson W. 1977. "Case-Mix Differences between Nonprofit and For-Profit Hospitals." *Inquiry* 14:17–21.

———. 1979. "Cost Comparisons of For-Profit and Nonprofit Hospitals." *Social Science and Medicine* 13C:219–25.

———. 1983. "Patterns of Hospital Growth: The Case of Profit Hospitals." *Medical Care* 21:850–57.

Bazzoli, Gloria J., Stephen M. Shortell, Nicole Dubbs, C. Chan, and Peter Kralovec. 1999. "A Taxonomy of Health Networks and Systems: Bringing Order Out of Chaos." *Health Services Research* 33:1683–1717.

Becker, Edmund R., and Frank A. Sloan. 1985. "Hospital Ownership and Performance." *Economic Inquiry* 23:21–36.

Bell, Judith E. 1996. "Saving Their Assets: How to Stop the Plunder at Blue Cross and Other Nonprofits." *American Prospect* 26:60–66.

Bell, Ralph, and Michael Krivich. 1990. "Effects of Type of Ownership of Skilled Nursing Facilities on Residents' Mortality Rates in Illinois." *Public Health Reports* 105:515–18.

Birnbaum, Howard, A. James Lee, Christine Bishop, and Gail Jensen. 1981. *Public Pricing of Nursing Home Care.* Cambridge, Mass.: Abt Books.

Bishop, Christine. 1980. "Nursing Home Cost Studies and Reimbursement Issues." *Health Care Financing Review* 2:47–64.

Blendon, Robert J., Mollyan Brodie, John M. Benson, Drew E. Altman, Larry Levitt, Tina Hoff, and Larry Hugick. 1998. "Understanding the Managed Care Backlash." *Health Affairs* 17:80–94.

Bloche, M. Gregg. 1998. "Should Government Intervene to Protect Nonprofits?" *Health Affairs* 17:7–25.

Blustein, Jan, and Emma C. Hoy. 2000. "Who Is Enrolled in For-Profit vs. Nonprofit Medicare HMOs?" *Health Affairs* 19:210–20.

Bond, C. A., Cynthia L. Raehl, Michael E. Pitterle, and Todd Franke. 1999. "Health Care Professional Staffing, Hospital Characteristics and Hospital Mortality Rates." *Pharmacotherapy* 19:130–38.

Booske, Bridget, Judith Lynch, and Gerald Riley. 2002. "Impact of Managed Care Market Withdrawal on Beneficiaries." *Health Care Financing Review* 24:95–115.

Born, Patricia H., and Carol J. Simon. 2001. "Patients and Profits: The Relationship between HMO Financial Performance and Quality of Care." *Health Affairs* 20:167–74.

Boscarino, Joseph A., and Jeani Chang. 2000. "Nontraditional Services Provided by Nonprofit and For-Profit Hospitals: Implications for Community Health." *Journal of Healthcare Management* 45:119–35.

Bradley, Elizabeth H., and Leslie C. Walker. 1998. "Education and Advance Care Planning in Nursing Homes: The Impact of Ownership Type." *Nonprofit and Voluntary Sector Quarterly* 27:239–57.

Brennan, Troyen, Liesi E. Herbert, Nan M. Laird, Ann G. Lawthers, Kenneth E. Thorpe, Lucian L. Leape, A. Russell Localio, Stuart R. Lipsitz, Joseph P. Newhouse, Paul C. Weiler, and Howard H. Hiatt. 1991. "Hospital Characteristics Associated with Adverse Events and Substandard Care." *Journal of the American Medical Association* 265:3265–69.

Brodie, Mollyann, Elizabeth C. Hamel, Drew E. Altman, Robert J. Blendon, and John M. Benson. 2003. "Health News and the American Public, 1995–2001." *Journal of Health Politics, Policy and Law* 28:927–50.

Broome, Sarah. 2002. "Market Characteristics and Hospital Organizational Factors that Affect Hospital Nursing Quality." Ph.D. dissertation, University of North Carolina.

Brotman, Billie Ann. 1995. "Hospital Indigent Care Expenditures." *Journal of Health Care Finance* 21:76–79.

Buchmueller, Thomas C., and Paul J. Feldstein. 1996. "Hospital Community Benefits Other Than Charity Care: Implications for Tax Exemption and Public Policy." *Hospital and Health Services Administration* 41:461–71.

Buczko, William. 1994. "Factors Affecting Charity Care and Bad Debt Charges in Washington Hospitals." *Hospital and Health Services Administration* 39:179–91.

Burgess, James F., and Paul W. Wilson. 1996. "Hospital Ownership and Technical Inefficiency." *Management Science* 42:110–23.

Campbell, Ellen S., and Melissa W. Ahern. 1993. "Have Procompetitive Changes Altered Hospital Provision of Indigent Care?" *Health Economics* 2:281–89.

Carter, Richard B., Lawrence J. Massa, and Mark L. Power. 1997. "An Examination of the Efficiency of Proprietary Hospital versus Non-Proprietary Hospital Ownership Structures." *Journal of Accounting and Public Policy* 16:63–87.

Castle, Nicholas G. 2000. "Differences in Nursing Homes with Increasing and Decreasing Use of Physical Restraints." *Medical Care* 38:1154–63.

Castle, Nicholas G., and Dennis G. Shea. 1998. "The Effects of For-Profit and Not-for-Profit Facility Status on the Quality of Care for Nursing Home Residents with Mental Illness." *Research on Aging* 20:246–63.

Caswell, Robert, and William Cleverly. 1983. "Cost Analysis of the Ohio Nursing Home Industry." *Health Services Research* 18:359–82.

Cerne, Frank. 1995. "Streetwise. Wall Street: Where Health Care Is Suddenly Hot." *Hospitals and Health Networks* 69:38–40, 42, 44–46.

Chattopadhyay, Sajal, and Subhash C. Ray. 1996. "Technical Scale and Size Efficiency in Nursing Home Care: A Nonparametric Analysis of Connecticut Homes." *Health Economics* 5:363–73.

Chillemi, Ottorino, and Benedetto Gui. 1991. "Uninformed Customers and Nonprofit Organizations: Modeling 'Contract Failure' Theory." *Economic Letters* 35:5–8.

Chiu, Kuanpin. 1999. "The Impact of Patient and Hospital Characteristics on the Quality of Maternity Care." Ph.D. dissertation, University of Maryland.

Chou, Shin-Yi. 2002. "Asymmetric Information, Ownership and Quality of Care: An Empirical Analysis of Nursing Homes." *Journal of Health Economics* 21:293–311.

Clark, Robin, Robert Dorwart, and Sherrie Epstein. 1994. "Managed Competition in Public and Private Mental Health Agencies: Implications for Services and Policy." *Milbank Quarterly* 72:653–78.

Clarke, Lee, and Carroll Estes. 1992. "Sociological and Economic Theories of Markets and Nonprofits: Evidence from Home Health Organizations." *American Journal of Sociology* 97:945–69.

Clarkson, Kenneth. 1972. "Some Implications of Property Rights in Hospital Management." *Journal of Law and Economics* 15:363–84.

Clement, Jan P., and Kyle L. Grazier. 2001. "HMO Penetration: Has It Hurt Public Hospitals?" *Journal of Health Care Finance* 28:25–38.

Clement, Jan P., Kenneth White, and Vivian Valdmanis. 2002. "Charity Care: Do Not-for-Profits Influence For-Profits?" *Medical Care Research and Review* 59:59–79.

Consumers Union. 1999. "How Does Your HMO Stack Up?" *Consumer Reports* 64:23–29.

Cowing, T. G., and A. G. Holtmann. 1983. "Hospital Cost Analysis: A Survey and Evaluation of Recent Studies." *Advances in Health Economics and Health Services Research* 4:257–303.

Cromwell, Jerry, and James R. Kanak. 1982. "The Effects of Prospective Reimbursement Programs on Hospital Adoption and Service Sharing." *Health Care Financing Review* 4:89–101.

Cunningham, Robert, III and Robert M. Cunningham Jr. 1997. *The Blues: A History of the Blue Cross and Blue Shield System.* DeKalb: Northern Illinois University Press.

Custer, William S., and Richard J. Willke. 1991. "Teaching Hospital Costs: The Effects of Medical Staff Characteristics." *Health Services Research* 25:831–57.

Cutler, David M., and Jill R. Horwitz. 2000. "Converting Hospitals from Not-for-Profit to For-Profit Status: Why and What Effects?" Pp. 45–79 in *The Changing Hospital Industry,* edited by D. Cutler. Chicago: University of Chicago Press.

Davis, Mark A. 1991. "On Nursing Home Quality: A Review and Analysis." *Medical Care Review* 48:129–66.

———. 1993. "Nursing Home Ownership Revisited: Market, Cost and Quality Relationships." *Medical Care* 31:1062–68.

de Lissovoy, Gregory, Neil R. Powe, Robert I. Griffiths, A. J. Watson, Gerard F. Anderson, J. W. Greer, Robert J. Herbert, Paul W. Eggers, R. A. Milam, and Paul K. Whelton. 1994. "The Relationship of Provider Organizational Status and Erythropoietin Dosing in End Stage Renal Disease Patients." *Medical Care* 32:130–40.

Desai, Kamal R., Gary J. Young, and Carol VanDeusen Lukas. 1998. "Hospital Conversions from For-Profit to Nonprofit Status: The Other Side of the Story." *Medical Care Research and Review* 55:298–308.

Devereaux, P. J., Peter T. L. Choi, Christina Lacchetti, Bruce Weaver, Holger J. Schunemann, Ted Haines, John N. Lavis, Brydon J. B. Grant, David R. S. Haslam, Mohit Bhandari, Terrence Sullivan, Deborah J. Cook, Stephen D. Walter, Maureen Meade, Humaira Khan, Neera Bhatnagar, and Gordon H. Guyatt. 2002. "A Systematic Review and Meta-Analysis of Studies Comparing Mortality Rates of Private For-Profit and Private Not-for-Profit Hospitals." *Canadian Medical Association Journal* 166:1399–1406.

DiMaggio, Paul J., and Helmut K. Anheier. 1990. "The Sociology of Nonprofit Organizations and Sectors." *Annual Review of Sociology* 16:137–59.

DiMaggio, Paul J., and Walter W. Powell. 1983. "The Iron Cage Revisited: Institutional Isomorphism and Collective Rationality in Organizational Fields." *American Sociological Review* 48:147–60.

Dorwart, Robert A., and Mark Schlesinger. 1988. "Privatization of Psychiatric Services." *American Journal of Psychiatry* 145:543–53.

Dranove, David, Michael Shanley, and Carol Simon. 1992. "Is Hospital Competition Wasteful?" *RAND Journal of Economics* 23:247–62.

Duggan, Mark. 2002. "Hospital Market Structure and the Behavior of Not-for-Profit Hospitals." *RAND Journal of Economics* 33:433–46.

Durso, Katherine A. 1992. "Profit Status in the Early History of Health Maintenance Organizations." Ph.D. dissertation, Department of Epidemiology and Public Health, Yale University.

Eakin, B. Kelly. 1991. "Allocative Inefficiency in the Production of Hospital Services." *Southern Economic Journal* 58:240–48.

Easley, David, and Maureen O'Hara. 1988. "Contracts and Asymmetric Information in the Theory of the Firm." *Journal of Economic Behavior and Organization* 9:229–46.

Eskoz, R., and K. Michael Peddecord. 1985. "The Relationship of Hospital Ownership and Service Composition to Hospital Charges." *Health Care Financing Review* 6:51–58.

Ettner, Susan L., and Richard C. Hermann. 2001. "The Role of Profit Status under Imperfect Information: Evidence from the Treatment Patterns of Elderly Medicare Beneficiaries Hospitalized for Psychiatric Diagnoses." *Journal of Health Economics* 20:23–49.

Evans, Robert. 1984. *Strained Mercy: The Economics of Canadian Health Care.* Toronto: Butterworths.

Ferrier, Gary D., and Vivian G. Valdmanis. 1996. "Rural Hospital Performance and Its Correlates." *Journal of Productivity Analysis* 7:63–80.

Ferris, James M., and Elizabeth A. Graddy. 1999. "Structural Changes in the Hospital Industry, Charity Care and the Nonprofit Role in Health Care." *Nonprofit and Voluntary Sector Quarterly* 28:18–31.

Fizel, John L., and T. S. Nunnikhoven. 1992. "Technical Efficiency of For-Profit and Non-Profit Nursing Homes." *Managerial and Decision Economics* 13:429–39.

Flood, Ann B. 1994. "The Impact of Organizational and Managerial Factors on the Quality of Care in Health Care Organizations." *Medical Care Review* 51:381–428.

Frank, Richard G., and David S. Salkever. 1991. "The Supply of Charity Services by Nonprofit Hospitals: Motives and Market Structure." *RAND Journal of Economics* 22:430–45.

———. 1994. "Nonprofit Organizations in the Health Sector." *Journal of Economic Perspectives* 8:129–144.

Frank, Richard G., David S. Salkever, and Jean Mitchell. 1990. "Market Forces and the Public Good: Competition among Hospitals and Provision of Indigent Care." Pp. 159–84 in *Advances in Health Economics and Health Services Research,* vol. 11, edited by R. M. Scheffler and L. F. Rossiter. Greenwich, Conn.: JAI Press.

Frank, Richard G., David S. Salkever, and Fitzhugh Mullan. 1990. "Hospital Ownership and the Care of Uninsured and Medicaid Patients: Findings from the National Hospital Discharge Survey, 1979–84." *Health Policy* 14:1–11.

Frankenfield, Diane, Jonathan Sugarman, Rodney Presley, Steven Pelgerson, and Michael Rocco. 2000. "Impact of Facility Size and Profit Status on Intermediate Outcomes in Chronic

Dialysis Patients." *American Journal of Kidney Disease* 36:318–25.

Frech, H. E., and Paul B. Ginsburg. 1981. "The Cost of Nursing Home Care in the United States: Government Financing, Ownership and Efficiency." Pp. 76–81 in *Health, Economics, and Health Economics,* edited by J. van der Gaag and M. Perlman. New York: North Holland.

Friedman, Bernard S., Paul A. Hattis, and Richard J. Bogue. 1990. "Tax Exemption and Community Benefits of Not-for-Profit Hospitals." Pp. 131–58 in *Advances in Health Economics and Health Services Research,* vol. 10, edited by R. M. Scheffler and L. F. Rossiter. Greenwich, Conn.: JAI Press.

Friedman, Bernard, and Stephen M. Shortell. 1988. "The Financial Performance of Selected Investor-Owned and Not-for-Profit System Hospitals before and after Medicare Prospective Payment." *Health Services Research* 23:237–67.

Friedman, Peter D., Jeffrey A. Alexander, and Thomas A. D'Aunno. 1998. "Organizational Correlates of Access to Primary Care and Mental Health Services in Drug Abuse Treatment Units." *Journal of Substance Abuse Treatment* 16:71–80.

Garg, Pushkal P., Kevin D. Frick, Marie Diener-West, and Neil R. Powe. 1999. "Effect of Ownership of Dialysis Facilities on Patients' Survival and Referral for Transplantation." *New England Journal of Medicine* 341:1653–60.

Gaumer, Gary. 1986. "Medicare Patient Outcomes and Hospital Organizational Mission." Pp. 354–74 in *For-Profit Enterprise in Health Care,* edited by B. H. Gray. Washington, D.C.: National Academy Press.

Gelijns, Annetine C., Joshua F. Zivin, and Richard R. Nelson. 2001. "Uncertainty and Technological Change in Medicine." *Journal of Health Politics, Policy and Law* 26:913–24.

Gesten, Foster. 1999. *Managed Care Quality Measurement in New York State, 1994–1997.* Albany: New York State Department of Health, Office of Managed Care.

Glavin, Mitchell, Christopher Tompkins, Stanley Wallack, and Stuart Altman. 2002/3. "An Examination of the Factors in the Withdrawal of Managed Care Plans from the Medicare+Choice Program." *Inquiry* 39:341–54.

Goddeeris, John H., and Burton A. Weisbrod. 1998. "Conversion from Nonprofit to For-Profit Legal Status: Why Does It Happen and Should Anyone Care?" Pp. 129–50 in *To Profit or Not to Profit: The Commercial Transformation of the Nonprofit Sector,* edited by B. Weisbrod. New York: Cambridge University Press.

Grabowski, David, and Richard Hirth. 2003. "Competitive Spillovers across Non-Profit and For-Profit Nursing Homes." *Journal of Health Economics* 22:1–22.

Grannemann, Thomas W., Randall S. Brown, and Mark V. Pauly. 1986. "Estimating Hospital Costs: A Multiple Output Analysis." *Journal of Health Economics* 5:107–27.

Gray, Bradford H., ed. 1986. *For-Profit Enterprise in Health Care.* Washington, D.C.: National Academy Press.

———. 1991. *The Profit Motive and Patient Care: The Changing Accountability of Doctors and Hospitals.* Cambridge, Mass.: Harvard University Press.

———. 1992. "Why Nonprofits? Hospitals and the Future of American Health Care." *Frontiers of Health Services Management* 8:3–32.

———. 1993. "Ownership Matters: Health Reform and the Future of Nonprofit Health Care." *Inquiry* 30:352–61.

———. 1997. "Conversion of HMOs and Hospitals: What's At Stake?" *Health Affairs* 16:29–47.

Gray, Bradford H., and Mark Schlesinger. 2002. "Health." Pp. 65–106 in *The State of Nonprofit America,* edited by L. Salamon. New York: Oxford University Press.

Greene, J. 1998. "Blue Skies or Black Eyes? HEDIS Puts Not-for-Profit Plans on Top." *Hospitals and Hospital Networks* 72:26–30.

Greenwald, S., and M. Linn. 1971. "Intercorrelation of Data on Nursing Homes." *The Gerontologist* 11:337–40.

Griffiths, Robert I., Neil R. Powe, Darrell J. Gaskin, Gerard F. Anderson, Gregory V. de Lissovoy, and Paul K. Whelton. 1994. "The Production of Dialysis by For-Profit versus Not-for-Profit Freestanding Renal Dialysis Centers." *Health Services Research* 29:473–87.

Gruber, Jonathan. 1994. "The Effect of Competitive Pressure on Charity: Hospital Responses to Price Shopping in California." *Journal of Health Economics* 13:183–212.

Hamilton, James A. 1961 *Patterns of Hospital Ownership and Control.* Minneapolis: University of Minnesota Press.

Hansmann, Henry B. 1980. "The Role of Nonprofit Enterprise." *Yale Law Journal* 89:835–901.

———. 1987. "The Effect of Tax Exemption and Other Factors on the Market Share of Nonprofit versus For-Profit Firms." *National Tax Journal* 40:71–82.

Hansmann, Henry, Daniel Kessler, and Mark McClellan. 2003. "Ownership Form and Trapped Capital in the Hospital Industry." Pp. 45–69 in *The Governance of Not-for-Profit Organizations,* edited by E. Glaeser. Chicago: University of Chicago Press.

Hargraves, J. Lee, and Sally Trude. 2002. "Obstacles to Employers' Pursuit of Health Care Quality." *Health Affairs* 21:194–200.

Harrington, Charlene, Steffie Woolhandler, Joseph Mullan, Helen Carrillo, and David U. Himmelstein. 2001. "Does Investor Ownership of Nursing Homes Compromise the Quality of Care?" *American Journal of Public Health* 91:1452–55.

Harris, Jeffrey E. 1977. "The Internal Organization of Hospitals: Some Economic Implications." *Bell Journal of Economics* 8:467–82.

Hartz, Arthur J., Henry Krakauer, Evelyn M. Kuhn, Mark Young, Steven J. Jacobsen, Greer Gay, Larry Muenz, Myron Katzoff, R. Clifton Bailey, and Alfred A. Rimm. 1989. "Hospital Characteristics and Mortality Rates." *New England Journal of Medicine* 321:1720–25.

Hawes, Catherine, and Charles D. Phillips. 1986. "The Changing Structure of the Nursing Home Industry and the Impact of Ownership on Quality, Cost and Access." Pp. 492–541 in *For-Profit Enterprise in Health Care,* edited by B. H. Gray. Washington, D.C.: National Academy Press.

Held, Philip J., Nathan Levin, Randall R. Bovbjerg, Mark V. Pauly, and Louis Diamond. 1991. "Mortality and Duration of Hemodialysis Treatment." *Journal of the American Medical Association* 265:871–75.

Held, Philip J., Mark V. Pauly, and Louis Diamond. 1987. "Survival Analysis of Patients Undergoing Dialysis." *Journal of the American Medical Association* 257:645–50.

Himmelstein, David U., Steffie Woolhandler, Ida Hellander, and Sidney M. Wolfe. 1999. "Quality of Care in Investor-Owned vs. Not-for-Profit HMOs." *Journal of the American Medical Association* 282:159–63.

Hirth, Richard A. 1997. "Competition between For-Profit and Nonprofit Health Care Providers: Can It Help Achieve Social Goals?" *Medical Care Research and Review* 54:414–38.

———. 1999. "Consumer Information and Competition between Nonprofit and For-Profit Nursing Homes." *Journal of Health Economics* 18:219–40.

Hirth, Richard A., Michael E. Chernew, and Sean M. Orzol. 2000. "Ownership, Competition, and the Adoption of New Technologies and Cost-Saving Practices in a Fixed-Price Environment." *Inquiry* 37:282–94.

Holmberg, R. Hopkins, and Nancy N. Anderson. 1968. "Implications of Ownership for Nursing Home Care." *Medical Care* 6:300–307.

Holmes, Julia Shaw. 1996. "The Effects of Ownership and Ownership Change on Nursing Home Industry Costs." *Health Services Research* 31:327–46.

Holtmann, Alphonse, and Todd Idson. 1991. "Why Nonprofit Nursing Homes Pay Higher Nurses' Salaries." *Nonprofit Management and Leadership* 2:3–12.

Holtmann, Alphonse, and Steven G. Ullmann. 1993. "Transaction Costs, Uncertainty and Not-for-Profit Organizations: The Case of Nursing Homes." Pp. 149–59 in *The Nonprofit Sector in the Mixed Economy,* edited by A. Ben-Ner and B. Gui. Ann Arbor: University of Michigan Press.

Homer, Carl G., Douglas D. Bradham, and Mark Rushefsky. 1984. "Investor-Owned and Not-for-Profit Hospitals: Beyond the Cost and Revenue Debate." *Health Affairs* 3:133–36.

Horwitz, Jill R. 2003. "Why We Need the Independent Sector: The Behavior, Law and Ethics of Not-for-Profit Hospitals." *UCLA Law Review* 50:1–72.

———. 2005. "Does Corporate Ownership Matter? Service Provision in the Hospital Industry." NBER working paper #11376. Cambridge, Mass.: National Bureau of Economic Research.

Hoy, Elizabeth W., Richard Curtis, and Tom Rice. 1991. "Change and Growth in Managed Care." *Health Affairs* 10:18–36.

Hoy, Elizabeth W., and Bradford H. Gray. 1986. "Growth Trends of the Major Hospital Companies." Pp. 250–59 in *For-Profit Enterprise in Health Care,* edited by B. H. Gray. Washington, D.C.: National Academy Press.

Hughes, Armel M., Kate L. Lapane, and Vincent Mor. 2000. "Influence of Facility Characteristics on Use of Antipsychotic Medications in Nursing Homes." *Medical Care* 38:1164–73.

Hughes, Robert G., and Harold S. Luft. 1990. "Keeping Up with the Joneses: The Influence of Public and Proprietary Neighbors on Voluntary Hospitals." *Health Services Management Research* 3:173–81.

Hyatt, Thomas K., and Bruce R. Hopkins. 2001. *The Law of Tax-Exempt Healthcare Organizations.* New York: John Wiley.

Immerwahr, John, Jean Johnson, and Adam Kernan-Schloss. 1992. *Faulty Diagnosis: Public Misconceptions about Health Care Reform.* New York: Public Agenda Foundation.

Irvin, Renee A. 2000. "Should St. Merciful Hospital Become CorpHealth, Inc.? Ownership and Quality in U.S. Health Care Organizations." *Nonprofit Management and Leadership* 11:3–20.

Jacobs, Larry R., and Robert Y. Shapiro. 1999. "The American Public's Pragmatic Liberalism Meets Its Philosophical Conservatism." *Journal of Health Politics, Policy and Law* 24:1021–31.

Japsen, Bruce. 1996. "Investor-Owned Chains Seek Rich Rural Harvest." *Modern Healthcare* 26:32–37.

Johnson, Jean, C. McKeen Cowles, and Samuel J. Simmens. 1996. "Quality of Care and Nursing Staff in Nursing Homes." Pp. 426–52 in *Nursing Staff in Hospitals and Nursing Homes: Is It Adequate?* edited by G. S. Wunderlich, F. A. Sloan, and C. K. Davis. Washington, D.C.: National Academy Press.

Kaiser Family Foundation. 1995. *Kaiser Foundation Family Survey of Americans' Perceptions about For-Profit and Not-for-Profit Health Care.* Menlo Park, Calif.: Kaiser Family Foundation.

———. 1998. *For-Profit Health Care Companies: Trends and Issues.* Menlo Park, Calif.: Kaiser Family Foundation.

Kane, Nancy M., and William H. Wubbenhorst. 2000. "Alternative Funding Policies for the Uninsured: Exploring the Value of Hospital Tax Exemption." *Milbank Quarterly* 78:185–212.

Kayser-Jones, J. S., Carolyn L. Wiener, and Joseph C. Barbaccia. 1989. "Factors Contributing to the Hospitalization of Nursing Home Patients." *The Gerontologist* 29:502–10.

Keeler, Emmett B., Glenn Melnick, and Jack Zwanziger. 1998. "The Changing Effects of Competition on Non-Profit and For-Profit Hospital Pricing Behavior." *Journal of Health Economics* 18:69–86.

Keeler, Emmett B., Lisa Rubenstein, Katherine L. Kahn, David Draper, Ellen R. Harrison, Michael J. McGinty, William H. Rogers, and Robert H. Brook. 1992. "Hospital Characteristics and Quality of Care." *Journal of the American Medical Association* 268:1709–14.

Kessler, Daniel, and Mark McClellan. 2001. "The Effects of Hospital Ownership on Medical Productivity." NBER working paper #8537. Cambridge, Mass.: National Bureau of Economic Research.

Khoury, Amal J., Carol S. Weisman, and Chad M. Jarjoura. 2001. "Ownership Type and Community Benefits in Women's Health Centers." *Medical Care Research and Review* 58:76–99.

Knox, Kris Joseph, Eric C. Blankmeyer, and J. R. Stutzman. 1999. "Relative Economic Efficiency in Texas Nursing Facilities: A Profit Function Analysis." *Journal of Economics and Finance* 23:199–213.

Koetting, Michael. 1980. *Nursing-Home Organization and Efficiency.* Lexington, Mass.: Lexington Books.

Kovner, Christine T., and Peter J. Gergen. 1998. "Nursing Staff Levels and Adverse Events following Surgery." *Image: Journal of Nursing Scholarship* 30:315–21.

Kramer, Ralph M. 2000. "A Third Sector in the Third Millennium?" *Voluntas* 11:1–23.

Krause, Elliot A. 1996. *Death of the Guilds: Professions, States and the Advance of Capitalism: 1930 to the Present.* New Haven, Conn.: Yale University Press.

Kuhn, Evelyn M., Arthur J. Hartz, Henry Krakauer, R. Clifton Bailey, and Alfred A. Rimm. 1994. "The Relationship of

Hospital Ownership and Teaching Status to 30- and 180-Day Adjusted Mortality Rates." *Medical Care* 32:1098–1108.

Kultgen, John. 1988. *Ethics and Professionalism.* Philadelphia: University of Pennsylvania Press.

Kushman, John E., and Carole F. Nuckton. 1977. "Further Evidence on the Relative Performance of Proprietary and Nonproprietary Hospitals." *Medical Care* 15:189–204.

Kuttner, Robert. 1996a. "Columbia/HCA and the Resurgence of the For-Profit Hospital Business, Part 1 of 2." *New England Journal of Medicine* 335:362–67.

———. 1996b. "Columbia/HCA and the Resurgence of the For-Profit Hospital Business, Part 2 of 2." *New England Journal of Medicine* 335:446–51.

Landon, Bruce E., and Arnold M. Epstein. 2001. "For-Profit and Not-for-Profit Health Plans Participating in Medicaid." *Health Affairs* 20:162–71.

Landon, Bruce E., Alan M. Zaslavsky, Nancy D. Beaulieu, James A. Shaul, and Paul D. Cleary. 2001. "Health Plan Characteristics and Consumers' Assessments of Quality." *Health Affairs* 20:274–86.

Lanska, Douglas J., and Richard J. Kryscio. 1998a. "In-Hospital Mortality Following Carotid Endarterectomy." *Neurology* 51:440–47.

———. 1998b. "Stroke and Intracranial Venous Thrombosis during Pregnancy and Puerperium." *Neurology* 51:1622–28.

Lave, Judith, and Lester Lave. 1974. *The Hospital Construction Act.* Washington, D.C.: American Enterprise Institute.

Law, Sylvia A. 1976. *Blue Cross: What Went Wrong?* 2nd ed. New Haven, Conn.: Yale University Press.

Lawrence, Carol M. 1990. "The Effect of Ownership Structure and Accounting System Type on Hospital Costs." *Research on Governmental and Nonprofit Accounting* 6:35–60.

Lee, Yong S. 1984. "Nursing Homes and Quality of Health Care: The First Year Result of an Outcome-Oriented Survey." *Journal of Health and Human Resources Administration* 7:32–60.

Lee, Yong S., Jeffrey A. Alexander, and Gloria J. Bazzoli. 2003. "Whom Do They Serve? Community Responsiveness among Hospitals Affiliated with Health Systems and Networks." *Medical Care* 41:165–79.

Lewin, Lawrence, Richard Derzon, and Robert Margulies. 1981. "Investor-Owneds and Nonprofits Differ in Economic Performance." *Hospitals* 56:52–58.

Lewin, Lawrence, Timothy Eckels, and Linda Miller. 1988. "The Provision of Uncompensated Care by Not-for-Profit Hospitals." *New England Journal of Medicine* 318:1212–15.

Lomas, Jonathan. 1997. "Reluctant Rationers: Public Input to Health Care Priorities." *Journal of Health Services Research and Policy* 2:103–11.

Long, Sharon K., and Alshadye Yemane. 2005. "Commercial Plans in Medicaid Managed Care: Understanding Who Stays and Who Leaves." *Health Affairs* 24:1084–94.

Luft, Harold. 1981. *Health Maintenance Organizations: Dimensions of Performance.* New York: Wiley.

Luksetich, William, Mary E. Edwards, and Thomas M. Carroll. 2000. "Organizational Form and Nursing Home Behavior." *Nonprofit and Voluntary Sector Quarterly* 29:255–79.

Lynk, William J. 1995. "Nonprofit Hospital Mergers and the Exercise of Market Power." *Journal of Law and Economics* 38:437–61.

Majone, Giandomenico. 1984. "Professionalism and Nonprofit Organizations." *Journal of Health Politics, Policy and Law* 8:639–59.

Malani, Anup, Tomas Philipson, and Guy David. 2003. "Theories of Firm Behavior in the Nonprofit Sector: A Synthesis and Empirical Evaluation." Pp. 181–215 in *The Governance of Not-for-Profit Organizations,* edited by E. Glaeser. Chicago: University of Chicago Press.

Manheim, Larry M., Joe Feinglass, Stephen M. Shortell, and Edward F. X. Hughes. 1992. "Regional Variation in Medicare Hospital Mortality." *Inquiry* 29:55–66.

Mark, Tami L. 1996. "Psychiatric Hospital Ownership and Performance: Do Nonprofit Organizations Offer Advantages in Markets Characterized by Asymmetric Information?" *Journal of Human Resources* 31:631–49.

Marmor, Theodore, Mark Schlesinger, and Richard Smithey. 1987. "Nonprofit Organizations and Health Care." Pp. 221–39 in *The Nonprofit Sector: A Research Handbook,* edited by W. W. Powell. 1st ed. New Haven, Conn.: Yale University Press.

Marsteller, Jill A., Randall R. Bovbjerg, and Len M. Nichols. 1998. "Nonprofit Conversion: Theory, Evidence, and State Policy Options." *Health Services Research* 33:1495–1535.

Mather, David. 1990. "Differences between For-Profit and Nonprofit Nursing Homes on Several Dimensions of Performance." Ph.D. dissertation, University of California, Berkeley.

Mays, Glen P., Paul K. Halverson, and Rachel Stevens. 2001. "The Contributions of Managed Care Plans to Public Health Practice: Evidence from the Nation's Largest Local Health Departments." *Public Health Practice* 116 (Suppl. 1): 50–67.

McClellan, Mark, and Douglas Staiger. 2000. "Comparing Hospital Quality at For-Profit and Not-for-Profit Hospitals." Pp. 93–112 in *The Changing Hospital Industry: Comparing Not-for-Profit and For-Profit Institutions,* edited by D. M. Cutler. Chicago: University of Chicago Press.

McClellan, William M., J. Michael Soucie, and W. Dana Flanders. 1998. "Mortality in End-Stage Renal Disease Is Associated with Facility-to-Facility Differences in Adequacy of Hemodialysis." *Journal of the American Society of Nephrology* 9:1940–47.

McCue, Michael J., and Jon M. Thompson. 1997. "Association of Ownership and System Affiliation with the Financial Performance of Rehabilitation Hospitals." *Health Services Management Research* 10:13–23.

Melnick, Glenn A., Emmett Keeler, and Jack Zwanziger. 1999. "Market Power and Hospital Pricing: Are Nonprofits Different?" *Health Affairs* 18:167–73.

Menke, Terri J. 1997. "The Effect of Chain Membership on Hospital Costs." *Health Services Research* 32:177–96.

Meurer, John R., Evelyn M. Kuhn, Varghese George, Jennifer S. Yauck, and Peter M. Layde. 1998. "Charges for Childhood Asthma by Hospital Characteristics." *Pediatrics* 102:E70–77.

Mobley, Lee R., and W. David Bradford. 1997. "Behavioral Differences among Hospitals: Is It Ownership, or Location?" *Applied Economics* 29:1125–38.

Modern Healthcare. 1995. "Former Charter Exec Sentenced to Prison Term." *Modern Healthcare* 25:32.

Morrisey, Michael A., Gerald J. Wedig, and Mahmud Hassan. 1996. "Do Nonprofit Hospitals Pay Their Way?" *Health Affairs* 15:132–44.

Moseley, Charles B. 1994. "Nursing Home Ownership and Quality of Care." *Journal of Applied Gerontology* 13:386–97.

Mukamel, Dana B. 1997. "Risk-Adjusted Outcome Measures and Quality of Care in Nursing Homes." *Medical Care* 35:367–85.

Mukamel, Dana B., Jack Zwanziger, and Kenneth J. Tomaszewski. 2001. "HMO Penetration, Competition, and Risk-Adjusted Hospital Mortality." *Health Services Research* 36:1019–35.

Mullner, Ross, and Jack Hadley. 1984. "Interstate Variations in the Growth of Chain-Operated Proprietary Hospitals, 1973–82." *Inquiry* 21:144–57.

Musacchio, Robert A., Stephen Zuckerman, Lynn E. Jensen, and Larry Freshnock. 1986. "Hospital Ownership and the Practice of Medicine: Evidence from the Physician's Perspective." Pp. 385–401 in *For-Profit Enterprise in Health Care,* edited by B. H. Gray. Washington, D.C.: National Academy Press.

Needleman, Jack. 2001. "The Role of Nonprofits in Health Care." *Journal of Health Politics, Policy and Law* 26:1113–30.

Newhouse, Joseph. 1970. "Toward a Theory of Nonprofit Institutions: An Economic Model of a Hospital." *American Economic Review* 60:64–74.

Nicholson, Sean, Mark V. Pauly, Lawton Burns, Agnieshka Baumritter, and David A. Asch. 2000. "Measuring Community Benefits Provided by For-Profit and Nonprofit Hospitals." *Health Affairs* 19:168–77.

Norton, Edward C., and Douglas O. Staiger. 1994. "How Hospital Ownership Affects Access to Care for the Uninsured." *RAND Journal of Economics* 25:171–85.

Nyman, John A., and Dennis L. Bricker. 1989. "Profit Incentives and Technical Efficiency in the Production of Nursing Home Care." *Review of Economics and Statistics* 71:586–94.

Oberlander, Jonathan. 2000. "Is Premium Support the Right Medicine for Medicare?" *Health Affairs* 19:84–99.

O'Brien, John. 1988. "The Three Sector Nursing Home Industry." Ph.D. dissertation, University of Washington.

Olfson, Mark, and David Mechanic. 1996. "Mental Disorders in Public, Private Nonprofit, and Proprietary General Hospitals." *American Journal of Psychiatry* 153:1613–19.

Ortmann, Andreas, and Mark Schlesinger. 1997. "Trust, Repute and the Role of Nonprofit Enterprise." *Voluntas* 8:97–119.

Ozcan, Yasar A., and Roice D. Luke. 1993. "A National Study of the Efficiency of Hospitals in Urban Markets." *Health Services Research* 27:719–39.

Ozcan, Yasar A., Roice D. Luke, and Cengiz Haksever. 1992. "Ownership and Organizational Performance: A Comparison of Technical Efficiency across Hospital Types." *Medical Care* 30:781–94.

Ozcan, Yasar A., Stephen E. Wogen, and Li Wen Mau. 1998. "Efficiency Evaluation of Skilled Nursing Facilities." *Journal of Medical Systems* 22:211–24.

Palmiter, Sharon. 1998. "Factors Associated with HEDIS Scores for Selected Preventive Services in HMOs." Ph.D. dissertation, University of Rochester.

Patterson, Carol. 1997. "For-Profit versus Nonprofit Health Maintenance Organizations: Efficiency and Efficacy." Ph.D. dissertation, University of California, Berkeley.

Pattison, Robert V., and Hallie M. Katz. 1983. "Investor-Owned and Not-for-Profit Hospitals: A Comparison Based on California Data." *New England Journal of Medicine* 309:347–53.

Pauly, Mark V. 1987. "Nonprofit Firms in Medical Markets." *American Economic Review* 77:257–62.

———. 1988. "Is Medical Care Different? Old Questions, New Answers." *Journal of Health Politics, Policy and Law* 13:1019–32.

———. 1996. "Health Systems Ownership: Can Regulation Preserve Community Benefits?" *Frontiers of Health Services Management* 12:3–34.

Pauly, Mark V., and Michael Redisch. 1973. "The Not-for-Profit Hospital as a Physician Cooperative." *American Economic Review* 63:87–100.

Philipson, Tomas. 2000. "Asymmetric Information and the Not-for-Profit Sector: Does Its Output Sell at a Premium?" Pp. 325–45 in *The Changing Hospital Industry: Comparing Not-for-Profit and For-Profit Institutions,* edited by D. Cutler. Chicago: University of Chicago Press.

Pitterle, Michael E., C. A. Bond, Cynthia L. Raehl, and Todd Franke. 1994. "Hospital and Pharmacy Characteristics Associated with Mortality Rates in United States Hospitals." *Pharmacotherapy* 14:620–30.

Placek, Paul J., Selma Taffel, and Mary Moien. 1983. "Cesarean Section Delivery Rates, 1981." *American Journal of Public Health* 73:861–62.

Porrell Frank, Francis G. Caro, Ajith Silva, and Mark Moname. 1998. "A Longitudinal Analysis of Nursing Home Outcomes." *Health Services Research* 33:835–65.

Potter, Sharyn J. 2001. "A Longitudinal Analysis of the Distinction between For-Profit and Not-for-Profit Hospitals in America." *Journal of Health and Social Behavior* 42:17–44.

Proenca, E. Jose, Michael D. Rosko, and Jacqueline S. Zinn. 2000. "Community Orientation in Hospitals: An Institutional and Resource Dependence Perspective." *Health Services Research* 35:1011–35.

———. 2003. "Correlates of Hospital Provision of Prevention and Health Promotion Services." *Medical Care Research and Review* 60:56–78.

Prospective Payment Assessment Commission. 1994. *Enrollment and Disenrollment Experience in the Medicare Risk Program.* Washington D.C.: Prospective Payment Assessment Commission.

Register, Charles A., and Edward Bruning. 1986. "Profit Incentives and Technical Efficiency in the Production of Hospital Care." *Southern Economic Journal* 53:899–914.

Register, Charles A., Ansel M. Sharp, and Lonnie K. Stevans. 1988. "Profit Incentives and the Hospital Industry: Some New Evidence." *Atlantic Economic Journal* 16:25–58.

Reinhardt, Uwe E. 2000. "The Economics of For-Profit and Not-for-Profit Hospitals." *Health Affairs* 19:178–86.

Reis, Bernard, and Jon B. Christianson. 1977. *Nursing Home Costs in Montana: Analysis and Policy Applications.* Research report #117, Montana Agricultural Experiment Station, Montana State University, Bozeman.

Rettig, Richard A., and Norman G. Levinsky, eds. 1991. *Kidney Failure and the Federal Government.* Washington, D.C.: National Academy Press.

Reynolds, Roger A., and Robert L. Ohsfeldt, eds. 1984. *Socio-Economic Characteristics of Medical Practice, 1984.* Chicago: American Medical Association.

Riley, Gerald F., Melvin J. Ingber, and Cynthia G. Tudor. 1997. "Disenrollment of Medicare Beneficiaries from HMOs." *Health Affairs* 16:117–24.

Riportella-Mueller, Roberta, and Doris Slesinger. 1982. "The Relationship of Ownership and Size to Quality of Care in Wisconsin Nursing Homes." *The Gerontologist* 22:429–34.

Robinson, James C. 2000. "Capital Finance and Ownership Conversions in Health Care." *Health Affairs* 19:56–71.

Robinson, James C., and Harold S. Luft. 1985. "The Impact of Hospital Market Structure on Patient Volume, Average Length of Stay, and the Cost of Care." *Journal of Health Economics* 4:333–56.

Roemer, Milton, A. R. Moustafa, and Carl E. Hopkins. 1968. "A Proposed Hospital Quality Index: Hospital Death Rates Adjusted for Case Severity." *Health Services Research* 3:96–111.

Roos, Noralou P., and Leslie L. Roos. 1994. "Small Area Variations, Practice Style and Quality of Care." Pp. 231–52 in *Why Are Some People Healthy and Others Not? The Determinants of Health of Populations,* edited by R. G. Evans, M. L. Barer, and T. R. Marmor. New York: Aldine de Gruyter.

Rose-Ackerman, Susan. 1997. "Altruism, Ideological Entrepreneurs and the Non-Profit Firm." *Voluntas* 8:120–35.

Rosenberg, Charles. 1987. *The Care of Strangers: The Rise of America's Hospital System.* New York: Basic Books.

Rosenman, Robert, Kris Siddharthan, and Melissa Ahern. 1997. "Output Efficiency of Health Maintenance Organizations in Florida." *Health Economics* 6:295–302.

Rosenthal, Gary E., Amrik Shah, Lynne E. Way, and Dwain L. Harper. 1998. "Variations in Standardized Hospital Mortality Rates for Six Common Medical Diagnoses." *Medical Care* 36:955–64.

Rosko, Michael D., Jon A. Chilingerian, Jackie S. Zinn, and William E. Aaronson. 1995. "The Effects of Ownership, Operating Environment, and Strategic Choices on Nursing Home Efficiency." *Medical Care* 33:1001–21.

Rossiter, Louis F., Kathryn Langwell, Thomas T. Wan, and Margaret Rivnyak. 1989. "Patient Satisfaction among Elderly Enrollees and Disenrollees in Medicare Health Maintenance Organizations: Results from the National Medicare Competition Evaluation." *Journal of the American Medical Association* 262:57–63.

Ruchlin, Hirsch S., and S. Levey. 1972. "Nursing Home Cost Analysis: A Case Study." *Inquiry* 9:3–15.

Ruchlin, Hirsch S., Dennis D. Pointer, and Lloyd L. Cannedy. 1973. "A Comparison of For-Profit Investor-Owned Chain and Nonprofit Hospitals." *Inquiry* 10:13–23.

Russell, Louise. 1978. *Technology in Hospitals: Medical Advances and Their Diffusion.* Washington, D.C.: Brookings Institution Press.

Salkever, David S., and Richard G. Frank. 1992. "Health Services." Pp. 24–54 in *Who Benefits from the Nonprofit Sector?* edited by C. S. Clotfelter. Chicago: University of Chicago Press.

Saphir, Ann. 2000. "Vencor Walloped for $1.3 Billion." *Modern Healthcare* 30:8.

Schlesinger, Mark. 1997. "Paradigm Lost: The Persisting Search for Community in American Health Policy." *Journal of Health Politics, Policy and Law* 22:937–92.

———. 1998. "Mismeasuring the Consequences of Ownership: External Influences and the Comparative Performance of Public, For-Profit and Nonprofit Organizations." Pp. 85–113 in *Private Action and the Public Good,* edited by W. W. Powell and E. S. Clemens. New Haven, Conn.: Yale University Press.

———. 2002. "A Loss of Faith: The Sources of Reduced Political Legitimacy for the American Medical Profession." *Milbank Quarterly* 80:1–45.

Schlesinger, Mark, Judith D. Bentkover, David Blumenthal, William S. Custer, Robert Musacchio, and J. Willer. 1986. "The Growth of Multi-Facility Health Care Systems and Access to Medical Services." Pp. 121–40 in *Advances in Health Services Research,* edited by L. Rossiter and G. Wilensky. Greenwich, Conn.: JAI Press.

Schlesinger, Mark, Judith D. Bentkover, David Blumenthal, Robert Musacchio, and Janet Willer. 1987. "The Privatization of Health Care and Physicians' Perceptions of Access to Hospital Services." *Milbank Quarterly* 65:25–58.

Schlesinger, Mark, Paul D. Cleary, and David Blumenthal. 1989. "The Ownership of Health Facilities and Clinical Decisionmaking: The Case of the ESRD Industry." *Medical Care* 27:244–58.

Schlesinger, Mark, Robert A. Dorwart, and Sherrie Epstein. 1996. "Managed Care Constraints on Psychiatrists' Hospital Practices: Bargaining Power and Professional Autonomy." *American Journal of Psychiatry* 153:256–60.

Schlesinger, Mark, Robert A. Dorwart, Claudia Hoover, and Sherrie Epstein. 1997a. "Competition and Access to Hospital Services: Evidence from Psychiatric Hospitals." *Medical Care* 35:974–92.

———. 1997b. "The Determinants of Dumping: A National Study of Economically Motivated Transfers Involving Mental Health Care." *Health Services Research* 32:561–90.

Schlesinger, Mark, Benjamin Druss, and Tracey Thomas. 1999. "No Exit? The Effect of Health Status on Dissatisfaction and Disenrollment from Health Plans." *Health Services Research* 34:547–76.

Schlesinger, Mark, and Bradford H. Gray. 1999. "Institutional Change and Organizational Performance in the Mental Health Service System." Pp. 427–48 in *Sociology and Mental Health,* edited by A. V. Horwitz. New York: Cambridge University Press.

Schlesinger, Mark, Bradford H. Gray, and Elizabeth Bradley. 1996. "Charity and Community: The Role of Nonprofit Ownership in a Managed Health Care System." *Journal of Health Politics, Policy and Law* 21:697–752.

Schlesinger, Mark, Bradford H. Gray, Gerard Carrino, Mary Duncan, Michael K. Gusmano, Vincent Antonelli, and Jennifer Stuber. 1998. "A Broader Vision for Managed Care, Part 2: A Typology of Community Benefits." *Health Affairs* 17:26–49.

Schlesinger, Mark, Bradford H. Gray, and Michael K.

Gusmano. 2004. "A Broader Vision for Managed Care, Part 3: The Scope and Determinants of Community Benefits Currently Provided by HMOs." *Health Affairs* 23:210–21.

Schlesinger, Mark, Bradford H. Gray, and Krista Perreira. 1997. "Medical Professionalism under Managed Care: The Pros and Cons of Utilization Review." *Health Affairs* 16:106–24.

Schlesinger, Mark, Shannon Mitchell, and Bradford H. Gray. 2003. "Measuring Community Benefits Provided by Nonprofit and For-Profit HMOs." *Inquiry* 40:114–32.

———. 2004. "Public Expectations of Nonprofit and For-Profit Ownership in American Medicine: Clarifications and Implications." *Health Affairs* 23:181–91.

Schlesinger, Mark, Nicole Quon, Matthew Wynia, Deborah Cummins, and Bradford Gray. 2005. "Profit-Seeking, Corporate Control, and the Trustworthiness of Health Care Organizations: Assessments of Health Plan Performance by Their Affiliated Physicians." *Health Services Research* 40:605–45.

Schneider, Eric, Alan Zaslavsky, and Arnold Epstein. 2004. "Use of High-Cost Operative Procedures by Medicare Beneficiaries Enrolled in For-Profit and Not-for-Profit Health Plans." *New England Journal of Medicine* 350:143–50.

Seidman, Robert L., and Susan B. Pollock. 1991. "Trends in Hospital Deductions from Revenues." *Hospital Topics* 69:19–26.

Sharma, Rajiv. 1998. "Competition, Market Structure and Incentives in the Health Care Industry." Ph.D. dissertation, University of Florida.

Shen, Yu-Chu. 2001. "The Effect of Market Reforms and Ownership Choice on the Quality of Care in Hospitals." Ph.D. dissertation, Harvard University.

Shortell, Stephen M. 1985. "The Effect of Hospital Ownership on Nontraditional Services." *Health Affairs* 5:97–111.

Shortell, Stephen M., and Edward F. X. Hughes. 1988. "The Effects of Regulation, Competition and Ownership on Mortality Rates among Hospital Inpatients." *New England Journal of Medicine* 318:1100–1107.

Shukla, Ramesh K., John Pestian, and Jan P. Clement. 1997. "A Comparative Analysis of Revenue and Cost-Management Strategies of Not-for-Profit and For-Profit Hospitals." *Hospitals and Health Services Administration* 42:117–34.

Silverman, Elaine, and Jonathan Skinner. 2001. "Are For-Profit Hospitals Really Different? Medicare Upcoding and Market Structure." NBER working paper #8133. Cambridge, Mass.: National Bureau of Economic Research.

Sloan, Frank A. 1998. "Commercialism in Nonprofit Hospitals." Pp. 151–68 in *To Profit or Not to Profit: The Commercial Transformation of the Nonprofit Sector,* edited by B. Weisbrod. New York: Cambridge University Press.

Sloan, Frank A., Michael A Morrisey, and James Valvona. 1988. "Hospital Care for the 'Self-Pay' Patient." *Journal of Health Politics, Policy and Law* 13:83–102.

Sloan, Frank A., Gabriel A. Picone, Donald H. Taylor, and Shin-Yi Chou. 2001. "Hospital Ownership and Cost and Quality of Care: Is There a Dime's Worth of Difference?" *Journal of Health Economics* 20:1–21.

Sloan, Frank A., Donald H. Taylor, and Christopher J. Conover. 2000. "Hospital Conversions: Is the Purchase Price Too Low?" Pp. 13–44 in *The Changing Hospital Industry,* edited by D. Cutler. Chicago: University of Chicago Press.

Sloan, Frank A., and Robert A. Vraciu. 1983. "Investor-Owned and Not-for-Profit Hospitals: Addressing Some Issues." *Health Affairs* 2:25–37.

Spann, Robert. 1977. "Rates of Productivity Change and the Growth of State and Local Government Expenditures." Pp. 100–129 in *Budgets and Bureaucrats: The Source of Government Growth,* edited by T. Borcherding. Durham, N.C.: Duke University Press.

Sparrow, Malcolm. 2000. *License to Steal: How Fraud Bleeds America's Health Care System.* Boulder, Colo.: Westview Press.

Spector, William D., Thomas M. Selden, and Joel W. Cohen. 1998. "The Impact of Ownership Type on Nursing Home Outcomes." *Health Economics* 7:639–53.

Spitz, Bruce. 1980. *Medicaid Nursing Home Reimbursement in New York.* Washington, D.C.: Urban Institute Press.

Spitz, Bruce, and Jane Weeks. 1980. *Medicaid Nursing Home Reimbursement in Illinois.* Washington, D.C.: Urban Institute Press.

Starr, Paul. 1982. *The Social Transformation of American Medicine.* New York: Basic Books.

Steinberg, Richard, and Bradford H. Gray. 1993. "'The Role of Nonprofit Enterprise' in 1993: Hansmann Revisited." *Nonprofit and Voluntary Sector Quarterly* 22:297–316.

Steinwald, Bruce, and Duncan Neuhauser. 1970. "The Role of the Proprietary Hospital." *Journal of Law and Contemporary Problems* 35:817–38.

Stevens, Rosemary. 1982. "A Poor Sort of Memory: Voluntary Hospitals and the Government before the Depression." *Milbank Memorial Fund Quarterly* 60:551–84.

———. 1989. *In Sickness and in Wealth: American Hospitals in the Twentieth Century.* New York: Basic Books.

Stone, Deborah. 2000. *Reframing Home Health-Care Policy.* Cambridge, Mass.: Radcliffe Public Policy Center.

Sullivan, T. J., and Bradley E. Karlin. 1999. "State Community Benefit Needs Assessment, Planning and Reporting Laws." *Tax Exempt Organization Tax Review* 23:285–92.

Taylor, Mark. 2000. "Insurers Pile On in Fresenius Case." *Modern Healthcare* 30:9.

Thorpe, Kenneth, and Charles Brecher. 1987. "Improved Access to Care for the Uninsured Poor in Large Cities: Do Public Hospitals Make a Difference?" *Journal of Health Politics, Policy and Law* 12:313–24.

Towers Perrin. 1995. *Navigating the Changing Health Care System: The Towers Perrin Survey of What Americans Know and Need to Know.* New York: Louis Harris Associates.

Troyer, Jennifer L., and Herbert G. Thompson Jr. 2004. "The Impact of Litigation on Nursing Home Quality." *Journal of Health Politics, Policy and Law* 29:11–42.

Tu, Ha T., and James D. Reschovsky. 2002. "Assessments of Medical Care by Enrollees in For-Profit and Nonprofit Health Maintenance Organizations." *New England Journal of Medicine* 346:1288–93.

Ullmann, Steven G. 1987. "Ownership, Regulation, Quality Assessment, and Performance in the Long-Term Health Care Industry." *The Gerontologist* 27:233–39.

U.S. Department of Health, Education and Welfare. 1977. *Health: United States, 1976–77.* DHEW publication no. (HRA) 77–1232. Washington, D.C.: Government Printing Office.

U.S. General Accounting Office. 1990. *Nonprofit Hospitals:*

Better Standards Needed for Tax Exemption. GAO/HRD-90–84. Washington, D.C.: General Accounting Office.

Valdmanis, Vivian G. 1990. "Ownership and Technical Efficiency of Hospitals." *Medical Care* 28:552–61.

Vandenburgh, Henry. 1996. "Organizational Deviance in For-Profit Psychiatric Hospital Business Practices." Ph.D. dissertation, University of Texas.

Vita, Michael G. 1990. "Exploring Hospital Production Relationships with Flexible Functional Forms." *Journal of Health Economics* 9:1–21.

Vitaliano, Donald F., and Mark Toren. 1994. "Cost and Efficiency in Nursing Homes: A Stochastic Frontier Approach." *Journal of Health Economics* 13:281–300.

Vladeck, Bruce. 1980. *Unloving Care: The Nursing Home Tragedy.* New York: Basic Books.

Wall Street Journal Online. 2003. "Most People Uncomfortable with Profit Motive in Health Care." *Wall Street Journal Online / Harris Interactive Health-Care Poll* 2, no. 12 (December 4): 1–3.

Watt, J. Michael, Steven C. Renn, James S. Hahn, Robert A. Derzon, and Carl J. Schramm. 1986. "The Effects of Ownership and Multihospital System Membership on Hospital Functional Strategies and Economic Performance." Pp. 260–89 in *For-Profit Enterprise in Health Care,* edited by B. H. Gray. Washington, D. C.: National Academy Press.

Weinstein, Rachel. 1997. "Medical and Economic Determinants of Cesarean Delivery in California." Ph.D. dissertation, Princeton University.

Weisbrod, Burton A. 1988. *The Nonprofit Economy.* Cambridge, Mass.: Harvard University Press.

———. 1991. "The Health Care Quadrilemma: An Essay on Technological Change, Insurance, Quality of Care and Cost Containment." *Journal of Economic Literature* 29:523–52.

———, ed. 1998a. *To Profit or Not to Profit: The Commercial Transformation of the Nonprofit Sector.* New York: Cambridge University Press.

———. 1998b. "Institutional Form and Organizational Behavior." Pp. 69–84 in *Private Action and the Public Good,* edited by W. W. Powell and E. S. Clemens. New Haven, Conn.: Yale University Press.

Weisbrod, Burton A., and Mark Schlesinger. 1986. "Ownership Form and Behavior in Regulated Markets with Asymmetric Information." Pp. 133–51 in *The Nonprofit Sector: Economic Theory and Public Policy,* edited by S. Rose-Ackerman. New York: Oxford University Press.

Wennberg, John E., Elliott S. Fisher, and Jonathan S. Skinner. 2004. "Geography and the Debate over Medicare Reform." *Health Affairs* (Web exclusive): W86–114.

White, Kenneth R. 2000. "Hospitals Sponsored by the Roman Catholic Church: Separate, Equal, Distinct?" *Milbank Quarterly* 78:213–40.

White, Kenneth R., and James W. Begun. 1998/99. "How Does Catholic Hospital Sponsorship Affect Services Provided?" *Inquiry* 35:398–407.

White, Kenneth R., and Yasar A. Ozcan. 1996. "Church Ownership and Hospital Efficiency." *Hospital and Health Services Administration* 41:297–310.

Wolff, Nancy, and Mark Schlesinger. 1998. "Ownership, Competition and Access to Health Care." *Nonprofit and Voluntary Sector Quarterly* 27:203–36.

Woolhandler, Steffie, and David U. Himmelstein. 1997. "Costs of Care and Administration at For-Profit and Other Hospitals in the United States." *New England Journal of Medicine* 336:769–74.

Young, Gary J., Kamal R. Desai, and Fred J. Hellinger. 2000. "Community Control and Pricing Patterns of Nonprofit Hospitals: An Antitrust Analysis." *Journal of Health Care Politics, Policy and Law* 25:1051–81.

Yuan, Zhong, Gregory S. Cooper, Douglas Einstadter, Randall D. Cebul, and Alfred A. Rimm. 2000. "The Association between Hospital Type and Mortality and Length of Stay: A Study of 16.9 Million Hospitalized Medicare Beneficiaries." *Medical Care* 38:231–45.

Zeckhauser, Richard, Jayenda Patel, and Jack Needleman. 1995. "The Economic Behavior of For-Profit and Nonprofit Hospitals: The Impact of Ownership on Responses to Changing Reimbursement and Market Environments." Report to the Robert Wood Johnson Foundation. John F. Kennedy School of Government, Harvard University.

Zinn, Jacqueline S., William E. Aaronson, and Michael D. Rosko. 1993. "Variations in the Outcomes of Care Provided in Pennsylvania Nursing Homes: Facility and Environmental Correlates." *Medical Care* 31:475–87.

Zuckerman, Stephen, Jack Hadley, and Lisa Iezzoni. 1994. "Measuring Hospital Efficiency with Frontier Cost Functions." *Journal of Health Economics* 13:255–80.

17

Social Care and the Nonprofit Sector in the Western Developed World

JEREMY KENDALL
MARTIN KNAPP
JULIEN FORDER

Interest in nonprofit sector organizations providing social care has increased dramatically in recent years, a development generated both because of their institutional form (nonprofit sector) and because of the growing salience of formally organized social care as a policy field, stimulated by demographic and economic trends and changes in family structure (Organisation for Economic Co-operation and Development 1996).[1] The aging of the world's population is especially pertinent, for older people account for the largest share of social-care resources. Increases in the proportion of older people living alone, linked to rises in divorce/separation and remarriage rates, and continued increases in the proportion of women participating in the labor market are likely to limit the capacity of the informal sector to meet social-care needs. Caring responsibilities will necessarily shift to formal organizations (Wittenberg et al. 1998). Moreover, the dual-earner or single-working-parent households that are increasingly prevalent in the twenty-first century are ever more willing and able to buy services such as child day care (Randall 2000) and domiciliary support services for coresident adult children with disabilities.

Many of the agencies meeting these needs or demands are organized as nonprofit institutions. Indeed, prior to the building of state welfare systems and the growth in reliance on market mechanisms to deliver welfare in the last century, the nonprofit sector was second only to family and friends in the breadth and depth of its responsibilities for meeting needs that would now be labeled social care, including those described at the time as poverty alleviation (Jutte 1994; van Leeuwen 1994). In premodern times, at least in western Europe, the charity of local elites, especially organized through religious foundations, and the more mutualistic support of lay and religious guilds were the wellsprings of care for those who could not rely upon the informal sector (Chesterman 1979; J. Smith and Borgmann 2001).

Against the backdrop of the dynastic and revolutionary struggles that were the catalysts for the birth of modern Western nation-states—which ultimately made the idea of national welfare systems possible—various state-church accommodations were reached, often after prolonged conflict between and within sectors (Cunningham and Innes 1998). In social care, the nonprofit sector often remained relatively free from state intervention, in part because of gaps between national intentions and local implementation, and in part because its activities were viewed as less politically significant than fields such as education (Innes 1998).

Under modern welfare arrangements, while the involvement of public authorities has altered the landscape dramatically, a relative lack of state penetration compared with other public policy fields such as education and health continued to characterize social care even into the late twentieth century. National and subnational governments have sought to rebalance systems away from institutional forms of care (including many residential and nursing home settings) toward community-based options involving care at home or in homelike environments (Organisation for Economic Co-operation and Development 1996)—but often without involving an extension of state ownership of assets or extensive regulatory controls. In some locales, the arrival of for-profit providers has recently relegated the nonprofit sector to third or even fourth place in terms of economic contribution, in the sense that agencies organized under profit-distributing auspices now account for more economic activity than nonprofits. Although this new pattern of ownership and control has been established in many countries, the nonprofit sector has remained the primary organizational supplier of social care.

In this chapter we first discuss the nature of social care. This is a necessary prerequisite for our account of how and why the nonprofit sector contributes to social care in such significant ways, and what lies behind the patterns of international variation in the extent and nature of these contributions. Next the nonprofit sector's historical and current roles are set within a comparative perspective, both internationally and by contrasting social care's development with other welfare fields, and the broad contours of the sector today are mapped. We then turn to arguably the most prominent discipline in nonprofit theorizing at the current time—economics—in an attempt to tease out some of the micro technical or technological factors that may lie behind these patterns. The aim is to supplement the more macro political style of argument that characterizes the preceding sections. The penultimate section then examines the evaluation of nonprofit-sector social-care performance, before we conclude with suggestions for future research.

THE NATURE OF SOCIAL CARE: GOALS, PROCESSES, AND OUTCOMES

In many policy fields, international conventions provide a starting point for specifying the conceptual terrain. For example, economic policy analysts are able to call upon International Labour Organization and United Nations definitions of "economic activity," and there are agreed industrial and occupational classificatory schema. Health policy analysts can build on the World Health Organization's widely cited definition of "good health" and international classifications of disease, although there remain cultural differences that also pervade the associated understanding of what constitutes a health service.

In social care, however, it is much harder to draw boundaries and to specify actors with confidence (Alber 1995; Anttonen and Sipila 1996; Anheier 2001). It is misleading to conflate the multifarious social-care professions, semiprofessions, and other caregiver or worker (paid and unpaid) activities with the single category of "social work," as in some national interpretations of the Standard Industrial Classification, and the Nomenclature générale des activités économiques dans les Communautés européennes (NACE) system.

With no clear single de facto industrial or professional (i.e., inputs) basis for proceeding, we could instead define social care in terms of its primary processes and its primary goals. We consider these in turn. Care involves a process and relationship geared toward socially realized autonomy (Brechin 1998). A mutually rewarding and sustainable interpersonal caring dynamic between provider and user lies at its heart, although social participation is viewed by older people in particular as conducive to their welfare, even when not explicitly labeled as, or oriented toward, caring per se (Netten et al. 2000).

The character of social care depends not just on the amount of labor mobilized to deliver it but also on the *motivation* of care suppliers: there is a "relational" aspect to care. A care recipient perceiving that services are delivered purely on the basis of instrumental, narrow self-interest or coercion gains less welfare-generating emotional reward and personal recognition, other things being equal, than one for whom support is perceived to be driven by motives of an affective, empathic, and trust-generating nature. Folbre and Weisskopf (1998:180) refer to the latter as "caring labor," to be distinguished analytically from "labor services providing care," which include all activities provided and packaged as care, regardless of the underlying motives. By definition, only caring labor involves both "confirmation to the care recipients that someone cares about them" and the carer commitment necessary to fulfill the developmental aims of social care. The motives that can generate this joint product are altruism; an internalized (but potentially reversible) sense of duty and obligation; intrinsic enjoyment, essentially meaning "caring is its own reward"; and "expectation of an informal *quid pro quo*," where that expectation is predicated upon mutual intimacy and trust rather than contractually specified (ibid.:174–76; see also Vesterlund, this volume). Evidence as to the prevalence of these motives in social care is rare, but recent studies in England demonstrate the significance of empathic and intrinsic motivations in the case of managers and proprietors (Kendall 2001a; Kendall et al. 2003).

Evandrou and Falkingham (1998:192) argue that social care ultimately has two aims: "social control, protecting societies' members from danger, discomfort and distress . . . [and] social integration amongst individuals or groups in society who would otherwise be marginalized or socially excluded. More specifically, [the aim] is to promote individual personal well being in the face of a disabling condition." Such activities, or the outcomes they generate, are collective goods because social control and integration benefit communities and not just service users. The largest client groups are therefore those people for whom society deems social control and proactive integration to be appropriate policy responses: vulnerable older people, children, people with physical or intellectual disabilities, and people with mental health problems.

As with many other human services, the desired outcomes tend to be intangible, difficult to measure, and often of long gestation. But social care may also be distinctive in terms of the sheer ubiquity of these complexities. Moreover, it often involves the prevention or management of welfare deterioration ("social maintenance") rather than the improvements in status and personal development character-

TABLE 17.1. THE MIXED ECONOMY MATRIX, WITH EXAMPLES OF TRANSACTION TYPES

	Sector of provision (ownership of production)			
Resourcing (funding)	Public sector	Nonprofit sector	For-profit sector	Informal sector
Taxation or social insurance	Hierarchies, internal "quasi-markets"[a]	Contracting out, external "quasi-markets,"[a] grants, and subsidies		Support for caregivers
Charitable giving	Foundation "top ups"[b]	Traditional private fund-raising charity; foundation support for nonprofit bodies	Foundation "top ups"[b]	Grants to support social-care mutualism, informal support networks
Corporate	—	Private markets		Paid leave for caregivers
Personal, out-of-pocket	User charges for state services			Informal economy activities supported by cash payments
Personal, from private insurance				—
Donations of time	Social-care volunteers mediated by formal organizations			Nonmonetary caring interaction, unfunded informal support networks

Source: Adapted from Knapp 1984.
[a] Resource allocation involving public finance but mixed forms of ownership on the supply side, wherein policy is designed to increase market forces.
[b] Grant-making trusts step in to make up the gap between providers' charges for care and users' ability to pay for that care.

izing other human services such as mainstream health and education (Davies and Knapp 1981).

In toto, social care is, then, the means by which social externalities (that is, the effects of provision of service to the client on society more generally)—the production of social integration and protection—are addressed. Just as health *care* is an element in the production of *health,* social *care* is an element in the production of *social well-being.* It involves the processes, motivated actors, and resources set up and arranged to achieve social goals. If kinship and friendship-based support constitute an "informal sector," this leaves the state (public), market (for-profit) and nonprofit sectors as the institutions that formally employ workers and deliver services.

These provider sectors are supported in various ways, some from taxation or compulsory social insurance fund revenues, some from donations (either collectively organized through nonprofit bodies or contributed as individual, one-to-one gifts), some by corporate (for-profit) bodies (for example, providing services for their employees and families), and some from payments by service users (either out-of-pocket or through private insurance). Donations of time are another important resource. Commonly, social-care providers are supported from multiple sources, and certainly all social-care systems rely on a mix of resources. Cross-classifying provider sector by the source of support—in the "mixed economy matrix" (table 17.1)—shows the plethora of transaction arrangements in use and the associated breadth of policy issues to be addressed.

THE HISTORICAL DEVELOPMENT OF NONPROFIT SOCIAL CARE

Welfare State Formation and the Persistence of Nonprofit Sector Dominance

The shift to recognizably modern patterns of extensive state responsibility for human services took place largely in the hundred years between the mid-nineteenth and mid-twentieth centuries, when modern nation-states came of age. This evolution involved a rebalancing of the formally organized element of the mixed economy away from heavy reliance on charity toward public-sector finance and control. Societies were (at different rates) undergoing restructuring associated with urbanization and industrialization. Contemporary research pointed to the human impact of these transformations, and the problems of poverty were discussed extensively by politicians, in popular novels, and in the press. There was also growing consciousness that modern welfare problems generated complex interdependencies, which implied the need for more extensive collective action and proactive policy (de Swaan 1988).

By the second half of the nineteenth century, for the first time national governments were well aware of these transformations, and they *potentially* had the political and technical capabilities to act as equal or dominant partners when engaging with the nonprofit sector in responding to them (Perkin 1989, 1996). What marked out social care from other welfare domains was the extent to which, in the ensuing period of modern welfare-state formation, public-sector authorities adopted a relatively hands-off approach (with the major exception of social-care policies that overlapped with acute "deviance" and vagrancy concerns). What is remarkable is how little state intervention (funding from taxation, regulation, or outright public ownership) took place, in comparison with the classic fields of welfare policy, mainstream education, health, and social security (income maintenance).

Why was this the case? One factor was the absence of political-economic motives for state engagement. Among the reasons for state interest in welfare domains were aspirations to improve national efficiency, strengthening the populace for armed struggle or to compete in overseas commodity markets (Rimlinger 1963; Thane 1996). By definition, with few exceptions, the clientele for social care was unlikely to contribute to competition on the battlefield or in the marketplace.

Second, there was a lack of enduring electoral or affective rationales for involvement in social care. Concerns about the voting preferences and loyalties of working-class employees were paramount for many elites, whose urgent priority (not always realized) was often to avoid the coming to power of extremists of the Left or Right. During armed conflicts such as World War I, politicians often promised servicemen better access to social security, health, education, and housing. To the extent that old age was considered a problem by such voters or by politicians, it was probably seen as essentially an issue of income maintenance, not social-care guarantees, presumably because family or other informal care providers were expected to meet those needs. Also, of course, some potential beneficiaries of widening state involvement would often have lacked either legal enfranchisement or the capability to vote by the very nature of their conditions. There were few votes to win by promising to improve social care.

Third, there was no hegemonic profession within social care and certainly no equivalent to the powerful doctors' and teachers' associations to press for relative income security, operational autonomy, or privilege. Social work, weakened by internal epistemic disputes, struggled to assert its identity and professional credentials in the late nineteenth and early twentieth centuries on either side of the Atlantic and was divided in continental Europe, too (Woodroofe 1962; Lorenz 1994). It lacked the significant core of uncontested scientific knowledge possessed by medical, teaching, and allied professions (de Swaan 1988) and was therefore short on legitimacy. Even if the state had been inclined to interventionism, it was not obvious with whom negotiations could or should be conducted in the absence of an authoritative profession. Social work was fragmented, dominated by female volunteers, and often provided at local levels without coordination by regional or national associations. In countries with diverse religious and ideological denominational bases, there was much internal rivalry both for resources and as part of a wider competition to secure or strengthen legitimacy (Prochaska 1988). For political and structural reasons, therefore, public-sector commitments to social care tended to be relatively small-scale, insecure, and intermittent compared with those to other human-service fields.

In some parts of continental Europe, although the public resources allocated to social care were still quite limited compared with the funding of other welfare fields, public support for the nonprofit sector was perhaps more systematic and less erratic than in the United States or the United Kingdom. To a degree, this support was ideologically associated with and lent legitimacy by the Catholic social doctrine of *subsidiarity,* situating welfare responsibilities as closely to the "natural" family unit as possible. Many nonprofit social-care institutions, as outgrowths or affiliates of churches, and heavily reliant on female labor, were regarded as the most appropriate alternatives when family was not an option. If public involvement was deemed appropriate, the situation need not call for state provision but rather for a combination of public funding and nonprofit-sector supply.

Even here, however, state intervention still tended not to be seen as appropriate in the first place. Under the most influential Catholic formulations of subsidiarity developed during the late nineteenth and early twentieth centuries, including statements from the Vatican, the pursuit of effectiveness was recognized as *the* fundamental rationale for "upscaling," in turn equated with state intervention. Assuming this was understood, at least in part, as involving an economic dimension, then it was essentially shorthand for cost-effectiveness. There were fewer obvious economies of scale in social care than in education or health, yielding less reason for state involvement on these terms (see also the discussion of demand and supply below).

Common Postwar Social and Political Influences

Moving into the second half of the twentieth century, social care gradually began to find a place on mainstream political agendas, and states began to intervene extensively for the first time. However, it becomes increasingly difficult to tell a general story about this process in the developed world. The forms that these state involvements took reflected ideological factors and were strongly influenced by the distinctive national arrangements that were coevolving in other social-welfare domains such as health and education. The result was that the mixed economies of social care developed differently from country to country (and by client group).

With this caveat in mind, we can nevertheless suggest that a number of factors—some external to the nonprofit sector, some internal—contributed to social care's finding a firmer footing on policy agendas in the first place, and have established parameters within which nonprofit organizations have subsequently operated.

External Pressures

While the informal sector continues to be the main source of support for many people with social-care needs, familial and demographic changes have generated historically exceptional demands for formal care services (Esping-Andersen 1999), with both political and economic implications. If the preferences of male (particularly industrial) workers as voters were uppermost in politicians' minds in the era of welfare-state formation, in part thanks to the labor movement, this dominance could now no longer be taken for granted. Electoral success was increasingly contingent on responding to the aspirations of working women and older people, as they formed ever increasing shares of the electorate. These and other social-care constituencies, such as people with disabilities or mental health problems, were forming their own groups to assert their identities and social entitlements and to demand equality and empowerment.

Social work was somewhat successful in extending its influence. The career structures gradually emerging earlier in the century were consolidated. Although social work typically remained far behind the classic welfare professions in status, continued to lack popular legitimacy, and was often attacked as interfering and pretentious by the political Right, it was nevertheless reasonably firmly established in terms of resources in most countries by the second half of the twentieth century. It gained institutional footholds in subnational governments and public agencies, and national professional associations were sometimes effective representatives. The trappings of respectability were acquired, particularly by expanding an array of generic and specialist courses, training methods, and associated qualifications (Webb and Wistow 1987:chap. 9; Lorenz 1994).

Unlike other welfare fields, social care also recognized and encouraged volunteer mobilization. In continental European traditions, this was historically linked with church-perpetuated principles of subsidiarity and charity; since the 1960s it has more generally been linked with the social change–oriented voluntarism of the new social movements (Lorenz 1994). In the Anglo-Saxon world, as part of what have traditionally been referred to as the "social group," "social group work," "community organization," or "community work" aspects of the social-work corpus, appropriate nonprofit agency involvement has been promoted as good practice and an important route to client empowerment.

As previously noted, many countries have witnessed attempts to reallocate resources from essentially health-care establishments, including acute hospitals and nursing homes, to community-based social-care environments. There are several reasons for these efforts. Social workers, allied professionals, and new social movements have played some role in encouraging this deinstitutionalization process. Human rights arguments have played a part, particularly in relation to people with intellectual disabilities and mental health problems. But at least as important have been pressures from other actors to contain costs and improve effectiveness. Politicians, public servants, and insurers have been seeking to counter perverse incentives (that is, when new policies have inadvertently generated pressures for actions incompatible with their designers' original intentions) and to economize on spiraling long-term care costs. At the same time, researchers have increasingly been demonstrating the avoidable costs, welfare shortfalls, and myriad institutional failures and limitations associated with the social-care status quo ante. (Important work of this kind has been undertaken at the Personal Social Services Research Unit, now based at three sites: the University of Kent at Canterbury; the London School of Economics and Political Science; and the University of Manchester.)

The search for efficiency gains has been associated with conscious efforts to redesign social-care governance. In western Europe various attempts have been made to engineer change (Forder 2002). Property rights have been changed to make systems more marketlike and less hierarchical, usually involving a policy preference for decentralization of budgets and the expansion of user choice, as in the United Kingdom and Germany (Schunk 1998). Reimbursement arrangements have been altered so as to realign incentives and influence prices. There has been greater readiness to contract with independent nongovernmental providers and a concomitant shift in some countries away from public ownership. Supply-side regulation has been developed to protect users and improve service quality.

Another external pressure has been yet more pervasive "spillover" into social care from functionally related policy fields—that is, when policies designed essentially with other domains in mind have had a significant influence on social care. The policy boundaries between health care, social security, education, housing, and social care are notoriously permeable and ill-defined. Social care–relevant joint budgeting arrangements and complex funding streams involving arrays of agencies and different layers of the state have proliferated (Evers and Svetlik 1993; Grønbjerg 1993). When policy spheres and competencies overlap in this way, the gray areas that result have been disproportionately important for social care in resource terms. This is because dedicated social care–specific public budgets, while much larger now than at the mid-century, still tend to be tiny in comparison with those of proximate policy programs, with their more powerful professional promoters and firmer historical bases. Moreover, whereas social-care systems have often been organized at the subnational government level (albeit often with supporting programs of national or federal grants), in some countries those adjacent fields have been structured and funded on a national (or federal) basis, giving them greater access to economic and political resources.[2]

Common Internal Factors

There have been internal as well as external influences on the position of social care. The sector itself has been an actor in shaping policy. Kramer et al. (1993) refer particularly to the growth in numbers and types of organizations. This trend has partly reflected the conversion of new social-movement pressures into formal organizations, but other forms coming to prominence have been self-help initiatives that did not originate as politically oriented (Borkman 1999). Increases in the supply of nonprofit-sector initiative have been particularly associated, in Kramer's analysis, with increased government funding for these organizations, leading in turn to their greater overall dependence on the state. Some of these changes have been associated with the systemic shift toward contracting out services in the search for gains in efficiency and economy (Judge 1982; Gilbert 1984). Kramer et al. (1993:114–16) argue that while a "good" reason for this trend might be the "ideology of voluntarism," the "real" reason has been a reduction in government expenditures, on the assumption that contracting with nonprofits can achieve the same service levels for lower financial outlays.

In fact, while selective budgetary cutbacks in the 1980s affected some specific forms of income maintenance and social-care services (S. Smith 2003; Kendall and Anheier 2001), overall social care–specific public expenditures certainly increased in the second half of the twentieth century to historically unprecedented degrees in most developed countries. This was probably due to the spillover influences and external pressures outlined earlier, although reliable comparative data do not exist to demonstrate or refute this.[3] Where Kramer et al. (1993) are more on target is that, at least from the 1960s onward, the unprecedented public funding opportunities were often seized by existing organizations, as well as by a generation of "new social entrepreneurship" agencies that could not have been formed without public funding.

Many parts of Europe also witnessed the rapid growth of new forms of hybrid and cooperative organizations initiated by volunteers and subsequently involving new alliances of care professionals unwilling or unable to work in the public or for-profit sectors. When legislatures redesigned public-welfare systems, in southern Europe in the 1980s in particular, they encouraged nonprofit organization as a way of handling devolved social-care statutory responsibilities (6 and Vidal 1994; 6 and Kendall 1997; Borzaga and Santuari 2000). These and allied organizations typically thrived on the creative exploitation of funding from different tiers and departments of the state, giving them parallels with the new generation of "government-sponsored agencies" that were also emerging in the United States (S. Smith and Lipsky 1993).

Kramer et al.'s (1993:116) final European generalization concerns the trend of modernization, involving "tendencies . . . at the organizational and societal levels," including "greater formalization, bureaucratization, and professionalization; more rationalization and restructuring of organizations, emphasizing greater efficiency and effectiveness; and toward the increased secularization of functions originally under religious auspices" (see also Kramer 2000). At least some of these changes were the consequences of the external influences discussed earlier. In his review of recent developments in the United States, S. Smith (2003) refers to similar developments, although unsurprisingly, given America's uniquely high and sustained levels of religiosity by developed-world standards, the emphasis on secularization is absent.

The sector therefore comprises a diverse mix of organizations. The crude typology in box 17.1 captures the main organizational distinctions to emerge from these historical forces. Evidence on the relative contributions of each type is not available, but this stylized summary reminds us of the inherent diversity of the sector and warns against overgeneralization in analyzing its roles.

THE BROAD CONTOURS OF NONPROFIT SOCIAL CARE

In most developed countries, the pressures and influences described above have led over the past fifty years to historically unprecedented government involvement in social care, albeit from an extremely low base and still quite limited by comparison with health, education, and social security. With the notable exception of the Scandinavian countries,[4] the mixed economy of social care has tended to involve comparatively limited public-sector penetration when set alongside other welfare services, especially education and health (which we now use as comparators).[5] Typically the nonprofit sector has retained its historically leading role. Table 17.2 illustrates that, on average, just over half of all full-time paid employment in social care is accounted for by nonprofit sector organizations across a range of European Union and other developed countries. This is usually a higher proportion than in education or health. In addition, notwithstanding the recent reforming putsch referred to earlier, in most countries state regulatory involvement has been relatively light, and the autonomy of nonprofit sector providers has been respected even when quite heavily reliant on public funds (Alber 1995; Forder 2002).

Table 17.3 underlines the nonprofit sector's significance by pooling "market share" data by sector, based upon activity levels for the only two forms of social care for which comparative information is available—residential care and preschool day care. In fact, these data underrepresent the nonprofit sector's market share in social care overall, because they relate to services toward the more institutionalized end of the spectrum, where there have been atypically high levels of penetration by either the state or the for-profit sector (depending on the country). Thus, the main reason why the nonprofit sector percentages in table 17.2 are higher than in table 17.3 is that the latter table reflects the nonprofit sector's disproportionate role for most countries in providing for smaller and less well-established client groups and in less institutional forms of care: services for people with alcohol or substance dependency, care for victims of domestic violence, befriending, advocacy, and help-line services for various adult client groups. Moreover, in such areas the nonprofit sector is often demonstrating its now well-recognized public roles as experimenter, pioneer, and specialist (Knapp, Robertson, and Thomason 1990).

There are also well-established community-based activities, long recognized as central to care systems and commanding significant public investment, where the nonprofit sector is often the dominant provider, such as domiciliary

Box 17.1. Major Types of Social-Care Nonprofit-Sector Organizations

Traditional generalist social-service agencies with services for people in financial or social need were often originally founded to address poverty, broadly defined (predating state income maintenance). With origins in the premodern eras, these tend to be strongly connected to religious denominations, to occupational, trade, or professional groupings, or to older social movements (including the labor movement). They maintain a wide variety of structures and connections with the founding entities. They have mixed funding (their relationships with the public sector vary significantly by country), but they often rely on substantial endowments or property-related monies—income earned on historically inherited assets and accumulated financial reserves—and on private giving.

Specialist social-care and support groups, or groups oriented de facto to particular client groups, were typically founded from the late nineteenth century onward under individual philanthropic or associative impetus. They often have fewer direct links with religious or political founding bodies, and their federal structures are looser. They may specialize in particular personal-care services and/or in information, advocacy, and policy issues. Some, especially those with deeper historical roots, may have significant endowments, property-related income, and private giving.

Advocacy groups are organized specifically to lobby for the interests and rights of users. They are often portrayed as "new social movement" organizations, but sometimes they later diversify into services and consequently draw in service professional support. Membership dues and charges tend to dominate their revenue streams, while endowment and private giving tend to be limited.

"New" nonprofit social entrepreneurship and hybrid organizations were founded or expanded from the 1960s onward in direct response to the availability of public funds, particularly for social-care schemes. They also strategically secured funding from adjacent government programs (e.g., employment creation, housing, health) for social-care ends. When politically aligned, they tend to be associated with new social movements or with new social movement–labor or religious movement alliances (not the latter in isolation). These may or may not specialize by client group, may develop national structures from typically local or regional origins, and often remain heavily reliant on public funding and user contributions.

Finally, there are *self-help and community groups* (geographically or ethnically identified) not covered in the above categories. They have mixed funding. Their main distinguishing resource characteristic is their small scale and limited scope of activities.

TABLE 17.2. NONPROFIT SECTOR FULL-TIME EQUIVALENT PAID EMPLOYMENT AS SHARE OF TOTAL EMPLOYMENT IN EDUCATION, HEALTH, AND SOCIAL CARE, BY COUNTRY, 1995

Region	Country	Education (%)	Health (%)	Social services (%)
European Union	Austria	6.3	15.0	62.4
	Belgium	58.2	77.8	40.3
	Finland	15.0	12.4	12.7
	France	11.7	12.4	41.4
	Germany	10.4	23.1	55.3
	Italy (1991)	8.5	6.0	78.9
	Ireland	72.4	40.9	100.0
	Netherlands	65.3	70.4	71.0
	Spain	17.0	9.5	84.0
	Sweden (1992)	5.7	0.7	3.3
	United Kingdom	35.6	4.2	21.6
European Union average		27.8	24.8	51.9
Other developed countries	Australia	20.6	17.3	60.8
	Israel	36.5	43.7	29.4
	Japan	25.2	59.7	56.1
	United States	21.5	46.6	54.0
Other developed country average		26.0	41.8	50.1

Source: Unpublished data, Johns Hopkins Comparative Nonprofit Sector Project database.

TABLE 17.3. NONPROFIT SECTOR MARKET SHARES IN RESIDENTIAL CARE AND DAY CARE FOR CHILDREN (AROUND 1990, PRECISE YEARS VARY)

Country/Region	Service[a]	Nonprofit (%)	Public (%)	For-profit (%)
Austria	Residential care (older people)	22	76	2
	Nursery places	25	72	3
Catalonia	Residential care (older people)	31	30	40
France	Residential care (older people)	29	58	13
Germany	Residential care (all client groups)	60	26	13
	Preschool day care	35	64	1
Italy	Residential care (all client groups)	81	19	0
Japan	Residential care (all client groups)	43	56	1
	Preschool day care	36	56	8
Norway	Preschool nursery and homes for problem children	32	68	0
Sweden	Preschool day care	7	92	< 1
England	Residential care (older people)	15	39	47
	Preschool day care	82	12	6
United States	Residential care (all client groups)	19	3	77
	Preschool day care	59	0	41

Sources: Salamon et al. 1996, Badelt 1997, Mauser 1998, Ranci 2002.

[a] Unit of analysis for activity varies: where available the proportion of places is used; otherwise, the proportion of paid employees; otherwise, the proportion of establishments. It is not clear whether care outside "public systems," including care not funded or regulated by public authorities, has always been included.

and day care for older people (Forder 2002; Laville and Nyssens 2001). Noteworthy exceptions are the Scandinavian countries, with their public-sector dominance, and the United Kingdom and United States, with their private-sector dominance.

As with education and health, fees from users and other commercial income are more important nonpublic sources of income than private giving (Salamon et al. 1996), while public-sector support is the single largest source. Putting this in comparative "industry" context, however, highlights the extent to which nonprofit sector social care tends to be relatively less dependent on the state than education or health.

Although it is not shown in these tables, we know that social care is also relatively more dependent on voluntarism in terms of human resources: volunteers form a much more significant part of the workforce here than in other welfare domains, and in many countries they outnumber their paid counterparts in full-time equivalent terms. Factoring these variables into the equation renders the social-care nonprofit sector larger, on average, than the education and health-care nonprofit sectors (Salamon et al. 1999).

Our historical narrative suggested a range of factors that shaped the developmental path of nonprofit social care, leaving it with less state provision, funding, and regulation than education or health. At least some are still relevant today:

- *The historical lack of incentives for engagement by governing elites.* The impact of the relatively recent higher political profile of social care has been limited in part because many policy actions are heavily constrained by inherited policy frameworks (Rose and Davies 1994). The legacy of sustained and extensive state intervention found elsewhere is generally less marked in social care, so any new policy proactivity has a less well-established historical grounding.
- *The willingness and ability of the nonprofit sector, continually reinventing itself, to supply social care* (see box 17.1). At just the time when the state might have been expected to take fuller responsibility, due to declining religiosity (in Europe) and an all-time-high level of popular enthusiasm for the capabilities of the modern state, not only did many older forms adapt and persist (most conspicuously, via the "negotiated continuity" of Catholicism, in which providers retained an important service provision role even as state systems were reformed), but there also was a remarkable flowering of newer, secular forms of activity.
- *The absence of a single powerful profession to compete for scarce resources in the public sphere.* Recent injections of public funds, often spilling over from adjacent fields almost incidentally, have not strengthened the power base of any one profession. The various social-care professional specialties have remained relatively insecure and unstable, leaving the field heterogeneous and fragmented.
- *The extent to which rights exist in social care is contested and problematic.* While certain rights have been established as the basis for access to social care in some countries for some client groups, in broad terms they have not been consolidated in this domain to the same degree that they have been in other welfare domains. Social-care systems tend to be less universal—in both theory and practice—than systems in health and education, for example. Thus, means-tested access to services remains a feature of social-care services in many countries, and to the extent that state interven-

tion is seen to involve an affinity with universalism, this leaves more political space for laissez-faire approaches.

- *The existence of social care–specific ideologies, arguing for the encouragement rather than the suppression of appropriate volunteer contributions, alongside informal care inputs.* For example, as previously mentioned, various philosophies of social work have often looked at the sector as an important form of social support, because of its capacity to mobilize volunteers as carriers of progressive values and beliefs.

As we argue below, economic and related theorizing may also be useful in understanding why the nonprofit sector is now particularly prominent in social care; appropriately elaborated, such studies can help us begin to make sense of changes over time. Political sociology and related "regime" approaches, which have been employed to explain patterns of variation by country, have focused on social security, education, and health (Esping-Andersen 1990, 1999). Attempts to examine social care per se are rare and underplay the leading role of nonprofits (Alber 1995; Antonnen and Sipila 1996). The exception is Ranci (2002), who starts with empirical data on market shares (table 17.3), which he combines with the nonprofit sector's funding base to describe four options (table 17.4). Thus the rows simplify the market-share patterns by distinguishing settings where most care is in the hands of nonprofits from activities where it is not, while the columns differentiate between settings on the basis of state control over finance.

Ranci's *nonprofit sector–dominant model* involves religious nonprofit sector organizations particularly prominently. The *subsidiarity model* involves "an intermediate balance between direct provision of services and care performed by the family" and considerable autonomy for nonprofits, while the *state-dominant model* involves Norway's social care as "most representative," but based upon these data would include French residential care, too. Finally, the *market-dominated model* involves an unusually high degree of market influence in terms of both funding and provision.

Using the same sample, Ranci finds patterns of relationships between these models and overall enrollment rates for formal services (older people's home care and preschool day care); familial dependence (as reflected in the proportion of older people living with their children); and economy-wide female participation in the labor force. The nonprofit sector–dominant model tends to involve high dependence on informal sector care, low-paying female employment, limited state responsibility for finance and regulation, and relatively fragmented services with limited professionalization. The state-dominant model involves precisely the opposite in each respect, alongside extensive public ownership and control of mainstream social care services. The subsidiarity model involves an intermediate situation associated with extensive state responsibility for finance but only limited state control and regulation. The market-dominant situation combines relatively low informal-sector dependence (although Ranci's data seem to show levels similar to those of the subsidiarity case) with a state that is austere in terms of welfare entitlements, plus a large for-profit supply as the result of unsatisfied demand.

Ranci's approach is an imaginative first attempt to draw together diverse financial, relational, and societal aspects of the nonprofit sector's role in social care, although arguably it ultimately fails to simplify sufficiently for analytic purposes.

ECONOMIC THEORIZING

While many economic theories have examined residential care for older people and preschool day care as prototypical nonprofit-sector industries and testing grounds (see the chapters in this volume by Anheier and Salamon; Steinberg; S. Smith and Grønbjerg; Prewitt; and Schlesinger and Gray), they have not examined social care comparatively by analyzing its situation relative to other welfare fields. This gap needs addressing. In this section we consider the extent to which economic and related arguments may help us to compare the economic character of social care with that of better-studied fields, particularly health care and education.[6]

The Structure of Demand and Supply

James (1987:413), the pioneering international comparative researcher, claims that "many but not all" of her ideas developed and tested with reference to education also apply to social and health care—but without actually demonstrating that this is the case. As with education, she argues, social services are quasi-public; they involve both government and nonprofit provision, with the latter "providing a service that

TABLE 17.4. SOCIAL-CARE POLICY MODELS

	Degree of state funding	
Role of nonprofit sector	Total (> 60%)	Partial (= 60%)
Dominant (> 50%)	Subsidiary model Germany	Nonprofit sector–dominant model Italy, France (child care), United Kingdom (child care)
Complementary (= 50%)	State-dominant model Norway, France (residential care)	Market-dominant model United Kingdom (residential care), Catalonia (Spain) (residential care)

Source: Ranci 2002.

is not being provided in type or amount by the government"; and "public funding of the nonprofit sector is important." Yet she also claims that "there are major differences in the nature of demand for these services, in the relative supply of the nonprofit form, and in the welfare evaluation of public versus private." Despite this passing recognition, she only really develops her argument in relation to health, leaving the impression that similarities with education are what matter: "I would argue for the importance of religious motivations, both for founding and donating. . . . [Nonprofit] sector growth and government subsidies usually go hand in hand . . . but they also enable government to extract concessions in return in the form of regulations over inputs, outputs, and other characteristics that satisfy diverse constituencies."

In the light of the evidence reviewed earlier, it seems plausible to broadly accept the transportability to social care of James's emphasis on both the significance of religion and the complementarity between government engagement and nonprofit-sector growth. However, religious heterogeneity or diversity is less clearly linked to sector scope and scale. After all, Italy, Spain, and Ireland all enjoy extensive nonprofit sectors in social care as well as in other domains, yet they have relatively homogeneous Catholic populations, which are responsible to a large degree for these welfare services and which face little "religious competition" in so doing.

There may be further economic differences between social care and education that might help explain the comparatively large role of the nonprofit social-care sector. State intervention in social care developed later and progressed less systematically than in education for the political and social reasons identified earlier—a developmental trajectory with important economic implications in the present. In keeping with James's logic, because social care typically remains less dependent upon the state financially and involves far greater reliance on volunteer labor, regulatory activity has been lower. More voluntarism lowers production costs. Limited regulation lowers transaction costs by sidestepping the need to commit resources to inspection and monitoring activities, while also potentially avoiding some of the "perverse impacts" that characterize heavily regulated education and health-care systems (James 1987:411–12). On the other hand, the social-care status quo would therefore be characterized by a dearth of public information on quality and performance, so actual efficiency levels would remain unknown. Moreover, with multiple tiers of the state involved (which we have argued is more likely to be the case in social care), *total* transaction costs could be higher for recipient organizations, even if the costs of any single public body's rules and regulations are relatively low (Grønbjerg 1993).

Second, for a given level of religious, linguistic, or ethnic heterogeneity, the supply organized on a nonprofit basis is likely to be more abundant in social care than other human services. Stakeholders with little capital can easily engage in such "low-intensity" activities as neighborhood visiting, befriending, and advice giving, whereas launching a school or hospital (or traditional institutional social-care establishment) requires substantial capital investment. Indeed, for some activities monetary transactions play a relatively minor role, thus limiting profit-generating opportunities, because demand or need is not backed by ability to pay. Poor, small, or less well-established religiously or ethnically distinctive communities might aspire to develop their own education, health, and social-care services but, initially at least, may only have the economic ability to provide the latter. The lack of a hegemonic profession in social care further lowers barriers to entry in terms of professional qualifications and regulatory requirements. For-profit entry may be limited, not least because long-term profit opportunities appear modest. In toto, low start-up or entry costs, lack of scale economies, low barriers to entry, and lack of opportunities for sustainable profit tend in combination to create an economic situation favorable to nonprofit activity.[7]

For similar economic reasons, some of the hybrid forms of entrepreneurship summarized in the bottom half of box 17.1 may be relatively more important in social care than elsewhere. Nonprofits as coalitions of volunteers, professionals, and other workers appear to be particularly prominent in social care in part because only relatively small capital outlays are required to initiate the community-based programs they typically organize. The reliance on external lending institutions or shareholders typical of for-profit enterprises can often be avoided.

Information Asymmetry, Trust, and Relational Aspects

Theories of trust and information asymmetry are also useful frames of reference. The for-profit sector's tendency to remain a quite peripheral player in social-care markets in most of the developed world in the 1980s and 1990s could have reflected the preemptive ideological choices and preferences of policy communities, as well as any economic or technical reasons for a lack of involvement. For example, political parties, trade unions, and social-worker groups in Austria have explicitly referred to the profit motive as exploitative, or incompatible with care in the case of social services, while apparently accepting it in health care where there are self-employed physicians (Badelt 1997).

An important feature of some recent social-care reforms in Europe has been legislation proscribing some for-profit activities, while simultaneously encouraging nonprofit activity. Even in the United States, supposedly exceptionally tolerant of a for-profit orientation, many of the major public funding programs from which social-care nonprofit organizations have benefited were, at least prior to Reaganite reforms, deliberately designed to exclude the for-profit sector (S. Smith and Lipsky 1993; S. Smith 2003). At the level of implementation in England, Wistow et al. (1996) found that, partly because of the difficulties of measuring quality of service (the information asymmetry problem) and associated fears of inappropriate profiteering, local public purchasers often preferred to contract with nonprofit rather than for-profit providers. This preference for the nonprofit sector also reflected perceptions of value compatibility and shared histories of dealing with social needs and problems. The size of the "trust differential" between the sectors has narrowed as mutual learning about motivations has progressed (Kendall 2001b) and perhaps also with the tendency to develop third-party monitoring.

The empirical facts that trust is predicated on a wider range of factors than sector alone, and can be vested in contrasting ways at different points in time, suggest that we need to develop a richer understanding of the causes and consequences of trust. It is helpful to distinguish between "competence trust" and "goodwill trust," where the former is predicated on perceived know-how and skills while the latter is based upon the presence of the right kind of motivation (from the perspective of the demander). The two forms do not necessarily go hand in hand (Kendall and Knapp 2000; Sako 1992). Trust may be sustained by different institutions in different client groups or between different types of social care. Religious and other motivations may be brought into the analysis not only in terms of entrepreneurship as per James's (1987) account, but also by asking whether there is anything about faith-based charities that inspires or undermines trust and its elements (Anheier and Kendall 2002; Cadge and Wuthnow, this volume).

A further distinctive aspect of social care is its labor intensity, a qualitative consideration that ties in with the discussion of process earlier in the chapter. From an economic perspective, it is "relational." The production of relational goods is said to involve local public-good properties generated by interpersonal interactions in social networks. Under this formulation, productive activity is said to "extend beyond the mere exchange of contractible items; these public goods can be enjoyed only by participating in a social process" (Ben-Ner and Gui 2003:14). Markets could fail in these cases because of the usual free-rider problem and because valued relationships can be generated only by interpersonal interaction: "What matters to a person with demand for a relational good is not only the objective behavior of others but also their attitude, and even their perceived motivations" (ibid.:15). This contingency of user satisfaction on supplier motivation is clearly analogous to Folbre and Weisskopf's (1998) distinction between caring labor and labor services providing care, where only when the former is involved is relational demand effectively met.

While the nondistribution constraint alone may not provide a convincing basis for trusting nonprofits, trust can be engendered when participants in transactions have motivations that are at least partially aligned. Entrepreneurial sorting theories suggest that individuals self-sort into particular industries according to the characteristics of each industry (Young 1983). Social-care industries arguably have characteristics that attract people with more caring, less financially oriented motivations. Consequently, sustaining high-trust, mutually supportive relationships with purchasers who share these motivations is more likely.[8]

Ben-Ner and Gui (2003:16) suggest that the nonprofit sector might be better placed than other forms to respond to relational demands because "the constraint on the appropriation of residual income keeps in check some conflicts of interest that hinder the development of shared cooperative attitudes." Organizations based on some form of mutuality are particularly well placed, because by "being members of the organization, these stakeholders have greater opportunity for expressing their intentions, opinions, and desires, which facilitates communication and coordination among them. Furthermore, participation enhances stakeholders' emotional involvement, which usually favors stability and continuity of relationships" (ibid.). To the extent that volunteers are concentrated in the nonprofit sector, this could signal to potential relational demanders the relative prevalence of caring labor because it at least implies the relative insignificance of selfish pecuniary motives. (It does not, of course, rule out selfish, nonpecuniary motives.) Where opportunities for communication are rich, as per Ben-Ner and Gui's second claim, it should be easier for relational demanders to gauge suppliers' *actual* motives.

But the contribution of volunteers can be of significance in social care not only because of signaling effects (already noticed by Hansmann [1980]) and the relatively rich interactive learning opportunities about motivations. Social-care volunteers can also be preferred by users to professionals at the level of one-to-one relationships (Kendall 2001b). One reason is that voluntarism could be mutually understood as meaning the volunteer is there primarily through free choice, whereas a conventional wage could be an obstacle to emotional investment and intimacy. Second, volunteers may be less likely than their paid counterparts to have formal qualifications or to project themselves as professionals, opening up the possibility for empathy (Quilgars 2000:chap. 5). Third, intimacy may flourish if the volunteer shares with the user certain needs-relevant attributes, including disabilities or experiences, and is therefore considered a peer. There could also be greater willingness to organize care through volunteer support as opposed to professional intervention because the historic doubts about the basic legitimacy of social work as a profession continue to generate mixed feelings within communities about its appropriateness.

EVALUATION AND PERFORMANCE

At the broadest level, two approaches can be discerned to evaluating the performance of the nonprofit sector. The strategy of those working within the rationalist social science mode of analysis draws on tools and concepts modeled on those of natural science in the positivist tradition, and attempts to reach objectively defensible conclusions against well-specified criteria. By contrast, those who adopt a more constructionist approach explore the sensitivities at stake in the actual process of evaluation to reveal the multiple, often contested meanings attached by stakeholders to criteria such as effectiveness, examining how such differences might be linked with stakeholders' social and political situations. Here we focus on the former approach (for a review of some evidence on the latter, see Kendall and Knapp 1999 and Ostrower and Stone, this volume).

Positivist evaluations should take care to account, as far as is feasible, for the complex features of social care discussed in earlier sections of this chapter. External effects and quasi-public good properties mean that costs and benefits are not reflected in orthodox accounting measures. The relational or personal aspect of many social-care transactions adds to the difficulties of evaluation. These considerations are all relevant when evaluating performance against such apparently straightforward criteria as economy, efficiency, or effectiveness. When considering equity, participation, choice, or advocacy criteria, the exercise becomes potentially more challenging still. In our necessarily selective review, we concentrate on the first three criteria, both to maintain our focus on service provision and because more evidence has been gathered regarding them.[9]

A prerequisite for a systematic approach to evaluating economy, efficiency, and effectiveness is a logical understanding of the relationships between costs and consequences. A helpful framework is offered by the *production of welfare* approach (Davies and Knapp 1981), which represents nonprofit-sector action as involving resource deployment that, mediated through "technology" (summarizing a host of often complex processes), generates what are often termed "outputs" (volumes of services delivered and their quantity, taking account of user case mix) and "outcomes" (changes over time in the well-being or quality of life of service users and their carers). Of course, the technology of social care is less tangible and less amenable to measurement and evaluation than the technology of, say, an industrial process. One reason is that staff attitudes and the social milieu of a care setting are likely to be important influences on the well-being of service users, but they do not have a readily identified cost. Moreover, the outcomes—met needs and enhanced quality of life for users—are notoriously hard to measure (Knapp 1984).

Examination of the facets of social-care "production" that are easiest to measure—the resource inputs to care (such as staff numbers and expenditure levels) and outputs (volume and quantity of services)—is sometimes a first step toward examining comparative effectiveness, but it can create perverse incentives (Weisbrod and Schlesinger 1986). Unsurprisingly, given the labor-intensive nature of social care, human resources are also a major preoccupation. There is evaluative evidence to suggest some intersectoral differences. For example, nonprofit-sector care homes apparently have lower staff turnover rates than for-profit homes in England (Local Government Management Board and Central Council for Education and Training in Social Work 1997). In social care more generally, there is a lower prevalence of very low pay and a higher average rate of pay in the nonprofit sector compared with the for-profit sector, but the public sector performs better on both counts (Almond and Kendall 2001). In North America, staff turnover rates in licensed child care are considerably lower in the nonprofit than the for-profit sector (Kisker and Piper 1992). That study also found higher levels of qualifications among nonprofit-sector staff, while Fletcher et al. (1994) report findings of higher average wages and superior fringe benefits in the nonprofit compared with the for-profit sector.

Some differences in labor input characteristics can be attributed to sector. Controlling statistically for a number of other factors, the nonprofit sector in Austria performed better in terms of staff-client ratios and staff qualifications in retirement homes, and class sizes were smaller in nonprofits' preschool day care (Badelt and Weiss 1990; Badelt 1997).[10] Weisbrod (1998) reports differences between the nonprofit and for-profit sectors in the mix of labor inputs in residential care for people with learning (intellectual) disabilities in the United States, with significantly higher staff-user ratios in the nonprofit sector.[11]

Acutely aware of the relational nature of social care, policymakers often assume that staff qualities are an overriding consideration in shaping the quality of care and even in user outcomes. This assumption is in keeping with regulator and practitioner beliefs that continuity of care and opportunities for sustained attention from trained staff are crucial ingredients. But labor is but one facet of the multifaceted social-care process, so that we cannot simply judge care quality purely on the basis of workers' on-paper caliber. It is the joint interaction of resource factors and nonresource factors, such as the social environment of care with user characteristics, which matters in determining effectiveness.

Empirical studies underscore the nondeterministic relationship between purely input-gauged performance and comparisons of differences that are closer to user-level outcomes. For example, the input differences referred to earlier in residential care for older people in England do not feed through into what might be interpreted as better quality (Netten et al. 2000). In his study of retirement homes, Badelt (1997:154) found that "many of the results were ambiguous, and it is much more difficult to draw any conclusion about differences in quality by sector," citing evidence on the relatively limited availability of opportunities for creative leisure apparently available in the nonprofit sector. In contrast, Weisbrod (1998), using a battery of measures of family members' satisfaction, found that the nonprofit sector, and particularly church-related organizations, systematically rated higher than the for-profit sector, although the differences were quite small. Similarly, Mauser (1998) reported parental perceptions of rather limited quality differences in favor of the nonprofit over the for-profit sector in U.S. child day care; religiously based providers were regarded as superior to their secular counterparts within the nonprofit sector. Krashinsky's (1998) study of child day care in Canada—while uncovering major intrasectoral variation and the crucial role of state funding and policies in impacting upon quality (cf. Schlesinger 1998)—found that, on average, regulators rated overall quality as highest in the public sector and lowest in the for-profit sector, with the nonprofit sector in between. However, parental perceptions, after controlling for provincial variations and income, suggested that sector of ownership generally made no difference. Similar conclusions were reached by Morris and Helburn (2000): sector does not make a difference to quality, but only when the regulatory environment is comparatively strict (see also Brown and Slivinski, this volume).

Some U.K. studies have examined cost differences, controlling for some measures of service volume and quality. Comparing public- and nonprofit-sector day care for older people, and standardizing cost differences for (some) user characteristics and other factors, one study suggested that nonprofit day-care centers were more cost-effective in service output terms, largely because of their access to volunteers, although this advantage might be lost if they moved toward the public-sector scale of operation (Knapp and Missiakoulis 1982). A related study, reviewing the costs of residential child care before and after standardization for situational factors and the characteristics of children accommodated, also comparing the quality of the care environment, found that the nonprofit sector appeared to perform relatively well (Knapp 1986). A more recent investigation found nonprofit providers of residential mental health care to be more cost-effective than their public and for-profit counterparts—now combining comprehensive cost measures with user outcomes and again standardizing for differences in users' needs and other characteristics (Knapp et al. 1999). Forder (2000) concluded that nonprofit and public-sector providers have higher market power than for-profit providers, but a lower propensity to use that power to make profits. In a previous study, accounting for motivational differences, Forder (1997) found nonprofit-sector providers of residential care for older people to be less inclined to exploit informational advantages: specifically, they were less likely to misreport cost-relevant user characteristics (that is, portraying clients as more dependent than their observable characteristics would seem to suggest) for financial gain.

In sum, while input, output, and cost comparisons often suggest superior average performance by the nonprofit sector as compared with the for-profit sector—in countries as diverse as Austria, Canada, the United Kingdom, and the United States, and for a number of service types—a cloudier picture emerges when considering measures closer to user outcomes. Averages may also mask significant intrasector variations. At least as important as sector of ownership in accounting for supply-side "performance" can be scale, local funding and regulatory environments, religious/secular affiliation, competitiveness, and use of volunteers.

We have considered nonprofit-sector social care in both its historical and present-day contexts, drawing on relevant theoretical approaches to help understand the sector's contours and the nature of its contributors. It is clear that our current understanding falls some distance short of our aspirations. We have had to be rather loose with many of our definitions, concepts, and categories, partly because of the contested nature of the material and, more mundanely, also because the paucity of empirical evidence does not allow more confident claims to be made about theory or practice in this field. We have also, of course, had to focus on those parts of the developing world in which research investigation is most advanced—Western Europe and North America. Within these constraints, we have endeavored to explore the connections between social care and the nonprofit sector by carefully tracing the field's development over time, emphasizing its theoretical distinctiveness from economic, social, and political perspectives and noting how evaluative concerns have been addressed.

One obvious challenge for future researchers is to collect—in a theoretically informed way—more systematic quantitative and qualitative information regarding social care at the system, client-group, and service-type levels. We conclude this chapter with the following list of some of the most obvious points that need both theoretical and empirical investigation:

- Indicators of aggregate expenditure and supply, and patterns of supply-side diversity, increasingly capturing community-based and not just institutional types of care; the latter should include the sectoral division of labor and also measures of the internal composition of the nonprofit sector (for example, along the lines of box 17.1)
- The financial structure of social-care systems and their elements: quantification of the public-private balance of funding, as well as indicators of the sources and character of such flows and the nature of transactions
- The regulatory structure and its elements; the extent of integration or separation between funding and regulation; nonprofit-sector involvement in regulatory design; intensity of regulatory arrangements; differences in requirements and implementation according to sector
- The original, and subsequently evolving, political relationship between the state and faith-based organizations; how societal institutions have developed to accommodate or provide political space for new social movements in alliance with, or separately from, the traditional churches and the labor movement
- The nature of policy elites' responses to the pressures created by demographic change and familial transformation, and how sector-specific solutions reflect national ideological and institutional factors
- The national dynamic of intragovernmental relations, including the evolving relationships among different levels of the state, the political situation of social-care responsibilities vis-à-vis other policy fields including health, and the involvement of the nonprofit sector at each of these levels and junctures
- The range of social, economic, and political factors affecting the relative influence of care professionals (including social workers) or semiprofessionals in both institutional processes and substantive outcomes of relevance to nonprofits, and the nature of their relationships with other paid employees and with volunteers

NOTES

1. Following the Organisation for Economic Co-operation and Development (1996:4), our working definition of social care is "assistance with the normal activities of daily life, including personal functioning, domestic maintenance and social activities." In many countries the categories of user that account for most social-care resources are vulnerable older people, children, and people with physical or intellectual disabilities. In the interests of manageability, this chapter will focus particularly on the first two client groups. We also focus primarily on the sector's delivery of care and support services, only attending to its important overtly political advocacy or campaigning roles in passing (on the latter, see, for example, Walker and Naegele 1999). In addition, we do not differentiate between established citizens and migrants without citizenship within countries, although it is important to acknowledge that the nonprofit sector has had a particularly important role in meeting the needs of the latter group. Our final scope limitation is geographical: reflecting a cultural bias in the English-language research corpus, our narrative focuses essentially on evidence and argument from western European countries, the United States, and Australia (although the data sources deployed also include Israel and Japan).

2. Prime examples are the Medicare and Medicaid programs in the United States (health) and, until recently, income support in the United Kingdom (social security).

3. It is difficult to measure aggregate resourcing in most countries because of fragmented delivery systems and blurred policy boundaries, but some trends can be identified. Tellingly, despite the United Kingdom's reputation for being vulnerable to public-sector budgetary cuts at times of fiscal austerity, the generic policy climate change from "welfare optimism" to "pessimism" in the mid-1970s (George 1996) did *not* result in social-care expenditure reductions. Instead there were large increases in real public funding levels. Between 1973–74 and 1995–96, the annual inflation-adjusted growth in personal social-services public expenditures was 4 percent (Evandrou and Falkingham 1998).

4. In terms of the proportion of gross domestic product (GDP) social care absorbs, the Organisation for Economic Co-operation and Development and European Union (EU) comparative systemic data suggest that Sweden's, Denmark's, and Finland's public expenditures on "family services" and "elderly and disabled services," accounting for 1.8 percent and 2.7 percent of GDP, respectively, are nearly three times the EU average (Ferrera, Hemerijck, and Rhodes 2000:table 3.3). Equally staggering are the gaps between Scandinavia (now including Norway) and fourteen other developed countries in the percentage of children covered by public-sector day care (28 percent compared to 5 percent) and the proportion of older people receiving publicly provided home help (20 percent compared with 4 percent).

5. Taken together, education, health, and social care account for over three-quarters of all paid full-time equivalent (FTE) employment, and just under two-thirds of all (paid and unpaid) FTE employment, in the nonprofit sectors of developed countries. The remainder of nonprofit-sector activity includes culture, recreation, environmental activities, development, housing, advocacy, philanthropic intermediation, international activities, and trade union and professional associations (see Salamon et al. 1999; Salamon and Anheier, this volume). (These figures do not include personnel employed by religious congregations for primarily sacramental purposes.)

6. Another comparative question worthy of attention is why the nonprofit sector varies in scope and scale in different subcategories of social care. Kendall (2000) uses a variant of regime theory to explain why the nonprofit sector is a particularly significant actor in day care for older people in England but is less prominent in residential care and relatively marginal in domiciliary care services.

7. This set of factors is most obviously relevant in "community-based" forms of social care. However, even in more institutional forms of care, as with residential care homes for older people, barriers to entry may be comparatively low and scale economies relatively limited in comparison with those of health and education services (Darton and Knapp 1984; Norton 2000).

8. Steinberg (1993) argues for the endogeneity of motivations to support the idea of predictable sorting by stakeholders.

9. Elsewhere (Kendall and Knapp 2000) we have extended the conceptual model discussed in the following text to include these other criteria, suggesting indicators for performance evaluation of nonprofit organizations.

10. The choice of variables treated as "exogenous" when making comparisons has implications. Theoretically, only factors bound up with the existence and essential character of the sector should be treated as endogenous, and all other variation attributed to exogenous influences. However, with no consensus on the theoretical foundations of the nonprofit sector, different assumptions are made, with size an example of a factor variously regarded as exogenous or endogenous. Schlesinger (1998), Weisbrod (1998), and Schlesinger and Gray (this volume) discuss the implications.

11. Weisbrod also reports that volunteers were only rarely used as substitutes for paid labor and were "essentially independent inputs" (p. 80), presumably involved primarily in fund-raising and/or governance. This tendency not to use volunteers mirrors the English experience in residential care for older people.

REFERENCES

Alber, Jens. 1995. "A Framework for the Comparative Study of Social Services." *Journal of European Social Policy* 5:131–49.

Almond, Stephen, and Jeremy Kendall. 2001. "Low Pay in the UK: The Case for a Three Sector Comparative Approach." *Annals of Public and Cooperative Economics* 72:45–76.

Anheier, Helmut K., ed. 2001. *Social Services in Europe: Annotated Bibliography.* Frankfurt: Observatory for the Development of Social Services in Europe.

Anheier, Helmut K., and Jeremy Kendall. 2002. "Interpersonal Trust and Voluntary Associations: Examining Three Approaches." *British Journal of Sociology* 53:343–62.

Anttonen, Anneli, and Jorma Sipila. 1996. "European Social Care Services: Is It Possible to Identify Models?" *Journal of European Social Policy* 6:87–100.

Badelt, Christoph. 1997. "Contracting and Institutional Choice in Austria." Pp. 149–61 in *The Contract Culture in Public Services: Studies from Britain, Europe and the USA,* edited by Perri 6 and Jeremy Kendall. Aldershot, U.K.: Ashgate.

Badelt, Christoph, and Peter Weiss. 1990 "Non-Profit, For-Profit and Government Organizations in Social Service Provision: Comparison of Behavioral Patterns for Austria." *Voluntas* 1:77–96.

Ben-Ner, Avner, and Benedetto Gui. 2003. "The Theory of Nonprofit Organizations Revisited." Pp. 3–26 in *The Study of Nonprofit Enterprise: Theories and Approaches,* edited by Avner Ben-Ner and Helmut Anheier. New York: Kluwer/Plenum.

Borkman, Thomasina J. 1999. *Understanding Self-Help/Mutual Aid: Experiential Learning in the Commons.* Piscataway, N.J.: Rutgers University Press.

Borzaga, Carlo, and Alceste Santuari. 2000. "Social Enterprises in Italy: The Experience of Social Co-operatives." Working paper #15, Institute for Development Studies of Non Profit Enterprises, University of Trento, Italy.

Brechin, Ann. 1998. "What Makes for Good Care?" Pp. 170–89 in *Care Matters: Concepts, Practice and Research in Health and Social Care,* edited by Ann Brechin, Jan Walmsley, Jeanne Katz, and Sheila Peace. London: Sage Publications.

Chesterman, Michael R. 1979. *Charities, Trusts and Social Welfare.* London: Weidenfeld and Nicholson.

Cunningham, Hugh, and Joanne Innes, eds. 1998. *Charity, Philanthropy and Reform: From the 1690s to 1850.* London: Macmillan.

Darton, Robin A., and Martin Knapp. 1984. "The Cost of Residential Care for the Elderly: The Effects of Dependency, Design and Social Environment." *Ageing and Society* 4:157–83.

Davies, Bleddyn, and Martin Knapp. 1981. *Old People's Homes and the Production of Welfare.* London: Routledge.

de Swaan, Abram. 1988. *In Care of the State: Health Care, Education and Welfare in Europe and the USA in the Modern Era.* Cambridge: Polity Press.

Esping-Andersen, Gosta. 1990. *The Three Worlds of Welfare Capitalism.* Cambridge: Polity Press.

———. 1999. *Social Foundations of Postindustrial Economies.* Oxford: Oxford University Press.

Evandrou, Maria, and Jane Falkingham. 1998. "The Personal Social Services." Pp. 189–256 in *The State of Welfare: The Economics of Social Spending,* edited by Howard Glennerster and John Hills. Oxford: Oxford University Press.

Evers, Adalbert, and Ivan Svetlik, eds. 1993. *Balancing Pluralism: New Welfare Mixes in Care for the Elderly.* Aldershot, U.K.: Ashgate.

Ferrera, Maurizio, Anton Hemerijck, and Martin Rhodes. 2000. "The Future of Social Europe: Recasting Work and Welfare in the New Economy." Report prepared for the Portuguese Presidency of the European Union.

Fletcher, Janice, Teresa P. Gordon, Thomas Nunamaker, and Sherrill Richarz. 1994. "Competing for Tots: Operating Objectives and Characteristics of For-Profit and Not-for-Profit Child Care Centers in the Pacific Northwest." *Voluntas* 5:59–85.

Folbre, Nancy, and Thomas E. Weisskopf. 1998. "Did Father Know Best? Families, Markets and the Supply of Caring Labor." Pp. 171–206 in *Economics, Values, and Organization,* edited by Avner Ben-Ner and Louis G. Putterman. Cambridge: Cambridge University Press.

Forder, Julien. 1997. "Contracts and Purchaser-Provider Relationships in Community Care." *Journal of Health Economics* 16:517–42.

———. 2000. "Mental Health: Market Power and Governance." *Journal of Health Economics* 19:877–905.

———. 2002. "Regulating Entrepreneurial Behaviour in Social Care." Pp. 163–78 in *Regulating Entrepreneurial Behaviour in European Health Care Systems,* edited by Richard B. Saltman, Reinhard Busse, and Elias Mossialos. Buckingham, U.K.: Open University Press.

George, Victor. 1996. "The Future of the Welfare State." Pp. 1–31 in *European Welfare Policy: Squaring the Welfare Circle,* edited by Victor George and Peter Taylor-Gooby. Basingstoke, U.K.: Macmillan.

Gilbert, Neil. 1984. "Welfare for Profit: Moral, Empirical and Theoretical Perspectives." *Journal of Social Policy* 13:63–74.

Grønbjerg, Kirsten A. 1993. *Understanding Nonprofit Funding: Managing Revenues in Social Services and Community Development Organizations.* San Francisco: Jossey-Bass.

Hansmann, Henry. 1980. "The Role of Nonprofit Enterprises." *Yale Law Journal* 89:835–98.

Innes, Joanna. 1998. "State, Church and Voluntarism in European Welfare, 1690–1850." Pp. 15–61 in *Charity, Philanthropy and Reform: From the 1690s to 1850,* edited by Hugh Cunningham and Joanna Innes. London: Macmillan.

James, Estelle. 1987. "The Nonprofit Sector in Comparative Perspective." Pp. 397–415 in *The Nonprofit Sector: A Research Handbook,* edited by Walter W. Powell. 1st ed. New Haven, Conn.: Yale University Press.

Judge, Ken. 1982. "The Public Purchase of Social Care: British Confirmation of the American Experience." *Policy and Politics* 10:397–416.

Jutte, Robert. 1994. *Poverty and Deviance in Early Modern Europe: New Approaches to European History.* Cambridge: Cambridge University Press.

Kendall, Jeremy. 2000. "The Third Sector and Social Care for Older People in England: Towards an Explanation of Its Contrasting Contributions in Residential Care, Domiciliary Care and Day Care." Civil Society Working Paper #8, Centre for Civil Society, London School of Economics and Political Science, London.

———. 2001a. "Of Knights, Knaves and Merchants: The Case of Residential Care for Older People in England in the Late 1990s." *Social Policy and Administration* 35:360–75.

———. 2001b. "Grand-Bretagne: Une économie plurielle de soins bouleversée par les 'quasi-marchés.'" Pp. 91–117 in *Les services sociaux entre associations, Etat et marché,* edited by Jean-Louis Laville and Marthe Nyssens. Paris: La Découverte/MAUSS/CRIDA.

Kendall, Jeremy, and Helmut K. Anheier. 2001. "Conclusion: The Nonprofit Sector at the Crossroads: Social, Political and Economic Dynamics." Pp. 228–51 in *Nonprofit Sector Policy at the Crossroads: An International Nonprofit Analysis,* edited by Helmut K. Anheier and Jeremy Kendall. London: Routledge.

Kendall, Jeremy, and Martin Knapp. 1999. "Evolution and the Voluntary (Nonprofit) Sector: Emerging Issues." Pp. 202–21 in *International Prospects on Voluntary Action,* edited by David Lewis. London: Earthscan.

———. 2000. "Measuring the Performance of Voluntary Organizations." *Public Management* 2:106–32.

Kendall, Jeremy, Tihana Matosevic, Julien Forder, Martin Knapp, Brian Hardy, and Patricia Ware. 2003. "The Motivations of Domiciliary Care Providers in England: New Concepts, New Findings." *Journal of Social Policy* 32:489–511.

Kisker, Ellen E., and Valerie Piper. 1992. *A Profile of Child Care Settings: Center-Based Programs.* Los Altos, Calif.: Sociometrics Corporation, American Family Data Archive.

Knapp, Martin. 1984. *The Economics of Social Care.* Basingstoke, U.K.: Macmillan.

———. 1986. "The Relative Cost-Effectiveness of Public, Voluntary and Private Providers of Residential Child Care." Pp. 171–99 in *Public and Private Health Services,* edited by Anthony Culyer and Bengt Jönsson. Oxford: Basil Blackwell.

Knapp, Martin, Angela Hallam, Jennifer Beecham, and Barry Baines. 1999. "Private, Voluntary or Public? Comparative Cost-Effectiveness in Community Mental Health Care." *Policy and Politics* 27:25–41.

Knapp, Martin, and Spiros Missiakoulis. 1982. "Inter-Sectoral Cost Comparisons: Day Care for the Elderly." *Journal of Social Policy* 11:335–54.

Knapp, Martin, Eileen Robertson, and Corinne Thomason. 1990. "Public Money, Voluntary Action: Whose Welfare?" Pp. 183–218 in *The Nonprofit Sector: International and Comparative Perspectives,* edited by Helmut K. Anheier and Wolfgang Seibel. Berlin: de Gruyter.

Kramer, Ralph M. 2000. "A Third Sector for the Third Millennium?" *Voluntas* 11:1–23.

Kramer, Ralph M., Håkon Lorentzen, Willem B. Melief, and Sergio Pasquinelli. 1993. *Privatization in Four European Countries: Comparative Studies in Government-Nonprofit Sector Relationships.* Armonk, N.Y.: M. E. Sharpe.

Krashinsky, Michael. 1998. "Does Auspice Matter? The Case of Day Care for Children in Canada." Pp. 114–24 in *Private Action and the Public Good,* edited by Elisabeth S. Clemens and Walter W. Powell. New Haven, Conn.: Yale University Press.

Laville, Jean-Louis, and Marthe Nyssens, eds. 2001. *Les services sociaux entre associations, Etat et marché.* Paris: La Découverte/MAUSS/CRIDA.

Local Government Management Board and Central Council for Education and Training in Social Work. 1997. *Independent Sector Workforce Survey, 1996.* London: LGMB and CCETSW.

Lorenz, Walter. 1994. *Social Work in a Changing Europe.* London: Routledge.

Mauser, Elizabeth. 1998. "The Importance of Organizational Form: Parent Perceptions and Reality in the Day Care Industry." Pp. 124–37 in *Private Action and the Public Good,* edited by Walter W. Powell and Elisabeth S. Clemens. New Haven, Conn.: Yale University Press.

Morris, John R., and Suzanne W. Helburn. 2000. "Child Care Quality of Differences: The Role of Profit Status, Client Preferences and Trust." *Nonprofit and Voluntary Sector Quarterly* 29:377–99.

Netten, Ann, Mandy Ryan, Paul Smith, Diane Skatun, Andrew T. Healey, Martin R. J. Knapp, and Til Wykes. 2000. "The Development of a Measure of Social Care Outcome for Older People." Discussion paper #1690, Personal Social Services Research Unit, University of Kent at Canterbury, U.K.

Norton, Edward. 2000. "Long-Term Care." Pp. 955–94 in *Handbook of Health Economics,* edited by Anthony J. Culyer and Joseph P. Newhouse. Amsterdam: North-Holland.

Organisation for Economic Co-operation and Development. 1996. *Caring for Frail Elderly People: Policies in Evolution.* Paris: Organisation for Economic Co-operation and Development.

Perkin, Harold J. 1989. *The Rise of Professional Society: England since 1880.* London: Routledge.

———. 1996. *The Third Revolution: Professional Elites in the Modern World.* London: Routledge.

Prochaska, Frank. 1988. *The Voluntary Impulse: Philanthropy in Modern Britain.* London: Faber and Faber.

Quilgars, Deborah. 2000. *Low Intensity Support Services: A Systematic Review of Their Effectiveness.* Bristol, U.K.: Policy Press.

Ranci, Costanzo. 2002. "The Mixed Economy of Social Care in Europe." Pp. 25–45 in *Dilemmas of the Welfare Mix: The New Structure of Welfare in an Era of Privatization,* edited by Ugo Ascoli and Costanzo Ranci. New York: Kluwer.

Randall, Vicki. 2000. "Childcare Policy in the European States: Limits to Convergence." *Journal of European Public Policy* 7:346–68.

Rimlinger, Gaston V. 1963. "Welfare Policy and Economic Development: A Comparative Historical Perspective." *Journal of Economic History* 26:556–71.

Rose, Richard, and Phillip L. Davies. 1994. *Inheritance in Public Policy: Change without Choice in Britain.* New Haven, Conn.: Yale University Press.

Sako, Mari. 1992. *Prices, Quality and Trust.* Cambridge: Cambridge University Press.

Salamon, Lester M., Helmut K. Anheier, Reyinn List, Stefan Toepler, Wojciech Sokolowski, and Associates. 1999. "Global Civil Society: Dimensions of the Nonprofit Sector." Center for Civil Society Studies, Johns Hopkins University, Baltimore.

Salamon, Lester M., Helmut K. Anheier, Wojtek Sokolowski, and Associates. 1996. "The Emerging Sector: A Statistical Supplement." Institute for Policy Studies, Johns Hopkins University, Baltimore.

Schlesinger, Mark. 1998. "Mismeasuring the Consequences of Ownership: External Influences and the Comparative Performance of Public, For-Profit, and Private Nonprofit Organizations." Pp. 85–114 in *Private Action and the Public Good,* edited by Elisabeth S. Clemens and Walter W. Powell. New Haven, Conn.: Yale University Press.

Schunk, Michaela. 1998. "The Social Insurance Model of Care

for Older People in Germany." In *Rights and Realities: Comparing New Developments in Long-Term Care for Older People,* edited by Caroline Glendinning. Bristol, U.K.: Policy Press.

6, Perri, and Isabel Vidal. 1994. *Delivering Welfare: Repositioning Non-Profit and Co-operative Action in Western European Welfare States.* Barcelona: Centre d'Iniciatives de l'Economia Social.

6, Perri, and Jeremy Kendall, eds. 1997. *The Contract Culture in Public Services: Studies from Britain, Europe and the USA.* Aldershot, U.K.: Ashgate.

Smith, James A., and Karsten Borgmann. 2001. "Foundations in Europe: The Historical Context." Pp. 2–35 in *Foundations in Europe: Society, Management and Law,* edited by Andreas Schluter, Volker Then, and Peter Walkenhorst. London: Directory of Social Change.

Smith, Steven R. 2003. "Social Services." Pp. 149–86 in *The State of Nonprofit America,* edited by Lester M. Salamon. Washington D.C.: Brookings Institution Press.

Smith, Steven R., and Michael Lipsky. 1993. *Nonprofits for Hire: The Welfare State in the Age of Contracting.* Cambridge, Mass.: Harvard University Press.

Steinberg, Richard. 1993. "Public Policy and the Performance of Nonprofit Organizations: A General Framework." *Nonprofit and Voluntary Sector Quarterly* 22:13–31.

Thane, Pat. 1996. *The Foundations of the Welfare State.* Harlow, U.K.: Longman.

van Leeuwen, Marco H. D. 1994. "Logic of Charity: Poor Relief in Preindustrial Europe." *Journal of Interdisciplinary History* 24:589–613.

Walker, Alan, and Gerhard Naegele, eds. 1999. *The Politics of Old Age in Europe.* Buckingham, U.K.: Open University Press.

Webb, Adrian, and Gerald Wistow. 1987. *Social Work, Social Care and Social Planning: The Personal Social Services since Seebohm.* London: Longman.

Weisbrod, Burton. 1998. "Institutional Form and Organizational Behavior." Pp. 69–85 in *Private Action and the Public Good,* edited by Elisabeth S. Clemens and Walter W. Powell. New Haven, Conn.: Yale University Press.

Weisbrod, Burton, and Mark Schlesinger. 1986. "Public, Private, Nonprofit Ownership and the Response to Asymmetric Information: The Case of Nursing Homes." Pp. 133–50 in *The Economics of Nonprofit Institutions,* edited by Susan Rose-Ackerman. Oxford: Oxford University Press.

Wistow, Gerald, Martin Knapp, Brian Hardy, Julien Forder, Jeremy Kendall, and Rob Manning. 1996. *Social Care Markets: Progress and Prospects.* Buckingham, U.K.: Open University Press.

Wittenberg, Raphael, Linda Pickard, Adelina Comas-Herrera, Bleddyn Davies, and Robin A. Darton. 1998. *Demand for Long-Term Care: Projections of Long-Term Care Finance for Elderly People.* London: Personal Social Services Research Unit, London School of Economics and Political Science.

Woodroofe, Kathleen. 1962. *From Charity to Social Work in England and the United States.* London: Routledge.

Young, Dennis R. 1983. *If Not for Profit, for What?* Lexington, Mass.: Heath.

18

Nonprofit Organizations and the Intersectoral Division of Labor in the Arts

PAUL DIMAGGIO

This chapter takes stock of what we know about the role of nonprofit enterprise in the production and distribution of the arts (broadly defined), primarily in the United States. After briefly discussing measurement, I present data about the extent of nonprofit activity in a range of cultural subfields. I then review theoretical explanations of the prevalence of nonprofits in cultural industries and discuss some puzzles that existing theories do not adequately solve. After reviewing research and theory about behavioral differences between nonprofit and for-profit arts firms, I explore how the arts and culture sector is evolving in the face of demographic change, the weakening of cultural hierarchy, and the emergence of new production and distribution technologies. I conclude with a research agenda.

My perspective is ecological in that I believe that the nonprofit sector's role can best be understood in the context of the intersectoral division of labor. I define the arts very broadly to include works associated with high, popular, and folk cultures: *Othello,* the *Drew Cary Show,* and outdoor religious drama; *Swan Lake,* clogging, and Las Vegas chorus lines; and the works of Rembrandt, the products of Native American craft artists, and the poker-playing dogs of Cassius Marcellus Coolidge. This chapter does *not* cover types of culture excluded from the arts so defined, such as science, religion, law, cuisine, industrial design, architecture, and the humanities.

Organizations in the field of culture and the arts represent a small share of total nonprofit activity (2.3 percent of revenues and 1.9 percent of employment; Weitzman et al. 2002:xxxiii). Moreover, they tend to include more very small organizations and fewer large ones than most other nonprofit fields (Seley and Wolpert 2002:14). But the nonprofit arts sector has been growing: rates of increase in both employment and revenues between 1987 and 1997 exceeded those in the fields of health, education, religion, social services, civic associations, and private foundations (Weitzman et al. 2002:xxxiii, 42). The number of nonprofit arts-and-cultural organizations filing returns with the Internal Revenue Service also rose sharply (though not more than nonprofits in other fields) during the 1990s, from 17,290 in 1992 to 23,779 in 1998 (Weitzman et al. 2002, table 5.6).[1] Nonprofit cultural organizations are distinctive in that they rely more on individual donations (and on volunteering) and less on government grants and contracts than do nonprofits in most other fields (Brooks 2006). Especially in the performing arts, earned income also accounts for a large share of revenue.

WHERE ARE NONPROFIT SECTORS PREVALENT?

In what industries is the nonprofit sector prevalent? This question is more complex than it seems, especially if we wish to compare the roles of nonprofit and commercial entities engaged in providing broadly similar artistic services.

Dilemmas of Measurement and Enumeration

Before presenting the evidence we must take a brief detour into measurement and methodology. As we illuminate sectors of the arts that statistical systems ordinarily obscure, we shall begin to see the nonprofit arts sector as less professional and more participatory, less restricted to high culture and more widely spread throughout the cultural hierarchy, and less limited to the grand museum or concert hall and more ubiquitously integrated into our homes, schools, churches, and everyday lives.

Several methodological problems cloud our vision of the sector. First, for historical reasons, data about nonprofit and for-profit cultural organizations are often collected separately and are therefore difficult to compare. Second, nonprofit and commercial cultural enterprises are typically organized in different ways, which also makes comparison difficult. (Nonprofit arts organizations tend to internalize functions that the commercial sector accomplishes through contracting among separate entities [Heilbrun and Gray 2001].)

Finally, institutional factors render some organizations more likely to be counted than others even when their structures are comparable. Weakly institutionalized organizational forms and organizations that depart from accepted forms in arts fields that *are* strongly institutionalized are often socially and statistically invisible. Nonprofit cultural programs embedded within organizations that are not generally considered producers or distributors of the arts pose a special problem. Churches and universities are active arts presenters, often the most important outside of metropolitan areas. The 1999 National Congregational Survey reported that large majorities of U.S congregations sponsor regularly performing choirs or other musical groups. Many churches present theater performances, sponsor book circles, organize trips to performing arts events, or provide rehearsal space for performing arts groups in the wider community (Chaves 1999; Chaves and Marsden 2000). But because their artistic programs are small relative to their many other functions, church arts programs, like those of universities, rarely show up when cultural activity is measured. Community-based arts activities are likewise often sponsored by nonprofit organizations with broader mandates (for example, community-development or youth-assistance programs) and are therefore undercounted in canvasses of arts providers as well (Grams and Warr 2002).

The most elusive cultural organizations from the standpoint of enumeration are "minimalist organizations": unincorporated associations with minimal or intermittent program activities, part-time or volunteer staff, and tiny budgets (Halliday et al. 1987). Such tiny groups play important roles in many fields: training young artists, presenting difficult or innovative work, or serving audiences that may not ordinarily attend events run by more established arts nonprofits (Jeffri 1980). Much informal activity—that by musicians who enjoy playing together, then name themselves and perform an occasional public concert, or that by the collector who opens his or her home and collection to strangers for a few hours each week—edges almost imperceptibly into formal organization and may just as easily edge out again. The problem is not unique to the arts; similarly fluid boundaries divide informal temporary childcare and organized daycare centers. But it is especially pervasive in much of the art world (Stern and Seifert 2000b).

How Many Organizations Do Standard Data Sources Miss?

How many nonprofit arts organizations would we discover if we had as reliable data about embedded and minimalist organizations as about more well-established nonprofit entities? A few local studies that made heroic efforts to enumerate less visible regions of the nonprofit sector provide a basis for rough estimation. One study based on IRS Form 990 data about nonprofit theaters, opera companies, and orchestras that were members of their respective service organizations found that 20 percent of the theaters and opera companies and 40 percent of the orchestras were missing from the IRS files. The researchers attributed much of the difference to cases "in which the organization was part of another nonprofit institution" (Bowen et al. 1994:219), a problem that would affect Census of Business counts as well. A study of section 501(c)(3) nonprofit organizations in three large metropolitan areas that produce and exhibit the arts collected information about embedded as well as freestanding nonprofits from many sources. These researchers enumerated more than twice as many nonprofit entities as appeared in the same categories in the IRS Business Master File (Kaple et al. 1996:165). A contemporaneous study of one of the cities (Philadelphia) went further to collect data about small, unincorporated, community-based associations, which swell the roster of nonprofit cultural entities even more (Stern 2000:table 1).[2]

It may be useful to think of the nonprofit arts and cultural sector as comprising three rings (figure 18.1). The inner core includes arts-and-cultural organizations (as classified under the National Taxonomy of Exempt Entities [NTEE]) that are incorporated under section 501(c)(3) of the Internal Revenue Code. The second ring adds arts-and-cultural organizations or programs embedded in 501(c)(3) nonprofits that fall outside of the NTEE's "arts and culture" heading. The third ring includes unincorporated associations that share the purposes and the noncommercial orientation of their incorporated counterparts. If Philadelphia is typical, the number of entities doubles and the distributions of size, sponsorship, and mission change at each step outward from the core. Because organizations in the core are better documented than those in the outer circles, we must keep the latter in mind lest we propagate a distorted view of the nonprofit arts sector and its social role.

The Nonprofit Role by Subsector

The best comparative data about the roles of nonprofit and for-profit organizations in different arts-and-cultural industries and subsectors come from the 1997 U.S. Economic Census, which distinguishes between tax-exempt (including nonprofit and some public entities) and taxable (for-profit) establishments in several fields. The census is not a perfect source by any means: in addition to missing embedded, minimalist, and poorly institutionalized organizations, it lumps

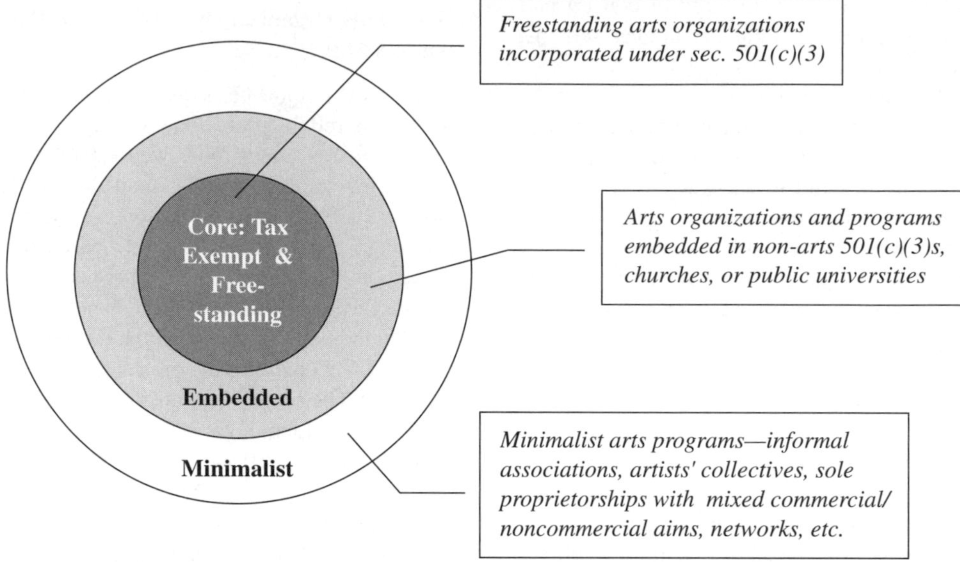

FIGURE 18.1. THE WORLD OF NONCOMMERCIAL ARTS ACTIVITIES

together public and private nonprofits, some categories (for example, museums) are aggregated at higher levels than we might wish, and it assumes (without asking) that firms in some industries are all for-profit. I draw on other sources of information throughout this chapter, but, as long as we remain aware of its limitations, the census provides the best single overview.[3]

Table 18.1 and figure 18.2 report the percentage of producers and distributors that are nonprofit organizations in each of several broadly defined arts industries, as well as the nonprofit share of revenues where such information is available. I present these data, first, to describe the broad outlines of the nonprofit sector's role in the arts and, second, to establish a set of cases that we can use to evaluate theories that attempt to explain variation among industries in the intersectoral division of labor.

Figure 18.2 provides an overview at a glance. To the right, we see industries that are almost entirely nonprofit: resident theaters, symphony orchestras, opera companies, chamber music groups, modern dance companies, historic sites (actually mixed nonprofit and public-sector), and community theater, all more than 90 percent nonprofit. Nonprofit organizations also dominate the fields of ballet, art museums (again, mixed public and private), choral music, stock theater, and children's theater.

By contrast, commercial enterprise accounts for more than 90 percent of dinner theaters, dance schools, dance or stage bands, jazz ensembles, and other music groups and artists. For-profit companies also dominate Broadway theater productions, touring theater companies, and circuses.[4] Art, drama, and music schools, Off-Broadway theater companies, folk-ethnic dance companies, and Off-Off Broadway theater groups are mixed in organizational form.

For the most part, whichever form dominates in number of establishments is even more dominant in its share of receipts. There are three notable exceptions to this rule, however. Nonprofits account for just 39 percent of art, drama, and music schools but 58 percent of revenues in this field. Commercial entities account for just 12 percent of choral groups, but these relatively few for-profit companies absorb more than half of the field's revenues. Similarly, just one in four ethnic dance companies is for-profit, but these garner almost 80 percent of the revenues. Smaller biases favor for-profits in the Off-Broadway and Off-Off Broadway theater.

To summarize, nonprofit (and public) organizations are hegemonic in the fields of art and historic exhibition, and nonprofits have a lock on the most prestigious regions of the performing arts. Other fields within the performing arts—for the most part those which, like jazz or ethnic dance, have won critical respect and scholarly attention relatively recently or, like pop music or dinner theater, still await it—are dominated by for-profit firms. In still other fields—arts education, circuses, several kinds of theaters—commercial and nonprofit enterprises compete. Although nonprofits compete with for-profits in some fields and with public enterprises in others, in no industry do we find concentrations of public and commercial enterprise without large nonprofit sectors.

How might these patterns be explained? Let us examine some theories that together can cast light on this complex array of statistics.

Three Explanations for the Intersectoral Division of Labor in the Arts

There are three kinds of scholarly accounts of the division of labor between nonprofit and for-profit organizations in the arts. One emphasizes the failure of markets to provide sufficient incentive for capitalists to invest in cultural enterprises that produce socially valued goods and services, and the need for philanthropic and government subsidization to

TABLE 18.1. PERCENTAGE OF ARTS FIRMS THAT ARE TAX-EXEMPT AND PERCENTAGE OF TAX-EXEMPT FIRMS' RECEIPTS/REVENUES BY CATEGORY*

NAICS Code	Category	Subcategory	Number of establishments	Receipts/ revenues ($1,000s)	Establishments that are tax-exempt (%)	Receipts/ revenues for tax-exempts (%)
7111102	Producers of live theatrical productions[a]		2,893	3,225,537	51.8	36.6
	Self-designated:	Resident theaters[a]	140	385,837	97.1	99.5
		Stock theaters[a]	102	72,969	81.4	89.4
		Broadway and traveling productions[a]	167	**	18.6	**
		Off-Broadway productions[a]	79	97,498	62.0	43.6
		Off-Off-Broadway productions[a]	131	114,774	77.1	57.2
		Children's theaters[a]	187	77,458	78.1	
		Dinner theaters[a]	45	**	2.2	**
		Community theaters[a]	478	131,550	91.2	89.5
		Other theatrical presentations[a]	309	241,698	35.3	22.4
	Not self-designated:	All other producers of live theatrical presentations[a]	1,255	1,082,151	32.5	22.9
711 pt.	Other theatrical producers and services[a]		3,479	4,912,754	18.0	21.1
7111200	Dance groups and artists[a]		530	432,690	68.5	74.7
	Self-designated:	Ballet companies[a]	146	184,745	89.7	99.0
		Modern dance companies[a]	96	51,423	93.8	95.9
		Folk/ethnic dance companies[a]	23	14,861	73.9	21.6
		Other dance groups, artists, presentations[a]	69	44,795	20.3	6.4
	Not self-designated:	All other dance groups and artists[a]	196	136,866	60.7	62.2
71111 pt.	Symphony orchestras, opera companies, chamber music organizations[a]		975	**	86.2	**
	Self-designated:	Opera companies[a]	122	539,986	94.3	99.7
		Symphony orchestras[a]	451	896,370	94.7	98.3
		Chamber music organizations[a]	150	69,164	94.0	98.9
	Not self-designated:	All other symphony orchestras, opera companies, chamber music organizations[a]	252	**	64.3	**
7111309	Other music groups and artists[a]		3,775	2,248,281	13.6	5.2
	Self-designated:	Dance or stage bands or orchestras[a]	279	85,801	5.7	2.6
		Choral groups[a]	239	85,353	88.3	46.6
		Jazz groups or artists[a]	159	69,254	7.5	11.0
		Other music groups, artists, or presentations[a]	1,326	1,233,131	4.6	1.6

TABLE 18.1 (CONTINUED)

NAICS Code	Category	Subcategory	Number of establishments	Receipts/ revenues ($1,000s)	Establishments that are tax-exempt (%)	Receipts/ revenues for tax-exempts (%)
	Not self-designated:	All other music groups and artists[a]	1,772	774,742	12.0	5.9
711 pt.	Other entertainers and entertainment groups[a]		4,018	3,076,520	1.7	0.8
7111901	Circuses[b]		87	289,048	19.5	7.2
71211	Museums and art galleries[b]		3,860	4,788,424	89.0	94.6
71212	Historic sites[b]		892	370,068	91.3	92.6
6116101	Dance schools[c]		5,367	781,732	5.0	8.4
6116102	Art, drama, and music schools[c]		1,887	560,803	39.2	57.6

*Number of establishments reflects those in business at any time in 1997. Revenues for taxable establishments are receipts; for tax-exempts, revenues. Self-designated establishments are those that responded to a mailed inquiry. Information on non-self-designated firms was gathered from administrative records.

**Data were suppressed by the Census Bureau owing to the risk of identifying a particular establishment.

[a] *Source:* Data are based on special tabulations from the 1997 Economic Census, prepared by the Census Bureau for the National Endowment for the Arts, Research Division, with the generous permission of whom they are reproduced here.

[b] *Source:* U.S. Census Bureau 2001a.

[c] *Source:* U.S. Census Bureau 2001b.

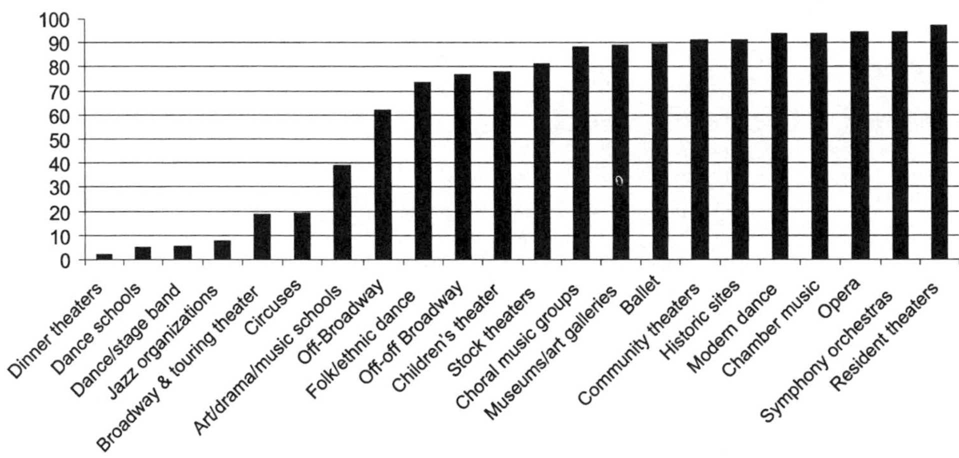

FIGURE 18.2. PERCENTAGE OF NONPROFIT ESTABLISHMENTS BY FIELD
Source: 1997 *U.S. Economic Census.* Various reports and special tabulations produced for the National Endowment for the Arts, Research Division, and graciously shared with the author.

which such market failure leads. The second set focuses less on the need for subsidies than on the way the organization of production and contracting in the arts poses specific problems that nonprofit organizations are well equipped to solve. The third perspective takes a historical approach, emphasizing the varying uses to which entrepreneurial artists and patrons have sought to put the nonprofit form in different eras.

Market-Failure and Related Approaches

The most venerable explanation for the prevalence of nonprofit organizations in some sectors of the arts is also the central justification for government subsidization: namely, that the best art costs more to produce or exhibit than people are willing to pay. For most exhibiting institutions, the economics behind this assertion is clear: art museums face huge fixed costs for building maintenance, security, conservation, and exhibition. For large urban art museums there is no price at which the number of visitors would generate sufficient revenue to cover these costs. The same is true of the live performing arts, as well: symphony orchestra concerts and Wagnerian opera, for example, are inherently expensive to produce, at least in the style to which audiences and critics are accustomed. Again, there is no price, it is argued, at which revenues will meet costs. Given this, so the story goes, it is crucial for government to promote the public good by subsidizing arts organizations so that their survival becomes economically feasible.

One may well ask (and some skeptics *have* asked) why this poses a problem. There are many goods and services for which demand is insufficient to produce viable markets, and few tears are shed at their demise. What makes the inadequacy of proprietary markets to sustain the arts so lamentable?

One argument is not about market failure so much as it is about *consumer* failure, that is, about the failure of consumers to demand as much art as they should. According to this view, the arts should be subsidized because they are "merit goods" whose intrinsic value justifies public action on their behalf (Netzer 1978). A variant of this argument holds that there *may* be sufficient demand to sustain production, but only if arts organizations priced their concerts and exhibits above what most of the public could pay, thus depriving potential consumers of what are believed to be the beneficial effects of exposure to the arts.

Other observers, however, argue that the nonprofit role in the arts really *is* rooted in market failure: that is, arts firms produce goods for which demand is sufficient but for which markets fail adequately to supply the full amount for which the public is willing to pay. (In practice, arts scholars seem to worry most about the market failures that reduce the supply of goods of which they approve.)

The argument is complicated because "market failure" is held to apply to the production of "public goods," goods for which consumption is *nonexcludable* and *nonrival* (see Steinberg, this volume). But arts organizations produce not public goods per se but what economists call "mixed goods," which have private and public components. The private-goods components (for example, a ticket buyer's experiences of concerts or exhibitions) are excludable (you can keep people from attending a concert or viewing an exhibit if they do not have tickets) and rival (two people cannot occupy the same seat or stand in the same position relative to an artwork). The public-goods components (educational spillovers, conservation of cultural heritage from which future generations may benefit, civic pride, and so on) are nonexcludable and nonrival. (See Throsby 2001 for a discussion of these public-good aspects of the arts.)

From this perspective, the arts are characterized by two kinds of market failure. The first reflects information problems that make it impossible for for-profit producers to exploit opportunities for price discrimination adequately to maximize revenues. The second derives from a producer's inability to charge anything at all for pure public-goods components of the arts product—for example, civic pride or heritage preservation. (For a more thorough discussion of the theories of collective goods and market failure as applied to the arts, see Steinberg, this volume.) Because of these market failures, then, for-profit firms either tend to produce too little of certain kinds of art or else do not enter the market at all.

An ingenious variant of the economic case for the nonviability of for-profit enterprise in much of the arts industry is the *cost-disease* theory that the economists William Baumol and William Bowen put forward in their landmark study *The Performing Arts: The Economic Dilemma.* In their account, the plight of performing arts firms can only worsen. The largest component of a performing arts organization's budget comprises labor costs for performers, technicians, set designers, and other highly skilled workers. Because live performances take place in real time and in one location, there are few ways to increase productivity. Yet arts organizations compete for employees in the same labor market as firms that can and do use technology to boost productivity, and these latter pass on some of the gains to employees in the form of higher wages. Constrained to keep up with rising labor costs in the economy at large but unable to boost revenues by raising productivity, performing arts groups fall ever further behind (Baumol and Bowen 1966).

Such economic accounts explain why, given stable aesthetic conventions, nonprofit arts organizations require subsidies in order to survive. They do not, however, explain why arts organizations *get* the subsidies they need. Demand for many artistic goods and services (most touring light-opera productions, slides for kinetoscopes, mechanical player pianos) has fallen below the level necessary to support the survival of firms that produce them. How, then, can we explain the persistence of nonprofit arts organizations in the face of adverse market conditions?

For that we need a theory of demand for public goods. We find such a theory in an explanation that addresses not simply the question of why the market does not work but also the issue of why we have private nonprofit as well as public provision of cultural goods and services. According to this argument, noncommercial organizations (including arts organizations) provide "collective consumption goods," the benefits of which cannot be limited to those who pay for them. As noted above, most arts programs (exhibits, performances, community projects) are "mixed goods" with both private and collective features. People who buy tickets to orchestra concerts or participate in neighborhood mural projects, for example, capture some unique benefits (such as entertainment or artistic training). But the rest of us benefit (whether we pay or not) from the survival of orchestras and the music they play or from the presence of murals in our communities (Throsby 2001). Because most ticket buyers will pay a price that covers only their private benefit, revenues fail to reflect the true value (private plus collective) of a performance. Only government, with its power to tax, can step in to make up the difference with subsidies (Weisbrod 1990).

According to public-choice theory, democratic governments provide subsidies that reflect the demand for public or mixed goods (or services) of the "median voter": the person in the middle of the range of values that voters place on the good in question. Where demand for a good or service develops gradually, the first citizens who care about it will create voluntary associations to satisfy their demand. As incomes rise and demand increases to the point at which the median voter desires the good or service, government enters the picture. At this point, citizens who want more than the median voter does will continue to subsidize private voluntary organizations to supplement the quantity or quality of government production. As people get wealthier still, they may substitute private goods for collective goods (Weisbrod 1990), as occurred when many U.S. cities stopped supporting municipal bands as sales of phonograph records increased in the 1920 and 1930s.

The public-choice model can be generalized to heterogeneity not only in the amount of demand but in the nature of demand, as well. Thus ethnic, religious, or political heterogeneity may induce nonprofit rather than public supply of collective goods if members of different groups want different types of programming (James 1987). Locational variation may matter, as well: where demand is geographically lumpy, the role of local government will exceed that of national government, and regional differences in the role of nonprofit sectors will also be greater.

Industrial-Organization Approaches

If we grant that (again given conventionally accepted standards of quality and craft) many nonprofit arts organizations cannot support their activities with earned revenues and that, furthermore, heterogeneity of demand means that government will supply fewer exhibitions, classes, and performances than many citizens desire, we still need to explain what it is about the nonprofit form that makes it such an attractive instrument for bringing demand and supply into balance. The availability of subsidization is an obvious answer, but many nonprofits in the arts sector get relatively little by way of government or foundation aid, especially compared to the money they raise from private individuals. Moreover, we still need to explain why government chooses to give grants to nonprofits (and to provide the tax deductibility that subsidizes private contributions to them) in the first place.

Economists who study organization and contracting have proposed additional reasons why the nonprofit form solves the problems of cultural organizations, especially those in the performing arts. These arguments emphasize the ways in which the nonprofit form enables arts organizations to make credible commitments to, and thereby induce the trust of, contributors and volunteers.

Hansmann (1981) argues that performing arts organizations facing insufficient revenues to mount work of the quality to which they aspire use the nonprofit form to take advantage of variability in demand for their product. Whereas starving music students labor to find $20 for standing room, wealthy patrons who believe that opera's survival is essential for civilization will pay much more. One can tap a limited portion of this variability by charging different prices for different types of seat. But one can exploit much more of it by operating two markets: one for tickets and one for contributions (often sold as memberships of different kinds, pegged to the size of annual gifts). Hansmann argues that arts groups must adopt the nonprofit form to assure subscribers and patrons that they will use contributed funds for program purposes rather than to line their own pockets.[5]

Caves (2000:225ff.) suggests an additional mechanism that helps explain the prevalence of nonprofits in some performing arts industries. Performing arts companies compete for the services of the most talented performers. Many such artists, Caves argues, are as concerned with working conditions (especially the amount of creative control that they can exercise over their work) as with income. It is difficult to specify contractually the relative voice of artists and businesspeople in making decisions that affect artistic quality. Nonprofit status serves as a signal to artists that a performing arts firm will be more likely to accord artistic values high importance. In other words, because patrons and artists perceive nonprofits as sharing their own values and interests to a greater degree than do businesses, nonprofits have privileged access to each of these groups.

Still other economists, drawing on "club theory," view governance as the key to understanding the effectiveness of the nonprofit form (Kuan 2001). A relatively small number of committed stakeholders provide most of the contributed income or labor power (or both) for many cultural organizations, especially small ones. Such stakeholders—who may be customers with a strong preference for quality levels that a profit-maximizing entrepreneur would not provide or artists who are committed to work for which a large market does not yet exist—create nonprofits to meet this demand. By forming a board comprising themselves or like-minded persons, they ensure that their aesthetic preferences will constrain business decisions and, at the same time, create a structure for inducing ongoing contributions.

New forms of cultural nonprofits emerge in response to new organizational problems. Thus Frey (1994) explains explosive growth in the number of nonprofit performing arts festivals in Europe during the 1980s and 1990s as the result of attractive organizational properties that solved economic and regulatory problems that weighed heavily on government-sponsored performing arts groups. In addition to benefiting from tourism (by locating in attractive travel destinations), nonprofit festivals employ the for-profit technique of short-term contracting for artistic talent (which they can do because they operate in the summer, when other organizations are dark) in order to reduce fixed costs, minimize risk, and avoid unions and government regulation.

Historical and Political Approaches

Market-failure theories explain why some arts organizations require subsidization. The industrial-organization literature explains the advantages that the nonprofit form presents to organizations whose managers hope to attract grants or contributions. But neither explains the particular cultural fields in which nonprofit entrepreneurs have been active or the reasons for their success.

In order to understand such patterns we need to attend to history and politics. History is important because opportunities for successful entrepreneurship vary over time and because the sequence in which different types of artists and patrons adopted the nonprofit form both created models and limited opportunities for their successors. Politics matters because the ability of artistic communities to take advantage of the nonprofit form depends on power and influence as much as on need. Seen from a historical perspective, intersectoral divisions of labor that appear natural today reflect the past capacity of particular groups to mobilize entrepreneurial resources.

In the nineteenth century, urban upper classes in the United States found trustee-governed nonprofit arts organizations to be useful tools for defining a prestigious status culture to which they and their children would have privileged access. For these emerging elites, symphony orchestras and art museums were important components of an institutional complex that included preparatory schools, universities, private libraries, and exclusive social clubs.[6] The nonprofit form (which, as Hall, this volume, demonstrates, was less clearly differentiated from its proprietary counterpart in the late nineteenth century than it is today) was attractive to museum and orchestra founders because it provided a stable framework for an arduous process of clarifying the distinctions between art, on one hand, and entertainment and fashion, on the other, and because trustee governance ensured that the founders would remain securely in control. As I have argued elsewhere (DiMaggio 1982; see also Levine 1990), the very strength of the conceptual distinction between high culture and popular entertainment throughout much of the twentieth century was itself a product of the institutional differentiation of nonprofit and proprietary enterprise.

The first part of the twentieth century witnessed a diffusion of the trustee-governed nonprofit arts, first to smaller cities across the United States and then to certain arts (opera, theater, contemporary art, the dance) that had previously been organized along commercial lines. Entrepreneurial patrons in these disciplines, often excluded by virtue of religion, ethnicity, or gender from the elite networks from whom the trustees of orchestras and encyclopedic art museums were selected, explicitly emulated the institutional design of the museums and orchestras, though for many years they were unable to attain the same degree of wealth, prestige, or stability (DiMaggio 1992).

Artists, especially artists of color, were notably absent from the ranks of nonprofit cultural entrepreneurs during the first half of the twentieth century. Nor did such new art forms as film and photography receive much nonprofit sponsorship at first. Yet the nonprofit form was not solely the reserve of the wealthy. During the late nineteenth and early twentieth centuries, immigrant groups created many voluntary associations devoted to communal cultural practice (for instance, the ubiquitous *turnervereins* of the German immigrant communities) or commercial enterprises with cultural missions (the Yiddish theaters, parts of the immigrant press) that provided communal vehicles for artistic and cultural expression. Established charities (for example, Chicago's Hull House and other settlements) and associations (for example, the National Federation of Women's Clubs) were also active in the arts.

By the 1950s the contours of the intersectoral division of labor in the arts were well defined. All that remained was to fill them in, a project epitomized by the Ford Foundation's arts program, which in the 1960s and 1970s engaged in massive institution-building efforts in the fields of theater and dance. The expansion of the role of the federal government in the 1960s and 1970s disrupted what turned out to be a surprisingly fragile equilibrium, however, by providing incentives and opportunities for adoption of the nonprofit form by groups that had been unable to use it in the past. By the time the tide of federal expansion was turned back in the 1980s, an institutional framework of state and local arts agencies, private foundations, and corporate grant makers had emerged to sustain a range of purposes that were foreign to the aesthetic traditionalism that had characterized most U.S. art patronage (with some notable exceptions in New York and a few other urban centers) until 1960.

The rise of institutional patronage coincided with the unintended production of a mass market for serious art due to the largest expansion of schooling in American history during the 1960s. Education has been the best predictor of interest in the sorts of arts experiences that nonprofits provide for as long as anyone has studied the topic, so the doubling of the percentage of Americans attending college provided a major demand-side stimulus at precisely the moment when an unprecedented infusion of grants and contracts bolstered the supply side. The expansion of higher education (and the concomitantly greater role of universities as arts presenters) also contributed to an overproduction of artists (relative to previous numbers and to the market for their services) during the post-Vietnam era. Not only were artists underemployed but, being college-educated, they had the skills to create and administer nonprofit organizations and, in some cases, the networks to receive modest but important grant support from state or local arts agencies. These factors contributed to an unprecedented increase in the number of nonprofit cultural organizations.

Institutional patronage worked in at least four ways to expand the scope of the nonprofit arts after the 1960s. First, it provided direct incentives to adopt the nonprofit form in industries where small enterprises became eligible for government and foundation grants that could make a big difference. For example, whereas almost all small presses were proprietary before the 1970s, new literary presses often incorporated as nonprofits (and some old ones converted to the nonprofit form) in order to become eligible for grants. Second, institutional patronage provided legitimacy to art forms that had been effectively shut out of the nonprofit sector because of their lack of access to philanthropic capital. Whereas private donors may spend their money however they want, government must justify its funding priorities. Ignoring jazz, craft and folk art, and other parts of the American living cultural heritage was difficult to justify. Moreover, such art forms were attractive investments for arts agencies in states that had few orchestras, art museums, and theater companies. Although the amount of funding going to organizations in such fields was a drop in the bucket compared to grants to orchestras, museums, and theater and dance companies, institutional patronage opened the door to nonprofit entrepreneurs in these areas.

Third, the scope and client base of nonprofit arts programs grew in response to what Lester Salamon (1987) has called "third-party government": the choice by governments to pay nonprofits to carry out programs that public agencies might otherwise have undertaken. The expansion of federal social programs in the 1970s (and of state programs later on) provided funds for arts programs that emphasized the utility of the arts for such purposes as community empowerment, economic development, and the salvation of "at-risk youth." Finally, the rise of institutional subsidization led to a mobilization of arts constituencies that enhanced the capacity of artists and their supporters to pursue shared interests. An early priority of the National Endowment for the Arts was to create a network that would support its requests for larger appropriations, for which purpose it employed congressionally mandated pass-through grants to any state that created a state arts agency. By the early 1970s all the states had done so, and many of these agencies were themselves encouraging the proliferation of local arts agencies throughout their states, as well as advocacy groups (in which staff or trustees of their grantees often played central roles). Although attempts to influence the legislative process were often ineffective, a by-product of these efforts was the production of a discourse that highlighted the instrumental value of the arts and justified the missions of nonprofits that used the arts in the service of education and community building.

For all these reasons—the expansion of government's role (and the shift from direct government service provision to contracting with nonprofit third parties), the rise of public and other forms of institutional funding of the arts, the explosion of higher education, and the oversupply of artists—the groups that were interested in and capable of using the nonprofit form to pursue artistic missions, and the nature of these missions, became markedly more diverse during the last third of the twentieth century.

We can draw five general lessons from this narrative. First, we should be cautious in modeling the division of labor between nonprofit and commercial enterprise as a consequence of organizational choices based on characteristics of organizations and arts forms as they currently exist. The kinds of art that nonprofit cultural organizations exhibit or present and the way they present it have coevolved over time with their organizational forms and therefore cannot be presumed to have caused the organizational peculiarities of nonprofit arts providers. Second, the nonprofit legal form is to some extent an empty shell that can be employed for an almost unlimited range of noncommercial (and some commercial) purposes, depending on who has the motivation and capacity to use it. Third, government plays a critical role in defining the scope of nonprofit activity by altering the incentives for entrepreneurs to use the nonprofit form. Fourth, a significant predictor of the extent of nonprofit activity in specific cultural subfields is the capacity of those who stand to benefit from it to organize and to overcome free-rider problems. Fifth, it follows from the first four points that we should not be surprised if the nonprofit sector's cultural role changes markedly over time.

Remaining Conundrums

Each of the explanations reviewed here casts light on the role of nonprofit organizations in the intersectoral division of labor, and together they do better than each one does on its own. As with any kind of mystery, finding the right solution requires that we identify motive, opportunity, and means. The *market-failure* approach goes far to solve the problem of *motive;* the *industrial-organization* view explains *opportunity;* and the *historical and political* perspective helps us understand the *means* by which entrepreneurs succeeded in making nonprofits effective vehicles for the purposes they pursued.

These theories account reasonably well for the intersectoral division of labor we observe today. That division of labor has several striking features. First, the relative importance of the nonprofit form varies less between artistic media (visual, musical, dramatic, literary) or organizational functions (exhibition, presentation) than within them. Most arts industries (broadly defined) have islands of nonprofit activity: scholarly and poetry presses, classical music presenters, art museums, resident theaters, and ballet or modern dance companies. Nonprofit organizations are responsible for live presentation and exhibition of most of what has traditionally been regarded as "high culture." For-profit concerns are dominant in the mechanical or digital distribution of all art forms and in live presentations and exhibitions that appeal to large and educationally heterogeneous audiences. For the most part, nonprofit sectors promote objectives—conserving a permanent collection of great art, keeping many musicians on long-term contract, developing and educating a committed audience—that require relatively large investments and enough organizational stability to see them bear fruit. By contrast, for-profit enterprise dominates sectors that rely on technology to keep variable costs very low and attempt to reach huge audiences through broadcasting and retail channels.

With respect to the division of labor between public and nonprofit organizations, the data are roughly consistent with the public-choice story. The few surveys that have asked Americans about their willingness to spend tax dollars on particular kinds of culture suggest that most people support assistance to institutions that are perceived as serving a broad educational function (museums, libraries, arts programs in the schools) whereas fewer favor support for performing arts groups or individual artists (DiMaggio and Pettit 1997). Consistent with this, the public sector is best represented in the former areas. Within the arts per se, between 70 and 75 percent of art museums are nonprofit, a proportion that has been stable for decades (Macro Systems

1979; Schuster 1998:table 3; Heilbrun and Gray 2001:187). Moreover, approximately one in five nonprofit art museums, including some of the largest, such as New York's Metropolitan Museum of Art and the Philadelphia Museum, are hybrids in which local government owns the buildings and grounds but nonprofit entities control collections and endowments (Schuster 1998:tables 7, 8). Consistent with public-choice theory, public and hybrid art museums appear to be concentrated among generalist museums in large cities, whereas specialized museums and those in small places are predominantly nonprofits.[7]

Nonetheless, there are patterns for which our theories do not account and which therefore represent areas of opportunity for research and theory development. In highlighting these opportunities, I expand the range of variation beyond the kinds of organizations that show up in the Census of Business by examining data about embedded and minimalist organizations and by looking more closely at industries that the Census assumes are entirely proprietary for signs of nonprofit life.[8]

Efficient Boundaries

A particular gap in research and theory concerning arts organizations has been the relative absence of work that addresses the issue of what economists call "efficient boundaries"—that is, the question of which activities fall within the boundaries of the firm and which are either excluded or incorporated through contracting. Most theories take the structure and activities of firms as givens from which one can deduce which organizational form is most appropriate. By contrast, I believe that we must endogenize organizational structure and activities if we are to understand the intersectoral division of labor. This is the case in at least two ways.

First, we need to understand why some performing arts activities are articulated by contract whereas others are internalized within single organizations. As we have seen, when numerous activities—the acquisition of talent by means of long-term contracts, facilities management, and marketing—are internalized in a single firm, the nonprofit form is more likely to prevail. But in many performing arts fields—from Hollywood movie production and Broadway theater to jazz clubs and rock concerts—artistic activities and management are articulated by means of contract rather than hierarchy, an approach that economists sometimes refer to as "flexible specialization" (Storper 1989; Scott 2002).

Jazz is the outstanding puzzle in this regard, for the genre has all the hallmarks of high culture—critical respect, a highly educated audience, representation in university music departments, and eligibility for government and foundation grants—*except* a dominant role for nonprofit organizations in its presentation (Peterson 1972; Lopes 2002). Why are jazz quartets for-profit and chamber quartets nonprofit? Jazz artists' work is labor-intensive, only a handful benefit from recording contracts and, consequently, technological economies of scale, and only a few can cross-subsidize their artistic work with teaching appointments in universities (Heckathorn and Jeffri 2003). Typically, jazz artists, like popular music artists, enter into short-term performance contracts with proprietors of commercial nightclubs, drinking establishments, or concert halls.

One explanation lies in the availability of grant support. For organizations in art forms that gained a foothold in the system of philanthropic support when the window of opportunity was open (DiMaggio 1992), the nonprofit form is an effective way for managers and artists to limit risk. By contrast, in genres for which contributed funds are rarely available, risk is handled by decoupling performance and presentation. Most performance contracts in popular music protect the proprietor from long-term risk, transferring it instead to performers, who ordinarily work for a small fee and a percentage of the admissions charges. (Broadway and many Off- and Off-Off Broadway theaters employ a similar system, except that the risk in the former is shared with investors rather than entirely assumed by the artists.) In effect, artists subsidize the artistic performance with proceeds from "day jobs" or family resources (Kreidler 1996; Alper and Wassall 2000).

Another explanation may be related to the distribution of talent. The founders of America's orchestras (and the creators of nonprofit theaters who emulated them decades later) sought an alternative to short-term artists' contracts because they believed (with good reason) that they could not achieve satisfactory levels of quality unless, first, they created long-term relationships among artists, who could achieve ensemble skills, and, second, they created long-term relationships with audiences, whom they could educate to appreciate the qualitative superiority they hoped to achieve. Similarly, art museums (compared to earlier for-profit museums) eventually sought to create significant permanent collections, which in turn required long-term commitments to facilities.

Given advances in the training of performing artists and increases in the number of talented, committed artists, short-term contracting may have become a more efficient means of organizing, for presenters if not for artists. Recording studios, for example, can contract with studio musicians by the session because they have immensely skilled labor pools from whom to choose (Peterson and White 1979). Similarly, members of small ensembles in every musical genre subsidize production in order to keep quality high. If this explanation is correct, then we might expect increases in the quality of performers (which may be indexed by local measures of artists' population density) to be associated with more contracting in such fields as classical music and theater. We might also find contracting more common when for-profit organizations can benefit parasitically from nonprofits' investments (for example, when small clubs or restaurants can contract with musicians who have learned to play together in a nonprofit orchestra or university jazz band).

The second efficient-boundary issue has to do with the ways in which for-profit media companies' choices provide opportunities for nonprofit entrepreneurs. For-profit cultural sectors, even the most concentrated and capital-intensive media industries, spawn oases of nonprofit activity. Public television emerged from the frustration of intellectuals and educators with the quality of commercial broadcasting. Nonprofit poetry and fiction magazines respond to the difficulties that young writers face in finding an audience. Most university presses publish works of scholarship (and in some cases, of fiction or poetry) for audiences too small to justify production by commercial publishers. Nonprofit media arts centers and public and private universities present independent and foreign films (although their numbers and importance have diminished with the spread of pay cable movie channels and video and DVD rentals). In many cases, efforts by publicly held media companies to slough off activities that, though profitable, produced poor margins account for the role of the nonprofit sector in these fields. (Public television emerged as a significant broadcast alternative only in the 1960s, after network executives stopped worrying about intellectual respectability and abandoned earnest public-affairs and dramatic programming.)[9] A theory that focused exclusively on the nonprofit sector (as opposed to the broader ecology of media and cultural production) would be hard pressed to explain such developments.

Is the Cost Disease Curable?

The cost-disease hypothesis is consistent with the results of analyses of change over time in performing arts institutions' cost structures, for labor costs have indeed increased more quickly than other expenses, consuming an ever greater share of performing arts budgets (Caves 2000; Heilbrun and Gray 2001). Yet it is not clear that the cost-disease hypothesis *explains* this trend. First, the nonprofit arts have expanded dramatically in the past thirty years. Many organizational deficits reflect increased fixed costs as a result of imprudent expansion (sometimes encouraged by donors or grant makers; McDaniel and Thorn 1991); others reflect reduced market share due to greater competition. Second, structural change in the U.S. economy—a prolonged decline in the manufacturing sector, where productivity growth through technological advance is easiest to achieve—should have reduced the cost disease's severity. Third, where deficits do reflect higher wages, the cost disease is not always responsible: in some cases, as when orchestra salaries rose precipitously in response to large investments by the Ford Foundation during the 1970s, foundation grants and government subsidies cause, rather than respond to, such increases (Caves 2000:254; Frey 1996).[10]

Fourth, performing arts organizations *have* found ways to boost productivity: for-profit theaters produce lavish shows with several casts and send them out on the road to increase the ratio of variable to fixed costs (Frey 1996); nonprofit theaters mount plays with smaller casts and less elaborate stage designs; studio ensembles (and some live pop performers) employ drum machines or replace string sections with synthesizers (Colonna et al. 1993). That they can do this demonstrates the principle that cost structures in the arts reflect conventions of the craft—shared ideas about what constitutes good practice—more than technical necessities (Becker 1982). Whatever we think of the aesthetic results of such devices, they represent economically viable means of fighting the cost disease.

Embedded Programs and Organizations

It is tempting to discount embedded organizations as messy exceptions that can be ignored in efforts to explain the nonprofit role. But if, as I have argued, embedded arts organizations and programs are all around us—in schools and universities, in churches, in community action agencies—then any theory of nonprofit origins must take them into account. None of our theories do.

The publishing industry (newspapers, magazines, and books) illustrates this well. Most of the field's nonprofits are embedded in other organizations, with the result that the nonprofit presence deviates from what one would predict on the basis of theories of market failure or public choice. The collective goods produced by newspapers are arguably as valuable as those produced, for example, by modern dance companies, and many observers believe that greater diversity and competition in that industry would enhance democratic debate. Yet all or almost all daily and weekly newspapers enumerated in the Census (U.S. Census Bureau 2001c) are proprietary in form. Like performing arts organizations, newspaper staffs are populated by professionals (journalists) with professional standards; also like performing arts organizations, they cannot convince consumers to pay prices that would cover the costs of living up to those standards. As Jencks (1986) observed, all this should make the newspaper industry ripe for the nonprofit presence it lacks.

By contrast, there is a greater, albeit still small, nonprofit presence among periodical publishers, even though the greater diversity of perspectives among national magazines and the relatively less daunting economics of the industry (compared to newspaper publishing) might lead us to expect very few. One might anticipate that nonprofits would be found primarily among literary and poetry magazines, the least commercially viable subsector and one that promotes a valued social function. Yet literary magazines are rarely tax-exempt (except when opportunities for government or foundation grants provide incentives): most of the nation's roughly five hundred poetry magazines are formally for-profit, mom-and-pop operations.[11] A few freestanding large-circulation periodicals devoted to serious debate or minority viewpoints—for example, *Ms., Harper's,* and the *Nation*—are nonprofit, but they are not typical. Most nonprofits that publish magazines do so to support such missions as running churches or trade unions, representing professional or industry groups *(Museum News),* or providing services to their members *(Modern Maturity).* In other words, we have nonprofit magazines because larger nonprofit entities believe they can help them pursue their broader goals.

The same is also true of book publishers. Because the trade publishing industry has experienced much recent consolidation (only two major proprietary U.S. trade publishers have escaped absorption by a handful of multinational media firms), many observers believe that the nonprofit subsector's role has become more important than it used to be (Miller 1997; Greco 2000). The core of nonprofit book publishing includes slightly more than one hundred university presses, which publish scholarly (and sometimes literary) works insufficiently commercial to interest large proprietary houses (Powell 1985).[12] In addition, there are approximately two hundred other nonprofit presses, including a few independent literary publishers and a larger number of embedded enterprises, such as the New England Science Fiction Association Press and Gospel Literature International.[13] Once again, much of the nonprofit role in publishing reflects the embeddedness of book publishing in such other nonprofits as universities and voluntary associations.

Embeddedness complicates our understanding and obscures our view of the field of performing arts presentation in a different way. *Presenters,* by which I refer to organizations that specialize in booking acts into venues and selling tickets to the public (as opposed to organizations that employ artists on long-term contract), have long occupied an important specialized role in the performing arts. Early in the twentieth century, women's clubs and music clubs formed a network of local presenters that sponsored performances of touring orchestras throughout the United States. By the 1920s, for-profit promoters such as Arthur Judson's Columbia Concert Management had learned to use such nonprofit associations so effectively that some contemporaries cried "monopoly" (Kirstein 1938:50).

Significant contemporary presenters run a wide gamut from proprietary nightclubs to municipal arenas to nonprofit performing arts centers. A large portion of the auditorium business is controlled by Clear Channel, a Texas-based entertainment conglomerate with large holdings in radio and outdoor advertising. Many nonprofit organizations are also in the presenting business: performing arts facilities, fairs and festivals, university-sponsored concert series, and churches, theaters, and orchestras that book outside acts into their own spaces when they are not using them (Hager and Pollak 2002). The public sector, almost always in the form of municipal government, also plays an active role, building, owning, and sometimes managing performing sites (Strom 2001).

Much of the for-profit sector's role in music presentation is invisible because it is embedded in restaurants and bars, as well as in the nation's more than 250 gambling casinos (U.S. Census Bureau 2001e).[14] Embeddedness also obscures the role of large public and nonprofit universities, most of which present touring performing arts presentations, as do many smaller institutions. Less visible are the hundreds of churches and community associations that present performing arts events and art exhibitions. Corporations also have embedded arts programs: about four hundred have art collections, many of which are sometimes exhibited to the public (Martorella 1990), and corporate contracts sustain more than three hundred firms that specialize in producing "industrials" (business-themed theatrical events for corporate management and sales meetings; Bell 1987).

Consideration of the role of the public sector in the arts is complicated by the importance of arts programs embedded in universities, many of them public, and is further complicated by the fact that public and private universities are so similar in their programming. Although we ordinarily do not think of government as an important part of the U.S. music business, the public sector produces much classical music via the orchestras of state universities (and much popular music as well, via high school, college, and military bands). This state of affairs has more to do with institutionalized expectations of universities than with the kinds of factors to which economic theories call attention.

The role of nonprofits in arts education also looks different once embedded organizations are taken into account. For example, 95 percent of 5,367 dance schools reported in the Census of Business (table 18.1) are proprietary. But the Census fails to measure dance instruction provided in colleges and universities. Women's colleges were the first U.S. institutions to treat the dance as a respectable activity, albeit often as part of their physical education programs (Kendall 1979), and many institutions of higher education remain involved in dance training.

I am aware of no research that attempts to explain systematically the kinds of artistic programs that entities outside the arts choose to organize and incorporate or attempts to analyze the economics of embedded nonprofits. Many of the cases reviewed here share one of two things: cross-subsidization of marketing and facilities expenses for arts activities out of fixed costs of the sponsoring institutions (for example, in churches, cocktail lounges, or universities) and opportunities to subsidize fixed costs with grants awarded in support of arts programs (for example, in community agencies and other nonprofits that depend on soft money). In addition, some arts programming appears to be expected of certain kinds of organizations (for instance, church choirs or university theaters) or to serve as a market signal for unobservable qualities (for example, the fad for gamelan orchestras in elite liberal arts colleges).

Issues related to size, capital intensity, and fixed costs.

Existing theories do not account for what appears to be a ∩-shaped relation between capital-intensiveness and form. As noted above, the cultural producers with the greatest fixed costs—television networks, book publishers, record companies, and so on—are predominantly for-profit, relying on economies of scale and scope to produce profits. Within arts fields that are predominantly nonprofit, however, this relation is reversed, and the nonprofit form is more commonly used by organizations that have relatively high fixed costs, for example, performing arts organizations that combine presentation and performance (especially those that own facilities) and museums, which must keep up facilities and conserve collections. Organizations with low fixed costs (jazz ensembles, chamber quartets, Off-Off-Broadway theater companies) are less likely to incorporate as 501(c)(3)s, even when their missions are consistent with nonprofit status.

Many "minimalist" organizations never make it into the official statistics. In classical music, volunteer-run, intermittently performing community orchestras and amateur chamber groups are ubiquitous, and only the more organized have acquired 501(c)(3) status. Unincorporated chamber ensembles outnumber chamber groups that are incorporated as nonprofits or that operate as formal subunits of symphony orchestras or of university or conservatory music programs (King 1980). In all fields, much performing is done by individual artists (unincorporated sole proprietorships, as it were).

Unincorporated associations are also active elsewhere in the performing arts. The Unified Database of Arts Organizations (UDAO, a comprehensive database produced by the Urban Institute and the National Assembly of State Arts Agencies; see note 8) lists more than five thousand theater groups and thirty-five hundred dance groups not counted by the Census. Although it classifies them as "nonprofit," one suspects that relatively few have their own tax exemptions. Approximately two thousand are amateur community groups, and more than one thousand are college or university ensembles. Most craft artists, painters, and sculptors are solo practitioners operating directly in the marketplace rather than creating artworks as employees of organizations (Jeffri and Greenblatt 1994). Many hold day jobs in schools, art centers, or other nonprofit or public institutions that provide both a living wage and access to studio space. (At the opposite extreme, the representational artist Thomas Kinkade formed a corporation, the Media Arts Group, which owns or franchises a national chain called Thomas Kinkade Signature Galleries that is traded on the New York Stock Exchange [Orlean 2001], and pop singer David Bowie incorporated himself in order to sell "Bowie Bonds" secured against his future royalties [Steyn 1997].) Finally, although no one has tried to count them, literally thousands of commercial bars, restaurants, and retail establishments (not to mention public airports and nonprofit schools and hospitals) maintain small exhibition spaces that, in the aggregate, serve numerous patrons.

Our theories of nonprofit organization make little room for the populous smallest end of the size distribution, where individuals shade into informal clubs and associations and informal groups occasionally become formal organizations. Yet such entities, like larger and more visible firms, make (or avoid) choices about organizational form. And, together, they embody many values and pursue many missions associated with the nonprofit cultural sector as a whole.

Questions about the public-private division of labor.

Public-choice models focus on goods for which demand rises over time and posit a dynamic in which government and nonprofits cede some of their role to commercial substitutes as incomes rise. Yet if one discounts activities embedded in public schools and universities, there are few cultural sectors in which government and commercial firms coexist: perhaps only broadcasting (where nonprofits and public stations constitute the public broadcasting system), museums (where commercial entities are a small and poorly understood minority), and performing arts presentation. Public enterprises are surprisingly absent from cultural sectors that are predominantly for-profit. In virtually all such fields, nonprofit organizations constitute the noncommercial minority.[15] The reasons for this pattern are not well understood.

The respective roles of public and nonprofit sectors in community cultural leadership warrant further study. In 2000 there were approximately four thousand local arts agencies, of which twelve hundred had paid professional staff. Formerly called "arts councils," local arts agencies present arts events, sponsor arts-education programs, make grants, manage facilities, provide services to artists, and engage in community cultural planning. The public sector is dominant in cities with populations greater than five hundred thousand, whereas the 75 percent of local arts agencies that are private nonprofits prevail in smaller places (Davidson 2001). It is not clear that public-choice theory would predict this pattern, which probably reflects the fact that the roles available to local arts agencies in large cities entail greater responsibility for tax dollars.[16]

Dynamic predictions of public-choice theories would seem to receive mixed support. Rising educational levels should increase government spending on the arts as demand from the median voter rises. This was the case in the United States (especially if one views the charitable deduction as a tax subsidy [Feld et al. 1983]), yet the opposite occurred in Europe, which experienced a trend toward greater nonprofit (as opposed to government) activity beginning in the 1980s (Kawashima 1999). Whether increasing religious and ethnic heterogeneity in much of Europe can explain this trend or whether it represents a failure of public-choice theory is a question that research has yet to answer.

Hybrids and network organizations.

We also lack powerful theories about the increasingly important phenomena of hybrid organizations, which contain elements of at least two organizational forms, and projects that are accomplished less by individual entities than by networks of organizations in different sectors. I have already referred to the large minority of important art museums in which governance is divided between the public sector, which controls the physical plant, and a nonprofit organization that controls collections and endowment. Still other private museums guarantee by charter that public officials are represented on their governing boards. Schuster (1998) contends that the proportion of all museums that are hybrids grew during the last quarter of the twentieth century. One can find similar arrangements in the performing arts (for example, Washington, D.C.'s Lincoln Theater, whose building is owned and maintained by local government and whose artistic programming is carried out by a nonprofit organization).

Artistic work is also carried out by partnerships that involve participants from all three sectors. The creation of large urban performing arts centers typically involves legislative sponsorship and fiscal stimulus from the government, private investment, and participation by the nonprofit arts organizations that occupy the structures; their management often involves public-private collaboration as well (Strom 2001).

Whereas such centers are among the largest arts entities, partnerships between nonprofit and for-profit entities are visible at the other end of the size distribution as well. A study of arts activities in ten low-income Chicago neighborhoods noted that much artistic vitality stemmed from interactions among networks of small groups, some for-profit, a few nonprofit, and many unincorporated or informal. One racially integrated neighborhood of sixty-five thousand residents boasted thirty-five arts entities, many of them clustered within a radius of just a few blocks. Major sites of this activity were a proprietary restaurant and bar that included a small bookstore, as well as a stage and exhibition space, which were available to local artists and performers. When this kind of network is successful, it may have substantial advantages over conventional nonprofit firms: the ability to engage readily participants from many types of organization; low capital costs owing to an infrastructure based on reciprocity rather than hierarchy; resilience in the face of staff turnover; and the robustness of a loosely coupled system of autonomous but interdependent parts (Grams and Warr 2002; for a different city, see Stern and Seifert 2000a; for the social services field, see Milofsky 1987; for biotechnology and related fields, see Powell 2001).

Broadcasting: A three-sector industry.

A few fields present special opportunities for comparative research because of the coexistence of multiple sectors within them. Of these, none is more intriguing than broadcasting, which is characterized by enormous diversity in organizational form, including networks as opposed to independent stations and embedded as opposed to freestanding stations. At the end of 2001, noncommercial entities controlled approximately one-sixth of U.S. radio stations and slightly more than one in five full-signal television stations (Reed Business Information 2003:xxxii). Noncommercial radio stations were underrepresented among those with the strongest signals; nonprofit television broadcasters constituted a larger share of UHF than of VHF outlets. Most nonprofit television stations and slightly fewer than one in three noncommercial radio stations are affiliated with the Public Broadcasting System (a public-private hybrid). In addition, the nonprofit broadcasting sector includes independent and Christian stations (although many other Christian stations are proprietary), as well as numerous college, university, and secondary-school stations (Reed Business Information 2003:B-134, D-545).

Radio is particularly intriguing because the noncommercial and the proprietary sectors occupy distinct niches marked by well-defined programming formats. Noncommercial stations dominate classical music and jazz formats, as well as the alternative and progressive rock formats favored by many college radio station managers. They also constitute the majority of stations with diversified formats and almost all those that describe themselves as educational. Commercial broadcasters, by contrast, rule mainstream pop radio, with well over 90 percent of stations in the adult contemporary, country, oldies, classic rock, and middle-of-the-road formats (ibid.).

Noncommercial and for-profit stations share some format niches. Nonprofits are prominent among religious broadcasters, comprising nearly 50 percent of Christian, religious, and inspirational stations (but slightly more than 10 percent of stations offering gospel programming). Noncommercial broadcasters also represent a large minority of stations with youth-oriented and African American formats (approximately 30 percent and almost 20 percent, respectively). In some cases the nonprofit-commercial divide is marked by relatively small differences in self-description: more than half of news stations are nonprofit, but almost 90 percent of stations boasting news-talk or talk formats are for-profit (ibid.:D661–62).

DOES ORGANIZATIONAL FORM MAKE A DIFFERENCE?

As readers of this handbook are aware, students of nonprofit and for-profit hospitals, nursing homes, and day care facilities have conducted many comparative studies of the behavioral differences that flow from organizational form. Students of cultural organizations have done little of this work.

In part, this is because there are few cases in which nonprofit and for-profit entities are similar enough in form and function to make statistical comparison sensible. How would one compare a nonprofit resident theater that maintains a facility, mounts several productions per year, books in jazz concerts and dance performances, and provides services to its community's schools to a Broadway production company whose only purpose is to produce one show as skillfully as possible until the end of its run? Is the appropriate comparison group for nonprofit art museums the relatively few small proprietary museums or the broader category of theme parks? What is the for-profit counterpart of the poets' collective, the arts-in-education program at a local community center, or a neighborhood mural project?

To be sure, there are select organizations between which fruitful behavioral comparisons *could* be made: between municipal and private museums or public and nonprofit local arts agencies, between for-profit art galleries and artists' cooperatives, or between nonprofit and for-profit literary presses, music schools, Christian radio stations, and circuses. If there are empirical studies of any of these topics but the first, I am unaware of them.

Without empirical guidance from systematic comparative research, students of nonprofit arts organizations must rely on case studies and theory. There are three basic kinds of theory, the first (primarily produced by economists, who value abstraction and parsimony) positing that behavioral differences flow from differences in the ordered preferences ("objective functions") of decision makers in nonprofit and for-profit firms, the second attributing behavioral differences to structural differences that influence decision making at the organizational level, and the third viewing behavioral differences as contingent on the particular niches that for-profit and nonprofit cultural producers occupy in particular fields.

Preference-Centered Explanations

Economics explains phenomena by aggregating upward from the more-or-less rational behavior of individuals who pursue their interests as they define them. Because people with varying preferences for different outcomes will behave in ways calculated to maximize their "objective functions," organizations run by such people will exhibit behavioral differences accordingly. The preferences of for-profit cultural producers are clear enough: they want to maximize profits.[17] By contrast, the objective functions of nonprofit decision makers are more varied. Economists ordinarily make stylized assumptions about what the nonprofit arts manager wants in lieu of maximizing net revenue. The two most popular assumptions are that nonprofit arts managers seek to maximize artistic excellence (if they share the values of artists) or audience size (if they want as many people as possible to receive the benefits of the work they produce). Some observers suggest that nonprofit managers may also want to maximize growth (in order to enhance their power, their salaries, or both; Hansmann 1981; Throsby and Withers 1979; Heilbrun and Gray 2001).

These assumptions are reasonable, especially when they are applied to conventional performing arts organizations or museums. Because most arts managers earn relatively low salaries and are prohibited from sharing in net revenues to stakeholders, the field is unlikely to attract managers who place financial outcomes first. Moreover, people who choose to work with artists, often in what are perceived to be support roles, are likely to sympathize with artists' perspectives and values. And managers who believe in what they are doing are likely to want to share the product with a large public.

Alas, there is little empirical support for these assumptions. Several ingenious studies have sought to reveal arts organizations' objective functions by seeing what such organizations do more of when their discretionary revenues increase. Results vary sharply from sample to sample (Luksetich and Lange 1995). Case studies of actual arts organizations, which, however atypical they may be, represent the bulk of the evidence available to us, are equally inconclusive.

To be sure, key decision makers in many arts nonprofits are committed to artistic excellence as they perceive it. Small performing groups that operate de jure or de facto as cooperatives are often quality maximizers (especially when members have viable day jobs; Murnighan and Conlon 1991). But even where quality maximization is the goal, it is an imprecise guide to behavior because there are so many dimensions to, and definitions of, artistic quality, including skill, daring or disturbing content, innovative production technique, virtuoso performances, and seamless ensemble work. Moreover, many small for-profit arts producers (for example, independent recording companies and poetry presses) seem equally artist-identified and committed to artistic values.

Similarly, the meaning of commitment to audience development varies markedly from manager to manager. Conservative arts institutions may prefer their audiences small and socially exclusive, if trustees and patrons value intimacy and social comfort. Arian (1971) contended that the Philadelphia Orchestra pursued this policy in the 1960s, and they were certainly not alone. Budgetary expansion, often associated with capital investments that raise fixed costs, has made some of the most staid of institutions, especially museums, seek larger audiences. Even so, nonprofit cultural organizations' pursuit of larger audiences is almost always constrained by ideas about appropriate repertoire or exhibition content or by considerations of organizational prestige (Ostrower 2002).

Some decision makers appear more interested in audience quality, often defined as audience commitment to the value of artistic risk-taking and willingness to be challenged, than in audience quantity. Even managers who want to increase audience size rarely act as if they are deeply committed to audience diversity: in the 1890s, the managers of the Chicago Symphony Orchestra failed to advertise concerts in the German-language press (which reached what would have been the largest market for symphonic music). In the 1990s, performing arts managers sought foundation grants in order to attract more ethnically diverse audiences only to abandon their efforts when the grants expired. Overall, the notion that arts managers are interested in reaching out to new publics (as opposed to using standardized marketing techniques to clone the audiences they already have) receives little empirical support.[18] Moreover, the assertion that audience expansion is an important objective of cultural organizations is belied by the low status of education and outreach programs in most established art museums and performing arts organizations (Eisner and Dobbs 1986; National Task Force for the American Orchestra 1993). Indeed, one study of art museums found that, controlling for exhibition space, collection budgets, and city characteristics, nonprofit museums drew significantly fewer visitors than their public counterparts (Oster and Goetzmann 2002:17).

The notion that nonprofit arts organizations seek growth has received much anecdotal support. The fact that arts managers cannot distribute profits does not mean that financial objectives do not guide their behavior. Many arts managers are *deficit optimizers* rather than profit maximizers. That is, they seek the deficit that will maximize the sum of earned and contributed revenues by inducing additional contributions at the margin. Growth is attractive to arts institutions and their managers for many reasons. Most mundanely, given the high correlation between budget size and managerial salaries in nonprofit arts firms (Hallock 2002:395), budgetary expansion is the best strategy a manager can employ to boost her or his income and prestige.

Expansion can also be a means to other ends. In the 1930s the Brooklyn Museum's director sought to open a chain of branch museums across Long Island as a means of using his collection more efficiently to reach a larger public, and in recent years New York's Guggenheim Museum created a worldwide chain of Guggenheim-branded museums (with dire financial consequences) for the same purpose (DiMaggio 1991c). Finally, growth is, to some extent, a strongly institutionalized cultural value: an anthropologist who studied arts organizations in a small Pennsylvania city reported that growth was a pervasive concern for managers, trustees, and donors because they regarded it as a sign of "vitality and good management" (Cameron 1991:232).

Behind the notion of an organizational or managerial objective function lies much ambiguity about whose objectives count. Ultimately, trustees have the authority to set organizational goals. Attempting to model the objective functions of large nonprofit arts organizations without reference to patrons and trustees is futile, not only because of their legal authority but because, compared to wealthy patrons in other fields, those in the arts are more specialized in their philanthropy, make larger gifts, are more personally involved with the organizations they support, and are more likely to be affiliated with upper-class social institutions (Ostrower 1995:92–95). Nonetheless, in many arts organizations, especially smaller ones, managers or artistic directors exert great influence over their boards. In some organizations (ordinarily large ones that depend on earned income for most of their revenues), artists are subordinate to managers. In others (ordinarily small ones that subsist on grants and contributed labor), artists may dominate managers. And for some purposes the objectives of grant makers may be as consequential as those of museum decision makers (Alexander 1996).

Organization-Centered Explanations

Such heterogeneity is at the center of organization-centered explanations. According to this view, differences between nonprofit and for-profit arts firms reflect not arts managers' preferences but rather decision-making processes peculiar to nonprofit (and public) enterprise. Whereas preference-based models may be more illuminating for small, artist-led nonprofits than for large and complex ones, the opposite is true of organization-centered explanations, which start from the premise that decisions represent the interaction of conflicting and incommensurable agendas rather than the objective function of any single actor.

From this perspective, the major difference between for-profit and nonprofit firms is that, whereas the former has one legitimate goal (profit maximization) to which all participants must at least publicly subscribe, nonprofit firms are intrinsically multiple-objective, multiple-stakeholder organizations (Blaug 2001:127; Tschirhart 1996). The encyclopedic urban art museum is the outstanding example, as much a confederation of professional departments, each with its own distinctive objective function, as a single organization (DiMaggio 1991b; for a similar view of theaters, see Voss et al. 2000). Curators focus on collecting and exhibiting objects, which they value for their own sake; exhibition specialists and educators emphasize the quality of the museum experience; marketing managers care about numbers, development specialists about cultivating donors, government-affairs directors about demonstrating enough public-spiritedness to justify subsidization (Zolberg 1981). The director (depending on background and inclinations) seeks some balance among all these objectives, often while working actively to snare the next big exhibition, perhaps while readying plans for a new wing. The board of trustees, which is supposed to adjudicate among these agendas, consists of men and women with agendas of their own. No wonder two perceptive observers remarked that the major job of the art museum director is to conceal the museum's true objective function (Frey and Pommerehne 1980).

In some ways, large cultural nonprofits are more like political coalitions—groups of stakeholders with diverse objectives who find potential value in cooperation—than they are like bureaucracies. Heterogeneity of objectives produces *not* characteristic decisions (these will vary from coalition to coalition) but characteristic organizational cultures and management styles. These include ambiguous goals, flexible rule systems with many exceptions, and a pervasive sense that decision making is a "political" rather than a purely rational activity (March 1962; Tschirhart 1996). Decision making itself is likely to be episodic: unable to articulate a clear objective function without alienating critical constituencies, managers will lurch from objective to objective one at a time, often responding to crises rather than initiating strategies in advance.[19] Planning will focus on facilities and programming; strategic planning will be largely symbolic. Elements of this description apply to many for-profits, as well. But in large cultural nonprofits, goal ambiguity is not a problem to be solved but a fundamental condition of organizational life.

Other differences between nonprofit and proprietary work settings flow from organizational features peculiar to particular industries. In the classical field, for example, commercial music jobs pay better, are less interesting musically, and require more extraordinary feats of sight-reading (to economize on studio or rehearsal time). By contrast, small-ensemble nonprofit settings provide poorer wages and more interesting music and require more tonal creativity and emotional range (Allen 1998).

Environmental Contingency Models

By *contingency models* I refer to models that view behavioral differences between nonprofit and for-profit firms as contextually variable, depending on the relative positions of such firms in a given industry (for examples from other industries, see Weisbrod 1990) and in their local communities. Such models represent the application of such theoretical approaches from sociology and organization science as resource-dependence theory, neoinstitutional theory, and organizational ecology. Common to all of them is the view that in order to predict differences in the behavior of nonprofits and for-profits in a given field, we must understand both the field's competitive dynamics (including the niches that for-profits and nonprofits occupy) and the network of cooperative relationships in which nonprofits are enmeshed. Decision makers' preferences matter in this view. But those preferences can be predicted if one knows the environment the organization faces, because organizations recruit managers whose preferences are suited to the environments in which they must operate.

Although most nonprofit arts organizations give lip service to the value of cooperation, they are in fact subject to intense competitive pressures. A study from the mid-1990s found that almost one in seven arts organizations became inactive within five years (Hager 2001; see also Bowen et al. 1994). Such failure rates indicate that selection pressures constrain the ability of trustees or managers to pursue objectives for which resources (market demand, grants or donations, contributed services) are unavailable, thus limiting the utility of models of nonprofit behavior based on assumptions about managers' or trustees' objective functions.

As we have seen, in relatively few fields do nonprofit arts organizations compete directly with similar for-profit firms. In most places, if one wants to visit a large art exhibit, one goes to a nonprofit (or public) museum, and if one buys a subscription to a series of performing arts events, it will probably be from a nonprofit organization as well. Within these fields, the behavior of a particular nonprofit will vary with the extent to which it holds a local monopoly. Where there are several nonprofit theaters, orchestras, art museums, or public radio stations, one is often the "generalist" (Hannan and Freeman 1989)—a full-service provider with a much larger budget than the rest, offering a diverse set of programs to a broad range of publics, with special attention to middle-class members or subscribers and wealthy patrons—and the others ordinarily specialize in particular kinds of artistic work (often with artists or curators playing more important decision-making roles than in larger institutions; DiMaggio and Stenberg 1985b).

In a long-term study of nonprofit organizations in the Twin Cities, Galaskiewicz (1997) reported that more competition among nonprofits in a particular field led to greater inequality, with the largest organizations increasing both earned and contributed income and the smallest forced to specialize and innovate in order to survive. By contrast, in remote places with relatively little commercial entertainment, the ecological perspective predicts that nonprofit arts presenters will offer repertoires that are decidedly more middlebrow than in communities with active for-profit commercial venues.

When arts nonprofits *do* compete directly with for-profit counterparts, nonprofits may attempt to differentiate their services as being of higher quality, whereas for-profits will compete in terms of price and convenience (a pattern that one observes in competition for young music students among for-profit music schools and nonprofit conservatories). Where competition is between community-based nonprofits and for-profit entities with fewer community ties (for example, between nonprofit theaters and traveling commercial shows oriented to African American audiences or between Hispanic-oriented commercial broadcasters and local nonprofits with Spanish-language programming), nonprofits are more likely to compete by emphasizing collective identity, political awareness, and special local services. Some community-based for-profits—such as local bookstores competing with chains or local nightclubs—also multiply services (for example, presenting readings by local authors or permitting local performing groups to use their stage for rehearsal, respectively) in order to underscore their community ties.

Endemic expansion and institutionalization have increased the intensity of competition among nonprofit arts organizations (and between them and for-profit substitutes) for the consumer dollar (McDaniel and Thorn 1991). In particular, many art museums have expanded their scope of operations (and with it, their fixed costs) to the point at which traditional sources of public and private patronage must be supplemented by additional forms of earned income, a development that has pushed most of the largest museums toward special exhibitions and retailing (Rudenstine 1991; Anheier and Toepfler 1998; Alexander 1996). Expansion has also increased commercial demands on performing arts organizations, the reliance of which on the subscription system has exerted a conservative influence on repertoire (DiMaggio and Stenberg 1985a; Hager 2001:387; Heilbrun 2001; O'Hagan and Neligan 2002). Under these circumstances, the openness of a field to artistic innovation depends on keeping entry barriers low, so that creatively fertile if short-lived small experimental organizations can operate at the field's artistic cutting edge.

The behavior of nonprofit arts organizations is a function not simply of their competitive environment but also of the network of cooperative relations in which they are enmeshed (Grams and Warr 2002; Backer 2002). Arts nonprofits engage in a wide range of exchanges with other actors (organizations and individuals), and much of their behavior can be explained analytically as an effort to maintain the commitment of actors on whom they depend (Galaskiewicz 1985; Stern and Seifert 2000a). Many small nonprofits, for example, survive by inducing artists to participate at below-market wages; in exchange for forgone income, such groups are likely to offer some combination of artistic voice (either directly, through participatory decision making, or by proxy through the dominance of an artistic leader whose vision participants respect), professional training, and access to valuable social networks.

The behavior of embedded nonprofits reflects the demands of the organizations that sponsor them. University-based performing arts institutions ordinarily devote more time to training young musicians than do other ensembles. College art museums devote more space to educational programs than do their public or freestanding nonprofit counterparts but have fewer visitors per square foot of exhibition space (Oster and Goetzmann 2002:7, 9). Community organizations' arts programs tend to reflect their sponsor's political orientation and social ethos, just as church-based arts programs may mirror the religious faith and communal orientation of the denominations that sponsor them.

Even freestanding nonprofit organizations are influenced by the network of relationships that sustain them. Where these relationships are formal (for example, when arts groups share a performance facility [Freedman 1986] or participate in a united fund-raising campaign [Shanahan 1989]) such ties can be highly constraining. Some collaborative relations, such as partnerships between nonprofit resident theaters that develop new plays and Broadway producers who commercialize them, induce nonprofits to behave more like commercial entities. In other cases, such as the positive impact of the expansion of university music programs on the number of new composers whose works are entering U.S. orchestras' repertoires, relationships stimulate artistic risk-taking by reducing its cost (Dowd 2002).

The same is true at the community level. Informal relations among trustees may also influence the opportunities available to nonprofit arts organizations as well as the constraints they face. Trustees of major arts nonprofits are more likely than those of other types to be involved in business associations that promote local economic development (Whitt and Lammers 1991). These ties may enhance the likelihood that such organizations cooperate with development plans and will be included in them.

No generalization can characterize the objective function of nonprofit arts firms in a way that enables us to predict their behavior (either as a group or in contrast to a stylized for-profit competitor), for three reasons. First, arts organizations' missions (and the objective functions of decision makers they recruit to accomplish these missions) reflect the niches they occupy in a broader community cultural ecology. Those niches vary over time, across communities, and among different arts fields. Second, the very notion that the large, complex nonprofit arts organization *has* a consistent objective function is itself problematic. Such institutions are sites at which trustees, managers, and professional staff members with distinct and often inconsistent objective functions struggle under ambiguous terms of engagement with results that resemble temporary truces more closely than sustained strategies. Third, in some cases, arts organizations' behavior reflects *other people's* objective functions—those of the churches, universities, or community groups that sponsor them, the managers of performing arts centers on which they depend for performance space, foundation program officers or local legislators on whom they rely for grants or subsidies, or the network of collaborating artists and organizations in which they participate. Under these circumstances, the best we can do is point to general principles or mechanisms that will help us analyze particular cases based on patterns that emerge from comparative analyses.

THE CHANGING NONPROFIT CULTURAL SECTOR

The role of nonprofit organizations in the arts has evolved steadily since the creation of America's first nonprofit art museums and orchestras in the nineteenth century. For the most part, the story has been one of expanding functions, resulting from two different processes. On one hand, the orchestras' and museums' model of trustee governance, donative support, and commitment to artistic values spread gradually to other art forms—opera, theater, the dance, and jazz. On the other, since the 1960s other kinds of nonprofits—community organizations, human services agencies, universities, and churches—have spawned arts programs, creating a separate nonprofit arts sector committed to different roles for the arts and based on somewhat different organizational principals.

Barring long-term economic recession that undercuts opportunities for contributed income or legislative action that makes the nonprofit form less attractive, we can expect to see the nonprofit sector bear the principal responsibility for live performance and exhibition of an expanding range of art forms and genres and for programs that use the arts to pursue social-welfare agendas, while gradually extending into new niches that are opened by industrial concentration and technological change.

Economic and Demographic Factors

The enormous boom in the nonprofit arts during the final third of the twentieth century, and especially in the creation of nonprofit museums and performing arts institutions in large and mid-sized cities around the United States, has arguably led to, if not oversupply, at least the satiation of demand. The forces that fueled that expansion—the coming of age of the baby boom generation, the simultaneous state-financed expansion of higher education, and the rapid rise in government arts funding—are spent. Although new enterprises will enter the picture as old ones fail, nonprofit theaters, museums, orchestras, and opera and dance companies constitute mature industries with relatively little potential for continuing growth and some risk of attrition in the middle ranks (Wolf Organization 1992).

Much growth in the nonprofit arts was facilitated by low wages due to the overproduction of artists during the 1970s and 1980s, a period during which the number of artists in the labor force increased rapidly as their median earnings markedly declined (Kreidler 1996). Because most arts have what the economist Robert Frank (Frank and Cook 1995; Rosen 1981) calls "winner-take-all" labor markets—career tracks where a few people reap extraordinary rewards while most others, including men and women of great talent, receive meager if any returns—graduates of arts programs have constituted a reserve army of the underemployed on which many nonprofits (as well as for-profit ad agencies, interior design firms, and proprietary schools [Stern 2000]) have depended for workers and managers alike. In the 1990s the rate of increase in the artistic labor force began to slow, falling slightly behind the growth rate for professional occupations as a whole (Cultural Policy and the Arts National Data Archive 2003). If the decline continues, an important foundation of the nonprofit arts economy may be placed in jeopardy.

By contrast, the new immigration will engender a boom in arts organizations devoted to the cultures and ambitions of newcomers from Latin America and Asia. Students of voluntary organizations in comparative cross-national perspective have long noted a positive association between ethnic and religious heterogeneity and the size of nonprofit sectors (Weisbrod 1997; James 1987). Whether demand for immigrant culture is absorbed by for-profit entrepreneurs or whether immigrant arts will become a nonprofit growth area during the first decades of the twenty-first century remains to be seen. To some extent it will depend on such imponderables as the rate of assimilation of new immigrants into the pan-ethnic middle class, the demand of immigrants for arts programs that emphasize fine points of shared culture and identity as opposed to those that market efficiently a mass-oriented version of indigenous art forms, and the fit between the U.S. nonprofit form and modes of organizing artistic activity prevalent in immigrant artists' countries of origin.

The rise of evangelical Christianity poses an analogous opportunity and challenge to the nonprofit arts sector. Conservative Christians have increased their share of the U.S. population substantially over the past four decades and, at the same time, have become more similar to other Americans in educational attainment, income, and regional distribution (Hout et al. 2001). Some Christian entrepreneurs have created new forms of identity-based, for-profit enterprise that elicit commitment, including donations of time or money, from customers based on shared identity or faith. The most notable examples at present are broadcast enterprises owned by evangelical Christians who portray their business interests as incidental to their mission to spread the Gospel. Like immigrant-based enterprises that produce collective goods without benefit of nonprofit charter, the key mechanism is the use of shared faith or identity as a substitute for the trust inspired by the nondistribution constraint. Eventually such entrepreneurs may gravitate to the nonprofit form, or they may present a challenge to it.

Ultimately, the challenges posed by demographic change will lead nonprofit arts organizations to search for new efficient boundaries to define their missions and activities. The key question is: What functions fit within the framework of the nonprofit arts firm (or of the larger nonprofit entity in which arts activities are embedded), and which ones will stay outside it? Galaskiewicz (1997) has pointed to the versatility of hospitals at bundling additional functions and services while preserving their core missions. Since the 1970s many large arts nonprofits have likewise bundled new services (educational programs, community outreach, presentation of performing arts, food services, retail operations) into their portfolio (Throsby and Withers 1979:48). Whether conventional arts nonprofits—theater companies, art museums, symphony orchestras, and so on—become arts mega-enterprises or leave new markets and missions to more agile competitors remains to be seen. At the same time, we may see new combinations of enterprise—for example, artists' cooperatives that branch into rights management or distribution of digital images, or cultural centers devoted to particular immigrant cultures that begin to present artists of other nations—occupy important roles.

The Eroding Boundary Between High and Popular Culture and the Nonprofit Arts Sector's Broadening Scope

The past half-century has witnessed dramatic change in beliefs about the appropriate role of the arts within society. The most important shift, from the standpoint of the nonprofit arts, has been the gradual erosion of the hierarchical model of culture—with European high culture at the top and other cultural forms arrayed beneath it—that animated (and was in turn instantiated in) the creation of America's first nonprofit orchestras and art museums in the late nineteenth century (Gans 1985; DiMaggio 1991a).[20]

The decline of the hierarchical model reflects not only a cognitive change but also a weakening of cognitive and institutional boundaries between high and popular culture. Since the 1970s observers have noted a trend toward more popular-culture programming on the part of many traditional arts nonprofits (Peterson 1990). A more recent and potentially equally important development is the entry of community-based commercial arts providers into networks that produce high-culture programming. For example, in 2003, a Trenton nightclub that ordinarily features edgy pop music acts hosted a series of films, piano soloists, and academic-style panels as part of a festival celebrating the life and work of the modernist composer George Antheil.[21] It is possible that some community-based nightspots will ultimately migrate to the nonprofit sector. But it seems more likely that small for-profits may usurp portions of the nonprofit sector's traditional role.

The expansion of the nonprofit arts. The decline of cultural hierarchy opens the nonprofit arts sector to a wider range of genres and styles. Some relatively new entrants are hybrids between high-culture art worlds and popular traditions. Performance art, for example, features solo or ensemble performers who combine elements of drama, comedy, dance, or visual art into novel performances (Wheeler 1999; Pagani 2001). It originated in the visual arts world but evolved to include participants with roots in theater, comedy, and music as well. The nonprofit sector's role in this field is largely that of presenter, providing venues in which these artists perform.

The nonprofit arts sector has also embraced "media arts," of which there have been two waves. The first used film and video to create installations that incorporated moving images into static assemblies. Although some projects required large exhibition spaces like the retooled factory that houses the Massachusetts Museum of Contemporary Art, smaller video loops and similar creations fit easily into ordinary museum spaces. The second wave has employed digital technologies with more radical consequences for exhibit organization owing to the suitability of the Internet for broadcasting digital works. Another case of intersectoral drift is the once entirely proprietary field of circus entertainment, which now includes a significant nonprofit minority, the most prominent of which, like Big Apple Circus and the Circus Center of San Francisco, boast more sophisticated self-presentations and more upscale, urban audiences than the Big Top's traditional denizens.

The art world has also become increasingly open to nonprofit organizations that promote distinctly American-based folk or popular culture. Two genres, craft art and jazz, were at the forefront of this development. A recent canvass of craft organizations enumerates 1,329 nonprofits devoted to craft art, including 88 museums, 315 galleries, and 105 festivals or craft art centers.[22] For jazz, nonprofit and philanthropic sponsorship has lagged behind critical esteem and academic respectability. Although more than 90 percent of the jazz groups enumerated in the Census are commercial, the nonprofit sector is making inroads, with jazz societies, service organizations and museums, and some jazz ensembles.[23] Jazz performers who employ the nonprofit form include a few typical small ensembles, performing groups affiliated with college or university music departments, and groups sponsored by organizations devoted to fostering African American cultural identity. Some of the largest are preservationist, devoted, like the first symphony orchestras, to defining and preserving a musical canon. A few large ensembles, like the Nebraska Jazz Orchestra (2002), have adopted all the institutional trappings of symphony orchestras.[24]

More recently, organizations that present musical forms associated with a wide range of ethnic identities have adopted the nonprofit form; for example, the Minnesota Chinese Music Ensemble, the Baltimore Klezmer Orchestra, the Irish Heritage Festival in West Virginia and an Omaha, Nebraska, mariachi orchestra.[25] The nonprofit form has also migrated to older popular American forms such as bluegrass music and rural blues. Nonprofit enterprise and government enterprise (for example, the Smithsonian Institution's Center for Folklife and Cultural Heritage) are also evident in the small but important field dedicated to preserving the recorded heritage by transferring at-risk recordings to new media.

The nonprofit sector is even represented (more faintly) in pop culture fields that are younger (the nonprofit Urban Think Tank publishes the *Journal of Rap Music and Hip Hop Culture*) or of doubtful repute (California's Exotic World Burlesque Museum commemorates and honors nude dancing, burlesque, and striptease [Kellogg 2002]). The nonprofit cutting edge often involves efforts to impart academic respectability or historical legitimacy to genres that have possessed neither. Other examples of early nonprofit ventures dedicated to conservation and consecration are Nashville's Country Music Museum and Hall of Fame and Mississippi's Delta Blues Museum.

Less distinct lines between nonprofit and commercial cultural organizations. At the same time that the weakening of cultural hierarchy has expanded the nonprofit arts sector's scope, it has made nonprofit cultural organizations more vulnerable to the imposition of values and methods imported from the proprietary sector. Increasingly, the language of commerce is permeating the boardrooms and hallways of traditional arts organizations as nonprofit managers adopt for-profit planning models and marketing techniques in order to placate trustees and corporate donors (Stone 1989; Alexander 1996). Although many arts organizations have benefited from adopting business management tools, others have wasted time and resources on symbolic gestures, and some have imported not only techniques but also vocabularies of motive, including "bottom-line" justifications for program decisions, from the for-profit sector (Kenyon 1995).

Similarly, erosion of the cognitive boundary between high and popular culture reduces resistance to the commercialization of nonprofit arts organizations. Early high-culture institutions shunned the market, lest they profane their sacred mission (DiMaggio 1982). In recent years, however, museums, performing arts organizations, and public broadcasters have embraced commercialism in many ways (Silverman 1986; Powell and Friedkin 1986; Wu 2001). Although in theory business activities cross-subsidize core missions, commercial success often becomes a goal in itself, competing with artistic objectives. Moreover, commercial successes may paradoxically undermine the rationale for government and philanthropic subsidization (DiMaggio 1986; Toepler 2001). Under such circumstances, policy makers who care about the arts have searched for new rationales to justify continued subsidization.

Two such rationales have become prominent, each representing a growth area for nonprofit cultural entrepreneurship. The arts have long played a key role in many urban development projects (Lincoln Center, or for that matter Boston's Museum of Fine Arts, which was originally sited near the public library in the Back Bay, at the heart of America's first culturally anchored urban development scheme). The practice accelerated toward the end of the twentieth century (Whitt 1987; Strom 1999), bolstered by the success of such projects as Newark's NJPAC (New Jersey Performing Arts Center), the efforts of arts advocates, and some evidence from academic researchers that the presence of artists and cultural organizations is associated with urban prosperity (Florida 2002) and neighborhood stability (Stern 2000).

Cultural policy analysts have also devoted attention to issues of "cultural heritage." Whereas *heritage* was once code for the preservation of stately homes, its referents are now far broader, including nineteenth-century workers' housing, public buildings of architectural value, and the nonbuilt heritage of musical recordings, choreography, and folklore. Although class politics invariably enters into allocation, as a general criterion for cultural subvention heritage is politically attractive for its democratic thrust. And the rationale for heritage preservation has been deepened by scholars who have probed the analogy between the cultural and the natural environments (Throsby 2001).

Technological Change and Economic Concentration

A dramatic increase in the media industries' concentration has narrowed distribution channels at the same time that the rise of digital recording and communications technology has reduced barriers to entry and challenged business models that have sustained for-profit culture industries for decades. When the dust clears, for-profit firms may provide some services that nonprofits do today, while nonprofits take over niches hitherto restricted to the proprietary sector.

New digital technologies undermine old business models in several ways. Most notably, any recording (of a piece of music, a film, or a photograph or other artwork) can be almost instantaneously transmitted at virtually no variable cost. First the recording industry and now Hollywood have seen their latest products distributed freely worldwide, sometimes before the official release date. The entertainment conglomerates have responded vigorously with lawsuits and technical fixes, but at this writing, the hackers have stayed one step ahead. The big companies will have to find a new business model that includes distribution for profit over the Internet. The effect this quest will have on the intersectoral division of labor remains to be seen. But it seems likely to give a boost to nonprofit distribution systems that promote the work of artists who use some variant of Creative Commons licensing, which, in its most common form, permits others to use creative products freely as long as they provide credit to the creator and do not extract a profit from its use (Lessig 2004:283ff.). Drawing on the model of open-source software, the organizations—almost all nonprofit—that promote the use of such rights protection schemes view them as a means to expand the readily available supply of cultural goods and to permit a wider range of creative endeavors (for example, by permitting "mashups" that recombine material from several copyrighted works into a single new production).

By reducing inventory costs nearly to zero, the digitization of cultural "content" extends the commercial viability of works that would in the past have gone out of print (Anderson 2004). The public has not benefited fully from this change in the economics of distribution, however, because many "orphaned works" (books, films, television programs) cannot now be reissued because their rights histories would cost more to untangle than their production and sale would earn. The nonprofit sector may have a larger role to play in the development of compulsory-licensing schemes that could potentially ameliorate this problem by maintaining rights information and routinizing the licensing and fee-collection process. The field of music composition, where songwriters and composers license their work to one of several nonprofit mutual-benefit membership associations such as ASCAP (the American Society of Composers, Authors, and Publishers) or BMI (Broadcast Music, Inc.), provides a useful model. Anyone who wishes to perform publicly or record a song is free to do so without negotiation, so long as standard royalties or fees are paid to the association, which passes them on to the composer or songwriter.

An equally important effect of the digital revolution has been a dramatic reduction of barriers to entry in many fields, continuing a trend originating in declining prices in the electronics market that antedated the Internet's rise. Sound recordings that would have absorbed thousands of dollars' worth of studio time a few years ago can be cut on relatively inexpensive equipment in a teenager's basement today. Costs have likewise fallen for magazine publishing and, to a lesser extent, photography, film, and animation. Yet the democratization of artistic production occurred alongside a concentration of the means of distribution. The Internet solves the technical distribution problem by reducing variable cost to almost nothing. But in so doing it creates an economy of attention scarcity that disadvantages artists without the marketing power the media giants possess.

The combination of an unprecedented abundance of product with a corporate media sector that is concentrated to an unprecedented degree creates an opportunity for nonprofit organizations in the field of distribution. In some cases, such organizations will operate in the physical world, as do several grant-supported organizations devoted to marketing and distributing small-press fiction, a field in which the concentration of commercial publishing has made small literary presses the primary publishers of first novels by talented young writers. One can imagine the nonprofit form moving further downstream to the consumer, as well, with nonprofit bookstores and record stores joining nonprofit art film houses, museum stores, and cafes in an enlarged arena of nonprofit cultural retailing.

Indeed, nonprofits have long been active in some forms of distribution and retailing; museum shops and college bookstores are significant examples (National Association of College Stores 2003). Nonprofit galleries, often artists' cooperatives, have emerged as significant alternatives to for-profit galleries in the fine arts and, especially, crafts.[26] And although independent bookstores have not yet used the nonprofit form, under pressure by chains and online bookstores, many of the surviving independents have taken on some functions of libraries (offering public programs, sponsoring reading groups, and so on). It seems a small step for some to reincorporate as nonprofit institutions, selling books as a "related business activity" that supports broader educational functions.

In other fields, virtual nonprofits may serve to link artists and potential publics. The Internet's advantage for cultural intermediation is its ability to harness the power of distributed intelligence using peer rating systems. The combination of peer reviews and network algorithms that online businesses such as Amazon and Netflix use to recommend books and films are readily applicable to organizing smaller markets for artistically ambitious alternatives to the products of media conglomerates.

Whether nonprofits will occupy this niche remains unclear. In some cases new network-based enterprises that are *not* organized as 501(c)(3)s have begun to organize the production of collective goods. Take, for example, an independent music site that provides a free space for bands to advertise their recordings or tour dates, gains the trust of Web surfers willing to donate a few minutes of their time to write reviews or edifying dialogue, and offers free Web-based information services to aspiring musicians (while also using the Web site to sell recordings of bands that its owners keep under contract, t-shirts, and related paraphernalia). The key mechanism is the ability of networks to compile and share information at very low cost: many people may contribute content to such sites not from any deep faith in the proprietors but because it is easy and fun to do so. The Internet ensures that very limited commitment can go a long way if it is shared by thousands of people.

At present, the relation between legal form and self-presentation online appears to be blurred, with many Web sites devoted to the production of public goods (for example, information exchange among digital artists or restaurant aficionados) describing themselves as "nonprofit" and soliciting donations to help keep their sites online, apparently without benefit of 501(c)(3) registration. Such sites as digitalart.org, Chowhound.com, and indiegrrl.com are, by all accounts, genuinely nonprofit in ethos. It is likely that they are organized as, in effect, sole proprietorships for the same reason that other minimalist organizations retain that form: they control few assets and lack realistic prospects for significant philanthropic fundraising, so they would not find the trouble or expense of incorporation worthwhile. It seems possible that the Internet culture (Castells 2001) has produced an alternative model that elides the line between charitable and mutual-benefit associations and between nonprofit and for-profit enterprise.[27]

In the nondigital world, industrial concentration has created opportunities for new enterprises that sell works that, though profitable, are not profitable enough for the giants. In the popular music industry, industrial concentration may have enhanced innovation as conglomerates have designed strategies that sustain diversity while opening niches for small independent companies ("indies") that record a wide range of talented artists working in and across every genre (Dowd 2004). Although they are financial dwarfs, the hundreds of independent record companies are an artistically vital part of the industry. Moreover, many operate with a nonprofit ethos, forgoing commercial success in the interest of substantive aesthetic ends (Gray 1988). They ordinarily adopt the nonprofit form, however, only when sound recording follows from a broader mission. For example, Appalshop, an entrepreneurial nonprofit multi-arts program in rural Kentucky, has created a subsidiary, Appal Records, which records Appalachian folk singers, and the Electronic Music Foundation, which promotes the work of serious composers using electronic media, has created a record label in order to publish important but unavailable works. If other states' arts councils follow New York's in offering grants to nonprofit record companies, such companies' numbers will increase (New York State Council for the Arts 2002). In states that do not offer the promise of grants from government agencies or private foundations, few small record companies have had reason to incorporate as 501(c)(3)s. Time will tell whether the indies evolve into a nonprofit sector of the recording industry or continue to pursue value-rational purposes by other means.

CONCLUSION: RESEARCH PRIORITIES

Whether one's interests are driven by theory development, substantive curiosity, or policy relevance, research opportunities abound. Whereas many kinds of rigorous empirical research on nonprofit arts organizations, especially comparative research across nonprofit and other sectors, were once virtually impossible, recent efforts to improve data quality and availability make the quest for rigor less quixotic. A sustained commitment by the Research Division of the National Endowment for the Arts, supplemented by programs of the Pew Charitable Trusts and other foundations, have paid off in several improvements. Notable among them are the enhanced quality of cultural data in the Census of Business, the Urban Institute's success in building databases from IRS Form 990s (including its collaboration with the National Assembly of State Arts Agencies to create the Uniform Database on Arts Organizations), and Princeton University's establishment of the Cultural Policy and the Arts Data Archive, which permits online analysis or downloading of dozens of data sets relevant to arts and cultural policy studies.

Theory Testing and Theory Development

I have already identified a series of theoretical challenges. Why are some performing arts activities articulated by contract whereas others are organized via hierarchy? To what extent do endemic deficits in nonprofit arts organizations reflect the cost disease, and to what extent do they stem from organizational expansion or other managerial choices? What explains the presence of embedded arts programs in organizations outside the arts, and how might our understanding of the origins of nonprofit cultural enterprise change once we take these into account? How can we understand the division of labor among the sectors in the few fields—for example, performing arts presentation and radio broadcasting—where all three are present? What accounts for the increase in hybrid arts organizations and interorganizational (and sometimes intersectoral) collaborations? What theories can provide the greatest purchase on minimalist arts organizations, including sole proprietorships and very small multi-person firms? Is it more productive to view them as for-profits (which they are as a legal matter), nonprofits (when they are nonprofit in ethos), or means for workers to survive difficult labor markets? Why do public and for-profit cultural firms rarely coexist in the same fields? How do size, capital-intensiveness, and cost structures interact to influence the intersectoral division of labor? Why are there for-profit art museums and nonprofit circuses?

In order to address such questions we need to develop more sophisticated and rigorous analytic methods. Too often we have been forced to test theories about the origins of nonprofit enterprise by anecdote and example or, at best, by cross-sectional comparisons. Yet our best theories are both probabilistic (they identify important and pervasive tendencies, not iron laws) and evolutionary (they make predictions, at least implicitly, about conditions influencing the relative rates of birth and death of nonprofit, as opposed to for-profit or government, firms). In order to give public-choice, market-failure, and other theories a fair hearing, we must develop over-time population data that enable us to test them in the context of realistic models of population dynamics (DiMaggio 2003).

Substantive Issues: Understanding Organizational Change

Other research priorities, although theoretically relevant, are matters of greater practical concern. Exploratory research concerning new nonprofit roles in the arts and culture is necessary in order to illuminate emerging nonprofit fields about which standardized data systems do not yet report. We need to better understand the emergence of nonprofit enterprise in the presentation and exhibition of art forms that have in the past been largely commercial: Who are the pioneers, what causes them to choose the nonprofit form, and how do their organizations' structures and missions differ from those of their for-profit counterparts? We need similar studies of the role of nonprofit and commercial organizations in identity-based cultural organizations, for example, those associated with new immigrant groups and emerging faith communities. Finally, we need systematic research concerning the organizational forms that are developing (online and off) to address new dilemmas in marketing and distribution. What are the advantages and disadvantages of the nonprofit form in the retailing and distribution of mechanically and digitally reproduced artworks, and what role might nonprofits play in bringing diverse products to the attention of audiences who otherwise would not encounter them?

Policy Studies

Although many of the topics I have mentioned will be of interest to cultural policy makers in the public and the philanthropic sectors, two policy research priorities are particularly urgent. First, we need research that will enable grant makers to assess the relation between organizational form and behavioral differences that are relevant to the values—for example, artistic excellence, education and access, innovation, and diversity—that cultural policy makers ordinarily wish to promote. Emphasis should be placed on rigorous comparisons that explore the conditions under which organizational form influences such behavioral differences, either directly or through elements of strategy and structure with respect to which different forms vary. Furthermore, such studies should go beyond mere comparison in two ways. They should explain *why* observed differences exist, and, therefore, provide guidance as to whether such patterns are replicable by means of policy incentives. And they should define organizational form more broadly than "nonprofit" versus "for-profit," including comparisons between pure types, on one hand, and hybrid and embedded organizations, on the other.

Second, we need community cultural-resource studies that view arts organizations as interrelated parts of coherent systems. Increasingly, grant makers seek not simply to sustain significant institutions but also to enhance the role of the arts in community life. From this perspective, it is important that we learn not only about institutions (or artists) but also about the relationships that sustain a community's arts institutions and link them to other arenas of public life. In particular, we need studies that can reveal the ways in which cultural organizations in different sectors—freestanding nonprofits, embedded nonprofits, government, commercial entities, and unincorporated associations—interact to produce collective goods. What is the relation, for example, between the robustness of informal neighborhood arts associations and arts schools, on one hand, and the vitality of professional institutions, on the other? In what ways do different kinds of art organization compete, and in what ways do their programs reinforce one another by building audiences, training artists, or enhancing the attractiveness of the arts to philanthropists?

These research priorities, like this chapter as a whole, reflect two premises that, although they are increasingly shared, are still somewhat controversial. First, one can understand the nonprofit sector only by comparing its scope and behavior to that of the public and commercial sectors. Second, understanding the current and likely future importance of the nonprofit arts sector involves focusing on a broader range of cultural nonprofits, including embedded and minimalist arts organizations, than analysts ordinarily take into account. Such nonprofits as museums, orchestras, and dance and theater companies will remain central to the sector. But the rate of growth in these fields will continue to slow. If we want to grasp the dynamism of the nonprofit sector in art and culture, we must focus on the less well institutionalized portions of the organizational universe from which new functions and future directions continually emerge.

ACKNOWLEDGMENTS

Research for this paper was supported by the Andrew W. Mellon Foundation and the Pew Charitable Trusts through grants to the Princeton University Center for Arts and Cultural Policy Studies. Institutional support from the center is gratefully acknowledged, as is the patience of the editors. I am also deeply grateful to Tom Bradshaw, director of the Research Division of the National Endowment for the Arts, for sharing and giving permission to use special Census tabulations prepared for the Research Division, and to Tom Pollak of the Urban Institute for access to and help in interpreting the Unified Arts Database. Thanks to Arthur Brooks,

Jennifer Kuan, Woody Powell, Mark Schuster, and Rich Steinberg for helpful editorial suggestions.

NOTES

1. Such estimates are intrinsically debatable. It makes sense to include only organizations that file, because many of the organizations in the IRS lists that do not file are inactive; at the same time, this does lead to the exclusion of some active organizations that are not required to file because they have annual budgets of less than $25,000 (Bowen et al. 1994). This figure also fails to count arts and cultural programs mounted by nonprofit organizations categorized under other headings (for example, private foundations that fund the arts; universities that support theater groups or film series, present concerts, and provide arts education; community groups that sponsor murals, use the arts in work with youth, and sponsor concerts and exhibitions in public parks; or churches that organize theater trips or whose choirs sing at festivals throughout their communities). It also leaves out the myriad informal, unincorporated groups (chamber groups, book circles, immigrant cultural societies, and so on) that pursue artistic or other cultural ends and neither seek nor distribute positive net revenues but lack legal standing as nonprofit entities. In other words, the size of the sector depends on how one defines it.

2. Kaple et al. (1996:165) went beyond the usual data sources to identify all 501(c)(3)s with at least one professional employee that presented performances or exhibited art, including organizations whose artistic programs were ancillary to a larger purpose. Although Kaple et al. included "embedded" cultural organizations, unlike Stern, they did not try to count freestanding associations without incorporated nonprofit status. Stern found 1,204 "nonprofit arts and cultural providers," but for comparative purposes I have only used fields covered by Kaple et al. (excluding history, humanities, libraries, science, and design arts) and organizations that mount their own performances or exhibitions (to which Kaple et al.'s organizations were limited). In this comparison, adding freestanding unincorporated associations increased the count of organizations in Philadelphia from 309 to 650. Even allowing for Stern's more intensive data-collection effort, it is clear that including the informal, unincorporated arts sector greatly increases the nonprofit cultural sector's size.

3. This problem is less acute for the performing arts because the Research Division of the National Endowment for the Arts has graciously shared special tabulations that the Census Bureau produced at the endowment's request. Interpretation of the less aggregated measures is complicated by the fact that detailed self-designations are available only for establishments that responded directly to the Census and not for organizations for which data were gleaned only from administrative sources. (Establishments that were part of multiestablishment firms and establishments that employed more than a certain number of employees [which varied by industry] received questionnaires in the mail. Smaller employers did not, and data about "firms" that employed no one during the previous year [a group that probably included most individual artists who define themselves as businesses for tax purposes] were excluded from published tabulations.)

4. The for-profit sector is so preponderant in manufacturing and distribution of instruments, supplies, and mechanically reproduced or broadcast music and drama that the Census simply assumes without asking that firms are proprietary. Motion picture distributors are corporate studios; most films are produced by ad hoc partnerships (Baker and Faulkner 1991) and distributed by large commercial firms. Most television drama and comedy programs are produced by a few for-profit companies (Bielby and Bielby 1994). Arts service industries that are exclusively or predominantly for-profit include music publishers, talent agencies and artists' representation firms, advertising agencies that employ graphic artists and musicians (U.S. Census Bureau 2001d), graphic design services, photography studios, and software publishers. Also overwhelmingly for-profit are retail establishments that sell musical instruments and sheet music and stores that specialize in selling new CDs, records, and tapes. The major exception to this rule, for recordings and books, comprises retail establishments embedded in nonprofit or government organizations—military commissaries, museum shops, and almost twenty-five hundred college and university bookstores that are owned and run by the institutions. Because retail operations are ancillary to such organizations' major missions, such establishments rarely show up in the Economic Census. (All figures in this paragraph are from U.S. Census 2002, except for the number of college and university stores, which comes from National Association of College Stores 2003.)

5. In the context of a continuing game (i.e., arts organizations hoping that this year's donors will give again next year), the nondistribution constraint is attractive because it is difficult for donors to monitor critical aspects of the product or the production process. Compared to the classic case of services purchased from nonprofits by third parties on behalf of clients who cannot easily evaluate or report those services' quality (e.g., young children, the infirm elderly, hospital patients with complex diseases), the arts organizations' exhibits and performances are highly visible; however, the processes that bring them to the stage or gallery are often not visible at all. For example, donors may need assurance that nonprofits will not use their gifts to boost the incomes of managers at the expense of working conditions for artists or services to the community.

6. The relation between function and motive is complex. Much elite entrepreneurship was motivated by a pragmatic interest in educating designers and craftsmen (art museums) or by an ideological commitment to the value of classical music (the orchestras). For more nuanced treatments of motivation see DiMaggio 1982, 1991a, 1992.

7. The 1997 Census of Business reports that 11 percent of museums (of all kinds) are not tax-exempt.

8. I am fortunate to have had use of a beta version of the Unified Database of Arts Organizations (UDAO), a valuable new resource created by the Urban Institute and the National Assembly of State Arts Agencies (NASAA) under contract to the Research Division of the National Endowment for the Arts. This database, which is the closest thing we have had to a complete listing of nonprofit arts organizations (as well as a few for-profits), represents the union of data from IRS Form 990s (which all nonprofit organizations with annual revenues of $25,000 or more are required to file annually) with NASAA's database of grantee lists and other lists provided annually by the fifty-seven state and territorial arts agencies of the United States (Lampkin and Boris 2002; Kaple 2002). The UDAO is particularly valuable for three reasons. First, the IRS 990s provide unusually comprehensive listings of nonprofit organizations compared to alternative sources (Kaple et al. 1998; Grønbjerg 2002). Second, the database permits some cross-walking between the serviceable but coarse-grained typology of organizations used by IRS and the National Center for Charitable Statistics, on one hand, and the more refined, arts-focused typology that NASAA employs. Third, the database identifies the organizations so that researchers can add data and cases of their own. The UDAO data are not comparable to Census tabulations, first, because the system does not yet have NAIC codes (the classification system that the Census uses to sort establishments by industry) for most entries and, second, because it does not yet include systematically collected data about proprietary entities. But although the UDAO cannot be used for intersectoral comparison, it is well equipped for more in-depth looks at the Census's "tax-exempt" categories and for studying the extent to which nonprofit organizations are becoming active in new arenas.

9. Organizational theorists refer to the process by which industrial concentration opens new markets to small firms as "niche partitioning" (Carroll 1985).

10. Brooks (2006) notes that labor costs in the arts have risen faster

in the United States than in other advanced industrial nations, a result that the theory would not predict (given the relatively small size of the U.S. manufacturing sector).

11. In order to estimate the number of poetry magazines, I consulted the electronic *Ulrich's Periodical Directory* in January 2003 and selected poetry magazines (www.ulrichsweb.com), of which Ulrich's listed 2,153. I sampled the first 250 of these and found that 49 are published in the United States and still listed as active. Because many listings are designated "researched/unresolved," I inflated the total estimate by about 20 percent above the figure that one would obtain by extrapolating from my sample to the whole.

12. The rise of public funding for poetry and serious fiction during the 1970s contributed to an increase in the number of presses taking the nonprofit form (in order to make themselves eligible for grants from public arts agencies or foundations). Despite the presence of a few exemplars (e.g., the New Press, founded as a nonprofit with an explicit public-benefit mission, and Graywolf Press, which adopted the nonprofit form to become eligible for grants in the 1970s), by 2000 this tendency appeared to have stalled in the face of more cautious grant making by public arts agencies eager to avoid controversial grants that attract legislative retribution (Mitchell 1985).

13. The UDAO F_Inst field lists 658 organizations classified as nonprofit independent presses, but my inspection of a sample of 30 of these organizations suggests that only about half are properly classified because the list includes some organizations that are not presses and some presses that are not nonprofit in form (though some may be nonprofit in mission).

14. When dining establishments present plays they are classified under "arts establishments" as dinner theaters; when they present musicians, the Census classifies them as dining establishments.

15. The only case in which for-profits and public agencies compete *without* nonprofits playing a more important role than at least one of the others is in the lending of feature films by public libraries in order to supplement provision by retail video lenders (from whom the practice elicits cries of unfair competition). This exception represents the complementarity of this function to libraries' major role as lenders of books and recorded music, fields that public and nonprofit libraries monopolize.

16. On one hand, demand for the arts in large cities is more heterogeneous than demand in smaller places, which should make the nonprofit sector more important. On the other hand, demand for the arts may be higher in cities, and public-choice theory would predict that this would increase the awarding of public grants to arts groups, which is consistent with the observed facts. A study of the relation between cultural philanthropy (a measure of demand) and the form and behavior of arts agencies would be illuminating.

17. This assumption applies better to managers of firms that are accountable to investors than to the owner of an art-house movie theater or to a chamber trio that performs at weddings and dinner parties, of course.

18. A 1993 task force of the American Symphony Orchestra League placed "orchestra leadership" near the top of a list of barriers to "achieving cultural diversity," writing that "many orchestra boards have become large, entrenched structures that include people who have not kept abreast of changing community dynamics and values" (National Task Force for the America Orchestra 1993:41).

19. See Cohen and March (1986) for a similar argument about universities on which I have drawn.

20. The influence of this trend in the United States (which has lagged behind Europe and the Commonwealth countries) is evident in the 1997 report of the American Assembly, titled "The Arts and the Public Purpose," a consensus document from a conference of leading nonprofit arts practitioners, with some representation of commercial interests and cultural grant makers. In the report's opening sentences, the authors make two claims that are strikingly different from the themes of previous pronouncements of this kind: "The 92nd American Assembly defined the arts inclusively—in a spectrum from commercial to not-for-profit to volunteer, resisting the conventional dichotomies of high and low, fine and folk, professional and amateur, pop and classic. This Assembly affirmed the interdependence of these art forms and the artists and enterprises that create, produce, present, distribute and preserve them, and underscored, in particular, the interdependence of the commercial and not-for-profit arts" (American Assembly 1997:5). Both of these premises are analytically sensible. They are also rhetorically powerful, for an arts sector that includes everything is, first, larger and more important and, second, can no longer be dismissed as an elite preserve. At the same time, this statement of formal equality and interdependence among all forms of art implicitly rejects the moral privileging of Euro-American high culture that was the dominant rationale for nonprofit enterprise in the arts for most of the twentieth century.

21. See www.paristransatlantic.com/antheil/frameset.html. Last accessed March 17, 2003. Antheil was a Trenton native. The celebration was organized by an association of New Jersey composers and supported by local corporations, among others.

22. The UDAO institution code 117 indicates "business corporation," which suggests that these groups are misclassified as nonprofits or that they have incorrect institution codes. Visits to some Web sites of organizations so designated suggest that the former is the case.

23. The UDAO lists 432 nonprofit organizations in the jazz discipline (twice as many jazz organizations of any kind and about thirty-five times as many nonprofit jazz organizations as were included in the Economic Census's mail survey). This reflects the fact that the Census restricts its coverage to performing organizations, whereas the UDAO includes jazz societies, service organizations, and jazz museums. Nonetheless, the UDAO classified almost one-half of the entries in the category as regular performing groups and another 14 percent as amateur, youth, or school-affiliated performing organizations. (It seems likely that the Census includes most of the nonprofit jazz performing organizations identified by the UDAO in nonspecific "musical performer" categories.) Jazz organizations are identified using the discipline codes (F_DISC), and types within this classification are distinguished by cross-classifying F_DISC against the UDAO's institution codes (F_INST). Visual inspection of organization names and consultation of their home pages suggest that some of these organizations are misclassified, either because they are actually blues bands or because they are really associations that sponsor concerts rather than actual performing groups.

24. An interesting subset of jazz nonprofits comprises associations of middle-class, middle-aged white musical amateurs who perform together in public but also promote occasional concerts by professional jazz artists. (One Web site lists fourteen such associations in the Los Angeles area alone, scheduling regular concerts or jam sessions at venues that include a local community college, Elks Club lodges, American Legion halls, and an International House of Pancakes [Valley Jazz Club 2002].)

25. The UDAO lists 377 nonprofits in the "ethnic" music field.

26. Based on UDAO lists and classifications, I estimate that there are roughly nine hundred to twelve hundred nonprofit galleries and artists' cooperatives—considerably fewer than their proprietary counterparts, but a significant proportion (perhaps 20 percent) nonetheless. This rough estimate is based on my analysis of Web pages of a sample of thirty galleries that the UDAO lists as nonprofit visual art galleries (as distinguished from museums). Of these, approximately one-third appeared to be proprietary art galleries misclassified as nonprofit, so I deducted one-third (as well as a few extra, based on other forms of misclassification) from the total reported in this category, but then added an estimated two hundred to three hundred gallery-type operations listed under other headings. It is likely that many such galleries are nonprofit mutual-benefit associations rather than 501(c)(3) nonprofits.

27. The field of software design and publishing adds plausibility to

such speculation. Most software is produced commercially by firms that sell it for profit. But some very important and successful software programs, such as Linux and Apache, have been produced by informal networks of cooperating programmers, whose collective work is facilitated by networks both physical (the Internet) and reputational. Although economists might predict that most people would freeride on the efforts of others (or else withhold their own contributions lest other designers profit from their efforts), such networks have been enormously effective although they lack the credibility provided by formal organizations and nonprofit charters. Indeed, new legal instruments—for example, so-called copylefts, by means of which software producers appropriate rights and then assign them to any user for free, with the sole condition that all further development remain in the public domain—may provide an institutional basis for new forms of cultural production. Even its advocates acknowledge that open source is not appropriate for every software project. Yet the open source movement suggests that, for some purposes, extensive, diffusely connected, online peer-to-peer networks may present a viable organizational alternative to conventional nonprofit organizations (Raymond 2001).

REFERENCES

Alexander, Victoria. 1996. *Museums and Money: The Impact of Funding on Exhibitions, Scholarship and Management.* Bloomington: Indiana University Press.

Allen, Susan. 1998. "Nonprofit and Commercial Music: Three Musicians' Experience." *Journal of Arts Management and Law* 28:145–54.

Alper, Neil, and Gregory Wassall. 2000. *More Than Once in a Blue Moon: Multiple Jobholdings by American Artists.* Santa Ana, Calif.: Seven Locks Press.

American Assembly. 1997. "The Arts and the Public Purpose." Final Report of the 92nd American Assembly, May 29–June 1, 1997. New York: American Assembly.

Anderson, Chris. 2004. "The Long Tail." *Wired* 12: 170–77.

Anheier, Helmut, and Stefan Toepler. 1998. "Commerce and the Muse: Are Art Museums Becoming Commercial?" Pp. 233–48 in *To Profit or Not to Profit: The Commercial Transformation of the Nonprofit Sector,* ed. Burton Weisbrod. New York: Cambridge University Press.

Arian, Edward. 1971. *Bach, Beethoven and Bureaucracy: The Case of the Philadelphia Orchestra.* University: University of Alabama Press.

Backer, Thomas E. 2002. *Partnership as an Art Form: What Works and What Doesn't in Nonprofit Arts Partnerships.* Report to the John S. and James L. Knight Foundation. Encino, Calif: Human Interaction Research Institute.

Baker, Wayne, and Robert Faulkner. 1991. "Role as Resource in the Hollywood Film Industry." *American Journal of Sociology* 97:279–309.

Baumol, William J., and William G. Bowen. 1966. *The Performing Arts: The Economic Dilemma.* Cambridge: MIT Press.

Becker, Howard S. 1982. *Art Worlds.* Berkeley: University of California Press.

Bell, John. 1987. "Industrials: American Business Theatre in the '80s." *Drama Review* 31:22–43.

Bielby, William T., and Denise D. Bielby. 1994. "'All hits are flukes': Institutionalized Decision Making and the Rhetoric of Network Prime-Time Program Development." *American Journal of Sociology* 59:1287–1313.

Blaug, Mark. 2001. "Cultural Economics." *Journal of Economic Surveys* 15:123–43.

Bourdieu, Pierre. 1977. *Reproduction: In Education, Culture, Society.* Beverly Hills: Sage.

Bowen, William G., Thomas I. Nygren, Sarah E. Turner, and Elizabeth A. Duffy. 1994. *The Charitable Nonprofits.* San Francisco: Jossey-Bass.

Brooks, Arthur. 2006. "Nonprofit Firms in the Performing Arts." *Handbook of the Economics of Art and Culture,* ed. Victor Ginsburgh. Amsterdam: Elsevier.

Cameron, Catherine M. 1991. "The New Arts Industry: Non-Profits in an Age of Competition." *Human Organization* 50:225–34.

Carroll, Glenn R. 1985. "Concentration and Specialization: Dynamics of Niche Width in Populations of Organizations." *American Journal of Sociology* 90:1263–83.

Castells, Manuel. 2001. *The Internet Galaxy: Reflections on the Internet, Business and Society.* New York: Oxford University Press.

Caves, Richard E. 2000. *Creative Industries: Contracts Between Art and Commerce.* Cambridge: Harvard University Press.

Chaves, Mark A. 1999. *How Do We Worship?* Washington, D.C.: Alban Institute.

Chaves, Mark A., and Peter V. Marsden. 2000. Congregations and cultural capital: Religious variations in arts activity. Paper presented at the annual meeting of the American Sociological Association, Washington, D.C.

Cohen, Michael D., and James G. March. 1986. *Leadership and Ambiguity: The American College President.* 2d ed. Boston: Harvard Business School Press.

Colonna, Carl M., Patricia M. Kearns, and John E. Anderson. 1993. "Electronically Produced Music and Its Economic Effects on the Performing Musician and the Music Industry." *Journal of Cultural Economics* 17:69–76.

Cultural Policy and the Arts National Data Archive (CPANDA). 2003. "National Trends in Artists' Occupations: Artists Compared to Other Occupations, 1970–2001." http//artsdata .Princeton.edu/arts-culture-facts/artists/brfrcothoccu.html. Last visited June 26, 2003.

Davidson, Benjamin. 2001. *Local Arts Agency Facts: Fiscal Year 2000.* Washington, D.C.: Americans for the Arts.

DiMaggio, Paul. 1982. "Cultural Entrepreneurship in Nineteenth-Century Boston." Pt. 1: "The Creation of an Organizational Base for High Culture in America"; pt. 2: "Cultural Entrepreneurship in Nineteenth-Century Boston, Part II: The Classification and Framing of American Art." *Media, Culture and Society* 4:33–50, 303–22.

———. 1986. "Can Culture Survive the Marketplace?" Pp. 65–92 in *Nonprofit Enterprise in the Arts: Studies in Mission and Constraint,* ed. Paul DiMaggio. New York: Oxford University Press.

———. 1991a. "Social Structure, Institutions, and Cultural Goods: The Case of the U.S." Pp. 133–55 in *Social Theory for a Changing Society,* ed. Pierre Bourdieu and James Coleman. Boulder, Colo.: Westview.

———. 1991b. "Notes on the Relationship Between Art Museums and Their Publics." Pp. 39–50 in *The Economics of Art Museums,* ed. Martin Feldstein. Chicago: University of Chicago Press.

———. 1991c. "Constructing an Organizational Field as a Professional Project: The Case of U.S. Art Museums." Pp. 267–92 in *The New Institutionalism in Organizational Analysis.* Chicago: University of Chicago Press.

———. 1992. "Cultural Boundaries and Structural Change: The Extension of the High-Culture Model to Theatre, Opera, and the Dance, 1900–1940." Pp. 21–57 in *Cultivating Differences: Symbolic Boundaries and the Making of Inequality,* ed. Michèle Lamont and Marcel Fournier. Chicago: University of Chicago Press.

———. 2003. "An Ecological Perspective on Nonprofit Research." Pp. 311–20 in *The Study of Nonprofit Enterprise: Theories and Approaches*, ed. Helmut K. Anheier and Avner Ben-Ner. New York: Kluwer Academic/Plenum.

DiMaggio, Paul, and Becky Pettit. 1997. *Public Sentiments Towards the Arts: A Critical Reanalysis of 13 Public Opinion Surveys.* Report to Pew Charitable Trusts. Princeton: Princeton University Center for Arts and Cultural Policy Studies.

DiMaggio, Paul, and Kristen Stenberg. 1985a. "Conformity and Diversity in American Resident Theatres." Pp. 116–60 in *Art, Ideology and Politics,* ed. Judith H. Balfe and Margaret Jane Wyszomirski. New York: Praeger.

———. 1985b. "Why Do Some Theatres Innovate More Than Others?" *Poetics* 14:107–22.

Dowd, Timothy J. 2002. "Organizing the Musical Canon: The Repertoires of Major U.S. Symphony Orchestras, 1842 to 1969." *Poetics* 30:35–61.

———. 2004. "Concentration and Diversity Revisited: Production Logics and the U.S. Mainstream Recording Market." *Social Forces* 82:1411–55.

Eisner, Elliot W., and Stephen M. Dobbs. 1986. *The Uncertain Profession: Observations on the State of Museum Education in Twenty American Art Museums.* Report to the Getty Center for Education in the Arts, Los Angeles.

Feld, Alan L., Michael O'Hare, and J. Mark Davidson Schuster. 1983. *Patrons Despite Themselves: Taxpayers and Arts Policy.* New York: New York University Press.

Florida, Richard. 2002. "Bohemia and Economic Geography." *Journal of Economic Geography* 2:55–71.

Frank, Robert H., and Philip J. Cook. 1995. *The Winner-Take-All Society.* New York: Free Press.

Freedman, Marc R. 1986. "The Elusive Promise of Management Cooperation in the Performing Arts." Pp. 299–313 in *Nonprofit Enterprise in the Arts: Studies in Mission and Constraint,* ed. Paul DiMaggio. New York: Oxford University Press.

Frey, Bruno. 1994. "The Economics of Music Festivals." *Journal of Cultural Economics* 18:29–39.

———. 1996. "Has Baumol's Cost Disease Disappeared in the Performing Arts?" *Ricerche Economiche* 50:173–82.

Frey, Bruno S., and Werner W. Pommerehne. 1980. "An Economic Analysis of the Museum." Pp. 248–59 in *Economic Policy for the Arts,* ed. William Hendon, James Shanahan, and Alice MacDonald. Cambridge, Mass.: Abt.

Galaskiewicz, Joseph. 1985. *The Social Organization of an Urban Grants Economy.* Orlando, Fla.: Academic.

———. 1997. "Niche Position and the Growth and Decline of Nonprofit Organizations." MS, University of Minnesota.

Gans, Herbert. 1985. "American Popular Culture and High Culture in a Changing Class Structure." *Prospects* 10:17–37.

Grams, Diane, and Michael Warr. 2002. *Leveraging Assets: How Small Budget Arts Activities Benefit Neighborhoods.* Report to the Richard H. Driehaus Foundation and the John D. and Catherine T. MacArthur Foundation. MS, DePaul University.

Gray, Herman. 1988. *Producing Jazz: The Experience of an Independent Record Company.* Philadelphia: Temple University Press.

Greco, Albert N. 2000. "Market Concentration Levels in the U.S. Consumer Book Industry: 1995–1996." *Journal of Cultural Economics* 24:321–36.

Grønbjerg, Kirsten A. 2002. "Evaluating Nonprofit Databases." *American Behavioral Scientist* 45:1741–77.

Hager, Mark A. 2001. "Financial Vulnerability Among Arts Organizations: A Test of the Tuckman-Change Measures." *Nonprofit and Voluntary Sector Quarterly* 30:376–92.

Hager, Mark A., and Thomas H. Pollak. 2002. *The Capacity of Performing Arts Presenting Organizations.* Washington, D.C.: Urban Institute.

Hall, Peter Dobkin. 1992. *Inventing the Nonprofit Sector.* Baltimore: Johns Hopkins University Press.

Halliday, Terence C., M. J. Powell, and M. W. Granfors. 1987. "Minimalist Organizations: Vital Events in State Bar Associations, 1870–1930." *American Sociological Review* 52:456–71.

Hallock, Kevin F. 2002. "Managerial Pay and Governance in American Nonprofits." *Industrial Relations* 41:377–406.

Hannan, Michael, and John Freeman. 1989. *Organizational Ecology.* Cambridge: Harvard University Press.

Hansmann, Henry. 1981. "Nonprofit Enterprise in the Performing Arts." *Bell Journal of Economics* 12(2):341–61.

Heckathorn, Douglas, and Joan Jeffri. 2003. "Patterns of Affiliation in Two Jazz Musician Communities." Paper presented at the annual meeting of the American Sociological Association, August.

Heilbrun, James. 2001. "Empirical Evidence of a Decline in Repertory Diversity Among American Opera Companies, 1991/92 to 1997/98." *Journal of Cultural Economics* 25:63–72.

Heilbrun, James, and Charles M. Gray. 2001. *The Economics of Art and Culture.* 2d edition. New York: Cambridge University Press.

Hout, Michael, Andrew Greeley, and Melissa J. Wilde. 2001. "The Demography of Religious Change in the United States." *American Journal of Sociology* 107:468–500.

James, Estelle. 1987. "The Nonprofit Sector in Comparative Perspective." Pp. 397–415 in *The Nonprofit Sector: A Research Handbook,* 1st ed., ed. Walter W. Powell. New Haven: Yale University Press.

Jeffri, Joan. 1980. *The Emerging Arts: Management, Survival and Growth.* New York: Praeger.

Jeffri, Joan, and Robert Greenblatt. 1994. "Artists Who Work with Their Hands: Painters, Sculptors, Craftspeople and Artist Printmakers; A Trend Report, 1970–1990." *Artists in the Workforce.* Research Report no. 37. Washington, D.C.: National Endowment for the Arts.

Jencks, Christopher. 1986. "Should the News Be Sold for Profit?" Pp. 279–84 in *Nonprofit Enterprise in the Arts: Studies in Mission and Constraint,* ed. Paul DiMaggio. New York: Oxford University Press.

Kaple, Deborah. 2002. "Current Data Resources on Nonprofit Arts Organizations." *American Behavioral Scientist* 45:1592–1612.

Kaple, Deborah A., Lori Morris, Ziggy Rivkin-Fish, and Paul DiMaggio. 1996. *Data on Arts Organizations: A Review and Needs Assessment, with Design Implications.* Report to the National Endowment for the Arts, Research Division. Princeton: Center for Arts and Cultural Policy Studies.

Kaple, Deborah, Ziggy Rivkin-Fish, Hugh Louch, Lori Morris, and Paul DiMaggio. 1998. "Comparing Sample Frames for Research on Arts Organizations: Results of a Study in Three Metropolitan Areas." *Journal of Arts Management, Law and Society* 28:41–66.

Kawashima, Nobuko. 1999. "Privatizing Museum Services in UK Local Authorities: New Managerialism in Action?" *Public Management* 1:157–77.

Kellogg, Stuart. 2002. "Vavoom." *Victorville (CA) Daily Press.* http://www.vvdailypress.com/living/vavoom/ Last accessed August 24, 2002.

Kendall, Elizabeth. 1979. *Where She Danced.* New York: Knopf.

Kenyon, Gerald S. 1995. "Market Economy Discourse in Nonprofit High-Status Art Worlds." *Journal of Arts Management and Law* 25:109–24.

King, Millie Mei-Vung. 1980. "Through the Eyes of Boston: The State of Chamber Music Today." MS, Yale University.

Kirstein, Lincoln. 1938. *Blast at Ballet: A Corrective for the American Audience.* Reprinted in Lincoln Kirstein, *Three Pamphlets Collected.* New York: Dance Horizons, 1967.

Kreidler, John. 1996. "Leverage Lost: The Nonprofit Arts in the Post-Ford Era." *Journal of Arts Management, Law and Society* 26:79–100.

Kuan, Jennifer. 2001. "The Phantom Profits of the Opera: Nonprofit Ownership in the Arts as a Make-Buy Decision." *Journal of Law and Economic Organization* 17:507–20.

Lampkin, Linda M., and Elizabeth T. Boris. 2002. "Nonprofit Organizations Data: What We Have and What We Need. *American Behavioral Scientist* 11:1675–1715.

Lessig, Lawrence. 2004. *Free Culture.* New York: Penguin.

Levine, Lawrence. 1990. *Highbrow/Lowbrow: The Emergence of Cultural Hierarchy in America.* Cambridge: Harvard University Press.

Lopes, Paul D. 2002. *The Rise of a Jazz Art World.* New York: Cambridge University Press.

Luksetich, William A., and Mark D. Lange. 1995. "A Simultaneous Model of Nonprofit Symphony Orchestra Behavior." *Journal of Cultural Economics* 19:49–68.

Macro Systems. 1979. *Contractor Report: Museums Program Survey 1979.* Washington, D.C.: National Center for Educational Statistics.

March, James G. 1962. "The Business Firm as a Political Coalition." *Journal of Politics* 24:662–78.

Martorella, Rosanne. 1990. *Corporate Art.* New Brunswick, N.J.: Rutgers University Press.

McDaniel, Nello, and George Thorn. 1991. *The Quiet Crisis in the Arts.* New York: FEDAPT.

Miller, Mark Crispin. 1997. "The Publishing Industry." Pp. 107–34 in *Conglomerates and the Media,* ed. Erik Barnouw. New York: New Press.

Milofsky, Carl. 1987. "Neighborhood-Based Organizations: A Market Analogy." Pp. 277–95 in *The Nonprofit Sector: A Research Handbook,* 1st ed., ed. Walter W. Powell. New Haven: Yale University Press.

Mitchell, Caroline A. 1986. "Graywolf Press." MS, Yale School of Organization and Management.

Murnighan, J. Keith, and D. E. Conlon. 1991. "The Dynamics of Intense Work Groups: A Study of British String Quartets." *Administrative Science Quarterly* 36:165–86.

National Association of College Stores. 2003. "Industry Information." http://www.nacs. org/public/research/higher_ed_retail.asp. Last visited January 28, 2003.

National Task Force for the American Orchestra. 1993. *Americanizing the American Orchestra.* Washington, D.C.: American Symphony Orchestra League.

Nebraska Jazz Orchestra. 2002. Nebraska Jazz Orchestra website. http://artsincorporated.org/njo/. Last accessed August 26, 2002.

Netzer, Dick. 1978. *The Subsidized Muse.* New York: Cambridge University Press.

New York State Council for the Arts. 2002. Guidelines, "Recording: Category 69 (Competitive Category)," p. 102. http://www.nysca.org/guidelines/102.htm. Last visited August 24, 2002.

O'Hagan, John, and Adriana Neligan. 2002. "The Determinants of Repertoire Diversity in the Non-Profit English Theatre Sector: An Econometric Analysis." MS, Trinity College, Dublin.

Orlean, Susan. 2001. "Art for Everybody: How Thomas Kinkade Turned Painting into Big Business." *New Yorker,* October 15, pp. 124ff.

Oster, Sharon, and William N. Goetzmann. 2002. "Does Governance Matter? The Case of Art Museums." Paper prepared for the National Bureau of Economic Research Workshop on Not-for-Profit Institutions. New Haven: Yale School of Management.

Ostrower, Francie. 1995. *Why the Wealthy Give: The Culture of Elite Philanthropy.* Princeton: Princeton University Press.

———. 2002. *Trustees of Culture: Power, Wealth, and Status on Elite Arts Boards.* Chicago: University of Chicago Press.

Pagani, Jacqualine. 2001. "Mixing Art and Life: The Conundrum of the Avant-Garde's Autonomous Status in the Performance Art World of Los Angeles." *Sociological Quarterly* 42:175–203.

Peterson, Richard A. 1972. "A Process Model of the Folk, Pop, and Fine Art Phases of Jazz." Pp. 135–51 in *American Music: From Storyville to Woodstock,* ed. Charles Nanry. New Brunswick, N.J.: Trans-Action Books and E. P. Dutton.

———. 1990. "Audience and Industry Origins of the Crisis in Classical Music Programming: Toward World Music." Pp. 207–23 in *The Future of the Arts: Public Policy and Arts Research,* ed. David B. Pankratz and Valerie Morris. New York: Praeger.

Peterson, Richard A., and Howard G. White. 1979. "The Simplex Located in Art Worlds." *Urban Life* 7:411–39.

Powell, Walter W. 1985. *Getting into Print: The Decision-Making Process in Scholarly Publishing.* Chicago: University of Chicago Press.

———. 2001. "The Capitalist Firm in the Twenty-First Century: Emerging Patterns in Western Enterprise." Pp. 33–68 in *The Twenty-First-Century Firm: Changing Economic Organization in International Perspective,* ed. Paul DiMaggio. Princeton: Princeton University Press.

Powell, Walter W., and Rebecca Friedkin. 1986. "Politics and Programs: Organizational Factors in Public Television Decision Making." Pp. 245–69 in *Nonprofit Enterprise in the Arts: Studies in Mission and Constraint,* ed. Paul DiMaggio. New York: Oxford University Press.

Raymond, Eric S. 2001. *The Cathedral and the Bazaar: Musings on Linux and Open Source by an Accidental Revolutionary.* Sebastopol, Calif.: O'Reilly & Associates.

Reed Business Information. 2003. *Broadcasting and Cable Yearbook.* New York: Broadcasting & Cable.

Roper Starch Worldwide. 1998. *1998 National Survey: Business Support to the Arts.* New York: Business Committee for the Arts.

Rosen, Sherwin. 1981. "The Economics of Superstars." *American Economic Review* 71:845–58.

Rudenstine, Neil. 1991. "Museum Finances." Pp. 73–86 in *The Economics of Art Museums,* ed. Martin Feldstein. Chicago: University of Chicago Press.

Salamon, Lester. 1987. "On Market Failure, Voluntary Failure, and Third Party Government." *Journal of Voluntary Action Research* 16:29–49.

Schuster, J. Mark. 1998. "Neither Public Nor Private: The Hybridization of Museums." *Journal of Cultural Economics* 22: 127–50.

Scott, Allen J. 2002. "A New Map of Hollywood: The Production and Distribution of American Motion Pictures." *Regional Studies* 36:957–75.

Seley, John E., and Julian Wolpert. 2002. *New York City's Nonprofit Sector.* New York: Community Studies of New York and the Nonprofit Coordinating Committee of New York.

Shanahan, James L. 1989. "Private Support for the Arts in U.S. Metropolitan Areas with United Arts Funds." *Journal of Cultural Economics* 13:35–51.

Silverman, Debora. 1986. *Selling Culture: Bloomingdale's, Diana Vreeland, and the New Aristocracy of Taste in Reagan's America.* New York: Pantheon.

Stern, Mark J. 2000. "The Geography of Cultural Production in Metropolitan Philadelphia." Working Paper no. 10 of the Social Impact of the Arts Project, University of Pennsylvania School of Social Work. http://www.sp2.upenn.edu/SIAP/wp10txt.pdf. Last accessed December 24, 2005.

Stern, Mark J., and Susan C. Seifert. 2000a. "Cultural Organizations in the Network Society." Working Paper no. 11 of the Social Impact of the Arts Project, University of Pennsylvania School of Social Work. http://www.sp2.upenn.edu/SIAP/wp11sum.pdf. Last accessed December 24, 2005.

———. 2000b. "'Irrational Organizations': Why Community-Based Organizations Are Really Social Movements." Working Paper no. 12 of the Social Impact of the Arts Project, University of Pennsylvania School of Social Work. http://www.sp2.upenn.edu/SIAP/wp12txt.pdf. Last accessed December 24, 2005.

Steyn, Mark. 1997. "After the Ball: Bowie Bonds." *Slate,* posted Thursday, May 8, 1997.

Stone, Melissa M. 1989. "Planning as Strategy in Nonprofit Organizations: An Exploratory Study." *Nonprofit and Voluntary Sector Quarterly* 18:297–315.

Storper, Michael. 1989. "The Transition to Flexible Specialisation in the US Film Industry: External Economies, the Division of Labour, and the Crossing of Industrial Divides." *Cambridge Journal of Economics* 13:273–305.

Strom, Elizabeth. 1999. "Let's Put on a Show: Performing Arts and Urban Revitalization in Newark, New Jersey." *Journal of Urban Affairs* 21:423–36.

———. 2001. "Converting Pork into Porcelain: Cultural Institutions and Downtown Development." MS, Rutgers University.

Throsby, David. 2001. *Economics and Culture.* Cambridge: Cambridge University Press.

Throsby, David, and Glenn A. Withers. 1979. *The Economics of the Performing Arts.* New York: St. Martin's.

Toepler, Stefan. 2001. "Culture, Commerce and Civil Society: Rethinking Support for the Arts." *Administration and Society* 33:508–22.

Tschirhart, Mary. 1996. *Artful Leadership: Managing Stakeholder Problems in Nonprofit Arts Organizations.* Bloomington: Indiana University Press.

U.S. Census Bureau—U.S. Department of Commerce, Economics and Statistics Administration. 2000. *Economic Census 1997: (Subject Series) Retail Trade: Establishment and Firm Size Including Legal Form of Organization* (NAICS Sector 44). Economic Census—EC97R44S-SZ. Washington, D.C.: Government Printing Office.

———. 2001a. *Economic Census 1997: (Subject Series) Art, Entertainment and Recreation* (NAICS Sector 71). Economic Census—EC97S71S-SM. Washington, D.C.: Government Printing Office.

———. 2001b. *Economic Census 1997: (Subject Series) Educational Services* (NAICS Sector 61). Economic Census—EC97S61S-SM. Washington, D.C.: Government Printing Office.

———. 2001c. *Economic Census 1997: (Subject Series) Information* (NAICS Sector 51). Economic Census—EC97S51S-SM. Washington, D.C.: Government Printing Office.

———. 2001d. *Economic Census 1997: (Subject Series) Professional, Scientific, and Technical Services* (NAICS Sector 54). Economic Census—EC97S54S-SM. Washington, D.C.: Government Printing Office.

———. 2001e. *Economic Census 1997: (Subject Series) Accommodation and Food Services* (NAICS Sector 72). Economic Census—EC97R72S-SM. Washington, D.C.: Government Printing Office.

———. 2001f. *Economic Census 1997: (General Summary) Manufacturing* (NAICS Sector 31). Economic Census—EC97M31S-GS. Washington, D.C.: Government Printing Office.

———. 2002. 1997 economic census, retail trade, United States. http://www.census.gov/epcd/ec97/us/US000_44.HTM#N451. Last accessed August 25, 2002.

Valley Jazz Club. 2002. Los Angeles area nonprofit jazz clubs. http://www.valleyjazzclub.org/Jazz_Clubs/jazz_clubs.html. Last accessed August 26, 2002.

Voss, Glenn, Daniel M. Cable, and Zannie Giraud Voss. 2000. "Linking Organizational Values to Relationships with External Constituents: A Study of Nonprofit Professional Theatres." *Organization Science* 11:330–47.

Weisbrod, Burton A. 1990. *The Nonprofit Economy.* Cambridge: Harvard University Press.

———. 1997. "The Future of the Nonprofit Sector: Its Entwining with Private Enterprise and Government." *Journal of Policy Analysis and Management* 16:541–55.

Weitzman, Murray S., Nadine T. Jalandoni, Linda M. Lampkin, and Thomas H. Pollak. 2002. *The New Nonprofit Almanac and Desk Reference.* San Francisco: Jossey-Bass.

Wheeler, Britta. 1999. "The Institutionalization of Performance Art." Paper presented at the annual meeting of the American Sociological Association, Washington, D.C.

Whitt, J. Allen. 1987. "Mozart in the Metropolis: The Arts Coalition and the Urban Growth Machine." *Urban Affairs Quarterly* 23:15–36.

Whitt, J. Allen, and John Lammers. 1991. "The Art of Growth: Ties Between Development Organizations and the Performing Arts." *Urban Affairs Quarterly* 26:376–93.

Wolf Organization. 1992. *The Financial Condition of Symphony Orchestras.* Washington, D.C.: American Symphony Orchestra League.

Wu, Chin-Tao. 2001. *Privatising Culture: Corporate Art Intervention Since the 1980s.* New York: Verso.

Zolberg, Vera. 1981. "Conflicting Visions of American Art Museums." *Theory and Society* 10:103–25.

19

Higher Education: Evolving Forms and Emerging Markets

PATRICIA J. GUMPORT
STUART K. SNYDMAN

Comparing and contrasting private nonprofit organizations with for-profit and government organizations can bring into clearer focus various functions and behaviors of the different organizational forms. According to economists, nonprofits provide a more trustworthy alternative organizational form for the respective consumers in industries where performance and quality are difficult to evaluate. Differences in behavior are attributed to the absence of a profit motive and to professional norms that value prestige and other nonpecuniary rewards (Hansmann 1980, 1987). Political scientists emphasize the roles and behaviors of nonprofit organizations in relation to governmental provision of public services. Private nonprofit sectors allow for greater diversification where democratic governments fail to provide services to marginal or specialized groups (Douglas 1987). An alternative perspective, which acknowledges the financial dependence of private nonprofits on government funding, suggests that nonprofit sectors emerge to provide public services without the constraints of government bureaucracy (Salamon 1987).

From a sociological perspective, however, such general distinctions can be problematic. DiMaggio and Anheier (1990) argue that prevailing differences among forms derive from a distinctive mix of state policies, professional interests, and institutional structures, as well as competitive and cooperative dynamics among different types of organizations. They suggest that an industry-level perspective—considering organizations within their respective industries—helps identify the ways in which differences in organizational form are related to specific industry contexts. Within these contexts, organizational forms may prove heterogeneous, with unclear boundaries among them, ambiguous goals, and multiple constituencies. They also argue that across countries, form-related differences vary as a result of unique national contexts wherein political interests, religious tradition, and legal legacies strongly influence the organizational landscape. Their analytical perspective is particularly apt for the study of form-related differences within higher education, where such industry- and nation-specific contours powerfully influence structural and behavioral differences among public, private nonprofit, and for-profit colleges and universities.

This chapter explores the ways in which activities in organizations long considered to be at the core of nonprofit purposes—institutions of education, in this case higher education in the United States—have shown an increasing trend toward commercialization and related hybridization such that the boundaries between nonprofits and for-profits in that domain have become indistinct. Postsecondary education provides a provocative setting for investigating distinctions between institutional forms. This is especially true for the United States system, which is the largest and most highly differentiated in the world, consisting of more than four thousand public, private nonprofit, and for-profit degree-granting organizations. From a comparative cross-national perspective, the magnitude, decentralized authority, and institutional heterogeneity of this organizational landscape have long been considered assets that enable the U.S. system to adapt to changing societal expectations (Clark 1993). At the same time, colleges and universities in the United States have been cited by organizational theorists for their many nonadaptive and nonrational features, including the persistent ambiguity emanating from poorly defined goals, multiple and at times competing demands from several constituencies, unclear domains of authority between faculty and administrators, and indistinguishable boundaries.

A core feature of U.S. higher education that makes it a

fruitful arena for examining theories of nonprofit organizations is that in the United States, higher education is both a public and a private good—a duality readily apparent across all types of colleges and universities. *Publicness* is inherent in the very identification of a college or university as an institution of higher education. This key social marker signals that postsecondary organizations are expected to fulfill one or more societal functions: to ensure access to educational opportunity, to provide workforce training and career preparation, to cultivate civic engagement, to advance knowledge, and to strengthen the economy. Yet higher education is also a private good, expected to accommodate the private interests of paying students and a wide range of sponsors. In terms of academic credentials, the value of undergraduate, graduate, technical, and professional degrees accrues in the form of economic and status returns to degree holders. Private interests are also served in that business partners generate revenue through their collaborations with universities, most notably, licensing revenue from patents. Thus higher education reflects a mélange of public goals and private interests.

This blend is reflected in the diversity of public and private organizational forms represented in the U.S. higher education system and tertiary systems worldwide. The forces of globalization, radically accelerating in the last decade of the twentieth century, have contributed to the increasing presence of private sectors in higher education systems (Currie and Newson 1998; Futures Project 2000). Competition in global labor markets, privatization of public services, cross-national collaborations, and innovations in information technology have begun to have major consequences for higher education, primarily the rise of global market forces as a means to allocate resources. One result of this trend is that nonstate providers are increasingly prominent, and postsecondary educational models in which public and private interests and organizations coexist—or commingle—are increasingly taken for granted. These circumstances may ultimately weaken public-sector providers, including public universities (Johnstone 2000).

The theoretical explanations for the rise of nonprofit sectors are consistent with the perspective of higher education scholars who have investigated the rise of private colleges and universities worldwide. Altbach (1999) characterizes private higher education as the fastest-growing sector worldwide, stemming largely from the inability of governments to fund expansion.[1] Geiger (1991) and Levy (2002) observe that private higher education's roles tend to evolve without foresight or planning, with opportunities appearing in niches that governments choose not to serve. At the same time, however, evidence shows that in many societies, government remains the largest source of revenue for private educational organizations (Salamon et al. 1999).

Although generalized theoretical approaches to the rise of nonprofit sectors find support in the higher education literature, they are less apt to account for the cross-national variation in the degree and circumstances of diversity within institutional forms.[2] Private nonprofit sectors have developed differently over time across national contexts. Geiger (1991) proposes three general patterns. In some countries, mass private sectors arise because governments restrict the provision of higher education to only a fraction of what the market demands. In other cases parallel private and public sectors emerge as a result of different cultural traditions that insist on separate institutions. Finally, small peripheral private sectors emerge in state-dominated higher education systems, where the government is the principal provider alongside private institutions that emerge in certain niches to serve distinctive demands.

Current theories of nonprofit organizations are less well suited to explain other contemporary trends in postsecondary education. For example, government failure theories presume that public and private sectors are complementary, one filling a gap in service created by the other. This does little to explain the pervasive competition in many countries between public and private colleges and universities. In addition, theories that tend to assume a clear distribution of roles between public and private sectors fail to account for the multiple forms of intersectoral collaboration evident in the United States and abroad. These include public-private consortia and hybrid organizations that blend features of both sectors. We argue that such trends put extant theories of nonprofits to the test.

Against this backdrop, this chapter examines the nature and distribution of organizational forms across the U.S. postsecondary landscape.[3] The U.S. case exemplifies a global trend toward convergence between public and private sectors. The first section provides the historical context necessary to understand how wider forces created a changing array of constraints and opportunities for colleges and universities. We cite major economic, political, and technological shifts that became salient for higher education in the second half of the twentieth century. The second section discusses differences between public and private nonprofit higher education, also noting the increasingly visible for-profit sector. We contrast organizational differences along three dimensions: finance, mission, and governance. Our analysis builds on the chapter by Daniel Levy (1987) in the first edition of this book. More historically oriented, our discussion identifies the ways in which some distinctions between public and private nonprofit educational organizations have faded in a context where economic, political, and technological forces have promoted convergence, and we characterize the ways market forces and competitive dynamics have heightened commercial activities throughout the postsecondary enterprise. The third section of the chapter identifies the hybridization of institutional forms—emerging organizations that display features of public and private institutions. We discuss commercial influences on administrative and academic activities, as well as new research and instructional arrangements that result from for-profit spin-offs and industry-university collaborations. The final section offers concluding remarks about the emerging consequences of these shifts and their implications for the distribution of forms within higher education.

U.S. HIGHER EDUCATION IN POST-INDUSTRIAL SOCIETY: HISTORICAL CONTEXT

The end of World War II marked a significant turning point in the organization of postsecondary education. Benchmark legislation, changing student demographics, and the acceleration of scientific and technological innovation facilitated the coevolution of new markets and organizational forms. These changes began with the passage of the Servicemen's Readjustment Act of 1944 (known as the GI Bill), which provided financial assistance to World War II veterans, enabling thousands of unemployed military personnel to afford a college education. This legislation established the entitlement of higher education for the masses and institutionalized universal access as a foundational principle of U.S. higher education. The overwhelming effectiveness of the GI Bill and subsequent financial aid mechanisms sharply increased the demand for higher education. In response, public and private nonprofit colleges and universities expanded their enrollment capacity and diversified their programmatic offerings. Booming enrollments resulted in the founding of new campuses and the dramatic expansion of community colleges (Brint and Karabel 1989, 1991) and specialized institutions (Carnegie Foundation 2001).

This increased demand for higher education was reinforced by enhanced social and economic returns on the value of a college degree. By the end of the twentieth century, postsecondary degrees and certificates all but replaced high school diplomas as the necessary currency for economic and professional advancement. As the economy shifted from manufacturing and agriculture to service and knowledge sectors, the burgeoning demand for undergraduate and professional degrees further compelled colleges and universities to extend their programmatic offerings. Between 1975 and 2000, employment in the manufacturing sector increased by roughly two hundred thousand jobs, or by 1 percent, while jobs in the service sector increased by approximately 26 million, or almost three times 1975 levels (U.S. Department of Labor 2001). These changes coincided with an influx of students, largely workers displaced from manufacturing jobs who returned to school for training in new professional or technical fields. Between 1975 and 1998, enrollment of adult students over the age of twenty-four at degree-granting institutions increased by 44 percent, while enrollment growth of students under twenty-four years of age increased only 22 percent (National Center for Education Statistics 2000).

This influx of adult learners and mid-career professionals, often referred to as the "new majority" of undergraduate students (Jacobs and Stoner-Eby 1998; Seftor and Turner 2002), combined with late twentieth-century labor market transformations to create a qualitative change in the nature of the demand for higher education. The frequency with which workers required retraining also increased, given the highly technical nature of jobs in the postindustrial economy. The rapid pace of technological innovation in recent years caused a decrease in the half-life of knowledge (the amount of time it takes for workers' knowledge to become obsolete) and created a continuous need for workers to upgrade their skills in order to remain competitive in the job market (Davis and Botkin 1994). These trends not only fed rising enrollments in traditional colleges and universities but also led to substantial growth in the corporate training market and other nontraditional educational alternatives (ibid.).

Changes in Public Policy

In addition to the wider economic context, changes in federal higher education policy have also contributed to major shifts in the institutional and ecological structure of higher education. Although education policy in the United States is primarily created at the state level, federal legislation has also been foundational to reshaping the contours of the U.S. higher education system. In the second half of the twentieth century, the Higher Education Act (HEA) of 1965 set guidelines for federal distribution of student aid. Periodic reauthorization of this act allows new government administrations to enact education agendas as well as to make necessary updates to regulations. The 1972 HEA reauthorization was particularly significant for the growth of a proprietary sector. For-profit educational organizations were made eligible to receive federally funded student aid, although significant restrictions to that eligibility applied. McPherson and Schapiro (1991) show that the size of Pell grant awards to students at for-profit institutions increased from 7 percent to 26.6 percent between 1973 and 1988. The 1998 revision of the HEA further helped remove barriers to founding new for-profit educational organizations by including proprietary schools in the official definition of "institutions of higher education" (Committee on Labor and Human Resources 1998).

The 1998 HEA also signaled the federal government's increased commitment to the viability of programs and schools that offer distance education by defining it as "an educational process that is characterized by the separation, in time or place, between instructor and student" (Committee on Labor and Human Resources 1998). This created a language for policy makers to use in discussing distance education. Regulations that had previously denied financial aid to students participating in such programs were removed, and—quite significant—accrediting agencies were authorized to review these programs (ibid.).

Another significant set of policy changes made during the past two decades has addressed the patenting and licensing of scientific discoveries. The Patent and Trademark Amendments of 1980 (also known as the Bayh-Dole Act) allowed universities and their faculty to apply for patents on scientific discoveries emerging from federally funded research projects. Along with legislation passed in 1984 that further loosened restrictions on commercializing research, the Bayh-Dole Act created new opportunities for collaboration between universities and industry. In reducing legal barriers to commercialization of publicly funded academic research, the act encouraged university administrators and faculty to consider the fruits of academic research as intellectual property with value in the marketplace.

Changes in Science and Technology

Also contributing to the changing landscape of postsecondary education was the pace of scientific and technological innovation, which quickened throughout the second half of the twentieth century. Significant federal investment in university-based research for defense-related technologies thrust U.S. higher education to the forefront of scientific research. Sustained government investment in university-based research led to accelerated innovations in computer sciences, engineering, aeronautics, and the life sciences. The era of modern computing began with the assembly of ENIAC at the University of Pennsylvania in 1945, and many of the innovations related to the space program in the 1950s and 1960s were rooted in university research. The 1970s and 1980s saw significant increases in health-related research in the life sciences, exemplified by Herbert Cohen and Stanley Boyer's discovery of recombinant DNA techniques (see below). These advances in science and technology established universities as valuable assets in advancing the frontiers of knowledge for the United States and the world.

The emergence of communications and information technologies provides further context for understanding the changing organizational landscape of U.S. higher education. Many educators and policy makers believe that information and communication technologies such as digital multimedia, computerized simulation, and the Internet have the potential to confer significantly greater learning benefits than traditional lecture and seminar formats and can extend access to quality instruction at reduced costs. Although there is little empirical evidence to support these claims, the use of new technologies in instruction has dramatically increased. For example, the percentage of classes using email for instruction rose 70 percent between 1994 and 2000 (Green 2000). The number of classes with course Web sites increased fourfold between 1994 and 2000. The use of the Internet to provide courses and degree programs remotely has also become widespread. By 1998 almost 80 percent of all public universities offered some distance education courses. Between 1995 and 1998 the number of private universities offering distance education courses almost doubled (Lewis, Snow, and Farris 1999).

The advent of new instructional technologies has several important consequences for the changing organizational landscape of U.S. higher education. First, the nature of digital technologies has helped transform instruction into a commodity that can be mass-produced, sold, and reused without the involvement of faculty. Unlike the textbook, often considered a supplementary tool of instruction, digital media blend text, sound, and video to create the appearance of a polished product that can be reproduced at very low cost. Information technologies create a new market for the design and sale of instructional materials, heightening awareness of the ambiguity and potential conflict between faculty and administrators over the ownership of intellectual property and professional compensation. Second, new information and communication technologies remove geography as a barrier to educational access. The place-bound residential college or commuter campus no longer represents the only option for degree attainment. Removing spatial limitations creates and expands markets of students living in remote locations or place-bound by employment, disability, or family responsibilities. Third, the ubiquity of information technologies facilitates new types of interorganizational collaboration, creating new options for organizing educational activities and services. For example, distant organizations with different competencies can more easily collaborate to provide a more complete range of academic programs or services. Fourth, the capacity of new technologies for economies of scale removes important barriers for new educational organizations. The high fixed costs of physical plants and salaries are significantly reduced in the provision of "virtual education." In expanding markets for distance education and lowering financial barriers, new information technologies change the behaviors of existing colleges and universities and stimulate the emergence of new types of providers.

This historical overview has depicted how forces in the wider context—specifically, policy, science, technology, and the economy—have incrementally altered the dynamics of the competitive landscape and opened up opportunities for colleges and universities. New markets and policies that affect financial streams prompt reconsideration of taken-for-granted practices in teaching and research. Many of these wider forces also promote similar behaviors across public, private nonprofit, and for-profit forms. It has also been noted that, at times, public and private nonprofits behave as for-profits do while retaining their nonprofit legal designation. This point echoes DiMaggio and Anheier's (1990) assertion that heterogeneity within an industry belies generalizable distinctions. The question remains, then, which distinctions between different sectors in higher education are noteworthy, and to what extent do those distinctions remain salient today?

Comparing Private Nonprofit, Public, and For-Profit Higher Education

For-profit colleges and universities. The United States is one of many countries with a prominent for-profit sector in higher education. Compared to other countries with notable for-profit sectors, the proprietary sector in the United States is quite mature. Except for estimates of enrollment, however, the paucity of data and research on for-profits in the United States and abroad does not allow for a systematic comparison of behavioral characteristics between them and their public and nonprofit counterparts. Instead, we briefly review the extant literature in order to characterize what is known about this sector.

Often referred to as "proprietary" colleges and universities, for-profits have a long history in U.S. education. Historically considered outside the mainstream of higher education, proprietary colleges and universities have, for many decades, offered instructional programs in trade and vocational fields. Common instructional programs include business (real estate, secretarial, travel, and tourism), personal services (cosmetology, massage), health services (nursing and medical assistance), technology (computer programming and data processing), and industrial trades (construction and auto mechanics). Programs tend to be of brief duration, and students tend to be younger and from lower-income backgrounds (Apling 1993).

The lion's share of research concerning for-profit institutions has focused on the composition of their enrollments as they compare to more traditional public and private nonprofit institutions (Apling 1993; Cheng and Levin 1995; Morris 1993). Researchers have documented disproportionately higher student loan default rates among students of proprietary schools (Apling 1993; Dynarski 1994; Grubb and Tuma 1991; Wilms, Moore, and Bolus 1987). High default rates on student loans have led critics to view for-profits with much skepticism and to lobby steadfastly for the exclusion of proprietary institutions from federal aid programs. Recent studies have investigated the apparent convergence of for-profit institutions with public community colleges (Bender 1991; Hyslop and Parsons 1995). Community colleges and other public and private nonprofit institutions have begun to adopt more market-oriented curriculum and business practices that resemble characteristics of the for-profit form. Conversely, proprietary institutions have increased efforts to appear more traditional, or mainstream, by applying for accreditation and expanding their curricula and degree offerings to include more general education and transferable credits (Bender 1991).

Although much of this research emphasizes lower-prestige vocational and trade schools, the last decade of the twentieth century saw the emergence of a new breed of for-profit colleges and universities, increasingly considered part of mainstream U.S. higher education. These consist primarily of large chains offering mainstream degrees and new for-profit ventures attempting to capitalize on the economies of scale afforded by distance education technologies (Davis and Botkin 1994; Katz et al. 1999). Examples of the chain model and distance education include the University of Phoenix, ITT Technical Institute, and DeVry University.[4] This new breed offers undergraduate and graduate degrees in high-demand professional fields such as business, computer science, psychology, and teacher education. Although some educators remain skeptical, distrusting profit-oriented colleges as "diploma mills" (Noble 2002), for-profits have gained legitimacy with accreditors and employers and have become popular among the growing number of adult students who seek relevant training that is both convenient and of good quality.

The for-profit sector's growing prominence is illustrated by data about the increased proportion of for-profit institutions in the national system and in their share of degree production at the undergraduate and the graduate levels. Breneman, Pusser, and Turner (2000) have compiled data showing that for-profits account for roughly half of all institutions of higher education,[5] although they grant only a small proportion of all degrees. For-profits remain heavily concentrated in the two-year, certificate-granting, and non–degree-granting domains and account for only a small share of all four-year and graduate degrees.[6] The data reveal, however, substantial changes in production of bachelor's and graduate degrees. Between 1980 and 1995, bachelor's degree production by for-profits increased 400 percent. This contrasts with the 20 percent increase in bachelor's degrees awarded by all public and private nonprofit colleges. Also, the number of master's degrees awarded by for-profits increased tenfold over the sixteen-year study period.

Research concerning competition between for-profits and the public or nonprofit sector in higher education is scarce, and preliminary evidence is mixed as to whether emergent for-profits ought to be considered competitors of established public and private nonprofit colleges and universities. For example, Raphael and Tobias (1997) report that competition from for-profit colleges in teacher preparation has raised concerns at state universities in Arizona. In interviews at public community colleges and for-profits offering similar degree programs, however, Bailey, Badway, and Gumport (2001) find little evidence that community college leaders perceive an immediate threat to their viability from local for-profits. Winston (1999) argues that traditional settings for higher education are not immediately exposed to competition from the for-profit sector, observing that only a subset of for-profit colleges can be meaningfully compared to nonprofit academic institutions. Given the size of endowments and government subsidies, public and private nonprofit institutions have historically attracted able students, recruited the most prestigious faculty, and maintained a breadth of programs by means of cross-subsidization. Particularly at the more elite levels of U.S. postsecondary education, Hansmann (1999) notes, students shop on the basis of institutional prestige and comparability of student peers, thus effectively limiting the ability of for-profits to compete.

Comparison of public and private nonprofit institutions. Far more data are available about public institutions (hereafter "publics") and private nonprofits. A descriptive overview of their respective sizes within the United States provides essential grounding.[7] In 1998–99, public colleges and universities accounted for 44 percent of degree-granting postsecondary institutions. Private nonprofits similarly accounted for 44 percent, and for-profits for 9 percent (see table 19.1). When disaggregated by type, publics dominate every category except for the baccalaureate colleges, 85 percent of which are private nonprofits. Of those, 70 percent are formally designated as having a religious affiliation, with the majority being of Catholic or Protestant denominations.[8] In fact, nearly all liberal arts colleges were founded with a religious affiliation and have to varying extents retained this institutional identity. Yet in terms of educational policies and practices, many of these became secularized during the twentieth century.

Of the approximately 14.8 million students enrolled in

TABLE 19.1. DEGREE-GRANTING INSTITUTIONS BY TYPE AND AFFILIATION

Carnegie institution type	Public	Private nonprofit independent	Private nonprofit religious	For-profit	NA	Row total[a]
All	1,539	667	910	315	92	3,523
AAC (two-year)	940	99	57	263	57	1,416
BC I and II	86	162	381	8	6	643
MCU I and II	277	84	171	0	1	533
RU II, DG I and II	92	30	25	0	0	147
RU I	59	28	2	0	0	89
Other	85	264	274	44	28	695

Source: U.S. Department of Education, National Center for Education Statistics 2000.

Note: Institution type reflects Carnegie classification: AAC = associate of arts colleges, BC I and II = baccalaureate colleges I and II, MCU I and II = master's-granting colleges and universities I and II, RU II and DG I and II = research university II and doctoral-granting universities I and II, RU I = research universities I.

[a] Data for institutions that were missing a Carnegie classification value were not included.

U.S. degree-granting postsecondary education in the fall of 1999, publics enrolled approximately 76 percent of the total, while private nonprofits enrolled 21 percent and for-profits about 3 percent. The larger institutions tend to be public. Approximately 90 percent of campuses with an enrollment of more than ten thousand students are public. Publics also grant more degrees, accounting for 66 percent of all degrees granted in 1999–2000, while private nonprofits accounted for 30 percent and for-profits 4 percent.

The private nonprofit sector in American higher education is the largest of any in the world (Geiger 1991). Enrolling students of all levels of ability, they do not lend themselves to generalizations except to note that the expansion of public higher education following World War II has resulted in the private sector's showing a steady decline in its share of total enrollment. In the United States private higher education reflects different roles fulfilled by different sets and subsets of institutions (Geiger 1991). Of all institutional types, the private research universities and liberal arts colleges deserve mention as having long-standing reputations, some for selectivity and others for serving a particular clientele (such as urban, female, or older students).

These data provide a sense of the scale of the degree-granting postsecondary landscape. We turn now to distinctions between publics and private nonprofits (which we refer to henceforth as "privates"), the two biggest segments of the system. We examine three domains of activity—finance, mission, and governance—and the ways in which wider economic and policy contexts have contributed to some convergences among the institutional forms.

Finance. In finance, the historical distinction between public and private nonprofit higher education is the revenue mix; specifically, the largest single source of revenue at publics is state appropriations. In reality, however, revenue at publics and privates derives from public funding (for example, revenue from student aid and sponsored research) and private funding (for example, revenue from research activities, tuition, and fees). Yet the rationale underlying the basic distinction is worth examining. The rationale for giving public funds to public colleges and universities is that they are state-controlled and thus provide a public good to the state, including equitable access to educational opportunity and economic benefit to society. Although this public value accrues to the society at the national level, as well as at the state and local levels, the federal government does not take direct responsibility for publicly financing institutions of higher education. Instead it funds the students by means of an extensive array of financial aid programs that offer grants and loans to students for their tuition and related expenses. As a result, much of this government funding ends up being distributed across public, private nonprofit, and for-profit institutions. Colleges and universities of all types have an enormous incentive to become and remain eligible for student financial aid programs, even though doing so requires that their practices comply with a multitude of federal regulations such as nondiscrimination, student privacy, and extensive recordkeeping. The overarching impact of these policies is to standardize, in that publics, nonprofits, and for-profits seeking eligibility for student aid dollars are all expected to comply with the same set of rules.

In addition to the policy context, a set of factors related to economic turbulence also shapes the behavior of all institutions. Although public colleges and universities have received the bulk of their funding from the state, in recent years, economic constraints and competing interests at the state level have resulted in the allocation of a declining proportion of state budgets to higher education. At the same time, the proportion of state revenue reflected in institutional budgets has declined, even though state appropriations remain the largest single revenue source for all publics (Gumport and Jennings 1999). Observers have cast this decline in political terms, in which public campuses shifted from being state-supported to state-assisted. In order to call attention to this alleged abandonment, some propose "state-located" as a more apt term (Duderstsadt 2000).

Though not mediated by the state, private nonprofits have also faced some economic turbulence. They are financed in large part by tuition and fees, voluntary support from alumni, and private funds from selected sources. For example, Catholic colleges and universities obtain substantial funding from their religious communities. Unlike the publics, private nonprofits set their own tuition levels as approved by their governing boards. Since the mid-1980s, private nonprofits have been heavily criticized for their tuition increases, catalyzing widespread media attention and legal action at the federal level. In spite of scrutiny, private nonprofits have fared well financially and continue to find ways to compete successfully against one another and with their public counterparts.

As publics and privates have weathered economic cycles of inflation and stock market fluctuations, they have made it a priority to cultivate a plurality of revenue sources in order to avoid dependence on a single source and to generate additional revenue for discretionary use. Publics and privates have launched capital campaigns for alumni, corporate, and foundation donations, and both have more actively developed intellectual property with commercial potential. The result has been an increase in private revenue dollars per full-time-equivalent student at publics and privates. The proportional increase at publics is larger across all levels of the system's hierarchy, suggesting that publics have indeed been successful in their attempts to generate nonstate revenue (see table 19.2).

Beyond the United States, several developed countries show signs of similar financial trends, although in varying degrees. Privatization has been in evidence since the late 1970s in most developed countries, especially where governments have faced constraints in public funds due to increased competition among demands from the public sector or declining tax revenues (Geiger 1991). In these contexts, public higher education has been expected to cultivate private revenue sources. One approach is to raise tuition and fees. The rationale is that students who receive the benefits should share in the costs of their higher education. In addition to the United States, the Netherlands, China, and Britain were all charging tuition at public colleges and universities by the end of the twentieth century. Another approach is to create revenue-generating academic units within public campuses and to adapt programs to respond to changes in market forces and changes in demands from a full range of consumers, including students, employers, and state governments themselves.[9] An example of this is the worldwide trend of establishing executive MBA programs, which charge higher levels of tuition to mid-career professionals whose companies often reimburse them for educational expenses. In addition to these specific strategies, colleges and universities are embracing academic management practices that seek to contain costs and carefully monitor resources in the name of efficiency and the economic bottom line.

Thus in the United States and abroad, the evidence of distinctions between publics and privates is mixed. On one hand, an enduring difference is that public colleges and universities do retain a stream of public funds. On the other, changes in the wider policy and economic contexts have necessitated that public and private funds flow to public and private colleges and universities. Some public funds derive from financial aid that students bring with them, and some private funds are derived from an array of nonstate sources. Each stream of funding entails a set of behavioral guidelines, either formally explicated (as in the case of requirements for student aid eligibility) or implicitly understood (as in the types of activities considered appropriate for generating revenue). Given that private higher education is in part publicly subsidized and that public institutions generate an increasing proportion of private revenue, this suggests some convergence in the financial profiles for both types of colleges and universities. In addition, prioritizing fiscal concerns in the management of publics and privates aligns them more closely with practices in the for-profit sector.

Mission. A college or university's mission sets its goals and, under constraints, its priorities. In postsecondary education, mission statements are notoriously broad and vacuous. Two dimensions of mission are most relevant to this chapter: the student populations served and the degree programs offered. The hierarchical nature of the U.S. system (from community colleges to research universities) produces more differences in mission *within* the publics and the privates than *between* them, because each level offers similar

TABLE 19.2. PRIVATE REVENUE PER FTE ENROLLMENT BY INSTITUTIONAL TYPE AND CONTROL, 1975–95

	Public institution dollars per FTE		Private institution dollars per FTE		Percentage change, 1975–95	
Institution type	1975	1995	1975	1995	Public	Private
All	348	694	3,105	4,012	100	29
AAC	40	88	1,275	1,688	122	34
BC I and II	135	244	2,756	3,077	82	12
MCU I and II	102	239	1,351	1,382	140	2
RU II and DG I and II	413	791	2,035	3,596	91	77
RU I	1,038	2,348	8,113	11,415	126	41

Source: Gumport and Jennings 1999.

Note: Amounts are given in constant 1997 dollars adjusted by the Higher Education Price Index. Institution type reflects Carnegie classification: AAC = associate of arts colleges, BC I and II = baccalaureate colleges I and II, MCU I and II = master's-granting colleges and universities I and II, RU II and DG I and II = research university II and doctoral-granting universities I and II, RUI = research universities I.

degrees and serves similar student clienteles. Nonetheless, setting aside this heterogeneity within each category, the basic difference in mission between publics and privates is that privates have more autonomy and discretion to set and modify their missions, to limit their student clientele, and to narrow program offerings for specific purposes.

With regard to students served, public colleges and universities have historically had impressive breadth in the name of providing access to educational opportunity. Their tuition is much lower than that of privates in order to permit affordable access (see table 19.3). Cross-nationally, however, the tuition charged by the public sector in the United States is the highest in the world. Public two-year colleges, referred to as "community colleges," have long been considered to constitute the primary mechanism for access. This ideal persists although scholars have provided evidence that only small proportions of students transfer out of community colleges to obtain higher degrees (Brint and Karabel 1989, 1991; Dougherty 1994). Ongoing concerns have been raised about the quality of lower-division education offered to these students and whether genuine access is being provided.

In contrast, private nonprofits tend to have more autonomy in setting selective admissions criteria. Whereas publics are mandated to admit students based on designated criteria and according to preestablished targets, privates set their own admissions criteria and make their own decisions, including whether to admit more or fewer students from any given year's applicant pool. The autonomy to determine which students to accept figures prominently in religiously affiliated institutions, women's colleges, and other private institutions that may seek uniformity in their student body based on a particular ideology or socioeconomic background.

Despite these differences between privates and publics, an overview of student background characteristics by institutional type indicates that student profiles at private nonprofit and public four-year institutions resemble one another more closely than do the profiles of students entering public two-year and public four-year institutions (see table 19.3). National data about characteristics of the three million first-time beginning postsecondary students in 1995–96 show that students entering public two-year institutions differed markedly from those enrolling in public four-year and private nonprofit four-year institutions (Kojaku and Nunez 1998). The students entering two-year publics were older, had lower scores on admissions tests, and came from families with less wealth (only 19 percent came from families with incomes of more than $70,000). Although there is less contrast between the characteristics of students entering private nonprofit four-years and public four-years, students enrolling in privates have higher test scores (43 percent in the highest quartile compared to 30 percent) and come from wealthier families (34 percent from families with incomes

TABLE 19.3. PERCENTAGE DISTRIBUTION OF BEGINNING POSTSECONDARY STUDENTS ACCORDING TO SELECTED CHARACTERISTICS, ACADEMIC YEAR 1995–96

	Public 2-year college	Public 4-year college	Private nonprofit 4-year college
Age			
18 or younger	38.3	59.7	62.4
19	22.7	25.6	24.9
20–23	13.2	9.3	6.7
24 or older	25.8	5.4	6
Dependency and 1994 income			
Dependent			
Lowest quartile (less than $25,000)	27.5	22.7	17.6
Middle quartiles ($25,000–$69,999)	53.4	50.5	48.3
Highest quartile ($70,000 or more)	19.2	26.8	34.1
Independent			
Lowest quartile (less than $6,000)	20.5	25.1	25.1
Middle quartiles ($6,000–$24,999)	51.4	50.9	51.7
Highest quartile ($25,000 or more)	28.1	24	23.2
Actual or derived SAT combined score			
Lowest quartile (400–700)	43	16.8	11.8
Middle quartiles (710–1020)	47.1	53.9	45.6
Highest quartile (1030–1600)	9.9	29.2	42.6
Parents' educational attainment			
High school diploma or less	51.5	37	26.9
Some postsecondary education	21.6	18.35	13.35
Bachelor's degree	18.4	24.95	25.7
Graduate or first professional degree	8.5	19.75	34.1
Tuition and fees (in current USD)			
Full-time, full year	$1,338	$3,862	$13,075
Part-time or part-year	$520	$1,822	$5,223

Source: Kojaku and Nunez 1998.

higher than $70,000 compared to 27 percent). Students, of course, also pay markedly different tuition for full-time study across these institutional types.[10]

In spite of these distinctions in student profiles, publics and privates must abide by state and federal policies that establish common guidelines for their admissions practices. For example, a U.S. Supreme Court ruling in 1978 established that they cannot use quotas in admissions, but they may select applicants on the basis of race in order to promote diversity. The use of racial preference in admissions has been so hotly contested over the past few decades that the courts have been asked to intervene to examine its legal foundations.

The second pertinent dimension of mission is the range of degree programs offered. Following the principle of access, the notion is that public colleges and universities should provide students with access to a comprehensive range of subjects, whether at community colleges or at research universities. Overall, publics are expected to cater to a wider range of student interests, employer needs, and state and regional requirements. The evolution of land grant universities illustrates this expectation. Initially created by landmark federal legislation (the Morrill Acts of 1862 and 1890) with a utilitarian focus, many land grant universities were fueled by institutional ambition to accommodate expanded enrollments throughout the twentieth century and establish a comprehensive array of program offerings.[11]

In contrast, the scope of programmatic offerings at private nonprofits has historically varied extensively: narrow or focused at some, but comprehensive at others. Yet among comprehensive private colleges, as Clark (1972) pointed out, some liberal arts colleges are noted for selective strength and financial investment in particular areas. Examples of this include music at Oberlin College, the arts at Bennington College, and languages at Middlebury College. Religiously affiliated colleges, many of which have become secularized, have the autonomy to weave nonsecular values and beliefs into their academic programs. Other private colleges unapologetically offer only a few degree programs that correspond with direct market demand. In other words, private nonprofits have greater discretion to offer a narrower range of programs in an effort to occupy a distinctive niche.

In recent years, publics and private nonprofits have engaged in mission differentiation in response to wider economic and political forces. This trend is noteworthy given that postsecondary organizations are known for continuity in their academic structures, whether due to inertia, entrenched professional interests, or a preponderance of tenured faculty positions.[12] Under the banner of restructuring and repositioning for the market, both types of campuses have sought cost savings and efficiency gains from eliminating and consolidating programs deemed weak as well as from selectively investing in programs deemed strong and profitable (Gumport 2000). Market-driven behavior is seen most clearly among for-profit colleges and universities, which unabashedly acknowledge their aim to "cherry-pick" the most profitable programs to correspond with demand (Kelly 2001).

In responding to and implementing academic restructuring, publics and private nonprofits have shifted their missions in slightly different ways. Privates have been able to pare down their offerings more dramatically and more quickly because they have fewer constraints imposed by state oversight. For example, a private liberal arts college of low selectivity plagued by financial constraints may eliminate cost-intensive programs, such as nursing, and refocus its mission to offer niche programs for students with a practical interest in obtaining skills for an occupation, such as dental hygiene or business. Mission change can be so extensive that what was once a residential college for students between the ages of 18 and 21 may become primarily a commuter campus that offers courses on a part-time basis for adults on evenings and weekends. Thus the legacy of comprehensive liberal arts is replaced with strategic repositioning for the market. Such mission redefinition in private nonprofits is not necessarily free from resistance, however, as alumni, students, and faculty may form a powerful constraint. For example, demonstrations at Mills College convinced the board of trustees to reverse their initial decision to become coeducational and retain the undergraduate mission of educating women (McCurdy 1990).

In public colleges and universities, shifts related to restructuring reflect additional layers of constraints due to state control, and proposed changes have often been contested by different stakeholders. For instance, the trustees of the City University of New York recently mandated that remedial programs be removed from its universities and instead offered only by community colleges, a policy change that overturned a legacy of open access to its universities, especially the City College of New York (Gumport and Bastedo 2001). In this case, mission differentiation in New York's public higher education was pursued by a coalition of conservative interests within and beyond the CUNY system. Thus, at publics, strategic moves to change degree program offerings occur not only at the campus level and locally but also at other levels throughout the state. Such changes at private nonprofits have tended to be much more circumscribed to particular campuses and the most proximate constituencies they serve.

At publics and privates, mission definition can change the configuration of students admitted and the academic programs offered, and marketing rhetoric reflects the intention of the institutions' positioning themselves to be more competitive in specific niches. Differences in the ways these processes unfold point to an enduring distinction: private nonprofits have the autonomy to set their missions, whereas publics are state-controlled and often find themselves mired in controversy over the appropriate organizational structures for achieving public higher education's egalitarian and meritocratic purposes. For both institutional types, however, the catalysts for mission change tend to be exogenous and primarily economic and political in nature.

Governance. In the early twenty-first century, governance of higher education worldwide has taken on a different hue. It has become deeply infused with both economic and political concerns. As periods of retrenchment have heightened concern about the way higher education manages its finances, external bodies have fortified the mechanisms for ensuring accountability. In an effort to make higher education systems and particular campus practices more transparent, state governments or their intermediaries have formalized accounting and auditing functions through performance indicators, not only for finance and operations but for a variety of research and student outcomes. This trend has been evident in the United States, the United Kingdom, the Netherlands, Germany, Hong Kong, Australia, and more recently in Eastern European countries. Although the particular forms vary from one country to the next, as do the relative inducements to become market-oriented, this general drive for accountability has become so tightly interwoven with resource allocations and political agendas that it has left no formal governing structure untouched.

Against this backdrop, in this chapter we address two dimensions of governance. First, we discuss the formal oversight provided by governing boards and by state, regional, and national agencies. Second, we discuss the role of campus leaders and faculty in managing campus affairs. As in the domains of finance and mission, structural distinctions in governance between publics and privates can be made. Wider political and economic factors, however, have contributed to some convergence between the forms.

In terms of formal oversight, the two major mechanisms in U.S. higher education are governing boards of trustees and an array of state, regional, and national agencies. More than fifty thousand trustees serve U.S. colleges and universities voluntarily. In their capacity as stewards, trustees provide oversight of the campus leadership and of a wide range of policies and practices, including admissions, financial aid, and financial and plant management. (For further discussion of board responsibilities, see Ostrower and Stone, this volume.) Fundraising is a major priority for individual trustees and for governing boards as a whole.

Publics and privates have shown some notable differences in board composition. Public boards have been smaller and more diverse than those of privates. In recent years, boards of both types have shown an increase in size and an increase in the proportion of women and minorities (see table 19.4). In addition, the age of trustees has increased, along with the proportion of business executives and retired business executives. Nonetheless, a basic distinction in size and demographic profiles has persisted.

The policymaking dynamics of boards also show differences between publics and privates. The governance of public colleges and universities has become both more structurally complex and more politicized. As Levy (1987) suggests, public college and university governance usually represents a wider array of special interests and stakeholder groups than does private governance, and accordingly, it more closely reflects the contested nature of campus purposes and practices. Ingram (1993:1) refers to such heterogeneity in public governing boards as "a gigantic kaleidoscope of conflicting values and ideologies." This is partly due to the fact that individuals who serve on governing boards for public colleges and universities may be either appointed or elected. Approximately half of all trustees are appointed, usually by the state's governor, and affirmed by the state legislature. The appointment and confirmation process brings political interests to center stage.

In contrast, the governing boards of privates tend to operate behind closed doors, and conflicts are not as apparent unless the media have identified a controversy that evokes broader public interest. Trustees for private colleges and universities are appointed and voted on by current board members, sometimes in consultation with a sitting president. In addition to providing oversight, they are expected to support the private institution financially with their own donations and fundraising efforts. Information about their governance or about the internal affairs of the institution is not mandated to be publicly available, as it is for public colleges and universities. The more accessible oversight mechanisms and greater uniformity of interests at the privates may make it easier for campus officials to work with their boards.

TABLE 19.4. COMPOSITION OF GOVERNING BOARDS OF PUBLIC AND PRIVATE COLLEGES AND UNIVERSITIES, 1977–97

	1977		1985		1997	
	Public	Private nonprofit	Public	Private nonprofit	Public	Private nonprofit
Total number of board members	7,044	43,493	6,528	45,135	NA	NA
Average board size	9	26.1	8.6	27.9	11.1	29.9
Female members (%)	17.7	14.7	23.1	19.6	30.1	26.4
Nonwhite members (%)	7.1	5.8	14.8	9.1	27.4	10.4
Having B.A. or less (%)	16.6	8.6	14.1	6.3	NA	NA
40 years old or younger (%)	12	9	12.6	8.3	7.8	5
60 years old or older (%)	21.9	32.7	28.2	32.9	30	36
Business executives (%)	NA	NA	39	42.3	40.7	47.3

Source: Anderson 1986; Madsen 1998.

Beyond formal oversight and fiduciary responsibilities, the second level of formal governance is the centralized state-level mechanism for coordination of policy and planning in higher education. The function of statewide coordination was regulative in the decades after World War II: it was to oversee expansion and ensure mission differentiation and planning across public colleges and universities (Berdahl 1971). In recent decades, through cycles of economic constraint, the state's priority was to ensure that resources were allocated efficiently rather than wasted in unnecessary program duplication and to provide incentives to compete for targeted funding on state-identified priority areas (such as teacher education). Since the 1990s, state boards have pushed public colleges and universities hard for accountability, particularly for assessing student learning and reviewing academic programs, leaving some to question whether their structures and staffs are suited to these tasks (Mingle and Epper 1997).

Publics and privates are subject to an additional layer of formal oversight that is voluntary in nature. Accreditation agencies conduct periodic reviews by external experts, typically doing so every ten years, although interim reviews are common. In preparation, campuses prepare extensive self-study documentation. Also, national-level programmatic accreditation is mandated for selected degrees in fields such as business, clinical psychology, and teacher education. The process of institutional and programmatic accreditation is a formidable force for conformity of curriculum, credit units required, instructional and advisory practices, and services provided to students. These two types of accreditation extend to for-profits as well if they seek degree-granting status and eligibility for federally funded student aid. The general principle of privates' having more autonomy than publics is superseded by such accrediting mechanisms.

Another major dimension of governance is the management of campus affairs, the activities and practices coordinated by top administrators, faculty, and staff in carrying out the organization's major functions (for example, reporting to external bodies, managing human resources, and internal decision making). In management—as in finance and mission—wider political and economic factors have contributed to similarities in many processes.

The daily management practices of publics and privates have historical distinctions that can be traced to their respective formal structures. For publics, the managerial structures and orientations have been more bureaucratic, with a hierarchy of offices (extending beyond the campus throughout the state) that call for standardized reporting procedures and specific guidelines for management practices. The multilevel structure of publics necessitates more layers for reporting and approval than at privates, as is evident in procedures for salary setting and faculty hiring. Publics must also make decisions in the face of uncertainty, of potential shifts or abrupt discontinuities in state funding and political climates (James 1990). In contrast, the locus of decision making and management in privates is local and less hierarchical, with a tendency toward considerable discretion in decisions about policies and resource allocation at the lower levels of departments, as well as at the upper levels occupied by the deans, the provost, and the president.

A campus's internal affairs are managed with similar norms for shared decision making and policy formulation. A major formal distinction between public and private nonprofits has been the opportunity for collective bargaining rights for full-time faculty. In 1980 the Supreme Court (in a 5–4 ruling) denied faculty at Yeshiva University, a private university, the right to bargain collectively under federal labor laws (*National Labor Relations Board v. Yeshiva University,* 444 U.S. 672 [1980]). The Court ruled that full-time faculty at private colleges and universities are not eligible to bargain under the National Labor Relations Act because they are managerial employees who participate in setting institutional policy. Although this ruling does not prevent faculty from organizing, it does mean that the administration is not obligated to recognize a union or to negotiate a collective bargaining contract. Its effect was substantial; it temporarily halted the unionizing efforts of full-time faculty in privates and chilling those efforts in publics, which generally gain recognition under state labor laws.[13] The ongoing effect of the Yeshiva University ruling also translates to public-private differences in the unionizing efforts of graduate students who work as teaching assistants and research assistants.[14]

Aside from these differences in formal arrangements, informal management of publics and privates does not follow a set pattern. Management can vary tremendously given a campus's distinctive legacies, such as whether the faculty senate has a history of strength and whether campus leaders tend to seek advice and consensus, as opposed to a top-down or autocratic leadership style. In more elite publics and privates, some acknowledge faculty buy-in as a critical factor in the success of major initiatives or of a campus leader's time in office. For-profits tend to have a far more circumscribed role for faculty, many of whom are hired as part-timers (Bailey, Badway, and Gumport 2001).

Although it may also be said that publics have been expected to respond to heightened pressure for accountability and demands for transparency, in the last quarter of the twentieth century the management of publics and privates became remarkably similar in terms of managerial rhetoric and strategy. Some of this can be seen as a standardization of practices attributable to regulations.[15] Similarly, publics and privates operate under long-standing shared presumptions about academic freedom according to which violations would likely result in censure by the American Association of University Professors. Beyond that, two significant trends that appeared during the last quarter of the twentieth century have cumulatively accounted for similar managerial approaches in publics and privates: the rise of a professional class of academic managers and the increased saliency of market forces.

Beginning in the mid-1970s, the watchwords used by campus managers were *enrollment management,* followed by *strategic planning* in the 1980s and by *downsizing* and *reengineering* in the 1990s. Aided by management science and imprinted by MBA programs, a growing class of professional academic managers carried out and further elaborated these prescriptions (Gumport 2000). Campuses expanded the number, types, and levels of administrative positions, although their salaries and work activities consumed additional resources (Gumport and Pusser 1995). Bolstered by the capacity to develop models from the decision sciences by means of advances in information technology, academic administrators tracked resources, planned for alternative future scenarios, and gathered centralized data that could be used to monitor several dimensions of teaching, research, and faculty workload. With the justification of adapting to changing contexts, academic administrators both monitored internal activities and scanned the environment, making critical linkages between budgeting and planning and between resource allocation and performance measures (Jedamus and Peterson 1980; Peterson, Dill, and Mets 1997). Though most faculty retained a sense of having authority over the academic domain and independence from administrative oversight (Rhoades 1998), academic administrators gained a central place in campus decision making and resource allocation within publics and privates.

As publics and privates were influenced by the ebb and flow of resources that accompanied cycles of enrollment shifts and funding changes, academic deans and campus officials reoriented their activities to blend fiscal and academic interests more directly, including consolidating academic units for retrenchment and, later, for restructuring (Gumport 1993; Gumport and Pusser 1997). Not surprisingly, nonprofits that were experiencing financial constraints came to behave as for-profits; raising revenue and reducing expenditures became the highest priorities, although nonprofits continued to engage in cross-subsidization (Massy 1996). This entrepreneurial orientation in publics and privates echoes their counterparts in public agencies and industry in pursuing such popularized strategies as downsizing, restructuring, and total quality management. In spite of criticism of these "management fads" (Birnbaum 2000), the presence of a professional class of academic managers and mandates to reengineer the enterprise have reinforced one another in publics and in private nonprofits. It is an understatement to say that an ethos of competition has become pervasive. Though most visible in the attempt to secure revenue from multiple sources, the discourse and rationale of market pressures show no signs of weakening. Nor does the entrepreneurial spirit of campus leaders and their governing boards.

The discussion above has outlined historical similarities and differences in finance, mission, and governance between public and private nonprofit colleges and universities. We have traced some behavioral distinctions between public and private nonprofits, many of which are structural. Yet we have also observed a trend toward convergence between the forms, particularly in countries with strong external demands for accountability, increased competition for government funds, and pervasive market ideologies. These observations led us to consider whether extant explanations of the distinctions among public, private nonprofit, and for-profit organizations effectively explain the higher education context. In the following section we consider the pressures to adapt organizational structures and practices to make them more competitive within changing markets, particularly within the research university sector, as illustrated by the commercialization of university research and instruction.

HYBRIDIZATION OF INSTITUTIONAL FORMS

In examining evidence of the distinctions between public and private nonprofit colleges and universities, we have also seen the ways in which these two institutional forms are converging. In this section we step back from a direct comparison across organizational forms and argue that the nomenclature and presumed distinctions among publics, nonprofits, and for-profits are becoming less useful for understanding higher education as a nonprofit sector. An industry-level view of higher education suggests the extent to which boundaries that distinguish traditional institutional forms are disappearing as hybrid organizational arrangements—blending features of public, private nonprofit, and for-profit forms—are emerging. In the research function, universities increasingly compete with government and corporate laboratories in producing scientific knowledge. We argue that increasing commercialization of science, university spin-offs, and industry-university collaborative arrangements confound the conventional distinctions between academic science and commercial science. In instructional activities at universities, boundaries are also disappearing with the emergence of virtual universities, instructional spin-offs, and corporate training organizations that compete directly with traditional colleges and universities. Once again, our primary example is the United States. As we will show, however, developments in the United States are illustrative of broader trends around the globe.

Commercialization of University Research

Throughout the history of the American university, the nature and role of scientific research has undergone significant changes. During the first half of the nineteenth century, higher education consisted mostly of small, elite private colleges that focused primarily on undergraduate teaching and professional training. In 1862 Congress passed the first Morrill Act, which established the importance of university-based research. The Morrill Acts allocated federal lands for the creation of state universities to serve local economic needs by means of research and training in technical and agricultural fields. Not only did the Morrill Act solidify the state's role in providing postsecondary education, but it legitimated the idea that academic research is an instrument for serving local economic needs. After the founding of Johns Hopkins University in 1876, the Humboldt model of the German research university, emphasizing scientific research, graduate education, and sharp distinctions between academic disciplines, gave further prominence to university research. In the early twentieth century the prominence of the research function grew slowly, with a small subset of universities excelling in the pursuit of basic scientific research, while research at public universities emphasized the practical concerns of their states. In the era prior to World War II, applied research dominated, and U.S. universities lagged behind European institutes and universities in the pursuit of more basic science.

After World War II, the university's role in conducting basic and applied research underwent a well-documented transformation (Rosenberg and Nelson 1994). Although primarily necessitated by wartime defense priorities, academic research in the postwar university received further investment for its anticipated contributions to the advancement of science. With funding from government agencies such as the National Science Foundation and the National Institutes of Health, investment in university-based research soared. A preponderance of star scientists and Nobel laureates were on U.S. campuses, and major discoveries in physics, engineering, and medicine occurred in their labs. Government laboratories remained vitally important and productive, especially in interdisciplinary research (Bozeman 2000), but additional funding for science and technology research was channeled to academic researchers because of the high standards of peer review and their role in training future scientists (National Academy of Sciences 1995). During this period, the pursuit of commercially viable discoveries remained the domain of corporate research and development (R&D) departments because universities rarely conducted research with immediate commercial application. In the conduct of basic and applied research, a division of labor seemed to be accepted by universities, government laboratories, and corporate R&D.[16]

A groundbreaking discovery by two scientists, one at a private university and the other at a public university, created a sea change in this relatively stable division of scientific labor. In 1973, Stanley Boyer of Stanford University and Herbert Cohen of the University of California developed a method of inserting recombined DNA into a living cell (Cohen et al. 1973; Kenney 1986). Recombinant DNA technology held great promise for serving the public good by enabling the creation of countless life-saving drugs and techniques, but it also had unlimited commercial potential. A key administrator at Stanford's Sponsored Projects Office, Niels Reimers, recognized this potential and persuaded the scientists, as well as the University of California, to apply for patent protection (Reimers 1998). By 1980, the first patent was granted. Defying the norm of openness in publicly funded medical research, the universities claimed proprietary ownership of a technology. The licensing revenues from the patents yielded impressive financial returns[17] and served notice to universities and scientists of the revenue-generating potential of university-based discoveries. More broadly, the Cohen-Boyer patent clearly established the university's potential as a prominent player in scientific and technological commercialization.

Not long after the Cohen-Boyer discovery, important shifts in U.S. science policy further facilitated patenting by universities and prompted changes in the nature and role of university research in general (Lee 1994). Slaughter and Rhoades have argued that as immediate national defense priorities for science waned, policy makers sought to emphasize industrial competitiveness in global markets. Coalitions of government, industry, and university interests drove a competitiveness agenda that resulted in a spate of legislative initiatives to stimulate the growth of technology-based industries through increased university-industry collaboration and deregulation (Slaughter and Rhoades 1996). Mowery and colleagues (2001) have argued that increased patenting in the 1970s and 1980s had less to do with specific public policy initiatives than with a general increase in the federal funding of biomedical research. Nonetheless, legislative initiatives such as the Bayh-Dole Act further reduced legal barriers to the commercialization of university-based research and facilitated the creation of new university-industry collaborations.

These changes in science policy were complemented by funding shifts for academic R&D. A robust government funding infrastructure had developed in the postwar era to fuel university research. Over the course of the next several decades, research funding from the federal government continued to rise (see figure 19.1).

Federal investments in research were substantial throughout the period; increases were both sizable and relatively consistent. Also notable were the proportional increases in expenditures by private industry. Between 1980 and 1998, industry expenditures on academic R&D increased almost eightfold, and they nearly doubled as a proportion of the total. When we compare the sources of R&D funding at public and private nonprofit universities, similar patterns are evident (see table 19.5).

Between 1977 and 1997, industry investment in academic R&D at private universities rose from $57.2 million to $555 million, almost a tenfold increase. By comparison, industry investment in academic R&D at public universities rose from $81.6 million to $1.16 billion, a fourteenfold increase. Throughout the twenty-year period, the percentage of all expenditures coming from private industry was roughly equal across the public and private universities.

Outside the United States, the funding environment for academic R&D has been similarly dominated by government resources. Trends in industry investment in academic R&D vary widely, however, owing to cultural and historical differences as well as to marked differences in national science and technology policies. Although no country has reached the R&D funding levels of the United States, many have attempted to stimulate industry investment in academic research.

Between 1994 and 1999, notable gains in industry investment in academic R&D were seen in Canada, France, Germany, Spain, Turkey, and the United Kingdom (see table 19.6). A notable exception is Japan, which experienced a 24

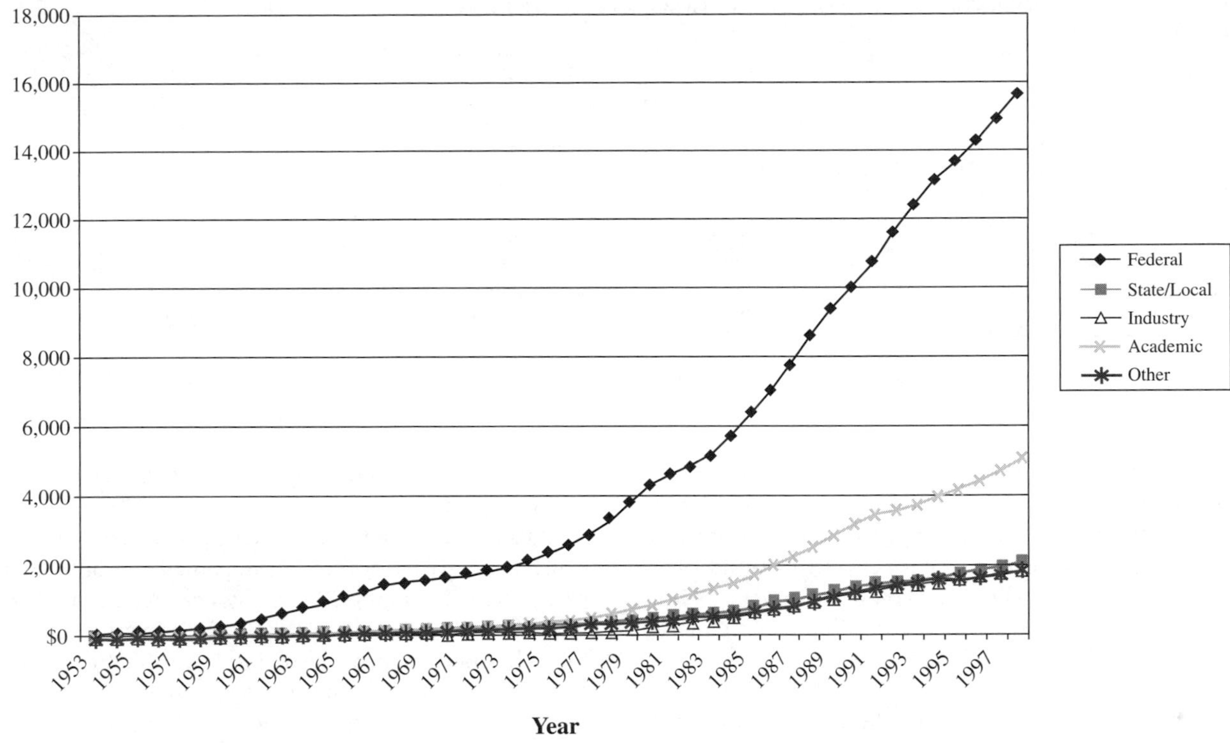

FIGURE 19.1. SUPPORT FOR ACADEMIC R&D BY SECTOR, 1953–98
Source: National Science Board 2000.

TABLE 19.5. SOURCES OF R&D FUNDS AT PUBLIC AND PRIVATE INSTITUTIONS, 1977–97 (IN MILLIONS OF CURRENT DOLLARS)

		Source of funds				
Year and institution type	Total	Federal government	State or local government	Industry	Academic institutions	Other sources
1977						
Private, total	1,448.9	1,120.4	33.9	57.2	92.6	144.9
Public, total	2,618.0	1,605.8	340.0	81.6	421.7	168.9
1987						
Private, total	4,251.9	3,163.5	96.9	295.8	365.8	330.0
Public, total	7,900.9	4,179.6	926.5	494.3	1,802.6	497.8
1997						
Private, total	7,957.2	5,750.0	167.4	555.0	806.8	678.0
Public, total	16,391.2	8,752.2	1,709.5	1,158.1	3,737.1	1,034.3

Source: National Science Board 2000:A-314.

percent decline in industry investment in academic R&D during this period. This is likely the result of the strength of the national university system and the education ministry's aggressive program of public investment (National Science Foundation 1997).

The Changing Organizational Ecology of University-Based Research

Increased collaboration on research among universities, industry, and government has resulted in the creation of new and hybrid organizational forms that blend the features of public, private nonprofit, and for-profit forms. University-based spin-offs, research joint ventures (RJVs), university-industry cooperative research centers (UICRCs), and a host of other organizational forms created to take advantage of technology transfer opportunities fuse the work practices, cultures, governance structures, and management styles of these different domains.

One of the most unambiguous cases of the dissolution of boundaries between organizational sectors is the creation of a for-profit spin-off from a nonprofit organization.[18] Start-up

TABLE 19.6. GROSS DOMESTIC EXPENDITURE ON ACADEMIC R&D BY BUSINESS ENTERPRISES, 1994–99

	Year						
	1994	1995	1996	1997	1998	1999	Change (%)
Canada	257.9	251.2	280.7	316.1	342.5	378.6	0.32
France	141.0	154.6	149.5	145.5	163.9	169.1	0.17
Germany	579.1	587.2	677.4	713.2	772.4	843.2	0.31
Japan	374.3	413.5	293.0	303.3	301.5	302.6	−0.24
Spain	88.1	129.1	122.3	109.9	126.3	142.2	0.38
Turkey	114.7	147.0	187.4	213.1	222.4	254.3	0.55
U.K.	245.3	259.7	278.7	295.0	309.0	330.5	0.26

Source: Basic Science and Technology Statistics (OECD 2001).
Note: Figures are given in constant 1995 millions of U.S. dollars.

firms emanating from the successful patenting of university-based research have become commonplace. More than 2,900 new companies were formed as a result of university-based research in the United States between 1980 and 1999 (Association of University Technology Managers 1999). The trend is also evident across Europe (European Commission 2002; Kinsella and McBrierty 1997) and in countries such as Israel (Meseri and Maital 2001) and Canada (Doutriaux 1987). Not only have these spin-offs created wealth and opportunity for faculty and students, but they are also (as vehicles for technology transfer) successful mechanisms for spillovers of localized knowledge and economic growth (Zucker, Darby, and Armstrong 1994). However, the frequency of spin-offs raises legitimate concerns that faculty and students will divert their attention and time to the work of the firm to the detriment of their university responsibilities.

A wide range of formal and informal collaborative arrangements brings together firms, universities, and government organizations. Often difficult to classify, these arrangements take a multitude of forms and vary in funding sources, oversight, duration, and goals. Two such arrangements, university-industry cooperative research centers and research joint ventures, inform much of what is known about formal research collaborations. Such collaborations account for the lion's share of all academic R&D expenditures and have proven effective conduits for technology transfer and knowledge spillovers between universities and partnering firms.[19] In the United States, RJVs are cooperative research organizations legalized by the National Cooperative Research Act of 1984, which protects R&D collaborations from antitrust liability provided that they foster technological innovation without harming competition (Baldwin 1996).[20] They vary widely in the types and number of organizations involved, as well as in the specific goals of the venture. Somewhat more formal in their structure are UICRCs, which are NSF-supported centers located on university campuses (Adams, Chang, and Starkey 2001; Cohen et al. 1998). Funding and oversight of UICRCs are shared among industry advisors, local and federal governments, and the universities themselves. Their research agendas include longer-term basic research as well as shorter-term projects with potential value to partnering firms.

Outside the United States, analogous university-industry collaborations have also emerged, particularly in the European Union. The European Commission created the Framework Programme (FWP) in 1984 as the primary mechanism for collaborative research involving universities, research institutes, firms, and government organizations across the European Union. The purpose of the FWP was both to create a common set of research priorities across the European Union and to stimulate collaboration across organizations and nations. The number of RJVs that include universities has increased steadily since the FWP's inception, constituting roughly two-thirds of all RJVs operating as a result of the FWP. Much like those in the United States, European universities have been most active in RJVs in the field of biotechnology (Caloghirou, Tsanikas, and Vonortas 2001).

These collaborations are of interest because they result in unique organizational forms that span the boundaries between universities and firms. Such relationships are more than mere financial transactions, because the governance and management of research projects are often shared. Agreements between firms and universities often include explicit terms regarding the ownership of intellectual property, disclosure of findings, and licensing rights of industry partners. Such arrangements, while stimulating technology transfer and supplying valuable resources to academic scientists, may affect the choice of projects, the articulation of research goals, and the nature of actual work at the bench. Indeed, depending on the degree of involvement of outside partners, collaborative arrangements can even affect such aspects of academic life as faculty hiring and curricular decisions.

Of particular interest is the impact of such collaborative arrangements on organizational culture and norms of professional practice. Packer and Webster (1996) note the emergence of a patenting culture on university campuses in which prestige is increasingly defined by one's ability to produce patentable research, as opposed to peer-reviewed publications. The climate of disclosure that typically accompanies the publication process may yield to a climate of secrecy required to protect the novelty of a patent claim. Faculty also must learn new skill sets that were not included in their academic training. They must learn to write in the language of patents and develop a sophisticated understanding of complicated intellectual property issues in order to navigate ownership agreements with industry partners and with their own universities. These normative and cultural changes in science cumulatively affect the trajectory of academic careers. The perceptions of scientists vary regarding the degree to which ties with industry threaten the academy and the degree to which academic and commercial science truly overlap (Owen-Smith and Powell 2001). The rhetoric of commercialization implies a distinctive shift away from an idealized separation between the public goals of academic science and the private interests of industry R&D. Alternatively, it may be more useful to think of these organizational transitions as a convergence of the knowledge creation and commercialization agendas, rather than a shift from one to the other (Etzkowitz et al. 2000).

Commercialization of Instruction

As with academic research, the roles of universities and the corporate sector are changing in the domain of instruction. There is little argument that public and private nonprofit colleges and universities remain the central providers of instruction in general education, professional certification, and vocational and technical training. The new educational requirements of a knowledge-centered, post-industrial economy have, however, expanded the demand for continuing education and retraining in technical and professional fields. Changes in information technology have enabled mass delivery of education to cohorts of students not traditionally served by residential or commuter institutions, and the market for instruction has substantially grown. Paralleling the for-profit educational sector's growth to accommodate new demand, managers within traditional colleges and universities see opportunities to expand continuing and adult education programs, while faculty assess opportunities in corporate education and distance learning. Furthermore, new and hybrid organizations have seen dramatic growth.

Changes in the context of postsecondary instruction have resulted in increasing commercialization within traditional postsecondary organizations. For example, universities have considered outsourcing instruction in less profitable fields such as introductory foreign languages (Gumport and Pusser 1997) and remedial education (Breneman and Haarlow 1999). Unless they reduce the costs associated with these socially and culturally valued programs, universities and colleges face the prospect of cutting them altogether. And at the same time institutions are externalizing low-margin instructional programs, they are increasing activities in more profitable domains typically left to the for-profit sector. For example, the most prominent universities are increasing their nondegree offerings to adult and continuing education students (Gose 1999). In 1999 Harvard University generated $150 million in revenue from continuing studies, accounting for nearly 10 percent of their $1.5 billion budget. As traditional universities have increased their revenue-generating activities through continuing education programs, training programs oriented toward improving the skills of employees have become standard in large and small corporations (Scott and Meyer 1994).

Nowhere is the disintegration of organizational boundaries more evident than in the case of information technology certification. With the rising demand for specialized information technology skills in the global labor market, an entire industry has emerged outside the mainstream of higher education to provide certification for technical skills. Certifications typically prove the holder's competency in working with specific products or technologies that have become standard in the information technology industry. The most prominent examples include Microsoft Certified Systems Engineer, Oracle Database Administrator, Certified Novell Administrator, and Certified Novell Engineer. For certain jobs, employers often consider these types of certification more important criteria for employment than undergraduate or graduate degrees.

In a groundbreaking study written for the U.S. Department of Education, Clifford Adelman (2000) has called this the emergence of a "parallel postsecondary universe" because it largely emerged outside the boundaries and norms of traditional higher education. Unlike traditional degrees, at least in the United States, certifications are determined by third-party testing agencies that operate throughout the world. Most striking, however, is that since the certification industry itself has proliferated, traditional public, private nonprofit, and for-profit colleges and universities have quickly entered the certification preparation market as formidable competitors. From large four-year research universities to small two-year community colleges, these traditional institutions offer certification courses to the public and often serve as contractors to firms to provide training to employees.

Table 19.7, taken from the Adelman (2000) report, lists the number of Microsoft Authorized Academic Training Providers (AATPs) as of August of 2000. Although it is telling that two-year colleges dominate, the number of four-year colleges and universities offering software certification courses is also noteworthy. Indeed, in this domain, four-year colleges and universities are in direct competition with a diverse array of corporate and small-business outfits providing instructional services and in most cases are offering an identical curriculum supplied or authorized by industry associations or software vendors.

It is also notable that this parallel postsecondary universe of information technology certification has quickly spread beyond the United States. Software vendors whose products require certification are multinational, and the demand for skilled information technology workers has continued to grow across the globe. The Adelman (2000) study reports that providers of certification training for products made by Cisco Corporation offer courses in nineteen languages, and

TABLE 19.7. DISTRIBUTION OF AATPS BY LEVEL AND CONTROL OF INSTITUTION, INCLUDING BRANCH CAMPUSES, AUGUST 2000

Category	Number	Percent of total	Comment
Four-year public and nonprofit	142	19	Approximately one-third are continuing education units
Four-year for-profit	42	6	Two-thirds are campuses of the University of Phoenix
Two-year public and nonprofit	298	40	Includes multiple campuses of large community college districts such as Houston and Allegheny (Pittsburgh)
Two-year for-profit	103	14	Includes multiple campuses of Heald, Herzing, and others
Indeterminable postsecondary status	39	5	Not listed in Barbett and Lin (1998) nor otherwise located
High school	129	17	More than half are technical or vocational high schools
Total	753	100	

Source: Adelman 2000.

of the roughly five thousand certified Cisco Internetworking Experts as of July 31, 2000, approximately 50 percent worked outside the United States.

Technology and the Changing Organizational Ecology of Instruction

Technology has been a major catalyst for changes in the division of labor and the related blurring of distinctions among public, private nonprofit, and for-profit education and training organizations. Innovations in information technology have removed the spatial and temporal boundaries of traditional educational organizations, enabling the creation of "virtual" or "online" universities, which do not require campuses, classrooms, fixed course schedules, or timelines. This reduction of the geographic constraints on educational organizing has also enhanced opportunities for interorganizational collaborations. Such collaborations involve agglomerations of universities, government agencies, and for-profit firms, sometimes resulting in the creation of a new commercial enterprise. Many new organizations have made the network form central to their design. Epper (1997) has shown how state university systems have responded to competition from new online ventures by creating statewide distance learning consortia to pool the resources and programs of several campuses. Several large regional consortia pool the online curricula from colleges and universities in neighboring states. Hybrid organizational forms are exemplified by for-profit subsidiaries or spin-offs by established public and private nonprofit universities. More prominent in the 1990s, spin-offs in the instructional domain have been created to compete in a variety of new markets, most commonly the marketing and distribution of online courses developed by faculty. University spin-offs have also been created to compete in emerging markets for online college preparatory classes and executive education.

For distance education organizations, as well as for other new hybrid forms, collaboration may make the decisive difference, particularly by pooling resources and expertise. Commercial activities can generate much-needed revenue. Hybridizing organizations with different missions, governance structures, and financial arrangements can also introduce new challenges, however. Such organizations may find it difficult to establish an organizational identity because affiliations with multiple institutions may put a strain on faculty and staff members' allegiances to their home institutions. When the new organization is a for-profit venture, faculty may be compelled to allocate more time to students in the commercial venture than to courses taught for their home institution. In addition to questions of organizational and professional identity, hybrid organizations also create ambiguities concerning the ownership of course material. Proprietary agreements between firms and universities may create scenarios in which firms are profiting from the work of faculty, who may in turn claim ownership of the course materials. Although such organizations typically develop explicit agreements for sharing profits with individual faculty members, collaborative arrangements involving computer-based instructional material have raised new questions about intellectual property rights to course materials. Finally, from the perspective of those who seek instruction via distance education and corporate training, a fundamental question arises as to how to ensure quality. Ultimately this question depends on whether accreditation mechanisms and criteria can be meaningfully mapped onto such ventures.[21] What is at stake is nothing less than the very inclusion of these entities as legitimate forms within higher education.

The preceding section portrays some of the ways in which classical notions of institutional form have less relevance in the contemporary technological era of U.S. higher education. New markets for research and instruction created by technological and scientific progress, as well as the pervasive influence of profit-making ideologies on traditional academic organizations, confound characterizations of public, private nonprofit, and for-profit colleges and universities as ideal types. Traditional public and nonprofit colleges and universities have adopted commercial behaviors and structures in an effort to respond to external pressures and exploit new markets. Similarly, firms have recognized the potential of burgeoning education markets and have become de facto competitors. Unprecedented collaborative relationships and spin-offs have resulted in new arrangements that blend the missions, financial arrangements, and governance models of multiple forms. Such contemporary trends suggest that higher education is an industry in even greater flux than observers have noted (Geiger 1986; Levy 1987).

In this chapter we have examined what is known about distinctions among forms in higher education. We have characterized the ways in which wider societal forces—economic, policy, and technological—have prompted changes within and across publics, private nonprofits, and for-profits. In attempting to reposition themselves within the new competitive landscape, all three have become increasingly similar in marketing activities, sharpening their missions, seeking private revenue, and heeding higher education policies at the state and federal levels. We have argued that emerging markets and competitive dynamics have simultaneously promoted this convergence among existing forms while creating incentives and opportunities for new organizational forms to emerge.

We have carefully considered the approach taken by the extant literature on nonprofits, which treats public, private nonprofit, and for-profit forms as intellectually distinct. We took our cues from Levy's (1987) work and investigated distinctions between forms in mission, finance, and governance across the increasingly complex organizational landscape of higher education. In the course of this investigation we arrived at a point of departure from conventional theories of nonprofits and argued that although form-related distinctions are evident, they do not effectively characterize the structure and behavior of postsecondary educational organizations. Other form-related dynamics are at work that beg attention from scholars of nonprofits.

These dynamics represent a paradox not addressed by nonprofit theory. On one hand, we found evidence of convergence in organizational structures and practices among government, private nonprofit, and commercial sectors. This connotes similarity between organizational forms along these dimensions. On the other, we found that intensified exchanges and intermingling between sectors have accelerated a hybridization of organizational forms. At the structural level, this hybridization has resulted in a more differentiated organizational ecology for postsecondary education.

In light of increased competition among sectors, the respective roles of public and private institutional forms in society warrant reexamination. The key question arises, whose interests are served by each form? Distinctions can no longer be presumed, nor can respective roles in fulfilling particular social functions. Mainly, as private interests gain further legitimacy within public institutions, this raises the obvious concern about whether public interests will be compromised. The question is not only whether public and private interests can be served simultaneously in the same form; it is whether the differences between forms should be preserved in order to better align their functions with different types of interests. Postsecondary education in the United States has no national mechanism for monitoring, let alone controlling, organizational drift. Although many observers and participants alike consider this decentralization to be a strength, it becomes problematic when market forces have come to the fore as a dominant rationale for postsecondary organizations to alter their practices.

These changes also have important implications for theoretical research about the competitive and collaborative dynamics of nonprofit organizations. As is the case for many other industries that are addressed by nonprofit theory, comparative research on public, private nonprofit, and for-profit educational organizations has identified the threatening implications of competition from corporate interests. What sets higher education apart, however, is that in postsecondary education, this competition is juxtaposed with pervasive collaboration across forms. Such collaboration is unique in that it is based on shared commitments to the advancement of knowledge that are powerfully reinforced by professional allegiances to academic disciplines. Unlike healthcare, for example, where new competitive dynamics resulted in wholesale conversions to for-profit forms, the dynamics of "collaborative competition" in higher education appear to result in greater differentiation rather than increased homogeneity. Thus, despite the influence of ongoing competition and commercialization as seen in other nonprofit industries, the concomitant shifts in the distribution of public, private, and for-profit forms within higher education may not be so predictable.

NOTES

1. Many countries once dominated by public provision have witnessed a sharp increase in enrollments in private nonprofit and for-profit universities (Altbach 1999). Throughout the latter part of the twentieth century, this occurred in Latin American countries such as Chile, Peru, Colombia, and Brazil and is also evident in Eastern Europe, Africa, and East and Southeast Asia (Giesecke 1999; Levy 2002).

2. See Geiger (1986, 1991) for different patterns of private higher education. Geiger observes that the expansion of enrollments was accommodated in the United States by public colleges and universities, whereas in Japan it was done through private colleges and universities. See Ramirez and Riddle (1991) for an overview of hypotheses and evidence regarding trends in the expansion of higher education.

3. This chapter does not provide in-depth cross-national comparison of public and private nonprofit higher education systems. DiMaggio and Anheier (1990) cite a number of challenges to cross-national comparisons of nonprofit sectors. These include the lack of organizational and sectoral equivalence, historical contingencies, and differences in political traditions and legal nomenclatures. Throughout the chapter we

present cross-national comparisons and international examples where they are appropriate. For extensive analyses of higher education in an international context, see, e.g., Clark (1983, 1984), Geiger (1986), and Altbach (1999).

4. DeVry University is part of DeVry, Inc. From 1968 to 2002 it was called DeVry Institute of Technology. We believe that the name change reflects their ambition to gain academic legitimacy.

5. Substantial challenges impede research on proprietary colleges and universities. One reason is that many do not complete the National Center for Educational Statistics surveys of institutional characteristics, on which most U.S. higher education researchers depend for their data.

6. Data provided by Breneman, Pusser, and Turner (2000) reveal that by 1995, for-profit colleges and universities accounted for less than 1 percent of all bachelor's and master's degrees granted in the United States.

7. The universe of postsecondary institutions includes more than 4,000 institutions that offer an associate's degree or higher and participated in Title IV federal student financial aid programs. Thousands of non–degree-granting for-profit organizations bring the total to 9,249, with estimates that the actual total is as much as 13 percent higher. More than four hundred thousand students are enrolled in non–degree-granting institutions, slightly fewer than half of them in for-profits.

8. An anomaly in the U.S. system is that private nonprofits are not the only ones to occupy niches with specific missions. Among publics, two categories are notable. As of 2000, of 103 historically black colleges in the United States, 52 are public and 51 are private nonprofit (National Center for Education Statistics 2001). Of 28 tribal colleges and universities existing in 2000, 22 are public and 6 are nonprofit (Carnegie Foundation 2001).

9. By the end of the twentieth century, observers characterized a growing consumer orientation in higher education (Gumport 2000). Students view themselves as consumers and behave accordingly in their choices of where to enroll and what courses to take. Managers of colleges and universities reorient their academic programs and services to correspond with student preferences. Researchers are also developing tools to accommodate this consumer orientation, constructing outcome measures of recent alumni to capture the distinctive profiles of colleges and universities. Zemsky, Shaman, and Shapiro (2001:74) assert that such tools will enable "student and parent consumers to make more informed choices, and . . . colleges and universities to make better investments in both the scope and quality of their educational programs."

10. The financial profile of the student clienteles for each institutional type warrants further examination. Patterns in higher education may be similar to those in the field of health care, where there is some concern about publics serving a disproportionately higher proportion of indigent patients (see Schlesinger and Gray, this volume.) Such patterns appear far less evident in higher education.

11. One check on this expansion in public higher education has been state oversight aimed at avoiding unnecessary program duplication in the same geographic area. The drift toward expanding degree offerings is evident among colleges as well. One indication of this is that during the 1990s, more than 120 public and private four-year colleges changed their names from "College" to "University" to signify a greater range of offerings (Morphew 2002).

12. Data from an exploratory study in a public comprehensive university suggest that the departmental infrastructure shows much continuity relative to degree programs (Gumport and Snydman 2002). It is possible that publics and privates show similar patterns of continuity and change in academic structure, although this has yet to be studied.

13. Several attempts have since been made to convince the National Labor Relations Board that the Yeshiva University ruling is not relevant on the basis of the claim that the full-time faculty are not managers but employees who play a narrower role. Some of these attempts have succeeded. Creative attempts to bypass the ruling have entailed organizing efforts by a separate group of full-time faculty, as seen most recently by musicians at the New School (Reynolds 1998).

14. Specifically, graduate students who work as teaching assistants and research assistants, usually doctoral students, perform these duties part-time while engaged in advanced study. The general ruling for privates has characterized them principally as students and not employees, whereas at publics they have gained the right to collective bargaining recognition and, as "graduate student-employees," can actively negotiate the terms of their work (salary, benefits, and workload).

15. Examples are guidelines in equal employment opportunity laws as set forth in federal regulations by the Department of Justice and administered by the Office of Civil Rights.

16. This distinction between the university as the primary arena for basic science and the corporate sector as the primary arena for applied science is far from perfect. Rosenberg and Nelson (1994) note that even if universities were conducting basic research with little direct commercial value, these discoveries often served industry needs. In the fields of engineering and computer science, for example, much of the basic science conducted at universities created the foundation for the emergence of the computer hardware and software industry. Fundamental biomedical research stimulated the meteoric rise of the biotechnology industry. Nevertheless, in the period immediately following World War II, universities on the whole favored the pursuit of more basic science, while industry was on its own in its pursuit of marketable products.

17. The Cohen-Boyer patent yielded nearly $400 million for Stanford and the University of California over the life of the patent.

18. The other unambiguous case, less common for established colleges and universities, is conversion of nonprofit organization to for-profit status.

19. In their 1990 study, Cohen and colleagues (1998) estimated that R&D expenditures by UICRCs constituted almost one-fifth of all academic R&D.

20. All RJVs must register with the U.S. Attorney General's office and the Federal Trade Commission in order to qualify for protection from antitrust litigation.

21. The Council for Higher Education Accreditation, a coordinating body for regional and specialized accrediting agencies, has taken a leadership role in ensuring quality in distance learning (Council for Higher Education Accreditation 2002). In an effort to develop standards, policies, and processes for evaluating distance learning, they focus on seven features of institutional operation: mission, resources, curriculum and instruction, faculty support, student support, and student outcomes.

REFERENCES

Adams, James D., Eric P. Chang, and Katara Starkey. 2001. "Industry-University Cooperative Research Centers." *Journal of Technology Transfer* 26:73–86.

Adelman, Clifford. 2000. "A Parallel Postsecondary Universe: The Certification System in Information Technology." Washington, D.C.: Office of Educational Research and Improvement, U.S. Department of Education.

Altbach, Phillip G., ed. 1999. *Private Prometheus: Private Higher Education and Development in the 21st Century.* Westport, Conn.: Greenwood.

Anderson, Charles J. 1986. *AGB Special Report: Composition of Governing Boards, 1985; A Survey of College and University Boards.* Washington, D.C: Association of Governing Boards of Universities and Colleges.

Apling, Richard N. 1993. "Proprietary Schools and Their Students." *Journal of Higher Education* 64:379–416.

Association of University Technology Managers. 1999. *AUTM Licensing Survey: FY 1999.* http://www.autm.net/events/File/Surveys/99AUTMLicSurveyPublic.pdf.

Bailey, Thomas, Norena Badway, and Patricia J. Gumport. 2001. "For-Profit Higher Education and Community Colleges." Technical Report Number NCPI-0400 for the U.S. Department of Education. http://www.stanford.edu/group/ncpi/documents/pdfs/forprofitandcc.pdf.

Baldwin, William L. 1996. "The U.S. Research University and the Joint Venture: Evolution of an Institution." *Review of Industrial Organization* 11:629–653.

Bender, Louis W. 1991. "Applied Associate Degree Transfer Phenomenon: Proprietaries and Publics." *Community College Review* 19:22–28.

Berdahl, Robert O. 1971. *Statewide Coordination in Higher Education.* Washington, D.C.: American Council on Education.

Birnbaum, Robert. 2000. *Management Fads in Higher Education: Where They Come From, What They Do, Why They Fail.* San Francisco: Jossey-Bass.

Bozeman, Barry. 2000. "Technology Transfer and Public Policy: A Review of Research and Theory." *Research Policy* 29:627–655.

Breneman, David W., and William N. Haarlow. 1999. "Establishing the Real Value of Remedial Education." *Chronicle of Higher Education,* 9 April, B6.

Breneman, David W., Brian Pusser, and Sarah E. Turner. 2000. "The Contemporary Provision of For-Profit Higher Education: Mapping the Competitive Market." Working Paper SWP-02, Curry School For-Profit Education Project, University of Virginia, Charlottesville.

Brint, Steven G., and Jerome Karabel. 1989. *The Diverted Dream: Community Colleges and the Promise of Educational Opportunity in America, 1900–1985.* New York: Oxford University Press.

———. 1991. "Institutional Origins and Transformations: The Case of American Community Colleges." Pp. 337–360 in *The New Institutionalism in Organizational Analysis,* edited by Walter W. Powell and Paul J. DiMaggio. Chicago: University of Chicago Press.

Caloghirou, Yannis, Aggelos Tsakanikas, and Nicholas S. Vonortas. 2001. "University-Industry Cooperation in the Context of the European Framework Programmes." *Journal of Technology Transfer* 26:153–161.

Carnegie Foundation for the Advancement of Teaching. 2001. *The Carnegie Classification of Institutions of Higher Education.* Menlo Park, Calif.: Carnegie Foundation for the Advancement of Teaching.

Cheng, Xing D., and Bernard H. Levin. 1995. "Who Are the Students at Community Colleges and Proprietary Schools?" *New Directions for Community Colleges* 23:51–60.

Clark, Burton R. 1972. "The Organizational Saga in Higher Education." *Administrative Science Quarterly* 17:178–184.

———. 1983. *The Higher Education System.* Berkeley: University of California Press.

———. 1984. *Perspectives on Higher Education: Eight Disciplinary and Comparative Views.* Berkeley: University of California Press.

———. 1993. "The Problem of Complexity in Modern Higher Education." Pp. 321–343 in *The European and American University Since 1800: Historical and Sociological Essays,* edited by Sheldon Rothblatt and Björn Wittrock. Cambridge: Cambridge University Press.

Cohen, Stanley N., Annie C. Y. Chang, Herbert W. Boyer, and Robert B. Helling. 1973. "Construction of Biologically Functional Bacterial Plasmids in Vitro." *Proceedings of the National Academy of Sciences of the United States of America* 70:3240–3244.

Cohen, Wesley M., Richard Florida, Lucien Randazzese, and John Walks. 1998. "Industry and the Academy: Uneasy Partners in the Cause of Technological Advance." Pp. 171–200 in *Challenges to Research Universities,* edited by Roger G. Noll. Washington, D.C.: Brookings Institution.

Committee on Labor and Human Resources, United States Senate. 1998. *Higher Education Act Amendments of 1998: Report of the Committee on Labor and Human Resources.* Washington, D.C.: Government Printing Office.

Council for Higher Education Accreditation. 2002. *Accreditation and Assuring Quality in Distance Learning.* CHEA Monograph Series no. 1. Washington, D.C.: Council for Higher Education Accreditation.

Currie, Jan, and Janice A. Newson, eds. 1998. *Universities and Globalization: Critical Perspectives.* Thousand Oaks, Calif.: Sage.

Davis, Stanley M., and Jim W. Botkin 1994. *The Monster Under the Bed: How Business Is Mastering the Opportunity of Knowledge for Profit.* New York: Simon and Schuster.

DiMaggio, Paul J., and Helmut K. Anheier. 1990. "The Sociology of Nonprofit Organizations and Sectors." *Annual Review of Sociology* 16:137–159.

Dougherty, Kevin J. 1994. *The Contradictory College: The Conflicting Origins, Impacts, and Futures of the Community College.* Albany: State University of New York Press.

Douglas, James. 1987. "Political Theories of Nonprofit Organization." Pp. 43–54 in *The Nonprofit Sector: A Research Handbook,* 1st ed., edited by Walter W. Powell. New Haven: Yale University Press.

Doutriaux, Jerome. 1987. "Growth Pattern of Academic Entrepreneurial Firms." *Journal of Business Venturing* 2:285–297.

Duderstadt, James J. *A University for the 21st Century.* Ann Arbor: University of Michigan Press.

Dynarski, Mark. 1994. "Who Defaults on Student Loans? Findings from the National Postsecondary Student Aid Study." *Economics of Education Review* 13:55–68.

Epper, Rhonda M. 1997. "Coordination and Competition in Postsecondary Distance Education: A Comparative Case Study of Statewide Policies." *Journal of Higher Education* 68:551–587.

Etzkowitz, Henry, Andrew Webster, Christine Gebhardt, and Branca R. Cantisano. 2000. "The Future of the University and the University of the Future: Evolution of Ivory Tower to Entrepreneurial Paradigm." *Research Policy* 29:313–330.

European Commission. 2002. "University Spin-Outs in Europe—Overview and Good Practice." Luxembourg: Office for Official Publications of the European Communities.

Futures Project. 2000. *The Universal Impact of Competition and Globalization in Higher Education.* http://www.futuresproject.org/publications/universal_impact.pdf.

Geiger, Roger L. 1986. *Private Sectors in Higher Education: Structure, Function and Change in Eight Countries.* Ann Arbor: University of Michigan Press.

———. 1991. "Private Higher Education." Pp. 1:233–246 in *International Higher Education: An Encyclopedia,* edited by Philip G. Altbach. New York: Garland.

Giesecke, Hans C. 1999. "The Rise of Private Higher Education in East Central Europe." *Society and Economy in Central and Eastern Europe* 21:132–156.

Gose, Ben. 1999. "Surge in Continuing Education Brings Profits for Universities." *Chronicle of Higher Education,* 19 February, A51.

Green, Kenneth C. 2000. *The Campus Computing Project.* http://www.campuscomputing.net.

Grubb, W. Norton, and John Tuma. 1991. "Who Gets Student Aid? Variations in Access to Aid." *Review of Higher Education* 14:359–382.

Gumport, Patricia J. 1993. "The Contested Terrain of Academic Program Reduction." *Journal of Higher Education* 64:283–311.

———. 2000. "Academic Restructuring: Organizational Change and Institutional Imperatives," *Higher Education* 39:67–91.

Gumport, Patricia J., and Michael N. Bastedo. 2001. "Academic Stratification and Endemic Conflict: Remedial Education Policy at CUNY." *Review of Higher Education* 24:333–349.

Gumport, Patricia J., and John D. Jennings. 1999. "Financial Challenges in Public Higher Education: A Trend Analysis." Technical Report Number NCPI-1320 for the U.S. Department of Education. Washington, D.C.: National Center for Postsecondary Improvement.

Gumport, Patricia J., and Brian Pusser. 1995. "A Case of Bureaucratic Accretion: Context and Consequences." *Journal of Higher Education* 66:493–520.

———. 1997. "Restructuring the Academic Environment." Pp. 453–478 in *Planning and Management for a Changing Environment: A Handbook on Redesigning Postsecondary Institutions,* edited by Marvin W. Peterson, David D. Dill, and Lisa A. Mets. San Francisco: Jossey-Bass.

Gumport, Patricia J., and Stuart K. Snydman. 2002. "The Formal Organization of Knowledge: An Analysis of Academic Structure." *Journal of Higher Education* 73:375–408.

Hansmann, Henry B. 1980. "The Role of Nonprofit Enterprise." *Yale Law Journal* 89:835–901.

———. 1987. "Economic Theories of Nonprofit Organization." Pp. 27–42 in *The Nonprofit Sector: A Research Handbook,* 1st ed., edited by Walter W. Powell. New Haven: Yale University Press.

———. 1999. "Higher Education as an Associative Good." Pp. 2:11–24 in *Forum Futures: 1999 Papers,* edited by Maureen E. Devlin and Joel W. Meyerson. Washington, D.C.: Foundation for the Future of Higher Education.

Hyslop, Cheryl, and Michael H. Parsons. 1995. "Curriculum as a Path to Convergence." *New Directions for Community Colleges* 23:41–49.

Ingram, Richard T. 1993. *Governing Public Colleges and Universities: A Handbook for Trustees, Chief Executives, and Other Campus Leaders.* San Francisco: Jossey-Bass.

Jacobs, Jerry A., and Scott Stoner-Eby. 1998. "Adult Enrollment and Educational Attainment." *Annals of the American Academy of Political and Social Sciences* 559:91–108.

James, Estelle. 1990. "Decision Processes and Priorities in Higher Education." Pp. 77–106 in *The Economics of American Universities: Management, Operations, and Fiscal Environment,* edited by Stephen A. Hoenack and Eileen L. Collins. Albany: State University of New York Press.

Jedamus, Paul, and Marvin W. Peterson. 1980. *Improving Academic Management.* San Francisco: Jossey-Bass.

Johnstone, D. Bruce. 2000. "Globalization and the Role of Universities." Keynote address to Universities Project of the Salzburg Seminar, Fifteenth Symposium, Salzburg, Austria, November.

Katz, Richard N., et al. 1999. *Dancing with the Devil: Information Technology and the New Competition in Higher Education.* San Francisco: Jossey-Bass.

Kelly, Kathleen F. 2001. "Meeting Needs and Making Profits: The Rise of For-Profit Degree-Granting Institutions." Denver: Education Commission of the States.

Kenney, Martin. 1986. *Biotechnology: The University-Industrial Complex.* New Haven: Yale University Press.

Kinsella, Ray, and Vincent McBrierty. 1997. "Campus Companies and the Emerging Techno-Academic Paradigm: The Irish Experience." *Technovation* 17:245–251.

Kojaku, Lawrence K., and Anne-Marie Nunez. 1998. "Descriptive Summary of 1995–1996 Beginning Postsecondary Students, with Profiles of Students Entering 2- and 4-Year Institutions; National Postsecondary Student Aid Study, 1995–96; Statistical Analysis Report." Washington, D.C.: National Center for Education Statistics.

Lee, Yong S. 1994. "Technology Transfer and Public Policy in an Age of Global Economic Competition." *Policy Studies Journal* 22:260–266.

Levy, Daniel C. 1987. "A Comparison of Private and Public Educational Organizations." Pp. 258–276 in *The Nonprofit Sector: A Research Handbook,* 1st ed., edited by Walter W. Powell. New Haven: Yale University Press.

———. 2002. "Unanticipated Development: Perspectives on Private Higher Education's Emerging Roles." Working Paper no. 1. Albany: University at Albany Program for Research on Private Higher Education.

Lewis, Laurie, Kyle Snow, and Elizabeth Farris. 1999. "Distance Education at Postsecondary Institutions, 1997–98." Washington, D.C.: U.S. Department of Education, National Center for Education Statistics.

Madsen, Holly. 1998. *Composition of Governing Boards of Public Colleges and Universities, 1997.* AGB Occasional Paper no. 37. Washington, D.C.: Association of Governing Boards of Universities and Colleges.

Massy, William F. 1996. "Productivity Issues in Higher Education." Pp. 49–86 in *Resource Allocation in Higher Education,* edited by William F. Massy. Ann Arbor: University of Michigan Press.

McCurdy, Jack. 1990. "Trustees of Mills College Reverse Decision to Admit Men." *Chronicle of Higher Education,* 30 May 1990.

McPherson, Michael S., and Morton O. Schapiro. 1991. *Keeping College Affordable: Government and Educational Opportunity.* Washington, D.C.: Brookings Institution.

Meseri, Ofer, and Shlomo Maital. 2001. "A Survey Analysis of University-Technology Transfer in Israel: Evaluation of Projects and Determinants of Success." *Journal of Technology Transfer* 26:115–125.

Mingle, James R., and Rhonda M. Epper. 1997. "State Coordination and Planning in an Age of Entrepreneurship." Pp. 45–65 in *Planning and Management for a Changing Environment: A Handbook on Redesigning Postsecondary Institutions,* edited by Marvin W. Peterson, David D. Dill, and Lisa A. Mets. San Francisco: Jossey-Bass.

Morphew, Christopher C. 2002. "'A Rose by Any Other Name': Which Colleges Became Universities." *Review of Higher Education* 25:207–223.

Morris, William V. 1993. "Avoiding Community Colleges: Students Who Attend Proprietary Vocational Schools." *Community College Journal of Research and Practice* 17:21–28.

Mowery, David C., Richard R. Nelson, Bhaven N. Sampat, and Arvids A. Ziedonis. 2001. "The Growth of Patenting and Licensing by U.S. Universities: An Assessment of the Effects of the Bayh-Dole Act of 1980." *Research Policy* 30:99–119.

National Academy of Sciences. 1995. *Allocating Federal Funds for Science and Technology: Report of the Committee on Criteria for Federal Support of Research and Development.* Washington, D.C.: National Academy Press.

National Center for Education Statistics. 2001. *Digest of Education Statistics.* Washington, D.C.: Government Printing Office.

National Science Board. 2000. *Science and Engineering Indicators—2000.* Arlington, Va.: National Science Foundation.

National Science Foundation, Division of Science Resources Studies. 1997. "The Science and Technology Resources of Japan: A Comparison with the United States." Special Report by Jean M. Johnson. NSF 97–324. Arlington, Va.: National Science Foundation.

Noble, David F. 2002. *Digital Diploma Mills: The Automation of Higher Education.* New York: Monthly Review Press.

Organization for Economic Cooperation and Development. 2001. Basic Science and Technology Statistics. Paris: Organization for Economic Cooperation and Development.

Owen-Smith, Jason, and Walter W. Powell. 2001. "Careers and Contradictions: Faculty Responses to the Transformation of Knowledge and Its Uses in the Life Sciences." *Research in the Sociology of Work* 10:109–140.

Packer, Kathryn, and Andrew Webster. 1996. "Patenting Culture in Science: Reinventing the Scientific Wheel of Credibility." *Science, Technology, and Human Values* 21:427–453.

Peterson, Marvin W., David D. Dill, and Lisa A. Mets. 1997. *Planning and Management for a Changing Environment: A Handbook on Redesigning Postsecondary Institutions.* San Francisco: Jossey-Bass.

Ramirez, Francisco O., and Phyllis Riddle. 1991. "The Expansion of Higher Education." Pp. 1:91–106 in *International Higher Education: An Encyclopedia.* New York: Garland.

Raphael, Jacqueline, and Sheila Tobias. 1997. "Profit-Making or Profiteering? Proprietaries Target Teacher Education." *Change* 29:44–49.

Reimers, Niels. 1998. "Stanford's Office of Technology Licensing and the Cohen/Boyer Cloning Patents." Oral history conducted in 1997 by Sally Smith Hughes, Regional Oral History Office, Bancroft Library, University of California, Berkeley.

Reynolds, Jason. 1998. "Jazz Professors at New School Vote to Form Union." *Chronicle of Higher Education,* 20 February.

Rhoades, Gary. 1998. *Managed Professionals: Unionized Faculty and Restructuring Academic Labor.* Albany: State University of New York Press.

Rosenberg, Nathan, and Richard R. Nelson. 1994. "American Universities and Technical Advance in Industry." *Research Policy* 23:323–348.

Salamon, Lester M. 1987. "Partners in Public Service: The Scope and Theory of Government-Nonprofit Relations." Pp. 99–117 in *The Nonprofit Sector: A Research Handbook,* 1st ed., edited by Walter W. Powell. New Haven: Yale University Press.

Salamon, Lester M., Helmut K. Anheier, Regina List, Stefan Toepler, and S. Wojciech Sokolowski. 1999. *Global Civil Society: Dimensions of the Nonprofit Sector.* Baltimore: Johns Hopkins Center for Civil Society Studies.

Scott, W. Richard, and John W. Meyer. 1994. "The Rise of Training Programs in Firms and Agencies." Pp. 228–254 in *Institutional Environments and Organizations: Structural Complexity and Individualism,* edited by W. Richard Scott and John W. Meyer. Thousand Oaks, Calif.: Sage.

Seftor, Neil S., and Sarah E. Turner. 2002. "Back to School: Federal Student Aid Policy and Adult College Enrollment." *Journal of Human Resources* 37:336–352.

Slaughter, Sheila, and Gary Rhoades. 1996. "The Emergence of a Competitiveness Research and Development Policy Coalition and the Commercialization of Academic Science and Technology." *Science, Technology, and Human Values* 21:303–339.

U.S. Department of Education, National Center for Education Statistics. 2000. *Integrated Postsecondary Education Data System (IPEDS): Institutional Characteristics, 1998–99.* Computer file. Washington, D.C.: U.S. Department of Education, National Center for Education Statistics.

U.S. Department of Labor. 2001. "Report on the American Workforce." 5th ed. Washington, D.C.: Government Printing Office.

Wilms, Wellford W., Richard W. Moore, and Roger E. Bolus. 1987. "Whose Fault Is Default? A Study of the Impact of Student Characteristics and Institutional Practices on Guaranteed Student Loan Default Rates in California." *Educational Evaluation and Policy Analysis* 9:41–54.

Winston, Gordon C. 1999. "For-Profit Higher Education: Godzilla or Chicken Little?" *Change* 31:12–19.

Zemsky, Robert, Susan Shaman, and Daniel B. Shapiro. 2001. "Higher Education as Competitive Enterprise: When Markets Matter." New Directions for Institutional Research, no. 111. San Francisco: Jossey-Bass.

Zucker, Lynne G., Michael R. Darby, and Jeff Armstrong. 1994. "Intellectual Capital and the Firm: The Technology of Geographically Localized Knowledge Spillovers." *NBER Working Paper no. 4946.* Cambridge, Mass.: National Bureau of Economic Research.

20

Religion and the Nonprofit Sector

WENDY CADGE
ROBERT WUTHNOW

The study of religion has a long history in the social sciences, figuring prominently in the work of Max Weber, Emile Durkheim, Karl Marx, Alexis de Tocqueville, William James, and Sigmund Freud, among others. Building on these early contributions, social scientists generally regard religion as one of society's core institutions, just as they do the family, the economy, or the system of government, rather than as part of the nonprofit sector. As a social institution, "religion" thus refers to such *organizations* as churches, mosques, temples, denominations, and religious movements and the *beliefs and practices* associated with these organizations, such as belief in God and the practice of participating in religious rituals. Broadly conceived, religion is oriented toward the attainment of meaningful understandings of and relationships with the transcendent. Religious activities and values are expressed in a wide variety of social spheres such as the home, government, business, entertainment, and the arts and in social movements as well as private devotional behavior. Whereas religious organizations generally fit the profile of voluntary associations that involve membership and support from members, they do not so easily fit definitions of nonprofit organizations based on registration with tax authorities (P. Hall 1999). In fact, the literature about religious organizations, beliefs, and practices has until recently paid relatively little attention to questions about nonprofits or the nonprofit sector. Thus, until at least the early 1990s, there was a notable disjuncture between studies of religion and research concerning the nonprofit sector. Only in recent years has this disjuncture been bridged.

Several reasons for the earlier neglect of religion's relation to the nonprofit sector can be noted. For many years, social scientists held the view that religion was of diminishing importance in modern societies. In some interpretations religious involvement itself was assumed to be declining, whereas in more thoughtful arguments religion was assumed to play a declining role in society as more specialized organizations developed (Chaves 1994; Gorski 2000). This assumption was particularly relevant to the way in which activities in the nonprofit sector were understood. For instance, textbooks about social welfare services generally acknowledged that religion had played a role in providing these services in earlier times but that they were now provided by specialized nonprofit and governmental organizations run by professionally trained specialists. Similarly, it was easy to assume that arts organizations, nonprofit hospitals, and private colleges had perhaps been associated with religion at the time of their founding but were no longer influenced by religion. Two related assumptions also help account for the lack of attention to religion in the literature concerning nonprofits. One is the view that as organizations become professionalized, they also become isomorphic. By implication, even nonprofit organizations that may have religious ties can thus be understood in the same terms that other organizations can, rather than requiring special treatment. The other assumption is that the issues of greatest concern have to do with nonprofit *management* and thus pertain less to religious organizations, since they are managed by clergy and lay committees, than to such nonprofits as museums, hospitals, and colleges.

All of these assumptions have been challenged during the past two decades in ways that make it imperative for religion to be understood as a vital aspect of the nonprofit sector. Approximately half of all philanthropic donations in the United States from individuals go to religious organizations, and participation in these organizations is a strong predictor of volunteering and other forms of community service. Researchers have begun to explore a wide range of questions about the relations between religion and the nonprofit sector: the historical role played by religion in the formation of the nonprofit sector, tensions between religious and nonreligious organizations within this sector, the ways in which religious organizations are being influenced by growth in the wider nonprofit sector, and relations between religious congregations and faith-based nonprofit organizations, to name a few. Interest in these questions has clearly been reinforced by public policy debates. Beginning with the welfare reforms of the mid-1990s, government leaders have called for greater public recognition of the role of religious organizations as service providers. New legislation and funding opportunities have emerged. In the process, scholars have paid more attention to the role that religious organizations were already playing in service provision. In addition, scholars have also challenged the received wisdom that religion could be understood chiefly in terms of congregations, denominational structures, and formal participation. One line of investigation suggested that "lived religion" happened outside of religious organizations, for instance, in homeless shelters, soup kitchens, and hospital rooms (D. Hall 1997). Another line of investigation suggested that growth of the nonprofit sector since the early 1960s was now affecting the structure and activities of religious organizations. For instance, they were increasingly spinning off nonprofit organizations of their own, developing ties with nonsectarian nonprofits, and becoming subject to tax laws and other public policies governing nonprofits (Ammerman 2005; Wuthnow 2004). In simplest terms, a local church that a few decades ago may have been an autonomous religious organization now functioned quite differently because it was part of a rich network of community agencies, initiated a nonprofit foster care program, received literature from special interest lobbying organizations, filed information about taxes and employee benefits, co-sponsored performances with the local arts council, and organized volunteers at a local hospital.

Because of these developments, it is probably safe to say that most scholars who are interested in the nonprofit sector now recognize the importance of taking religious organizations into consideration. Understanding the role of religion, though, presents a significant challenge. Although instances can be found of studies in which religion is valuably considered in simplistic ways (such as including a variable about religious participation in a survey), religions are complex sets of organizations and practices with long traditions, distinct languages, and specialists of their own. In the United States alone, for instance, twelve hundred separate denominations exist, and the diversity of American religion has increased dramatically in recent decades as a result of new immigration involving large numbers of Muslims, Hindus, Buddhists, and non-Western versions of Christianity (Wuthnow 2005). In addition to the many seminaries and theological schools that specialize in understanding the various religious traditions, a growing number of religious studies departments and research centers have been established in colleges and universities. Conversations with scholars interested in other aspects of the nonprofit sector suggest that their lack of attention to religion stems less from indifference than from a sense of being overwhelmed by the sheer amount of knowledge they would need in order to understand religion.

This chapter aims to provide an overview of the aspects of religion in the United States that are likely to be of greatest relevance to scholars interested in the nonprofit sector. There is a huge and growing literature, produced largely by sociologists of religion, on which to draw. Because this literature has remained separate from the literature about nonprofit organizations until fairly recently, we begin with a brief historical overview of the ways in which religion preceded and contributed to the rise of the nonprofit sector in the United States, especially through provision of social services, relief efforts, and hospitals. Throughout its history, religion in America has been influenced by the nation's tradition of church-state separation. This tradition made it possible for religious organizations to flourish but also shaped their role in providing social services. These relationships have become increasingly important in scholarship concerned with government provision of resources to the nonprofit sector. We thus include a section that traces some of the more important aspects of these complex relations between government and religion. Turning to the present, we then summarize research that shows how extensively religion is practiced in the United States, how it is organized, and how religious organizations relate to other nonprofit organizations. Subsequent sections take up the specific issues that have generated the greatest interest in recent years among scholars and practitioners concerned with the relations between religion and the nonprofit sector. These include faith-based service organizations and congregations, charitable choice legislation and welfare reform, religion and public advocacy, the transnational aspects of religious organizations, and the role of religion in facilitating giving and volunteering. Each of these topics has recently been the focus of considerable research. The chapter concludes by discussing some of the conceptual and empirical questions that need to be addressed in future research concerning religion and the nonprofit sector. No single theoretical perspective has emerged that unites the research that has been conducted regarding these various topics. It is nevertheless becoming evident that the organizational forms that characterize American religion are increasingly diverse and that this diversity is in part attributable to the increasingly complex relationships that have emerged between religious organizations and other aspects of the nonprofit sector. Thus, a secondary aim of the present chapter is to encourage scholars to pay greater attention to conceptual and theoretical insights that may emerge from bringing the study of religion and the study of nonprofit organizations into closer alignment. The chapter is primarily concerned with research about religion and the nonprofit sector in the United States. Readers are therefore cautioned that religion plays a much larger role in the United States than it does in many other industrialized societies. At the same time, organized religion appears to be growing in Latin America, Africa, and parts of

Asia, and this growth is not unrelated to the transnational activities of religious organizations in the United States (Jenkins 2002; Barrett, Kurian, and Johnson 2001).

THE SOCIAL HISTORY OF RELIGION AND THE NONPROFIT SECTOR

Research concerning ancient, late antique, medieval, and early modern societies indicates that religion played an important role in organizing the kinds of social services that are now provided by nonprofit organizations, for instance, assistance for the poor, emergency relief, hospital care, and managing orphanages. Provision for the poor was institutionalized in the Hebrew Scriptures and in rabbinic teachings (Weber 1952). Under Constantine, the early Christian church received alms and established hospitals, a practice that spread widely from that time until the high Middle Ages (Mollat 1986). In early modern Europe, the Protestant reformers took control of relief chests and worked closely with municipal authorities to regulate access to welfare provision (N. Davis 1968; Kingdon 1971; Jutte 1981). In early modern Japan, Buddhist temples provided legal asylum as well as social services in local villages (Vesey 1999). In several Muslim countries, *zakat* (poor's due) was a central teaching that required Muslims whose financial situation was above a specified minimum to pay two and a half percent of income and liquid assets to help support the impoverished and unemployed (Cizakca 2000).

In the American colonies, religious leaders admonished followers to be, in the words of John Winthrop, "models of Christian charity" and founded churches that supplied relief to the poor as well as places in which to hold public meetings (Hammack 1998). When Alexis de Tocqueville toured the United States in the 1830s, the nation was experiencing a resurgence of religious interest as a result of revivalist efforts on the expanding frontier in upstate New York, Ohio, and Kentucky (Cross 1950; P. Johnson 1978). Counties in which revivalism was present disproportionately became centers of abolitionist activity and showed distinctive voting patterns well after the Civil War (Hammond 1978). Religious organizations provided the impetus in these years for the first national benevolent societies and temperance crusades, efforts that not only addressed issues of public concern but also forged federations among voluntary associations (Rogers 1996; Young 2002). The associational activity that Tocqueville credited with tempering self-interest and undergirding American democracy was often located in church basements and fellowship halls (Tocqueville 1945). At the same time, religious communities engaged in conflict with one another, sought to keep out new immigrants, and often encouraged intolerance toward racial, ethnic, and religious minorities (Niebuhr 1929).

During the Civil War, religious organizations played a large role in the development of the U.S. Sanitary Commission and other relief organizations that were mobilized by ladies' auxiliaries to supply clothing, food, and medical supplies to military units (Wuthnow 1999). After the war, African American churches became important community centers and served as staging grounds for the subsequent exodus of many black Americans to northern industrial cities (Giggie 1997). African American churches played a significant role in giving women a voice in religious and community affairs through the formation of local and regional "sisterhoods" (Higginbotham 1993). More generally, churches and synagogues gained strength during the second half of the nineteenth century as a result of missionary or congregation-planting efforts and the founding of new immigrant congregations, as well as from the gradual formation of centralized denominational administrative structures. Between 1870 and the end of World War I, the number of local churches grew from little more than 70,000 to more than 225,000. During the same period, the number of church buildings increased from 63,000 to 203,000, and the total value of these buildings mushroomed from $354 million to nearly $1.7 billion, far outstripping growth in population or inflation rates (Wuthnow 1988:22). Historical research suggests that denominational competition, revivalism, and strong leadership were key elements in this growth (Finke and Stark 1992; Christiano 1987). Although this growth contributed to the religious vitality of European Americans, it often had less favorable implications for Native Americans, resulting, for instance, in displacement to new locations and efforts to resocialize youth in church-sponsored boarding schools (J. Martin 1999).

The rapid industrialization, urbanization, and immigration that took place between 1890 and 1920 were accompanied by renewed, albeit only partially effective, efforts by religious groups to address the growing needs of the urban poor (Hall 1990). The Salvation Army was one of the most notable of these efforts, utilizing full-time religious workers and holding innovative rallies and fundraisers to generate support (Winston 1999). Religious leaders also developed urban ministries through the YMCA and YWCA and through settlement house efforts, many of which were initiated or supported by churches (Weisenfeld 1998). As social needs became too great for private charities to address, religious leaders also turned increasingly to municipalities and other governmental agencies to supply welfare assistance (Olasky 1992; Kaufman 2002). Yet it was also in this period that many of the nation's religious architectural landmarks were built as lasting symbolic reminders of the presence of religion in the public square and the historic role of religion in encouraging sacred music and the visual arts (Chidester and Linenthal 1995; P. Williams 1997).

Although religious organizations drew an increasing proportion of the population as members during the first half of the twentieth century, this period also witnessed increasing competition from nonsectarian voluntary associations (Skocpol 1999; Putnam 2000; C. Smith 2003). Museums and orchestras emerged in larger cities, private foundations were established, and Masonic temples as well as such civic organizations as Rotary, Kiwanis, and the Federation of Women's Clubs offered alternatives to the churches (DiMaggio 1992). During the same period, the share of colleges and universities that were operated by religious organizations declined precipitously compared to the share of those sponsored by state governments, church-related colleges increasingly severed historic ties binding them closely to denominations, and hospitals run by religious organizations played a smaller role in healthcare delivery than did nonsectarian hospitals (Freeland 1992; Marsden 1994; Burtchaell 1998).

After World War II, religion in the United States competed increasingly with other phenomena—not only voluntary associations but also television, sports, and the entertainment industry—for the public's loyalties. But religion flourished during the 1950s and early 1960s in response to Cold War insecurities and as part of the postwar building boom; the large number of families with young children whose parents were apparently persuaded, with the popular slogan of the day, that the "family that prays together stays together" also appears to have added a "demographic factor" to this religious vitality (Wuthnow 1988, 1998). Membership in congregations and attendance at religious services grew to record numbers, and a kind of civic religion that equated God and country prevailed (Glock and Stark 1965:68–85; Bellah 1970:168–91). Critics suggested that religion in America was relatively shallow but saw participation in religion as an antidote to the mass culture that threatened to weaken American democracy (Herberg 1955).

Apart from the specific services provided by religious organizations, one of the most significant contributions to the growth of the nonprofit sector during the first two centuries of the nation's existence was an ethos of voluntarism or self-help and the development of a strong civic sphere that was only loosely associated with government (Stackhouse 1990). Whereas trade unions, socialist movements, and corporatist-style government encouraged more centralized polities in many European societies, the American tradition of locally oriented and denominationally pluralistic religion contributed to a more decentralized, associationalist system of government. At the same time, it is also apparent that many of the social functions currently attributed to the nonprofit sector—from services for the poor to the administration of colleges and hospitals, and from providing space for public meetings to supporting the arts—were at one time performed to a significant extent by religious organizations. Long before social scientists and policy makers identified "nonprofits" as composing a distinct social sector, religion offered ways of carrying out social activities that differed from those of either the marketplace or government (Watt 1991).

QUESTIONS ABOUT CHURCH AND STATE

The overall prominence (and, indeed, the growth) of religion in the United States during the nineteenth and twentieth centuries is often attributed to the fact that America, unlike many western European countries, has never had a state church. Separation of church and state is one of the nation's distinctive characteristics. It not only ensures that religious organizations have to compete with one another; it also influences religion's relation to the nonprofit sector. It is beyond the scope of this chapter to discuss rulings concerning church-state relations in detail; however, a brief summary shows that such rulings have played an important role in determining the extent of religious organizations' involvement in providing community services. As the role of federal government has expanded, church-state rulings have also governed the extent to which tax, employment, and nondiscrimination policies that apply to other nonprofit organizations would apply to religious ones. These rulings, in particular, serve as the context for recent policy initiatives involving so-called faith-based social service provision.

The First Amendment to the U.S. Constitution guarantees freedom of religious expression and protection against government establishment of religion. After much debate, the final formulation of this clause, "Congress shall make no law respecting an establishment of Religion or prohibiting the free exercise thereof," was presented in the first session of Congress in September 1789 and was ratified by the requisite number of states by December 1791. Although the meaning of these clauses has been contested from the beginning, the First Amendment has in practice created strong inhibitions against the mingling of religion and government. Separationists interpret these clauses to mean that the government may not benefit or burden religious expression and may not endorse or sponsor religious beliefs or activities; the government should consider religion when making policy to assure that religious organizations or individuals with certain religious beliefs are not singled out for differential treatment. Accommodationists, on the other hand, argue that the government should accept religion and religious groups as central parts of American society and should play the role of a "pragmatic reconciler" in the contested area of church-state relations (Fowler et al. 1999).

Before 1940, states were primarily responsible for granting religious rights and liberties within their boundaries. The First Amendment applied only to the federal government, and Congress passed few laws related to religious expression and establishment. The majority of state constitutions contained a clause protecting liberty or the right of conscience, and 25 states specifically included a free exercise clause. States without such constitutional protection, however, were free to discriminate on the basis of religion. The Supreme Court heard its first free exercise case, *Reynolds v. United States,* in 1879 and decided to uphold a federal law prohibiting polygamy, thereby denying a Mormon's free exercise claim.[1] In its first establishment clause case, *Bradfield v. Roberts* (1899), the Supreme Court also found no First Amendment violation, ruling that funds available from Congress to build new hospitals could be awarded to a nonprofit hospital incorporated and run by an order of nuns under the auspices of the Roman Catholic Church.[2] The Court also reviewed a number of state and local laws related to religion and ruled on church property and polity during this period (Witte 2000).[3]

After 1940 the Court applied the First Amendment's religion clause to the states, shifting responsibility for religious liberty from the states to the federal government. In a free exercise case, *Cantwell v. Connecticut* (1940), the Court first applied the religion clause of the First Amendment to a local ordinance in order to overturn an ordinance that prohibited Jehovah's Witnesses from proselytizing.[4] Court decisions in establishment clause cases changed markedly with the ruling in *Everson v. Board of Education* (1947).[5] Drawing from the First Amendment's religion clause and the Fourteenth Amendment's due process clause, the Court decided that states that provided bus service to children in religious and public schools were not establishing religion. Although public money could not be used to support religious organizations or programs directly, it could be used indirectly (Monsma 1996). The *Everson* decision was reinforced in *Lemon v. Kurtzman* (1971) when the Supreme Court ruled that public money could not be used to subsidize teachers in religious schools for teaching secular subjects.[6] These three decisions and others that followed made clear that the First Amendment applied both to the states and to the federal government. States also maintained a full docket of religion cases during this period, adjudicating them on the basis of state constitutions and the guidance of the Supreme Court.

Since 1940 the Supreme Court has handed down more than 150 decisions regarding free exercise and establishment clause cases, many of which apply directly to the workings of nonprofit organizations. In early cases, for example, the Court ruled that religious groups must have autonomy to decide internal disputes and that state courts must defer to the highest religious authorities in such cases.[7] In *Jones v. Wolf* (1979),[8] the Court reversed these decisions, however, ruling that intrachurch debates could be resolved using "neutral principles of law." In recent free exercise cases, the Supreme Court has come to a narrow reading of the free exercise clause. This reading was most evident in *Employment Division v. Smith* (1990).[9] In this case Smith, a Native American, consumed peyote as part of a rite performed in the Native American Church, to which he belonged. As a result, he was discharged from his job as a drug rehabilitation counselor and applied for unemployment benefits from the state of Oregon. The state denied his request, arguing that consuming peyote was illegal, and disqualified him from receiving benefits. The Supreme Court upheld the state's view, narrowly defining religious practices that are protected under the free exercise clause in the process. This narrow reading was challenged by Congress in the 1993 Religious Freedom Restoration Act, but in 1997 the Court struck down the act as it applies to the states.[10]

In establishment cases, the Court has moved in the opposite direction, shifting from a single narrow principle of church-state relations to a more multiprincipled reading. The Court struck down release-time programs for religious instruction in public schools,[11] prayer,[12] Bible reading,[13] and religious symbols[14] in early cases that focused largely on the public schools. Since 1980 the Court has broadened its establishment decisions to include new principles of religious equality, though Court decisions in this area remain particularly inconsistent.

State and federal legislation concerning taxes, financial reporting requirements, employment practices, and local zoning also influence the formation and functioning of religious and nonreligious nonprofit organizations. Some religious nonprofits, most notably churches, are treated differently from nonreligious nonprofits by the IRS, though both types of nonprofits are exempted from paying income tax. Federal and state governments have been hesitant to define "religion" for tax purposes, and their definitions have been much debated in state courts. The IRS asks two questions: Are the "particular religious beliefs of the organization . . . truly and sincerely held?" And are "the practices and rituals associated with the organizations' religious belief or creed . . . not illegal or contrary to clearly defined public policy?" (Internal Revenue Service 1999b). In 1983, for example, the Supreme Court upheld the IRS's decision to revoke the tax-exempt status of Bob Jones University because its discriminatory racial policies were contrary to public policy.[15] Despite their tax exemptions, churches have been required since 1969 to pay tax on unrelated business income or income from trades or businesses not substantially related to the basis of the organizations' exemption (Internal Revenue Service 1999c). Federal regulations also stipulate that many clergy members are exempt from certain wage and payroll taxes (Internal Revenue Service 1999a; Martin and Miller 1998). At the state level, tax regulations for churches and religious organizations vary. Property tax exemptions are granted by all states, though specific laws differ (Bookman 1992).

With respect to employment issues and zoning, some religious nonprofits, such as churches, are subject to specific regulations. The Civil Rights Act of 1964 and later amendments include an exemption that allows some religious groups to use religion as a criterion in employment decisions. This exemption was upheld in *Corporation of the Presiding Bishop of the Church of Jesus Christ of Latter Day Saints v. Amos* (1987)[16] when the Supreme Court ruled that a religious employer need not retain an employee who had lapsed from its faith (Witte 2000). Property zoning at the local level has also influenced the development and functioning of religious organizations, especially those new to American shores. Throughout Southeast Asia, for example, Buddhist temples are both religious gathering places and residences for monks. When Vietnamese Buddhists in California began to have religious gatherings in their homes in the 1980s and 1990s, neighbors complained about traffic and the sound of prayers and chants in the residential areas where these "home temples" were located. Private homes in these areas were not allowed to be used for religious gatherings without a conditional use permit and without meeting certain safety requirements (Dixon 1996; Breyer 1993). Other Buddhist temples and religious groups formed by recent immigrants present similar challenges to city councils and local zoning boards.

As these examples suggest, the laws and policies governing religious organizations in the United States are subject to differing interpretations and are frequently contested. The ebb and flow of restrictions and regulations influences in particular the competitive relationships that often exist in local communities between religious organizations and nonsectarian nonprofits. Nonsectarian organizations are sometimes at a competitive disadvantage because fewer restrictions apply to religious organizations. Conversely, religious organizations sometimes experience greater difficulty in applying for government funds than do organizations for which separation of church and state is less of an issue.

THE CONTOURS AND DYNAMICS OF AMERICAN RELIGION AND THE NONPROFIT SECTOR

A great deal of research has been conducted in the past half-century on the general contours and dynamics of American religion, including studies of the memberships of various denominations and religious traditions, the religious beliefs and attendance patterns of the public, alliances and divisions among various religious communities, trends in religious commitment, and comparisons with other countries. This research demonstrates that religious organizations are more numerous and command more time and financial contributions than any other kind of nonprofits do. It also demonstrates that religious organizations differ from many kinds of nonprofit organizations in depending on voluntary contributions instead of third-party payments. Although much of this research goes well beyond considerations of the nonprofit sector, the strength and character of American religion are of relevance to any consideration of the nonprofit sector (Biddle 1992; James and Ackerman 1986; James 1993; Corbin 1999).

According to figures from the Gallup Organization (which has examined religion over a longer period of time and in greater detail than any other research center), 59 percent of Americans identify their religious preference as Protestant, 27 percent as Catholic, and 1 percent each as Orthodox, Mormon, or Jewish; only 6 percent say they have no religious preference (Gallup and Lindsay 1999). Polls have thus far not provided reliable figures about membership in other religious organizations, although some estimates suggest that as many as four to six million Muslims, two to four million Buddhists, and more than one million Hindus live in the United States (T. Smith 2002; Committee on the Study of Religion 2005). Among Protestants, more than half are affiliated with evangelical denominations, the largest of which is the Southern Baptist Convention with approximately 16 million members, and the remainder including such groups as Assemblies of God, Church of Christ, and various Pentecostal, Holiness, and independent churches. Approximately one-third of Protestants belong to the historically mainline denominations (United Methodist, Evangelical Lutheran Church in America, Presbyterian Church USA, Episcopal, United Church of Christ, and American Baptist), and the remainder belong to predominately black denominations (such as African Methodist Episcopal, National Baptist Convention, and Churches of God in Christ).

During the 1970s and 1980s, membership in mainline denominations and in Jewish congregations declined by as much as one-quarter, largely because of demographic factors (fewer children and greater spacing between generations), while membership in evangelical denominations increased (Kelley 1986; Hout, Greeley, and Wilde 2001). During the late 1990s, in contrast, the rate of decline in mainline denominations diminished to near zero, and the rate of growth in most larger evangelical denominations was significantly smaller than in the earlier period (Wuthnow and Evans 2002). Among Catholics, the largest shift during the last third of the twentieth century was a substantial increase in the proportion of Hispanic and Latino or Latina members (estimated to be as high as one-quarter of American Catholics; Diaz-Stevens and Stevens-Arroyo 1998). Theological and subcultural boundaries continued to separate Protestants from Catholics, Christians from Jews, and black Christians from white Christians; however, these boundaries were also weakened by higher rates of intermarriage, new contexts for interaction (such as college campuses), declining commitment to creedal traditions, and interfaith coalitions.

More than two-thirds of adult Americans (69 percent) claim to be members of local congregations, a figure that has remained constant since the late 1970s but is slightly lower than it was in the 1940s and 1950s (Gallup and Lindsay 1999). Membership is higher among women than among men, among blacks than among whites, and among southerners and midwesterners than among northeasterners and westerners. According to the 1998 National Congregations Study (a sample of more than 1,200 congregations identified by referrals from a national survey of the adult population), "the median congregation has only 75 regular participants, but the median person is in a congregation with 400 regular participants[, and] only 10 percent of American congregations have more than 350 regular participants, but those congregations contain almost half of the religious service attenders in the country" (Chaves et al. 1999; see also Chaves 2004).

The proportion of Americans who regularly attend religious services is smaller than the proportion who claim membership in congregations, but researchers disagree about the exact figures (Hadaway, Marler, and Chaves 1993, 1998; Presser and Stinson 1998; Woodberry 1998). In Gallup surveys, approximately four adults in ten claim to have attended religious services in the seven days prior to being surveyed (Gallup and Lindsay 1999:15). Estimates from the General Social Survey place the figure at approximately 36 percent, or 28 percent if only worship services are considered (T. Smith 1998). Attendance is higher among women than among men, among evangelical Protestants than among mainline Protestants, Catholics, or Jews, and among older people than among younger people.

Besides attendance at services, participation in small groups sponsored by congregations plays a significant role in the religious lives of many Americans. According to a national study conducted in 1991, 40 percent of adults claimed to be involved in a small group that "meets regularly and provides caring and support for its members," and two-thirds of this number said their group was formally sponsored by a religious organization (Wuthnow 1994a). Approximately 18 to 22 million adults were estimated to be members of 800,000 Sunday school classes, 15 to 20 million were found to participate in 900,000 Bible studies and prayer fellowships, and 8 to 10 million were said to be members of 500,000 self-help groups (such as AA, Al-Anon, and ACOA). The average member had participated in his or her group for at least five years, attended every week for at least an hour and a half, and was highly satisfied with the group. Small groups of this kind are sometimes criticized for being short-lived and focusing on individual needs; however, such groups generate social capital in the form of networks and trust, much as community-based nonprofit organizations do (Wuthnow 2004).

In ideological terms, the U.S. public appears to be committed to a core of basic religious values, but specific beliefs show considerable variation. In Gallup surveys, 95 percent of adults claim belief in God or a higher power, 79 percent believe in miracles, and 67 percent believe in life after death (Gallup and Lindsay 1999). In General Social Surveys, 72 percent say they "feel God's presence" in their daily lives and 76 percent say they "desire to be closer to or in union with God" (Davis et al. 1998). Specific beliefs that show less consensus include beliefs about the Bible, which divide about equally between literalists and nonliteralists, and views of creation and evolution, each being favored by about 40 percent of the public (Gallup and Lindsay 1999). A number of studies conducted since the mid-1980s show that between one-fifth and one-quarter of the public identify their religious views as very conservative, and a roughly equal proportion identify their religious views as very liberal; moreover, religious conservatives and liberals hold negative images of each other and differ dramatically with regard to such issues as abortion and homosexuality (Wuthnow 1988, 1996). Some observers argue that there is a "culture war" in American religion between evangelical Christians and secular humanists (Hunter 1991); others suggest that ideological conflict is more visible in public life than in the beliefs and practices of individuals and congregations (R. Williams 1997; Wolfe 1998; Becker 1999). These religiously rooted ideological divisions influence attitudes toward a wide range of issues relevant to the nonprofit sector, including attitudes about artists and arts organizations, attitudes toward nonprofit organizations concerned with racial equality and sexual preference, and attitudes toward organizations engaged in social service provision (Hunter 1991).

One reason for the visibility of ideological conflict is that special-purpose groups play a greater role in American religion than they did a half-century ago, and many of these groups have aligned themselves with particular identities and ideologies (Wuthnow 1988). Examples range from the Moral Majority, founded by the evangelical preacher Jerry Falwell in the 1980s (Harding 2000), to the more recent Christian Coalition, headed by the television evangelist Pat Robertson, to more local or less influential groups such as the Black Mormon Caucus and the Women's Alliance for Theology, Ethics, and Ritual. Special-purpose groups often model themselves after other nonprofit organizations, work in concert with those organizations, and conform to the same tax codes and managerial styles.

The possibility that religious commitment is weakening has been much debated. Such weakening could have a wider impact on civil society, since religious involvement correlates positively with other forms of community participation and philanthropy. Arguments about secularization drawn from classical sociological theory suggest that the strength of religion diminishes as societies become more industrialized and pluralistic and better educated (B. Wilson 1966; D. Martin 1976). Yet alternative arguments suggest that religious vitality may be maintained by competition among religious groups or by sheer inertia. Gallup data regarding church attendance, using the largest samples for which such data are available, show no change since the early 1970s (Gallup and Lindsay 1999). Hout and Greeley (1998:118), analyzing General Social Survey data and organization data collected by other investigators, conclude, "Neither their data nor the survey record support the conjecture that church attendance rates in the United States have fallen in recent years." In contrast, Putnam (2000) and Inglehart and Baker (2000) estimate that church attendance has decreased by four or five percentage points in the past two or three decades. As Putnam observes, a decline of this magnitude is nevertheless quite small compared to the declines in other measures of community participation (such as visiting with neighbors and joining fraternal organizations).

Whether religion in the United States is weakening or holding steady, it is a significantly more influential social presence than in most other advanced industrialized societies. For instance, monthly attendance at religious services in the United States in the late 1990s was 30 percent higher than in Germany or Australia and 39 percent higher than in Sweden; the proportion saying that God was important in their lives was 29 percent higher in the United States than in Australia, 34 percent higher than in Germany, and 42 percent higher than in Sweden (Inglehart and Baker 2000).

On the whole, religious organizations in the United States make up a substantial share of the ways in which the public voluntarily participates in public life. They probably generate more grassroots participation and link this participation to wider networks of social organizations than any other segment of the nonprofit sector (Greeley 1997). Much of American religion has become "privatized," focusing on personal spiritual journeys and the pursuit of individual religious experiences within congregations (Wuthnow 1998; Roof 1999). Yet it is misleading to describe religion entirely in terms of either personal beliefs or local congregations.

Despite the influence of religion in the United States, researchers have only recently begun to investigate the ways in which religious and secular nonprofit organizations compare on a range of axes. The effectiveness of existing theories of nonprofit organization in explaining the organization and functioning of religious nonprofit organizations is an area where much future research is needed. Existing research reveals differences between religious and secular nonprofit organizations in terms of structure and in terms of service delivery and client satisfaction.

For instance, empirical studies show that religious and secular nonprofit organizations often behave differently.[17] Religious nursing homes are more likely than for-profit or secular nonprofit nursing homes, for example, to use waiting lists, an indicator of the extent to which religious nursing homes may refrain from acting as for-profit nursing homes do by raising prices until the market clears (Weisbrod 1988, 1998). Religious and secular nonprofits also differ in their approaches to employment and personnel matters. Church-related nonprofit nursing homes and facilities for mentally handicapped people, for example, are found to employ significantly more full- and part-time nurses, dieticians, and maintenance workers than are proprietary homes, perhaps suggesting more concern with patient care or less concern with profit maximization (Weisbrod 1998). Hiring criteria in religious and secular nonprofit organizations also differ. In a study of day care centers in Wisconsin, the directors of religious centers were found to have less management experience but more previous experience with children than were the directors of secular nonprofit centers (Mauser 1993, 1998). And in one study religious nursing homes were found to pay lower wages than secular or for-profit nursing homes (Borjas et al. 1983). Research also shows that trustees of large urban nonprofit hospitals are recruited differently depending on the religious affiliation of the hospital. Whereas Catholic and Jewish hospitals have continued to recruit trustees on the basis of religion and ethnicity, Protestant hospitals have become more like secular hospitals, in which trustees are rarely recruited for religious reasons (Swartz 1998).

Existing research also begins to suggest that service delivery and client satisfaction sometimes differ in religious and secular nonprofit organizations. In a study of nursing homes, Weisbrod found that among clients who were given sedatives, clients in secular nursing homes received significantly more medication than did those in church-owned nonprofit nursing homes. Coleman, Hoffer, and Kilgore (1982) found that comparable students learn somewhat more in nonprofit than in public schools, although effects differed by student type and for Catholic and other nonprofit schools. Weisbrod (1998) found customer satisfaction to be higher in religious nursing homes and facilities for the mentally handicapped than among clients in similar secular nonprofit organizations. Mauser also found that religious nonprofit day care providers offer higher quality care than do secular providers and that parents have more trust in them (1993, 1998). Morris and Helburn (2000) added further nuance to these results by examining religious, secular, public, and private day care providers. Much research about the distinctions between for-profit and nonprofit organization centers around the role of trust in organizational behavior and exchange. The way trust functions among religious as compared to secular nonprofit organizations is only now beginning to be studied. Wuthnow, Hackett, and Hsu (2004), for instance, compared perceptions of the trustworthiness of faith-based nonprofits, nonsectarian nonprofits, and congregations in a sample of more than two thousand recipients of assistance from these organizations. There were no significant differences between the perceptions of faith-based and nonsectarian nonprofits; however, congregations were perceived as being more trustworthy than the other organizations, and this difference remained when other factors were controlled.

Although it is possible to speculate about the relevance of nonprofit theory to religious organizations, empirical research is insufficient to confirm or disconfirm such speculation at this point. For instance, nonprofit theory suggests that religious organizations provide the kinds of services that are better supplied by nonprofit than by for-profit means: hard to define or measure, value-based services, such as meaning and belonging, assurance about an afterlife, and emotional support. Such services have traditionally been supported by general membership donations, which disconnect payments from specific outcomes. Yet fee-for-service provision has become increasingly popular in some congregations (where it is possible to find price lists indicating specific charges for prayers, funerals, wakes, weddings, choir lessons, and the like). Scholars have also suggested that a kind of market mentality governs religious shopping and that preferences for denominations can be understood in terms of rational-choice calculations. Cultural taboos against the commingling of God and mammon, as well as prevailing tax laws, deter religious organizations from functioning on a for-profit basis. But in actual practice the lines separating religious activities from for-profit or other nonprofit activities may be blurred.

FAITH-BASED NONPROFITS AND CONGREGATIONS

The topic that has generated more research in recent years about religion than almost any other concerns the role of so-called faith-based nonprofit organizations. Besides the more than three hundred thousand local congregations that presently exist in the United States, thousands of faith-based nonprofit organizations have been founded in recent years (Scott 2002).[18] These are specialized organizations that exist to fulfill such functions as operating homeless shelters and food banks, as opposed to the broad range of liturgical, ritual, and educational functions performed by most congregations. Faith-based service organizations are typically incorporated as 501(c)(3) nonprofits. Examples range from local organizations founded and sponsored by a coalition of congregations, such as a soup kitchen or a day care center, to such national organizations as Catholic Charities and Lutheran Social Services. Faith-based nonprofits are particularly significant in the present context because they, to a greater extent than congregations, function in cooperative and competitive relationships with other nonprofit organizations. They have many of the same managerial problems and conform to the same legal requirements. They are also more likely than congregations to receive government funding (Monsma 1996; Chaves 1999; Glenn 2000; Wuthnow 2004).

Many faith-based nonprofits are *multipurpose organizations* that include a range of activities or programs such as food banks, neighborhood centers, job training programs, and transportation programs and therefore are concerned with coordinating and supervising these various activities. *Church service agencies,* which are semiautonomous service arms of a single denomination or confessional tradition, are one kind of multipurpose faith-based organization. These include some of the nation's largest faith-based service providers. Even at the local level, the budgets of these organizations often exceed those of large congregations and may include substantial receipts from government agencies. *Ecumenical* or *interfaith coalitions* are another kind of multipurpose faith-based organization. These range from coalitions involving a few congregations in a single neighborhood to coalitions involving hundreds of congregations throughout a region or metropolitan area. Smaller coalitions often develop when single congregations cannot effectively deliver services; larger coalitions often receive government funding and work closely with nonsectarian nonprofit agencies.

Other faith-based nonprofits have emerged as *direct-service ministries,* which focus less on coordination or supervision than on immediate relationships with clients, often centered around a particular activity, such as a homeless shelter or a soup kitchen. Usually these are local organizations operating in specific neighborhoods, such as the Fifth Street Shelter in New York City or the Waco Cares Ministry in Waco, Texas. Within the larger category of direct-service ministries, *church-sponsored ministries* retain formal or informal connections with a religious organization and usually receive financial support from this organization and in turn include influences from that organization in the form of board memberships, overlapping staff, or bylaw restrictions. A Presbyterian church that runs a local nursing home is an example. In contrast, *church-initiated organizations* are more likely to have been started by a religious organization or by a pastor or lay member with strong ties to a religious organization but then become sufficiently autonomous that their mission and governance reflect religious values only informally. An AIDS counseling program that was started with help from a local church but that now operates independent of that church is an example.

Faith-based nonprofits form a significant complement to the informal service activities and social ministries that take place within congregations. The activities in which faith-based nonprofits engage generally require professional training, unlike the volunteer activities performed in congregations. Whereas congregations are concentrated in suburban areas, faith-based nonprofits appear more likely to be located in inner-city neighborhoods or in areas closer to clients (Wuthnow 2000b). In these areas, faith-based and secular nonprofits typically evolve a division of labor that minimizes duplication of effort and develop relationships with at least several congregations in the wider community that supply volunteers and funding or donations in kind (Cnaan 2002).

In one study conducted in northeastern Pennsylvania, faith-based service agencies and churches referred clients back and forth, shared information about them, and worked together to channel resources from larger programs to specific points of delivery in local neighborhoods. But service agencies characteristically handled clients that the churches were unable or unwilling to deal with and not the converse; that is, agencies appeared to be helping churches meet needs more than churches were helping agencies. This was one of the reasons that faith-based agencies had been established in the first place. Clergy members recognized that some people's needs required long-term or specialized attention, or they knew that too many needs were concentrated in some churches while other churches had resources to spare. Agency heads were generally pleased that churches were able to send them clients. Yet these administrators also complained that churches were sometimes doing too little to care for their own. The congregations that were most likely to have formal, mutually supportive relationships with faith-based agencies had larger memberships and budgets, were located closer to low-income neighborhoods, and were affiliated with mainline Protestant denominations (Wuthnow 2000b, 2004).

Because they often receive government funding, faith-based nonprofits typically develop strategies for managing possible conflicts of interest between their religiously oriented activities and other programs. These strategies include keeping separate budgets for different programs, housing programs in different facilities, and referring clients with religious interests to congregations. It is difficult to know, however, whether funds received to support specific services also contribute indirectly in some way to the larger religious purposes of the organizations. The effectiveness of these faith-based organizations is still being assessed (Johnson, Tompkins, and Webb 2002).

CHARITABLE CHOICE AND WELFARE REFORM

The relation between faith-based nonprofit organizations and the federal government changed with the passage of the charitable choice provision (section 104) of the 1996 welfare law (the Personal Responsibility and Work Reconciliation Act). This provision aimed to expand the involvement of community and faith-based organizations in public antipoverty efforts (Center for Public Justice 1997). Prior to passage of the charitable choice provision, faith-based organizations that administered social service programs generally formed separate nonprofit organizations in order to receive federal funds. They were also subject to a great deal of ambiguity about how religious the social services they provided could be. The 1996 charitable choice provision required states that contract with social service organizations to deliver services to the poor to allow faith-based organizations to also apply for those contracts. This provision applies to money distributed through the Temporary Assistance to Needy Families program, or TANF (the program that replaced AFDC), to the Supplementary Security Income program (SSI), and to food stamps and Medicaid programs that are administered through contracts or vouchers. Since the law's initial passage, charitable choice provisions have been extended by executive orders to other areas, such as low-income housing programs.

The charitable choice legislation lays out specific requirements for faith-based organizations and the government in these partnerships. First, as a condition of receiving a contract, the state cannot require a religious organization to "alter its form of internal governance" or "remove religious art, icons, scripture, or other symbols" from its buildings. Second, the religious organization retains its independence from federal, state, and local governments, including its "control over the definition, development, practice, and expression of its religious beliefs" throughout the duration of the contract. Third, religious organizations awarded a contract to provide social services can be audited, but they may receive the federal funds in a separate account so that only the "financial assistance provided with such funds shall be subject to audit." Fourth, funds received via the charitable choice provision may not be used for "sectarian worship, instruction, or proselytization." Fifth, faith-based organizations are prohibited from discriminating against individuals receiving their services on the "basis of religion, a religious belief, or refusal to actively participate in religious practice." Religious organizations do, however, retain their right (granted by an exemption clause to the 1964 Civil Rights Act) to hire program staff on the basis of their religious beliefs (although this right has been challenged in the courts). Finally, the charitable choice legislation stipulates that if a recipient of assistance objects to the religious nature of an organization providing services, the government must find an alternative service provider of the same quality within a reasonable amount of time (Center for Public Justice 1997). Although this legislation requires that states allow faith-based organizations to apply for these government contracts, it does not guarantee that they will be awarded contracts (it is not an affirmative action program).

Charitable choice was a hotly debated issue among religious leaders during the 1996 welfare policy discussions. Those who opposed it were concerned about increased entanglement between church and state and the possibility that organizations involved with charitable choice would drift from their core mission and goals. Some argued that the churches' critical stance toward government would change if they received government money, as would churches' relations with the poor. Others were concerned about excessive government delegation of powers and argued that churches do not have the resources to care for the poor. Many expressed concerns about the constitutionality of the legislation, in particular, the possibility of civil rights abuses occurring when government money is used by organizations that discriminate in employment. Those who supported charitable choice emphasized that it would expand their ability to provide social services to the poor, and some argued that religiously based social service programs are more effective than similar secular programs.

Since the charitable choice legislation was passed in 1996, responses from religious communities have been mixed. In an early nationally representative study, leaders of one-third of congregations in the United States expressed interest in applying for government funds to support social service activities. Very large congregations, Catholic churches, and theologically moderate and liberal Protestant congregations were among those most likely to want to apply. After taking into account other factors, African American congregations were five times more likely than other churches to express interest in public support for their social service activities (Chaves 1999). Fewer than half of congregations included in this study, however, were aware of charitable choice. Other studies also suggest that many religious groups and government officials remain ignorant of the law (Owens 2000; Sherman 2000; Winston 2000). There is also evidence to suggest that some faith-based organizations may not be interested in applying for federal funds via charitable choice because they already receive federal funds and have learned to accommodate their services to the old rules governing faith-based organizations (Loconte 2000; Winston 2000).

Researchers have only begun to draw preliminary conclusions about the effects of the charitable choice legislation on the provision of local social services. In a study released by the Center for Public Justice, Amy Sherman reported that charitable choice has resulted in "cooperative relationships between government and the faith community" in at least 23 states. In the 9 states on which she focused specifically, she found 84 new financial collaborations between government and religious social service providers and 41 new nonfinancial relationships formed since 1996. More than half of the financial relationships involved churches and other faith-based organizations that had not previously collaborated with government. These new programs focused largely on faith-based mentoring and job training. In Virginia, for example, the Norfolk Interfaith Partnership, a group of Catholic and Protestant congregations, partnered with the Norfolk Department of Human Services. Together they created the Norfolk Interfaith Partnership, which in part provides welfare-to-work mentoring for families receiving public assistance. In another case, Jewish Family Services in Monroe County, New York, received a grant to provide job training and placement services for TANF clients in their region. There were complaints in only two of the programs that Sherman examined. In both cases, clients felt subtly pressured to attend church, and in both cases the clients were transferred to appropriate secular service providers (Sherman 2000). Additional research points to some of the obstacles to implementing charitable choice. In one case in Philadelphia, Cookman United Methodist Church, its nonprofit service organization, Neighborhood Joy Ministries, and the state had to negotiate a range of issues and misunderstandings—in particular, program guidelines and payment schedules—as a program was implemented (Sinha 2000). Differences in quality between grant applications from religious and secular groups may also be an issue in charitable choice implementation (Farnsley 2001).

The larger point illustrated by the recent history of charitable choice and faith-based initiatives is that government is an important factor in the day-to-day activities of nonprofit organizations. Government provides a significant share of funding for nonprofit organizations, including faith-based organizations. As government funding is appropriated, expectations about the outcomes of nonprofit programs change. For instance, questions about efficiency and effectiveness are likely to be more important when public funds are involved than in, say, a small religious congregation that prides itself on promoting long-term, caring relationships. Although religious organizations may be said to compete with one another insofar as members and donations are concerned, competition is likely to be more important when these organizations write grants in order to secure funding from limited public pools. Indeed, the fact that larger and wealthier congregations and faith-based nonprofits appear to be the most successful at securing such funding suggests that comparative advantage does become increasingly important.

RELIGION AND PUBLIC ADVOCACY

Tax-exempt nonprofits are prohibited from engaging directly in public advocacy. The nonprofit sector, however, is widely regarded as a kind of free space in which critical ideas can germinate, and religious organizations have taken part. Since the abolitionist movement of the nineteenth century, religious groups in the United States have joined secular nonprofits' attempts to influence public policy at the state and national levels in a range of ways. Religious and nonreligious groups were active in the temperance movement, the civil rights movement, and, more recently, in the sanctuary movement's efforts to protect refugees from Central America (C. Smith 1996). Religious groups have also assisted in mobilizing nativist movements, survivalist organizations, and movements interested in restricting civil liberties (Lipset and Raab 1970; Barkun 1996). The way people vote in elections may be indirectly influenced by contact with poor people through religiously sponsored social service projects or conversations in temples or national denominational meetings. Church-based community organizing has also been a significant form of religious advocacy, mobilizing an estimated one to two million Americans involved in local issues concerned with inequality and social justice by means of intensive congregational education and accountability programs (Warren 2001). Such programs utilize the facilities, leadership, and values of religious organizations to nurture civic skills (Verba et al. 1995). Yet religious advocacy also raises ethical and policy concerns. Many church members believe that churches should provide services at the local level but steer clear of partisan politics for fear of violating the separation of church and state; others believe that advocacy should be done selectively and only after careful consideration within congregations (Wuthnow and Evans 2002). Others express concern about lobbying because of funding issues, though recent evidence drawn from religious and secular nonprofit organizations suggests that the levels of government funding current in most nonprofits do not suppress their political activities (Chaves, Stephens, and Galaskiewicz 2002).

In addition to congregational advocacy, religious groups have added their voices to national public policy debates by lobbying in Washington, D.C. The United Methodist Church became the first major religious presence in the nation's capital because of its support for Prohibition in 1916, and in 1943 the Quakers registered the first national religious lobby, the Friends Committee on National Legislation (Hertzke 1988). By 1950 at least 16 religious groups had offices in Washington, D.C., and by 2000 there were more than 100 religious lobbies representing Jewish, Catholic, liberal Protestant, evangelical, African American, and Muslim faiths (Fowler et al. 1999).

The media and the American public became increasingly interested in religious lobbying organizations with the rise of the Christian Right in the late 1970s and 1980s. The Christian Right includes a range of organizations that aim to mobilize conservative Protestants to political participation. These organizations' messages and constituencies overlapped during the 1980s, with the Moral Majority being the most visible. In 1989, after his failed run for the presidency, Pat Robertson founded the Christian Coalition. With more than 1.5 million members and 1,700 local chapters in all 50 states, the Christian Coalition quickly became one of the best-organized religious lobbying groups. The coalition's membership has largely consisted of white evangelicals but also includes some conservative Catholics. The group's lobbying strategy is twofold. First, it founded a Government Affairs Office in Washington, D.C., in 1993 and spent a significant amount of time and resources lobbying there, primarily regarding conservative economic issues. Second, the group became involved in every aspect of electoral politics. It worked to influence decisions about who received party nominations and then provided training for the candidate, his campaign manager, and his finance director. Most significant, the Christian Coalition sought to influence the outcome of elections by preparing and distributing voter guides and mobilizing voters at the grass roots. Although federal tax regulations stipulate that these guides must include each candidate's positions, it was often clear from the way the positions were presented which candidate the coalition supported (Moen 1992; Wilcox 1992; Watson 1997). Increasingly, this and other conservative Christian organizations have adopted a strategy of proliferating separate nonprofit organizations for specific purposes. For instance, a large, well-funded local congregation may have a separate nonprofit entity to support its television ministry, another nonprofit organization to solicit tax-deductible contributions for charitable programs, a nonprofit educational organization to train ministers, and a non-tax-exempt nonprofit through which to engage in lobbying. With tens of millions of dollars at their disposal, such organizations function more as national and international conglomerates do than as traditional congregations.

Following a more centralized model of organization, American Catholics have also added their voices to public dialogue, largely through the pastoral letters of American bishops. Before the Second Vatican Council took place in the early 1960s, Catholic bishops were involved in politics mostly at the local level. After World War I, the National Catholic Welfare Conference was formed in Washington, D.C., but it was not directly tied into the hierarchy of the

Catholic Church. After Vatican II, American bishops realized that they needed to strengthen their national presence if they wanted to have an impact on American politics. The National Conference of Catholic Bishops (NCCB) was subsequently created by the highest church authority, and all American bishops were required to join. The conference was granted authority apart from the authority of individual bishops (Byrnes 1991). The conference was active in the presidential elections of 1976 and 1984, and its antiabortion position has been advanced by many groups since *Roe v. Wade* was decided in 1973. In the 1980s the conference's most significant statements focused on modern war, nuclear weapons, and the U.S. economy. Drawing from the long tradition of Catholic social thought, *The Challenge of Peace* (1983) prohibited the first use of nuclear weapons and stressed deterrence as a step toward disarmament. In *Economic Justice for All: Catholic Teaching and the U.S. Economy* (1986), the bishops argued that "all people have a right to participate in the economic life of society" and "all members of society have a special obligation to the poor and vulnerable." The bishops also emphasized specific policy proposals such as coordinating fiscal monetary policy to achieve full employment and expanding job training programs. The 1983 statement led some American bishops to get involved in the 1984 presidential elections, and the 1986 statement was widely discussed among Catholics and non-Catholics alike. Statements made after Vatican II were generally more influential in American politics than those made before the council occurred because they had the full weight of the Catholic Church behind them (Byrnes 1991; Warner 1995).

Jewish lobbying groups have also enjoyed success, in part because of their resources and their access to political elites. A range of Jewish organizations such as the American Jewish Committee, the Anti-Defamation League, and the Union of American Hebrew Congregations are dedicated to presenting Jewish perspectives on a range of issues (Fowler et al. 1999). These groups have traditionally supported the strict separation of church and state and have been liberal with regard to civil liberties issues (Hertze 1988; Fowler et al. 1999). In a class by itself, the secular American Israel Public Affairs Committee (AIPAC) has worked since its founding in 1954 to "keep Israel safe and secure and strengthen the country's friendship with the United States" by "advancing the peace process, strengthening Israel through military and economic aid, and protecting Jerusalem as the capital of Israel."[19] At present, the group has a grassroots membership of 50,000, a staff of more than 100, several paid lobbyists, and a multimillion-dollar annual budget. The group works largely through key contacts and has exerted considerable influence on U.S. actions in Israel and the Middle East more broadly. The AIPAC and other Jewish groups exert considerable influence on the political process financially via political action committees (PACs) that donate money to candidates (Medding 1992).

Evangelical Christian, Catholic, Jewish, Muslim, and other religious lobbyist groups have been involved in politics primarily at the federal level. Like secular lobbyists, religious lobbyists aim to affect the political process by influencing the choice of issues that are up for congressional debate and mobilizing congressional and public opinion regarding those issues. Groups do this by publishing action alerts, newsletters, and magazines about their faith traditions and their work. The Council on American Islamic Relations, for example, publishes a quarterly newsletter, *Faith in Action.* Religious lobbyists also propose bills, testify before congressional committees, track legislation, provide information to Congress and the media on the effects of public policy, and mobilize their constituencies regarding relevant issues (Hertze 1988). With the exception of some Jewish groups, the majority do not contribute money to PACs (Fowler et al. 1998). At the judicial level, religious lobbies have also sometimes led the groups they represent to file amicus curiae, or friend of the court, briefs in relevant federal and state court cases.

As with secular advocacy organizations, the results of religious advocacy efforts at the national level have been mixed (Hertze 1988; Hofrenning 1995). The Christian Coalition significantly influenced electoral politics in the 1980s, and more recently mainline Protestant groups influenced actions concerning debt relief for poor nations through the Jubilee 2000 campaign. More recently, grassroots religious organizations have played an important role in federal policies involving so-called religious freedom in other countries, that is, monitoring foreign governments' policies toward Christian missionaries and various indigenous religious groups. The relation between the tax status of religious groups and their involvement in public advocacy has, of course, been a recurrent issue, as in the Supreme Court case *United States Catholic Conference et al. v. Abortion Rights Mobilization* (1988),[20] in which Abortion Rights Mobilization and others tried, unsuccessfully, to revoke the 501(c)(3) status of the Catholic Church because of what they perceived to be inconsistent enforcement across organizations of the rules governing the lobbying activities of 501(c)(3) organizations.

TRANSNATIONAL ASPECTS OF RELIGIOUS ORGANIZATIONS

In addition to their domestic concerns, international issues are important to many religious and nonreligious nonprofit organizations in the United States. Since the late eighteenth century, American religious organizations have sent people and funds abroad to spread religious messages and to provide social services, engage in political advocacy, and offer technical assistance. Institutional and local communication between religious groups in the United States and abroad is also an important component of the transnationalization of religious practice. At the institutional level, many religious groups in the United States are in contact with related groups abroad. The Episcopal Church in the United States, for example, is in contact with Episcopal churches around the world in regular meetings of the Anglican Communion of Churches. Other religious groups, such as the Thai Buddhist temple Wat Mongkoltepmunee, outside Philadelphia, are closely affiliated with religious organizations centered outside the United States. On the local level, immigration, especially since 1965, has encouraged the flow of ideas and practices between religious organizations in sending and receiving countries. Catholic parishes in Boston and parts of the Dominican Republic, for example, are increasingly related as individuals move between parishes in each location and religious practices converge with their movements (Levitt 1998). Because they have the economic wherewithal, a growing number of middle-class Americans also participate annually in short-term trips to other countries as part of church-sponsored mission and relief programs (Peterson, Aeschliman, and Sneed 2003). These programs are undoubtedly facilitated by the activities of international nongovernmental organizations, or INGOs (such as World Vision and Catholic Relief) and by the growing infrastructure of churches and humanitarian nonprofit organizations in developing countries (Jenkins 2002).

Nonprofit U.S.-based missions organizations have been involved in work abroad since the early nineteenth century. The Protestant American Board of Commissioners for Foreign Missions was founded in 1810 as the first and, for the next fifty years, the largest agency to send workers abroad. Clergy members were sent abroad first, and laypeople later joined the missionary force (Hutchison 1987). By the end of World War I, Christian missionaries were spread around the globe (Miller 1998). In addition to their work of spreading the Gospel, they built and supported schools, hospitals, and agricultural extension programs in their countries of residence (Burridge 1991). The religious affiliations of missionaries abroad changed significantly in the twentieth century. The number of mainline Protestant missions declined during the century while the number of Evangelical and Pentecostal missions increased dramatically, especially after 1960 (Hutchison 1987). Missionaries working with the Seventh-Day Adventists, the Church of Jesus Christ of Latter-Day Saints, and the Jehovah's Witnesses also increased in number during the second half of the century. At present, evangelical and Pentecostal groups dominate the mission landscape, although Protestant, Catholic, and Orthodox Christian groups in the United States continue to place religious workers abroad. The Southern Baptist Convention International Missions Board, a nonprofit organization based in the United States, currently is the largest American presence overseas as measured both by the number of persons placed (more than 4,000) and by its financial resources ($22.1 million; Siewert and Valdez 1997). Whereas local congregations formerly participated in such activities via denominational mission boards, more congregations currently send mission teams abroad directly to help build local churches, train indigenous clergy members, or engage in relief efforts (ibid.). Churches that do not send their own members abroad may support a specific missionary or collect money for a mission's organization.

The rise of evangelical Christianity in Latin America in the past 40 years is a vivid illustration of the involvement of U.S.-based religious organizations in missions there. Protestantism grew slowly in Latin America in the nineteenth and early twentieth centuries as a result of the efforts of European immigrants, American and British Bible societies, and missionaries from Protestant churches in the United States and Europe (Deiros 1991). As the religious right grew in the United States and political situations changed in Latin America in the 1970s and 1980s, evangelical and Pentecostal missions increased on the continent and gained large numbers of members, especially among the lower classes. By the 1980s, 10 percent of Latin Americans were evangelicals, with the percentage significantly higher in Brazil, Chile, and much of Central America (Stoll 1989; Garrard-Burnett and Stoll 1993). In Guatemala, for example, evangelicalism and Pentecostalism grew dramatically after the earthquake of 1976. Members of U.S. evangelical churches, relief and development organizations, and parachurch groups poured into the country to help with disaster relief, and many stayed or formed alliances with local groups before returning home. By the mid-1990s, 25 to 35 percent of Guatemalans were Protestant, and half of those were Pentecostal (Sherman 1997). Although most evangelical and Pentecostal churches in Latin America are currently led by Latin Americans, many remain strongly tied to North American organizations, most particularly to the Assemblies of God (Deiros 1991). North American organizations provide guidance, financial assistance, pastoral education, and televangelism to local churches, directly influencing Latin America's rapidly changing religious landscape (D. Martin 1990; Levine and Stoll 1997).

In addition to their mission activities abroad, religious organizations in the United States have been involved with church-affiliated relief and development organizations around the world. Following World War II, religious groups established nonprofit organizations such as the United Methodist Committee on Relief (formed in 1940), Catholic Relief Services (formed in 1943), Lutheran World Relief (formed in 1945), and Church World Service (formed in 1945) to resettle displaced people and help rebuild war-torn Europe (Nichols 1988; B. Smith 1990). By the 1950s, Catholic Relief Services had become the largest private relief agency in the world (Nichols 1988). These groups have continued to provide services and have shifted their focus from Europe to the developing world and from short-term emergency relief services to long-term development strategies (B. Smith 1998). The impact of these organizations has been significant. The organization USAID provides money for services in the developing world, often relying on religious and church-affiliated organizations because of their track records and their impartial distribution of services (B. Smith 1982). In 1981, in part because of USAID's support, church-affiliated nonprofits accounted for almost one-third of all nongovernmental overseas assistance that year ($1.4 billion of $4.5 billion; B. Smith 1998). In 1990, nearly 10 percent of Western nonprofits involved in work abroad were affiliated with a religious organization (ibid.). The activities of these nonprofits appear to be remarkably similar regardless of the faith tradition with which they are involved. Mainline Protestant and evangelical groups, for example, run their own programs and support indigenous programs in about equal numbers and do not seem to have programs that are of different sizes or have different foci. The groups do justify their programs differently, however, with evangelicals emphasizing individual responsibility and mainline Protestants often focusing on community responsibility more broadly (Kniss and Campbell 1997).

Research suggests that religious groups working transnationally can be categorized in various ways, for instance, according to their level of organization in the sending and receiving countries (local, regional, national, international), their orientation (evangelical missions, economic development), their funding (public, private), and their staff (professional or volunteer). Although researchers have begun to consider these issues for INGOs in general, the significance of a religion's founders and affiliations has not been adequately explored (Boli and Thomas 1997; Lindenberg and Dobel 1999). Research that specifically compares the ways religious and secular relief and development organizations do their work abroad will allow for a fuller understanding of the ways similarly structured religious and secular nonprofit organizations aim to create social change.

These examples illustrate some of the ways in which religion extends beyond the usual considerations raised in studies of local congregations and local communities. Nonprofit organizations that are affiliated with religious groups in the United States are centrally involved in the process of globalization. As transnational actors they have contributed and continue to contribute to globalization by spreading people, finances, and ideas around the world. In addition to instigating changes abroad, religious groups in the United States are being influenced on their own shores by the relatively recent growth of newly imported religious traditions. Hindu, Muslim, Buddhist, and Sikh religious centers dot the nation, and the dialogue between these centers and their countries of origin is changing the American religious landscape (Wuthnow 2005). Future research that describes the ways transnational religious organizations relate to their constituencies around the globe will add to our understanding of the ways religious groups function as transnational actors.

RELIGION, GIVING, AND VOLUNTEERING

Any survey of the relation between religion and the nonprofit sector must include the ways in which religious involvement influences the availability of resources on which nonprofit organizations depend. Although third-party payments and payments by clients are important to much of the nonprofit sector, voluntary contributions of time and money also remain significant. In the past decade, researchers have focused considerable attention on the relation between the religious beliefs and practices of individuals, on one hand, and their philanthropic giving and volunteering, on the other. Several national surveys have been conducted, and these have been supplemented with qualitative interviews and ethnographic observations (Wuthnow 1991; Hoge et al. 1996). Much of the research has been concerned with questions of motivation and opportunity.

Nearly all religious traditions emphasize some form of altruism, whether expressed as love of neighbor, care for the poor, hospitality, or service to fellow members of one's community. Several overlapping manifestations of altruistic values have been identified: humanitarianism, or the capacity to empathize with a needy person on grounds of sharing the basic fact of being members of the same species; the pursuit of happiness, or the belief that God wants all people to be happy and that individual happiness is optimized when others in one's social context are also happy; reciprocity, or the view that resources and talents are divine gifts that are intended to be shared with those who have fewer gifts; and self-realization, or the idea that personal fulfillment is a divine expectation that can best be achieved by putting oneself in challenging situations such as helping others (Wuthnow 1995; Monroe 1996). Most Americans subscribe to one or more of these rationales for altruistic behavior. They may differ, of course, in how they define the target groups toward which altruism is shown and in practice may be more driven by self-interest than by altruistic ideals.

Religious organizations absorb a significant share of Americans' altruistic behavior. By 2003, for example, financial giving to religious organizations had risen to more than $84 billion annually, and this figure accounted for more than half of all giving from private households (*U.S. Statistical Abstract* 2004). Most of this money is spent on clergy salaries and on the maintenance of buildings, but at least a small fraction goes toward wider community needs (Hoge et al. 1996; Wuthnow 2004). In the same period, volunteering for religious organizations was more common than for any other kind of organization (Hodgkinson and Weitzman 1994). The religiously involved are more likely than the religiously uninvolved to volunteer for other nonprofit organizations and to do volunteer work informally (Wuthnow 1991; Greeley 1997). Surveys also show that religious involvement encourages people to think about their responsibility to the poor and to say they want more from life than a good job and a comfortable lifestyle—attitudes that are in turn related to participation in charitable activities (Wuthnow 1994b).

Religious organizations vary in the extent to which they provide opportunities and incentives for giving and volunteering and in the kinds of volunteer activities in which members participate. At least 75 percent of those who attend services participate in congregations that sponsor social service activities of one kind or another, meaning that most congregants have opportunities to volunteer (Chaves 1999, 2004). But larger congregations typically have more of these activities than do smaller ones; thus members of larger congregations are also more likely to be involved in more volunteer activities than are members of smaller ones (Wuthnow 2001, 2004). The most notable differences in *kinds* of volunteering are those between evangelical Protestants and mainline Protestants: church involvement among the former is associated mainly with volunteering within the congregation, among the latter, with joining and volunteering for a wider variety of community organizations (Wuthnow 1999). Similar differences are evident in giving patterns (Iannacone 1998; Hoge et al. 1996; Hamilton and Ilchman 1995).

The content of sermons, discussions, and other group activities also influences parishioners' likelihood of engaging in giving and volunteering. In one study, church members who were involved in charitable activities were more likely than members not involved in charitable activities to have heard a stewardship sermon in the past year and participated in a small fellowship group (Wuthnow 1994b). In another study, members of small prayer and Bible study groups that discussed forgiveness were more likely than members of groups that did not discuss forgiveness to say they had worked to heal broken relationships and had engaged in volunteer activities at their church and in other community organizations (Wuthnow 2000a). Further research would be necessary, however, to establish causal relationships. Research concerning pastors shows that sermons about charitable (especially financial) giving are often preached reluctantly and in ways that may obscure their effectiveness (Wuthnow 1997). Pastors say they have not been trained well to preach about giving and sometimes report worrying that members will respond negatively if preaching focuses too much on giving.

Less research has been done on the *recipients* of altruistic behavior than on givers and volunteers, but in one national survey of working Americans 4 percent claimed to have received financial help from a religious organization within the past year. Eighty percent of these recipients were themselves church or synagogue members (compared to 56 percent of nonrecipients), and 61 percent belonged to religious fellowship groups (compared to 18 percent among nonrecipients). The recipients were disproportionately people in lower income brackets who had children and who had been laid off from their jobs or experienced pay cuts and had trouble paying their bills; nearly half had received religious counseling as well as financial assistance (Wuthnow 1994b). Further research would be needed to determine the extent to which religious networks provide an informal safety net that prevents people from having to seek formal assistance from government or nonprofit service agencies.

Qualitative research is also beginning to challenge the assumption that religion's role in promoting volunteering is always and necessarily beneficial. For instance, Lichterman (2003) shows that religious groups that encourage caring for needy individuals in their community often have difficulty understanding the collective character and identity of other groups *as groups,* especially when those groups differ in racial, ethnic, and religious composition. Questions also remain about the extent to which religious volunteering may encourage or discourage understanding of social justice.

Until relatively recently, research concerning religion and research about the nonprofit sector were conducted largely in isolation from one another. Only in the past few years has the extensive role of religion in the nonprofit sector begun to be appreciated within the academic community. As a result, many conceptual and empirical issues remain. For instance, quantitative and qualitative studies of congregations have flourished in recent years, greatly increasing our knowledge of the size, worship styles, and social ministries of congregations. Yet, in comparison, relatively little is known about other faith-based nonprofit organizations or the roles they play in relation to congregations. In the absence of more detailed research, the two general conclusions that emerge about the management of faith-based nonprofits are, first, that the challenges facing these organizations are in many ways similar to those facing other nonprofits, and, second, that religion poses several unique challenges for the nonprofit sector. The common challenges arise from competition within the nonprofit sector and between it and the for-profit sector for scarce resources. Because nonprofit organizations have generally been regarded as a positive feature of democratic societies and because religion appears to reinforce involvement in nonprofits, researchers have also tended to pay more attention to the positive contributions of religion than to its negative aspects.

Several specific challenges face the leaders of faith-based nonprofit organizations. These include developing and maintaining viable linkages between local, regional or state, and national organizations—linkages that may at one time have been less important to religious organizations or supplied by denominational structures. These linkages are likely to include and depend on strong relationships with federal, state, and local government agencies from which funding is received. Although many policy makers believe faith-based organizations can play a significant role in social service provision, few think that these organizations can effectively replace government programs (McCarthy and Castelli 1996; Cnaan 2002). At the local level, overcoming the spatial mismatch between the more affluent communities in which the majority of U.S. congregations are located and the more needy communities in which social services are lacking is an important challenge (Ramsay 1998). The organization and management of volunteers also becomes increasingly important, especially as volunteering becomes more sporadic, short-term, and specialized. Religious values may continue to encourage altruism, but the effective mobilization of altruism requires thoughtful planning and management.

Religious freedom entails protection for the expression of minority religious views, especially from infringement that may arise intentionally or inadvertently from government action or from the actions of religious organizations themselves. Insofar as government relies on religious organizations to carry out such social functions as education, treatment of the sick, and care of the poor, the rights and privileges of minority religious groups must be given special consideration (Wolfe 2003). The strength of religion in America has depended on the competition that prevails under a system of religious freedom, yet the considerable resources that religion has garnered as a result of this system make religion a logical ally in such wide-ranging social causes as education, healthcare reform, overcoming racial discrimination, and protecting the environment. At the same time, religious freedom—not to mention individuals and groups that are violating the law—permits darker aspects of the human spirit to flourish, as evidenced in clergy pedophilia, religiously motivated hate crimes and violence, and the misuse of religious funds (Juergensmeyer 2001). Religious freedom also encourages a kind of privatized expression of faith that leads to withdrawal from active participation in religious organizations in favor of more personalized forms of spirituality. Privatization of this kind reduces engagement with the voluntary organizations that are so much a part of the nonprofit sector.

NOTES

1. 98 U.S. 145 (1879).
2. 175 U.S. 291 (1899).
3. This section draws heavily on Witte (2000).
4. 310 U.S. 296 (1940).
5. 330 U.S. 1 (1947).
6. 403 U.S. 602 (1971).
7. *Kendroff v. Saint Nicholas Cathedral,* 344 U.S. 94 (1952); *Presbyterian Church in the United States v. Elizabeth Blue Hull Memorial Presbyterian Church,* 393 U.S. 440 (1969); *Serbian Orthodox Diocese v. Milivojevich,* 426 U.S. 696 (1976).
8. 443 U.S. 595 (1979).
9. 494 U.S. 872 (1990).
10. The Supreme Court struck down the Religious Freedom and Reconciliation Act in *City of Boerne v. Flores,* 521 U.S. 507 (1997).
11. *McCollum v. Board of Education,* 330 U.S. 203 (1948).
12. *Engel v. Vitale,* 370 U.S. 421 (1962).
13. *Abington School District v. Schempp,* 374 U.S. 203 (1963).
14. *Stone v. Graham,* 449 U.S. 39 (1980).
15. *Bob Jones University v. United States,* 461 U.S. 574 (1983).
16. 483 U.S. 327 (1987).
17. See also Schlesinger and Gray (this volume) for further discussion of empirical studies in health.
18. See also http://www.religionandsocialpolicy.org/.
19. American Israel Public Affairs Committee Web site: http://www.aipac.org/documents/unique.html (last accessed November 14, 2000).
20. 487 U.S. 72 (1988).

REFERENCES

Ammerman, Nancy Tatom. 2005. *Pillars of Faith: American Congregations and Their Partners.* Berkeley: University of California Press.

Barkun, Michael. 1996. *Religion and the Racist Right: The Origins of the Christian Identity Movement.* Chapel Hill: University of North Carolina Press.

Barrett, David B., George T. Kurian, and Todd M. Johnson. 2001. *World Christian Encyclopedia: A Comparative Survey of Churches and Religions in the Modern World,* 2d ed. New York: Oxford University Press.

Becker, Penny Edgell. 1999. *Congregations in Conflict: Cultural Models of Local Religious Life.* Cambridge: Cambridge University Press.

Bellah, Robert N. 1970. *Beyond Belief: Essays on Religion in a Post-Traditional World.* New York: Harper and Row.

Biddle, Jeff E. 1992. "Religious Organizations." Pp. 92–133 in *Who Benefits from the Nonprofit Sector?* edited by Charles T. Clotfelter. Chicago: University of Chicago Press.

Boli, John, and George M. Thomas. 1997. "World Culture in the World Polity: A Century of International Non-Governmental Organization." *American Sociological Review* 62:171–90.

Bookman, Mark. 1992. *Protecting Your Organization's Tax-Exempt Status: A Guide for Nonprofit Managers.* San Francisco: Jossey-Bass.

Borjas, G. H., H. Frech, and P. B. Ginsburg. 1983. "Property Rights and Wages: The Case of Nursing Homes." *Journal of Human Resources* 17:231–46.

Breyer, Chloe Anne. 1993. "Religious Liberty in Law and Practice: Vietnamese Home Temples and the First Amendment." *Journal of Church and State* 35:368–401.

Burridge, Kenelm. 1991. *In the Way: A Study of Christian Missionary Endeavors.* Vancouver: University of British Columbia Press.

Burtchaell, James Tunstead. 1998. *The Dying of the Light: The Disengagement of Colleges and Universities from Their Christian Churches.* Grand Rapids, Mich.: Eerdmans.

Byrnes, Timothy. 1991. *The Catholic Bishops in American Politics.* Princeton: Princeton University Press.

Center for Public Justice. 1997. *A Guide to Charitable Choice.* http://www.cpjustice.org/~cpjustice/CGuide/Guide.html.

The Challenge of Peace: God's Promise and Our Response; A Pastoral Letter on War and Peace. 1983. Washington D.C.: National Conference of Catholic Bishops.

Chaves, Mark. 1994. "Secularization as Declining Religious Authority." *Social Forces* 72:749–74.

———. 1999. "Religious Congregations and Welfare Reform: Who Will Take Advantage of 'Charitable Choice'?" *American Sociological Review* 64:836–46.

———. 2004. *Congregations in America.* Cambridge: Harvard University Press.

Chaves, Mark, Mary Ellen Konieczny, Kraig Beyerlien, and Emily Barman. 1999. "The National Congregations Study: Background, Methods, and Selected Results." *Journal for the Scientific Study of Religion* 38:458–76.

Chaves, Mark, Laura Stephens, and Joseph Galaskiewicz. 2002. "Does Government Funding Suppress Nonprofits' Political Activity?" Paper presented at the American Sociological Association Annual Meeting.

Chidester, David, and Edward Tabor Linenthal, eds. 1995. *American Sacred Space.* Bloomington: Indiana University Press.

Christiano, Kevin J. 1987. *Religious Diversity and Social Change: American Cities, 1890–1906.* Cambridge: Cambridge University Press.

Cizakca, Murat. 2000. *A History of Philanthropic Foundations: The Islamic World from the Seventh Century to the Present.* Istanbul: Bogazici University Press.

Cnaan, Ram A. 2002. *The Invisible Caring Hand: American Congregations and the Provision of Welfare.* New York: New York University Press, 2002.

Coleman, James, Thomas Hoffer, and Sally Kilgore. 1982. "Cognitive Outcomes in Public and Private Schools." *Sociology of Education* 55:65–76.

Committee on the Study of Religion. 2005. "Statistics." The Pluralism Project. http://www.pluralism.org/resources/statistics/index.php.

Corbin, John. 1999. "A Study of the Factors Influencing the Growth of Nonprofits in Social Services." *Nonprofit and Voluntary Sector Quarterly* 28:296–314.

Cross, Whitney R. 1950. *The Burned-Over District: The Social and Intellectual History of Enthusiastic Religion in Western New York, 1800–1850.* Ithaca, N.Y.: Cornell University Press.

Davis, James A., Tom W. Smith, and Peter V. Marsden. 1998. *General Social Surveys, 1972–1998: Cumulative Codebook.* Chicago: National Opinion Research Center.

Davis, Natalie Zemon. 1968. "Poor Relief, Humanism, and Heresy: The Case of Lyon." *Studies in Medieval and Renaissance History* 5:217–75.

Deiros, Pablo. 1991. "Protestant Fundamentalism in Latin America." Pp. 142–96 in *Fundamentalisms Observed,* edited by Martin E. Marty and R. Scott Appleby. Chicago: University of Chicago Press.

Diaz-Stevens, Ana Maria, and Anthony M. Stevens-Arroyo. 1998. *Recognizing the Latino Resurgence in U.S. Religion.* Boulder, Colo.: Westview.

DiMaggio, Paul. 1992. "Cultural Boundaries and Structural Change: The Extension of the High-Culture Model to Theatre, Opera, and the Dance, 1900–1940." Pp. 21–57 in *Cultivating Differences: Symbolic Boundaries and the Making of Inequality,* edited by Michele Lamont and Marcel Fournier. Chicago: University of Chicago Press.

Dixon, Lily. 1996. "Tranquil Temples Nettle O.C. Neighbors," *Los Angeles Times* (Orange County Edition), 7 October. Pp. 388–391 in *Asian Religions in America: A Documentary History,* edited by Thomas Tweed and Stephen Prothero. New York: Oxford University Press.

Economic Justice for All: Pastoral Letter on Catholic Social Teaching and the U.S. Economy. 1986. Washington, D.C.: National Conference of Catholic Bishops.

Farnsley, Arthur. 2001. "Can Faith-Based Organizations Compete?" *Nonprofit and Voluntary Sector Quarterly.* 30:99–111.

Finke, Roger, and Rodney Stark. 1992. *The Churching of America, 1776–1990: Winners and Losers in Our Religious Economy.* New Brunswick: Rutgers University Press.

Fowler, Robert, Alan Hertzke, and Laura Olson. 1999. *Religion and Politics in America: Faith and Strategic Choice.* Boulder, Colo.: Westview.

Freeland, Edward Patrick. 1992. "The Dynamics of Nonprofit and Public Organizational Growth in Health Care and Higher Education: A Study of U.S. States, 1910–1980." Ph.D. diss., Princeton University.

Gallup, George J., and D. Michael Lindsay. 1999. *Surveying the Religious Landscape: Trends in U.S. Beliefs.* Harrisburg, Pa.: Morehouse.

Garrard-Burnett, Virginia, and David Stoll. 1993. *Rethinking Protestantism in Latin America.* Philadelphia: Temple University Press.

Giggie, John Michael. 1997. "God's Long Journey: African Americans, Religion, and History in the Mississippi Delta, 1875–1915." Ph.D. diss., Princeton University.

Glenn, Charles L. 2000. *The Ambiguous Embrace: Government and Faith-Based Schools and Social Agencies.* Princeton: Princeton University Press.

Glock, Charles Y., and Rodney Stark. 1965. *Religion and Society in Tension.* Chicago: Rand McNally.

Gorski, Philip S. 2000. "Historicizing the Secularization Debate: Church, State, and Society in Late Medieval and Early Modern Europe (Ca. 1300 to 1700)." *American Sociological Review* 65:138–57.

Greeley, Andrew. 1997. "The Other Civic America: Religion and Volunteering." *American Prospect* 32:111–22.

Hadaway, C. Kirk, Penny Long Marler, and Mark Chaves. 1993. "What the Polls Don't Show: A Closer Look at U.S. Church Attendance." *American Sociological Review* 58:741–52.

———. 1998. "Overreporting Church Attendance in America: Evidence That Demands the Same Verdict." *American Sociological Review* 63:122–30.

Hall, David, ed. 1997. *Lived Religion in America: Toward a History of Practice.* Princeton: Princeton University Press.

Hall, Peter Dobkin. 1990. "The History of Religious Philanthropy in America." Pp. 38–62 in *Faith and Philanthropy in America,* edited by Robert Wuthnow and Virginia A. Hodgkinson. San Francisco: Jossey-Bass.

———. 1999. "Vital Signs: Organizational Population Trends and Civic Engagement in New Haven, Connecticut, 1850–1998." Pp. 211–48 in *Civic Engagement in American Democracy,* edited by Theda Skocpol and Morris P. Fiorina. Washington, D.C.: Brookings Institution Press; New York: Russell Sage Foundation.

Hamilton, Charles, and Warren Ilchman. 1995. *Cultures of Giving: How Region and Religion Influence Fundraising.* San Francisco: Jossey-Bass.

Hammack, David C., ed. 1998. *Making the Nonprofit Sector in the United States: A Reader.* Bloomington: Indiana University Press.

Hammond, John C. 1978. *The Politics of Benevolence.* New York: Ablex.

Harding, Susan Friend. 2000. *The Book of Jerry Falwell: Fundamentalist Language and Politics.* Princeton: Princeton University Press.

Herberg, Will. 1955. *Protestant-Catholic-Jew: An Essay in American Religious Sociology.* Garden City, N.Y.: Doubleday.

Hertzke, Alan. 1988. *Representing God in Washington: The Role of Religious Lobbies in the American Polity.* Knoxville: University of Tennessee Press.

Higginbotham, Evelyn Brooks. 1993. *Righteous Discontent: The Women's Movement in the Black Baptist Church, 1880–1920.* Cambridge: Harvard University Press.

Hodgkinson, Virginia A., and Murray Weitzman. 1994. *Giving and Volunteering in the United States: Findings from a National Survey.* Washington, D.C.: Independent Sector.

Hofrenning, Daniel. 1995. *In Washington but Not of It.* Philadelphia: Temple University Press.

Hoge, Dean R., et al. 1996. *Money Matters: Personal Giving in American Churches.* Louisville: Westminster John Knox Press.

Hout, Michael, and Andrew Greeley. 1998. "What Church Officials' Reports Don't Show: Another Look at Church Attendance Data." *American Sociological Review* 63:113–19.

Hout, Michael, Andrew Greeley, and Melissa J. Wilde. 2001. "The Demographic Imperative in Religious Change in the United States." *American Journal of Sociology* 107:468–500.

Hunter, James Davison. 1991. *Culture Wars: The Struggle to Define America.* New York: Basic Books.

Hutchison, William R. 1987. *Errand to the World: American Protestant Thought and Foreign Missions.* Chicago: University of Chicago Press.

Iannacone, Laurence R. 1998. "Why Strict Churches Are Strong." In *Sacred Companies: Organizational Aspects of Religion and Religious Aspects of Organizations,* edited by N. J. Demerath, Peter Dobkin Hall, Rhys Williams, and Terry Schmitt. New York: Oxford University Press.

Inglehart, Ronald, and Wayne E. Baker. 2000. "Modernization, Cultural Change, and the Persistence of Traditional Values." *American Sociological Review* 65:19–51.

Internal Revenue Service. 1999a. *Social Security and Other Information for Members of the Clergy and Other Religious Workers.* IRS Publication 517. Washington, D.C.: Government Printing Office.

———. 1999b. *Tax-Exempt Status for Your Organization.* IRS Publication 557. Washington, D.C.: Government Printing Office.

———. 1999c. *Tax on Unrelated Business Income of Exempt Organizations.* IRS Publication 598. Washington, D.C.: Government Printing Office.

James, Estelle. 1993. "Why Do Different Countries Choose a Different Public-Private Mix of Educational Services?" *Journal of Human Resources* 28:571–92.

James, Estelle, and Susan Rose Ackerman. 1986. *The Nonprofit Enterprise in Market Economies.* New York: Harwood Academic.

Jenkins, Philip. 2002. *The Next Christendom: The Coming of Global Christianity.* New York: Oxford University Press.

Johnson, Bryon R., Ralph Brett Tompkins, and Derek Webb. 2002. *Objective Hope: Assessing the Effectiveness of Faith-Based Organizations; A Review of the Literature.* Philadelphia: Center for Research on Religion and Urban Civil Society.

Johnson, Paul. 1978. *A Shopkeeper's Millennium: Society and Revivals in Rochester, New York, 1815–1837.* New York: Hill and Wang.

Juergensmeyer, Mark. 2001. *Terror in the Mind of God: The Global Rise of Religious Violence,* rev. ed. Berkeley: University of California Press.

Jutte, Robert. 1981. "Poor Relief and Social Discipline in Sixteenth-Century Europe." *European Studies Review* 11:25–52.

Kaufman, Jason. 2002. *For the Common Good: American Civic Life and the Golden Age of Fraternity.* New York: Oxford University Press.

Kelley, Dean M. 1986. *Why Conservative Churches Are Growing: A Study in Sociology of Religion.* Macon, Ga.: Mercer University Press.

Kingdon, Robert M. 1971. "Social Welfare in Calvin's Geneva." *American Historical Review* 76:50–69.

Kniss, Fred, and David Todd Campbell. 1997. "The Effect of Religious Orientation on International Relief and Development Organizations." *Journal for the Scientific Study of Religion* 36:93–103.

Kuzma, Abigail Lawlis. 2000. "Faith-Based Providers Partnering with Government: Opportunity and Temptation." *Journal of Church and State* 42: 38–67.

Levine, Daniel H., and David Stoll. 1997. "Bridging the Gap Between Empowerment and Power in Latin America." Pp. 63–103 in *Transnational Religion and Fading States,* edited by Susanne Hoeber Rudolph and James Piscatori. Boulder, Colo.: Westview.

Levitt, Peggy. 1998. "Local-Level Global Religion: The Case of U.S.-Dominican Migration." *Journal for the Scientific Study of Religion* 37:74–89.

Lichterman, Paul. 2003. *Elusive Togetherness: Religious Groups and Civic Engagement in America.* Princeton: Princeton University Press.

Lindenberg, Marc, and J. Patrick Dobel. 1999. "The Challenges of Globalization for Northern International Relief and Development NGOs." *Nonprofit and Voluntary Sector Quarterly* 28:4.

Lipset, Seymour Martin, and Earl Raab. 1970. *The Politics of Unreason: Right-Wing Extremism in America, 1790–1970.* New York: Harper and Row.

Loconte, Joe. 2000. "The Anxious Samaritan: Charitable Choice and the Mission of Catholic Charities." Charitable Choice Tracking Project. Annapolis: Center for Public Justice.

Marsden, George M. 1994. *The Soul of the American Univer-*

sity: From Protestant Establishment to Established Nonbelief. New York: Oxford University Press.

Martin, David. 1976. *A General Theory of Secularization.* New York: Harper and Row.

———. 1990. *Tongues of Fire: The Explosion of Protestantism in Latin America.* Oxford: Blackwell.

Martin, Joel. 1999. *Native American Religion.* New York: Oxford University Press.

Martin, Vernon Jr., and Sandra Miller. 1998. "The Clergy's Unique Tax Issues." *Tax Advisor.* August.

Mauser, Elizabeth. 1993. "Is Organizational Form Important to Consumers and Managers? An Application to the Day-Care Industry." Ph.D. diss., University of Wisconsin at Madison.

———. 1998. "The Importance of Organizational Form: Parent Perceptions Versus Reality in the Day Care Industry." Pp. 124–36 in *Private Action and the Public Good,* edited by Walter Powell and Elizabeth Clemens. New Haven: Yale University Press.

McCarthy, John D., and Jim Castelli. 1996. "Religion-Sponsored Social Service Providers: The Not-So-Independent Sector." Working paper, Aspen Institute, Washington, D.C.

Medding, Peter. 1992. "The 'New Jewish Politics' in the United States: Historical Perspectives." Pp. 105–18 in *The Quest for Utopia: Jewish Political Ideas and Institutions Through the Ages,* edited by Zvi Gitelman. Armonk, N.Y.: Sharpe.

Miller, Jon. 1998. "Missions." Pp. 523–31 in *Encyclopedia of Politics and Religion,* edited by Robert Wuthnow. London: Routledge.

Moen, Matthew. 1992. *The Transformation of the Christian Right.* Tuscaloosa: University of Alabama Press.

Mollat, Michel. 1986. *The Poor in the Middle Ages: An Essay in Social History,* translated by Arthur Goldhammer. New Haven: Yale University Press.

Monroe, Kristen Renwick. 1996. *The Heart of Altruism: Perceptions of a Common Humanity.* Princeton: Princeton University Press.

Monsma, Stephen V. 1996. *When Sacred and Secular Mix: Religious Nonprofit Organizations and Public Money.* Lanham, Md.: Rowman and Littlefield.

Morris, John, and Suzanne Helburn. 2000. "Child Care Center Quality Differences: The Role of Profit Status, Client Preferences, and Trust." *Nonprofit and Voluntary Sector Quarterly* 29:377–99.

Nichols, J. Bruce. 1988. *The Uneasy Alliance: Religion, Refugee Work, and U.S. Foreign Policy.* New York: Oxford University Press.

Niebuhr, H. Richard. 1929. *The Social Sources of Denominationalism.* Cleveland: World.

Nonprofit and Voluntary Sector Quarterly. 1997. Special issue. Vol. 26, supplemental.

Olasky, Marvin. 1992. *The Tragedy of American Compassion.* Washington, D.C.: Regnery.

Owens, Michael Lee. 2000. "Sectarian Institutions in State Welfare Reform: An Analysis of Charitable Choice." Albany: State University of New York, Nelson A. Rockefeller Institute of Government.

Peterson, Roger, Gordon Aeschliman, and R. Wayne Sneed. 2003. *Maximum Impact Short-Term Mission.* Minneapolis: Short-Term Evangelical Missions Press.

Presser, Stanley, and Linda Stinson. 1998. "Data Collection Mode and Social Desirability Bias in Self-Reported Religious Attendance." *American Sociological Review* 63:137–45.

Putnam, Robert E. 2000. *Bowling Alone: The Collapse and Revival of American Community.* New York: Simon and Schuster.

Ramsay, Meredith. 1998. "Redeeming the City: Exploring the Relationship Between Church and Metropolis." *Urban Affairs Review* 33:595–26.

Rogers, Richard Lee. 1996. "A Testimony to the Whole World: Evangelicalism and Millennialism in the Northeastern United States, 1790–1850." Ph.D. diss., Princeton University.

Roof, Wade Clark. 1999. *Spiritual Marketplace: Baby Boomers and the Remaking of American Religion.* Princeton: Princeton University Press.

Saxon-Harold, Susan, et al. 2000. *America's Religious Congregations: Measuring Their Contribution to Society.* Washington, D.C.: Independent Sector.

Scott, Jason. 2002. "The Scope and Scale of Activities Carried Out by Faith-Based Organizations: A Review of the Literature." Albany: Roundtable on Religion and Social Welfare Policy.

Sherman, Amy. 1997. *The Soul of Development: Biblical Christianity and Economic Transformation in Guatemala.* New York: Oxford University Press.

———. 2000. "The Growing Impact of Charitable Choice: A Catalogue of New Collaborations Between Government and Faith-Based Organizations in Nine States." Charitable Choice Tracking Project. Annapolis: Center for Public Justice.

Siewert, John, and Edna Valdez, eds. 1997. *Missions Handbook, 1998–2000: U.S. and Canadian Christian Churches Overseas.* Monrovia, Calif.: Marc.

Sinha, Jill Witmer. 2000. "Cookman United Methodist Church and Transitional Journey: A Case Study in Charitable Choice." Charitable Choice Tracking Project. Annapolis: Center for Public Justice.

Skocpol, Theda. 1999. "How Americans Became Civic." Pp. 27–80 in *Civic Engagement in American Democracy,* edited by Theda Skocpol and Morris P. Fiorina. Washington, D.C.: Brookings Institution Press; New York: Russell Sage Foundation.

Smith, Brian. 1982. "Churches as Development Institutions: The Case of Chile, 1973–1980." Working paper, Program on Non-Profit Organizations, Yale University.

———. 1990. *More Than Altruism: The Politics of Private Foreign Aid.* Princeton: Princeton University Press.

———. 1998. "Nongovernmental Organizations." Pp. 571–74 in *Encyclopedia of Politics and Religion,* edited by Robert Wuthnow. London: Routledge.

Smith, Christian. 1996. *Resisting Reagan: The U.S. Central American Peace Movement.* Chicago: University of Chicago Press.

———, ed. 2003. *The Secular Revolution: Power, Interests,*

and Conflict in the Secularization of American Public Life. Berkeley: University of California Press.

Smith, Tom W. 1998. "A Review of Church Attendance Measures." *American Sociological Review* 32:131–36.

———. 2002. "Religious Diversity in America: The Emergence of Muslims, Buddhists, Hindus, and Others." *Journal for the Scientific Study of Religion* 41(3):577–85.

Stackhouse, Max. 1990. "Religion and the Social Space for Voluntary Institutions." Pp. 22–37 in *Faith and Philanthropy in America: Exploring the Role of Religion in America's Voluntary Sector,* edited by Robert Wuthnow and Virginia A. Hodgkinson. San Francisco: Jossey-Bass.

Stoll, David. 1989. *Is Latin America Turning Protestant?* New York: Oxford University Press.

Swartz, David. 1998. "Secularization, Religion, and Isomorphism: A Study of Large Nonprofit Hospital Trustees." Pp. 323–39 in *Sacred Companies: Organizational Aspects of Religion and Religious Aspects of Organizations,* edited by N. J. Demerath, Peter Dobkin Hall, Terry Schmidt, and Rhys H. Williams. New York: Oxford University Press.

Tocqueville, Alexis de. 1945. *Democracy in America,* 2 vols. New York: Vintage.

U.S. Statistical Abstract. 2004. Washington, D.C.: Government Printing Office.

Verba, Sidney, Kay Lehman Schlozman, and Henry E. Brady. 1995. *Voice and Inequality: Civic Voluntarism in American Politics.* Cambridge: Harvard University Press.

Vesey, Alexander. 1999. "'Entering the Temple': Buddhist Temple Asylum in Early Modern Japan." Princeton: Princeton University.

Warner, Michael. 1995. *Changing Witness: Catholic Bishops and Public Policy, 1917–1994.* Washington, D.C.: Ethics and Public Policy Center.

Warren, Mark R. 2001. *Dry Bones Rattling: Community Building to Revitalize American Democracy.* Princeton: Princeton University Press.

Watson, Justin. 1997. *The Christian Coalition: Dreams of Restoration, Demands for Recognition.* New York: St. Martin's.

Watt, David Harrington. 1991. "United States: Cultural Challenges to the Voluntary Sector." Pp. 243–87 in *Between States and Markets: The Voluntary Sector in Comparative Perspective,* edited by Robert Wuthnow. Princeton: Princeton University Press.

Weber, Max. 1952. *Ancient Judaism.* New York: Free Press.

Weisbrod, Burton. 1988. *The Nonprofit Economy.* Cambridge: Harvard University Press.

———. 1998. "Institutional Form and Organizational Behavior." Pp. 69–84 in *Private Action and the Public Good,* edited by Walter Powell and Elizabeth Clemens. New Haven: Yale University Press.

Weisenfeld, Judith. 1998. *African American Women and Christian Activism: New York's Black YWCA, 1905–1945.* Cambridge: Harvard University Press.

Wilcox, Clyde. 1992. *God's Warriors: The Christian Right in 20th Century America.* Baltimore: Johns Hopkins University Press.

Williams, Peter W. 1997. *Houses of God: Region, Religion and Architecture in the United States.* Urbana: University of Illinois Press.

Williams, Rhys H., ed. 1997. *Cultural Wars in American Politics: Critical Reviews of a Popular Myth.* New York: Aldine de Gruyter.

Wilson, Bryan. 1966. *Religion in Secular Society.* Baltimore: Penguin.

Wilson, John. 2000. "Volunteering." *Annual Review of Sociology* 26: 215–40.

Winston, Diane. 1999. *Red-Hot and Righteous: The Urban Religion of the Salvation Army.* Cambridge: Harvard University Press.

———. 2000. "Soup, Soap, and Salvation: The Impact of Charitable Choice on the Salvation Army." Charitable Choice Tracking Project. Annapolis: Center for Public Justice.

Witte, John Jr. 2000. *Religion and the American Constitutional Experiment: Essential Rights and Liberties.* Boulder, Colo.: Westview.

Wolfe, Alan. 1998. *One Nation After All: What Americans Really Think About God, Country, Family, Racism, Welfare, Immigration, Homosexuality, Work, the Right, the Left, and Each Other.* New York: Viking.

———. ed. 2003. *School Choice: The Moral Debate.* Princeton: Princeton University Press.

Woodberry, Robert D. 1998. "When Surveys Lie and People Tell the Truth: How Surveys Oversample Church Attenders." *American Sociological Review* 63:119–22.

Wuthnow, Joel R. 1999. "The U.S. Sanitary Commission in the Civil War." Princeton: Princeton University.

Wuthnow, Robert. 1988. *The Restructuring of American Religion: Society and Faith Since World War II.* Princeton: Princeton University Press.

———. 1991. *Acts of Compassion: Caring for Others and Helping Ourselves.* Princeton: Princeton University Press.

———. 1994a. *Sharing the Journey: Support Groups and America's New Quest for Community.* New York: Free Press.

———. 1994b. *God and Mammon in America.* New York: Free Press.

———. 1995. *Learning to Care: Elementary Kindness in an Age of Indifference.* New York: Oxford.

———. 1996. "Restructuring of American Religion: Further Evidence." *Sociological Inquiry* 66:303–29.

———. 1997. *The Crisis in the Churches: Spiritual Malaise, Fiscal Woe.* New York: Oxford University Press.

———. 1998. *After Heaven: Spirituality in America Since the 1950s.* Berkeley: University of California Press.

———. 1999. "Mobilizing Civic Engagement: The Changing Impact of Religious Involvement." Pp. 331–65 in *Civic Engagement in American Democracy,* edited by Theda Skocpol and Morris P. Fiorina. Washington, D.C.: Brookings Institution Press; New York: Russell Sage Foundation.

———. 2000a. "How Religious Groups Promote Forgiving: A National Study." *Journal for the Scientific Study of Religion* 39:205–21.

———. 2000b. "Linkages Between Faith-Based Nonprofits and Congregations." Working paper, Aspen Institute, Washington, D.C.

———. 2001. "Reassembling the Civic Church: The Changing Role of Congregations in American Civil Society." Pp. 163–80 in *Meaning and Modernity: Religion, Polity, and Self,* edited by Richard Madsen, William Sullivan, Ann Swidler, Steven Tipton, and Robert Bellah. Berkeley: University of California Press.

———. 2004. *Saving America? Faith-Based Services and the Future of Civil Society.* Princeton: Princeton University Press.

———. 2005. *America and the Challenges of Religious Diversity.* Princeton: Princeton University Press.

Wuthnow, Robert, and John H. Evans, eds. 2002. *The Quiet Voice of God: Faith-Based Activism and Mainline Protestantism.* Berkeley: University of California Press.

Wuthnow, Robert, Conrad Hackett, and Becky Yang Hsu. 2004. "The Effectiveness and Trustworthiness of Faith-Based and Other Service Organizations: A Study of Recipients' Perceptions." *Journal for the Scientific Study of Religion* 42:651–67.

Young, Michael P. 2002. "Confessional Protest: The Religious Birth of U.S. National Social Movements." *American Sociological Review* 67:660–88.

21

Nonprofit Community Organizations in Poor Urban Settings: Bridging Institutional Gaps for Youth

SARAH DESCHENES
MILBREY MCLAUGHLIN
JENNIFER O'DONOGHUE

Young people growing up in poor urban communities confront the same developmental tasks as do other American youth: they must acquire the social skills, attitudes, mental and physical competencies, and values that will carry them forward to successful adulthood (National Research Council and Institute of Medicine 2002). But poor urban youth must accomplish these developmental goals in the context of failed institutions and political, economic, and social isolation. Youth from affluent neighborhoods know more, stay in school longer, get better jobs, and have fewer pregnancies and less trouble with the law than do youth from poor neighborhoods; research makes it clear that these are consequences of wealth, not race (Brooks-Gunn, Duncan, and Aber 1997a, 1997b; Danziger and Lin 2000; Jencks and Mayer 1990; National Research Council 1990). For some young people growing up in poor urban communities, though, neighborhood nonprofit organizations negotiate these institutional gaps and provide access to the tools, attitudes, competencies, and connections essential to healthy development. This chapter examines the role of nonprofits in supporting the positive development of young people who confront the myriad challenges of urban America. We show how nonprofit community organizations enable youth to navigate urban environments defined by the absence of sufficient or effective public services and a dearth of labor market possibilities. First we detail the social and institutional landscape of such communities and the consequences for youth who grow up there. Then we describe the ways in which nonprofit organizations fill institutional gaps for young people. We follow this descriptive account with an analysis of the roles that nonprofits are playing in disadvantaged communities and how and why they come to play these parts.

THE SOCIAL AND ORGANIZATIONAL LANDSCAPE FOR DISADVANTAGED YOUTH

Literature addressing disadvantaged urban youth exists at many levels; the individual, the neighborhood, and the city levels are prominent among them. Many government services for poor youth are delivered at the city or the county level, yet neighborhoods constitute crucial settings in which youth live, learn, and struggle. We focus on the neighborhood or community level because it allows for an intimate view of nonprofits and of a neighborhood's pivotal mediating role in the process by which various external forces—social, economic, political, and more—make their way into local environments.[1]

Neighborhood environments are critical to the individual development of low-income young people, who often are cut off from the larger community (Anderson 1990; Chaskin 1995; Furstenberg et al. 1999; Jargowsky 1997; Simon and Burns 1997; Sorin 1990; Wallis 1996). Although there are numerous ways in which poor urban neighborhoods can comprise detrimental environments for youth, including low employment, crime, drug use, and geographic isolation, neighborhoods can also support youth through social capital, networks, positive group socialization, and participation in neighborhood development (Sampson 1999; Slayton 1986; Wilson 1996; Wolpert 1999). Neighborhood organizations are often the entities facilitating these supports, and they can help mitigate manifestations of disadvantage such as transient lifestyles, problem behaviors among youth, negative school outcomes, and little attention to individual development (Blyth and Leffert 1995; Brooks-Gunn, Duncan, and Aber 1997a, 1997b; Duncan 1994; Elliott et al. 1996; Nettles 1991). In this tradition, we take a neighborhood-focused look at the social and institutional conditions of the nation's poor urban communities. Although the specific experiences of youth growing up in these settings differ across the country, common features characterize the social organization and institutional landscape that young people encounter in such neighborhoods.

Social Conditions in Disadvantaged Settings

Unemployment and high welfare dependency signal and perpetuate poverty in disadvantaged communities (National Research Council and Institute of Medicine 1996). Market shifts that have occurred since the 1970s in the location and nature of jobs available in urban settings exacerbate unemployment, concentrating it in inner cities, where residents are isolated from job networks and opportunities (Barclay-McLaughlin 2000; Jencks and Peterson 1991; Wilson 1996). William Dickens, for example, found that although national unemployment rates remain at about 5 percent, it is not uncommon for unemployment rates in some neighborhoods to exceed 25 percent (Dickens 1999:381). When work disappears in the neighborhood, so do many opportunities for meaningful experience and seeing everyday role models (Wilson 1987, 1996). Many inner-city youth want to believe in the American Dream but do not always see it enacted in their daily lives and have difficulty feeling as if they are a part of it.

Dilapidated, crowded housing, signs of neglect, and urban incivility pervade the landscape—littered streets, empty lots strewn with garbage, graffiti-abused walls, shells of burned-out stores and houses, the homeless. Families living in these settings often differ in many ways from those in advantaged America. Single-parent families are the norm; the number of zero-parent and grandmother-headed families is growing fast, as is the number of children and youth assigned to the state by the foster care system. Rates of teenage childbearing are highest in poor neighborhoods (Jencks and Mayer 1990; Crane 1991). The urban sociologist Elijah Anderson observes that having a baby is one of the only markers of adulthood for young women in poor neighborhoods—a rite of passage (1991).

Inner-city youth often have few caring adults in their lives because of either family dysfunction or institutional failures, and research shows that this lack of adult involvement is especially detrimental to youth growing up in poor communities (National Research Council and Institute of Medicine 2002). For example, a case study of African American high school girls growing up in a high-poverty Chicago neighborhood concluded: "Students cannot hold fast to their dreams without sufficient sponsorship" (O'Connor 2000:132).

Geographic isolation and neighborhood poverty are associated with heightened rates of crime and violence (National Research Council and Institute of Medicine 1996, 2002). Crime becomes an everyday occurrence as drug trafficking replaces legitimate exchange as a source of income (Anderson 1999). In the nation's worst-off communities, violence invades homes, streets, schools, and psyches; the presence of physical and emotional violence is "just the way it is" (McIntyre 2000:75; see also Anderson 1999; Children's Express 1993; Garbarino et al. 1992). Murder rates are more than twice as high in the nation's one hundred largest cities as they are in suburban America, and residents fall victim to violence twice as often as people living in other communities (Fitzpatrick and LaGory 2000:7). Furthermore, violence comes in many forms, from "being ignored to psychological abuse to physical abuse to sexual abuse—it's everywhere" (Children's Express 1993:89).

Institutional Landscape in Disadvantaged Settings

Society's institutions do little to buffer the social and developmental consequences of poverty for urban youth and in fact often exacerbate them. Disadvantaged communities are often marked by a lack of healthy public- and private-sector institutions. The Carnegie Council on Adolescent Development (1992:27) concluded that poor urban youth are "the most likely to attend inadequate schools, the most likely to face physical danger in their daily lives, . . . the most likely to spend large amounts of time without adult supervision and . . . the least likely to have access to the supports that youth development organizations can offer to them during the nonschool hours."

The school system, the main public institution for youth, is expected to educate them and prepare them to be good parents, citizens, and workers. Yet too often schools fail youth who grow up in poor neighborhoods. In more than one-quarter of urban high schools, the dropout rate is 50 percent or higher (Braddock and McPartland 1992). Deteriorating facilities, inadequate materials, and the scarcity of qualified teachers send clear signs to youth of the lack of support for their learning and even of hope for their futures (Anyon 1997; Darling-Hammond 1997; Fine 1991).

The so-called helping institutions also fall short in meeting the needs of poor children and youth and their families (Fitzpatrick and LaGory 2000; National Research Council and Institute of Medicine 1996). Healthcare facilities are frequently forbidding, impersonal bureaucratic mazes; social services such as foster care seem to ignore the developmental needs of children and youth. Inner-city youth and their families endure an "urban health penalty"; they experience the highest concentration of health risks—HIV, drugs, teen pregnancy, lead and other environmental toxins—yet have fewer medical or social resources to combat them than do individuals living in more advantaged settings (Fitzpatrick and LaGory 2000).

Moreover, poor urban youth often experience police not as protectors but as opponents or members of a rival gang (Anderson 1999; McLaughlin, Irby, and Langman 2001). Sociologists observe that violent disputes in inner-city settings often are efforts to achieve justice in a world where the aggrieved cannot rely on the formal justice system to help (Moore 1999:298). For example, participants in one citywide youth development initiative report that heavy police presence in their communities makes them feel *less* safe.

Youth growing up in America's poor urban communities lack access to the same range of recreational and cultural facilities—parks, libraries, and museums—that are available to advantaged youth (Furstenberg et al. 1999). Poor neighborhoods, barren of opportunities for positive leisure activities, locate youth on street corners and send signals of social disregard. In a study of urban youth, one young person quipped that the only public facility open in his neighborhood was the county jail (McLaughlin 2000). Lack of transportation further prevents poor youth from taking advantage of educational and recreational resources (Annie E. Casey Foundation 2000).

Government social service programs run into special problems in poor urban communities because of the high demand for services and the urgency of the need (National Research Council 1993). Ironically, this means that people living in impoverished inner-city neighborhoods often have less access to government services than do residents of nonpoor neighborhoods (National Research Council and Institute of Medicine 2002). Government cutbacks in recent years have compounded access issues. During the past several decades, neighborhood-based services have been stripped away by deep cuts in publicly funded institutions such as schools, recreation centers, healthcare organizations, and libraries, further compromising the ability of government to provide so much as adequate services and supports to poor communities (Danziger and Lin 2000; Furstenberg et al. 1999).

In the face of these institutional shortcomings, youth in disadvantaged neighborhoods are often marginalized politically, denied the opportunity to engage in democratic action that could effect change in the world around them. Growing poverty and inequality preclude access to opportunities for meaningful engagement with the public realm (Schlozman, Verba, and Brady 1999; Skocpol 1999). In fact, levels of political efficacy and poor youths' trust in government have steadily declined over the past several decades (Flanagan and Faison 2001).

The absence of meaningful market opportunities mirrors the inadequacies of public institutions in such communities. One consequence is the difficulty young people have in finding paid employment. Equally important, there are few adults to model steady employment and the habits it requires. African American males in particular are affected by the absence of role models. Growing up in a neighborhood with high welfare dependency reduces these young men's chances of finding well-paid jobs in adulthood (Jencks and Mayer 1990; National Research Council 1993; Sum and Fong 1990). In part, the lack of role models stymies labor market success, but poor youth are also hamstrung by attitudes of hopelessness and beliefs that "the future be dead" (McLaughlin et al. 2001:1). They are disadvantaged by the general absence of social networks or social capital that could introduce them to job opportunities and of schooling adequate to prepare them to take advantage of economic opportunities that might arise (Sampson 1999).

Nonprofits Fill Institutional Gaps for Poor Urban Youth

Nonprofit organizations play an important role in all communities. But for youth growing up in poor urban neighborhoods, nonprofits' role may be even more important. With the flight of the market and the shortfall of government services in many disadvantaged communities, the nonprofit sector not only has taken up the slack in providing resources to support positive development but has often been a proactive agent for change and in many instances functions as the resource of last resort for youth. In many poor communities, nonprofits provide the assets, supports, and safe havens that enable youth to navigate through and around the institutional challenges and potholes of their communities as well as become catalysts for change.

In terms of social service provision in particular, nonprofits are often referred to as "supplements" to government. Indeed, the nonprofit sector is often conceived of as a "social safety net" for disadvantaged communities. These organizations are, however, often working against traditional notions of social service delivery. They are involved in a process of deinstitutionalizing traditional ways of managing disadvantaged communities—such as neglecting residents' input, working from the outside in, and focusing on individualized problem definition and delivery of service—and are working toward establishing more constructive, proactive, and progressive working relationships.

The nonprofits that have stepped in to support disadvantaged youth are extraordinarily diverse, representing different missions, programs, structures, funding sources, financial capacity, and political affiliation. Some are freestanding grassroots organizations that reflect the energy and the passion of a dedicated adult; others are local affiliates of national organizations such as the Boys and Girls Clubs and the YMCA. Still others are faith-based organizations with deep roots in the community; yet others operate in partnership with local, state, or federal agencies. Some are also nonprofit-business partnerships that help youth create and run their own enterprises. National organizations such as the YMCA and the Boys and Girls Clubs are the largest nonprofit providers of youth programs, followed by multiservice organizations that have a focus on youth but often provide other community services as well (National Research Council and Institute of Medicine 2002).

There is little comprehensive information about the number, distribution, and focus of nonprofit organizations' efforts on behalf of youth. Data from the National Center for Charitable Statistics indicate that there were more than 17,000 youth organizations in the United States in 1990. No other national compilations have been conducted, however, and this assessment likely underestimates to a significant degree the number of nonprofit organizations engaged with poor urban youth (Carnegie Council on Adolescent Development 1992; National Research Council and Institute of Medicine 2002). Many grassroots organizations, for example, do not show up in community directories, tax rolls, or the yellow pages of the telephone book, and organizations with budgets of less than $25,000 do not have to file Form 990 with the IRS.

Programs and services offered by these organizations run the gamut from arts, sports, and recreation to leadership development, advocacy, community volunteerism, education, entrepreneurship, and personal development. Some are comprehensive in scope, and some focus on a single activity. Some focus on remediation, and some focus on development of interests and competencies. The East Palo Alto (California) Mural Project engages youth in designing and painting on school walls a series of colorful murals expressing the community's ethnic culture. The Children's Aid Society in New York City sponsors community schools that offer medical services, recreation, and supplemental teen and parent education programs. A group of young people in one of Chicago's most notorious housing projects meets almost daily in a converted firehouse where they can get involved in theater productions, community-service projects, tutoring, or just casual conversation. The Omega Boys Club in San Francisco provides support and resources to gang members, drug dealers, and incarcerated youth, getting them through school and in many cases into college (Marshall and Wheeler 1996). The Point, in the Bronx, aims to channel "the street corner skills of at-risk youth away from the underground economy and towards legitimate artistic, entrepreneurial and educational activities" through enterprise activities and advocacy (Butler and Wharton-Fields 1999:73).

Nonprofit organizations' efforts to fill gaps in services for youth also are diverse in structure and funding arrangements. Some, like the East Palo Alto Mural Project and the Omega Boys Club, are freestanding grassroots efforts. The Point and the Children's Aid Society operate with funding from a variety of public and private sources. The Children's Aid Society, like other community school efforts, represents a partnership between the nonprofit organization and the local board of education (Smith and Thomases 2002).

There has been almost no systematic or rigorous evaluation of the effects of these nonprofits on youth development outcomes (Carnegie Council on Adolescent Development 1992; National Research Council and Institute of Medicine 2002). Nonexperimental evidence and reports by youth workers and others working with community-based organizations, however, point to the positive contribution of nonprofits and their success in addressing the shortfalls in services, supports, and opportunities for youth (McLaughlin 2000; National Research Council and Institute of Medicine 2002). Moreover, growing evidence documents the essential and particular contributions of nonprofits to the lives of low-income youth (National Research Council and Institute of Medicine 2002; Pittman, Yohalem, and Tolman 2003; Pittman and Wright 1991).

A decade's research in 34 diverse disadvantaged communities, for example, shows that community organizations can make a powerful, positive difference in the lives of youth—that such organizations can help youth beat the odds associated with gaps in traditional institutional resources, most particularly schooling (McLaughlin 2000). This research shows that youth from poor communities who were part of community-based organizations generally achieved more in school than did "typical" American youth and held higher expectations for themselves as students and young adults. Those participating in these organizations' programs expressed high levels of self-confidence, civic engagement, and personal efficacy rather than defeatist attitudes and cynical forecasts. Little doubt exists in the minds of youth who participated in this research that the community organizations where they spent their time after school, on weekends, or in the summer months played a critical role in nurturing their development and in mediating the risk factors in their schools and neighborhoods and often in their families and peer groups.

Community development organizations, groups traditionally involved in economic development and housing, are expanding their involvement with youth and with community institutions that work with youth (Cahill 1997). A 1998 national survey of community development organizations, for example, found that all responding organizations reported being involved in youth development (Butler and Wharton-Fields 1999:19ff.). Furthermore, responding organizations indicated that they broadened their agenda to include youth in recognition of their communities' inadequate support for them. Although the majority of the programs have not evaluated their programs formally, they report progress in meeting the following benchmarks:

- improved self-esteem
- improved community involvement
- delayed pregnancy
- high school graduation
- development of goals and work preparation
- ability to formulate and advocate for their ideas. (ibid.:22)

Role of Nonprofits in Poor Urban Communities

Nonprofits operating in low-income communities attend to an array of functions, needs, and circumstances in a variety of ways. The nonprofit sector is in a unique position to be responsive to the neighborhood context. One of the greatest strengths of the nonprofit sector is its connection to place—to the culture and norms of a particular community (Smith and Lipsky 1993). Youth find this in many different ways in the organizations that we discuss. This sense of place also strengthens the voluntary sector's ability to work in disadvantaged neighborhoods; these organizations often provide a strong sense of community in neighborhoods that seem to lack one (Milofsky 1987; McNulty 1996). In poor urban communities, nonprofit organizations provide *safe havens, educational opportunities, employment opportunities, political resources, supports for community development,* and *capacity for change.* Because there is little literature about the role of nonprofits in the lives of urban youth to review (and most of it is fugitive literature), we make inductive arguments using examples from our own research and work with nonprofit community-based organizations to illustrate the way in which such organizations play these roles.

Safe havens. "Safe and off the streets" is a mantra for many community-based organizations for children and youth. The sheer practical value of safety cannot be underestimated in urban America. In many cases nonprofits provide the only alternatives to street corners or empty homes. The thick-walled stone church in a large Midwestern city that houses the literacy program Building Educational Strategies for Teens is such a place—literally a sanctuary in a neighborhood "where even grandmothers aren't safe." In communities that are so devoid of public facilities and so violent that "even the pizza man won't deliver," nonprofits provide secure refuge. Safe places for youth also enable caregivers to seek jobs, go to school, and attend community functions. Indeed, the importance for youth in high-poverty communities of having such safe havens has been underscored in numerous studies of youth organizations (Gambone and Arbreton 1997; McLaughlin, Irby, and Langman 2001; Moore 1999).

Nonprofit community organizations do more than simply provide physical safety within harsh urban corridors. They also can be emotional safe havens, providing a "free space"[2] in which young people can explore identity, self-expression, creativity, and their role in the community. In this sense, these organizations represent places for young people to confront what Fine et al. (2000) refer to as "harsh and humiliating public representations" of race, class, gender, sexuality, and youth. Nonprofits can be places to "critique what is, shelter themselves from what has been, redesign what might be, and/or imagine what could be" (ibid.:133). This type of safety allows youth to craft and assert understandings of themselves, their identities, their interests, and their realities that they may not be able to claim in spaces such as school or the home.

Youth can also be who they want to be in these safe places. At the Community School for Democracy (CSD) in another Midwestern city, an education and action initiative located in a historically poor immigrant community, youth can explore their Hmong American identity although this might not be possible at school or at home, where they are asked to have either a Hmong or an American identity (Lesch and O'Donoghue 1999:261). Similarly, HOME,[3] a youth-adult collaborative in Alameda, California, provides youth with a "teen space" in which they have a place to express themselves and feel heard—something they do not find in the "outside" world.

Educational opportunities. Recent research highlights nonprofits' role in creating strong learning opportunities for youth (National Research Council and Institute of Medicine 2002; Pittman, Yohalem, and Tolman 2003). In these community-based settings, youth can experiment with new skills, take on leadership roles, and learn from caring adults. These organizations tend to be more youth-centered than other institutions in disadvantaged communities, and as such they are more attractive to and hold the interest of youth more effectively. Perhaps most important, nonprofit community organizations give poor urban youth ways to learn mainstream skills that middle-class youth learn at home and that are not taught in most urban public schools; they also show youth the possibility of making it to high school graduation and even reaching college.

The "stuff" of education in youth organizations ranges from homework help and school-like classes to classes in subjects such as theater and dance that youth might not have the opportunity to experience at school to "life skills" such as teamwork and leadership—an "embedded curriculum."[4] At HOME, youth learn real-world skills by having authentic, hands-on learning experiences. They learn professional skills such as making phone calls, networking, using computers, writing letters, and giving presentations. Since opening a charter high school, HOME has worked to integrate academic subjects into the youths' community project–based work; they write papers about biodiversity, for example, while working to create a community garden or learn math by developing a budget for their Youth Media Studios (O'Donoghue et al. 2003). In "learning circles" youth at CSD learn about their own and other cultures, write poetry, and study traditional dance. Youth in the after-school programs at San Francisco's Jamestown Community Center are able to take classes in arts, dance, theater, and other subjects that their schools do not offer, and Jamestown runs these classes in more youth-focused ways than the school might, involving youth in the process of creating curricula in some instances and in making the classes relevant to youth experience in others.

Nonprofit organizations have been involved in creating educational opportunities for neighborhoods on a larger scale as well by negotiating larger contexts for urban families. In San Francisco's Tenderloin District, the Bay Area Women's and Children's Center was instrumental in the founding of the neighborhood's first public school by first surveying neighborhood parents about their needs and then lobbying the city and the school district extensively to make their vision a reality. This is also an example of nonprofits' ability to bring sectors together—in this case, the nonprofit and the public sectors—and bridge institutional gaps while dealing with very specific community concerns (Deschenes 2003).

Employment opportunities. Neighborhood community organizations also represent critical employment opportunities for poor urban youth and their families. As these organizations help youth with mainstream educational experiences, so do they provide youth with mainstream employment skills.

When private-sector employment is scarce, these nonprofits often provide financial security for youth and families struggling to survive. At the Center for Young Women's Development in San Francisco, the employment opportunities provided by the organization have allowed young women to leave behind work in the "street economies" while gaining competence in a variety of areas ranging from office skills to group facilitation and political advocacy.

Nonprofits often represent crucial "pathways to participation" for those living in poor communities (Smith and Lipsky 1993). For many youth, economic need can often preclude meaningful, voluntary engagement in a community organization. Nonprofits that provide paid positions for young people help ease this tension. The Jamestown Community Center, for example, supports the idea that youths' work should be treated as employment in their Youth Power group, in which middle school students receive a stipend for their community organizing and school reform work. This stipend acknowledges that the work they do is more than participation in an after-school program, and it fosters a sense of loyalty to the program. Other nonprofit programs also use stipends or points redeemable for food, clothing, books, CDs, or trips in order to make participation more feasible.

Nonprofit organizations provide a chance for youth to run their own businesses as well, creating market opportunities in neighborhoods often devoid of meaningful employment for youth. At the Sunrise Sidewalk Cleaners, a program of the San Francisco Boys and Girls Club, youth run all aspects of the business: soliciting clients and maintaining relationships, doing the accounting, performing the cleaning itself, and designing the business logo. Although these opportunities are still rare, the ownership of the work experience that Sunrise provides makes this employment much preferable to a fast food or retail job in which youth have little control over their experience.

Political resources. Nonprofit organizations are often catalysts or vehicles for efforts to effect social change or bring about social justice (Boris 1999; Hunter and Staggenborg 1988; Milofsky 1987). They are mobilizers, advocates, and sources of empowerment for youth and other community members. As the initiators or sites of public dialogue about issues of social justice, nonprofits can become means for residents of disadvantaged communities to work for social, economic, and political equality.

In addition, nonprofits also represent important components of civic life by providing spaces for community members to practice the arts of democracy, working with diverse people to address public issues and gaining important skills (public speaking, problem solving, collaboration) in the process. But beyond simply allowing for practice, nonprofits often create the avenues for youth to become powerful and creative actors in their communities. Youth at HOME, for example, get daily practice in public presentations and facilitating meetings within the organization; the real power of this learning comes when they are able to put their newly honed skills into action, as they did at school board hearings, where their efforts led to unanimous support for their charter school proposal. In another compelling example, youth from HOME presented concerns to the staff about the way the organization was operating and developed strategies for change; the adults in the organization praised the youth for their show of ownership and power rather than feeling threatened by this well-thought-out attempt to reform youth's role in HOME.

These political resources for social change help youth see the possibilities that can exist for them outside their challenging environments, while also giving youth the skills to change their circumstances in a more immediate way. If the public and private sectors are not available to them, youth who learn these political skills are more prepared to improve their own communities and lives.

Supports for community development. The community-building functions of nonprofit organizations occur across a variety of dimensions (Smith and Lipsky 1993; Harvey 1996; Kretzmann and McKnight 1996; McNulty 1996). First, these organizations can help knit neighborhoods together by creating local traditions and generating social life (Milofsky 1988). They often serve as a forum for the voices of residents, even becoming manifestations of the community, giving expression to its values (Smith and Lipsky 1993). Nonprofit organizations strengthen community by leveraging new resources—tapping into the talents and energies of youth, who are traditionally excluded by both the state and the market (Boris 1999). In addition, they build such aspects of community as social capital and civic infrastructure, creating collaborations and networks that provide important stability to disadvantaged areas.

After several Community School for Democracy members had experienced difficulties with the Immigration and Naturalization Service (INS), the school organized a meeting with the district director of the INS, hosted by the state attorney general's office, to give community members a chance to voice their concerns about their experiences with the INS and to propose solutions. At the meeting, school members brought up the idea of having nonparticipating observers present at citizenship examination interviews. Since this meeting, the school has continued the relationship with the INS, and currently all school participants taking the exam can be accompanied by an observer. As a result of this working relationship with the INS, youth from the CSD have met with testing supervisors, and the district director has visited the school and attended school events, including the premiere of the citizenship video. Those who attend the school see this relationship as the first step in holding the government accountable to the people and in changing the way the INS operates.

In a different type of community building, organizations in the Tenderloin District of San Francisco have tried to build shared cultural frames to support the work the neighborhood does on youth-related issues (Deschenes 2003).

Despite its diverse ethnic population and variety of cultural influences, the Tenderloin has created a sense of community with regard to youth from which its cultural understandings emerge. Youth are a community-wide concern and form a significant part of the common culture. Housing, for example, is talked about in terms of children and families, and the Boys and Girls Club recognizes and responds to the housing crisis the neighborhood is facing by being located in low-income housing and understanding the living situations of its members. Another important part of this is the framing of youth-related issues as social rather than individual; adults working on these issues are mindful not to blame all youths for the neighborhood's crime and drug problems, and the network of youth service providers gives them an opportunity to create alternative frameworks.

Capacity for change. Nonprofits also provide a forum for helping residents—even the youngest of them—gain the skills necessary to effect change in their neighborhoods. Researchers of community action point to the "persistent role" played by local neighborhood organizations in facilitating collective community action (Hunter and Staggenborg 1988). There are two components of this role: deciding what goals and issues are priorities and then actually networking and building capacity to act on these priorities. Many of the previous examples embody some piece of this process.

As part of its long-term planning, HOME held a series of "identity conversations" with stakeholders—youth participants, adult staff, adult volunteers, parents of participants, and other members of the community. These conversations provided the opportunity for people of diverse interests and backgrounds to share their thoughts about where the organization is and where it should go. These discussions afforded the time and space for people to think intentionally about the relation of the organization to the community, not only in the opportunities it offers for youth but also in its ability to create institutional change in the community as a whole.

Networks serve as important tools for community building in many disadvantaged areas. Youth organizations connect to one another and to other kinds of agencies and services through local networks. In the Tenderloin, these networks, according to participants, have strengthened relationships among agencies and have helped organizations achieve their goals. The Boys and Girls Club has been instrumental in creating an after-school program network and participates in other networks involved in police-youth relationships and services for children and families.

The networks developed by HOME during its Community Build—which brought people from city government, local unions and apprenticeship programs, colleges and universities, community businesses, parent groups, senior citizens' groups, and youth of all ages—have since provided HOME with connections that are useful in achieving its goals. This network allows participants to mobilize political support, as they did in their fight to get their charter school approved, as well as financial and material resources, as they are doing in their work to create a community garden. The network relationships are reciprocal, opening the doors for youth from the organization to move out into the community as well.

Organizations other than those directly involving young people also act to bridge institutional gaps in poor communities. Advocacy organizations, in particular, often play a critical role in bringing political and material assets to poor urban settings by creating capacity for social action. For example, the Texas Industrial Areas Foundation, a faith-based network, leveraged significant new resources for the Fort Worth and San Antonio public schools that serve poor Hispanic families (Shirley 1997; Warren 2001). Similarly, in Oakland, California, the Oakland Community Organizations, a faith-based community action group focused on the needs of youth and families living in the city's high-poverty Flatlands neighborhoods, organized parents' successful demand for new, small, autonomous schools (Cross City Campaign for Urban School Reform 2002; Wood 2002). Community-based advocacy groups such as these construct relational bridges between diverse professional, economic, cultural, and social groups in order to forge the political will necessary to direct new and different resources to poor residents. Following the politics of collective action, local advocacy organizations can give "grassroots citizenship" to politically weak residents and link them to local and state political systems (Warren 2001).

THE FUNCTIONS OF NONPROFITS: HOW THEY PLAY THESE ROLES

By influencing the social ecology of disadvantaged neighborhoods, nonprofits can affect the personal agency of youth and their families. Examining the roles nonprofits play in poor communities is the first step in gaining a deeper understanding of the importance of these organizations for youth. How do nonprofits fill these roles in poor communities? What is it about the functioning of these organizations that permits them to play these parts? We identify three general attributes that enable nonprofits to address the institutional gaps apparent in low-income communities: their *connection to place,* their *mediating between the community and larger institutions,* and their *responsiveness within intersectoral relationships.* The analysis in this section considers the functioning of nonprofits in the *ideal.* Not all organizations are able to play these roles effectively for youth in disadvantaged neighborhoods. Lack of funds, staff turnover, ineffective organizational structure, and unfriendly political and social climates are some of the reasons nonprofits can have trouble supporting youth in these communities or sustaining their programs. In the following section we take up the *why* question by examining the enabling and constraining conditions that influence the roles and functioning of nonprofit community organizations.

Connection to Place

Nonprofits, more easily than public agencies or market institutions, can provide known, stable, and situated resources for youth and the community. Grassroots organizations, most especially, are able to use local knowledge and contacts to the benefit of youth and adults, in part because they typically involve as paid and volunteer staff individuals with deep commitments to and roots in the community. These connections also mean that community-based nonprofits are often able to make better investments of human capital than are public or private agencies (Furstenberg et al. 1999; Jencks and Mayer 1990), though staff turnover is an endemic problem. The nonprofits we have discussed—local community-based organizations that support youth and their related groups and associations—take full advantage of the place in which they are located. They use knowledge of local culture, needs, beliefs, and the like to act with and for youth. Being tied to a place involves more than this, though. It also means that the organization is part of the fabric of an area—part of the lives of residents, the activities of the community, and the institutional structure of a neighborhood. Not all nonprofits can achieve this level of connectedness; often organizations are in a neighborhood but not of the neighborhood, as can be the case when a local affiliate of a national organization does not take local needs into account when designing programs for youth.

For example, nonprofits in San Francisco's Tenderloin District have used local culture to try to improve the image of their youth. Activists and organizers in the Tenderloin often lament the fact that neighborhood youth are seen as enemies and have actively worked to make youth part of the process of change in the community by soliciting their opinions, working with the police to strengthen relationships, and making youth issues visible. Youth workers in the Tenderloin also know well those they work with, their families, their friends, and the places where they spend time and can use these connections to be more effective in their efforts to improve opportunities for them. Youth working at HOME have led discussions and conducted surveys with community residents to ensure that their efforts both tap into local resources and reflect local values and interests. The curriculum of the charter school created by HOME, for example, is strongly tied to the local community. This connection to place has given them a strong base of support and contributed to their success. Furthermore, a number of youth organizations, such as the Tenderloin Unit of the San Francisco Boys and Girls Club, are located in low-income housing developments, providing automatic ties to families and home life on which these organizations can draw.

In contrast to the multitude of government programs that focus on individual deficits and community problems, area-based organizations, because of their connection to a place, can also build on residents' strengths and assets. These nonprofits know what residents and organizations in an area can do or have access to, and the sector as a whole is able to harness this local power. For example, when the Community School for Democracy was working to support the Hmong Veterans Bill, which would waive the English-language requirement for Hmong veterans and their spouses, they built on the extended-family culture of the local Hmong community. When public events came up, clan leaders were contacted in order to spread the word most quickly and mobilize the greatest number of people in the shortest period of time. For instance, in less than two days they mobilized more than three hundred people to attend a meeting with congressional representatives. Similarly, rather than relying solely on external support, HOME built on its ties to the local community to mobilize volunteer and material resources, first to build a skate park and then to undertake its Community Build.

Nonprofit organizations and networks are able to develop situated responses to individuals, in contrast to the state's routine application of rules and regulatory structures. They can often do so in a proactive way, not needing to cut through red tape or wait for the bureaucratic decisionmaking process to play out. This is because people in these organizations know the residents they are working with and because nonprofits have a flexibility and responsiveness that government structures do not typically have.

Mediating Between the Community and Larger Institutions

In addition to drawing on their connection to place, nonprofit organizations often function as links between individuals or the community and larger contexts. They serve as "mediating structures" or "brokering institutions" (Berger and Neuhaus 1977).[5] Although the boundaries between sectors often blur, the nonprofit sector plays an important role in connecting citizens to cities, funders, bureaucracies, or national policy makers (Deschenes 2003; Smith and Lipsky 1993; Warren 2001; Wuthnow 1998). Community-based nonprofits can strengthen families' and youths' capacities to manage the external world by connecting them to mainstream organizations and assisting them in navigating government bureaucracies. When such nonprofits serve as centers for health and social services, for example, they often also connect youth to an understanding network of caregivers. Connections such as these enable youth and their families to build the social capital needed to counter the isolation of their setting. On the other hand, some organizations choose not to connect to other contexts because they don't want to be involved with the government on principle or fear cooptation; connections and mediation might not be necessary if an organization is focused on creating safe places or helping youth learn mainstream socialization, but they become essential if an organization is dealing with health, education, or employment.

This mediating role is multidirectional, linking community members with the state and the market, providing a doorway into the community for the state, offering an opening into the community for market systems, and bringing together the local social capital necessary to engage political systems. With this kind of resource, communities are able to compensate to an extent for the absence of assistance from the state or the market. Implicit in these conceptualizations of mediating structures, though, is a focus on local structures, needs, and opportunities.

Examples from practice demonstrate how nonprofits can act as mediators. When youth and adults at the CSD became concerned with the process of naturalization, the school served as a means for them to connect with the Immigration and Naturalization Service. The Center for Young Women's Development in San Francisco connects young women from the "street economy" with educational, job training, and employment opportunities otherwise inaccessible to them. At HOME, youth have been linked with state and market systems. Because of their ongoing relationship with city government, one HOME youth explained, he was able to "just call up the mayor" to work out some issues related to the creation of a skate park. This organization also connects young people to internships with area businesses.

These nonprofits are creating opportunities for relationships between community members and broader government and market institutions that otherwise would not exist. Moreover, nonprofits can represent relatively stable places that can facilitate more fluid individual participation than can government agencies, though funding, staff turnover, and a lack of strong connections to other contexts can threaten this stability. Although individuals may be unable to commit constant and extended efforts to community action or involvement, nonprofit community organizations can provide the continuity that allows them to participate when they can. The CSD, for example, has created a permeable space that community members can access as they are able. This stability comes from the ongoing commitment of the school to create an open and democratic space for youth and their families.

Organizational Responsiveness Within Intersectoral Relationships

Traditional models have tended to view the private, public, and nonprofit sectors as relatively independent of one another (with the exception of government regulation). More recent theorists have pointed to problems with this view, positing a more interrelated model of sector relationships; Wuthnow (1991), Weisbrod (1997), and Salamon (1993, 1995, 1996) all point to the degree of overlap or the blurring of distinctions among these sectors. Although the sectors might provide the same or similar functions, they often approach them in different ways (Wuthnow 1991). There are, in addition, a growing number of types of alliances and partnerships among the sectors, including nonprofits that have for-profit arms and nonprofit-business partnerships that connect businesspeople and youth in order to start youth-run companies, not to mention the vast devolution of government services to nonprofit organizations.

The nonprofit sector, though, is often in a unique position to address the needs and interests of youth in disadvantaged communities, particularly with the flexibility and responsiveness of community organizations. Many nonprofits, not restricted by bureaucratic regulation or the need to turn a profit, have greater flexibility than the state or the market to respond to context and fill the institutional gaps left by those sectors. The growing overlap between the sectors often makes this flexibility a real challenge for nonprofits. Yet in the ideal, the flexibility afforded nonprofits allows them to create safe, educational, and empowering spaces that connect youth and their communities to the state and market sectors.

They are able to create these spaces not because of their separation from these sectors but rather because of their interrelatedness with them. For instance, state legislation and local school district funding have allowed HOME to create a charter high school that offers new flexibility in the education of the area's young people. Using its connection with public institutions, this nonprofit organization is able to expand its work and provide needed opportunities for youth, opportunities that might not exist if the relationship were dissolved. Similarly, through their connections with the juvenile justice system, the Center for Young Women's Development and the Omega Boys Club initiate contact with young people prior to their release from the California Youth Authority in order to construct a smooth transition to a supportive environment, legitimate employment, or training opportunities. The Bay Area Women's and Children's Center was able to create a school that is able to respond to community needs at the same time the organization is connected by this endeavor to the school district, a bureaucratic institution not usually known for flexibility.

FACTORS AFFECTING NONPROFITS' ROLES FOR YOUTH IN POOR COMMUNITIES

We have described some of the roles that nonprofit organizations working in disadvantaged communities can play for youth. Not all nonprofits can or do play all of these roles or function in these ways, however. The nonprofit sector generally is characterized by heterogeneity, and this is especially true of community-based organizations located in disadvantaged neighborhoods (Milofsky 1987, 1988; National Research Council and Institute of Medicine 2002). Few organizations working in such areas are able to play *all* of these roles, and some organizations, by design or default, may not be able play any of them. Various contextual, institutional, and organizational conditions enable or constrain what these nonprofits can do for and with youth.

Funding

Funding is one of the greatest influences in the lives of nonprofit organizations in all communities (Hunter and Staggenborg 1988; Milofsky 1987; Smith and Lipsky 1993). The level, nature, and source of funding can determine the types and quality of activities nonprofits can pursue, their stability, and their reach. Funding agencies, whether nonprofit, private, or public, impose requirements that strongly influence the work of community organizations. Funders may have timelines or priorities that do not necessarily match local needs, and the pressure to secure funding often forces nonprofits to change their work. Recent legislation supporting after-school tutoring, for example, led more than one community youth development initiative to move away from youth leadership and community involvement programs (for which funding was more difficult to procure) toward more traditional academic tutoring programs (which brought more stable funding). This highlights a tension for nonprofits that focus, for example, on capacity building, a central need in poor communities trying to survive in a funding environment that emphasizes service delivery. The small grassroots organizations that are so effective in their work with poor youth are much more vulnerable to funding vagaries tied to "flavor of the month" priorities established by government or philanthropies because they are less able or willing to change their focus or mission in response to changed funding goals.

The constant effort required to secure funds can also limit the roles nonprofits are able to play in communities. There are few funding guarantees in the nonprofit world. As a result, organizations are forced to dedicate the time and effort of knowledgeable staff to "chasing money" and meeting reporting requirements. Organizations benefit from having expert staff with knowledge and experience in grantwriting and fundraising to obtain necessary resources. Furthermore, the lack of stable funding can result in piecemeal programming, making it challenging for nonprofits to provide consistent programs for young people or their communities. Moreover, youth organizations report that they are constantly required to innovate because they are often funded not for their ongoing (and often successful) programs but for developing new ones. These constraints bedevil nonprofits in all settings, but they are particularly disruptive or paralyzing in poor communities where expertise, discretionary capital, and human resources are in short supply.

Likewise, evaluation and accountability requirements attached to funding complicate the lives of nonprofits everywhere but can be especially problematic for nonprofits in poor communities. For one thing, these nonprofits typically lack the infrastructure or expertise to comply with these reporting requirements. But just as important, nonprofits in poor communities often are held to "benchmarks" or "outcomes" that are not requested in more advantaged settings. As one community organizer likes to point out, "Ballet programs in rich communities aren't asked to show gains in student achievement to justify their existence and get their funding renewed" (Richard Murphy, pers. comm.). Yet nonprofit efforts in poor communities typically are held to narrow indicators of success that can interfere with the type of youth development programming many are trying to implement.

Social, Organizational, and Institutional Contexts

External factors relevant to the work of nonprofits may include community ecology, federal, state, or local policy, the configuration of intersectoral relationships within a given setting, the politicization of the community, or the presence of other community organizations. State charter school legislation, for example, opened the door for youth from HOME to create a high school that would better address the needs of young people in their community. Connections with public institutions may bring opportunity to nonprofits; some organizations, such as the Jamestown Community Center, have developed relationships with schools that allow them to locate their programs on school grounds. The extent to which these types of relationships represent reciprocal collaborations is often questionable, however, and some organizations have found that working closely with public institutions is actually more constraining than enabling. Similarly, some communities may be able to take advantage of greater levels of market integration than can others.

The external factors influencing organizations serving youth and their communities operate in complex ways. In one community a complete lack of access to public health or social services may push nonprofits to devote more of their time to providing basic services, while in another community a nonprofit might become a means for community residents to mobilize for increased access to public services. In many urban communities, the lack or expense of transportation limits the access of participants in nonprofits to resources such as parks, museums, and libraries that could enrich and extend programs.

Nonprofits in poor areas have been negatively affected by efforts to devolve responsibilities previously held by government to local communities. Ironically, the success of nonprofit community organizations is often used to justify the deinstitutionalization of essential resources and services. The nonprofit sector is held up as the alternative to "big government"—as nonprofits take on an ever larger share of the task of social service provision, government can relieve itself of this duty (Watt 1991). The 1980s and 1990s witnessed dramatic cutbacks in government spending on social services, especially for programs targeting the poor. Government devolution in this era was largely predicated on the belief that the voluntary sector would be able to provide needed services and opportunities, especially in disadvantaged communities.

Unfortunately, devolution simply serves to deinstitutionalize needed resources, forcing nonprofits to try to do more with less. This redeployment of government resources is especially difficult in neighborhoods already coping with depleted institutional resources. The assumption that nonprofits can pick up the slack left by government or by lack of market investment in poor communities is based on a misunderstanding of the relations among the sectors. The government is, in fact, by far the largest funder of nonprofit organizations. What happens in effect is that government cutbacks have increased "the *need* for nonprofit services while reducing the resources the sector has available to meet this need" (Salamon 1996:4; emphasis in original). The ironic result has been a shift in the composition of the voluntary sector toward provision of services for those able to pay, doubly disadvantaging residents of poor communities.

Deinstitutionalization of government resources has also led to the commercialization of the nonprofit sector and has further handicapped poor communities. As government funding has been cut (by 10 percent in 1996 alone) and private funding has remained stable, nonprofit organizations have increasingly turned to the market for revenue. This growing commercialization not only undermines the "fundamental justification for the special social and economic role played by nonprofit organizations" (Weisbrod 1997:548) but also constrains the ability of nonprofits to effectively play their roles in disadvantaged neighborhoods. In addition, by allocating resources at the local level through block grants and the like, devolution encourages localized solutions to problems with broader causes, resulting in "Band-aid" responses and further serving to isolate disadvantaged communities.

Devolution of public resources brings the relations between nonprofits working in poor communities and their external environments into stark relief. It demonstrates the way in which policy changes can disrupt intersectoral relationships, and in particular the flexibility of nonprofits within such relationships, thereby constraining the ability of community organizations to do much-needed work for youth in low-income neighborhoods. It also highlights the idea that effective nonprofits, those that are able to play needed roles in disadvantaged communities, will be those that have the internal resources to negotiate successfully their external environments.

Internal Organizational Factors

A variety of internal factors, such as mission, age, size, and location, will influence an organization's ability to play some or all of the roles outlined above. Deficiencies can almost always be traced to issues of capacity, and nonprofits operating in poor communities are chronically low on human capital and infrastructure. Nonprofits in such communities have an especially hard time attracting and retaining qualified staff—because of low pay and because of the perceived danger of working in the setting. This results in high staff turnover and staff members who often lack the skills or background necessary to maintain program quality. Nonprofits without stable staff or familiar adults on site are unable to provide the safe haven youth seek since the necessary trust and relationships cannot be established.[6] Nonprofits without the staff capacity needed to apply for grants, comply with state or foundation guidelines, or otherwise participate in mainstream funding opportunities effectively are cut out of the funding action.

Furthermore, the level of staff resources within an organization can determine its ability to buffer itself from an external environment that is often turbulent. Staff knowledge and expertise are frequently crucial, not only in providing high-quality programming for young people but also in building a healthy relationship with the external environment and managing the funding domain. The importance of having expert staff can, however, come into tension with the more democratic and community-building aims of many nonprofits.[7] These more professional staff members may be more effective in navigating the external environment, but the professionalization of nonprofits often brings with it exclusivity; many have become centralized and are controlled by an elite corps of professionals rather than a broad spectrum of community participants.[8] Effective organizations have to balance this tension between expert staff and a commitment to building capacity within the local community.

Nonprofits vary in their institutional structure, and these differences shape their roles and functions, especially in poor neighborhoods. They may be local affiliates of national organizations, such as the Boys and Girls Club, local organizations with strong institutional affiliations or collaborations with other organizations, such as the Jamestown Community Center, or autonomous community-based organizations that are more independent of other organizations or institutions, such as HOME or the Center for Young Women's Development. Each of these institutional forms brings with it opportunities and challenges for organizations' work in disadvantaged communities.

Being a local affiliate of a national organization brings stable funding and access to a broader research and knowledge base, scarce resources in poor neighborhoods. These types of organizations are often able to function as effective mediating institutions, connecting local residents to resources at the national level. This structural feature brings needed stability to nonprofits. Local affiliates, however, face the challenge of balancing national goals with the needs and interests of local contexts. One of the ways in which nonprofits are able to work effectively is by having a strong sense of place. For local affiliates, this means figuring out how to be responsive to and build from the strengths of local communities and youth within the context of a broader national mission. But transforming materials and procedures often is a struggle for poor communities where the assumptions or goals of the national program may not be applicable. For example, one local affiliate of a national organization had to discontinue the leadership program provided by the national office because its young people had neither the assumed material supplies (alarm clocks, telephones, bus fare) nor the family support required.

For nonprofit organizations that have strong ties with other institutions, the picture is also mixed. Institutional collaboration can bring resources that would otherwise be difficult to access. The Community School for Democracy, for example, is a collaboration that involves community groups and a large public university. Each of these partners brings resources to the organization that help it to reach its goals—the community groups bring legitimacy and local knowledge from their long history of working in the neighborhood, and the university brings financial and knowledge resources, student volunteers, and legitimacy of a different kind. Collaboration also facilitates nonprofits' mediating functions by connecting youth and other community residents to resources and institutions. These types of collaborations are not easy, however. The organizations involved often have competing missions or priorities. Moreover, the extent to which they actually share resources is often unclear. Several youth organizations report that their relationships with schools seem quite one-sided, with the schools viewing the community organization as a resource but not offering much in return.

For autonomous community-based organizations, the opportunities and the challenges stem from their independence from other organizations. These organizations potentially have the freedom and flexibility to be responsive to local needs. They are able to use the connection to place to its greatest advantage because they do not have to worry (at least not in the same way) about outside institutions or national offices. For example, churches and faith-based institutions have long played a key role in the lives of poor communities, enabled by their local knowledge and symbolic function as focal points of the community. Although these organizations tend to be more inclusive, they run the risk of becoming insular and overly parochial. Skocpol (1999), for example, points out that highly localized organizations may not fully understand the interconnections between problems and solutions. Efforts focused on change solely at the local level may ignore the roles of broader forces and of policy-making bodies at the state or national level. Many ethnic organizations, for example, while creating a supportive space for their members, are often opposed to mainstream integration or relationships with the state, the market, or other nonprofits. The result can be increased marginalization of members. In order to function as effective mediating institutions, then, autonomous organizations must work to develop and maintain external networks. This can be a time- and labor-intensive process, making it challenging for them to reach their goals.

In short, factors in the external, internal, and funding environments both enable and constrain nonprofits' work with youth in poor communities. These forces are complex and interrelated, presenting tensions and trade-offs that community organizations must work through and with in order to help youth effectively navigate the institutional gaps they face when growing up in disadvantaged neighborhoods. Ironically, the factors that enhance nonprofits' effectiveness for youth in such areas—deep community ties and autonomy—also are features that may check their effective functioning in larger social, organizational, and institutional contexts.

ACKNOWLEDGMENTS

We thank W. Richard Scott and Anne R. Newman for their helpful comments and feedback on this chapter.

NOTES

1. When the literature we review is located at the city level, we have focused for the most part on what this research says about the neighborhood level or what its implications for neighborhoods are. We have chosen to use the word "settings" to encompass these various levels.

2. Evans and Boyte (1986:17) define free spaces as "settings between private lives and large-scale institutions where ordinary citizens can act with dignity, independence, and vision." These free spaces are seen as having three common characteristics: they are grounded in the community, provide autonomy for participants, and are public in character. Evans and Boyte maintain that such spaces are critical sources of democratic renewal and change, allowing participants to gain "schooling in citizenship" and develop a vision of the common good through the discovery of their own dignity, self-respect, voice, and power.

3. HOME is not an acronym.

4. McLaughlin (2000) develops the concept of the "embedded curriculum" to refer to the ways in which a diverse range of competencies is built into programming. For example, a dance program may incorporate journal writing and sharing of reflection with the group or a basketball coach may facilitate discussions of sportsmanship; the explicit curriculum of the program (dance or basketball) is supplemented by an embedded curriculum (reading and writing or personal responsibility and teamwork).

5. The original conception of mediating structures (Berger and Neuhaus 1977) has taken on a decidedly conservative characteristic thanks to those that have interpreted it as antigovernmental. The voluntary sector can be seen, however, as a mediator without absolving government from its responsibilities to disadvantaged communities.

6. Ironically, volunteers from outside the community intending to fill those gaps sometimes only make matters worse when the "kindness of strangers" brings insensitivity to the values, life circumstances, or cultural perspectives that youth bring with them. Furthermore, volunteers traveling to poor urban neighborhoods are not typically accessible to youth because of either the hours volunteered or the distance from their neighborhood.

7. Skocpol (1999), for example, points out that although voluntary associations are often thought of as the "backbone" of democratic life, the past thirty years have seen a change in the nature of the nation's voluntary associations away from participatory membership organizations and toward professionalized advocacy groups.

8. Some argue that this broader community representation has rarely existed. DiMaggio and Anheier (1990), for example, point out that prior to the dominance of professionals, nonprofit organizations were frequently controlled by the urban elites who made up most nonprofit boards, not by the members of local communities.

REFERENCES

Anderson, Elijah. (1990). *Streetwise: Race, Class, and Change in an Urban Community.* Chicago: University of Chicago Press.

———. (1991). "Neighborhood Effects on Teenage Pregnancy." In *The Urban Underclass,* ed. Christopher Jencks and Paul E. Peterson. Washington, D.C.: Brookings Institution. Pp. 375–98.

———. (1999). *Code of the Street: Decency, Violence and the Moral Life of the Inner City.* New York: Norton.

Annie E. Casey Foundation. (2000). *Kids Count Data Book.* Baltimore, Md.: Annie E. Casey Foundation.

Anyon, Jean. (1997). *Ghetto Schooling: A Political Economy of Urban Educational Reform.* New York: Teachers College Press.

Barclay-McLaughlin, Gina. (2000). "Communal Isolation: Narrowing the Pathways to Goal Attainment and Work." In *Coping with Poverty: The Social Contexts of Neighborhood, Work and Family in the African-American Community,* ed. Sheldon Danziger and Ann Chih Lin. Ann Arbor: University of Michigan Press. Pp. 52–76.

Berger, Peter L., and Richard Neuhaus. (1977). *To Empower People: The Role of Mediating Structures in Public Policy.* Washington, D.C.: American Enterprise Institute for Public Policy Research.

Blyth, D. A., and N. Leffert. (1995). "Communities as Context for Adolescent Development: An Empirical Analysis." *Journal of Adolescent Research* 10(1): 64–87.

Boris, Elizabeth T. (1999). "The Nonprofit Sector in the 1990s." In *Philanthropy and the Nonprofit Sector in a Changing America,* ed. Charles T. Clotfelter and Thomas Ehrlich. Bloomington: Indiana University Press.

Braddock, Jomills Henry, and James M. McPartland. (1992). "Education of At-Risk Youth: Recent Trends, Current Status, and Future Needs." Commissioned paper for the Panel on High-Risk Youth, Commission on Behavioral and Social Sciences and Education, National Research Council, Washington, D.C.

Brooks-Gunn, Jeanne, Greg J. Duncan, and J. Lawrence Aber (eds.). (1997a). *Neighborhood Poverty.* Vol. 1, *Contexts and Consequences for Children.* New York: Russell Sage Foundation.

———. (1997b). *Neighborhood Poverty.* Vol. 2, *Policy Implications in Studying Poverty.* New York: Russell Sage Foundation.

Butler, Benjamin, and Donna Wharton-Fields. (1999). "Report on a National Survey of Community Development Organizations." In *Finding Common Agendas: How Young People Are Being Engaged in Community Change Efforts.* Community and Youth Development Series, Paper no. 4. Sponsored by the Ford Foundation and the International Youth Foundation–U.S.

Cahill, Michele. (1997). *Youth Development and Community Development: Promises and Challenges of Convergence.* Community and Youth Development Series, Paper no. 2. Sponsored by the Ford Foundation and the International Youth Foundation–U.S.

Carnegie Council on Adolescent Development. (1992). *A Matter of Time: Risk and Opportunity in the Nonschool Hours.* Report of the Task Force on Youth Development and Community Programs. New York: Carnegie Corporation of New York.

Chaskin, Robert. (1995). *Defining Neighborhood: History, Theory and Practice.* Chicago: Chapin Hall Center for Children.

Children's Express. (1993). *Voices from the Future: Our Children Tell Us About Violence in America.* Edited by Susan Goodwillie. New York: Crown.

Crane, Jonathan. (1991). "Effects of Neighborhoods on Dropping Out of School and Teenage Childbearing." In *The Urban Underclass,* ed. Christopher Jencks and Paul E. Peterson. Washington, D.C: Brookings Institution. Pp. 299–320.

Cross City Campaign for Urban School Reform. (2002). *Strong Neighborhoods, Strong Schools: Case Study: Oakland Community Organizations.* Chicago: Cross City Campaign for Urban School Reform.

Danziger, Sheldon, and Ann Chih Lin (eds.). (2000). *Coping with Poverty: The Social Contexts of Neighborhood, Work and Family in the African-American Community.* Ann Arbor: University of Michigan Press.

Darling-Hammond, Linda. (1997). *The Right to Learn: A Blueprint for Creating Schools That Work.* San Francisco: Jossey-Bass.

Deschenes, Sarah. (2003). Lessons from the Middle: Neighborhood Reform for Youth in San Francisco. Ph.D. diss., Stanford University.

Dickens, William T. (1999). "Rebuilding Urban Labor Markets: What Community Development Can Accomplish." In *Urban Problems and Community Development,* ed. Ronald F. Ferguson and William T. Dickens. Washington, D.C: Brookings Institution Press. Pp. 381–436.

DiMaggio, Paul J., and Helmut K. Anheier. (1990). "The Sociology of Nonprofit Organizations and Sectors." *Annual Review of Sociology* 16:137–59.

Duncan, Greg J. (1994). "Families and Neighbors as Sources of Disadvantage in the Schooling Decisions of Black and White Adolescents." *American Journal of Education* 103(1): 20–53.

Elliott, D. S., W. J. Wilson, D. Huisinga, R. J. Sampson, A. Elliott, and B. Rankin. (1996). "The Effects of Neighborhood Disadvantage on Adolescent Development." *Journal of Research on Crime and Delinquency* 33(4): 389–426.

Evans, Sara M., and Harry C. Boyte. (1986). *Free Spaces: The Sources of Democratic Change in America.* New York: Harper & Row.

Fine, Michelle. (1991). *Framing Dropouts: Notes on the Politics of an Urban Public High School.* Albany: State University of New York Press.

Fine, Michelle, Lois Weis, Craig Centrie, and Rosemarie Roberts (2000). "Educating Beyond the Borders of Schooling." *Anthropology and Education Quarterly* 31(2): 131–51.

Fitzpatrick, Kevin, and Mark LaGory. (2000). *Unhealthy Places: The Ecology of Risk in the Urban Landscape.* New York: Routledge.

Flanagan, Constance A., and Nakesha Faison. (2001). "Youth Civic Development: Implications of Research for Social Policy and Programs." *Social Policy Report: Giving Child and Youth Development Knowledge Away* 15(1): 1–15.

Furstenberg, Frank F., Thomas D. Cook, Jacquelynne Eccles, Glen H. Elder Jr., and Arnold Sameroff. (1999). *Managing to Make It: Urban Families and Adolescent Success.* Chicago: University of Chicago Press.

Gambone, Michelle, and Amy J. Arbreton. (1997). *Safe Havens: The Contributions of Youth Organizations to Healthy Adolescent Development.* Philadelphia: Public/Private Ventures.

Garbarino, James, Nancy Dubrow, Kathleen Kostelny, and Carol Pardo. (1992). *Children in Danger: Coping with the Consequences of Community Violence.* San Francisco: Jossey-Bass.

Harvey III, F. Barton. (1996). "Community Rebuilding: A Quiet Revolution." *National Civic Review* 85(4): 17–22.

Hunter, Albert, and Suzanne Staggenborg. (1988). "Local Communities and Organized Action." In *Community Organizations: Studies in Resource Mobilization and Exchange,* ed. Carl Milofsky. New York: Oxford University Press.

Jargowsky, Paul. (1997). *Poverty and Place: Ghettos, Barrios, and the American City.* New York: Russell Sage Foundation.

Jencks, Christopher, and Susan E. Mayer. (1990). "The Social Consequences of Growing Up in a Poor Neighborhood." In *Inner-City Poverty in the United States,* ed. Laurence E. Lynn Jr. and Michael G. H. McGeary. Washington, D.C.: National Academy Press. Pp. 187–222.

Jencks, Christopher, and Paul E. Peterson (eds.). (1991). *The Urban Underclass.* Washington, D.C.: Brookings Institution.

Kretzmann, John, and John P. McKnight (1996). "Assets-Based Community Development." *National Civic Review* 85(4): 23–29.

Lesch, D'Ann Urbaniak, and Jennifer L. O'Donoghue (eds.). (1999). *We Are the Freedom People: Sharing Our Stories, Creating a Vibrant America.* Minneapolis: Center for Democracy and Citizenship.

Marshall, Joseph, Jr., and Lonnie Wheeler. (1996). *Street Soldier: One Man's Struggle to Save a Generation—One Life at a Time.* New York: Delta.

McIntyre, Alice. (2000). *Inner-City Kids: Adolescents Confront Life and Violence in an Urban Community.* New York: New York University Press.

McLaughlin, Milbrey W. (2000). *Community Counts: How Youth Organizations Matter for Youth Development.* Washington, D.C.: Public Education Network.

McLaughlin, Milbrey W., Merita A. Irby, and Juliet Langman. (2001). *Urban Sanctuaries: Neighborhood Organizations in the Lives and Futures of Inner-City Youth.* San Francisco: Jossey-Bass.

McNulty, Robert. (1996). "Nonprofits, Culture, and Community Renewal." *National Civic Review* 85(4): 30–33.

Milofsky, Carl. (1987). "Neighborhood-Based Organizations: A Market Analogy." In *The Nonprofit Sector: A Research Handbook,* 1st ed., ed. Walter W. Powell. New Haven: Yale University Press. Pp. 277–95.

———. (1988). *Community Organizations: Studies in Resource Mobilization and Exchange.* New York: Oxford University Press.

Moore, Mark H. (1999). "Security and Community Development." In *Urban Problems and Community Development,* ed. Ronald F. Ferguson and William T. Dickens. Washington, D.C.: Brookings Institution Press. Pp. 293–338.

National Research Council. (1990). *Inner-City Poverty in the United States,* ed. Laurence E. Lynn Jr. and Michael G. H. McGeary. Washington, D.C.: National Academy Press.

———. (1993). *Losing Generations: Adolescents in High-Risk Settings.* Panel on High-Risk Youth. Commission on Behavioral and Social Sciences in Education. Washington, D.C.: National Academy Press.

National Research Council and Institute of Medicine. (1996). *Youth Development and Neighborhood Influences: Challenges and Opportunities,* Committee on Youth Development, ed. Rosemary Chalk and Debora H. Phillips. Washington, D.C.: National Academy Press.

———. (2002). *Community Programs to Promote Youth Development,* Committee on Community-Level Programs for Youth, ed. Jacquelynne Eccles and Jennifer A. Gootman. Washington, D.C.: National Academy Press.

Nettles, S. M. (1991). "Community Contributions to School Outcomes of African-American Students." *Education and Urban Society* 24 (1): 132–47.

O'Connor, Carla. (2000). "Dreamkeeping in the Inner City: Diminishing the Divide Between Aspirations and Expectations." In *Coping with Poverty: The Social Contexts of Neighborhood, Work and Family in the African-American Community,* ed. Sheldon Danziger and Ann Chih Lin. Ann Arbor: University of Michigan Press. Pp. 105–40.

O'Donoghue, Jennifer L., Sally Brown, William Dyckman, Heather Hughes, Juliet Stein, and Julie Lieberman Neale. (2003). HOME BASE Evaluation Report: Findings, Implications, and Questions, Pilot Year, 2001–02 [Alameda, Calif.].

Pittman, Karen, and Marlene Wright. (1991). "Bridging the Gap: A Rationale for Enhancing the Role of Community Organizations in Promoting Youth Development." Commissioned paper for the Center on Youth Development and Policy Research, Washington, D.C.

Pittman, Karen, Nicole Yohalem, and Joel Tolman (issue eds.). (2003). *When, Where, What and How Youth Learn: New Directions for Youth Development* (Spring).

Salamon, Lester M. (1993). "The Marketization of Welfare: Changing Nonprofit and For-Profit Roles in the American Welfare State." *Social Service Review* 67(1): 16–39.

———. (1995). *Partners in Public Service: Government-Nonprofit Relations in the Modern Welfare State.* Baltimore: Johns Hopkins University Press.

———. (1996). "The Crisis of the Nonprofit Sector and the Challenge of Renewal." *National Civic Review* 85(4): 3–16.

Sampson, Robert J. (1999). "What 'Community' Supplies." In *Urban Problems and Community Development,* ed. Ronald F. Ferguson and William T. Dickens. Washington, D.C.: Brookings Institution Press. Pp. 241–92.

Schlozman, Kay Lehman, Sidney Verba, and Henry E. Brady. (1999). "Civic Participation and the Equality Problem." In *Civic Engagement in American Democracy,* ed. Theda Skocpol and Morris P. Fiorina. Washington, D.C.: Brookings Institution Press.

Shirley, Dennis. (1997). *Community Organizing for Urban School Reform.* Austin: University of Texas Press.

Simon, David, and Edward Burns. (1997). *The Corner: A Year in the Life of an Inner-City Neighborhood.* New York: Broadway Books.

Skocpol, Theda. (1999). "Advocates Without Members: The Recent Transformation of American Civic Life." In *Civic Engagement in American Democracy,* ed. Theda Skocpol and Morris P. Fiorina. Washington, D.C.: Brookings Institution Press.

Slayton, Robert A. (1986). *Back of the Yards: The Making of a Local Democracy.* Chicago: University of Chicago Press.

Smith, Stephanie M., and Jean G. Thomases. (2002). *CBO Schools: Profiles in Transformational Education.* Washington, D.C.: Academy for Educational Development Center for Youth Development & Policy Research.

Smith, Steven Rathgeb, and Michael Lipsky. (1993). *Nonprofits for Hire: The Welfare State in the Age of Contracting.* Cambridge: Harvard University Press.

Sorin, Gerald. (1990). *The Nurturing Neighborhood: The Brownsville Boys Club and Jewish Community, 1940–1990.* New York: New York University Press.

Sum, Andrew, and Neal Fong. (1990). "The Changing Fortunes of Young Black Men in America." *Black Scholar* 12 (January–February): 47–55.

Wallis, Allan D. (1996). "Toward a Paradigm of Community-Making." *National Civic Review* 85(4): 34–47.

Warren, Mark R. (2001). *Dry Bones Rattling: Community Building to Revitalize Democracy.* Princeton: Princeton University Press.

Watt, David Harrington. (1991). "United States: Cultural Challenges to the Voluntary Sector." In *Between States and Markets: The Voluntary Sector in Comparative Perspective,* ed. Robert Wuthnow. Princeton: Princeton University Press.

Weisbrod, Burton A. (1997). "The Future of the Nonprofit Sector: Its Entwining with Private Enterprise and Government." *Journal of Policy Analysis and Management* 16(4): 541–55.

Wilson, William Julius. (1987). *The Truly Disadvantaged: The Inner City, the Underclass, and Public Policy.* Chicago: University of Chicago Press.

———. (1996). *When Work Disappears: The World of the New Urban Poor.* New York: Vintage.

Wolpert, Julian. (1999). "Communities, Networks, and the Future of Philanthropy." In *Philanthropy and the Nonprofit Sector in a Changing America,* ed. Charles T. Clotfelter and Thomas Ehrlich. Bloomington: Indiana University Press.

Wood, Richard L. (2002). *Faith in Action: Religion, Race and Democratic Organizing in America.* Chicago: University of Chicago Press.

Wuthnow, Robert. (1991). *Between States and Markets: The Voluntary Sector in Comparative Perspective.* Princeton: Princeton University Press.

———. (1998). *Loose Connections: Joining Together in America's Fragmented Communities.* Cambridge: Harvard University Press.

V

WHO PARTICIPATES IN THE NONPROFIT SECTOR AND WHY?

22

Nonprofit Membership Associations

MARY TSCHIRHART

Membership associations are a significant component of the nonprofit sector. Mutual benefit organizations, incorporated to serve their members' interests, compose 33 percent of the nonprofit organizations registered in the United States in 2004 (NCCS statistics 2005). If we include registered congregations, the percentage goes up to 60 percent of the registered nonprofit organizations. Though the prevalence of nonprofit membership associations varies across countries (Baer, Curtis, and Grabb 2001), they play important and varied roles in many societies. If we want to understand the nonprofit sector, we cannot ignore the aspects of the sector related to nonprofit organization membership.

Knoke (1986:2) defined a membership association as "a formally organized named group, most of whose members—whether persons or organizations—are not financially recompensed for their participation." Under this broad definition, associations include "labor unions, religious churches and sects, social movement organizations, political parties, professional societies, business and trade associations, fraternal and sororal associations, recreational clubs, civic service associations, philanthropies, social welfare councils, communes, cooperatives, and neighborhood organizations." Knowledge related to this highly diverse group of organizations is available in many academic disciplines. This chapter draws from the academic literature to examine ways to differentiate among nonprofit membership associations, discuss claims about the value of associations, link the claims to key research questions, and present theories and findings related to the research questions. In doing so, the chapter suggests opportunities for further scholarship on collective activity through nonprofit membership associations.

What distinguishes this chapter from others in this book is its focus on membership in a nonprofit. Many of the ideas in the other chapters apply to nonprofit membership associations. For example, nonprofit membership associations operate in a legal context, make decisions about commercial activity and the pursuit of charitable gifts, have governance bodies, and respond to government pressures. They do these activities and more in a context where individual members have rights and responsibilities. This chapter draws together scholars' thoughts on member entry, retention, and participation in nonprofit membership associations; as well as nonprofit membership association governance, structure, and trends.

To provide a context for the discussion to follow, table 22.1 provides statistics using 2004 data from the National Center for Charitable Statistics showing a breakdown by common types of nonprofit membership associations and the percentage change in each classification from 1996. The table indicates an overall decline of about 8 percent in the number of U.S. registered nonprofits under the main classifications for nonprofit membership associations, not including religious congregations and the miscellaneous category.

Few scholars attempt to generalize their conclusions to all types of nonprofit membership associations and there is no one typology of associations in use. Therefore, the classifications used in table 22.1 do not map onto all the published studies of associations. In addition, the table ignores the variety of classifications for membership associations in use outside the United States. Therefore, it seems helpful to present other categorization schemes for nonprofit membership associations. The next sections discuss categorizing associations by purpose and member type. Each of these categorization devices has variants, further illustrating the range of organizations under the nonprofit membership association label. After a discussion of categorization schemes, the chapter turns to a review of claims about the value of non-

TABLE 22.1. REGISTERED NONPROFIT MEMBERSHIP ASSOCIATIONS IN UNITED STATES IN 2004

	Number of registered nonprofits	Percent of all nonprofits	Percent change from 1996
All nonprofit organizations	1,397,263	100	28.8
Membership associations (breakdown below)	460,829	33.0	−8.2
Membership associations including congregations	846,703	60.6	—
Civic leagues, social welfare organizations, and local associations of employees	119,515	8.6	−6.3
Fraternal beneficiary societies and associations	87,833	6.3	−14.4
Business leagues, chambers of commerce, real estate boards, etc.	71,470	5.1	4.2
Labor, agricultural, and horticultural organizations	58,362	4.2	−5.5
Social and recreational clubs	56,494	4.0	−1.0
Post or organization of war veterans	35,097	2.5	14.8
Registered congregations	385,874	27.6	NA
All other mutual benefit nonprofit organizations	32,058	2.3	NA

Source: Adapted from National Center for Charitable Statistics, Urban Institute, http://nccsdataweb.urban.org/, downloaded March 11, 2005.

profit membership associations and then to research questions.

WAYS TO CATEGORIZE ASSOCIATIONS

Differentiating Associations by Their Purpose

Scholars often differentiate nonprofit membership associations according to their purpose (e.g., Bennett 1999; Stolle and Rochon 1998). One method is to look at whom an association exists to serve. Another way is to sort associations by whether they seek to support existing societal structures, undermine the structures, or provide alternative structures. A third way to use purpose to sort associations is to look at territorial base or scope. Each of the methods provides a lens to use in judging the generalizability of existing research findings and claims.

Nonprofit membership associations vary in the balance of their service to individual members, the member collectivity, and an external community made up primarily of nonmembers but which may also include members. Associations existing to satisfy the private interests of members have been called "expressive," while associations existing to achieve a condition or change in some segment of society—that is, that have goals focused outside of the organizations or the members—have been called "social influence" or "instrumental" associations (Gordon and Babchuk 1959). Hybrids have both expressive and instrumental goals.

It is not clear where associations whose main purpose is to regulate members in order to benefit the membership as a whole fit on an expressive–instrumental linear dimension. Consider a community association, a commune, and an accrediting society. With these types of associations, the main purpose often is to support the interests of the collectivity, even if that means subjugating individual needs to the needs of the whole. The community association may set rules prohibiting members from engaging in behaviors that change the look of the neighborhood. The commune may eject members who do not conform to group values and norms. An accrediting society may require members to uphold standards for professional practice, keeping the protection and promotion of the profession as the top priority.

Another challenge with sorting associations by service targets is where to put associations whose purpose is under debate, or where research reveals that the actual benefits provided are inconsistent with the stated mission and rhetoric of the association. For example, in deciding how the Jaycees should treat women, the State of Minnesota had to decide whether the Jaycees are a social club as presented by the male members or a public accommodation subject to regulation under the state's human rights law.

Another illustration of this dilemma is cooperatives. Producer and consumer cooperatives act to give members economic rewards unavailable to non-members. They may also provide substantial benefits to non-members as in the case of sugar cane cooperatives in Maharashtra, India, that started and operated temples, schools, colleges, and hospitals (Banerjee, Mookherjee, Munshi, and Ray 2001). Though these public service endeavors may have earned social approval and rents for controlling members of the cooperative, they also helped the general public. This directs us to see at least some cooperatives as benefiting members and non-members. To add to the complexity in how to categorize cooperatives, some argue that the foundation of cooperatives is religious or political, not merely economic, and their main purpose is to forward an ideology and create an alternative system in which members can operate (Mooney, Roahrig, and Gray 1996). For example, cooperatives operating under a directive to displace capitalism would primarily be serving the membership collectivity, not the individual interests of members.

In addition to categorizing nonprofit membership associations by targeted beneficiaries, we can sort nonprofit membership associations relative to societal norms and values. Associations differ according to whether they operate in a manner that supports or at least is compatible with status quo conditions, act to undermine the conditions, or attempt to isolate members from the conditions and provide alternative ones. Most nonprofit membership associations have no social change agenda and are comfortable operating within established societal parameters. Recreational clubs and fraternal societies fit into this category. Membership organizations that advocate for social change, such as the NAACP, are examples of associations that act to undermine the status quo. Examples of associations that offer alternative lifestyles for members include the Amish, Oneidas, and some communes and cooperatives.

We can also distinguish between associations operating overtly within legal guidelines and those that are covert with questionable or no legal status. Covert associations are likely to be working to undermine the status quo or to provide members with an alternative lifestyle. In the United States, and many other countries, the freedom to associate is limited, constraining the overt organization of membership groups, particularly those that are instrumental rather than expressive. For example, some U.S. states outlaw paramilitary associations such as citizen militias, considering them to be instrumental groups harmful to the public interest (Rosenblum 1998). By differentiating associations according to their relationship to established societal systems, we can begin to see the variety of roles they play in society.

A third aspect of purpose useful in differentiating associations relates to their localness—that is, their mission scope and size of budget and membership. By focusing on scope and size, we are less likely to forget grassroots associations whose activities are local with modest membership numbers and budgets and therefore exist under most researchers' radar screens. As D. Smith (2000) cautions, many nonprofit membership associations are missing from databases of registered nonprofit organizations.

Membership size objectives vary among associations. Witches' covens and some musical groups limit their size in order to carry out activities that are not possible with larger groups. Some religious congregations divide or create spinoffs whenever membership reaches a certain number so that they do not exceed a desired community size. Other associations may see large membership size as having a positive influence on their effectiveness, as in the case of social movement organizations wishing to sway votes through a large support base or professional service organizations dependent on member dues that see cost efficiencies with greater membership numbers. The use and level of member dues to support operations may influence membership size objectives. For some associations, size may not appear to be particularly worthy of special attention or procedures.

The broadness of the interests and backgrounds of members may affect the broadness of the mission. To limit the service base, selection rules for membership candidates may be applied. To join some nonprofit membership associations you must be elected, as in the American Association of Advertising Agencies, Elks, and some Greek fraternities and sororities. You might be restricted from joining an association even if you share the same interests as the members of an association and can contribute to the pursuit of its collective interests. This is the case for the Boy Scouts, which retained the right to refuse membership to avowed homosexuals, or Daughters of the American Revolution, which requires specified ancestry as a condition of membership. To continue as a member of some associations you may be required to prove your worth through continuing education, service to the association, or some other practice. Member selection mechanisms can help to create a homogeneous base of members who can agree on and work to maintain the boundaries of the service base (Tschirhart and Johnson 1998).

Some nonprofit membership associations serve as branches or affiliates of a head organization with a larger geographic service domain. Whether or not a nonprofit membership association is part of a larger structure has some bearing on its service base. Local and central units face environments that are likely to differ in their complexity, stability, and demands, and consequently the needs for flexibility and independence, as well as the benefits of affiliation (Grossman and Rangan 2001). A focus on service base helps us to compare the dynamics of federated associations with associations that are not embedded in larger associational systems.

Differentiating Associations by Their Membership

One characteristic that all associations must share is members holding rights to influence the affairs of the organization. Two aspects of member type receive special attention in this chapter: degree of member coercion and member identity. Each aspect provides a different way of mapping the world of nonprofit membership associations and can help in judging the generalizability of theories and findings.

Not all members of nonprofit associations join without coercion. History offers numerous examples of the coercive ability of associations. In the United States, every trade union prior to the Civil War was in favor of excluding nonmembers from employment (Stockton 1911). Up until a Supreme Court decision in 1978, occupational associations in the United States could demand that in order for an individual to be certified or licensed in a field, the individual had to be a member of the association *(National Society of Professional Engineers v. United States).* Not so direct, but still representing coercion, some individuals and organizations join associations to protect themselves from the setting of codes or regulations by the associations that could harm their lifestyle or business, or to prevent requirements for expensive investments needed for compliance with association standards. Some members of associations are born into them and raised by other members. They do not voluntarily choose to join and may be too dependent to leave until they reach adolescence or adulthood.

Most of the literature on associations examines associations with voluntary membership. In only a few cases do authors acknowledge that their ideas do not apply to coerced members. By explicitly considering whether claims about associations apply to those with coerced membership, we can begin to see how generic our theories about associations can be.

In addition to differentiating nonprofit membership associations by degree of member coercion, we can look at what interests members represent in the organization. Individuals may be participating in an association through their own independent, personal initiative or as the designated agent of another entity. As a member, they may be representing their own interests or those of others such as a family, firm, club, or state. Associations vary in the type of entities allowed membership status and how members' stakes and claims are communicated and managed. As support for the importance of considering member type, in King and Walker's (1992) study of non-coerced members of associations, individuals representing institutions are more likely than individuals representing themselves to value the pursuit of collective (purposive) goods. In addition to effects on the attractiveness to members of association activities and outcomes, the interests represented by members may influence other phenomena of interest to scholars, such as member retention and participation, and association governance and structure.

The roles given members as well as the interests represented by them vary among nonprofit membership associations. Members may or may not staff an association and there are various methods in use for designating officers. In some nonprofit membership associations, members fill specified seats and are expected to serve as representatives of their race, gender, occupation, or other identity group. Much of the literature on associations focuses on relatively large organizations with paid staff. The dynamics of these associations may be quite different from the less-structured hobby club, garden society, and other grassroots organizations that run entirely through the efforts of unpaid members (D. Smith 2000).

THE VALUE OF ASSOCIATIONS

Nonprofit membership associations are used to pursue a variety of ends and may have side benefits and effects. The main claims about association benefits are that they support democratic processes, give voice to special interests, regulate behaviors, develop and diffuse innovations, and provide psychological and social rewards. However, they can also support inequities, repress voices, and constrain freedoms. Associations may contribute to civic engagement and build social capital (Putnam 2000). In this section of the chapter, I review claims about the outcomes of nonprofit membership associations and link them to four research questions. The research topics are member entry into associations, member retention and participation in associations, dynamics of governance and structure in associations, and association growth and decline.

Much of the recent and enduring attention on the outcomes of associations has focused on their pluralistic function. They may help to check government by developing skills and tastes for democratic processes; in other words, by serving as a school of democratic virtue and self-government (Schlesinger 1944) and by stabilizing a democratic system by training participants to work well together (Tocqueville 1956). However, there are arguments that this skill building is selective, helping some association members more than others. For, example, Schwadel (2002) found that within Christian church congregations, the higher-income members receive more practice and training in civic skills than the lower-income members. Torpe (2003) also questioned whether associations are serving as schools of democracy. Looking at nonprofit membership associations in Denmark, he found that membership was associated with political involvement and competence but not with the civic virtue of political tolerance. A focus on the pluralistic function coupled with concerns about social equity and the democratic process raises questions about who is joining, participating in, and governing associations.

Other benefits associated with nonprofit membership associations are their service in giving voice to special interests that otherwise might not be heard, and as intermediaries between government and individual members. There are many accounts of the contributions of nonprofit membership associations to the passage of legislation. For illustrative works see Skocpol, Abend-Wein, Howard, and Lehman (1993) on the importance of women's associations in the enactment of mothers' pensions, and Kahane (1999) for the influence of the National Rifle Association on voting on the Brady Bill. Understanding who are the individuals and other entities involved in associations and how and why they are involved helps us look for possible inequities in the democratic process.

Nonprofit membership associations may play a role as instruments of government, useful in promotion of policies and political agendas (Bennett 1998; Monti 1993; Streeck and Schmitter 1985) and raising issues of social equity and political democracy (Amin and Thrift 1995). In their role as conveyers of interests to government, there are debates about whether association membership should be compulsory or voluntary. For an illustrative work see Marin (1983), who argues that the best system to maintain legitimacy and credibility is to have duplication of compulsory representative associations with voluntary associations that cover the same interest domains.

The extent to which nonprofit membership associations appear to be able to represent members' interests to governments and influence policy varies from setting to setting depending on both external and internal factors. For illustrative studies of representation of business interests through associations, see Baroudi (2000) for Lebanon, McBeath (1998) for Taiwan, Feldman and Nocken (1975) for Germany, and for Ontario, Canada, see Bradford (1988). In a cross-country comparison, Coleman and Grant (1988) explore how business associations' roles in the policy-making process are influenced by association structure. They suggest that the more centralized, concentrated, and representative the organization of business interests, the greater will be the association's voice in policy-making and its role in implementing policies.

Nonprofit membership associations are an alternative to markets, hierarchies, vertical integration, and states, but their effectiveness as regulators of their members is subject to a variety of challenges. Some scholars argue that associations regulating professions require the support of the state to be effective (e.g., Brockman 1998). Schneiberg (1999) discusses the following as problems to solve for collective self-regulation through trade associations: internal problems of bad faith and external problems of predation, legitimation, and institutional authorization. For example, the Norwegian Employers Associations were relatively successful in attracting members but less successful in coordinating wage-setting among members (Bowman 1998). In an analysis of ethical codes of conduct developed by professional business-related associations, Tucker, Stathakopolous, and Patti (1999) found that few association leaders strongly believe that their members adhere to the code, that the code has improved ethical conduct of members, and that the code is strictly enforced. This raises issues of how nonprofit membership associations can best be structured and governed to meet association objectives related to member regulation.

Membership in professional associations can have significant economic implications (Lawrence 2004). Associations can be influential in legitimizing and controlling professions, safeguarding specialized knowledge, and dictating who can practice the profession. In doing so, they can protect the incomes and social status of their members. Lawrence (2004) explores how members' interaction rituals can structure the boundaries of professional fields and differentially affect the power of members. Subfields of professions can be marginalized, while members of other subfields are privileged.

Nonprofit membership associations may serve important functions in the development and diffusion of innovations (Newell and Swan 1995; Swan, Newell, and Robertson 1999). Professional associations can bring diverse individuals together to brainstorm and share ideas. They can define best practices and set standards and benchmarks. Certain technologies can be promoted among members, encouraging their adoption over alternatives. Associations can be instrumental in the development of technologies and might even require their adoption by members. They may also force all members to accept innovations and comply with rules and regulations set by the most powerful members. Theories about membership dynamics and how decisions are made and enforced in associations can inform models of innovation and policy diffusion.

The value of nonprofit membership associations is frequently tied to psychological and social benefits to members. Benefits of association membership that are commonly claimed include satisfaction of psychological needs for fellowship, safety, and security; promotion of social mobility; prestige-enhancement; legitimation; advancement of political and economic interests; satisfaction of religious impulses; self-improvement; assistance with problem-solving; and development of group consciousness. Voluntary association membership has been negatively related to psychological distress (Rietschlin 1998).

Through nonprofit membership associations, members may affirm their beliefs and values, and develop positive self-identifications. Stanfield (1993) suggests that the aggrandizing function of associations is particularly important for African Americans in the United States, who turn to civic associations, fraternal orders, and churches partially in response to a rejecting dominant society. The associations give them an opportunity for advancement in power, rank, and honor. Some scholars studying women's associations note the self-esteem, organization skills development, and consciousness-building aspects of association membership, though how much women's associations contributed to the feminist movement and building of social capital is debated (Boylan 1984; Clemens 1999; Skocpol and Fiorina 1999).

Nonprofit membership associations can also serve as a lifeline for scared, otherwise isolated youth. This helps to explain the success of white supremacist organizations in targeting lonely, disconnected young adults. By channeling aggressive tendencies, these organizations may constrain potentially more dangerous and harmful inclinations of their members (Ezekial 1995; Rosenblum 1998).

Scholars following Hirschman (1982) posit that simply striving for a good, even if not obtained, can be a benefit to association members. In some cases, the participative process itself, rather than the achievement of any tangible or collective goods, is the greatest value of membership (Rosenblum 1998). The greatest benefit to members may not be the membership incentives and services offered in exchange for dues or other contributions but the identification with a group and pursuit of a cause greater than oneself.

In affirming members and promoting their interests, nonprofit membership associations have the potential to demean and disadvantage others. Through associations, members can consolidate their positions, maintain the status quo, and actively discriminate against others (Charles 1993; Clawson 1989; Massey and Denton 1993; Walzer 1991; D. Warren 1975). As Rosenblum (1998) explains in describing the moral importance of associations, "Associations mirror, reinforce, and actively create social inequalities." For example, blacks, Jews, and Catholics were commonly excluded from membership in established social and professional associations and in turn created their own exclusive organizations (Gamm and Putnam 1999). Kaufman (2002) argues that the growth of fraternal organizations exacerbated religious and ethnic intolerance in the United States. Some early women's auxiliary associations served as simple support structures for the more powerful male associations with which they were affiliated, mirroring the gender divisions in the society (Boylan 1984). Associations built through the network ties of members can be highly homogeneous, creating parallel and independent sets of societies with little in common, as in the case of early women's benevolent associations (Boylan 1984). Preexisting associations can prevent other more inclusive service groups from forming and developing solidarity, as we see in the history of the labor movement. For example, the strong identification of craft workers and their desire to retain a disproportionate amount of resources for skilled workers, encouraged by membership in preexisting craft associations, impeded the development of more broad-based labor unions (Conell and Voss 1990).

Some research suggests that not all members of the same nonprofit membership association receive the same benefits. Associations that have a diverse membership base can end up promoting the interests of their large, more dominant and powerful members, as in the case of trade associations in which big companies enforce their wishes sometimes to the detriment of the smaller firms in the association (Staber 1987). Labor unions have been criticized for disproportionately promoting the interests of subsets of workers; some workers gain while others lose (Freeman and Medoff 1984).

A review of the value of nonprofit membership associations raises a variety of concerns about equity and influence. Nonprofit membership associations operate in political and legal systems that differentially support their activities. This leads to questions about who is joining and staying in associations, how associations are governed, and how members' interests are being identified and addressed. It also leads to concerns about association trends. If claims about outcomes of association membership are valid, individuals and society are affected by the extent to which nonprofit membership associations are thriving or declining. However, it is unclear how we should identify and interpret trends at an aggregated level. Given the diversity of nonprofit membership associations and their effects it may make little sense to generalize about their virtues and harmful effects (M. Warren 2001). Is it even worthwhile to use one umbrella term for nonprofit membership associations that cover such diverse purposes and member types?

RESEARCH QUESTIONS

This section reviews the literature relevant to four research questions. I first turn to research on member entry into associations. The second research area reviewed is member retention and participation. The third research area addressed is governance and coordination. A discussion of research on association trends ends the section.

What Explains Member Entry into Associations?

To have a nonprofit association, you must have members, and according to Knoke's definition, these members cannot be financially recompensed for their participation. If they are not paid to participate, what are their motivations for joining? Why are some associations more successful than others in attracting members? Who is most likely to become a member? These questions are examined to varying extents in the association literature. Most studies addressing entry into nonprofit membership associations use at least one of the following three complementary approaches: cost-benefit, demographic and social-psychological, and environmental explanations.

Cost-benefit approaches. Most cost-benefit explanations are rooted in Mancur Olson's (1965) classic argument that individuals join organized groups to attain selective benefits that exceed the costs of membership. While scholars have rejected many of Olson's early assumptions, such as the idea that individuals have full information (Moe 1980a) and are interested only in economic rewards (Clark and Wilson 1961; Moe 1980a), the contention remains that joining an association is a calculated self-interested decision. Benefits are treated as falling into two broad categories, collective (available to members and nonmembers) and selective (available to members only). Clark and Wilson (1961) classified the types of incentives that attract members as material, solidary, and purposive. Material benefits are private, tangible rewards such as association-produced magazines and discounts on association events and catalog items. Solidary benefits are social in nature, derived from interactions through the association. For example, a member may join an association in order to make friends with like-minded individuals. Purposive benefits are intangible rewards associated with ideological interests tied to association values and goals. An example of a purposive benefit is the passage of legislation pursued by the association. Purposive benefits are collective while material and solidary benefits may be selective or collective.

Related to the question of why join is the question of how many will join. The research in this area seems to focus primarily on interest diversity as the key predictor of density—that is, the number of members in the association compared to the number of potential members. Under a cost-benefit framework, the larger the arena within which collective action occurs, the greater the potential diversity of interests and thus the lower the density of members within any one organization (Olson 1965).

A similar line of thought focuses specifically on associations that are economic clubs in that there is jointness in supply and consumption of goods and services with some exclusion possible (Isaacs and Laband 1999). Individuals vote with their feet; in other words, they enter and exit organizations until they find their optimal bundle of goods (Tiebout 1956). This suggests that the greater the heterogeneity of interests in a population, the greater the number of clubs to serve specific bundles of interests. Density of membership is inversely related to the diversity of interests of potential members. Increasing the size of the market for members reduces the market penetration—that is, the percentage of potential members actually brought into the nonprofit membership association.

Streeck (1991) compared the density of labor unions and business associations. He found that business associations have more narrow service scopes and density than labor unions and explained that it was due to the associations having more fragmented interests than the unions. This greater heterogeneity of capitalists' interests over workers' interests runs counter to what class theory (Offe and Wiesenthal 1980) suggests about the challenges of mobilizing workers and the supposed single-purposeness of capitalists. Empirical research is mixed on the relationship between market size and penetration (Kilbane and Beck 1990) and may be related to type of incentives provided and quantity of services offered by the associations (Bennett 1998).

Demographic and social psychological approaches. For decades, a focus on member characteristics has dominated the writings on nonprofit membership associations (Cress, McPherson, and Rotolo 1997; Knoke 1986). Demographic variables commonly used in studies of membership entry include income, age, gender, marital status, education, occupational status, religion, race, and socioeconomic class. Much of the research linking demographic variables to membership entry is either purely descriptive or makes arguments that are relatively specific to the demographic variable being used and the type of association under study. However, a common assumption, drawn from Blau (1977, 1994), is that people associate with others who are similar in character. Nonprofit membership associations tend to recruit through the network ties of their members, thus creating a relatively homogeneous membership base (Booth and Babchuk 1969; McPherson, Popielarz, and Drobnic 1992a). For example, numerous studies have shown that social networks are good predictors of recruitment into cults, sects, and mainstream churches (Stark and Bainbridge 1985).

Some of the most theory-rich demographic-based studies that are broad in types of associations addressed focus on race/ethnicity and/or minority status as predictors of membership. Ethnic community theory (Olsen 1970) is supported in several studies, including Guterbock and London's (1983) test of four competing models of racial participation. In ethnic community theory, members of an ethnic community develop cohesiveness and consciousness in response to pressures from an outside majority. This leads them to join associations. According to Olsen, blacks participate more in social change efforts than is predicted by social-economic status and other demographic variables due to higher than average levels of efficacy and distrust—that is, greater race consciousness. Assuming that social consciousness is stronger in the black church than in white churches, Secret et al. (1990) unsuccessfully attempted to show that religiosity helps explain association membership by blacks but not whites, but did show that religiosity is connected to membership.

Some common approaches using demographic predictors of membership are compensatory, isolation, and cultural inhibition theories. Compensatory theory contends that individuals in lower-status positions join associations for prestige, ego-enhancement, and achievement restricted or denied them in the larger society. On the other hand, isolation theory contends that individuals in minority groups are less likely than individuals in majority groups to participate in associations because the minorities are not as integrated into society, lack necessary skills, and are unaware of the benefits of association affiliation (Williams, Babchuk, and Johnson 1973). Peleman (2002), among others, uses isolation theory to explain the level of association involvement by women in some cultures. Culture-based or cultural inhibition theories suggest that some cultures promote values that do not encourage or constrain association participation for some subsets of society (e.g., Huber-Sperl 2002). In addition, nonprofit association membership is sometimes explained as an adaptive response to historical circumstances and environmental conditions faced by individuals sharing specific demographic characteristics such as sex and ethnicity (e.g., Walker 1983).

Wandersmith, Florin, Friedmann, and Meier (1987) argue that research employing demographic predictors is limited and that research directly using social-psychological variables is likely to be more fruitful. The more theoretically driven studies using demographic variables usually have underlying assumptions about social-psychological processes. The demographic variables are treated as proxies for values, norms, beliefs, attitudes, and behaviors shared by a set of individuals. They may even serve as a proxy for interest sets, as illustrated by Isaacs and Laband's (1999) use of income, race, and education categories to represent different sets of church-related interests. Some studies examining member entry directly incorporate psychological variables such as interpersonal capabilities; locus of control; self-esteem; sense of efficacy; ideology; perceptions of time and resource constraints; cynicism; and attitudes toward the association's cause, inducements, and collective goods. Expectations about other members and probability of success in achieving social change goals are predictors of membership decisions for instrumental associations (Klandermans 1984). In research on cults, social-psychological variables take center stage. For example, there are numerous studies demonstrating that the experience of transition has a positive relationship to recruitment as do psychosocial difficulties, low self-esteem, high self-doubt, anxiety, and depression (Robinson and Bradley 1998).

External environment approaches. Researchers look to environmental factors as well as psycho-sociological variables to explain entry into nonprofit membership associations. One of the founders within this broad area of research is Truman (1951), who argued that people join associations in response to disturbances in their environments. They are more likely to join an association in response to a threat than to prospects for gain. Truman's hypothesis about the relative importance of threats is widely discounted but still we find numerous studies linking association formation and growth to environmental threats. Hansen (1985) found that political and economic threats helped to explain membership in the American Farm Bureau Federation (State Farm), the League of Women Voters, and the National Association of Home Builders. In large-scale studies covering many types of associations, major crises such as wars and depression are linked to association formation (Gamm and Putnam 1999; Skocpol and Fiorina 1999; Skocpol, Ganz, and Munson 2000). Salamon (1995) argues that the global spread of associations is due to crises and revolutions that result in bottom-up mobilization of ordinary people; encouragement from churches, western private voluntary organizations, and official aid agencies; and pressures from national governments. Ashenfelter and Pencavel (1969) developed an argument involving environmental factors along with member cost-benefit analyses and worker discontent as the determinants of the growth of labor unions.

Some scholars look to the environment for more than threat explanations of member entry and association growth. While formation of nonprofit membership associations may be linked to single issues that mobilized the founders, continuation of the association once the organizing issue is settled relies on the development of a broader portfolio of member concerns. For example, land-use issues prompted the creation of neighborhood associations but not their continuation (Logan and Rabrenovic 1990). Some studies indicate that some types of associations are more likely to be founded and gain members when times are good rather than bad. For example, cooperatives are more likely to emerge and thrive during periods of economic prosperity and when there is support from government and other cooperatives (McLaughlin 1996). Industrialization, immigration, and urbanization are debated as factors explaining the growth and decline of associations in the United States (Walker 1991) though they receive little support as explanatory factors for some other countries (Curtis, Grabb, and Baer 1992). Some scholars link association entry and growth to general societal concerns rather than specific threats. For example, both labor unions (Tannebaum 1951) and service clubs (Charles 1993) have been seen as reactions to alienation and loss of community in increasingly bureaucratic, impersonal societies.

Depending on the type of nonprofit membership association studied, more specific environmental factors have been examined to explain association formation and member entry. To illustrate, for unions, explanations of unionization may bring in industry character, labor force size, and government type (Western 1994). For interest groups, many of which are membership associations, Walker (1991) claims that 80 percent of American interest groups arise from preexisting occupational or professional communities, mobilized either out of the immediate economic or professional interests of the members or through the efforts of social service professionals to protect their vulnerable constituents. The remaining 20 percent of interest groups emerge out of broad social movements to reform society, typically arising out of the educated middle class.

The financial support of outside actors plays a significant role in the creation and growth of some nonprofit membership associations. For example, some labor unions benefited from significant foundation support (Magat 1999), and Danish sports associations are dependent on local government (Klausen 1995). The principal source of income for Students for a Democratic Society was grants from a labor union, the United Auto Workers (Walker 1991). The Farm Bureau movement started when the federal and many state governments decided that no government money would be available to government-employed county agents hired to disseminate information to farmers unless the agents organized an association of farmers (Kile 1948). Growth of social movement organizations is linked to access to large amounts of capital through government subsidization, philanthropic patrons, or sliding-scale fee structures with a few large members subsidizing the remaining membership (Hansen 1985; King and Walker 1991; Logan and Rabrenovic 1990; Walker 1983). Despite the involvement of outside actors in encouraging the establishment and growth of certain types of associations, some research demonstrates that associations implanted from outside have a high failure rate and that indigenous local efforts are more likely to be successful (Monti 1993). In addition, patronage can backfire, as in the case of the National Student Association; it almost died after it became known that it received substantial and sustained financial aid from the Central Intelligence Agency (Meyer 1980; Walker 1983).

In additional to external financial resources, the availability of human resources and technology to reach potential members may encourage growth (McCarthy and Zald 1977). For example, the availability of mailing lists makes it possible for some associations to use direct-mail solicitation to fill the membership ranks with individuals who keep their distance from association affairs (Skocpol 1999). The Internet appears to be facilitating the organization and mobilization of individuals with similar interests (Ray 1999). Increases in the number of working women and female-headed households in the United States reduced the time available for women to participate in associations, spurring declines in membership in the PTA and other associations traditionally dependent on female members (Crawford and Levitt 1999). When more individuals are in life stages associated with stable financial position, free time, or external pressures for affiliation, conditions are more favorable for association growth (Babchuk and Booth 1969; Knoke and Thomson 1977; McAdam 1989).

Barriers to member entry. Nonprofit membership associations are not equally welcoming to potential new members. Established members may fear that new members could divert the mission of the association or require too many resources. A variety of mechanisms can be used to limit entry into an association (front door protections) and to limit new members' ability to influence association decision-making (decision control barriers) (Tschirhart and Johnson 1998). Examples of front door protections include sponsored membership programs in which potential members must be championed by an established member, rigorous and restrictive membership requirements, competition for limited membership openings, and secrecy about the membership process. These devices are most likely to be in place in associations with strong ideologies without evangelical missions, where members must compete among themselves for resources, and where association funds do not need continual renewal through new members' entrance fees.

Comment on research on member entry. The voluntary

decisions of individuals to join nonprofit membership associations appear to be at least partially driven by their interest in satisfying psychological and social needs. They may share these needs with others who have similar demographic and psychographic profiles, helping to explain homogeneity of members within associations. Individuals are likely to be recruited to associations through their social networks, helping to explain membership homogeneity given that social networks tend to be composed of people with similar characteristics. Environmental conditions may make joining an association attractive, as a way either to respond to threats or to take advantage of opportunities. Patterns in membership entry and restrictions can be linked to environmental and internal conditions that change the costs and benefits of participating, the configuration of social networks, basic psychological and social needs, the pool of potential members, and resources that can be devoted to member recruitment and satisfaction.

We know little about the relative importance of these factors across organizations with different service targets, aims, and bases. For example, is self-esteem as useful a predictor of a decision to join a hobby club as it is in explaining decisions to join a cult or gang? Are associations with local service bases more dependent on social networks for members than national associations? Is membership more likely to be restricted the narrower the purpose of the association or the greater the fear of takeover? While there are general predictions that can be made about membership entry for all types of associations, the relative power of specific explanations may be linked to association purpose.

It is unlikely that explanations of member entry hold equally strong across nonprofit membership associations that vary in their degree of coercion and member identities. For example, individuals brought into association membership by their parents are unlikely to search, at least as children, among associations for an optimal bundle of goods. Some cost-benefit theorists explicitly state that their models do not apply to coerced members (e.g., Olson 1965). The social-psychological theories reviewed in this section do a good job explaining member entry for individuals representing themselves in the association but seem less applicable when members are representing a principal such as firm, club, family, state, or some other entity. We know little about how the personal interests of individuals influence how they represent others. As an agent, a decision to join an association is likely to be based on what the membership can do for the principal, not what it can do for them personally. The promise of solidary benefits in attracting members is applicable to nonprofit membership associations whose members are humans with desires for social interaction but not for associations of groups or organizations for which only material and purposive inducements may be relevant.

Why Stay and Participate?

The literature on nonprofit membership associations addresses why members stay and participate in association activities. Theories developed to understand the persistence and participation of association members typically assume that membership is voluntary and that the factors that explain member entry may not be the same ones that explain member retention and active participation. Unlike the literature on member entry, which can relatively easily be sorted into three streams, the literature on retention and participation has less-distinct boundaries.

Studies of how associations experience declines in membership are few in comparison to studies looking at the successful retention of members. One rich case study of strategies under membership decline applies ideas from the business literature to decline in the Jesuit religious order (Ludwig 1993). The order used increased linkages and cooperation to address declines in membership and to some degree was able to protect its core. However, the changes may have had consequences on retained members' willingness to invest in the organization. Another interesting study related to member loss is by Dyke and Starke (1999), who studied the splitting off of new religious congregations from old ones and developed a process model describing how associations may split in response to conflict among members.

Many theorists attribute participation and persistence in nonprofit membership associations to members' commitment. While participation and commitment are often highly correlated, they are independent phenomena and one can occur without the other (Knoke 1988). More committed members will have higher levels of participation and longer persistence, and in a feedback loop, more participation will lead to greater commitment (Knoke and Wood 1981; Zurcher and Snow 1981). Scholars offer a range of predictors and associated explanations of commitment. Proposed ways to gain commitment include offering selective material and solidary incentives (Olson 1965), requiring investments and sacrifices (Kanter 1968, 1972), closing off of alternative options and demands for participation (Zurcher and Snow 1981), and providing opportunities to communicate with leaders and influence organizational decision-making (Knoke 1981; Houghland and Wood 1980). Member commitment is also proposed to be gained by having members in direct contact with other members (McCarthy and Zald 1977), with one method for achieving this being use of local groups as part of a federated structure (Barkan, Cohn, and Whitaker 1993). Perceptions of effectiveness and legitimacy may also enhance member commitment (Barkan, Cohn, and Whitaker 1993). In sum, this literature suggests that characteristics of the organization, the member, and interpersonal interactions of members all influence commitment.

Within the collective action literature, commitment is gained through incentives (Olson 1965). In Olson's (1965) by-product theory and Salisbury's (1969) exchange theory, members join and remain committed for the selective material or solidary incentives they receive. Later theorists found that receipt of collective benefits also encourages commitment (Sabatier 1992; Walker 1991). Moe (1980b) argues that individuals can miscalculate what they will need to contribute to an association in order to obtain desired benefits.

Perceptions of high efficacy in obtaining desired benefits influence individuals to join and stay in nonprofit membership associations. Rothenberg (1988) argues that individuals join associations to learn whether their membership is worthwhile. If they see that it is, they stay; otherwise they leave. With experience in the association, they better understand the true costs and benefits of membership, particularly related to non-economic costs and solidary and purposive benefits, and reevaluate the membership decision. Under this model, if costs and benefits remain stable, we should see that the longer-tenured members are the least likely to leave a nonprofit membership association given that their experiential searching reveals less new information over time.

Johnson (1987) presents a further twist on the decision to persist in a nonprofit membership association. He argues that membership should be viewed as a capital asset investment. Members stay in associations in anticipation of future benefits. When associations provide selective incentives based on seniority (for example, labor unions and the Freemasonry), members remain in order to preserve their seniority even if there are lapses in benefit provision.

Decisions to actively participate in an association rather than to free-ride are also addressed under the collective action framework. Free-riding is diminished when monitoring and bargaining costs to reduce this behavior are low and when there is a strong culture of support and social cohesion (Lane and Bachmann 1997). High levels of social cohesion and solidarity are strongest in associations that bring in all or a majority of the residents of an action arena but still have a small absolute number of members (Olson 1965). The possibility of having one's contributions be spurned by other members and the degree to which this is undesirable can also affect free-riding (Hirshman 1982).

Network connections explain participation and persistence in some studies. As Clemens (1999) found in her study of women's associations in the 1880s to the 1920s, individuals often join multiple associations affiliated with the same issue resulting in competing loyalties. For religious congregations, the importance of social attachments to other members in predicting entry and retention is referred to as social bond theory (Stark and Bainbridge 1985). The basic argument is that strong internal network ties reduce turnover, and connections outside the group increase turnover (McPherson, Popielarz, and Drobnic 1992b). Popielarz and McPherson (1995) find that members who are least similar to the group are likely to leave the fastest (the niche edge hypothesis) as are members who are subject to more competition for their membership from groups recruiting the same types of individuals (the niche overlap hypothesis). Members' positions in an area of social space influence the quality and quantity of their ties with fellow members and the demands put on them for their limited time and resources. The niche edge hypothesis argues that more and stronger ties of an individual to other members (i.e., a central position in the niche) leads to more contact of the individual with other niche members, leading to more importance placed on the membership by the individual and, consequently, the greater the individual's duration in the niche. In regions of denser overlap, there is heightened competition for members, greater options, and thus more movement of members from association to association. Members operating in a region with little overlap have affiliations of longer duration.

Cress, McPherson, and Rotolo (1997) found that members with lower rates of participation have longer membership durations. Attributing this to competition, they explain that associations that make greater demands on members are more likely to create conflicts with demands made on the members from other sources, and consequently lose the members due to the competitive pressures. Some associations can isolate members and cut off other demands. For these organizations, the higher level of sacrifice that members make for the association, the more value they are likely to place on the association and thus the higher their commitment to it (Kanter 1972).

Rather than look at what nonprofit membership associations demand from members, some theorists have looked at what members gain from the associations in a competitive environment. Finke and Stark (1998) argue that association leaders work harder to attract and retain members when their market share is low, and are more likely to be lazy and complacent when they face little competition for members. Consequently, participation of members will be higher in associations with smaller market share in reaction to the more aggressive nurturing of members.

Two competing perspectives related to member commitment can be found within the study of religion, but seem generalizable to other types of nonprofit membership associations (see Perl and Olson 2000 for a review and test of the perspectives). One argument is that the subcultural distinctiveness of a denomination, demonstrated by a small market share, helps to make members more dependent on each other for resources and more committed to their unique values and beliefs. On the other hand, taking a social isolation perspective, a small market share reflecting a relatively unique identity should be associated with low member commitment. Through exposure to non-members, members may perceive that their unique beliefs are less convincing than majority beliefs. Also, there are fewer fellow members to observe and sanction behaviors outside the minority belief system, thus allowing for lower commitment.

Comment on Member Retention and Participation

The theories used by researchers to explain member retention and participation are mostly complementary. The dominant explanation is that members make choices among competing opportunities in order to best serve their own interests and maintain their strongest ties. The value of this explanation to all associations is suspect. As Olson (1965) acknowledges, it is doubtful that interest-based explanations adequately explain the retention and participation dynamics in associations in which membership is coerced. They also may be less applicable to associations in which individuals represent others' interests, and the associations primarily serve the collectivity or outsiders rather than the interests of individual members. We also learn little about how the roles that members take in associations shape their interests, ties, and loyalties, though the discussion of centrality in a niche and competing demands for time may provide some insight. If associations are competing for members' time and other resources, can the competitive domains be identified? Are they bounded by similarities and differences in association purposes and member types? We know little about how competition for members may influence the claimed benefits and side effects of associations.

The bulk of the research under this topic is on member commitment and how commitment affects retention. What members do in associations is largely ignored, except in detailed case studies of specific associations. Cohen, Barkan, and Halteman's (2003) work is one of the notable exceptions, and they are careful to note that their findings are limited to one specific association. Knoke (1988) is one of the few scholars to attempt to provide an aggregated look at some forms of participation in associations. The collective action framework provides some attention to free-riding, but this work has a focus on predicting the lack of participation rather than seeing what predicts active participation. The internal dynamics of member involvement are largely unexplored. This leads us to the next section on association governance and structure, in which we can gather more insights on internal membership dynamics.

How Are Associations Governed and Structured?

Discussions of association structure are complicated by the fact that some nonprofit membership associations use a nesting of governance structures. They may have chapters, affiliates, franchises, or branches, and perhaps even divisions or interest groups within these units and an umbrella or head organization. In addition, associations may have multiple membership categories, each with its own rights and access to decision-making processes. Membership may be on an apprenticeship or probationary basis, with restricted rights for members who have not been approved for full membership. There may also be a hierarchy, with members ascending through the ranks, paying larger membership dues, or performing more volunteer hours to gain more influence in association matters.

A core question for nonprofit membership associations is how much power to give individual members. Not all associations operate on a one-vote-per-member principle. Leroy (1997) claims that only 77 percent of associations in the United States have members with direct voting privileges and these associations vary in what types of votes are brought before members. Association governance may involve boards, executive committees, delegate assemblies, section representatives, and other mechanisms for hearing member voices. It also may be largely autocratic, though in the United States, certain voting rights must be given to members of legally incorporated nonprofit membership associations.

Research on nonprofit membership association governance and coordination is thin and scattered across diverse fields. The literature presents a variety of factors that may predict structure for specific types of associations and under certain conditions, but there is little testing and replication of findings. Environmental factors presented as predictors include local resource density and environmental variation (Hudson and Bielefeld 1997) and composition of the potential membership base (Austin 1991). Internal factors tied to structure include territorial scope (Bennett 1998; D. Smith 2000), membership size (Akers and Campbell 1970; Staber 1987), members' personal interests (Barman and Chaves 2001), professionalization (Olson 1965), collectivist orientation and egalitarian norms (Knoke 1990; Mansbridge 1986; Milofsky 1988), transaction costs (Schneiberg and Hollingsworth 1990), and age and resource dependencies (Knoke 1990). For religious congregations, divine inspiration may play a role in determining strategy and structure (Harris 1995).

Most treatments of governance and structure are found in case studies or explorations of specific types of associations (e.g., Beito 2000, for fraternal orders). The bulk of the work on structure examines associations that have multiple units. Grossman and Rangan (2001) lay out a view of federated association units and members having identities, resource needs, reputational needs, and goals that may or may not be compatible and complementary. Local and central units face environments that may differ in their complexity, stability, and demands, and consequently the need for flexibility and independence, as well as the benefits of affiliation. This leads to tensions among units over allocation of resources, delivery of services, use of parent name, payments to headquarters, and governance of the system.

Structural form appears to determine how much autonomy is available to local units, and how the association system is self-regulated, as well as the types of goals emphasized. When local units have more autonomy, members can better regulate the national office (Young, Bania, and Bailey 1996); however, they may trade control for more resources from the central office (Young 1989). Control over local units can be critical to national associations that wish to pursue national goals (Freeman 1979) and need to protect their national reputation and compete for donations (Oster 1996). Given that part of a nonprofit's strategy is to define itself for multiple stakeholders, choice of structure is linked to self-concept (Young 2001), for both central and local units. Structure influences how an association is perceived and interacts with individuals and other organizations, including its members, and the perceptions and interactions influence the structure. Case studies of four national health associations (Standley 2001) help to illuminate this relationship. Though strategies varied, the national associations were able to change members' trust in them, allowing them to develop a more centralized structure that reinforced a national identity among members. Ideological mechanisms and strong psychological identification with an association may promote conformity of local units and members, as in the cases of Alcoholics Anonymous (Messer 1994), fraternal lodges (Knight 1984), and the Salvation Army (Winston 1999).

The literature examining nonprofit membership associations gives significant attention to the balancing of a desire for member influence with administrative needs. Knoke (1990) claims that associations rely on internal democratic systems to respond to environmental and internal imperatives. Associations can struggle over the desire to have democratic and inclusive structures, especially when there are inadequate membership resources to sustain them (see Strobel 1995 for a discussion of this challenge in women's associations). Democratic and inclusive structures also make associations more vulnerable to takeovers from those wishing to control, change, or undermine their purposes (Tschirhart and Johnson 1998), as found by the Sierra Club and dog clubs (Lanting 1992). Jarley, Fiorito, and Delaney (1997) reject what they say is the dominant view of unions, that administrative and representative systems are in conflict, with the elaboration of one system impeding the other. They find that a variety of factors influence administrative structures in unions and these are not the same factors that influence democratic structures. They also argue that democracy should not be viewed as an end in itself. Instead, an optimal level should be achieved.

In addition to the argument that administrative systems can undermine democratic ones, a wide body of literature suggests that operating in an authoritarian regime and having close linkages to the state can undermine the degree of democracy within an association (Foster 2001). Under this framework, if an association is linked to a non-democratic state through personnel, financial, decision-making, or operational procedures or arrangements, then state interests dominate member interests. This suggests that associations can be arrayed along a public-private continuum (Foster 2001) depending on the degree of domination. Foster (2001) argues that an association may choose to develop close ties to an authoritarian state in response to member demands and interests. He also argues that influence does not always merely flow top-down from authoritarian states to associations and that many associations in authoritarian regimes do little to help the state control members.

A concern when considering the governance of nonprofit membership associations is that leaders may not accurately represent the views of their association members. Leaders may present themselves as acting in the interests of the membership while actually pursuing their own elite interests (Cnaan 1991). To complicate the matter, members may not act in the common interest, especially if there are no incentives or coercion to do so (Olson 1965), making it difficult for leaders to understand and enforce a common membership interest. The larger the size of the association, the less influence members may feel that they have (Torpe 2003), though those who want influence are the most likely to report that they have influence.

Sabatier (1992) and Sabatier and McLaughlin (1990) review theories on the belief congruence of leaders and members, finding somewhat incompatible results. The exchange theory approach, as it has evolved from Salisbury's (1969) original formulation, argues that staff members will not attempt to push policy positions that will alienate a significant portion of their membership because they fear they will lose membership renewals. In organizations where purposive or collective policy benefits are important to members, leaders are likely to work hard to develop belief congruence in other types of associations; the extent of belief congruence is irrelevant to the maintenance of the association. This expanded exchange theory has some support in Sabatier (1992) and comes out well in Sabatier and McLaughlin (1990). Commitment theory, originating in work on political parties and political elites, predicts a greater distance between member and leader beliefs with leaders having more coherent, developed, and extreme views. This distance may not be problematic for association maintenance if membership is based primarily on selective, material incentives, there is low dependency on member dues, and members have incomplete information on the beliefs and activities of leaders. Commitment theory gets good reviews in Sabatier (1992) and Sabatier and McLaughlin (1990). Sabatier and McLaughlin reject a third theory, the moderating elite's perspective. This theory predicts that leaders of associations will have more moderate views than their members because of the leaders' greater interaction with opponents, concern with maintenance of the political system, and need to show how their position serves the common welfare. Sabatier (1992) finds no significant differences between members and leaders, leading him to reject Olson's by-product theory.

Ideology seems particularly pertinent in studies of the structures of purposive nonprofit membership associations such as feminist organizations and communes (Ethies 2000). Without ideological consensus, there is the possibility for conflict over organization form given that the form embodies normative ideals (Arnold 1995). The use of ideologically driven structures and practices that are outside the societal norm can also open associations to surveillance and attack such as the FBI oppression of the Chicago Women's Liberation Union (Aker 1995).

Comment on Research on Governance and Structure

The empirical research on governance and structure of nonprofit membership associations is thin relative to the research on member entry and retention. This is disappointing given that questions of governance and structure are critical when considering the value of associations to societies and members. Issues of representation and structure become even more complex when associations have multiple membership categories, and subunits with their own subpurposes, member identities, and roles.

We do not know how applicable the limited findings are across associations with different purposes and member types. The service base and aim seem particularly relevant to discussions of governance and structure but these are rarely explored by scholars. It is likely that some of the models of governance and structure applied to business and to nonprofit organizations other than associations can also be applied to associations. New models for specific types of nonprofit membership associations may be needed to increase our understanding of governance and structure dynamics.

What are the trends and what explains them? Humans

are long thought to have a natural propensity to form and join associations (e.g., Mosca 1939; Simmel 1950), and Americans in particular are heralded as a nation of joiners (Schlesinger 1944; Tocqueville 1956). In the past two decades, numerous studies have examined membership trends and cross-cultural patterns. The studies have provoked lively debate but little consensus. Baer, Curtis, and Grabb (2001) argue that, overall, nonprofit association membership has remained stable from the early 1980s to the early 1990s in fourteen out of fifteen countries, including the United States; only Spain shows a substantial decline.

On the side of growth in nonprofit association membership, scholars point to the explosive expansion of the American Association of Retired Persons (Baumgartner and Walker 1988) and homeowners and residential community associations (McKenzie 1994). Salamon (1995) proclaimed an "associational revolution" under way at the global level, with increasing founding of associations in both developed and developing countries. D. Smith (2000), looking at the little-studied small grassroots associations, argues that there is accumulating qualitative evidence for a long-term worldwide growth trend in grassroots membership and association prevalence.

Other scholars decry the loss of social capital and civic engagement over the last third of the twentieth century as evidenced by declines in participation in some types of nonprofit membership associations (e.g., Putnam 2000). There are membership declines in the American labor movement (Cornfield 1986; Dickens and Leonard 1985; Lipset 1986), with labor unions for private sector employees experiencing significant declines while unions for public sector employees are more stable (Kearney 2003). Examples of other nonprofit membership associations experiencing declines are the Rotary, Lions, and Kiwanis service clubs (Charles 1993); the Parent-Teacher Association (Crawford and Levitt 1999); and mainline Protestant churches (Roof and McKinney 1987; Hoge and Roozen 1979), not to forget bowling leagues (Putnam 2000). The mixed findings in the literature suggest that membership association trend lines are rarely straight and conclusions depend on specific associations and time periods examined.

Mapping the association world and conducting longitudinal or time-series studies are no easy tasks. Historical data are fragmented and difficult to triangulate. Research on association trends and patterns is sensitive to use of probes, wording of questions, and non-comparability across surveys, and context effects, helping to explain inconsistent findings across databases and problems with meta-analyses (T. Smith 1990). There are also challenges in deciding subcategories of associations to use in tracking trends (Selle and Oymyr 1992). Further complicating any historical mapping of the nonprofit sector is that many associations are part of the "dark matter" of the nonprofit sector, consisting of unincorporated organizations staffed by volunteers that do not make it into directories or leave records that can be used for historical analyses (D. Smith 2000). When the focus extends to the global level, methodological complexities increase (Curtis, Grabb, and Baer 1992), though there are rigorous cross-national studies incorporating historical trends and issues affecting nonprofit associations and membership numbers (e.g., Meister 1984).

Most scholars go beyond counting and attempt to explain patterns within and across nations and historical periods, producing some promising lines of research but no overarching framework to explain membership growth and decline, even within specific categories of nonprofit associations. There are ongoing debates about what are the most important forces in determining association patterns. For example, Gamm and Putnam (1999) critically review the widespread claim that greater participation in religious organizations explains Americans' ranking as the highest in association joiners (e.g., Curtis, Grabb, and Baer 1992), with religion and politics claimed to be the most important organizing force in the United States in the late eighteenth to early nineteenth centuries. Shofer and Fourcade-Gourinchas (2001) find that national polity characteristics (statism and corporateness) help explain differences in association membership across nations. As reviewed earlier in this chapter in the discussion of member entry, a wide range of environmental factors may help to explain association trends such as resource availability and threats.

Comment on Association Trends

The research on association trends leaves us with little confidence in what we know about nonprofit membership associations as a whole. There are substantial methodological difficulties in finding and tracking associations as well as debates over what explains patterns found. The diversity of purposes and member types under the association label makes it difficult to offer strong, highly generalized conclusions about the state of the association world. To evaluate claims about the benefits and harms of associations at an aggregated level, we need more theories and empirical work that help justify this aggregation. As we saw in the sections on member entry, retention and participation, and governance and structure, there are few findings that are likely to fit all types of nonprofit membership associations. Research on trends related to specific phenomena of relevance to all associations (as represented by the research areas discussed earlier in this chapter) would help to complement and inform research on trends in association numbers.

More than a decade ago, Knoke (1986:2) wrote, "Put bluntly, association research remains a largely unintegrated set of disparate findings, in dire need of a compelling theory to force greater coherence upon the enterprise. Without a common agreement about central concepts, problems, explanations, and analytical tools, students of associations and interest groups seem destined to leave their subject in scientific immaturity." Knoke's assessment of the literature on association varies little from another written decades earlier: "The research on voluntary associations represents discontinuous approaches without reference to systematic theory" (Gordon and Babchuk 1959:23).

This chapter demonstrates that for the most part these

earlier assessments still hold today. This is less of an indictment than an invitation. There are numerous opportunities for scholars to significantly advance the study of associations. Possibilities include integrating paradigms for specific types of membership associations—for example, grassroots organizations (D. Smith 2000); adding to the debates concerning the origins, maintenance, management, and transformations of associations; providing conceptual clarity for terms; and exploring enduring and new theories about the value of nonprofit membership associations.

This chapter's goal is to highlight key questions, theories, and findings and cite readings that can help in identifying related work. It also offers important questions concerning associations that need more attention. For example, we know little about predictors of member satisfaction, accountability to members' collective interests, and association life cycles and effectiveness. Structure and strategy are barely examined. We know more about why individuals and organizations join and leave associations than why they do not join in the first place. We also know more about the outcomes of association membership than outcomes of association disaffiliation, though at least in the area of cults, there is a substantial body of work on disaffiliation effects (e.g., Robinson and Bradley 1998).

The internal dynamics and cultures of associations are richly described in many of the historical accounts of specific associations and there are models speaking to what goes on inside associations that are scattered throughout the literature. There are ample opportunities for the development and testing of models that may be generalizable within and across specific types of associations. We have many of the puzzle pieces on the table. Given the prominence of nonprofit membership associations in many countries and claims about their benefits and harms, further work in this area is necessary and welcome.

The articles and books cited in this chapter are by academic scholars. There are numerous studies conducted by associations; perhaps most prominent among them is research by the American Society of Association Executives (ASAE). Though studies by associations offer insights on membership dynamics, comparisons across associations, and benchmarks, they rarely test theories and therefore are not emphasized in this chapter. The focus is on academic scholars' approaches to the study of associations and the identification of gaps in the research. Ideas are drawn from sociology, psychology, business, law, economics, labor studies, geography, urban studies, women's studies, religion, public administration, political science, and other disciplines. This large multidisciplinary base demonstrates scholars' fascination with studying associations but contributes to the challenge of summarizing what we have learned and building from the existing extensive and varied literature.

REFERENCES

Aker, Joan. 1995. "Feminist Goals and Organizing Processes." Pp. 137–144. *Feminist Organizations: Harvest of the New Women's Movement,* edited by Myra Marx Feree and Patricia Yancey Martin. Philadelphia: Temple University Press.

Akers, Ronald, and Frederick L. Campbell. 1970. "Size and the Administrative Component in Occupational Associations." *Pacific Sociological Review* (Fall): 241–251.

Amin, Ash, and Nigel Thrift. 1995. "Institutional Issues for the European Regions: From Markets and Plans to Socioeconomics and Powers of Association." *Economy and Society* 24(1):41–65.

Arnold, Gretchen. 1995. "Dilemmas of Feminist Coalitions: Collective Identity and Strategic Effectiveness in the Battered Women's Movement." Pp. 276–290. *Feminist Organizations: Harvest of the New Women's Movement,* edited by Myra Marx Feree and Patricia Yancey Martin. Philadelphia: Temple University Press.

Ashenfelter, Orley, and John H. Pencavel. 1969. "American Trade Union Growth: 1900–1960." *Quarterly Journal of Economics* 83:434–448.

Austin, Mark D. 1991. "Community Context and Complexity of Organizational Structure in Neighborhood Associations." *Administration and Society* 22:516–531.

Babchuk, Nicholas, and Alan Booth. 1969. "Voluntary Association Membership: A Longitudinal Analysis." *American Sociological Review* 34:31–45.

Baer, Douglas, James Curtis, and Edward Grabb. 2001. "Has Voluntary Association Activity Declined? Cross-National Analyses for Fifteen Countries." *Canadian Review of Sociology and Anthropology* 38:249–274.

Banerjee, Abhijit, Dilip Mookherjee, Kaivan Munshi, and Debraj Ray. 2001. "Inequality, Control Rights, and Rent-Seeking: Sugar Cooperatives in Maharashtra." *Journal of Political Economy* 109(1):138–190.

Barkan, Steven E., Steven E. Cohn, and William H. Whitaker. 1993. "Commitment across the Miles: Ideological and

Microstructural Sources of Support in a National Antihunger Organization." *Social Problems* 40(3):362–373.

Barman, Emily, and Mark Chaves. 2001. "Lessons for Multisite Nonprofits from the United Church of Christ." *Nonprofit and Voluntary Sector Quarterly* 11:339–370.

Baroudi, Sami E. 2000. "Business Associations and the Representation of Business Interests in Post-war Lebanon: The Case of the Association of Lebanese Industrialists." *Middle Eastern Studies* 36:23–51.

Baumgartner, Frank P., and Jack L. Walker. 1988. "Survey Research and Membership in Voluntary Associations." *American Journal of Political Science* 32:908–927.

Beito, David. 2000. *From Mutual Aid to Welfare State: Fraternal Societies and Social Services, 1890–1967.* Chapel Hill: University of North Carolina Press.

Bennett, R. J. 1998. "Explaining the Membership of Voluntary Local Business Associations: The Example of British Chambers of Commerce." *Regional Studies* 32:503–514.

———. 1999. "Explaining the Membership of Sectoral Business Associations." *Environment and Planning* 31:877–899.

Blau, Peter M. 1977. *Inequality and Heterogeneity: A Primitive Theory of Social Structure.* New York: Free Press.

———. 1994. *Structural Contexts of Opportunities.* Chicago: University of Chicago Press.

Booth, Alan, and Nicholas Babchuk. 1969. "Personal Influence Networks and Voluntary Association Affiliation." *Sociological Inquiry* 39:179–188.

Bowman, John R. 1998. "Achieving Capitalist Solidarity: Collective Action among Norwegian Employers." *Politics and Society* 26(3):303–336.

Boylan, Anne M. 1984. "Women in Groups: An Analysis of Women's Benevolent Organizations in New York and Boston, 1797–1840." *Journal of American History* 71:497–523.

Bradford, Neil. 1988. "Prospects for Associative Governance: Lessons from Ontario, Canada." *Politics and Society* 26(4):539–573.

Brockman, Joan. 1998. "Fortunate Enough to Obtain and Keep the Title of Profession: Self-Regulating Organizations and the Enforcement of Professional Monopolies." *Canadian Public Administration* 41(4):587–621.

Charles, Jeffrey A. 1993. *Service Clubs in American Society: Rotary, Kiwanis, and Lions.* Urbana: University of Illinois Press.

Clark, Peter B., and James Q. Wilson. 1961. "Incentive Systems: A Theory of Organization." *Administrative Science Quarterly* 6:129–166.

Clawson, Mary Ann. 1989. *Constructing Brotherhood: Class, Gender, and Fraternalism.* Princeton: Princeton University Press.

Clemens, Elisabeth S. 1999. "Securing Political Returns to Social Capital: Women's Associations in the United States, 1880s-1920s." *Journal of Interdisciplinary History* 25:613–638.

Cnaan, Ram A. 1991. "Neighborhood-Representing Organizations: How Democratic Are They?" *Social Service Review* (December): 614–634.

Cohen, Steven F., Steven E. Barkan, and William A. Halteman. 2003. "Dimensions of Participation in a Professional Social-Movement Organization." *Sociological Inquiry* 73:311–337.

Coleman, William, and Wyn Grant. 1988. "The Organizational Cohesion and Political Access of Business: A Study of Comprehensive Associations." *European Journal of Political Research* 16:467–487.

Conell, Carol, and Kim Voss. 1990. "Formal Organization and the Fate of Social Movements: Craft Association and Class Alliance in the Knights of Labor." *American Sociological Review* 55:255–269.

Cornfield, Daniel B. 1986. "Declining Union Membership in the Post–World War II Era: The United Furniture Workers of America, 1939–1982." *American Journal of Sociology* 91:1112–1153.

Crawford, Susan, and Peggy Levitt. 1999. "Social Change and Civic Engagement: The Case of the PTA." Pp. 249–296. *Civic Engagement in American Democracy,* edited by Theda Skocpol and Morris P. Fiorina. Washington, D.C.: Brookings Institution Press.

Cress, Daniel M., J. Miller McPherson, and Thomas Rotolo. 1997. "Competition and Commitment in Voluntary Memberships." *Sociological Perspectives* 40:61–79.

Curtis, James E., Edward G. Grabb, and Douglas E. Baer. 1992. "Voluntary Association Membership in Fifteen Countries: A Comparative Analysis." *American Sociological Review* 57:139–152.

Dickens, William T., and Jonathan S. Leonard. 1985. "Accounting for the Decline in Union Membership, 1950–1980." *Industrial and Labor Relations Review* 38:323–334.

Dyke, Bruno, and Frederick A. Starke. 1999. "The Formation of Breakaway Organizations: Observations and a Process Model." *Administrative Science Quarterly* 44:792–822.

Ethies, Clifford. 2000. "The Success of American Communes." *Southern Economic Journal* 67(1):186–199.

Ezekial, Raphael. 1995. *The Racist Mind.* Cambridge, Mass.: Harvard University Press.

Feldman, Gerald D., and Ulrich Nocken. 1975. "Trade Associations and Economic Power: Interest Group Development in the German Iron and Steel and Machine Building Industries, 1900–1933." *Business History Review* 49(4):413–445.

Finke, Roger, and Rodney Stark. 1998. "Reply to Olson: Religious Choice and Competition." *American Sociological Review* 63:761–766.

Foster, Kenneth W. 2001. "Associations in the Embrace of an Authoritarian State: State Domination of Society?" *Studies in Comparative International Development* 35(4):84–109.

Freeman, J. 1979. "Resource Mobilizational Strategy." Pp. 167–189. *The Dynamics of Social Movements* edited by M. N. Zald and J. D. McCarthy. Cambridge, Mass.: Winthrop Publishers.

Freeman, Richard B., and James L. Medoff. 1984. *What Do Unions Do?* New York: Basic Books.

Gamm, Gerald, and Robert D. Putnam. 1999. "The Growth of Voluntary Associations in America, 1840–1940." *Journal of Interdisciplinary History* 29:511–557.

Gordon, C. Wayne, and Nicholas Babchuk. 1959. "A Typology of Voluntary Associations." *American Sociological Review* 24:22–29.

Grossman, Allen, and V. Kasturi Rangan. 2001. "Managing

Multisite Nonprofits." *Nonprofit and Voluntary Sector Quarterly* 11:321–337.

Guterbock, Thomas M., and Bruce London. 1983. "Race, Political Orientation, and Participation: An Empirical Test of Four Competing Theories." *American Sociological Review* 48:439–453.

Hansen, John Mark. 1985. "The Political Economy of Group Membership." *American Political Science Review* 79:79–96.

Harris, Margaret. 1995. "The Organization of Religious Congregations: Tackling the Issues." *Nonprofit Management and Leadership* 5:261–274.

Hirschman, Albert O. 1982. *Shifting Involvements: Private Interest and Public Action.* Princeton, N.J.: Princeton University Press.

Hoge, Dean R., and David A. Roozen. 1979. *Understanding Church Growth and Decline, 1950–1978.* New York: Pilgrim Press.

Houghland, Jr., James G., and James R. Wood. 1980. "Control in Organizations and the Commitment of Members." *Social Forces* 59(1):85–105.

Huber-Sperl, Rita. 2002. "Organized Women and the Strong State: The Beginnings of Female Associational Activity in Germany, 1810–1840." *Journal of Women's History* 13(4):81–105.

Hudson, Bryant A., and Wolfgang Bielefeld. 1997. "Structures of Multinational Nonprofit Organizations." *Nonprofit Management and Leadership* 8:31–49.

Isaacs, Justin P., and David N. Laband. 1999. "Within-Group Heterogeneity and Exit in Religious Clubs." *Applied Economics Letters* 6:12, 805–808.

Jarley, Paul, Jack Fiorito, and John Thomas Delaney. 1997. "A Structural Contingency Approach to Bureaucracy and Democracy in U.S. National Unions." *Academy of Management Journal* 40(4):831–861.

Johnson, Paul Edward. 1987. "Foresight and Myopia in Organizational Membership." *Journal of Politics* 49:678–703.

Kahane, Leo H. 1999. "Gun Lobbies and Gun Control: Senate Voting Patterns on the Brady Bill and the Assault Weapons Ban." *Atlantic Economic Journal* 27(4):384–393.

Kanter, Rosabeth. 1968. "Commitment and Social Organization: A Study of Commitment Mechanisms in Utopian Communities." *American Sociological Review* 33:499–517.

———. 1972. *Commitment and Community: Communes and Utopias in Sociological Perspective.* Cambridge, Mass.: Harvard University Press.

Kaufman, Jason. 2002. *For the Common Good? American Civic Life and the Golden Age of Fraternity.* Oxford: Oxford University Press.

Kearney, Richard C. 2003. "Patterns of Union Decline and Growth: An Organizational Ecology Perspective." *Journal of Labor Research* 24:561–578.

Kilbane, Sally Conway, and John H. Beck. 1990. "Professional Associations and the Free Rider Problem: The Case of Optometry." *Public Choice* 65:181–187.

Kile, Orville Merton. 1948. *The Farm Bureau through Three Decades.* Baltimore: Waverly Press.

King, David C., and Jack L. Walker, Jr. 1991. "The Origins and Maintenance of Groups." Pp. 75–102. *Mobilizing Interest Groups in America: Patrons, Professions, and Social Movements,* edited by J. L. Walker, Jr. Ann Arbor: University of Michigan Press.

King, David C., and Jack L. Walker. 1992. "The Provision of Benefits by Interest Groups in the United States." *Journal of Politics* 54(2):394–426.

Klandermans, Bert. 1984. "Mobilization and Participation: Social-Psychological Expansions of Resource Mobilization Theory." *American Sociological Review* 49:583–600.

Klausen, Kurt Klaudi. 1995. "On the Malfunction of the Generic Approach in Small Voluntary Associations." *Nonprofit Management and Leadership* 5:275–290.

Knight, Stephen. 1984. *The Brotherhood: The Secret World of the Freemasons.* London: Dorset.

Knoke, David. 1981. "Commitment and Detachment in Voluntary Organizations." *American Sociological Review* 46:141–158.

———. 1986. "Associations and Interest Groups." *Annual Review of Sociology* 12:1–21.

———. 1988. "Incentives in Collective Action Organizations." *American Sociological Review* 53:311–329.

———. 1990. *Organizing for Collective Action: The Political Economies of Associations.* New York: Aldine de Gruyter.

Knoke, David, and Randall Thomson. 1977. "Voluntary Association Membership Trends and the Family Lifecycle." *Social Forces* 56:48–65.

Knoke, David, and James R. Wood. 1981. *Commitment in Voluntary Associations.* New Brunswick, N.J.: Rutgers University Press.

Lane, C., and R. Bachmann. 1997. "Cooperation in Inter-firm Relations in Britain and Germany: The Role of Social Institutions." *British Journal of Sociology* 42:226–254.

Lanting, F. 1992. "AKC Plans Hostile Takeover." *Dog World.* 77(2):121.

Lawrence, Thomas B. 2004. "Rituals and Resistance: Membership Dynamics in Professional Fields." *Human Relations* 57:115–143.

Leroy, Wayne E. 1997. "Association Governance and Structure." Pp. 1–10. *Professional Practices in Association Management,* edited by John B. Cox. Washington, D.C.: ASAE.

Lipset, Seymour Martin, ed. 1986. *Unions in Transition: Entering the Second Century.* San Francisco: ICS Press.

Logan, John R., and Gordana Rabrenovic. 1990. "Neighborhood Associations: Their Issues, Their Allies, and Their Opponents." *Urban Affairs Quarterly* 26:68–94.

Ludwig, Dean C. 1993. "Adapting to a Declining Environment: Lessons from a Religious Order." *Organization Science* 4(1):41–56.

Magat, Richard. 1999. *Unlikely Partners: Philanthropic Foundations and the Labor Movement.* Ithaca, N.Y.: Cornell University Press.

Mansbridge, Jane. 1986. *Why We Lost the ERA.* Chicago: University of Chicago Press.

Marin, Bernd. 1983. "Organizing Interests by Interest Organizations." *International Political Science Review* 4(2):197–216.

Massey, Douglas S., and Nancy A. Denton. 1993. *American Apartheid: Segregation and the Making of the Underclass.* Cambridge, Mass.: Harvard University Press.

McAdam, Doug. 1989. "The Biographical Consequences of Activism." *American Sociological Review* 54:744–760.

McBeath, Gerald A. 1998. "The Changing Role of Business Associations in Democratizing Taiwan." *Journal of Contemporary China* 7(18):303B.

McCarthy, John D., and Mayer Zald. 1977. "Resource Mobilization and Social Movements: A Partial Theory." *American Journal of Sociology* 82:1212–1242.

McKenzie, Evan. 1994. *Privatopia: Homeowner Associations and the Rise of Residential Private Government.* New Haven, Conn.: Yale University Press.

McLaughlin, Paul. 1996. "Resource Mobilization and Density Dependence in Cooperative Purchasing Associations in Saskatchewan, Canada." *Rural Sociology* 61:326–348.

McPherson, J. Miller, Pamela A. Popielarz, and Sonja Drobnic. 1992a. "Social Movements: Multiorganizational Fields and Recruitment to Mississippi Freedom Summer." *Sociological Forum* 3:357–832.

———. 1992b. "Social Networks and Organizational Dynamics." *American Sociological Review* 57:153–170.

Meister, Albert. 1984. *Participation, Associations, Development, and Change,* edited and translated by J. C. Ross. New Brunswick, N.J.: Transaction Books.

Messer, John G. 1994. "Emergent Organization as a Practical Strategy: Executing Trustee Functions in Alcoholics Anonymous." *Nonprofit and Voluntary Sector Quarterly* 23:293–307.

Meyer, C. 1980. *Facing Reality.* New York: Harper and Row.

Milofsky, Carl. 1988. *Community Organizations: Studies in Resource Mobilization and Exchange.* New York: Oxford University Press.

Moe, Terry M. 1980a. "A Calculus of Group Membership." *American Journal of Political Science* 24(4):593–632.

———. 1980b. *The Organization of Interests: Incentives and the Internal Dynamics of Political Interest Groups.* Chicago: University of Chicago Press.

Monti, Daniel J. 1993. "People in Control: A Comparison of Residents in Two U.S. Housing Developments." *Ownership, Control and the Future of Housing Policy,* edited by R. Allen Hays. Westport, Conn.: Greenwood.

Mooney, Patrick H., Jerry Roahrig, and Thomas W. Gray. 1996. "The De/Repoliticization of Cooperation and the Discourse of Conversion." *Rural Sociology* 61(4):559–576.

Mosca, Gaetano. 1939. *The Ruling Class.* New York: McGraw Hill.

Newell, Sue, and Jacky Swan. 1995. "Professional Associations as Important Mediators of the Innovation Process." *Science Communication* 16(4):371–387.

Offe, Claus, and Helmut Wiesenthal. 1980. "Two Logics of Collective Action: Theoretical Notes on Social Class and Organizational Form." *Political Power and Social Theory* 1:67–115.

Olsen, Marvin E. 1970. "Social and Political Participation of Blacks." *American Sociological Review* 35:682–692.

Olson, Mancur. 1965. *The Logic of Collective Action.* Cambridge, Mass.: Harvard University Press.

Oster, S. 1996. "Nonprofit Organizations and Their Local Affiliates: A Study in Organizational Forms." *Journal of Economic Behavior and Organization* 30:83–95.

Peleman, Kathleen. 2002. "The Impact of Residential Segregation on Participation in Associations: The Case of Moroccan Women in Belgium." *Urban Studies* 39(4):727–747.

Perl, Paul, and Daniel V. A. Olson. 2000. "Religious Market Share and Intensity of Church Involvement in Five Denominations." *Journal for the Scientific Study of Religion* 39:12–31.

Popielarz, Pamela A., and J. Miller McPherson. 1995. "On the Edge or In Between: Niche Position, Niche Overlap, and the Duration of Voluntary Association Memberships." *American Journal of Sociology* 101:698–720.

Putnam, Robert D. 2000. *Bowling Alone: The Collapse and Revival of American Community.* New York: Simon and Schuster.

Ray, Marcella Ridlen. 1999. "Technological Change and Associational Life." Pp. 297–330. *Civic Engagement in American Democracy,* edited by Theda Skocpol and Morris P. Fiorina. Washington, D.C.: Brookings Institution Press.

Rietschlin, John. 1998. "Voluntary Association Membership and Psychological Distress." *Journal of Health and Social Behavior* 39:348–355.

Robinson, Beth, and Loretta J. Bradley. 1998. "Adaptation to Transition: Implications for Working with Cult Members." *Journal of Humanistic Education and Development* 36(4):212–222.

Roof, Wade Clark, and William McKinney. 1987. *American Mainline Religion: Its Changing Shape and Future.* New Brunswick, N.J.: Rutgers University Press.

Rosenblum, Nancy L. 1998. *Membership and Morals: The Personal Uses of Pluralism in America.* Princeton, N.J.: Princeton University Press.

Rothenberg, Lawrence S. 1988. "Organizational Maintenance and the Retention Decision in Groups." *American Political Science Review* 82(4):1129–1152.

Sabatier, Paul A. 1992. "Interest Group Membership and Organizations: Multiple Theories." Pp. 99–129. *The Politics of Interests: Interest Groups Transformed,* edited by Mark P. Petracca. San Francisco: Westview Press.

Sabatier, Paul A., and Susan M. McLaughlin. 1990. "Belief Congruence between Interest-group Leaders and Members: An Empirical Analysis of Three Theories and a Suggested Synthesis." *Journal of Politics* 52(3):914–935.

Salamon, Lester M. 1995. *Partners in Public Service: Government—Nonprofit Relations in the Modern Welfare State.* Baltimore: Johns Hopkins University Press.

Salisbury, Robert H. 1969. "An Exchange Theory of Interest Groups." *Midwest Journal of Political Science* 13:1–32.

Schlesinger, Arthur M. 1944. "Biography of a Nation of Joiners." *American Historical Review* 50(1):1–25.

Schneiberg, Marc. 1999. "Political and Institutional Conditions for Governance by Private Association: Private Order and Price Controls in American Fire Insurance." *Politics and Society* 27(1):67–103.

Schneiberg, Marc, and J. Rogers Hollingsworth. 1990. "Can Transaction Cost Economics Explain Trade Associations?" Pp. 233–246. *The Firm as Nexus of Treaties,* edited by Masahiko Aoki, Bo Gustafsson, and Oliver E. Williamson. London: Sage.

Schwadel, Philip. 2002. "Testing the Promise of the Churches:

Income Inequality in the Opportunity to Learn Civic Skills in Christian Congregations." *Journal for the Scientific Study of Religion* 41(3):565–575.

Secret, Philip E., James B. Johnson, and Audrey W. Forrest. 1990. "The Impact of Religiosity on Political Participation and Membership in Voluntary Associations among Black and White Americans." *Journal of Black Studies* 21:87–102.

Selle, Per, and Bjarne Oymyr. 1992. "Explaining Changes in the Population of Voluntary Organizations: The Roles of Aggregate and Individual Level Data." *Nonprofit and Voluntary Sector Quarterly* 2:147–180.

Shofer, Evan, and Marion Fourcade-Gourinchas. 2001. "The Structural Contexts of Civic Engagement: Voluntary Association Membership in Comparative Perspective." *American Sociological Review* 66:806–828.

Simmel, Georg. 1950. *Conflict and the Web of Group Affiliations,* translated by Kurt Wolff and Reinhard Bendix. Glencoe, Ill.: Free Press.

Skocpol, Theda. 1999. "Advocates without Members: The Recent Transformation of Civic Life." Pp. 461–510. *Civic Engagement in American Democracy,* edited by Theda Skocpol and Morris P. Fiorina. Washington, D.C.: Brookings Institution Press.

Skocpol, Theda, Marjorie Abend-Wein, Christopher Howard, and Susan Goodrich Lehmann. 1993. "Women's Associations and the Enactment of Mothers' Pensions in the United States." *American Political Science Review* 87(3):686–701.

Skocpol, Theda, and Morris P. Fiorina. 1999. *Civic Engagement in American Democracy.* Washington, D.C.: Brookings Institution Press.

Skocpol, Theda, Marshall Ganz, and Ziad Munson. 2000. "A Nation of Organizers: The Institutional Origins of Civic Voluntarism in the United States." *American Political Science Review* 94:527–543.

Smith, David Horton. 2000. *Grassroots Associations.* Thousand Oaks, Calif.: Sage Publications.

Smith, Tom W. 1990. "Trends in Voluntary Group Membership: Comments on Baumgartner and Walker." *American Journal of Political Science* 34(3):646–661.

Staber, Udo. 1987. "Corporatism and the Governance Structure of American Trade Associations." *Political Studies* 35:278–288.

Standley, Anne P. 2001. "Reinventing a Large Nonprofit: Lessons from Four Voluntary Health Associations." *Nonprofit Management and Leadership* 11:305–320.

Stanfield II, John H. 1993. "African American Traditions of Civic Responsibility." *Nonprofit and Voluntary Sector Quarterly* 22:137–153.

Stark, Rodney, and William Sims Bainbridge. 1985. *The Future of Religion.* Berkeley: University of California Press.

Stockton, F. T. 1911. *The Closed Shop in American Trade Unions.* Baltimore: Johns Hopkins Press.

Stolle, Dietland, and Thomas R. Rochon. 1998. "Are All Associations Alike?" *American Behavioral Scientist* 42(1):47–66.

Streeck, Wolfgang. 1991. "Interest Heterogeneity and Organizing Capacity: Two Logics of Collective Action?" Pp. 161–197. *Political Choice: Institutions, Rules and the Limits of Rationality,* edited by Roldan Czada and Adrienne Windhoff. Boulder, Colo.: Westview.

Streeck, Wolfgang, and Phillippe C. Schmitter. 1985. *Private Interest Government: Beyond Market and State.* London: Sage.

Strobel, Margaret. 1995. "Organizational Learning in the Chicago Women's Liberation Union." Pp. 145–162. *Feminist Organizations: Harvest of the New Women's Movement,* edited by Myra Marx Feree and Patricia Yancey Martin. Philadelphia: Temple University Press.

Swan, Jacky, Sue Newell, and Maxine Robertson. 1999. "Central Agencies in the Diffusion and Design of Technology: A Comparison of the U.K. and Sweden." *Organization Studies* 20(6):905–932.

Tannenbaum, Frank. 1951. *A Philosophy of Labor.* New York: Alfred A. Knopf.

Tiebout, C. M. 1956. "A Pure Theory of Local Expenditures." *Journal of Political Economy* 64(5):416–424.

Tocqueville, de, Alexis. 1835–1840. *Democracy in America.* Reprint, New York: New American Library, 1956.

Torpe, Lars. 2003. "Democracy and Associations in Denmark: Changing Relationships between Individuals and Associations." *Nonprofit and Voluntary Sector Quarterly* 32:329–343.

Truman, David. 1951. *The Governmental Process.* New York: Knopf.

Tschirhart, Mary, and Jonathan L. Johnson. 1998. "Infidels at the Gate and Rebels in the Ranks: Protection from Takeovers in Nonprofit Membership Organizations." Paper presented at the Association for Research on Nonprofit Organizations and Voluntary Action. November 5–7.

Tucker, Lewis R., Vlasis Stathakapolous, and Charles H. Patti. 1999. "A Multidimensional Assessment of Ethical Codes: The Professional Business Association Perspective." *Journal of Business Ethics* 19:287–300.

Walker, Jr., Jack L. 1983. "The Origins and Maintenance of Interest Groups in America." *American Political Science Review* 77:390–406.

———. 1991. *Mobilizing Interest Groups in America: Patrons, Professions, and Social Movements.* Ann Arbor: University of Michigan Press.

Walzer, Michael. 1991. "The Idea of Civil Society: A Path to Social Reconstruction." *Dissent* (Spring): 293–404.

Wandersmith, Abraham, Paul Florin, Robert Friedmann, and Ron Meier. 1987. "Who Participates, Who Does Not, and Why? An Analysis of Voluntary Neighborhood Organizations in the United States and Israel." *Sociological Forum* 2(3):534–555.

Warren, Donald I. 1975. *Black Neighborhoods: An Assessment of Community Power.* Ann Arbor: University of Michigan Press.

Warren, Mark E. 2001. *Democracy and Association.* Princeton, N.J.: Princeton University Press.

Western, Bruce. 1994. "Institutional Mechanisms for Unionization in Sixteen OECD Countries: An Analysis of Social Survey Data." *Social Forces* 73(2):497–519.

Williams, Jr., J. Allen, Nicholas Babchuk, and David R. Johnson. 1973. "Voluntary Associations and Minority Status: A Comparative Analysis of Anglo, Black, and Mexican Americans." *American Sociological Review* 38:637–646.

Winston, Diane. 1999. *Red-Hot and Righteous: The Urban Re-*

ligion of the Salvation Army. Cambridge, Mass.: Harvard University Press.

Young, Dennis R. 1989. "Local Autonomy in a Franchise Age." *Nonprofit and Voluntary Sector Quarterly* 19:101–117.

———. 2001. "Organizational Identity and the Structure of Nonprofit Umbrella Organizations." *Nonprofit Management and Leadership* 11:289–304.

Young, Dennis R., N. Bania, and D. Bailey. 1996. "Structure and Accountability: A Study of National Nonprofit Organizations." *Nonprofit Management and Leadership* 6:347–365.

Zurcher, Louis, and David A. Snow. 1981. "Collective Behavior: Social Movements." Pp. 447–482. *Social Psychology,* edited by M. Rosenberg and R. Turner. New York: Basic Books.

23

Charitable Giving: How Much, by Whom, to What, and How?

JOHN J. HAVENS
MARY A. O'HERLIHY
PAUL G. SCHERVISH

In this chapter we discuss four aspects of charitable giving by individuals: how much is given in total; the patterns of giving broken down by demographic and behavioral characteristics; how much is given to various areas of need; and how donors are giving, that is, through outright cash gifts, or through more formal and strategic methods. We define individual charitable giving more broadly than simply as those contributions that are eligible for the charitable deduction according to the IRS—that is, gifts made to qualified nonprofit organizations. In addition to contributions to and through charitable organizations, we also discuss several aspects of informal giving, by which we mean gifts of money and goods made directly to other individuals living outside of the donor's household.[1] Finally, we consider not just inter vivos giving (giving during the donor's lifetime) but also charitable bequests—that is, posthumous gifts made to charitable organizations from the donor's estate.

We draw heavily, but not exclusively, on several well-established and rich sources of data on charitable giving in the United States: *Giving USA, Giving and Volunteering in the United States,* the *Nonprofit Almanac,* the *Center on Philanthropy Panel Study* in the *Panel Study of Income Dynamics* (COPP/PSID), the *Survey of Consumer Finances* (SCF), the *Statistics of Income* (SOI), and the *Consumer Expenditure Survey.*[2] These sources allow us to paint a general picture of philanthropy that is practiced by all economic and demographic groups and that has increased considerably in total amounts since 1990.

Unless otherwise noted, all dollar values in this chapter have been adjusted for inflation and are expressed in 2002 dollars; the values may differ from the cited sources due to this adjustment. When depicting more detailed patterns of giving, some sources are more valuable than others. In such instances, we present the most consistent findings, and when there is little consistency among the sources we present a range of findings.

HOW MUCH?

In this section we review broad trends and patterns in aggregate inter vivos giving to charitable organizations and needy individuals. We also review trends in bequest giving to nonprofits and raise some issues about how survey methodology affects the reported amounts of charitable giving.

Individuals give by far the largest share of charitable contributions to nonprofit organizations. In 2001 individuals accounted for $163.5 billion[3] (or 76 percent)[4] of total giving to charities (AAFRC Trust for Philanthropy 2002). An additional $16.3 billion (or 7.7 percent) was donated through charitable bequests. Taken together, approximately 84 percent of the $215.4 billion total contributed to nonprofit organizations across the nation came from individuals. If current growth trends continue, the future looks promising for philanthropy: we estimate that between 1998 and 2052, between $21 trillion and $55 trillion will be donated to charities. As shown in table 23.1, the total will be composed of between $6.6 trillion and $27.4 trillion from bequests and

TABLE 23.1. PROJECTIONS FOR CHARITABLE CONTRIBUTIONS IN THE PERIOD 1998–2052 (TRILLIONS OF 2002 DOLLARS)

Type of contribution	Low estimate (2% secular growth)[a] (1)	Middle estimate (3% secular growth)[a] (2)	High estimate (4% secular growth)[a] (3)
Bequests to charity[b]	$6.6	$12.8	$27.4
Inter vivos giving by individuals[c]	$14.6	$20.0	$28.0
Total charitable contributions	$21.2	$32.8	$55.4
Percent of total contributed by millionaires[d]	52.0	57.5	65.3

Source: Calculated by the Center on Wealth and Philanthropy at Boston College, http://www.bc.edu/swri.

[a] Calculated for secular trends of 2%, 3%, and 4% in real growth rates for both household wealth and individual inter vivos giving. The real growth rate in household wealth was 3.3% from 1950 to 2000; the real growth rate in individual inter vivos giving was 3.7% from 1985 to 2000.

[b] Bequests to charity were estimated by the Center on Wealth and Philanthropy at Boston College (Havens and Schervish 1999).

[c] Calculated by the Center on Wealth and Philanthropy at Boston College, based on estimates from AAFRC Trust for Philanthropy, 2002.

[d] Millionaires are defined as having at least $1 million of household net worth at the time of the contribution.

TABLE 23.2. AGGREGATE INTER VIVOS CHARITABLE CONTRIBUTIONS AS A PERCENTAGE OF GROSS DOMESTIC PRODUCT AND AVERAGE CONTRIBUTION PER HOUSEHOLD BY SOURCE AND YEAR

Data source (1)	Years (2)	Content of next columns (3)	Total amount (billions of 2002 dollars) (4)	Contributions as percent of GDP (5)	Average contribution per household (2002 dollars) (6)
Nonprofit Almanac	1990	Gifts by individuals and families	$110.59	1.35	$1,203
	1995		$118.60	1.36	$1,198
	1998		$152.50	1.57	$1,457
Giving and Volunteering (in the United States)[a]	1990	Household contributions	$90.29	1.17	$983
	1995		$81.86	0.95	$841
	2000		$154.76	1.51	$1,479
Giving USA	1990	Gifts by individuals and families	$111.46	1.45	$1,213
	1995		$112.54	1.30	$1,157
	2000		$166.05	1.62	$1,586
Survey of Consumer Finances (SCF)[b]	1990	Family contributions ($500 or more)	$97.85	1.27	$1,065
	1995		$111.56	1.29	$1,147
	2000		$188.52	1.84	$1,770
Consumer Expenditure Survey	1990	Consumer unit cash contributions	$109.08	1.42	$1,187
	1995		$112.64	1.30	$1,158
	2000		$145.05	1.41	$1,315
Statistics of Income (SOI)	1990	Itemized charitable deductions	$78.73	1.02	$856
	1995		$88.56	1.02	$910
	2000		$142.85	1.39	$1,364
Panel Study of Income Dynamics (PSID)	1990	Family contributions ($25 or more)			
	1995				
	2000		$157.38	1.53	$1,445

Source: Calculated and compiled by the Center on Wealth and Philanthropy at Boston College, http://www.bc.edu/swri.

[a] The *Giving and Volunteering Survey* adopted a telephone interview format and implemented other methodological changes between 1995 and 2000. The higher estimates for 2000 may reflect methodological improvements in the survey.

[b] Some wealthy households make large donations from time to time, which produces lumpiness in the time series of giving. The estimate for 2000 reflects an unusual number of large gifts during 2000 among the oversample of wealthy households.

between $14.6 trillion and $28 trillion from inter vivos gifts. Over 50 percent of the future trillions will be contributed by households at or above $1 million in net worth.

Participation in charitable giving is high, with nearly 90 percent of households making donations to charity on an annual basis. The average dollar amount contributed per household is approximately $1,479, representing 2.7 percent of income (Independent Sector 2002b:28). When informal giving is included, participation rates, average dollar amounts, and percentage of income contributed for the benefit of others are even higher.

Table 23.2 presents findings on giving to nonprofit organizations derived from a variety of data sources. A number of trends can be discerned from the data. First, aggregate giving, after adjustment for inflation, has increased during the period from 1990 to 2000 and rapidly so since 1995. Except for *Giving and Volunteering,* all sources imply a growth rate in aggregate giving of between 2 percent and 5 percent during the decade and between 5 percent and 9 percent from 1995 to 2000.[5] Second, as shown in column 6, households contributed substantial amounts to charity with estimates of average annual contributions per household ranging from approximately $850 to $1,800. Third, also shown in column 6, average contributions per household generally increased from 1990 to 2000. Moreover, as shown in column 5, household contributions grew faster than did gross domestic product during the 1990s, since from 1990 to 2000, within each data source the contributions as a percentage of GDP generally increased.

Findings on informal giving will be presented in some detail in a later section. Suffice it to say here that table 23.2 does not include the substantial amount of informal giving documented subsequently. The broad range of reported results for aggregate and household charitable giving reported in columns 4 and 6 reveals just how difficult it is to capture the complexity of inter vivos giving. There are substantial differences in estimates of aggregate inter vivos giving among sources that report on essentially the same population in the same year, which are due in part to the variety of measures, inconsistencies between sample design, and differing methodologies employed by each study. As for measures, *Giving USA* and the *Nonprofit Almanac* provide series with aggregate measures of inter vivos giving; the *Consumer Expenditure Survey* does not include in-kind giving; the SCF does not measure contributions of less than $500; the SOI ignores the charitable contributions of non-itemizers or charitable contributions that exceed legal limits on the level of charitable deduction; and the COPPS/PSID does not include contributions of less than $25 and, in comparison to the SCF, has a relatively sparse sample of very wealthy households. Sample design and survey methodology also influence the findings of research on charitable giving. Based in part on their experience of interviewing forty respondents weekly for thirteen months about their formal and informal giving in the Boston Area Diary Study, researchers Schervish and Havens made five recommendations in regard to improving survey data: first, that surveys sample households across the complete spectrum of income; second, that they interview the household member who knows the most about the household's giving, not necessarily the head of the household; third, that interviewers be well trained; fourth, that interviewers use a variety of prompts to aid respondent recall (Schervish and Havens 1998:241); and fifth, that surveys inquire about a broad range of voluntary giving to others in need so as to achieve the most complete and extensive findings possible on the landscape of financial care (Havens and Schervish 2001:548).

The latter propositions were recently confirmed by researchers at the Indiana University Center on Philanthropy, who, in *Indiana Gives 2000,* simultaneously tested a variety of survey methods ranging from a very short module ("Did you give last year? If so, how much?") to two longer modules, which in some cases took up to ninety minutes to complete since they prompted respondents by both area and method of giving. The most successful of the seven instruments tested were those that combined prompts to interviewees on the method of giving and the area of need to which they gave. Researchers Rooney, Steinberg, and Schervish conclude that: "The longer the module and the more detailed its prompts, the more likely a household was to recall making any charitable contribution and the higher the average level of its giving. These differences persisted even after controlling for differences in age, educational attainment, income, household status, race, and gender" (2001:551).[6]

Turning from lifetime giving in table 23.2 to the area of charitable bequests, our analysis is limited to a single data source, IRS estate tax filings. We know from the *National Survey on Planned Giving* (2001:6) that only one in ten households has named a charity in its will. Of these, only those that exceed the estate tax threshold, $675,000 in 2000, will show up in the federal estate tax data. Of the 108,322 estate tax forms filed in 2000, 52,000 estates (or 48 percent) were subject to tax, and of these, 10,959 (or 21 percent) made a charitable bequest, averaging $934,516 per bequesting estate, or $196,249 averaged over all taxable estates. The amount donated to charities represented 7.5 percent of the total assets of all taxable estates. The average number of charitable bequests is somewhat misleading since

TABLE 23.3. CHANGES IN VALUE AND ALLOCATION OF NET ESTATES[a] (BILLIONS OF 2002 DOLLARS)

Year	Value	Bequests to charity	Taxes	Bequests to heirs
1992	$80.29	$8.72	$16.93	$54.64
1995	$86.19	$10.27	$18.41	$57.51
1997	$115.60	$16.03	$24.67	$74.90
1999	$139.66	$15.77	$32.73	$91.17
2000	$144.68	$16.81	$33.98	$93.88
% Δ 92–00	80.2	92.9	100.8	71.8

Source: Calculated by the Center on Wealth and Philanthropy at Boston College based on data from Johnson and Mikow 1999 and Eller 1997 and from the Web site of the Statistics of Income Division of the IRS, www.irs.gov/taxstats/.

[a] Net estates are gross value of estates minus debt, estate fees, and surviving spouse deduction.

the data do not differentiate between estates that can take a spousal deduction and those with no surviving spouse, which make most of the charitable bequests. When the data are separated by the presence of a surviving spouse, radically different patterns appear for married versus single or widowed decedents. Only 7.4 percent of married decedents made a charitable bequest, with the vast majority (97.2 percent) transferring the estate to a surviving spouse.[7] In contrast, 43.3 percent of single estates and 25.4 percent of widowed estates made a charitable bequest, indicating that when the priority of looking after a surviving partner is removed, charity becomes important for a substantial proportion of estates (Eller 2001) and may be increasing as a priority, especially compared to heirs.

Charitable bequests have increased from 1992 to 2000, outpacing growth in both the value of estates and bequests to heirs, though not taxes. As shown in table 23.3, the value of all net estates (estates net of spousal deduction and estate fees) grew by 80.21 percent, from $80.3 billion to $144.7 billion; the value of estate tax revenue was up by more than 100 percent, from $16.9 billion to $34.0 billion; bequests to heirs increased by more than 70 percent, from $54.6 billion to $93.9 billion; and charitable bequests grew more than 90 percent, from $8.7 billion to $16.8 billion. If current growth trends continue, charitable bequests are projected to total between $6.6 and $27.4 trillion (2002 dollars) from 1998 to 2052, depending on the rate of real growth in wealth. Later in this chapter we will discuss the relations between bequest and inter vivos giving and outline some potential future trends.

WHO GIVES?

Decades of research indicate that higher levels of charitable giving are positively associated with higher income, higher wealth, greater religious participation, volunteerism, age, marriage, higher educational attainment, U.S. citizenship, higher proportion of earned wealth versus inherited wealth, and a greater level of financial security. How gender, ethnicity, or religion, among other demographic characteristics, affects participation in giving and amounts donated is more complex than simple bivariate analysis can describe. As a general point, due to cost restrictions in conducting surveys, simple random samples typically do not interview sufficient numbers of high-income and high-net-worth households or enough ethnically diverse households to accurately capture their giving patterns. In addition, there is frequently insufficient multivariate analysis that would enable us to determine to what extent an increase or decrease in charitable giving is due to a complex array of causes, rather than a single demographic characteristic.

One context for the findings presented in this section is that research shows that the most important predictor of charitable giving is "communities of participation," or groups and organizations in which the donor is a member or is otherwise involved. Based on a multivariate analysis of data from the Independent Sector's (1992) *Giving and Volunteering in the United States,* researchers Schervish and Havens conclude that the key indicators of a donor's giving are the "density and mix of opportunities and obligations for voluntary association" (Schervish and Havens 1997:256). Many of the demographic characteristics we explore here are proxies for associational capital or what Brown and Ferris (2002:ii) call a donor's "network-based social capital," the degree to which the donor is embedded socially, or involved and engaged in society. For example, greater income and wealth aside, a college graduate participates in a number of networks that a high school graduate might not, each of which may offer many opportunities for giving such as an alumni association, a professional membership organization, or a workplace giving program.

Income and Wealth

In regard to income and wealth, we first address the persistent misconception among the public and even some researchers on philanthropy that there is a U-shaped relation between the level of household income and charitable giving, with low-income households giving more to charity as a percentage of household income than do middle-income or high-income households. The myth of the U-shaped curve has existed at least from the mid-1980s and was reinforced through the early 1990s by findings derived from the Independent Sector (1992, 1996) surveys *Giving and Volunteering in the United States.* Research at the Boston College Center on Wealth and Philanthropy (formerly the Social Welfare Research Institute), however, revealed that the U-shaped curve pertained not to the entire population but only to households that contributed to charity, and even among this group excluded households with the highest incomes. The Boston College research produced several relevant findings (Schervish and Havens, 1995a, 1995b). First, as income and wealth increase, the participation rate of households in charitable giving increases; however, the U-shaped curve, which was based on contributing households only, left out of the calculations the relatively high proportions of low-income households that give nothing to charity. As shown in figure 23.1, when these "zeros" are included and the percentage of income is calculated for all households in the sample, the left-hand side of the U virtually disappears. What remains of the uptick at the lower end of the income spectrum can be explained by taking into account household wealth in addition to income (Savoie and Havens 1998). Finally, because *Giving and Volunteering in the United States* does not over-sample higher-income households, its findings pertain mainly to households with incomes of no more than $125,000. Although a sample with incomes up to this level covers most households (approximately 93 percent of the nation's households in 2000), it is unable to capture the giving patterns of households above that level (approximately 7 percent of households in 2000) that contribute half of individual inter vivos charitable giving. When the curve charting the relation between income and percentage of income contributed is extended to include that top 7 percent of house-

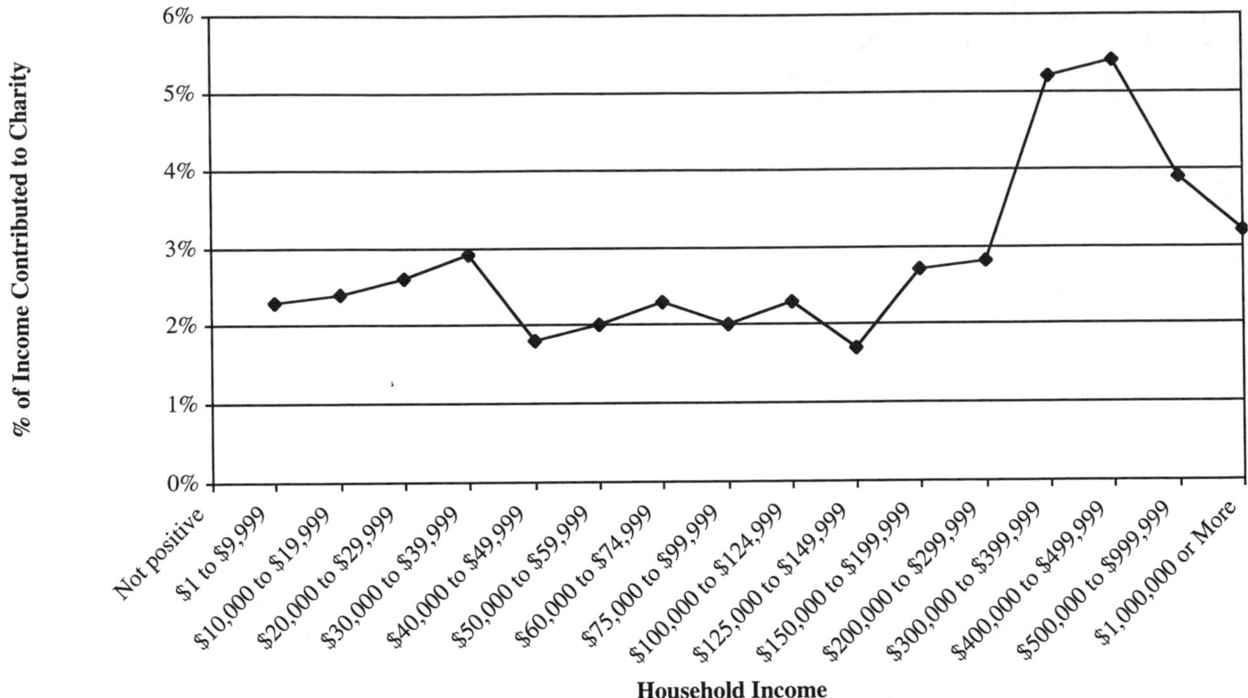

FIGURE 23.1. RELATION OF HOUSEHOLD INCOME TO PERCENTAGE OF INCOME CONTRIBUTED TO CHARITY
Source: Calculated at the Boston College Center on Wealth and Philanthropy, based on data from the 2001 *Survey of Consumer Finances* (Board of Governors of the Federal Reserve System 2001).

holds by income, an upswing in the right side of the curve appears. The original U-shaped curve did not reveal the dramatic upswing in giving among very high income households.

Tables 23.4 and 23.5 present additional important patterns of charitable giving by income and wealth based on data from the 2001 *Survey of Consumer Finances,* which, because of its over-sample of wealthy households, provides a basis for estimating giving at the upper ends of income and wealth distributions. First, except at the very highest levels, families at every level of income and wealth are about equally philanthropic in terms of the percentage of income contributed. Second, charitable giving is highly skewed toward the upper end of the wealth and income spectrums, with the small number of families at the highest end of the distributions of wealth and income contributing a dramatically high proportion of total annual charitable giving.[8] As a group, the 98 percent of families with incomes under $300,000 all tend to contribute about the same proportion of their income to charitable causes, roughly 2.3 percent. On average the highest-income families, those with incomes in excess of $300,000, represent just 2 percent of families nationwide, and contribute an average of 4.4 percent of their income to charitable causes and in aggregate approximately 37 percent of all charitable dollars (Board of Governors of the Federal Reserve System 2001).

The same pattern is true for wealth: at higher levels of wealth, families contribute more to charitable organizations as compared with families at lower wealth levels. The proportion of families that contribute at least $500 to the financial support of charitable organizations increases substantially as family wealth increases, from 8.3 percent of families with a net worth below $10,000 to 93 percent of families who have $10 million or more in net worth. Families with a net worth of $1 million or more represent 7 percent of all households nationwide but make 50 percent of all charitable contributions. Third, although the percentage of income contributed to charitable causes increases with wealth as well as with income (as shown in tables 23.4 and 23.5), the percentage of wealth contributed rises with income, but not with wealth (not shown in tables).

Charitable bequests relate positively to wealth, as shown in table 23.6. Even among affluent estates (the only estates for which tax data are available), bequests are more concentrated among wealthier decedents: estates worth $2.5 million or more, after subtracting estate fees and spousal deduction, constitute only 15 percent of those filing but contribute 80 percent of the approximately $16.8 billion gifted to charity annually through bequests (AAFRC Trust for Philanthropy 2002). Charitable bequests rise with the net worth of the estate while bequests to heirs decrease. In 2000, across all estates, charitable bequests were valued at 11.6 percent of the estate, taxes at 23.5 percent, and bequests to heirs at 64.9 percent. Among estates worth $20 million or more after subtracting estate fees and spousal deduction, the trend is skewed more toward charity and away from heirs, with charitable bequests at 33.2 percent, estate taxes at 39.1 percent, and heirs receiving 27.8 percent.

TABLE 23.4. 2000 CHARITABLE CONTRIBUTIONS BY FAMILY INCOME IN 2002 DOLLARS

Family income[a]	Percentage of families giving at least $500 (1)	Average family contribution[b] (2)	Average percentage of family income contributed (3)	Cumulative percentage of families (4)	Aggregate contribution[b] (millions) (5)	Percentage of total aggregate contribution (6)	Cumulative percentage of contributions (7)	Cumulative percentage of income of all families (8)
Not positive	7.2	$544	—	100.0	$200	0.1	100.0	—
$1–$9,999	7.4	$143	2.3	99.7	$1,467	0.7	99.9	100.0
$10,000–$19,999	18.2	$359	2.4	90.0	$5,304	2.6	99.2	99.1
$20,000–$29,999	26.8	$667	2.6	76.2	$10,209	5.1	96.5	96.1
$30,000–$39,999	32.9	$1,072	2.9	61.8	$14,159	7.0	91.5	90.9
$40,000–$49,999	36.1	$834	1.8	49.4	$7,739	3.8	84.5	84.7
$50,000–$59,999	43.7	$1,114	2.0	40.7	$9,445	4.7	80.6	79.0
$60,000–$74,999	51.7	$1,579	2.3	32.7	$15,991	7.9	76.0	72.7
$75,000–$99,999	60.6	$1,789	2.0	23.2	$17,668	8.7	68.1	63.3
$100,000–$124,999	71.6	$2,641	2.3	13.9	$14,977	7.4	59.3	51.7
$125,000–$149,999	69.1	$2,386	1.7	8.6	$6,389	3.2	51.9	43.0
$150,000–$199,999	79.1	$4,660	2.7	6.1	$11,431	5.7	48.7	37.9
$200,000–$299,999	82.9	$7,049	2.8	3.8	$12,538	6.2	43.1	32.1
$300,000–$399,999	97.0	$17,539	5.2	2.1	$14,204	7.0	36.8	26.3
$400,000–$499,999	94.2	$23,709	5.4	1.4	$8,135	4.0	29.8	22.4
$500,000–$999,999	85.3	$28,354	3.9	1.0	$19,441	9.6	25.8	20.3
$1,000,000 or more	98.6	$77,999	3.2	0.4	$32,627	16.2	16.2	13.8
All families	39.1	$1,896	2.4		$201,923	100.0		

Source: Calculated by the Center on Wealth and Philanthropy at Boston College based on data from the 2001 *Survey of Consumer Finances* (Board of Governors of the Federal Reserve System 2001).

[a] The term *family* in this table denotes the combination of families plus unrelated individuals living together.

[b] Contributions of less than $500 were imputed based on data from the *General Social Survey* (National Opinion Research Center 2001).

Note: Columns 3, 7, and 8 cumulate from high-income categories to low-income categories.

TABLE 23.5. 2000 CHARITABLE CONTRIBUTIONS BY FAMILY NET WORTH IN 2002 DOLLARS

Family net worth[a]	Percentage of families giving at least $500 (1)	Average family contribution[b] (2)	Average percentage of family income contributed (3)	Cumulative percentage of families (4)	Aggregate contribution[b] (millions) (5)	Percentage of total aggregate contribution (6)	Cumulative percentage of contributions (7)	Cumulative percentage of net worth of all families (8)
Not positive	8.7	$262	1.1	100.0	$2,678	1.3	100.0	—
$1–$9,999	8.3	$237	1.1	90.4	$3,349	1.7	98.7	100.0
$10,000–$19,999	17.0	$439	2.3	77.2	$2,731	1.4	97.0	99.9
$20,000–$29,999	21.4	$542	1.6	71.4	$2,512	1.2	95.7	99.7
$30,000–$39,999	22.7	$650	1.6	67.0	$2,894	1.4	94.4	99.4
$40,000–$49,999	37.4	$683	1.9	62.8	$2,201	1.1	93.0	99.0
$50,000–$59,999	33.9	$668	2.2	59.8	$2,231	1.1	91.9	98.7
$60,000–$74,999	32.3	$736	1.9	56.7	$2,938	1.5	90.8	98.3
$75,000–$99,999	34.6	$1,048	2.6	52.9	$6,553	3.2	89.3	97.6
$100,000–$124,999	43.9	$1,139	2.8	47.0	$6,146	3.0	86.1	96.3
$125,000–$149,999	39.4	$1,477	2.1	42.0	$5,803	2.9	83.0	94.9
$150,000–$199,999	49.8	$1,159	2.4	38.3	$7,335	3.6	80.2	93.6
$200,000–$299,999	53.5	$1,603	3.0	32.3	$14,353	7.1	76.5	91.0
$300,000–$399,999	66.3	$2,356	4.3	23.9	$13,020	6.4	69.4	85.8
$400,000–$499,999	65.3	$1,748	2.6	18.7	$7,204	3.6	63.0	81.2
$500,000–$999,999	73.6	$2,378	3.4	14.9	$19,861	9.8	59.4	76.9
$1,000,000–$4,999,999	82.9	$7,055	3.7	7.0	$43,501	21.5	49.6	63.1
$5,000,000–$9,999,999	95.9	$17,592	4.3	1.2	$15,289	7.6	28.0	35.4
$10,000,000 or more	92.8	$94,966	12.3	0.4	$41,324	20.5	20.5	21.1
All families	39.1	$1,896	2.4		$201,923	100.0		

Source: Calculated by the Center on Wealth and Philanthropy at Boston College based on data from the 2001 *Survey of Consumer Finances* (Board of Governors of the Federal Reserve System 2001).

[a] The term *family* in this table denotes the combination of families plus unrelated individuals living together.

[b] Contributions of less than $500 were imputed based on data from the *General Social Survey* (National Opinion Research Center 2001).

Note: Columns 3, 7, and 8 cumulate from high-net-worth categories to low-net-worth categories.

TABLE 23.6. ESTATES AND CHARITABLE BEQUESTS. FEDERAL ESTATE RETURNS FILED IN 2000 (2002 DOLLARS)

	Gross estate			Estate funds available for distribution		Charitable deduction		Taxes		Heirs and others	
Gross estate category	# Returns (thousands)	Assets (billions)	Net worth[a] (billions)	Fees & surviving spouse (billions)	Net estate available[b] (billions)	Amount (billions)	Percentage of available	Amount (billions)	Percentage of available	Amount (billions)	Percentage of available
.6 M–1M	47.8	$40.3	$39.2	$7.8	$31.4	$0.9	3.0	$1.4	4.3	$29.1	92.7
1 M–2.5 M	45.2	$69.9	$67.6	$21.5	$46.1	$2.7	5.8	$7.3	16.0	$36.1	78.2
2.5 M–5 M	10.0	$35.6	$34.3	$13.1	$21.2	$2.2	10.3	$6.6	30.9	$12.4	58.7
5 M–10 M	3.4	$24.3	$23.3	$8.7	$14.5	$2.1	14.3	$6.0	40.6	$6.6	45.1
10 M–20 M	1.1	$16.0	$15.3	$6.0	$9.3	$1.6	17.1	$4.2	44.3	$3.6	38.6
20 M or more	0.7	$41.0	$39.4	$17.2	$22.2	$7.3	33.2	$8.7	39.1	$6.2	27.8
Total	108.3	$227.2	$219.0	$74.3	$144.7	$16.8	11.6	$34.0	23.5	$93.8	64.9

Source: Calculated by the Center on Wealth and Philanthropy at Boston College based on tabulated data available on the Web site of the Statistics of Income Division of the IRS, www.irs.gov/taxstats/.

[a] The net worth is calculated by subtracting liabilities against the estate from assets.

[b] Net estate available is the net worth of the estate minus estate fees and spousal deduction.

Religious Affiliation

Religious affiliation and attendance at religious services have historically been positively correlated with charitable giving. In 2000 the average contribution of households where the respondent belonged to a religious organization was more than twice that of households where the respondent reported no religious affiliation, and the average amount of income donated was also more than double (Independent Sector 2002b:85). *Giving and Volunteering in the United States* reports that "more respondents in contributing households belong to religious organizations than do those in non-contributing households (68.8% versus 43.1% respectively)" (84). The same pattern holds for frequency of attendance: those who go to church at least once a month give almost twice as many dollars, and almost three times as much as a percentage of income, as those who attend services less frequently (86).

Not only do religiously affiliated households give more to religion, as one would expect, they also give more to secular causes. The 52 percent of households that give to both religious and secular causes give more to secular organizations than do the 28 percent of households that give to secular organizations only, $1,001 versus $651 respectively. In fact, households that give to religion give 88 percent of total charitable contributions (Independent Sector 2002a:11–12). Religious giving is an example of the most prevalent type of giving: what might be called consumption philanthropy—that is, charitable giving that supports causes from which the donors themselves benefit (Schervish 2000:20–21). Furthermore, as a great many churches and houses of worship are also involved in providing social services to members and a wider community, membership in a congregation tends to embed a donor further in the community, increasing the potential number of "communities of participation" in which the donor is involved, and thereby increasing opportunities for charitable giving.

While the Independent Sector's bivariate analysis shows that religiously affiliated households give more to secular causes, recent multivariate analysis by researchers at the University of San Francisco based on data from *Giving and Volunteering in California* (O'Neill and Silverman 2002) has somewhat complicated the picture of how religious affiliation and spirituality relate to charitable giving. The researchers conclude that for Californians "religious affiliation makes no difference with regard to either the rate or level of giving and volunteering to *secular* [emphasis added] agencies" (7). They also find that in regard to *religious* giving and volunteering, it is frequency of attendance at services, rather than simple affiliation that, after income, is the strongest predictor of giving. The researchers summarize their findings as follows: "While the California data confirm the general significance of religious affiliation and activity to charitable behavior, they also make clear that there is no clear and simple connection between the two," since other demographics—income, age, ethnicity, and immigration status—play a role in participation and amount in charitable giving among religiously affiliated households (25).

Volunteer Status

If we consider that the degree to which a donor is involved and engaged in social networks increases charitable giving, it follows that those who volunteer also give more money to charity than those who do not. Volunteer giving is always associated with charitable contributions that are two to four times higher than that of non-volunteers (Independent Sector 2002b). Not only do households where members volunteer give larger dollar amounts to charity, they also have higher participation rates in charitable giving (94 percent versus 82 percent), and contributing households where members volunteer give more than twice the percentage of income to charity (2.5 percent versus 1.2 percent).[9]

Despite research on the substitutability of volunteer time for charitable donations (Duncan 1999), the zero-sum notion of how volunteering and charitable giving interact belies the degree to which either volunteer time or charitable donations can lead to increased contributions of the other. Volunteering and charitable giving bring donors into contact with an organization, give them a better knowledge of the needs of the organization, and make them more likely over time to identify with and support the mission of the organization. Previous donors are more likely to be asked by the nonprofit organization to contribute either time or money. As a volunteer, proximity to the organization allows the donor to see in person just how the organization is utilizing funds, thereby gaining confidence in an organization. *Giving and Volunteering in the United States* reports that in 2000, 67.1 percent of volunteering households agreed that most charitable institutions are honest in their use of donated funds, versus 57.7 percent of non-volunteering households (Independent Sector 2002b:69). However, it is also the case that many interested and strategic donors carefully read annual reports and information on how an organization is using their money to meet social needs, and thus it may be the case that it is giving that leads to greater volunteering, or that giving and volunteering are mutually reinforcing activities.

Age

Charitable giving is found to increase with age up to approximately age sixty-five, at which point there is a drop in the dollar amount of annual charitable giving. *Giving and Volunteering in the U.S.* shows that the average dollar contribution increases from age twenty-one to sixty-four from a minimum of $698 to a maximum average of $1,781 and from a minimum of 1.7 percent of income to 2.8 percent of income per household. After age sixty-five, while the average amount contributed drops to $1,551, the average percentage of income contributed jumps to 4.1 percent (Independent Sector 2002b).

Gender

Are women more generous than men? Are men more generous than women? This question posed to any roomful of people is guaranteed to elicit a wide variety of responses and lively discussion, but what do the data reveal about gender and charitable giving?

The Independent Sector (2002b) finds no significant differences in household participation between male and female respondents but reports higher average charitable contributions by male respondents than female respondents, $1,858 versus $1,594 for contributing households, or $1,617 versus $1,393 for all households. It should be noted that as in the majority of other surveys, the *Giving and Volunteering* survey respondents are answering for the *household,* but the data are frequently interpreted as revealing something about giving patterns by the *gender* of the respondent. Much of the difference reported by the Independent Sector may be due to differences in income, with male respondents reporting significantly higher household income than female respondents ($63,265 versus $51,330). Translating the contributions into a percentage of household income, we find that male and female respondents report very similar levels of household giving, both among all households 2.7 percent versus 2.8 percent of income respectively, as well as among contributing households 3.1 percent of income versus 3.2 percent respectively. As the wage gap between men and women continues to narrow[10] and as business ownership by women continues to increase,[11] we expect in the future that income and wealth disparities between men and women will decrease and the dollar amounts of inter vivos charitable giving equalize. Thus in analyzing the Independent Sector results, "the most definitive thing that one can say . . . is that women say their households give a little less than men say" (Kaplan and Hayes 1993:11).

Reviewing the literature from 1998, Mary Ellen S. Capek (2001:2) summarizes: "much existing research is based on stereotypes about gender that generate the wrong questions and hence the wrong answers. In fact, once other variables such as age, level of income, number of dependents, and health are taken into account, few discernible differences between men and women donors remain. The data reveal, however, that some differences do exist. Women have less wealth than men, earn less, and have to spend more on day-to-day expenses. Yet women do give and give generously."

Recent multivariate analysis by researchers at Indiana University, however, begins to develop a theory of the relation between gender and giving, which implies there may be some substantive differences in giving patterns. The researchers cite sociological and psychological research on gender differences in altruism and empathy, as well as evidence that women are "socialized to conceive of themselves as connected to others and socialized to reflect a strong concern of care to others" (Mesch, Rooney, Chin, and Steinberg 2002:66). Their analysis indicates that there may be differences in the giving patterns of single women as compared with single men: breaking out single males and single females from a sample of 885 Indiana households and performing regression analysis, the researchers find that "after controlling for differences in age, educational attainment, and research methodologies,[12] single females were 14 percent more likely to donate than were single men" and, "after controlling for differences in income, education, and methodologies, single females gave $330 more than single men did" (72).

When it comes to bequests, we find more women making charitable bequests, 60 percent versus only 40 percent of male decedents. Life expectancy rates for women in the United States continue to be higher than men, thus, widows often end up bequeathing the final estate; "the majority of female estate tax decedents were widowed—with no spouse as a potential heir—and therefore more likely to contribute to charity. The majority of male tax decedents were married" (Eller 1997:175). Hence the simple fact of making a charitable bequest cannot reveal whether the gifts from final estates by widowed women represent their personal desire to leave a charitable bequest, their husband's wish to do so, or their joint plan as a couple to leave a bequest to charity.

Marital Status

In the United States the majority of households (60.3 percent) are headed by married couples (Board of Governors of the Federal Reserve System 2001), who have a higher rate of participation in charitable giving than do single, widowed, divorced, and separated households (92.5 percent versus a range of 82.2 percent to 87.5 percent for the other groups), and higher average household contribution ($2,299 versus a range of $887 to $1,246) than the other groups. Many of these differences are partly due to the fact that marriage seems to be an engine of wealth formation. For reasons perhaps to do with more efficient division of labor and costs, the combined net worth of a married couple is 40 percent more than that of two single people and the combined income of a married couple is 35 percent more than two single people. Married households represent 60.3 percent of households, but make 79.1 percent of the income, hold 81.9 percent of wealth, and give 76.2 percent of charitable contributions (Independent Sector 2002b).

Region

Charitable giving is often thought to be a way of redistributing wealth, but if it is true that most giving is local and supports causes that the donor or the donor's family and friends identify with, or benefit from, what effect does the ongoing geographic segregation of the United States both ethnically and socioeconomically have on both the idea and reality of philanthropy as a great equalizer?

Julian Wolpert describes in his research the uneven distribution of nonprofits across the country, with a majority concentrated in metropolitan areas, and numbers growing faster in the suburbs nationwide than in city centers. Wolpert (1996:9) terms this a "dislocation effect," creating an enormous fundraising burden on inner-city charities serving low-income constituents, while suburban dollars are creating nonprofits locally to meet a more affluent community's needs.

In regions around the country, a great deal of research has been sponsored by community foundations, local associations of grant makers, and other consortia of nonprofits. However, again it is difficult to truly say whether one area of the country is more or less generous than another, since due to differences in survey design and methodology, cross-comparisons between regions are almost impossible, and the vast majority of the studies lack the rigor to make their data reliable. Researchers who conducted the *Giving and Volunteering in California* study have acknowledged that the significantly higher rates of giving and participation in giving in California reported in the study, as compared with the national trends reported by the Independent Sector, might have less to do with Californian generosity and more to do with study design (O'Neill and Roberts 2000:3).

Employment Status

It would seem clear that due to higher income and financial security, employment would correlate strongly with giving. This is indeed the case for participation rates and for the amount contributed, but not for the percentage of income contributed. The percentage of households contributing to charity is higher if the respondent is employed than if the respondent is unemployed (90 percent versus 86 percent respectively) and, in terms of donation amounts, employed households donate 17 percent more than unemployed households ($1,558 versus $1,336 respectively). However, as a percentage of household income, unemployed households contribute more than employed households (3.2 percent versus 2.5 percent respectively) (Independent Sector 2002b:133–134).

Two explanations for the difference in percentage income seem plausible. First, unemployed households have lower household income and if their charitable contributions do not decline proportionately, their percentage of income contributed will be higher than it was when the respondent was employed. Second, the Independent Sector includes retirees as unemployed respondents. Data from the 2001 SCF show that the retirement status of the head of household is highly correlated with both larger dollar amounts contributed to charity and larger percentage of income contributed. According to the SCF, retiree-headed households make 16 percent of total income, hold 31.4 percent of the net worth, but make charitable contributions that are more than one and a half times larger than those made by households where no one is retired (Board of Governors of the Federal Reserve System 2001).

Periods of unemployment negatively impact giving, not just because of loss of income and the drawing down of savings, but, as economist Arthur Brooks's research shows, because welfare payments tend to depress giving. Brooks (2002:12) finds that a 10 percent increase in welfare payments is correlated with an average drop of 1.4 percent in charitable giving. He emphasizes that while the impact on levels of funding is low, the findings have public policy implications in terms of the impact on civic participation.

Educational Attainment

Even without a specific curriculum on philanthropy, education increases participation in charitable giving, as well as the average contribution, and average percent of income contributed. Sixty-eight percent of households gave to charity where the respondent had less than a high school education, compared to 86 percent of households with a high school diploma, and 95 percent of households where the respondent was a college graduate (Independent Sector 2002b:134–135). Even controlling for income, education has "an independent, positive effect on how much a person gives to charitable causes" (Brown 1999:218). Income among households where the respondent was a college graduate is more than two and a half times greater than that of households where the respondent had not graduated from high school ($80,551 versus $28,870 respectively), but charitable contributions were four and a half times higher ($2,432 versus $541 respectively) (Independent Sector 2002b:134–135). Brown and Ferris (2002:13–14) suggest that education is "a socializing influence as well as an occasion for making contacts. Education lowers the costs of identifying specific avenues of participation and, perhaps through increased efficacy, increases the benefits of engagement."

Ethnicity

There are methodological difficulties in measuring charitable giving by ethnic group. The lack of large enough sample sizes, of culturally sensitive survey methodologies, and of multivariate analysis on the interactions of ethnicity with factors such as income, wealth, communities of participation, and so on are insufficiencies that all have a tendency to cloud findings on the philanthropic practices of various ethnic groups. The Independent Sector's (2002b) *Giving and Volunteering* for 2001 finds that whites were more likely to contribute to charity (90.3 percent) compared to blacks (80.6 percent), Hispanics (85.2 percent), and other racial/ethnic groups (77.6 percent), with some significant differences also reported in the amounts contributed (127). For example, when averaged over all households, whites had contributions that were one and a half times larger than those of Hispanics, and despite differences in income, with white households having incomes 27 percent higher than Hispanic households, Hispanic households contributed significantly less to charity as a percentage of income, 1.9 percent versus 2.9 percent for whites.

If formal philanthropy is something that whites are involved in more than members of other ethnicities, what are the implications of these findings for nonprofits in a country where in the coming decades, whites will increasingly constitute a minority of the population in many cities and states across the country? The impact on nonprofits can be reduced if they manage to suitably engage donors of diverse cultures. The Independent Sector considers the "power of the ask" as one of the strongest motivators of charitable giving. Quite simply, people give because they are asked to do so. In the 1997 *National Survey on Philanthropy (*Institute for Social Inquiry and Roper Center for National Commission on Philanthropy and Civic Renewal 1997), 67 percent of Hispanic households and 68 percent of black households said that the biggest reason they had not volunteered or made a charitable contribution was that they were not asked to do so. Only 44 percent of white households said not being asked had been an obstacle to participation. Given that housing is increasingly segregated socioeconomically and that black households, for example, tend to have on average only one-fifth to one-quarter of the wealth of white households (Altonji, Dorazelski, and Segal 2000:1), it is not surprising that direct mail campaigns or telephone fundraisers, which tend to target affluent areas, fail to engage ethnically diverse donors.

Giving and Volunteering in California is a useful touchstone regarding the relative generosity of different ethnic groups since in its design and methodology it included a special effort to assess the relation between race/ethnicity and charitable behavior for Black/African American, Latino/Hispanic, Asian/Pacific Islander, and White/Caucasian households. The survey contained a module on informal giving and volunteering, which the authors, based on prior research, believed might be "particularly important in some demographic groups, e.g. immigrant, minority, and low-income people" (O'Neill and Roberts 2000:6). Looking at informal giving to individuals as a percentage of income, *Giving and Volunteering in California* found, for example, that Latino/Hispanic households were giving nearly twice as much informally as a percentage of income than were white households (4.0 percent versus 1.9 percent respectively). Moreover, when informal and formal giving were combined, multivariate analysis revealed that "when the effects of income, education, and immigration status are statistically taken into account, differences in charitable behavior among whites, Latinos, Asian/Pacific Islanders, and African Americans virtually disappear" (56).

Obstacles to the engagement of donors from different socioeconomic and cultural backgrounds take on even more importance when we consider that more than one in ten Americans is foreign-born, presenting an additional challenge to nonprofit organizations that would seek to engage them.

Immigrant/Citizenship Status

One of the first things that Americans tend to claim about philanthropy is that it is a uniquely American phenomenon, though there is little evidence to compare helping behavior across cultures. Nonetheless, it is the case that families with at least one member born in the United States contribute approximately twice as much to charity as do families composed entirely of immigrants. The Independent Sector reports that among households where the respondent was born in the United States, the average charitable contribution was 59 percent greater ($1,529 versus $898 respectively) than among immigrant households. Participation rates are slightly higher where the respondent is U.S.-born: 88.9 percent versus 79.6 percent of households where the respondent was not U.S.-born. Differences in charitable contributions cannot be explained by income alone, since income was only 9 percent greater among households where the respondent had been born in the United States ($56,191 versus $51,476 respectively). Research has shown time and again that charitable giving is connected to a donor's involvement in various social networks, to opportunities for participation, and to identifying with a cause (Schervish and Havens 1997; Havens and Schervish 2002; Putnam 2000; Brown and Ferris 2002). The fact that immigrant households do not give as much to charitable causes as U.S. citizens may have to do with: first, a lack of connection between immigrants, especially new immigrants, and American society; second, immigrants' origins in societies, such as Europe, where higher taxes provide many social services that philanthropy supports in the United States; or third, immigrants leaving societies where gifts are typically made to others directly, rather than through charitable organizations.

Of course, differences in reported giving may be artifacts of survey methodology: small proportions of immigrant households in survey samples, lack of emphasis on informal giving, and language and conceptual barriers in the survey process. Certainly one significant aspect of immigrant giving that is rarely specified in surveys is immigrant remittances, typically informal gifts of money and goods to relatives, friends, and other needy individuals in the donor's country of origin.[13] Though not comprehensive, estimates of remittances are extremely high for certain immigrant groups, up to 10 percent of immigrants' household income in some cases (de la Garza 1999:58). The Multilateral Investment Fund estimates that Latin American and Caribbean (LAC) immigrants to the United States remit $250 between eight and ten times a year, reaching an estimated $20 billion in 2000 (Multilateral Investment Fund of the Inter-American Development Bank 2001:6). The Bank of Mexico reports that Mexican emigrants remit as much as 1.5 percent of Mexican GDP annually (Rapoport and Docquier 2006). Although only one in six households surveyed by *Giving and Volunteering in California* made such direct transfers abroad, the actual dollar amounts as a mean for the group ($1,276) were more than the mean contributed to charitable organizations averaged across all households ($1,235) (O'Neill and Roberts 2000:5,7).

Though, as we noted above, there are ongoing differences in giving behaviors among ethnic groups, there is also some evidence to support the theory that the longer immigrants remain in the United States, the more cultural norms they adopt, including formal philanthropy. A multivariate regression analysis using data from the Latino National Political Survey and Independent Sector finds that "after controlling for nativity, income, and education, as well as how confident an individual is in an organization, there are no statistically significant differences between Mexican Americans and Anglos . . . [in terms of] rates of giving and volunteering" (de la Garza 1999:64). De la Garza concludes therefore that these behaviors are learned in one generation. Using the Panel Study of Income Dynamics, Osili and Du (2005) also find that immigrant status has an insignificant impact on the incidence and levels of charitable giving once controls for permanent income are introduced, suggesting that immigrants adapt rapidly to U.S. charitable institutions over time. However, results on private transfers present a striking contrast: immigrant households are significantly more likely to participate in informal giving to non-household members, compared to similar natives.

Currently, the foreign-born represent 28.4 million, or 10 percent, of the total U.S. population and have doubled in number since 1970. Among those born outside the United States, 14.5 million hail from Latin America, 7.2 million from Asia, and 4.4 million from Europe (Census Bureau 2002). Given that immigration to the United States will certainly continue in the future, more research is needed on how to involve immigrants in philanthropy in the United States, or on how to increase U.S. international philanthropy so that acculturation and increased ties to one's local community in the United States need not necessarily imply the abandonment of social, economic, and human development in those countries from which the United States draws much of its labor and markets in a global economy.

Inherited and Earned Wealth

We have learned that wealth is a strong correlate of charitable giving, and that the multi-trillion dollar wealth transfer that will take place over the next fifty-five years will make wealthy heirs of some of the baby boomers' children. While much interest is currently focused on how the legacy of the boomers will be divided between heirs, taxes, and charity, an equally pertinent question is, what portion of their inheritance will the heirs of the boomers give to charity? Are donors more generous when the source of their wealth is inherited, or when it is earned?

The *Survey of Consumer Finances* gathers data on whether a household has ever received an inheritance. The data reveal some interesting patterns. First, only about 20 percent of households report having received an inheritance, and these recipients are concentrated among households with high income and wealth. The 7 percent of households with a net worth of $1 million or more are more than twice as likely to have received an inheritance as households below $1 million, and the same pattern holds true for income. Households that have received an inheritance[14] give more to charity than households that have never received an inheritance: the mean charitable contribution of households that have received an inheritance is almost double that of households which have not received an inheritance ($3,003 versus $1,656 respectively) (Board of Governors of the Federal Reserve System 2001). But this is due in no small part to higher income and wealth among inheritors: the average income of inheritors is over 40 percent more than non-inheritors ($93,833 versus $65,059); the net worth of households that received an inheritance is almost two and a half times that of non-inheritors ($791,022 versus $317,791). Inherited wealth is currently significant for less than one-tenth of wealthy households. However, with the overwhelming majority of millionaire households (93 percent) having earned most of their net worth through their own skills and efforts during their lifetime (including investments),[15] it is important to note that even a small inheritance can provide the seed capital for a business, or graduate education, the cornerstones of wealth formation.

What happens when we compare a dollar of earned wealth to a dollar of inherited wealth? Is it true that money is money in terms of charitable giving? One research finding suggests that donors have a greater propensity—up to six times greater—to give from earned wealth than from inherited wealth, with the average person giving $4.56 to charity each year for every $1,000 of non-inherited wealth, but only $0.76 out of inherited wealth (Avery 1994:29). Preliminary results from researchers at Indiana University and Pomona College tentatively confirm that non-inherited wealth has a substantially positive effect on charitable giving "that is larger than that of inherited wealth, earned income, or transfer income" (Steinberg, Wilhelm, Rooney, and Brown 2002:14). Ongoing research on how donors spend differently the dollars they earn through salary, investment, inheritance, windfalls, and so on has the potential to shed light on the psychological aspects of another key correlate of giving: financial security.

Financial Security

We are all familiar with stories of Americans, who, having lived through the Depression and led lives of extreme frugality, indeed ascetism, surprise everyone, especially the charitable beneficiaries of their estates, by leaving vast bequests from nest eggs that they accumulated virtually untouched over a lifetime. Clearly the experience of living through the Depression greatly impacted a generation's sense of the amount of income and wealth necessary to feel financially secure. Though today we live in much more fortunate times, preliminary research shows an intense human anxiety concerning personal financial security or economic self-confidence at all levels of income and net worth that substantially impacts charitable giving.

The Independent Sector's *Giving and Volunteering in the United States* asks respondents whether they are worried about having enough money for the future. In 2001, the majority of contributing households (57.5 percent) reported being worried about their financial future and gave a little more than half the amount to charitable causes as did the 42.5 percent of contributing households who said they were not worried about their financial security ($1,255 versus $2,306 respectively).

While a sense of security about one's financial future increases monotonically with income, age, and education (Independent Sector 2002b:64), other exploratory research has revealed that even at very high levels of net worth ($5 million or more) and income, insecurity around finances continues to have a strong psychological hold. Although 98 percent of the pentamillionaires who responded to a study conducted jointly by the Center on Wealth and Philanthropy at Boston College and Deutsche Bank Private Banking placed themselves above the midpoint on a scale from zero to ten (from not at all secure to extremely secure), only a relatively low 36 percent felt completely financially secure.

The median amount needed for financial security was $20 million (or 67 percent) more than their current wealth. Even respondents who rated themselves as a relatively high eight or nine on the scale indicated that they would require an average additional 60 percent of their current net worth in order to feel completely financially secure, and respondents who rated themselves lower than eight on the scale indicated they would require an average increase of 285 percent in their net worth to feel completely secure. Table 23.7 summarizes the results: the more financially secure a respondent feels, the more is given to charity, not just in absolute amounts but also as a percentage of income and net worth. Despite the small sample size, the findings are striking enough, especially in the context of *Giving and Volunteering in the United States,* to warrant further investigation.

How can fundraisers and nonprofits work with donors on this issue of perceived financial security so as to increase charitable giving? According to Thomas B. Murphy (2001) one way to have this happen is for wealth holders to clarify their expected stream of resources and their expected stream of expenditures for self, family, investments, and other purposes. The extent of positive difference between the stream of resources and the stream of desired expenditures quantifies the level of financial security and the stream of discretionary resources available for philanthropy. The extent to which this positive difference "is perceived as permanent strengthens the case for allocating some of the resources for philanthropy. The extent to which the difference is positive, permanent, and growing in magnitude enhances the philanthropic allocation" (35).

Wealth holder Claude Rosenberg of the New Tithing Group has sought to develop a formula for giving that donors can use to determine that third stream of financial resources, one which is conservative enough to ensure that the donor feels secure. Rosenberg (1994:7) saw the need for such a formula when he recognized that he himself was "virtually flying blind with [my] finances." While tables 23.4 and 23.5 above outline the amount and percentage of income contributed by various income and net worth categories, and Rosenberg's formula implies a strictly scientific approach to financial security, no quota or "one-size-fits-all" approach is likely to create a confident giver. Rather, the data on financial security suggest the benefits of donor and fundraiser working jointly with a financial planner to go through the reckoning needed to establish the amount and timing of charitable giving in the context of a larger financial biography.

TO WHAT?

The distribution of charitable giving among different types of nonprofit organizations provides an insight into the priorities and cultural imperatives of our society. By this criterion religious organizations are held in high social esteem since the greatest percentage of individual giving goes to religion. Among the wealthy, education is the number-one giving priority. In this section we will report on total giving by recipient organization, and review patterns in both inter vivos giving and bequest giving, including both formal and informal giving and their interrelationship. Given the disproportion-

TABLE 23.7. CHARITABLE GIVING BY NET WORTH AND FINANCIAL SECURITY

Panel A. Net worth of $15 million or less

	Less than 8/10 financial security[a]	8/10 or 9/10 financial security	Complete (10/10) financial security	All levels of financial security
Mean charitable contribution	$36,000	$77,389	$414,521	$130,908
Mean % income contributed	5.0	6.6	23.4	9.5
Mean % net worth contributed	0.4	0.5	3.0	1.0

Panel B. Net worth of more than $15 million

	Less than 8/10 financial security[a]	8/10 or 9/10 financial security	Complete (10/10) financial security	All levels of financial security
Mean charitable contribution	$255,961	$1,170,621	$4,236,437	$2,505,077
Mean % income contributed	7.6	19.2	51.0	32.9
Mean % net worth contributed	0.7	2.0	3.9	2.8

Panel C. All levels of net worth

	Less than 8/10 financial security[a]	8/10 or 9/10 financial security	Complete (10/10) financial security	All levels of financial security
Mean charitable contribution	$65,996	$676,904	$2,913,466	$1,242,861
Mean % income contributed	5.4	13.5	41.5	20.4
Mean % net worth contributed	0.5	1.3	3.6	1.8

Source: Calculated by the Center on Wealth and Philanthropy at Boston College based on data from the Deutsche Bank *Wealth with Responsibility Study/2000* (Havens and Schervish 2000). This table reprinted from Munnell and Sunden 2003:145.

[a] Respondents were asked to rate their sense of financial security on a scale of 0–10, from completely insecure to completely secure.

ate percentage of charitable dollars contributed by a small number of wealthy households, we will also focus on recipients of giving by the wealthy, which differs somewhat from the general population.

Recipients of Inter Vivos and Bequest Giving

According to *Giving USA (*AAFRC Trust for Philanthropy 2002), religion receives the greatest percentage of total charitable giving. This represents giving from all sources, including individuals, bequests, corporations, and foundations; however, since individual giving constitutes the vast majority of contributions, the proportions reported by *Giving USA* generally reflect individual giving. As shown in figure 23.2, the largest amount of giving goes to religion, 38.2 percent, or $82.3 billion, of total contributions; with the second largest category, education, receiving 15.0 percent, or $32.3 billion, of total giving; followed by gifts to foundations and unallocated gifts 12.1 percent; human services 9.8 percent; health 8.7 percent; arts, culture, and humanities 5.7 percent; public-society benefit 5.6 percent; environment 3.0 percent; and international affairs 2.0 percent. Independent Sector (2002b) data on the distribution of household giving (the percentage of households giving to an organization type rather than the percentage of total giving by organization type) confirm these general trends: in 2001, 53.3 percent of total contributions went to religion, 10.1 percent to education, 7.8 percent to human services, 5.9 percent to youth development, 5.8 percent to health, with the remaining split among other types of charitable organization.

The data on the beneficiaries of charitable bequests from the estates of wealthy decedents reveal a quite different pattern. Based on data from estate filings of the wealthy decedents, only 11 percent of bequests are made to religion, with 30.6 percent of bequests going to public-society benefit, 18.7 percent to educational institutions, and 10.4 percent to health, and the remaining to other types of charitable causes (AAFRC Trust for Philanthropy 2002:75, citing Joulfaian 2002).

Individual Recipients of Giving

Formal philanthropy, giving to nonprofit organizations, is only one aspect of care that individuals provide to others. Informal philanthropy, giving directly to other individuals, constitutes a large secondary component of care. There is a great deal of truth to the old adage that charity begins at home, and that the care that people provide directly to indi-

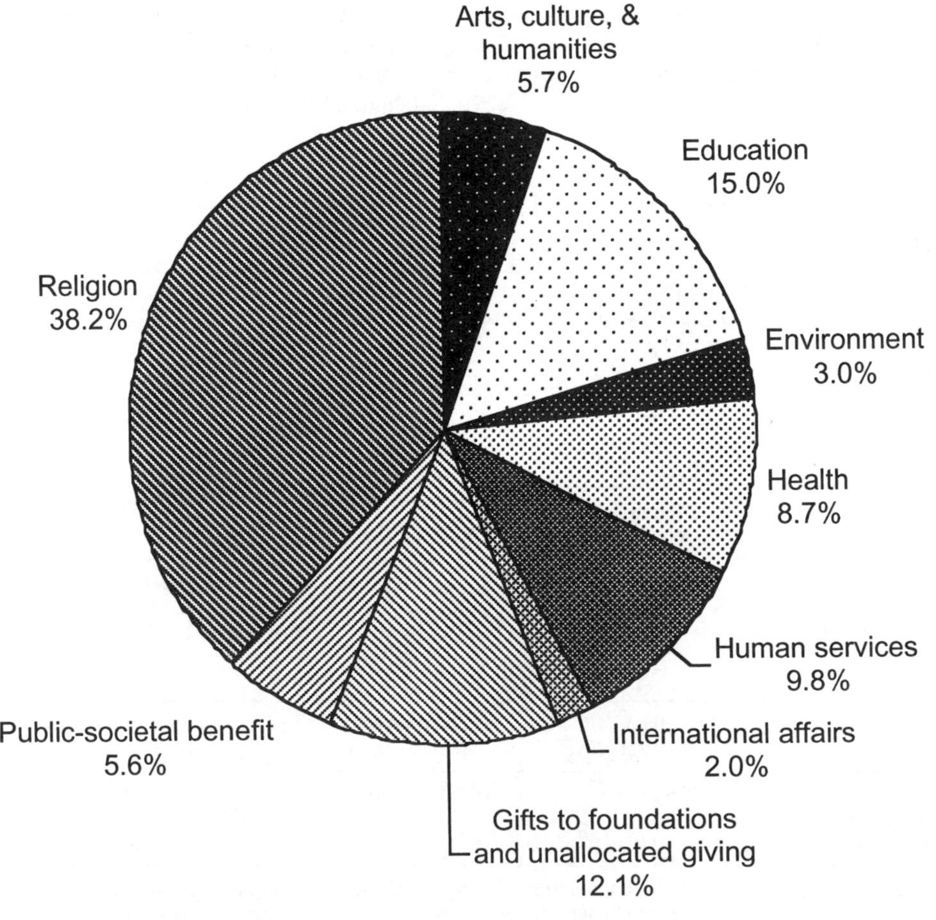

FIGURE 23.2. TOTAL GIVING BY ORGANIZATION TYPE
Source: AAFRC Trust for Philanthropy 2002.

TABLE 23.8. 1997 CHARITABLE CONTRIBUTIONS AND TRANSFERS TO RELATIVES AND FRIENDS BY FAMILY INCOME (2002 DOLLARS)

Family income	Number of families	Percentage of families	Charitable contributions[a] averaged over all families	Transfers to relatives and friends averaged over all families	Charitable contributions[a] averaged over contributing families	Transfers to relatives and friends averaged over gifting families
Negative	1,339,813	1.3	$379	$420	$3,245	$3,708
$1–$9,999	11,936,824	11.6	$92	$65	$1,270	$1,921
$10,000–$19,999	16,829,531	16.4	$208	$185	$1,418	$2,291
$20,000–$29,999	15,903,313	15.5	$449	$321	$1,865	$2,366
$30,000–$39,999	12,911,943	12.6	$476	$360	$1,641	$3,172
$40,000–$49,999	9,369,095	9.1	$926	$545	$2,387	$4,310
$50,000–$59,999	8,574,005	8.4	$1,093	$572	$2,344	$4,139
$60,000–$74,999	9,270,570	9.0	$1,493	$954	$2,583	$7,101
$75,000–$99,999	7,806,849	7.6	$1,727	$1,303	$2,852	$9,288
$100,000–$124,999	3,296,579	3.2	$2,507	$1,558	$3,542	$9,257
$125,000–$149,999	1,273,740	1.2	$3,240	$2,249	$4,281	$9,164
$150,000–$199,999	1,642,334	1.6	$4,588	$2,910	$5,624	$18,482
$200,000–$299,999	1,131,882	1.1	$7,957	$4,693	$9,625	$27,173
$300,000–$399,999	433,042	0.4	$10,383	$3,952	$11,931	$19,514
$400,000–$499,999	274,971	0.3	$8,914	$4,109	$11,562	$14,596
$500,000–$999,999	327,098	0.3	$22,788	$6,461	$25,279	$29,239
$1,000,000 or more	227,253	0.2	$72,454	$17,519	$76,833	$62,708
Total	102,548,843	100.0	$1,204	$686	$3,485	$5,916

Source: Calculated by the Center on Wealth and Philanthropy at Boston College based on data from the 1998 *Survey of Consumer Finances* (Board of Governors of the Federal Reserve System 1998).

[a] Contributions of less than $500 are counted as zero.

viduals is, from their viewpoint, inseparable from the care that they provide through nonprofits to alleviate needs. Many of the same patterns that hold for formal giving are reiterated in informal giving. As tables 23.8 and 23.9 show, as wealth and income increase, the value of charitable contributions averaged over all households and the value of transfers to relatives and friends, similarly averaged over all households, also increases.

There is a good deal of variation in estimates of informal giving from different data sources. Data from the *Center on Philanthropy Panel Study* module in the *Panel Study of Income Dynamics* (COPPS/PSID) (Survey Research Center 2001) indicate that informal giving (defined by the survey simply as money given directly to others) represents $58.4 billion, while the SCF (Board of Governors of the Federal Reserve System 2001) finds informal giving (defined by the survey as financial support to others outside the household) topping $102 billion. According to the SCF, fewer households make interpersonal transfers than contribute to charity, but their average transfer is substantially larger than the average contribution of households that give to charity. Twelve million households reported making interpersonal transfers in 1997 with an average annual transfer of $6,007 per gifting household. During the same period 35 million households reported making a charitable contribution of at least $500, with an average annual gift of $3,539 per contributing household. Children were the most frequent recipients of gifts (48 percent), followed by parents (26 percent), and then by siblings (19 percent) (Board of Governors of the Federal Reserve System 1998).

Table 23.10 summarizes findings on informal giving from a number of surveys. The data reflect our methodological conclusions from the first section: studies that have included a stronger focus and more detailed questions on informal giving have generally found higher participation rates and amounts of informal giving. *Giving and Volunteering in the United States* asks two questions on informal giving and finds that 52 percent of households made informal contributions and that the average contribution was $1,130 (Independent Sector 2002b:35). This amount is quite substantial given that the average contribution to charitable organizations was $1,479. In other words, transfers to individuals were almost two-thirds as large as contributions to charity. *Giving and Volunteering in California* (O'Neill and Roberts 2000) also included a specific focus on informal giving and found that 57 percent of households gave money and goods to individuals outside the immediate family, including homeless persons, needy neighbors, friends and relatives, and struggling individuals outside the United States. The mean contribution was $636 across all households and $1,109 among contributing households, relative to $1,235 mean giving to charitable organizations across all households or $1,374 among contributing households. The Boston Area Diary Study (BADS), which interviewed respondents weekly for more than a year about all the money, goods, time, and skills donated, not just to charitable organizations but also directly to other people, found almost universal participation in giving to others (98 percent of households). Table 23.11 summarizes the annual contributions of money and goods reported by participants in BADS. On average respondents gave $9,183, or 7.4 percent, of family income to others directly, versus $1,759, or 2.2 percent, of family income through organizations. Thus, the amount of money devoted to caring directly was more than five times the cor-

TABLE 23.9. 1997 CHARITABLE CONTRIBUTIONS AND TRANSFERS TO RELATIVES AND FRIENDS BY FAMILY NET WORTH (2002 DOLLARS)

Family net worth	Number of families	Percentage of families	Charitable contributions[a] averaged over all families	Transfers to relatives and friends averaged over all families	Charitable contributions[a] averaged over contributing families	Transfers to relatives and friends averaged over gifting families
Negative	8,076,719	7.9	$261	$192	$1,835	$1,989
$0	2,669,138	2.6	$0	$33	$0	$1,007
$1–$9,999	15,096,872	14.7	$162	$148	$1,682	$1,666
$10,000–$19,999	6,121,852	6.0	$312	$405	$2,411	$3,612
$20,000–$29,999	5,352,651	5.2	$275	$431	$1,562	$3,140
$30,000–$39,999	3,882,414	3.8	$454	$317	$1,911	$2,892
$40,000–$49,999	3,338,656	3.3	$467	$348	$1,463	$3,631
$50,000–$59,999	3,123,843	3.1	$482	$406	$1,681	$4,020
$60,000–$74,999	4,574,088	4.5	$546	$254	$1,785	$2,320
$75,000–$99,999	7,393,811	7.2	$722	$244	$2,126	$2,366
$100,000–$124,999	5,815,093	5.7	$792	$785	$1,788	$4,819
$125,000–$149,999	4,027,848	3.9	$858	$645	$2,178	$5,730
$150,000–$199,999	6,979,877	6.8	$942	$277	$2,098	$3,747
$200,000–$299,999	7,942,895	7.8	$1,155	$572	$2,219	$4,317
$300,000–$399,999	5,110,244	5.0	$2,100	$843	$3,108	$7,550
$400,000–$499,999	3,066,877	3.0	$1,703	$1,633	$2,791	$10,246
$500,000–$999,999	5,370,002	5.2	$2,395	$1,256	$3,497	$8,358
$1,000,000–$4,999,999	3,916,854	3.8	$5,954	$4,723	$7,177	$20,924
$5,000,000–$9,999,999	479,300	0.5	$16,623	$5,717	$18,247	$24,852
$10,000,000 or more	212,809	0.2	$89,545	$19,003	$91,688	$44,789
Total	102,548,843	100.0	$1,204	$686	$3,485	$5,916

Source: Calculated by the Center on Wealth and Philanthropy at Boston College based on data from the 1998 *Survey of Consumer Finances* (Board of Governors of the Federal Reserve System 1998).

[a] Contributions of less than $500 are counted as zero.

responding amounts devoted to indirect caring for others through charitable organizations and causes (Schervish and Havens 2002; Havens and Schervish 2001). The BADS findings suggest that informal giving is prominent among the population in general, and reinforces the notion that the care provided to friends, family members, and others in need can be extended beyond this narrow circle if nonprofits can succeed in increasing the "familiarity" of the donor-beneficiary relationship

Recipients of Philanthropy by the Wealthy

A small number of U.S. households disproportionately shape philanthropy, with 7 percent of households donating 50 percent of charitable dollars in the year 2000. Stereotypes of wealthy philanthropists as being driven by a desire to endow buildings and capital projects are belied by leadership on the part of younger donors in funding experimentation and innovation. For example, billionaire Bill Gates's 2003 donation of $51 million to the New York Public Schools goes to support innovative models that reduce school size, thereby increasing attendance and standards. As hyper-agents, wealth holders shape our society by their choices of which needs get priority, and how social problems are solved. In this section we will review data concerning giving by wealthy households. The data sources include the SCF (Board of Governors of the Federal Reserve System 2001), with its over-sample of wealthy households, and surveys published by U.S. Trust, Deutsche Bank Private Banking, Fidelity, HNW Digital, and the Spectrem Group.

Figure 23.3 compares patterns of giving by the wealthy with those of the total population. As indicated in the figure, giving to religion is not as high a priority among the wealthy as among all households. As a percentage of giving, the wealthy contribute about 29.5 percent to religious causes and congregations versus 45.8 percent of giving nationally. However, the wealthy do give more than twice as much to education, human services, and arts and cultural organizations as does the general population.

Numerous other studies about the wealthy confirm that education is the number-one priority in their charitable giving. In a study that asked wealth holders about the policy issues they would like to influence, the highest-ranking policy area was improvement of education (mentioned by 60 percent of respondents), followed by policies to do with poverty, inequality, hunger, affordable housing, health care for the uninsured (49 percent), and arts and culture (33 percent) (Havens and Schervish 2000). The Spectrem Group's (2002) report, *Charitable Giving and the Ultra-High-Net-Worth: Reaching the Wealthy Donor,* found that the greatest amount of charitable donations in the previous three years went to education: $120,600,[16] or almost three times the amount that went to religion, more than six times the amount that went to hospitals, health care, and curative causes, and more than eight times the amount that went to social service organizations (7).

TABLE 23.10. INFORMAL GIVING COMPARED TO FORMAL GIVING FROM A VARIETY OF DATA SOURCES (2002 DOLLARS)

	Panel Study of Income Dynamics[a] (Survey Research Center 2001)	Survey of Consumer Finances (National Opinion Research Center 2001)	Giving and volunteering in the U.S. (Independent Sector 2001)	Giving and volunteering in California (O'Neill and Roberts 2000)	Indiana Gives 2000 IU Area-Method	Indiana Gives 2000 IU Method-Area	Boston Area Diary Study
Definition of informal giving	Money	Financial support	Money, property, or the cash equivalent of property	Money or goods	—	—	Money and goods
Informal giving participation rate	10%	12.70%	51.60%	57%	71.40%	69.40%	98%
Formal giving participation rate	67.8%[a]	39.10%[b]	89%	89.90%	97.60%	93.50%	100%
Average informal contribution	$540.12	$957.58	$1,081	$641.78	$1,484.77	$524.80	$9,137
Average formal contribution	$1,445	$1,896[c]	$1,415	$1,904.22	$1,578.71	$2,522.49	$1,750
Average percent of income contributed as informal giving	Less than 1%	1.80%	2.40%	1%	N/A	N/A	7.40%
Average percent of income contributed as formal giving	2.50%	2.40%	2.70%	3%	N/A	N/A	2.20%

Source: Compiled by the Center on Wealth and Philanthropy at Boston College, 2002.

[a] The *Panel Study of Income Dynamics* asks respondents only about charitable contributions in excess of $25.

[b] This rate is the percentage of households with charitable contributions of $500 or more, since the *Survey of Consumer Finances* only asks about contributions of $500 or more.

[c] Charitable contributions less than $500 in the *Survey of Consumer Finances* imputed from the *General Social Survey.*

TABLE 23.11. BOSTON AREA DIARY STUDY: AVERAGE ANNUAL CONTRIBUTIONS OF MONEY AND GOODS (2002 DOLLARS)

Category of organization or person	Participation rate	Average annual contribution	Contributions as percentage of income
All organizations	100%	$1,759	2.20
Religious	75%	$875	1.30
Non-religious	95%	$885	0.90
All interpersonal	98%	$9,183	7.40
Recipient is relative	93%	$8,372	6.10
Adult child/grandchild	50%	$5,706	3.80
Parent	52%	$347	0.60
Other relative	93%	$2,318	1.60
Recipient is non-relative	98%	$811	1.30
Total money and goods	100%	$10,942	9.60

Source: Calculated at the Center on Wealth and Philanthropy at Boston College based on data from the Boston Area Diary Study (Havens and Schervish 2001).

That the wealthy place so much emphasis on education is due in part to the increasing trend in philanthropy toward donor interest in tackling the root cause of social problems rather than ameliorating them. In almost all cases, wealth holders have derived a great deal of their wealth from their education, and they identify strongly both with their alma mater and with the notion that equality of education is one of the main ways of reducing inequality in a society (Havens and Schervish 2001). As we will discuss in the next section, the high-tech boom of the 1990s created a great deal of wealth, especially among younger donors, whose entrepreneurial, investment orientation shaped the timing and form of their charitable giving.

AND HOW?

Perhaps the greatest change that has taken place in philanthropy over the past decade is how business and investment practices have reshaped philanthropy through the creation of vehicles of giving that meet the personal financial needs of donors, especially affluent donors, as well as societal needs. The involvement of financial planners in philanthropy as partners with the donors in a more holistic view of their financial portfolios is in part the result of donor demand for a more strategic than reactive philanthropy. In this section, we review growth in the inter vivos giving to intermediary organizations, such as family and private foundations,[17] as well as to such other vehicles as donor-advised funds,[18] charitable gift annuities,[19] and charitable trusts.[20]

At the current time, only a small percentage of the general population has made planned gifts other than a bequest. There are a dearth of data around participation rates in planned giving, but, as an example of how few planned givers there currently are, the National Committee of Planned Giving (2001:6) estimates that only 2 percent of the population have established a charitable remainder trust. Due to the cost of setting up many of these planned giving vehicles, ranging from $10,000 for a donor-advised fund to $500,000 for a family or private foundation, it seems likely that the one in fifty planned givers is a wealth holder. This is confirmed by the findings of *Wealth with Responsibility Study / 2000* (Havens and Schervish 2000), which found substantial participation in planned giving among respondents worth $1 million or more, with 67 percent of respondents making contributions to trusts, gift funds, and foundations, averaging $844,017 per household or 63 percent of total charitable contributions.

The growth in wealth over the past twenty years has been matched by a growth in the size and number of family and private foundations that, in 1998, represented nearly two-fifths of U.S. foundations, numbering 18,300 and holding $170.6 billion in assets. The Foundation Center and National Center for Family Philanthropy (2001:2) reports that two-thirds of larger family foundations were formed in the 1980s and 1990s, and the largest share of them were founded in the western part of the United States (Foundation Center 2002b:1), suggesting that many recent foundations are the fruit of entrepreneurial and investment wealth accrued during the high-tech boom of the late1990s. As is the pattern with individual giving, foundation giving is highly skewed toward the upper end of net worth, with the top 1 percent of foundations providing half of the $7.9 billion dollars (in 2002 dollars) given in 1998 (Foundation Center and National Center for Family Philanthropy 2001:1–2). Despite the recent downturn in the economy, the Foundation Center (2002a:3) reports that while new gifts into foundations slipped from $34.7 billion in 1999 to $28.8 billion in 2000 (both amounts in 2002 dollars), they helped to offset market losses and boost giving in 2001. Another subset of individual giving vehicles, private foundations, also showed rapid growth in the 1990s, growing between 1992 and 1998 by about 5 percent annually, and increasing 33.6 percent in number over the period from 42,000 to 57,000 organizations, which represent $438 billion in assets and $23 billion in charitable contributions in 1998 (Whitten 2002).

Private and family foundations represent quite a substantial investment on the part of the donor in terms of time and money, not just in setup and annual maintenance costs, but also due to the annual 5 percent payout regulation. In the 1990s, Fidelity Investments led the way in creating a vehicle that offers many of the advantages of a family foundation, but at a much lower financial threshold, leading some to re-

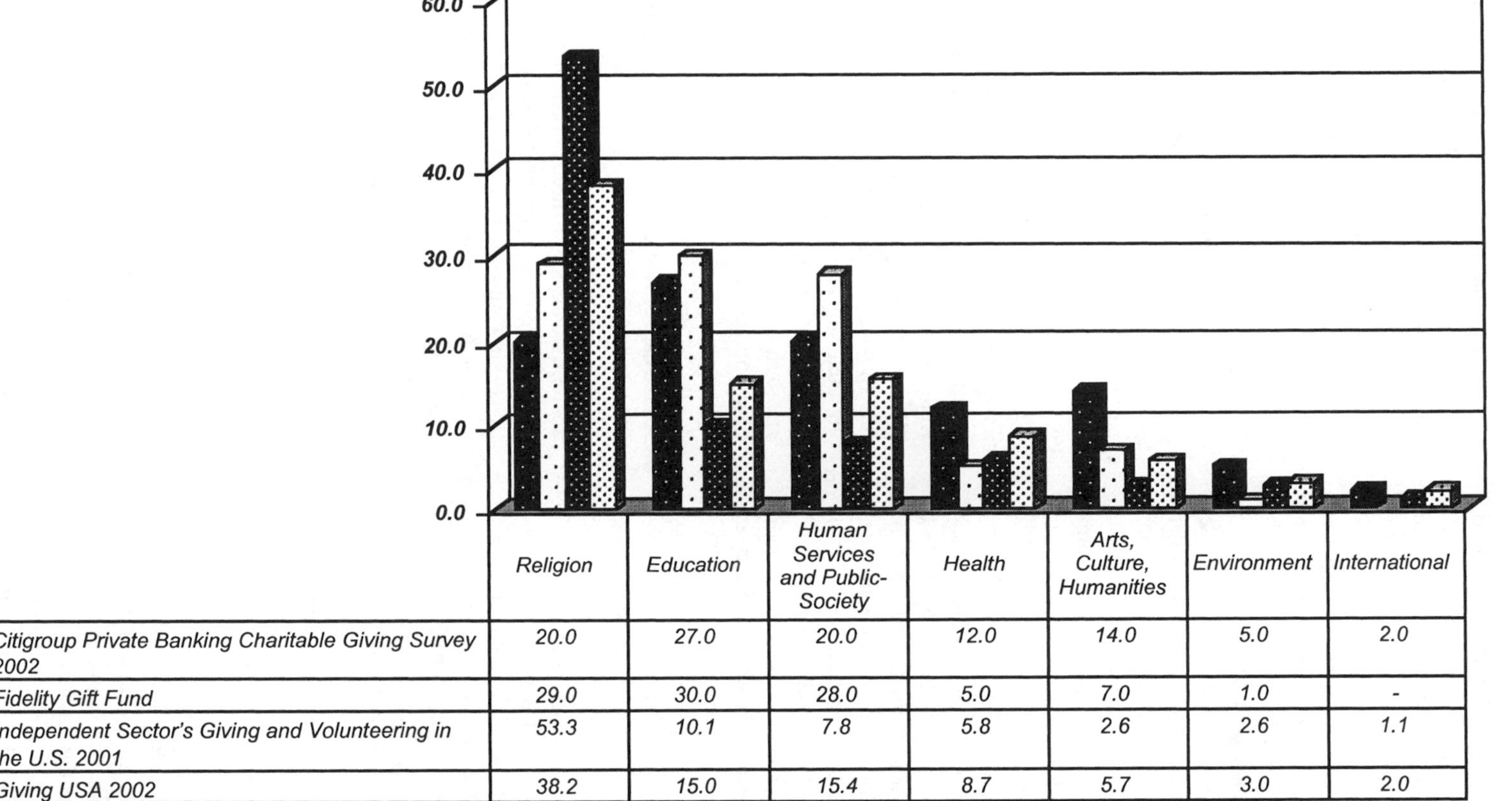

	Religion	Education	Human Services and Public-Society	Health	Arts, Culture, Humanities	Environment	International
■ Citigroup Private Banking Charitable Giving Survey 2002	20.0	27.0	20.0	12.0	14.0	5.0	2.0
□ Fidelity Gift Fund	29.0	30.0	28.0	5.0	7.0	1.0	-
▪ Independent Sector's Giving and Volunteering in the U.S. 2001	53.3	10.1	7.8	5.8	2.6	2.6	1.1
▫ Giving USA 2002	38.2	15.0	15.4	8.7	5.7	3.0	2.0

FIGURE 23.3. PERCENTAGE OF GIVING BY RECIPIENT ORGANIZATION FOR THE WEALTHY AND THE TOTAL POPULATION

Source: Citigroup Private Banking Charitable Giving Survey 2002 (survey distributed in magazines sent to high net worth clients and at a high net worth event; high net worth respondents had $3 million or more in net worth); Fidelity Gift Fund Web site (www.charitablegift.org). We are assuming that donations from the donor-advised funds represent giving trends by the wealthy since the cost of setting up a fund is $10,000; Independent Sector 2002b:35 (Table 1.6). Note that Environment includes animal welfare; AAFRC Trust for Philanthropy 2002.

fer to it as the "poor man's foundation." With an initial tax-deductible minimum investment of $10,000, a donor can start a donor-advised fund, name it as a personal charitable entity, and make self-directed contributions to charity without the same burdens of annual reporting, required distributions, recordkeeping, or personal liability as a personal foundation (Smith 2001). The Fidelity Charitable Gift Fund has seen exponential growth and, in 2000, became the fifth largest charity in the United States with 30,000 funds. This same year two other commercial providers of donor-advised funds also joined the Philanthropy 400 (Chronicle of Philanthropy 2001). Nationally, numbers of for-profit and nonprofit providers of donor-advised funds have grown. A 2002 survey of seventy-five donor-advised funds found the number of funds had increased 24.9 percent in the space of a year, from 42,653 in 2000 to 53,275 in 2001, with total assets increasing to $12.5 billion, and $2 billion distributed in grants in 2001 (Larose 2002). Part of the reason for the success of donor-advised funds is that they allow the donor to make a substantial commitment to philanthropy today, but the freedom to explore the landscape of philanthropy over a longer period, a landscape that newcomers can find "very intimidating" due to the vast range of social needs, seemingly infinite ways of addressing them, and large number of undifferentiated organizations doing so (Havens and Schervish 2001). The opportunity for initial exploration of social problems and solutions, as well as the desire for a buffer between the donor and the nonprofit world, is also a factor in the phenomenal success of the Social Venture Partnership model, which has grown since 1997 from the founding organization in Seattle to more than twenty-three across the country. In exchange for an initial investment of between $5,000 and $10,000, donors can participate in a philanthropic experiment of jointly committing time, money, and expertise to charitable causes (Havens and Schervish 2001).

Despite the current low participation rate in planned giving, some surveys indicate that there is a strong inclination among affluent households in formalizing their philanthropy. A study by Giving Capital (2000) found that among households with assets of $100,000 or more, interest was almost three times as high as utilization, with 27.3 percent of households having made planned gifts, but 74.6 percent interested in doing so in the future. Regarding the wealthy, studies have found that as wealth grows, so too does planned giving. Among those aged over thirty-five and with investable assets of $250,000 or more, one in twenty-five has established trusts with a charity as the beneficiary (Lincoln Financial Advisors 2001); among business owners that figure is closer to one in twelve (National Foundation for Women Business Owners 2000); and among households with an income of $250,000 or more or a net worth of $3 million or more, almost one in six respondents had set up a charitable remainder trust and almost one in six said he or she was likely to do so in the future (U.S. Trust 1998); and at $5 million or more in net worth, one in four respondents reported having charitable trusts (Spectrem Group 2002).

While community foundations are one sector of the nonprofit world that has responded to the challenge posed by commercial providers by offering donors a similar array of planned giving vehicles, higher education is probably the most competitive sector in terms of the planned giving options provided to donors. Donations to colleges and universities are still primarily made through outright gifts (gifts from individuals and from family and private foundations), representing $6.8 billion (66 percent) of total individual giving. Bequests are in the region of $2.2 billion (22 percent) of total individual giving, while deferred gifts (e.g., charitable remainder trusts, charitable lead trusts, charitable gift annuities, pooled income funds, etc.) total $1.3 billion (13 percent) of total individual charitable giving. Total individual giving to higher education has grown rapidly during the past decade at an average annual rate of 8.7 percent. From 1998 to 2001, new commitments for bequests declined from an average face value of $2.9 million to $2.6 million per institution, while new pledges for planned gifts have grown from an average of $7 million to $7.7 million per institution (Council for Aid to Education 2002). It is difficult to tell if this five-year trend is an indication that donors are moving their substantial giving from their estates during their lifetime, but even if this is not the case, the data on the increase in interest and utilization of planned giving vehicles have implications for nonprofits and how they interact with donors.

All the data presented here reveal aspects of donor behavior; indeed, numbers *are* behavior. As such, there are areas of philanthropy where more quantitative research needs to be done on trends and patterns in charitable giving both to increase the reliability and usefulness of data on familiar questions—how much is given by wealth and income?—as well as to address complex donor behaviors that current data sources hint at, but do not explain—do donors spend a dollar of inherited wealth differently from a dollar of earned wealth? Here we focus on four main topics for future research: improvement of survey methodology, wealth and philanthropy, informal giving, and planned giving.

We have noted the great strides that survey methodology has made toward completing the picture of charitable giving: for example, by including questions on informal giving, trying to get at asset composition, asking culturally sensitive questions about giving, and attempting to sample high income and high wealth as well as ethnically diverse households. The SCF and the COPPS/PSID, currently the best sources of data on charitable giving, could be improved by expansion of their modules: in the case of the SCF, to include questions about causes and organizations that are the recipients of giving, and in the case of the COPPS/PSID, to include a greater set of questions and prompts about the components of household wealth. Both data sources would also benefit from an expansion of the set of questions on giving, to include, for example, planned giving vehicles.

Two major issues remain outstanding in regard to wealth: the "lumpiness" of giving patterns and how the composition of wealth affects philanthropy. "Lumpiness" of giving refers to the fact that wealthy households tend to give large amounts to charity but relatively infrequently. Their donations are often large enough to add a noticeable amount to the total charitable donations for the year, bulging the distributions of giving by income, wealth, and other demographic characteristics. A glance at the wealth of the Forbes 400 over a couple of years shows dramatic changes in wealth for individuals on the list, and for the group as a whole. Research that would map the "lumpiness" of philanthropy by the wealthy, both at an individual level and as a group, and how this relates to the unevenness of wealth in a given period, would shed some light on the financial biography of wealth holders and how it affects accumulation and allocation. In regard to the composition of wealth, research has begun, and should be ongoing, on how the different sources and forms of wealth and income relate to charitable giving: for example, whether giving patterns from earned wealth are different from giving from inherited wealth; and whether donors are more generous from investment income components such as dividends, interest, rent, and capital gains or from earned income, wage and salary, and self-employment income. We surmise that ebbs and flows of wealth and income, as well as composition changes in portfolios, impact the donor's perception of his or her financial security. Better data on the financial aspects of economic self-confidence will provide a basis for exploration of the psychological component of this significant variable.

With regard to informal giving, the vast amounts of person-to-person aid documented in this chapter show that further exploration of expressions of care, including remittances, informal giving to others, and interpersonal transfers to family and friends outside the household, is necessary. Most important, the interaction of formal and informal giving needs further research that will enable us to distinguish where, and under what conditions, they are complements or substitutes. There are also some fundamental data gaps when it comes to informal and in-kind giving: for example, there is no comprehensive data source available on the recipients of such giving, among them religious organizations that receive a great deal of support from their congregants and communities in the form of in-kind gifts of goods and services. Furthermore, there is a large foreign-born population in the United States that sends remittances to home countries around the globe. Data on the frequency and amounts of these remittances are needed to complete the picture of charitable giving in the United States.

Finally, for a variety of reasons the landscape of philanthropy has changed in recent decades from a relatively reactive to a relatively strategic enterprise. As yet, however, there are no data sources documenting how much planned giving is occurring and few surveys that involve charitable intermediaries, such as financial planners or fundraisers, in the survey process.

The goal of future research on philanthropy should be to help donors and nonprofits alike to better grasp the knowledge and self-knowledge that inspires people to allocate their resources for the care of others.

ACKNOWLEDGMENTS

The authors thank Richard S. Steinberg and Walter W. Powell, editors of this handbook, for inviting us to author this chapter and for their subsequent suggestions and patient encouragement. We also thank Caroline Noonan, Todd Fitzpatrick, Cheryl Stults, and Rosa Ortiz, staff members of the Center on Wealth and Philanthropy at Boston College, for their considerable assistance in compiling material, editing drafts, proofreading text, and providing general assistance in developing the chapter.

The Center on Wealth and Philanthropy is generously supported by the T. B. Murphy Foundation Charitable Trust and the Lilly Endowment, Inc., whose funding supported the development of this chapter.

The authors are listed in alphabetical order to represent the fully collaborative nature of the chapter.

NOTES

1. And although they are not tax deductible, to the extent that their motivation is similar to philanthropy, we also consider as charitable giving gifts to political parties and advocacy groups.

2. An annotated description of these sources can be found on our Web site: http://www.bc.edu/cwp.

3. All dollars throughout the chapter are 2002 dollars and have been updated where necessary.

4. Percentages reported are valid only for the year of analysis and are not likely to be stable for subsequent years. However, they do indicate trends.

5. The substantially higher estimates of giving reported in *Giving and Volunteering in the United States 2001,* which utilized a revised survey methodology, suggest that the estimates reported in the prior G&V series may have been biased downward in unknown ways.

6. This questionnaire has been employed in the national survey *America Gives* (Steinberg and Rooney 2005), for which data collection was complete at the time of going to press.

7. Since 7.4 percent plus 97.2 percent adds up to 104.6 percent, we presume that 2.8 percent of married decedents made a charitable bequest but left no inheritance to their surviving spouse, 4.6 percent of married decedents made a charitable bequest and also left an inheritance to their surviving spouse, and 92.6 percent of married decedents made no charitable bequest but left their estates to their surviving spouse.

8. Some very wealthy households make multimillion dollar contributions, but relatively infrequently. In any given year there are several of these large contributions, whose number and value make the distribution of charitable giving lumpy among higher-income households. Moreover, estimates based on household surveys, even those with oversamples of wealthy households, tend to magnify the lumpiness in the population distribution through the application of weights to project results to the population. This lumpiness in the distribution and estimates may affect aggregate and even average estimates based on the SCF (Board of Governors of the Federal Reserve System 2001).

9. Because the 2001 Independent Sector report does not provide data on the relation between giving and volunteering, we used earlier data on this relation from the IS Web site: http://www.independentsector.org/GandV/s_rela.htm.

10. A report by the Bureau of Labor Statistics shows that the gap between men's and women's wages narrowed for most major age groups between 1979 and 2001; furthermore, among younger workers, the wage difference was much lower than for middle-aged and older

workers, with nineteen- to twenty-four-year-old women earning 90.2 percent as much as their male counterparts, versus women aged forty-five to fifty-four, who, though the gap had closed considerably from 56.9 percent in 1979, still earned only 73.6 percent of men's earnings in the same age group (Bureau of Labor Statistics 2002).

11. Between 1997 and 2002, the Center for Women's Business Research (2002) estimates that the number of women-owned firms increased by 14 percent nationwide, or at twice the rate of all firms.

12. The researchers use data from the Indiana Gives study in which a variety of different questionnaires were used.

13. Since remittances are so significant to many countries—some estimates are that remittances to Mexico will reach $100 billion before 2012—there have been efforts to promote the use of remittances by communities. In the United States, Mexican immigrants have hometown associations that have been successful in aggregating immigrant remittances to build local infrastructures and setting up government matching schemes in Mexico for dollars remitted (Public-Private Infrastructure Advisory Facility 2002).

14. These are aggregate data and so do not take into account the timing or amount of the inheritance, merely the fact of having received an inheritance of any amount at any time.

15. These estimates are based on data from the 1998 SCF (Board of Governors of the Federal Reserve System 1998), which asked respondents detailed questions concerning inheritance. The current value of all inheritances was estimated by adjusting the value of inheritances received for inflation and by assuming a real secular growth rate of 3 percent. This value was at least 50 percent of current total net worth for only 7 percent of families whose net worth was $1 million or more.

16. Because this figure is an aggregate of three years, we did not adjust it to 2002 dollars.

17. The Foundation Center defines a private foundation (including a family foundation) as "[a] non-governmental, nonprofit organization with an endowment (usually donated from a single source, such as an individual, family, or corporation) and program managed by its own trustees or directors. Private foundations are established to maintain or aid social, educational, religious, or other charitable activities serving the common welfare, primarily through the making of grants" (http://fdncenter.org/funders/grantmaker).

18. "A donor-advised fund is a specially segregated donation to a public charity. The fund is distributed based on the donor's wishes" (Kennedy, Capassakis, and Wagman 2002). A donor-advised fund is a less-costly alternative to a private foundation, because of both the considerable initial investment required and the comparatively low level of reporting and administration required. Donor-advised funds are typically managed by community foundations or commercial providers.

19. The American Council on Gift Annuities defines them as follows: "A Gift Annuity (also known as a 'charitable Gift Annuity' or 'CGA') is a contract (not a 'trust'), under which a charity, in return for a transfer of cash, marketable securities or other property, agrees to pay a fixed sum of money (payments) for a period measured only by one or two lives (not a term of years)." The ACGA's Web site (http://www.acga-web.org) gives further detailed information on various subtypes of annuities.

20. Charitable trusts include various kinds of Charitable Remainder Trusts, where a trust is set up by a transfer of assets with a current charitable deduction and that pay income to beneficiaries with the remaining assets transferred to the charity when the terms of the trust end (Kennedy, Capassakis, and Wagman 2002:51–59), as well as a variety of Charitable Lead Trusts that provide income payments to the charity with the remainder in the trust going to a non-charitable beneficiary or individual (61–64).

REFERENCES

AAFRC Trust for Philanthropy. 2002. *Giving USA 2002: The Annual Report on Philanthropy for the Year 2001.* Indianapolis, Ind.

Altonji, Joseph G., Ulrich Dorazelski, and Lewis Segal. 2000. "Black/White Differences in Wealth." Economic Perspectives. Federal Reserve Bank of Chicago. http://www.chicagofed.org/publications/economicperspectives/2000/Epart3.pdf.

American Council on Gift Annuities. 2003. "What Is a Gift Annuity?" http://www.acga-web.org/whatisga.html.

Avery, Robert B. 1994. "The Pending Intergenerational Transfer." *Philanthropy* 8(1):5, 28–29.

Brooks, Arthur C. 2002. "Welfare Receipt and Private Charity." *Public Budgeting and Finance.* 22(3):101–114.

Brown, Eleanor. 1999. "Patterns and Purposes of Philanthropic Giving." In *Philanthropy and the Nonprofit Sector in a Changing America,* ed. Charles T. Clotfelter and Thomas Ehrlich. Indianapolis: Indiana University Press. 224–226.

Brown, Eleanor, and James M. Ferris. 2002. "Social Capital in Los Angeles: Findings from the Social Capital Community Benchmark Survey." Los Angeles: Center on Philanthropy and Public Policy. http://www.usc.edu/schools/sppd/philanthropy/pdf/soc_cap_final.pdf.

Board of Governors of the Federal Reserve System. 1998. Survey of Consumer Finances. http://www.federalreserve.gov/pubs/oss/oss2/scfindex.html.

———. 2001. *Survey of Consumer Finances.* Board of Governors of the Federal Reserve System. http://www.federalreserve.gov/pubs/oss/oss2/scfindex.html.

Bureau of Labor Statistics. 1990. *Consumer Expenditure Survey.* Washington, D.C.: U.S. Department of Labor. Available at http://www.bls.gov/cex/home.htm.

———. 1995. *Consumer Expenditure Survey.* Washington, D.C.: U.S. Department of Labor. http://www.bls.gov/cex/home.htm.

———. 2000. *Consumer Expenditure Survey.* Washington,

D.C.: U.S. Department of Labor. http://www.bls.gov/cex/home.htm.

———. 2002. *Highlights of Women's Earnings in 2001: Report no. 960.* Washington, D.C.: Bureau of Labor Statistics. Available at http://www.bls.gov/bls/blsnew02.htm#May%202002.

Capek, Mary Ellen S. 2001. *Women and Philanthropy: Old Stereotypes, New Challenges,* vol. 1. San Francisco, Calif.: Women's Funding Network.

Catalogue for Philanthropy. 2002. *Generosity Index.* Boston, Mass. Available at http://www.catalogueforphilanthropy.org.

Center for Women's Business Research. 2002. "Women-Owned Businesses in the United States 2002: A Fact Sheet." Washington, D.C. Available at http://www.nfwbo.org or http://www.womensbusinessresearch.org.

Chronicle of Philanthropy. 2002. "The Philanthropy 400." Washington, D.C. October 28, 2001Available at http://philanthropy.com/premium/stats/philanthropy400/2002.

Citigroup Private Bank. 2002. *CPB Charitable Giving Survey: Final Report,* ed. Peg Dwan. New York.

Clotfelter, Charles T. 1997. "The Economics of Giving." Terry Sanford Institute of Public Policy, Duke University. Available at http://www.pubpol.duke.edu/people/faculty/clotfelter.

Council for Aid to Education. 2002. *Voluntary Support of Education Survey.* New York.

De la Garza, Rodolfo O., and Fujia Lu. 1999. "Explorations into Latino Voluntarism." In *Nuevos Senderos: Reflections on Hispanics and Philanthropy,* ed. Diana Campoamor, William A. Diaz, and Henry A. J. Ramos. Houston: Arte Publico Press. 55–77.

DeSipio, Louis. 2000. "Sending Money Home . . . For Now: Remittances and Immigrant Adaptation in the United States." Washington, D.C.: Inter-American Dialogue and Tomas Rivera Policy Institute. Available at http://www.iadialog.org/publications/DeSipio.html.

Duncan, Brian. 1999. "Modeling Charitable Contributions of Time and Money." *Journal of Public Economics* 72:213–242.

Eller, Martha B. 1997. "Federal Taxation of Wealth Transfers, 1992–1995." *Statistics of Income Bulletin* 16(3):8–63.

———. 2001. "Charitable Bequests: Evidence from Federal Estate Tax Returns, 1995." *Statistics of Income Bulletin* (Spring): 174–190. http://www.irs.gov/pub/irs-soi/95escbar.pdf.

Foundation Center and National Center for Family Philanthropy. 2001. *Family Foundations: A Profile of Funders and Trends.* Washington, D.C.: Foundation Center. http://www.ncfp.org/program-research-execsummary-FFTrends.pdf.

Foundation Center. 2002a. *Foundation Growth and Giving Estimates: 2001 Preview.* Washington, D.C.: Foundation Center. http://fdncenter.org/research/trends_analysis/pdf/fgge02.pdf.

———. 2002b. *Highlights of the Foundation Center's Foundation Yearbook.* Downloaded September 3. http://fdncenter.org/research/trends_analysis/pdf/fgge02.pdf.

———. 2002c. "Profile of the Funding Community. Foundations Today: Tutorial." September 3. http://fdncenter.org/learn/classroom/ft_tutorial/ftt_part1_q2.html.

Giving Capital. 2000. *Giving Wisely: How Financial Advisors Can Meet the Charitable Needs of Affluent Donors.* New York.

Havens, John J., and Paul G. Schervish. 1999. "Millionaires and the Millennium: New Estimates of the Forthcoming Wealth Transfer and the Prospects for a Golden Age of Philanthropy." Center on Wealth and Philanthropy, Boston College. Available at http://www.bc.edu/cwp.

———. 2000. "Wealth with Responsibility Study / 2000." Center on Wealth and Philanthropy, Boston College. Bankers Trust Private Banking, Deutsche Bank Group. Available at http://www.bc.edu/cwp.

———. 2001. "The Methods and Metrics of the Boston Area Diary Study." *Nonprofit and Voluntary Sector Quarterly* 30(3):524–550.

HNW Digital. 2001. *Survey of Wealth and Giving.* New York: HNW Digital, Inc. Available at http://www.hnw.com.

Independent Sector. 1992. *Giving and Volunteering in the United States: A National Survey.* Washington, D.C: Independent Sector.

———. 1996. *Giving and Volunteering in the United States: A National Survey.* Washington, D.C: Independent Sector.

———. 2002a. *Faith and Philanthropy: The Connection Between Charitable Behavior and Giving to Religion.* Washington, D.C.: Independent Sector. http://www.independentsector.org/programs/research/faithphilanthropy.html.

———. 2002b. *Giving and Volunteering in the United States 2001: Findings from a National Survey.* Washington, D.C.: Independent Sector. http://www.independentsector.org.

Institute for Social Inquiry and Roper Center for National Commission on Philanthropy and Civic Renewal. 1997. *National Survey on Philanthropy.* Roper Center for Public Opinion Research, University of Connecticut.

Johnson, Barry W., and Jacob M. Mikow. 1999. "Federal Estate Tax Returns, 1995–1997." *Statistics of Income Bulletin* 19(1):69–129.

Joulfaian, David. 2002, "Basic Facts on Charitable Giving." Unpublished mimeo. U.S. Department of Treasury, May. Washington D.C.

Kaplan, Ann E., and M. Joanne Hayes. 1993. "What We Know About Women as Donors." In *New Directions in Philanthropic Fundraising: Women as Donors, Women as Philanthropists,* ed. Abbie J. Von Schlegell and Joan M. Fisher. San Francisco: Jossey-Bass.

Kennedy, Michael B., Evelyn M. Capassakis, and Richard S. Wagman. 2002. *PriceWaterhouseCoopers Guide to Charitable Giving.* Hoboken, N.J.: Wiley.

Larose, Marni D. 2002. "Assets of Donor-Advised Funds Totaled $12.3 Billion Last Year, Survey Finds." *Chronicle of Philanthropy,* May 30. Washington, D.C.

Lincoln Financial Advisors. 2001. *Financial Planning Among America's Wealthy.* https://www.bisysinsurance.com/PDFShare/mktg/lincoln.pdf.

Mesch, Debra J., Patrick Michael Rooney, William Chin, and Kathryn S. Steinberg. 2002. "Race and Gender Differences in Philanthropy: Indiana as a Test Case." In *New Directions in Philanthropic Fundraising: Fundraising in Diverse Cultural and Giving Environments,* ed. Robert E. Fogal, (37):65–77.

Minton, Frank. 2000. *Report and Comments on the American Council on Gift Annuities 1999 Survey of Charitable Gift Annuities.* Indianapolis. Available at http://www.acga-web.org.

Multilateral Investment Fund of the Inter-American Development Bank. 2001. "Remittances to Latin America and the Carribbean: Comparative Statistics." Unpublished report presented at the conference, "Remittances as a Development Tool: A Regional Conference," Inter-American Bank Headquarters, Washington, D.C., May 17–18, 2001.

Munnell, Alicia H., and Sundén, Annika, eds. 2003. *Death and Dollars: The Role of Gifts and Bequests in America.* Washington, D.C.: Brookings Institution Press.

Murphy, Thomas B. 2001. "Financial and Psychological Determinants of Donor's Capacity to Give." In *New Directions in Philanthropic Fundraising: Understanding the Needs of Donors: The Supply-Side of Charitable Giving,* ed. Eugene R. Tempel and Dwight F. Burlingame, (28):33–49.

National Foundation for Women Business Owners. 2000. *Leaders in Business and Community: The Philanthropic Contributions of Women and Men Business Owners.* November. Washington, D.C.: NFWBO. Available at http://www.nfwbo.org.

National Committee on Planned Giving. 2001. *Planned Giving in the United States: A Survey of Donors 2000.* Indianapolis, Ind.: National Committee on Planned Giving.

National Opinion Research Center. 1998. *General Social Survey.* University of Chicago, National Opinion Research Center. Available at www.norc.uchicago.edu/projects/gensoc.asp.

———. 2001. *General Social Survey.* University of Chicago, National Opinion Research Center. Available at www.norc.uchicago.edu/projects/gensoc.asp.

O'Neill, Michael, and William L. Roberts. 2000. *Giving and Volunteering in California.* San Francisco: Institute for Nonprofit Management.

O'Neill, Michael, and Carol Silverman. 2002. "Varieties of Religious and Charitable Experience." Paper presented at the ARNOVA conference, Montreal, Canada, November.

Osili, Una Okonkwo, and Dan Du. 2005. "Do Immigrants Free Ride?: New Evidence from Charitable Giving and Volunteering." Working paper, Department of Economics, Indiana University–Purdue University at Indianapolis.

Public-Private Infrastructure Advisory Facility. 2002. "Migrants' Capital for Small-Scale Infrastructure and Small Enterprise Development in Mexico." Project Report to Public-Private Infrastructure Advisory Facility, World Bank, Washington, D.C.

Putnam, Robert D. 2000. *Bowling Alone: The Collapse and Revival of American Community.* New York: Simon & Schuster.

Rapoport, Hillel, and Frederic Docquier. 2006. "The Economics of Migrants' Remittances." In *Handbook of the Economics of Giving, Altruism, and Reciprocity,* ed. J. Mercier-Ythier and S. C. Kolm. Amsterdam: Elsevier-North Holland.

Rooney, Patrick M., Kathryn S. Steinberg, and Paul G. Schervish. 2001. "A Methodological Comparison of Giving Surveys: Indiana as a Test Case." *Nonprofit and Voluntary Sector Quarterly* 30(3):551–568.

Rosenberg, Claude, Jr. 1994. *Wealthy and Wise: How You and America Can Get the Most Out of Your Giving.* Boston: Little, Brown.

Savoie, Anthony J., and John J. Havens. 1998. "The High Giving Poor: Who Are the Low Income People Who Make High Contributions?" Paper presented at the annual meeting of the Association for Research on Nonprofit Organizations and Voluntary Action, Seattle.

Schervish, Paul G. 2000. "The Modern Medici: Patterns, Motivations, and Giving Strategies of the Wealthy." Paper presented at "What Is 'New' About New Philanthropy?" University of Southern California Nonprofit Studies Center, Los Angeles. Available at http://www.bc.edu/cwp.

Schervish, Paul G., and John J. Havens. 1995a. "Do the Poor Pay More: Is the U-Shaped Curve Correct?" *Nonprofit and Voluntary Sector Quarterly* 24 (1):79–70.

———. 1995b. "Explaining the U in the U-Shaped Curve." *Voluntas: International Journal of Voluntary and Nonprofit Organizations* 6(2):202–225.

———. 1997. "Social Participation and Charitable Giving: A Multivariate Analysis." *Voluntas: International Journal of Voluntary and Nonprofit Organizations* 8 (3):235–260.

———. 1998. "Embarking on a Republic of Benevolence: New Survey Finding on Charitable Giving." *Nonprofit and Voluntary Sector Quarterly* 27(2): 237–242.

———. 2001. "The Mind of the Millionaire: Findings from a National Study on Wealth with Responsibility." *New Directions in Philanthropic Fundraising: Understanding Donor Dynamics: The Organizational Side of Charitable Giving,* ed. Eugene R. Tempel, 32 (Summer): 75–107.

———. 2002. "The Boston Area Diary Study and the Moral Citizenship of Care." *Voluntas: International Journal of Nonprofit and Voluntary Organizations.* 13(1):47–71.

Schervish, Paul G., Mary A. O'Herlihy, and John J. Havens. 2001. "Agent-Animated Wealth and Philanthropy: The Dynamics of Accumulation and Allocation Among High-Tech Donors." Center on Wealth and Philanthropy, Boston College. Available at http://www.bc.edu/cwp.

Smith, Eric L. 2001. "An Introduction to Donor Advised Funds." In *Fundraising on the Internet: The ePhilanthropy Foundation's Guide to Success Online,* ed. Mal Warwick, Ted Hart, and Nick Allen. San Francisco: Jossey-Bass. 95–104.

Spectrem Group. 2002. *Charitable Giving and the Ultra High Net Worth: Reaching the Wealthy Donor.* Available at http://www.spectremgroup.com.

Steinberg, Kathryn S., and Patrick M. Rooney. 2005. "America Gives: A Survey of Americans' Generosity after September 11." *Nonprofit and Voluntary Sector Quarterly* 34(1):101–135.

Steinberg, Richard, Mark Wilhelm, Patrick Rooney, and Eleanor Brown. 2002. "Inheritance and Charitable Donations." Department of Economics, Indiana University.

Survey Research Center. 2001. *Panel Study of Income Dynamics.* Institute for Social Research, University of Michigan.

U.S. Census Bureau. 2002. "Coming to America: A Profile of the Nation's Foreign Born (2000 Update)." Census Brief: Current Population Survey. February. Available at http://www.census.gov/prod/2002pubs/, listed under cenbr01-1.pdf.

U.S. Trust. 1998. *U.S. Trust Survey of Affluent Americans,* vol. 15. November.

Weitzman, Murray S., Nadine T. Jalandoni, Linda M. Lampkin, and Thomas H. Pollak. 2002. *The New Nonprofit Almanac and Desk Reference: The Essential Facts and Figures for Managers, Researchers, and Volunteers.* Washington, D.C.: Independent Sector.

Whitten, Melissa. 2002. "Domestic Foundations and Charitable Trusts, 1998." *Statistics of Income Bulletin* (Winter): 45–82. http://www.irs.gov/pub/irs-soi/98pfctar.pdf.

Wolpert, Julian. 1996. "How Federal Cutbacks Affect the Charitable Sector." *Nonprofit Research Fund.* Spring. Working Paper Series.

24

Why Do People Give?

LISE VESTERLUND

The vast majority of Americans make charitable contributions. In 2000, 90 percent of U.S. households donated on average $1,623 to nonprofit organizations.[1] Why do so many people choose to give their hard-earned income away? What motivates them to behave in this altruistic or seemingly altruistic manner? The objective of this chapter is to present a short summary of what economists have learned about the motivations for individual charitable giving.[2] This is a question of substantial importance, as individual contributions account for more than 80 percent of total dollars given.[3] If we do not understand why people give, then how can we encourage them to become donors or to increase their contributions, and how can we predict the effect changes in the economic environment will have on giving?

One way to think about charitable giving is that it is just like the purchase of any other commodity. That is, we expect contributions to depend on how much we earn and how costly it is to give. In the first part of the chapter I examine how the individual's income and the price of giving affect her contribution. Determining how individuals respond to these factors is crucial not only for predicting how total donations respond to changes in tax policy and how fundraisers can take advantage of these changes, but also for determining how the government best can design subsidies such as the tax deductibility of donations to nonprofits.[4]

While the similarity with ordinary commodities is clear when we examine responses to changes in income and prices, it is less so when we want to determine what motivates us to make such a purchase or contribution. What is it that we get in return from these transactions? What tradeoffs do we face when we give our money away? In the second part of the chapter I discuss the potential benefits of giving. There are many types of benefits and they vary with both the individual and the organization. Economists typically classify them into two groups. One group is public in nature because both the donor and other individuals benefit. For example, while a donor may care about the provision of the nonprofit's output, this same output may simultaneously benefit other individuals. The second group is private in nature. Giving may make you feel better about yourself, it may make you feel like you have done your share and perhaps paid back to the community, or it may give you prestige or an acknowledgment that you would not otherwise get. Since no one but the donor can enjoy these aspects of giving, we characterize them as private benefits.

Why does it matter whether the benefit from giving accrues solely to the donor or affects the well-being of other donors as well? The reason is, in part, that the characteristics of the benefit help us determine whether voluntary contributions are likely to result in the "right," or optimal, level of contributions. If everyone views the benefit from giving as entirely private then each individual will contribute an amount that reflects her valuation of the nonprofit, and as a result the voluntary provision level will be optimal. If on the other hand the benefit is public, then the contribution by another donor provides the exact same benefit as one made by yourself, and since it is costly for you to contribute you have an incentive to free-ride off the contribution of others. In the presence of other donors an individual who is motivated by the public benefit will choose to contribute less than she would absent these donors. When the benefit is public we predict that too little of the public good will be provided.

To determine whether benefits from giving are primarily public or private, economists have examined the following distinct predictions of these two alternatives: an increase in the contribution of others is expected to decrease an individual's contribution when the benefit of giving is public, and it is expected to cause no change in giving when the benefit is private. Most empirical studies of survey or donation data find that on average the benefit appears to be private in nature. This suggests that the last dollar that we give to charity is not motivated by the nonprofit's output. This is an extreme result, and one may question whether the nonprofit's output truly can be irrelevant for our decision to give an additional dollar to charity. In the final section of the chapter I investigate the possibility that perhaps the economic interpretation of the empirical results is misled by the assumptions we impose on the model of giving. I relax the assumptions and examine if this alters the crucial prediction that donors who are concerned about the nonprofit's output decrease their personal donations when the donations of others increase. In particular I consider environments where donors take account of the effect that their donation will have on the contributions of others, as well as those where donors not only maximize their well-being but are also restricted by social norms or rules. I show that in some circumstances these altered assumptions change the predictions of the model.

THE EFFECTS OF PRICE AND INCOME ON GIVING

It is natural to expect charitable giving to increase with income and decrease with the price of giving. But what exactly is meant by the price of giving? Typically the price of an object refers to what we have to pay to obtain a particular good. For charitable giving the price of giving refers to what it costs us to give the organization an additional dollar. Since charitable contributions are deductible for those who itemize, the price of giving depends on the individual's marginal tax rate.[5] Suppose, for example, that an itemizing taxpayer faces a marginal tax rate of 28 percent. Then, by giving $1, the donor will pay $0.28 less in taxes for a net price of $0.72. Thus someone with a marginal tax rate of 15 percent is faced with a price of $0.85 per dollar given. Further reductions in tax liability can be attained if the donor decides to contribute an appreciated asset. In this case the donor can deduct the market value of the asset and does not have to pay taxes on the accrued capital gain.[6]

Data from a survey of 200 big donors are suggestive of the impact that taxes have on giving (Prince and File 1994). This study revealed that "awareness of tax advantages" was ranked the third most important motivator for making a charitable donation.[7] Does such awareness cause charitable giving to respond to changes in the tax rate? Often aggregate data suggest little if any response to price changes. For example, despite the substantial changes in the marginal tax rates during the 1980s the share of income donated remained fairly constant. However, one must be cautious when interpreting such aggregate statistics. We first have to account for other simultaneous changes in the economy and for the fact that not all contributors experienced the same changes in the marginal tax rate. A possible way of incorporating both of these effects is to determine whether those who were presented with a higher price of giving decreased their contributions relative to those who did not face a higher price.[8] Clotfelter (1990) and Auten, Cilke, and Randolph (1992) examine this question and find that in the aftermath of the 1986 Tax Reform Act, giving for those faced with a lower marginal tax rate decreased relative to those who did not face a different marginal tax rate. Thus a more careful analysis suggests that people do respond to the price of giving.

For the past three decades economists have tried to determine exactly how sensitive giving is to price and income. The measures of interest have generally been the income and price elasticities of demand, which is the percentage change in the amount given associated with a 1 percent change in income and price, respectively. Because the income elasticity measures the responsiveness of gifts to changes in income, we expect that the measure is positive.[9] If, for example, the income elasticity of demand is 1.50 then a 1 percent increase in income increases giving by 1.5 percent. The price elasticity of demand measures responsiveness to price and is therefore expected to be less than zero. That is, an increase in price is likely to decrease donations.

To examine if it is a good idea for charitable contributions to be tax deductible, researchers have been particularly interested in determining whether the price elasticity, in absolute value, is larger or smaller than one. It has been argued that for deductions to be effective, the deductibility provision must increase charitable contributions by an amount that exceeds the government's cost of the provision. The reason is that the government instead of allowing contributions to be tax deductible could transfer the funds spent on this provision directly to the charity. When donations are tax deductible, each dollar received by the charity is in part financed by the donor and in part by the government's lost tax revenue.

To see that the threshold for the "treasury efficient" price elasticity equals one, in absolute value, consider the unit elastic case.[10] If, in this case, the marginal tax rate increases to reduce the price of giving by 1 percent, then the individual's contribution also increases by 1 percent. While the individual's total cost of giving remains the same as prior to the tax increase, the government's cost increases. In fact the 1 percent increase in charitable giving is financed entirely by the lost tax revenue associated with deducting contributions at a higher tax rate. In the unit elastic case the government's lost revenue is therefore transferred directly to the charity.[11] If the price elasticity of demand is above one, in absolute value, then the nonprofit sector will receive contributions that exceed the government's lost revenue, while the opposite holds when the elasticity is below one.

Knowing how sensitive charitable giving is to income and price not only enables us to determine how changes in the economy will affect charitable giving but can also help us design better tax policies for the future.

While researchers agree that giving responds to changes in income and price, there is disagreement on how much it responds to these factors. The first analyses of this question estimated the price and income elasticities using cross-sectional data. While the precise estimates varied from study to study, the general consensus was that giving was price elastic (that is, the elasticity is greater than one in absolute value) and income inelastic (that is, the elasticity is smaller than one). Most estimates on the price elasticity were in the range of -0.5 to -1.75, whereas the estimates on the income elasticity were in the range of 0.4 to 0.8.[12] As representative of these earlier studies Clotfelter (1990) uses measures of 0.79 for the income elasticity, and -1.27 for the price elasticity, with the latter clearly demonstrating that personal deductions of donations do have the intended positive effect on charitable giving.[13]

One of the drawbacks of the cross-sectional data is that with only one year of data it is difficult to identify separately the effect of changes in income from that of prices. Since the marginal tax rate increases with income, one cannot determine whether a positive correlation between giving and income is caused by people giving more when they face a higher income or when they face a lower price.[14] More recent studies have used panel data to separate these effects. In panel data the same individuals are observed over a series of years, hence if tax rates change over the observed period then the panel can provide independent observations of income and price variations. Initial studies of panel data suggest that the cross-sectional evidence may not have correctly identified the price and income effects. For example, Randolph (1995) examines giving in a ten-year panel of tax-return data and finds results that differ substantially from those of the previous cross-sectional studies. His study reveals that people smooth their consumption. In particular, an income change causes people to change their consumption a little bit over many years, rather than immediately changing their consumption a lot. Thus an individual's consumption does not respond much to temporary changes in income. In contrast, giving is quite sensitive to permanent changes in income. The opposite pattern holds for prices. Donors appear to time their giving to take advantage of temporary changes in the tax prices, whereas permanent changes in price have but a small effect.[15]

An important policy question raised by the substantial sensitivity to temporary price changes and limited sensitivity to permanent price changes is whether the current tax incentives merely affect the timing of giving rather than, as intended, the level of giving. A large temporary price elasticity also has important implications for practitioners. If giving is very sensitive to temporary changes in the tax code then it is crucial that fundraisers are aware of such changes. For example, prior to the tax reductions of 1981 there is substantial evidence that donors were anticipating an increase in the price of giving and chose to substitute current giving for future giving. Organizations who fail to anticipate such changes are likely to miss opportunities, and they may inappropriately blame or praise their development staff for failures and successes beyond their control.

Auten, Sieg, and Clotfelter (2002) use an alternative approach to distinguish between temporary and permanent changes.[16] Opposite of Randolph's finding, they estimate a substantial permanent price elasticity and a very small temporary effect. However, they confirm the finding that the permanent income elasticity exceeds that of the temporary one.[17] Given this recent study, it is still unclear how much changes in price affect charitable giving. More research using panel data will be needed to definitively answer this difficult and important question.[18]

Recently, economists have begun to study the effects of income and price using techniques from experimental economics. While the standard economic approach examines responses from surveys or data on actual donations, experimental economists design the environment that they are interested in studying and invite volunteers to a controlled setting to observe how they respond to the provided monetary incentives. The benefit of experimental economics is that it allows researchers a large degree of control over the examined environment.[19] Despite the often abstract setting, this relatively new economic tool has proven useful in shedding light on a number of important economic questions.

For example, one question of interest is whether men and women respond differently to tax incentives for giving. It is difficult to answer this question using natural data because most data come from households where the decision may be jointly made, and data from single-member households confound gender effects with personality traits or other factors that lead one to be single (i.e., women are more likely to be the surviving spouse). In the laboratory, we control for these factors by testing a random sample of male and female respondents. Andreoni and Vesterlund (2001) examine such gender differences in giving in an experimental setting using undergraduates.[20] To ensure a simple environment, they ask participants to make decisions in a dictator game. A dictator game is a decision problem where one of two players (the dictator) is given an initial sum of money of, say, \$10 and must decide how much he or she wants to give to the other player (the recipient). While this game differs substantially from the traditional charitable giving environment, transfers from the dictator suggest that he or she is altruistic, and hence we may be able to study altruism and charitable giving in this simple game. The experimental setting is generally one of complete anonymity. The identity of the participant is not known to the experimenter or to the other participants. This helps reduce unmeasurable effects such as social pressure, acceptance, and so on.

To examine the effect of changes in income and price, Andreoni and Vesterlund look at contribution decisions in a modified dictator game where both the initial allocation and the price of giving are varied. For example, they ask dictators to decide how much they want to transfer to the recipient when they have an initial sum of \$6 and each dollar they decide to give away results in \$2 being given to the recipient. In this case, the price of giving a dollar is experimentally set at \$0.50.[21] Examining a series of choices, they determine average male and female gifts as a function of price and income.

Their results show that although neither gender is more generous than the other; there are significant gender differences in the way that they respond to changes in the price of giving. While an increase in the price of giving causes both men and women to give less, the decrease in the amount given is much larger for men than it is for women. More precisely, female giving is found to be price inelastic, while that of the males is elastic, and the male and female giving schedules as a function of price of giving are found to intersect. This shows that men will be more generous than women when it is cheap to give, and that women are more generous than men when it is more expensive to give. If this result extends to charitable giving, then it may have important implications for practitioners. For example, charities who match contributions to decrease the price of giving may be well advised to be aware of the gender composition of their donor base.

Although the experimental environment studied by Andreoni and Vesterlund differs substantially from that of charitable giving, these results have shed light on a phenomenon that researchers had not previously thought to investigate with traditional data sets. The lesson to be learned from this study is not merely one on charitable giving, but also one on the research approach taken to examine giving. If behaviors in the controlled laboratory are consistent with those outside of the lab, then this is a simple and attractive way of studying charitable giving and the rules that govern it.

Despite difficulties in analyzing actual giving data it is reassuring that a recent study has shown that the experimental results of Andreoni and Vesterlund do extend to actual charitable giving. Andreoni, Brown, and Rischall (2003) examine the 1992 and 1994 surveys by the Independent Sector and show that one can reject the hypothesis that single men and single women have the same patterns of annual giving. They show that the male demand for giving is more elastic than that of females, and that the two demand curves for giving intersect. The same results are found when comparing giving by male and female "deciders" in married households, where the decider is the spouse who is reported to be primarily responsible for the charitable giving decisions. Again, married male deciders are far more price elastic than married female deciders.

Another experimental study on the response to price is that of Eckel and Grossman (2003). They use a method similar to that of Andreoni and Vesterlund to investigate how donors respond to variation in their initial income and price of giving. However, rather than asking a dictator to make a contribution to an anonymous recipient, they ask the dictator to allocate an amount of money between herself and a charity of her choice. To examine the effect of tax deductions they present experimental participants with a series of different subsidies. The clever feature of this study is that they also examine an alternative framing where instead of a subsidy, the participant is presented with an equivalent offer of a matching contribution. Thus, they observe donations when, for example, the subsidy is 50 percent, and when the match is 100 percent. As these subsidies and matches are mirror images of one another they should trigger the same response.

Interestingly, Eckel and Grossman find substantial differences between the match and subsidy. Donors presented with a match contribute 1.2 to 2 times more than those presented with the equivalent subsidy.

Eckel and Grossman are now extending the study to field experiments. In contrast to the standard laboratory experiment, a field experiment is one that is conducted with individuals in a natural setting; for example, the experimenter may intervene in a preexisting economic institution to observe how the actual participants of that institution may respond.[22] In the new study they will examine the effect of matches and subsidies on actual contributions to Minnesota Public Radio and other nonprofit organizations. If the field studies confirm this initial finding then the consequences may be substantial; not only does it suggest that the current fundraising and corporate practices of providing matched contributions is the right one, but it also suggests that perhaps we can generate even larger charitable contributions if we replace the personal deduction of donations with a government matching provision.

Many more research questions lie ahead. We are only beginning to understand how people respond to the price of giving. However, past studies make clear that donors do respond to the price of giving and as a result charities are well advised to anticipate future changes in these prices, as well as potential differences in price sensitivity among their contributors.

PUBLIC VERSUS PRIVATE BENEFIT FROM CHARITABLE GIVING

Although taxes influence an individual's incentive to give, they do not reduce the price of giving to zero, and thus for anyone to contribute it must be that they get some type of benefit from doing so.[23] In this section I describe some of the many benefits donors may get from giving. It is important to keep in mind that I am examining motivations for donations to a broad and heterogeneous set of institutions. These institutions vary in their purpose, philosophies, and objectives. While some organizations have a clientele far removed from the donor, there are other cases in which the donor is the client. Therefore it should be no surprise that the motives for making donations to the different organizations vary as well.

In some cases one needs to make the actual contribution to derive benefits from it, and in others one can enjoy these benefits even when the contribution is made by someone else.[24] In the first case we characterize the benefit as private and in the second as public.[25] Individual contributions will be distinctly different depending on the types of benefits that motivate them. I describe these differences and review the substantial empirical literature that has tried to determine whether the marginal benefit from giving is either public or private.

Public Benefit

The most obvious benefit from giving is the output produced by the relevant nonprofit organization. The motive for giving may simply be a wish to increase the organization's services or provision level, be it to increase the frequency or quality of art exhibits, a desire to increase the number of children fed or educated in developing countries, or simply wanting to increase the income of those less fortunate. The literature on charitable giving frequently refers to individuals who benefit from the nonprofit's output as being altruistic.

Fundraising practices seem consistent with donors benefiting from the nonprofit's output. For example, many charities now provide the donor with specific information on the potential value of contributions: UNICEF informs potential donors that $17 can immunize a child against the six major childhood diseases and $40 can provide large wool blankets to protect ten children from the cold/winter weather during an emergency, Doctors Without Borders states that $35 will buy two high-energy meals a day to two hundred children and $100 can pay for infection-fighting antibiotics to treat nearly forty wounded children.[26] Similarly, one may view the concern for organizations' fundraising and administration costs as evidence of a desire to increase the provision level. In fact, most organizations now post their overhead costs. For example, the Make-a-Wish Foundation reports that 83 percent of total support and revenues go to program services, whereas the Mercy Corps reports that 94 percent go to program services, and more recently the September 11th Fund has been faced with demands that 100 percent of funds raised during a national telethon be used to help the victims and families of the terrorist attacks.[27]

While the charity's output is a compelling motive for giving, it is unlikely that it is the primary explanation. The reason is that although many charities provide services to specific clients, the benefit of knowing that someone is being fed or clothed is not limited to a few individuals.[28] In particular, it is not possible to prevent noncontributors from benefiting as well, nor is there a cost associated with others enjoying these benefits. This implies that the nonprofit's output is nonexclusive and nonrival in consumption.[29] Goods with such characteristics are referred to as public goods. A concrete example is that of National Public Radio. Once a program has been produced and is being broadcast there are no additional costs associated with increasing the number of listeners (nonrival), nor is it possible at a reasonable cost to exclude noncontributors from listening (nonexclusive). If the benefits from giving are identical to those of a public good, then an individual benefits fully from another contributor's donation, and few will want to give on their own.[30] Specifically, someone who is concerned solely for the nonprofit's output should never give if she is unable to distinguish between the quality provided in the presence and absence of her donation. For many charities like NPR most donors should therefore choose to free-ride. This strong incentive to free-ride has brought researchers to argue that benefits other than the nonprofit's output must be the reason why practically all U.S. households choose to make charitable contributions.

Theoretical analysis of the public motive also casts doubt on it being the primary contribution motive. A model where the nonprofit's output is the sole motive for giving simply generates unrealistic predictions. Consider the classical model of charitable giving. Here it is assumed that individuals benefit solely from their private consumption and the nonprofit's output, and that each individual takes the contributions of others as given. One of the extreme predictions of this model is that an increase in taxes to fund government support of an organization will have no effect on total funding to the charity. The reason is that donors are indifferent toward the source of nonprofit funding and hence will nullify the tax by reducing their contribution to the charity dollar-for-dollar (Bergstrom, Blume, and Varian 1986; Roberts 1984, 1987; Warr 1982, 1983). This result is referred to as the complete crowding-out result since it predicts that the government's contribution will crowd out private contributions.

Bergstrom et al. (1986) show that two conditions for the complete crowd-out prediction are that the tax is limited to those who contribute to the charity, and that none of the present contributors stop giving after the tax. To see why, consider the case where the government funds its contribution to charity through a tax levied solely on noncontributors. In this case the government's contribution will have the same effect as an increase in income. Once the government has contributed, a donor can decrease her contribution to the charity, enjoy the same level of nonprofit output, and still have money left to spend. If increases in income are normally spent on both private consumption and donations to the charity, then the individual does not reduce her donation dollar-for-dollar, and total contributions to the charity may increase.

Interestingly, the possibility of increasing total contributions does not exist when there are many potential contributors. Sugden (1982) argues that when there are many donors, then an increase in one person's contribution is almost completely offset by decreases in other peoples' contributions.[31] Andreoni (1988) extends and formalizes this argument using the classical model, and he proves that when there are many donors it is not possible for a charity to increase funding by finding new funding sources. The reason is that an increase in contributions by others leads each current donor to decrease her contribution a little bit. Thus if the sole motive for giving is a concern for the charity's output, then government grants can affect the quantity provided only when there are no individual contributors.[32]

Other predictions from the classical model of giving are equally extreme. As mentioned earlier, the level of services experienced with and without the individual donation is almost the same, hence the individual has but a small incentive to give and would rather free-ride. Andreoni (1988) shows that when there are many donors this implies that both the proportion of the population donating and the average donation will go to zero. In large economies we should observe only the wealthiest donors contributing. This is clearly not what we observe in the data, where most people give and there is little variation in the percentage of income given across income levels.

Private Benefit

To better explain charitable giving it has been argued that in addition to the nonprofit's output there are many benefits that only the contributor experiences (Arrow 1974; Andreoni 1989; Cornes and Sandler 1984; Steinberg 1987; Schiff 1990). These benefits are private, as they are unique to the person who contributes to the organization. If individuals derive private benefits from giving, then they will no longer view the donations by others as a perfect substitute for their private donation, and hence they will not generally prefer that donations are made by others. As this was the primary reason for the extreme free-riding and neutrality results of the classical model, these two results are weakened when donors also get private benefits from giving. In particular, it will no longer be the case that an increase in government contributions will result in a dollar-for-dollar crowd-out of private donations.

The literature has proposed a number of private benefits that individuals may experience when donating. At the most extreme level the private benefit of donating is no different from that of purchasing any other private good. Some charities offer the donor actual gifts in return for the donation—for example, recognition, welcoming or thank-you gifts, membership benefits like free tickets to events, updates on shows and exhibits, and so on.[33] Similarly, large contributors may have buildings named after them, receive exclusive dinner invites, be invited to have lunch with powerful politicians, and so on. In many instances these goods can be acquired only by making donations to the charity, and one may view part of the motivation for the donation as a mere purchase of the associated "rewards." Others may choose to contribute because doing so enables the donor to become a member of a club or a certain social circle. In these cases the donation can be seen as equivalent to the payment of a "membership fee" to be part of the community surrounding the charity. Certainly donations to the donor's house of worship carry some element of a membership fee.

Other private benefits of donating may be less tangible. For example, Tullock (1966) argues that in determining their level of giving, individuals take into consideration their evaluation of how the gift will affect their reputation. Becker (1974) suggests that charitable behavior can be motivated by a desire to avoid the scorn of others or to receive social acclaim. According to Glazer and Konrad (1996), individuals may contribute to a charity because it enables them to signal their wealth in a socially acceptable way.[34] Finally, Harbaugh (1998b) models a preference for prestige and suggests that charities, by publishing donations in ranges, actively affect the prestige associated with a gift.[35] He argues that prestige can be valuable to individuals either because it directly enters the individual's utility or because being known as a generous donor increases income and business opportunities.[36] To analyze this hypothesis Harbaugh (1998a) examines alumni donations to a prestigious law school. The law school used to report all donations but changed its policy to reporting only the categories of contributions. Consistent with the prestige and reputation argument, he finds that donors responded strongly to the change in announcements. The change to category reporting increased the proportion of donations made at the minimum amount necessary to get into a category and decreased the proportion of donations made at other amounts.

Private benefits from donating may also be more intrinsic in nature. Arrow (1974:17) argues that "the welfare of each individual depends not only on the utilities of himself and others but also on his contributions to the utilities of others." That is, "welfare is derived not merely from an increase in someone else's satisfaction but from the fact that the individual himself has contributed to that satisfaction."[37] Andreoni (1989, 1990) suggests that people may experience a "warm glow" from having done their bit. Perhaps the emphasis on sending thank-you notes is evidence that fundraisers try to maximize the warm glow the individual feels from having made a contribution. Other reasons for giving may be that it alleviates a sense of guilt. Sen (1977) suggests that contributors are motivated by "commitment" rather than sympathy. Donors may want to feel that they are doing their share, or that they are able to give back to society for the fortune that has met them. Or perhaps individuals are motivated by a "buying-in" mentality whereby they are prevented from feeling good about a charitable program unless they have made a fair-share contribution to it (Rose-Ackerman 1982).

Although these benefits differ from one another, they are all private in the sense that only the individual responsible for the donation gets to experience the benefit. Typically the approach used to model these incentives for giving is to assume that the individual's private benefit is unaffected by the donation made by others.[38] Thus donors who are solely motivated by private benefits should not respond to changes in the contributions made by others, and in particular we should observe essentially no crowd-out of individual donations when government contributions increase.

Empirical Evidence on the Motive for Giving

A substantial empirical literature seeks to determine whether the benefit of the last dollar given can be characterized as being either public or private. The typical empirical approach is to examine how an increase in government grants to nonprofits will affect giving by individuals. If the benefit is purely private, then we should observe no effect, and if the benefit is purely public, then we should see dollar-for-dollar crowd-out when the economy is large. Perhaps the most natural a priori assumption is that the benefit of giving has both private and public characteristics. The degree of crowd-out for these mixed-motive preferences has been carefully examined by Andreoni (1989), Cornes and Sandler (1984), Posnett and Sandler (1986), and Steinberg (1987).[39] Depending on the strength of the two, the degree of crowd-out will lie somewhere between complete and no crowd-out.[40] Recently Ribar and Wilhelm (2002) demonstrated that this prediction needs to be modified when there are many donors. In this case the motive for the last contributed dollar will be either public or private but not both. Thus we should observe either complete or no crowd-out, but should not expect to see incomplete crowd-out.[41]

I first review the empirical literature that has used the crowd-out hypothesis to determine why people give. While the vast majority of this work relies on actual giving data, more recent work has tested the crowd-out hypothesis using experimental methods. After I review the primary findings on crowding out, I conclude the section by discussing a series of experimental studies that move beyond the crowd-out hypothesis and more directly test the motives for giving.

I begin by examining the literature that uses either survey, giving, or tax data to determine how changes in government grants to nonprofits affect private giving to the nonprofit sector. For example, using tax data, Abrams and Schmitz (1978, 1984) show that government grants crowd out private contributions at the rate of about 28 percent; thus if the nonprofit sector were to receive an additional $100 in government grants, then individual contributions would decrease by $28. Using similar data, Clotfelter (1985) estimates that crowd-out is only 5 percent. The degree of crowd-out found in both of these studies suggests that a concern for the nonprofit's output is not the primary reason for giving.

One of the difficulties in examining tax data is that only the average degree of crowd-out across nonprofits can be determined. Alternatively, Kingma (1989) examines data on giving to National Public Radio. Using these data he is able to directly connect giving to the local NPR station to the grants that were given. Interestingly, the degree of crowd-out found in these data does not differ substantially from that found in larger data sets. The estimated crowd-out is merely 13.5 percent.[42] Kingma and McClelland (1995) reanalyze the same data using more sophisticated methods and come to the same conclusion, that there is very limited crowd-out.[43]

Surveying the literature on crowd-out estimates, Steinberg (1991) concludes that most studies have rejected the hypothesis of complete crowd-out and found the degree of crowd-out to range from 0.5 percent to 35 percent per unit of government spending.[44] One reason why the evidence speaks so strongly in favor of a private benefit from giving may be that many of the examined charities are national charities. Perhaps the private motive will be smaller if we examine nonprofits that have a clientele far removed from the donor, such as international relief organizations. If anything, one would expect that the concern for the charity's output is larger in this case. Recent evidence, however, suggests that this is not the case. In a very careful econometric study Ribar and Wilhelm (2002) examine a 1986–1992 panel of donations and government funding from the United States to 125 international relief and development organizations. The evidence suggests that the benefit that drives people to increase their contribution is private. They find that private donations at most decrease by thirteen cents for every dollar increase in government funding; however, in most cases they cannot reject the hypothesis that an increase in government funding has no effect on private giving. They conclude as others before them that the motive for giving an additional dollar is private, and that on the margin individuals are not concerned about the charity's provision level.[45]

One of the difficulties in drawing inferences from surveys or data on actual donations is that the data do not reveal whether the limited degree of crowd-out is driven by donors not being concerned for the provision of the nonprofit's output, or by the model not accurately describing the giving environment. For example, the lack of a response may signify a lack of information more than a private motive for giving. If donors are not informed of the government's donation to the organization then how can they respond to changes in the government's grants?

One environment with more control over such factors is the experimental lab. Here the experimenter controls the information, and hence the lab may present a cleaner environment in which to test the crowd-out hypothesis and thus to examine motives for giving. The primary difficulty is, of course, to determine the extent to which the experimental results extend to the real world.[46]

The experimental studies on crowd-out tend to find stronger evidence of a public motive for giving than those using survey or tax data. Typically, two different games have been used to examine crowd-out in the lab. One is the dictator game, and the other is the public good game. In the latter subjects are paired anonymously in small groups of, say, four individuals. Every individual in the group is given an allocation of money and asked to choose how much she wants to contribute to a public good and how much she wants to spend on a private good. Purchases of the private good benefit only the individual, whereas contributions to the public good benefit every member of the group. For example, each dollar in the private good may result in the individual earning one dollar, while each dollar contributed to the public good by any member generates an earning of fifty cents to that member and every other member of the group. Obviously an individual who is concerned solely with maximizing her private payoff will not contribute anything to the public good in this example. However, an individual may appreciate that although a contribution to the public good will cost her fifty cents, it will also increase the payoffs to each of the other group members by fifty cents. Someone who is altruistic and concerned for the payoff of others may decide that this payoff warrants a contribution.[47]

Andreoni (1993) is the first experimental study to assess motives for giving by looking at crowding-out behavior. This study relies on a modified version of the above public good game in which even subjects who care only about their own monetary returns would contribute some amount to the public good. He compares contributions in two different public good games. In one game donors are free to contribute any amount between zero and seven units, and in the second they are forced to contribute a minimum of two units and can choose any additional contribution between zero and five. The latter game is meant to simulate the situation where all contributors are faced with a tax that subsequently is contributed to the public good. If all donors contribute in both treatments then complete crowd-out implies that we should see no difference in total contribution levels between the two environments. If, for example, the average contribution level is 3.5 in the first treatment, then we would expect to see average individual donations decrease to 1.5 in the second treatment. However, if participants also derive a private benefit in the form of, say, a warm glow, then the forced donation is not a perfect substitute for the private donation, and we expect to see larger total contributions in the latter case. That is, we may see individual donations falling to, say, 2 instead of 1.5. Andreoni (1993) finds that total contributions in the second environment exceed those of the first—however, not by as much as one would have expected based on the previous empirical studies. He finds an average crowd-out of 71.5 percent over all rounds of the game and finds crowd-out of 84 percent in the last period of the game.[48] Relative to the previous crowd-out experiments, this suggests that in the experiment subjects are much more concerned about the size of the public good.

Bolton and Katok (1998) examine crowding-out by comparing donations in two different dictator games.[49] In one game the dictator is given $15 and the recipient is given $5, and in the other game the dictator is given $18 while the recipient has $2. By comparing contributions in the two games the authors determine whether donors take account of the amount of money given to the recipient. Complete crowding-out predicts that donors who gave more than $3 in the $18/$2 treatment would decrease their contributions by $3, and donors who gave less than $3 are expected to make no transfer in the $15/$5 treatment. By examining the average transfer in the two treatments Bolton and Katok (1998) find that 60 percent of the original transfers were crowded out when the original allocation to the recipients was increased by $3.[50] Thus they too find larger evidence of crowd-out in the lab.

Eckel, Grossman, and Johnston (2005) recently extended Bolton and Katok's study to real charities. Rather than having individuals transfer funds to an anonymous participant in the experiment they asked subjects to transfer funds to a charity of their choice. They considered two different frames; in one subjects were simply informed of the initial allocation ($18/$2 or $15/$5), and in the other the subjects were told that of their initial $20 entitlement $2 or $5 had already been taxed and given to the charity. Their results reveal great sensitivity to framing. In the neutral frame they observed essentially no crowd-out and in the tax frame they found complete crowd-out.

Finally, some experimental studies do not rely on the crowd-out hypothesis to determine the motives for giving. Palfrey and Prisbrey (1996, 1997) examine a series of public good experiments where the payoff from the public good is the same for all members of the group, while the payoff from the private good varies from person to person. By varying the relative benefits from the private and public good the authors can determine whether individuals donate primarily because they are confused, or because they derive either a private or public benefit from giving.[51] In contrast to other experimental evidence Palfrey and Prisbrey find that altruism cannot help explain the observed contribution patterns. Instead, it appears that error and warm glow both play a significant role in explaining giving patterns; however, the warm-glow effect is found to be low in magnitude.[52]

Using an alternative procedure Goeree, Holt, and Laury (2002) also examine charitable contributions in a series of situations where the return from the public and the private good varies.[53] In contrast to Palfrey and Prisbrey they find that contributions are increasing in the return to others and in the size of the group. Both of these findings are consistent with an altruistic motive, as increasing the size of the group and holding the individual's return from the public good constant suggests that at a fixed cost more people are receiving the benefit from the public good. In estimating the motive for giving they find that behavior is consistent with a strong public motive, whereas there is no evidence for a private motive for giving.

Although the experimental evidence is somewhat mixed, most studies find stronger evidence of public motives for donating than that observed when using survey or actual donation data. How do we reconcile these opposing findings? The most obvious explanation focuses on the many differences between actual donations and those of the experiment. One explanation for the different behaviors may be that the available information varies substantially between the two environments. Another is provided by Ribar and Wilhelm (2002), who cleverly suggest that a reason for the contradictory evidence may be that while there are only a few contributors in an experimental study, there are many contributors in the empirical studies. They show that when donors derive both public and private benefits from giving, incomplete crowd-out is predicted only when there are a small number of donors. If, however, there are many donors, the prediction is that one motive will dominate on the margin. That is, the motive for giving the last dollar will be either private or public. This implies that we should observe incomplete crowd-out only when the population size is small. The conflicting evidence may suggest that while the benefit of contributing in small groups has both private and public characteristics, the benefit from individual donations in large groups has only private characteristics.

In making comparisons between the experimental and nonexperimental environments it is important also to be aware that sometimes the definitions of the public benefit vary between the two. For example, the standard empirical and theoretical approach assumes that the public benefit is the benefit the individual donor gets from the nonprofit's output. In contrast, the experimental literature occasionally argues that the public benefit also depends on the benefit that others derive from the public good.[54]

The implication of the Ribar and Wilhelm result is substantial as for most charities there are many donors, and taken at face value this result suggests that these donors do not contribute out of a concern for the charity's output. Combined with the extreme and unrealistic neutrality results of the classical model of charitable giving it is not surprising that many doubt that donors contribute because they have publicly motivated or altruistic preferences. While we may critique the empirical findings on grounds of lack of information, it is harder to get around the extreme theoretical predictions of the model. The fact is that many people contribute to charities, and this observation is inconsistent with the prediction of the classical model of charitable giving.

So, is it really the case that donors do not care about the nonprofit's output? One possible explanation of the extreme predictions of the classical model may be that the results rely heavily on a few perhaps strict and unrealistic assumptions. In the next section I briefly review some of the work that has relaxed the underlying assumptions of the classical model of giving.

RELAXING THE ASSUMPTIONS OF THE CLASSICAL MODEL

While one would expect there to be private benefits from giving, it is surprising that public benefits appear to have no influence on giving. How is it possible that the incentive to give does not depend on the quantity of the nonprofit's output? It is certainly not consistent with the surveys on donor motivations, which find that individuals contribute because they care for the nonprofit's mission, project, or program.[55] Are donors simply wrong about what motivates them to give? In this section I relax assumptions of the classical model to see if we can maintain that contributions are due to a concern for the nonprofit's output while generating less extreme free-riding predictions.

I focus on cases that modify the standard prediction of negative correlation between individual contributions—that is, the prediction that an increase in one individual's contribution decreases that of another. First I consider the possibility that social norms and rules may cause individual contributions to be positively correlated. Second I relax the assumption that individuals take the donations of others as given. Charitable funds are often raised over time, and in these cases individuals may very well account for the effect their donation has on others. I conclude the section by discussing a couple of fundraising mechanisms, such as matches and raffles, that also help reduce the negative correlation between individual contributions.

Overall, the reviewed literature has yet to be subjected to the same degree of scrutiny as the literature examined earlier. However, preliminary results suggest that there are cases where donors are concerned about the nonprofit's output, yet an increase in a donor's contribution need not decrease that of others; in fact, it may even increase it. This is a crucial finding as it may weaken the extreme neutrality and free-riding results of the classical model.

Social Norms and Rules

The economics literature generally assumes that individuals are free to choose as they please as long as it is within their financial means. This is also the assumption of the classical model on charitable giving; however, some have argued that it is less appropriate because giving decisions often are guided by social norms and rules. If that is the case then the charitable giving model needs to account for the constraints imposed by the norms by which people abide.[56] The literature has proposed a number of alternatives. One of these has often been referred to as the "Kantian" rule (see, e.g., Laffont 1975).[57] This rule requires that those individuals who care about the services provided by a nonprofit will choose a contribution that equals the amount they would most prefer that the other members of the group should contribute. The implications of the Kantian rule are just as extreme and unrealistic as those of the classic model. Instead of extreme free-riding we should see everyone contributing a socially optimal amount to the charity, and instead of individual contributions decreasing with increases in those of others, we now predict that the individual's contribution level is independent of that of others.

Alternatively, Sugden (1984) proposes that individuals subscribe to a principle of reciprocity.[58] He questions that we follow a norm which dictates that we contribute irrespective of what others are doing. Why would we help someone who refuses to help us? Instead, Sugden suggests a principle of conditional commitment that does not require that you always contribute to the public good, but rather that you must do so if everyone else in your reference group does. Specifically, if the donor's preferred contribution level by the other members of the group is no smaller than the current minimum contribution, then the donor must contribute an amount that is at least as large as the minimum contribution in the reference group.[59] The individual's reference group is any group of individuals who benefit from provision of the same public good. While people who abide by the principle of reciprocity may contribute a socially optimal amount, they may just as well provide less than the optimal level. In contrast to both the classical model and that of the Kantian rule, Sugden's model predicts that an individual's contribution will increase when people in his or her reference group increase their contributions.

Interestingly, a positive effect of the contributions of others is consistent with evidence from Andreoni and Scholz (1998).[60] They examine data from the 1985 Consumer Expenditure Survey to determine whether donors respond positively to an increase in donations by others in their reference group. Given the available data they are limited to defining a reference group in a socioeconomic sense and cannot take account of geographic proximity. They find a positive effect of an increase in donations by others in the same "social reference space," which is defined as those of similar age, education, occupation, and residence (urban or rural). Specifically, they show that a 10 percent increase in donations by others in the reference group will cause the individual's donation to increase by 2 percent to 3 percent.[61]

The work on norms typically does not analyze how a certain norm or rule may develop; however, Holländer (1990) shows that when individuals care about social approval and this approval is a function of the extent to which the individual deviates from the average contribution among her peers, then approval or disapproval may be what triggers the individual to feel that the norm applies to her.[62]

The literature on norms suggests that incorporating them into the classical model may weaken the predictions of the model. However, before adopting these rules it is important that we gain empirical evidence in their favor. When should we expect such norms to be in effect? When will they constrain behavior? In the next section we present experimental results that test for the effect of reciprocity and find that in some environments reciprocity appears to play a small role, if any.

Accounting for the Contribution Behavior of Others

The classical model of charitable giving relies on the assumption that people make a one-time contribution and that in doing so they take the behavior of others as given. This implies that individuals do not account for the effect that their contribution may have on that of others. There are many situations, however, where this is not a reasonable assumption. For example, if people jointly contribute to the same charity more than once then they may consider the effect their current donation will have on the future donations of others. As a simple illustration consider the case where a group of neighbors all benefit from a nearby park. To maintain the park they each voluntarily contribute $40 for maintenance per month. If an individual fails to contribute in a particular month then it is quite possible that this will affect future maintenance contributions. Hence in choosing the preferred contribution now, the individual may take into account how her decision affects the future behavior of others.

This section examines a series of studies that point to environments where donors naturally are aware of the interdependencies between contributions. I start by discussing the effect of repeated interaction among donors. I then examine another case where donors naturally anticipate the effect their contribution will have on that of others. In particular, I review a recent study on the effect of publicly announcing past contributions to future donors. A public announcement may influence the amount given by subsequent donors, and it is likely that current donors take this effect into account prior to contributing. Both repetition and public announcements may reduce, remove, or reverse the negative correlation between individual contributions. I finish the section by showing that fundraising mechanisms, such as matches and raffles, also can cause individual contributions to be positively correlated. Throughout the section I focus on whether the predictions from the classical model (where donors are solely concerned with the nonprofit's output) are sustained. Of particular interest is whether an increase in an individual's donation may increase the amount contributed by others.

Repeated interaction. Donating to charity is rarely a one-time event; rather, people typically contribute to the same charity year after year. Whether repeated interaction affects the predictions of the classical model depends on the time horizon of the interaction. If donors believe that they may always contribute to the charity then the contribution game is one of infinite repetition, and the predictions of the classical model are quite different. In particular, the extreme free-riding result need not hold. With infinite repetition it is possible for contributors to threaten potential noncontributors with punishments that are large enough that individuals prefer to contribute despite their short-run incentive to free-ride.[63] For example, if donors choose to punish free-riders by withholding all future contributions, the long-term cost of free-riding may exceed the short-term benefit, and it will be possible to sustain cooperation.[64] However, if everyone recognizes that these interactions will eventually end, then such a strategy is not sufficient. To see why, consider the last period of the interaction. At this time donors recognize that there is no possibility of future punishments, and accounting for their last period incentives they choose to free-ride. With no cooperation in the last period, there is no threat of punishment in the second-to-last period either, hence people will free-ride in that period as well as in any period before that. Thus, cooperation collapses if the interaction is finitely repeated. Since finite repetition by itself has no effect on the predictions of the classical model we generally view the assumption of one-shot interaction as a simplifying one.

Marx and Matthews (2000) show that the effect of finite repetition is sensitive to the characteristics of the nonprofit's output. The assumption in the models I have examined so far was that a small increase in contributions also results in a small increase in the benefit from the nonprofit's output; however, this is not always the case.

Marx and Matthews consider instead the case where completion of a project results in a discrete jump in the project's benefit. While every contribution is beneficial in and of itself, the donation that completes the project derives a benefit that exceeds that of any donation before it. For example, there are benefits from helping members of a poor community, but the full benefit may only be enjoyed when the community becomes self-sufficient. Similarly, there were benefits of every shot of smallpox vaccination, but the benefit of the shot that secured that enough were vaccinated and the virus was unviable was greater than any before it.

When the nonprofit's output exhibits discrete jumps then repeated contribution to the project can result in outcomes that reduce or even remove the free-riding result of the one-shot interaction. Repetition allows the use of a "little-by-little" mechanism whereby donors can complete the project over several rounds. Although donors may not be willing to contribute to the charity when everyone makes one-time and simultaneous contributions to the project, it may be possible to raise sufficient funds when donations are raised a little at a time.

To see why several contribution rounds may secure provision of the public good, consider a case where the desired threshold for the project may be reachable if the fundraiser decides to raise a third of the project at a time. As in my earlier example, donors may choose to contribute as long as one-third of the donations were raised in the last period, and they may stop contributing if insufficient funds were raised in the previous period. If this threat of punishment is large enough donors may choose to cooperate. A sufficiently large discrete payoff jump secures that a contribution level can be reached where a donor is willing to complete the project although there is no threat of future punishments. This little-by-little mechanism can succeed in providing the project because gradual commitment of other donors and the reduction in the donor's per-period obligation both reduces the benefit and increases the cost of free-riding, and makes it worthwhile for individuals to continue to contribute to secure completion of the project.[65] When funds are raised over several rounds and there is a discrete benefit jump at completion then the extreme free-riding prediction from the classical model need not hold.

Public announcements of past contributions. Another case where individuals may consider how their contribution affects that of others is when donations are announced to potential future donors. The practice of announcing contributions is quite common. For instance, during fund drives potential donors may be informed of past contributions and in particular of major individual contributions. Capital campaigns are typically launched by the announcement of a large "leadership" contribution, and new donors and their pledged amounts are made public throughout the campaign. Similarly, churches collect contributions in open baskets, and recurring fundraising campaigns inform donors of previous contributions made in the local community or at the latest charity event.[66] Empirical evidence on announcements helps us understand why fundraisers may prefer this strategy. For example, Silverman et al. (1984) examine data from a national telethon in which three different funding schemes were employed. Their results show that announcing the names of individuals pledging money and the amount of money pledged resulted in greater contributions than when they were not announced.

The literature on announcements has primarily focused on explaining why announcements may increase contributions. We maintain this emphasis, but also examine whether the results are likely to alter the crucial prediction that individual donations decrease when those of others increase.

The reason why economists have been interested in announcements is that simple extensions of the classical model cannot explain the phenomenon. Comparing contributions without announcements to those that arise with announcements, Varian (1994) shows that private contributions are largest when donors are uninformed of the contributions made by others. The reason is that the initial donors will make a small initial contribution and thereby leave it up to those who follow to contribute to the charity. Thus the initial contributors will free-ride off subsequent contributors. This result, however, relies on the assumption that the donors can commit to giving only once. Relaxing this assumption, predicted contribution levels with and without an announcement are identical.[67] Thus, extending the classical model to account for the sequential contributions does not enable us to understand why announcements may increase contributions.

I consider a number of modifications to the model that may help us understand why fundraisers announce past contributions. I examine whether the success of announcements may be due to the private benefits of giving, the characteristics of the nonprofit's output, uncertainty about the quality of the nonprofit, reciprocity, or a concern for the status of the nonprofit's other donors.

Perhaps the classical model's failure in explaining announcements is just additional evidence that we need to extend the motives for giving to incorporate a private benefit. Announcements may be effective because they increase the donor's private benefit from giving; for example, announcements may provide the donor with prestige or the ability to signal her success or wealth.[68] While compelling, this argument is not a sufficient explanation of the announcement phenomenon. The reason is that announcements are viewed to be effective because they may increase the donations not only of those who have their contribution announced but also of those who follow. For instance, characteristic of Brook Astor's philanthropic endeavors is that others tend to copy her contribution after news about her donation. "When she gave one donation to the New York Library, for example, three other major gifts—from Bill Blass, Dorothy and Lewis B. Cullman, and Sandra and Fred Rose—all followed, with her generosity cited as the inspiration."[69] The chairman of the trustees of Johns Hopkins University explains that the reason that the university asks donors for permission to announce their gifts is that "fundamentally we are all followers. If I can get somebody to be the leader, others will follow. I can leverage that gift many times over."[70] This suggests that a large initial contribution can increase the donations of those who follow. This is exactly opposite of the predicted negative effect of the classical model. Explaining announcements may therefore also improve our understanding of public motives for giving.

One case where announcements may affect the contributions of others is when a certain threshold of funds must be collected before any of the nonprofit's output can be produced; this would be the case if there is a fixed cost associated with the production of the project. Such a project is referred to as a threshold project. Under the assumption that donors derive solely a public benefit from giving, Andreoni (1998) shows that the lack of announcements may result in two possible outcomes: the project either is or is not provided. He makes the point that announcements provide donors with an inexpensive method of coordinating on the positive provision outcome. Thus when the project is of the threshold type, announcements may increase contributions of both the leader and those who follow.[71]

What about the classical case where an increase in contributions always increases the nonprofit's output? The evidence by Silverman et al. (1984) suggests that announcements also are effective in this case, and both List and Lucking-Reiley (2002) and Shang and Croson (2003) show that in such cases individuals contribute more when the announced contribution is large.[72] Romano and Yildirim (2001) suggest that we consider the broader interaction between the private and public benefit to better understand this effect of announcements. They show that announcements increase overall contributions if individuals benefit from the donations of others and the benefits from giving are such that followers increase their contributions when those of leaders increase. The reason is that the leader will take the positive response into account when contributing first, and increase the contribution relative to when it is not announced. Announcements may therefore increase contributions to the charity.

One explanation for the positive correlation between initial and subsequent contributions is that past contributions may serve as a signal of the nonprofit's quality. In particular, large initial contributions may suggest to future donors that this is a charity worth supporting. While the literature on nonprofits generally assumes that donors know how productive or efficient a nonprofit may be, there are many circumstances where this is not the case.[73] But why are initial contributions needed to convince future donors of the quality? Can't the nonprofit simply reveal its quality to the donors? The reason why contributions are a good signal of quality is that all fundraisers have an incentive to convince donors that they are representing a high-quality charity, thus unverifiable information provided by the fundraiser will not be credible. In contrast, announcing past contributions is a credible way for the fundraiser to reveal the nonprofit's quality.[74]

Vesterlund (2003) examines an environment where past contributions are used as a signal of quality. She shows that an initial donor, who knows that his contribution will be announced, will investigate the quality of the charity before donating, and that the donor subsequently reveals the quality through his contribution.[75] A sufficiently large initial contribution informs future donors that the charity is of high quality and they too will make a large contribution. Announcements enable the high-quality charity to reveal its type and secure a higher contribution level than would arise absent announcements. High-quality charities will therefore always choose to announce past contributions. To not reveal their quality, low-quality charities will also announce past contributions. Thus in environments where there is uncertainty about the quality of the charity, we should expect fundraisers to announce past contributions.

Relaxing the assumptions that everyone contributes simultaneously to a nonprofit organization of well-known quality not only helps explain why announcements may be effective, but it also shows that even when donors care only about the nonprofit's output, an increase in one donor's contribution may increase that of others. As the announcement serves as a signal of quality we refer to this as the signaling hypothesis for announcements.

An interesting insight of the signaling model is that contributions to the high-quality charity exceed the level that results when the charity's quality is common knowledge. Thus announcements not only help high-quality charities to be recognized as being worthwhile, but also help them reduce the traditional free-rider problem. Furthermore, an implication of this model is that contributions are larger when the fundraiser solicits the wealthier donors first. The model therefore provides an interesting explanation for a phenomenon that is often observed but not well understood.[76]

Another explanation for the effectiveness of announcements may be that they trigger a social norm of reciprocity (see my earlier description). Seeing that someone contributes a large amount to the nonprofit may make others feel obligated to behave with similar kindness.[77] Thus reciprocity may create a positive correlation between contributions, and fundraisers may be able to trigger this reciprocity norm by publicly announcing previous contributions.

While the reciprocity and signaling hypotheses complement each other in explaining why announcements are successful, it is of interest to determine whether there are environments where we can distinguish between the two. Of particular concern is the signaling hypothesis. Donors need to be quite clever for signaling to work, and one may wonder not only whether future donors use past contributions to infer the nonprofit's quality, but also whether the initial donor anticipates this response.

Potters, Sefton, and Vesterlund (2001) examine responses in two-person public good experiments to distinguish between the signaling and reciprocity hypotheses and to determine if signaling may be a likely explanation for announcements. They ask two questions: first, when only the initial donor knows the value of the public good, do announcements cause contributions to increase? Second, if contributions are higher with announcements, could this be due to reciprocity rather than signaling? To answer these questions they study behavior of undergraduates in four simple treatments. In two of them the first potential donor, but not the second, is informed of the quality of the public good, and the authors examine the effect of informing the follower of the leader's contribution. According to the signaling hypothesis, higher contributions are predicted when the leader's contribution is announced. To assess the extent to which reciprocity, rather than signaling, causes contributions to increase they conduct two additional treatments to examine the effect of announcements when both donors are fully informed of the quality of the public good. These four treatments allow them to test the predictive force of the signaling hypothesis and also to calibrate the effect of reciprocity considerations.

Their results are broadly consistent with the signaling hypothesis. Followers in the asymmetric-information treatment tend to mimic the leaders' contributions, and leaders anticipate this inference. Thus leaders internalize the response of subsequent donors, so that the leader's private incentives become aligned with those of the group. As a result, announcements cause a substantial increase in contributions. In contrast, announcements have a negligible effect on contributions when the quality of the public good is known by both players. Combined, the two results suggest that the observed success of announcements is unlikely to be caused by reciprocity, and it does not appear that the interaction between private and public benefits of giving results in an individual generally increasing contributions with those of others. Ruled out in this experiment is also the possibility that the observed increase in contributions from announcements is due to a concern for status. For example, there is no evidence in the complete information treatment that announcements provide the leader with status, and that the followers subsequently give to get status as well.[78]

While status does not appear to affect behavior in the neutral experimental study, there is ample anecdotal evidence to suggest that actual donations are influenced by concerns for status. For example, charities often launch a campaign by announcing which high-status donors are on board, suggesting that we may prefer to give to charities that have a high-status donor base. Perhaps the decisions of Blass, Cullman, and Rose to follow Brook Astor's lead in contributing to the New York Library were motivated as much by status as the uncertainty about the quality of the library.

Kumru and Vesterlund (2003) examine whether it is optimal to announce contributions when donors are concerned about the status of other donors to the charity. Following the work by Ball et al. (2001) they assume that donors exogenously are given status, and that they prefer to be associated with individuals who have higher status than themselves. They show that it is optimal to announce contributions in such an environment, and that the high-status donor should be the first to give. While a high-status donor prefers not to be associated with low-status donors, these donors will subsequently mimic his donation and contribute an amount large enough to entice the high-status donor to contribute first. Thus the prediction is once again that we may observe a positive correlation among individual donations.

Since the theoretical result is sensitive to how concerned donors are with status, one may question the real-world implications of this model. To study the effect of status on charitable giving Kumru and Vesterlund conducted a series of two-person public good experiments. Following Ball et al. they induced status by asking participants to take a short quiz. Participants were then assigned to either a star or a no-star group, and were informed that in each round of the experiment they would be paired with a member of the other group. All contributions were done sequentially. In one treatment members of the star group were first to give, and in the second they were last to give. The authors find that overall contributions to the public good double when members of the star group contribute before the no-star group. As predicted by the theory, they find a strong positive correlation between individual contributions when members of the star group are first to give.

Matches and raffles. While announcing contributions is one method fundraisers can use to reduce the negative correlation among individual donations, another obvious one is to design the campaign such that the contributions by some donors are matched by those of others. If a donor is willing to contribute the same amount through a match as through a direct monetary contribution, then it is clear that the organization should prefer that the money be given as a match. While a direct contribution decreases the contributions of others, a match increases it.[79]

Another procedure that may reduce the free-rider problem is to raise contributions through a fixed-prize raffle. Morgan (2000) compares the contribution level that results from a raffle to that of direct voluntary contributions. He finds that contributions always are larger with a raffle, and that they increase with the size of the prize.[80] The reason is that the chance of winning is reduced every time someone buys a raffle ticket, hence to maintain the same likelihood of winning the individual has to buy more tickets. The increased competition to win the raffle counteracts the decrease in the incentive to contribute to the charity. Experimental results by Morgan and Sefton (2000) confirm that contributions are larger with a raffle than through voluntary contributions, even after accounting for the cost of the raffle prize. Duncan (2002) objects that Morgan's results are sensitive to some of the assumptions he makes.[81] He shows that the prize may be so large that people contribute less with a raffle than without it. However, although larger prizes do not always cause people to buy more tickets, Duncan demonstrates that there is always a prize such that contributions are larger with a raffle than without it.

The results presented in this section still need to be extended to more general environments; however, they suggest that realistic extensions of the classical model may alter the critical prediction that individual donations decrease when those of others increase. As this is the driving force for the extreme predictions of the classical model, this avenue of research is promising for determining whether it is unrealistic to assume that donors benefit from the nonprofit's output.

In this chapter I have provided a brief review of what economists have learned about why people contribute to nonprofits. While many questions have been answered, many others lie ahead. On one hand there is agreement that people give more when it is cheap to give and when their income is large, but on the other hand there is disagreement on how sensitive giving is to temporary and permanent changes in these variables. Future research using panel data is needed to settle this dispute. There appears to be more agreement among those who examine the motives for giving. I argued that the benefits from giving have either private or public characteristics. That is, some benefits can be experienced only by the individual contributing, while others can be enjoyed even when the contribution is made by other donors. Researchers typically rely on the predictions of the classical model of charitable giving when determining whether the benefits from giving have private or public characteristics. The vast majority of the empirical research on this topic has found that private benefits are the primary motive for giving. As a result most researchers agree that there is limited evidence to support the common belief that donors give because they care about the nonprofit's output. This finding is puzzling and surprising because most donors claim to contribute in part because they want to affect the nonprofit's output. One possible explanation for this extreme finding is that the predictions of the classical model mislead us when we interpret the data.

The classical model of charitable giving relies on a series of assumptions, some of which may be a poor approximation to the environment in which giving takes place. We relax some of these to see if we can maintain the assumption that contributions are driven by a concern for the nonprofit's output while generating less-extreme free-riding predictions. We find that a number of factors may reverse the prediction that an increase in a donor's contribution causes those of others to decrease. In particular, the prediction is sensitive to social norms, the extent to which we may interact with other donors again, the characteristics of the nonprofit's output, the benefits from giving, the uncertainty regarding the quality of the charity, and the status of other contributors. Much of this literature is still in its infancy and the full implications of these modifications are not well understood. However, by incorporating these features into more general models we may be able to better describe actual giving behaviors, and to understand what motivates individuals to contribute.

Another approach that may prove useful for future research is to more carefully model the public benefits of giving. While the common assumption is that the benefit from the nonprofit's output is independent of the number of people who benefit from it, the experimental literature has begun to view the individual's benefit from the public good as increasing the number of people who derive the benefit. That is, the benefit we get from contributing to public radio may depend both on the quantity and quality of public radio and on the number of people who get to experience it. While the literature has not acknowledged these two types of public benefits, this distinction may be important when modeling how people contribute, and in particular when we use the generated predictions to empirically determine why they contribute.

NOTES

1. Independent Sector (2001).

2. Similar to donating money or goods, volunteering also requires that individuals make resources that belong to them available to others. That is, both acts require a voluntary transfer of property. While similar, analysis of volunteering involves a different set of tools and is covered in Leete (this volume). If the objective is to examine the combined effect on giving and volunteering then one should be careful about separating these two (see Duncan 1999). Note also that the broad social and cognitive psychological literatures on motivation, attitudes and behavior, and decision-making and help-giving behavior are not included herein.

3. Corporations and foundations account for 16.5 percent of total dollars given (U.S. Census Bureau 2002).

4. The government's objective in using tax subsidies is not merely one of maximizing contributions (this could always be done at 100 percent subsidy). Rather, an optimal subsidy is characterized by the fact that marginal social benefits equal the marginal social costs. This is discussed more generally later in this chapter, and Simon, Dale, and Chisolm (this volume) provide a careful discussion of these design issues.

5. The marginal tax rate is the tax rate levied on the last dollar earned.

6. Relative to a cash transfer the donation of an appreciated asset is preferable; the reason is that no tax is assessed on the capital gain that would arise had the asset been sold. See Simon, Dale, and Chisolm (this volume) for a review of tax laws that affect giving.

7. The seven motivations were in descending order of importance: (1) pragmatic considerations of personal and community benefits; (2) devotion to religious principles and institutions; (3) awareness of tax advantages; (4) interest in social functions and networks attached to charitable activities; (5) perceived obligation to repay an institution for past services received; (6) altruism as a moral imperative; and (7) desire to continue family tradition of giving (Prince and File 1994).

8. To determine the overall effect on giving one needs to account for how taxes affect both income and price of giving; for example, decreasing the marginal tax rate will not only increase the price of giving but will also increase the donor's disposable income.

9. The proportion of income given as a function of income typically decreases with income at small income levels, and increases with income at higher income levels. Thus it is U-shaped, with the largest proportion of income given by low- and high-income households. See O'Herlihy, Havens, and Schervish (this volume) for a careful discussion of what may cause this U-shaped pattern.

10. If the government is less efficient in providing for public goods than the private sector then the threshold for efficiency could be closer to zero (see Feldstein 1980). Necessary for a unit elastic demand to be the threshold for efficiency is also that individuals truly make the contributions they report on the tax form, and that the government is able to make a direct transfer without adversely affecting the contributions by others. Slemrod (1989) emphasizes that if contributors deduct amounts larger than their actual contributions then a larger revenue is lost, thereby indicating that the price elasticity needs to be above one, in absolute value. Roberts (1987), on the other hand, argues that if an increase in government donations decreases donations of others then the efficiency threshold for the price elasticity needs to be below one in absolute value.

11. See Roberts (1987) and Schiff (1990) for careful illustrations of this point.

12. See Clotfelter (1985, 1997) and Steinberg (1990).

13. European studies generally find that giving is less sensitive to price.

14. To separate the income and price effect, Feenberg (1987) examines data that include information on the taxpayer's residency. This allows him to also incorporate differences in state income taxes, and hence he observes similar individuals with the same income and different prices, thereby allowing him to identify the two effects.

15. More precisely, Randolph (1995) finds that the permanent income elasticity is 1.14 and that the temporary income elasticity is 0.58; thus the previous cross-sectional studies appear to underestimate the permanent income elasticity. In contrast, the price elasticity appears to have been overestimated. He estimates the temporary price elasticity to be -1.55.

16. See also Barrett, McGuirk, and Steinberg (1997), who examine the short- versus long-run reaction to a change in price or income experienced during a specific year.

17. The estimates on permanent income elasticity range between 0.40 and 0.87, and the estimated temporary elasticity ranges from 0.29 to 0.45. The estimates on the permanent price elasticity range from -0.79 to -1.26, and that of the transitory range from -0.4 to -0.61.

18. Some studies suggest that it is important to simultaneously estimate the effect of taxes on volunteering and giving of money. Menchik and Weisbrod (1987), Brown and Lankford (1992), and Andreoni, Gale, and Scholz (1996) find that volunteering and gifts of money are complements; hence we may be underestimating the net effect of taxes when examining solely the effect of taxes on dollars given.

19. See Kagel and Roth (1995) for a general review of experimental economics.

20. To be able to replicate experimental results easily, researchers tend to rely on undergraduate subject pools. Typically the concern is whether the qualitative rather than the quantitative results extend to other populations. Studies that have examined this question tend to find that the undergraduate sample is a reasonably representative one. A

subsequent study by Andreoni, Brown, and Rischall (2003) reveals that the gender results of Andreoni and Vesterlund (2001) do extend to individuals who are not undergraduates.

21. At the extreme, allocations of $6 to self or $12 to the recipient were available; however, any allocation in between was available as well, e.g., $4 to each player.

22. Harrison and List (2004) propose six factors that can be used to identify the field context of an experiment: the nature of the subject pool, the nature of the information that the subjects bring to the task, the nature of the commodity, the nature of the task or trading rules applied, the nature of the stakes, and the environment that subjects operate in.

23. This result relies on the fundamental economic assumption that people are self-interested, thus individuals make costly charitable contributions only because they have a preference for doing so. Note that the selfishness assumption need not imply that the individual simply aims to maximize her material payoff.

24. I will not discuss why an individual may have a preference for giving. However, Schervish and Havens (1997) suggest that it may be caused by an experience in one's youth. Boris (1987) concludes that it is associated with religious heritage, personal philosophy, social responsibility, and political beliefs. Others have shown that donors must be asked to contribute (Hodgkinson and Weitzman 1996).

25. Alternative to the private and public motives for giving is codependent philanthropy. Duncan (2002) argues that some donors contribute because they want to make a difference. The interesting consequence of this motive is that donors are worse off when contributions of others increase ("an impact philanthropist cannot enjoy saving children if other philanthropists save them first" [p. 2.]). Another interesting implication of Duncan's model is that increased government contributions to a nonprofit may increase the individual's contribution.

26. See https://www.unicefusa.org/site/apps/ka/ct/contactus.asp?c=duLRI8O0H&b=36041 and http://www.doctorswithoutborders.org/donate/what.cfm.

27. There are substantial variations in how organizations determine administration and fundraising costs. The Urban Institute and the Center of Philanthropy have conducted research on this topic—see http://nccsdataweb.urban.org/FAQ/index.php?category=40.

28. Note that while economists generally work under the assumption that individuals make choices to maximize their well-being, this does not contradict the possibility that an individual's well-being may be a function of that of others. See, for example, Arrow (1974), who states that the welfare of each individual depends both on his own satisfaction and on the satisfactions obtained by others. Similarly, Becker (1974:1083) states that "charitable behavior can be motivated by a desire to improve the general well-being of recipients."

29. Nonexclusive implies that no one can be excluded from consuming the good, and being nonrival means that the consumption of one individual does not affect the consumption possibilities of any other potential consumers.

30. Samuelson (1954) examines a public goods environment and argues that free-riding will result in an inefficiently low provision of the public goods. Donors who are concerned for the nonprofit's output are often described as being altruistic; however, as pointed out by Rose-Ackerman (1996) it is misleading to refer to the public-motivated donors as being altruistic as such donors generally will be free-riding.

31. A similar argument is made by Margolis (1982).

32. This prediction relies on the assumption that the individual's benefit from the nonprofit's output depends only on the size of this output and not on the size of the population.

33. While gifts received from nonprofits are not tax deductible they may nonetheless be motives for contributing.

34. Consistently, Ostrower (1997) finds that philanthropy is what defines the boundaries of elite life.

35. Rose-Ackerman (1996:714) comments that "one can obtain prestige from making a gift only if others view one's actions as worthy. If the narrow private benefits of gift giving are too obvious and large, gift givers will not be praised for their self-sacrifice." Frank (2004) suggests that nonprofits want to appear charitable not only to attract donors who care about the nonprofit's output but also to attract those who want the prestige associated with giving to a charitable organization.

36. As the flip side of Harbaugh's argument, Long (1976) argues that publishing names and contributions in alumni magazines imposes social pressure on the contributor, and hence donations are made to relieve social pressure.

37. Interestingly, Arrow (1974) argues that this motivation is necessary since otherwise a purely altruistic individual would prefer that the action be taken by someone else, while an individual that is motivated by both might prefer to give.

38. Exceptions are Holländer (1990), who examines an environment where social approval is a function of the donations made by others. We will examine his and related models in the last section of the paper. A different approach is taken by Duncan (2002), who develops a model of codependent altruism in which a donor derives a private benefit from his or her donation if it makes a difference. In such a model donors prefer that others not contribute to their charity.

39. The model is frequently referred to as an impure altruism model.

40. Steinberg (1987) argues that the response can be more extreme. In particular, the individual's contribution may decrease more than the increase in contributions by others (super crowd-out), or it may increase (crowd-in).

41. Ribar and Wilhelm (2002) show that incomplete levels of crowd-out are possible—however, only as a knife-edge case.

42. Subsequent research has followed a similar approach and examined private and public donations on an organization-by-organization basis.

43. Controlling for quantity of public radio consumed (directly and through instruments) and trying three alternatives to deal with the nonnormality of the censored errors, they conclude that a single household's giving would be between fifteen and nineteen cents lower if government expenditures increased by $10,000. Based on a comparison of crowd-out and income effects they reject the null hypothesis that altruism is pure.

44. A few studies, however, have not found any degree of crowd-out. Posnett and Sandler (1989) examine donations to U.K. charities in 1985 and find that government grants to nonprofits increase rather than decrease individual donations to the charity. Thus increased government donations augment the charities' ability to attract private donations. Similarly, Khanna, Posnett, and Sandler (1995) examine a panel of 159 U.K. charities and find that government grants encourage rather than decrease private giving. Using panel data on U.S. charities Payne (1998) reaches the opposite conclusion, however, using panel data from U.S. universities. Payne (2001) does find evidence of crowd-in. See Steinberg (2003) for a summary of recent crowd-out studies.

45. Duncan (1999) cannot reject that there is complete crowd-out when including the joint effect on contributions of time and money.

46. Alston and Nowell (1996) are among the few who have tried to extend an experimental study to a field experiment.

47. This game has been well studied by experimental economists, political scientists, psychologists, and sociologists. The results generally show that while some participants choose to give nothing, others choose to give a lot. On average, individual contributions typically lie between 40 and 60 percent of the amount of money participants are given. By varying the parameters of the environment, economists have shown that the amount contributed responds in the manner one would expect. Contributions tend to decrease with repetition, increase with face-to-face interaction, and increase when the marginal return from giving increases. See Ledyard (1995) for an excellent review of experiments on public goods.

48. Chan et al. (2002) replicate Andreoni's results and show that

crowd-out increases as the involuntary transfer increases. See also Gronberg, Luccasen, and Van Huyck (2003).

49. Bolton and Katok make the point that Andreoni's crowd-out analysis relies on the assumption that individuals care only about their own payoff. If instead participants are altruistic and also derive utility from increasing the payoffs of others then there may be multiple allocations that are equilibria of the game, and as a result many different contribution levels may be consistent with complete crowd-out.

50. Conversations with the authors revealed a small error in the original article where the stated degree of crowd-out was 73.7 percent. Average giving in $18/$2 was $3.48; taking account of those who contributed less than $3, this generates the complete crowd-out prediction that giving should be $1.83 in $15/$5. However, average giving in $15/$5 was $2.49. Thus crowd-out is (3.48 − 2.49)/(3.48 − 1.83) = 60 percent.

51. For example, a participant who is solely concerned about his own payoff will choose to free-ride and not to contribute to the public good if her private return exceeds that of the public good. Palfrey and Prisbrey argue that the utility of a publicly motivated or altruistic donor will be increasing in his or her own payoff as well as that of others, whereas the privately motivated donor's benefit from giving will be independent of how the donation affects the group payoff.

52. Sefton and Steinberg (1996) and Andreoni (1995) find less evidence of confusion. In contrast to Palfrey and Prisbrey (1996) they do not try to determine whether individuals are motivated by private or public motives.

53. There are several differences relative to the Palfrey and Prisbrey studies. First, the participants are fully informed of the return that other participants in their group are facing, second, to avoid any repeated game effects they examine only one-shot interaction, and third, they allow the return from the public good to vary for the donor and the other participants in the group. This latter addition helps identify whether donations might be altruistically motivated. In the Palfrey and Prisbrey experiment a change in the return from the public good causes two simultaneous changes. First, it increases the benefit of the contribution received by others, and second, it decreases the individual's cost of making the contribution. By holding the donor's return of the public good constant and increasing that of the other donors, it is possible to determine whether altruism may be the motivation for giving.

54. For example, Goeree et al. (2002) found that donations increase when the group size increases. The reason is that as the group size increases more people benefit from provision of the public good. If individuals take into account the benefit that other donors get from the public good then the limiting arguments of Andreoni (1989) and Ribar and Wilhelm (2000) are not correct, as they rely on the assumption that the public benefit depends only on the dollars contributed and thus are independent of the population size. This raises two important questions for future research. First, it may be of interest to examine an experimental environment that better approximates the classical definition of the public benefit. This could potentially be done in a modified dictator game where the number of potential dictators varies. Second, it is important to determine what donors consider to be the public benefit of their contribution. If donors care about both the effect that their donation has on total output as well as the effect that it has on other donors then the classical crowd-out analysis is misleading and must be modified.

55. See, e.g., Panas (1984), Prince and File (1994).

56. Norms may be modeled either as determining individual preferences (e.g., Fehr and Schmidt 1999; Bolton and Ockenfels 2000), or as a constraint on the objective along the lines of a budget constraint (e.g., Sugden 1984).

57. Arrow's (1974) interpretation of the Kantian categorical imperative is closer to one of serial reciprocity or social exchange. He suggests that "perhaps one gives good things in exchange for a generalized obligation on the part of fellow men to help in other circumstances if needed." See also Bilodeau and Gravelle (2004).

58. For a substantial review on reciprocity see Moody (1994).

59. Sugden (1984) uses the phrase *effort level* rather than *contribution.* He refers to effort as measuring labor time, absolute monetary contribution, or contribution as percentage of income.

60. This prediction is also consistent with Schervish and Haven's (1997) finding that communities of participation induce charitable giving.

61. It is not clear that the positive coefficient should be interpreted as interdependent preferences. As argued by Andreoni and Scholz (1998), "our estimation method could also be interpreted as a very complex fixed-effects model, hence it is possible that individual heterogeneity could be mistakenly attributed to interdependent preferences."

62. Holländer argues that individuals obtain approval only from their reference group, meaning friends, kin, acquaintances, neighbors, etc. While his model predicts a positive correlation between individual gifts, it also predicts that government contribution reduces the approval from giving and hence increases in government giving may result in individual gifts being crowded out.

63. Consider, for example, the case where everyone contributes, say, $100 to a certain charity in every period, as long as everyone else contributed $100 in the last period. If someone fails to make a contribution in one period, then the result is that no one will contribute in subsequent periods.

64. See Fudenberg and Tirole (1992) for a careful discussion of repeated games and the folk theorem.

65. While the dynamic game may result in equilibria that complete the project there will also be equilibria that fail to do so. Thus the set of equilibria for the dynamic game is larger than that of the static game. Duffy, Ochs, and Vesterlund (2003) compare contributions in the static and dynamic games to see if this expanded set of equilibria changes behavior. As predicted they find that contributions are larger in the dynamic than in the static game. However, in contrast to the theory by Marx and Matthews they show that dynamic play increases contributions even when there is no discrete increase in payoffs upon completion of the project.

66. Edles (1993) recommends that fundraisers inform future donors of the number of donors and the total amount that they have contributed.

67. See Vesterlund (2003).

68. Andreoni (1988, 1990), Harbaugh (1998b), Glazer and Konrad (1996), and Olson (1965).

69. *New York Times,* March 30, 2002, p. A13.

70. *New York Times,* February 2, 1997, p. 10.

71. Bagnoli and Lipman (1989) propose an alternative method of securing the positive provision outcome. If the fundraiser offers to refund donations short of the threshold then the positive provision outcome is always reached. See also Morelli and Vesterlund (2000) for a model where the fundraiser strategically chooses the threshold.

72. List and Lucking-Reiley (2002) find that increasing the initial contribution from 10 percent to 67 percent of the campaign goal produces nearly a sixfold increase in subsequent contributions. While the objective for each solicitation was to provide funds for a computer, the letter made clear that insufficient or excessive funds would be put to alternative use within the organization. Thus provision was increasing with contributions. Consistent with the continuous production technology is the fact that their results are the same when contributions are refunded when they are short of the goal (see Bagnoli and Lipman 1989; Pecorino and Temimi 2001). Interestingly, a recent follow-up experiment by List and Rondeau (2003) does not find a strong effect of announcement. One explanation for the differing results may be that in the lab there is no uncertainty about the charity, hence announcements do not serve as a signal of high quality. Another explanation may be that it is easier for donors to coordinate on a positive provision outcome in the lab than it is in the real world. Shang and Croson (2003) examine the effect of informing donors to a public

radio station of the contributions made by others. They find that contributions increase with the size of the previously announced contributions.

73. Considering that in 2005 there were more than 600,000 charities and another 30,000 join their ranks every year, it seems plausible that contributors do not have perfect information about the quality of the organizations. While contributors may be informed about the quality of some organizations, charities continually introduce "new products" and it may be difficult prior to the provision of a specific good to evaluate how useful that good will be.

74. Government grants and contracts may also provide signals of a nonprofit's quality (see Rose-Ackerman 1981; Payne 2001).

75. It is not an assumption of the model that only the first mover can purchase information. Rather, all donors are free to purchase information, but the followers choose not to because they realize that the first contribution will reveal this information to them free of charge. The result easily extends to a case where smaller donors do not have the option of purchasing the information.

76. See also Komai (2004).

77. In sequential games it has frequently been shown that people tend to be kind to those who have been kind to them and unkind to those who have been unkind. See Fehr and Gächter (2000) for references and an overview of the importance of reciprocity.

78. For example, it may be argued that status plays a role when Bill Blass, Dorothy and Lewis B. Cullman, and Sandra and Fred Rose all follow Brook Astor's contribution to the New York Library (*New York Times,* March 30, 2002, p. A13). See Ball et al. (2001) for some interesting status experiments.

79. For a match to have the intended positive effect, donors must believe that the match is paid only when the requested donation is made. If the donor commits to matching up to a certain point and this contribution is made independent of whether the challenge is reached, then the match is equivalent to a standard donation, and should be viewed as such.

80. For these results to hold it is necessary that the prize be fixed and the probability of winning increases with the contribution. For example, Morgan (2000) shows that it does not hold when the prize depends on the number of tickets purchased, and Duncan (2002) shows that it does not hold if the probability is fixed, such as with a door prize.

81. Duncan shows that Morgan's result depends on the assumption that the benefit of the nonprofit's output is independent of the consumption of all other goods.

REFERENCES

Abrams, Burton A., and Mark D. Schmitz. 1978. "The Crowding-out Effect of Governmental Transfers on Private Charitable Contributions." Pp. 303–312 in *The Economics of Nonprofit Institutions: Studies in Structure and Policy,* edited by Susan Rose-Ackerman. Yale Studies on Nonprofit Organizations series. New York and Oxford: Oxford University Press.

———. 1984. "The Crowding-Out Effect of Governmental Transfers on Private Charitable Contributions: Cross-Section Evidence." *National Tax Journal* 37(4):563–568.

Alston, Richard, and Clifford Nowell. 1996. "Implementing the Voluntary Contribution Game: A Field Experiment." *Journal of Economic Behavior and Organization* 31:357–368.

Andreoni, James. 1988. "Privately Provided Public Goods in a Large Economy: The Limits of Altruism." *Journal of Public Economics* 35:57–73.

———. 1989. "Giving with Impure Altruism: Applications to Charity and Ricardian Equivalence." *Journal of Political Economy* 97:1447–1458.

———. 1990. "Impure Altruism and Donations to Public Goods: A Theory of Warm-Glow Giving" *Economic Journal* 100:464–77.

———. 1993. "An Experimental Test of the Public-Goods Crowding-Out Hypothesis." *American Economic Review* 83:1317–27.

———. 1995. "Cooperation in Public Goods Experiments: Kindness or Confusion?" *American Economic Review* 85:891–904.

———. 1998. "Toward a Theory of Charitable Fundraising." *Journal of Political Economy* 106:1186–1213.

Andreoni, James, Eleanor Brown, and Isaac Rischall. 2003. "Charitable Giving by Married Couples: Who Decides and Why Does It Matter?" *Journal of Human Resources* 38:111–133.

Andreoni, James, William G. Gale, and John K. Scholz. 1996. "Charitable Contributions of Time and Money." Unpublished manuscript.

Andreoni, James, and John K. Scholz. 1998. "An Econometric Analysis of Charitable Giving with Interdependent Preferences." *Economic Inquiry* 36:410–428.

Andreoni, James, and Lise Vesterlund. 2001. "Which Is the Fair Sex? On Male-Female Differences in Altruism." *Quarterly Journal of Economics* 116 (February):293–312.

Arrow, Kenneth. 1974. "Gifts and Exchanges." *Philosophy and Public Affairs* 1(4):343–362.

Auten, Gerald, James Cilke, and William Randolph. 1992. "The Effects of Tax Reform on Charitable Contributions." *National Tax Journal* 45:267–290.

Auten, Gerald, Holger Sieg, and Charles Clotfelter. 2002. "Charitable Giving, Income, and Taxes: An Analysis of Panel Data." *American Economic Review* 92:371–382.

Bagnoli, Mark, and Barton Lipman. 1989. "Provision of Public

Goods: Fully Implementing the Core through Private Contributions." *Review of Economic Studies* 56(4):583–601.

Ball, Sheryl, Catherine Eckel, Philip Grossman, and William Zame. 2001. "Status in Markets." *The Quarterly Journal of Economics* 16(1):161–188.

Barrett, Kevin, Anya McGuirk, and Richard Steinberg. 1997. "Further Evidence on the Dynamic Impact of Taxes on Charitable Giving." *National Tax Journal* 50:312–334.

Becker, Gary S. 1974. "Theory of Social Interaction." *Journal of Political Economy* 82(6):1064–1093.

Bergstrom, Ted, Lawrence Blume, and Hal Varian. 1986. "On the Private Provision of Public Goods." *Journal of Public Economics* 29(1):25–49.

Bilodeau, Marc, and Nicolas Gravel. 2004. "Voluntary Provision of a Public Good and Individual Morality." *Journal of Public Economics* 88(3–4): 645–666.

Bolton, Gary, and Elena Katok. 1998. "An Experimental Test of the Crowding-Out Hypothesis: The Nature of Beneficent Behavior." *Journal of Economic Behavior and Organization* 37:315–331.

Bolton, Gary, and Axel Ockenfels. 2000. "ERC, A Theory of Equity, Reciprocity and Competition." *American Economic Review* 90(1):166–193.

Boris, Elizabeth. 1987. "Creation and Growth: A Survey of Private Foundations." Pp. 65–126 in *America's Wealthy and the Future of Foundations,* edited by Teresa Odendahl. New York: Foundation Center.

Brown, Eleanor, and Hamilton Lankford. 1992. "Gifts of Money and Gifts of Time: Estimating the Effects of Tax Prices and Available Time." *Journal of Public Economics* 47(3):321–341.

Chan, Kenneth, Rob Godby, Stuart Mestleman, and R. Andrew Muller. 2002. "Crowding Out Voluntary Contributions to Public Goods." *Journal of Economic Behavior and Organization* 48:305–317.

Clotfelter, Charles. 1985. *Federal Tax Policy and Charitable Giving.* Chicago: University of Chicago Press.

———. 1990. "The Impact of Tax Reform on Charitable Giving: A 1989 Perspective." In *Do Taxes Matter?* edited by Joel Slemrod. Cambridge, Mass.: MIT Press.

———. 1997. "The Economics of Giving." Pp. 31–55 in *Giving Better, Giving Smarter: Working Papers of the National Commission on Philanthropy and Civic Renewal,* edited by John W. Barry and Bruno V. Manno. Washington, D.C.: National Commission on Philanthropy and Civic Renewal.

Cornes, Richard, and Todd Sandler. 1984. "Easy Riders, Joint Production and Public Goods." *Economic Journal* 94:580–598.

Duffy, John, Jack Ochs, and Lise Vesterlund. 2003. "Do Contributions Increase When Funds Are Raised Little-by-Little?" Unpublished manuscript.

Duncan, Brian. 1999. "Modeling Charitable Contributions of Time and Money." *Journal of Public Economics* 72:213–242.

———. 2002. "Pumpkin Pies and Public Goods: The Raffle Fundraising Strategy." *Public Choice* 111:49–71.

———. 2004. "A Theory of Impact Philanthropy." *Journal of Public Economics* 88:2159–2180.

Eckel, Catherine, and Philip Grossman. 2003. "Rebate versus Matching: Does How We Subsidize Charitable Contributions Matter?" *Journal of Public Economics* 87:681–701.

Eckel, Catherine, Philip Grossman, and Rachel Johnston. 2005. "Crowding Out Private Charitable Giving: An Experimental Test." *Journal of Public Economics 89(8):1543–1560.*

Edles, L. Peter. 1993. *Fundraising: Hands-on Tactics for Nonprofit Groups.* New York: McGraw Hill.

Feenberg, Daniel. 1987. "Are Tax Price Models Really Identified?: The Case of Charitable Giving." *National Tax Journal* 40:629–633.

Fehr, Ernst, and Simon Gächter. 2000. "Cooperation and Punishment in Public Goods Experiments." *American Economic Review* 90(4):980–994.

Fehr, Ernst, and Klaus Schmidt. 1999. "A Theory of Fairness, Competition and Cooperation." *Quarterly Journal of Economics* 114:817–868.

Feldstein, Martin. 1980. "A Contribution to the Theory of Tax Expenditures: The Case of Charitable Giving." Pp. 99–122 in *The Economics of Taxation,* edited by H. J. Aaron and M. Boskin. Washington, D.C.: Brookings Institution.

Frank, Robert. 2004. *What Price the Moral High Ground? Ethical Dilemmas in Competitive Environments.* Princeton, N.J.: Princeton University Press.

Fudenberg, Drew, and Jean Tirole. 1992. *Game Theory.* Cambridge, Mass.: MIT Press.

Glazer, Amihai, and Kai Konrad. 1996. "A Signaling Explanation for Charity." *American Economic Review* 86:1019–1028.

Goeree, Jacob, Charles Holt, and Susan Laury. 2002. "Private Costs and Public Benefits: Unraveling the Effects of Altruism and Noisy Behavior." *Journal of Public Economics* 83:225–276.

Gronberg, Timothy, Andrew Luccasen, and John Van Huyck. 2003. "Contributions and Crowd-Out of Public Goods: Competing Models and Experimental Evidence." Unpublished manuscript.

Harbaugh, William. 1998a. "The Prestige Motive for Making Charitable Transfers." *American Economic Review, Papers and Proceedings* 88:277–282.

———. 1998b. "What Do Gifts Buy? A Model of Philanthropy and Tithing Based on Prestige and Warm Glow." *Journal of Public Economics* 67:269–284.

Harrison, Glenn, and John List. 2004. "Field Experiments." *Journal of Economic Literature* 42(4):1013–1059.

Hodgkinson, Virginia, and Murray Weitzman. 1996. *Giving and Volunteering in the United States.* Washington, D.C.: Independent Sector.

Holländer, Heinz. 1990. "A Social Exchange Approach to Voluntary Cooperation." *American Economic Review* 80:1157–1167.

Independent Sector. 2002. Giving and Volunteering in the United States. Washington, D.C.: Independent Sector.

Kagel, John H., and Alvin E. Roth. 1995. *The Handbook of Experimental Economics.* Princeton, N.J.: Princeton University Press.

Khanna, Jyoti, John Posnett, and Todd Sandler. 1995. "Charity Donations in the U.K.: New Evidence Based on Panel Data." *Journal of Public Economics* 56:257–272.

Kingma, Bruce. 1989. "An Accurate Measurement of the Crowd-Out Effect, Income Effect, and Price Effect for Charitable Contributions." *Journal of Political Economy* 97:1197–1207.

Kingma, Bruce, and Robert McClelland. 1995. "Public Radio Stations Are Really, Really Not Public Goods." *Annals of Public and Cooperative Economics* 66(1):65–76.

Komai, Mana. 2004. "An Economic Theory of Leadership." Dissertation, Virginia Polytechnic Institute and State University.

Kumru, Cagri, and Lise Vesterlund. 2003. "The Effect of Status on Charitable Giving." Unpublished manuscript.

Laffont, Jean J. 1975. "Macroeconomic Constraints, Economic Efficiency and Ethics: An Introduction to Kantian Economics." *Economica* 42:430–437.

Ledyard, John O. 1995. "Public Goods: A Survey of Experimental Research." Pp. 111–194 in *The Handbook of Experimental Economics,* edited by John H. Kagel and Alvin E. Roth. Princeton, N.J.: Princeton University Press.

List, John, and David Lucking-Reiley. 2002. "The Effects of Seed Money and Refunds on Charitable Giving: Experimental Evidence from a University Capital Campaign." *Journal of Political Economy* 110(1):215–233.

List, John, and Daniel Rondeau. 2003. "The Impact of Challenge Gifts on Charitable Giving: An Experimental Investigation." *Economics Letters* 79:153–159.

Long, Stephen H. 1976. "Social Pressure and Contributions to Health Charities," *Public Choice* 28:55–56.

Margolis, Howard. 1982. *Selfishness, Altruism and Rationality.* Cambridge: Cambridge University Press.

Marx, Leslie, and Steven Matthews. 2000. "Dynamic Voluntary Contribution to a Public Project." *Review of Economic Studies* 67:327–358.

Menchik, Paul, and Burton Weisbrod. 1987. "Volunteer Labor Supply." *Journal of Public Economics* 32:159–183.

Moody, Michael. 1994. *Pass It On: Serial Reciprocity as a Principle of Philanthropy.* Indianapolis: Indiana University Center on Philanthropy.

Morelli, Massimo, and Lise Vesterlund. 2000. "Over Provision of Public Goods." Unpublished manuscript.

Morgan, John. 2000. "Financing Public Goods by Means of Lotteries." *Review of Economic Studies* 67:761–784.

Morgan, John, and Martin Sefton. 2000. "Funding Public Goods with Lotteries: An Experiment." *Review of Economic Studies* 67:785–810.

Olson, Mancur. 1965. *The Logic of Collective Action.* Cambridge, Mass.: Harvard University Press.

Ostrower, Francie. 1997. *Why the Wealthy Give: The Culture of Elite Philanthropy.* Princeton, N.J.: Princeton University Press.

Palfrey, Thomas and Jeffrey Prisbrey. 1996. "Altruism, Reputation and Noise in Linear Public Goods Experiments." *Journal of Public Economics* 61:409–27.

———. 1997. "Anomalous Behavior in Public Goods Experiments: How Much and Why?" *American Economic Review* 87:829–846.

Panas, Jerold. 1984. *Megagifts: Who Gives Them, Who Gets Them.* Chicago, Ill.: Pluribus Press.

Payne, Abigail. 1998. "Does the Government Crowd-Out Private Donations? New Evidence from a Sample of Non-profit Firms." *Journal of Public Economics* 69:323–345.

———. 2001. "Measuring the Effect of Federal Research Funding on Private Donations at Research Universities: Is Federal Research Funding More than a Substitute for Private Donations?" *International Tax and Public Finance* 8(5):731–751.

Pecorino, Paul, and Akram Temimi. 2001. "A Note on the Theory of Charitable Fundraising: The Role of Refunds." *Journal of Public Economic Theory* 3:341–345.

Posnett, John, and Todd Sandler. 1986. "Joint Supply and the Finance of Charitable Activity." *Public Finance Quarterly* 14:209–222.

———. 1989. "Demand for Charity Donations in Private Nonprofit Markets." *Journal of Public Economics* 40:187–200.

Potters, Jan, Martin Sefton, and Lise Vesterlund. 2001. "Why Announce Leadership Contributions? An Experimental Study of the Signaling and Reciprocity Hypotheses." Unpublished manuscript, http://www.pitt.edu/~vester/leadingbyexample.pdf.

Prince, Russ, and Karen File. 1994. *The Seven Faces of Philanthropy: A New Approach to Cultivating Major Donors.* San Francisco: Jossey-Bass.

Randolph, William. 1995. "Dynamic Income, Progressive Taxes, and the Timing of Charitable Contributions." *Journal of Political Economy* 103:709–738.

Ribar, David C., and Mark O. Wilhelm. 2002. "Altruistic and Joy-of-Giving Motivations in Charitable Behavior." *Journal of Political Economy* 110:425–457.

Roberts, Russell D. 1984. "A Positive Model of Private Charity and Public Transfers." *Journal of Political Economy* 92(1):136–148.

———. 1987. "Financing Public Goods." *Journal of Political Economy* 92:420–437.

Romano, Richard, and Huseyim Yildirim. 2001. "Why Charities Announce Donations: A Positive Perspective." *Journal of Public Economics* 81:423–447.

Rose-Ackerman, Susan. 1981. "Do Government Grants to Charity Reduce Private Donations?" Altruism, Nonprofits, and Economic Theory." Pp. 95–114 in *Nonprofit Firms in a Three-Sector Economy,* edited by Michelle White. COUPE Papers in Public Economics #6.Washington, D.C.: Urban Institute.

———. 1982. "Charitable Giving and 'Excessive' Fundraising." *Quarterly Journal of Economics* 96:193–212.

———. 1996. "Altruism, Nonprofits, and Economic Theory." *Journal of Economic Literature* 34:701–786.

Samuelson, Paul A. 1954. "The Pure Theory of Public Expenditure." *Review of Economics and Statistics* 36:387–389.

Schervish, Paul G., and John J. Havens. 1997. "Social Participation and Charitable Giving: A Multivariate Analysis." *Voluntas* 8(3):235–260.

Schiff, Jerald. 1990. *Charitable Giving and Government Policy: An Economic Analysis.* Westport, Conn.: Greenwood.

Sefton, Martin, and Richard Steinberg. 1996. "Reward Structures in Public Good Experiments." *Journal of Public Economics* 61:263–287.

Sen, Amartya K. 1977. "Rational Fools: A Critique of the Behavioural Foundations of Economic Theory." *Philosophy and Public Affairs* 6:317–344.

Shang, Jen, and Rachel Croson. 2003. "Social Comparison and Public Good Provision." Paper presented at Economic Science Association North American Regional Meeting, Tucson, Arizona, October 30–November 2.

Silverman, Wendy, Steven Robertson, Jimmy Middlebrook, and Ronald Drabman. 1984. "An Investigation of Pledging Behavior to a National Charitable Telethon." *Behavior Therapy* 15:304–311.

Slemrod, Joel. 1989. "Are Estimated Tax Elasticities Really Just Tax Evasion Elasticities? The Case of Charitable Contributions." *Review of Economics and Statistics* 71:517–522.

Sugden, Robert. 1982. "On the Economics of Philanthropy." *Economic Journal* 92:341–350.

———. 1984. "Reciprocity: The Supply of Public Goods through Voluntary Contribution." *Economic Journal* 94:772–787.

Steinberg, Richard. 1987. "Voluntary Donations and Public Expenditures in a Federalist System." *American Economic Review* 77:24–36.

———. 1990. "Taxes and Giving: New Findings." *Voluntas* 1:61–79.

———. 1991. "Does Government Spending Crowd Out Donations? Interpreting the Evidence." *Annals of Public and Cooperative Economics* 62:591–617.

———. 2003. "Economic Theories of Nonprofit Organizations: An Evaluation." In *Study of the NonProfit Enterprise: Theories and Approaches,* edited by Helmut Anheier and Avner Ben-Ner. New York: Springer-Verlag.

Tullock, Gordon. 1966. "Information without Profit." Pp. 141–159 in *Papers on Non-Market Decision Making,* edited by Gordon Tullock. Thomas Jefferson Center of Political Economy, University of Virginia.

U.S. Census Bureau. 2002. Statistical Abstract of the United States. Washington, D.C.: Government Printing Office.

Varian, Hal R. 1994. "Sequential Provision of Public Goods." *Journal of Public Economics* 53:165–186.

Vesterlund, Lise. 2003. "The Informational Value of Sequential Fundraising." *Journal of Public Economics* 87:627–658.

Warr, Peter G. 1982. "Pareto Optimal Redistributions and Private Charity." *Journal of Public Economics* 19:131–138.

———. 1983. "The Private Provision of a Public Good Is Independent of the Distribution of Income." *Economics Letters* 13:207–211.

Wynne-Edwards, Vero C. 1962. *Animal Dispersion in Relation to Social Behavior.* New York: Hafner Press.

VI

MISSION AND GOVERNANCE

25

Nonprofit Mission: Constancy, Responsiveness, or Deflection?

DEBRA C. MINKOFF
WALTER W. POWELL

INTRODUCTION: WHY MISSION LOOMS LARGE

In a simple, elemental fashion, a mission is a clarion call for nonprofit organizations. The goals or agendas attached to a mission serve to rally, engage, and enroll workers, volunteers, and donors. They also serve as guidelines for how to go about the business of contributing to the public good, arguably the primary principle that motivates the nonprofit enterprise. In this sense, nonprofit mission operates as an inducement and, as a long tradition of organization theory stresses, inducements are essential for motivating participants to contribute to organizations (Barnard 1938; Simon 1947).

Nonprofit organizations have both instrumental and expressive dimensions (Frumkin 2002). Thus a core feature of nonprofit activity is affording individuals the opportunity to express their beliefs through work and donations. As Frumkin (2002:23) observes, "the very act of attempting to address a need or fight for a cause can be a satisfying end in itself, regardless of the outcome." Nonprofit mission looms large in the context of such expressive activity because an organization's goals provide workers and donors with the satisfaction that their values are being put into action. Organizational mission also drives founders to start an organization, and it provides a sense of purpose that energizes and justifies organizational existence. In an important sense, mission serves to signal what a nonprofit organization regards as good and important, and through that signal induces supporters to invest their time, energy, and resources.

Oster (1995) contends that mission plays a much larger role in nonprofits than in proprietary enterprises. She argues that a distinctive advantage of nonprofits is their ability to motivate staff on the basis of an organization's fidelity to a cause. That engagement hinges on issues of trust, commitment, and reputation. Many nonprofits, whether religious or secular, are ideological organizations, and their passion or faith is their rationale for existence. A clear mandate or calling creates allegiance and trust among employees, clients, and donors. For ideologically oriented nonprofits, mission both attracts and compels staff and supporters.

The mechanisms of trust and assurance underline the major theoretical accounts of nonprofit activity, including contract failure (Hansmann 1980), median voter or government failure (Weisbrod 1988), and worker control (Pauly and Redisch 1973; Glaeser 2003). These literatures are discussed extensively elsewhere in this volume, so we need not review them at length here. We simply want to note how mission functions in each approach. Contract failure arguments rest on the idea that in circumstances where there are strong informational asymmetries between the provider of a service and a good, and thus abundant opportunities for the former to exploit the latter, nonprofit status is an assurance that such incentives are mitigated. Devotion to a mission wraps the consumer in a blanket of trust, so to speak.

Government provision of goods and services is typically targeted to the mainstream, to a stylized median voter. Nonprofits, in response, cater to more specialized, distinctive, or passionate niches. Oster (1995) argues that nonprofits specialize in the more controversial ends of the public goods spectrum. And it is in precisely these areas where participants have a strong allegiance to an activity or a constant need for a service; hence the signal of a nonprofit's adherence or commitment to a mission is critical.

A third view of nonprofit activity stresses that the form is well suited for the realization of professional goals. Nonprofit mission dovetails nicely with a professional calling or purpose and helps foster professional sovereignty as well. Pauly and Redisch (1973) suggested that hospitals may, at one time, have functioned as doctors' cooperatives. Glaeser (2003) extends this idea to art museums, private universities, and other settings where elite, well-educated workers control the governance of nonprofits. In such settings, staff dominance works to ensure that nonprofits focus on missions that are closely aligned with professional mandates.

The centrality of mission is apparent, then, in each of the major theoretical accounts of nonprofit activity. But while mission serves as organizational purpose or compass, nonprofits are also buffeted by environmental contingencies and challenged by external mandates. Our goal in this chapter is to enhance understanding of the interplay of mission, mandates, and external constraints and opportunities. Our approach is informed by neoinstitutional theories of organizational behavior (Powell and DiMaggio 1991), which emphasize the need for organizations to conform with externally determined normative, cognitive, and regulatory expectations regarding their structure and functioning. Pressures toward conformity are especially strong for nonprofits that are highly dependent on external sources for both legitimacy and support. The decisions and choices that members of organizations make are thus constrained by considerations of appropriateness that are widely shared among members of the institutional field. Further, given our conceptualization of mission as tied to both individual and collective inducements, we focus on nonprofit organizations that are more reliant on solidaristic or cause-related incentives, in contrast with more utilitarian calculations, to attract and reward participants (Clark and Wilson 1961). This somewhat broad category includes voluntary associations, human service agencies, social movement organizations, religious organizations, and cultural or lifestyle groups, while excluding nonprofits such as universities, foundations, and hospitals that load higher on the dimension of instrumental inducements. While mission shift can—and often does—occur in all types of nonprofits, our interest here is in those organizations that we expect to experience the most acute disruption when the group's original mission no longer aligns with the expectations of members, outside supporters, or political decision makers. This set of organizations is presumed to be more subject to internal and external scrutiny and to the need for acceptance by powerful participants. Many of these organizations also articulate ideological or political agendas that are difficult to achieve, and this struggle exacerbates the problem of providing inducements and maintaining commitment over the long haul (W. R. Scott 2003:176–77).

We begin with a general discussion of key forces that might trigger or compel mission deflection or adherence. We then provide detailed capsule summaries of a set of rich organizational case studies that focus on nonprofit mission or goals. These cases, which cover a wide terrain that includes voluntary social service agencies, local and national feminist groups, community-based AIDS organizations, cultural and religious organizations, and public-interest science organizations, among others, form the empirical core of our chapter. We conclude with reflections on the challenges of responsiveness in the nonprofit sector.

EXPLAINING CHANGES IN NONPROFIT MISSION

In the first edition of this handbook, this chapter was entitled "Organizational Change in Nonprofit Organizations." Our goal in revising and expanding the chapter is not merely to update the research, which has grown considerably, but also to tackle the interesting question about the saliency of nonprofit mission more directly. We consider nonprofit mission as both a charter and a constraint. Mission motivates activity and also limits the menu of possible actions. But mission interacts, in powerful ways, with external contingencies. Rangan (2004) captures the twin pulls of fidelity to mission and the need for survival with the labels "mission stickiness" and "market stretchiness." "Mission creep" and "mission drift" are other phrases that reflect the process through which organizational goals can be deflected or sacrificed in the interests of organizational survival, or as the result of a loss of focus. Mission stretch or drift reflects the core challenges of maintaining solvency and purpose.

In a series of interviews with the executive directors of San Francisco Bay Area nonprofits, we asked about the difficulties of juggling fidelity to a mission with achieving fiscal stability. Several responses were quite relevant to the analytical aims of this chapter. The director of a human services organization for developmentally challenged children and adults commented:

> You get a nonprofit in a financial situation like we are, and you tell yourselves it's okay to change our mission somewhat to include the possibility of operating a for-profit grocery store to generate some revenues. So then the mission changes and the reason the agency was originally started has gotten watered down. You learn that you've changed the whole nature of the organization without really knowing it, and the mission has become much more diffuse. It happens a lot, it's very seductive.

The director of a large arts organization is struggling with his board of directors over issues of mission, values, and vision. He observed that

> Whenever there is a financial problem, the board's first response is, "The problem is with all this new, weird work that nobody wants to see. So if we do less of it, we'll do better, right?" The board says to me, "We love your commitment to the arts, but right now you have to be more commercially focused." So I say, "Okay, take dance, we've been losing all this money on dance, so we're going to do less dance." But if we do less dance, then we have even less people coming to see it, and then that means we do even less. And the next thing you know, it's gone.

These comments reflect a core question: what factors push nonprofits, poised at a critical juncture, in one direction or another? To tackle this vexing question, we need to consider external influences as well as the internal dynamics of nonprofit organizations. We hope to provide an analytically nuanced portrait of the internal organizational dilemmas that different kinds of nonprofit organizations face. Our goal is a richer understanding of how internal organizational processes interact with both the interpretation of and the responses to external circumstances. As a starting point, we highlight four critical influences and describe what we think are the central challenges that nonprofits face in negotiating pressures for change.

Critical Influences

Organizational Life Cycle

The size and age of a nonprofit organization may strongly influence the extent to which it maintains its fidelity to a mission. Several factors, however, are at play in considerations of the influence of organizational demography. Very small organizations, which DiMaggio (this volume) characterizes as minimalist, are often highly fluid and flexible. In contrast, larger, established organizations are much more formal and procedural. The attachment to organizational policies may supplant passion for a mission in hierarchical organizations, while the participatory nature of small organizations may promote zeal for a mission. Similarly, Glaeser (2003) argues that donor control over established, well-to-do nonprofits is weak, and thus donors who want their funds spent in specific ways may opt to start their own foundations or engage with a limited number of smaller nonprofits whose behavior they can strongly influence. Such a calculus seems to motivate many of the practices of the so-called new venture philanthropy.

In contrast, however, smaller, younger nonprofits are often in vulnerable financial positions, while larger, established nonprofits have a more secure and diversified funding base. Thus cash-starved small nonprofits typically have to chase after funds, and such money is frequently tied more closely to a donor's interests than to a nonprofit's mission. Rangan (2004) argues that this kind of struggle for support can be "addictive," as the funds obtained usually cover only direct costs and do not contribute to overhead or infrastructure. Hence the organization must search again for other funds, and in so doing the mission becomes ever more diluted.

One further life-cycle factor that may influence adherence to or deflection from an organization's mission is the departure of the founder or early charismatic leader. To the extent that a group's original mission is not widely institutionalized in organizational practices or that participation and external support is mainly a function of a single individual's standing both inside and outside of the group, the loss of a key leader is likely to make mission constancy much more difficult to achieve. In more general terms, generational or demographic turnover in leaders and members has the potential to introduce new ideas and challenges regarding an organization's structure and objectives. Turnover seems to be particularly disruptive for social movement groups that gain visibility and new members who then are accommodated (or ignored). Gitlin (1980), for example, documents such a life-cycle effect for the Students for a Democratic Society, as does Polletta's (2002) research on the Student Nonviolent Coordinating Committee, although we expect that this dilemma confronts all nonprofits that operate along less (or non-) bureaucratized lines.

Volunteerism versus Professionalism

Nonprofits that are volunteer-based are built from the grass roots on the basis of strong commitment. Such organizations are often highly purposive, with specific goals as the abiding passion of the participants. Fidelity to mission is critical in order to sustain participation. Nonprofits with more professionalized staff may also be motivated by a sense of purpose, but that calling is tempered by concerns with public accountability, the dictates of professional responsibility, and an awareness of the requirements that professional service providers must follow. Increased professionalism may inevitably lead such nonprofits to "bend more with the wind" because professionals are more cognizant of external contingencies that influence work practices and organizational goals.

Mission versus Mandate

A mission is concerned with creating social value or contributing to the public good, although opinions certainly differ on the definition of what is "good" or "valuable" (Mansbridge 1998). Promoting a more equitable or open society, reviving traditional family values, eradicating disease, preserving the remaining pristine places on the planet, or working to reduce the scope of government are aspirations, not requirements. Mandates, in contrast, are imposed by external bodies, be they funders, governments, or standard-setting or accreditation agencies. Such organizations frequently dictate the "musts" a nonprofit is required to observe or practice in order to receive funding, approval, or certification. The tension between mission and mandate underscores how divergent internal and external influences can be. External demands can be viewed internally as, at worst, attempts at control or co-optation designed to thwart an organization's desires and aims. In contrast, funders or standards bodies may see their efforts as reasonable attempts to influence or cajole nonprofits to specify what constitutes success and to set measurable standards for its attainment.

Changing Relations with Government

In many industrial democracies, a fundamental change in social welfare provision is under way. Whether this shift is ascribed to neoliberalism, to the legacies of Margaret Thatcher and Ronald Reagan, or to the rise of new public management, governments are rethinking the provision of social services and turning to private entities—nonprofits and commercial firms—and relying on market mechanisms for service provision. The United States has a long history of this relationship, dubbed third-party government (Salamon 1987), but such tendencies have been amplified over the past two decades, so much so that some have decried the devolution of government and the rise of nonprofit services as a form of codependence or vendorism (Frumkin 2002:71–78). These changes have made nonprofit organizations more noted as social service providers than as policy innovators or social critics (Salamon 1995). Indeed, in our interviews with executive directors of San Francisco Bay Area nonprofits, managers reported that government grants were both the most procedural and the most demanding funding sources to account for, but were also highly unreliable year in and year out. Such trends toward privatization can be highly corrosive of nonprofit mission and programmatic values. Consequently, some ideological nonprofits do not accept state funding precisely because it restricts their autonomy and fidelity to mission.

Critical Challenges

Viewed broadly, purposive nonprofit organizations are influenced by a number of internal and external circumstances that often pressure them into pursuing more conservative activities and adopting more conventional organizational structures. As posited by neoinstitutional theory, the need for external legitimacy and survival tends to provide incentives for groups to compromise the missions that may have originally motivated them. Advocacy and community-based organizations, for example, may retreat from their distinctive commitment to the public good, opting for a more legitimate and comfortable service role as they become more invested in organizational survival, pursuing individual-level solutions to social problems such as providing services to the elderly, disabled, welfare recipients, or people with AIDS. Thus, at various points in their life cycles, nonprofits face a choice between taking a more cautious or conservative interpretation of their mission versus pursuing a more flexible or innovative orientation.

Faced with this characterization, nonprofit agency staff are likely to throw up their hands and cry foul. How are they expected to do any "good deeds" if they can't stay in business? How are they supposed to obtain funding for critical programs and services if they try to innovate or engage in controversial advocacy? Staff who view themselves as trained professionals not only need to follow established standards of client treatment; they have also made significant investments in specific programs and technologies that are not easily altered. Can't we see how risky it would be to undertake any kind of fundamental change in what an organization does when there is so much competition for funding clients? Isn't it obvious that legitimacy can be compromised if an organization strays from the presumption that nonprofits should be motivated solely by service or charitable agendas? By the same token, staff in social movement and cultural organizations are likely to take offense at the characterization of themselves as unable to maintain their original commitments in the face of increasing competition for resources and legitimacy, or they may balk at the suggestion that altering their mix of activities is tantamount to compromise or co-optation.

In one sense, these complaints are certainly justified. Political and resource conditions clearly raise the stakes of increased advocacy. All organizations, not just nonprofit service agencies, are more or less constrained by the need to conform to acceptable modes of doing business. And any kind of organizational change is disruptive and exposes organizations to higher risks of failure, especially when the resulting change places the organization in a new relationship with the state and other critical sources of support (Hannan and Freeman 1984; Minkoff 1999). Shifting from advocacy toward more individual-oriented service provision confers survival advantages as organizations conform more closely with institutional rules and expectations about appropriate methods of organization (DiMaggio and Powell 1983) and with dominant views of the moral worth of the constituency served (Hasenfeld 2000). In contrast, when service organizations try to adopt an advocacy agenda, they move closer to the terrain of political activism, possibly jeopardizing their survival chances. Such a change may signal an objection to or questioning of public policy, with the potential consequence that the group will sacrifice some degree of institutional support and face a greater risk of failure.

Clearly, then, one of the most fundamental challenges that nonprofit organizations face is to be responsive to environmental shifts—in the availability of funding from private and public sources, in support and resistance from key stakeholders and political elites, and in issue salience—while remaining consistent with their original organizational missions and accountable to their internal bases of support. In this sense, nonprofits are constrained by their commitment to a mission that defines appropriate forms of organization, the degree of autonomy from the state, and the extent of accountability to the constituencies they serve or represent. At the same time, in a number of circumstances, a nonprofit organization may need to redefine the mission itself in a way that enables an interpretation of organizational change as continuous with the group's avowed goals and identity. This is no small task, however, as a variety of factors—including mission, ideology, and collective identities—establish an outer boundary for what models of organization and types of activities are tenable.

PATHWAYS TO ORGANIZATIONAL CHANGE

Our characterization of nonprofit organizations suggests both a heightened vulnerability and a need to be flexible in the face of changes in the political and social context. There are any number of external and internal organizational barriers to adaptation and an increased risk of failure when movement groups alter their core organizational missions or identities, regardless of whether such changes move the group in more or less conventional directions.

The important point, from our perspective, is that there is no single trajectory that organizations follow in response to environmental pressures. Rather, as we seek to demonstrate in this section, changes in nonprofit mission can take one of a variety of forms: (a) conservative transformation or accommodation; (b) proactive change, in particular turning from a more conventional mission to a more challenging role despite pressures to conform; (c) resistance to change, that is, holding fast to the group's mission even when it includes more challenging goals; (d) shifting priorities as a response to changing external circumstances, while renewing or reorienting the mission to focus on or enhance a core animating belief; or (e) mission displacement, largely as a result of pursuing new funding sources in hopes that they may allow some vestige of an original identity to persist and enable organizational survival in perilous times. Despite a great deal of diversity within and across the nonprofit sector, the cases we discuss demonstrate that organizational responsiveness, as well as how much internal conflict is generated as a result, are both constrained and enabled by mission.

Accommodation

There is a long tradition of research on organizational change in voluntary associations and nonprofit agencies that, building on Michels's ([1915] 1962) discussion of the "iron law of oligarchy," posits that nonprofit agencies tend over time to become more conservative and to shy away from controversy for the sake of organizational survival. Although Michels's thesis has been critiqued (e.g., Zald and Ash 1966; Clemens and Minkoff 2004), it has become almost a truism that, to the extent to which nonprofits undergo change, it is in the direction of political or institutional accommodation. As the cases we review here demonstrate, organizations as varied as mass-based social movements, neighborhood groups, feminist service agencies, and community-based AIDS organizations have a tendency to succumb to external pressures for accommodation—although not without a fair amount of reluctance or resistance to alterations in organizational structure and mission.

Messinger's analysis (1955) of the transformation of the Townsend movement is often held up as the archetypal story of accommodation or mission deflection, a case in which the organizational apparatus remained intact long after the social movement lost its original impetus. The Townsend movement was founded as a network of membership clubs in the 1930s to advocate national pensions for the elderly as a mechanism for economic recovery. One might even think of it as a precursor to the American Association of Retired Persons. Following the Depression and later World War II, the Townsend clubs remained firmly committed to a specific program of pensions and economic reconstruction. But their failure to respond to changing social conditions led to a steep decline in membership, even as pension issues gained political visibility in the 1950s. From a national membership of 2,250,000 in 1936, the movement shrank to 56,656 by 1951. The decreasing political relevance of the Townsend plan halted recruitment of new members, and the advanced ages of existing members rapidly depleted the membership base. Moreover, other organizations, which did a more effective job of mobilizing political support for economic aid to the elderly, attracted many Townsend members to their ranks.

A key consequence of the sharp drop in Townsend club membership was financial difficulty. In what Messinger refers to as a "tendency to salesmanship," the movement began lending its name to consumer products (candy bars and soaps) in order to raise new funds. The purchase of these items—unlike those in previous sales efforts, such as bumper stickers with political slogans—implied no commitment to the movement. These activities focused organizational efforts on the business of raising money rather than on the pursuit of political goals. Potential new members ceased to be regarded as converts and came to be seen as customers. The leaders of the Townsend movement shifted their goals from a political agenda to a concern with organizational maintenance, even to the point that this change entailed the death of the original mission. Membership involvement was altered, turning "what were once the incidental rewards of participation into its only meaning." A politically active, value-oriented social movement was transformed into a recreation network, offering dances and card games for its remaining elderly members. The demise of the Townsend movement serves as a clear warning for contemporary nonprofits that turn to aggressive revenue generation with little consideration of how such activities may engage members.

In a more recent example, various local feminist organizations offer a lesson in how even those groups that are keenly attentive to the risks of seeking external funding find it difficult to resist external mandates. The contemporary feminist movement has encompassed a number of ideological positions and has supported diverse organizational forms, addressing such issues as economic equality, reproductive rights, domestic violence, and rape through both national and community-level organizations and activism. Efforts at the local level have tended to be concentrated in smaller, collectively structured groups committed to a more progressive ideology grounded in an analysis of the structural sources of women's oppression and focused as much on collective empowerment as policy change. Nancy Matthews's (1994, 1995) analyses of rape crisis centers in Los Angeles illustrate many of the central tensions faced by feminist "social movement agencies" that have "an ideational duality that encompasses both social movement and human service orientations" (Hyde 1992:122). In the 1980s the increasing reliance of rape crisis centers on state funding had the twin effect of enabling organizational survival and compromising the pursuit of feminist goals. Comparing the trajectories of six centers, Matthews documents the "transformation from grassroots activism to professionalized social service provision" that had taken place in the movement by 1990.

A particularly telling example of this transformation is the Los Angeles Commission on Assaults against Women (LACAAW), the first rape crisis hotline in the area. LACAAW was created in 1973 by feminists from two local women's centers that were already involved in consciousness-raising activities and antirape work (providing informal counseling and engaging in marches, demonstrations, and direct confrontations with known perpetrators). The founding members of LACAAW were primarily white leftist activists committed to collectivist organizational ideals and autonomy from the state, both hallmarks of radical feminism. We discuss this case in some depth, since it vividly illustrates a path from partial to full accommodation.

From the start, LACAAW confronted the question of whether to pursue federal financial support, in this case from the Law Enforcement Assistance Administration. Although very much in need of the funding, LACAAW members ultimately decided that the compromises involved would be too great, even though the decision generated significant internal conflict. In 1976, however, LACAAW accepted a two-year grant from the National Institutes for Mental Health (NIMH) for community-based rape prevention education. This funding enabled the center to increase its staff, but it also came with various requirements for program and product development. The formalization entailed by such programs, however, conflicted with the center's founding ideology. LACAAW's resolution was to continue to operate by consensus with respect to major policies, while decisions regarding the day-to-day operation of the hotline were made by key staff. Such "apparent accommodation" (Matthews 1995) was carried out with reluctance by the founding members, who remained committed to egalitarian ideals; nonetheless, they moved the center toward greater formalization.

The most dramatic change in organizational structure and operations took place in 1979, soon after the NIMH grant ran out and LACAAW was barely able to secure additional funding. At this juncture, when the hotline was close to folding and the center was besieged by internal conflicts and the resignation of key leaders, the decision was made to adopt a more conventional bureaucratic structure in order to attract external funding. On the initiative of a new director—a longtime volunteer who undertook the task of reviving LACAAW on an unpaid basis—the most significant restructuring involved establishing an independent working board of directors. Since most of the new board members were women with traditional volunteer backgrounds and little or no experience in antirape or feminist activism, the new director pursued training and consciousness-raising with board members, while also constituting an informal "council of elders" that debated policies using consensus procedures prior to their submission to the board for approval. Thus the organization made a concerted effort to retain some elements of the shelter's original principles, while at the same time moving toward greater formalization.

The second critical restructuring event was receipt of an emergency grant and subsequent funding from the California Office of Criminal Justice Planning (OCJP) in 1980. This was a significant departure for LACAAW, given its early rejection of support from the criminal justice/law enforcement system. An OCJP mandate to collect detailed information on the calls received (such as information on the race and ethnicity of victims) obliged staff to supervise volunteers in order to produce the required paperwork and took valuable time away from pursuing movement-related objectives. OCJP-funded rape crisis centers were monitored for compliance through regular site visits by auditors who checked organizational bylaws, operations, and records. Reporting and accountability structures also consolidated a broader trend in the rape crisis movement toward a service-oriented therapeutic perspective, which treated rape as a problem of individual mental health. At every step of the way, activist members resisted the imposition of conventional structures and ideas, and they attempted to devise mechanisms to protect their original commitment to feminist ideals and practice. Ultimately, however, organizational survival hinged on conformity to institutional conventions.

The overall pattern of organizational development within the AIDS activist movement has followed a similar trajectory of organizational growth, bureaucratization, and depoliticization (Cain 1993, 1995; Rosenthal 1996). Community-based AIDS service organizations (ASOs) in North America developed initially from the gay and lesbian community's outrage at the lack of government response to the epidemic. The first initiatives were mainly small volunteer efforts to develop support services such as hotlines, buddy programs, prevention brochures, and education campaigns, combined with political advocacy aimed at improving medical research, treatment, and services for people infected with HIV. The Gay Men's Health Crisis (GMHC), founded in New York City in 1981, was the first such organization and served as a model for community-based AIDS response (Chambré 1997; Kayal 1991). More generally, early ASOs were characterized by informal, nonhierarchical structures that were thought to be more responsive to, and representative of, the concerns of people living with HIV/AIDS. These organizations also operated with a broader social-change agenda that sought to situate HIV infection within the context of homophobia and heterosexism, sexism, and racism and to empower people living with HIV/AIDS through volunteer participation and involvement in ASO program development (Cain 1995).

Given the immediacy of the AIDS crisis, supportive service provision necessarily took precedence over grassroots advocacy, and ASOs were quick to professionalize, hiring paid staff and successfully seeking external funding. For example, although only a few of the sixteen New York City–based ASOs studied by Chambré (1997) followed the "classic pattern" of volunteer to paid labor and private to public funding, formalization was still the dominant route. Rosenthal (1996) also documents that the bulk of community service projects sponsored by New York State's AIDS Institute shifted from more participatory structures to a more hierarchical client services model, a transition also evident in the Ontario-based AIDS Network (Cain 1993). As Cain (1993, 1995) argues, this move toward formalization effectively depoliticized these organizations—a charge leveled early on at GMHC, leading to the formation of the direct-action group AIDS Coalition to Unleash Power (ACT UP) in 1987 (Wolfe 1994).

Although the development of community-based AIDS organizations appears to mirror the trajectory of feminist groups toward formalization and professionalization, most studies provide little evidence of the same level of internal organizational conflict or serious risk to organizational survival. In fact, it appears that the impetus for professionalization reflected self-conscious "impression management" and the desire for external legitimacy (Elsbach and Sutton 1992; Cain 1994). Specifically, ASOs explicitly sought to distance themselves from their origins in the gay and lesbian community by presenting themselves as professional service agencies serving the general public. In the AIDS Network, for example, efforts to appear "respectable" took the form of establishing a board of directors composed of nongay professional and community leaders, favoring staff hires based on technical and administrative experience rather than political commitment, and appropriating the language of professional agencies (Cain 1993:675).

These examples of accommodation by community-based feminist and AIDS organizations have strong parallels to the dilemmas that faced more politicized nonprofits in the 1960s. Helfgot's (1974) study of Mobilization for Youth (MFY) documents a case where resource availability and a commitment to social change first promoted the group's transformation from a service agency to a radical community action program. As funding became more restrictive and a culture-of-poverty perspective became dominant, MFY returned to a manpower development agency that stressed personal adjustment via vocational training. Hasenfeld's (1974) analysis of the failure of Community Action Centers points in a similar direction: despite a strong ideological commitment to the urban poor and some success in employing members of the community and giving their clients a voice in decision making, each center studied "experienced organizational difficulties that seriously jeopardized its mission and led it to assume the same characteristics as those of the agencies it wished to modify" (Hasenfeld 1974:697).

As a final example of what we have referred to as accommodation, Cooper (1980) analyzed the development and subsequent bureaucratic transformation of a community organization in the Pico-Union neighborhood of Los Angeles. The Pico-Union Neighborhood Council (PUNC) was founded in 1966. The product of organizing efforts of a small group of community residents, PUNC enjoyed some early, visible successes such as improved street lighting and cleaning, but it was unable to make progress in the area it had targeted for action: housing. When both a private developer and the Los Angeles Community Redevelopment Agency (CRA) expressed interest in Pico-Union as a redevelopment site, PUNC entered its second phase. It sought assistance in developing expertise in housing and redevelopment and greatly expanded its membership. During the height of community participation, PUNC had a small paid staff and about five hundred members. The group effectively mobilized community residents, involved them in decision making, and established itself as a legitimate representative of community interests. Subsequently, however, active community involvement dwindled, replaced by passive and often tacit support for a professional, bureaucratic organization.

The Pico-Union Neighborhood Council is fairly unusual among our case studies because financial pressures appear to have been an insignificant factor in its development. A local foundation was the sole funder of PUNC, but it attached few strings to its money. Cooper argues that it was not financial dependence but the necessity of interacting with external organizations whose perspectives were different from those of a grassroots community organization, as well as the technical and legal nature of the projects that PUNC undertook, that ultimately drove PUNC's transformation. In a similar fashion, Swidler's (1979) study of a "free" school in Berkeley, California, founded with the mission of alternative educational programs, chronicles increasing bureaucratization not because of fiscal concerns, but out of the necessity of interacting with key external authorities such as school boards and accreditation agencies.

The two organizations with which PUNC established ongoing relationships were the CRA and the University of California at Los Angeles (UCLA). Although the nature of these relationships was initially different—the CRA and PUNC battled over control of the redevelopment process, whereas UCLA assumed more of an advocacy role—both organizations contributed to PUNC's professionalization and bureaucratization. Faculty members at UCLA were instrumental in helping PUNC obtain funding, develop a base of technical expertise, and solicit and articulate community preferences. Independent funding required PUNC's incorporation as a nonprofit organization and the hiring of staff, thus introducing bureaucratic and legal elements into its structure and facilitating its interaction with other organizations. Although these steps were necessary for PUNC to have influence in the redevelopment process, they also contributed to its formalization and professionalization. Similarly, the CRA's official control of the redevelopment process necessitated that, if PUNC was to remain substantively involved, the two organizations would interact within a framework largely defined by the CRA.

The nature of the tasks undertaken by PUNC was also responsible for the organization's transformation. The group became increasingly involved in projects requiring high levels of technical expertise and legal accountability. PUNC's initial housing success was a detailed plan for community redevelopment. Although the council required considerable technical assistance on this project, its distinctive area of expertise was its coherent presentation of informed community opinion. The development and construction of low-income housing, PUNC's next major project, required far more technical, legal, and bureaucratic knowledge; consequently, active community participation declined considerably, while expert involvement became paramount.

The cases reviewed in this section suggest that there is no uniform path to accommodation and, by extension, to organizational survival. The Townsend movement is a classic case of goal displacement caused by the group's unwillingness to adapt to changing social conditions. In order to compensate for membership decline, the Townsend clubs substituted purposive incentives with selective inducements, trading off the political goals that originally defined their coalition. In contrast, the trajectories of LACAAW, community-based AIDS organizations, and PUNC illustrate the difficulties that politically oriented service providers and neighborhood advocacy groups encounter in maintaining their commitment to member involvement and less formalized structures. The extended discussion of LACAAW shows an intermediate step of "apparent accommodation" on the road to formalization and acceptance of client-based service delivery that was driven by resource dependence on the federal government. Facing similar funding constraints, AIDS organizations seemed more willing to accommodate preemptively, which may have been less internally disruptive given the immediacy of the health crisis and the fact that moves toward professionalization took place shortly after the groups were established. In the case of the Pico-Union Neighborhood Council, the replacement of membership mobilization by professional staff reflects a different set of causal influences, namely interactions with key authorities and the need to develop new technical competencies that required expertise as opposed to member enthusiasm.

Proactive Change

While Michels has argued that organizational change is typically inherently conservative, in some cases control of an organization by its staff does lead to greater militancy or more intense commitment to espoused goals. One example of a radical transformation of organizational mission is provided by Jenkins's study (1977) of the National Council of Churches (NCC). He analyzed the history of the NCC, focusing on its increasing involvement in broad social-change movements in the 1960s. His detailed analysis of the Migrant Ministry, an agency of the NCC, shows that it was so completely transformed that it essentially merged with the California farm workers' movement.

The NCC was founded as a federation of about thirty Protestant denominations, which contributed to the council proportionate to their congregational membership. The council provided member services, such as educational programs and literature, and sponsored agencies concerned with specific programs, including giving aid to migrant farm workers (the initial goal of the Migrant Ministry). The NCC's social involvement had traditionally been limited to charitable social work and teaching—a social gospel approach. In the late 1950s some agencies, including the Migrant Ministry, began to take a more activist approach to serving their clientele. By the early 1960s the mission of the NCC had evolved toward fundamental social change, particularly racial equality, in spite of the more conservative attitudes held by most congregation members—the nominal constituency of the NCC. Such activities as lobbying, community organizing, and political advocacy became important NCC undertakings.

As these activist programs became publicly visible, the NCC came under attack from its conservative laity. As a result, automatic contributions to NCC agencies were discontinued and denominations were allowed to select those activities to which they would contribute. Lay opposition did not result in pulling back from the activist mission, however, although expansion was curbed and some existing programs were consolidated. Jenkins notes that the NCC continued to provide valuable services to the denominations and that denominational leaders, for prestige and career reasons, favored continued association with the NCC, thus helping to keep the council together. The general radicalization of the NCC continued despite the criticism. In fact, the withdrawal of automatic contributions to the Migrant Ministry seemed to hasten its radicalization by lessening the ministry's dependence on "hostile" funding sources and thus increasing its autonomy. Although budgetary reductions were required, the Migrant Ministry invested all its effort in the Farm Workers' Union; as a result, the Migrant Ministry and the farm workers' movement soon became inseparable.

Several factors help explain the NCC's transformation. The growth of Protestant churches in the 1950s was important in several respects. Increasing membership meant more funds available for the NCC and its agencies. A surge in professional training for the clergy and the development of liberation theology contributed to the growth of a radical definition of the clergy's mission. A combination of self-selection and church personnel policies aimed at avoiding open conflict within the church channeled activist clergy into the NCC, which became a relatively insulated arena in which radicalism could flourish. In addition, the NCC's reward structure emphasized mission over money, encouraging staff members to develop programs in which they believed strongly.

The growth of the NCC required a larger administrative staff and increasing reliance on trained professionals, which gave the staff considerable control over decision making. Jenkins identifies several mechanisms through which this transfer of power occurred. For example, the volunteer status of members of the board of directors and the professional training of staff and executives encouraged an expert-client relationship between the NCC staff and its board. In addition, NCC executives held voting rights on the board, giving them ample opportunity to push their arguments at board meetings. Several reorganizations were intended to increase the accountability of the NCC to its board and the constituent denominations by centralizing budgetary control and increasing communications. In fact, executive control over the agencies and influence over volunteer board members increased, and NCC executives could push virtually any program through the board as long as the program did not entail any decrease in services available to the denominations. In addition, the dependence of NCC agencies on denominational funds declined as monies became available from foundations, investments, individual donors, and non-denominational agencies. As a result, the NCC found itself relatively affluent. The combination of ample resources, organizational control by the staff, and a secure domain were the principal factors that enabled the NCC to pursue radical goals that were divergent from the interests of its conservative lay constituency.

Another brief example of a nonprofit that was able to redefine its mission in a more institutionally challenging direction is the National Urban League (NUL). When it was established in 1910, the NUL characterized itself as a direct-service agency operating with the express goal of improving the status of African Americans through the provision of educational, economic, and social welfare services. By the early 1960s, as the civil rights movement gathered momentum at the national level, the NUL began to take a more activist stance. Despite initial reservations among its executive committee, the league became both a sponsor of and participant in the 1963 March on Washington. This step marked the "transformation of the league from a social service agency to a civil rights organization without abandoning any of its historic commitments to the promotion of the economic and social welfare of black Americans" (Weiss 1989:124). Here was an instance of an executive staff responding to new political circumstances that made it difficult to remain nonpolitical at a time when its constituency, broadly construed, became more committed to activism and social change.

Spalter-Roth and Schreiber's (1995) analysis of how national women's organizations survived the hostile Reagan-Bush years demonstrates an alternative scenario: proactive responsiveness when a politically oriented mission becomes increasingly risky. Although many of these groups opted to employ more professionalized "insider tactics" such as legislative lobbying, litigation, and media campaigns, adopting the tools and language of mainstream politics did not necessarily result in decreased commitment to feminist objectives. In some instances, feminist organizations even became willing to take on more controversial issues. For example, when members and staff pressured the American Association of University Women (AAUW) and the Women's Equity Action League (WEAL), both organizations became active in the abortion rights lobby despite their earlier resistance. Organizations also sometimes withdrew from formal coalitions because they were unwilling to accept legislative compromises. The National Organization for Women (NOW), for example, quit a coalition formed by the Leadership Conference on Civil Rights when it was willing to accept a cap on damages in sex discrimination suits; the AAUW initiated an independent child-care coalition when the Children's Defense Fund accepted a provision that would have enabled government funding for day-care centers operated by religious groups. In another example, in 1985 the National Coalition against Domestic Violence (NCADV) received a grant from the U.S. Department of Justice; when the agency refused to allow the words "lesbian" and "woman abuse" in the organization's publications, NCADV rejected the federal contract for its second year.

This limited sample of cases suggests the importance of executive control in reorienting nonprofits toward more proactive social-change agendas. In the case of the NCC, the combination of ample resources, a secure operating domain, and a set of changes that centralized power among the administrative staff enabled the organization to pursue a more radical mission in spite of opposition on the part of member churches—many of which remained in the council because they continued to receive valuable services. The willingness to tolerate budget reductions when faced with the loss of member contributions enabled the NCC to decrease its dependence on supporters who objected to the organization's new direction. In the case of the NUL and national women's organizations, executive responsiveness to member and staff demands for more radical action (both in response to more favorable and hostile political conditions) was critical.

Resistance to Change

The sort of successful, proactive adaptation demonstrated by organizations such as the National Council of Churches, the National Urban League, and national feminist groups is somewhat surprising, given that organizations with strong ideological commitments are often expected to be less flexible than professional nonprofits with more instrumental orientations or pragmatic objectives (Hasenfeld and English 1974). The very process of considering changes in mission is also likely to engender more conflict in ideologically motivated organizations, heightening the risks associated with change (Zald and Ash 1966). As the cases reviewed in this section demonstrate, however, it is not simply a matter of political or ideological commitment, but how narrowly organizations define themselves and their missions, which in turn places sharp limits on their ability and willingness to adapt to changed external conditions.

Gusfield's analysis (1955, 1963) of the Women's Christian Temperance Union (WCTU) portrays an organization in decline because its original goals and strategies were adhered to even in the face of significant social change. After the repeal of Prohibition, the WCTU faced an increasingly hostile environment but continued to strongly oppose drinking. Gusfield's explanation for this inability to adapt focuses on the WCTU leadership. During its heyday, the WCTU occupied a prestigious position in middle-class society. The social status of its leadership provided some legitimation for its reformist posture, which was directed largely at the lower classes. With the end of Prohibition, however, these middle-class members left the organization and the social status of WCTU leadership declined. As the leadership came to be rooted in the lower and lower-middle strata, the WCTU could no longer maintain a "superior," reformist posture. Instead there was a growing resentment of the middle-class Americans who had abandoned the movement, and WCTU rhetoric became increasingly marked by moral indignation.

A second important factor in the decline of the WCTU was the rate of leadership turnover. Presidential tenure was rather long, and the slow pipeline to top positions groomed future leaders in terms of present politics. Although some members were well aware of their organization's waning popularity and tried to recruit and develop younger members and to support new leaders, the continuing presence of the old guard negated their efforts.

Moore's (1993) research on public interest science organizations provides a more recent example of a movement organization constrained by its founding mission and unable to adapt to changing political conditions. Science for the People (SftP) was established at the annual meeting of the American Physical Society in 1969 to oppose the Vietnam War; SftP defined itself in radical opposition to other science groups and mainstream professional science practices. Its antiwar stance was embedded in a systemic critique of capitalism and the links between academic science and the military-industrial complex. SftP, like its companion New Left groups, was based on egalitarian principles, and its various local groups were linked through informal cooperation. The activities of the locals (represented in forty cities by 1972) included providing technical assistance to the Black Panthers, defusing bombs at bomb factories in Philadelphia, direct protest at Livermore Laboratories in California, and public education campaigns. Financial needs were minimal, and the group never received substantial external funding. The most labor- and resource-intensive activity was publication of the magazine *Science for the People,* which was largely self-sustaining through the efforts of the Boston chapter.

In 1972, after a period of fairly rapid growth, SftP confronted an identity crisis that took the form of conflict over the question of what role scientists should play in a radical movement. The egalitarian emphasis of SftP placed a premium on critical self-reflection, and the groups' energies became absorbed with the (apparently never-ending) process of deciding "*how to go about* deciding *who* they were, rather than focusing their discussions on who they were" (Moore 1993:193, emphasis in original). This inward-looking project came at the expense of developing strategies for responding to a changed political environment, particularly the end of the Vietnam War and with the emergence of feminist and third world movements that provided members with alternative venues for activism. In addition, SftP was never able to provide a means for activists to reconcile the demands of their dual identities as scientists and radical activists. According to Moore, SftP's narrow mission as a radical political organization left few avenues open to it and undermined its ability to respond quickly or effectively to changed circumstances. Although the organization tried a variety of strategies to revitalize itself during the 1970s and 1980s (including creating a national office), it was ultimately unable to incorporate new issues or innovative practices that might have enhanced the group's survival prospects, and SftP finally collapsed due to financial reasons in 1989. (Some members of the original SftP launched a listserv by the same name in 1998.)

Whereas adherence to ideological missions ultimately undermined efforts by the WCTU and SftP to revitalize, the brief existence of the San Fernando Valley Hotline illustrates a somewhat different organizational response, what Matthews (1994) refers to as "overt opposition." This hotline was founded as a radical feminist collective in 1980 in response to the mainstreaming of older rape crisis centers. Although initiated with a grant from the California Department of Social Services, the hotline embodied the conflict between feminist and official definitions of rape crisis work. When, shortly after the collective was founded, the administration of rape crisis funding was transferred to the state's Office of Criminal Justice Planning (OCJP), the Valley Hotline set itself apart from other centers such as the LACAAW by refusing to apply for funding. It also became a vocal critic of OCJP reporting mandates. Matthews argues that the Valley Hotline was more ideologically defined from the beginning because the group came together out of a common commitment to feminist activism and then adopted antirape work as the vehicle. The fact that the collective had a clear ideological mission lent coherence to the project, but it also meant that members were less flexible about the kinds of pragmatic issues to which other groups succumbed. By 1986 the Valley Hotline was defunct. In another example, the feminist-run Santa Cruz Women against Rape (SCWAR) accepted OCJP funding but actively protested the reporting requirements, filling in "unknown" where they felt questions on the forms were inappropriate. Within months the agency withdrew its funding, which sent a clear warning to other California centers.

The strong ideological commitments initially articulated in the missions of the WCTU, SftP, and the San Fernando Valley Hotline clearly led to significant resistance to change. Provisionally, we would also argue that it was the narrowness of each organization's mission—Prohibition, opposition to the Vietnam War, and radical antirape work, combined with the highly articulated collective identities of members and staff—that made it especially difficult to redefine these organizations' missions. In the case of the WCTU, this choice led to severe constraints on recruiting new members; in SftP, it created an internal group orientation that limited consideration of new options; and in the case of the Valley Hotline, it led to a rejection of critical funding to the detriment of carrying out the group's work. In each case, these organizations refused to change course and then were not able to sustain themselves, even when there was interest in remaining active.

Reorientation

The three trajectories we have discussed so far—accommodation, proactive transformation, and adherence to mission at the expense of organizational survival—illustrate the fairly dramatic challenges that nonprofits can face as the conditions around them change and they get caught up in conflicting demands from stakeholders both within and outside the organization. These cases point to relatively extreme consequences, namely either a wholesale reconfiguration of mission and structure or organizational demise. In this section, we explore an alternative set of responses that, although they may involve a reorientation in founding mission, do not fundamentally alter a nonprofit's identity.

Sills's classic study (1957) of the National Foundation for Infantile Paralysis is an account not of goal transformation but rather of the successful achievement of the foundation's major objective—the eradication of polio. Instead of subsequently closing up shop, however, the foundation used its effective organizational structure and volunteer corps to broaden its mission to include research on all birth defects. In 1958 the name was changed to the National Foundation, dropping "for Infantile Paralysis." Two decades later, in 1979, the name was changed again to the March of Dimes Birth Defects Foundation.

Sills argues that the organizational structure of the foundation was essential in keeping its activities centered on its stated mission, and facilitated its subsequent decision to pursue related goals once polio was conquered. The foundation's structure was corporate in nature, with a national headquarters and local branches rather than a federation of semiautonomous affiliates. Thus ultimate control for foundation policy and the direction of its activities was retained by the national headquarters. This centralization was balanced, however, by a clear-cut division of responsibility. The foundation engaged in three distinct activities, each of which was the main purview of a separate part of the foundation: fund-raising, the disbursement of funds in communities to aid victims of infantile paralysis, and research to eliminate the disease. The research function was administered by the national headquarters.

The foundation is perhaps best known for its annual fund-raising drive, the March of Dimes. This massive effort is the responsibility of local March of Dimes organizations, which are temporary in nature, rather than of the local foundation chapters, although the chapters participate in the drive. The march is directed by the national headquarters, which appoints campaign directors for each community. The position of director does not entail year-round effort, and new directors are often appointed each year. A huge number of volunteers is mobilized and then dispersed upon completion of the drive. The local chapters of the foundation are primarily concerned with patient care. Half the money raised by the March of Dimes is returned to the chapters for disbursement in their communities, primarily to give financial assistance to victims of polio.

Although the foundation is a large organization, the size of local chapters is kept small, and members are kept actively involved through a system of assigning them specific tasks. The temporary nature of the March of Dimes organizations focuses volunteer involvement on the task at hand, namely fund-raising. In addition, the high turnover among March of Dimes volunteers seems to sustain enthusiasm. Responsibility for chapter affairs remains with volunteers, largely because chapters are prohibited from electing physicians or public health professionals as chairs. Professional guidance is available when needed from a medical advisory committee and from the state representative, a national headquarters employee.

Sills contends that the foundation was successful largely because of its organizational structure, which allowed volunteers to become actively involved in the organization but not in such a way as to displace the mission, and which permitted headquarters staff to retain responsive control over the local chapters. The strong corporate structure was also important in the foundation's decision to broaden its purpose in the late 1950s. A record of success, local involvement combined with a lean and effective national leadership, and a clear delegation of functions made the search for a new organizational purpose much easier than would have been the case in many other voluntary organizations, where the group's continued existence might have been perceived as solely in the interest of the paid staff, not the larger public.

Zald's studies (1970; Zald and Denton 1963) of the Young Men's Christian Association (YMCA) in the United States offer a contrasting analysis of a successful organizational transformation. We regard this change as successful because, although the organization's activities and efforts were altered in important ways, the changes enabled it to reach a larger audience without sacrificing its basic mission. Zald analyzed the history of the YMCA from its founding in the mid-1800s to the mid-1960s and developed a case study of the large Chicago YMCA from 1961 to 1967.

Founded as an interdenominational Protestant organization to provide Christian fellowship for young men, the YMCA quickly took on a strong evangelical character as revivalism grew in the late 1850s. After the Civil War, there were disagreements within the federation over the appropriateness and visibility of evangelism in the YMCA. The New York association adopted a model of general service to young men, and by 1889 the International Committee (the national executives' committee for the federation) officially opposed evangelism as a YMCA goal. The New York model gradually spread throughout the country, changing the YMCA from an organization dedicated to the moral salvation of young Protestant men to a more secular, broad-based, fee-for-service organization that pursued general character development.

Four main factors underlay the transformation of the YMCA's mission from evangelism to general service. First, the group's economic base as a religious organization was unstable. Resembling a Protestant denomination in its activities and the incentives offered to its members, the YMCA competed with churches for members and contributions and was vulnerable to the ups and downs of both revivalism and business cycles. This financial insecurity made clear the need for alternative funding sources. Three programmatic innovations also helped change the character of the YMCA. Various fee-for-service programs, such as lecture series and vocational education programs, were easy to implement and could be discontinued if demand declined. The widespread construction of dormitory residences, beginning in the 1870s, was a second innovation. These hostels provided income for the association and were widely perceived as a general public service. Finally, the development in 1885 of YMCA gymnasiums proved to be effective in recruiting members. These innovations moved the organization toward acquiring a diversified economic base, supported by fees for various services. The residences and gymnasiums represented large capital investments and, in turn, programmatic commitments, making the YMCA a building-centered organization. Perhaps more important for future changes in programs and goals, the developing enrollment economy linked YMCA programs to the demands of its clientele.

Changes in the availability of resources, then, were clearly a driving force in the transformation of the YMCA, but an exclusive focus on resources would miss elements of the organization's structure and political processes that also facilitated its ability to adapt. From the 1890s, the association pursued a rather broad mission. Providing for the welfare of the whole man—physical, intellectual, social, and spiritual—permitted various emphases and allowed considerable latitude in developing or rejecting programs. Although the organization's goals were originally religious in purpose, several factors prevented religious dominance of the YMCA. An interdenominational emphasis, the use of lay rather than clerical leadership, and the focus on association and fellowship rather than church activities alone minimized theological influence in the YMCA's early days, thus maintaining options for future development.

In contrast with Sills's analysis of the National Foundation for Infantile Paralysis, Zald maintains that the YMCA's federated structure permitted flexibility and responsiveness to local needs. Zald (1970:64) argues that "it was the ability of local Associations to command the support of their own communities that accounted for the YMCA's staying power, not the limited power of the national association." The autonomy of the local associations is evidenced by the fact that they often ignored national directives with impunity. Their importance is indicated by the observation that some local policies, such as admitting women to membership, were originally opposed at the national level but later became the norm.

The final facilitating factor in the YMCA's successful evolution was its reliance on lay rather than professional control. The organization's history emphasized democratic lay control, and policymaking was traditionally deemed the responsibility of the board rather than the secretary (the top-level administrator). This ideology was reinforced by a committee structure developed to involve laypeople in specific program areas, as well as in overall policy direction. The historic importance of laypeople, however, did not necessarily ensure their continued dominance. Zald argues that several factors tended to reduce conflict between secretaries and their boards and to support board control of policy development. The secretaries did not belong to a professional association or ascribe to a professional ideology that might compete with the YMCA for their allegiance; hence, they could not lay claim to a specialized skill or knowledge base from which to buttress their policy positions. As a result, the YMCA has been dominated not by its national professional staff but by local members.

Two public interest science organizations studied by Moore (1993)—the Union of Concerned Scientists (UCS) and Scientists' Institute for Public Information (SIPI)—represent cases where reliance on professional staff was itself key to mission reorientation and organizational maintenance. Formed in 1969 by MIT faculty and graduate students, the UCS remained relatively close to its original form and mission as a politically neutral lobbying group, funded by individual donations, that promoted the use of scientific information to address social and environmental problems. From the outset, UCS defined itself as a moderate group, and within its first few years it began a process of formalization by hiring a paid staff person. In the early 1980s, as the nuclear energy agenda that had motivated the group in the 1970s waned, UCS shifted its attention to the arms race and by the middle of the 1980s it had established itself as a respected watchdog group and political insider. UCS also built a solid financial base, maintained largely through individual contributions but with some outside grants. UCS was never confronted with internal conflicts of the sort that beset the more radical Science for the People, and it continued to run smoothly even as it grew to include a full-time financial manager, researchers, legal staff, and a Washington-based lobbying office. Over time, the operation of the UCS remained substantially the same, with separate research groups producing reports on specific issues of concern. UCS's original structure as a public interest lobbying group with no partisan agenda enabled it to orient itself externally and successfully take advantage of new opportunities for activism. UCS was thus able to change its substantive focus without undermining the group's core mission. Significantly, the activities of UCS remained consistent with the routines of scientific practice, thereby reinforcing rather than challenging its members' identities as scientists.

SIPI, created in 1963 by Barry Commoner, took a somewhat rockier path, with a more dramatic change from its original structure as a coalition of twenty-three local science information groups, run by two charismatic leaders (Commoner and Margaret Mead), to a $2.5 million organization with no local affiliates, administered by a staff of fifteen and governed by a board of directors that nonetheless continued to follow its original mission: to provide the public with unbiased scientific information. In its first few years of operation, SIPI remained "committed to the principle of avoiding centralization and professionalization as threats to local initiative and volunteer participation" (Moore 1993:209) and employed only two paid staff in the national office. The first significant organizational change took place in early 1964, when SIPI changed its emphasis from the genetic and environmental effects of radiation to environmental issues more generally. The transition occurred smoothly, largely because it was framed as consistent with the group's founding mission and was broad enough to accommodate the interests of its board and volunteer members.

In 1971, after an internal crisis that revolved around the relationship between the national office and local chapters and the respective roles of scientists and nonscientists in the organization, SIPI undertook other significant organizational changes: the group reconstituted its board to include nonscientist community members; created a new field organizer staff position; hired a new director who had a science background but was by trade a professional administrator; appointed a committee to outline the group's new goals; and voted to open the organization to nonscientists as dues-paying members. The organization also considered adopting a federated structure but opted to continue with less formal ties between local chapters and the national office. Again, these changes were explicitly framed as consistent with the group's original intention; that is, they were conceptualized as the best means of enhancing the organization's mission to find the most innovative and relevant means of providing scientific information on issues of public concern.

After this point, the national office became more strongly involved in its own projects, departing from its early role of facilitating the activities and information dissemination of local chapters. Another critical moment came in the late 1970s, when Mead died and the executive director orchestrated the departure of Commoner, who was beginning to be considered a political and financial liability because of his political outspokenness. The shifting of power from these two charismatic leaders to a professional administrator guaranteed that organizational survival would become a central concern. Finally, the elimination of local chapters and nonscientist members, which could have undermined organizational stability since they did, in fact, contradict SIPI's founding identity, was accomplished through "benign neglect"—absent strong national leadership, the local groups simply disappeared or transformed themselves into independent organizations. Moore attributes SIPI's ability to be both adaptive and organizationally stable to its early formalization efforts, which included incorporating as a nonprofit and hiring a full-time director who was a professional administrator. These features contributed to SIPI's ability to capitalize on the public's interest in environmental issues in an ongoing manner, as well as to make changes in the organization's structure, without undermining the group's core mission.

In contrast to a focus on the consequences of external mandates or changes in the political environment, Barman's (2002) analysis of the Chicago-based United Way/Crusade of Mercy (UW/CM) draws attention to the role of increased interorganizational competition in provoking strategic change. In this particular case, the UW/CM consciously pursued a strategy of differentiation vis-à-vis its new competitors, whereas it had previously been oriented to defining itself with respect to the dual standards of efficiency/effectiveness and external accountability.

The UW/CM was formed in 1934 and, like other United Ways, it had a widely representative board and employed both staff and volunteers. Its mission was "to increase the capacity of organized community health and human-service needs of people in the Greater Chicago area" (quoted in Barman 2002:1204) by assisting local agencies through volunteer-based planning and workplace fund-raising. Donated funds were distributed to the local agencies that were deemed to be the most worthy recipients dealing with the most pressing community issues.

Throughout the first fifty-plus years of its existence, the UW/CM was effectively the only game in town. UW/MC's operating environment became increasingly competitive in the late 1980s, however. After a series of legal challenges to the monopoly status of the United Way fund-raising campaigns in government workplaces, in 1987 the federal government opened the door to participation of other nonprofits in its Combined Federal Campaign (see also Brilliant 1990). Subsequent legal decisions at the state and local levels led to the proliferation of federated workplace giving programs or alternative funds, many of which have missions organized around shared identities or interests. Compounding the challenges associated with the entry of rivals into the field, local United Ways sustained a blow to their credibility in 1992, when the media reported that the CEO of United Way of America was involved in fraudulent activities (he was later sentenced to seven years in prison for charges ranging from tax fraud to conspiracy).

UW/MC responded to this competitive new environment with a strategy of differentiation, which entailed both a programmatic shift and rhetorical claims regarding the organization's uniqueness and greater worth compared with others in the field. In 1994, after a period of initial reluctance among key individuals within the organization, the agency formally adopted a policy of donor choice that gave contributors the ability to designate whether they wanted their donations to go to the United Way for distribution according to traditional practice, to a constituency of the donor's choice, or to a specific agency in the community. This shift to donor choice represented a fundamental challenge to the traditional mission of the UW/MC, and one senior volunteer referred to it as "a threat . . . of the highest order and beyond" (quoted in Barman 2002:1207). Specifically, donor choice reduces the organization's central role as a coordinating agency (and therefore fund-raiser) for member charities; it privileges donor preferences over the systematic community needs assessment that has long served as a key dimension of the agency's legitimacy; and it "weakens the institutionalized role of the UW/CM as an accountability mechanism for the nonprofit field, one that guarantees the quality of recipient charities through the bestowal of a 'Good Housekeeping' seal of approval . . . [which] turns the United Way into a mere processor and pass-through point for donors' contributions to any and all recipient organizations" (Barman 2002:1207).

In effect, UW/MC chose to prioritize donor needs and demands over community or member charity needs. This fundamental shift, however, was accompanied by a conscious strategy of positioning the agency as both unique and superior to other workplace fund-raising drives. Rather than redefining its original mission, UW/MC linked the new policy to its historic role by stressing the benefits of its traditional methods of allocating resources, which it renamed the Community Fund and reframed with an analogy to mutual funds that are able to generate a higher "return" and broader impact than targeted alternative funds. Drawing on its long experience with needs assessment and monitoring of local charities, the agency effectively offered its services as a credible financial advisor. Thus, in addition to giving donors the ability to direct their giving to specific groups or charities, the UW/MC gave them a stronger rationale and inducement for giving in the traditional way, based on the assurance that their donation would get the most bang for the buck.

According to Barman, the strategy worked: the proportion of donor-designated dollars, which had increased from 3 percent in 1993 to 18 percent in 1998, seems to be holding and possibly even declining (Barman 2002, 2004). Significantly, the UW/MC's choice of how to adapt was delimited both by its organizational structure and by the nature of its competitors. Given the identity- and interest-based missions of most of the newer alternative funds, UW/MC was able to credibly emphasize its traditionally broad and community-based focus. And, given its dependence on support from member charities, it had little choice but to find a way to maintain its role as a coordinating agency and shore up its traditional allocation methods in order to ensure that member groups continued to receive funding and remained within the fold. UW/MC's ability to differentiate itself from its competitors effectively enabled it to diversify without losing its traditional base of legitimacy and support.

Some common themes are discernible across the diverse set of cases discussed in this section. One commonality that the March of Dimes, the YMCA, the United Way, UCS, and SIPI share is a broad mission that has lent itself to active redefinition by a responsive staff. Although Sills and Zald differ in their interpretations of the benefits of relying on centralized structures and professional staff, we would argue that the key in each of these cases was some degree of centralization that promoted flexibility and accountability to the membership base. The federated structure of the YMCA and the reliance on small local chapters in the March of Dimes also provided members with avenues for active involvement and, by extension, for their considerable investment in organizational continuity. One notable feature of UCS's ability to adapt was its political neutrality and reliance on professional staff, which offset the ideological narrowness that undermined more radical groups such as SftP. SIPI was different in this regard, in that its activist founders initially articulated their political commitments in their choice of organizational structure, but it was still able to implement changes in issue focus and operating procedures by framing such adaptations as consistent with the group's mission—a process not unlike UW/MC's realignment of its emphasis from member agencies to donors, which it backed up with tangible benefits for both constituencies. Significantly, all these organizations reoriented their priorities in ways that were broad enough to encompass the interests of both insiders and outsiders and to extend the organization's base of support. Diversification and differentiation—of issues, activities, and resources—were central to successful adaptation, survival, and growth.

Mission Displacement

One final pathway to change, which we refer to as mission displacement, represents perhaps an even more dramatic form of organizational change than either accommodation or the kind of reorientations described in the last section. In an effort to secure their survival chances, the service and cultural organizations we describe in this section were almost immediately confronted with—and gave in to—the need to move away from their founding principles.

In his analysis of social service organizations for the blind, R. A. Scott (1967) found that, although the stated agency goals were to enhance the welfare of the blind, factors other than client need often strongly influenced service delivery, distorting the stated mission of these agencies. Organizational persistence and the interests of key benefactors were the primary forces that Scott identified as responsible for mission deflection. Although most blind people are female, elderly, and only partially blind, the majority of services have been directed at children and employable adults. When services for the blind were first provided over a hundred years ago, children and otherwise healthy adults composed the needy population, and organizations for the blind thus addressed the problems of education and employability. That these emphases have endured is partly attributable to the institutionalization of early programs.

Fund-raising considerations, however, also explain the lack of attention paid to the majority of the blind population. Blind children evoke more sympathy from funders than do the elderly blind, and programs to employ younger blind adults appeal to widely shared values of personal independence. Agency administrators perceive, whether accurately or not, that programs for the young, educable, and employable will enjoy better funding than those for the elderly.

This focus on service delivery to a small segment of the blind population has obviously been detrimental to the majority of the blind people whom these agencies are ostensibly intended to serve. Programs that are targeted to the young and employable force the agencies to compete for those who can take advantage of these services. These "marketable" blind persons assist the organizations in their fund-raising efforts. The process of mission displacement is completed when, rather than fostering independence, the agencies guard their "desirable" blind and increase their clients' dependence by providing housing, employment, and recreation.

A second example of mission displacement is the California Institute of the Arts (CalArts), founded as an avant-garde, utopian community in which artists of all media could experiment and create, and intended to be unhindered by market pressures or lay opinion (Adler 1979). From its inception, however, CalArts labored under twin pressures: ideological and financial. Within two years of its establishment, CalArts was largely transformed into a more conventional and conservative private art school. Within five years, public statements of philosophy espoused a new, more professional direction, and utopian proclamations were increasingly out of favor. Numerous adherents of the original institute agreed that the dream had died.

Ideologically, two major conflicts contributed to the demise of the initial mission. From the start there was a divergence of opinion between the trustees and artists. The former were concerned that they fulfill the dreams of Walt Disney, the institute's primary benefactor, who died shortly before final plans were approved. The Disney legacy was typified by elaborate public events. The artists' conception of the institute was also grand, but in the service of artists, with little concern for public consumption. In CalArts's early days its participants reveled in the "joke" they had pulled on conservative funders, who had committed apparently unlimited monies for a spectacularly equipped artists' playground. It soon became apparent, however, that the joke was on the artists, as the trustees began to exercise their considerable control. The extent of this control became clear when the board refused to approve leftist philosopher Herbert Marcuse for a position in the School of Critical Studies.

There was also a fundamental contradiction in the premise on which the institute was founded. CalArts's planners were advocates of the 1960s' avant-garde culture, which was inherently anarchistic and called for the destruction of institutionalization. Artists were lured to a utopian community based on total freedom from constraints of any kind, a promise that proved impossible to fulfill. For example, the initial philosophy stressed collegial relations between faculty and students and opposed a formal curriculum. Pressures soon mounted for a more traditional curriculum, however, as faculty members found it difficult to limit student access to their time, as students failed to meet the faculty's inflated expectations, and as the distinctions between professional and amateur were increasingly blurred. Similarly, many artists were attracted to CalArts in part by the opportunity to work closely with artists of other media in a community of art professionals. In practice, however, many faculty members expected to have easy access to other artists but not to have to provide support in return. Although CalArts survived as a school, its avant-garde characteristics soon disappeared.

Financial difficulties also plagued CalArts even before the campus was built; hence, from the outset, many activities were evaluated in terms of their impact on the school's economy. Owing to lavish plans and cost overruns, the entire fund allotted by Disney for CalArts was used up well before construction was completed. This shortfall increased the school's already strong dependence on the Disney family and created a perpetual atmosphere of insecurity and crisis. Board members were selected on the basis of personal and financial ties to the Disney family rather than for their abilities to raise and maintain a sufficient endowment. High-level artistic administrators exacerbated the financial problems by nominating board members who were sympathetic to their academic disciplines, while paying little, if any, attention to their fund-raising ability.

As the extent of the financial crisis became evident, faculty members who had purchased expensive homes with steep mortgages or who had given up secure tenured positions at other schools became less willing to experiment artistically or to rock the boat. Control of the purse strings soon translated into control over educational policy, as those arts most useful in fund-raising, such as classical music and dance and conventional theater, grew in favor with the trustees, while less marketable arts were severely cut back or eliminated. The lay staff also facilitated the work of artists of whom they approved (those whose work required discipline, scheduling, and coordination and whose products they appreciated) through their control of access to technical facilities and their selection of artists to appear in public events or display. As financial pressures increased, the utopian character of the institute dissipated and values originally scorned became the keys to survival. Professionalism, originally dismissed in favor of vanguardism, was now perceived by the artists to be their only source of power vis-à-vis the trustees. Similarly, market success, which was to have been discarded in favor of recognition by colleagues, became legitimate currency at CalArts.

On the surface, service agencies for the blind and avant-garde cultural institutes could not seem more distinct, especially in terms of their missions, structures, and stakeholders. What links these two types of organizations, however, is the way that financial insecurity in the face of high costs of service delivery (broadly defined) led almost directly to takeover and control by key benefactors and trustees. Other needy beneficiaries, in the case of service agencies, and avant-garde artistic and educational ideals, in the case of CalArts, were displaced by the search for stable sources of support. Both the "marketable blind" and "marketable art" were privileged at the expense of the more expansive missions that initially animated these organizations.

LESSONS FROM THE CASES

Across a range of nonprofit organizations—social movements, community-based organizations, nonprofit service agencies, and traditional voluntary associations—we observe the dual role of mission as both charter and constraint. As charter, mission serves to direct an organization toward specific combinations of ideology, organizational structure, and relations with members and sponsors. Mission also operates as a constraint with respect to how an organization responds to changed circumstances.

A common element across the cases we have presented is that identity and mission are "provoked" when nonprofits become involved with various funding sources that have divergent interests. This interaction impinges upon organizational autonomy and, in turn, triggers an array of responses. This provocation is especially salient for social movement organizations that become increasingly involved with the very government agencies and officials they intend to challenge. Adding to the complexity is the need for such organizations to present themselves as both credible advocates and serious service providers.

Interaction with government is not the only contested relationship fraught with tension around organizational mission, however. Relations between local and national offices, between volunteer and professional staff, and with key funding sources all trigger considerations of goals and strategies. Indeed, many of the cases illustrate a familiar pattern of internal versus external expectations, and the accommodations that are reached as organizations evolve from volunteer to paid labor, private to public funding, and informal, minimalist organizations to more formal, hierarchical entities.

In the social movements arena, a dominant trajectory toward greater formalization and professionalization at the expense of initial ideological commitments has been often identified. The cases we have reviewed, however, stress the need to consider the *content* of organizational formalization on a continuum of reactive to preemptive responses. At one extreme, movement organizations such as the Los Angeles Commission on Assaults against Women formalized reactively as early activists struggled to remain faithful to feminist ideology and practice. Despite their best (and often creative) efforts to resist the imposition of a conventional social service model, they ultimately ceded to pressures for institutional conformity. In contrast, AIDS service organizations have apparently attempted to consciously leverage the service agency model in order to preempt the perceived reluctance of public and private sponsors to support activism on behalf of stigmatized social groups.

A critical factor in terms of the constancy, responsiveness, or deflection of organizational mission is the nature of the coupling between organizational structure and ideology. Those organizations that are committed to an alternative vision of the social order—whether in the political, creative, or lifestyle realms—are typically concerned with how their internal organization reflects the kind of world they are striving for. For such organizations, making accommodations or instrumental changes in the organization of work sullies the vision of the kind of society they want to create. Such a close auditing of internal processes may make these organizations correspondingly less effective or less willing to monitor and respond to external events. Organizations with a mission that is less radical or broader (in the sense that a range of goals can fit comfortably within its purview) experience much less difficulty juggling the fit between internal practices and external contingencies. Indeed, we see in the cases of the YWCA and the March of Dimes that general-purpose missions greatly facilitated organizational adaptability.

Nonprofits with a strong ideological purpose often face tensions from attempting to involve and integrate staff, volunteers, and board members. These disparate groups often do not share the same commitments or identities that motivated the founding of the organization. Again, less ideologically charged organizations with broader identities are better able to juggle diverse interests, and indeed can use them to attend to a differentiated environment; the strategy of the Union of Concerned Scientists offers a good illustration. An alternative approach for more ideologically grounded nonprofits is to consciously work to diversify their base of support, while holding to their original identities. The ability to simultaneously continue a connection with original stakeholders and enroll new supporters who understand the continued commitment to a strong mission may enable a nonprofit to resist pressures for formalization and to mitigate the many efforts of funders to channel the organization into more mainstream pursuits (Jenkins 1998).

The reality of nonprofit life, however, is that many organizations operate within a context of constant financial pressures. The need to diversify the funding base is a continuing challenge for many nonprofits. Such efforts are fraught with the danger of mission dilution, as funders bring their own set of agendas. In some cases it may be possible to balance competing demands by essentially playing funders off against one another, though such an approach may be short-lived. In an analysis of the 1976 public television series *Dance in America,* Powell and Friedkin (1986) show how program staff and dance professionals managed to juggle the divergent demands for a classic repertoire from corporate funders with a diverse, inclusive agenda from government endowments and avant-garde aspirations on the part of choreographers and arts funders. This balancing act led to a highly successful and innovative public television series that eventually met a premature end as the various constituencies broke apart. The performance and broadcast of dance was greatly helped by this series and soon flourished on commercial cable television, but public broadcasting lost one of its signature programs.

An open question is what the implications of such diversifying processes are for the representation of more activist voices and practices in the realm of public ideas. Groups such as Science for the People, advocating a critical analysis of the relationship between science and politics, appear more likely to face internal conflict and eventually to become defunct in response to the efforts to expand their base of support. The San Fernando Valley Hotline, which rejected state funding in order to maintain its identity as a radical feminist collective, met a similar fate within a much shorter time. More generally, national women's and civil rights organizations that espouse radical social change have a higher likelihood of failure than reform-oriented associations (Minkoff 1999). In addition, moving toward the dominant service model appears to decrease the direct advocacy component of community-based organizations.

The challenge, then, is how nonprofits can broaden inclusiveness inside their existing organizations. Expanding and consolidating an existing base of support is clearly a less daunting task than convincing political authorities and influential external sponsors to moderate their demands for ideological and structural accommodations. The task of responding to shifting external conditions while retaining the enthusiasm of core constituents depends on the ability to convince members and supporters that changes will remain broadly congruent with the mission. In several of the cases presented here, nonprofits were able both to give existing supporters an important role as new activities were being pursued and to educate new constituencies about the organization's original identity.

IMPLICATIONS

The detailed cases we have reviewed suggest several broad patterns of organizational change. Most notably, there is a common life cycle for nonprofits as they move from advocacy to service. This pathway entails not only surrendering political objectives in favor of a less confrontational service role, but also attention to the hard work of formalization—that is, developing procedures and structures that will enable tasks to be performed regularly and that will afford continuity even in the face of leadership change (Staggenborg 1988). Professionalization goes hand in hand with formalization, as paid staff replace volunteers, and these employees not only make a career out of work in the sector (McCarthy and Zald 1977) but also are committed to maintaining the long-term presence of the organization. For many types of service provision, this commitment is essential for patients, clients, and the needy and dispossessed.

But we also find examples of organizations that have taken on more activist objectives, even in the face of pressures for accommodation. Thus, the core implication from our survey is that nonprofit organizations evince a good bit of flexibility in response to changes in internal and external circumstances. The cases suggest that nonprofits, far from being lumbering, inert entities, have considerable capacities for change. But the direction and efficacy of change remain open questions. There is good reason to expect that core changes in organizational mission are likely to be disruptive indeed.

For example, research on a population of Toronto-based voluntary social service organizations found that service area shifts, such as from providing legal services to sociorehabilitative or education services, were associated with a higher risk of organizational failure (Singh, Tucker, and Meinhard 1991). Research on shifts between protest, advocacy, and service provision by national women's and racial minority organizations also documents a higher rate of failure associated with organizational change (Minkoff 1999). Such studies confirm that recently redefined groups face a "liability of newness" that is characteristic of newly formed organizations: namely the need to reconstruct both internal routines and relationships with the environment (Stinchcombe 1965). The negative consequences of undertaking change may, however, be mitigated by the characteristics of the organizations undertaking them. For example, more established organizations—those that are larger and more professionalized, that have survived longer, or that adopt more conventional and familiar operating structures—may be better able to withstand the potential disruptions associated with organizational change.

Several key factors help account for the capacity of some nonprofit organizations to make changes in their strategy while retaining fidelity to their mission. In our view, organizational mission serves as a barometer to test alternative strategies. An organization's mission is based on what its participants regard as valuable and important. Organizational strategies speak to the instrumentality of survival. In many organizations, strategies for survival evolve into the mission, and this evolution can drain the organization of a sense of purpose. The challenge, then, is how to adapt to changing circumstances without robbing a nonprofit of its compass and values.

Much contemporary organizational research emphasizes the extent to which organizations become ossified with age and as they grow larger. Whether stressing accountability and inertia (Hannan and Freeman 1984), concerns with legitimacy (DiMaggio and Powell 1983), or learning traps and technological lock-in (Christensen 1997), the general view in the literature is that organizations become more conservative as they age and grow. We wonder, however, if these arguments are primarily suited for production-driven organizations with well-established routines intended to facilitate both reproducibility and accountability. Perhaps ideologically driven organizations operate differently. We raise this conjecture because there is suggestive evidence that nonprofits may be better able to experiment with change if they are older and equipped with the necessary resources.

Consider a standard array of organizational attributes—age, size, administrative structure, identity, and resource environment. Older organizations are regarded as less responsive to pressures for change because they must be attentive to the expectations of current stakeholders. But an early study of program change over five years in sixteen social welfare organizations did not find any evidence of a significant association between age and change or lack of change, although the authors had expected older organizations to be less flexible (Hage and Aiken 1974). More recent studies of changes in the populations of voluntary social service organizations and day-care centers report that nonprofit organizations are in fact more likely to experiment with change as they age (cited in Kelly and Amburgey 1991). Anecdotal evidence that social service organizations may become more flexible as they grow older was provided earlier: the National Urban League had been active for over fifty years when it added civil rights advocacy to its original mission. Minkoff (1999) demonstrates, in research on national women's and racial minority organizations, that older organizations are more likely to make changes in strategy. Moreover, there is also no evidence that older organizations are more likely to make conservative changes, defined as shifts from protest or advocacy to service provision. Although core change reexposes organizations to the kinds of liabilities that confront newly established groups as they seek out resources and legitimacy, the disruptive effects diminish somewhat over time. Older nonprofit organizations may be, in general, more stable and less likely to fail.

Other standard organizational hypotheses are that increasing size means more centralization and formalization, and that such features are associated with organizational inertia. Again, the bulk of the supporting evidence is drawn from for-profits, while research on nonprofits offers a possible alternative view. Hage and Aiken's (1974) study of social welfare organizations revealed a positive correlation between the size of the organization (measured in terms of number of employees) and higher rates of program change. Minkoff (1999) found that organizational formalization, indexed by the number of paid staff, was correlated with flexibility. Organizations with larger paid staff were more likely to make changes in strategy, particularly to and from advocacy and service. Staff size was also positively correlated with survival. This finding has been corroborated by research on voluntary social service organizations in Toronto, which showed that social service agencies with larger boards at the time of founding were more likely to engage in service area and goal changes, and that such organizations were also less likely to fail (Singh, Tucker, and Meinhard 1991).

Many of the standard accounts of the development of the social work field emphasize its evolution from a commitment to social reform to a focus on professionalization and case work (Cloward and Epstein 1965; Lubove [1965] 1980). This tendency for human-service professionals to invest in identities as experts is well established and clearly has been a key factor in the distancing of service-delivery organizations from advocacy on behalf of the poor. But that historical development impinges much less on contemporary organizations than on agencies that developed early in the twentieth century. Given that their identities as expert service providers are secure, members and staff of contemporary nonprofits are much more buffered from perceived losses in status that might follow from changes in organizational practice. Again, such protection is likely to be most efficacious in established nonprofits.

We have stressed that many nonprofit organizations exist in environments that impose contradictory demands. Such multiple pulls can generate internal conflicts or external contention between supporters and representatives and officials to whom an organization is accountable. Location in competing spheres can impede consideration of thoughtful responses to multiple pressures. Nevertheless, larger, more established nonprofits may find it easier to prioritize competing demands. In particular, one response available to mature organizations is to pursue hybrid strategies that permit varied responses to divergent institutional pressures.

In a study of mental health centers that diversified to provide drug abuse treatment centers, D'Aunno, Sutton, and Price (1991) focus on how organizational units responded to new external demands that conflicted with their traditional practices. The need to operate in both traditional and new institutional environments led hybrid agencies to rank their new practices in terms of a hierarchy of institutional demands; they effectively adopted or combined practices on the basis of their visibility to external groups. This emphasis on visibility represents an adaptive strategy for addressing conflicting external expectations. Similarly, service agencies that integrate advocacy are likely to find themselves in a contradictory relationship with their institutional environment. By virtue of their political nature, advocacy/service organizations may be as vulnerable as advocacy organizations to changes, especially restrictions, in the political climate. From the perspective of authorities and sponsors, however, the combination of forms may be seen as an acceptable compromise between the traditional form of service and the more overt political advocacy form (Minkoff 2002b).

We close, then, with a conjecture that prospects for organizational adaptation operate differently in the nonprofit world than in the proprietary sector. Small, minimalist nonprofits, especially those that are volunteer supported, may fly below the radar screen of external influences, and they are so deeply engaged in day-to-day survival that they are possibly shielded from or unaware of many external pressures. Larger, more established nonprofits that are more professionalized are most likely to be able to undertake significant modifications in strategy and activities *and* to withstand the disruptive effects of organizational change. Medium-sized nonprofits appear to be the most vulnerable to external pressures and most likely to chase after new funding sources. In our study of San Francisco Bay Area nonprofits, we found that it was precisely these mid-sized organizations that were engaging most often in earned-income activities, juggling multiple demands, and tailoring their missions to meet funders' demands. The encouraging news is that it is precisely those organizations that many scholars consider most likely to be complacent that are most capable of considered, thoughtful, and responsive change. The discouraging news is that these established nonprofits are a minority of the nonprofit field.

ACKNOWLEDGMENTS

The authors would like to thank Lisa Berlinger, past director of the Program on Nonprofit Organizations at Yale University, for early research support and Andy Gersick for helpful research assistance. We also appreciate research support provided by the Center on Social Innovation at the Graduate School of Business at Stanford University. We are grateful to Caroline Simard, David Suarez, Richard Steinberg, and Mayer Zald for very helpful suggestions on an early draft. We draw on material that was previously published in Powell and Friedkin (1987) and Minkoff (2002a).

REFERENCES

Adler, Judith E. 1979. *Artists in Offices: An Ethnography of an Academic Art Scene.* New Brunswick, N.J.: Transaction Books.

Barman, Emily. 2002. "Asserting Difference: The Strategic Response of Nonprofit Organizations to Competition." *Social Forces* 80:1191–1222.

———. 2004. "Satisfying Donors or Clients: New Pressures on Nonprofits." *Snapshots: Research Highlights from the Nonprofit Sector Research Fund.* January/February, no. 33.

Barnard, Chester. 1938. *Functions of the Executive.* Cambridge, Mass.: Harvard University Press.

Brilliant, Eleanor. 1990. *The United Way: Dilemmas of Organized Charity.* New York: Columbia University Press.

Cain, Roy. 1993. "Community-Based Services: Formalization and Depoliticization." *International Journal of Health Services* 23:665–84.

———. 1994. "Managing Impressions of an AIDS Service Organization: Into the Mainstream or Out of the Closet?" *Qualitative Sociology* 17:43–61.

———. 1995. "Community-Based AIDS Organizations and the State: Dilemmas of Dependence." *AIDS and Public Policy Journal* 10:83–93.

Chambré, Susan M. 1997. "Civil Society, Differential Resources, and Organizational Development: HIV/AIDS Organizations in New York City, 1982–1992." *Nonprofit and Voluntary Sector Quarterly* 26:466–88.

Christensen, Clayton M. 1997. *The Innovator's Dilemma: When New Technologies Cause Great Firms to Fail.* Boston: Harvard Business School Press.

Clark, Peter B., and James Q. Wilson. 1961. "Incentive Systems: A Theory of Organizations." *Administrative Science Quarterly* 17:178–84.

Clemens, Elisabeth S., and Debra C. Minkoff. 2004. "Beyond the Iron Law: Rethinking the Place of Organizations in Social Movement Research." Pp. 155–70 in *The Blackwell Companion to Social Movements,* edited by D. Snow, S. Soule, and H. Kriesi. Malden, Mass.: Blackwell Publishers.

Cloward, Richard A., and Irwin Epstein. 1965. "Private Social Welfare's Disengagement from the Poor: The Case of Family Adjustment Agencies." Reprinted in pp. 623–43 of *Social Welfare Institutions: A Sociological Reader,* edited by M. Zald. New York: John Wiley.

Cooper, Terry L. 1980. "Bureaucracy and Community Organization: The Metamorphosis of a Relationship." *Administration and Society* 11:411–44.

D'Aunno, Thomas, Robert I. Sutton, and Richard Price. 1991. "Isomorphism and External Support in Conflicting Institutional Environments: A Study of Drug Abuse Treatment Centers." *Academy of Management Journal* 34:636–61.

DiMaggio, Paul J., and Walter W. Powell. 1983. "The Iron Cage Revisited: Institutional Isomorphism and Collective Rationality in Organizational Fields." *American Sociological Review* 48:147–60.

Elsbach, Kimberly, and Robert Sutton. 1992. "Acquiring Organizational Legitimacy through Illegitimate Actions: A Marriage of Institutional and Impression Management Theories." *Academy of Management Journal* 35:699–738.

Frumkin, Peter. 2002. *On Being Nonprofit.* Cambridge, Mass.: Harvard University Press.

Gitlin, Todd. 1980. *The Whole World Is Watching: Mass Media in the Making and Unmaking of the New Left.* Berkeley: University of California Press.

Glaeser, Edward L. 2003. "Introduction." Pp. 1–44 in *The Governance of Not-for-Profit Organizations,* edited by E. L. Glaeser. Chicago: University of Chicago Press.

Gusfield, Joseph R. 1955. "Social Structure and Moral Reform: A Study of the Women's Christian Temperance Union." *American Sociological Review* 50:639–58.

———. 1963. *Symbolic Crusade: Status Politics and the American Temperance Movement.* Urbana: University of Illinois Press.

Hage, Jerald, and Michael Aiken. 1974. "Program Change and Organizational Properties." Pp. 720–42 in *Human Service Organizations: A Book of Readings,* edited by Y. Hasenfeld and R. A. English. Ann Arbor: University of Michigan Press.

Hannan, Michael, and John Freeman. 1984. "Structural Inertia and Organizational Change." *American Sociological Review* 49:149–64.

Hansmann, Henry. 1980. "The Role of Nonprofit Enterprise." *Yale Law Journal* 89:835–902.

Hasenfeld, Yeheskel. 1974. "Organizational Dilemmas in Innovating Social Services: The Case of Community Action Centers." Pp. 685–97 in *Human Service Organizations: A Book of Readings,* edited by Y. Hasenfeld and R. A. English. Ann Arbor: University of Michigan Press.

———. 2000. "Organizational Forms as Moral Practices: The Case of Welfare Departments." *Social Science Review* 74:329–51.

Hasenfeld, Yeheskel, and Richard A. English. 1974. "Human Service Organizations: A Conceptual Overview." Pp. 1–23 in *Human Service Organizations: A Book of Readings,* edited by Y. Hasenfeld and R. A. English. Ann Arbor: University of Michigan Press.

Helfgot, Joseph. 1974. "Professional Reform Organizations and the Symbolic Representation of the Poor." *American Sociological Review* 39:465–91.

Hyde, Cheryl. 1992. "The Ideational System of Social Movement Agencies: An Examination of Feminist Health Centers." Pp. 121–44 in *Human Services as Complex Organizations,* edited by Y. Hasenfeld. Newbury Park, Calif.: Sage Publications.

Jenkins, J. Craig. 1977. "Radical Transformation of Organizational Goals." *Administrative Science Quarterly* 22:568–86.

———. 1998. "Channeling Social Protest: Foundation Patronage of Contemporary Social Movements." Pp. 206–16 in *Private Action and the Public Good,* edited by W. W. Powell and E. S. Clemens. New Haven, Conn.: Yale University Press.

Kayal, Philip M. 1991. "Gay AIDS Voluntarism as Political Activity." *Nonprofit and Voluntary Sector Quarterly* 20:289–311.

Kelly, Dawn, and Terry L. Amburgey. 1991. "Organizational Inertia and Momentum: A Dynamic Model of Strategic Change." *Academy of Management Journal* 34:591–612.

Lubove, Roy. [1965] 1980. *The Professional Altruist.* New York: Atheneum.

Mansbridge, Jane. 1998. "On the Contested Nature of the Public Good." Pp. 3–19 in *Private Action and the Public Good,* edited by W. W. Powell and E. S. Clemens. New Haven, Conn.: Yale University Press.

Matthews, Nancy A. 1994. *Confronting Rape: The Feminist Anti-Rape Movement and the State.* New York: Routledge.

———. 1995. "Feminist Clashes with the State: Tactical Choices by State-Funded Rape Crisis Centers." Pp. 291–305 in *Feminist Organizations: Harvest of the New Women's Movement,* edited by M. Ferree and P. Martin. Philadelphia: Temple University Press.

McCarthy, John, and Mayer N. Zald. 1977. "Resource Mobilization and Social Movements." *American Journal of Sociology* 82:1212–41.

Messinger, Sheldon. 1955. "Organizational Transformation: A Case Study of a Declining Social Movement." *American Sociological Review* 20:3–10.

Michels, Robert. [1915] 1962. *Political Parties: A Sociological Study of the Oligarchical Tendencies of Modern Democracy.* New York: Free Press.

Minkoff, Debra C. 1999. "Bending with the Wind: Strategic Change and Adaptation by Women's and Racial-Minority Organizations." *American Journal of Sociology* 104:1666–1703.

———. 2002a. "Walking a Political Tightrope: Responsiveness and Internal Accountability in Social Movement Organizations." Pp. 33–48 in *Exploring Organizations and Advocacy: Governance and Accountability,* edited by E. Reid and M. Montilla. Nonprofit Advocacy and the Policy Process, vol. 2., no. 2. Washington, D.C.: Urban Institute Press.

———. 2002b. "The Emergence of Hybrid Organizational Forms: Combining Identity-Based Service Provision and Political Action." *Nonprofit and Voluntary Sector Quarterly* 31:377–401.

Moore, Kelly. 1993. "Doing Good While Doing Science: The Origins and Consequences of Public Interest Science Organizations in America, 1945–1980." Ph.D. dissertation, University of Arizona.

Oster, Sharon. 1995. *Strategic Management for Nonprofit Organizations.* New York: Oxford University Press.

Pauly, Mark, and Mark Redisch. 1973. "The Not-for-Profit Hospital as a Physicians' Cooperative." *American Economic Review* 63:87–99.

Polletta, Francesca. 2002. *Freedom Is an Endless Meeting: Democracy in American Social Movements.* Chicago: University of Chicago Press.

Powell, Walter W., and Paul J. DiMaggio, eds. 1991. *The New Institutionalism in Organizational Analysis.* Chicago: University of Chicago Press.

Powell, Walter W., and Rebecca Friedkin. 1986. "Politics and Programs: Organizational Factors in Public Television Decision-Making." Pp. 245–69 in *Nonprofit Enterprise in the Arts,* edited by P. DiMaggio. New York: Oxford University Press.

———. 1987. "Organizational Change in Nonprofit Organizations." Pp. 180–92 in *The Nonprofit Sector: A Research Handbook,* edited by W. W. Powell. 1st ed. New Haven, Conn.: Yale University Press.

Rangan, V. Kasturi. 2004. "Lofty Missions, Down-to-Earth Plans." *Harvard Business Review* March:112–19.

Rosenthal, Donald B. 1996. "Who 'Owns' AIDS Service Organizations? Governance Accountability in Non-Profit Organizations." *Polity* 29:97–118.

Salamon, Lester. 1987. "Partners in Public Service: The Scope and Theory of Government-Nonprofit Relations." Pp. 99–117 in *The Nonprofit Sector: A Research Handbook,* edited by W. W. Powell. 1st ed. New Haven, Conn.: Yale University Press.

———. 1995. *Partners in Public Service.* Baltimore: Johns Hopkins University Press.

Scott, Robert A. 1967. "The Selection of Clients by Social Welfare Agencies: The Case of the Blind." *Social Problems* 14:248–57.

Scott, W. Richard. 2003. *Organizations: Rational, Natural and Open Systems.* 5th ed. Upper Saddle River, N.J.: Prentice-Hall.

Sills, David L. 1957. *The Volunteers: Means and Ends in a National Organization.* Glencoe, Ill.: Free Press.

Simon, Herbert. 1947. *Administrative Behavior.* Glencoe, Ill.: Free Press.

Singh, Jitendra V., David J. Tucker, and Agnes G. Meinhard. 1991. "Institutional Change and Organizational Dynamics." Pp. 390–442 in *The New Institutionalism in Organizational Analysis,* edited by Walter W. Powell and Paul J. DiMaggio. Chicago: University of Chicago Press.

Spalter-Roth, Roberta, and Ronnee Schreiber. 1995. "Outsider Issues and Insider Tactics: Strategic Tensions in the Women's Policy Network during the 1980s." Pp. 105–27 in *Feminist*

Organizations: Harvest of the New Women's Movement, edited by M. Ferree and P. Martin. Philadelphia: Temple University Press.

Staggenborg, Suzanne. 1988. "The Consequences of Professionalization and Formalization in the Pro-Choice Movement." *American Sociological Review* 53:585–606.

Stinchcombe, Arthur. 1965. "Social Structure and Organizations." Pp. 142–93 in *Handbook of Organizations,* edited by James G. March. Chicago: Rand McNally.

Swidler, Ann. 1979. *Organization without Authority.* Cambridge, Mass.: Harvard University Press.

Weisbrod, Burton. 1988. *The Nonprofit Economy.* Cambridge, Mass.: Harvard University Press.

Weiss, Nancy J. 1989. *Whitney M. Young, Jr., and the Struggle for Civil Rights.* Princeton, N.J.: Princeton University Press.

Wolfe, Maxine. 1994. "The AIDS Coalition to Unleash Power (ACT UP): A Direct Model of Community Research for AIDS Prevention." Pp. 217–47 in *AIDS Prevention and Services: Community Based Research,* edited by J. P. Van Vugt. Westport, Conn.: Bergin and Garvey.

Zald, Mayer. 1970. *Organizational Change: The Political Economy of the YMCA.* Chicago: University of Chicago Press.

Zald, Mayer, and Roberta Ash. 1966. "Social Movement Organizations: Growth, Decay, and Change." *Social Forces* 44:327–41.

Zald, Mayer, and Patricia Denton. 1963. "From Evangelism to General Service: The Transformation of the YMCA." *Administrative Science Quarterly* 8:214–34.

26

Governance: Research Trends, Gaps, and Future Prospects

FRANCIE OSTROWER
MELISSA M. STONE

Boards are charged with ultimate responsibility for the nonprofit organizations that they oversee. Within the nonprofit world, they serve as an important channel for civic participation and play a critical role in connecting individual institutions to their larger environment. Accordingly, boards are a subject of enormous importance for those with scholarly, managerial, and public policy interests in the nonprofit sector. In 1987, however, a major assessment of the governance literature found that empirical studies and scholarly analyses of nonprofit boards were scarce (Middleton 1987). Twenty years later, major gaps in our theoretical and empirical knowledge about boards continue to exist, but the research literature is growing, and there is an evident increase in the level of attention and interest concerning nonprofit boards. There is now a small but identifiable subfield of board research, and all evidence suggests that interest in boards will only continue to grow. This chapter provides an overview of the primary approaches, assumptions, questions, and emphases that characterize this emerging literature; it also identifies remaining gaps.

Two themes run throughout this chapter. First, boards are complex entities that defy sweeping generalizations. They are heterogeneous, subject to internal shifts, and respond to multiple—and sometimes conflicting—influences. Explicitly and implicitly, the emerging consensus in the literature is that there is no "one size fits all" model of boards. Second, boards are deeply influenced by the context in which they operate. They are part of both the organization and its environment (Middleton 1987), and therefore governance research must explicate both internal and external contingencies. The two themes are related because contextual differences are sources of variation among boards. We contend that a pressing task for future research is to develop the implication of these conclusions. Toward that end, we further suggest that while it is important to develop a distinct body of knowledge about boards, it is also critical that board research not isolate itself from wider disciplinary and theoretical concerns. Rather, drawing on such concerns and perspectives will both enhance our understanding of boards and strengthen the ability of board research to contribute to our overall knowledge of philanthropy, nonprofit organizations, and civic participation.

The boundaries in the scope of this review are also important to keep in mind. This chapter deals primarily with boards of larger 501(c)(3) organizations in health and human services in the United States because these are the types of organizations commonly discussed in the literature. We found, for instance, far less literature on boards of grassroots organizations than of larger, better established organizations, and little on nonprofit boards outside of the United States, with the exception of research on boards in Canada and the United Kingdom by scholars from those countries. However, our review was confined to English-language publications that were referenced in documents and databases in the United States. A review of the research from sources outside of the United States would complement this one and might uncover other themes and emphases.

THE LEGAL CONTEXT

The boards of charitable corporations exist in a legal context that is sometimes informed by the law of trusts and more often, by the law of business corporations (Brody 1998; Middleton 1987). The law of trusts maintains stringent standards prohibiting self-dealing and delegation of management responsibilities and holds trustees liable for simple errors of judgment. The law of business corporations allows self-dealing with proper disclosure, delegation with proper oversight, and liability only for gross negligence. While corporate legal standards of governance are more frequently applied to nonprofit organizations, the underlying questions of to whom and for what nonprofit boards are accountable remain difficult to answer (for further discussion of the legal dimensions of trusteeship, see Brody, this volume).

The Question of Accountability

Principal-agent theory focuses on issues of roles and responsibilities when ownership is separate from control of an enterprise (Fama and Jensen 1983; Eisenhardt 1989). The principal-agent problem is how owners (the principals) who do not have direct control over daily operations can ensure that managers (the agents) operate in a manner that benefits the interests and goals of the owners. In for-profit firms, stockholders, as owners, delegate responsibilities for managerial oversight to a board of directors. In theory (though not necessarily in practice), the voting power of stockholders plus the discipline of the market monitor the board's decision making and help guard against capture of the board by opportunistic managers.

In the nonprofit world, it is unclear who should be regarded as the principal (Ben-Ner and Van Hoomissen 1994; Fama and Jensen 1983; Miller 2002; Oster 1995). First, there are no owners in the sense of stockholders, and second, there is no market to provide additional safeguards. Ben-Ner and Van Hoomissen contend that founding stakeholders constitute the nonprofit's owners, but that subsequent parties can readily usurp their power and pursue different interests and goals. This ambiguity concerning who constitutes the "principal" heightens the difficulty of defining the nature and scope of nonprofit accountability. In practice, the major constituency of accountability is the state attorney general who acts as *parens patriae,* speaking for the beneficiaries to ensure that the charitable corporation uses funds and property to fulfill its original purpose (American Bar Association 1993). Most state attorneys general, however, infrequently use their power to call nonprofit boards to account for abuses because they lack adequate staff to provide oversight, face a political climate that discourages investigation into a particular charity, or are reluctant to pursue those thought to be well-meaning volunteers (Hansmann 1981; Brody 1998, this volume). This situation, along with abuses periodically covered in the media, continues to prompt questions and debates about the adequacy of accountability mechanisms under the current system of nonprofit governance.

Duties of Loyalty, Care, and Obedience

To satisfy basic dimensions of accountability, a board and individual directors must fulfill three duties. First, the duty of loyalty requires directors to exercise their power in the interests of the nonprofit corporation and not in their, or someone else's, self-interest. Conflicts of interest that are not fully disclosed prior to board action are the primary concern here. Second, the duty of care requires a board of directors to participate in decision making, to be informed about the matters that come before the board, and to exercise independent judgment based on the good faith and care that an ordinarily prudent person would use in similar circumstances (American Bar Association 1993). Third, the duty of obedience concerns loyalty to the purpose for which the organization was created. Smith (1992, 1995) strongly argues that this duty is one of the primary moral principles that should guide *and constrain* trustee behavior. He suggests that boards act as "communities of interpretation," looking back to the original founding purpose (similar to Ben-Ner and Van Hoomissen's point) and reinterpreting that purpose in light of current notions of the common good.

Traditional notions of board responsibilities follow directly from these basic legal standards and comprise a common set of elements (see, for example, Bowen 1994; Harris 1989; Houle 1989; Kramer 1981; and Widmer 1993):

- ensuring that the activities of the organization align with its mission
- making long-range plans and establishing major organizational policies
- overseeing financial management and ensuring that adequate resources are in place
- ensuring that basic legal and ethical responsibilities are met
- hiring and overseeing the chief executive officer
- representing the organization to the environment in general as well as to key constituencies

Despite these common elements, the legal context provides few answers for boards concerning the actual implementation of their duties in concrete board roles and responsibilities. As will be discussed later (see "Roles and Responsibilities of Boards of Directors"), the gap between what boards are supposed to do and what they actually do is considerable.

BOARD COMPOSITION

Board composition is one of the topics that accounts for much of the growth in the nonprofit board literature since 1987. Research on who sits on boards connects to a range of issues concerning governance, nonprofit institutions, and their relationship to society at large. Such issues pertain to organizational effectiveness and mission and to the ways power is exercised in, and through, nonprofit institutions. Thus, board composition has also attracted attention because it is assumed that who serves on the board makes a difference.

Diverse types of research suggest that some elements of board composition, including board homogeneity/heterogeneity, have an influence on board and organizational culture, emphases, policy, and effectiveness (Bradshaw, Murray, and Wolpin 1996; Gittell and Covington 1994; Middleton 1989; Odendahl and Youmans 1994; Ostrander 1984; Ostrower 2002; Siciliano 1996). At the same time, evidence strongly warns against making assumptions about trustees' attitudes, roles, and actions based on particular demographic characteristics (Brown 2002; Oster and O'Regan 2002; Ostrower 2002; Widmer 1989). Moreover, it is vital that simultaneous consideration be given to different aspects of board composition, including interactions between race, gender, and class (Odendahl and Youmans 1994; Ostrower 1995, 2002; Widmer 1989).

The following discussion of the disparate material on nonprofit board composition is organized in terms of three separate, but related, questions. One question, descriptive in nature, concerns the characteristics of trustees, although we must emphasize that we lack adequate data to provide a reliable and general portrait of board composition in the United States. The two other questions, analytic in nature, focus on the relationship between board composition and other variables. One concerns the *determinants* of board composition, such as factors that lead boards to have more or less balanced gender ratios. The other question concerns the *consequences* of board composition, and asks whether and how board composition matters—to trustees, boards, institutions, and the community.

Board Composition

In the absence of a representative sample of boards, we lack the data needed to generalize about board composition and differences among boards. The largest set of data comes from a survey of 1,347 organizations published in 2000 by the National Center for Nonprofit Boards (NCNB; now BoardSource), which asks about gender, race, ethnicity, and age (but not education, profession, or income). As NCNB cautions, the sample is not a representative one, but is drawn from their database of members, publication buyers, and other contacts. Numerous other studies provide data on aspects of board composition in other samples and have been incorporated as relevant. Before turning to address the individual dimensions of board composition, we offer the following summary of the overall conclusions that emerge with respect to the descriptive aspect of our analysis:

- We know more about the composition of larger, more affluent institutions than we do about the membership of smaller, community-based organizations. Studies of board composition of institutions with varied asset levels are critical in order to determine how much our current picture of board composition may be "biased" toward larger organizations.
- Nonprofit boards are larger than corporate boards (Bowen 1994; Oster 1995; Ostrower 2002). Bowen (1994) observes that nonprofit boards typically include twelve to thirty members, as compared with the ten to fifteen members on a corporate board. The NCNB (2000) found an average nonprofit board size of nineteen, but boards can be considerably larger, and their size appears to increase with organizational size and be related to important board characteristics (Cornforth and Simpson 2002).[1] One reason that nonprofit boards are large is to allow them to include members of their multiple constituencies (Abzug et al. 1993; Bowen 1994; Kang and Cnaan 1995). Fundraising concerns also contribute to large board size, certainly among elite institutions, which use prestigious board seats to encourage and reward large donors. Large boards have drawbacks and can prove unwieldy for carrying out governance functions, however, prompting some boards to seek additional ways to incorporate large donors (Bowen 1994; Kaplan 2004; Ostrower 1995, 2002).
- Studies find that the vast majority of trustees are white, more trustees are male than female, and boards draw their members disproportionately from members of the upper-middle and upper classes (see, for example, Abzug 1996; Abzug et al. 1993; Abzug and Galaskiewicz 2001; DiMaggio and Useem 1982; Kang and Cnaan 1995; Middleton 1987, 1989; Moore and Whitt 2000; NCNB 2000; Odendahl and Youmans 1994; Ostrower 1995, 2002; Zald 1967). Still, most of our information about board composition is based on larger and more affluent institutions of the type that attract elite participation. It is quite likely that boards of other types of institutions are different in composition.
- Boards are becoming more demographically diverse, but at a very uneven pace (Abzug 1996; Abzug et al. 1993; Abzug and Galaskiewicz 2001; Kang and Cnaan 1995; Ostrower 1995, 2002).
- Elements of board diversity must be addressed individually and scrutinized in relation to one another. Boards can, for instance, become dramatically more diverse with respect to gender or race while remaining quite homogeneous with respect to class (Odendahl and Youmans 1994; Ostrower 1995, 2002; Widmer 1989).
- Board composition varies among institutions of different types. Data suggest that organizational size, prestige, and area of activity are important variables (Abzug 1996; Abzug et al. 1993; DiMaggio and Useem 1982; Kang and Cnaan 1995; Middleton 1987; Moore and Whitt 2000; NCNB 2000; Odendahl and Youmans 1994; Ostrower 1995, 2002; Zald 1967). More research is needed to ascertain the degree and nature of variations in board composition and also to examine the importance of other potentially important variables.
- More research is needed on board diversity of all types, but considerably more attention has been given to gender than to ethnic and racial diversity.
- Available data indicate that board composition does have consequences for trustees, boards as a whole, organizations, and even the wider community. Much remains to be learned, however, about the degree and nature of these consequences, and the mechanisms through which they operate.

Gender

The issue of gender, women, and boards is a subject of growing prominence. Gender ratios on boards are presented in several studies (see, for example, Abzug et al. 1993; Abzug and Beaudin 1994; Bradshaw, Murray, and Wolpin 1996; Covelli 1989; Daniels 1988; Gittell and Covington 1994; McCarthy 1990; Odendahl and Youmans 1994; Ostrander 1984; Ostrower 1995, 2002; Ross 1954; Siciliano 1996; Moore and Whitt 2000; Whitt et al. 1993). Although the studies have different purposes and use varied samples, taken together they allow us to identify certain common patterns and their implications. Overall, the research indicates that men outnumber women on nonprofit boards. Thus, the NCNB (2000) finds that women constitute 43 percent of trustees, a figure very close to the 40 percent found among Canadian nonprofit boards (Bradshaw, Murray, and Wolpin 1996). Clearly, women are a far greater presence on nonprofit boards than on corporate ones, where, for instance, women held fewer than 7 percent of all Fortune 1000 directorships and fully 42 percent of companies had *no* female directors as recently as 1994. (Figures from the organization Catalyst's census of women board directors cited in Zweigenhaft and Domhoff 1998:45.) This is consistent with historian Kathleen McCarthy's (1990) observation that the nonprofit sector has historically provided an arena for women to pursue opportunities for leadership and participation not available to them elsewhere.

Further scrutiny, however, reveals considerable variation in gender diversity among different nonprofit institutions. Organizational size and field of activity are two apparent sources of this variation, with women more likely to serve on the boards of smaller and less prestigious nonprofit institutions (Babchuk, Massey, and Gordon 1960; Bradshaw, Murray, and Wolpin 1996; Middleton 1987; Moore and Whitt 2000; NCNB 2000; Odendahl and Youmans 1994; McPherson and Smith-Lovin 1986; Zald 1969). Still, the generalization does not hold for all types of institutions, such as large and prestigious arts organizations (Moore and Whitt 2000).

Differences in gender ratios are also found across different fields of activity. Fewer women are found on the boards of hospitals, colleges and universities, and policy-related organizations, by comparison with human service and cultural boards (Abzug 1996; Kang and Cnaan 1995; Middleton 1987; Moore and Whitt 2000; Ostrower 1995). There is, however, also variation within field of activity. For instance, overall 34.4 percent of foundation trustees are women, but the figure is higher for family foundations (43.3 percent) and lower for other private independent foundations (25.6 percent; Council on Foundations 2002). Interestingly, women who serve on multiple boards may also be more likely than comparable men to specialize within a field (Moore and Whitt 2000; Ostrower 2002).

Comparisons over time show that boards are becoming more diverse with respect to gender, but the pace of change is uneven across fields of activity (Abzug 1996; Abzug et al. 1993; Ostrower 1995). Comparing the composition of a group of boards of large nonprofits in 1931, 1961, and 1991, the "Six Cities" study found an overall increase in the percentage of women, from 28 percent to 35 percent, but growth in particular subfields was sometimes dramatic (Abzug 1996; Kang and Cnaan 1995). For example, while the educational boards were entirely male in 1931, and over 95 percent male in 1961, by 1991 they were almost 20 percent female.

What explains the gender ratios and patterns that we observe on nonprofit boards? Odendahl and Youmans (1994) argue that "the homogeneous composition of traditional governing boards . . . established and maintains a model for pervasive class, ethnic or racial, and sex discrimination throughout society" (188), and that "a strong case can be made that there is institutionalized sex discrimination in the nonprofit system" (194). Another point of view is that nonprofit boards *reflect* the wider discrimination in society. For instance, Ostrower's (1995) findings suggest that gender per se may not be a determinant of trusteeship among men and women who command the requisite resources—but women are less likely to be in that position. In short, power, wealth, and status in the community and the business world provide an advantage in gaining access to seats on prestigious nonprofit boards (DiMaggio and Useem 1982; Middleton 1987; Ostrower 1995, 2002; Ratcliff, Gallagher, and Ratcliff 1979; Useem 1984; Zald 1967).

Increasing attention has been given to the consequences of gender for trustee roles, boards as a whole, and organizations. Evidence suggests that gender does have an impact, but much work needs to be done before the nature, extent, and reasons for that impact are understood. One line of research focuses on the impact of the board's gender ratio on board and organizational functioning. Gittell and Covington (1994) argue that the gender composition of boards influences organizational policy and program content. In a study of neighborhood development organizations, they find that gender ratios influenced the approach to community development taken and the "provision of women friendly programs" (11). In a study of 240 YMCA organizations, Siciliano (1996) found that gender diversity was positively related to social performance levels (fulfillment of social mission) and negatively related to levels of money raised, but it had no relationship to operating efficiency. Bradshaw, Murray, and Wolpin (1996) also examined the impact of gender ratios on organizational effectiveness, with mixed results. They found relationships using *subjective* measures of performance, but not with their *objective* measure, annual budget change. They also found associations between gender composition and process variables (such as hours spent on board work by officeholders, number of full board meetings, and adoption of a power-sharing governance model). Gender diversity was negatively associated with budget size (and extent of linkages with other organizations, such as engaging in joint planning) but positively associated with government funding. As authors of both these studies (Siciliano 1996; Bradshaw, Murray, and Wolpin 1996) point out, however, the cross-sectional nature of their data precludes establishing the direction of causality. Oster and O'Regan (2002) find that female trustees spend significantly more time on board matters than their male counterparts, but that gender is not related to personal giving or monitoring responsibilities.

Another focus in the research has been the impact of gender on the allocation of roles and influence within boards among male and female trustees. There is some evidence that on elite boards, the roles of male and female trustees reflect traditional upper-class gender roles, in which men hold elite economic positions while women coordinate the social life of their class (see, for example, Collins 1992; Daniels 1988; Domhoff 1970; Hacker 1975; McCarthy 1990; Odendahl 1990; Odendahl and Youmans 1994; Ostrower 1995, 2002; Ostrander 1984; Tickamyer 1981; Whitt et al. 1993). This is perhaps most evident in female volunteers' creation of social fundraising events (Daniels 1988; Odendahl and Youmans 1994; Ostrower 1995, 2002). Considerably more research is needed, however, to compare the actual activities of male and female trustees (Odendahl and Youmans 1994) and to control for other variables such as occupation.

Race and Ethnicity

Less information exists on the racial and ethnic composition of boards (and the consequences of ethnic composition) than on gender, and this topic represents one of the largest gaps in the literature. Existing research finds that boards are overwhelmingly white. The NCNB (2000) found that among trustees, 86 percent were Caucasian, 9 percent were African American, and Hispanics/Latinos and Asian Americans constituted 3 and 2 percent, respectively. Foundation boards appear to be even more racially homogeneous, according to Council on Foundation research (2002) that places the percentage of white trustees at 89.5 percent (African Americans, at 6.3 percent, again constitute the largest minority group). Other studies similarly find racial and ethnic homogeneity on boards (Abzug 1996; Ostrower 2002; Siciliano 1996; Widmer 1989). The little data that are available suggest that there has been an increase in the presence of minorities on boards (Abzug 1996; Kang and Cnaan 1995). One study found an eightfold increase in African American board membership between 1961 and 1991, but starting percentages were so low that in 1991 African Americans still composed fewer than 10 percent of trustees (Abzug 1996:106).

A subject on which far more information is needed concerns what types of boards are more or less racially and ethnically homogeneous, and why. Abzug et al. (1993) found that ethnic composition was associated with field of activity, with United Way (UW) trustees being more diverse than those of hospitals, which in turn were more diverse than those of art museums. Kang and Cnaan cite the influence of environmental factors on board diversity, observing that "the dependency of UW on a wide task-environment explains why UW boards have, on the average, more minority members" than other human service agencies (1995:40). Ostrower (2002) found that greater attention to diversity by arts boards was prompted by external demographic changes in the community and trustees' perception that greater diversity was critical to organizational survival in this changing environment.

Class

Studies consistently find that trustees are drawn from higher socioeconomic groups. They also find that socially and economically prominent community members select, and are selected by, prominent boards of affluent institutions (Abzug et al. 1993; Babchuk, Massey, and Gordon 1960; Dain 1991; Middleton 1987, 1989; DiMaggio and Useem 1982; Moore and Whitt 2000; Odendahl 1990; Ostrander 1984; Ostrower 1995, 1998, 2002; Ratcliff, Gallagher, and Ratcliff 1979; Salzmann and Domhoff 1983; Zald 1967). In many cities, local upper-class boards were also deeply involved in founding the nonprofit institutions they governed (DiMaggio 1982; Hall 1982; Zolberg 1981). Since more attention has been given to boards of larger and comparatively financially better off institutions, we need to determine just how much higher in socioeconomic status trustees are when compared to the general population at large and their specific constituencies. It may also be precisely among the less-studied, smaller, and grassroots organization boards that we are more likely to find trustees with less elite or upper middle-class backgrounds (Middleton 1987).

Class composition is also associated with field of activity. Prestigious arts boards, for instance, are particularly likely to attract those with elite affiliations (Abzug et al. 1993; DiMaggio and Useem 1982; Middleton 1987; Moore and Whitt 2000; Ostrower 1995). Once again, we also find variation within fields. Thus, a study of human service organizations found a larger elite presence on United Way boards than on the boards of YMCAs or YWCAs or family service organizations (Kang and Cnaan 1995). The types of elites recruited to boards may also be changing, with more trustees selected on the basis of their corporate position (rather than familial ties), and the importance of various types of elite status (such as economic versus social) may vary in different fields of activity (DiMaggio and Anheier 1990; DiMaggio and Useem 1982; Ostrower 1995, 2002).

The class composition of boards may have consequences for individual trustee behavior, for the functioning of the board and the organization, and also for the wider community. Handy (1995) argues that high status trustees provide their reputation to nonprofits "as collateral," and that trustees' exposure to the potential loss of this collateral enhances consumer and donor trust in nonprofits. Researchers have argued that boards play a role among elites, positing that board service enhances elite status, cohesion, and influence (DiMaggio 1982; DiMaggio and Useem 1982; Hall 1975, 1982; Middleton 1987, 1989; Odendahl 1990; Ostrander 1984; Ostrower 1995, 1998, 2002). Power structure theorists argue that nonprofit board membership perpetuates upper-class power (Domhoff 1983; Odendahl 1990; Ostrander

1984). For instance, Ostrander (1984) argues that upper-class womens' volunteer work "is essential to upholding the power and privilege of the upper class" (129), and that "it is important to directing policy and exercising control over the paid professionals" (131). Another perspective, taken by Ostrower (2002) in a study of elite arts boards, is that boards are subject to the dual, and often conflicting, influences of class and organizational factors. On this view, organizational factors and professionals serve to modify the impact of class power.

BOARD-STAFF RELATIONS

Typical prescriptive models of the board-executive relationship within nonprofit organizations often describe this relationship as either a harmonious partnership within the leadership core or a hierarchical authority relationship with the board in a superordinate position (see, for example, Carver 1990; Houle 1989). The notion that participants within the leadership core are a "team of equals," perhaps concentrating on different tasks, is common to the partnership model (Drucker 1990:10). Problems between boards and managers, for example, can be solved if each partner has clearly articulated roles, responsibilities, and expectations. The hierarchical authority model of governance clearly places the board in a superordinate position relative to the rest of the organization. The model, termed by some a "heroic" ideal for the role of the board (Herman 1989), places ultimate responsibility and accountability for fiscal integrity and organizational direction with the board. Statutory requirements and the courts have held to the hierarchical authority model of governance where, in fact, boards are held legally responsible for these functions.

For scholars trying to understand, rather than prescribe, behaviors or dynamics within the leadership core, both models are inadequate (Golensky 1993; Harris 1989; Heimovics and Herman 1990; Kramer 1981; Murray, Bradshaw, and Wolpin 1992). First, tensions are embedded within the nature of governance responsibilities that will not be resolved permanently in favor of one party. As Kramer (1987) describes, the partnership concept belies what exists in practice—a system of "parallel governance" that establishes the authority of both lay volunteers and professionals in the decision making of nonprofit organizations. The relationship between these two types of authority is fluid and complex, and the partnership model is likely to overstate the degree of integration among the parties. Similarly, Golensky (1993) argues that the primary power relationship in nonprofit organizations is between the board and the executive director and that power in this relationship shifts over time. The partnership model does not recognize power relations.

Second, it is likely that the roles, responsibilities, and power of boards, executive directors, and top managers follow more of an evolutionary cycle as described by Wood (1992). After a nonrecurring founding period, the operational style of the board moves through three sequential phases as the board becomes less intensely involved in the mission and operations of the nonprofit and more interested in bureaucratic procedures associated with governance. An internal or external crisis initiates the cycle all over again. Similarly, Boris (1989) identifies a developmental life cycle in the balance of board and staff roles and responsibilities in foundations that is associated with age, size, and distance from the original donor.

Most recent research on board-CEO relationships has recognized the problems with prescriptive models. One stream has directly questioned the managed-systems approach to governance, which assumes the board to be in a hierarchical relationship with the rest of the organization (see, for example, Herman and Heimovics 1990; Heimovics and Herman 1990; Heimovics, Herman, and Jurkiewicz 1995). Indeed, researchers found that both executive directors and board presidents saw executive directors as responsible for most critical events in their organizations, including those with successful and unsuccessful outcomes. Because CEOs occupy a place of "psychological centrality" in nonprofit organizations (Herman and Heimovics 1990:171), they should work to see that boards fulfill their legal, organizational, and public roles. Furthermore, the most effective CEOs in terms of reputation provided "board-centered leadership" (Heimovics, Herman, and Jurkiewicz 1995:236), guiding the board to fulfill its governing role.

Patterns of Board-Staff Relations and Their Determinants

A complementary stream of research concerns shifting patterns of board-CEO dominance. For example, studies of arts boards identified complex and shifting patterns of board-staff power: DiMaggio and Useem (1978) observe that the emergence of professional arts managers challenged elite control, Zolberg (1981) finds a shifting balance of influence among elite museum boards and professional staff, and Ostrower (2002) finds that contemporary elite trustees give up a measure of their authority in order to secure top professionals. Two major themes emerge from research on board-CEO dominance: first, there are a number of distinct patterns that describe relationships between boards and executive directors; and second, these patterns vary depending on a wide range of variables.

The starkest patterns uncovered involve board versus CEO dominance, which were first explored by Kramer in 1965 and Zald in 1969. Kramer later established a more refined set of patterns that included not only highly concentrated power by either the CEO or board president but also dispersed power within board or CEO leadership (1981, 1987). More recently, a large-scale study in Canada by Murray, Bradshaw, and Wolpin (1992) found five dominant patterns. In addition to CEO-dominated and chair-dominated boards, they also describe a fragmented power arrangement, where power is dispersed among several groups or individuals; a power-sharing pattern, in which power is widely dispersed but joined together by ideological consensus; and a powerless board, where no group or individual seems to have power. Among the five, only the power-sharing pattern comes close to describing the partnership model depicted in the prescriptive literature.

Some research indicates that the particular relationship between the board and CEO at any one point in time depends on a number of personal characteristics of the leadership core, and on organizational and environmental variables. Common across studies are the following variables:

Individual/personal

- gender, where women board members are associated with less influential boards (Babchuk et al. 1960; Zald 1969) which may translate to chair or CEO-dominated boards (Murray, Bradshaw, and Wolpin 1992)
- prestige or wealth, where greater socioeconomic status of board members is associated with greater power (Zald 1969; Kramer 1965)
- CEO tenure, where greater CEO seniority is related to more power (Kramer 1985)
- professional credentials, where CEOs with high credentials can lead to greater CEO power (Zald 1967, 1969; Kramer 1981, 1987)

Organizational

- age of organization, where younger nonprofits are more likely to be dominated by the board (Zald 1969)
- size of the nonprofit, where larger nonprofits are more likely to be dominated by their CEOs (Kramer 1985)
- complexity and degree of bureaucratization, where greater degrees of both lead to CEO dominance (Kramer 1985; Zald 1969)

Environmental

- interorganizational relationships, where ties to many different types of constituencies lead to greater fragmentation of power between the board and staff (Zald 1969)
- type of financial dependence, where the extent to which the board controls or represents critical financial resources will be related to its power (Pfeffer 1973; Provan 1980; Kramer 1981; Zald 1969)
- external stability, where stability is related to less board power (Kramer 1981; Zald 1969) and turbulence or crisis is related to more board power (Wood 1992; Zald 1969)
- funding source, where greater dependence on government resources is related to less board power (Kramer 1981, 1987; Smith and Lipsky 1993)

A study by Murray, Bradshaw, and Wolpin (1992) of over 400 Canadian health and human-service nonprofits related some of these variables to the five patterns of board–executive director dominance described above. The study's major findings were that the individual background characteristics of board members related most strongly to the five patterns. For example, higher percentages of women and younger board members were positively associated with power-sharing boards, and higher percentages of women board members were negatively associated with CEO-dominated boards. A higher percentage of board members over sixty years of age was associated with chair-dominated and powerless boards and negatively associated with power-sharing boards. Weaker relationships were found between organizational and environmental characteristics and patterns of dominance.

The relative statistical weakness of all these relationships (correlation coefficients never exceeded 0.27 in the Murray, Bradshaw, and Wolpin study) leads us to argue that one cannot predict patterns of board-CEO dominance simply based on cross-sectional variables. As Perrow (1963) and Zald (1969) argued decades ago, one must also examine key contingencies, such as developmental phases of organizational life and certain organizational crises or major events, and how these contingencies interact with the cross-sectional variables above. A strategic-contingencies view argues that organizations will be controlled by those individuals or groups who successfully cope with uncertainty, performing the most critical tasks needed by the organization when it faces a distinctive problem (Hickson et al. 1971). Power, therefore, shifts over time among key groups. For example, in his study of a voluntary general hospital, Perrow found four shifts in power, including domination by trustees, then by the medical staff, then by the administration, and, finally, a stage of multiple leadership. These power shifts related to which group was best able to respond to the critical tasks facing the hospital at that time.

Hult and Walcott (1990) state that governance is concerned with significant issues, such as decisions regarding organizational mission, major activities, the right to participate in decision making, and general relations with the external environment. The research examined above strongly suggests that which group or groups take on governance responsibilities for a nonprofit organization will change over time. It is likely, therefore, that governance reaches beyond the role of the board to include activities of the executive director, top management, informal groups of individual board members and staff, and so forth (Harris 1989; Kramer 1981; Middleton 1989; Saidel 1998; Zald 1967).

ROLES AND RESPONSIBILITIES OF BOARDS IN THE RESEARCH

Despite common assumptions of what boards should do (described earlier as "traditional responsibilities"), the research literature has established that there is much variation across and within nonprofit boards regarding which roles and responsibilities are more likely to be performed. For example, Wood's original study of college trustees (1983) found three dominant styles (or roles) played by these boards, including participatory, ratifying, and corporate styles. Later, in a 1992 study of human-service organizations, Wood refined this argument by mapping particular board styles onto phases of development experienced by boards. Recent research also indicates that governance practices differ when a founder leads a nonprofit (Block and Rosenberg 2002).

Recent studies have also addressed the impact of government contracting on the role and authority of nonprofit boards, though these present complex and often contradictory pictures. Some studies suggest that boards become more marginal in organizations that function as part of government-contracting regimes (Bernstein 1991; Fink 1991; Grønbjerg 1990; Smith and Lipsky 1993), while others find boards performing substantial and active roles (Harlan and Saidel 1994). A later study by Saidel and Harlan (1998), however, found that key governance functions were shared between the board and the executive and that, in some cases, boards were simply bystanders when it came to issues concerning the relationship between government-contracting agencies and nonprofit providers. Although the final verdict on the impact of government is not in, and may well vary depending on other factors, this literature reminds us that the role of a nonprofit board is subject to change as the external environment undergoes transformation.

Differing Expectations

In addition to describing multiple roles performed by nonprofit boards, the research literature presents evidence that what boards do in practice often differs from the traditional responsibilities. For example, Holland (2002) found that few boards developed sustained efforts to deal with ongoing accountability issues, and Miller (2002) found that boards often neglected their monitoring role over the executive and the organization. Moreover, different perceptions of board roles exist between board members themselves and staff. Harris's study of Citizens Advice Bureaux in the United Kingdom (1989) reports two major findings. First, a big gap exists between the official functions of local boards and what they do in reality. For example, board members report that they do not view their official resource acquisition role as anything more than a formality and that they take a casual attitude toward their staff oversight responsibilities. Second, Harris reports differences in perceptions of the governing role between board members and staff. Fenn's 1971 study of over four hundred business executives who served on nonprofit boards produced a similar finding—that boards and staff differ significantly in their perceptions of what are important board responsibilities. For example, these board members wanted to be involved in the operational details of their organizations and to follow the direction of staff in initiating new programs. By contrast, staff members wanted trustees to play more of a leadership role in initiating projects.[2]

Differing Perceptions of Individual Roles

While the research above focused on the roles of the board as a whole, Widmer's work (1991, 1993) examines roles played by individual trustees. She finds several important dynamics in place within boards that may shed light on why expectations of governing roles often differ and why a gap exists between prescribed trustee responsibilities and how these are actually practiced. Her 1993 findings suggest that (1) some but not all trustees play the traditional role of trustee; (2) other commonly practiced roles include that of worker, expert, representative, and figurehead; and (3) these roles often conflict with each other and with the traditional trustee role. Widmer (1991) also finds that role differences among individual trustees are related to how those individuals view the essential functions of a board. Not surprisingly, a trustee who sees herself as playing the role of financial expert views financial oversight as the most important board responsibility. A board member who describes his role as representative of a particular constituency is likely to perceive the board's responsibility to the stakeholders as most important.

BOARD EFFECTIVENESS: DETERMINANTS AND CONSEQUENCES

As the nonprofit sector has grown in size and economic impact, increasing attention has been paid to nonprofit performance and accountability. Indeed, most of the literature on nonprofit boards has been prescriptive in nature, offering advice on ways to improve board performance. Recent years have also witnessed a growth in the scholarly literature on board effectiveness. This includes an interest in both the determinants of board effectiveness and the consequences of board effectiveness for organizational effectiveness. Some attention has also been given to empirically assessing the success of intentional efforts to improve board effectiveness (Brudney and Murray 1998; Holland and Jackson 1998). The study of board effectiveness, and its links to organizational performance, speaks directly to whether, how, and why boards make a difference. As such, it is an area of major theoretical and practical importance—but one that presents numerous challenges.

The Difficulty of Studying "Effectiveness"

"Effectiveness" has proven a difficult, elusive, and contentious concept to define and measure in relation to boards and to organizations more generally (Bradshaw, Murray, and Wolpin 1992; Forbes 1998; Green and Griesinger 1996; Herman and Renz 1999; Herman, Renz, and Heimovics 1997; Stone and Cutcher-Gershenfeld 2002). One group of effectiveness researchers concluded, "The major challenge in the study of board effectiveness is the lack of criteria for defining and measuring board effectiveness. The elusiveness of board effectiveness is further aggravated by the elusiveness of organizational effectiveness for nonprofit organizations" (Herman, Renz, and Heimovics 1997:374). Perhaps it is not surprising, then, that reviews commonly find an absence of shared measures of board and organizational effectiveness (Bradshaw, Murray, and Wolpin 1992). A fundamental challenge arises from researchers' efforts to objectively and empirically examine an inherently evaluative concept that can be ascertained only in relation to some (or someone's) specific criteria. But whose judgment and what criteria are to be used? A common strategy has been to use subjective measures based on self-reports by organizational members, but that approach has also been subject to various limitations and challenges. Furthermore, most studies focus on human-service organizations, and most employ cross-sectional data drawn from survey questionnaires. This has prevented researchers from determining the direction of causality between board effectiveness, organizational effectiveness, and other variables.

Determinants of Board Effectiveness

Many studies focus on effectiveness as judged by organizational executives, draw on the normative literature to develop survey items and measures, and rely on surveys and cross-sectional data. In two studies of health and human-service agencies, Fletcher (1992) developed measures of board effectiveness by gathering CEO assessments of board practices through questionnaires. She found that higher attendance at board meetings and longer CEO experience were associated with "good boards" as perceived by CEOs. Other variables, such as number of female trustees, were significant in only one sample, emphasizing that much remains to be done to establish the generality of relationships found in any particular study.

Using survey data from a sample of Canadian nonprofits (mostly social services and health agencies), Bradshaw, Murray, and Wolpin (1992) found that board involvement in strategic planning was particularly important to perceptions of board effectiveness among CEOs.[3] Other significant variables included a common vision for the organization, good meeting management, avoidance of board-staff conflict, the existence of a core group that acts as a positive force for change, and elements of board formalization. These authors also drew from the normative literature to identify the set of board characteristics to be examined.

Herman, Renz, and Heimovics (1997) also focus on perceptions of board effectiveness, but they emphasize the need to consider perceptions of multiple stakeholders, not the CEO alone. Theoretically, they advocate a social constructionist approach to board effectiveness, according to which "there is no independently real board (or organizational) effectiveness . . . there are only judgments of effectiveness" (375). This perspective implies that different stakeholders may have different judgments about effectiveness, and indeed they find only "a rather modest correlation" ($r = 0.32$) between CEO judgments and those of other stakeholders, namely funders and trustees (381). Apparently, different stakeholders also employ different criteria to assess board effectiveness. Thus, the board's use of various prescribed practices was modestly related to CEO judgments of board effectiveness but not to judgments made by funders or trustees.[4] These findings underscore the problematic and variable nature of effectiveness judgments and the importance of expanding effectiveness research beyond CEO judgments.

A major question that arises from the social constructionist perspective, however, is whether there is any meaningful distinction between the study of board effectiveness and the study of stakeholder perceptions of effectiveness. Forbes observes that the theoretical significance of social constructionist studies "derives not from their capacity to actually represent organizational effectiveness but rather from their potential to illuminate the way that effectiveness is conceived of, negotiated, and measured" (1998:196). The work of Herman, Renz, and Heimovics, however, emphasizes that there is no "real" organizational effectiveness—in their words, "effectiveness is judgment" (1997:375; see also Herman and Renz 1997, 1999). Whatever the reality accorded to such judgments, the fact is that the literature has been dominated by approaches that focus on CEO assessments of effectiveness. Herman, Renz, and Heimovics have challenged this focus and included additional organizational participants, but they continue to measure effectiveness by soliciting stakeholder assessments (and indeed challenge the notion that there is any other "effectiveness").

Are there other strategies for measuring organizational effectiveness? One line of research by Chait, Holland, Jackson, and Taylor differs from most of the other literature in this area (Chait, Holland, and Taylor 1991; Holland and Jackson 1998; Taylor, Chait, and Holland 1991). Using an inductive, grounded-theory approach, they conducted interviews with college presidents, board chairs, and other trustees, questioning them in detail about situations in which they felt their boards had performed effectively. A research team then analyzed the actual board behaviors identified in the interviews and identified a set of six competencies necessary for performing these behaviors (e.g., understands institutional context, recognizes complexities and nuances). Using these competencies and a numerical rating system, researchers score boards for their effectiveness (Taylor, Chait, and Holland 1991). Distinguishing between effective and ineffective boards, Taylor, Chait, and Holland find that effectiveness in private college boards is related to trustees' motivations, with trustees of effective boards more likely to have institution-specific and institution-centered motives for joining and serving. In another study, Holland and Jackson (1998) developed a board development program using these six competencies and tested its success in a multiyear quasi-experimental research design. They conclude that "focused and sustained efforts to improve board performance can realize measurable gains" (133). It would be of interest to see the differences and similarities in the competencies yielded by repeating this approach with boards of organizations in other fields of activity.

Boards and Organizational Effectiveness

Studies that explore the relationship between board and organizational effectiveness are confronted with the problems facing "effectiveness" research in both their dependent and independent variables. As with the literature discussed above, data are typically survey-based, correlational, and cross-sectional in nature. Organizational effectiveness is also often measured using organizational participants' assessments, although some research also examines the impact of the board on such objective measures as budgets and deficits (Bradshaw, Murray, and Wolpin 1992, 1996; Pfeffer 1973; Siciliano 1996). Existing research has found significant relationships between board and organizational effectiveness, but much work remains to be done to establish the nature, bases, and causal direction of these relationships (Herman and Renz 1999; Stone and Cutcher-Gershenfeld 2002). One relationship to repeatedly emerge is between board involvement in strategic planning and organizational effectiveness (Bradshaw, Murray, and Wolpin 1996; Green and Griesinger 1996; Siciliano and Floyd 1993, cited in Stone and Cutcher-Gershenfeld 2002). As noted earlier (see "Board Composition"), some studies have linked elements of board composition, such as gender diversity, to organizational effectiveness (Bradshaw, Murray, and Wolpin 1996; Pfeffer 1973; Siciliano 1996). Siciliano found that occupational diversity was positively related to social performance and fund-raising but not to financial performance. Age diversity was somewhat linked to higher donation levels but not to social or financial performance.

In a study of sixteen nonprofits serving developmentally disabled adults, Green and Griesinger (1996) find a significant relationship between board performance and organizational effectiveness, defined as quality and sustainability of services to clients. They conclude that boards of effective organizations are more involved in policy formation, strategic planning, program review, board development, resource development, financial planning and control, and dispute resolution. While board performance was correlated with organizational effectiveness in both CEO- and trustee-derived data, relationships were considerably stronger in the former case (and sometimes not significant in the case of the latter). Sometimes the findings differed. Their findings support the social constructionists' argument concerning the variability of effectiveness judgments among different stakeholders.

Bradshaw, Murray, and Wolpin (1992) found significant relationships between board processes (and other structural characteristics) and CEO perceptions of organizational effectiveness, including board involvement in strategic planning, a common vision of organizational activities, the CEO as the source of that vision, and, depending on the effectiveness measure used, board formalization and board size. Overall, however, the research found a relatively small relationship between board practices and objective measurements (e.g., change in annual budget, deficit as part of total budget).

Herman and Renz (1997), again using a social constructionist perspective, examine multiple stakeholders' judgment of organizational effectiveness in samples of health and welfare organizations and organizations serving individuals with developmental disabilities. They find that judgments of a single organization's effectiveness can vary considerably among different stakeholders (CEOs, funders, trustees), and that different stakeholders use some similar and some different criteria in reaching judgments about an organization's effectiveness. Among all stakeholders, however, perceived board effectiveness was the most important determinant of perceived organizational effectiveness.

Some Thoughts on Future Directions in the Study of Effectiveness

In reviewing the literature, we believe that there are several strategies that would help to expand and further research on boards and effectiveness. First, a significant development in the field is the recognition that effectiveness is a contingent concept—and that no one model of effectiveness will be suitable for all organizations or even for one organization at different points of time (Fletcher 1992; Bradshaw, Murray, and Wolpin 1992; Herman 1989). Yet this point of view needs to be more fully incorporated into the actual research design of effectiveness studies. For instance, if there is no "one size fits all" or single model of effectiveness, then context, including organizational context, is critical. Second, we need data that permit testing of causal relationships, which is not possible with the cross-sectional data commonly used. This is a problem for many research areas but is particularly pressing for effectiveness studies, whose interest is so clearly in establishing causality. Helpful methods would be to collect the type of survey data currently compiled but at multiple points in time, and to employ experimental designs. Third, the field also needs more historical, qualitative, and case studies of effectiveness to shed light on contextual factors and to help further develop and refine survey questionnaires. Indeed, we suggest that there is a discrepancy between the way that the literature is moving (in terms of its conclusions and arguments) and the methods and approaches that predominate.

THE CASE OF GOVERNANCE IN HEALTH CARE ORGANIZATIONS

Our analysis of the general literature on nonprofit boards has emphasized the need for research to pay closer attention to contextual influences, such as legal and environmental factors and particular subsector characteristics. Below, we illustrate and emphasize this point by considering research on governance in health-care organizations. This is not an exhaustive review but one that highlights how significant changes in context have affected governance in one specific subsector.

Historical Overview

The power and importance of hospital boards, medical staff, and administrators have fluctuated over time (see, for example, Fennell and Alexander 1989; Perrow 1963). During the mid- to late nineteenth century, hospital trustees were critical to hospital survival because they provided the legitimacy and capital needed to transform almshouses for the poor into medical institutions. Advances in medical technology in the late 1800s enhanced the role of medical staff such that it was common practice for physicians to occupy places on hospital boards. The entrance of government as a major regulator and purchaser of health care and increasing internal complexity of hospital systems by the mid-twentieth century expanded the scope of administrators' responsibilities and power. For example, beginning in the early 1980s, government enacted various prospective payment systems (PPS) to control spiraling health-care costs. PPS limited reimbursement for hospital and medical care and, more generally, spawned a new emphasis on managed care, competition for patients, and a reconfiguration of health-care delivery systems, all of which heightened the importance of health-care management. At the same time, legal changes have been a crucial part of this shifting landscape (Weiner and Alexander 1993a) and have contributed to an expanded role for boards. Following the landmark cases of *Darling v. Charleston Community Memorial Hospital* (211 NE 2d 253 [IL 1965]) and *Stern v. Lucy Webb Hayes National Training School* (381 F. Supp. 1003 [D. DC 1974]), commonly referred to as the *Sibley Hospital* case, boards were now held responsible for oversight of the hospital's medical staff, for ensuring the quality of care, and for proper hospital management (Molinari et al. 1995). Since the 1980s, then, boards of both hospitals and health-care systems have reemerged as important actors, playing critical roles in how these institutions contend with issues of internal efficiency and quality as well as external competition, regulation, and legal standards of accountability.

Governance Models

Conflicting pressures, internal and external, have stimulated vigorous debates over what models of governance hospital boards should follow. Two basic models dominate this debate—the corporate model of governance and the philanthropic, or stewardship, model (Judge and Zeithaml 1992). A relatively small board, few committees, less diversity of board members' occupational backgrounds, a substantial proportion of insider members, and an emphasis on strategic activities characterize the corporate governance model. Proponents of this model argue that the health-care environment is a highly competitive one that demands rapid decision-making capabilities, risk taking, and a strategic focus that is expertise-driven and results-oriented (Kovner 1990; Shortell 1989). On the other hand, relatively larger board size, more occupational diversity and community representatives, more committees, and an emphasis on asset preservation characterize the philanthropic model. This model conforms to pressures from the institutional environment to demonstrate both voluntaristic control of hospitals and established links between hospitals and local communities (Weiner and Alexander 1993b).

In an empirical study of nearly sixteen hundred nonprofit community hospitals, Weiner and Alexander (1993b) found no examples of "pure" corporate or philanthropic boards. Most were hybrid forms. For example, boards that followed a predominantly corporate model were still large and maintained many committees and high levels of occupational heterogeneity. As Weiner and Alexander argue, the hybrid form may be the most adaptive because it reflects the fact that hospitals exist in environments that are *both* highly institutional and competitive.

Hospital Board Composition and Its Link to Performance

Several studies analyze whether changes in board composition improve a health-care organization's position within its competitive and institutional environments. Most of these studies have examined the relative influence of insider members on boards, including the CEO and medical staff. In general, insiders are positively related to hospital performance, although the role of medical staff insiders presents a more mixed picture.

One study looked broadly at the question of the relationship between insiders on the board and a board's ability to engage in strategic change, including service additions, service divestitures, and corporate reorganization (Gautam and Goodstein 1996). Data were drawn from over three hundred proprietary and nonproprietary hospitals in California for the years 1983–1986. For the sample overall, indicators of strategic change were related to having insiders on the hospital board. Looked at separately, however, insiders were related to strategic change for nonprofit but not proprietary hospitals, suggesting that the role of insiders may be more significant for nonprofit hospital boards than for the boards of proprietary hospitals.

Two other studies (Molinari et al. 1993; Molinari, Hendryx, and Goodstein 1997) examined the relationship between insiders on the board and various measures of financial performance and occupancy rates. Both tested two prevalent theories of governance, the managerialist and the agency-theory perspectives. The managerialist view holds that organizations will perform better if their boards include insider members because of higher quality decision-making information provided by insiders. Agency theorists contend that insiders can use their special knowledge opportunistically to the disadvantage of organizations. In one study, Molinari and colleagues (1993), using 1985 data on 190 short-term general hospitals in California, found that boards with both CEO and medical staff insiders performed better than those with no insider participation. The other study focused solely on the influence of the CEO-board relationship on financial performance and used data from ninety acute-care hospitals (nonprofit, for-profit, and public) in California that provided governance data in 1985 and again in 1989. This study found that CEO involvement on hospital boards was related to higher hospital operating margins (Molinari, Hendryx, and Goodstein, 1997). In both studies, Molinari and colleagues argue that these findings support a managerialist perspective of hospital governance that advocates for insider participation on boards.

The commitment of medical staff to cost containment and to improving operating efficiencies is of particular importance to hospitals. Some estimate that physicians directly influence up to 80 percent of all expenditures on health care

(Chilingerian and Sherman 1990, as cited in Goes and Zhan 1995), and there is some indication that having medical staff actively involved with the board has a greater positive impact on financial performance than having the CEO on the board (Molinari et al. 1993). Hospitals have experimented with numerous ways of aligning the interests of medical staff and hospital trustees through strategies such as physician involvement on governing boards, physician ownership of hospitals, and various financial integration schemes. Overall, findings are particularly mixed regarding the influence of insider medical staff on hospital performance.

One study (Molinari et al. 1995), conducted in California for the time period 1985–1988, found that those hospitals with some physician involvement (either insider or outsider) on the board performed better than those with no physician involvement but that those hospitals with only insider medical staff (and no outside medical staff) on their boards had the best performance, measured as hospital operating margins.

Goes and Zhan's research (1995) presents a more variable picture of the relationship between physician integration strategies and hospital performance. Their study of the relationship between integration strategies and hospital performance was longitudinal, relying on ten years' worth of data from 1981 to 1990, and included three hundred acute-care hospitals in California. The study's time period permitted analysis of relationships both before and after California's prospective payment system (PPS) went into effect in 1983. Goes and Zhan found that having medical staff on hospital boards was related to higher occupancy rates but not lowered costs; only financial integration strategies, such as those associated with managed care, lowered costs, and only for the post-PPS period.

In an attempt to reconcile the inconsistent findings regarding whether physician/insider involvement on hospital boards leads to greater commitment by medical staff to cost containment and higher operating efficiencies, Succi and Alexander (1999) conducted a telephone survey in 1993 of over twelve hundred community hospitals drawn from a national sample. They found that higher levels of physician involvement on boards was associated with greater hospital *inefficiencies* but that this effect was moderated by several staff structure and composition variables, including the size of the medical staff, the number of specialties, and the number of salaried physicians on staff.

Lessons for Research on Governance in Nonprofit Organizations

While there is inconclusive evidence linking governance characteristics to health-care performance, the research suggests several important lessons about studying governance more generally. First, the studies presented here clearly specified aspects of the external environment and its impact on internal organizational systems and actions that led them to particular research questions, hypotheses, and variables. Second, several used competing theoretical perspectives, again related to their assessment of the external environment, which added rigor to the hypotheses posed, the variables used, and the conclusions drawn. Third, governance themes in this work are likely to have relevance for other types of nonprofit organizations, including the rapid impact of changes in legal standards on governance behavior, competing models of governance, existence of hybrid models, the extent to which insiders are included on boards, and their impact on organizational performance.

Since 1987, the research on nonprofit boards has expanded, and a distinct body of research on the topic now exists. The literature has not only grown, it has changed in focus. Twenty years ago, the scant scholarly work available was primarily the product of researchers interested in boards as organizational mechanisms for dealing with environmental uncertainties (Middleton 1987). That characterization would not apply to the field today. Environmental concerns are no longer at the fore, and boards have become more a focus of interest in and of themselves, rather than as aspects of, or vehicles for testing, other concerns about organizational functioning.

By contrast, the two predominant areas of growth in board research have been (1) the determinants and consequences of board composition, and (2) the sources, nature, and consequences of board effectiveness. In this regard, the scholarly literature has moved closer to the prescriptive literature, which has long been concerned with effectiveness. There is every indication that board composition and effectiveness (and the relation between the two) will continue to be major areas of attention, and much remains to be done in each. For instance, we have seen considerable recent research on gender, but race has received virtually no attention. Available evidence clearly indicates that board composition matters—but additional research is needed for us to understand how, when, and why. Likewise, major questions remain about the meaning and measurement of effectiveness, and the direction and nature of the relationship between board and organizational effectiveness. To understand these areas, we argue, will require not only additional data but also additional theory, to help guide the framing of the research and the development of hypotheses.

If there is one generalization that emerges from our review of the literature, it is that boards are heterogeneous entities that defy easy generalization. The overwhelming evidence from the literature underscores the inadequacy of any "one size fits all" model of boards. Perhaps the major challenge for future research will be to integrate that recognition into the ways that actual studies are conducted and designed. If boards are heterogeneous and influenced by their context, then we must carefully delineate contextual factors as we construct our hypotheses, collect our data, and interpret our findings. Similarly, a major challenge for the field is to specify both similarities and differences among boards, and to establish the reasons for variations that do exist. Broadly, this review of the literature indicates the importance of the following variables in relation to board heterogeneity: organizational field of activity or subsector (e.g., art, social services), organizational size, organizational complexity (e.g., bureaucratization, professionalization), organizational age and life cycle, and environmental characteristics and interorganizational relations. In this review, we have referred often to strategic contingency theory, which reminds us that we must always study the board in context—with reference to the fundamental mission and tasks that face the institution it oversees.

In terms of understanding board heterogeneity, we will need to expand our research to include additional types of institutions. In particular, we know very little about boards of smaller, community-based organizations. While such boards may be similar to those of larger organizations, they may also be radically different in some ways, forcing us to rethink and refine current assumptions. We would argue, moreover, that research should be focused not only on the most dramatic and readily apparent differences (e.g., one board spends more time on financial oversight, another on advocacy), but also on the more subtle, but possibly critical, variations in the ways that multiple boards approach and carry out the same activities. The study of variation, however, should not eclipse our sensitivity to the very real similarities that may cut across boards.

A further finding that emerges from the literature is that boards are not isolated entities, and that governance itself is often undertaken jointly by boards in connection with other parties, notably top management. Accordingly, additional research on board-staff relationships is needed to understand the variety of arrangements that exist and why they vary among organizations and in the same institutions over time. In analyzing the board's level of active involvement in governance activities, we should not equate board passivity with insignificance. As social theorists have long emphasized, nondecisions and failure to act by those with influence can be as consequential as forceful action. Whatever the power-sharing arrangements in which boards engage, ultimate responsibility and accountability continue to reside with the board. While research shows that some boards may be passive and slow to react, organizational experience (and highly publicized scandals and crises in nonprofit organizations) shows that this can lead to serious trouble for the organization.

To fill the gaps in our current knowledge will require both additional data and theory of multiple types. To this day, we continue to lack the large-scale, representative sample of organizations that is so vital to establishing what are (and are not) general and variable characteristics of boards and to determining patterns of variation. The absence of panel data remains a major barrier to testing causal hypotheses, as we have seen above. And considerably more in-depth, qualitative research will be needed that can provide the contextual and holistic picture of boards that evidence shows is so important to their analysis. We believe, however, that major advances in the field will come not only through the gathering of additional data, but through the development and application of additional, *theoretically grounded* perspectives to the analysis and interpretation of the data.

Board research has become a distinct and identifiable area of research interest. We would strongly argue, however, that it should not become an isolated subfield but remain connected to wider disciplinary and theoretical concerns. This is particularly important since there is a considerable amount of descriptive literature in the field that would benefit from being placed within a larger analytical framework. Boards are complex, and we do not believe that any single theory of boards would be adequate. By bringing various disciplinary and theoretical concerns to bear on boards, we will not only further our understanding of governance, but the study of boards will contribute to our overall understanding of nonprofit institutions, philanthropy, and civic participation.

NOTES

1. Foundation boards are smaller than nonprofit boards in general, averaging just over eleven members (Council on Foundations 2002). Community and public foundations, however, have much larger boards than do private independent foundations. This difference supports the idea that large board size is a way to respond to multiple constituencies. Community and public foundations must pass a public support test, and thus must rely on a larger and broader group of supporters; this is reflected in the larger size of their boards.

2. A recent survey undertaken by the NCNB (2000) found that both trustees and chief executive officers most often saw the board in a policy-making role. Since NCNB's sample is drawn from a database of members, customers, and contacts, it may also disproportionately include those who are more familiar with literature about board roles, including the definition of the board as a policy-making entity that should avoid interference in daily matters.

3. Two types of subjective measures were used: (1) CEO ratings of their satisfaction with the board, and (2) a multi-item scale constructed by gathering CEO ratings of the board's performance on its most important functions (as seen by the CEO).

4. Perceptions of board effectiveness were measured through the use of items drawn from a self-assessment tool widely used by boards. Samples were drawn from Kansas City–area health and welfare institutions and from nonprofits providing services to people with developmental disabilities.

REFERENCES

Abzug, Rikki. 1996. "The Evolution of Trusteeship in the United States: A Roundup of Findings from Six Cities." *Nonprofit Management and Leadership* 7:101–111.

Abzug, Rikki, and Christy Beaudin. 1994. "Women on Board: Parallel and Subordinate Power Structures/Cultures in Voluntarism and Trusteeship." Working Paper 211, Program on Non-Profit Organizations, Yale University.

Abzug, Rikki, Paul J. DiMaggio, Bradford H. Gray, Chul Hee Kang, and Michael Useem. 1993. "Variations in Trusteeship: Cases from Boston and Cleveland, 1925–1985." *Voluntas* 4:271–300.

Abzug, Rikki, and Joseph Galaskiewicz. 2001. "Nonprofit Boards: Crucibles of Expertise or Symbols of Local Identities?" *Nonprofit and Voluntary Sector Quarterly* 30:51–73.

American Bar Association. 1993. *Guidebook for Directors of Nonprofit Corporations.* Chicago: Section of Business Law, American Bar Association.

Babchuk, Nicholas, Ruth Massey, and C. Wayne Gordon. 1960. "Men and Women in Community Agencies: A Note on Power and Prestige." *American Sociological Review* 25:399–403.

Ben-Ner, Avner, and Theresa Van Hoomissen. 1994. "The Governance of Nonprofit Organizations: Law and Public Policy." *Nonprofit Management and Leadership* 4:393–414.

Bernstein, Susan R. 1991. "Contracted Services: Issues for the Nonprofit Agency Manager." *Nonprofit and Voluntary Sector Quarterly* 20:429–443.

Block, Stephen R., and Steven Rosenberg. 2002. "Toward an Understanding of Founder's Syndrome: An Assessment of Power and Privilege among Founders of Nonprofit Organizations." *Nonprofit Management and Leadership* 12:353–368.

Boris, Elizabeth T. 1989. "Working in Philanthropic Foundations." In *Philanthropic Giving,* edited by Richard Magat, 200–218. New York: Oxford University Press.

Bowen, William G. 1994. *Inside the Boardroom: Governance by Directors and Trustees.* New York: John Wiley.

Bradshaw, Pat, Vic Murray, and Jacob Wolpin. 1992. "Do Nonprofit Boards Make a Difference? An Exploration of the Relationships among Board Structure, Process, and Effectiveness." *Nonprofit and Voluntary Sector Quarterly* 21:227–249.

———. 1996. "Women on Boards of Nonprofits: What Difference Do They Make?" *Nonprofit and Voluntary Sector Quarterly* 6:241–254.

Brody, Evelyn. 1998. "The Limits of Charity Law." *Maryland Law Review* 54:1400–1501.

Brown, William A. 2002. "Inclusive Governance Practices in Nonprofit Organizations and Implications for Practice." *Nonprofit Management and Leadership* 12:369–385.

Brudney, Jeffrey L., and Victor V. Murray. 1998. "Do Intentional Efforts to Improve Boards Really Work?" *Nonprofit Management and Leadership* 8:333–348.

Carver, John. 1990. *Boards That Make a Difference.* San Francisco: Jossey-Bass.

Chait, Richard, Thomas Holland, and Barbara Taylor. 1991. *The Effective Board of Trustees.* New York: Macmillan.

Chilingerian, Jon, and H. Sherman. 1990. "Managing Physician Efficiency and Effectiveness in Providing Hospital Services." *Health Services Management Research* 3:3–15.

Collins, Randall. 1992. "Women and the Production of Status Cultures." In *Cultivating Differences,* edited by M. Lamont and M. Fournier, 213–231. Chicago: University of Chicago Press.

Cornforth, Chris, and Claire Simpson. 2002. "Change and Continuity in the Governance of Nonprofit Organizations in the United Kingdom: The Impact of Organizational Size." *Nonprofit Management and Governance* 12:451–470.

Council on Foundations. 2002. *Foundation Management Series,* 10th ed., vol. 2. Washington, DC: Council on Foundations.

Covelli, Lucille. 1989. "Dominant Class Culture and Legitimation: Female Volunteer Directors." In *Nonprofit Boards of Directors,* edited by R. D. Herman and J. Van Til, 24–35. New Brunswick, NJ: Transaction Publisher.

Dain, Phyllis. 1991. "Public Library Governance and a Changing New York City." *Libraries and Culture* 26:219–250.

Daniels, Arlene K. 1988. *Invisible Careers: Women Civic Leaders from the Volunteer World.* Chicago: University of Chicago Press.

DiMaggio, Paul. 1982. "Cultural Entrepreneurship in Nineteenth-Century Boston, I: The Creation of an Organizational Base for High Culture in America." *Media, Culture and Society* 4:33–50.

DiMaggio, Paul, and Helmut Anheier. 1990. "The Sociology of Nonprofit Organizations and Sectors." *Annual Review of Sociology* 16:137–159.

DiMaggio, Paul, and Michael Useem. 1978. "Cultural Democracy in a Period of Cultural Expansion: The Social Composition of Arts Audiences in the United States." *Social Problems* 25:179–197.

———. 1982. "The Arts in Class Reproduction." In *Cultural and Economic Reproduction in Education,* edited by Michael W. Apple, 181–201. London: Routledge and Kegan Paul.

Domhoff, G. William. 1970. *The Higher Circles: The Governing Class in America.* New York: Vintage Books.

———. 1983. *Who Rules America Now? A View for the Eighties.* Englewood Cliffs: Prentice-Hall.

Drucker, Peter F. 1990. "Lessons for Successful Nonprofit Governance." *Nonprofit Management and Leadership* 1:7–13.

Eisenhardt, Kathleen. 1989. "Agency Theory: An Assessment and Review." *Academy of Management Review* 14:57–74.

Fama, Eugene, and Michael Jensen. 1983. "Separation of Ownership and Control." *Journal of Law and Economics* 26:301–325.

Fenn, Dan H. 1971. "Executives and Community Volunteers." *Harvard Business Review* 49:4ff.

Fennell, Mary L., and Jeffrey A. Alexander. 1989. "Governing

Boards and Profound Organizational Change in Hospitals." *Medical Care Review* 46:157–187.

Fink, Justin. 1991. "Leadership and Equity in Voluntary Organizations." Spring Research Forum Working Papers. Washington, DC: Independent Sector.

Fletcher, Kathleen. 1992. "Effective Boards: How Executive Directors Define Them and Develop Them." *Nonprofit Management and Leadership* 2:283–293.

Forbes, Daniel. 1998. "Measuring the Unmeasurable: Empirical Studies of Nonprofit Organization Effectiveness from 1977–1997." *Nonprofit and Voluntary Sector Quarterly* 27:183–202.

Gautam, Kanak, and Jerry Goodstein. 1996. "Insiders and Business Directors on Hospital Boards and Strategic Change." *Hospital and Health Services Administration* 41:423–440.

Gittell, Marilyn, and Sally Covington with Jill Gross. 1994. "The Difference Gender Makes: Women in Neighborhood Development Organizations." Howard Samuels State Management and Policy Center Graduate School and University Center, City University of New York.

Goes, James B., and ChunLiu Zhan. 1995. "The Effects of Hospital-Physician Integration Strategies on Hospital Financial Performance." *Health Services Research* 30:507–530.

Golensky, Martha. 1993. "The Board-Executive Relationship in Nonprofit Organizations: Partnership or Power Struggle?" *Nonprofit Management and Leadership* 4:177–191.

Green, Jack C., and Donald W. Griesinger. 1996. "Board Performance and Organizational Effectiveness in Nonprofit Social Services Organizations." *Nonprofit Management and Leadership* 6:381–402.

Grønbjerg, Kirsten. 1990. "Managing Nonprofit Funding Relations: Case Studies of Six Human Service Organizations." Working Paper 156, Program on Non-Profit Organizations, Yale University.

Hacker, Helen Mayer. 1975. "Class and Race Differences in Gender Roles." In *Gender and Sex in Society,* edited by Lucile Duberman, 134–184. New York: Praeger.

Handy, Femida. 1995. "Reputation as Collateral: An Economic Analysis of the Role of Trustees on Nonprofits." *Nonprofit and Voluntary Sector Quarterly* 24:295–305.

Hansmann, Henry. 1981. "Reforming Nonprofit Corporation Law." *University of Pennsylvania Law Review* 129:500–623.

Hall, Peter Dobkin. 1975. "The Model of Boston Charity: A Theory of Charitable Benevolence and Class Development." *Science and Society* 38:464–477.

———. 1982. *The Organization of American Culture, 1700–1900: Private Institutions, Elites, and the Origins of American Nationality.* New York: New York University Press.

———. 1997. "A History of Nonprofit Boards in the United States." Washington, DC: National Center for Nonprofit Boards.

———. 1999. "Resolving the Dilemmas of Democratic Governance: The Historical Development of Trusteeship in America, 1636–1996." In *Philanthropic Foundations: New Scholarship, New Possibilities,* edited by Ellen Condliffe Lagemann, 3–42. Bloomington: Indiana University Press.

Harlan, Sharon, and Judith Saidel. 1994. "Board Members' Influence on the Government-Nonprofit Relationship." *Nonprofit Management and Leadership* 5:173–196.

Harris, Margaret. 1989. "The Governing Body Role: Problems and Perceptions in Implementation." *Nonprofit and Voluntary Sector Quarterly* 18:317–333.

Heimovics, Richard, and Robert D. Herman. 1990. "Responsibility for Critical Events in Nonprofit Organizations." *Nonprofit and Voluntary Sector Quarterly* 19:59–85.

Heimovics, Richard D., Robert D. Herman, and Carole L. Jurkiewicz. 1995. "The Political Dimension of Effective Nonprofit Executive Leadership." *Nonprofit Management and Leadership* 5:233–248.

Herman, Robert D. 1989. "Board Functions and Board-Staff Relations in Nonprofit Organizations: An Introduction." In *Nonprofit Boards of Directors: Analyses and Applications,* edited by Robert D. Herman and Jon Van Til, 1–7. New Brunswick, NJ: Transaction.

Herman, Robert D., and Richard D. Heimovics. 1990. "The Effective Nonprofit Executive: Leader of the Board." *Nonprofit Management and Leadership* 1:167–180.

Herman, Robert D., and David O. Renz. 1997. "Multiple Constituencies and the Social Construction of Nonprofit Organization Effectiveness." *Nonprofit and Voluntary Sector Quarterly* 26:185–206.

———. 1998. "Theses on Nonprofit Organizational Effectiveness." *Nonprofit and Voluntary Sector Quarterly* 28:107–126.

———. 1999. "Board Practices of Especially Effective and Less Effective Local Nonprofit Organizations." *American Review of Public Administration* 30:146–160.

Herman, Robert D., David O. Renz, and Richard D. Heimovics. 1997. "Board Practices and Board Effectiveness in Local Nonprofit Organizations." *Nonprofit Management and Leadership* 7:373–385.

Hickson, David J., C. R. Hinings, C. A. Lee, R. E. Schneck, and J. M. Pennings. 1971. "A Strategic Contingencies Theory of Intraorganizational Power." *Administrative Science Quarterly* 16:216–229.

Holland, Thomas. 2002. "Board Accountability: Lessons from the Field." *Nonprofit Management and Leadership* 12:409–428.

Holland, Thomas P., and Douglas K. Jackson. 1998. "Strengthening Board Performance: Findings and Lessons from Demonstration Projects." *Nonprofit Management and Leadership* 9:121–134.

Houle, Cyril O. 1989. *Governing Boards.* San Francisco: Jossey-Bass.

Hult, Karen M., and Charles Walcott. 1990. *Governing Public Organizations: Politics, Structures and Institutional Design.* Pacific Grove, CA: Brooks/Cole.

Judge, William Q., and Carl P. Zeithaml. 1992. "An Empirical Comparison between the Board's Strategic Role in Nonprofit Hospitals and in For-Profit Industrial Firms." *Health Services Research* 27:47–64.

Kang, Chul Hee, and Ram Cnaan. 1995. "New Findings on Large Social Service Organization Boards of Trustees." *Administration in Social Work* 19:17–44.

Kaplan, Gabriel. 2004. "How Academic Ships Actually Navigate: A Report from the 2001 Survey on Higher Education Governance." In *Governing Academia,* edited by Ronald Ehrenberg. Ithaca, NY: Cornell University Press.

King, Karen N., and J. Allen Whitt. 1997. "Princes and Paupers: Network Ties and Financial Contributions among Nonprofit Organizations." *Journal of Nonprofit and Public Sector Marketing* 5:65–74.

Kovner, Anthony. 1990. "Improving Hospital Board Effectiveness: An Update." *Frontiers of Health Services Management* 6:3–27.

Kramer, Ralph. 1965. "Ideology, States and Power in Board-Executive Relationships." *Social Work* 10:107–114.

———. 1981. *Voluntary Agencies in the Welfare State.* Berkeley: University of California Press.

———. 1985. "Toward a Contingency Model of Board-Executive Relations in Non-Profit Organizations." Working Paper 86, Program on Non-Profit Organizations, Yale University.

———. 1987. "Voluntary Agencies and the Personal Social Services." In *The Nonprofit Sector: A Research Handbook,* 1st ed., edited by W. W. Powell, 240–257. New Haven: Yale University Press.

Lipsky, Michael, and Steven Rathgeb Smith. 1989. "Nonprofit Organizations, Government, and the Welfare State." *Political Science Quarterly* 104:625–648.

McCarthy, Kathleen D. 1990. "Parallel Power Structures: Women and the Voluntary Sphere." In *Lady Bountiful Revisited: Women, Philanthropy, and Power,* edited by Kathleen D. McCarthy, 1–31. New Brunswick, NJ: Rutgers University Press.

McPherson, Miller, and Lynn Smith-Lovin. 1986. "Sex Segregration in Voluntary Associations." *American Sociological Review* 51:61–79.

Middleton, Melissa. 1987. "Nonprofit Boards of Directors: Beyond the Governance Function." In *The Nonprofit Sector: A Research Handbook,* 1st ed., edited by W. W. Powell, 141–153. New Haven: Yale University Press.

———. 1989. "The Characteristics and Influence of Intraboard Networks: A Case Study of a Nonprofit Board of Directors. In *Nonprofit Boards of Directors: Analyses and Applications,* edited by Robert D. Herman and Jon Van Til, 160–192. New Brunswick, NJ: Transaction.

Miller, Judith L. 2002. "The Board as Monitor of Organizational Activity: The Applicability of Agency Theory to Nonprofit Boards." *Nonprofit Management and Leadership* 12:429–450.

Molinari, Carol, Jeffrey Alexander, Laura Morlock, and C. Alan Lyles. 1995. "Does the Hospital Need a Doctor?" *Medical Care* 33:170–184.

Molinari, Carol, Michael Hendryx, and Jerry Goodstein. 1997. "The Effects of CEO-Board Relations on Hospital Performance." *Health Care Management Review* 22:7–15.

Molinari, Carol, Laura Morlock, Jeffrey Alexander, and C. Alan Lyles. 1993. "Hospital Board Effectiveness: Relationships between Governing Board Composition and Hospital Financial Viability." *Health Services Research* 28:357–377.

Moore, Gwen, and J. Allen Whitt. 2000. "Gender and Networks in a Local Voluntary-Sector Elite." *Voluntas* 11:309–328.

Murray, Victor, V. Patricia Bradshaw, and Jacob Wolpin. 1992. "Power in and around Nonprofit Boards: A Neglected Dimension of Governance." *Nonprofit Management and Leadership* 3:165–182.

National Center for Nonprofit Boards (NCNB). 2000. *The Nonprofit Governance Index.* A joint project with the Stanford University Graduate School of Business. Washington, DC: National Center for Nonprofit Boards.

Odendahl, Teresa. 1990. *Charity Begins at Home: Generosity and Self-Interest among the Philanthropic Elite.* New York: Basic Books.

Odendahl, Teresa, and Sabrina Youmans. 1994. "Women on Nonprofit Boards." In *Women and Power in the Nonprofit Sector,* edited by Teresa Odendahl and Michael O'Neill, 183–221. San Francisco: Jossey-Bass.

Oster, Sharon. 1995. *Strategic Management of Nonprofit Organizations.* New York: Oxford University Press.

Oster, Sharon M., and Katherine M. O'Regan. 2002. "Does the Structure and Composition of the Board Matter? The Case of Nonprofit Organizations." Yale School of Management Working Paper 4, Politics of Management.

Ostrander, Susan A. 1984. *Women of the Upper Class.* Philadelphia: Temple University.

Ostrower, Francie. 1995. *Why the Wealthy Give.* Princeton, NJ: Princeton University.

———. 1998. "The Arts as Cultural Capital among Elites: Bourdieu's Theory Reconsidered." *Poetics* 26:43–53.

———. 2002. *Trustees of Culture: Power, Wealth, and Status on Elite Arts Boards.* Chicago: University of Chicago Press.

Perrow, Charles. 1963. "Goals and Power Structures: A Historical Case Study." In *The Hospital in Modern Society,* edited by Eliot Friedson. New York: Macmillan.

Pfeffer, Jeffrey. 1973. "Size, Composition, and Function of Hospital Boards of Directors: A Study of Organization-Environment Linkage." *Administrative Science Quarterly* 18:349–363.

———. 1987. "A Resource Dependence Perspective on Intercorporate Relations." In *Intercorporate Relations: The Structural Analysis of Business,* edited by Mark S. Muzruchi and Michael Schwartz, 25–55. Cambridge: Cambridge University.

Provan, Keith. 1980. "Board Power and Organizational Effectiveness among Human Service Organizations." *Academy of Management Journal* 23:221–236.

Ratcliff, Richard E., Mary Elizabeth Gallagher, and Kathryn Strother Ratcliff. 1979. "The Civic Involvement of Bankers: An Analysis of the Influence of Economic Power and Social Prominence in the Command of Civic Policy Positions." *Social Problems* 26:298–303.

Ross, Aileen. 1954. "Philanthropic Activity and the Business Career." *Social Forces* 32:274–280.

Saidel, Judith. 1998. "Expanding the Governance Construct: Functions and Contributions of Nonprofit Advisory Groups." *Nonprofit and Voluntary Sector Quarterly* 27:421–436.

Saidel, Judith, and Sharon Harlan. 1998. "Contracting and Patterns of Nonprofit Governance." *Nonprofit Management and Leadership* 8:243–259.

Salzman, Harold, and G. William Domhoff. 1983. "Nonprofit Organizations and the Corporate Community." *Social Science History* 7:205–216.

Shortell, Stephen M. 1989. "New Directions in Hospital Governance." *Hospital and Health Services Administration* 34:7–22.

Siciliano, Julie I. 1996. "The Relationship of Board Member

Diversity to Organizational Performance." *Journal of Business Ethics* 15:1313–1320.

———. 1997. "The Relationship between Formal Planning and Performance in Nonprofit Organizations." *Nonprofit Management and Leadership* 7:387–403.

Siciliano, Julie, and Floyd, Steven. 1993. "Nonprofit Boards, Strategic Management, and Organizational Performance: An Empirical Study of YMCA Organizations." Working Paper 182, Program on Non-Profit Organizations, Yale University.

Smith, David H. 1992. "Moral Responsibilities of Trustees: Some First Thoughts." *Nonprofit Management and Leadership* 2:351–362.

———. 1995. *Entrusted: The Moral Dimension of Trusteeship.* Bloomington: Indiana University Press.

Smith, Steven Rathgeb, and Michael Lipsky. 1993. *Nonprofits for Hire.* Cambridge, MA: Harvard University Press.

Stone, Melissa M., and Susan Cutcher-Gershenfeld. 2002. "The Challenges of Measuring Performance in Nonprofit Organizations." In *Measuring the Impact of the Nonprofit Sector,* edited by V. A. Hodgkinson and P. Flynn, 33–57. New York: Kluwer Academic/Plenum.

Succi, Melissa J., and Jeffrey A. Alexander. 1999. "Physician Involvement in Management and Governance: The Moderating Effects of Staff Structure and Composition." *Health Care Management Review* 24:33–44.

Taylor, Barbara E., Richard P. Chait, and Thomas P. Holland. 1991. "Trustee Motivation and Board Effectiveness." *Nonprofit and Voluntary Sector Quarterly* 20:207–224.

Tickamyer, Ann R. 1981. "Wealth and Power: A Comparison of Men and Women in the Property Elite." *Social Forces* 60:463–481.

Useem, Michael. 1984. *The Inner Circle: Large Corporations and the Rise of Business Political Activity in the US and UK.* New York: Oxford University Press.

Weiner, Bryan J., and Jeffrey A. Alexander. 1993a. "Hospital Governance and Quality of Care: A Critical Review of Transitional Roles." *Medical Care Review* 20:375–409.

———. 1993b. "Corporate and Philanthropic Models of Hospital Governance: A Taxonomic Evaluation." *Health Services Research* 28:325–355.

Whitt, J. Allen, Gwen Moore, Cynthia Negrey, Karen King, and Deborah White. 1993. "The Inner Circle of Local Nonprofit Trustees: A Comparison of Attitudes and Backgrounds of Women and Men Board Members." Working Paper 192, Program on Non-Profit Organizations, Yale University.

Widmer, Candace. 1989. "Minority Participation on Boards of Directors of Human Service Agencies: Some Evidence and Suggestions." In *Nonprofit Boards of Directors: Analyses and Applications,* edited by Robert D. Herman and Jon Van Til, 139–151. New Brunswick, NJ: Transaction.

———. 1991. "What Do They Think They Are Doing?" Paper presented at the 1991 ARNOVA Conference, Chicago, October.

———. 1993. "Role Conflict, Role Ambiguity, and Role Overload on Boards of Directors of Nonprofit Human Service Organizations." *Nonprofit and Voluntary Sector Quarterly* 22:339–356.

Wood, Miriam M. 1983. "What Role for College Trustees?" *Harvard Business Review,* May–June: 52–57.

———. 1992. "Is Governing Board Behavior Cyclical?" *Nonprofit Management and Leadership* 3:139–163.

Zald, Mayer. 1967. "Urban Differentiation, Characteristics of Boards of Directors, and Organizational Effectiveness." *American Journal of Sociology* 73:261–272.

———. 1969. "The Power and Functions of Boards and Directors: A Theoretical Synthesis." *American Journal of Sociology* 75:97–111.

Zolberg, Vera L. 1981. "Conflicting Visions in American Art Museums." *Theory and Society* 10:81–102.

Zweigenhaft, Richard, and G. William Domhoff. 1998. *Diversity in the Power Elite: Have Women and Minorities Reached the Top?* New Haven: Yale University.

27

Commercial Activity, Technological Change, and Nonprofit Mission

HOWARD P. TUCKMAN
CYRIL F. CHANG

Many nonprofit organizations engage in commercial activities. Some sell goods or services as a sideline to supplement their main income from donations and government subsidies. Others have evolved to rely almost exclusively on commercial activities for revenue (Hansmann 1988). Still others engage in moneymaking pursuits to gain a more diversified revenue flow and reduce their vulnerability to external shocks such as a downturn in the economy or a drastic decline in government support (Tuckman and Chang 1991; Chang and Tuckman 1994). No matter what the motivation or degree of involvement is, commercialization can significantly impact the behavior of the nonprofits that engage in it. It can erode the public trust on which nonprofits rely to raise donations and garner public support, and it can cause nonprofits to drift from their original missions (Weisbrod 1998; Nelson and Zeckhauser 2002). Especially in an age of rapid technological change, with new for-profit opportunities growing, the implications of the relationship between commercial activity and nonprofit mission warrant careful attention.

THE FOR-PROFIT PURSUITS OF NONPROFITS

Nonprofit scholars have long noted the paradox of the pursuit of profits by nonprofits. James (1983, 1998) hypothesizes that nonprofits exist to provide goods and services not offered by the private sector and that nonprofit decision makers prefer donations to commercial revenues. In James's model, nonprofits engage in commercial activity when other revenue sources become less available, with the goal of using commercial revenues to cross-subsidize the goods and services they prefer. For example, nonprofit museums open glitzy retail shops, which generate revenue that is now a larger percentage of operating income than that from federal funding or admissions and membership (Dobrzynski 1997). Cash flows from sales of goods and services enable museums to keep admission charges low and operating hours long. Universities have increasingly formed research alliances with private, for-profit firms to market research results for income (Kolata 1997). They create joint ventures to further their research and education missions by cross-subsidizing unprofitable activities with moneys earned from profitable ones.

Chang and Tuckman (1990) and Tuckman and Chang (1993) offer additional insights as to the reasons nonprofits pursue profits. Hypothesizing that nonprofits pursue profits to accumulate equity (i.e., the excess of assets over liabilities), they show that nonprofits such as hospitals and other health-related organizations earn profits when they can and channel surpluses to accumulate equity. These profitable nonprofits, along with many well-endowed universities and asset-rich foundations and associations, have come under media criticism for not spending enough of the proceeds from their investment on mission-related activities—for example, negative reaction to the American Red Cross's accumulation of surpluses from the World Trade Center tragedy on September 11, 2001, suggests that the public is not always in accord with this use of funds.

The Crowding-Out Effect

Commercialization has an interesting side effect: it can potentially "crowd out" other revenues from donations, bequests, and grants. Theoretically, increases in commercial revenues can have either positive or negative effects on these revenues by stimulating funding from donors who wish to reward entrepreneurial endeavors while causing others to reduce their giving based on the assumption that the new revenue makes these entities more self-sufficient and less deserving.

The two-way relationship between donations and program-service income has been the focus of several studies. Examining the relationships among donations, sales, costs, and pricing for a local chapter of the American Red Cross, Kingma (1995) finds that increases in profits from sales of Red Cross goods and services lead to a decrease in donations, supporting the crowding-out hypothesis. Increases in donations, on the other hand, decrease profits by raising costs and lowering the "community prices" (i.e., subsidized prices) of Red Cross services such as health and safety classes. Kingma finds no effect from donations on either full-service prices or prices charged by "authorized providers" of Red Cross services. In contrast, Okten and Weisbrod (2000) find no evidence of crowding-out from either government grants or an organization's own program services when data from seven different nonprofit industries are analyzed. The findings of Yetman and Yetman (2003) imply that the phenomenon may be related to mission type; no evidence of crowding-out is found for educational and medical nonprofits, although such effect is found for charitable organizations such as arts, culture, and public-benefit organizations. Additional work is needed before the full effects of "crowding out" are known.

The Rise in Commercial Activity

Several studies—Weisbrod (1998), Cordes and Weisbrod (1998), and Steuerle (2000)—find that nonprofit commercial sales of services have been increasing since the late 1980s and early 1990s in the United States. In part, this is because nonprofit managers are becoming increasingly creative in identifying ways to commercialize their outputs (Anderson, Dees, and Emerson 2002). Art museums use galleries as sellable sites for after-hours receptions and parties, zoos use their best visual settings for similar events as well as for weddings, and planetariums offer weekend laser and sound shows. While these activities may differ from those initially envisioned for nonprofits, they are not obviously antithetical to nor inconsistent with nonprofits' missions—for example, after-hours parties in galleries expose more members of the public to great works of art than might otherwise be the case (Andreasen 1996).

While some nonprofits are unable to sell products commercially, at least some of those who are able to do avail themselves of the opportunity. Universities and other nonprofit research institutions commercialize their outputs by creating revenue-yielding alliances with biotech, chemical, engineering, medical, and pharmaceutical firms (Powell and Owen-Smith 1998). Large disease-oriented nonprofits such as the American Lung Association add revenues through partnerships with the for-profit sector. Likewise, the National Jewish Medical and Research Center increased its revenues by conducting clinical trials for private companies and by licensing its technology.

Commercialization is likely fueled by the increased presence of for-profit competitors. In areas like health care and disease-related research, for-profits have increased their presence in industries traditionally dominated by nonprofits. Competition from for-profit hospital chains such as Colombia HCA and Tenet Health System has caused nonprofit managers to minimize costs and mimic the behavior of for-profit competitors. Nonprofit hospitals have also set up for-profit subsidiaries, created new businesses in adjacent market segments, and engaged in unrelated businesses to capture economies of scope (Sloan 1998). Hospital nonprofits also acquired for-profit pharmaceutical companies, medical equipment vendors, health clubs, and parking garages, which gave the nonprofits greater freedom to earn profits and enhanced their ability to survive unanticipated financial exigencies (Chang and Tuckman 1994).

Necessary Conditions for Successful Commercialization

Several necessary conditions must exist for a nonprofit to successfully commercialize its outputs. First, it must feel a need for additional revenues and perceive that the sale of its outputs will provide a viable means to realize its financial goals. Well-endowed national nonprofits (e.g., St. Jude Children's Research Hospital) may be able to forgo commercial activity in order to focus on their missions, but many other nonprofits cannot afford to.

The need for additional revenues, while necessary, is not a sufficient condition. A second necessary condition is that a nonprofit must have opportunities. Advocacy organizations usually have limited chances to market their main products because pricing of political ideas and causes is difficult and outcomes inherently uncertain. Such organizations may sell small items such as T-shirts, banners, and posters to supplement membership dues and donations, but commercial sale of services to feed children in Africa is difficult. It is important to recognize that a limited portion of the nonprofit sector has substantial commercial opportunities and, in some cases, sale of products runs counter to organizational goals (Steinberg and Weisbrod 1998). When a price is charged, this has the effect of reducing the quantity demanded for that good or service; the extent of the exclusion is dependent on the elasticity or price responsiveness of consumer demand (Oster 2000).

A third condition is that a nonprofit's governing board must decide that pursuit of commercial activities is both consistent with (or at least does not substantially interfere with) its mission and is likely to be profitable (Young 2002). In making this decision, the board has a choice either of undertaking a commercial activity consistent with its mission or of developing an unrelated activity. In the latter case, it must then decide whether to operate the activity within the existing nonprofit and subject to the strict limits set by the Internal Revenue Service (IRS) or whether to develop a separate entity (Brody and Cordes 2001; Steurle 2000). Either way, the board must be amenable and business savvy. Some nonprofit governing boards may decide that the imposition of a price on the use of existing services goes against their mission (e.g., housing for the poor) because price acts as a barrier to access. For others, the additional benefits to the target population may outweigh the costs (e.g., a private university using a service fee to cover the cost of a new health facility; Brinckerhoff 2000). Still others may choose a voluntary fee (e.g., a museum that "strongly recommends" a voluntary admissions fee) that does not limit use by those who cannot afford to pay.

Clearly, these options are available only if products are suitable for sale and consumers wish to purchase them—the fourth necessary condition. The services or products of many nonprofits are unsuitable since their target consumers cannot afford to pay for what they produce and they can find no other items to market. Consider the prospects for sale of custodial services for at-risk juveniles from low-income families, for abused teenagers, or for teaching reading to those with learning disabilities. In these cases, the conditions do not exist to sustain a marketplace in which commercial transactions are feasible. The obverse of this is interesting; when the conditions for a market develop, private competitors may find it attractive to enter the marketplace (Sloan 1998).

When the conditions exist to sustain nonprofit activity, a structure must be found to support it. Mission-related activities may fit within the existing nonprofit entity, although it is not always most advantageous to do so. When engaging in unrelated business-income activities, nonprofits run the risk that excessive activity will endanger their charitable status. In both instances, the question arises as to whether to establish a separate vehicle to contain the commercial activity. Steuerle (2000) reports that panelists at the Hauser Center for Nonprofit Organizations at Harvard identified several reasons for creating a taxable entity, including the following: to gain financial capital or access to human capital, to ultimately cash in and sell a new venture, to address tax aspects of the activity itself, to simplify tax filing for certain activities, and to make payments in lieu of taxes. The fact that new legal forms may be required may serve as a deterrent to some nonprofit boards.

APPROPRIATE DEFINITIONS OF COMMERCIAL ACTIVITY

We have discussed the fact that several forms of commercial activity exist in the nonprofit sector and that this, together with the lack of a suitable vocabulary, complicates the task of identifying and quantifying this activity in the nonprofit sector. Increased media and scholarly attention to nonprofit activity has failed to produce a consensus as to what constitutes commercial activity, in part because of the diversity in the missions pursued by nonprofits and the types of goods and services they provide and in part because the appropriate definition depends on the question(s) under discussion. Consequently, we have developed several definitions that reflect various ways that commercial activity has been defined by scholars, the IRS, and other policy makers in the field. Consider the following characterizations.

The first definition relates to whether the *primary outputs of nonprofits (namely, those that nonprofits were established to provide) are given away or sold.* In its most stringent form, if *any* portion of the primary goods or services of a nonprofit is sold, a nonprofit is engaged in commercial activity. Anderson, Dees, and Emerson argue that "social entrepreneurship is about finding new and better ways to create and sustain social value" using funding strategies as a means to serve mission (2002:191). For them, funding strategies are a means to that end and earned income should be pursued only to improve an organization's social impact. Within this context, a decision to charge for a service previously offered at no cost can be justified. Under this definition, nonprofits offering subsidized rents to low-income tenants, hospitals charging for inpatient or outpatient health services, or universities offering scholarship-subsidized education are engaged in commercial activity (Hansmann 1987:30–31). Whether the nonprofit sells its primary services at a loss or gain is irrelevant.

This definition can also be less stringent; under this variant commercial nonprofits are firms that derive income primarily or exclusively from sales of goods and services. Nonprofits such as the American Red Cross and March of Dimes are *not* regarded as engaging in commercial activity because their revenues come primarily from donations and not from the sale of goods and services. In contrast, hospitals, nursing homes, and the Jewish Community Centers are commercial nonprofits because their main source of income is program services, although these organizations do provide free services occasionally to select groups of individuals.

The second definition focuses on what a nonprofit does in relation to its primary mission. A nonprofit is defined as engaged in commercial activity *if it earns any income unrelated to its primary mission.* The IRS uses the "unrelated" definition to determine whether revenue is subject to the Unrelated Business Income Tax (UBIT). It defines unrelated business income as income derived from any "trade or business" that is "regularly carried on" by a nonprofit and not "substantially related to" the nonprofit's exempt purpose or function (Simon 1987; Hansmann 1989). Thus, a hospital's highly profitable cardiac unit can earn tax-free profits because treating patients with heart problems is part of the primary mission of hospitals, but on-site gift shops and restaurants cannot because these are "ancillary" services unrelated to a hospital's core mission. In 1999, a panel of experts concluded that the UBIT had the effect of a voluntary tax and was "at most an intermediate sanction against charities earning too much commercial income" (Brody and Cordes

2001:2). Because of the large subjective element involved in this definition, its usefulness is uncertain.

Unlike the preceding definitions that focus on the concept of "relatedness," the third definition of commercial activity focuses on the blurring of borders that traditionally separate nonprofit and for-profit firms. In markets populated by both for-profits and nonprofits, competition from the nonprofit side is deemed "unfair" because nonprofits are exempt from federal, state, and local taxes while the for-profit competitors are not (Rose-Ackerman 1982; Hansmann 1989; Steinberg 1991). Thus a nonprofit can be defined as engaged in commercial activity if *its activity is similar to that of a for-profit enterprise* (Bennett and Rudney 1987) *or it charges for services that can be provided by a tax-paying for-profit* (Hansmann 1988). Under this definition, a nonprofit hospital may be regarded as engaging in commercial activity if it competes with for-profit hospitals in the provision of patient care services even though such services are the core purpose of both types of hospitals.

The last definition focuses on whether, in sum, a nonprofit's activities produce revenues exceeding its costs, irrespective of how surpluses are used. Thus, *a nonprofit that earns persistent profits* can be defined as engaged in commercial activity in the sense that at least a portion of its efforts appear to benefit the organization rather than its clients. This seems to be the definition used by the media when they periodically report on nonprofits earning large profits. It also corresponds with a literal definition of the term "nonprofit" that refers to a charitable organization that is, by design, constantly broke. Such a definition may be problematic, however, in the case of an organization such as a symphony orchestra that earns surpluses for several years and then begins to run deficits. Alternatively, it can be argued that since the goal of for-profit firms is to produce profits, nonprofits consistently producing profits from program services operate like commercial enterprises. Chang and Tuckman (1990) and Tuckman and Chang (1993) argue that profits are a major source of endowment growth that can be important both in insuring the long-term survival of an organization and enabling it to engage in investment and growth strategies.

Clearly, multiple definitions of commercial activity make sense depending on the specific issues under discussion and the perspective of the discussants. For example, donors, taxpayers, and other observers of the nonprofit scene may find the first two definitions useful because they focus on the primary mission of nonprofits. Mission is the soul of nonprofit organizations, while money is the facilitating agent that enables them to carry out their work. When nonprofits drift from their original missions, however noble the cause or extraneous the circumstance, they risk losing public trust and support.

Congress and tax authorities are particularly interested in the second definition—that is, the definition that the IRS uses to collect UBIT dollars from nonprofits that engage in "unrelated" business activities. Congressional concern rests on two key desires: to extract potential tax dollars from commercial activity and to eliminate "unfair competition" between tax-paying businesses and tax-exempt entities. Tax authorities, as agencies of government and enforcers of the law, need clarity as to what constitutes taxable income to make tax collection easier and less controversial. Thus, this definition is frequently the focus of debates in Congress, the legislatures, and the courts.

For-profit firms that compete with nonprofits may find the second and third definitions of nonprofit commercial activity particularly useful because they draw attention to turf disputes and other fairness-related issues that affect for-profits' market shares and profit margins. Some for-profit firms may wish to enter markets traditionally dominated by nonprofits (e.g., health care and social services), while others face competition from nonprofit entrants searching for business opportunities. Competition, while beneficial to the economy as a whole, makes life tough for for-profits. For-profit managers and stockholders find the attention drawn to the alleged "unfair competition" from nonprofits helpful in their efforts to "level the playing field."

Finally, two groups of nonprofit stakeholders may find the fourth definition, which focuses on the persistent profits of nonprofits, particularly useful. These are nonprofit managers wishing to cross-subsidize unprofitable activities and advocates who monitor the nonprofit sector for their clients. Nonprofit managers earn acclaim during financial tough times through innovative business practices that enable them to use monies earned from unconventional sources to support worthy causes that cannot support themselves. Persistent profits provide stable income streams that ease budgetary stress, make cross-subsidization possible, and increase the ability of nonprofit decision makers to fulfill their goals unobstructed by donor preferences (Tuckman and Chang 1993). Persistent profits may also suggest, however, that these "rich" nonprofits are not doing enough for their target populations. Thus the fourth definition frequently functions as a canary in the mine, signaling the emergence of a problem.

INTERNALIZATION OF COMMERCIAL ACTIVITY: OUTSOURCING

Production of nonprofit goods and services has long had a commercial side (Schiff and Weisbrod 1991; Hammack and Young 1993; Preston 1993). Nonprofits engage in private market transactions by buying advertising, hiring consultants and employees, paying to ship their goods, and contracting for a wide range of commercially produced goods and services in a variety of markets. Some nonprofits contract with for-profits to perform tasks previously done internally while others form for-profit subsidiaries to provide services to both themselves and others. Nonprofit theaters outsource ticket sales to for-profit agents, while nonprofit hospitals use for-profit subsidiaries to manage office buildings, satellite clinics, and even, in one case, an automobile dealership (Starkweather 1996:114).

Management theorists focus on the importance of identifying core competencies and outsourcing non-core activities to third parties (Hammel and Prahalad 1994). For-profits frequently outsource media work to external advertising agencies, storage and distribution functions to warehousing and freight-forwarding companies, and Web site construction to Web-design and content-management firms. Considerable efficiencies are attainable by using outside experts to perform those tasks in which they have competitive advantage. Outsourcing is not new to the nonprofit sector, but opportunities are now available that either did not exist or were not economical to pursue previously. These include but are not limited to human resource administration, events planning, executive search, identification and solicitation of donor contributions, information technology consulting, investing and managing nonprofit assets, membership management, pension and health-plan administration, and Web hosting (Carbone 1993:299–301). A number of authors have written on the advantages of this approach (see Abelson 1998).

Nonprofits are showing increased interest in outsourcing a portion of their activities, as evidenced by the growth in external vendors offering such services as asset management, online membership enrollment, and donor solicitation (Ben-Ner 2004). Outsourcing of the internal activities of nonprofits can have a substantial impact on the way that nonprofit services are delivered. For example, it can reduce the need for internal staff, alter the nature of fund-raising and investment strategies, and change the fund-raising solicitation processes. It can also blur the line between what is distinctly nonprofit and what is commercial. Four related research questions warrant further discussion.

First, outsourcing donor solicitation may alter the nature of the relationship between donors and nonprofit service providers. One issue involves the ethical practices of fund-raisers (Carbone 1993). A second involves "resource dependency" (overreliance on a single source of a particular resource) and its effect (Grønbjerg 1993:32–33). How the introduction of for-profit intermediaries alters relationships with donors remains an unanswered question.

Second, outsourcing may affect volunteerism, particularly at the board level. For example, many boards use volunteers from the business world on investment committees. Outsourcing investment to professional managers may reduce both the number of volunteers on a nonprofit board and the incentive to give. Ben-Ner and Van Hoomissen note that "stakeholder control is a sine qua non for the existence of nonprofits because it avails the trust required for patronizing the organization" (1993:52). Control over the outsource function by boards may become increasingly important in retaining stakeholder support for nonprofits. We know little about how outsourcing affects board behavior in nonprofits.

Third, we also lack knowledge about how outsourcing affects a nonprofit's mission on the revenue side. Grant writing, events planning and execution, and collection of user fees may be outsourced over the Internet, but we do not know how this form of contracting affects which activities nonprofits may choose to engage in. Nor do we know whether outsourcing revenue-generating activities would strengthen or weaken the organization's pursuit of its mission. It is possible that the mission becomes less embedded in grant writing and events planning, both because the contractee has less knowledge of (and commitment to) the mission and because the nonprofit personnel are not forced, by their employment function, to constantly consider the relationship between these activities and the mission and so may become less concerned with what to ask the contractee to do. On the other hand, outsourcing allows the board and staff to specialize in carrying out the core mission activities, potentially enhancing efficiency.

Finally, on the cost-saving side, outsourcing of some activities, such as benefits administration, likely has less mission impact than outsourcing service delivery. Outsourcing service-delivery functions leads to the logical question of why the nonprofit form is needed and to a loss of uniqueness for the organization. If donors and consumers are indifferent to who produces and delivers services, then other factors are needed to justify the unique legal status of the nonprofit. Following up on the notion of trust, Ben-Ner and Van Hoomissen suggest three elements that establish confidence in a nonprofit: absence of ownership shares, the nondistribution constraint, and an open-books policy (1993:53).

MISSION STATEMENTS, COMMERCIAL ACTIVITY, AND MISSION DRIFT

General Mission Statement

Mission statements can be found in the chartering documents of nonprofits. Frequently lofty and attractive in an ideological and pragmatic sense, these statements have one or more of the following impacts:

- legitimate provision of services designed to meet a wide variety of constituent demands
- make it easier for nonprofits to "sell" their mission to a wide variety of participants with divergent views on how best to accomplish a given goal
- provide flexibility for administrators to be creative and propose activities that appeal to donors
- inspire volunteers and administrators to fulfill the organization's goals and pursue multiple approaches in meeting these goals
- allow nonprofits to perform a variety of activities without having to alter their mission statement each time they undertake a new activity

These statements, when written in broad, unfocused, and sometimes all-encompassing terms, make it difficult to tell when the activities of a nonprofit are drifting from its intended purpose. Specifically, a mission statement written broadly enough to encompass both nonprofit and for-profit activities can give moneymaking priority over the original mission. The following organizations' mission statements illustrate the difficulties of identifying mission drift when a statement is too general.

American Association of Retired Persons (AARP): The AARP offers the following *vision statement* (frequently a part of the overall mission statement of an organization):

"AARP excels as a dynamic presence in every community, shaping and enriching the experience of aging for each member and for society" (Novelli 2002). This statement appears to include any activity remotely related to the aged.

Monterey Bay Aquarium: "to inspire conservation of the ocean" (www.mbayaq.org/aa/trustees.asp). This mission appears to include any activities related to the ocean and its surrounding shores.

National Audubon Society: "to conserve and restore national ecosystems, focusing on birds and other wildlife for the benefit of humanity and earth's biological diversity" (www.audobon.org/nas/about.html). This mission encompasses birds, world ecosystems, and a broad array of biological entities.

KaBOOM!: "to inspire individuals, organizations, and business to join together to build much needed, safe, and accessible playgrounds" (www.kaboom.org). This statement is so general that a casual reader might wonder whether it belongs to a nonprofit or a for-profit.

Mission statements framed in general terms are not limited to the nonprofit sector. Albrecht provides the following example of the mission statement for Levi Strauss: "The mission of Levi Strauss is to sustain profitable and responsible commercial success by marketing jeans and selected casual apparel under the Levi's brand" (1994:153). For Albrecht, this mission fails to dramatize customer need, offers no insight into the value the organization creates in meeting customer need, and lacks any insight into what makes the organization special. General mission statements mask mission drift by making its detection difficult. What differentiates a for-profit from a nonprofit is that the former is in the business of pursuing profits for stockholders while the latter is not. Normally, a nonprofit engages in commercial activity with the purpose of earning a profit to cross-subsidize current nonprofit activities (James 1983) or to increase its endowment (Tuckman and Chang 1993). Neither earning a profit nor developing an endowment is a goal usually reflected in the mission statement of a nonprofit. Indeed, an extensive search of nonprofit mission statements failed to reveal a single nonprofit mission statement containing either goal. When a nonprofit pursues a growth or profit strategy and, in the process, gives moneymaking priority over service delivery, mission drift becomes a distinct possibility.

Overly general nonprofit mission statements also create a different problem by facilitating a situation where "managerial preferences . . . may interact with organization constraints to produce a managerial sorting process that determines nonprofit organization objectives and behavior. . . . Nonprofits' goals may be multiple and in conflict and there is no simple measure of the trade-offs being made among goals" (Weisbrod 1998:50). The AARP statement above encompasses many forms of commercial activities under its umbrella, as does the mission of a pediatric hospital that exists "to serve the health needs of children." Given the general nature of mission statements, other factors such as organization-specific articles of incorporation and corporate bylaws, the legal provision of nondistribution of surplus funds to individuals, and public opinion are relied upon to determine the limits on nonprofit expansion in commercial activity.

Additional Factors Affecting Mission Drift

While general mission statements provide an opportunity for nonprofits to engage in commercial activity, a decision to do so still needs to be made by individuals with the decision-making responsibility. It is interesting and useful to explore both the incentives that motivate decision makers and the circumstances under which the direction of an organization is changed.

Mission drift can be intentional, as when a nonprofit chooses to consciously redirect its activities in new directions, or unintentional, as when the new direction is driven by forces such as market competition, donor demands, or financial exigency. Drift can occur on a voluntary basis, as when a nonprofit willingly chooses to adopt a new activity in order to obtain a government grant, or it may be induced by the persuasive powers of a powerful grantee or a cash-flow crisis (Grønbjerg 1993:33). Of particular interest is the drift caused by the pursuit of commercial activity when nonprofits consider profit the main goal. This situation may lead to behaviors less desirable than those pursued by nonprofit administrators untouched by a profit motive (Sheth 1993:386).

The notion that commercial activity will lead to self-interested behavior is one of several concerns. An issue arises as to whether increased time spent on commercial activities by the head of a nonprofit and by the senior staff diverts time and energy away from the primary mission of the nonprofit. Another issue is that commercial activities attract business-oriented managers, and this sorting of managerial talents can change the organizational focus away from the original mission. If commercial activities involve primary mission activities, they are less likely to cause drift than if they involve time spent on unrelated activities. In the latter case, extensive commitment to commercialization can raise serious questions as to whether a nonprofit can continue to fulfill the terms under which it received its charter. But such drift is also easier to detect. Less difficult to identify but of equal concern is the situation that arises when adoption of commercial activities leads to a reduction in the charitable activities or actions previously performed by a nonprofit. These may be subtle but mission affecting, as in the reduction of business to minority contractors or the elimination of informational events that have small audiences.

How to Detect Mission Drift?

Commercial activity by itself is neither good/bad nor ethical/unethical; it is simply a way of raising money (Brinckerhoff 2000). It becomes a concern when it diverts a nonprofit from accomplishing its mission (Anderson, Dees, and Emerson 2002). The public has an interest in knowing when a nonprofit moves so far away from its mission that its ability to deliver charitable activities is compromised. It also needs a mechanism for knowing when commercial activity adds significantly to the surplus of a nonprofit.

No meaningful performance indicators have been developed to capture mission drift, and this is not an easy task to accomplish. In the best of circumstances, mission drift is difficult to identify because alternative activities can support the same mission and because, in some cases, the same mission may be accomplished by either nonprofit or for-profit entities. The appropriateness of nonprofit versus for-profit methods for achieving a mission may not be easy to discern, and limits on commercial activity may not be readily definable. Over time, additional guidelines will be needed to regulate commercial activity, particularly where nonprofits have broadly defined missions. Currently, the IRS limits its regulations in terms of (1) whether an activity is an unrelated business, (2) the accounting method used to calculate taxable income, and (3) which activities may justify withdrawal of tax-exempt status (Weisbrod 1998:289).

Consider the problem of how to measure drift from the AARP mission statement. The sale of insurance or mutual funds to the population aged fifty and over is not a drift from the primary AARP mission, because access to stable and reasonably priced insurance benefits the aged, particularly if the provider offers enhanced consultative services. Where should the line be drawn to separate appropriate business activities from those that divert a nonprofit from its intended mission? If *any* activity that benefits the aged is mission related, the AARP can engage in a wide range of activities including automobile sales, home sales, hotel and motel rental, movie theaters, nursing homes, pharmacies, and travel agencies. When, if at all, should society become concerned? Is the intervention point when a nonprofit is competing unfairly with the for-profit sector, when it has too many commercial activities, or when it is earning too much money (presumably defined as some subjective limit) from tangential activities? Does the answer change if these activities are primarily partnerships with for-profits rather than nonprofit-produced services?

These are difficult questions with no simple answers. Weisbrod notes that the effects of commercialization cannot be evaluated without assessing a nonprofit's success in achieving its social goals. He further notes that "until operational measures of nonprofits' outputs . . . are developed and standardized, the debate will continue over how to operationalize such allegedly negative influences" of commercialization (1998:292). Note that the behaviors of nonprofits and their administrators are at least as important as the social value of programs in determining the need for public action. Several phenomena should be a cause for public concern:

- The administrators are driven by personal gain to spend so much time on for-profit activities that they lose sight of "the central role of providing socially valuable but privately unprofitable services," a concept referred to as *bonoficing* by Weisbrod (1998:52).
- The administrators increase time and effort devoted to commercial activities while reducing the time they spend on charitable activity.
- Pressures from for-profit competition cause a nonprofit to charge unaffordable amounts for its services, to neglect significant segments of the served population, or to reduce the quality of the services provided.
- A serious conflict of interest develops between the goals of the nonprofit and the goals of its commercial endeavor.
- Dollars raised for charitable purposes are used as venture capital to start risky moneymaking activities.
- Charitable dollars are used by administrators to bail out failed businesses or projects.

More Specific Mission Statements

In contrast to general mission statements, specific mission statements are focused and thus more clearly define what nonprofits should do. Consider the following:

The Ad Council: "to identify a select number of significant public issues and stimulate actions on these issues through communication programs that make a measurable degree of difference in our society" (Ad Council 1999:2).

MIT Technology Licensing Office: "to benefit the public by moving the results of MIT research into societal use via technology licensing, through a process which is consistent with academic principles, demonstrates a concern for the welfare of students and faculty, and conforms to the highest ethical standards" (http://web.mit.edu/tlo/www/ directions.html).

Natural History Museum of Los Angeles County, Department of Mineral Sciences: "to develop and conserve collections of minerals, rocks, and gems to make these available to the scientific community and the public, to interpret mineralogical and gemological materials and concepts for the public through exhibits and other types of public programming, and to conduct research in the interests of furthering the science of mineralogy and providing useful new information to the community at large" (http://www.lam.mus.ca.us/research/minsci/index.htm).

Each of the above statements provides a focus for nonprofit activity and at least some indication of how the adopting entity's mission is to be carried out. They provide sufficient detail to make a subjective determination of when mission drift occurs but not necessarily to determine when commercial activity is inappropriate. Weisbrod notes that if "it were entirely clear that certain commercial activities were in conflict with nonprofits' pursuit of their tax-exempt missions, the IRS would be revoking tax-exempt status far more often. . . . We have found that in light of their mission vagueness, it is understandable that nonprofits typically claim that there is no conflict" (1998:289). Indeed Steuerle identifies several reasons why a nonprofit may establish a for-profit entity to meet its objectives: to ensure accountability to the IRS, to maintain accountability to the nonprofit's board and its members, to limit the nonprofit's liability, and to gain some flexibility in compensation (2000:3).

COMMERCIAL ACTIVITY AND NEW TECHNOLOGIES

The evolving technological environment has made it feasible for nonprofits that previously did not engage in commercial activity to do so. It also made it easier to outsource many managerial and revenue-generating functions to external vendors. Among the technological changes opening commercial vistas for nonprofits are the growth of the Internet; evolution of the audio, visual, and communication technologies into digital form; the biotechnology revolution, and the emphasis on very small (nano) technologies. The development of new software opened marketing and management opportunities to nonprofits that previously could not afford them. Rapid changes in the 1990s and early 2000s made it possible for nonprofits to share information with others at substantially lower costs than in the past and to offer products for sale across time and space. This section explores the effects of these developments on the commercial potential of nonprofits.

New Product Creation

The digital revolution permits nonprofits to offer products that were financially impractical to sell in the past (Tiernan 2001). These new products create the potential for an important stream of revenue. For example, the cost of recording and storing music is reduced by CD technology, enabling symphony orchestras and opera companies to reach wider audiences while selling their products at prices kept low by reasonable distribution and production costs. Similarly, some universities are offering asynchronous distance-learning courses to reach students who want to control both when they learn and the intensity of their learning experience. Cornell University has set up a wholly owned online learning company to serve "the executive and professional development needs of individuals and organizations through exceptional online education programs developed by the faculty of Cornell." Its staff and user-experience designers "work closely with faculty experts at Cornell University to develop and deliver learning experiences that are both engaging and effective" (http://www.ecornell.com/about/who/). For Tiernan, "successful companies operate within a set of strategies that influence their position in the marketplace positively" (2001:31).

The potential for nonprofits to sell the products of third parties has also increased. Especially popular are Web sites that enable nonprofits to partner with private vendors to both earn revenue and serve the constituency (e.g., Sagenonprofit.com, Schoolpop.com, and Greatergood.com). The National Rifle Association's online store sells apparel, books, coins, decoys, gun cases, knives, optics, prints, sporting equipment, and wooden items (www.nrafoundation.org/store). Likewise, Associated Builders and Contractors offers construction, health insurance, and retirement planning online (www.abc.org). This modest sampling illustrates the rich increase in sales opportunities made feasible by the World Wide Web.

Elimination of Exclusion

According to Weisbrod's well-known theory, nonprofit organizations emerge to meet individuals' unmet demand for government services (1975). These include services that for-profit firms typically do not provide (e.g., basic research that has no immediate applications), as well as services that for-profits do provide but from which many individuals are excluded because of price or other factors (e.g., health care, ballet performances, and operas). Nonprofits emerge to fill the void by providing the service at an affordable price (Hansmann 1981; Ben-Ner 1986), or at a price below the average total cost with patrons making up the deficit with donations (Bilodeau and Steinberg 1997).

Digital technology enables nonprofits to bring many services to individuals previously excluded from receiving them because of geographic barriers or the high transaction costs of seeking and discovering information (Tiernan 2001:283–286). Eliminating that exclusion creates an opportunity to charge for these goods; that is, those who do not pay remain excluded while those who pay can avail themselves. Worldwide deployment of the Web, powerful search engines, growing user access, and burgeoning databases create opportunities for vendors to supply information quickly, interactively, and with low transaction costs. For-profit firms earn substantial profits in this market by offering services to those who can pay, but the new technologies and the resulting lower costs have offered nonprofits new opportunities to supply information to previously excluded clients (Tiernan 2001, chap. 9).

Changing Delivery Costs

Digital delivery of information usually involves high fixed and low variable costs. Fixed costs refer to a firm's overhead costs that do not vary with the volume of service. Variable costs, on the other hand, are the carrying costs (such as costs of raw materials and energy) that increase when the firm produces more. The high fixed costs associated with the delivery of digital information offer the opportunity for nonprofits to take information they already produce and offer it to clients at low marginal cost. For example, Alcoholics Anonymous incurs costs in preparing, printing, and distributing brochures. The cost of producing an additional brochure is minimal once the typesetting costs are paid. But the distributional costs continue to grow, particularly when the goal is national distribution. Internet delivery of the material, however, can be accomplished with a server and a limited technical staff. The fixed cost can thus be distributed across a wide variety of publications and other online applications, causing the variable cost to fall to a fraction of the cost of producing and delivering paper-based materials. Internet delivery also makes it feasible to deliver a range of new member services.

Today, advocacy organizations can construct a modest Web site for a few thousand dollars, enabling rapid two-way communication with members. The Coalition for a Better Waterfront provides news and updates, member exchanges, information to members, and links to relevant databases (www.betterwaterfront.com). The National Center for Nonprofit Boards offers a bookstore, consulting, workshops, and information on global programs on its Web site (www.ncnb.org). The American College of Cardiology (www.acc.org) provides a wide variety of enhanced services, including access to information on the latest clinical trials; legislative information; a calendar of scientific sessions; and a confidential service for cardiologists, hospitals, and catheterization labs enabling participation in nationwide data collection and benchmarking effort. These one-stop shopping sites reduce transaction costs for members of nonprofits and enhance their ability to deliver services. These also facilitate commercial partnerships and alliances. But these cost advantages made possible by the Internet may be offset by certain disadvantages. For example, although it is cheaper to circulate an advocate's message, it is also cheaper for the opposing advocates to circulate counter messages. And lower information costs can lead to traffic overload in cyberspace, potentially reducing the benefits of Web sites to owners and users alike. Finally, building and maintaining a high-quality Web site can be expensive and require expertise that many nonprofits cannot afford (Chatterjee, Muha, and Tuckman 2004).

Service Delivery Channel

Because of the broad range of activities in the nonprofit sector, service delivery takes many new forms. In the case of specific disease-oriented nonprofits, the World Wide Web expedites several forms of delivery including information on new medications, care treatment plans for individuals, e-mail care programs enabling individuals to self-treat their condition, support of local physician care plans, and current information on environmental conditions that bear on the disease (see, for example, the National Jewish Medical and Research Center Web site at www.njc.org/consumer). Disease-specific nonprofits also have the potential to commercialize services in several ways: provision of services to businesses (e.g., clinical trials and patient contracts), other health-care institutions (consultative and managed care) and managed care organizations (care delivery and advisory), and licensing and clinical trial partnerships with for-profits. Mothers Against Drunk Driving (MADD) offers booklets helping students deal with the death of a classmate and, for adults, giving advice on how best to assist the family when an employee is killed or injured. It also provides training packages for law enforcement agencies, clergy, mental health counselors, and medical personnel who deal with death. The MADD Web site offers these deliverables for a small fee to an audience that reaches far beyond the constituency group (www.madd.org/victims). Low-cost Web communication makes it feasible for these entities to expand their service delivery to new clients. Because commercial opportunities are sometimes not immediately obvious, many additional ventures remain to be discovered.

Digital Technologies and Global Mission

Some nonprofit missions involve outreach to clients on a global basis, and increased Web access enables realization of this goal in ways that have only recently become feasible. The Web site of the State Hermitage Museum in St. Petersburg, Russia, enables Web users all over the world to view its collection online using elaborate IBM software (www.hermitagemuseum.org). Museum artworks and artifacts have also been marketed worldwide by the Museum of Modern Art, which maintains both a nonprofit and a commercial Web site, with the latter selling a variety of products (www.momastore-online.com). Global outreach enables advocacy nonprofits to keep global members apprised of the progress of campaigns and to permit like-minded individuals to develop strategies and legislative campaigns. The Marine Animal Rescue Society uses its Web site to provide information on rescue and rehabilitation activities, to promote worldwide volunteering, and to create links to related sites (www.marineanimalrescue.org). Greenpeace International uses its Web site to notify its constituents of campaign events dealing with toxics, forests, climate, ocean dumping, genetic engineering, and other topics (www.greenpeace.org/International/). Expansion of the web increases the influence of nonprofits, enabling advocacy to expand worldwide; the commercial opportunities arising from this trend depend on whether these organizations develop viable products for sale. Anderson, Dees, and Emerson (2000) provide critical success factors relevant to accomplishing this goal.

Sale of By-products

Low-cost Web delivery makes it possible to sell by-products of nonprofits' operations. A nonprofit hospital can sell patient records software, a nonprofit data-collection entity its databases, and a nonprofit opera its scenery. Mailing lists of nonprofit members have value to those interested in developing a database on individual preferences; for example, *Newsweek* and *U.S. News and World Report* use the AARP membership list to customize the editions they mail to those aged fifty and above, highlighting medical products. Much of this information is in electronic form that enhances the value to users by reducing the time needed to use it. Important ethical and privacy issues are involved, however, and they warrant further exploration.

Increased Research Reach

New technologies enable researchers in a variety of locations to exchange data, acquire knowledge of new and ongoing products, share discoveries, and act as consultants. Web sites provide abstracts on basic and applied research, working papers, and information on partnerships and collaborations. Some nonprofits charge full price for access to their data, others use grants and financial aid to offer free use of information, and still others charge moderate fees (Brinckerhoff 2000). Some are quite elaborate, such as the Conference Board, which maintains and updates the Leading Economic Indicators data series that business firms in every industry and market segment use for planning and forecasting (www.conferenceboard.org). Some sites also offer access to press releases, answers to frequently asked questions, media guides, and postings of research results, and they sometimes serve as an information clearinghouse for research publications, ongoing studies, and consulting services (e.g., Rand.org, Flynnresearch.com). Because the Internet often indicates whether a nonprofit is interested in commercial partnerships, it also facilitates formation of commercial ventures and hastens development of new projects.

Outsourcing Nonessential Functions

The Internet enables outsourcing of nonprofit activities such as fund-raising, event planning, and providing third-party accounting services (e.g., eCharity.com, Donation.com, and Sagenonprofit.com). The scope of coverage for some of these entities is impressive. Donation.com's database contains listings of over 600,000 charities. Similar dot-org and dot-com companies service nonprofit Web sites and offer an assortment of service packages aimed at improving nonprofit administrative functions. These sites reinforce adoption of business-based practices among nonprofits, permit substitution of computer applications for staff time, and enable nonprofits to modify their supply chain to link more closely with suppliers, deliverers, and clients. However, the potential negative effects of outsourcing such as those discussed earlier in the "Outsourcing" section must be carefully identified to ensure that they are minimal and do not outweigh the benefits of these new technologies. Moreover, it is clear that use of the Internet is both limited in the nonprofit sector and more likely to be found among wealthier nonprofit organizations (Chatterjee, Muha, and Tuckman 2004).

Negative Aspects of Technological Change

Some changes created by technology can hurt the nonprofit sector. Internet solicitation of donations, while increasing the reach of a fund-raising nonprofit, may force the nonprofit to comply with the rules and regulations of many states and hence cost them money. Online solicitation also raises international law and homeland safety issues when foreign donations are involved.

Another example of negative effects involves the discoveries that enable nonprofits to pursue new commercial opportunities. Once discovered and made available on the Web, the new information and knowledge usually become available to for-profits, causing increased competition between the two sectors in areas where they did not compete in the past. An example of this is for-profits supplying health-care information to consumers through sites like Medscape.com, Dietwatch.com, and iVillage.com. Although some of these entities existed prior to the development of the Internet, they were less visible then and arguably less effective. The presence of for-profits (and the increased competition they bring), while good for consumer choice, may crowd out donations to nonprofits. It can be argued that nonprofits have the advantage of consumer trust (Hansmann 1987), but for-profits have the advantage of being able to expand more rapidly because of access to capital markets (Weisbrod 1998:297). To the extent that the latter provides greater competitive advantage than the former, nonprofits may find competition frustrating and difficult. Early experience suggests partnerships and alliances may provide a desirable alternative to direct competition between the sectors, as in the case of the AARP's alliance with Monster.com, a leading global online career site and flagship brand of Monster Worldwide, Inc. Steuerle notes that nonprofit regulation is made more difficult because of the inexpensive and universal marketing opportunities available through the Internet (2000:5).

New technologies may also reduce the advantages provided by the nonprofit form. To date most states do not collect sales taxes from for-profits on the Internet, and this differential tax treatment reduces the tax-free advantage that nonprofits enjoy over for-profits. Similarly, when for-profits forgo brick-and-mortar facilities in favor of online operations, the property tax advantage enjoyed by nonprofits is reduced, just as subsidized postage rates for nonprofits yield less competitive advantage when for-profits opt to deliver information via the Web. Tiernan also identifies the clicks-over-bricks advantages as speed, technological expertise, and knowledge of customer needs (2001:47). Companies that hire a more technically competent workforce have a competitive advantage over less tech-savvy competitors, but nonprofits with limited access to funding may find it difficult to compete for talents. Some benefits, such as tax deductibility of contributions, limited regulation, and access to grants, are largely unaffected.

Increased Blurring of the Nonprofit/For-Profit Border

Nonprofits have long cohabited with for-profits in health care, education, and the delivery of social services (Simon 1987), and a further blurring of the nonprofit/for-profit border seems inevitable over time. The Internet, together with the trend toward strategic partnerships and alliances, has created new structures that blur the labels "nonprofit" and "for-profit" (Hammel and Prahalad 1994). Consider the following examples:

- *Web sites focused on economic, environmental, political, public health, and social concerns.* These perform many information functions of a nonprofit but they may involve a single person or a group of loosely associated individuals.
- *Chat rooms that play an informational, issues-oriented, or advocacy role.* These entities provide a forum for information exchange between two or more individuals (e.g., disease-specific, issue-specific, politically oriented). While they have no formal mission, their de facto informational goals resemble those of a nonprofit.
- *For-profit–sponsored Web sites providing services within the domain of nonprofits.* Web sites of many pharmaceutical companies offer information on specific diseases and drugs, women's health issues, minority outreach, etc. Linked with kindred sites, these create a mini-network of information targeted at specific consumers at little or no cost to the customer.
- *Nonprofit Web sites that provide no distinction between mission-related services and those offered commercially,* either by the nonprofit or in partnership with for-profits. The National Rifle Association's Web site (www.nra.org), like others, makes no effort to distinguish between commercial products and mission-related products.

What remains unclear is how the activities, entities, and structures that are erasing the nonprofit/for-profit border affect public perception of nonprofits' role in society. While there are not specific signs of concern, pressure exists for nonprofits to justify continued special treatment, particularly where commercialization is substantial. As Steuerle notes, the structuring of activities that would normally be exempt from taxation raises important regulatory, competitive, and structural issues that increase the difficulty state attorneys general face in measuring and monitoring nonprofit activity (2000:5). At a minimum, these issues suggest that the public will demand greater accountability from the sector and that this will persist over time (Independent Sector 2005).

COMMERCIAL ACTIVITY AND MISSION EXPANSION

This section focuses on three situations in which commercial activity either augments or is inextricably bound with the mission of nonprofits: distance education, technology transfer, and business incubation.

Distance Education

According to the U.S. Distance Learning Association, the provision of education over long distances has been around a long time. The technology has varied from the use of correspondence courses to radio, satellite, and most recently the Web, and it has captured attention even in developing countries (Tuckman and Nas 1987). Distance education enhances the educational mission by enabling nonprofits to educate larger numbers of students without the high fixed costs of bricks and mortar. The opportunity to reach world markets is great, particularly when an institution has world-class faculty able to attract bright and eager students. New technologies make it feasible to attract top students without requiring full-time residence on campus.

For example, the MBA programs of Duke University and other well-known universities offers a chance for nonprofits to charge high prices for the added convenience of asynchronous learning, to use fewer classrooms, to operate in multiple locations, and to create a global perspective for students. From a student's perspective, these programs offer latitude in determining when and how long to listen to a lecture, when and where to complete assignments, and when and how to interact with other students. In states and regions served by a limited number of institutions, it may not be feasible to reach students through a brick-and-mortar facility; distance learning brings education to students in such areas. Distance learning also provides top faculty the opportunity to educate in a global marketplace, raising their visibility and offering them the potential for substantial remuneration. These and other considerations support adoption of distance programs.

The decision to enhance educational mission through distance learning raises several issues. The modern version of distance education involves interactive delivery over the Web. This can take considerably more effort from the professor than traditional delivery techniques, and keeping a Web site staffed 24 hours a day, 7 days a week, requires an infrastructure. Technology is not self-explanatory, and quality assurance concerns require the availability of service support for faculty. Moreover, competition from high quality for-profit vendors can raise the cost of delivering a first-rate course, especially in university programs for degrees such as an MBA. Intellectual property issues, such as who owns the online material, further complicate the world of those who would exploit the new technology.

These considerations have led some universities (e.g., New York University, University of Maryland) to create a for-profit venture to implement distance education. The decision to move to a for-profit form is of interest because it illustrates the flexibility that this form offers in certain contexts. According to Gerry Heeger, the first dean of the School of Continuing and Professional Studies at NYU and later fourth president of the University of Maryland University College, large capital reserves are needed to produce a first-class product, and for-profit status facilitates collaboration with dot-coms, venture capitalist firms, and private investors (2000:9). Nonprofit educators have seen large sums expended by for-profit companies such as University Access. Universities can counter this by developing for-profit subsidiaries to seek capital on the same basis as their for-profit competitors. But the benefits of building a for-profit distance education program will come at a price. First, universities may face a loss of control to the private stockholders who share ownership of the for-profit subsidiary. This loss of control, if not monitored and managed diligently, can lead to a shift of the university's core mission. It thus remains to be seen if these for-profit ventures will prove to be successful adjuncts to the educational goals of a university over time.

Second, many nonprofit educational institutions have rules that preclude effective competition with for-profit providers. These place limits on how money is spent, on bidding procedures, on who can be hired as a consultant, and on who approves curriculum changes. Given these constraints, some universities find creation of a for-profit necessary in order to compete effectively. Here again, the benefits of flexibility and financial returns afforded by for-profit subsidiaries must be balanced by the potential cost of mission drift and loss of purpose that might be experienced by the parent entity.

Third, creation of a for-profit enables nonprofit administrators unfamiliar with most up-to-date accounting procedures and management techniques to gain a better understanding and control of their costs. It becomes possible to identify course development costs, teaching costs, and control over scheduling in a manner not customarily conducted in a public or nonprofit context. It also allows closer attention to student services, library services, career placement, and so on. The end result is an infrastructure different from the one used in nonprofit and public universities and colleges. While this form of commercial activity is mission enhancing for educational nonprofits, its effect on mission drift is unclear. Heeger notes that asynchronous education at exclusive liberal arts colleges is different from that at lesser-known regional institutions; for example, Harvard's mission is different from that of a small Catholic college (2000:49). Self-analysis is required to define the type of business model that best serves the mission of the institution, and the danger is that in the rush to enhance their missions, nonprofit educational institutions will unintentionally alter them. If an institution imposes a model inconsistent with its mission, Heeger argues, there is a distinct risk they will be "foredoomed to fail."

Technology Transfer

The major public and private universities embrace creation of new knowledge as an important element of their mission. In practice, the actual development of discoveries coming from basic research is accomplished by forming alliances and partnerships, as well as through licensing and client sharing with external entities such as the National Science Foundation, National Institutes of Health, as well as private foundations, corporations, and firms large and small. There is a growing recognition that the research universities should play a large and direct role in assisting industry (Powell 1982; Powell and Owen-Smith 1998). Badaracco (1991) identifies increased corporate reliance on external sources of expertise, induced in part by global competitive pressures, as well as multiple sources of new discoveries across both fields and institutions. Take the biopharmaceutical field, for example, where a complex relationship exists between universities, government, small firms, and large firms. The forces pushing universities to play a critical role in basic research are encouraged by potential users of the research, as well as by the belief that universities should play a critical role in economic development and in creating the foundation for centers of competitive advantage such as Silicon Valley (Feller 1990).

An important difference exists between the talents required to develop new research and those that lead to commercial development. In recognition of this, the research universities have created technology transfer offices to take research from the discovery stage through to the creation of patents and licensing, as well as to facilitate collaborations with industry. The California Institute of Technology's Office of Technology Transfer reports that over 800 U.S. patents were issued to the university between 1980 and 2005, with 120 granted in 2000 alone (www.ott.caltech.edu). Harvard University's Office of Technology Development (OTD) reported 133 inventions, filed 64 patent applications, had 55 patents issued, and earned $16.6 million in the 2000 fiscal year. An additional 153 active licenses produced revenues of $649,000 (http://www.techtransfer.harvard.edu/files/OTD_AR2000.pdf). The mission of Harvard's OTD is "to bring University-generated intellectual property into public use as rapidly as possible while protecting academic freedoms and generating a financial return to the University, inventors and their departments; to serve as a resource to faculty and staff on interactions with industry; and to protect against unauthorized third-party use of the University's various trademarks worldwide and to license their use on approved merchandise, generating income for support of undergraduate financial aid" (http://www.techtransfer.harvard.edu/MissionStatement.html). In contrast to distance education, where some for-profit subsidiaries were created, the technological transfer function largely nests within the nonprofit or public structure, primarily because the function is to outsource commercial activity.

Commercialization is clearly within the purview of the mission statements of these research institutions. It can produce additional revenues for basic research and other uses, supplement faculty salaries enabling universities to attract higher quality talent, facilitate university–private industry collaboration, and result in quicker entry of university-created knowledge into the public domain. A question arises as to whether it also leads to mission drift. Powell and Owen-Smith argue that in life sciences research, commercialization can create a conflict between researchers wanting accessible, open licenses that maximize knowledge dissemination and universities seeking more lucrative and exclusive terms (1998:189). Zolla-Pazner highlights the cultural change that occurs when scientists must learn the language of business: "The academic scientist finds herself taking a crash course in business and law. The demands of negotiating agreements and writing patents drain time and energy. Some research activities are redirected from basic science toward more immediately practical goals" (1994:20). Powell and Owen-Smith conclude that "a profound blurring of the roles of universities and private industry is developing. These changes are, in large part, irreversible because they reflect a significant transformation in the nature of knowledge" (1998:189). Feller (1990) observes that some academic teams become quasi-firms as R&D focuses on programs leading to commercial applications. The mission of institutions that engage in technology transfers is both enhanced and, to some degree, transformed.

Business Incubators

Business incubators are entities that promote and foster the start-up and growth of small businesses with promising futures. They provide reasonably priced office and lab space, access to business support resources, informational networks, and sources of financial capital. The plan is to provide services that improve the chance to grow and mature in the critical initial years of a new business so it can leave the program as a financially viable entity. The National Business Incubation Association estimates the number of incubators at 800, up from 12 in 1980 (www.nbia.org); 75 percent are nonprofit and the other 25 percent for-profit. Many nonprofit incubators are public-private joint ventures with federal, state, and local governments joining forces with private for-profit entities to promote job growth and revitalization of urban centers. A primary reason for nonprofit provision of these services is that incubators require large amounts of risk capital not always forthcoming from the private sector.

The logic for using the nonprofit vehicle as the legal entity for developing incubation programs rests with the assumption of significant benefits accruing to the larger community (Feller 1990). Incubation programs are expected to attract new industries to an economy, create the potential for new jobs, breed skilled entrepreneurs, and diversify the economy. Like technology transfer programs, which some incubator companies emerge from, they speed the pace of commercialization of new ideas and inventions but their success is affected by access to venture capital.

If the benefits from creating an incubator are perceived as large enough to exceed its costs, including the degree of risk inherent in subsidizing new companies, a likelihood exists that it will be developed and run by private individuals, real-estate firms, or even venture-capital firms. The calculus used to decide when to create an incubator is different for a nonprofit than a for-profit. The former takes into account the anticipated gains to society while the latter focuses primarily on the benefits that it receives (Audretsch and Stephan 1996). Prior to 1998, more nonprofits than for-profits were willing to provide incubator services. From 1998 to mid-2000, however, the rapid growth of technology start-ups sharply increased for-profit interest in incubators, particularly when incubator services could be traded for participatory stock options. In the year 2000, new for-profit incubators opened at a rate of four per week, many serving as a vehicle for owner investment in a group of companies (www.nbia.org). But a largely disinterested stock market, an increase in startup failures, and the subsequent drying up of venture capital are likely to increase the market share of nonprofits.

Nonprofit incubators' mission is to create an environment that enables startups within their orbit to succeed. But mission drift can occur when nonprofits share in the successes of their clients, if only through the modest payments they receive for their services. For example, tight budgets cause administrators to choose companies with a strong potential to succeed, even if this does not necessarily reflect the highest social priorities. Similarly, companies may be chosen based on their willingness to issue participatory stock shares or because of the potential they have to pay the full cost of the services they use. Moreover, the potential for personal gains may cloud the judgment of nonprofit decision makers. Nonetheless, in the case of nonprofit business incubators, involvement with commercial activities is essential to mission realization. These include furnishing space and some services for at least partial remuneration.

The new information age has seen a great increase in internal and external commercialization in the nonprofit sector. For external commercialization to succeed, a nonprofit must feel a need for additional revenues, perceive that sale of its outputs provides a viable means to realize its financial goals, decide that the pursuit of profits is consistent with its mission, and have a product suitable for sale in the marketplace. Internal commercialization occurs through decisions to adopt practices that encourage a more businesslike orientation, including improved accounting and finance systems, fund-raising using modern marketing techniques, information systems that allow for a flexible and swift response to changing market conditions, and modern management techniques. The adoption of these methods and techniques is fostered both by the growing outsourcing of some activities as well as by stakeholders' demands for strategic and entrepreneurial practice, and for greater accountability from donors and government agencies.

Technological changes are lifting the constraints on nonprofits, making it feasible for many organizations that previously did not engage in commercial activities to do so. Many of these activities have gone unnoticed, both because of the vastness of the Internet (where they have grown phenomenally) and because of the inadequate means for measuring them. Meanwhile, many benefits have been gained by nonprofits that capitalize on the new technology. These include reduced delivery costs, new service delivery channels, greater global outreach, the ability to sell by-products, increased research outreach, and greater outsourcing. The new technology has made it feasible for more nonprofits to take greater advantage of commercial opportunities in new ways unimaginable only a few years ago. These changes have the potential for contributing to the increased efficiency of the sector, but the slow pace of adoption, particularly among small nonprofits, is likely to mean that these benefits will be realized over time rather than immediately. The analysis in this chapter suggests that increased commercialization is inevitable, resulting in further blurring of the border between the nonprofit and for-profit sector. However, the evidence to date indicates that the growth of online commercialization has been restricted to a fraction of the sector (Chatterjee, Muha, and Tuckman 2004).

Nonprofits with secure internal finances, a financially strong donor base (secured in some cases through revenues from commercialization of services), or an appealing mission have the best opportunity to avail themselves of the new technologies. Small nonprofits living hand to mouth with limited mission appeal may need to find a financially strong donor to fully participate. The potential for mission drift caused by commercialization is real. In areas where mission success involves commercialization, such as with nonprofit incubators, the drift may be minimal, while in other areas, such as distance learning, it may cause goal conflict. Without better performance monitors, much of the monitoring of this drift remains anecdotal and legalistic. As the potential of the Internet increases the ability of nonprofits to earn revenues, the IRS will increasingly be called upon to make judgment calls as to how much commercialization is too much. Meanwhile, new and exciting methods of financing and delivering nonprofit products will continue to develop to meet consumer demand for charitable activities. It is extremely likely that the need for rigorous research on the effects of the commercialization of the nonprofit sector will grow through time, increasing the value of scholarship in this area.

REFERENCES

Abelson, Reed. 1998. "Charities Use For-Profit Units to Avoid Disclosing Finances," *New York Times,* February 9.

Ad Council. 1999. *Annual Report.* Obtained from the Ad Council Web site, http://www.adcouncil.org/campaigns/.

Albrecht, Kurt. 1994. *The North Star.* New York: American Management Association.

Anderson, Beth Battle, J. Gregory Dees, and Jed Emerson. 2002. "Developing Viable Earned Income Strategies." In J. Gregory Dees, Jed Emerson, and Peter Economy, eds., *Strategic Tools for Social Entrepreneurs: Enhancing the Performance of Your Enterprising Nonprofit.* New York: Wiley.

Andreasen, A. R. 1996. "Profits for Nonprofits: Find a Corporate Partner," *Harvard Business Review* (November–December): 47–59.

Audretsch, David B., and Paula E. Stephan. 1996. "Company-Scientist Locational Links: The Case of Biotechnology," *American Economic Review* 86 (3): 641–652.

Badaracco, Joseph. 1991. *The Knowledge Link.* Boston: Harvard Business School Press.

Ben-Ner, Avner. 1986. "Nonprofit Organizations: Why Do They Exist in Market Economies?" In Susan Rose-Ackerman, ed., *The Economics of Nonprofit Institutions: Studies in Structure and Policy,* 94–113. New York: Oxford University Press.

———. 2004. "Outsourcing by Nonprofit Organizations." In Dennis Young, ed., *Effective Economic Decision Making by Nonprofit Organizations.* New York: Foundation Center.

Ben-Ner, Avner, and Theresa Van Hoomissen. 1993. "Nonprofit Organizations in the Mixed Economy: A Demand and Supply Analysis." In Avner Ben-Ner and Benedetto Gui, eds., *The Nonprofit Sector in a Mixed Economy,* 27–58. Ann Arbor: University of Michigan Press.

Bennett, James, and Gabriel Rudney. 1987. "A Commerciality Test to Resolve the Commercial Nonprofit Issue," *Tax Notes* (September 14): 1095–1098.

Bilodeau, Marc, and Richard Steinberg. 1997. "Ransom of the Opera." Photocopy, Department of Economics, Indiana University–Purdue University at Indianapolis.

Brinckerhoff, Peter C. 2000. *Social Entrepreneurship: The Art of Mission-Based Venture Development.* New York: Wiley.

Brody, Evelyn, and Joseph Cordes. 2001. "The Unrelated Business Income Tax: All Bark and No Bite?" Emerging Issues in Philanthropy seminar series, 1–3, the Urban Institute and the Hauser Center.

California Institute of Technology, Office of Technology Transfer. http://www.ott.caltech.edu/ (accessed December 14, 2005).

Carbone, Robert F., 1993. "Marketplace Practices and Fundraising Ethics." In David C. Hammack and Dennis R. Young, eds., *Nonprofit Organizations in a Market Economy,* 294–318. San Francisco: Jossey-Bass.

Chang, Cyril F. and Howard P. Tuckman. 1990. "Why Do Nonprofit Managers Accumulate Surpluses, and How Much Do They Accumulate?" *Nonprofit Management and Leadership* 1 (2): 117–135.

———. 1991. "Financial Vulnerability and Attrition as Measures of Nonprofit Performance," *Annals of Public and Cooperative Economics* 62 (4): 655–672.

———. 1994. "Revenue Diversification among Nonprofit Organizations," *Voluntas* 5 (3): 273–290.

Chatterjee, Patrali, David Muha, and Howard P. Tuckman. 2004. "Nonprofit Websites: Prevalence, Usage, and Commercial Activity," *Journal of Nonprofit and Public Sector Marketing* 12 (1): 49–68.

Cordes, Joseph L., and Burton A. Weisbrod. 1998. "Differential Taxation of Nonprofits and the Commercialization of Nonprofit Revenues," *Journal of Policy Analysis and Management* 17 (2): 195–214.

Cornell University. "Who Is eCornell?" http://www.ecornell.com/about/who/ (accessed February 7, 2006).

Dobrzynski, Judith. 1997. "Art (?) to Go: Museum Shops Broaden Wares, at a Profit," *New York Times,* December 10.

Feller, Irwin. 1990. "Universities as Engines of R&D Based Economic Growth: They Think They Can," *Research Policy* 19:333–348.

Grønbjerg, Kirsten A. 1993. *Understanding Nonprofit Funding.* San Francisco: Jossey-Bass.

Hammack, David C., and Dennis R. Young. 1993. *Nonprofit Organizations in a Market Economy.* San Francisco: Jossey-Bass.

Hammel, Gary, and C. K. Prahalad. 1994. *Competing for the Future.* Boston: Harvard Business School Press.

Hansmann, H. 1981. "Nonprofit Enterprise in the Performing Arts," *Bell Journal of Economics* 12:341–361.

———. 1987. "Economic Theories of Nonprofit Organizations." In W. W. Powell, ed., *The Nonprofit Sector: A Research Handbook,* 1st ed., 27–42. New Haven: Yale University Press.

———. 1988. "The Two Independent Sectors." In *Proceedings of the 1988 Spring Research Forum of the Independent Sector, San Francisco, Calif.,* 15–24.

———. 1989. "Unfair Competition and the Unrelated Business Income Tax," *Virginia Law Review* 75:605–635.

Harvard University, Office of Technology Development. "The OTD Mission." http://www.techtransfer.harvard.edu/MissionStatement.html (accessed February 7, 2006).

———. 2000. "Annual Report to the Committee on Patents and Copyrights: Fiscal Year 2000." http://www.techtransfer.harvard.edu/files/OTD_AR2000.pdf (accessed February 7, 2006).

Heeger, Gerry. 2000. "Gerry Heeger Goes the Distance," *University Business* (September).

Independent Sector, Panel on the Nonprofit Sector. 2005. *Strengthening Transparency, Governance, and Accountability of Charitable Organizations: A Final Report to the Congress and the Nonprofit Sector, June 2005.* Washington, DC: Independent Sector.

James, Estelle. 1983. "How Nonprofits Grow: A Model," *Journal of Policy Analysis and Management* 2 (Spring): 350–365.

———. 1998. "Commercialism among Nonprofits: Objectives, Opportunities, and Constraints." In Burton A. Weisbrod, ed., *To Profit or Not to Profit,* 271–286. Cambridge: Cambridge University Press.

KaBoom! "Vision and Mission." http://www.kaboom.org/About_KaBOOM/Vision_and_Mission.html (accessed December 14, 2005).

Kingma, Bruce R. 1995. "Do Profits Crowd Out Donations, or Vice Versa? The Impact of Revenue from Sales on Donations to Local Chapters of the American Red Cross," *Nonprofit Management and Leadership* 6 (no. 1, Fall): 21–38.

Kolata, Gina. 1997. "Safeguards Urged for Researchers: Aim Is to Keep Vested Interests from Suppressing Discoveries," *New York Times,* April 17.

MIT Technology Licensing Office. "Mission Statement." http://web.mit.edu/tlo/www/mission.html (accessed December 14, 2005).

Monterey Bay Aquarium. "About Us." http://www.mbayaq.org/aa/trustees.asp (accessed December 14, 2005).

Mullen, William. 1997. "Museum, Zoo Shops Putting on Glitz, Raking in Profits," *Chicago Tribune,* June 11.

National Audubon Society. "About Audubon." http://www.audubon.org/nas/ (accessed December 14, 2005).

National Business Incubation Association. www.nbia.org (accessed December 14, 2005).

Natural History Museum of Los Angeles County. "Mineral Sciences." http://www.lam.mus.ca.us/research/minsci/index.htm (accessed December 14, 2005).

Nelson, Jonathan K., and Richard J. Zeckhauser. 2002. "A Renaissance Instrument to Support Nonprofits: The Sale of Private Chapels in Florentine Churches." In Edward L. Glaeser, ed., *The Governance of Not-for-Profit Organizations.* Chicago: University of Chicago Press.

Novelli, William D. 2002. "Connecting a Valued Past with Possibilities for Our Future." AARP Web site. http://www.aarp.org/about_aarp/aarp_leadership/on_issues/aging_issues/connecting_a_valued_past_with_the_possibilities_fo.html (accessed December 14, 2005).

Okten, Cagla, and Burton A. Weisbrod. 2000. "Determinants of Donations in Private Nonprofit Markets," *Journal of Public Economics* 75:255–272.

Oster, Sharon. 2000. "Pricing in the Nonprofit Sector," *Nonprofit Times,* October 15, 26–27.

Powell, W. W. 1982. "Adapting to Tight Money and New Opportunities," *Scholarly Publishing* 14 (no. 1, October).

Powell, W. W. and Jason Owen-Smith. 1998. "Universities as Creators and Retailers of Intellectual Property: Life-Sciences Research and Commercial Development." In Burton A. Weisbrod, ed., *To Profit or Not to Profit,* 169–194. Cambridge: Cambridge University Press.

Preston, Anne E. 1993. "The Market for Human Resources: Comparing Professional Careers in the Public, Private and Nonprofit Sectors." In David C. Hammack and Dennis R. Young, eds., *Nonprofit Organizations in a Market Economy,* 177–202. San Francisco: Jossey-Bass.

Rose-Ackerman, Susan. 1982. "Unfair Competition and Corporate Income Taxation," *Stanford Law Review* 34:1017–1036.

Schiff, Jerald, and Burton A. Weisbrod. 1991. "Competition between For-Profit and Nonprofit Organizations in Commercial Markets," *Annals of Public and Cooperative Economics* 62 (4): 619–39.

Sheth, Jagdish N. 1993. "User-Oriented Marketing for Nonprofit Organizations." In David C. Hammack and Dennis R. Young, eds., *Nonprofit Organizations in a Market Economy,* 378–398. San Francisco: Jossey-Bass.

Simon, John G. 1987. "The Tax Treatment of Nonprofit Organizations: A Review of Federal and State Policies." In W. W. Powell, ed., *The Nonprofit Sector: A Research Handbook,* 1st ed., 67–98. New Haven: Yale University Press.

Sloan, Frank A. 1998. "Commercialism in Nonprofit Hospitals." In Burton A. Weisbrod, ed., *To Profit or Not to Profit,* 151–168. Cambridge: Cambridge University Press.

Starkweather, David. 1996. "Profit Making in Nonprofit Hospitals." In David C. Hammack and Dennis R. Young, eds., *Nonprofit Organizations in a Market Economy,* 105–137. San Francisco: Jossey-Bass.

Steinberg, Richard. 1991. "Unfair Competition by Nonprofits and Tax Policy," *National Tax Journal* 44:351–363.

Steinberg, Richard and Burton A. Weisbrod. 1998. "Pricing and Rationing by Nonprofit Organizations with Distributional Objectives." In Burton A. Weisbrod, ed., *To Profit or Not to Profit: The Commercial Transformation of the Nonprofit Sector,* 65–82. Cambridge: Cambridge University Press.

Steuerle, Eugene. 2000. "When Nonprofits Conduct Exempt Activities as Taxable Enterprises," Emerging Issues in Philanthropy seminar series, 1–5, the Urban Institute and the Hauser Center.

Tiernan, Bernadette. 2001. *The Hybrid Company.* Chicago: Dearborn.

Tuckman, Howard P., and Cyril F. Chang. 1991. "A Methodology for Measuring Charitable Nonprofit Organization Financial Vulnerability," *Nonprofit and Voluntary Sector Quarterly* 20 (4): 445–460.

———. 1993. "Accumulating Financial Surpluses in Nonprofit Organizations." In Dennis R. Young, ed., *Governing, Leading and Managing Nonprofit Organizations,* 253–278. San Francisco: Jossey-Bass.

Tuckman, Howard P., and Tevfik F. Nas. 1987. *Educational Technology in Developing Countries.* Allahabad, India: Chugh.

U.S. Distance Learning Association. http://www.usdla.org/ (accessed December 14, 2005).

Weisbrod, Burton A. 1975. "Toward a Theory of the Voluntary Nonprofit Sector in a Three-Sector Economy." In Edmund S. Phelps, ed., *Altruism, Morality, and Economic Theory,* 171–195. New York: Russell Sage Foundation.

———. 1998. *To Profit or Not to Profit: The Commercial Transformation of the Nonprofit Sector.* Cambridge: Cambridge University Press.

Yetman, Michelle H., and Robert J. Yetman. 2003. "The Effect of Nonprofits' Taxable Activities on the Supply of Private Donations," *National Tax Journal* 56 (no. 1, part 2, March): 243–258.

Young, Dennis R. 2002. "Corporate Partnerships: A Guide for the Nonprofit Manager." Photocopy, Case Western Reserve University, Cleveland, Ohio.

Zolla-Pazner, Susan. 1994. "The Professor, the University, and Industry," *Scientific American* 268 (no. 3, September): 72–77.

About the Contributors

Helmut K. Anheier (Ph.D., Yale University, 1986) is professor at the School of Public Policy and Social Research, University of California–Los Angeles, where he is also director of the Center for Civil Society. From 1998 to 2002 he was founding director of the Centre for Civil Society at the London School of Economics and a member of LSE's Department of Social Policy, where he now holds the title of Centennial Professor. Prior to this he was a senior research associate and project co-director at the Johns Hopkins University Institute for Policy Studies, and associate professor of sociology at Rutgers University. Dr. Anheier's work has focused on civil society, the nonprofit sector, organizational studies, policy analysis, and comparative methodology.

John Boli is professor and chair of the department of sociology at Emory University. A native Californian and Stanford graduate, he has published work on world culture and global organizations, education, citizenship, and state power and authority in the world polity. Recent publications include *World Culture: Origins and Consequences* (with Frank Lechner), *The Globalization Reader,* 2nd ed. (also with Frank Lechner), and *Constructing World Culture: International Nongovernmental Organizations Since 1875* (with George Thomas).

Elizabeth T. Boris is founding director of the Center on Nonprofits and Philanthropy (CNP) at the Urban Institute in Washington, D.C. CNP conducts research on issues affecting the nonprofit sector and houses the National Center for Charitable Statistics. From 1991 to 1996, Dr. Boris was founding director of the Aspen Institute's Nonprofit Sector Research Fund. Dr. Boris was also vice president for research at the Council on Foundations. She has a doctorate in political science from Rutgers University.

Evelyn Brody is a professor at Chicago-Kent College of Law, Illinois Institute of Technology, and has visited at Penn, Duke, and NYU law schools. She teaches courses on taxation and nonprofit law. She is the author of "Accountability and Public Trust," in *The State of Nonprofit America* (ed. Lester Salamon), as well as work on the similarities between nonprofit and for-profit organizations; charitable endowments; the effects of tax reform on charities; nonprofit fiduciary law; and the constitutional bounds of the right of association.

Eleanor Brown received her doctorate in economics from Princeton University in 1981. After teaching at the University of Florida and Princeton University, she moved to Pomona College in 1986, where she is now the James Irvine Professor of Economics. Professor Brown's research centers on charitable giving, volunteer labor, and nonprofit organizations.

Wendy Cadge received her doctorate in sociology at Princeton University in 2002. She is assistant professor of sociology in the department of sociology and anthropology at Bowdoin College. Her research interests center on religious pluralism, immigration, gender and sexuality, medicine, and their intersections in the contemporary United States. Her first book, *Heartwood: The First Generation of Theravada Buddhism in America,* is an ethnographic study of a Thai Buddhist temple in Philadelphia and a convert Buddhist center in Cambridge, Massachusetts.

Cyril F. Chang is a professor of economics at the Fogelman College of Business and Economics, University of Memphis, where he also serves as director of the Methodist LeBonheur Center for Healthcare Economics. He received his doctorate in economics from the University of Virginia in 1979 and has taught at the University of Memphis since 1981. In 2004, Dr. Chang won the University of Memphis Board of Visitors Eminent Faculty Award, the highest distinction given annually to one faculty member who has made sustained contributions to scholarly and creative activity, teaching, and service. Dr. Chang's primary teaching interests are in health economics and nonprofit organizations.

Laura Chisolm is professor of law at Case Western Reserve University School of Law, where she has been on the faculty since 1984. She teaches courses in the law of nonprofit organizations at the law school and in the Mandel Center for Nonprofit Organizations Master of Nonprofit Organizations program. Her research focuses on advocacy activities of nonprofit organizations and charity governance issues.

Elisabeth S. Clemens is associate professor of sociology at the University of Chicago. Building on organizational theory and political sociology, her research has addressed the role of social movements and voluntary organizations in processes of institutional change. Her first book, *The People's Lobby: Organizational Innovation and the Rise of Interest Group Politics in the United States, 1890–1925,* received the 1998 Max Weber Award and the award for the best book in political sociology in 1997–98. She is also coeditor of *Private Action and the Public Good* and *Remaking Modernity: Politics, History and Sociology.*

Michelle Sinclair Colman's academic research and work focuses on corporate social responsibility and nonprofit management, particularly information transfer through best practices. With master's degrees from the London School of Economics and the University of Minnesota, she has helped a number of nonprofits improve their performance through best practices. She is also the author of *Urban Babies Wear Black.*

Harvey Dale is University Professor of Philanthropy and the Law at New York University, where he has been on the faculty since 1977. He is director of the National Center on Philanthropy and the Law, and founding president and director of the Atlantic Philanthropies. He is a member of the Visiting Committee to the Harvard Law School and the Visiting Committee to the Duke Law School, a consultant to the American Law Institute's Project on Nonprofit Organizations, a member of the American Academy of Arts and Sciences, and a fellow of the American College of Tax Counsel.

Sarah Deschenes has been a postdoctoral fellow at the John W. Gardner Center for Youth and Their Communities at Stanford University and is an education policy consultant. Her research has focused on the learning environments of youth development organizations and nonprofit organizations' roles in community development. Her dissertation was titled *Lessons from the Middle: Neighborhood Reform for Youth in San Francisco.* She holds a doctorate in administration and policy analysis from the Stanford University School of Education.

Paul DiMaggio is professor of sociology at Princeton University, where he also serves as research director of the Center for Arts and Cultural Policy Studies. Formerly executive director of the Program on Non-Profit Organizations at Yale University, he has written widely about culture and the arts, as well as organizational and economic sociology. DiMaggio is editor of several books, including *Nonprofit Enterprise in the Arts: Studies in Mission and Constraint* and *The Twenty-first Century Firm.*

Julien Forder is an economist at LSE Health and Social Care, London School of Economics. His research interests include industrial and organizational economics relating to health and social care systems. Current research topics concern social care governance issues, such as contracts and incentive mechanisms, and the role of nonprofit organizations, and the use of quasi-markets or hierarchies.

Joseph Galaskiewicz is professor of sociology at the University of Arizona and served as president of the Association for Research on Nonprofit Organizations and Voluntary Action from 2002 to 2004. He is currently doing research on the market for youth services in Phoenix, Arizona, focusing on household consumption and the competition between nonprofit, for-profit, government, and faith-based organizations. He is the author of several books including *Nonprofits in an Age of Uncertainty* (with Wolfgang Bielefeld), *Social Organization of an Urban Grants Economy,* and *Exchange Networks and Community Politics.*

Bradford H. Gray is a principal research associate at the Urban Institute in Washington, D.C., and editor of the *Milbank Quarterly,* an interdisciplinary journal of health policy and population health. From 1989 to 1996, he was director of the Program on Non-Profit Organizations at Yale University. He has collaborated with coauthor Mark Schlesinger for the past decade and has written about for-profit and nonprofit health care for more than twenty years. At the Institute of Medicine of the National Academy of Sciences, he edited *The New Health Care for Profit* and directed the IOM study "For-Profit Enterprise in Health Care." He holds a doctorate in sociology from Yale University. He is a member of the Institute of Medicine of the National Academy of Sciences.

Kirsten A. Grønbjerg, still intrigued by the peculiarities of the U.S. system of welfare and stance toward the role of government, has spent many years examining the nonprofit sector with particular attention to how it elucidates those topics. Her previous research and publications have focused on nonprofit databases, nonprofit funding relations, the facility needs of nonprofit human-service organizations, the nonprofit child-welfare system, longitudinal changes in the grants and contract system of a large state human-service agency, public and philanthropic planning and funding structures in human services. She holds the Efroymson Chair in Philanthropy at the Center on Philanthropy and is professor in the School of Public and Environmental Affairs at Indiana University.

Patricia J. Gumport is professor of education and director of the Stanford Institute for Higher Education Research. Dr. Gumport's research addresses key changes in the academic landscape and organizational character of American higher education. She has spent much of the past fifteen years studying how institutional practices and organizational contexts reshape the content, structure, practice, and relative legitimacy of academic fields. She is writing a book on academic restructuring, portraying the ascendance of an industry logic and its consequences within public higher education during the last quarter of the twentieth century.

Peter Dobkin Hall is Hauser Lecturer on Nonprofit Organizations at Harvard's John F. Kennedy School of Government and Visiting Research Fellow at the Yale Divinity School. His published work includes *The Organization of American Culture, 1700–1900, Inventing the Nonprofit Sector, Lives in Trust,* and *Sacred Companies.* He is author (with Colin B. Burke) of the chapter on voluntary, nonprofit, and religious entities and activities in the forthcoming "Millennial Edition" of *Historical Statistics of the United States.*

John J. Havens received his training in mathematics, economics, and physics at Yale University and his graduate training in economics at the Massachusetts Institute of Technology. For the past twenty years, Havens has participated in the study of philanthropy at the Social Welfare Research Institute, Boston College. His current research explores the associations among philanthropy, income, and wealth; the organizational and moral determinants of giving and volunteering; and the implications for fundraising and philanthropy.

J. Craig Jenkins is professor of sociology and political science at Ohio State University. His major interests focus on the politics of social protest, nonprofit political advocacy, comparative studies of political conflict and instability, and the early warning of humanitarian disasters. He is author of *The Politics of Insurgency: The Farm Worker Movement of the 1960s, The Politics of Social Protest: Comparative Perspectives on States and Social Movements* (with Bert Klandermans), and numerous articles and chapters.

Jeremy Kendall is research fellow at the Personal Social Services Research Unit, LSE Health and Social Care, and at the Centre for Civil Society, both at the London School of Economics. His background is in economics. His main topics of study include social care services, particularly for older people; economic, political, and social aspects of the U.K. voluntary sector; and "third sector" European policy. Recent books include *Third Sector Policy at the Crossroads? An International Nonprofit Analysis* (coedited with Helmut Anheier), and *The Voluntary Sector: Comparative Perspectives in the UK.*

Martin Knapp is professor of social policy at the London School of Economics, where he is also chair of LSE Health and Social Care and director of the Personal Social Services Research Unit. He is also professor of health economics at the Institute of Psychiatry in London. He has been an active researcher in the social care and mental health fields for many years, including work on the nonprofit sector's roles and performance. His books include *The Voluntary Sector in the UK* (with Jeremy Kendall), *Social Care Markets* (with Gerald Wistow et al.), and an edited volume, *Long-Term Care: Matching Resources and Need* (with José-Luis Fernández et al.).

Laura Leete is the Fred H. Paulus Director of the Public Policy Research Center and associate professor of economics and public policy at Willamette University. She has written and taught on topics relating to low-wage labor markets and occupational mobility, nonprofit labor markets, gender and race discrimination, family/work issues and welfare reform, and labor market access. Dr. Leete holds a doctorate in economics from Harvard University.

Milbrey McLaughlin is the David Jacks Professor of Education and Public Policy at Stanford University. McLaughlin also is executive director of the John W. Gardner Center for Youth and Their Communities, a partnership between Stanford University and Bay Area communities to build new practices, knowledge, and capacity for youth development and learning both in communities and at Stanford. She is the author or coauthor of books, articles, and chapters on education policy issues, contexts for teaching and learning, productive environments for youth, and community-based organizations.

Debra C. Minkoff joined the faculty of Barnard College in fall 2005; prior to that she was associate professor of sociology at the University of Washington. Her work explores the ecological and institutional dynamics of contemporary American social movements. She is the author of *Organizing for Equality: The Evolution of Women's and Racial-Ethnic Organizations in America, 1955–1985* and a number of articles on such topics as the structure of protest cycles in the United States, organizational adaptation and survival, and the role of national social movements in American civil society. Her current research examines the field of national organizations representing a broad range of domestic social movements in the United States (civil rights, feminist, peace, environmental, pro-choice, pro-life, and others) in the hopes of uncovering sources of activist potential in the highly institutionalized national social movement sector.

Jennifer O'Donoghue is a doctoral student at the Stanford University School of Education. Her research interests include community-based education and public engagement of traditionally marginalized groups, youth participation and development, and citizenship and democracy. She is currently studying the characteristics of community-based youth organizations that mediate urban youth's engagement in social or community change efforts.

Mary A. O'Herlihy is director of the Irish Institute, the executive education arm of Boston College's Center for Irish Programs. A native of Cork, Ireland, O'Herlihy graduated from the National University of Ireland–Cork in 1994 with a bachelor's degree in English and German, and in 1996 with a master's in English. She attended Boston College from 1998 to 2000 as the Fr. Martin Harney Doctoral Fellow in English.

Francie Ostrower is senior research associate at the Urban Institute's Center on Nonprofits and Philanthropy, where she is conducting studies on foundations, governance, and cultural participation. Prior to joining the Urban Institute in 2000, she was a sociology faculty member at Harvard University. Dr. Ostrower received her doctorate in sociology from Yale University, where she also served as associate director of the Program on Non-Profit Organizations. Dr. Ostrower is the author of *Trustees of Culture* and *Why the Wealthy Give.*

Walter W. Powell is professor of education and (by courtesy) sociology, organizational behavior, communication, and management science at Stanford University and an external faculty member at the Santa Fe Institute. Powell's initial involvement in research on nonprofits came at the behest of John Simon at Yale University's Program on Non-Profit Organizations back in the early 1980s. Powell was the editor of the first edition of *The Nonprofit Sector.* With Elisabeth Clemens, he coedited *Private Action and the Public Good.* He is currently involved in research on the professionalization of the nonprofit sector, analyzing the transfer of managerial practices across sectors in the San Francisco Bay Area nonprofit community.

Kenneth Prewitt is the Carnegie Professor of Public Affairs, School of International and Public Affairs at Columbia University. Previous positions include director of the U.S. Census Bureau, president of the Social Science Research Council, professor of political science and director of NORC (National Opinion Research Center) at the University of Chicago, and, for ten years, senior vice president of the Rockefeller Foundation, where he served on numerous boards, opined about foundations, and otherwise collected experiences that helped in the writing of his chapter for this handbook.

Kevin C. Robbins is an associate professor of history and philanthropic studies at Indiana University–Purdue University at Indianapolis. Over the last decade, he has developed undergraduate and graduate courses in the comparative cultural history of philanthropy within the context of Western civilization from ancient to modern times. Among his current research interests are the history of charity hospitals, the contentious development of charity law in the West, and sharp debates on the necessity of government regulation over endowed philanthropies in early modern Europe.

Lester M. Salamon is a professor at Johns Hopkins University and director of the Center for Civil Society Studies at the Johns Hopkins Institute for Policy Studies. He previously served as director of the Center for Governance and Management Research at the Urban Institute in Washington, D.C. Dr. Salamon's 1982 book *The Federal Budget and the Nonprofit Sector* was the first to document the scale of the American nonprofit sector. His *Partners in Public Service: Government-Nonprofit Relations in the Modern Welfare State* won the 1996 ARNOVA Book Award. Dr. Salamon has extended his work to the international sphere, producing the first comparative empirical assessment ever undertaken of the size and structure of the sector. The results of this work have been published in *The Emerging Sector, Global Civil Society: Dimensions of the Nonprofit Sector,* and an entire series of books on the international nonprofit sector published by Manchester University Press. Dr. Salamon is also the author of *America's Nonprofit Sector: A Primer* and *The State of Nonprofit America.*

Paul G. Schervish is professor of sociology and director of the Center on Wealth and Philanthropy at Boston College, and national research fellow at the Indiana University Center on Philanthropy. He is also senior adviser to the John Templeton Foundation and to the Wealth and Giving Forum, a national organization dedicated to increasing the amount and significance of philanthropy among the ultra-wealthy. He received his doctorate in sociology from the University of Wisconsin–Madison. He has been selected five times to the *NonProfit Times*'s annual "Power and Influence Top 50," a list which acknowledges the most effective leaders in the nonprofit world. Along with John J. Havens, he authored the report *Millionaires and the Millennium: New Estimates of the Forthcoming Wealth Transfer and the Prospects for a Golden Age of Philanthropy.*

Mark Schlesinger, Ph.D., is professor at the School of Medicine at Yale University, a fellow at the Institute for Social and Policy Studies at Yale, and a visiting research professor at the Institute for Health, Health Care Policy, and Aging Research at Rutgers University. He is the current editor of the *Journal of Health Politics, Policy and Law.* Dr. Schlesinger has previously taught at the Kennedy School of Government and Harvard Medical School. He received his doctorate in economics from the University of Wisconsin. Dr. Schlesinger's research falls under two broad topics: (1) the determinants of public attitudes toward complex social policy, and (2) evaluating the consequences of various ongoing trends in the American health-care system. His research on political attitudes explores the sources of public understanding about policies and the factors that increase public legitimacy for government interventions.

John Simon is Augustus Lines Professor Emeritus of Law and former deputy and acting dean, Yale Law School, and founding director of Yale University's Program on Non-Profit Organizations. He has been engaged in teaching and writing (and testifying) on philanthropy and the nonprofit sector since 1963. He has also served as officer or trustee of a number of nonprofit groups, including the Taconic Foundation (president), Cooperative Assistance Fund (founding chairman), Open Society Institute–New York (trustee), the Foundation Center (trustee), and the Council on Foundations (trustee); he also served on the Internal Revenue Commissioner's Advisory Committee on Exempt Organizations.

Al Slivinski earned a doctorate in Economics from Purdue University in 1980. He is currently associate professor and chair of the economics department at the University of Western Ontario. He has served as a member of the Research Advisory Board at Independent Sector, and held visiting faculty positions with the Indiana University Center on Philanthropy, the University of Toronto economics department, and the Wallis Institute for Political Economy at the University of Rochester.

Steven Rathgeb Smith is professor of public affairs and associate dean at the Daniel J. Evans School of Public Affairs at the University of Washington. He also is the director of the Nancy Bell Evans Center on Nonprofits and Philanthropy at the Evans School. Smith is coauthor of *Nonprofits for Hire: The Welfare State in the Age of Contracting and Adjusting the Balance: Federal Policy and Victim Services.* He was the editor of the *Nonprofit and Voluntary Sector Quarterly (NVSQ)* from 1998 to 2004. His recent publications examine the government-nonprofit relationship, the development of social services in the United States and abroad, the role of faith-related agencies in the provision of social welfare services, and the implications for citizenship of the growing importance of nonprofit organizations in providing public services.

Stuart K. Snydman is a doctoral candidate in the administration and policy analysis program at the Stanford University School of Education. His research examines the impact of evolving computer and information technologies on the organization of colleges and universities. Mr. Snydman is also an authority on the emergence of online libraries and has participated in the development of the Stanford University Libraries' digital library program.

Richard Steinberg is professor of economics, philanthropic studies, and public affairs at Indiana University–Purdue University at Indianapolis. He was lured to this institution by the Indiana University Center on Philanthropy. As a graduate student, he attracted the attention of first Henry Hansmann (who invited him to present his work at Yale University's Program on Non-Profit Organizations) and then Walter W. Powell (who invited him to write a chapter in the first edition of this book). Since then, he has had the good fortune to befriend many of the authors of this volume and serve as co-president of ARNOVA with one of them (Kirsten Grønbjerg). His other books include *Economics for Nonprofit Managers* (with Dennis R. Young) and the edited volume *The Economics of Nonprofit Enterprises.* He has served as assistant then associate professor of economics at Virginia Tech, and he has held visiting appointments at Northwestern University and Queensland University of Technology.

C. Eugene Steuerle is a senior fellow at the Urban Institute, a columnist for *Tax Notes Magazine,* and a co-director the Urban-Brookings Tax Policy Center. Among other positions, he has served as Deputy Assistant Secretary of the Treasury for Tax Analysis (1987–89), president of the National Tax Association (2001–02), chair of the 1999 Technical Panel advising Social Security on its methods and assumptions, and economic coordinator and original organizer of the 1984 Treasury study that led to the Tax Reform Act of 1986. He is the author, coauthor, or coeditor of over 150 articles, reports, and testimonies, 650 briefs, and 11 books, including *Nonprofits and Government: Collaboration and Conflict* (with Elizabeth Boris). His research on charity and philanthropy includes studies on the patterns of giving by the wealthy (for the Council on Foundations), the effect of taxes on charitable giving, payout rates for foundations (for the Filer Commission), and ways of simplifying and reforming tax rules for charitable contributions and charitable giving.

Melissa M. Stone is associate professor of Public Affairs and Planning and the Gross Family Professor of Nonprofit Management at the Humphrey Institute, University of Minnesota. Stone is director of the institute's Public and Nonprofit Leadership Center. She has published widely on the strategic management and governance of nonprofit organizations. Her current research examines the use of public-private partnerships to implement public policy, such as social welfare reform. Stone holds a doctorate in organizational behavior from Yale University. Prior to pursuing her graduate degree, she founded two nonprofit organizations that worked with youth and families in crisis.

Mary Tschirhart is an associate professor of public administration at Syracuse University's Maxwell School of Citizenship and Public Affairs and Senior Research Associate at the Campbell Public Affairs Institute. Her research addresses management and strategic issues in public and nonprofit organizations. Current projects examine legitimization and branding strategies, stakeholder management, membership dynamics, diversity in organizations, and service and volunteer behavior. She has published in a variety of journals and edited books, and is the author of *Artful Leadership: Managing Stakeholder Problems in Nonprofit Arts Organizations.*

Howard P. Tuckman, Ph.D., is dean of Rutgers Business School–Newark and New Brunswick at Rutgers University and a P2 professor in the department of finance and economics. Previously, he was dean of the School of Business at Virginia Commonwealth University and the interim dean of the Fogelman College of Business and Economics at the University of Memphis. During his tenure as Distinguished Professor of Economics at the University of Memphis, he was recipient of both the University Distinguished Teaching Award and the University Distinguished Research Award. He is the author of eight books and over 100 journal articles. He has served as a consultant to many private, nonprofit, and government entities and is on a variety of nonprofit and for-profit boards of directors.

Lise Vesterlund is a Danish national who received her doctorate from the University of Wisconsin–Madison and is currently an associate professor in economics at the University of Pittsburgh. She has previously been at Iowa State University and has held visiting professorships at the Center on Philanthropy at Indiana University–Purdue University at Indianapolis and the Harvard Business School. Her current research interest is in the development of economic models of charitable giving, from the perspective of both the individual contributor and the strategies employed by fund-raisers.

Robert Wuthnow grew up in Kansas, did his graduate work at Berkeley, and currently teaches sociology and directs the Center for the Study of Religion at Princeton University. He has written many books about American religion and culture, civil society, and voluntary action, including *Loose Connections: Joining Together in America's Fragmented Communities.*

Index